Merriam-Webster's COMPACT 5-LANGUAGE VISUAL Dictionary

ENGLISH | SPANISH | FRENCH | GERMAN | ITALIAN

Jean-Claude **Corbeil**
Ariane **Archambault**

Merriam-Webster, Incorporated
SPRINGFIELD, MASSACHUSETTS
USA

Merriam-Webster Inc.
www.Merriam-Webster.com
www.LearnersDictionary.com
www.VisualDictionaryOnline.com

Merriam-Webster's 5-Language Compact Visual Dictionary
was created and produced by

QA International
329, rue de la Commune Ouest, 3e étage
Montréal (Québec) H2Y 2E1 Canada
T: 514.499.3000 F: 514.499.3010
www.qa-international.com

Published by Merriam-Webster Inc. 2010

ISBN: 978-0-87779-291-8

Printed and bound in China
10 9 8 7 6 5 4 3 2 1 13 12 11 10
www.qa-international.com
414 Version 3.5.3

ACKNOWLEDGMENTS

Our deepest gratitude to the individuals, institutions, companies and businesses that have provided us with the latest technical documentation for use in preparing *The Compact Multilingual Visual Dictionary.*

Arcand, Denys (motion picture director); Audet, Nathalie (Radio Canada); Beaudouin, Yves (Université du Québec à Montréal); Beaudry, Jean (Longeuil Police Department); Beaulieu, Jacques (Sainte-Thérèse Automotive Vocational Training Center); Bordeleau, André (astronomer); Bugnet-Buchwalter, Marie-Odile (Music Librarian, Université de Montréal); Butler, Philip (Stewart Museum); Christian, Ève (meteorology consultant); Delorme, Michel (Montreal Biodôme); Deschamps, Laurent; Desjardins, Jean-Pierre (Université du Québec à Montréal); Doray, Francine (Hydro-Québec); Doyon, Philippe (Ministry of Natural Resources, Wildlife, and Parks); Dupré, Céline (terminologist); Dupuis, Laval (Montreal Trade School of Motorized Equipment); Faucher, Claude (Communications Transcript); Fournier, Jacques (Éditions Roselin); Gagnon, Roger (astronomer); Garceau, Gaétan (Sainte-Thérèse Automotive Vocational Training Center); Harou, Jérôme (Montreal School of Construction Trades); Lachapelle, Jacques (School of Architecture, Université de Montréal); Lafleur, Claude (science journalist); Lapierre, Robert (chief machinist); Le Tirant, Stéphane (Montreal Insectarium); Lemay, Lucille (Leclerc Weaving Center); Lemieux-Bérubé, Louise (Montreal Center of Contemporary Textiles); Lévesque, Georges (ER doctor); Marc, Daniel (Montreal School of Construction Trades); Marchand, Raymond G. (Université Laval); Martel, Félix (information technology consultant); McEvoy, Louise (Air Canada Linguistic Services); Michotte, Pierre (Maritime Institute of Quebec); Morin, Nadia (Montreal Fire Department Training Center); Mosimann, François (Université de Sherbrooke); Neveu, Bernard (Université du Québec à Trois-Rivières); Normand, Denis (telecommunications consultant); Ouellet, Joseph (Montreal School of Construction Trades); Ouellet, Rosaire (Cowansville Vocational Education Training Center); Papillon, Mélanie (aeronautical engineer); Paquette, Luc (Montreal Trade School of Motorized Equipment); Paradis, Serge (Pratt & Whitney); Parent, Serge (Montreal Biodôme); Prichonnet, Gilbert (Université du Québec à Montréal); Rancourt, Claude (Montreal Trade School of Motorized Equipment); Revéret, Jean-Pierre (Université du Québec à Montréal); Robitaille, Jean-François (Laurentian University, Ontario); Ruel, Jean-Pierre (Correctional Service Canada); Thériault, Joël.

EDITORIAL STAFF

Editor: Jacques Fortin
Authors: Jean-Claude Corbeil and Ariane Archambault
Editorial Director: François Fortin
Editor-in-Chief: Anne Rouleau
Graphic Designer: Anne Tremblay

PRODUCTION

Nathalie Fréchette
Josée Gagnon

TERMINOLOGICAL RESEARCH

Jean Beaumont
Catherine Briand
Nathalie Guillo

ILLUSTRATIONS

Artistic Direction: Jocelyn Gardner
Jean-Yves Ahern
Rielle Lévesque
Alain Lemire
Mélanie Boivin
Yan Bohler
Claude Thivierge
Pascal Bilodeau
Michel Rouleau
Anouk Noël
Carl Pelletier
Raymond Martin

LAYOUT

Pascal Goyette
Danielle Quinty
Émilie Corriveau
Preliminary layout: Émilie Bellemare
Sonia Charette

DOCUMENTATION

Gilles Vézina
Kathleen Wynd
Stéphane Batigne
Sylvain Robichaud
Jessie Daigle

DATA MANAGEMENT

Programmer: Éric Gagnon
Josée Gagnon

REVISION

Veronica Schami
Jo Howard
Marie-Nicole Cimon
Liliane Michaud

PREPRESS

Julien Brisebois
François Hénault
Karine Lévesque
Patrick Mercure

MERRIAM-WEBSTER EDITORS

C. Roger Davis
Caroline Wilcox Reul
Peter A. Sokolowski
Erica I. Walch

CONTRIBUTIONS

QA International wishes to extend a special thank you to the following people for their contribution to this book:
Jean-Louis Martin, Marc Lalumière, Jacques Perrault, Stéphane Roy, Alice Comtois, Michel Blais, Christiane Beauregard, Mamadou Togola, Annie Maurice, Charles Campeau, Mivil Deschênes, Jonathan Jacques, Martin Lortie, Frédérick Simard, Yan Tremblay, Mathieu Blouin, Sébastien Dallaire, Hoang Khanh Le, Martin Desrosiers, Nicolas Oroc, François Escalmel, Danièle Lemay, Pierre Savoie, Benoît Bourdeau, Marie-Andrée Lemieux, Caroline Soucy, Yves Chabot, Anne-Marie Ouellette, Anne-Marie Villeneuve, Anne-Marie Brault, Nancy Lepage, Daniel Provost, François Vézina, Guylaine Houle, Daniel Beaulieu, Sophie Pellerin, Tony O'Riley, Mac Thien Nguyen Hoang, Serge D'Amico.

Introduction

Merriam-Webster's Compact 5-Language Visual Dictionary is designed to meet the needs of users who speak, are learning, or need to understand words in English, Spanish, French, German, or Italian. Every image in the dictionary is named in each of the five languages to help users identify and understand a particular object and words associated with that object or its parts. In addition, the dictionary can serve as a vocabulary-building resource for each of the five languages, as users will find vocabulary they need to master in regard to many aspects of life, such as food, clothing, transportation, science, and sports.

The aim of this dictionary has been to bring together in one volume the technical and the everyday terms required to understand the contemporary world and the specialized fields that shape our daily experience. In effect, it provides an inventory of our physical environment for users who need to know and understand general and specialized terms in a wide variety of fields.

EDITORIAL POLICY

Each word in this dictionary has been carefully selected after consulting authoritative information sources containing the appropriate level of specialization. In some instances, the sources consulted reveal that different words are used to name the same item. In such cases, the word most frequently used by the most authoritative sources has been chosen.

STRUCTURE

This book has three sections: the preliminary pages, including the table of contents, which lists the themes and subthemes; the body of the text (i.e., the detailed treatment of each theme); and the index. Throughout each chapter, information is presented moving from the most abstract to the most concrete: theme, subtheme, title, illustration, terminology.

HOW TO CONSULT THIS DICTIONARY

Users may gain access to the contents of this dictionary in a variety of ways:

- From the table of contents, the user can locate the section that is of interest.
- The index can be consulted to locate a specific term, and by examining the illustration cited, the user can see what corresponds to the word.
- The user can examine the illustrations in the relevant sections of the dictionary. The great strength of this dictionary is the fact that the illustrations enable the user to find a word even if he or she only has a vague idea of what it is.

AUTHORS

Jean-Claude Corbell is an expert in linguistic planning, with a world-wide reputation in the fields of comparative terminology and socio-linguistics. He serves as a consultant to various international organizations and governments.

Ariane Archambault, a specialist in applied linguistics, has taught foreign languages and is now a terminologist and editor of dictionaries and reference books.

TITLE

It is highlighted in the edition's main language, while the other languages are placed underneath in smaller characters. If the title runs over a number of pages, it is printed in gray on the pages subsequent to the first page on which it appears.

SUBTHEME

All of the themes are subdivided into subthemes.

THEME

These are shown at the end of the preliminary pages. They are then repeated on each page of the section.

TERM

Each term appears in the index with a reference to the pages on which it appears. It is given in all languages.

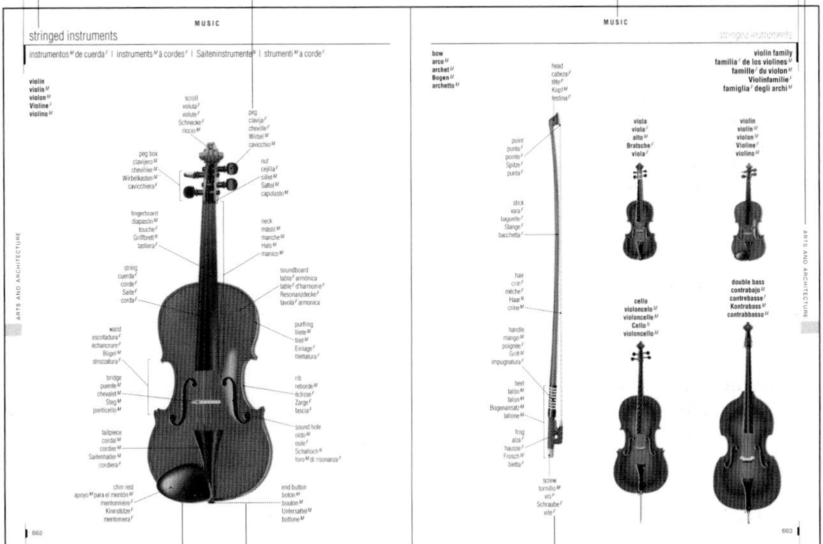

MUSIC
stringed instruments
instrumentos M de cuerda F | instruments M à cordes F | Saiteninstrumente N | strumenti M a corde F
violin
violín M
violon M
Violine F
violino M
bow
arco M
archet M
Bogen M
archetto M
violin family
familia F de los violines M
famille F du violon M
Violinfamilie F
famiglia F degli archi M
viola
violin
cello
double bass
ARTS AND ARCHITECTURE
662
663

ILLUSTRATION

It is an integral part of the visual definition for each of the terms that refer to it.

NARROW LINES

These link the word to the item indicated. Where too many lines would make reading difficult, they have been replaced by color codes with captions or, in rare cases, by numbers.

GENDER INDICATION

The gender of each word in a term is indicated.

F: feminine M: masculine N: neuter

The people shown in the dictionary may be men or women when the function illustrated can be fulfilled by either. In these cases, the gender assigned to the word depends on the illustration; in fact, the word is either masculine or feminine depending on the sex of the person.

CONTENTS

SPORTS AND GAMES

LIST OF CHAPTERS

solar system

sistema^M solar | système^M solaire | Sonnensystem^N | sistema^M solare

outer planets
planetas^M externos
planètes^F externes
äußere Planeten^M
pianeti^M esterni

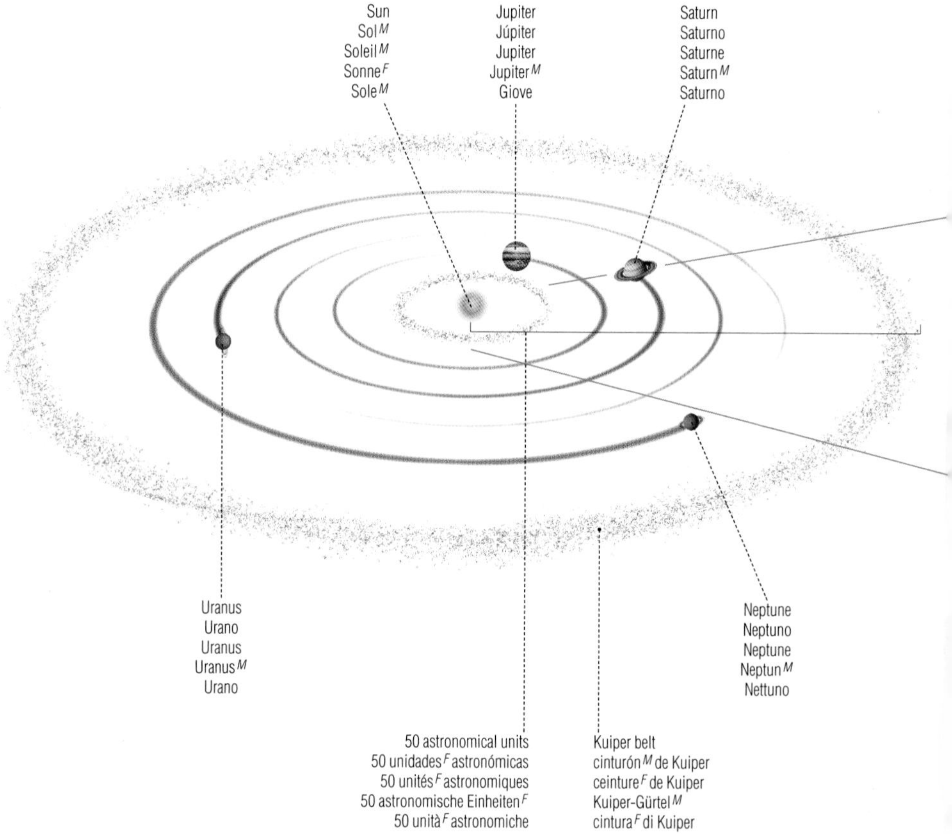
Sun
Sol M
Soleil M
Sonne F
Sole M
Jupiter
Júpiter
Jupiter
Jupiter M
Giove
Saturn
Saturno
Saturne
Saturn M
Saturno
Uranus
Urano
Uranus
Uranus M
Urano
Neptune
Neptuno
Neptune
Neptun M
Nettuno
50 astronomical units
50 unidades F astronómicas
50 unités F astronomiques
50 astronomische Einheiten F
50 unità F astronomiche
Kuiper belt
cinturón M de Kuiper
ceinture F de Kuiper
Kuiper-Gürtel M
cintura F di Kuiper

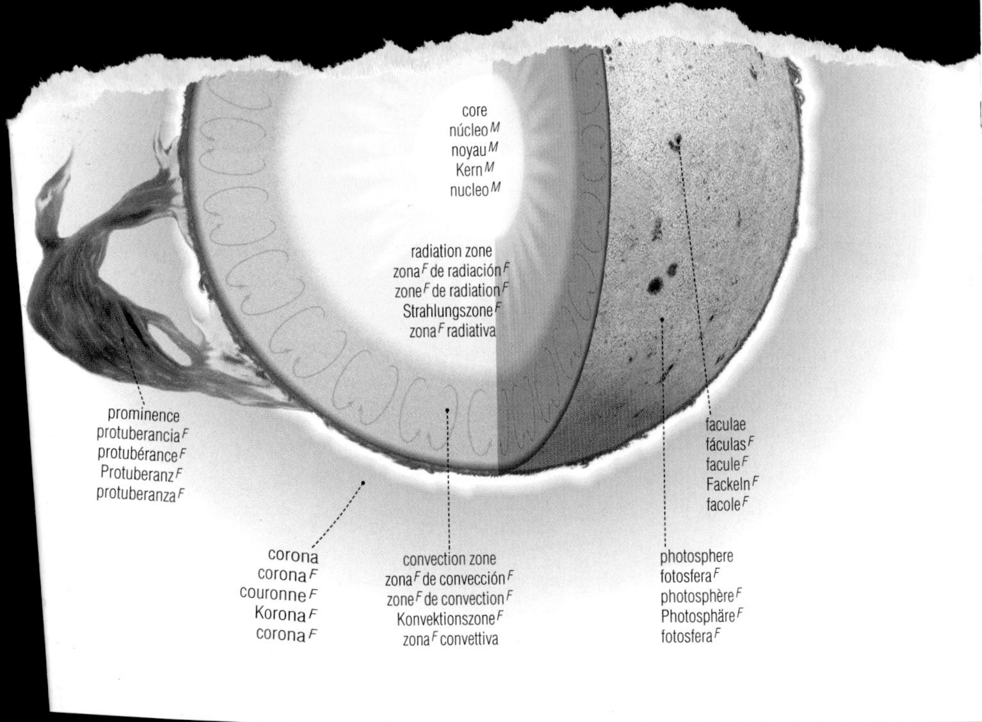
core
núcleo ^{M}
noyau ^{M}
Kern ^{M}
nucleo ^{M}
radiation zone
zona ^{F} de radiación ^{F}
zone ^{F} de radiation ^{F}
Strahlungszone ^{F}
zona ^{F} radiativa
prominence
protuberancia ^{F}
protubérance ^{F}
Protuberanz ^{F}
protuberanza ^{F}
faculae
fáculas ^{F}
facule ^{F}
Fackeln ^{F}
facole ^{F}
corona
corona ^{F}
couronne ^{F}
Korona ^{F}
corona ^{F}
convection zone
zona ^{F} de convección ^{F}
zone ^{F} de convection ^{F}
Konvektionszone ^{F}
zona ^{F} convettiva
photosphere
fotosfera ^{F}
photosphère ^{F}
Photosphäre ^{F}
fotosfera ^{F}

inner planets
planetas ^{M} internos
planètes ^{F} internes
innere Planeten ^{M}
pianeti ^{M} interni

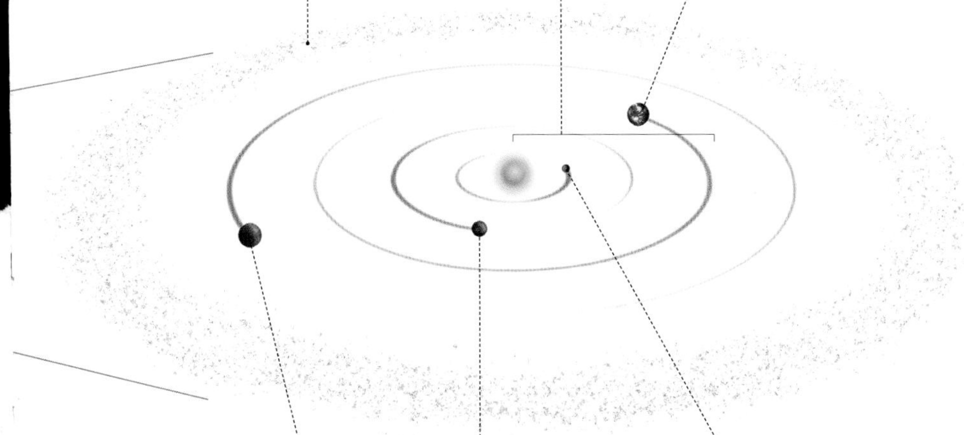
asteroid belt
cinturón ^{M} de asteroides ^{M}
ceinture ^{F} d'astéroïdes ^{M}
Asteroidengürtel ^{M}
fascia ^{F} degli asteroidi ^{M}
1 astronomical unit
1 unidad ^{F} astronómica
1 unité ^{F} astronomique
1 astronomische Einheit ^{F}
1 unità ^{F} astronomica
Earth
Tierra ^{F}
Terre ^{F}
Erde ^{F}
Terra ^{F}
Mars
Marte
Mars
Mars ^{M}
Marte
Venus
Venus
Vénus
Venus ^{F}
Venere
Mercury
Mercurio
Mercure
Merkur ^{M}
Mercurio

planets and satellites

planetas[M] y satélites[M] | planètes[F] et satellites[M] | Planeten[M] und Monde[M] | pianeti[M] e satelliti[M]

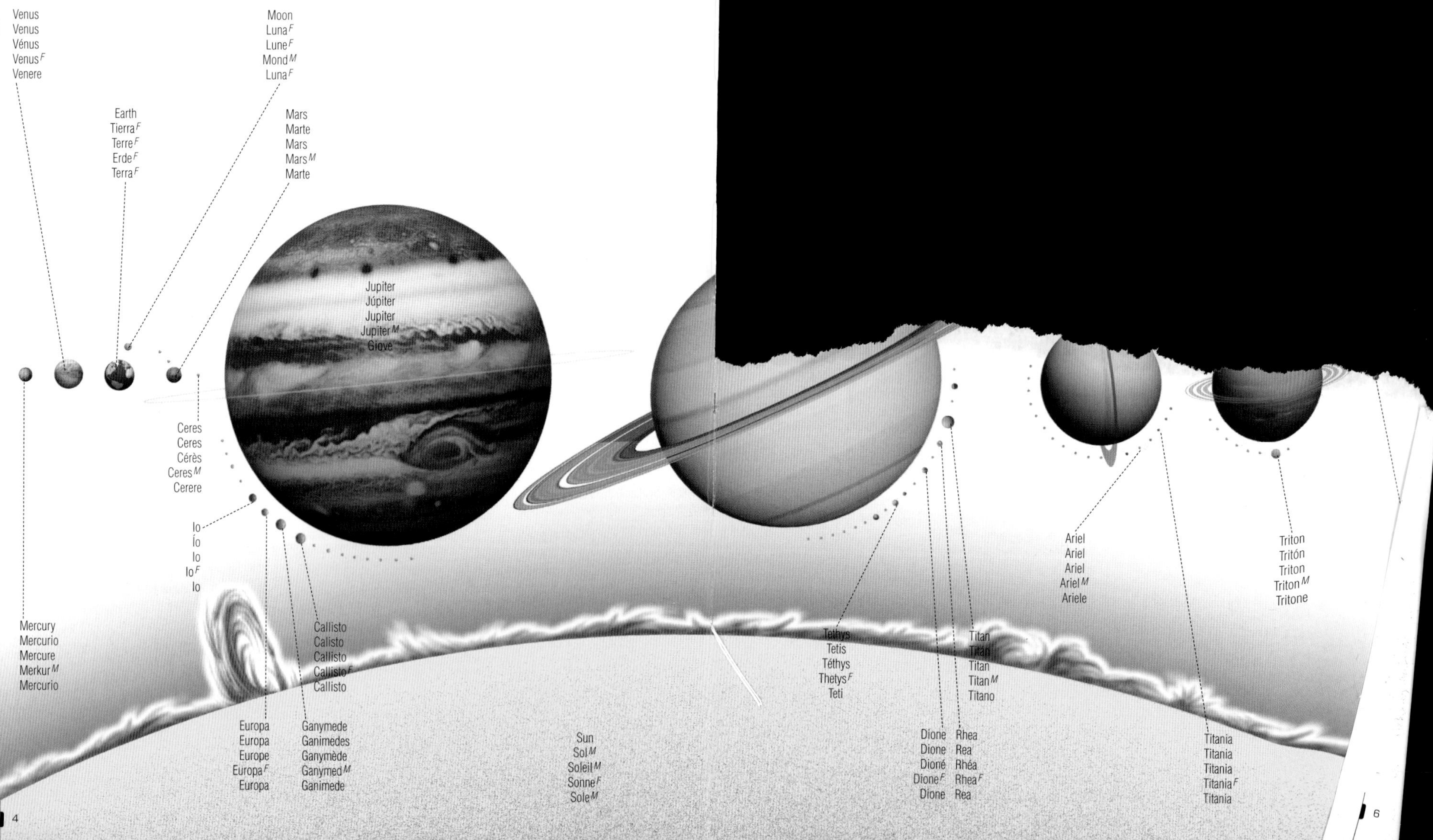

Venus
Venus
Vénus
Venus[F]
Venere
Moon
Luna[F]
Lune[F]
Mond[M]
Luna[F]
Earth
Tierra[F]
Terre[F]
Erde[F]
Terra[F]
Mars
Marte
Mars
Mars[M]
Marte
Jupiter
Júpiter
Jupiter
Jupiter[M]
Giove
Ceres
Ceres
Cérès
Ceres[M]
Cerere
Io
Ío
Io
Io[F]
Io
Mercury
Mercurio
Mercure
Merkur[M]
Mercurio
Callisto
Calisto
Callisto
Callisto[F]
Callisto
Europa
Europa
Europe
Europa[F]
Europa
Ganymede
Ganimedes
Ganymède
Ganymed[M]
Ganimede
Sun
Sol[M]
Soleil[M]
Sonne[F]
Sole[M]
Tethys
Tetis
Téthys
Thetys[F]
Teti
Titan
Titán
Titan
Titan[M]
Titano
Dione
Dione
Dioné
Dione[F]
Dione
Rhea
Rea
Rhéa
Rhea[F]
Rea
Ariel
Ariel
Ariel
Ariel[M]
Ariele
Triton
Tritón
Triton
Triton[M]
Tritone
Titania
Titania
Titania
Titania[F]
Titania

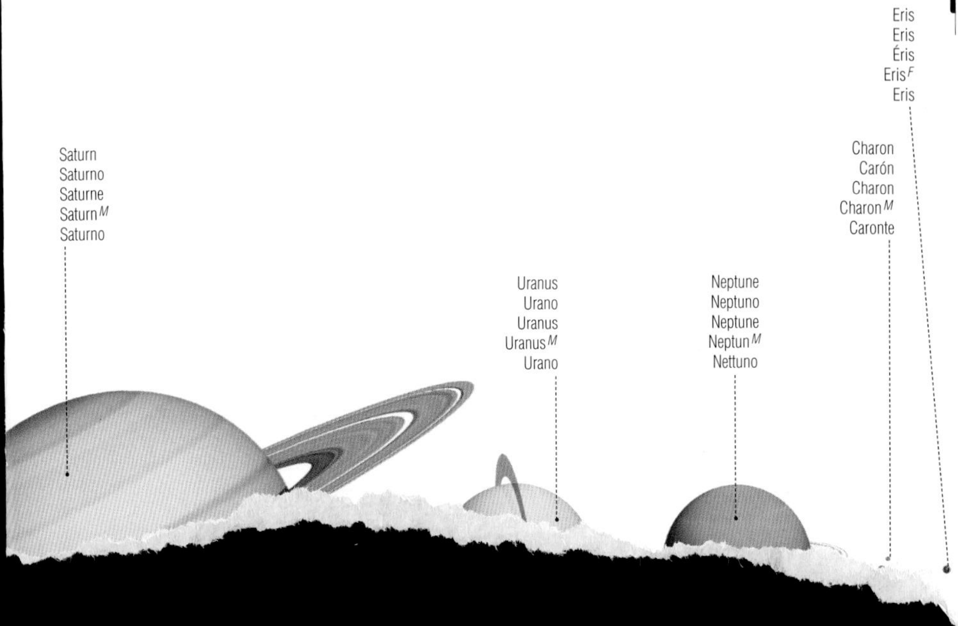
Eris
Eris
Éris
Eris F
Eris
Saturn
Saturno
Saturne
Saturn M
Saturno
Charon
Carón
Charon
Charon M
Caronte
Uranus
Urano
Uranus
Uranus M
Urano
Neptune
Neptuno
Neptune
Neptun M
Nettuno

Sun

Sol^M | Soleil^M | Sonne^F | Sole^M

structure of the Sun
estructura^F del Sol^M
structure^F du Soleil^M
Aufbau^M der Sonne^F
struttura^F del Sole^M

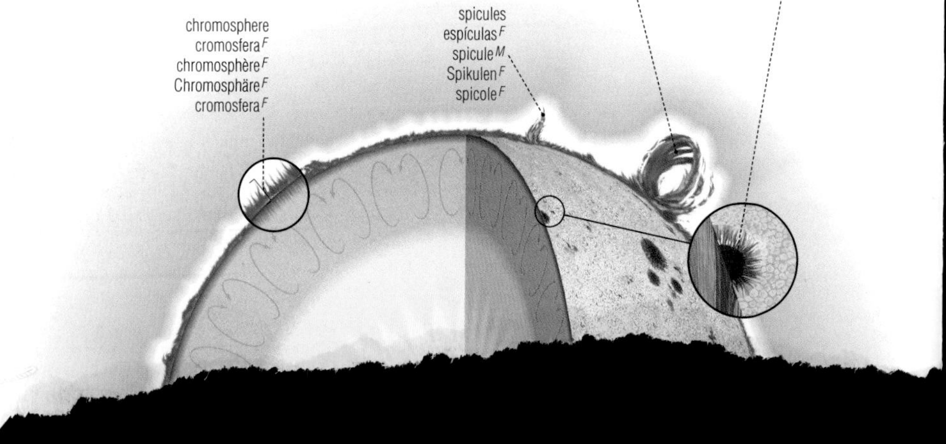

flare
erupción^F
éruption^F
Flare^F
brillamento^M
sunspot
mancha^F solar
tache^F
Sonnenfleck^M
macchia^F solare
chromosphere
cromosfera^F
chromosphère^F
Chromosphäre^F
cromosfera^F
spicules
espículas^F
spicule^M
Spikulen^F
spicole^F

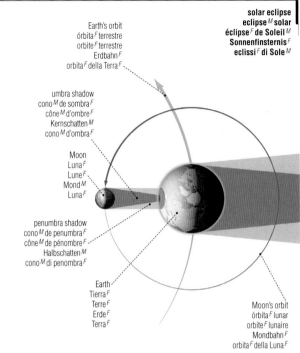

solar eclipse
eclipse M solar
éclipse F de Soleil M
Sonnenfinsternis F
eclissi F di Sole M

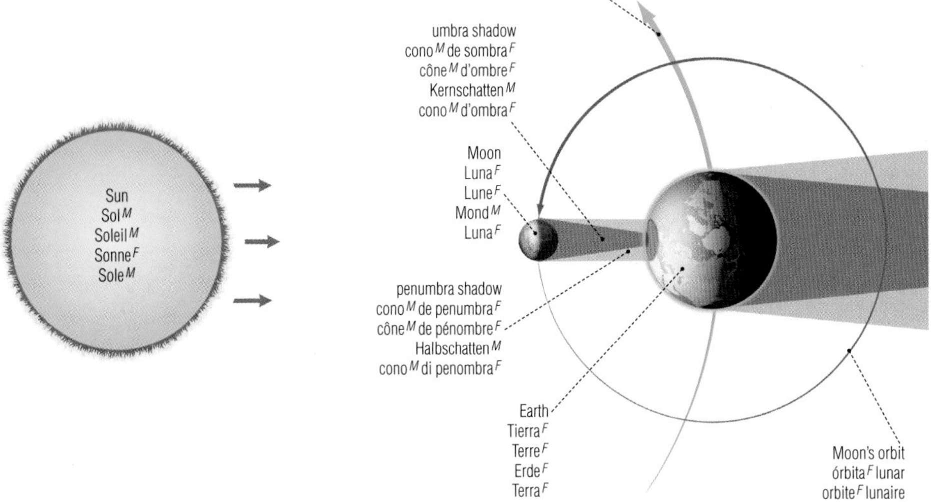
Earth's orbit
órbita F terrestre
orbite F terrestre
Erdbahn F
orbita F della Terra F
umbra shadow
cono M de sombra F
cône M d'ombre F
Kernschatten M
cono M d'ombra F
Moon
Luna F
Lune F
Mond M
Luna F
Sun
Sol M
Soleil M
Sonne F
Sole M
penumbra shadow
cono M de penumbra F
cône M de pénombre F
Halbschatten M
cono M di penombra F
Earth
Tierra F
Terre F
Erde F
Terra F
Moon's orbit
órbita F lunar
orbite F lunaire
Mondbahn F
orbita F della Luna F

types of eclipses
tipos M de eclipses M
types M d'éclipses F
Finsternisarten F
tipi M di eclissi F

eclipse
anular
ulaire
ternis F
re

partial eclipse
eclipse M parcial
éclipse F partielle
partielle Finsternis F
eclissi F parziale

total eclipse
eclipse M total
éclipse F totale
totale Finsternis F
eclissi F totale

Moon

Luna^F | Lune^F | Mond^M | Luna^F

lunar features
superficie^F lunar
relief^M lunaire
Mondoberfläche^F
caratteristiche^F della Luna^F

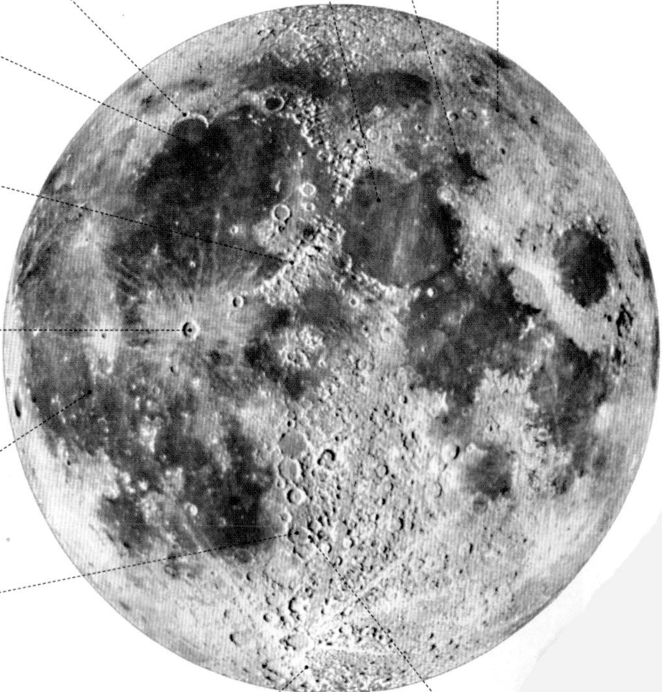

lake
lago^M
lac^M
See^M
lago^M

highland
continente^M
continent^M
Hochland^N
altopiano^M

cliff
risco^M
falaise^F
Felsen^M
scarpata^F

sea
mar^M
mer^F
Meer^N, Mare^N
mare^M

bay
bahía^F
baie^F
Bucht^F
baia^F

mountain range
cordillera^F
chaîne^F de montagnes^F
Bergkette^F
catena^F montuosa

crater
cráter^M
cratère^M
Kraterstrahl^M
cratere^M

ocean
océano^M
océan^M
Ozean^M
oceano^M

cirque
circo^M
cirque^M
Kar^N
circo^M

crater ray
estela^F luminosa del cráter^M
traînée^F lumineuse
Kraterstrahlen^M
scia^F luminosa del cratere^M

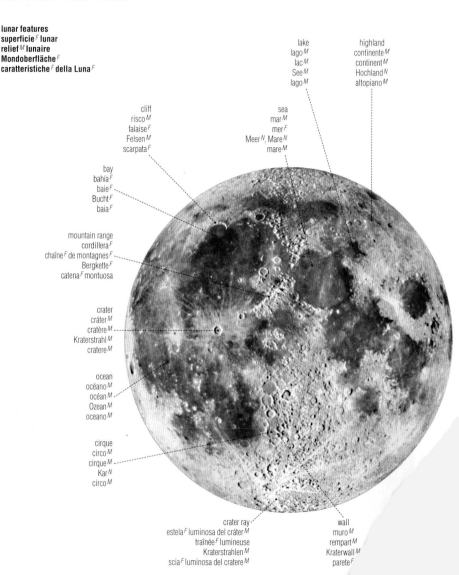

wall
muro^M
rempart^M
Kraterwall^M
parete^F

lunar eclipse
eclipse^M de Luna^F
éclipse^F de Lune^F
Mondfinsternis^F
eclissi^F di Luna^F

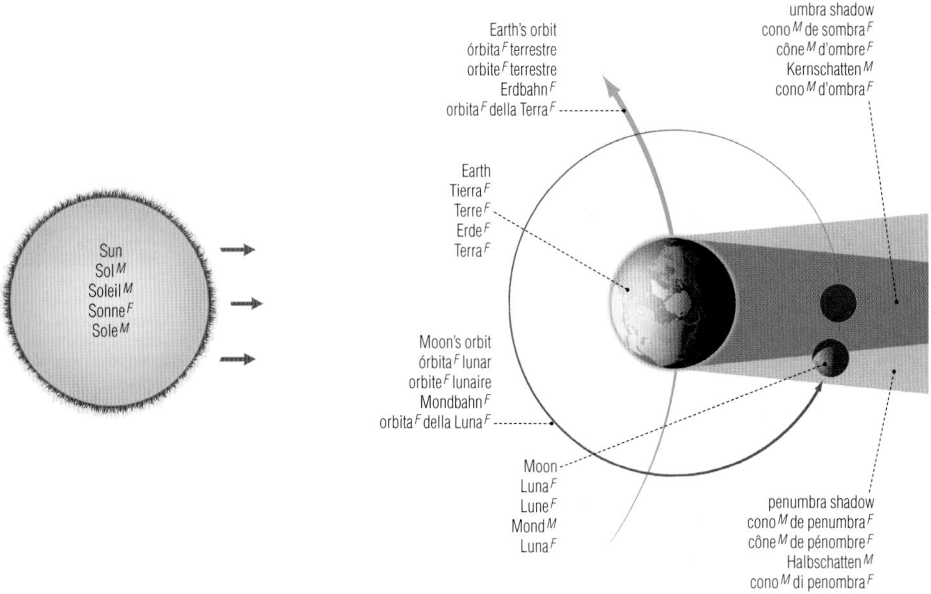
Sun
Sol M
Soleil M
Sonne F
Sole M
Earth's orbit
órbita F terrestre
orbite F terrestre
Erdbahn F
orbita F della Terra F
Earth
Tierra F
Terre F
Erde F
Terra F
Moon's orbit
órbita F lunar
orbite F lunaire
Mondbahn F
orbita F della Luna F
Moon
Luna F
Lune F
Mond M
Luna F
umbra shadow
cono M de sombra F
cône M d'ombre F
Kernschatten M
cono M d'ombra F
penumbra shadow
cono M de penumbra F
cône M de pénombre F
Halbschatten M
cono M di penombra F

types of eclipses
tipos^M de eclipses^M
types^M d'éclipses^F
Finsternisarten^F
tipi^M di eclissi^F

total eclipse
eclipse^M total
éclipse^F totale
totale Finsternis^F
eclissi^F totale

partial eclipse
eclipse^M parcial
éclipse^F partielle
partielle Finsternis^F
eclissi^F parziale

Moon

phases of the Moon
fases^{F} de la Luna^{F}
phases^{F} de la Lune^{F}
Mondphasen^{F}
fasi^{F} della Luna^{F}

new moon
Luna^{F} nueva
nouvelle Lune^{F}
Neumond^{M}
Luna^{F} nuova

new crescent
Luna^{F} creciente
premier croissant^{M}
zunehmende Mondsichel^{F}
Luna^{F} crescente

first quarter
cuarto^{M} creciente
premier quartier^{M}
erstes Viertel^{N}
primo quarto^{M}

waxing gibbous
quinto octante^{M}
gibbeuse^{F} croissante
zunehmender Mond^{M}
Luna^{F} gibbosa crescente

comet

cometa^{M} | comète^{F} | Komet^{M} | cometa^{F}

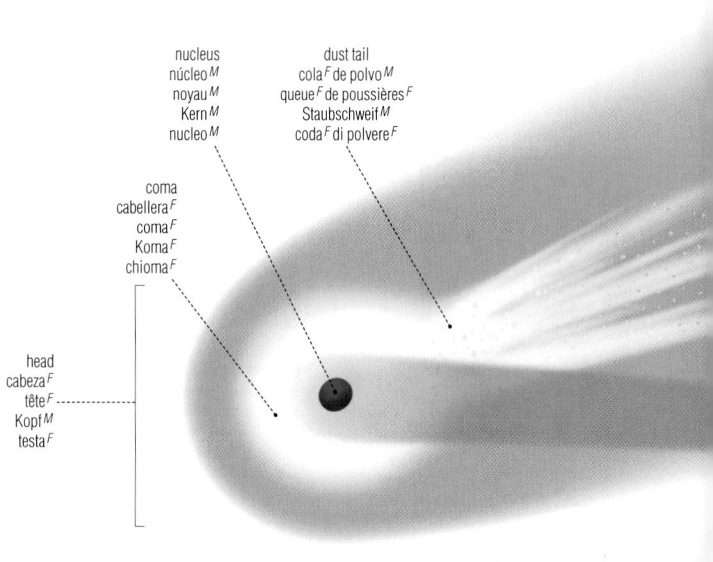
nucleus
núcleo^{M}
noyau^{M}
Kern^{M}
nucleo^{M}
dust tail
cola^{F} de polvo^{M}
queue^{F} de poussières^{F}
Staubschweif^{M}
coda^{F} di polvere^{F}
coma
cabellera^{F}
coma^{F}
Koma^{F}
chioma^{F}
head
cabeza^{F}
tête^{F}
Kopf^{M}
testa^{F}

Moon

full moon
Luna^F llena
pleine Lune^F
Vollmond^M
Luna^F piena

waning gibbous
tercer octante^M
gibbeuse^F décroissante
abnehmender Mond^M
Luna^F gibbosa calante

last quarter
cuarto^M menguante
dernier quartier^M
letztes Viertel^N
ultimo quarto^M

old crescent
Luna^F menguante
dernier croissant^M
abnehmende Mondsichel^F
Luna^F calante

comet

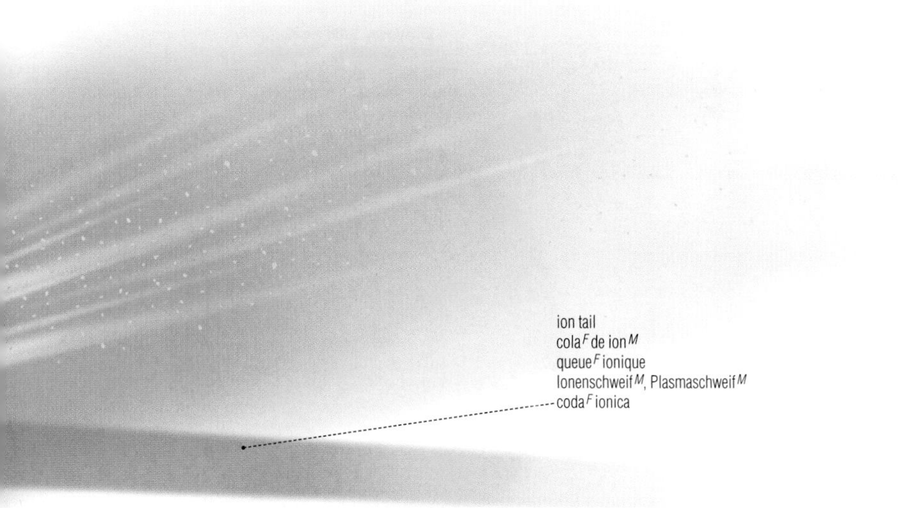
ion tail
cola^F de ion^M
queue^F ionique
Ionenschweif^M, Plasmaschweif^M
coda^F ionica

galaxy

galaxia[F] | galaxie[F] | Galaxie[F] | galassia[F]

Milky Way
Vía[F] Láctea
Voie[F] lactée
Milchstraße[F]
Via[F] Lattea

Milky Way (seen from above)
Vía[F] Láctea (vista[F] desde arriba)
Voie[F] lactée (vue[F] de dessus[M])
Milchstraße[F] (Ansicht[F] von oben)
Via[F] Lattea (vista[F] dall'alto)

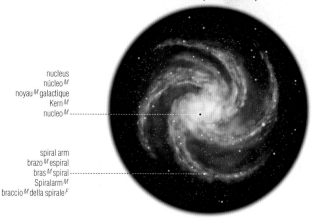

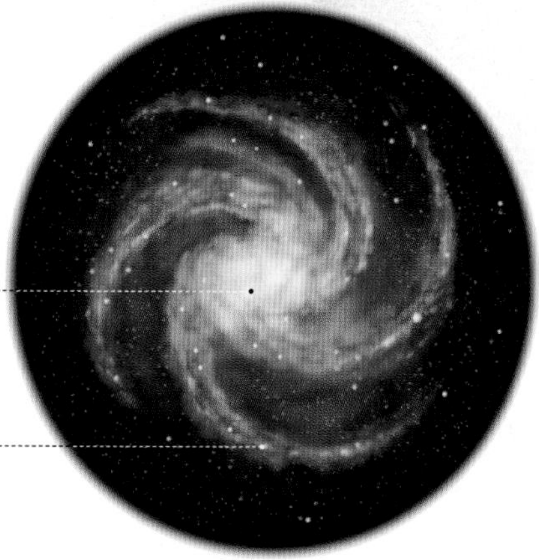
nucleus
núcleo[M]
noyau[M] galactique
Kern[M]
nucleo[M]
spiral arm
brazo[M] espiral
bras[M] spiral
Spiralarm[M]
braccio[M] della spirale[F]

Milky Way (side view)
Vía[F] Láctea (vista[F] lateral)
Voie[F] lactée (vue[F] de profil[M])
Milchstraße[F] (Seitenansicht[F])
Via[F] Lattea (vista[F] laterale)

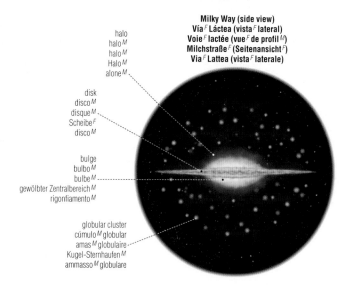

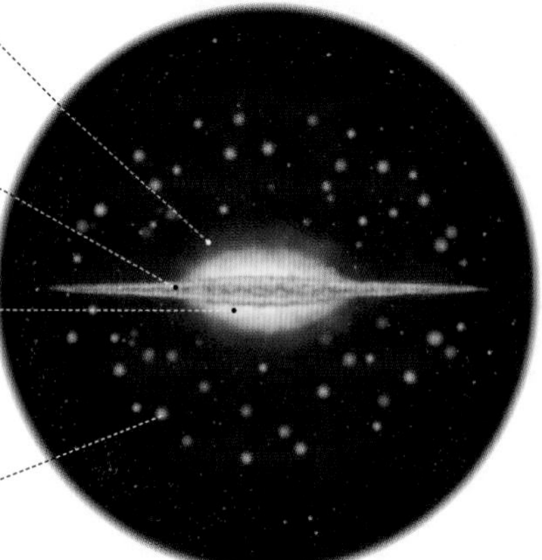
halo
halo[M]
halo[M]
Halo[M]
alone[M]
disk
disco[M]
disque[M]
Scheibe[F]
disco[M]
bulge
bulbo[M]
bulbe[M]
gewölbter Zentralbereich[M]
rigonfiamento[M]
globular cluster
cúmulo[M] globular
amas[M] globulaire
Kugel-Sternhaufen[M]
ammasso[M] globulare

Hubble's classification
clasificación *F* de Hubble
classification *F* de Hubble
Hubblesche Klassifikation *F*
classificazione *F* di Hubble

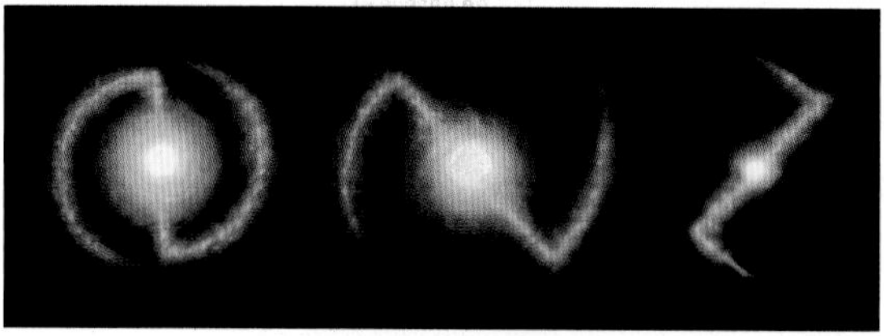

barred spiral galaxy
galaxia *F* espiral barrada
galaxie *F* spirale barrée
Balkenspiralgalaxie *F*
galassia *F* a spirale *F* barrata

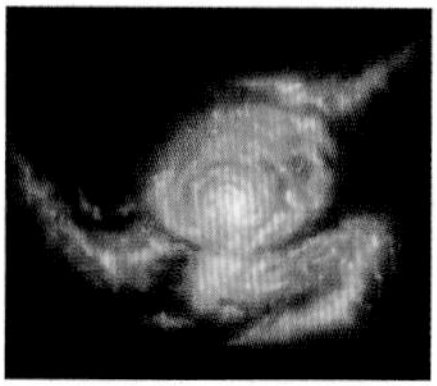

type I irregular galaxy
galaxia *F* irregular de tipo *M* I
galaxie *F* irrégulière de type *M* I
irreguläre Galaxie *F* Typ *M* I
galassia *F* irregolare di tipo *M* I

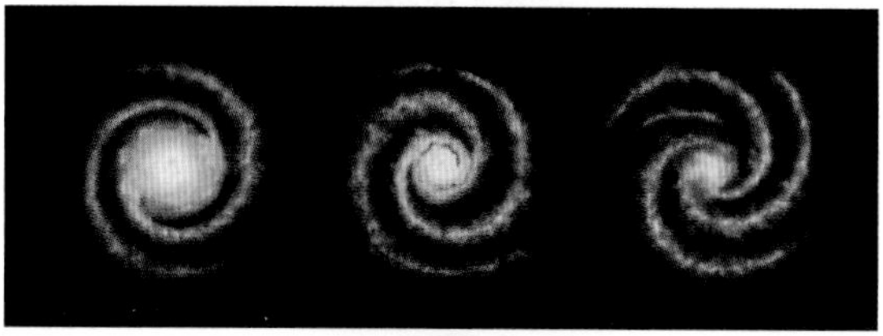

normal spiral galaxy
galaxia *F* espiral normal
galaxie *F* spirale normale
normale Spiralgalaxie *F*
galassia *F* a spirale *F* normale

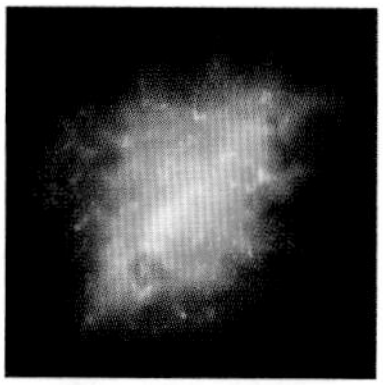

type II irregular galaxy
galaxia *F* irregular de tipo *M* II
galaxie *F* irrégulière de type *M* II
irreguläre Galaxie *F* Typ *M* II
galassia *F* irregolare di tipo *M* II

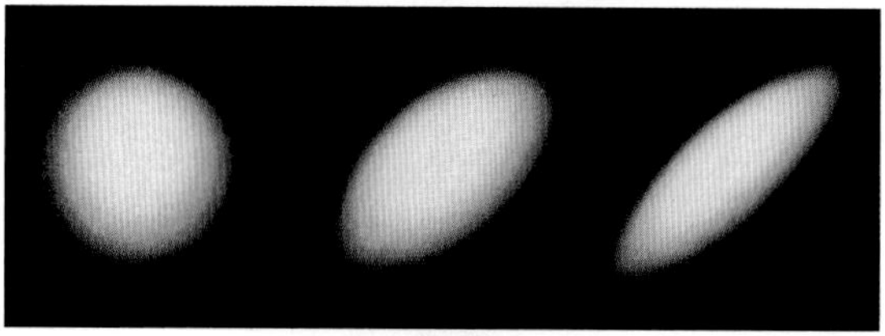

elliptical galaxy
galaxia *F* elíptica
galaxie *F* elliptique
elliptische Galaxie *F*
galassia *F* ellittica

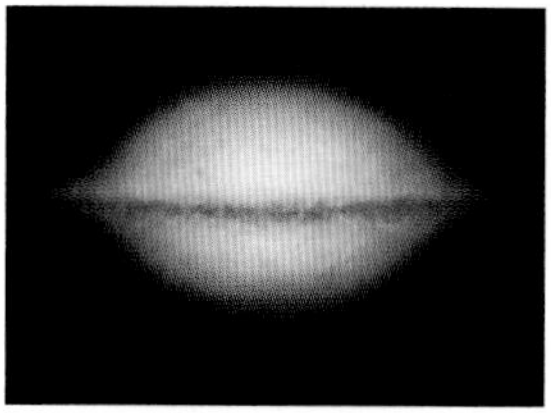

lenticular galaxy
galaxia *F* lenticular
galaxie *F* lenticulaire
linsenförmige Galaxie *F*
galassia *F* lenticolare

reflecting telescope

telescopio[M] reflector | télescope[M] | Spiegelteleskop[N] | telescopio[M]

eyepiece
ocular[M]
oculaire[M]
Okular[N]
oculare[M]
right ascension setting scale
anillo[M] graduado de ascensión[F] recta
cercle[M] d'ascension[F] droite
Einstellung der Rektaszensionsachse[F]
cerchio[M] graduato dell'ascensione[F] retta
finderscope
anteojo[M] buscador
chercheur[M]
Suchfernrohr[N]
cannocchiale[M] cercatore
main tube
tubo[M] principal
tube[M]
Tubus[M]
tubo[M] principale
focusing knob
botón[M] de enfoque[M]
bouton[M] de mise[F] au point[M]
Scharfeinstellung[F]
manopola[F] della messa[F] a fuoco[M]
declination setting scale
anillo[M] graduado de declinación[F]
cercle[M] de déclinaison[F]
Einstellung[F] der Deklinationsachse[F]
cerchio[M] graduato della declinazione[F]
azimuth clamp
palanca[F] de bloqueo[M] del acimut[M]
vis[F] de blocage[M] (azimut[M])
Azimutfeststeller[M]
leva[F] di bloccaggio[M] dell'asse[M] orizzontale
altitude clamp
palanca[F] de bloqueo[M] de la altura[F]
vis[F] de blocage[M] (latitude[F])
Höhenfeststeller[M]
leva[F] di bloccaggio[M] dell'altezza[F]
altitude fine adjustment
ajuste[M] fino de la altura[F]
réglage[M] micrométrique (latitude[F])
Höhenfeineinstellung[F]
regolazione[F] micrometrica dell'altezza[F]
azimuth fine adjustment
ajuste[M] fino del acimut[M]
réglage[M] micrométrique (azimut[M])
Azimutfeineinstellung[F]
regolazione[F] micrometrica dell'asse[M] orizzontale

refracting telescope

telescopio^{M} refractor | lunette^{F} astronomique | Linsenfernrohr^{N} | cannocchiale^{M}

eyepiece
ocular^{M}
oculaire^{M}
Okular^{N}
oculare^{M}
finderscope
anteojo^{M} buscador
chercheur^{M}
Suchfernrohr^{N}
cannocchiale^{M} cercatore
main tube
tubo^{M} principal
tube^{M}
Tubus^{M}
tubo^{M} principale
declination setting scale
círculo^{M} graduado de declinación^{F}
cercle^{M} de déclinaison^{F}
Einstellung^{F} der Deklinationsachse^{F}
cerchio^{M} graduato della declinazione^{F}
azimuth clamp
palanca^{F} de bloqueo^{M} del acimut^{M}
vis^{F} de blocage^{M} (azimut^{M})
Azimutfesteller^{M}
leva^{F} di bloccaggio^{M} dell'asse^{M} orizzontale
altitude clamp
palanca^{F} de bloqueo^{M} de la altura^{F}
vis^{F} de blocage^{M} (latitude^{F})
Höhenfeststeller^{M}
leva^{F} di bloccaggio^{M} dell'altezza^{F}
right ascension setting scale
anillo^{M} graduado de ascensión^{F} recta
cercle^{M} d'ascension^{F} droite
Einstellung^{F} der Rektaszensionsachse^{F}
cerchio^{M} graduato dell'ascensione^{F} retta
tripod
trípode^{M}
trépied^{M}
Stativ^{N}
treppiede^{M}
azimuth fine adjustment
ajuste^{M} fino del acimut^{M}
réglage^{M} micrométrique (azimut^{M})
Azimutfeineinstellung^{F}
regolazione^{F} micrometrica dell'asse^{M} orizzontale
altitude fine adjustment
ajuste^{M} fino de la altura^{F}
réglage^{M} micrométrique (latitude^{F})
Höhenfeineinstellung^{F}
regolazione^{F} micrometrica dell'altezza^{F}

astronomical observatory

observatorio[M] astronómico | observatoire[M] astronomique | Sternwarte[F] | osservatorio[M] astronomico

cross section of an astronomical observatory
sección[F] transversal de un observatorio[M] astronómico
coupe[F] d'un observatoire[M] astronomique
Querschnitt[M] durch eine Sternwarte[F]
sezione[F] trasversale di un osservatorio[M] astronomico

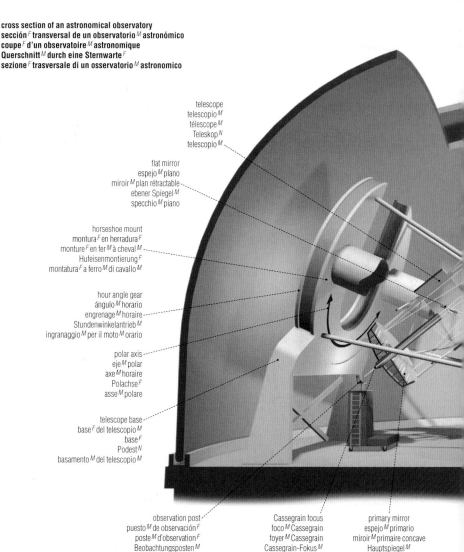

telescope
telescopio[M]
télescope[M]
Teleskop[N]
telescopio[M]
flat mirror
espejo[M] plano
miroir[M] plan rétractable
ebener Spiegel[M]
specchio[M] piano
horseshoe mount
montura[F] en herradura[F]
monture[F] en fer[M] à cheval[M]
Hufeisenmontierung[F]
montatura[F] a ferro[M] di cavallo[M]
hour angle gear
ángulo[M] horario
engrenage[M] horaire
Stundenwinkelantrieb[M]
ingranaggio[M] per il moto[M] orario
polar axis
eje[M] polar
axe[M] horaire
Polachse[F]
asse[M] polare
telescope base
base[F] del telescopio[M]
base[F]
Podest[N]
basamento[M] del telescopio[M]
observation post
puesto[M] de observación[F]
poste[M] d'observation[F]
Beobachtungsposten[M]
punto[M] di osservazione[F]
Cassegrain focus
foco[M] Cassegrain
foyer[M] Cassegrain
Cassegrain-Fokus[M]
fuoco[M] Cassegrain
primary mirror
espejo[M] primario
miroir[M] primaire concave
Hauptspiegel[M]
specchio[M] primario

observatory
observatorio[M]
observatoire[M]
Sternwarte[F]
osservatorio[M]
dome shutter
obturador[M] de la cúpula[F]
cimier[M] mobile
Kuppelspaltabdeckung[F]
portellone[M] della cupola[F]
rotating dome
cúpula[F] giratoria
coupole[F] rotative
Drehkuppel[F]
cupola[F] rotante

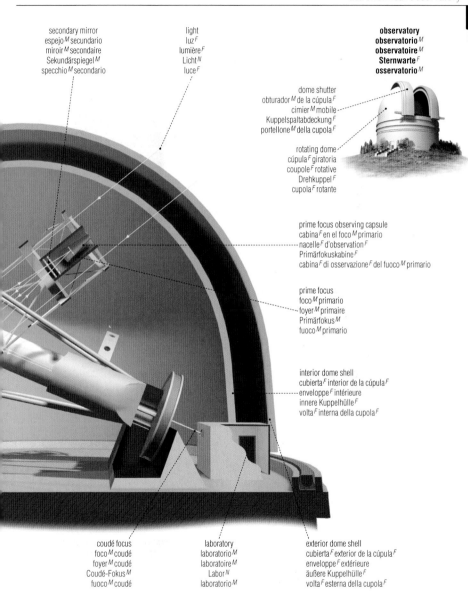

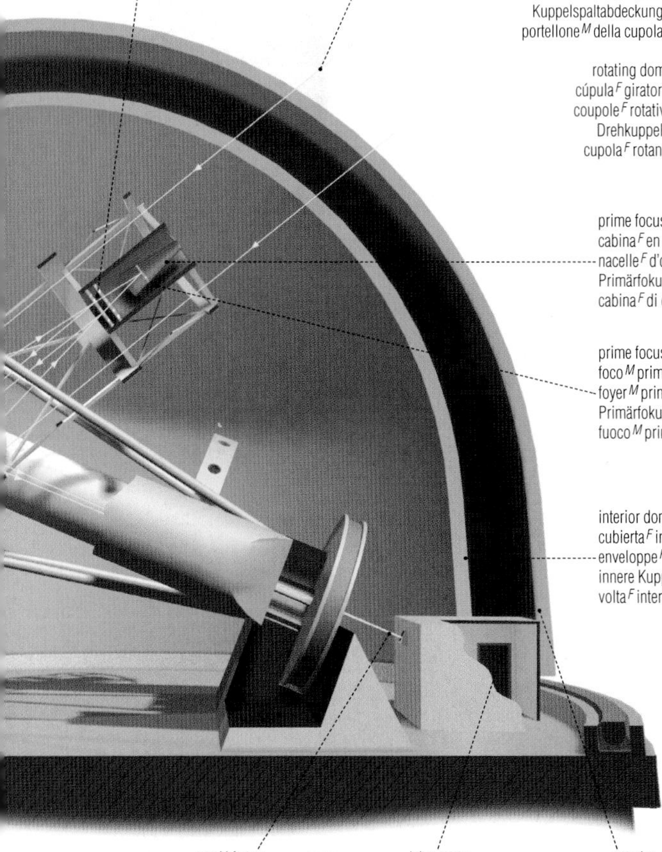
secondary mirror
espejo[M] secundario
miroir[M] secondaire
Sekundärspiegel[M]
specchio[M] secondario
light
luz[F]
lumière[F]
Licht[N]
luce[F]
prime focus observing capsule
cabina[F] en el foco[M] primario
nacelle[F] d'observation[F]
Primärfokuskabine[F]
cabina[F] di osservazione[F] del fuoco[M] primario
prime focus
foco[M] primario
foyer[M] primaire
Primärfokus[M]
fuoco[M] primario
interior dome shell
cubierta[F] interior de la cúpula[F]
enveloppe[F] intérieure
innere Kuppelhülle[F]
volta[F] interna della cupola[F]
coudé focus
foco[M] coudé
foyer[M] coudé
Coudé-Fokus[M]
fuoco[M] coudé
laboratory
laboratorio[M]
laboratoire[M]
Labor[N]
laboratorio[M]
exterior dome shell
cubierta[F] exterior de la cúpula[F]
enveloppe[F] extérieure
äußere Kuppelhülle[F]
volta[F] esterna della cupola[F]

Hubble space telescope

telescopio^{M} espacial Hubble | télescope^{M} spatial Hubble | Hubble-Weltraumteleskop^{N} | telescopio^{M} spaziale Hubble

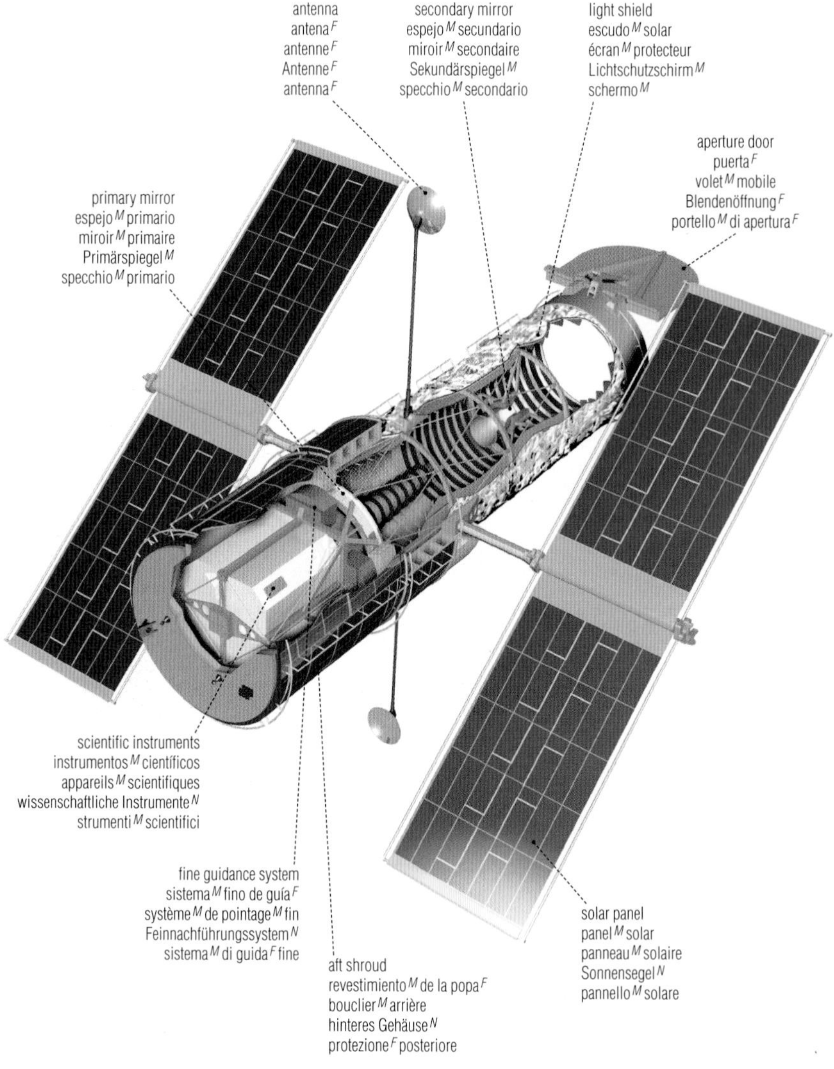
antenna
antena F
antenne F
Antenne F
antenna F
secondary mirror
espejo M secundario
miroir M secondaire
Sekundärspiegel M
specchio M secondario
light shield
escudo M solar
écran M protecteur
Lichtschutzschirm M
schermo M
aperture door
puerta F
volet M mobile
Blendenöffnung F
portello M di apertura F
primary mirror
espejo M primario
miroir M primaire
Primärspiegel M
specchio M primario
scientific instruments
instrumentos M científicos
appareils M scientifiques
wissenschaftliche Instrumente N
strumenti M scientifici
fine guidance system
sistema M fino de guía F
système M de pointage M fin
Feinnachführungssystem N
sistema M di guida F fine
solar panel
panel M solar
panneau M solaire
Sonnensegel N
pannello M solare
aft shroud
revestimiento M de la popa F
bouclier M arrière
hinteres Gehäuse N
protezione F posteriore

celestial coordinate system

sistema^M de coordenadas^F astronómicas | coordonnées^F célestes | Koordinatensystem^N der Himmelskugel^F | sistema^M di coordinate^F celesti

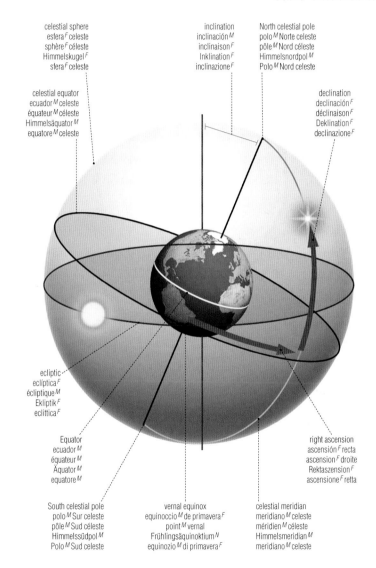

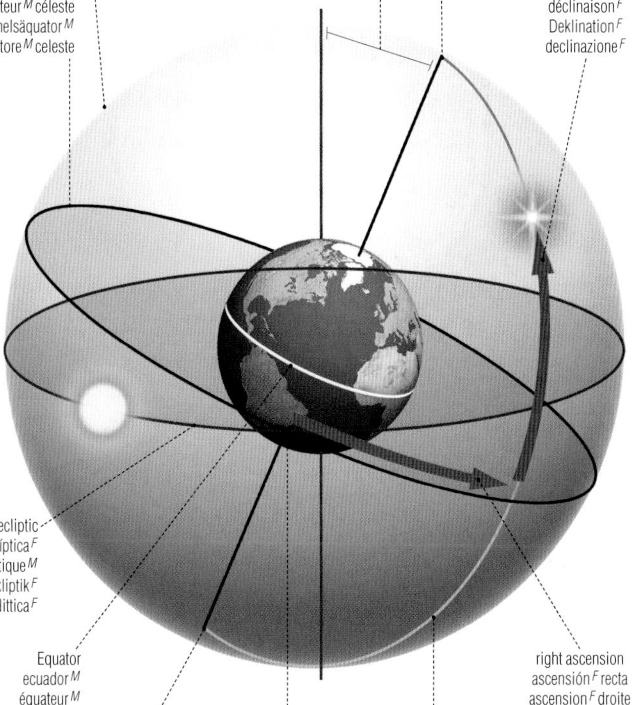
celestial sphere
esfera^F celeste
sphère^F céleste
Himmelskugel^F
sfera^F celeste
inclination
inclinación^M
inclinaison^F
Inklination^F
inclinazione^F
North celestial pole
polo^M Norte celeste
pôle^M Nord céleste
Himmelsnordpol^M
Polo^M Nord celeste
celestial equator
ecuador^M celeste
équateur^M céleste
Himmelsäquator^M
equatore^M celeste
declination
declinación^F
déclinaison^F
Deklination^F
declinazione^F
ecliptic
eclíptica^F
écliptique^M
Ekliptik^F
eclittica^F
Equator
ecuador^M
équateur^M
Äquator^M
equatore^M
right ascension
ascensión^F recta
ascension^F droite
Rektaszension^F
ascensione^F retta
South celestial pole
polo^M Sur celeste
pôle^M Sud céleste
Himmelssüdpol^M
Polo^M Sud celeste
vernal equinox
equinoccio^M de primavera^F
point^M vernal
Frühlingsäquinoktium^N
equinozio^M di primavera^F
celestial meridian
meridiano^M celeste
méridien^M céleste
Himmelsmeridian^M
meridiano^M celeste

spacesuit

traje^{M} espacial | scaphandre^{M} spatial | Raumanzug^{M} | tuta^{F} spaziale

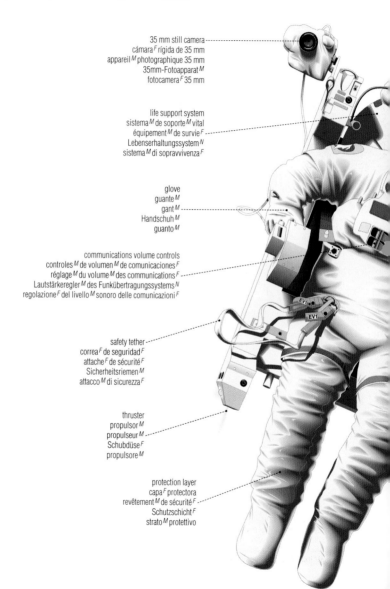

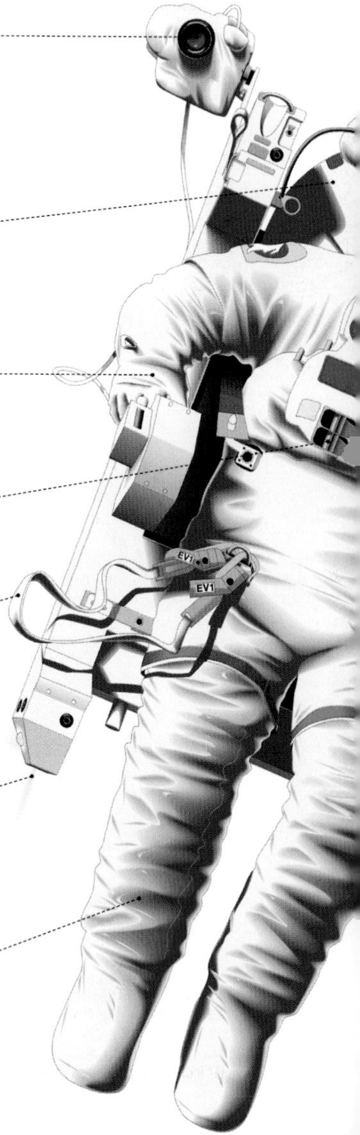
35 mm still camera
cámara^{F} rígida de 35 mm
appareil^{M} photographique 35 mm
35mm-Fotoapparat^{M}
fotocamera^{F} 35 mm
life support system
sistema^{M} de soporte^{M} vital
équipement^{M} de survie^{F}
Lebenserhaltungssystem^{N}
sistema^{M} di sopravvivenza^{F}
glove
guante^{M}
gant^{M}
Handschuh^{M}
guanto^{M}
communications volume controls
controles^{M} de volumen^{M} de comunicaciones^{F}
réglage^{M} du volume^{M} des communications^{F}
Lautstärkeregler^{M} des Funkübertragungssystems^{N}
regolazione^{F} del livello^{M} sonoro delle comunicazioni^{F}
safety tether
correa^{F} de seguridad^{F}
attache^{F} de sécurité^{F}
Sicherheitsriemen^{M}
attacco^{M} di sicurezza^{F}
thruster
propulsor^{M}
propulseur^{M}
Schubdüse^{F}
propulsore^{M}
protection layer
capa^{F} protectora
revêtement^{M} de sécurité^{F}
Schutzschicht^{F}
strato^{M} protettivo
EV1
EV1

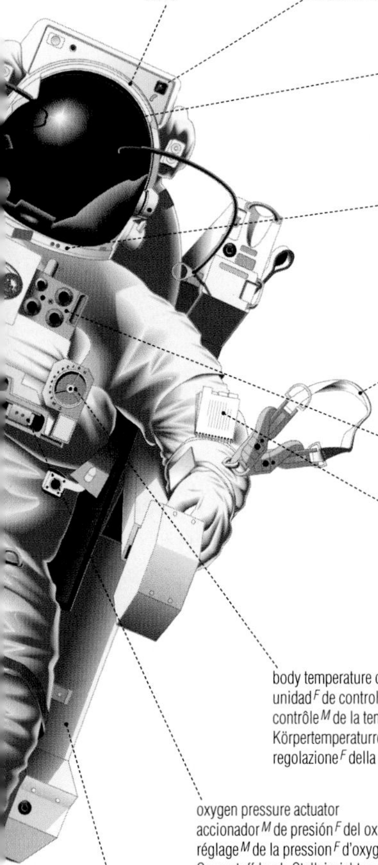

helmet
casco M
casque M
Helm M
casco M

color television camera
cámara F de televisión F en color M
caméra F de télévision F couleur F
Farbfernsehkamera F
telecamera F a colori M

solar shield
protector M solar
visière F antisolaire
Sonnenschutzschicht F
visiera F antisolare

helmet ring
anillo M de unión F del casco M
collier M de serrage M du casque M
Ringverschluss M
collare M di chiusura F del casco M

tool tether
correa F para herramientas F
attache F pour outils M
Werkzeughalter M
attacco M per attrezzi M

life support system controls
controles M del sistema M de soporte M vital
contrôles M de l'équipement M de survie F
Steuerung F des Lebenserhaltungssystems N
regolazione F del sistema M di sopravvivenza F

procedure checklist
lista F de procedimientos M
aide-mémoire M des procédures F
Checkliste F
lista F di controllo M delle procedure F

body temperature control unit
unidad F de control M de la temperatura F del cuerpo M
contrôle M de la température F du corps M
Körpertemperaturregelung F
regolazione F della temperatura F corporea

oxygen pressure actuator
accionador M de presión F del oxígeno M
réglage M de la pression F d'oxygène M
Sauerstoffdruck-Stelleinrichtung F
regolazione F della pressione F dell'ossigeno M

manned maneuvering unit
unidad F para maniobras F en el espacio M
véhicule M spatial autonome
bemannte Manövriereinheit F
unità F individuale di propulsione F e manovra F

international space station

estación[F] espacial internacional | station[F] spatiale internationale | internationale Raumstation[F] | stazione[F] spaziale internazionale

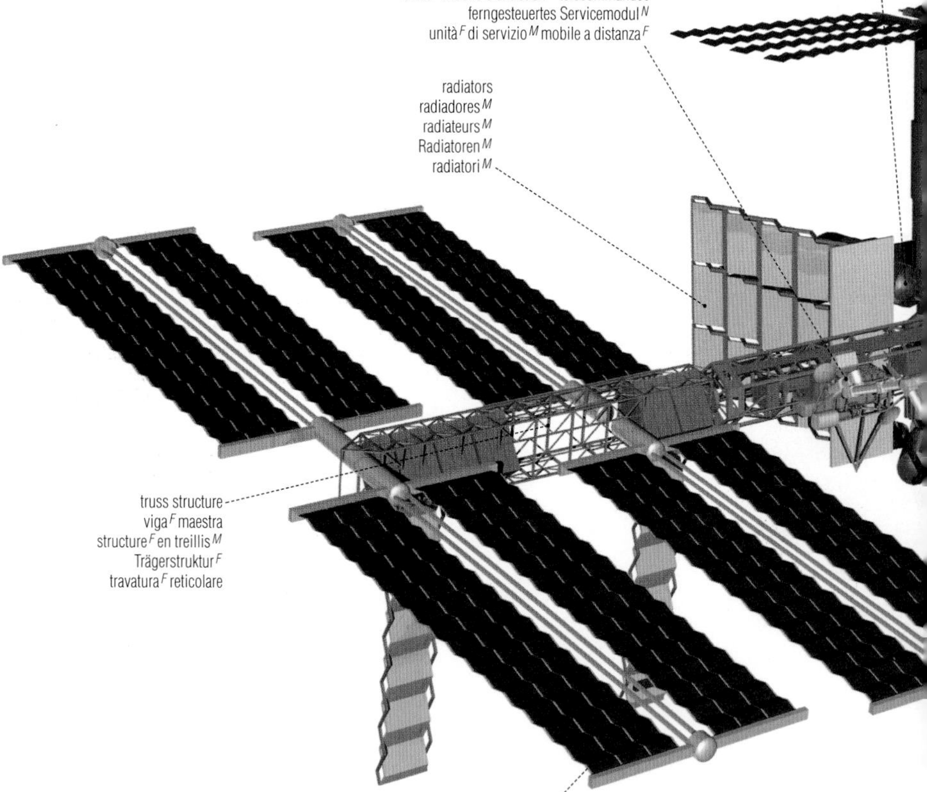

Russian module
módulo[M] ruso
module[M] russe
russisches Modul[N]
modulo[M] russo
mobile remote servicer
unidad[F] móvil de servicio[M] por control[M] remoto
unité[F] mobile d'entretien[M] télécommandée
ferngesteuertes Servicemodul[N]
unità[F] di servizio[M] mobile a distanza[F]
radiators
radiadores[M]
radiateurs[M]
Radiatoren[M]
radiatori[M]
truss structure
viga[F] maestra
structure[F] en treillis[M]
Trägerstruktur[F]
travatura[F] reticolare
photovoltaic arrays
paneles[M] fotovoltaicos
panneaux[M] solaires
Solarzellengenerator[M]
moduli[M] fotovoltaici

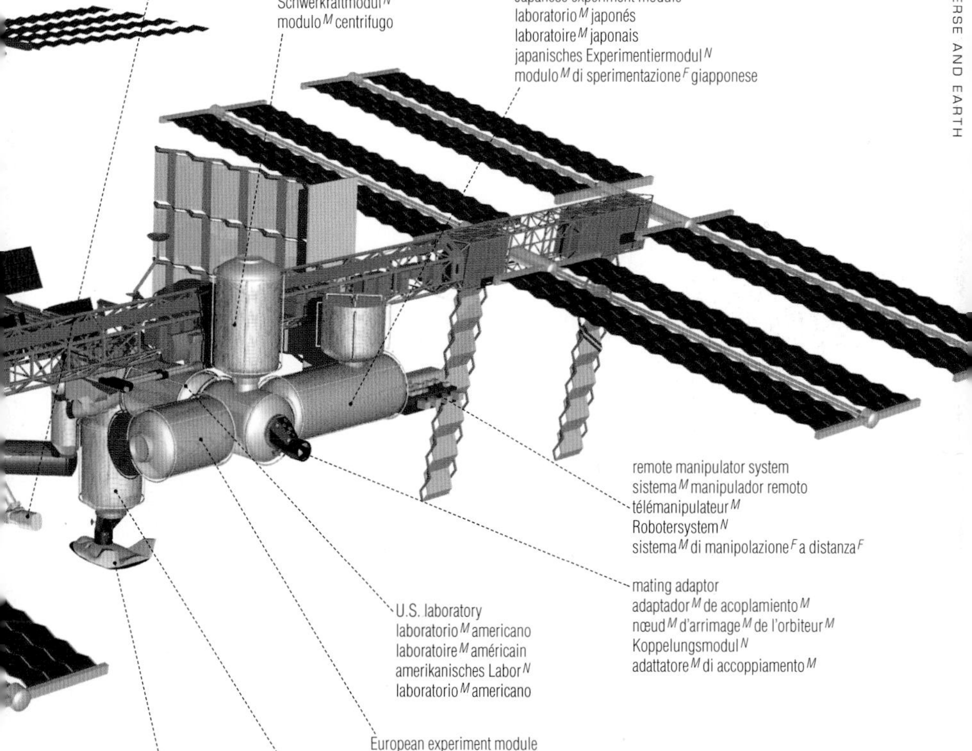
remote manipulator system
brazo[M] por control[M] remoto
télémanipulateur[M]
Roboterarm[M]
braccio[M] telecomandato
centrifuge module
módulo[M] centrífugo
centrifugeuse[F]
Schwerkraftmodul[N]
modulo[M] centrifugo
Japanese experiment module
laboratorio[M] japonés
laboratoire[M] japonais
japanisches Experimentiermodul[N]
modulo[M] di sperimentazione[F] giapponese
remote manipulator system
sistema[M] manipulador remoto
télémanipulateur[M]
Robotersystem[N]
sistema[M] di manipolazione[F] a distanza[F]
mating adaptor
adaptador[M] de acoplamiento[M]
nœud[M] d'arrimage[M] de l'orbiteur[M]
Koppelungsmodul[N]
adattatore[M] di accoppiamento[M]
U.S. laboratory
laboratorio[M] americano
laboratoire[M] américain
amerikanisches Labor[N]
laboratorio[M] americano
European experiment module
laboratorio[M] europeo
laboratoire[M] européen
europäisches Experimentiermodul[N]
modulo[M] di sperimentazione[F] europeo
crew return vehicle
vehículo[M] de emergencia[F] para los tripulantes[M]
véhicule[M] de sauvetage[M]
Evakuierungskapsel[F]
veicolo[M] d'emergenza[F] per l'equipaggio[M]
U.S. habitation module
módulo[M] de habitación[F] americano
module[M] d'habitation[F] américain
amerikanisches Wohnmodul[N]
modulo[M] abitativo americano

space shuttle

transbordador^{M} espacial | navette^{F} spatiale | Raumfähre^{F} | navetta^{F} spaziale

orbiter
orbitador^{M}
orbiteur^{M}
Orbiter^{M}
orbiter^{M}

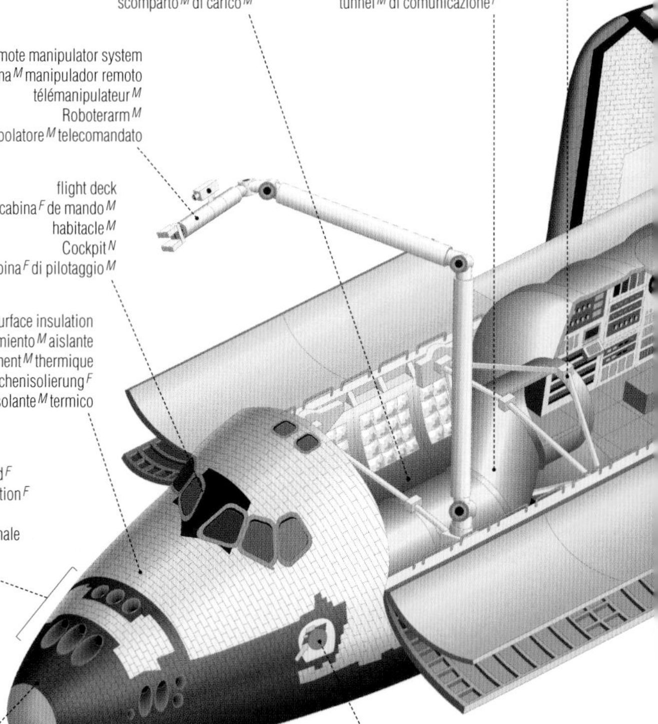

hatch
escotilla F
écoutille F
Einstiegsluke F
boccaporto M
cargo bay
bodega F de carga F
soute F
Nutzlastraum M
scomparto M di carico M
communication tunnel
túnel M de comunicación F
tunnel M de communication F
Verbindungstunnel M
tunnel M di comunicazione F
remote manipulator system
sistema M manipulador remoto
télémanipulateur M
Roboterarm M
braccio M manipolatore M telecomandato
flight deck
cabina F de mando M
habitacle M
Cockpit N
cabina F di pilotaggio M
surface insulation
recubrimiento M aislante
revêtement M thermique
Oberflächenisolierung F
isolante M termico
attitude control thrusters
propulsores M de control M de actitud F
propulseurs M de commande F d'orientation F
vorderes Rückstoßtriebwerk N
propulsori M per il controllo M direzionale
heat shield
cubierta F térmica
bouclier M thermique
Hitzeschild N
scudo M termico
side hatch
escotilla F
écoutille F d'accès M
Seitenluke F
portellone M laterale

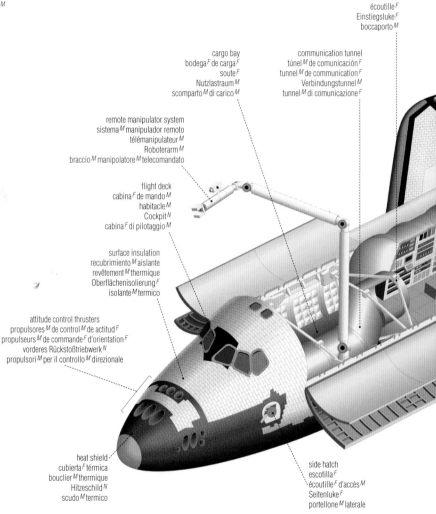

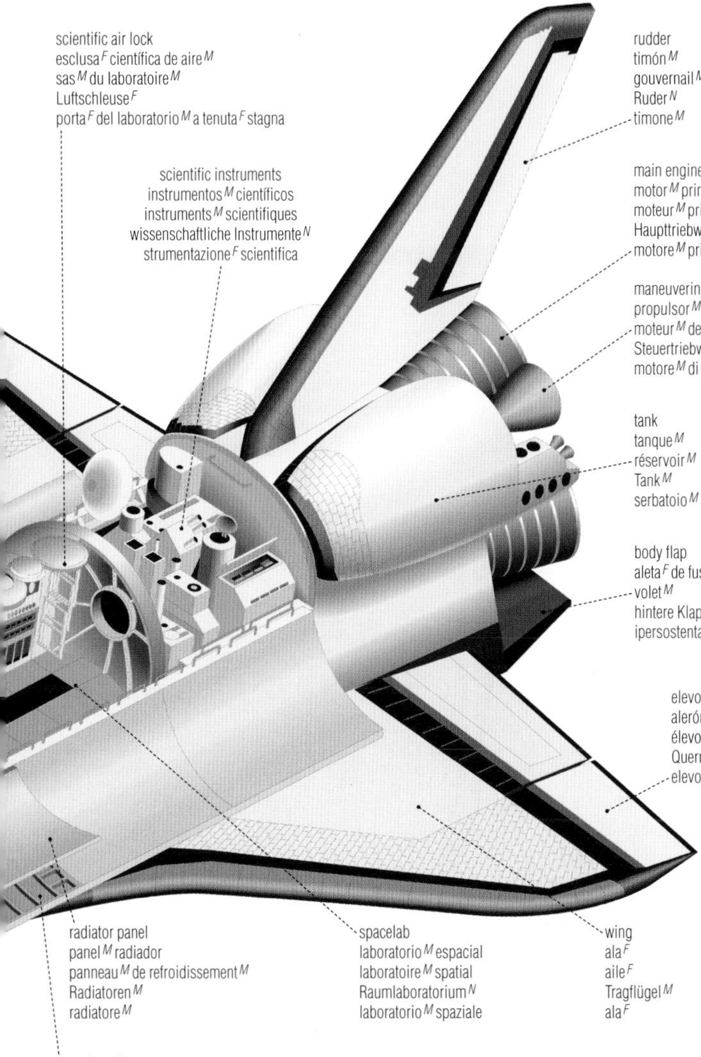
scientific air lock
esclusa F científica de aire M
sas M du laboratoire M
Luftschleuse F
porta F del laboratorio M a tenuta F stagna
scientific instruments
instrumentos M científicos
instruments M scientifiques
wissenschaftliche Instrumente N
strumentazione F scientifica
rudder
timón M
gouvernail M
Ruder N
timone M
main engine
motor M principal
moteur M principal
Haupttriebwerk N
motore M principale
maneuvering engine
propulsor M de maniobras F
moteur M de manœuvre F
Steuertriebwerk N
motore M di manovra F
tank
tanque M
réservoir M
Tank M
serbatoio M
body flap
aleta F de fuselaje M
volet M
hintere Klappe F
ipersostentatore M
elevon
alerón M
élevon M
Querruder N
elevone M
radiator panel
panel M radiador
panneau M de refroidissement M
Radiatoren M
radiatore M
spacelab
laboratorio M espacial
laboratoire M spatial
Raumlaboratorium N
laboratorio M spaziale
wing
ala F
aile F
Tragflügel M
ala F
cargo bay door
puerta F de la bodega F de carga F
porte F de la soute F
Tür F zum Nutzlastraum M
portellone M dello scomparto M di carico M

space shuttle

space shuttle at takeoff
transbordador^{M} espacial en posición^{F} de lanzamiento^{M}
navette^{F} spatiale au décollage^{M}
Raumfähre^{F} beim Start^{M}
navetta^{F} spaziale al decollo^{M}

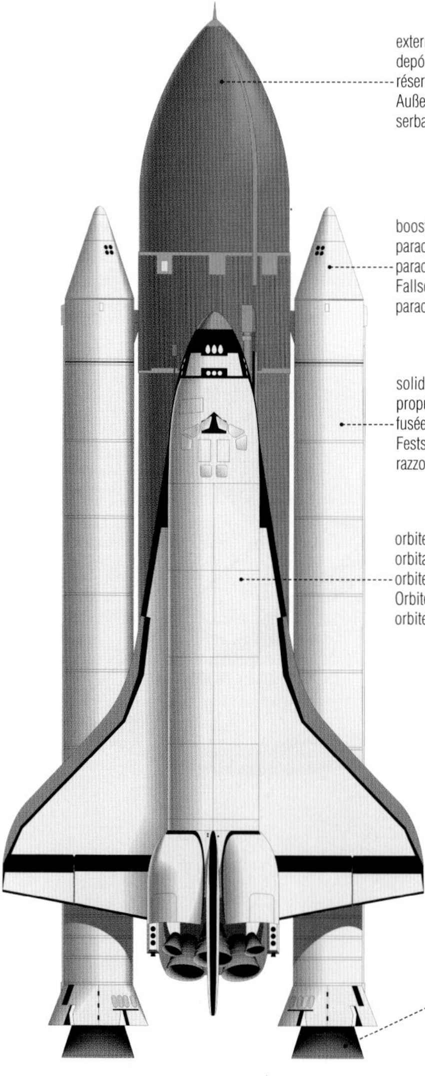

external fuel tank
depósito^{M} externo de combustible^{M}
réservoir^{M} externe
Außentank^{M}
serbatoio^{M} esterno del combustibile^{M}
booster parachute
paracaídas^{M} auxiliar
parachute^{M}
Fallschirm^{M} für die Feststoffrakete^{F}
paracadute^{M} del booster^{M}
solid rocket booster
propulsor^{M} sólido
fusée^{F} à propergol^{M} solide
Feststoff^{M}-Booster^{M}
razzo^{M} a propellente^{M} solido
orbiter
orbitador^{M}
orbiteur^{M}
Orbiter^{M}
orbiter^{M}
nozzle
propulsor^{M}
tuyère^{F}
Düse^{F}
ugello^{M}

space launcher

cohete^{M} espacial | lanceur^{M} spatial | Trägerrakete^{F} | razzo^{M} spaziale

examples of space launchers
ejemplos^{M} de lanzadores^{M} espaciales
exemples^{M} de lanceurs^{M} spatiaux
Beispiele^{N} für Trägerraketen^{F}
esempi^{M} di razzi^{M} spaziali

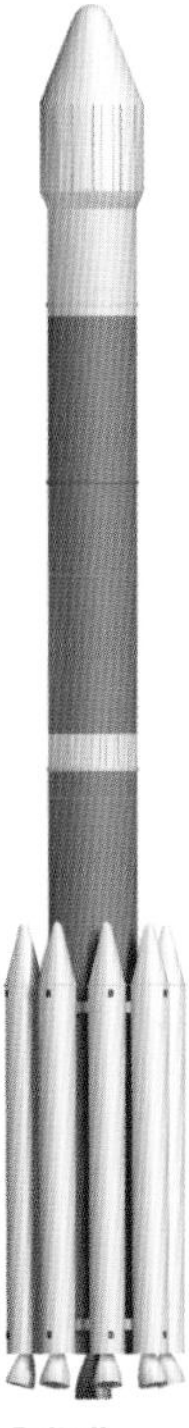

Delta II
Delta II
Delta II
Delta II
Delta II

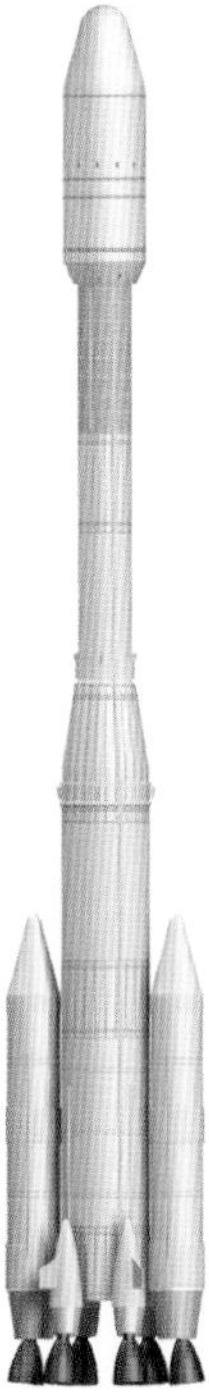

Ariane IV
Ariane IV
Ariane IV
Ariane IV
Ariane IV

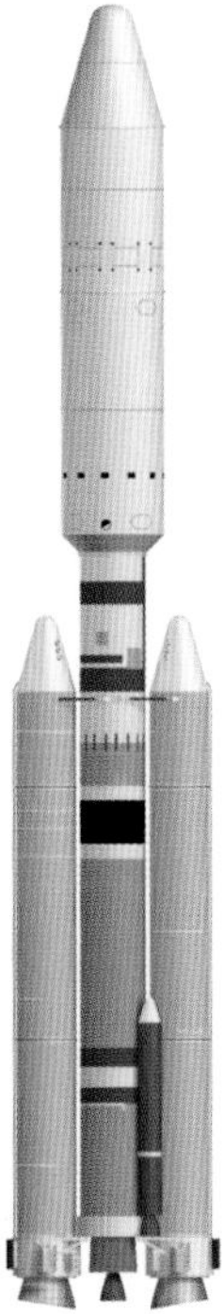

Titan IV
Titan IV
Titan IV
Titan IV
Titan IV

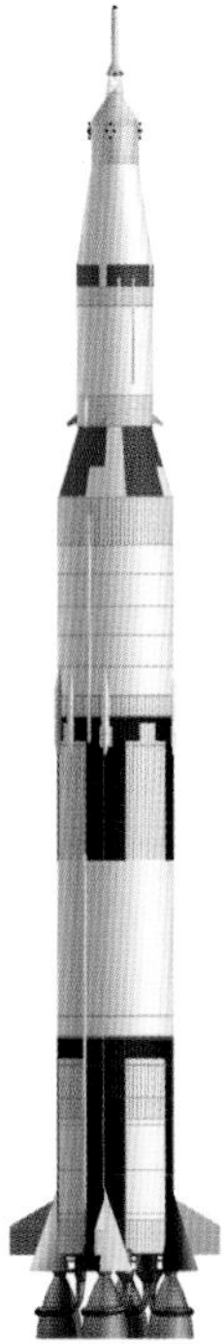

Saturn V
Saturno V
Saturn V
Saturn V
Saturn V

configuration of the continents

configuración^{F} de los continentes^{M} | configuration^{F} des continents^{M} | Lage^{F} der Kontinente^{M} | carta^{F} dei continenti^{M}

planisphere
planisferio^{M}
planisphère^{M}
Erdoberfläche^{F}
planisfero^{M}

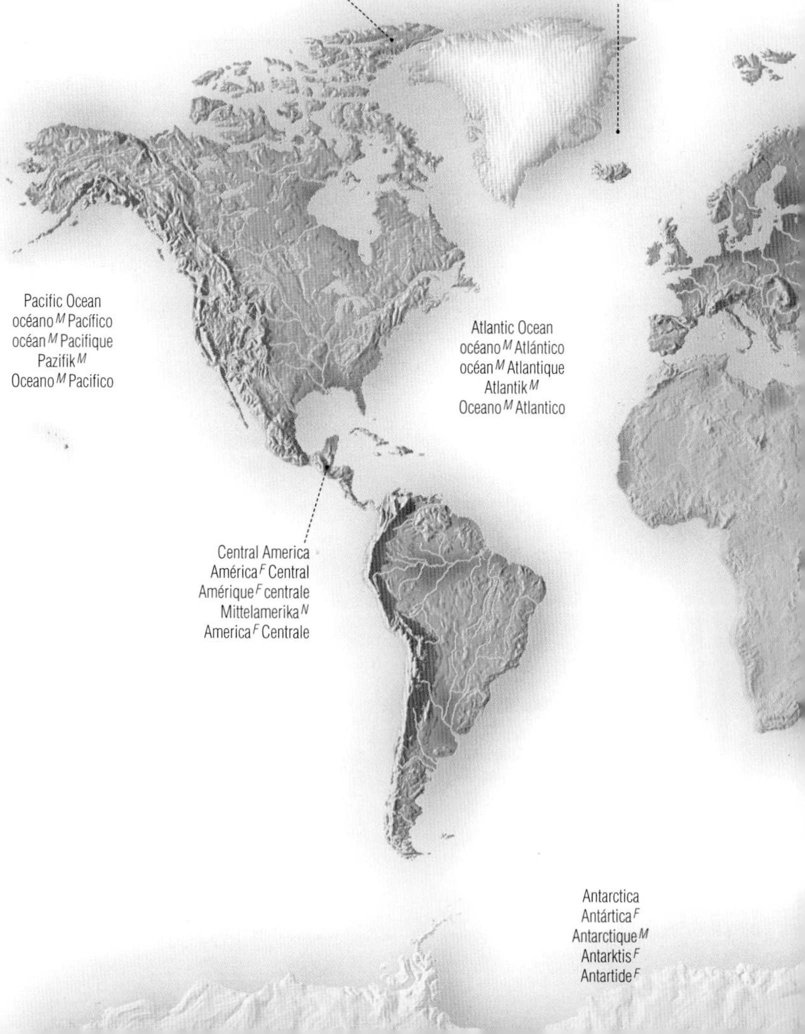

Arctic
Ártico^{M}
Arctique^{M}
Arktis^{F}
Artide^{F}
Greenland Sea
mar^{M} de Groenlandia^{F}
mer^{F} du Groenland^{M}
Grönlandsee^{F}
Mar^{M} di Groenlandia^{F}
Pacific Ocean
océano^{M} Pacífico
océan^{M} Pacifique
Pazifik^{M}
Oceano^{M} Pacifico
Atlantic Ocean
océano^{M} Atlántico
océan^{M} Atlantique
Atlantik^{M}
Oceano^{M} Atlantico
Central America
América^{F} Central
Amérique^{F} centrale
Mittelamerika^{N}
America^{F} Centrale
Antarctica
Antártica^{F}
Antarctique^{M}
Antarktis^{F}
Antartide^{F}

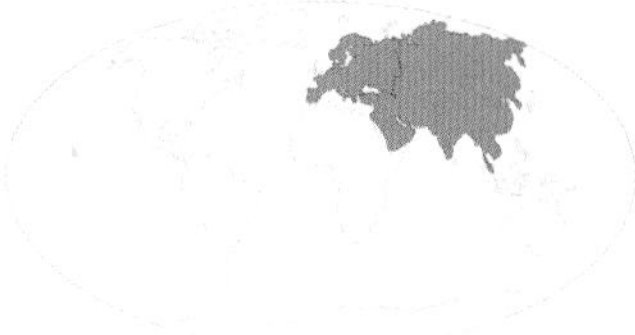

Eurasia
Eurasia *F*
Eurasie *F*
Eurasien *N*
Eurasia *F*

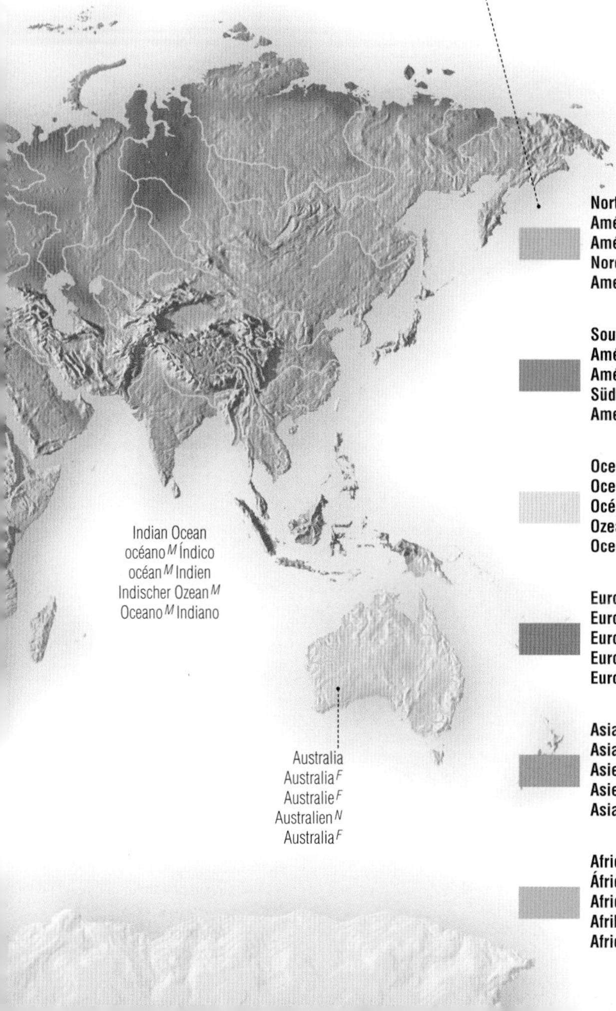
Arctic Ocean
océano *M* Glacial Ártico
océan *M* Arctique
Nordpolarmeer *N*
Mar *M* Glaciale Artico
Bering Sea
mar *M* de Bering
mer *F* de Béring
Beringsee *F*
Mar *M* di Bering
Indian Ocean
océano *M* Índico
océan *M* Indien
Indischer Ozean *M*
Oceano *M* Indiano
Australia
Australia *F*
Australie *F*
Australien *N*
Australia *F*

North America
América *F* **del Norte**
Amérique *F* **du Nord** *M*
Nordamerika *N*
America *F* **Settentrionale**

South America
América *F* **del Sur**
Amérique *F* **du Sud** *M*
Südamerika *N*
America *F* **Meridionale**

Oceania
Oceanía *F*
Océanie *F*
Ozeanien *N*
Oceania *F*

Europe
Europa *F*
Europe *F*
Europa *N*
Europa *F*

Asia
Asia *F*
Asie *F*
Asien *N*
Asia *F*

Africa
África *F*
Afrique *F*
Afrika *N*
Africa *F*

cartography

cartografía[F] | cartographie[F] | Kartographie[F] | cartografia[F]

Earth coordinate system
sistema[M] de coordenadas[F] terrestres
coordonnées[F] terrestres
Koordinatensystem[N] der Erdkugel[F]
sistema[M] di coordinate[F] terrestri

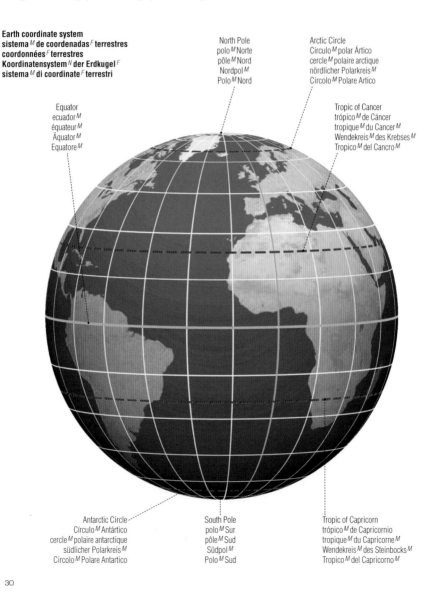

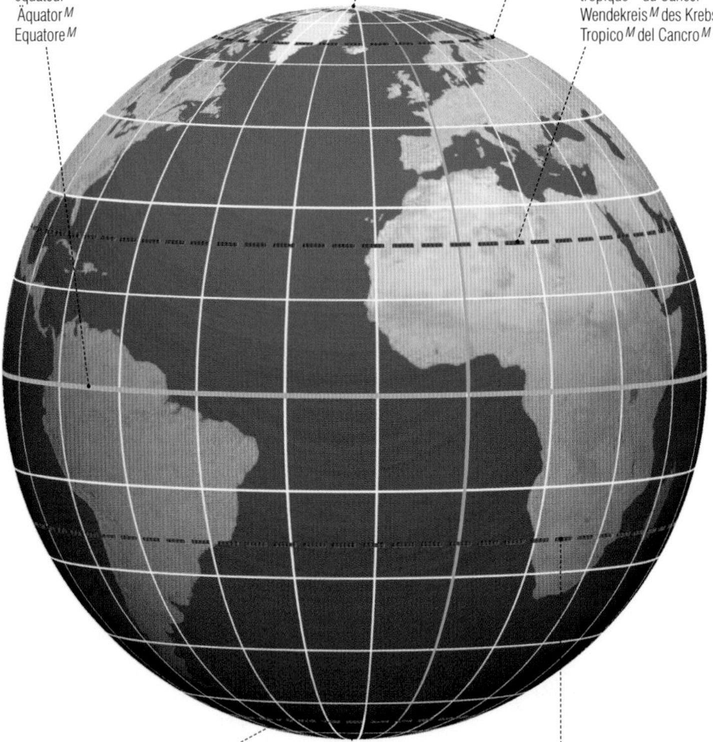
North Pole
polo[M] Norte
pôle[M] Nord
Nordpol[M]
Polo[M] Nord
Arctic Circle
Círculo[M] polar Ártico
cercle[M] polaire arctique
nördlicher Polarkreis[M]
Circolo[M] Polare Artico
Equator
ecuador[M]
équateur[M]
Äquator[M]
Equatore[M]
Tropic of Cancer
trópico[M] de Cáncer
tropique[M] du Cancer[M]
Wendekreis[M] des Krebses[M]
Tropico[M] del Cancro[M]
Antarctic Circle
Círculo[M] Antártico
cercle[M] polaire antarctique
südlicher Polarkreis[M]
Circolo[M] Polare Antartico
South Pole
polo[M] Sur
pôle[M] Sud
Südpol[M]
Polo[M] Sud
Tropic of Capricorn
trópico[M] de Capricornio
tropique[M] du Capricorne[M]
Wendekreis[M] des Steinbocks[M]
Tropico[M] del Capricorno[M]

hemispheres
hemisferios *M*
hémisphères *M*
Hemisphären *F*
emisferi *M*

Northern Hemisphere
hemisferio *M* **Norte**
hémisphère *M* **boréal**
nördliche Hemisphäre *F*
emisfero *M* **settentrionale**

Southern Hemisphere
hemisferio *M* **Sur**
hémisphère *M* **austral**
südliche Hemisphäre *F*
emisfero *M* **meridionale**

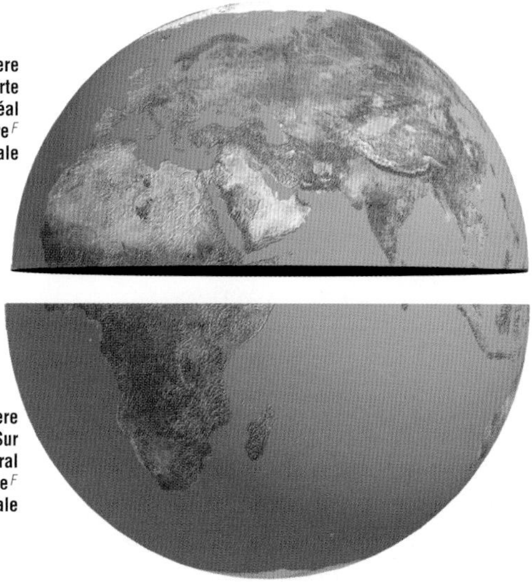

Western Hemisphere
hemisferio *M* **occidental**
hémisphère *M* **occidental**
westliche Hemisphäre *F*
emisfero *M* **occidentale**

Eastern Hemisphere
hemisferio *M* **oriental**
hémisphère *M* **oriental**
östliche Hemisphäre *F*
emisfero *M* **orientale**

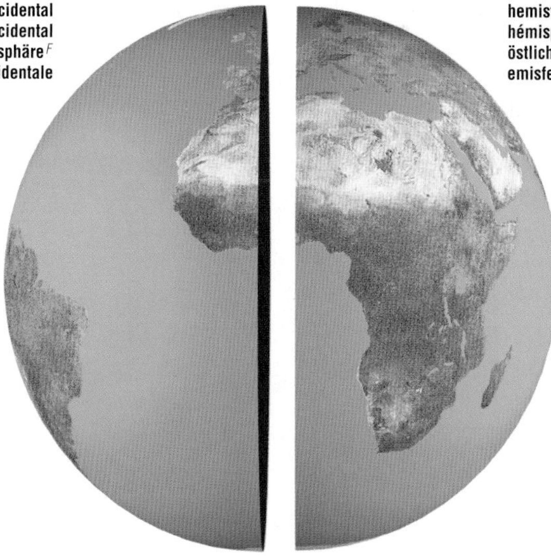

grid system
sistema^M de retícula^F
divisions^F cartographiques
Gradnetz^N
reticolato^M geografico

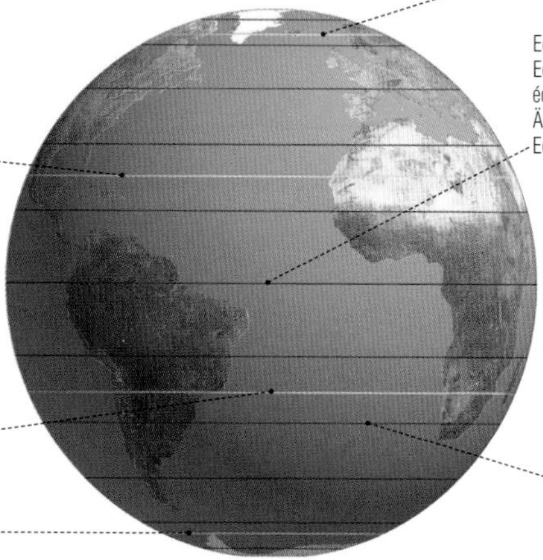
line of latitude
líneas^F de latitud^F
latitude^F
Breitengrade^M
latitudine^F
Arctic Circle
Círculo^M polar Ártico
cercle^M polaire arctique
nördlicher Polarkreis^M
Circolo^M Polare Artico
Tropic of Cancer
trópico^M de Cáncer
tropique^M du Cancer^M
Wendekreis^M des Krebses^M
Tropico^M del Cancro^M
Equator
Ecuador^M
équateur^M
Äquator^M
Equatore^M
Tropic of Capricorn
trópico^M de Capricornio
tropique^M du Capricorne^M
Wendekreis^M des Steinbocks^M
Tropico^M del Capricorno^M
parallel
paralelo^M
parallèle^M
Breitenkreis^M
parallelo^M
Antarctic Circle
Círculo^M Antártico
cercle^M polaire antarctique
südlicher Polarkreis^M
Circolo^M Polare Antartico

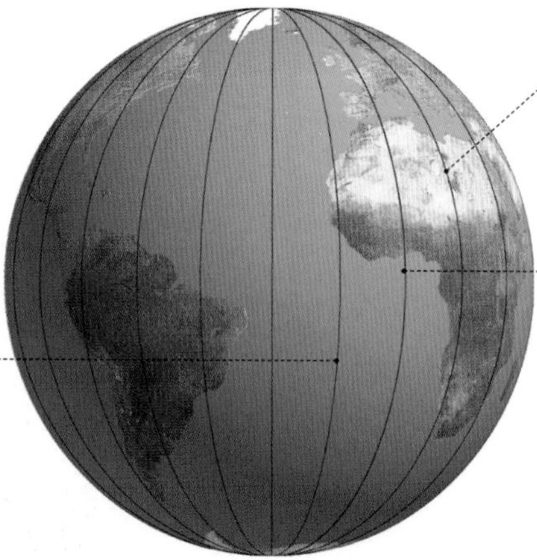
line of longitude
líneas^F de longitud^F
longitude^F
Längengrade^M
longitudine^F
Eastern meridian
meridiano^M oriental
méridien^M est
östlicher Meridian^M
meridiano^M orientale
prime meridian
meridiano^M principal
méridien^M de Greenwich
Nullmeridian^M
meridiano^M fondamentale
Western meridian
meridiano^M occidental
méridien^M ouest
westlicher Meridian^M
meridiano^M occidentale

map projections
proyecciones[F] cartográficas
projections[F] cartographiques
Kartendarstellungen[F]
proiezioni[F] cartografiche

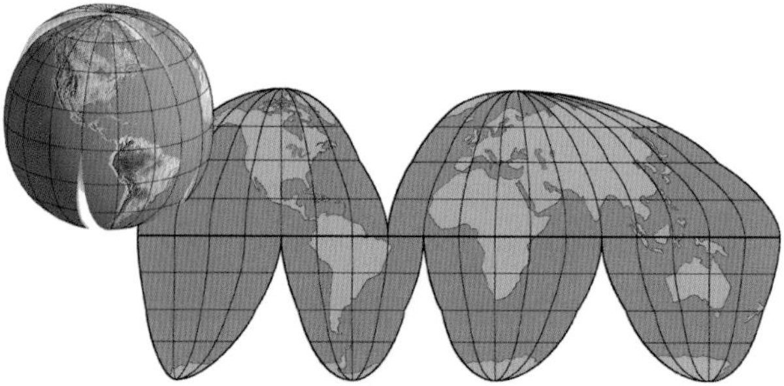

interrupted projection
proyección[F] interrumpida
projection[F] interrompue
zerlappte Projektion[F]
proiezione[F] interrotta

cylindrical projection
proyección[F] cilíndrica
projection[F] cylindrique
Zylinderprojektion[F]
proiezione[F] cilindrica

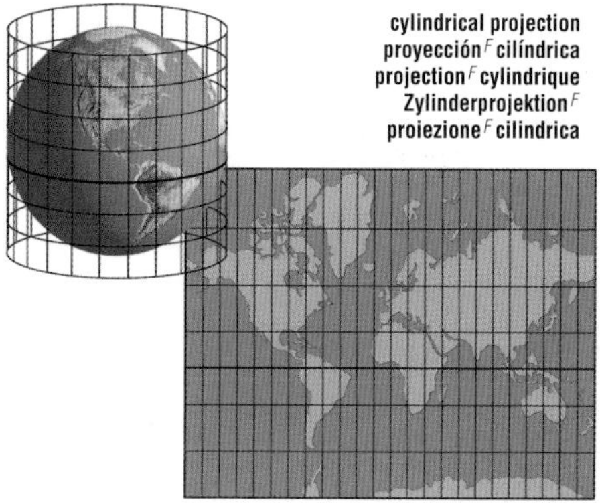

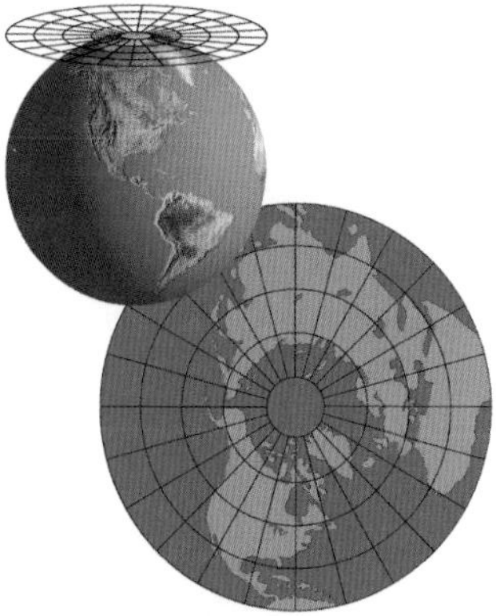

plane projection
proyección[F] plana
projection[F] horizontale
Azimutalprojektion[F]
proiezione[F] piana

conic projection
proyección[F] cónica
projection[F] conique
Kegelprojektion[F]
proiezione[F] conica

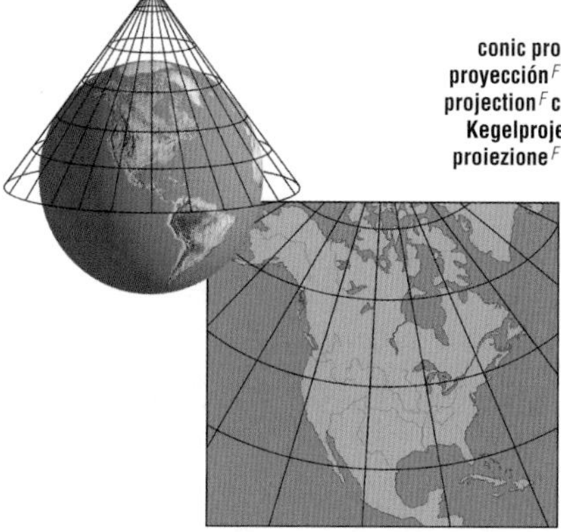

cartography

physical map
mapa[M] físico
carte[F] physique
physische Karte[F]
carta[F] fisica

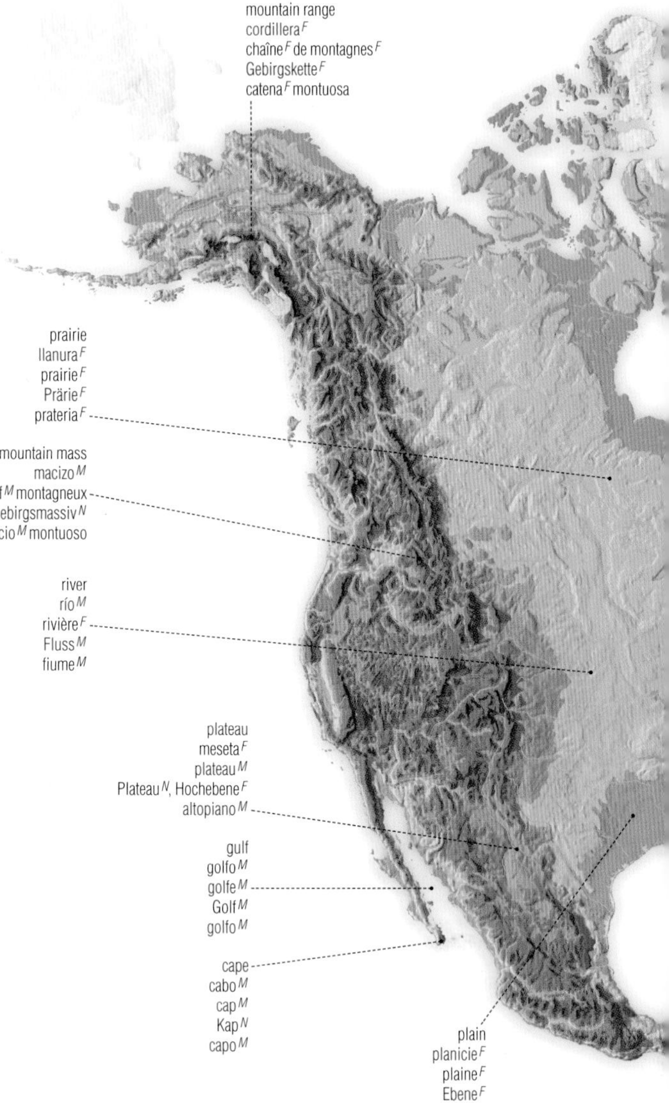
mountain range
cordillera[F]
chaîne[F] de montagnes[F]
Gebirgskette[F]
catena[F] montuosa
prairie
llanura[F]
prairie[F]
Prärie[F]
prateria[F]
mountain mass
macizo[M]
massif[M] montagneux
Gebirgsmassiv[N]
massiccio[M] montuoso
river
río[M]
rivière[F]
Fluss[M]
fiume[M]
plateau
meseta[F]
plateau[M]
Plateau[N], Hochebene[F]
altopiano[M]
gulf
golfo[M]
golfe[M]
Golf[M]
golfo[M]
cape
cabo[M]
cap[M]
Kap[N]
capo[M]
plain
planicie[F]
plaine[F]
Ebene[F]
pianura[F]

sea
mar M
mer F
Meer N
mare M
strait
estrecho M
détroit M
Meerenge F
stretto M
bay
bahía F
baie F
Bucht F
baia F
island
isla F
île F
Insel F
isola F
estuary
estuario M
estuaire M
Flussmündung F
estuario M
river
río M
fleuve M
Fluss M
fiume M
lake
lago M
lac M
See M
lago M
peninsula
península F
péninsule F
Halbinsel F
penisola F
ocean
océano M
océan M
Ozean M
oceano M
archipelago
archipiélago M
archipel M
Archipel M
arcipelago M
isthmus
istmo M
isthme M
Landenge F
istmo M

section of the Earth's crust

corte^M de la corteza^F terrestre | coupe^F de la croûte^F terrestre | Erdkruste^F im Querschnitt^M | sezione^F della crosta^F terrestre

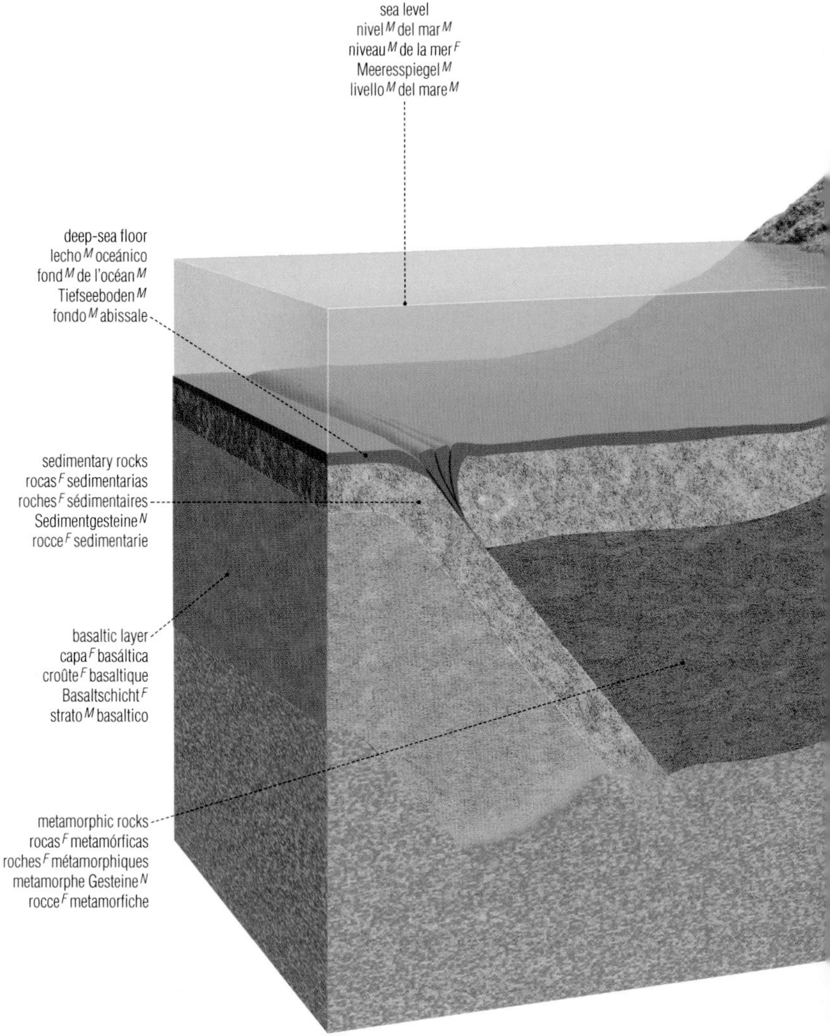

sea level
nivel^M del mar^M
niveau^M de la mer^F
Meeresspiegel^M
livello^M del mare^M
deep-sea floor
lecho^M oceánico
fond^M de l'océan^M
Tiefseeboden^M
fondo^M abissale
sedimentary rocks
rocas^F sedimentarias
roches^F sédimentaires
Sedimentgesteine^N
rocce^F sedimentarie
basaltic layer
capa^F basáltica
croûte^F basaltique
Basaltschicht^F
strato^M basaltico
metamorphic rocks
rocas^F metamórficas
roches^F métamorphiques
metamorphe Gesteine^N
rocce^F metamorfiche

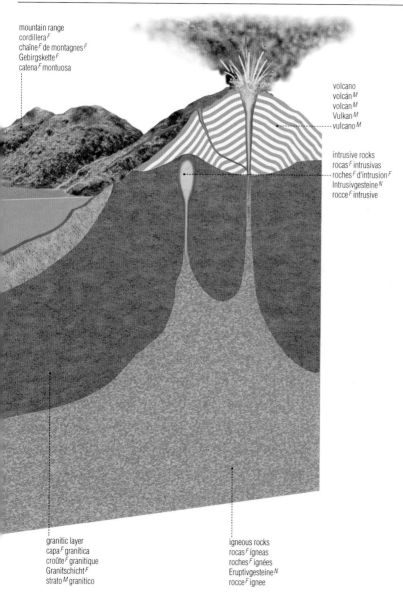

mountain range
cordillera F
chaîne F de montagnes F
Gebirgskette F
catena F montuosa
volcano
volcán M
volcan M
Vulkan M
vulcano M
intrusive rocks
rocas F intrusivas
roches F d'intrusion F
Intrusivgesteine N
rocce F intrusive
granitic layer
capa F granítica
croûte F granitique
Granitschicht F
strato M granitico
igneous rocks
rocas F ígneas
roches F ignées
Eruptivgesteine N
rocce F ignee

structure of the Earth

estructura^F de la Tierra^F | structure^F de la Terre^F | Erdaufbau^M | struttura^F della Terra^F

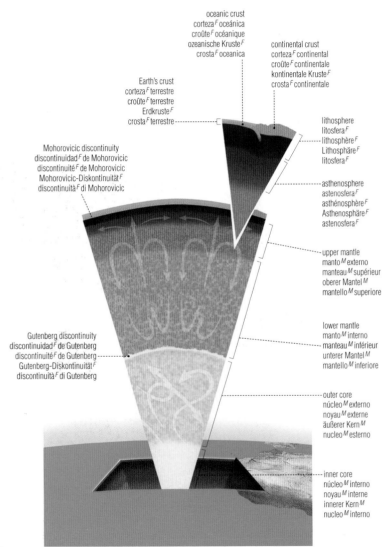

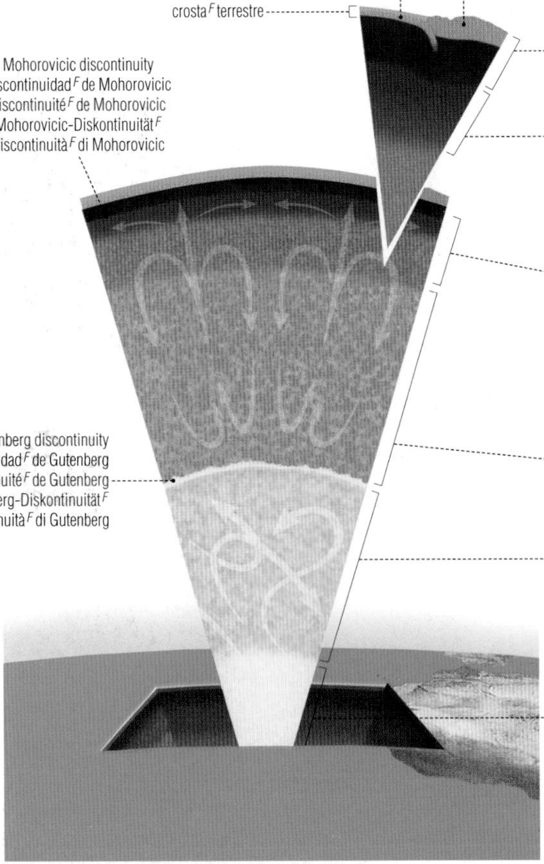
oceanic crust
corteza^F oceánica
croûte^F océanique
ozeanische Kruste^F
crosta^F oceanica
continental crust
corteza^F continental
croûte^F continentale
kontinentale Kruste^F
crosta^F continentale
Earth's crust
corteza^F terrestre
croûte^F terrestre
Erdkruste^F
crosta^F terrestre
lithosphere
litosfera^F
lithosphère^F
Lithosphäre^F
litosfera^F
Mohorovicic discontinuity
discontinuidad^F de Mohorovicic
discontinuité^F de Mohorovicic
Mohorovicic-Diskontinuität^F
discontinuità^F di Mohorovicic
asthenosphere
astenosfera^F
asthénosphère^F
Asthenosphäre^F
astenosfera^F
upper mantle
manto^M externo
manteau^M supérieur
oberer Mantel^M
mantello^M superiore
lower mantle
manto^M interno
manteau^M inférieur
unterer Mantel^M
mantello^M inferiore
Gutenberg discontinuity
discontinuidad^F de Gutenberg
discontinuité^F de Gutenberg
Gutenberg-Diskontinuität^F
discontinuità^F di Gutenberg
outer core
núcleo^M externo
noyau^M externe
äußerer Kern^M
nucleo^M esterno
inner core
núcleo^M interno
noyau^M interne
innerer Kern^M
nucleo^M interno

earthquake

terremoto M | séisme M | Erdbeben N | terremoto M

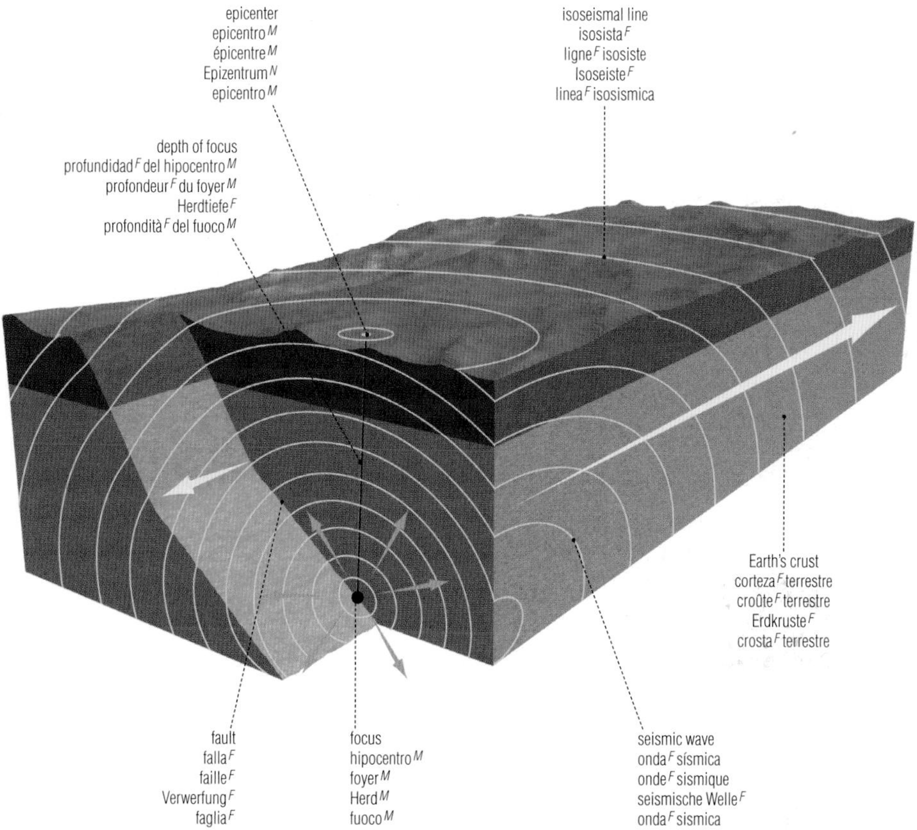
epicenter
epicentro M
épicentre M
Epizentrum N
epicentro M
isoseismal line
isosista F
ligne F isosiste
Isoseiste F
linea F isosismica
depth of focus
profundidad F del hipocentro M
profondeur F du foyer M
Herdtiefe F
profondità F del fuoco M
Earth's crust
corteza F terrestre
croûte F terrestre
Erdkruste F
crosta F terrestre
fault
falla F
faille F
Verwerfung F
faglia F
focus
hipocentro M
foyer M
Herd M
fuoco M
seismic wave
onda F sísmica
onde F sismique
seismische Welle F
onda F sismica

tectonic plates

placas[F] tectónicas | plaques[F] tectoniques | tektonische Platten[F] | placche[F] tettoniche

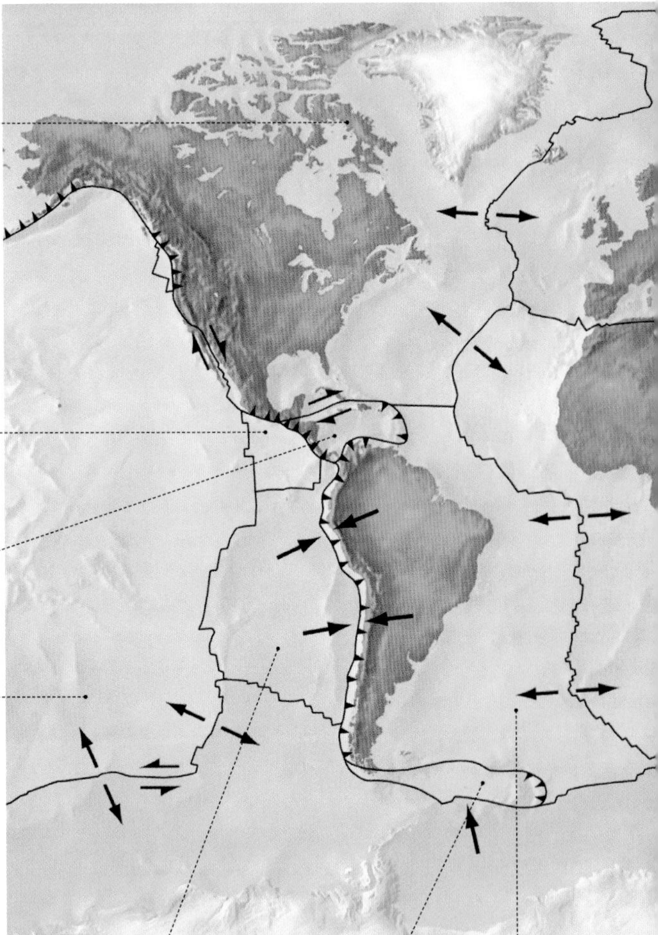
North American Plate
placa[F] norteamericana
plaque[F] nord-américaine
Nordamerikanische Platte[F]
placca[F] nordamericana
Cocos Plate
placa[F] de Cocos
plaque[F] des îles[F] Cocos
Cocos-Platte[F]
placca[F] delle Cocos
Caribbean Plate
placa[F] del Caribe
plaque[F] des Caraïbes
Karibische Platte[F]
placca[F] caribica
Pacific Plate
placa[F] del Pacífico
plaque[F] pacifique
Pazifische Platte[F]
placca[F] del Pacifico[M]
Nazca Plate
placa[F] de Nazca
plaque[F] Nazca
Nazca-Platte[F]
placca[F] di Nazca
Scotia Plate
placa[F] de Escocia
plaque[F] Scotia
Scotia-Platte[F]
placca[F] di Scozia[F]
South American Plate
placa[F] sudamericana
plaque[F] sud-américaine
Südamerikanische Platte[F]
placca[F] sudamericana

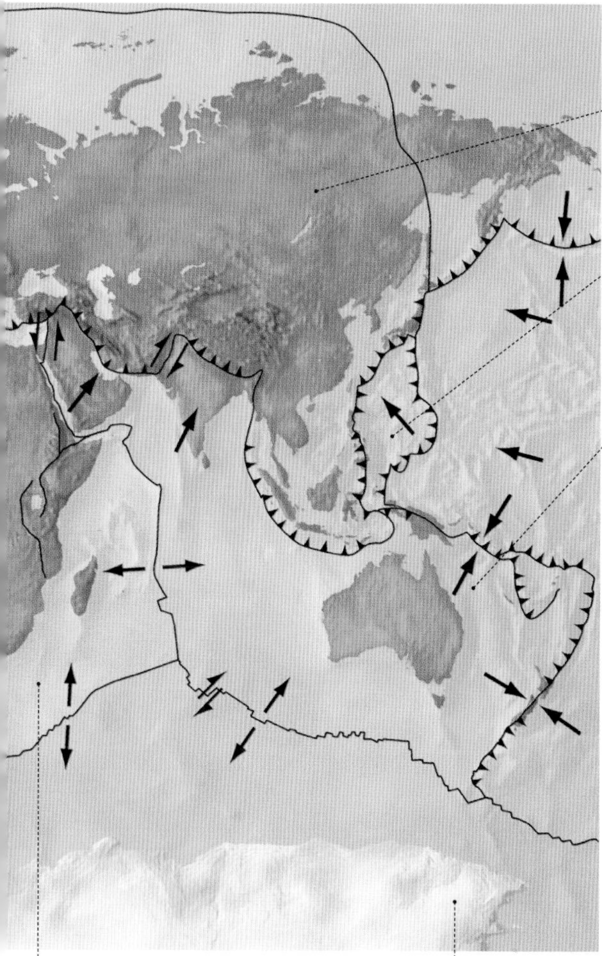

Eurasian Plate
placa[F] euroasiática
plaque[F] eurasiatique
Eurasiatische Platte[F]
placca[F] euroasiatica

Philippine Plate
placa[F] de Filipinas
plaque[F] philippine
Philippinen-Platte[F]
placca[F] filippina

Australian-Indian Plate
placa[F] indoaustraliana
plaque[F] indo-australienne
Indisch-Australische Platte[F]
placca[F] indoaustraliana

subduction
subducción[F]
subduction[F]
Subduktionszone[F]
subduzione[F]

transform plate boundaries
fallas[F] transformantes
plaques[F] transformantes
Transformstörungen[F]
placche[F] trasformi

convergent plate boundaries
placas[F] convergentes
plaques[F] convergentes
konvergierende Plattengrenzen[F]
placche[F] convergenti

divergent plate boundaries
placas[F] divergentes
plaques[F] divergentes
divergierende Plattengrenzen[F]
placche[F] divergenti

African Plate
placa[F] africana
plaque[F] africaine
Afrikanische Platte[F]
placca[F] africana

Antarctic Plate
placa[F] antártica
plaque[F] antarctique
Antarktische Platte[F]
placca[F] antartica

volcano

volcán^{M} | volcan^{M} | Vulkan^{M} | vulcano^{M}

volcano during eruption
volcán^{M} en erupción^{F}
volcan^{M} en éruption^{F}
Vulkan^{M} mit Ausbruchstätigkeit^{F}
vulcano^{M} in eruzione^{F}

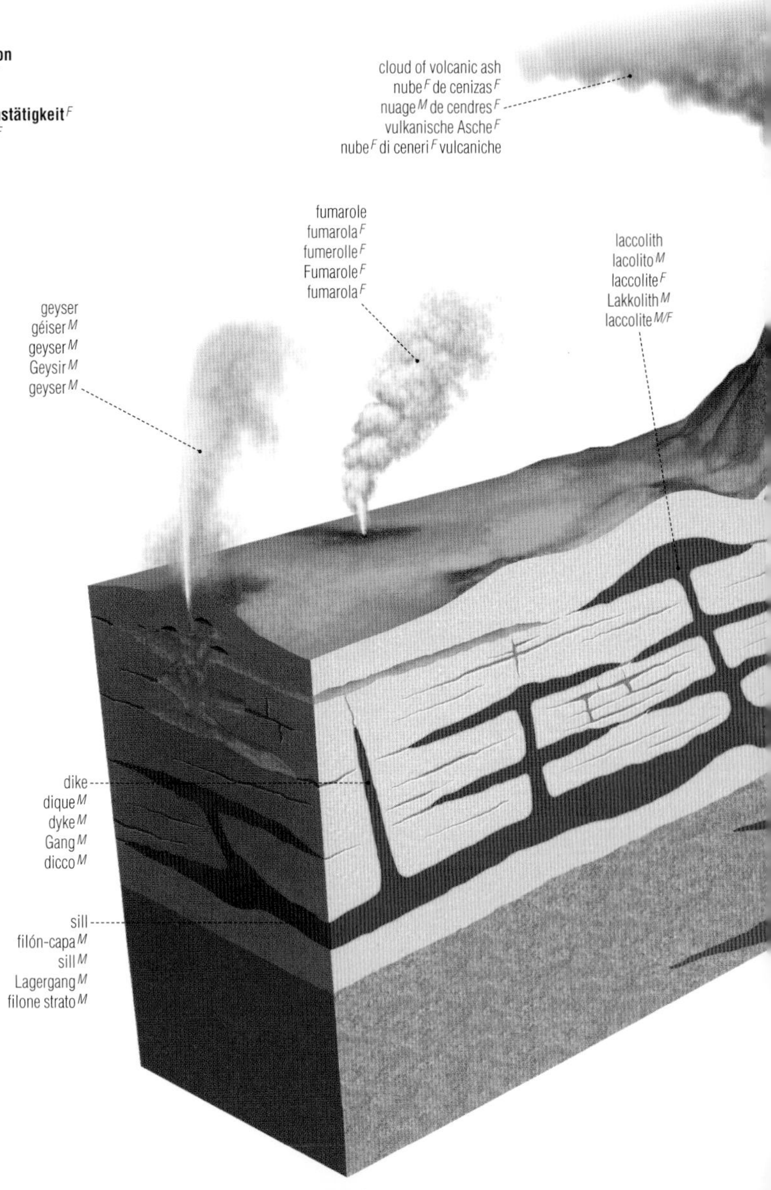

cloud of volcanic ash
nube^{F} de cenizas^{F}
nuage^{M} de cendres^{F}
vulkanische Asche^{F}
nube^{F} di ceneri^{F} vulcaniche
fumarole
fumarola^{F}
fumerolle^{F}
Fumarole^{F}
fumarola^{F}
laccolith
lacolito^{M}
laccolite^{F}
Lakkolith^{M}
laccolite$^{M/F}$
geyser
géiser^{M}
geyser^{M}
Geysir^{M}
geyser^{M}
dike
dique^{M}
dyke^{M}
Gang^{M}
dicco^{M}
sill
filón-capa^{M}
sill^{M}
Lagergang^{M}
filone strato^{M}

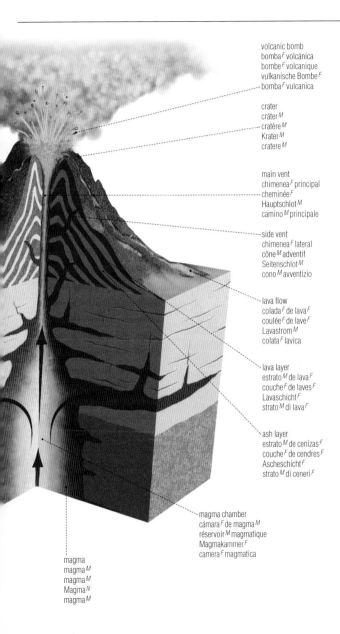

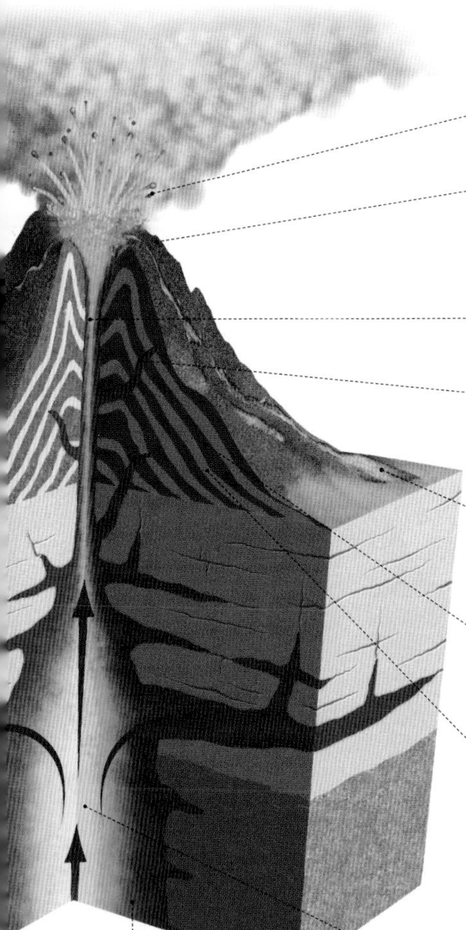
volcanic bomb
bomba[F] volcánica
bombe[F] volcanique
vulkanische Bombe[F]
bomba[F] vulcanica
crater
cráter[M]
cratère[M]
Krater[M]
cratere[M]
main vent
chimenea[F] principal
cheminée[F]
Hauptschlot[M]
camino[M] principale
side vent
chimenea[F] lateral
cône[M] adventif
Seitenschlot[M]
cono[M] avventizio
lava flow
colada[F] de lava[F]
coulée[F] de lave[F]
Lavastrom[M]
colata[F] lavica
lava layer
estrato[M] de lava[F]
couche[F] de laves[F]
Lavaschicht[F]
strato[M] di lava[F]
ash layer
estrato[M] de cenizas[F]
couche[F] de cendres[F]
Ascheschicht[F]
strato[M] di ceneri[F]
magma chamber
cámara[F] de magma[M]
réservoir[M] magmatique
Magmakammer[F]
camera[F] magmatica
magma
magma[M]
magma[M]
Magma[N]
magma[M]

mountain

montaña F | montagne F | Berg M | montagna F

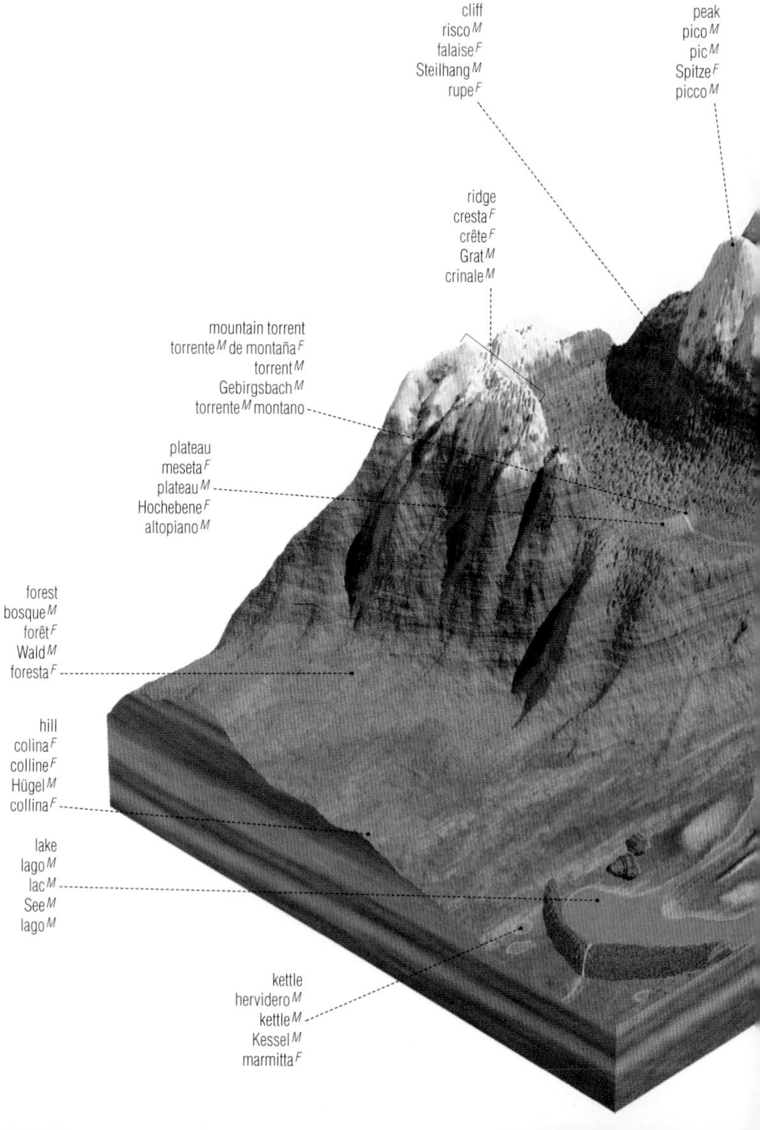
cliff
risco M
falaise F
Steilhang M
rupe F
peak
pico M
pic M
Spitze F
picco M
ridge
cresta F
crête F
Grat M
crinale M
mountain torrent
torrente M de montaña F
torrent M
Gebirgsbach M
torrente M montano
plateau
meseta F
plateau M
Hochebene F
altopiano M
forest
bosque M
forêt F
Wald M
foresta F
hill
colina F
colline F
Hügel M
collina F
lake
lago M
lac M
See M
lago M
kettle
hervidero M
kettle M
Kessel M
marmitta F

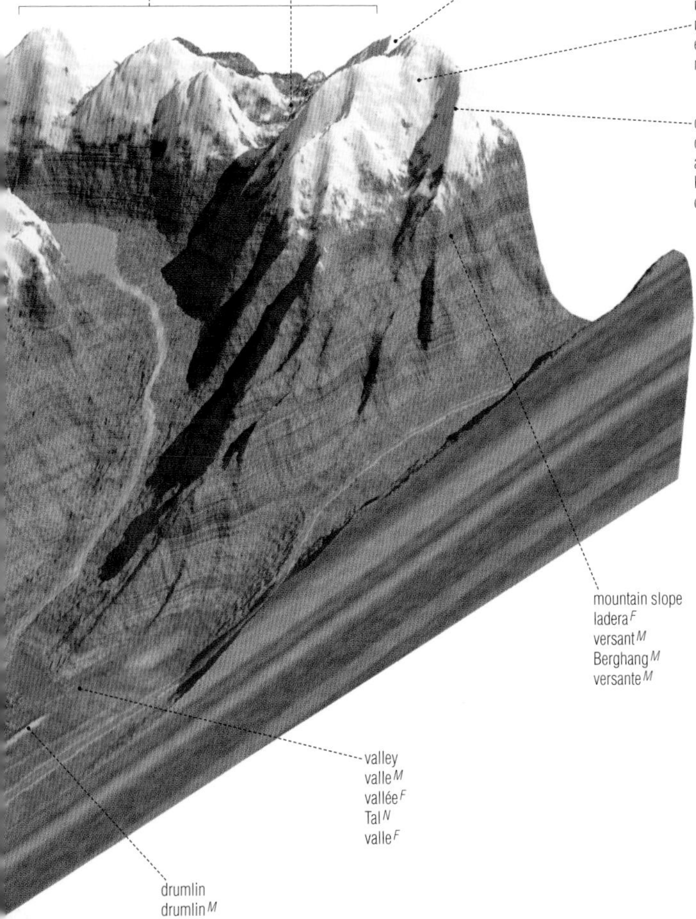
spur
estribación F
contrefort M
Vorsprung M
sperone M
pass
paso M
col M
Pass M
passo M
summit
cima F
sommet M
Gipfel M
cima F
perpetual snows
nieves F perpetuas
neiges F éternelles
ewiger Schnee M
nevi F perenni
crest
cresta F
arête F
Kamm M
cresta F
mountain slope
ladera F
versant M
Berghang M
versante M
valley
valle M
vallée F
Tal N
valle F
drumlin
drumlin M
drumlin M
Drumlin M
drumlin M

glacier

glaciar^M | glacier^M | Gletscher^M | ghiacciaio^M

bergschrund
rimaya F
rimaye F
Bergschrund M
crepaccio M terminale
firn
neviza F
névé M
Firn M
nevato M
glacial cirque
circo M glaciar
cirque M glaciaire
Kar N
circo M glaciale
rock basin
ombligo M
ombilic M
Felsenbecken N
ombelico M
riegel
umbral M
verrou M
Riegel M
soglia F glaciale
glacier tongue
lengua F glaciar
langue F glaciaire
Gletscherzunge F
lingua F glaciale
crevasse
grieta F
crevasse F
Gletscherspalte F
crepaccio M
medial moraine
morrena F central
moraine F médiane
Mittelmoräne F
morena F mediana
ground moraine
morrena F de fondo M
moraine F de fond M
Grundmoräne F
morena F di fondo M

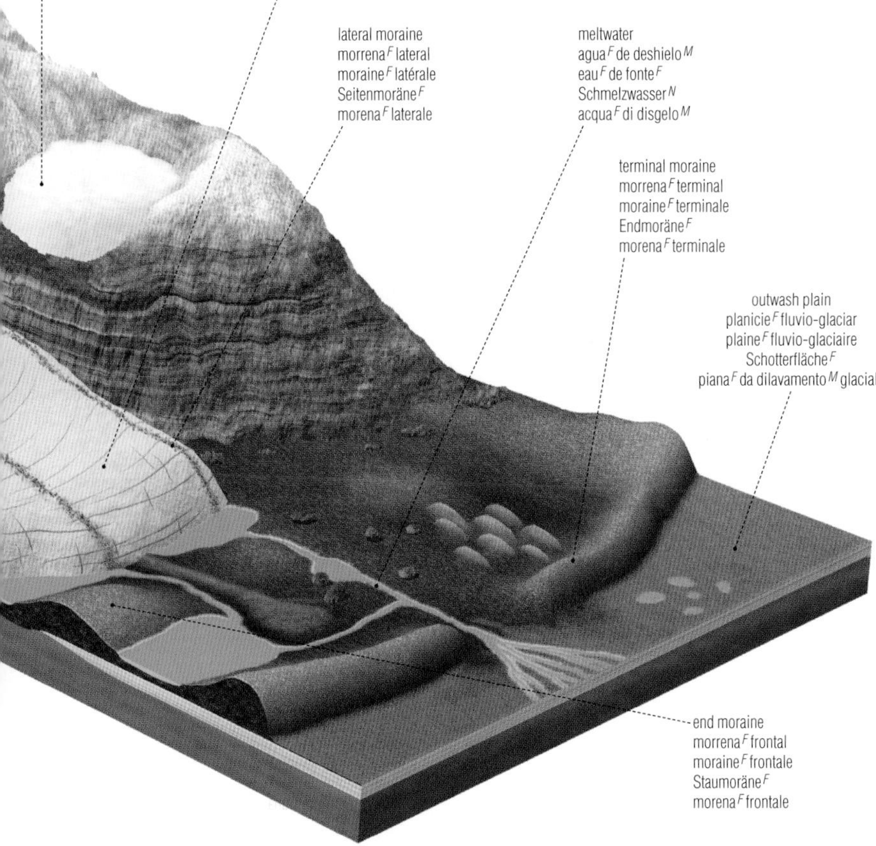
hanging glacier
glaciar[M] suspendido
glacier[M] suspendu
Hängegletscher[M]
vedretta[F]
serac
serac[M]
sérac[M]
Serac[M]
seracco[M]
lateral moraine
morrena[F] lateral
moraine[F] latérale
Seitenmoräne[F]
morena[F] laterale
meltwater
agua[F] de deshielo[M]
eau[F] de fonte[F]
Schmelzwasser[N]
acqua[F] di disgelo[M]
terminal moraine
morrena[F] terminal
moraine[F] terminale
Endmoräne[F]
morena[F] terminale
outwash plain
planicie[F] fluvio-glaciar
plaine[F] fluvio-glaciaire
Schotterfläche[F]
piana[F] da dilavamento[M] glaciale
end moraine
morrena[F] frontal
moraine[F] frontale
Staumoräne[F]
morena[F] frontale

cave

gruta^F | grotte^F | Höhle^F | grotta^F

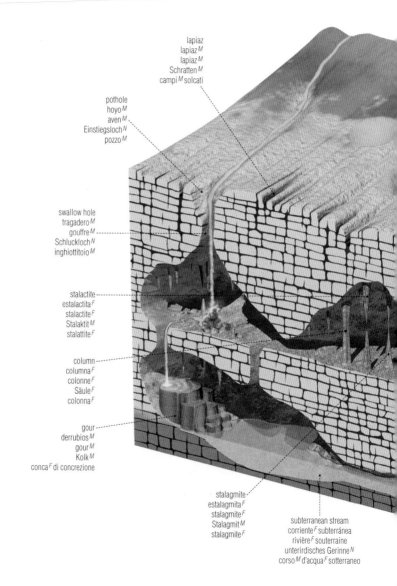

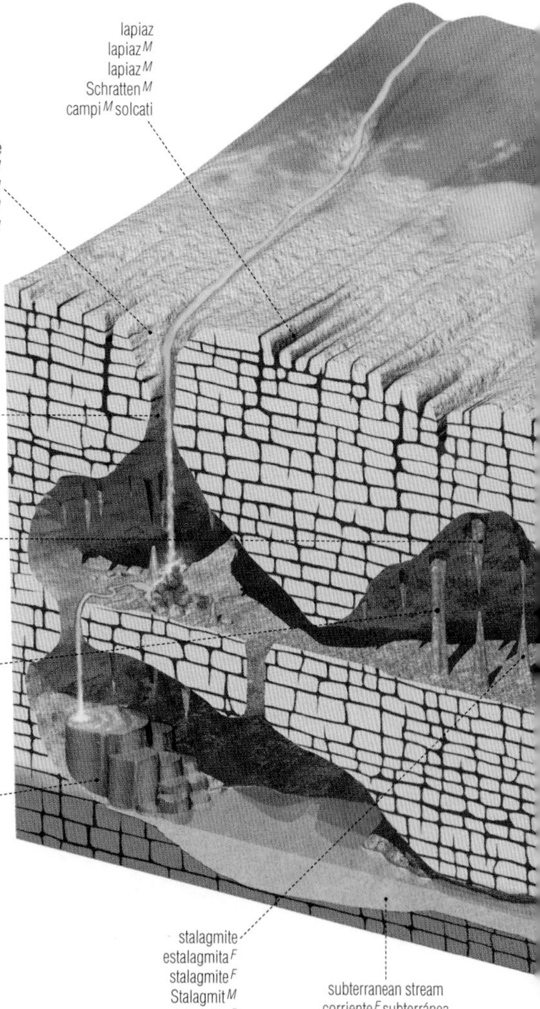
lapiaz
lapiaz^M
lapiaz^M
Schratten^M
campi^M solcati
pothole
hoyo^M
aven^M
Einstiegsloch^N
pozzo^M
swallow hole
tragadero^M
gouffre^M
Schluckloch^N
inghiottitoio^M
stalactite
estalactita^F
stalactite^F
Stalaktit^M
stalattite^F
column
columna^F
colonne^F
Säule^F
colonna^F
gour
derrubios^M
gour^M
Kolk^M
conca^F di concrezione
stalagmite
estalagmita^F
stalagmite^F
Stalagmit^M
stalagmite^F
subterranean stream
corriente^F subterránea
rivière^F souterraine
unterirdisches Gerinne^N
corso^M d'acqua^F sotterraneo

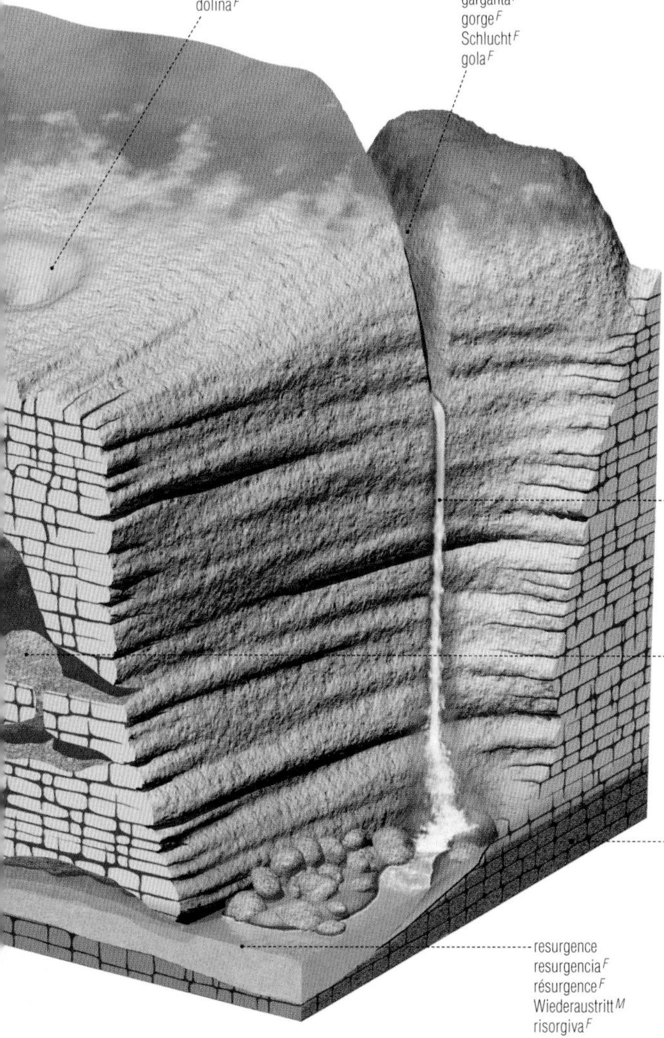
sinkhole
torca F
doline F
Doline F
dolina F
gorge
garganta F
gorge F
Schlucht F
gola F
waterfall
cascada F
chute F
Wasserfall M
cascata F
dry gallery
galería F seca
galerie F sèche
trocken liegender Höhlenraum M
galleria F secca
water table
nivel M freático
nappe F phréatique
Grundwasserspiegel M
superficie F freatica
resurgence
resurgencia F
résurgence F
Wiederaustritt M
risorgiva F

watercourse

corriente^F de agua^F | cours^M d'eau^F | Flusslandschaft^F | corso^M d'acqua^F

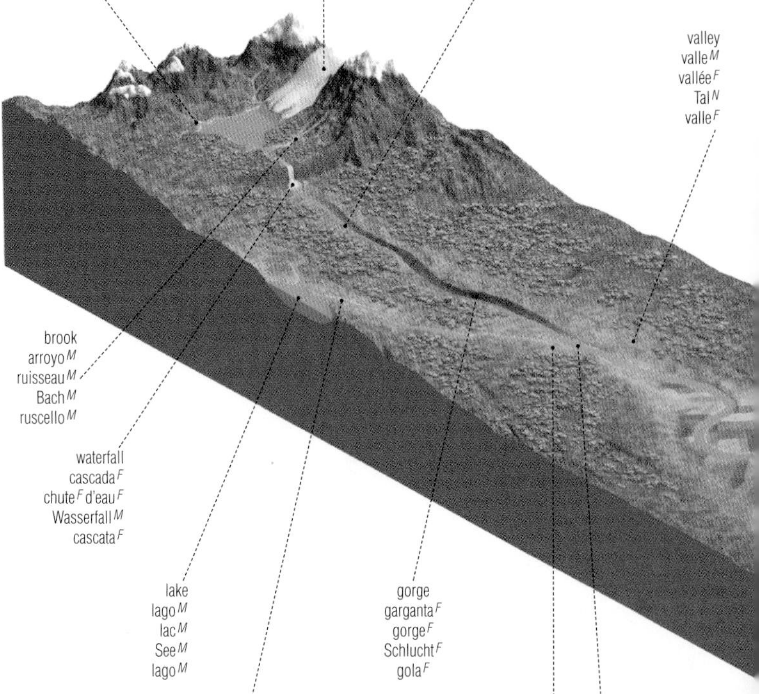
spring
fuente F
source F
Quelle F
sorgente F
glacier
glaciar M
glacier M
Gletscher M
ghiacciaio M
river
río M
rivière F
Fluss M
fiume M
valley
valle M
vallée F
Tal N
valle F
brook
arroyo M
ruisseau M
Bach M
ruscello M
waterfall
cascada F
chute F d'eau F
Wasserfall M
cascata F
lake
lago M
lac M
See M
lago M
gorge
garganta F
gorge F
Schlucht F
gola F
effluent
efluente M
effluent M
Abfluss M
emissario M
affluent
afluente M
affluent M
Zufluss M
affluente M
confluence
confluente M
confluent M
Zusammenfluss M
confluente M

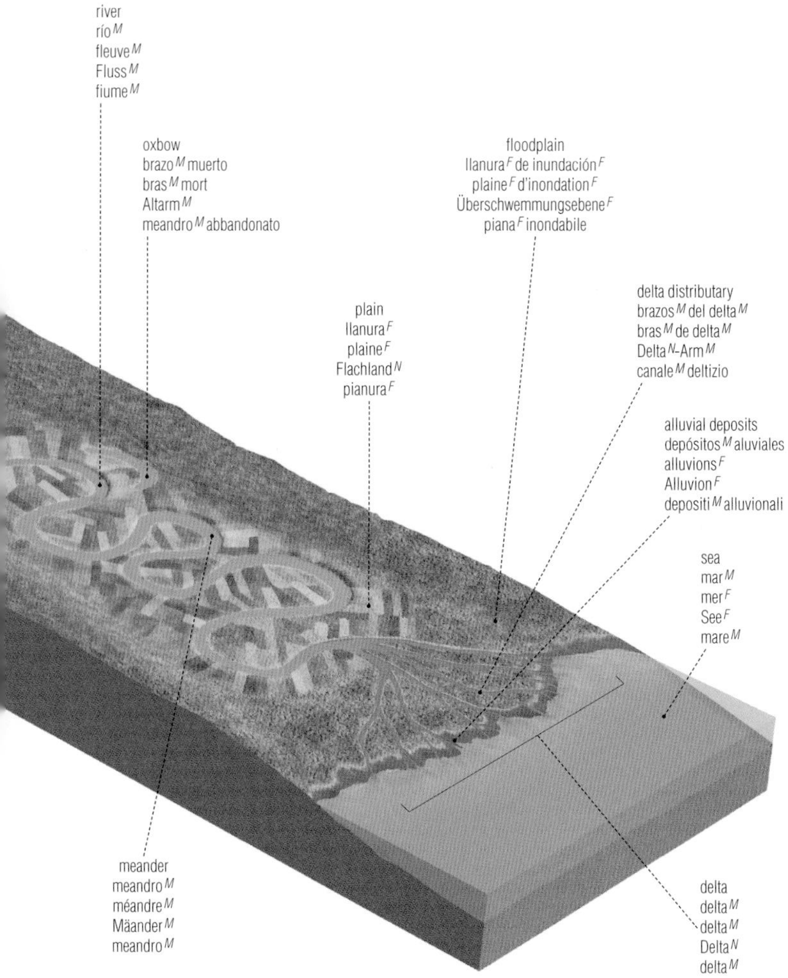
river
río M
fleuve M
Fluss M
fiume M
oxbow
brazo M muerto
bras M mort
Altarm M
meandro M abbandonato
floodplain
llanura F de inundación F
plaine F d'inondation F
Überschwemmungsebene F
piana F inondabile
plain
llanura F
plaine F
Flachland N
pianura F
delta distributary
brazos M del delta M
bras M de delta M
Delta N-Arm M
canale M deltizio
alluvial deposits
depósitos M aluviales
alluvions F
Alluvion F
depositi M alluvionali
sea
mar M
mer F
See F
mare M
meander
meandro M
méandre M
Mäander M
meandro M
delta
delta M
delta M
Delta N
delta M

wave

ola[F] | vague[F] | Welle[F] | onda[F]

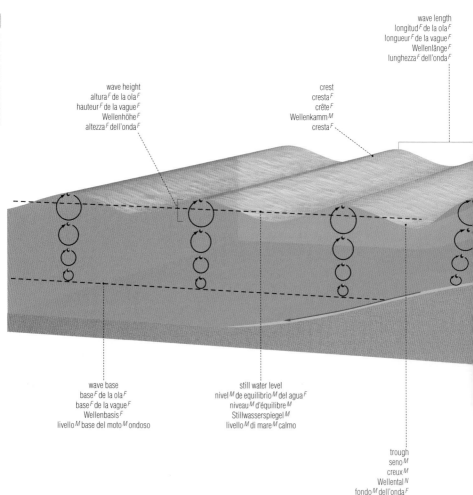

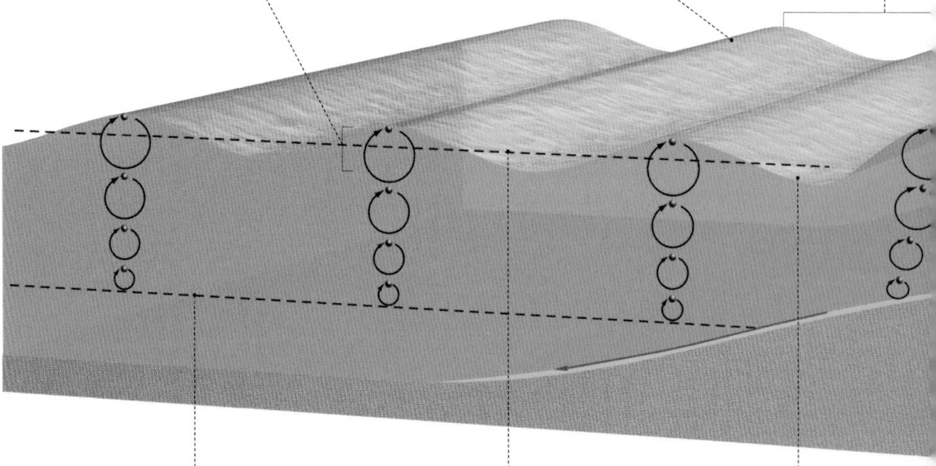
wave length
longitud[F] de la ola[F]
longueur[F] de la vague[F]
Wellenlänge[F]
lunghezza[F] dell'onda[F]
wave height
altura[F] de la ola[F]
hauteur[F] de la vague[F]
Wellenhöhe[F]
altezza[F] dell'onda[F]
crest
cresta[F]
crête[F]
Wellenkamm[M]
cresta[F]
wave base
base[F] de la ola[F]
base[F] de la vague[F]
Wellenbasis[F]
livello[M] base del moto[M] ondoso
still water level
nivel[M] de equilibrio[M] del agua[F]
niveau[M] d'équilibre[M]
Stillwasserspiegel[M]
livello[M] di mare[M] calmo
trough
seno[M]
creux[M]
Wellental[N]
fondo[M] dell'onda[F]

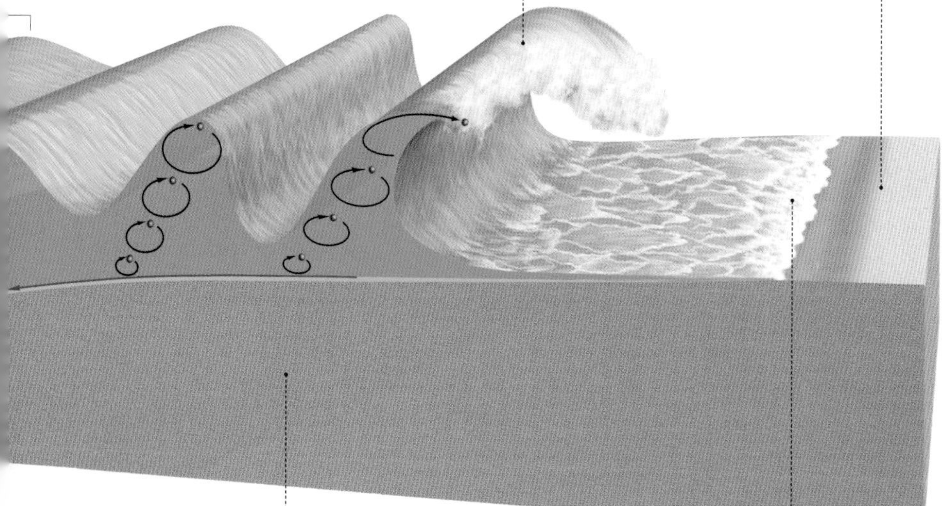
breaker
rompiente M
vague F déferlante
Brecher M
frangente M
shore
costa F
côte F
Küste F
costa F
sand bar
banco M de arena F
banc M de sable M
Sandbank F
banco M di sabbia F
foam
espuma F
écume F
Schaum M
schiuma F

ocean floor

fondo^M oceánico | fond^M de l'océan^M | Meeresboden^M | fondale^M oceanico

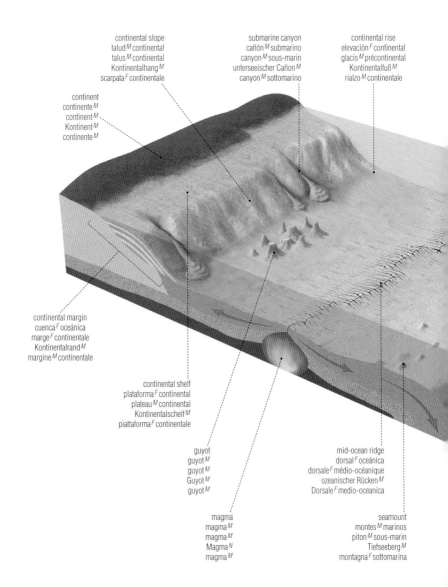

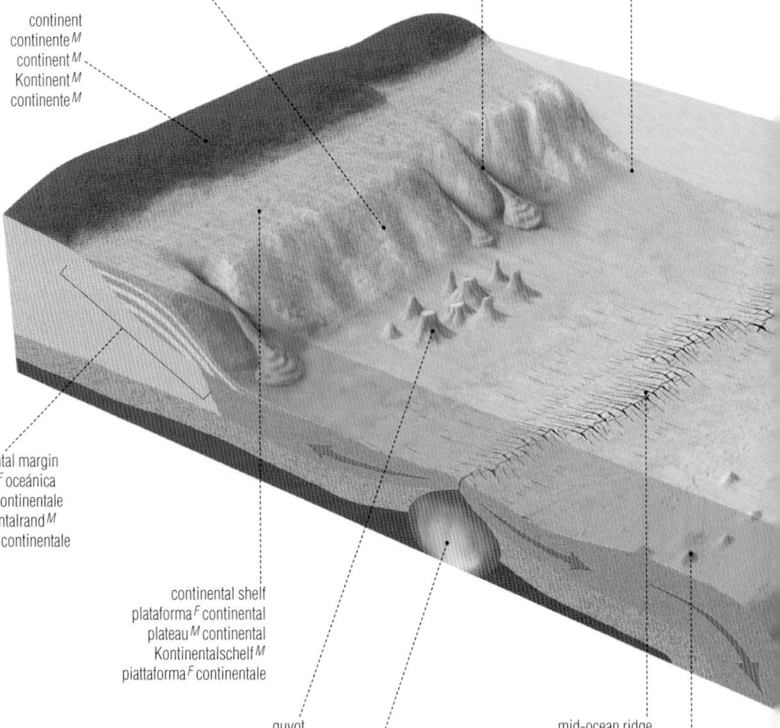
continental slope
talud^M continental
talus^M continental
Kontinentalhang^M
scarpata^F continentale
submarine canyon
cañón^M submarino
canyon^M sous-marin
unterseeischer Cañon^M
canyon^M sottomarino
continental rise
elevación^F continental
glacis^M précontinental
Kontinentalfuß^M
rialzo^M continentale
continent
continente^M
continent^M
Kontinent^M
continente^M
continental margin
cuenca^F oceánica
marge^F continentale
Kontinentalrand^M
margine^M continentale
continental shelf
plataforma^F continental
plateau^M continental
Kontinentalschelf^M
piattaforma^F continentale
guyot
guyot^M
guyot^M
Guyot^M
guyot^M
mid-ocean ridge
dorsal^F oceánica
dorsale^F médio-océanique
ozeanischer Rücken^M
Dorsale^F medio-oceanica
magma
magma^M
magma^M
Magma^N
magma^M
seamount
montes^M marinos
piton^M sous-marin
Tiefseeberg^M
montagna^F sottomarina

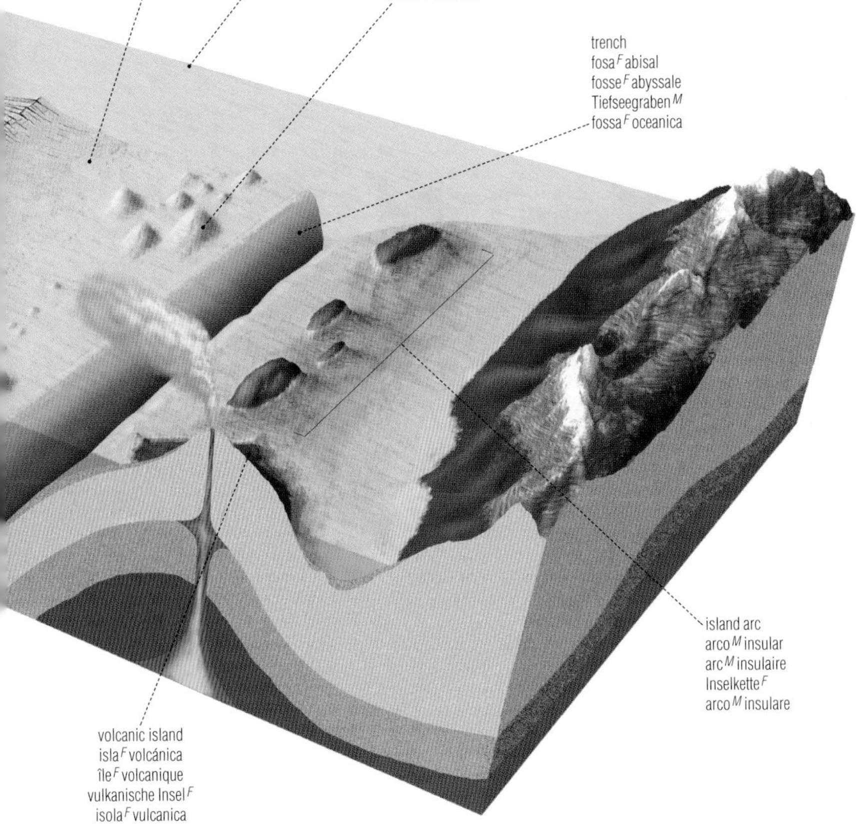
abyssal plain
llanura F abisal
plaine F abyssale
Tiefsee-Ebene F
pianura F abissale
sea level
nivel M del mar M
niveau M de la mer F
Meeresspiegel M
livello M del mare M
abyssal hill
colina F abisal
colline F abyssale
Tiefseehügel M
collina F abissale
trench
fosa F abisal
fosse F abyssale
Tiefseegraben M
fossa F oceanica
island arc
arco M insular
arc M insulaire
Inselkette F
arco M insulare
volcanic island
isla F volcánica
île F volcanique
vulkanische Insel F
isola F vulcanica

common coastal features

configuración^F del litoral^M | configuration^F du littoral^M | typische Küstenformen^F | caratteristiche^F della costa^F

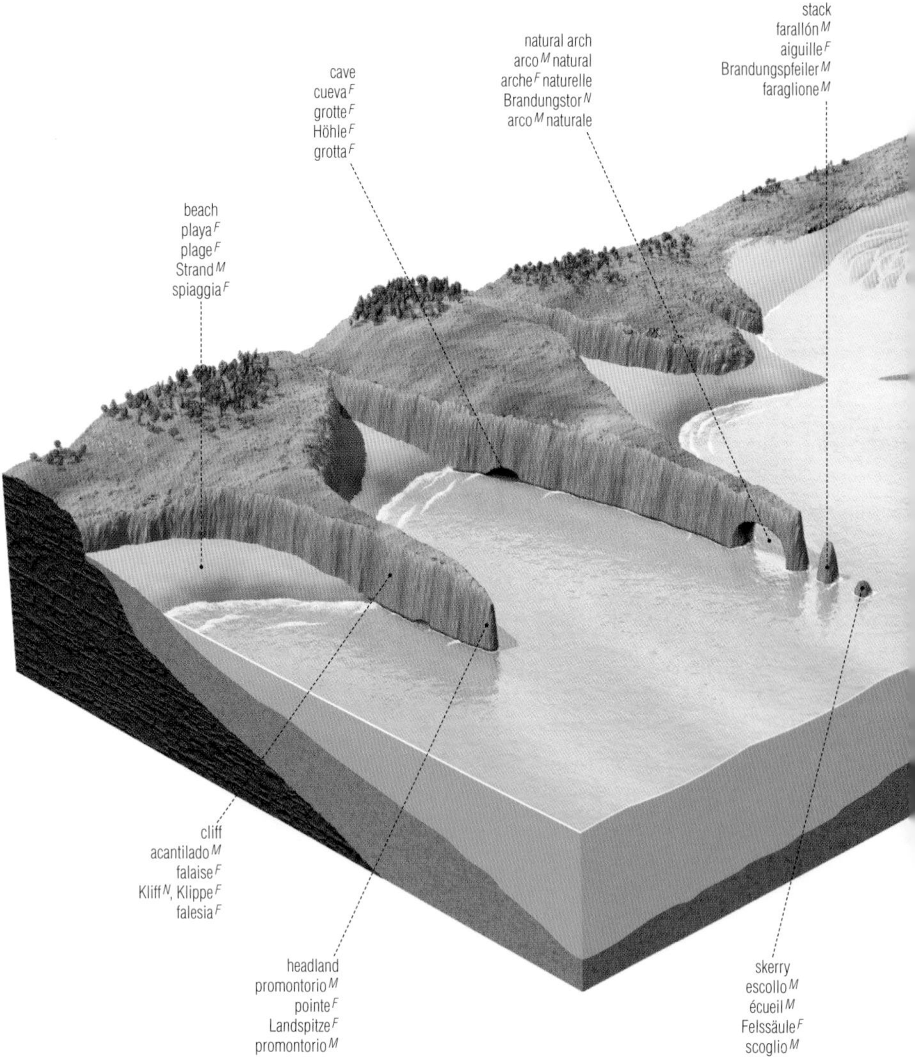

stack
farallón M
aiguille F
Brandungspfeiler M
faraglione M
natural arch
arco M natural
arche F naturelle
Brandungstor N
arco M naturale
cave
cueva F
grotte F
Höhle F
grotta F
beach
playa F
plage F
Strand M
spiaggia F
cliff
acantilado M
falaise F
Kliff N, Klippe F
falesia F
headland
promontorio M
pointe F
Landspitze F
promontorio M
skerry
escollo M
écueil M
Felssäule F
scoglio M

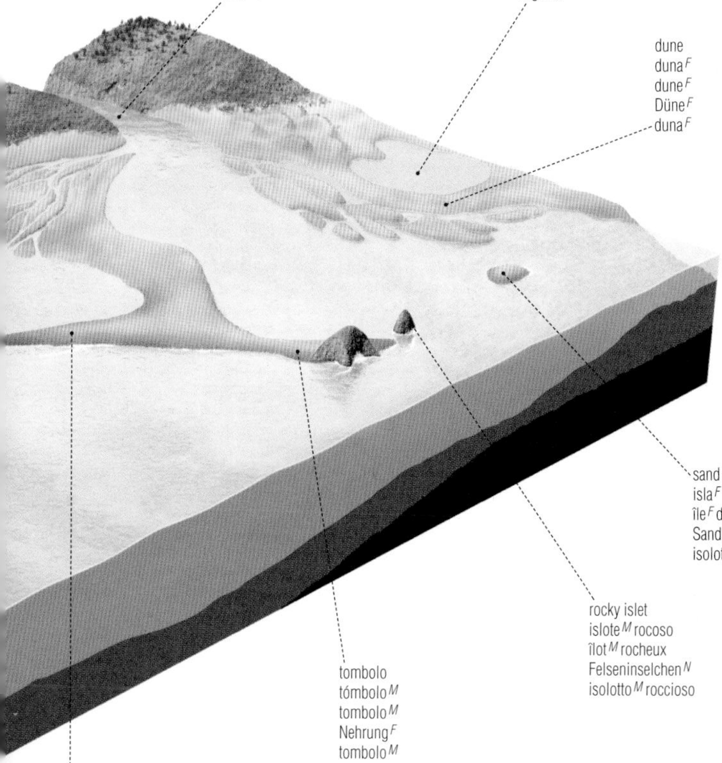
estuary
estuario M
estuaire M
Flussmündung F
estuario M
lagoon
laguna F
lagune F
Lagune F
laguna F
dune
duna F
dune F
Düne F
duna F
sand island
isla F de arena F
île F de sable M
Sandinsel F
isolotto M sabbioso
rocky islet
islote M rocoso
îlot M rocheux
Felseninselchen N
isolotto M roccioso
tombolo
tómbolo M
tombolo M
Nehrung F
tombolo M
spit
barra F
flèche F littorale
Landzunge F
lingua F di terra F

examples of shorelines
ejemplos^M de costas^F
exemples^M de côtes^F
Küstenformen^F
esempi^M di linee^F di costa^F

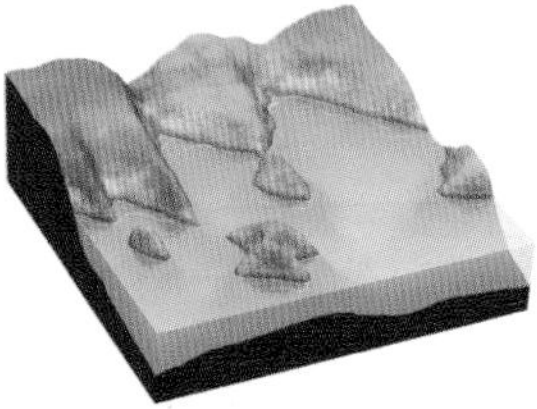

rias
rías^F
rias^F
Riasküste^F
costa^F a rias^F

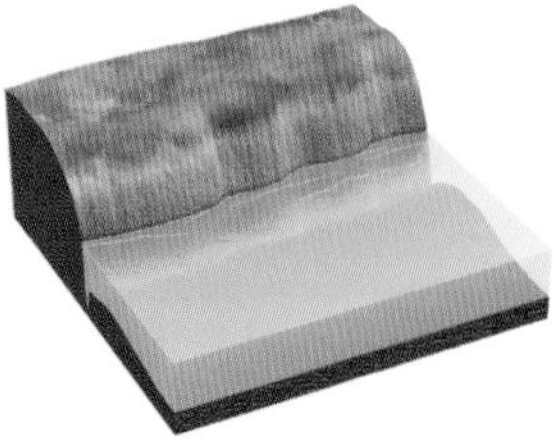

shore cliff
acantilado^M
falaise^F côtière
Steilküste^F
falesia^F costiera

delta
delta^M
delta^M
Delta^N
delta^M

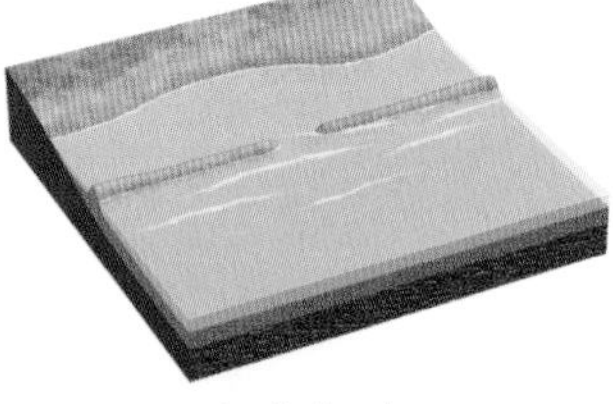

barrier beach
cordón^M litoral
cordon^M littoral
Riffküste^F
cordone^M litorale

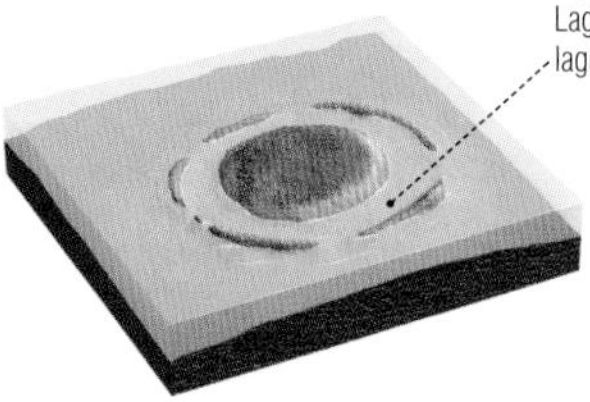
lagoon
laguna^F
lagon^M
Lagune^F
laguna^F

atoll
atolón^M
atoll^M
Atoll^N
atollo^M

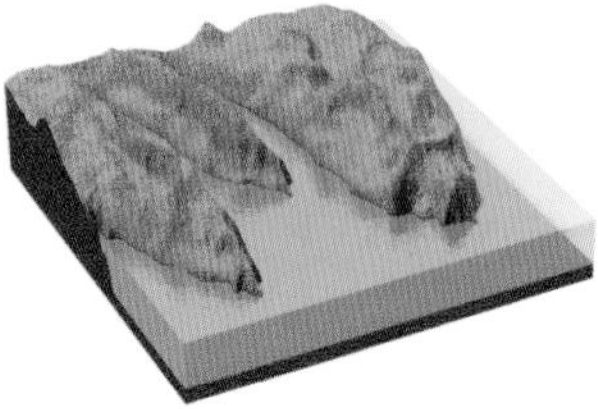

fjords
fiordo^M
fjords^M
Fjordküste^F
fiordi^M

desert

desierto[M] | désert[M] | Wüste[F] | deserto[M]

examples of dunes
ejemplos[M] de dunas[F]
exemples[M] de dunes[F]
Dünenformen[F]
esempi[M] di dune[F]

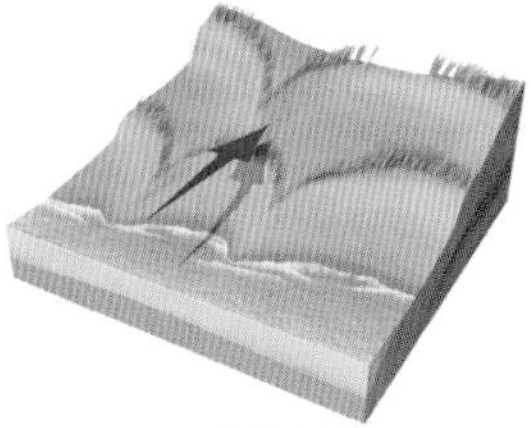

parabolic dune
duna[F] parabólica
dune[F] parabolique
Parabeldüne[F]
duna[F] parabolica

complex dune
duna[F] compleja
dune[F] complexe
komplexe Düne[F]
duna[F] complessa

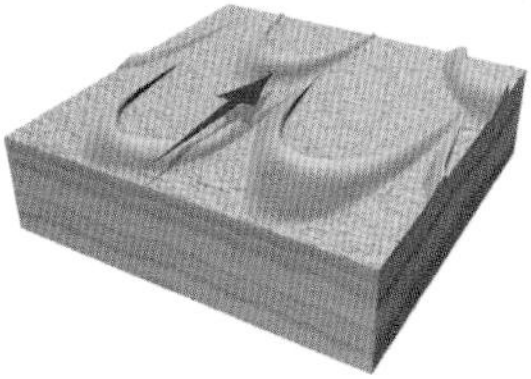

crescentic dune
barján[M]
dune[F] en croissant[M]
Sicheldüne[F]
barcana[F]

chain of dunes
cadena[F] de dunas[F]
cordon[M] de dunes[F]
Dünenzug[M]
catena[F] di dune[F]

transverse dunes
dunas[F] transversales
dunes[F] transversales
Querdünen[F]
dune[F] trasversali

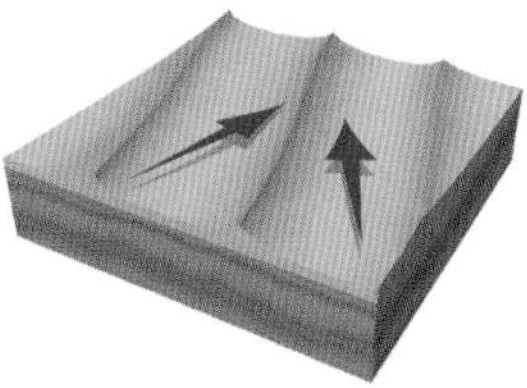

longitudinal dunes
dunas[F] longitudinales
dunes[F] longitudinales
Längsdünen[F]
dune[F] longitudinali

desert

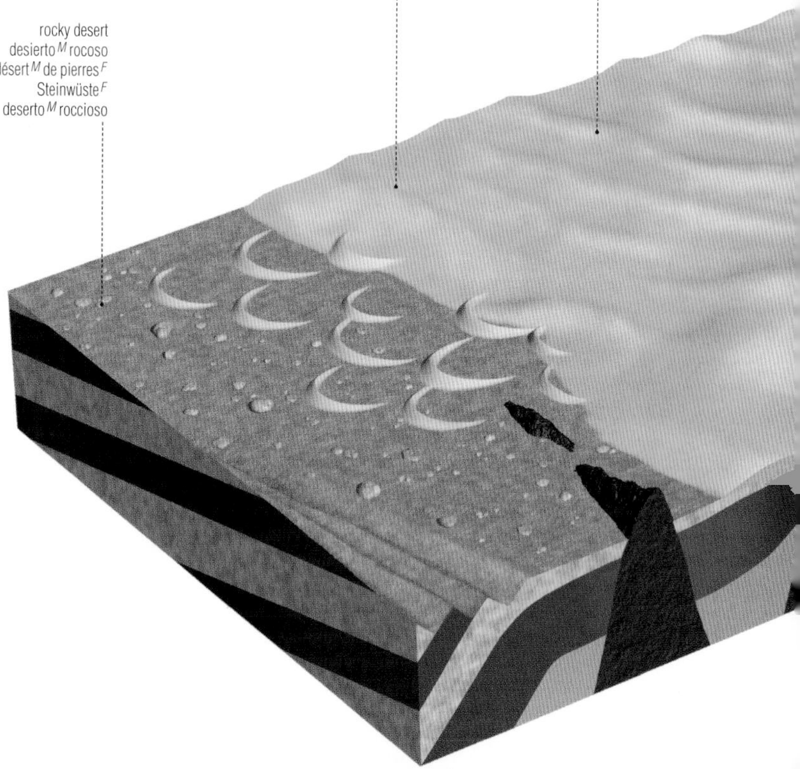
dune
duna F
dune F
Düne F
duna F
sandy desert
desierto M arenoso
désert M de sable M
Sandwüste F
deserto M sabbioso
rocky desert
desierto M rocoso
désert M de pierres F
Steinwüste F
deserto M roccioso

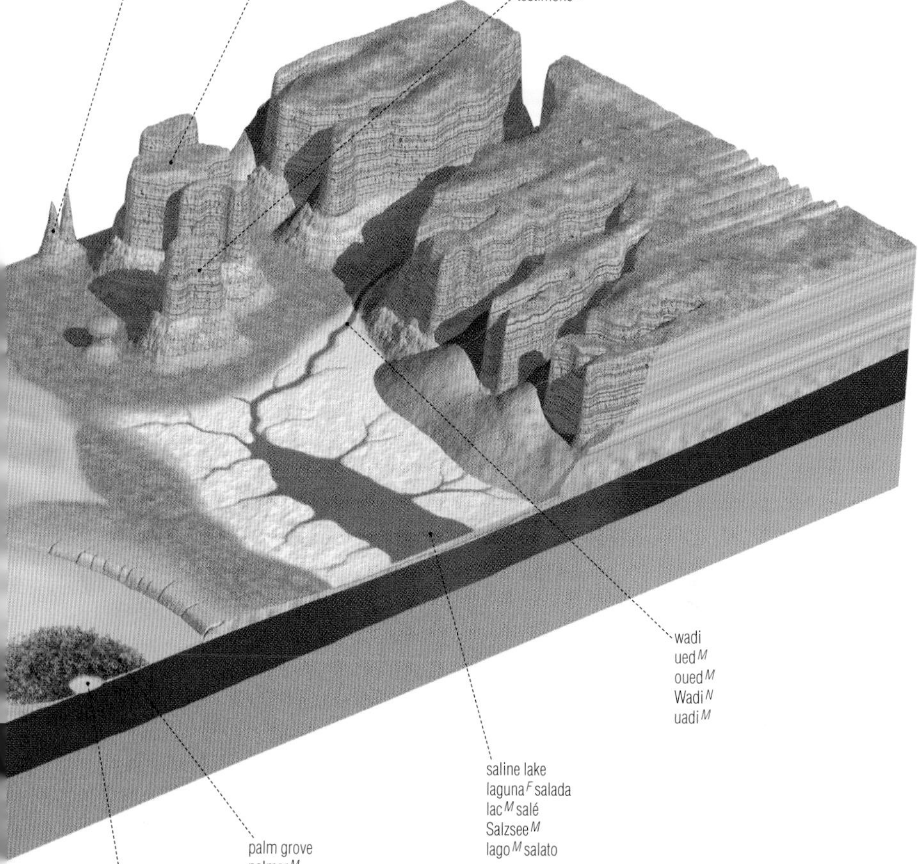
needle
aguja [F]
aiguille [F]
Nadel [F]
guglia [F]
mesa
mesa [F]
mesa [F]
Tafelberg [M]
mesa [F]
butte
hamada [F]
butte [F]
Zeugenberg [M]
testimone [M]
wadi
ued [M]
oued [M]
Wadi [N]
uadi [M]
saline lake
laguna [F] salada
lac [M] salé
Salzsee [M]
lago [M] salato
palm grove
palmar [M]
palmeraie [F]
Palmenhain [M]
palmeto [M]
oasis
oasis [M]
oasis [F]
Oase [F]
oasi [F]

profile of the Earth's atmosphere

corte[M] de la atmósfera[F] terrestre | coupe[F] de l'atmosphère[F] terrestre | Erdatmosphäre[F] im Querschnitt[M] | profilo[M] dell'atmosfera[F] terrestre

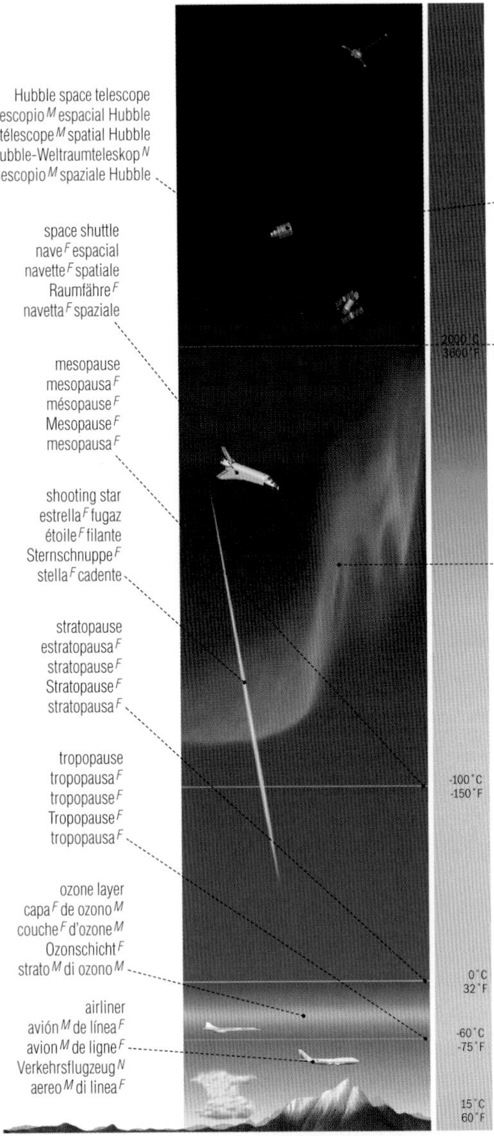
2000°C
3600°F
500 km
310 mi
-100°C
-150°F
80 km
50 mi
0°C
32°F
50 km
30 mi
-60°C
-75°F
15 km
10 mi
15°C
60°F

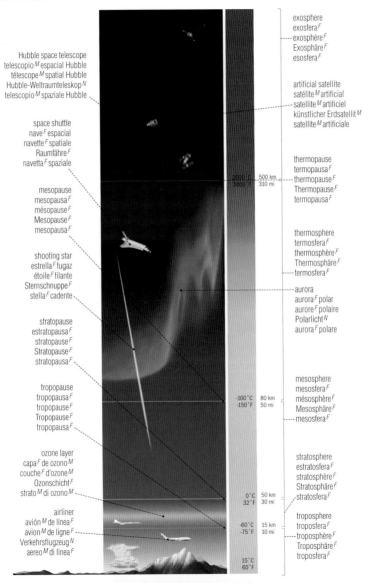

Hubble space telescope
telescopio[M] espacial Hubble
télescope[M] spatial Hubble
Hubble-Weltraumteleskop[N]
telescopio[M] spaziale Hubble

space shuttle
nave[F] espacial
navette[F] spatiale
Raumfähre[F]
navetta[F] spaziale

mesopause
mesopausa[F]
mésopause[F]
Mesopause[F]
mesopausa[F]

shooting star
estrella[F] fugaz
étoile[F] filante
Sternschnuppe[F]
stella[F] cadente

stratopause
estratopausa[F]
stratopause[F]
Stratopause[F]
stratopausa[F]

tropopause
tropopausa[F]
tropopause[F]
Tropopause[F]
tropopausa[F]

ozone layer
capa[F] de ozono[M]
couche[F] d'ozone[M]
Ozonschicht[F]
strato[M] di ozono[M]

airliner
avión[M] de línea[F]
avion[M] de ligne[F]
Verkehrsflugzeug[N]
aereo[M] di linea[F]

exosphere
exosfera[F]
exosphère[F]
Exosphäre[F]
esosfera[F]

artificial satellite
satélite[M] artificial
satellite[M] artificiel
künstlicher Erdsatellit[M]
satellite[M] artificiale

thermopause
termopausa[F]
thermopause[F]
Thermopause[F]
termopausa[F]

thermosphere
termosfera[F]
thermosphère[F]
Thermosphäre[F]
termosfera[F]

aurora
aurora[F] polar
aurore[F] polaire
Polarlicht[N]
aurora[F] polare

mesosphere
mesosfera[F]
mésosphère[F]
Mesosphäre[F]
mesosfera[F]

stratosphere
estratosfera[F]
stratosphère[F]
Stratosphäre[F]
stratosfera[F]

troposphere
troposfera[F]
troposphère[F]
Troposphäre[F]
troposfera[F]

seasons of the year

estaciones F del año M | cycle M des saisons F | Jahreszeiten F | stagioni F dell'anno M

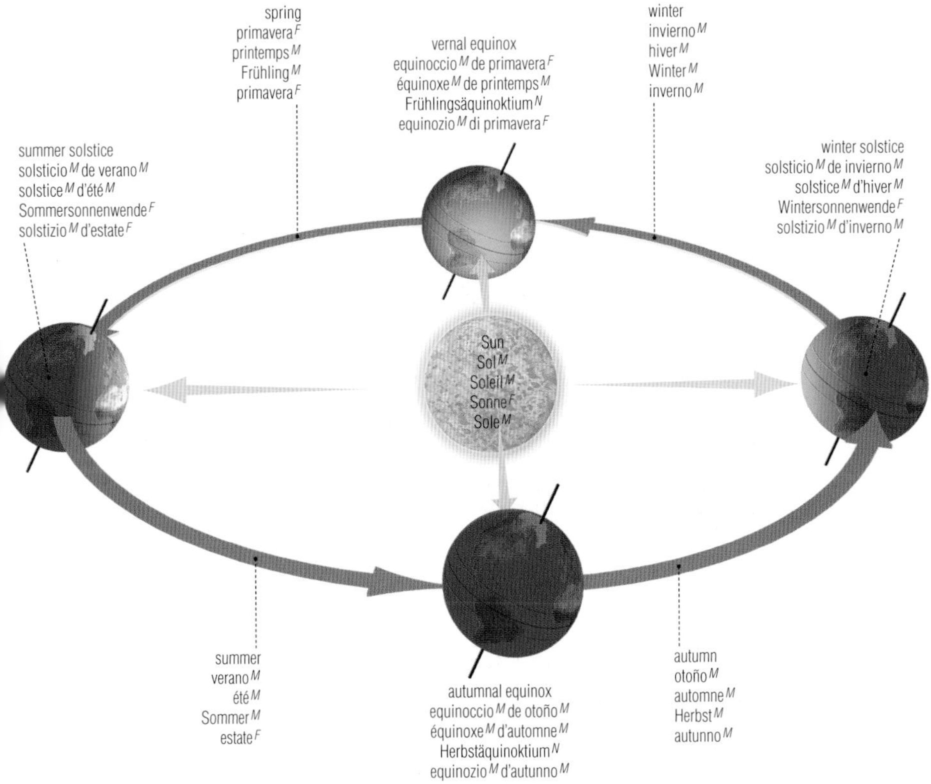
spring
primavera F
printemps M
Frühling M
primavera F
vernal equinox
equinoccio M de primavera F
équinoxe M de printemps M
Frühlingsäquinoktium N
equinozio M di primavera F
winter
invierno M
hiver M
Winter M
inverno M
summer solstice
solsticio M de verano M
solstice M d'été M
Sommersonnenwende F
solstizio M d'estate F
winter solstice
solsticio M de invierno M
solstice M d'hiver M
Wintersonnenwende F
solstizio M d'inverno M
Sun
Sol M
Soleil M
Sonne F
Sole M
summer
verano M
été M
Sommer M
estate F
autumnal equinox
equinoccio M de otoño M
équinoxe M d'automne M
Herbstäquinoktium N
equinozio M d'autunno M
autumn
otoño M
automne M
Herbst M
autunno M

climates of the world

climas[M] del mundo[M] | climats[M] du monde[M] | Klimate[N] der Welt[F] | climi[M] del mondo[M]

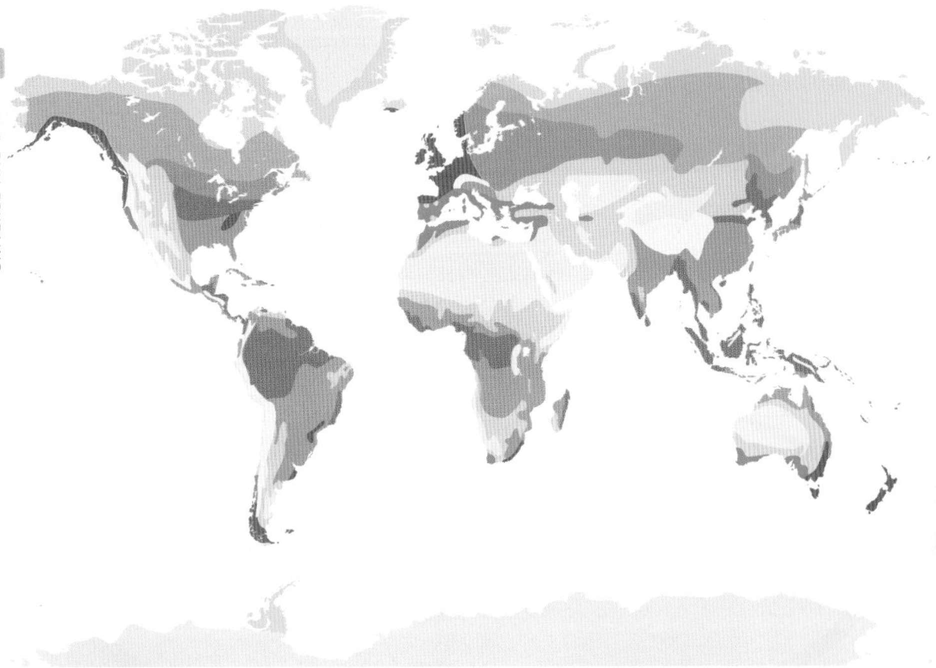

tropical climates
climas[M] tropicales
climats[M] tropicaux
tropische Klimate[N]
climi[M] tropicali

tropical rain forest
tropical[M] lluvioso
tropical humide
tropischer Regenwald[M]
tropicale della foresta[F] pluviale

tropical wet-and-dry (savanna)
tropical[M] húmedo y seco (sabana[F])
tropical humide et sec (savane[F])
tropisch feucht und trocken (Savanne[F])
tropicale umido e secco (savana[F])

highland climates
climas[M] de alta montaña[F]
climats[M] de montagne[F]
Hochlandklimate[N]
climi[M] di montagna[F]

highland
climas[M] de montaña[F]
climats[M] de montagne[F]
Hochgebirge[N]
di montagna[F]

cold temperate climates
climas[M] templados fríos
climats[M] tempérés froids
kaltgemäßigte Klimate[N]
climi[M] temperati freddi

humid continental-hot summer
continental[M] húmedo - verano[M] tórrido
continental humide, à été[M] chaud
feucht-kontinental - heißer Sommer[M]
continentale umido - estate[F] torrida

humid continental-warm summer
continental[M] húmedo - verano[M] fresco
continental humide, à été[M] frais
feucht-kontinental - warmer Sommer[M]
continentale umido - estate[F] calda

subarctic
subártico
subarctique
subarktisch
subartico

polar climates
climas[M] polares
climats[M] polaires
Polarklimate[N]
climi[M] polari

polar tundra
tundra[F]
toundra[F]
Polartundra[F]
della tundra[F] polare

polar ice cap
hielos[M] perpetuos
calotte[F] glaciaire
Eiskappe[F]
della calotta[F] polare

warm temperate climates
climas[M] templados cálidos
climats[M] tempérés chauds
warmgemäßigte Klimate[N]
climi[M] temperati caldi

humid subtropical
subtropical húmedo
subtropical humide
feucht subtropisch
subtropicale umido

Mediterranean subtropical
subtropical mediterráneo
méditerranéen
mediterran subtropisch
subtropicale mediterraneo

marine
marítimo
océanique
maritim
marino

dry climates
climas[M] áridos
climats[M] arides
Trockenklimate[N]
climi[M] aridi

steppe
estepario
steppe[F]
Steppe[F]
steppico

desert
desértico
désert[M]
Wüste[F]
desertico

clouds

nubes[F] | nuages[M] | Wolken[F] | nuvole[F]

high clouds
nubes[F] altas
nuages[M] de haute altitude[F]
hohe Wolken[F]
nubi[F] alte

cirrostratus
cirrostratos[M]
cirro-stratus[M]
Zirrostratus[M]
cirrostrato[M]

middle clouds
nubes[F] medias
nuages[M] de moyenne altitude[F]
mittelhohe Wolken[F]
nubi[F] medie

altostratus
altostratos[M]
alto-stratus[M]
Altostratus[M]
altostrato[M]

altocumulus
altocúmulos[M]
alto-cumulus[M]
Altokumulus[M]
altocumulo[M]

low clouds
nubes[F] bajas
nuages[M] de basse altitude[F]
tiefe Wolken[F]
nubi[F] basse

stratocumulus
estratocúmulos[M]
strato-cumulus[M]
Stratokumulus[M]
stratocumulo[M]

nimbostratus
nimbostratos[M]
nimbo-stratus[M]
Nimbostratus[M]
nembostrato[M]

stratus
estratos[M]
stratus[M]
Stratus[M]
strato[M]

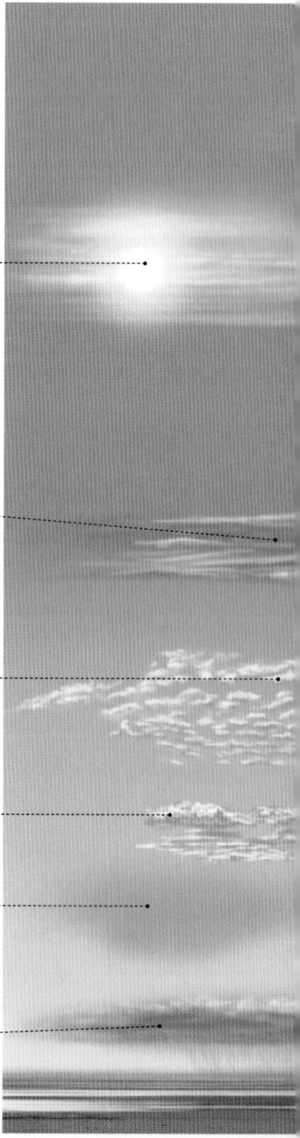

cirrocumulus
cirrocúmulos [M]
cirro-cumulus [M]
Zirrokumulus [M]
cirrocumulo [M]

cirrus
cirros [M]
cirrus [M]
Zirrus [M]
cirro [M]

clouds of vertical development
nubes [F] de desarrollo [M] vertical
nuages [M] à développement [M] vertical
Quellwolken [F]
nubi [F] a sviluppo [M] verticale

cumulonimbus
cumulonimbos [M]
cumulo-nimbus [M]
Kumulonimbus [M]
cumulonembo [M]

cumulus
cúmulos [M]
cumulus [M]
Kumulus [M]
cumulo [M]

tropical cyclone

ciclón[M] tropical | cyclone[M] tropical | tropischer Wirbelsturm[M] | ciclone[M] tropicale

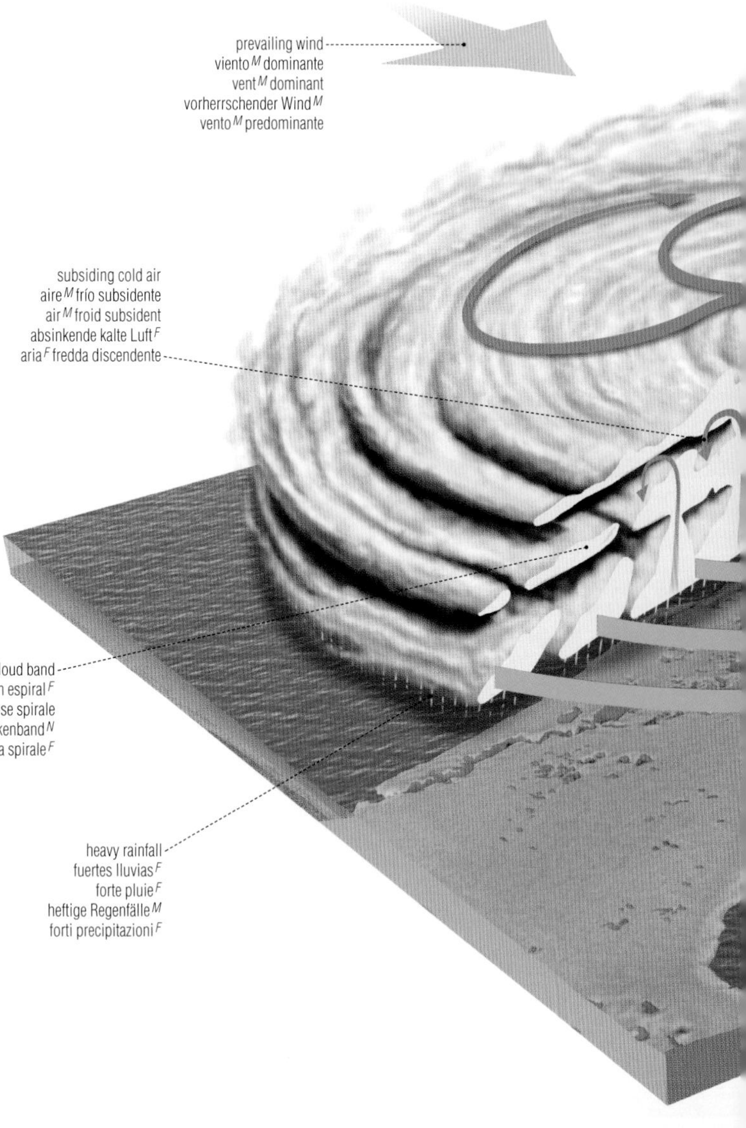
prevailing wind
viento[M] dominante
vent[M] dominant
vorherrschender Wind[M]
vento[M] predominante
subsiding cold air
aire[M] frío subsidente
air[M] froid subsident
absinkende kalte Luft[F]
aria[F] fredda discendente
spiral cloud band
banda[F] nubosa en espiral[F]
bande[F] nuageuse spirale
spiralförmiges Wolkenband[N]
banda[F] nuvolosa a spirale[F]
heavy rainfall
fuertes lluvias[F]
forte pluie[F]
heftige Regenfälle[M]
forti precipitazioni[F]

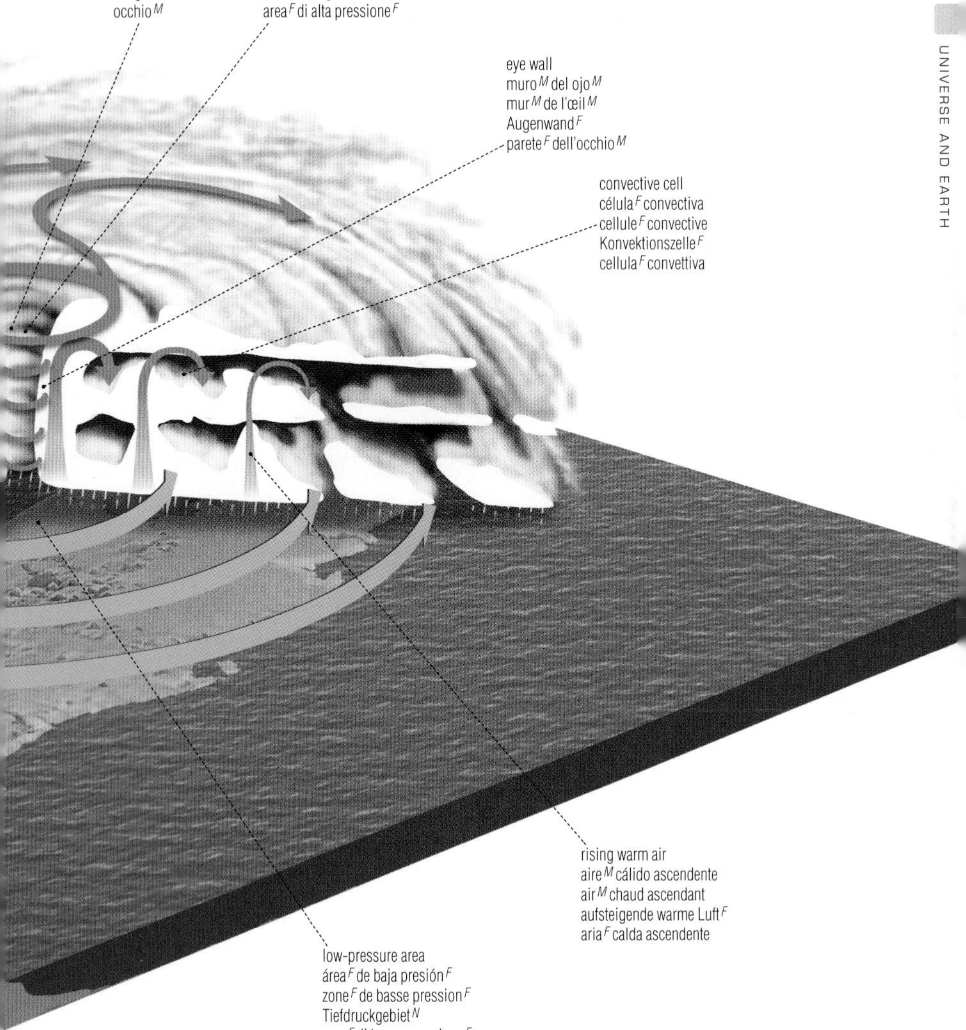
eye
ojo M
œil M
Auge N
occhio M
high-pressure area
área F de alta presión F
zone F de haute pression F
Hochdruckgebiet N
area F di alta pressione F
eye wall
muro M del ojo M
mur M de l'œil M
Augenwand F
parete F dell'occhio M
convective cell
célula F convectiva
cellule F convective
Konvektionszelle F
cellula F convettiva
rising warm air
aire M cálido ascendente
air M chaud ascendant
aufsteigende warme Luft F
aria F calda ascendente
low-pressure area
área F de baja presión F
zone F de basse pression F
Tiefdruckgebiet N
area F di bassa pressione F

tornado and waterspout

tornado^M y tromba^F marina | tornade^F et trombe^F marine | Tornado^M und Wasserhose^F | tornado^M e tromba^F marina

waterspout
tromba^F marina
trombe^F marine
Wasserhose^F
tromba^F marina

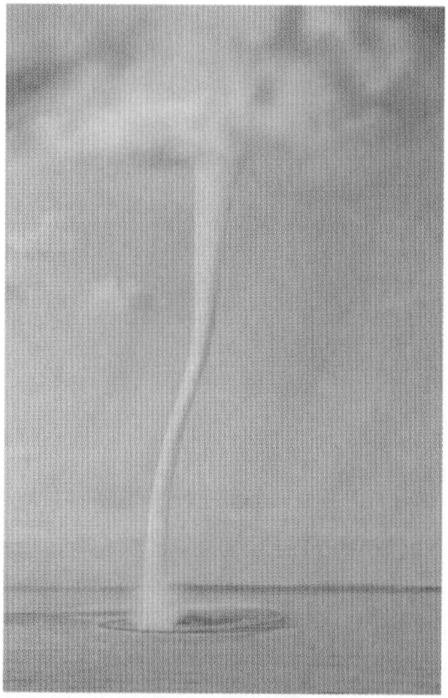

tornado
tornado^M
tornade^F
Tornado^M
tornado^M

wall cloud
muro^M de nubes^F
mur^M de nuages^M
Gewitterwolken^F
parete^F di nuvole^F

funnel cloud
nube^F en forma^F de embudo^M
nuage^M en entonnoir^M
Wolkentrichter^M
nube^F a proboscide^F

debris
detritos^M
buisson^M
aufgewirbelter Staub^M
detriti^M

precipitation

precipitaciones^{F} | précipitations^{F} | Niederschläge^{M} | precipitazioni^{F}

rain forms
formas^{F} de lluvia^{F}
formes^{F} de pluie^{F}
Regenarten^{F}
tipologie^{F} di pioggia^{F}

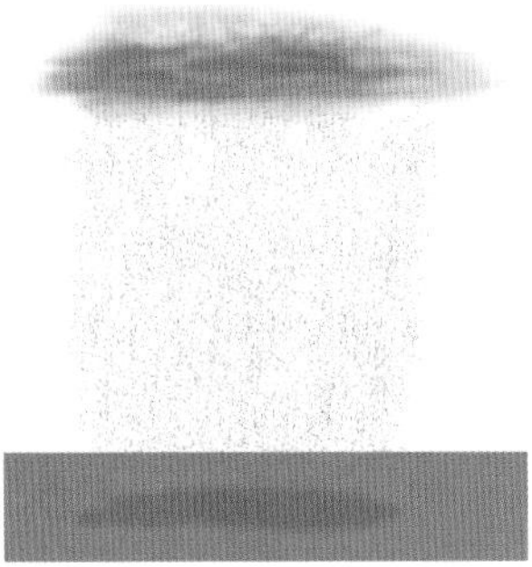

drizzle
llovizna^{F}
bruine^{F}
Sprühregen^{M}
pioviggine^{F}

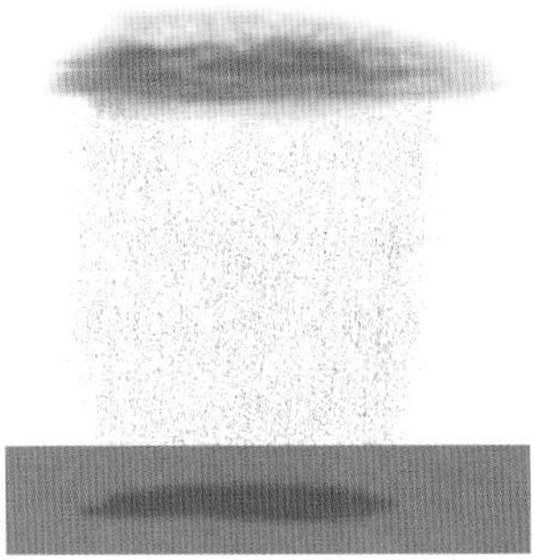

light rain
lluvia^{F} ligera
pluie^{F} faible
leichter Regen^{M}
pioggia^{F} leggera

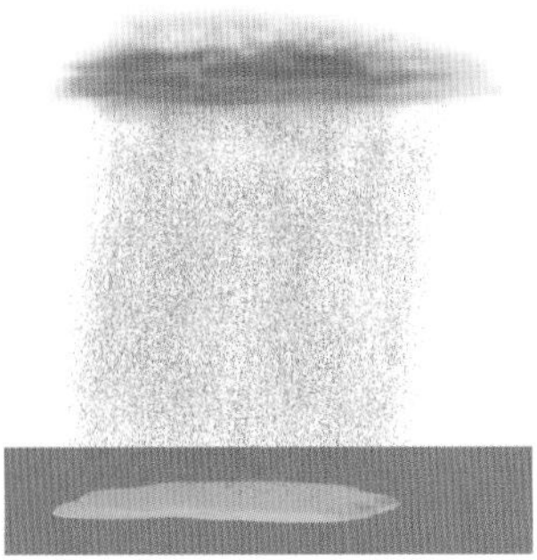

moderate rain
lluvia^{F} moderada
pluie^{F} modérée
mäßiger Regen^{M}
pioggia^{F} moderata

heavy rain
lluvia^{F} intensa
pluie^{F} forte
starker Regen^{M}
pioggia^{F} forte

precipitation

snow crystals
cristales^{M} de nieve^{F}
cristaux^{M} de neige^{F}
Schneekristalle^{M}
cristalli^{M} di neve^{F}

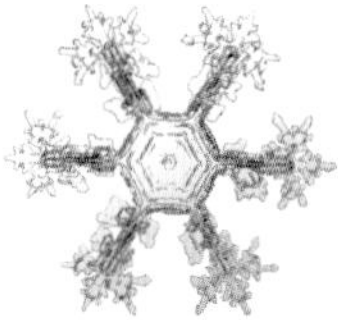

stellar crystal
estrella^{F}
étoile^{F}
Stern^{M}
cristallo^{M} stellare

hail
granizo^{M}
grêlon^{M}
Hagel^{M}
grandine^{F}

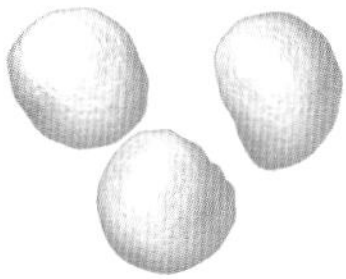

sleet
cellisca^{F}
grésil^{M}
Eiskörnchen^{N}
nevischio^{M}

snow pellet
copo^{M} de nieve^{F}
neige^{F} roulée
Reif- und Frostgraupel^{F}
pallottoline^{F} di neve^{F}

winter precipitations
precipitaciones^{F} invernales
précipitations^{F} hivernales
Winterniederschläge^{M}
precipitazioni^{F} invernali

freezing rain
lluvia^{F} helada
pluie^{F} verglaçante
gefrierender Regen^{M}
pioggia^{F} congelantesi

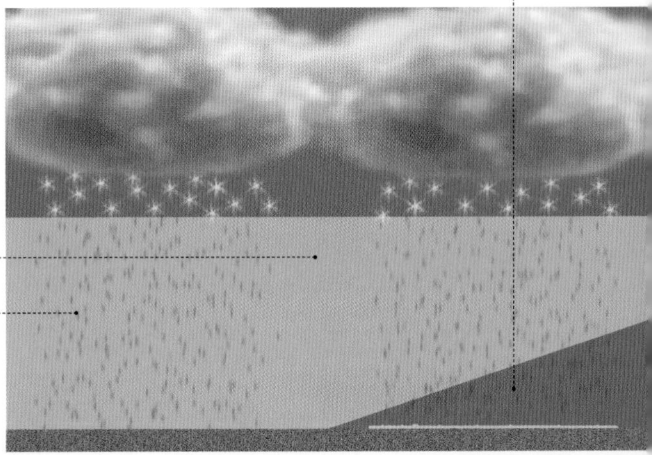

warm air
aire^{M} caliente
air^{M} chaud
warme Luft^{F}
aria^{F} calda

rain
lluvia^{F}
pluie^{F}
Regen^{M}
pioggia^{F}

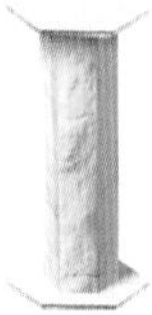

capped column
columna F con capuchón M
colonne F avec capuchon M
bedeckte Säule F
colonna F con lamelle F terminali

irregular crystal
cristales M irregulares
cristaux M irréguliers
irreguläres Aggregat N
cristallo M irregolare

spatial dendrite
dendrita F espacial
dendrite F spatiale
räumlicher Dendrit M
cristallo M dendritico spaziale

plate crystal
placa F de hielo M
plaquette F
Plättchen N
cristallo M lamellare

column
columna F
colonne F
Säule F
colonna F

needle
aguja F
aiguille F
Nadel F
ago M

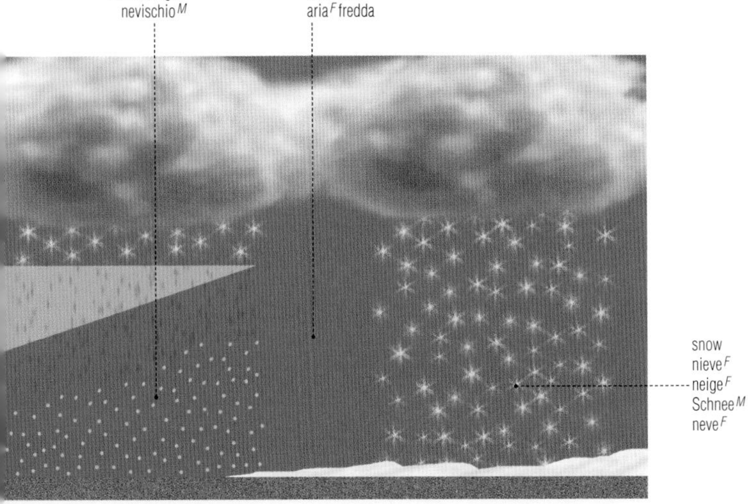
sleet
aguanieve M
grésil M
Schneeregen M
nevischio M
cold air
aire M frío
air M froid
kalte Luft F
aria F fredda
snow
nieve F
neige F
Schnee M
neve F

precipitation

stormy sky
cielo[M] **turbulento**
ciel[M] **d'orage**[M]
stürmischer Himmel[M]
cielo[M] **tempestoso**

lightning
rayo[M]
éclair[M]
Blitz[M]
fulmine[M]

cloud
nube[F]
nuage[M]
Wolke[F]
nube[F]

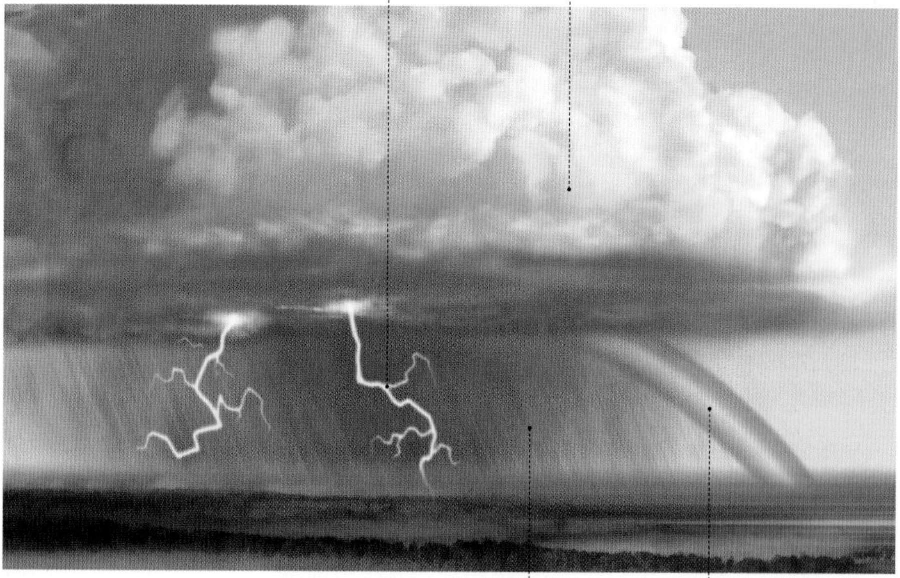

rain
lluvia[F]
pluie[F]
Regen[M]
pioggia[F]

rainbow
arco[M] iris
arc-en-ciel[M]
Regenbogen[M]
arcobaleno[M]

dew
rocío M
rosée F
Tau M
rugiada F

rime
escarcha F
givre M
Reif M
brina F

mist
neblina F
brume F
Dunst M
foschia F

fog
niebla F
brouillard M
Nebel M
nebbia F

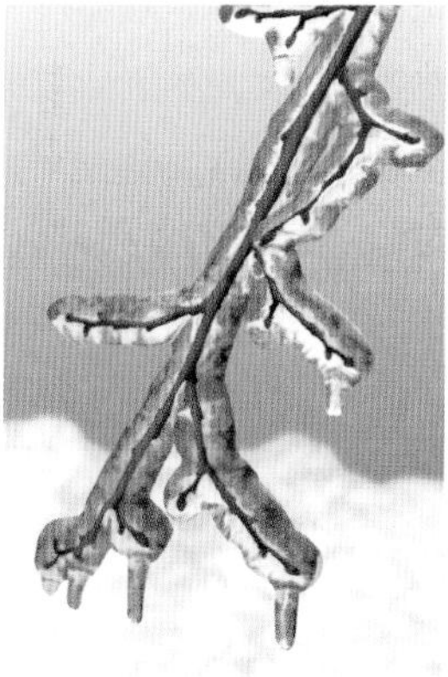

frost
hielo M
verglas M
Raureif M
vetrone M

hydrologic cycle

ciclo[M] hidrológico | cycle[M] de l'eau[F] | Wasserkreislauf[M] | ciclo[M] idrologico

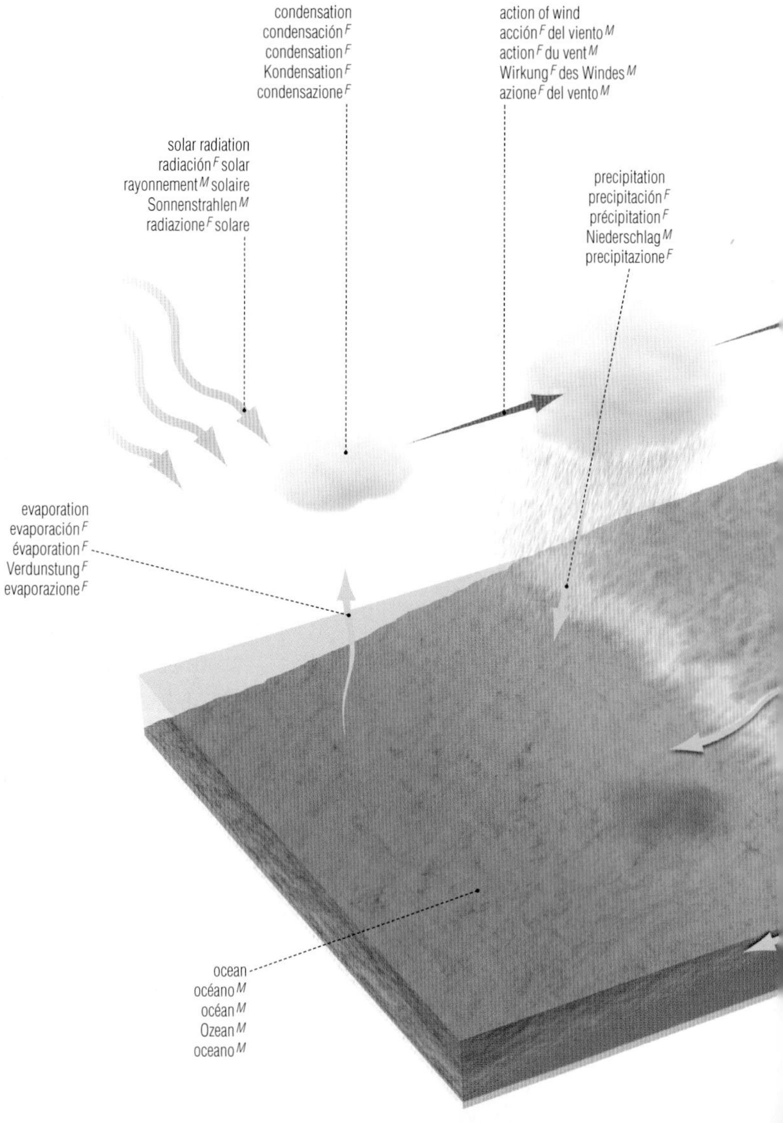
condensation
condensación F
condensation F
Kondensation F
condensazione F
action of wind
acción F del viento M
action F du vent M
Wirkung F des Windes M
azione F del vento M
solar radiation
radiación F solar
rayonnement M solaire
Sonnenstrahlen M
radiazione F solare
precipitation
precipitación F
précipitation F
Niederschlag M
precipitazione F
evaporation
evaporación F
évaporation F
Verdunstung F
evaporazione F
ocean
océano M
océan M
Ozean M
oceano M

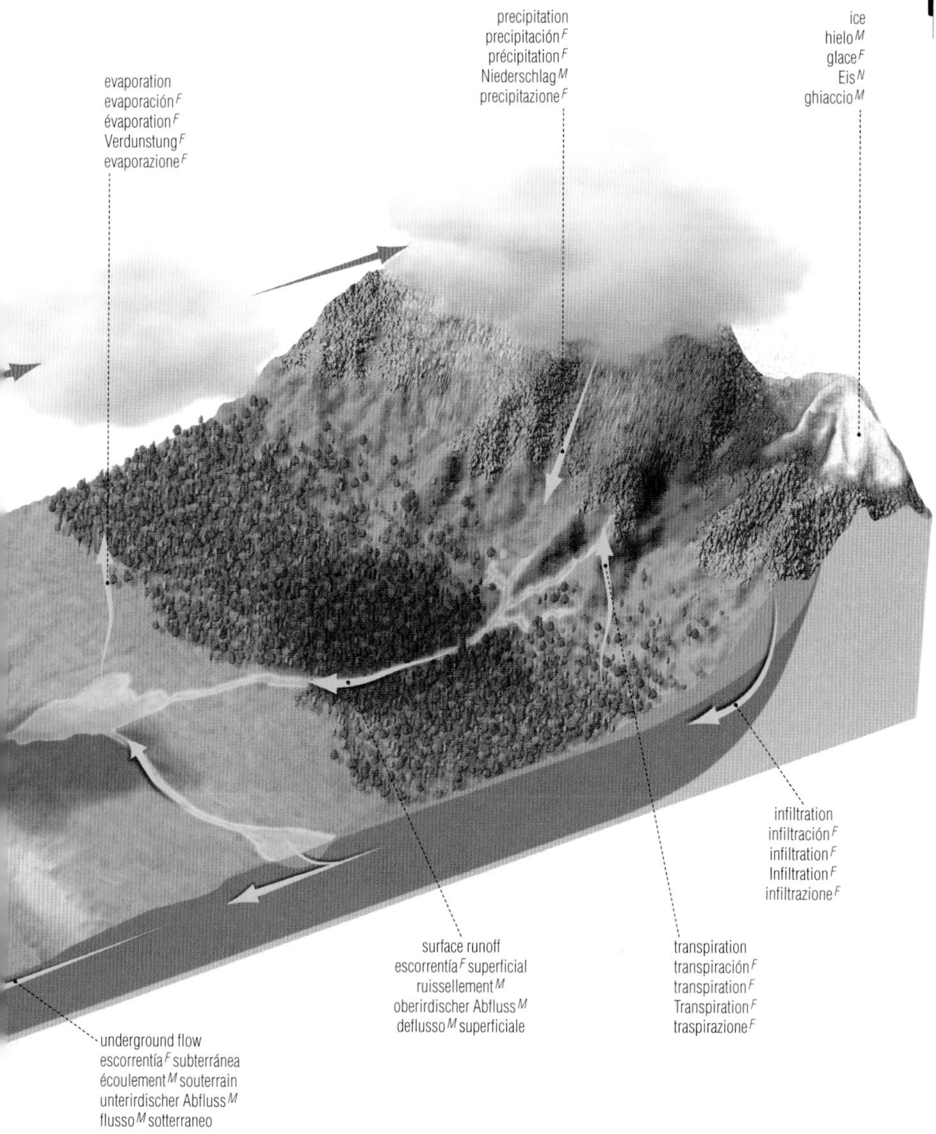
precipitation
precipitación F
précipitation F
Niederschlag M
precipitazione F
ice
hielo M
glace F
Eis N
ghiaccio M
evaporation
evaporación F
évaporation F
Verdunstung F
evaporazione F
infiltration
infiltración F
infiltration F
Infiltration F
infiltrazione F
surface runoff
escorrentía F superficial
ruissellement M
oberirdischer Abfluss M
deflusso M superficiale
transpiration
transpiración F
transpiration F
Transpiration F
traspirazione F
underground flow
escorrentía F subterránea
écoulement M souterrain
unterirdischer Abfluss M
flusso M sotterraneo

greenhouse effect

efecto^M invernadero^M | effet^M de serre^F | Treibhauseffekt^M | effetto^M serra^F

natural greenhouse effect
efecto^M invernadero^M natural
effet^M de serre^F naturel
natürlicher Treibhauseffekt^M
effetto^M serra^F naturale

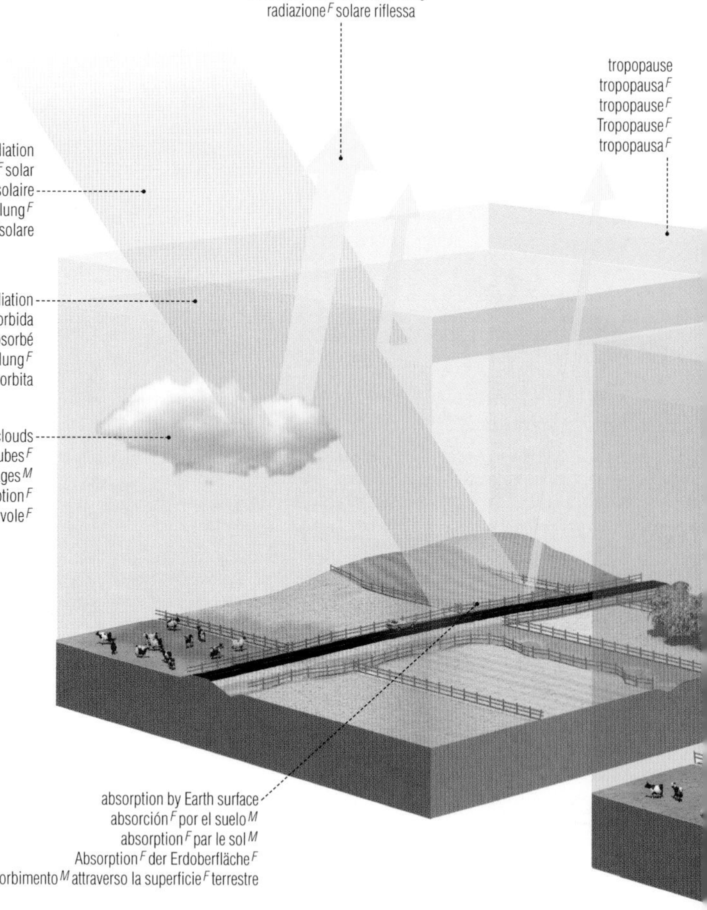

reflected solar radiation
radiación^F solar refleja
rayonnement^M solaire réfléchi
reflektierte Sonneneinstrahlung^F
radiazione^F solare riflessa
tropopause
tropopausa^F
tropopause^F
Tropopause^F
tropopausa^F
solar radiation
radiación^F solar
rayonnement^M solaire
Sonneneinstrahlung^F
radiazione^F solare
absorbed solar radiation
radiación^F solar absorbida
rayonnement^M solaire absorbé
absorbierte Sonneneinstrahlung^F
radiazione^F solare assorbita
absorption by clouds
absorción^F por las nubes^F
absorption^F par les nuages^M
Wolkenabsorption^F
assorbimento^M attraverso le nuvole^F
absorption by Earth surface
absorción^F por el suelo^M
absorption^F par le sol^M
Absorption^F der Erdoberfläche^F
assorbimento^M attraverso la superficie^F terrestre

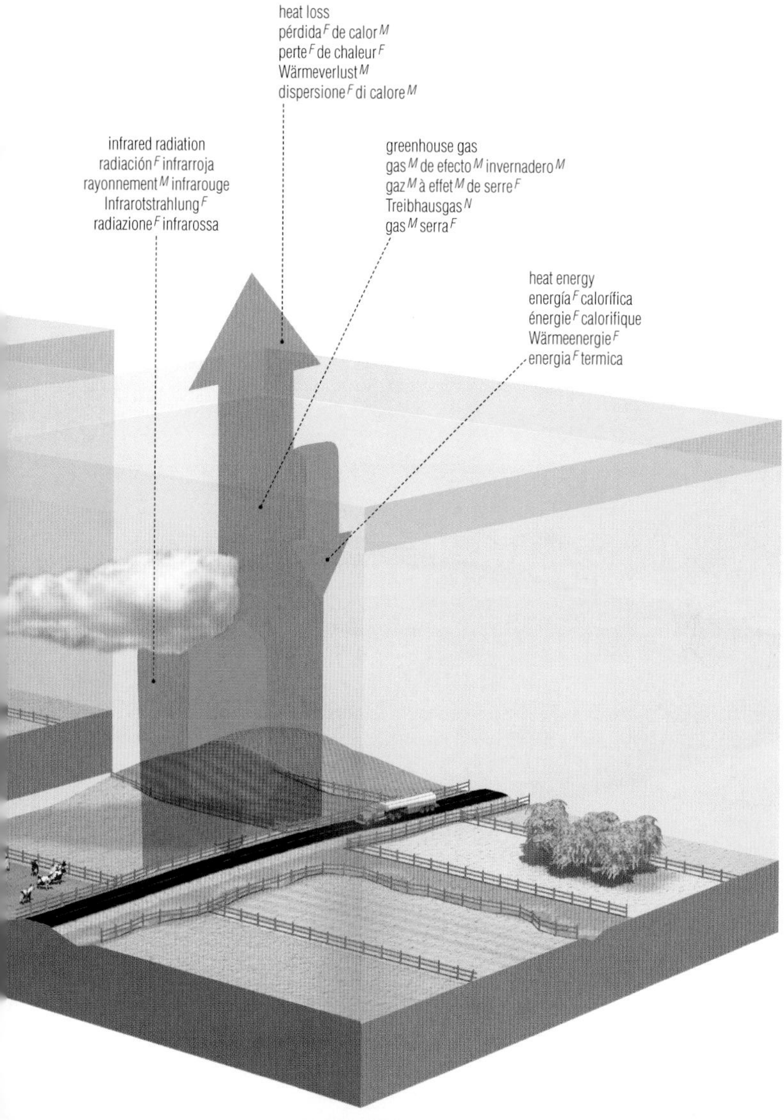
heat loss
pérdida F de calor M
perte F de chaleur F
Wärmeverlust M
dispersione F di calore M
infrared radiation
radiación F infrarroja
rayonnement M infrarouge
Infrarotstrahlung F
radiazione F infrarossa
greenhouse gas
gas M de efecto M invernadero M
gaz M à effet M de serre F
Treibhausgas N
gas M serra F
heat energy
energía F calorífica
énergie F calorifique
Wärmeenergie F
energia F termica

greenhouse effect

enhanced greenhouse effect
aumento M del efecto M invernadero M
augmentation F de l'effet M de serre F
anthropogener Treibhauseffekt M
incremento M dell'effetto M serra F

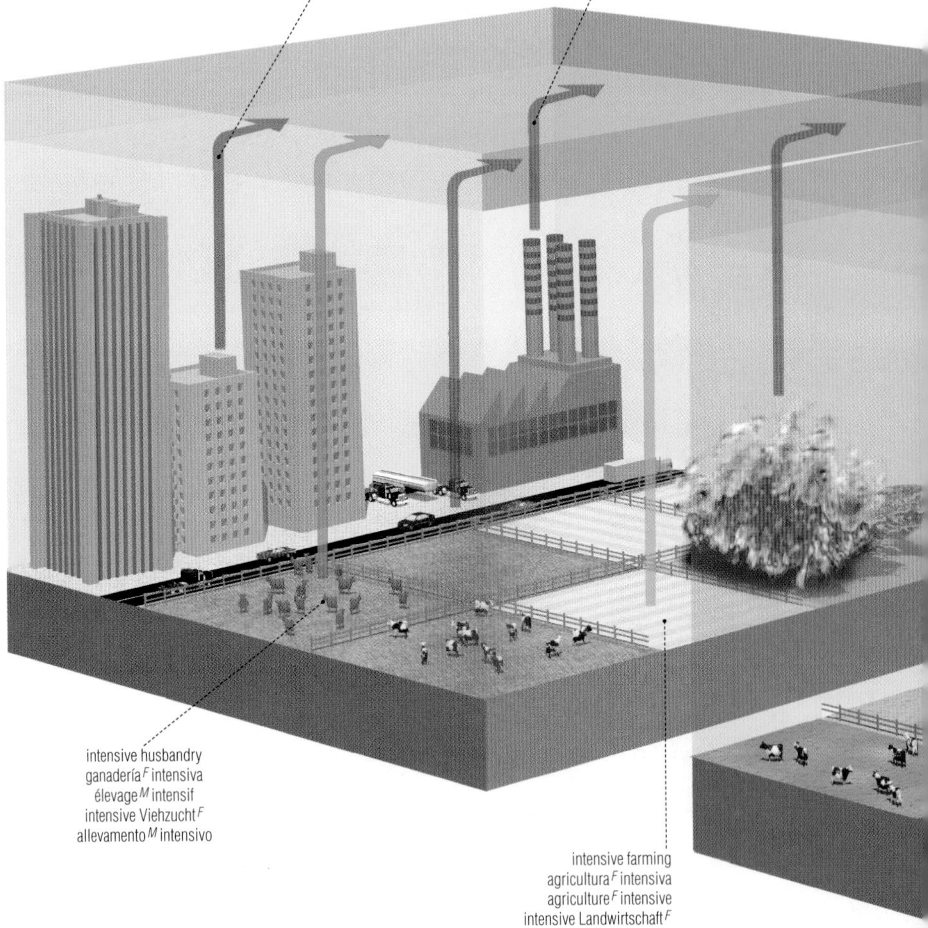
air conditioning system
sistema M de aire M acondicionado
système M de climatisation F
Klimaanlage F
sistema M di climatizzazione F
fossil fuel
combustible M fósil
combustible M fossile
fossiler Brennstoff M
combustibile M fossile
intensive husbandry
ganadería F intensiva
élevage M intensif
intensive Viehzucht F
allevamento M intensivo
intensive farming
agricultura F intensiva
agriculture F intensive
intensive Landwirtschaft F
agricoltura F intensiva

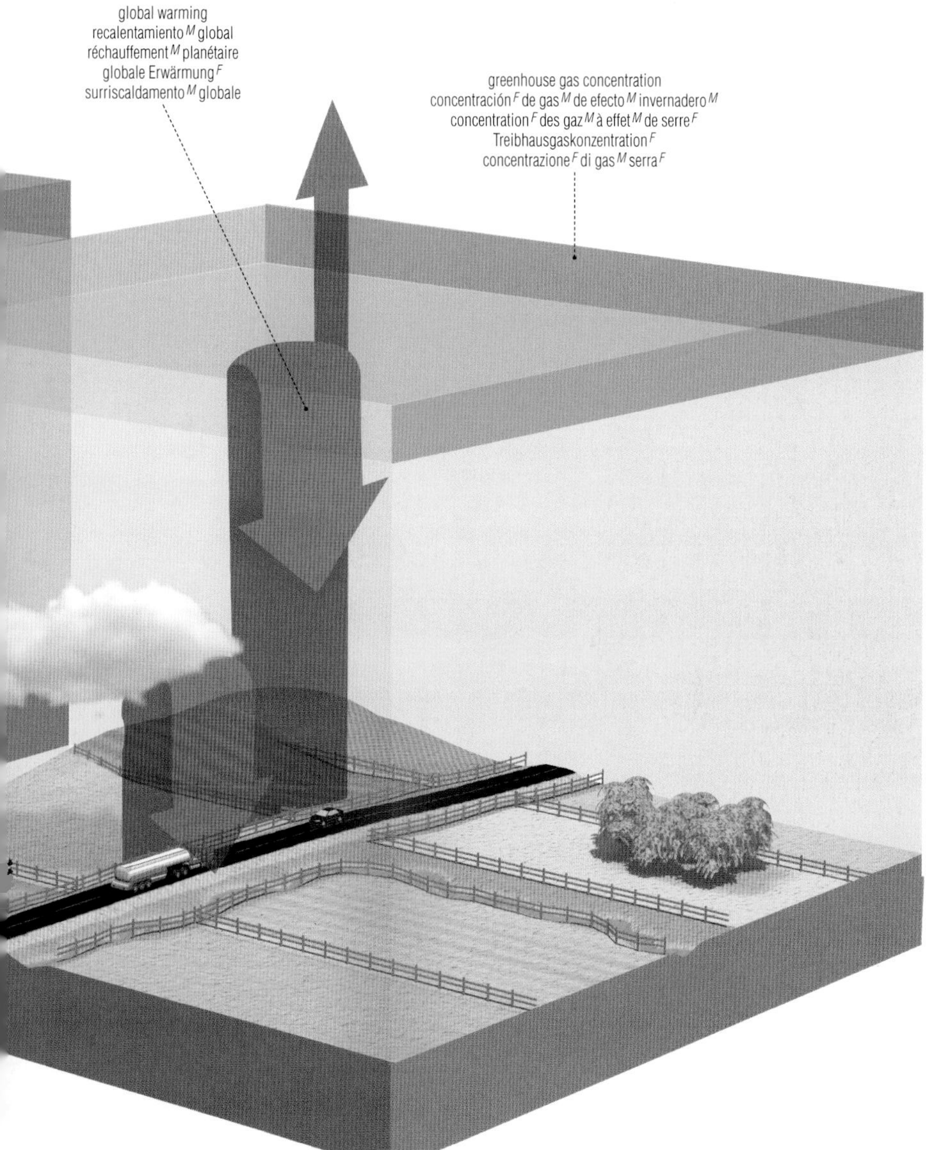
global warming
recalentamiento M global
réchauffement M planétaire
globale Erwärmung F
surriscaldamento M globale
greenhouse gas concentration
concentración F de gas M de efecto M invernadero M
concentration F des gaz M à effet M de serre F
Treibhausgaskonzentration F
concentrazione F di gas M serra F

acid rain

lluvia[F] ácida | pluies[F] acides | saurer Regen[M] | piogge[F] acide

cloudwater
agua[F] de nubes[F]
eau[F] des nuages[M]
Wolkenwasser[N]
umidità[F] contenuta nelle nuvole[F]
nitric acid emission
emisión[F] de ácido[M] nítrico
émission[F] d'acide[M] nitrique
Emission[F] von Salpetersäure[F]
emissione[F] di acido[M] nitrico
sulfuric acid emission
emisión[F] de ácido[M] sulfúrico
émission[F] d'acide[M] sulfurique
Emission[F] von Schwefelsäure[F]
emissione[F] di acido[M] solforico
nitrogen oxide emission
emisión[F] de óxido[M] de nitrógeno[M]
émission[F] d'oxyde[M] d'azote[M]
Emission[F] von Stickoxiden[N]
emissione[F] di ossido[M] d'azoto[M]
sulfur dioxide emission
emisión[F] de dióxido[M] de sulfuro[M]
émission[F] de dioxyde[M] de soufre[M]
Emission[F] von Schwefeldioxid[N]
emissione[F] di anidride[F] solforosa
fossil fuel
combustible[M] fósil
combustible[M] fossile
fossiler Brennstoff[M]
combustibile[M] fossile
watercourse
corriente[F] de agua[F]
cours[M] d'eau[F]
Wasserlauf[M]
corso[M] d'acqua[F]
soil
suelo[M]
sol[M]
Boden[M]
suolo[M]

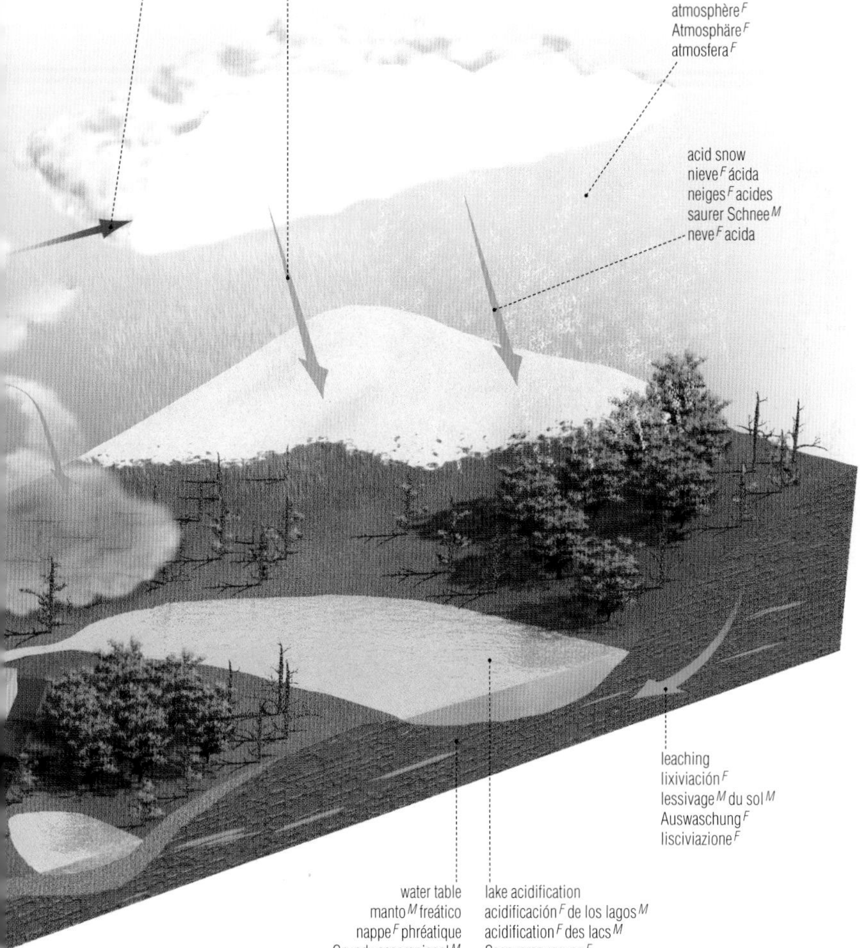
wind
viento M
vent M
Wind M
vento M
acid rain
lluvia F ácida
pluies F acides
saurer Regen M
piogge F acide
atmosphere
atmósfera F
atmosphère F
Atmosphäre F
atmosfera F
acid snow
nieve F ácida
neiges F acides
saurer Schnee M
neve F acida
leaching
lixiviación F
lessivage M du sol M
Auswaschung F
lisciviazione F
water table
manto M freático
nappe F phréatique
Grundwasserspiegel M
falda F freatica
lake acidification
acidificación F de los lagos M
acidification F des lacs M
Seenversauerung F
acidificazione F dei laghi M

plant cell

célula^F vegetal | cellule^F végétale | Pflanzenzelle^F | cellula^F vegetale

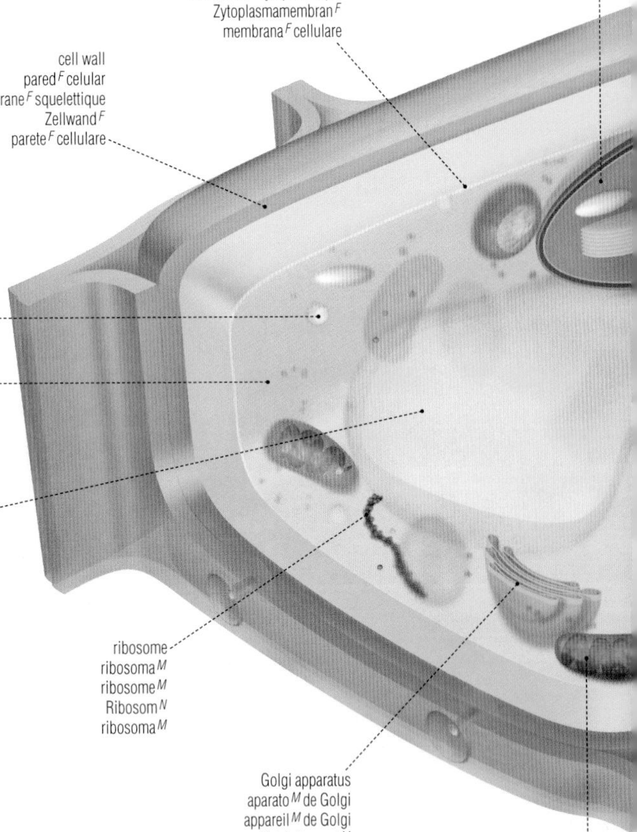
chloroplast
cloroplasto M
chloroplaste M
Chloroplast M
cloroplasto M
cell membrane
membrana F celular
membrane F cytoplasmique
Zytoplasmamembran F
membrana F cellulare
cell wall
pared F celular
membrane F squelettique
Zellwand F
parete F cellulare
lipid droplet
gránulo M de lípido M
gouttelette F lipidique
Fett-Tröpfchen N
granulo M lipidico
cytoplasm
citoplasma M
cytoplasme M
Zytoplasma N
citoplasma M
vacuole
vacuola F
vacuole F
Vakuole F
vacuolo M
ribosome
ribosoma M
ribosome M
Ribosom N
ribosoma M
Golgi apparatus
aparato M de Golgi
appareil M de Golgi
Golgi-Apparat M
apparato M del Golgi
mitochondrion
mitocondria F
mitochondrie F
Mitochondrium N
mitocondrio M

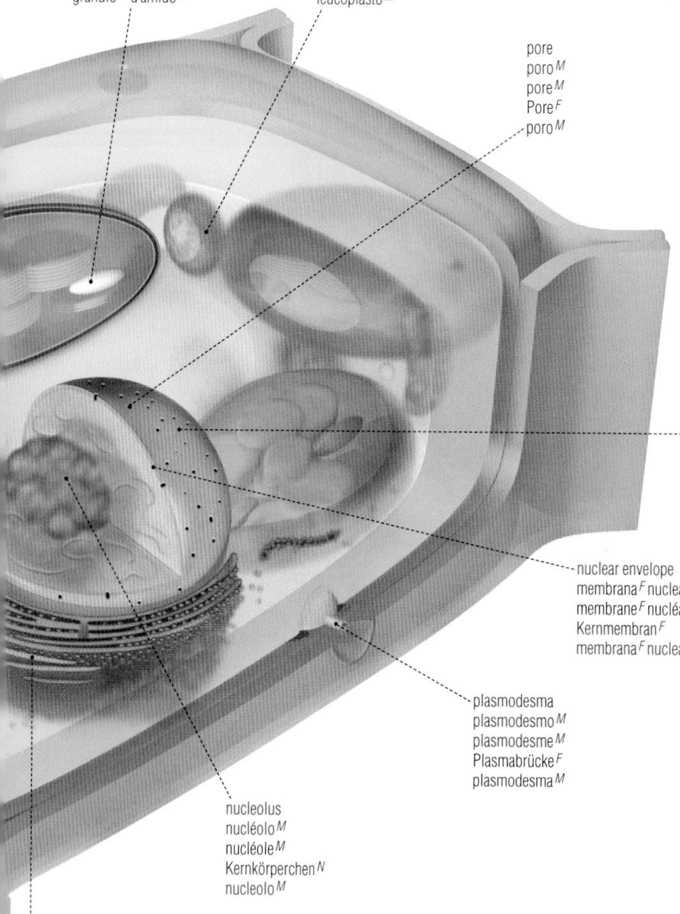
starch granule
grano M de almidón M
grain M d'amidon M
Stärkekörnchen N
granulo M d'amido M
leucoplast
leucoplasto M
leucoplaste M
Leukoplast M
leucoplasto M
pore
poro M
pore M
Pore F
poro M
nucleus
núcleo M
noyau M
Zellkern M
nucleo M
nuclear envelope
membrana F nuclear
membrane F nucléaire
Kernmembran F
membrana F nucleare
plasmodesma
plasmodesmo M
plasmodesme M
Plasmabrücke F
plasmodesma M
nucleolus
nucléolo M
nucléole M
Kernkörperchen N
nucleolo M
endoplasmic reticulum
retículo M endoplasmático
réticulum M endoplasmique
endoplasmatisches Retikulum N
reticolo M endoplasmatico

lichen

liquen[M] | lichen[M] | Flechte[F] | lichene[M]

structure of a lichen
estructura[F] de un liquen[M]
structure[F] d'un lichen[M]
Aufbau[M] einer Flechte[F]
struttura[F] di un lichene[M]

apothecium
apotecio[M]
apothécie[F]
Fruchtkörper[M]
apotecio[M]
thallus
talo[M]
thalle[M]
Thallus[M]
tallo[M]

examples of lichens
ejemplos[M] de líquenes[M]
exemples[M] de lichens[M]
Beispiele[N] für Flechten[F]
esempi[M] di licheni[M]

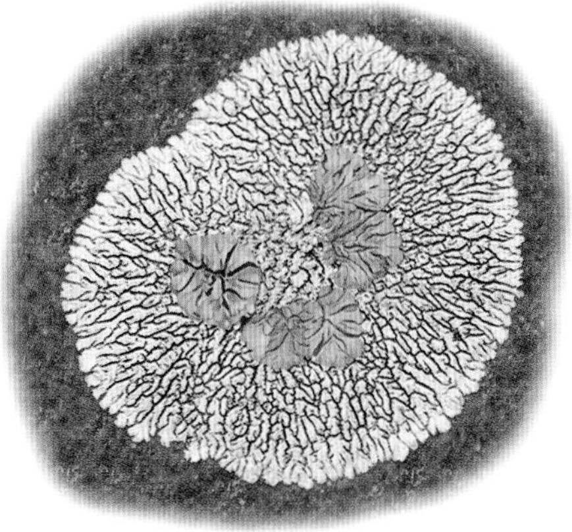

crustose lichen
liquen[M] custráceo
lichen[M] crustacé
Krustenflechte[F]
lichene[M] crostoso

fruticose lichen
liquen[M] fruticuloso
lichen[M] fruticuleux
Strauchflechte[F]
lichene[M] fruticoso

foliose lichen
liquen[M] foliáceo
lichen[M] foliacé
Laubflechte[F]
lichene[M] fogliaceo

moss

musgo*M* | mousse*F* | Moos*N* | muschio*M*

structure of a moss
estructura*F* de un musgo*M*
structure*F* d'une mousse*F*
Aufbau*M* eines Mooses*N*
struttura*F* di un muschio*M*

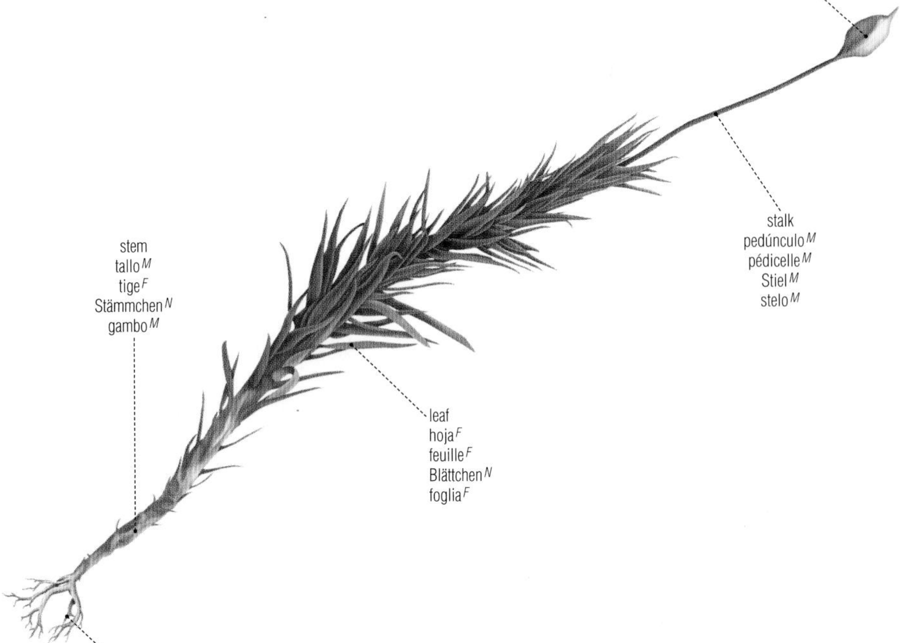
capsule
cápsula F
capsule F
Kapsel F
capsula F
stalk
pedúnculo M
pédicelle M
Stiel M
stelo M
stem
tallo M
tige F
Stämmchen N
gambo M
leaf
hoja F
feuille F
Blättchen N
foglia F
rhizoid
rizoide M
rhizoïde M
Rhizoid N
rizoide M

examples of mosses
ejemplos[M] de musgos[M]
exemples[M] de mousses[F]
Beispiele[N] für Moose[N]
esempi[M] di muschi[M]

prickly sphagnum
esfagno[M]
sphaigne[F] squarreuse
sparriges Torfmoos[N]
sfagno[M] pungente

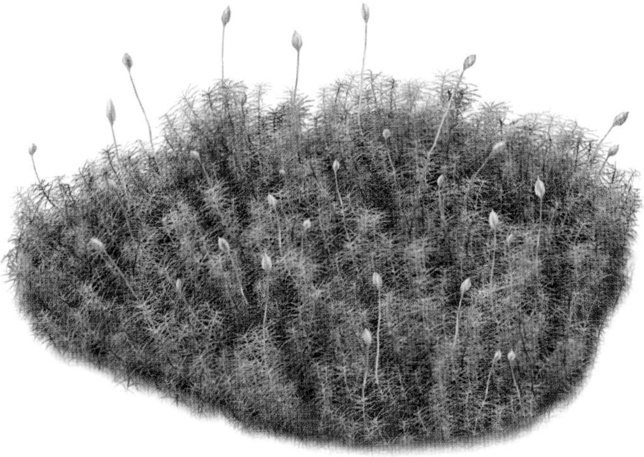

common hair cap moss
polítrico[M]
polytric[M] commun
gemeines Widertonmoos[N]
politrico[M] comune

alga

alga^F | algue^F | Alge^F | alga^F

structure of an alga
estructura^F de un alga^F
structure^F d'une algue^F
Aufbau^M einer Alge^F
struttura^F di un'alga^F

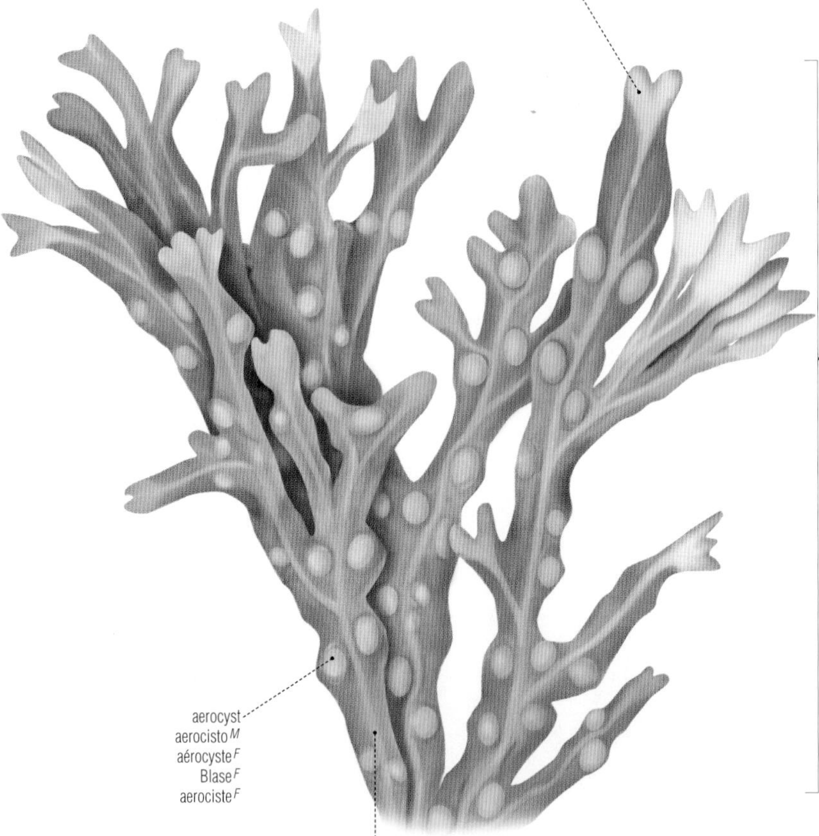

receptacle
receptáculo^M
réceptacle^M
Rezeptakel^N
ricettacolo^M
thallus
talo^M
thalle^M
Thallus^M
tallo^M
aerocyst
aerocisto^M
aérocyste^F
Blase^F
aerociste^F
midrib
nervio^M central
nervure^F médiane
Mittelrippe^F
nervatura^F centrale

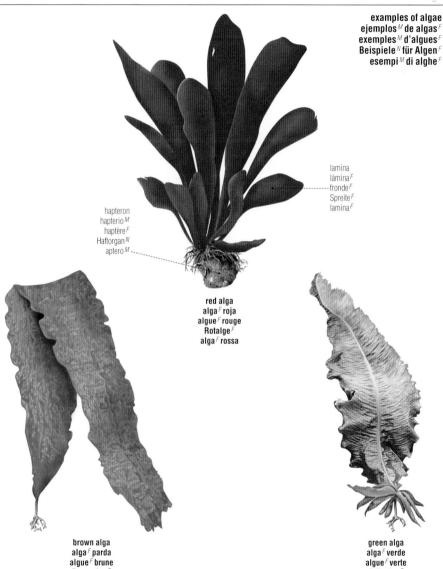

examples of algae
ejemplos^M de algas^F
exemples^M d'algues^F
Beispiele^N für Algen^F
esempi^M di alghe^F

lamina
lámina F
fronde F
Spreite F
lamina F
hapteron
hapterio M
haptère F
Haftorgan N
aptero M

red alga
alga^F roja
algue^F rouge
Rotalge^F
alga^F rossa

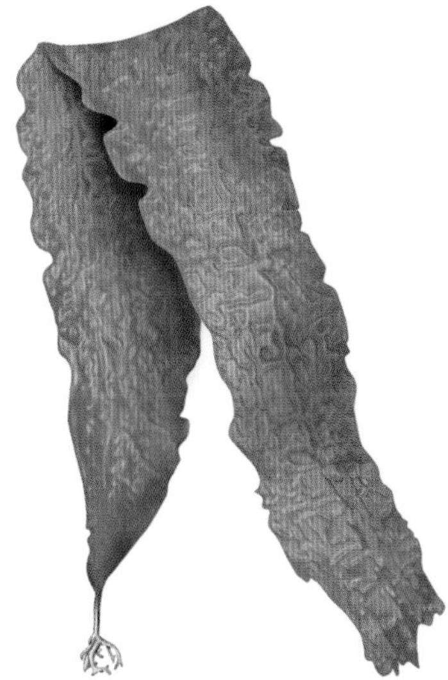

brown alga
alga^F parda
algue^F brune
Braunalge^F
alga^F bruna

green alga
alga^F verde
algue^F verte
Grünalge^F
alga^F verde

fern

helecho M | fougère F | Farn M | felce F

structure of a fern
estructura F de un helecho M
structure F d'une fougère F
Aufbau M eines Farns M
struttura F di una felce F

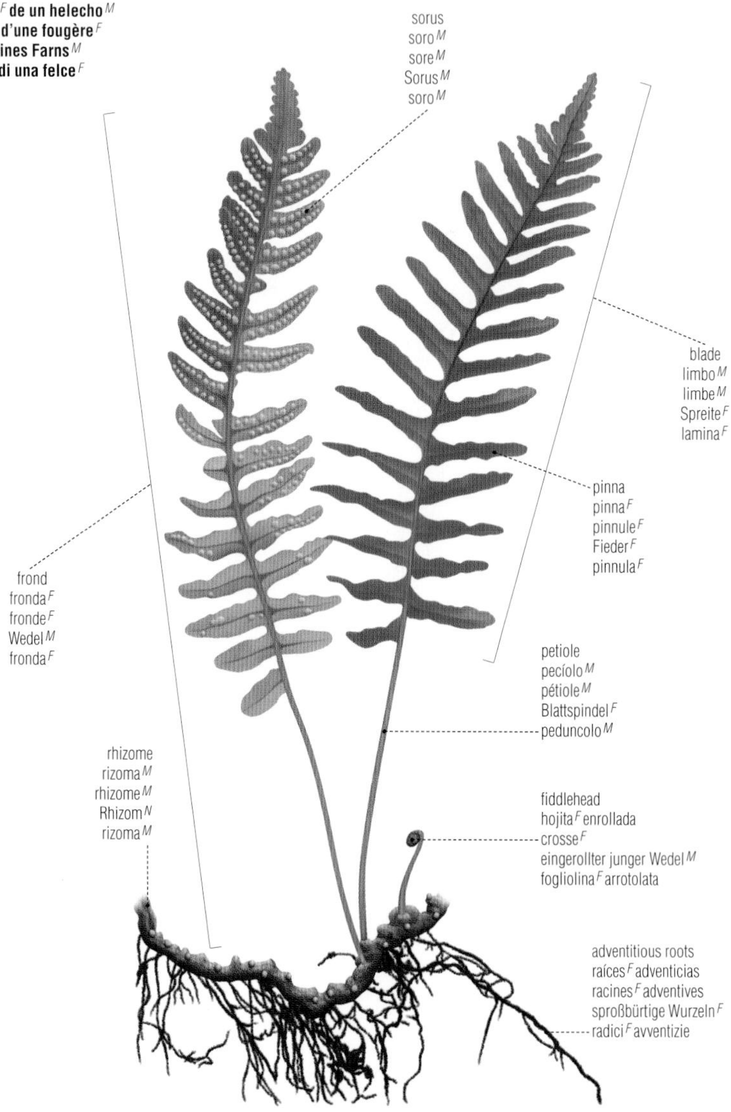
sorus
soro M
sore M
Sorus M
soro M
blade
limbo M
limbe M
Spreite F
lamina F
pinna
pinna F
pinnule F
Fieder F
pinnula F
frond
fronda F
fronde F
Wedel M
fronda F
petiole
pecíolo M
pétiole M
Blattspindel F
peduncolo M
rhizome
rizoma M
rhizome M
Rhizom N
rizoma M
fiddlehead
hojita F enrollada
crosse F
eingerollter junger Wedel M
fogliolina F arrotolata
adventitious roots
raíces F adventicias
racines F adventives
sproßbürtige Wurzeln F
radici F avventizie

examples of ferns
ejemplos[M] de helechos[M]
exemples[M] de fougères[F]
Beispiele[N] für Farne[M]
esempi[M] di felci[F]

trunk
tronco[M]
tronc[M]
Stamm[M]
tronco[M]

tree fern
helecho[M] arbóreo
fougère[F] arborescente
Baumfarn[M]
felce[F] arborea

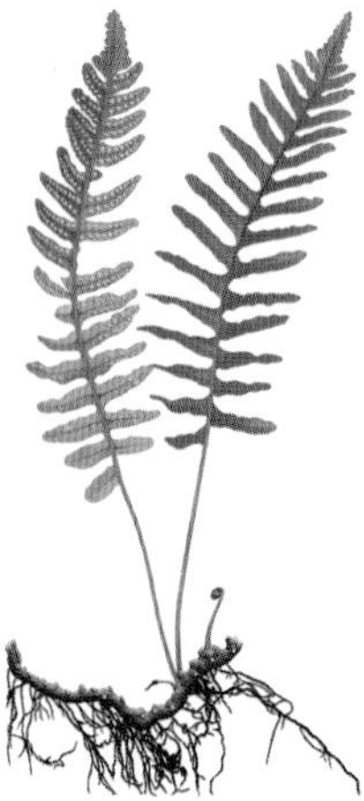

common polypody
polipodio[M] común
polypode[M] commun
gemeiner Tüpfelfarn[M]
polipodio[M] comune

bird's nest fern
helecho[M] nido[M] de pájaro[M]
fougère[F] nid[M] d'oiseau[M]
Nestfarn[M]
lingua[F] di cervo[M]

mushroom

hongo M | champignon M | Pilz M | fungo M

structure of a mushroom
anatomía F de un hongo M
structure F d'un champignon M
Aufbau M eines Pilzes M
struttura F di un fungo M

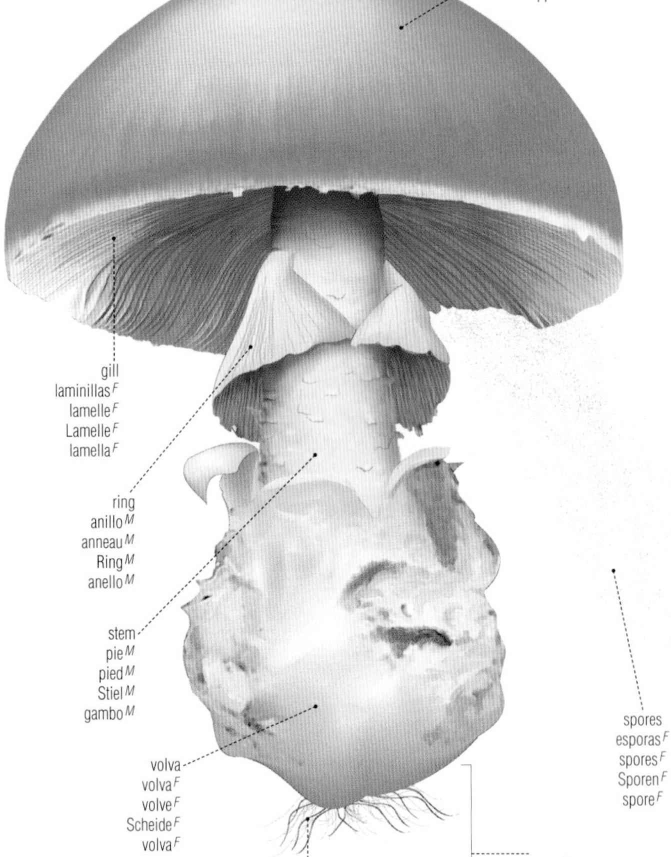
cap
sombrero M
chapeau M
Hut M
cappello M
gill
laminillas F
lamelle F
Lamelle F
lamella F
ring
anillo M
anneau M
Ring M
anello M
stem
pie M
pied M
Stiel M
gambo M
volva
volva F
volve F
Scheide F
volva F
hypha
hifa F
hyphe M
Pilzfaden M
ifa F
mycelium
micelio M
mycélium M
Myzel N
micelio M
spores
esporas F
spores F
Sporen F
spore F

deadly poisonous mushroom
hongo M mortal
champignon M mortel
tödlich giftiger Pilz M
fungo M velenoso e mortale

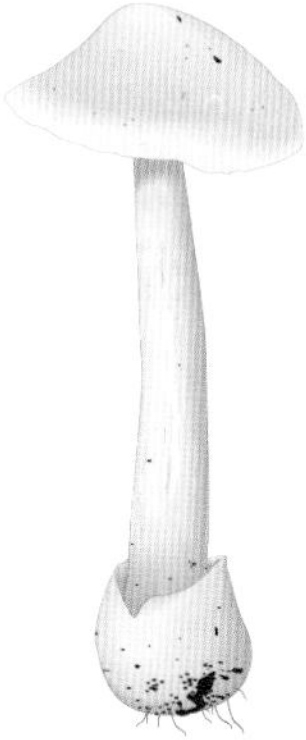

destroying angel
amanita F virosa
amanite F vireuse
Knollenblätterpilz M
amanita F virosa

poisonous mushroom
hongo M venenoso
champignon M vénéneux
Giftpilz M
fungo M velenoso

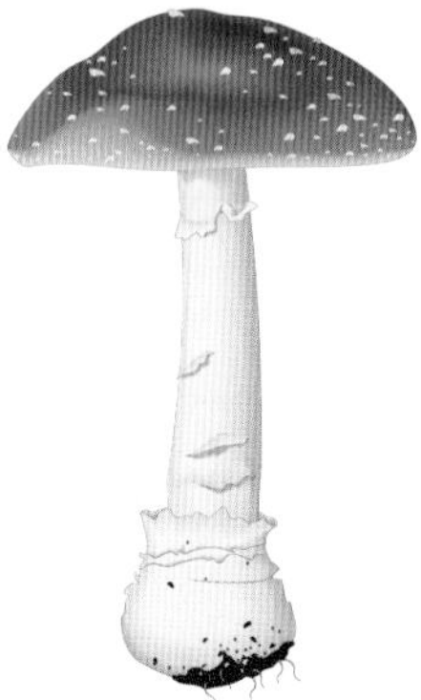

fly agaric
falsa oronja F
fausse oronge F
Fliegenpilz M
amanita F muscaria

edible mushrooms
setas F comestibles
champignons M comestibles
Speisepilze M
funghi M commestibili

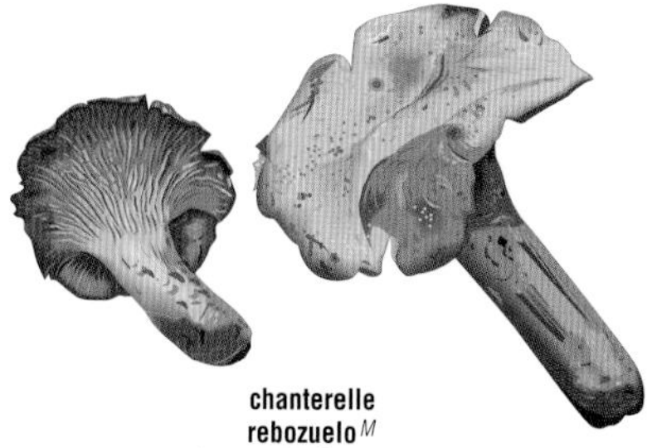

chanterelle
rebozuelo M
chanterelle F commune
Pfifferling M
cantarello M

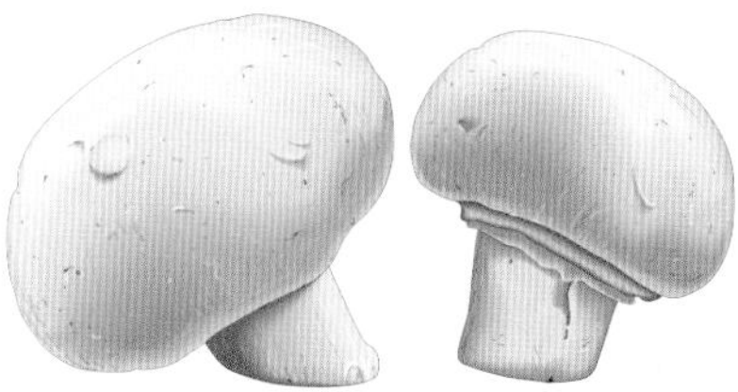

cultivated mushroom
champiñón M
champignon M de couche F
Zuchtchampignon M
fungo M coltivato

plant

planta^F | plante^F | Pflanze^F | pianta^F

structure of a plant
anatomía^F de una planta^F
structure^F d'une plante^F
Aufbau^M einer Pflanze^F
struttura^F di una pianta^F

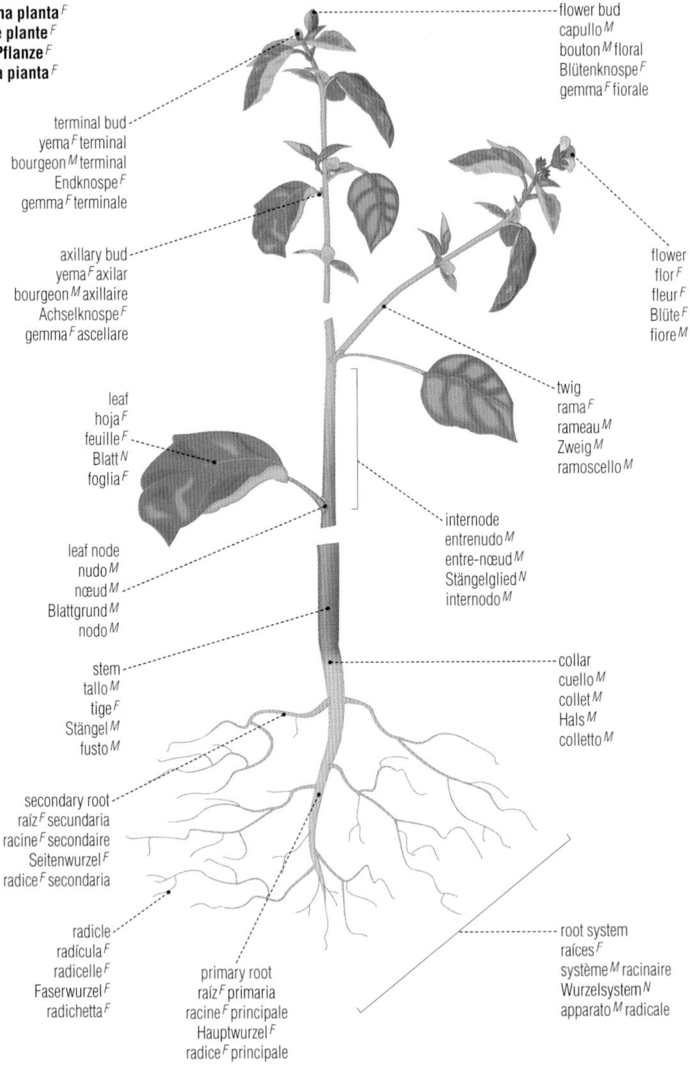
flower bud
capullo^M
bouton^M floral
Blütenknospe^F
gemma^F fiorale
terminal bud
yema^F terminal
bourgeon^M terminal
Endknospe^F
gemma^F terminale
axillary bud
yema^F axilar
bourgeon^M axillaire
Achselknospe^F
gemma^F ascellare
flower
flor^F
fleur^F
Blüte^F
fiore^M
twig
rama^F
rameau^M
Zweig^M
ramoscello^M
leaf
hoja^F
feuille^F
Blatt^N
foglia^F
internode
entrenudo^M
entre-nœud^M
Stängelglied^N
internodo^M
leaf node
nudo^M
nœud^M
Blattgrund^M
nodo^M
stem
tallo^M
tige^F
Stängel^M
fusto^M
collar
cuello^M
collet^M
Hals^M
colletto^M
secondary root
raíz^F secundaria
racine^F secondaire
Seitenwurzel^F
radice^F secondaria
radicle
radícula^F
radicelle^F
Faserwurzel^F
radichetta^F
primary root
raíz^F primaria
racine^F principale
Hauptwurzel^F
radice^F principale
root system
raíces^F
système^M racinaire
Wurzelsystem^N
apparato^M radicale

soil profile
perfil *M* **del suelo** *M*
profil *M* **du sol** *M*
Bodenprofil *N*
profilo *M* **del suolo** *M*

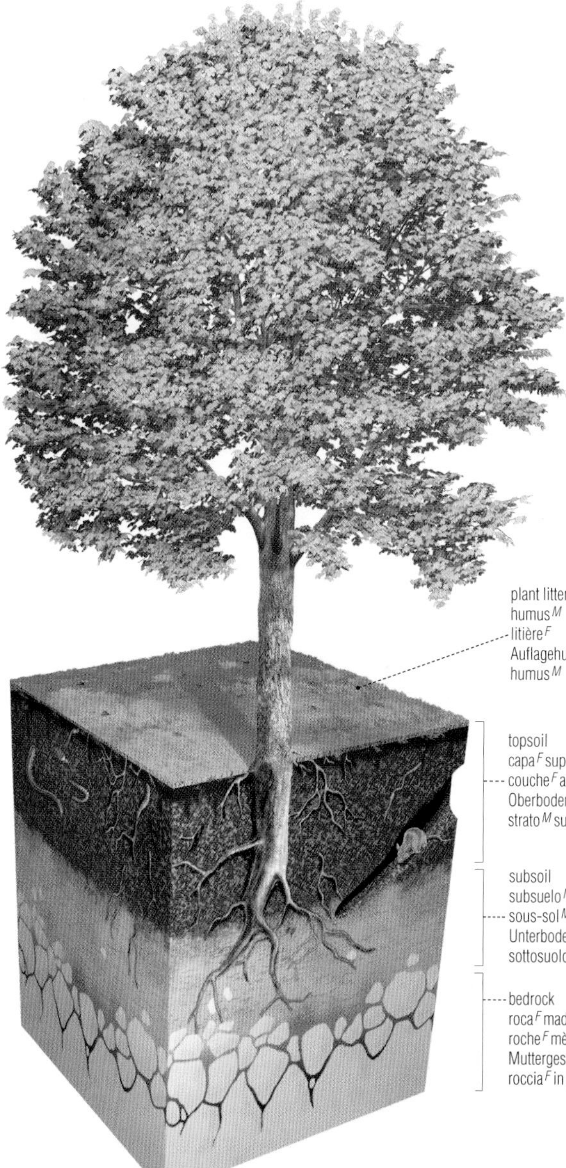
plant litter
humus M
litière F
Auflagehumus M
humus M
topsoil
capa F superficial del suelo M
couche F arable
Oberboden M
strato M superficiale del suolo M
subsoil
subsuelo M
sous-sol M
Unterboden M
sottosuolo M
bedrock
roca F madre
roche F mère F
Muttergestein N
roccia F in posto M

plant

photosynthesis
fotosíntesis F
photosynthèse F
Photosynthese F
fotosintesi F

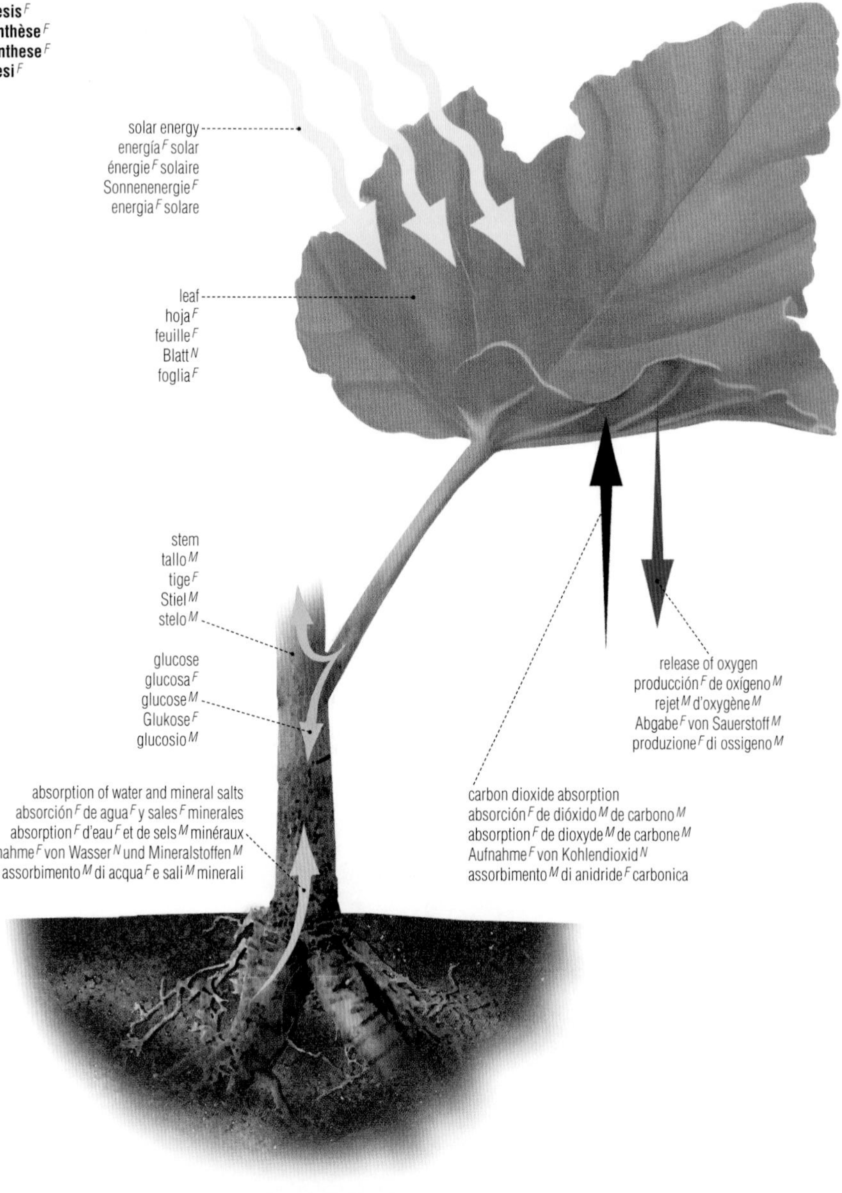
solar energy
energía F solar
énergie F solaire
Sonnenenergie F
energia F solare
leaf
hoja F
feuille F
Blatt N
foglia F
stem
tallo M
tige F
Stiel M
stelo M
glucose
glucosa F
glucose M
Glukose F
glucosio M
absorption of water and mineral salts
absorción F de agua F y sales F minerales
absorption F d'eau F et de sels M minéraux
Aufnahme F von Wasser N und Mineralstoffen M
assorbimento M di acqua F e sali M minerali
release of oxygen
producción F de oxígeno M
rejet M d'oxygène M
Abgabe F von Sauerstoff M
produzione F di ossigeno M
carbon dioxide absorption
absorción F de dióxido M de carbono M
absorption F de dioxyde M de carbone M
Aufnahme F von Kohlendioxid N
assorbimento M di anidride F carbonica

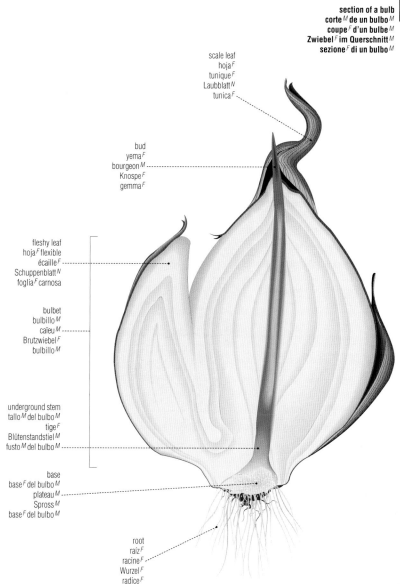

section of a bulb
corte [M] de un bulbo [M]
coupe [F] d'un bulbe [M]
Zwiebel [F] im Querschnitt [M]
sezione [F] di un bulbo [M]

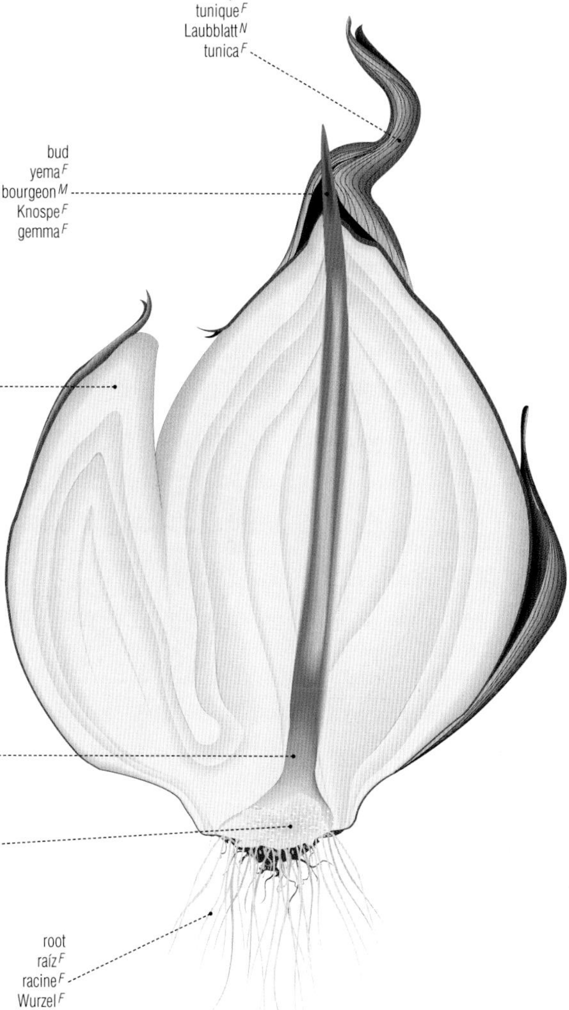
scale leaf
hoja [F]
tunique [F]
Laubblatt [N]
tunica [F]
bud
yema [F]
bourgeon [M]
Knospe [F]
gemma [F]
fleshy leaf
hoja [F] flexible
écaille [F]
Schuppenblatt [N]
foglia [F] carnosa
bulbet
bulbillo [M]
caïeu [M]
Brutzwiebel [F]
bulbillo [M]
underground stem
tallo [M] del bulbo [M]
tige [F]
Blütenstandstiel [M]
fusto [M] del bulbo [M]
base
base [F] del bulbo [M]
plateau [M]
Spross [M]
base [F] del bulbo [M]
root
raíz [F]
racine [F]
Wurzel [F]
radice [F]

leaf

hoja^F | feuille^F | Blatt^N | foglia^F

structure of a leaf
estructura^F de una hoja^F
structure^F d'une feuille^F
Aufbau^M eines Blatts^N
struttura^F di una foglia^F

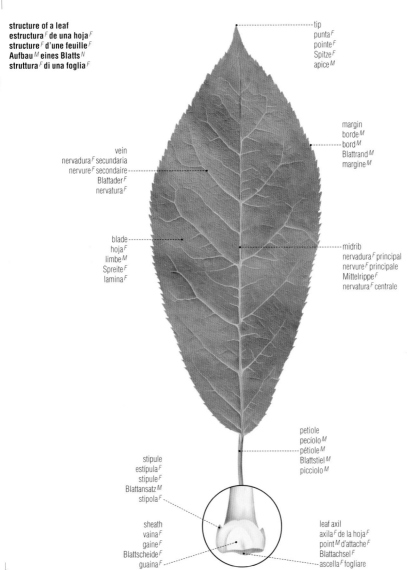

tip
punta^F
pointe^F
Spitze^F
apice^M
margin
borde^M
bord^M
Blattrand^M
margine^M
vein
nervadura^F secundaria
nervure^F secondaire
Blattader^F
nervatura^F
blade
hoja^F
limbe^M
Spreite^F
lamina^F
midrib
nervadura^F principal
nervure^F principale
Mittelrippe^F
nervatura^F centrale
petiole
pecíolo^M
pétiole^M
Blattstiel^M
picciolo^M
stipule
estípula^F
stipule^F
Blattansatz^M
stipola^F
sheath
vaina^F
gaine^F
Blattscheide^F
guaina^F
leaf axil
axila^F de la hoja^F
point^M d'attache^F
Blattachsel^F
ascella^F fogliare

compound leaves
hojas[F] compuestas
feuilles[F] composées
zusammengesetzte Blätter[N]
foglie[F] composte

abruptly pinnate
paripinnada
paripennée
paarig gefiedert
paripennata

pinnatifid
pinatífida
pennée
fiederteilig
pennatifida

odd pinnate
imparipinnada
imparipennée
unpaarig gefiedert
imparipennata

trifoliolate
trifoliada
trifoliée
dreizählig
trifogliata

palmate
palmeada
palmée
handförmig
palmata

simple leaves
hojas[F] simples
feuilles[F] simples
einfache Blätter[N]
foglie[F] semplici

orbiculate
orbicular
arrondie
rund
orbicolare

spatulate
espatulada
spatulée
spatelförmig
spatolata

cordate
acorazonada
cordée
herzförmig
cordata

reniform
reniforme
réniforme
nierenförmig
reniforme

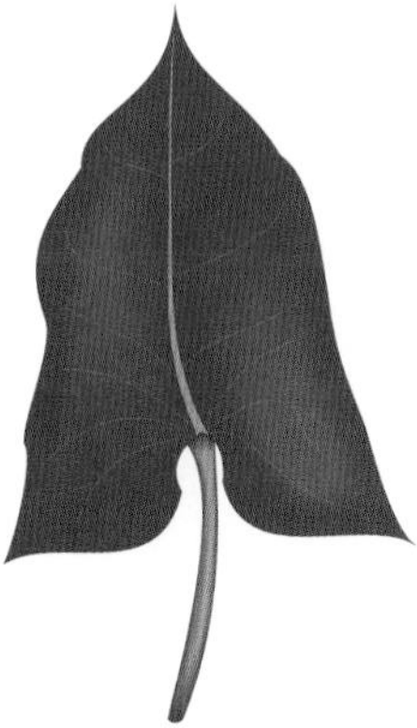

hastate
astada
hastée
pfeilförmig
astata

lanceolate
lanceolada
lancéolée
lanzettförmig
lanceolata

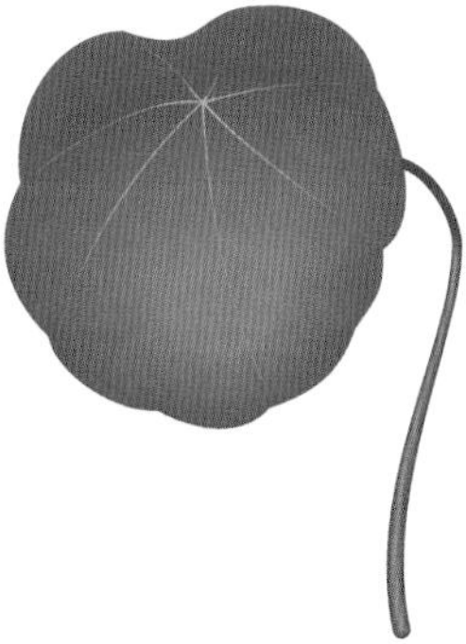

peltate
peltada
peltée
schildförmig
peltata

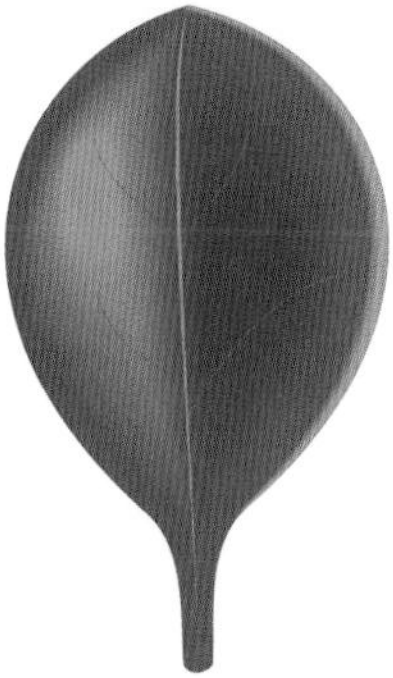

ovate
aovada
ovoïde
eiförmig
ovata

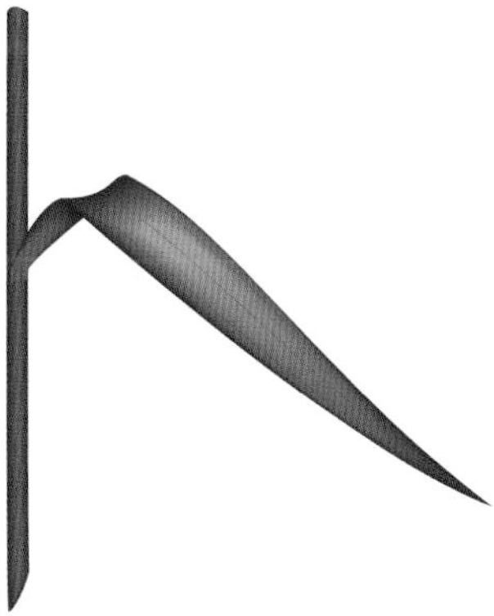

linear
acicular
linéaire
linealisch
lineare

flower

flor[F] | fleur[F] | Blüte[F] | fiore[M]

structure of a flower
estructura[F] de una flor[F]
structure[F] d'une fleur[F]
Aufbau[M] einer Blume[F]
struttura[F] di un fiore[M]

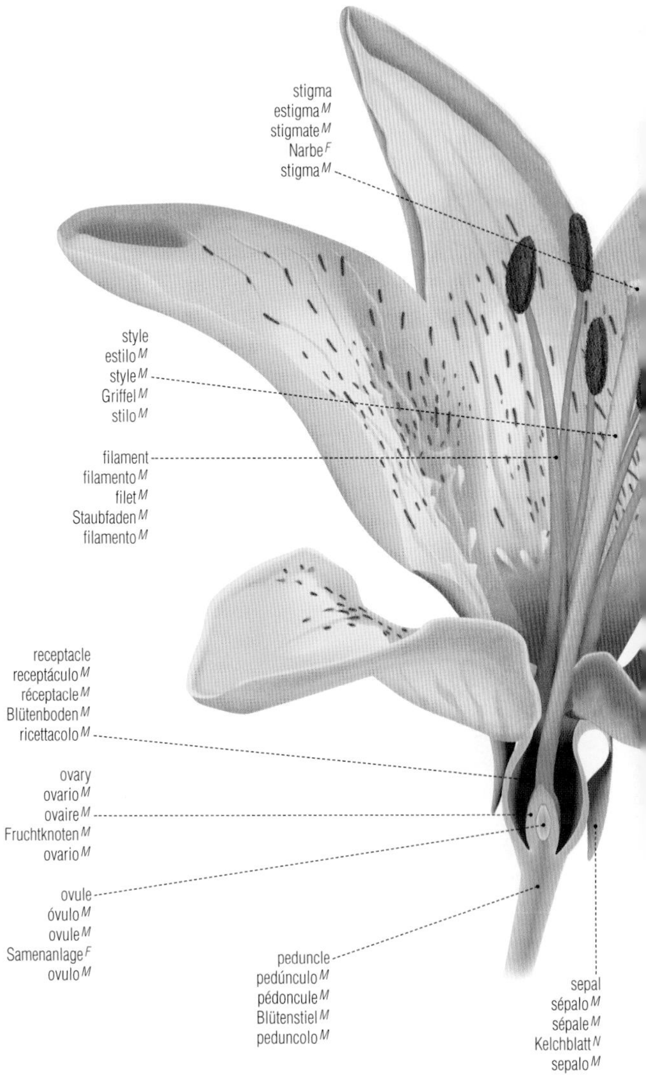

stigma
estigma M
stigmate M
Narbe F
stigma M
style
estilo M
style M
Griffel M
stilo M
filament
filamento M
filet M
Staubfaden M
filamento M
receptacle
receptáculo M
réceptacle M
Blütenboden M
ricettacolo M
ovary
ovario M
ovaire M
Fruchtknoten M
ovario M
ovule
óvulo M
ovule M
Samenanlage F
ovulo M
peduncle
pedúnculo M
pédoncule M
Blütenstiel M
peduncolo M
sepal
sépalo M
sépale M
Kelchblatt N
sepalo M

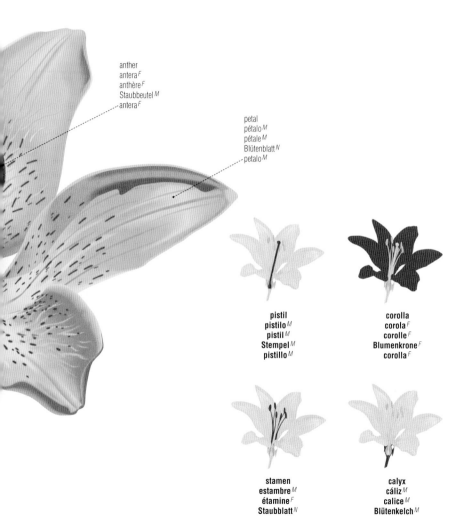

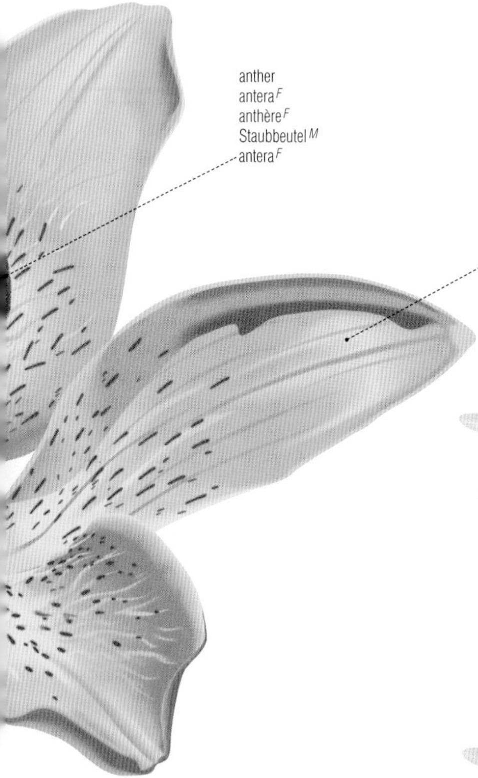
anther
antera^F
anthère^F
Staubbeutel^M
antera^F
petal
pétalo^M
pétale^M
Blütenblatt^N
petalo^M

pistil
pistilo^M
pistil^M
Stempel^M
pistillo^M

corolla
corola^F
corolle^F
Blumenkrone^F
corolla^F

stamen
estambre^M
étamine^F
Staubblatt^N
stame^M

calyx
cáliz^M
calice^M
Blütenkelch^M
calice^M

examples of flowers
ejemplos[M] de flores[F]
exemples[M] de fleurs[F]
Beispiele[N] für Blumen[F]
esempi[M] di fiori[M]

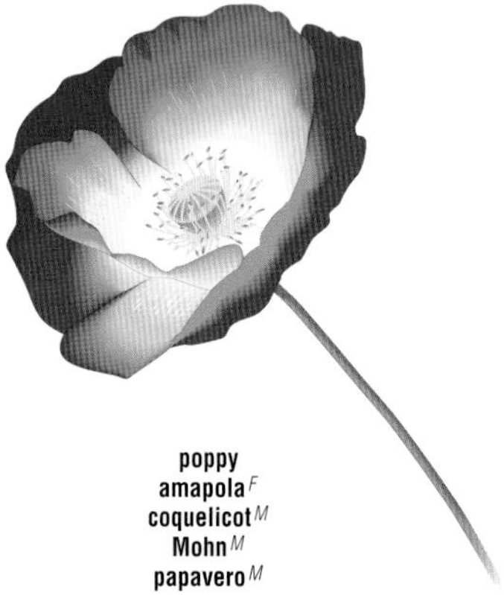

poppy
amapola[F]
coquelicot[M]
Mohn[M]
papavero[M]

carnation
clavel[M]
œillet[M]
Nelke[F]
garofano[M]

orchid
orquídea[F]
orchidée[F]
Orchidee[F]
orchidea[F]

tulip
tulipán[M]
tulipe[F]
Tulpe[F]
tulipano[M]

violet
violeta F
violette F
Veilchen N
viola F

lily of the valley
muguete M
muguet M
Maiglöckchen N
mughetto M

begonia
begonia F
bégonia M
Begonie F
begonia F

lily
azucena F
lis M
Lilie F
giglio M

flower

rose
rosa ^{F}
rose ^{F}
Rose ^{F}
rosa ^{F}

crocus
croco ^{M}
crocus ^{M}
Krokus ^{M}
croco ^{M}

daffodil
narciso ^{M}
jonquille ^{F}
Narzisse ^{F}
trombone ^{M}

buttercup
ranúnculo ^{M}
bouton ^{M} d'or ^{M}
Hahnenfuß ^{M}
botton ^{M} d'oro ^{M}

sunflower
girasol ^{M}
tournesol ^{M}
Sonnenblume ^{F}
girasole ^{M}

primrose
prímula [F]
primevère [F]
Primel [F]
primula [F]

daisy
margarita [F]
marguerite [F]
Gänseblümchen [N]
margherita [F]

dandelion
diente [M] de león [M]
pissenlit [M]
Löwenzahn [M]
dente [M] di leone [M]

thistle
cardo [M]
chardon [M]
Distel [F]
cardo [M]

fruits

frutos M | fruits M | Früchte F | frutti M

stone fleshy fruit
drupa F
fruit M charnu à noyau M
fleischige Steinfrucht F
drupa F

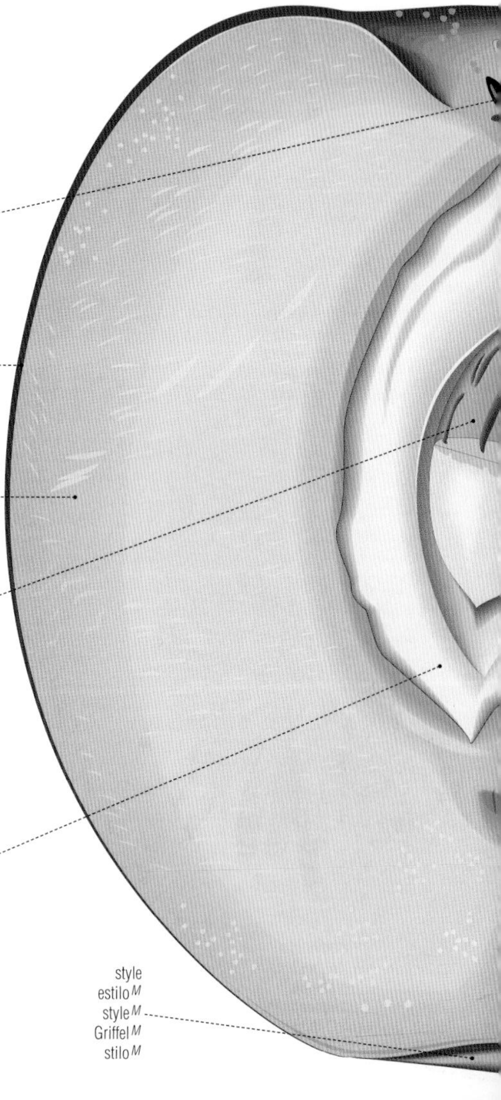

technical terms
términos M técnicos
termes M techniques
wissenschaftliche Bezeichnungen F
termini M tecnici

peduncle
pedúnculo M
pédoncule M
Stiel M
peduncolo M

exocarp
epicarpio M
épicarpe M
Exokarp N
esocarpo M

mesocarp
mesocarpio M
mésocarpe M
Mesokarp N
mesocarpo M

seed coat
tegumento M de la semilla F
tégument M de la graine F
Samenmantel M
tegumento M del seme M

endocarp
endocarpio M
endocarpe M
Endokarp N
endocarpo M

style
estilo M
style M
Griffel M
stilo M

section of a peach
corte M de un melocotón M
coupe F d'une pêche F
Pfirsich M im Querschnitt M
sezione F di una pesca F

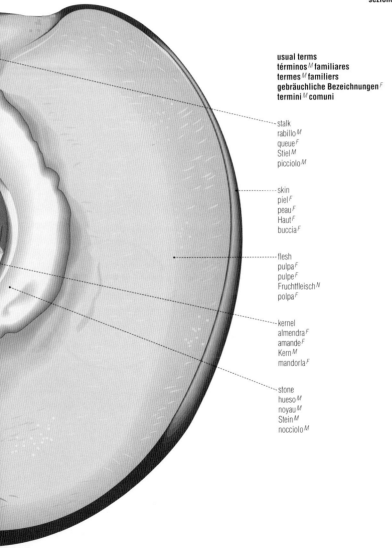

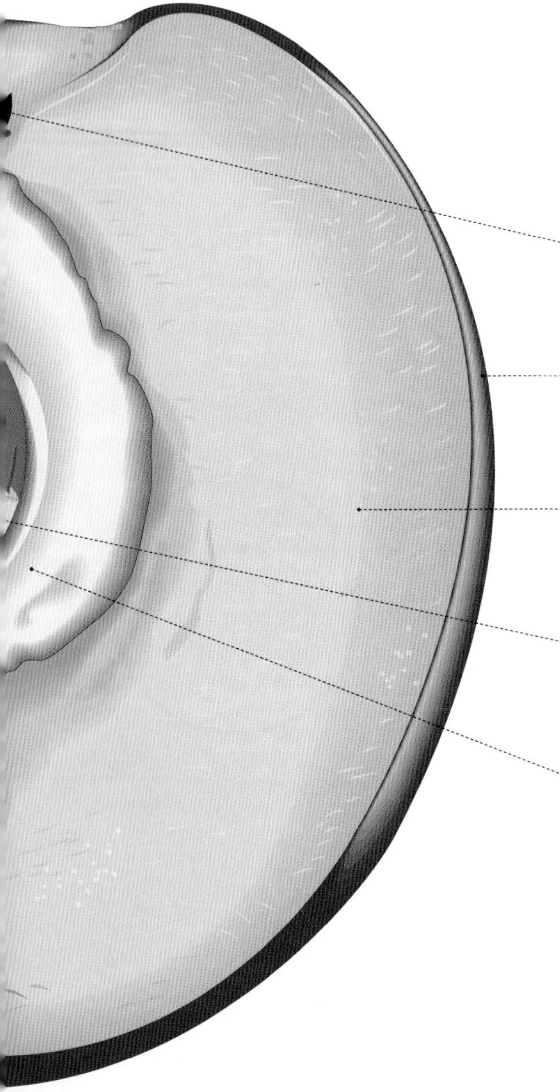
usual terms
términos M familiares
termes M familiers
gebräuchliche Bezeichnungen F
termini M comuni
stalk
rabillo M
queue F
Stiel M
picciolo M
skin
piel F
peau F
Haut F
buccia F
flesh
pulpa F
pulpe F
Fruchtfleisch N
polpa F
kernel
almendra F
amande F
Kern M
mandorla F
stone
hueso M
noyau M
Stein M
nocciolo M

fleshy fruit: citrus fruit
fruto[M] carnoso: cítrico[M]
fruit[M] charnu : agrume[M]
fleischige Frucht[F]: Zitrusfrucht[F]
frutto[M] carnoso: agrume[M]

technical terms
términos[M] técnicos
termes[M] techniques
wissenschaftliche Bezeichnungen[F]
termini[M] tecnici

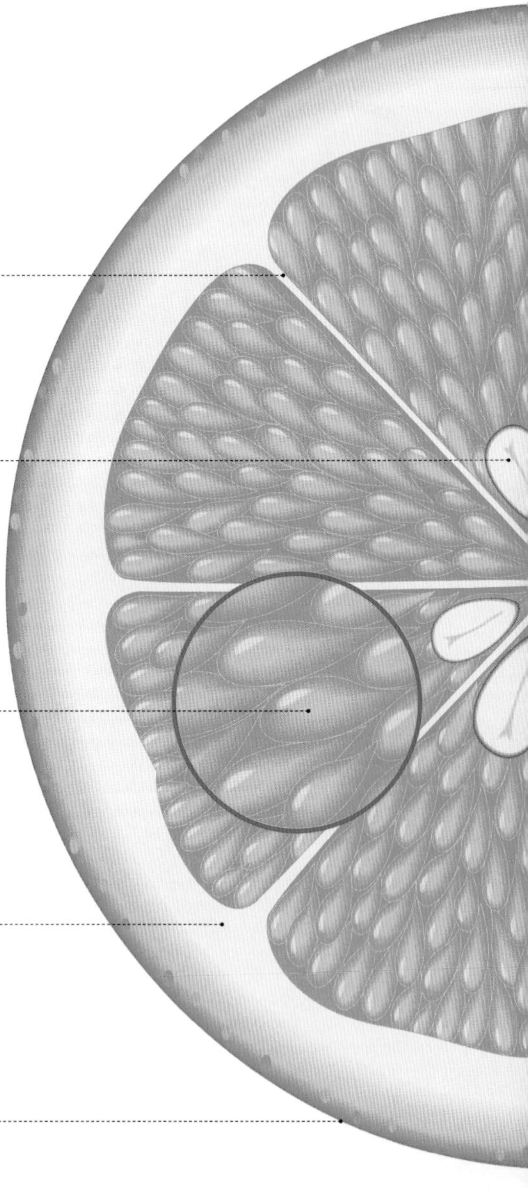

wall
membrana[F]
cloison[F]
Scheidewand[F]
parete[F]

seed
semilla[F]
graine[F]
Samen[M]
seme[M]

juice sac
celdilla[F]
loge[F]
Fruchtfach[N]
cellula[F] del succo[M]

mesocarp
mesocarpio[M]
mésocarpe[M]
Mesokarp[N]
mesocarpo[M]

exocarp
epicarpio[M]
épicarpe[M]
Exokarp[N]
epicarpo[M]

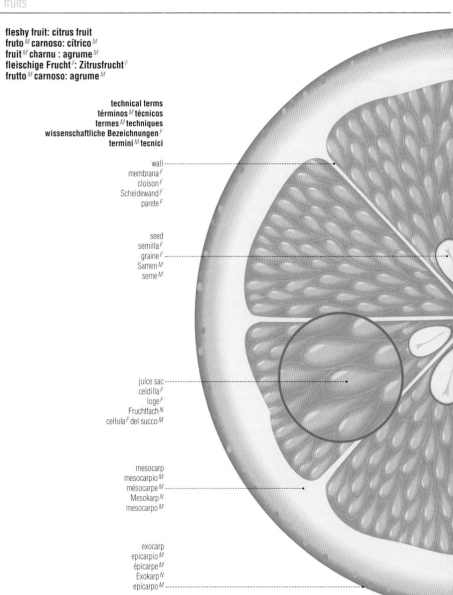

section of an orange
corte[M] de una naranja[F]
coupe[F] d'une orange[F]
Orange[F] im Querschnitt[M]
sezione[F] di un'arancia[F]

usual terms
términos[M] familiares
termes[M] familiers
gebräuchliche Bezeichnungen[F]
termini[M] comuni

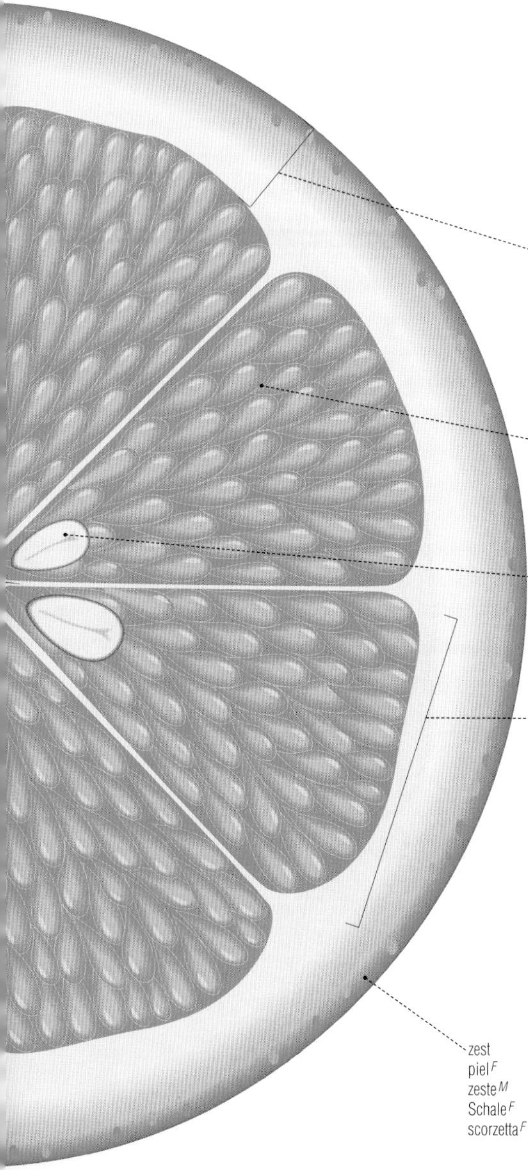
rind
corteza[F]
écorce[F]
Fruchtwand[F]
scorza[F]
pulp
pulpa[F]
pulpe[F]
Fruchtfleisch[N]
polpa[F]
pip
pepita[F]
pépin[M]
Kern[M]
seme[M]
segment
gajo[M]
quartier[M]
Spalt[M]
spicchio[M]
zest
piel[F]
zeste[M]
Schale[F]
scorzetta[F]

fleshy fruit: berry fruit
fruto[M] carnoso: baya[F]
fruit[M] charnu : baie[F]
fleischige Frucht[F]: Beere[F]
frutto[M] carnoso: bacca[F]

technical terms
términos[M] técnicos
termes[M] techniques
wissenschaftliche Bezeichnungen[F]
termini[M] tecnici

pedicel
pedúnculo[M]
pédicelle[M]
Stiel[M]
peduncolo[M]

exocarp
epicarpio[M]
épicarpe[M]
Exokarp[N]
esocarpo[M]

funiculus
funículo[M]
funicule[M]
Nabelstrang[M]
funicolo[M]

seed
semilla[F]
graine[F]
Samen[M]
seme[M]

mesocarp
mesocarpio[M]
mésocarpe[M]
Mesokarp[N]
mesocarpo[M]

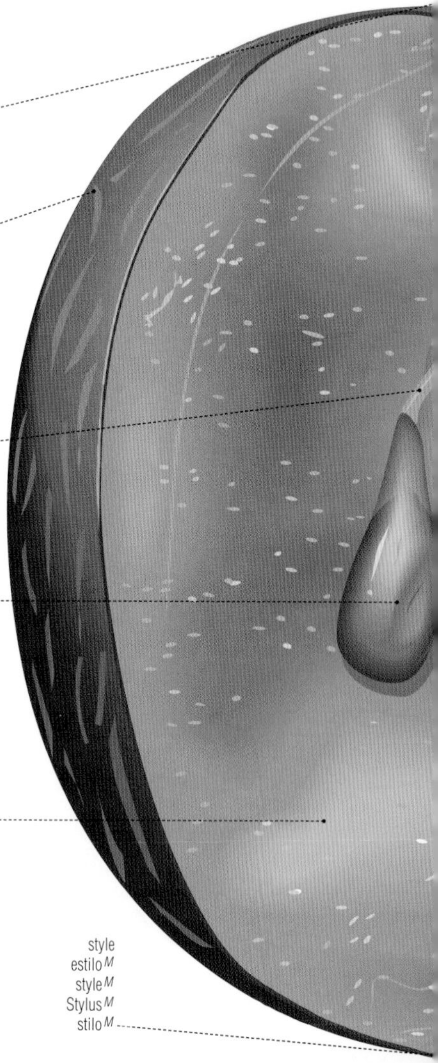

style
estilo[M]
style[M]
Stylus[M]
stilo[M]

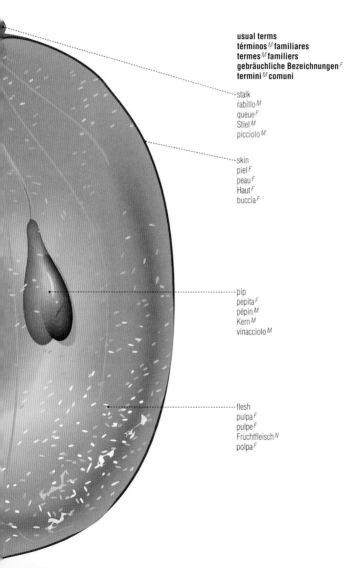

section of a grape
corte^M de una uva^F
coupe^F d'un raisin^M
Weintraube^F im Querschnitt^M
sezione^F di un acino^M

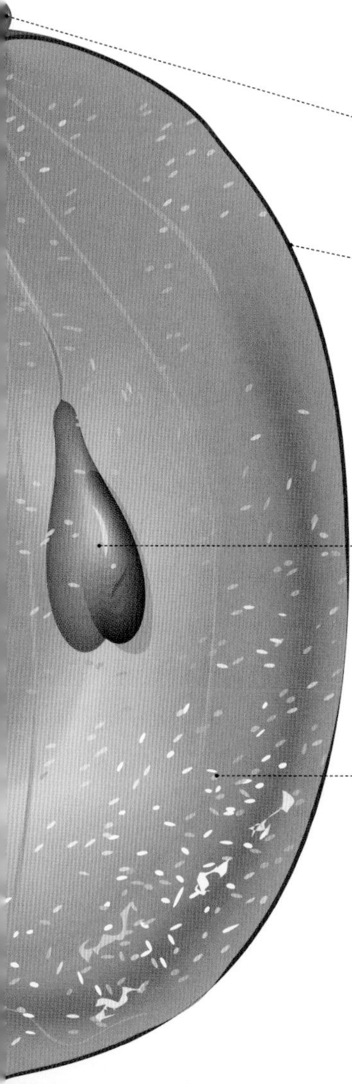
usual terms
términos^M familiares
termes^M familiers
gebräuchliche Bezeichnungen^F
termini^M comuni

stalk
rabillo^M
queue^F
Stiel^M
picciolo^M

skin
piel^F
peau^F
Haut^F
buccia^F

pip
pepita^F
pépin^M
Kern^M
vinacciolo^M

flesh
pulpa^F
pulpe^F
Fruchtfleisch^N
polpa^F

fleshy fruit: berry fruit

section of a strawberry
corte M de una fresa F
coupe F d'une fraise F
Erdbeere F im Querschnitt M
sezione F di una fragola F

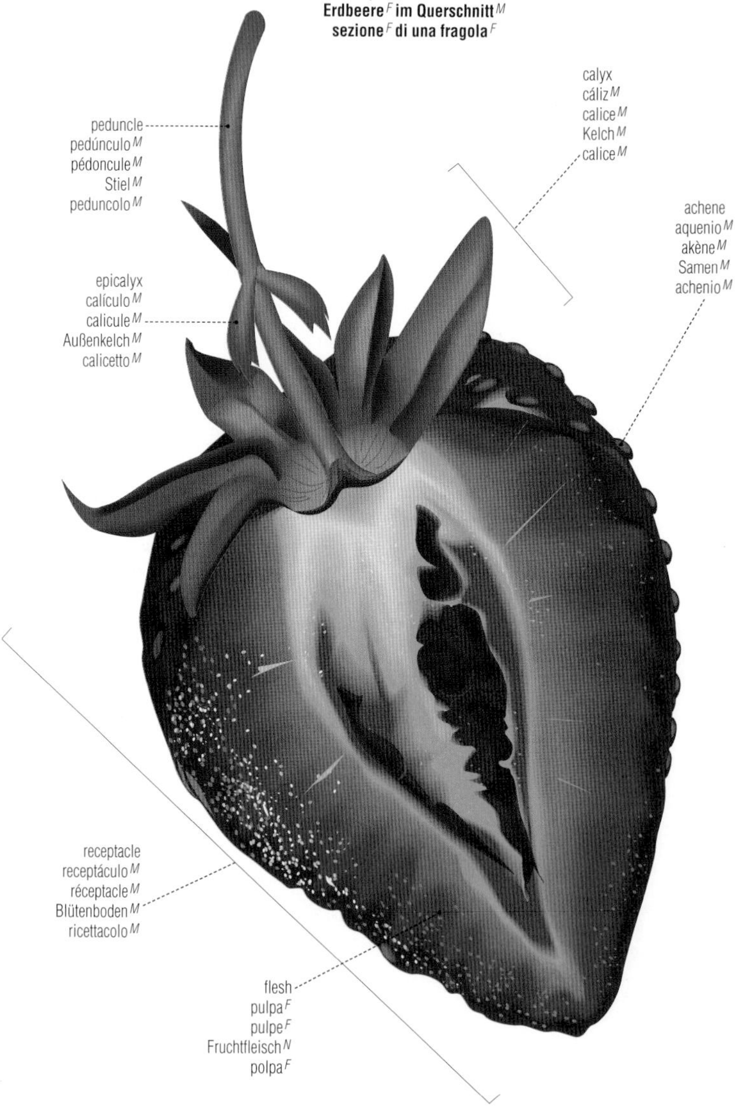
peduncle
pedúnculo M
pédoncule M
Stiel M
peduncolo M
epicalyx
calículo M
calicule M
Außenkelch M
calicetto M
calyx
cáliz M
calice M
Kelch M
calice M
achene
aquenio M
akène M
Samen M
achenio M
receptacle
receptáculo M
réceptacle M
Blütenboden M
ricettacolo M
flesh
pulpa F
pulpe F
Fruchtfleisch N
polpa F

section of a raspberry
corte M de una frambuesa F
coupe F d'une framboise F
Himbeere F im Querschnitt M
sezione F di un lampone M

peduncle
pedúnculo M
pédoncule M
Stiel M
peduncolo M
sepal
sépalo M
sépale M
Kelchblatt N
sepalo M
seed
semilla F
graine F
Samen M
seme M
receptacle
receptáculo M
réceptacle M
Blütenboden M
ricettacolo M
drupelet
drupéola F
drupéole F
Steinfrüchtchen N
drupeola F

pome fleshy fruit
pomo M carnoso
fruit M charnu à pépins M
fleischige Apfelfrucht F
frutto M carnoso: mela F

technical terms
términos M técnicos
termes M techniques
wissenschaftliche Bezeichnungen F
termini M tecnici

peduncle
pedúnculo M
pédoncule M
Stiel M
peduncolo M

loculus
lóculo M
loge F
Fruchtknotenfach N
loculo M

seed
semilla F
graine F
Samen M
seme M

mesocarp
mesocarpio M
mésocarpe M
Mesokarp N
mesocarpo M

endocarp
endocarpio M
endocarpe M
Endokarp N
endocarpo M

exocarp
epicarpio M
épicarpe M
Exokarp N
esocarpo M

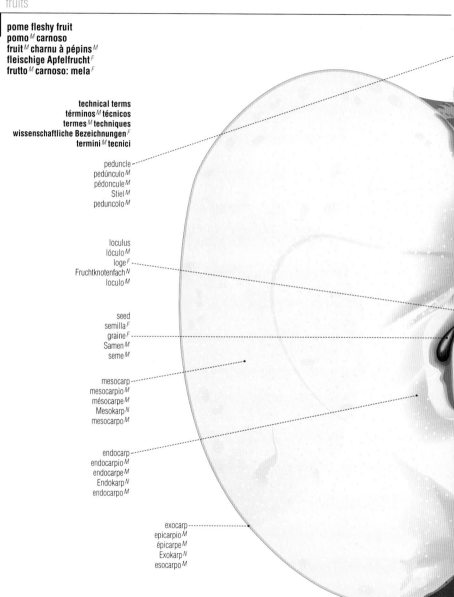

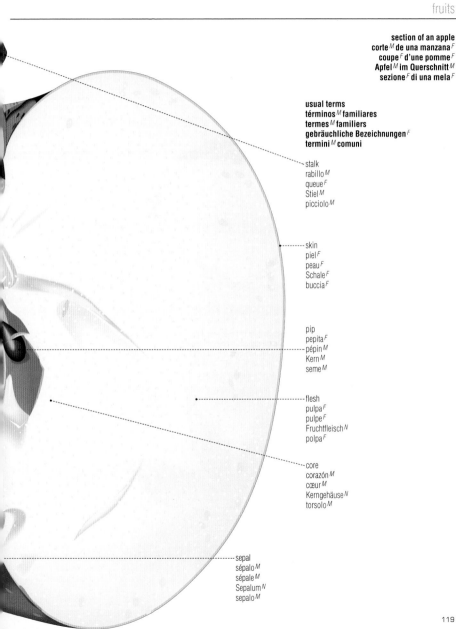

section of an apple
corte[M] de una manzana[F]
coupe[F] d'une pomme[F]
Apfel[M] im Querschnitt[M]
sezione[F] di una mela[F]

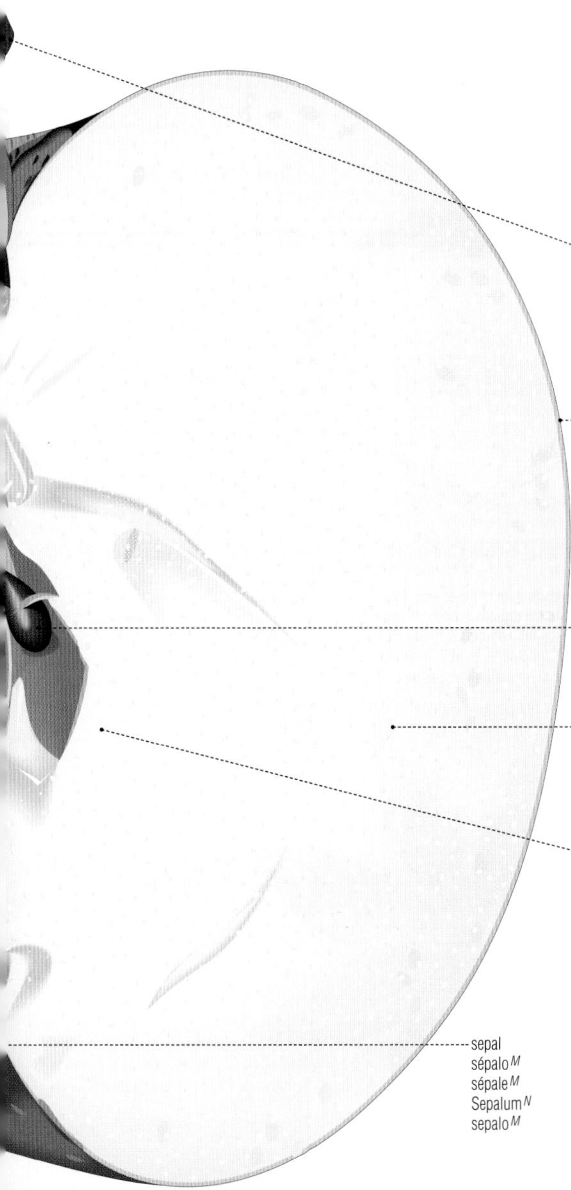

usual terms
términos[M] familiares
termes[M] familiers
gebräuchliche Bezeichnungen[F]
termini[M] comuni

stalk
rabillo[M]
queue[F]
Stiel[M]
picciolo[M]

skin
piel[F]
peau[F]
Schale[F]
buccia[F]

pip
pepita[F]
pépin[M]
Kern[M]
seme[M]

flesh
pulpa[F]
pulpe[F]
Fruchtfleisch[N]
polpa[F]

core
corazón[M]
cœur[M]
Kerngehäuse[N]
torsolo[M]

sepal
sépalo[M]
sépale[M]
Sepalum[N]
sepalo[M]

dry fruits
frutos[M] secos
fruits[M] secs
Trockenfrüchte[F]
frutti[M] secchi

section of a hazelnut
corte[M] de una avellana[F]
coupe[F] d'une noisette[F]
Längsschnitt[M] durch eine Haselnuss[F]
sezione[F] di una nocciola[F]

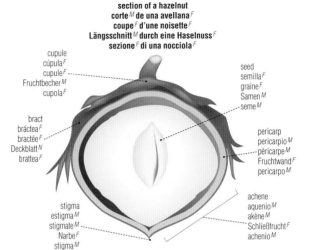

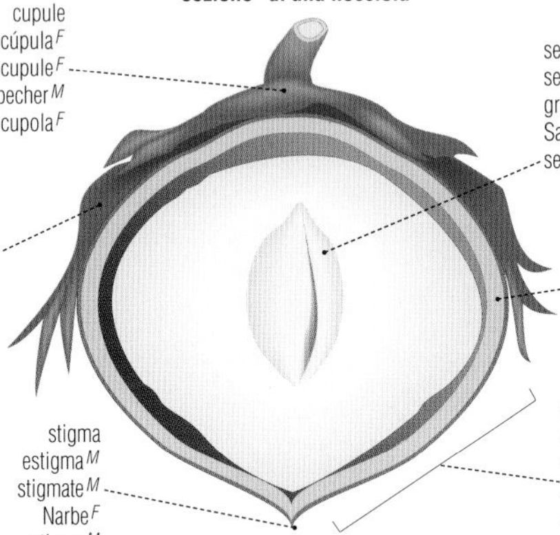
cupule
cúpula[F]
cupule[F]
Fruchtbecher[M]
cupola[F]
seed
semilla[F]
graine[F]
Samen[M]
seme[M]
bract
bráctea[F]
bractée[F]
Deckblatt[N]
brattea[F]
pericarp
pericarpio[M]
péricarpe[M]
Fruchtwand[F]
pericarpo[M]
achene
aquenio[M]
akène[M]
Schließfrucht[F]
achenio[M]
stigma
estigma[M]
stigmate[M]
Narbe[F]
stigma[M]

section of a follicle: star anise
corte[M] de un folículo[M] : anís[M] estrellado
coupe[F] d'un follicule[M] : anis[M] étoilé
Balg[M] im Querschnitt[M]: Sternanis[M]
sezione[F] di un follicolo[M]: anice[M] stellato

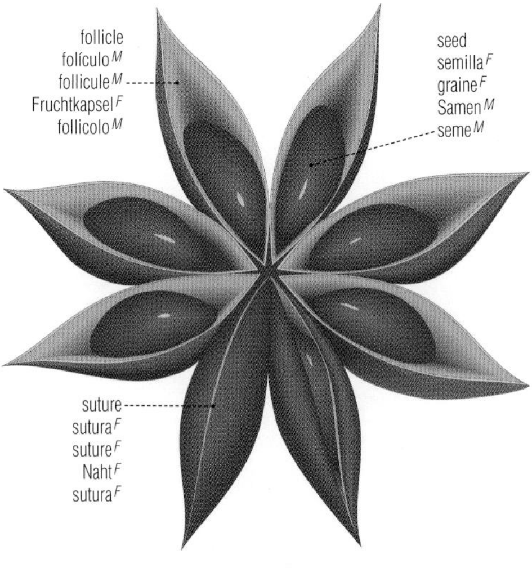
follicle
folículo[M]
follicule[M]
Fruchtkapsel[F]
follicolo[M]
seed
semilla[F]
graine[F]
Samen[M]
seme[M]
suture
sutura[F]
suture[F]
Naht[F]
sutura[F]

section of a silique: mustard
corte M de una silicua F : mostaza F
coupe F d'une silique F : moutarde F
Schote F im Querschnitt M: Senf M
sezione F di una siliqua F: senape F nera

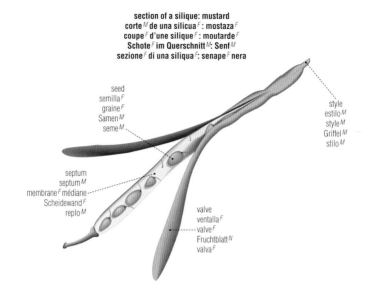

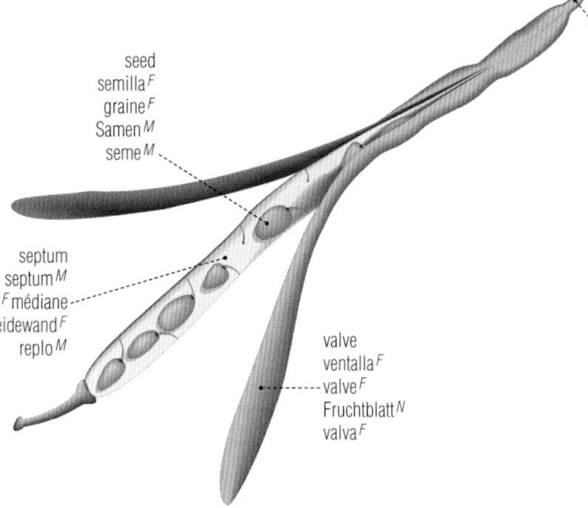
seed
semilla F
graine F
Samen M
seme M
style
estilo M
style M
Griffel M
stilo M
septum
septum M
membrane F médiane
Scheidewand F
replo M
valve
ventalla F
valve F
Fruchtblatt N
valva F

section of a capsule: poppy
corte M de una cápsula F : amapola F
coupe F d'une capsule F : pavot M
Fruchtkapsel F im Querschnitt M: Mohn M
sezione F di una capsula F: papavero M

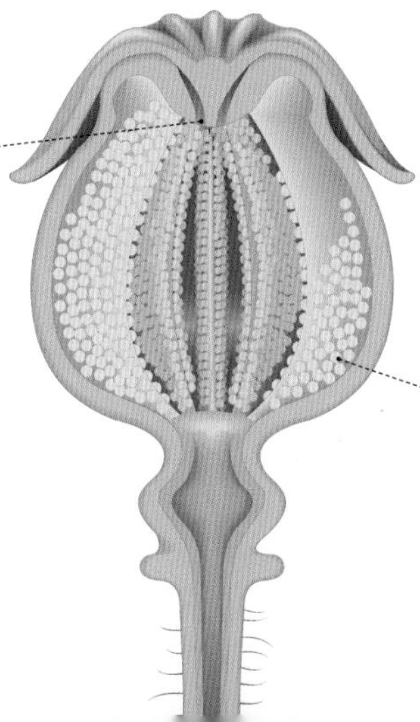
pore
poro M
pore M
Pore F
poro M
seed
semilla F
graine F
Samen M
seme M

cereals

cereales[M] | céréales[F] | Getreide[N] | cereali[M]

section of a grain of wheat
corte[M] de un grano[M] de trigo[M]
coupe[F] d'un grain[M] de blé[M]
Längsschnitt[M] durch ein Weizenkorn[N]
sezione[F] di un chicco[M] di grano[M]

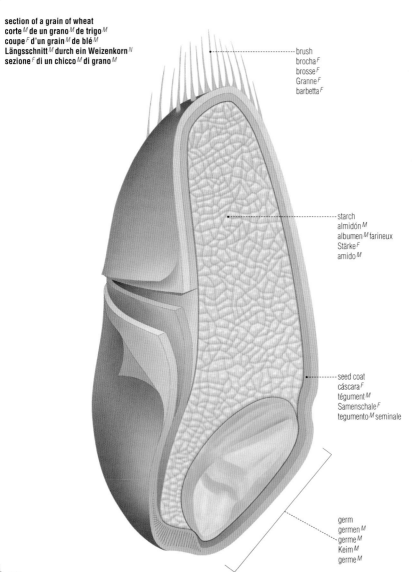

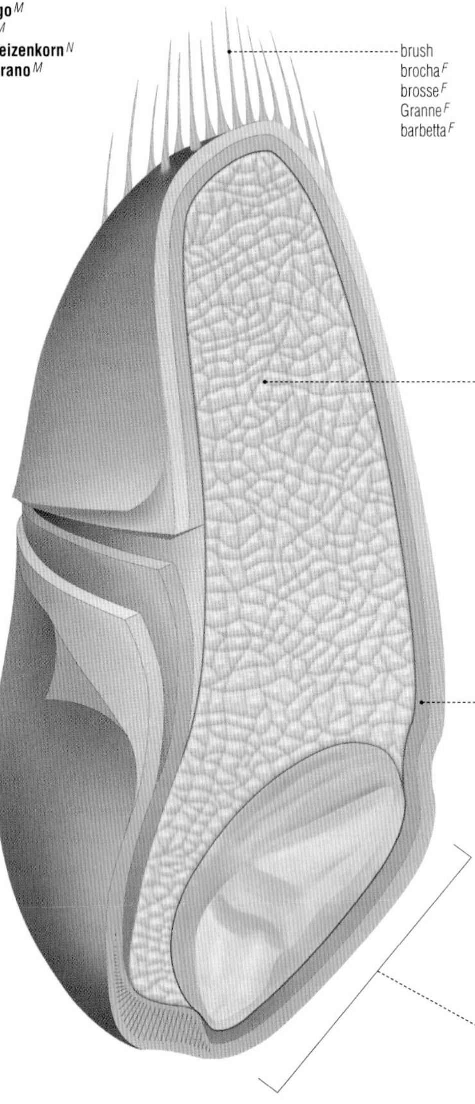
brush
brocha[F]
brosse[F]
Granne[F]
barbetta[F]
starch
almidón[M]
albumen[M] farineux
Stärke[F]
amido[M]
seed coat
cáscara[F]
tégument[M]
Samenschale[F]
tegumento[M] seminale
germ
germen[M]
germe[M]
Keim[M]
germe[M]

wheat: spike
trigo *M* **: espiga** *F*
blé *M* **: épi** *M*
Weizen *M***: Ähre** *F*
grano *M***: spiga** *F*

wheat
trigo *M*
blé *M*
Weizen *M*
grano *M*

barley: spike
cebada *F* **: espiga** *F*
orge *F* **: épi** *M*
Gerste *F***: Ähre** *F*
orzo *M***: spiga** *F*

barley
cebada *F*
orge *F*
Gerste *F*
orzo *M*

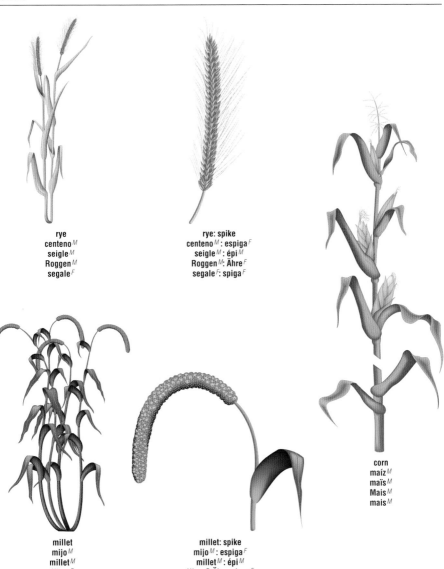

rye
centeno *M*
seigle *M*
Roggen *M*
segale *F*

rye: spike
centeno *M* **: espiga** *F*
seigle *M* **: épi** *M*
Roggen *M***: Ähre** *F*
segale *F***: spiga** *F*

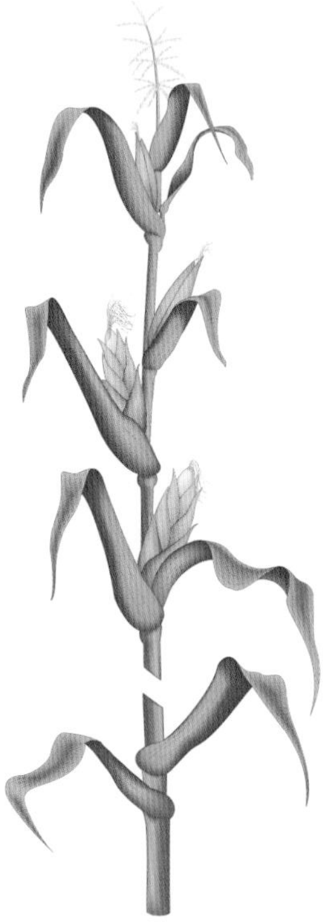

corn
maíz *M*
maïs *M*
Mais *M*
mais *M*

millet
mijo *M*
millet *M*
Hirse *F*
miglio *M*

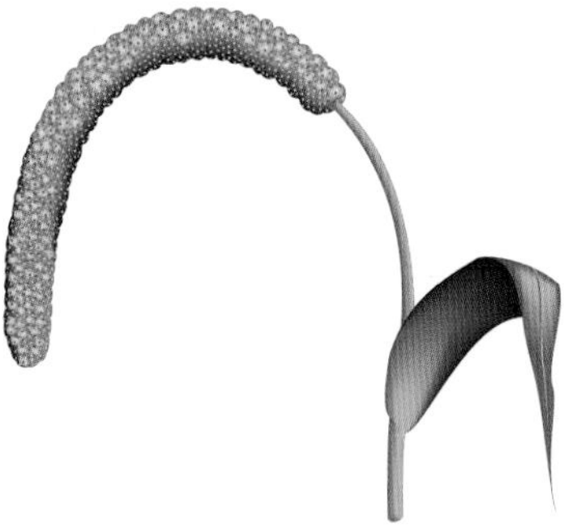

millet: spike
mijo *M* **: espiga** *F*
millet *M* **: épi** *M*
Hirse *F***: Ährenrispe** *F*
miglio *M***: spiga** *F*

corn: cob
maíz^M : mazorca^F
maïs^M : épi^M
Mais^M: Kolben^M
mais^M: pannocchia^F

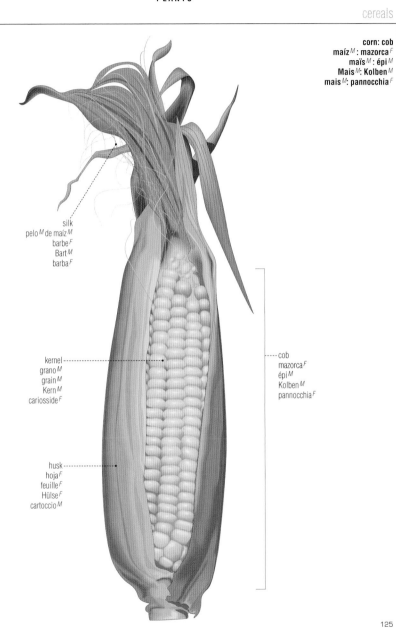

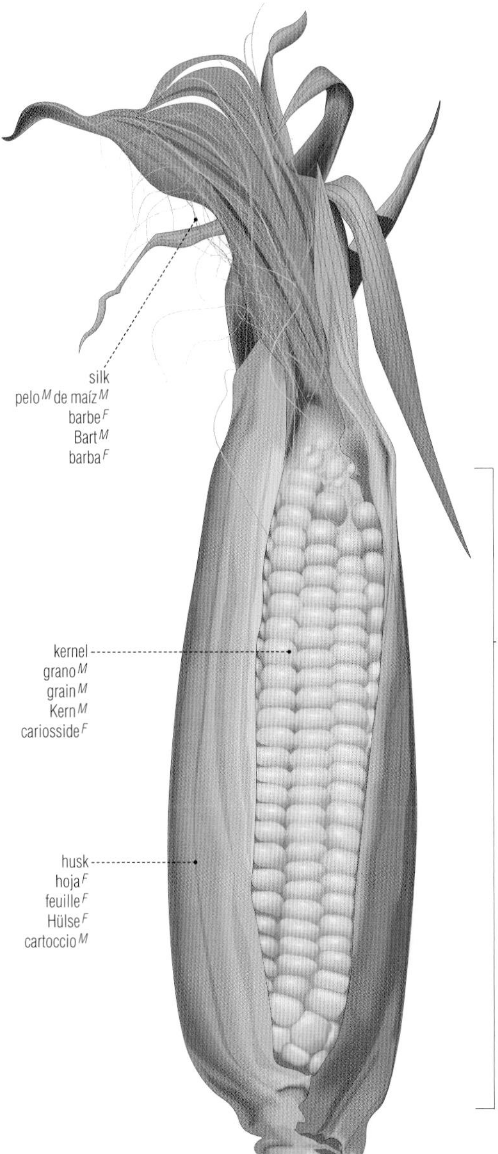
silk
pelo M de maíz M
barbe F
Bart M
barba F
kernel
grano M
grain M
Kern M
cariosside F
husk
hoja F
feuille F
Hülse F
cartoccio M
cob
mazorca F
épi M
Kolben M
pannocchia F

oats
avena [F]
avoine [F]
Hafer [M]
avena [F]

oats: panicle
avena [F] **: panícula** [F]
avoine [F] **: panicule** [F]
Hafer [M]**: Ährchen** [N]
avena [F]**: pannocchia** [F]

buckwheat
trigo [M] **sarraceno**
sarrasin [M]
Buchweizen [M]
grano [M] **saraceno**

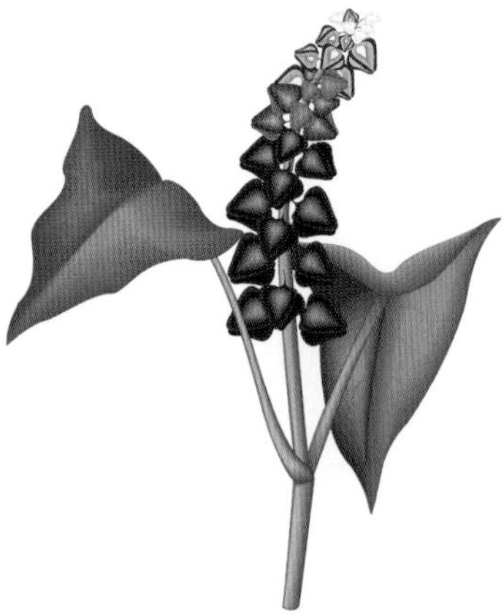

buckwheat: raceme
trigo [M] **sarraceno: racimo** [M]
sarrasin [M] **: grappe** [F]
Buchweizen [M]**: Doldenrispe** [F]
grano [M] **saraceno: racemo** [M]

rice
arroz *M*
riz *M*
Reis *M*
riso *M*

rice: panicle
arroz *M*: **panícula** *F*
riz *M* : **panicule** *F*
Reis *M*: **Rispe** *F*
riso *M*: **pannocchia** *F*

sorghum
sorgo *M*
sorgho *M*
Mohrenhirse *F*
sorgo *M*

sorghum: panicle
sorgo *M* : **panícula** *F*
sorgho *M* : **panicule** *F*
Mohrenhirse *F*: **Rispe** *F*
sorgo *M*: **pannocchia** *F*

tree

árbol M | arbre M | Baum M | albero M

structure of a tree
anatomía F de un árbol M
structure F d'un arbre M
Aufbau M eines Baumes M
struttura F di un albero M

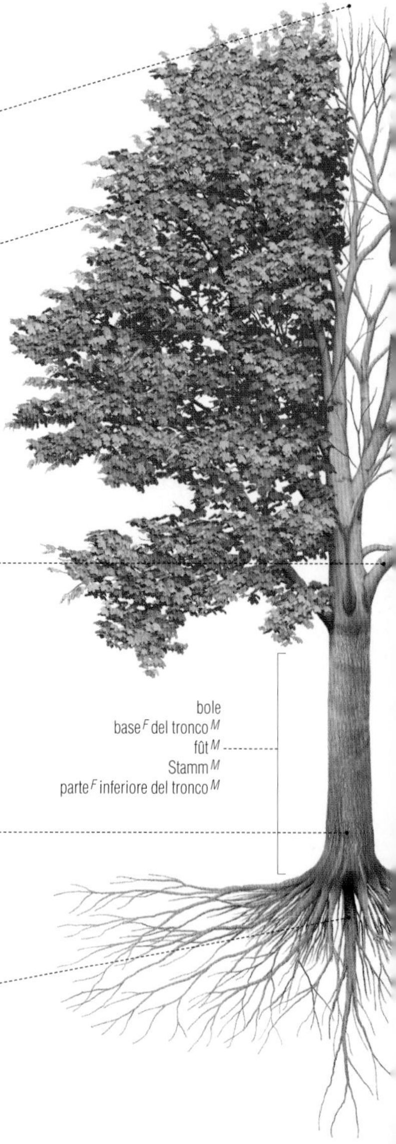

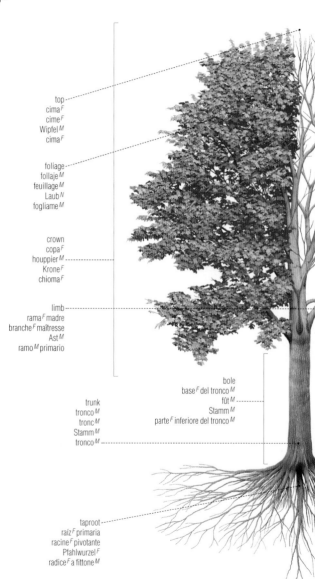

top
cima F
cime F
Wipfel M
cima F
foliage
follaje M
feuillage M
Laub N
fogliame M
crown
copa F
houppier M
Krone F
chioma F
limb
rama F madre
branche F maîtresse
Ast M
ramo M primario
bole
base F del tronco M
fût M
Stamm M
parte F inferiore del tronco M
trunk
tronco M
tronc M
Stamm M
tronco M
taproot
raíz F primaria
racine F pivotante
Pfahlwurzel F
radice F a fittone M

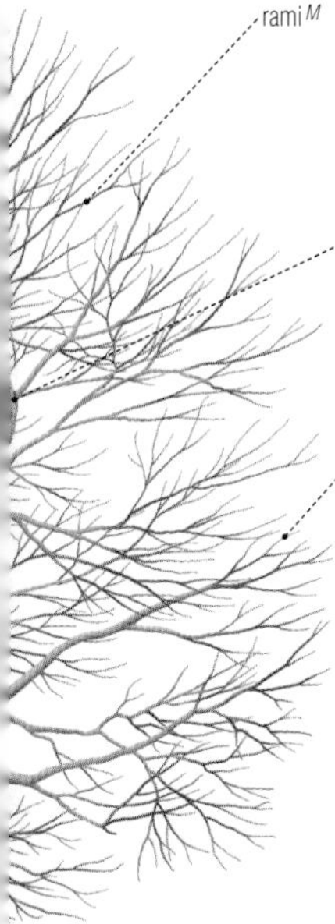

branches
ramaje[M]
ramure[F]
Äste[M]
rami[M]

branch
rama[F]
rameau[M]
Ast[M]
ramo[M]

twig
ramilla[F]
ramille[F]
Zweig[M]
ramo[M] secondario

stump
tocón[M]
souche[F]
Stumpf[M]
ceppo[M]

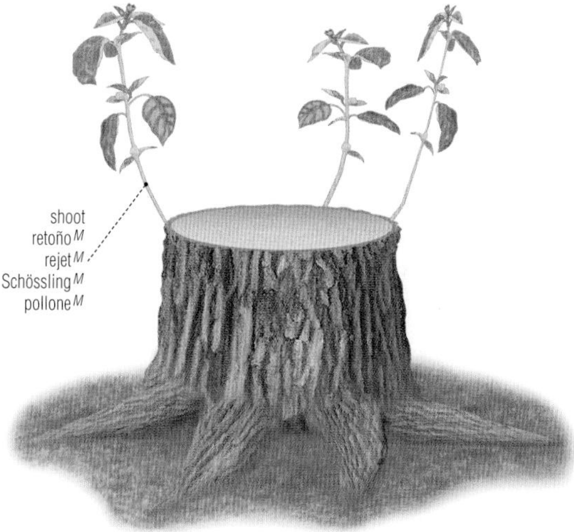

shoot
retoño[M]
rejet[M]
Schössling[M]
pollone[M]

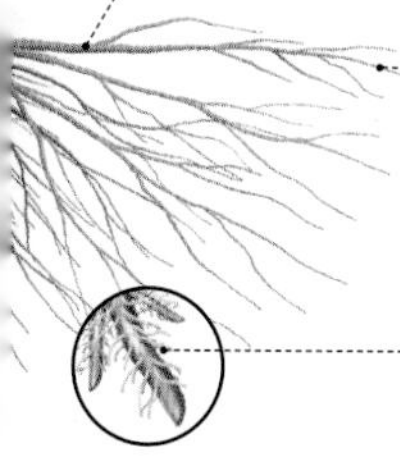

shallow root
raíces[F] superficiales
racine[F] traçante
Flachwurzel[F]
radice[F] superficiale

radicle
radícula[F]
radicelle[F]
Faserwurzel[F]
radichetta[F]

root-hair zone
zona[F] de pelos[M] absorbentes
chevelu[M]
Wurzelhaarzone[F]
regione[F] pilifera

examples of broadleaved trees
ejemplos[M] de latifolios[M]
exemples[M] d'arbres[M] feuillus
Beispiele[N] für Laubhölzer[N]
esempi[M] di latifoglie[F]

lilac
lilas[F]
lilas[M]
Flieder[M]
lillà[M]

birch
abedul[M]
bouleau[M]
Birke[F]
betulla[F]

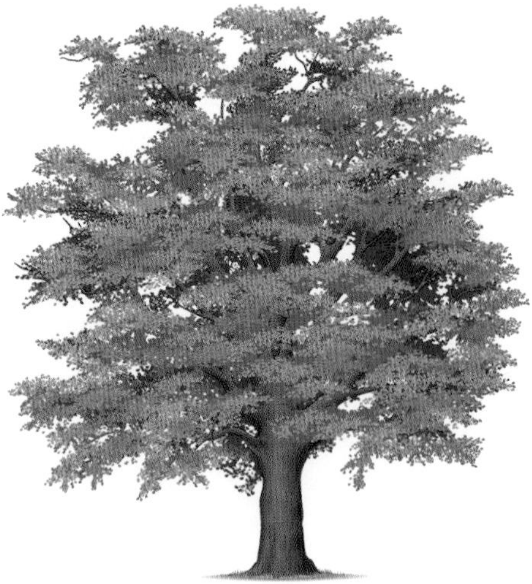

oak
roble[M]
chêne[M]
Eiche[F]
quercia[F]

beech
haya F
hêtre M
Buche F
faggio M

weeping willow
sauce M llorón
saule M pleureur
Trauerweide F
salice M piangente

palm tree
palmera F
palmier M
Palme F
palma F

examples of broadleaved trees

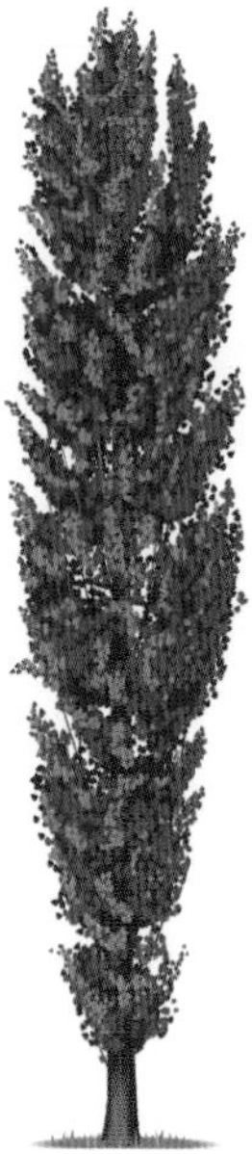

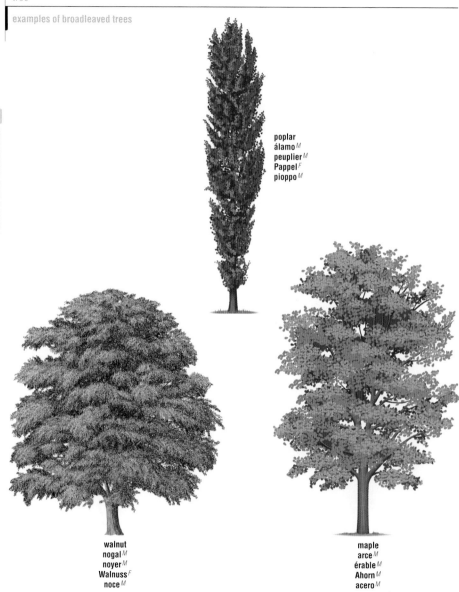

poplar
álamo *M*
peuplier *M*
Pappel *F*
pioppo *M*

walnut
nogal *M*
noyer *M*
Walnuss *F*
noce *M*

maple
arce *M*
érable *M*
Ahorn *M*
acero *M*

conifer

conífera F | conifère M | Nadelbaum M | conifera F

structure of a conifer
estructura F de una conífera F
structure F d'un conifère M
Struktur F einer Konifere F
struttura F di una conifera F

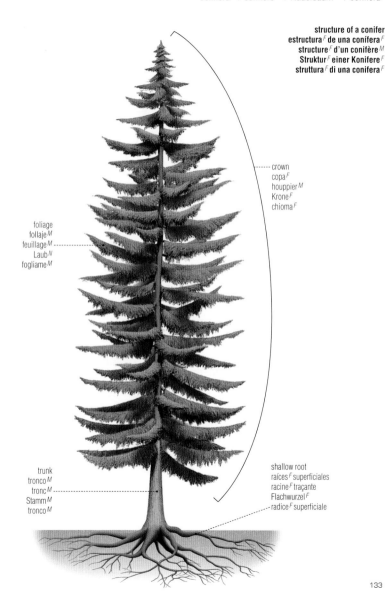

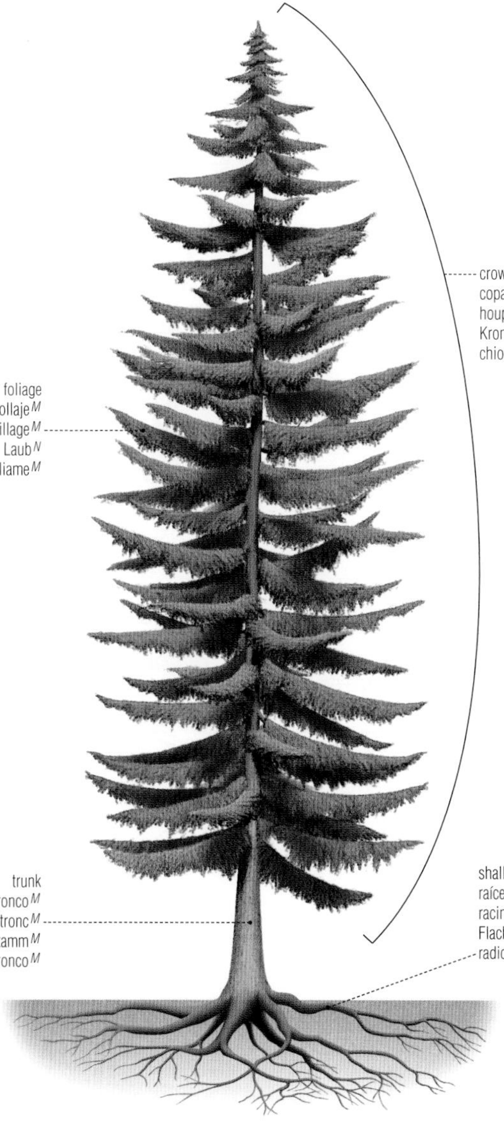
crown
copa F
houppier M
Krone F
chioma F
foliage
follaje M
feuillage M
Laub N
fogliame M
trunk
tronco M
tronc M
Stamm M
tronco M
shallow root
raíces F superficiales
racine F traçante
Flachwurzel F
radice F superficiale

conifer

examples of conifers
ejemplos[M] de coníferas[F]
exemples[M] de conifères[M]
Beispiele[N] für Nadelhölzer[N]
esempi[M] di conifere[F]

umbrella pine
pino[M] piñonero
pin[M] parasol[M]
Pinie[F]
pino[M] domestico

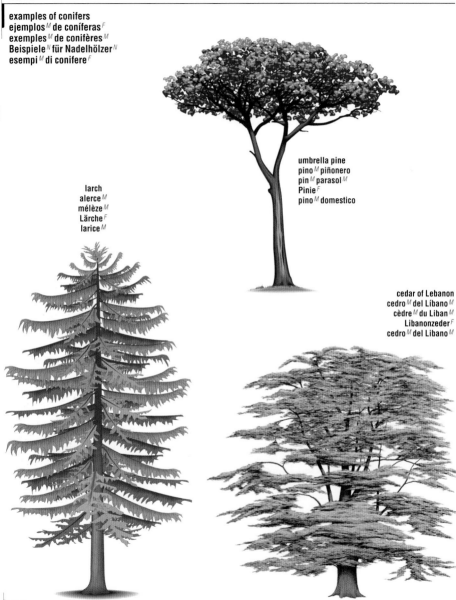

larch
alerce[M]
mélèze[M]
Lärche[F]
larice[M]

cedar of Lebanon
cedro[M] del Líbano[M]
cèdre[M] du Liban[M]
Libanonzeder[F]
cedro[M] del Libano[M]

spruce
pícea *F*
épicéa *M*
Fichte *F*
picea *F*

fir
abeto *M*
sapin *M*
Tanne *F*
abete *M*

vegetation and biosphere

vegetación^F y biosfera^F | végétation^F et biosphère^F | Vegetation^F und Biosphäre^F | vegetazione^F e biosfera^F

vegetation regions
distribución^F de la vegetación^F
distribution^F de la végétation^F
Vegetationszonen^F
distribuzione^F della vegetazione^F

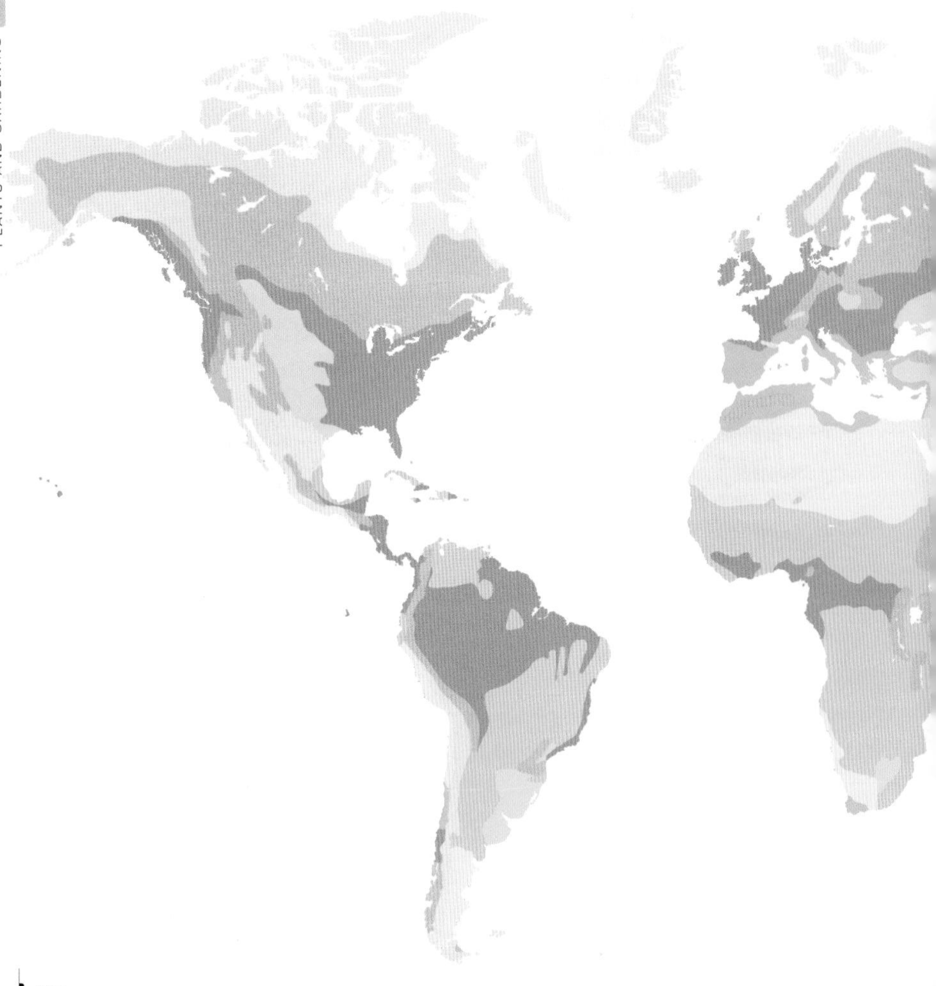

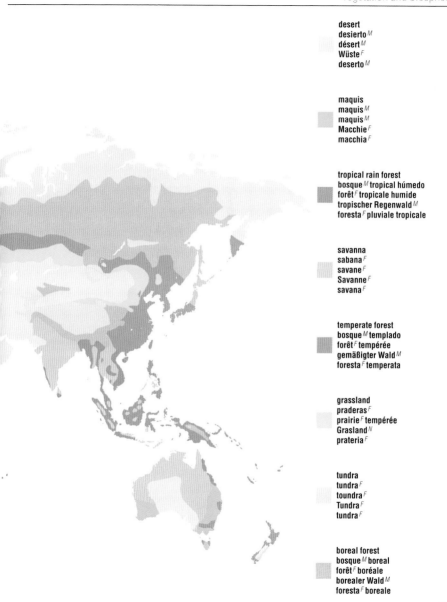

desert
desierto [M]
désert [M]
Wüste [F]
deserto [M]

maquis
maquis [M]
maquis [M]
Macchie [F]
macchia [F]

tropical rain forest
bosque [M] **tropical húmedo**
forêt [F] **tropicale humide**
tropischer Regenwald [M]
foresta [F] **pluviale tropicale**

savanna
sabana [F]
savane [F]
Savanne [F]
savana [F]

temperate forest
bosque [M] **templado**
forêt [F] **tempérée**
gemäßigter Wald [M]
foresta [F] **temperata**

grassland
praderas [F]
prairie [F] **tempérée**
Grasland [N]
prateria [F]

tundra
tundra [F]
toundra [F]
Tundra [F]
tundra [F]

boreal forest
bosque [M] **boreal**
forêt [F] **boréale**
borealer Wald [M]
foresta [F] **boreale**

pleasure garden

jardín M | jardin M d'agrément M | Ziergarten M | giardino M

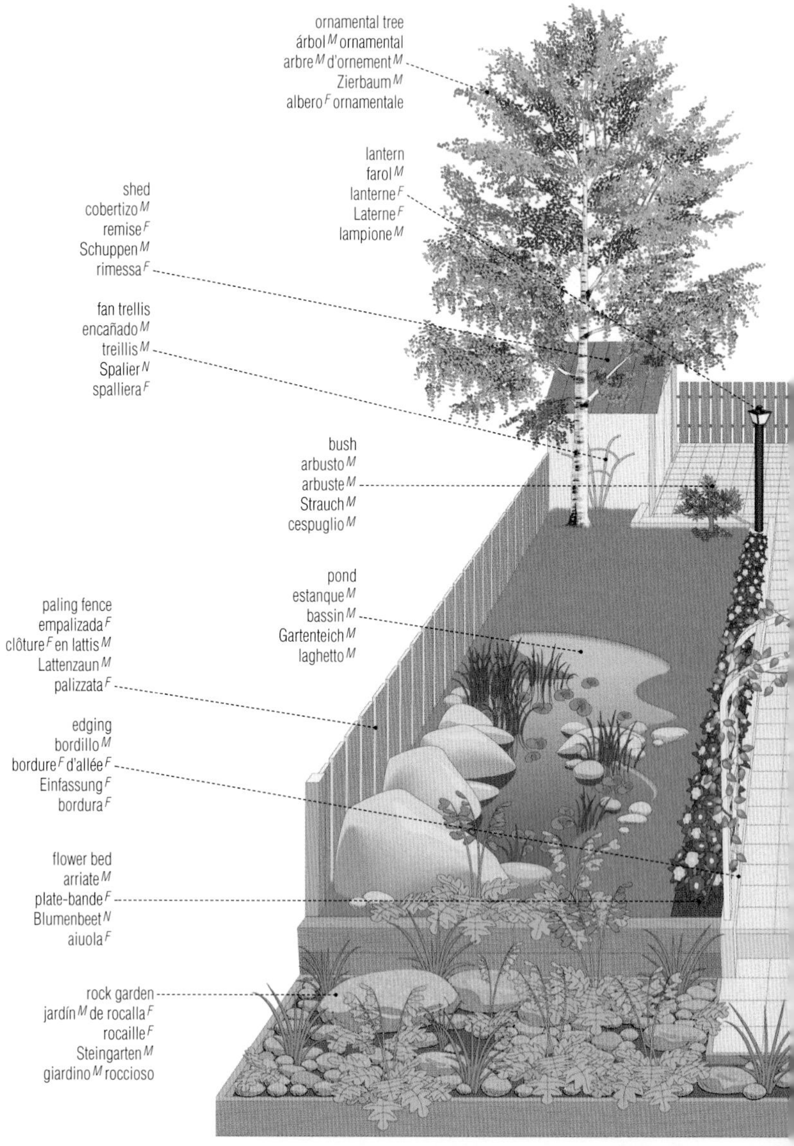
ornamental tree
árbol M ornamental
arbre M d'ornement M
Zierbaum M
albero F ornamentale
lantern
farol M
lanterne F
Laterne F
lampione M
shed
cobertizo M
remise F
Schuppen M
rimessa F
fan trellis
encañado M
treillis M
Spalier N
spalliera F
bush
arbusto M
arbuste M
Strauch M
cespuglio M
pond
estanque M
bassin M
Gartenteich M
laghetto M
paling fence
empalizada F
clôture F en lattis M
Lattenzaun M
palizzata F
edging
bordillo M
bordure F d'allée F
Einfassung F
bordura F
flower bed
arriate M
plate-bande F
Blumenbeet N
aiuola F
rock garden
jardín M de rocalla F
rocaille F
Steingarten M
giardino M roccioso

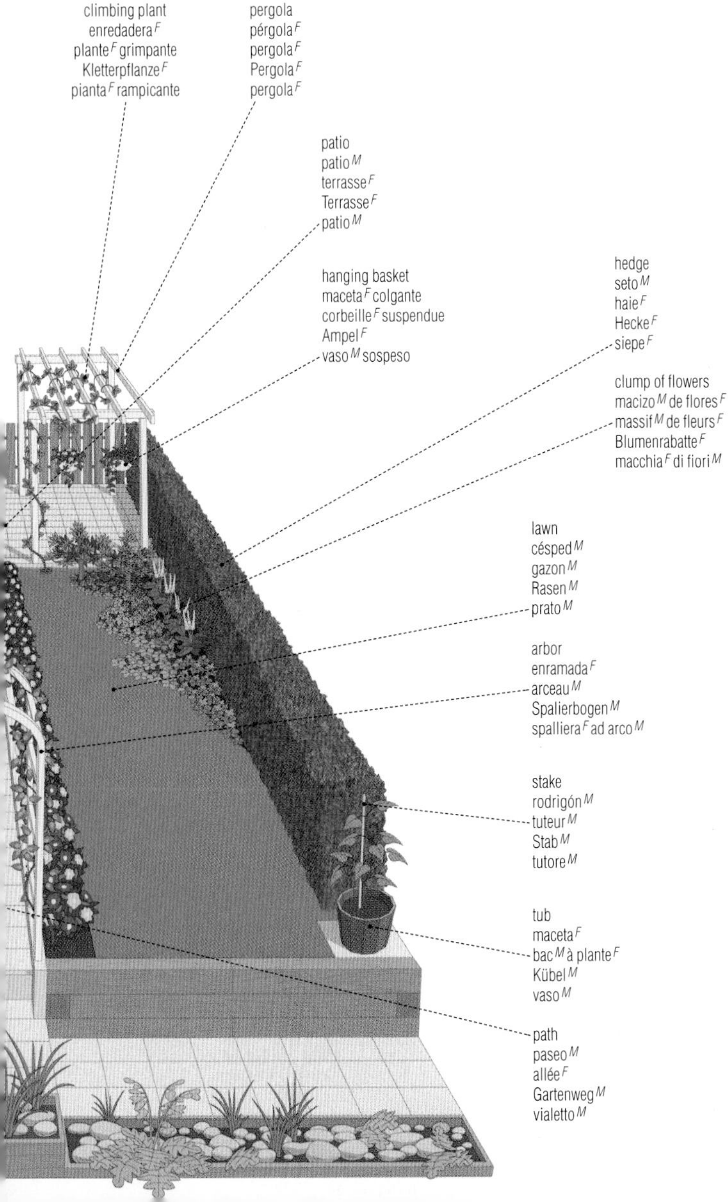
climbing plant
enredadera F
plante F grimpante
Kletterpflanze F
pianta F rampicante
pergola
pérgola F
pergola F
Pergola F
pergola F
patio
patio M
terrasse F
Terrasse F
patio M
hanging basket
maceta F colgante
corbeille F suspendue
Ampel F
vaso M sospeso
hedge
seto M
haie F
Hecke F
siepe F
clump of flowers
macizo M de flores F
massif M de fleurs F
Blumenrabatte F
macchia F di fiori M
lawn
césped M
gazon M
Rasen M
prato M
arbor
enramada F
arceau M
Spalierbogen M
spalliera F ad arco M
stake
rodrigón M
tuteur M
Stab M
tutore M
tub
maceta F
bac M à plante F
Kübel M
vaso M
path
paseo M
allée F
Gartenweg M
vialetto M

seeding and planting tools

herramientas^F para sembrar y plantar | outils^M pour semer et planter | Werkzeuge^N zum Säen^N und Pflanzen^N | attrezzi^M per seminare e piantare

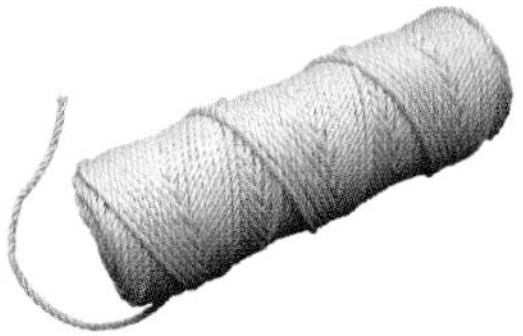

garden line
cuerda F
cordeau M
Pflanzschnur F
filo M **da giardino** M

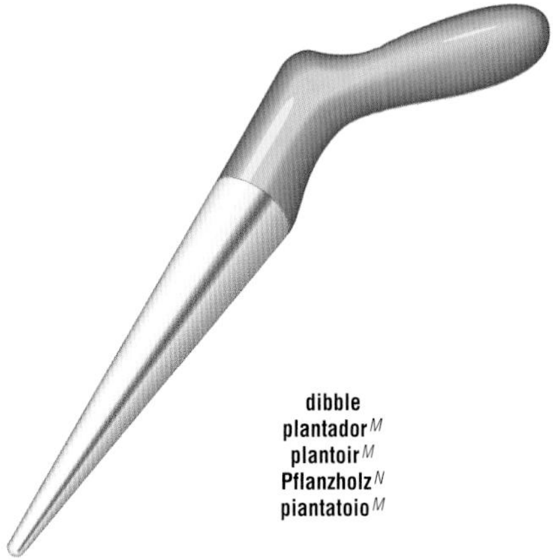

dibble
plantador M
plantoir M
Pflanzholz N
piantatoio M

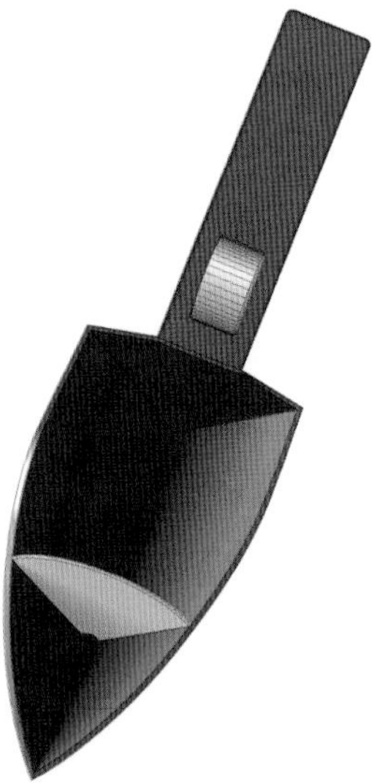

seeder
sembradora F **de mano** F
semoir M **à main** F
Säkelle F
seminatoio M **a mano** F

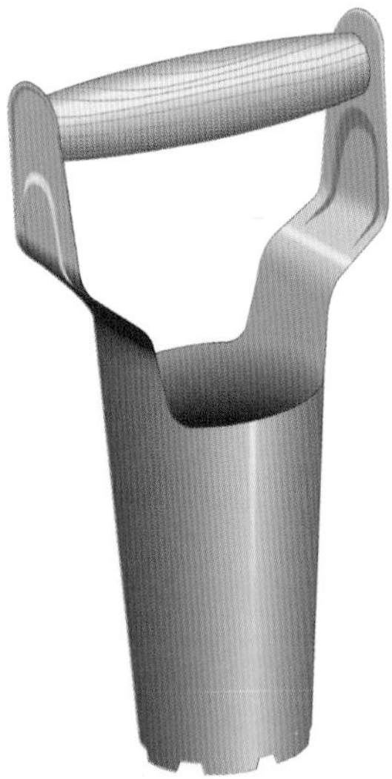

bulb dibble
plantador M **de bulbos** M
plantoir M **à bulbes** M
Pflanzlochstecher M
piantabulbi M

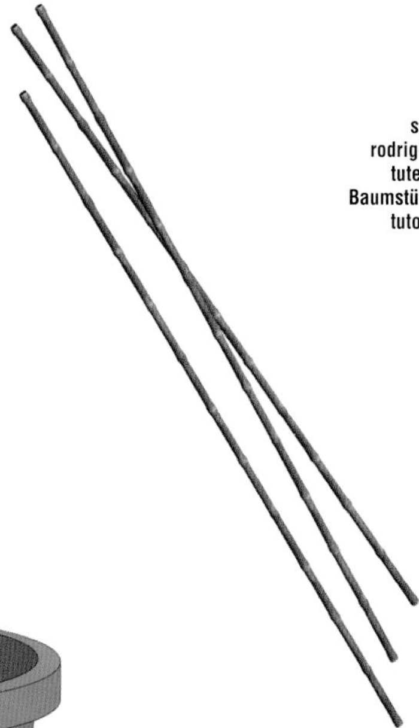
stake
rodrigón M
tuteur M
Baumstütze F
tutore M

spreader
esparcidora F de abono M
épandeur M
Düngerstreuer M
spandiconcime M
wheel
rueda F
roue F
Rad N
ruota F

tools for loosening the earth

herramientas[F] para remover la tierra[F] | outils[M] pour remuer la terre[F] | Geräte[N] zur Erdbewegung[F] | attrezzi[M] per smuovere la terra[F]

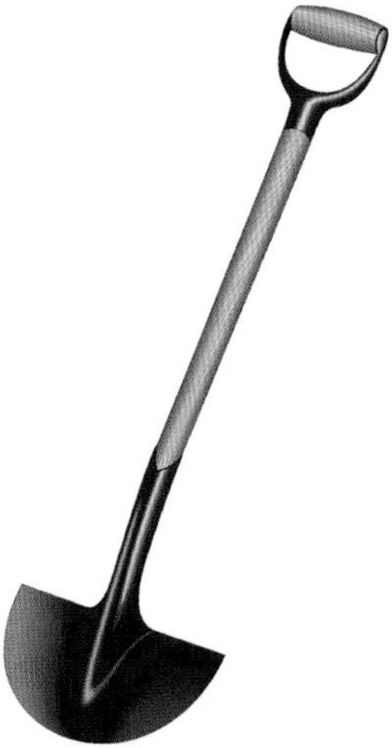

lawn edger
cuchilla[F] para delimitar el césped[M]
coupe-bordures[M]
Kantenstecher[M]
tagliabordi[M]

shovel
pala[F]
pelle[F]
Grabschaufel[F]
badile[M]

spading fork
horca[F]
fourche[F] à bêcher
Grabgabel[F]
forcone[F]

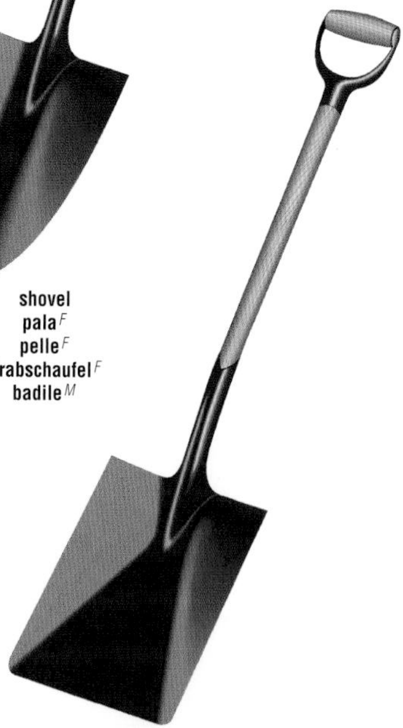

spade
laya[F]
bêche[F]
Spaten[M]
vanga[F]

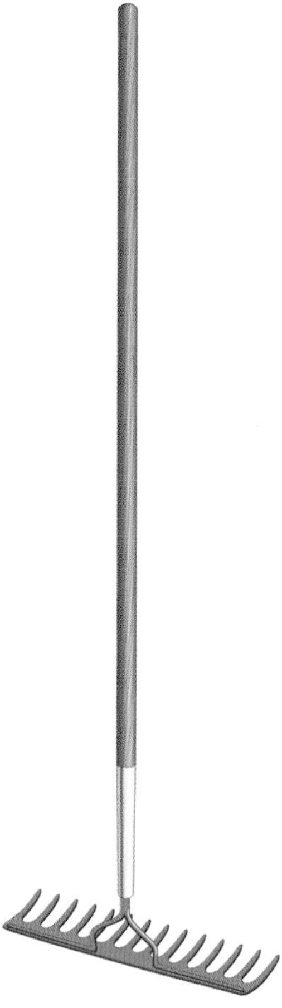

rake
rastrillo M
râteau M
Rechen M
rastrello M

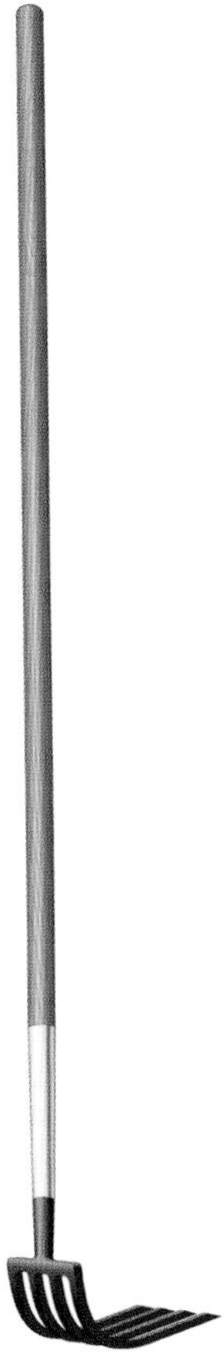

hook
garabato M
croc M à défricher
Krail M
zappa F a quattro denti M

hoe
azadón M
houe F
Rodehacke F
zappa F

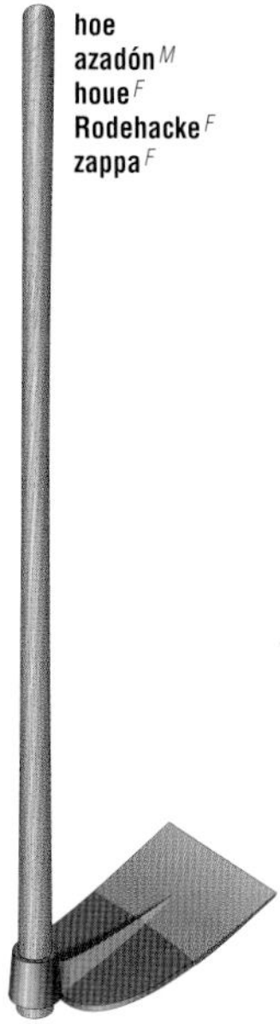

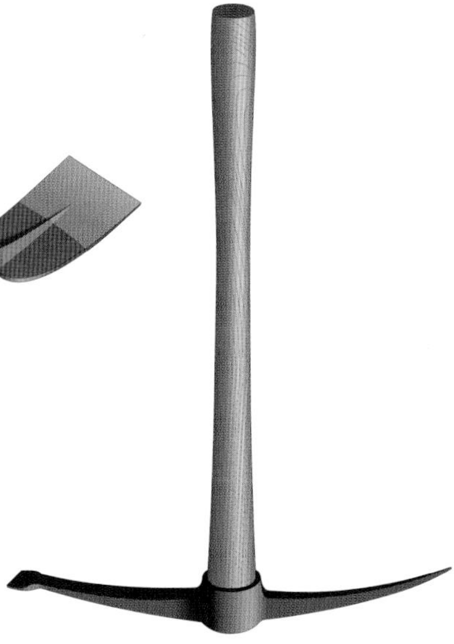

pick
pico M
pioche F
Kreuzhacke F
piccone M

tools for loosening the earth

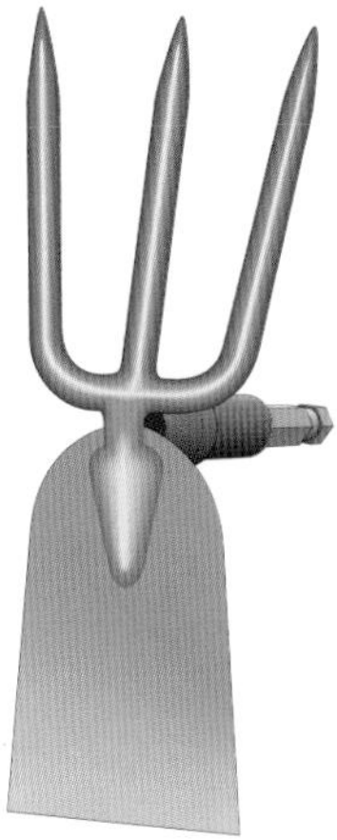

hoe-fork
azuela[F]
serfouette[F]
Kombihacke[F]
zappetta[F] **tridente**

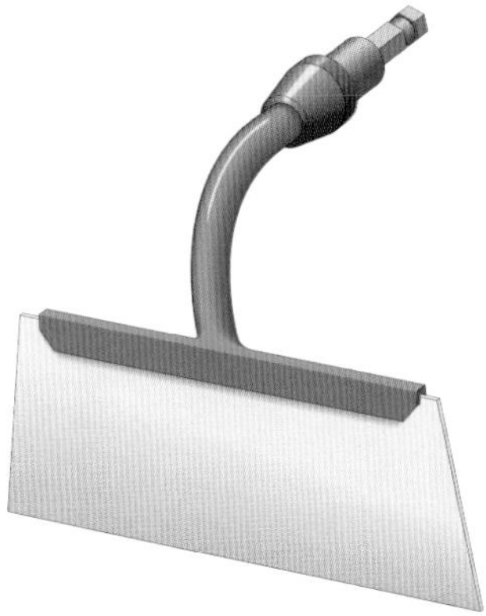

draw hoe
azada[F]
binette[F]
Rübenhacke[F]
sarchiello[M]

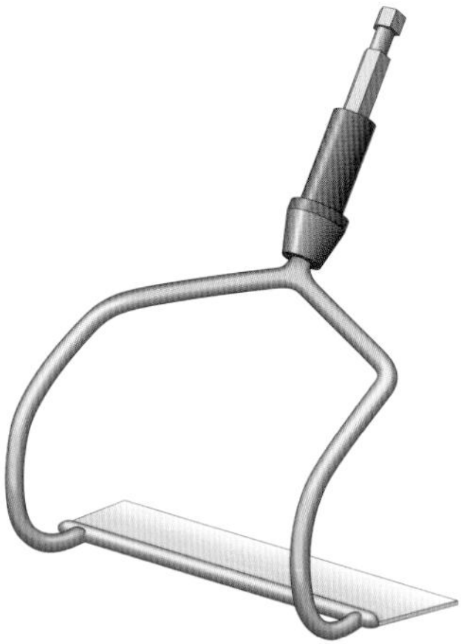

collinear hoe
azada[F] **de doble filo**[M]
ratissoire[F]
Ziehhacke[F]
sarchio[M]

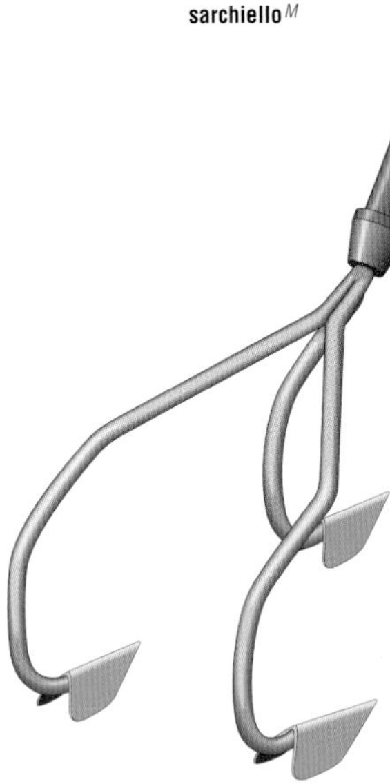

weeding hoe
cultivador[M]
sarcloir[M]
Handkultivator[M]
coltivatore[M]

tiller
motocultor M
motoculteur M
Gartenfräse F
motocoltivatore M

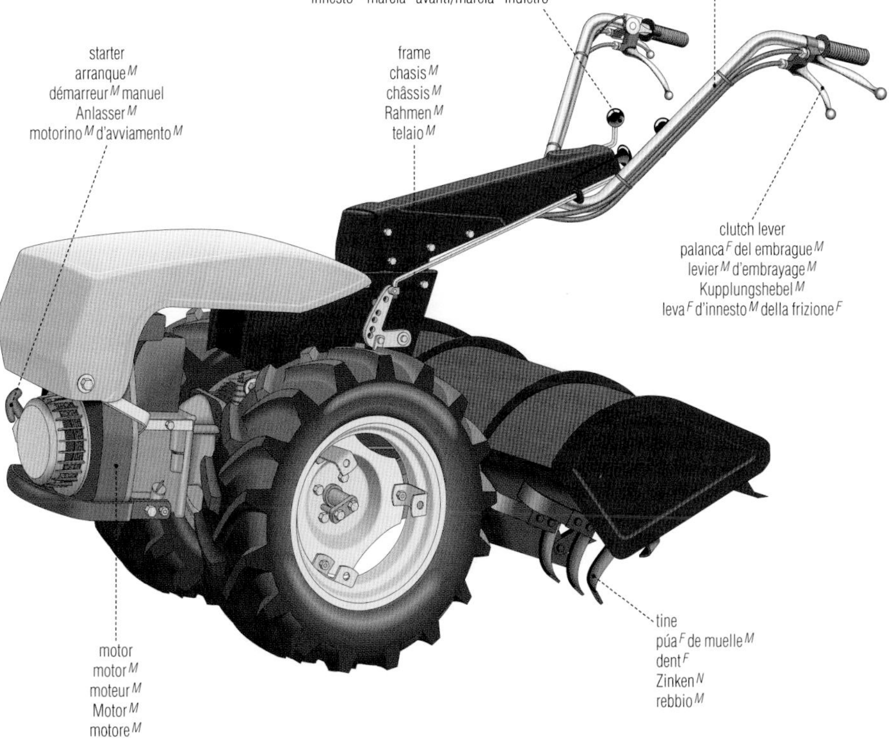
handlebar
manillar F
mancheron M
Lenkholm M
manubrio M
forward/reverse
palanca F de avance M/marcha F atrás
marche F avant/marche F arrière
vorwärts/rückwärts
innesto M marcia F avanti/marcia F indietro
starter
arranque M
démarreur M manuel
Anlasser M
motorino M d'avviamento M
frame
chasis M
châssis M
Rahmen M
telaio M
clutch lever
palanca F del embrague M
levier M d'embrayage M
Kupplungshebel M
leva F d'innesto M della frizione F
tine
púa F de muelle M
dent F
Zinken N
rebbio M
motor
motor M
moteur M
Motor M
motore M

watering tools

herramientas F para regar | outils M pour arroser | Gießgeräte N | attrezzi M per annaffiare

hose trolley
carretilla F para manguera F
dévidoir M sur roues F
Schlauchwagen M
carrello M avvolgitubo

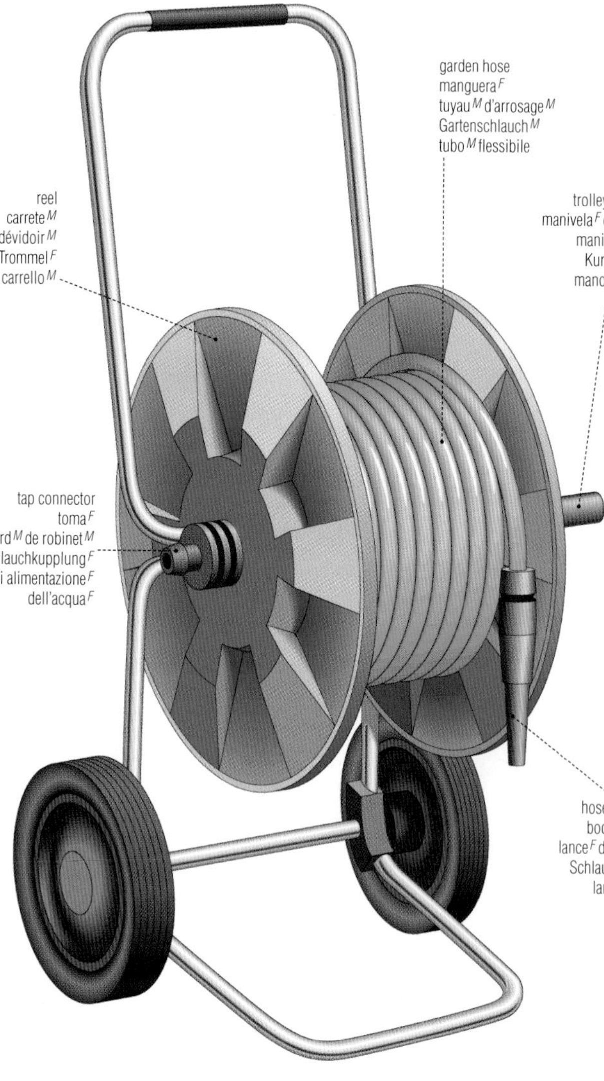
garden hose
manguera F
tuyau M d'arrosage M
Gartenschlauch M
tubo M flessibile
reel
carrete M
dévidoir M
Trommel F
carrello M
trolley crank
manivela F del carrete M
manivelle F
Kurbel F
manovella F
tap connector
toma F
raccord M de robinet M
Schlauchkupplung F
attacco M del tubo M di alimentazione F dell'acqua F
hose nozzle
boquilla F
lance F d'arrosage M
Schlauchdüse F
lancia F

watering can
regadera *F*
arrosoir *M*
Gießkanne *F*
annaffiatoio *M*

handle
asa *F*
anse *F*
Griff *M*
manico *M*

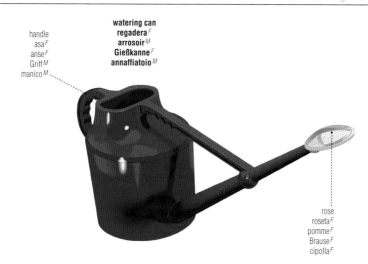

rose
roseta *F*
pomme *F*
Brause *F*
cipolla *F*

tank sprayer
pulverizador *M*
pulvérisateur *M*
Gartenspritze *F*
atomizzatore *M*

sprinkler hose
manguera *F* **de riego** *M*
tuyau *M* **perforé**
Regnerschlauch *M*
tubo *M* **per irrigazione** *F*

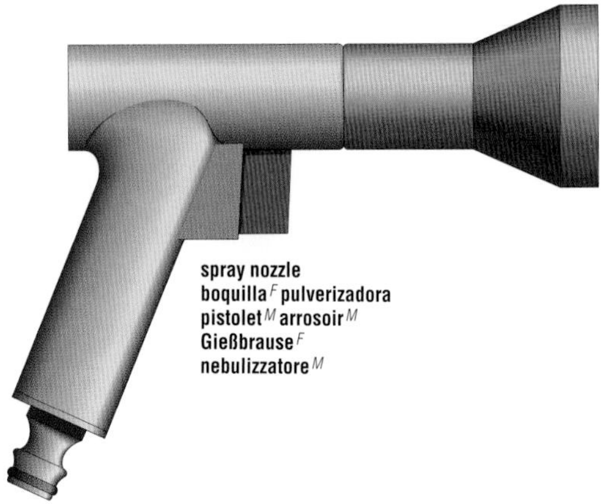

spray nozzle
boquilla[F] pulverizadora
pistolet[M] arrosoir[M]
Gießbrause[F]
nebulizzatore[M]

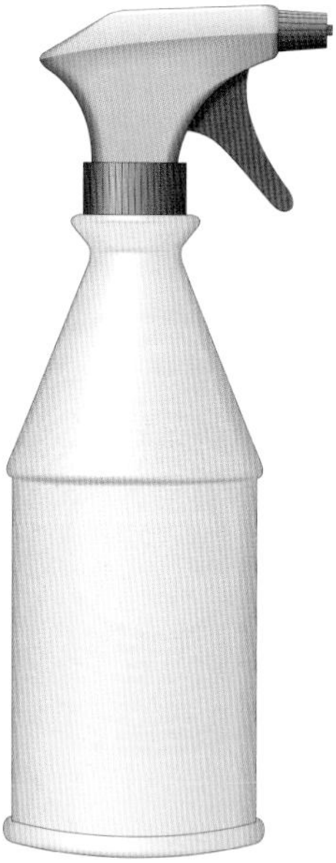

sprayer
pulverizador[M]
vaporisateur[M]
Sprühflasche[F]
spruzzatore[M]

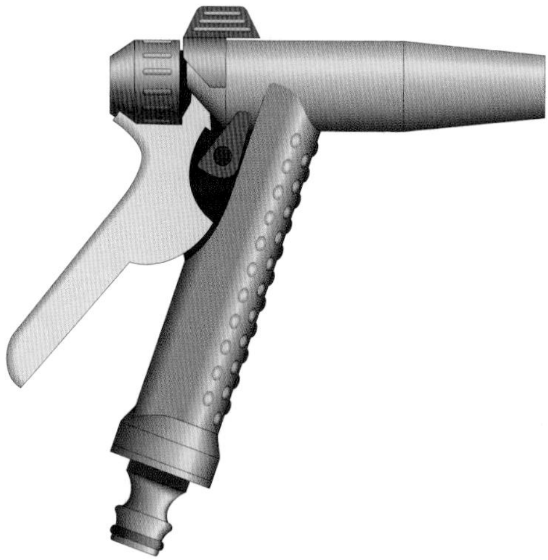

pistol nozzle
pistola[F] pulverizadora
pistolet[M] d'arrosage[M]
Gießpistole[F]
polverizzatore[M] a pistola[F]

revolving sprinkler
irrigador^M giratorio
arroseur^M rotatif
Kreisregner^M
irrigatore^M rotativo a pioggia^F

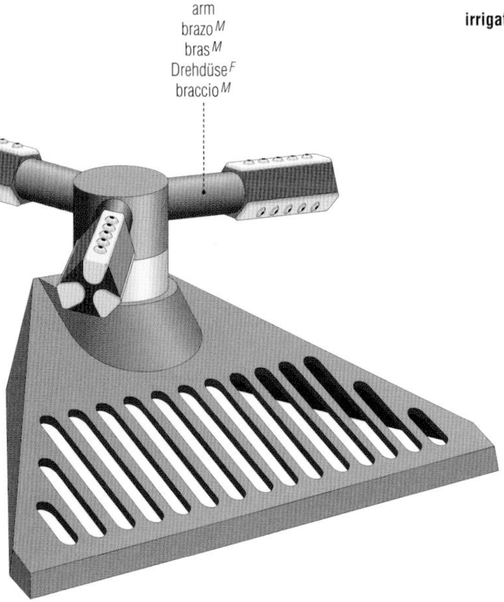
arm
brazo M
bras M
Drehdüse F
braccio M

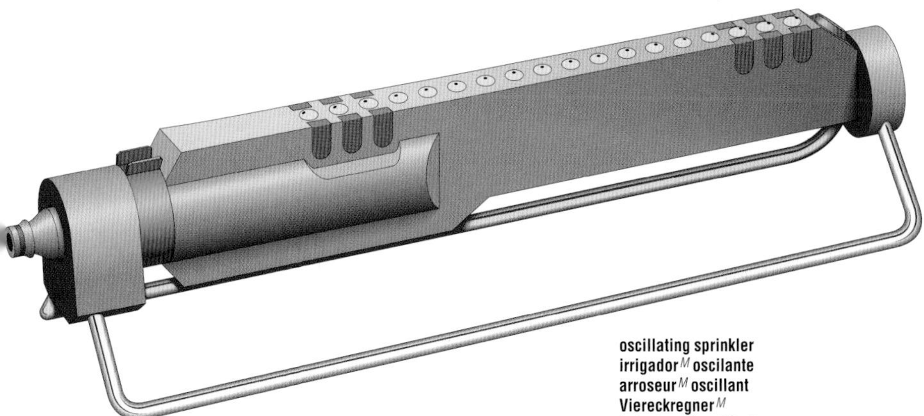

oscillating sprinkler
irrigador^M oscilante
arroseur^M oscillant
Viereckregner^M
irrigatore^M oscillante

watering tools

impulse sprinkler
irrigador *M* **de impulso** *M*
arroseur *M* **canon** *M*
Impulsregner *M*
irrigatore *M* **a impulsi** *M*

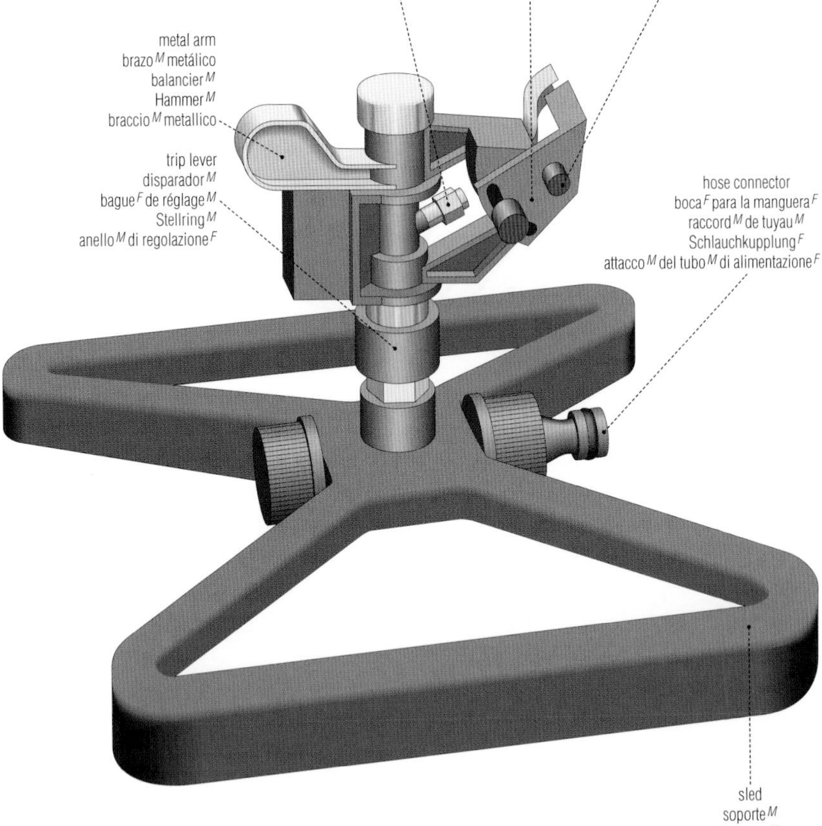
nozzle
boquilla F
buse F
Düse F
ugello M
deflector
deflector M
déflecteur M
Strahlstörer M
deflettore M
diffuser pin
perno M difusor
brise-jet M
Zerstäuberstift M
vite F rompigetto
metal arm
brazo M metálico
balancier M
Hammer M
braccio M metallico
trip lever
disparador M
bague F de réglage M
Stellring M
anello M di regolazione F
hose connector
boca F para la manguera F
raccord M de tuyau M
Schlauchkupplung F
attacco M del tubo M di alimentazione F dell'acqua F
sled
soporte M
traîneau M
Fuß M
slitta F

pruning and cutting tools

herramientas^F para cortar | outils^M pour couper | Schneidwerkzeuge^N | attrezzi^M per potare e tagliare

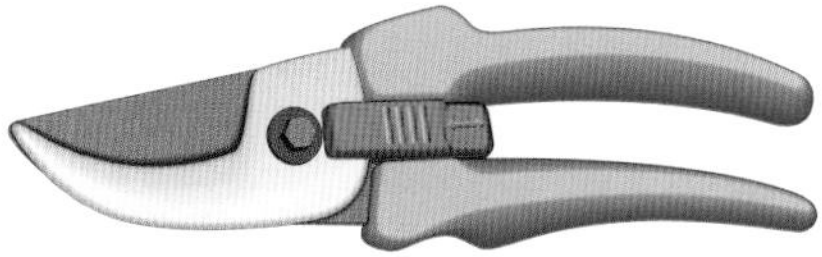

pruning shears
tijeras^F de podar
sécateur^M
Baumschere^F
cesoie^F da giardino^M

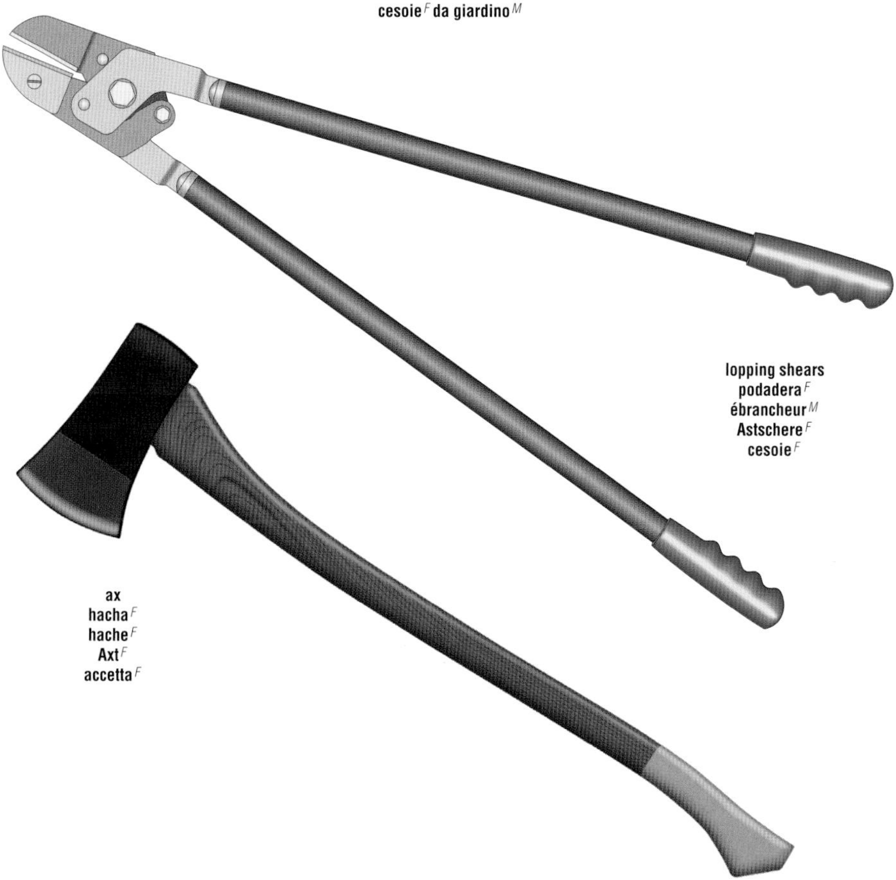

lopping shears
podadera^F
ébrancheur^M
Astschere^F
cesoie^F

ax
hacha^F
hache^F
Axt^F
accetta^F

pruning and cutting tools

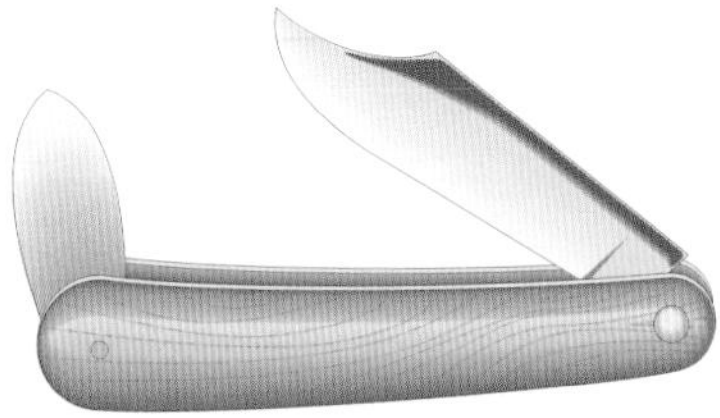

grafting knife
navaja *F* de injertar
greffoir *M*
Veredelungsmesser *N*
innestatoio *M*

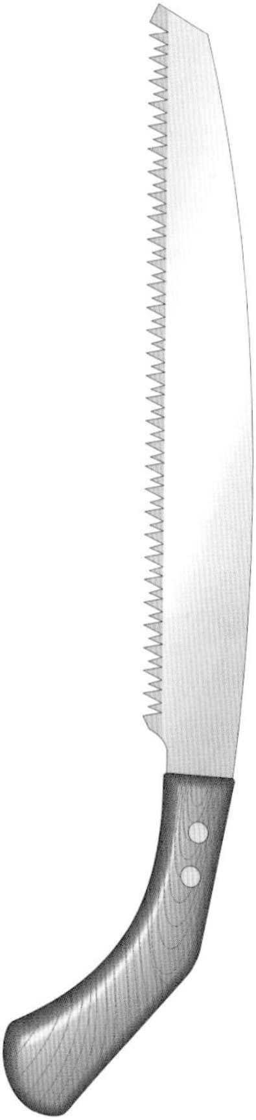

pruning saw
sierra *F* de podar
scie *F* d'élagage *M*
Baumsäge *F*
sega *F* da giardiniere *M*

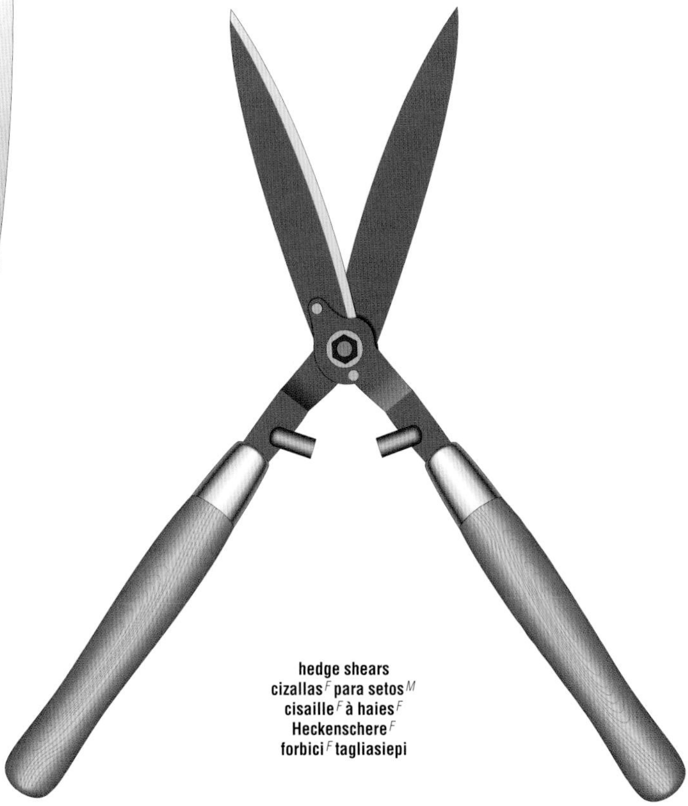

hedge shears
cizallas *F* para setos *M*
cisaille *F* à haies *F*
Heckenschere *F*
forbici *F* tagliasiepi

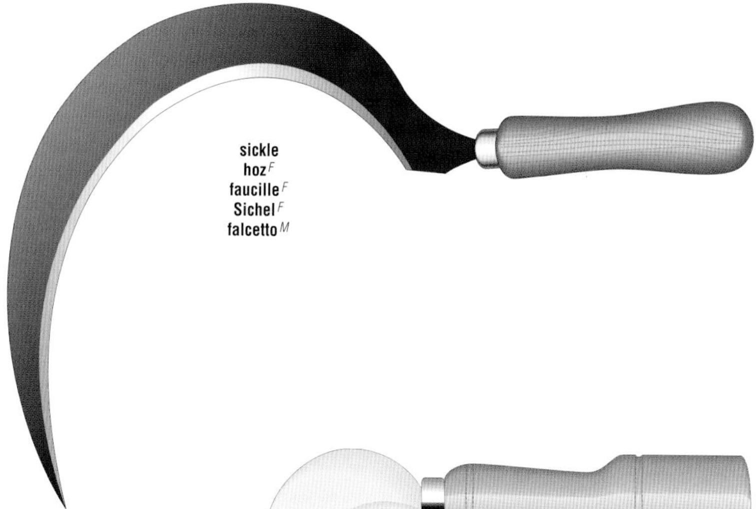

sickle
hoz *F*
faucille *F*
Sichel *F*
falcetto *M*

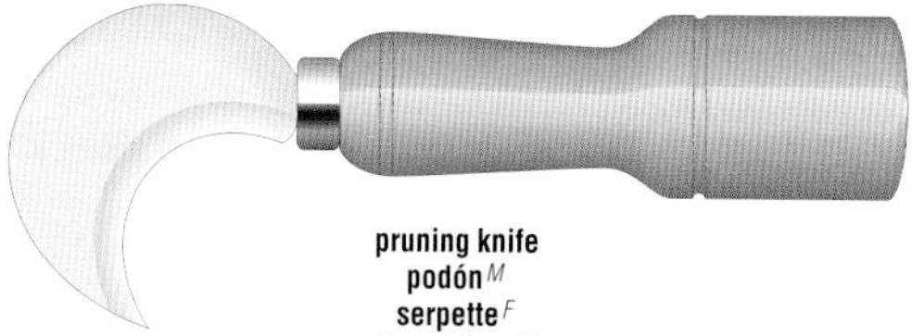

pruning knife
podón *M*
serpette *F*
Baumhippe *F*
potatoio *M*

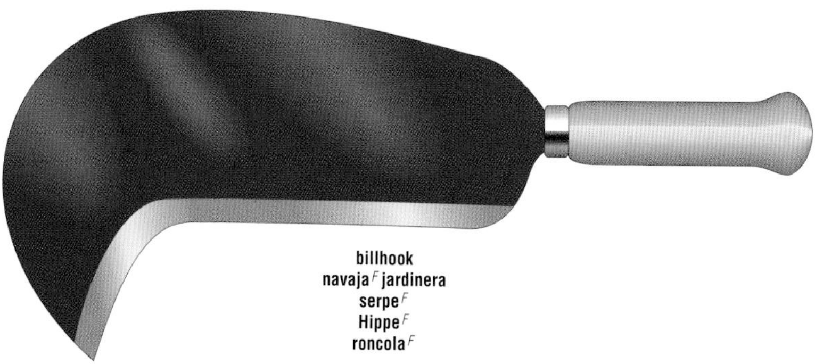

billhook
navaja *F* **jardinera**
serpe *F*
Hippe *F*
roncola *F*

pruning and cutting tools

chainsaw
sierra *F* **de cadena** *F*
tronçonneuse *F*
Kettensäge *F*
motosega *F*

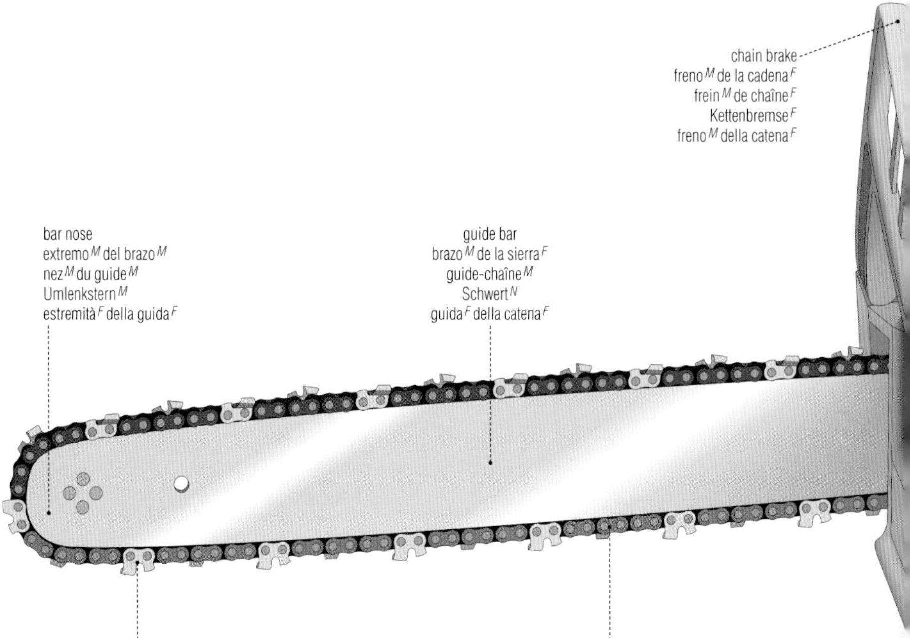

chain brake
freno M de la cadena F
frein M de chaîne F
Kettenbremse F
freno M della catena F
bar nose
extremo M del brazo M
nez M du guide M
Umlenkstern M
estremità F della guida F
guide bar
brazo M de la sierra F
guide-chaîne M
Schwert N
guida F della catena F
cutter link
eslabón M de corte M
maillon M-gouge F
Hobelzahn M
maglia F dentata
chainsaw chain
cadena F
chaîne F coupante
Sägekette F
catena F trinciante

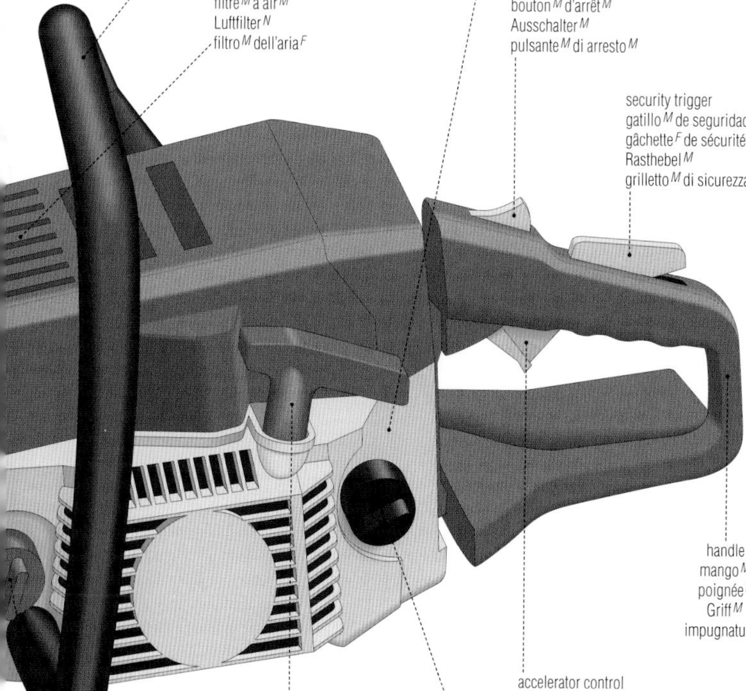
antivibration handle
barra[F] antivibración
poignée[F] antivibrations[F]
schwingungsdämpfender Bügelgriff[M]
impugnatura[F] con sistema[M] antivibrazione[F]

engine housing
caja[F] del motor[M]
boîtier[M] du moteur[M]
Motorgehäuse[N]
rivestimento[M] del motore[M]

air filter
filtro[M] de aire[M]
filtre[M] à air[M]
Luftfilter[N]
filtro[M] dell'aria[F]

stop button
botón[M] de apagado[M]
bouton[M] d'arrêt[M]
Ausschalter[M]
pulsante[M] di arresto[M]

security trigger
gatillo[M] de seguridad[F]
gâchette[F] de sécurité[F]
Rasthebel[M]
grilletto[M] di sicurezza[F]

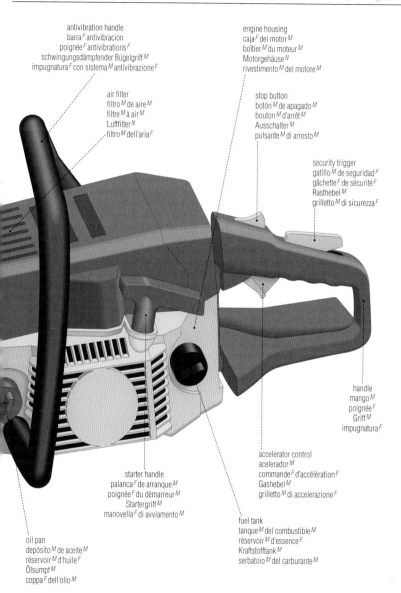

handle
mango[M]
poignée[F]
Griff[M]
impugnatura[F]

accelerator control
acelerador[M]
commande[F] d'accélération[F]
Gashebel[M]
grilletto[M] di accelerazione[F]

starter handle
palanca[F] de arranque[M]
poignée[F] du démarreur[M]
Startergriff[M]
manovella[F] di avviamento[M]

fuel tank
tanque[M] del combustible[M]
réservoir[M] d'essence[F]
Kraftstofftank[M]
serbatoio[M] del carburante[M]

oil pan
depósito[M] de aceite[M]
réservoir[M] d'huile[F]
Ölsumpf[M]
coppa[F] dell'olio[M]

lawn care

cuidado M del césped M | soins M de la pelouse F | Rasenpflege F | cura F del prato M

lawn trimmer
podadora F **de bordes** M
taille-bordures M
Rasentrimmer M
tagliabordi M

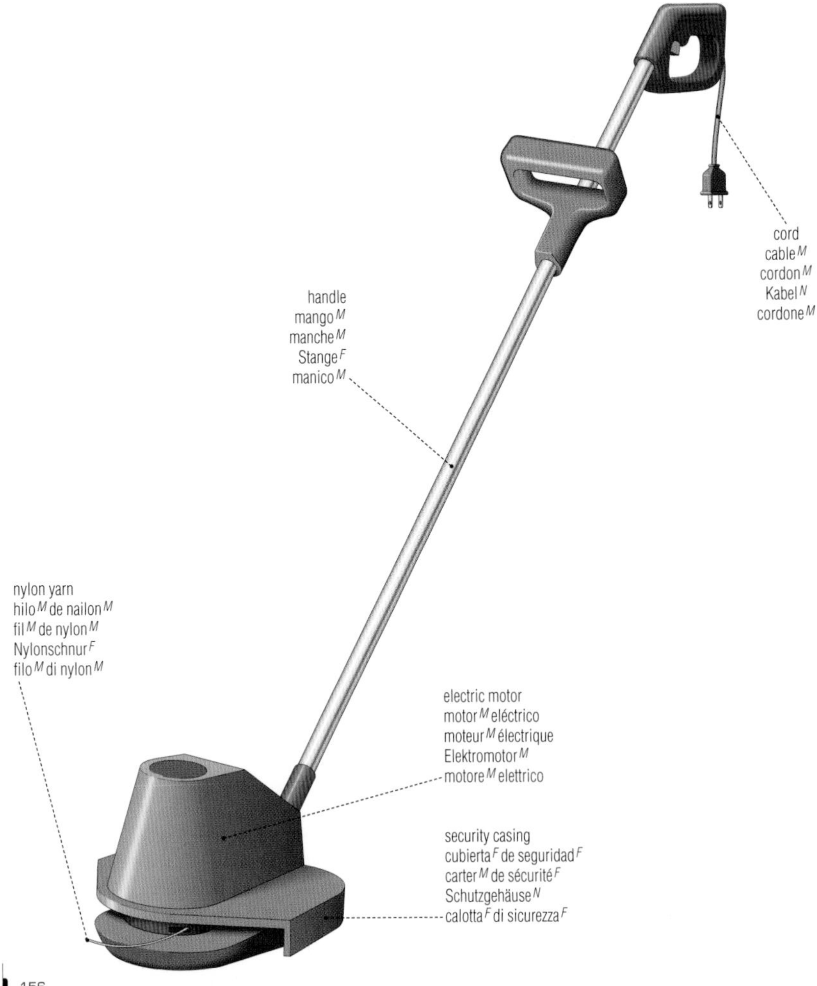
cord
cable M
cordon M
Kabel N
cordone M
handle
mango M
manche M
Stange F
manico M
nylon yarn
hilo M de nailon M
fil M de nylon M
Nylonschnur F
filo M di nylon M
electric motor
motor M eléctrico
moteur M électrique
Elektromotor M
motore M elettrico
security casing
cubierta F de seguridad F
carter M de sécurité F
Schutzgehäuse N
calotta F di sicurezza F

power mower
cortacésped M con motor M
tondeuse F à moteur M
Motorrasenmäher M
motofalciatrice F

handle
barra F
guidon M
Griff M
impugnatura F
safety handle
palanca F de seguridad F
poignée F de sécurité F
Sicherheitsgriff M
impugnatura F di sicurezza F
starter
motor M de arranque M
démarreur M manuel
Anlasser M
motorino M d'avviamento M
filler cap
boca F del depósito M
bouchon M de remplissage M
Einfüllstutzen M
bocchetta F del serbatoio M
motor
motor M
moteur M
Motor M
motore M
grass catcher
recogedor M
bac M de ramassage M
Grasfang M
raccoglierba M
casing
caja F
carter M
Gehäuse N
scocca F
deflector
deflector M
déflecteur M
Schwadenblech N
deflettore M

animal cell

célula[F] animal | cellule[F] animale | tierische Zelle[F] | cellula[F] animale

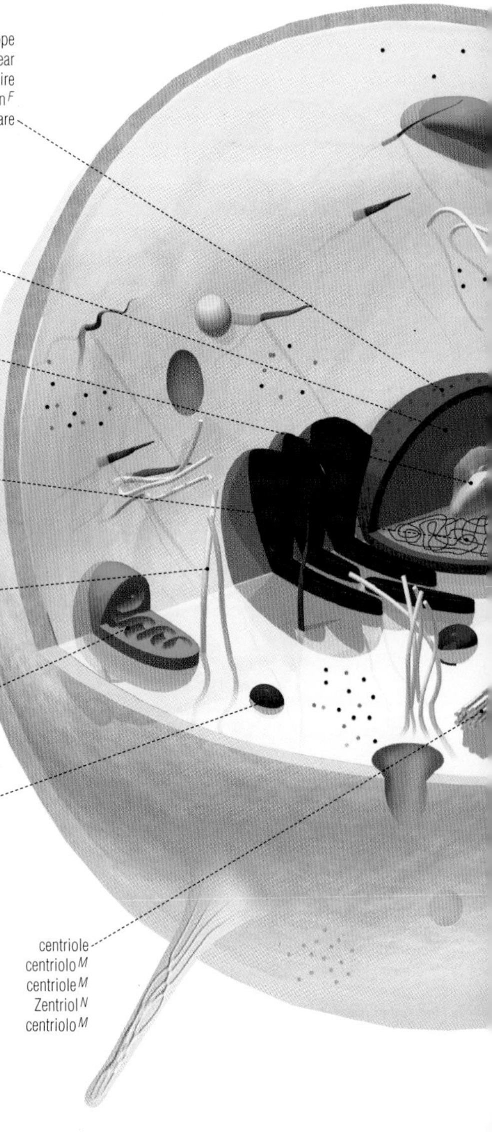
nuclear envelope
membrana[F] nuclear
membrane[F] nucléaire
Kernmembran[F]
membrana[F] nucleare
nucleus
núcleo[M]
noyau[M]
Zellkern[M]
nucleo[M]
nucleolus
nucléolo[M]
nucléole[M]
Nukleolus[M]
nucleolo[M]
chromatin
cromatina[F]
chromatine[F]
Chromatin[N]
cromatina[F]
microtubule
microtúbulo[M]
microtubule[M]
Mikrotubulus[M]
microtubulo[M]
mitochondrion
mitocondrio[M]
mitochondrie[F]
Mitochondrium[N]
mitocondrio[M]
peroxisome
peroxisoma[M]
peroxysome[M]
Peroxysom[N]
perossisoma[M]
centriole
centriolo[M]
centriole[M]
Zentriol[N]
centriolo[M]

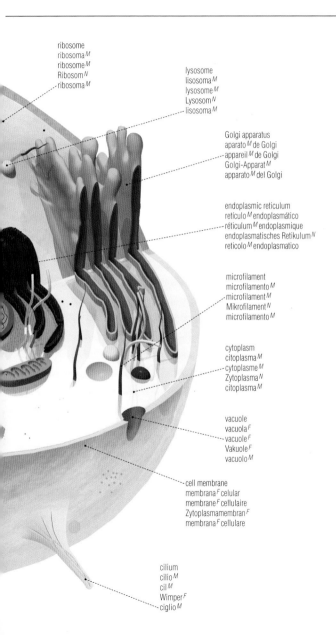

ribosome
ribosoma[M]
ribosome[M]
Ribosom[N]
ribosoma[M]

lysosome
lisosoma[M]
lysosome[M]
Lysosom[N]
lisosoma[M]

Golgi apparatus
aparato[M] de Golgi
appareil[M] de Golgi
Golgi-Apparat[M]
apparato[M] del Golgi

endoplasmic reticulum
retículo[M] endoplasmático
réticulum[M] endoplasmique
endoplasmatisches Retikulum[N]
reticolo[M] endoplasmatico

microfilament
microfilamento[M]
microfilament[M]
Mikrofilament[N]
microfilamento[M]

cytoplasm
citoplasma[M]
cytoplasme[M]
Zytoplasma[N]
citoplasma[M]

vacuole
vacuola[F]
vacuole[F]
Vakuole[F]
vacuolo[M]

cell membrane
membrana[F] celular
membrane[F] cellulaire
Zytoplasmamembran[F]
membrana[F] cellulare

cilium
cilio[M]
cil[M]
Wimper[F]
ciglio[M]

unicellulars

unicelulares M | unicellulaires M | Einzeller M | unicellulari M

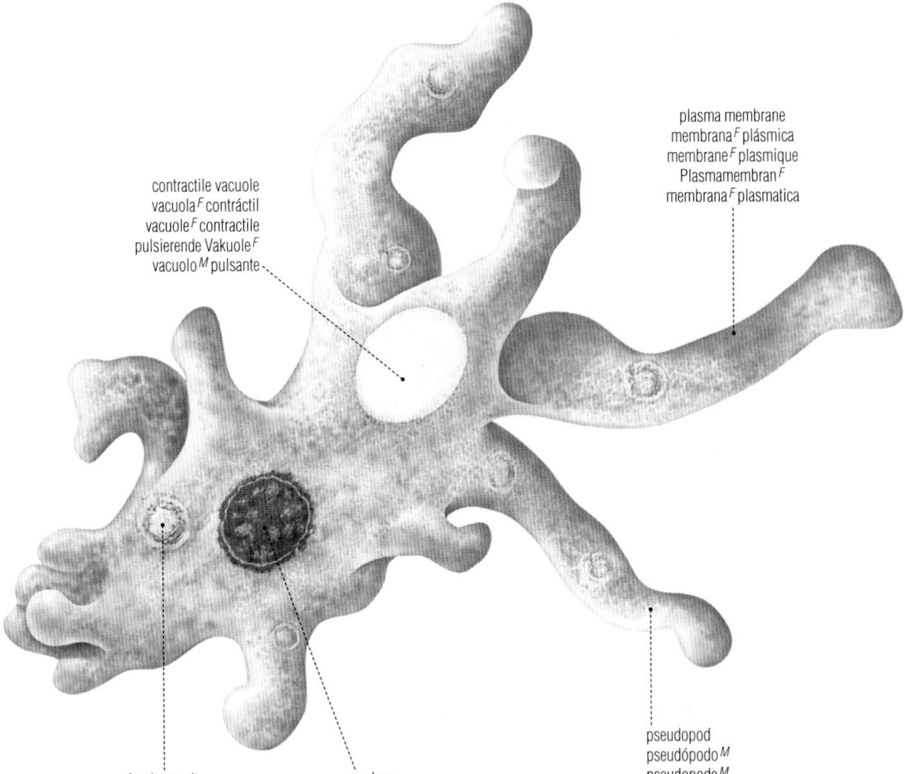

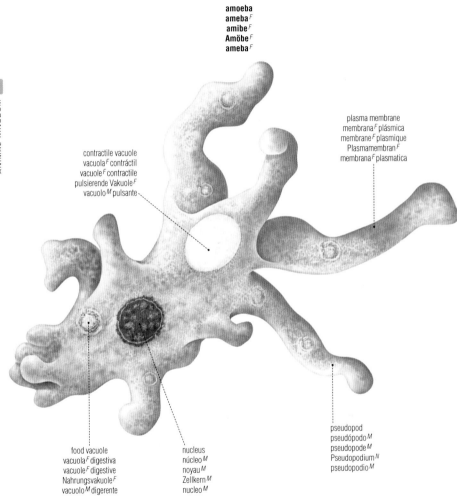

amoeba
ameba F
amibe F
Amöbe F
ameba F
plasma membrane
membrana F plásmica
membrane F plasmique
Plasmamembran F
membrana F plasmatica
contractile vacuole
vacuola F contráctil
vacuole F contractile
pulsierende Vakuole F
vacuolo M pulsante
food vacuole
vacuola F digestiva
vacuole F digestive
Nahrungsvakuole F
vacuolo M digerente
nucleus
núcleo M
noyau M
Zellkern M
nucleo M
pseudopod
pseudópodo M
pseudopode M
Pseudopodium N
pseudopodio M

paramecium
paramecio^{M}
paramécie^{F}
Paramecium^{N}
paramecio^{M}

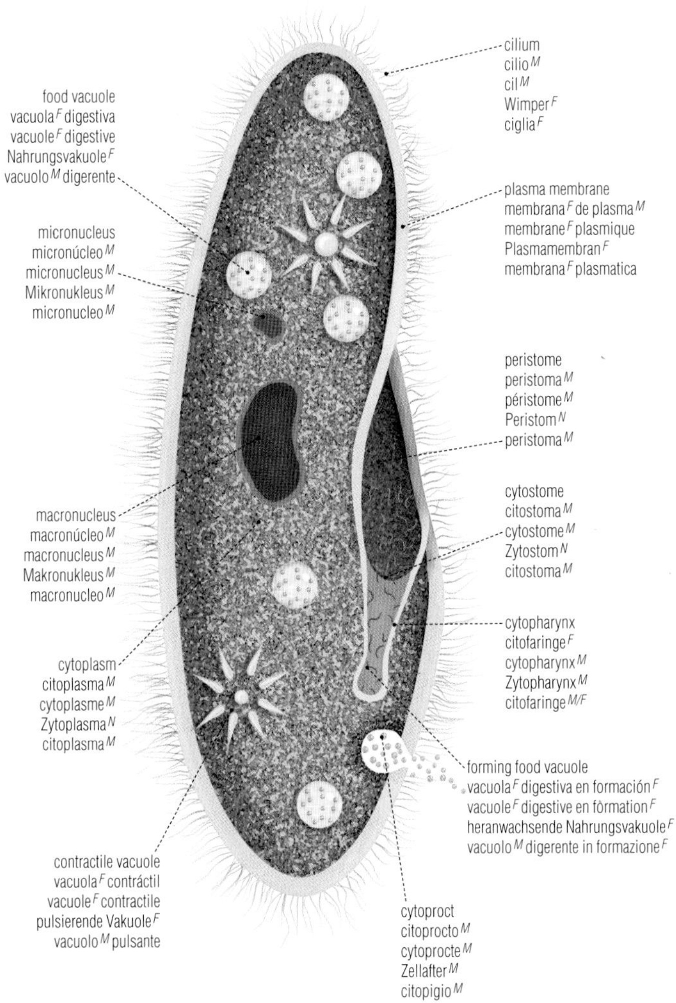
cilium
cilio M
cil M
Wimper F
ciglia F
food vacuole
vacuola F digestiva
vacuole F digestive
Nahrungsvakuole F
vacuolo M digerente
plasma membrane
membrana F de plasma M
membrane F plasmique
Plasmamembran F
membrana F plasmatica
micronucleus
micronúcleo M
micronucleus M
Mikronukleus M
micronucleo M
peristome
peristoma M
péristome M
Peristom N
peristoma M
macronucleus
macronúcleo M
macronucleus M
Makronukleus M
macronucleo M
cytostome
citostoma M
cytostome M
Zytostom N
citostoma M
cytopharynx
citofaringe F
cytopharynx M
Zytopharynx M
citofaringe M/F
cytoplasm
citoplasma M
cytoplasme M
Zytoplasma N
citoplasma M
forming food vacuole
vacuola F digestiva en formación F
vacuole F digestive en formation F
heranwachsende Nahrungsvakuole F
vacuolo M digerente in formazione F
contractile vacuole
vacuola F contráctil
vacuole F contractile
pulsierende Vakuole F
vacuolo M pulsante
cytoproct
citoprocto M
cytoprocte M
Zellafter M
citopigio M

sponge

esponja^F | éponge^F | Schwamm^M | spugna^F

calcareous sponge
esponja^F calcárea
éponge^F calcaire
Kalkschwamm^M
spugna^F calcarea

anatomy of a sponge
anatomía^F de una esponja^F
anatomie^F de l'éponge^F
Anatomie^F eines Schwamms^M
anatomia^F di una spugna^F

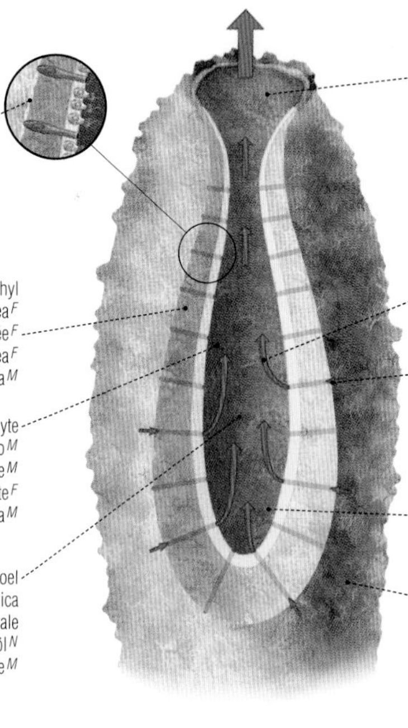
pinacocyte
pinacocito^M
pinacocyte^M
Pinakocyte^F
pinacocita^M
mesohyl
mesoglea^F
mésoglée^F
Mesogloea^F
mesenchima^M
choanocyte
coanocito^M
choanocyte^M
Choanocyte^F
coanocita^M
spongocoel
cavidad^F gástrica
cavité^F gastrale
Spongozöl^N
spongocele^M
osculum
ósculo^M
oscule^M
Osculum^N
osculo^M
water flow
flujo^M de agua^F
circulation^F de l'eau^F
Wasserfluss^M
flusso^M d'acqua^F
incurrent pore
poro^M inhalante
pore^M inhalant
Porenzelle^F
poro^M inalante
endoderm
endodermo^M
endoderme^M
Entoderm^N
endoderma^M
ectoderm
ectodermo^M
ectoderme^M
Ektoderm^N
ectoderma^M

echinoderms

equinodermos M | échinodermes M | Echinodermen M | echinodermi M

morphology of a starfish
morfología F de una estrella F de mar M
morphologie F de l'étoile F de mer F
äußere Merkmale N eines Seesterns M
morfologia F di una stella F marina

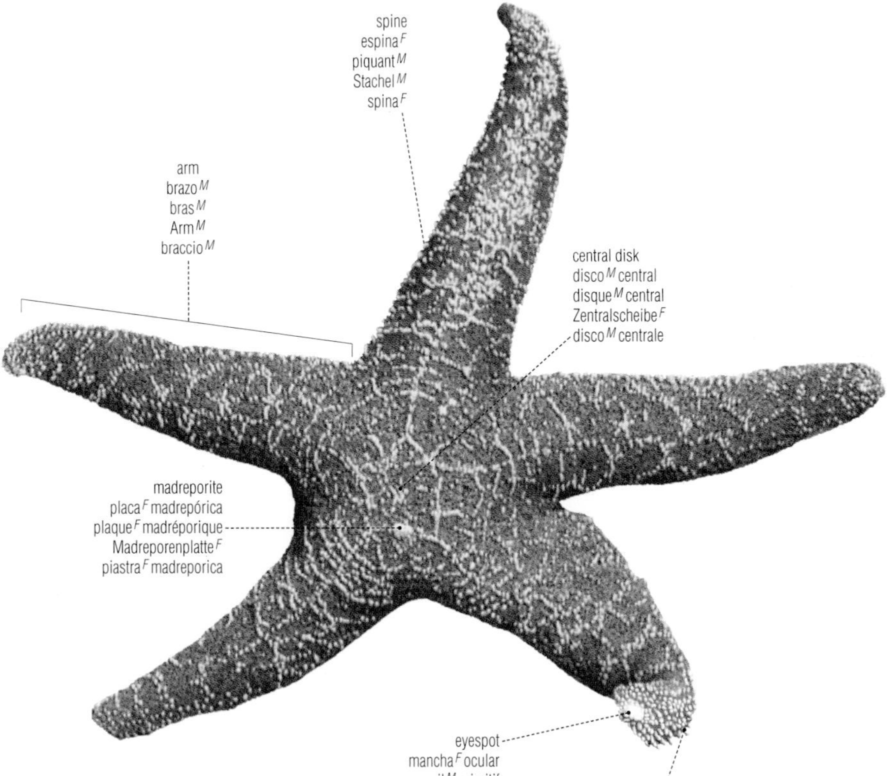
spine
espina F
piquant M
Stachel M
spina F
arm
brazo M
bras M
Arm M
braccio M
central disk
disco M central
disque M central
Zentralscheibe F
disco M centrale
madreporite
placa F madrepórica
plaque F madréporique
Madreporenplatte F
piastra F madreporica
eyespot
mancha F ocular
œil M primitif
einfaches Auge N
macchia F oculare
tube foot
pie M ambulacral
pied M ambulacraire
Ambulakralfüßchen N
pedicello M ambulacrale

butterfly

mariposa F | papillon M | Schmetterling M | farfalla F

morphology of a butterfly
morfología F de una mariposa F
morphologie F du papillon M
äußere Merkmale N eines Schmetterlings M
morfologia F di una farfalla F

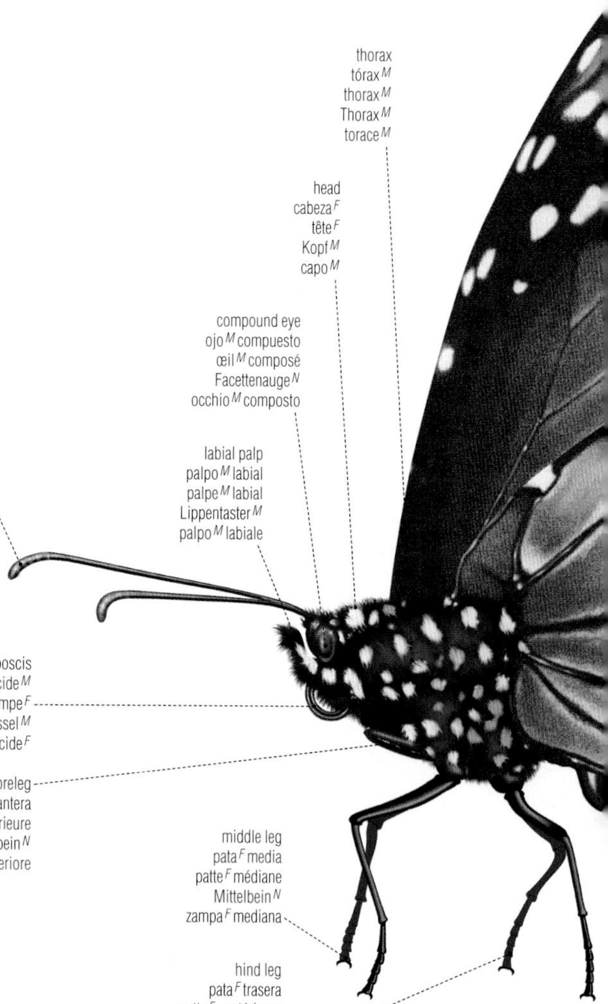
thorax
tórax M
thorax M
Thorax M
torace M
head
cabeza F
tête F
Kopf M
capo M
compound eye
ojo M compuesto
œil M composé
Facettenauge N
occhio M composto
antenna
antena F
antenne F
Antenne F
antenna F
labial palp
palpo M labial
palpe M labial
Lippentaster M
palpo M labiale
proboscis
probóscide M
trompe F
Rüssel M
proboscide F
foreleg
pata F delantera
patte F antérieure
Vorderbein N
zampa F anteriore
middle leg
pata F media
patte F médiane
Mittelbein N
zampa F mediana
hind leg
pata F trasera
patte F postérieure
Hinterbein N
zampa F posteriore

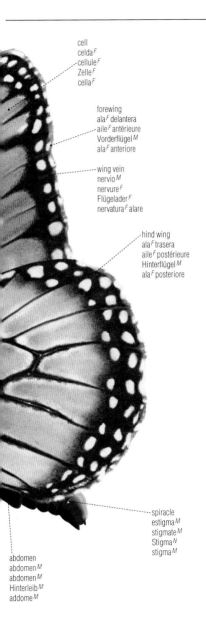

cell
celda[F]
cellule[F]
Zelle[F]
cella[F]
forewing
ala[F] delantera
aile[F] antérieure
Vorderflügel[M]
ala[F] anteriore
wing vein
nervio[M]
nervure[F]
Flügelader[F]
nervatura[F] alare
hind wing
ala[F] trasera
aile[F] postérieure
Hinterflügel[M]
ala[F] posteriore
spiracle
estigma[M]
stigmate[M]
Stigma[N]
stigma[M]
abdomen
abdomen[M]
abdomen[M]
Hinterleib[M]
addome[M]

hind leg
pata[F] trasera
patte[F] postérieure
Hinterbein[N]
zampa[F] posteriore

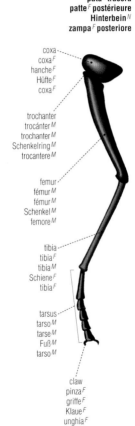

coxa
coxa[F]
hanche[F]
Hüfte[F]
coxa[F]
trochanter
trocánter[M]
trochanter[M]
Schenkelring[M]
trocantere[M]
femur
fémur[M]
fémur[M]
Schenkel[M]
femore[M]
tibia
tibia[F]
tibia[M]
Schiene[F]
tibia[F]
tarsus
tarso[M]
tarse[M]
Fuß[M]
tarso[M]
claw
pinza[F]
griffe[F]
Klaue[F]
unghia[F]

honeybee

abeja^F | abeille^F | Honigbiene^F | ape^F

morphology of a honeybee: worker
morfología^F de una abeja^F trabajadora
morphologie^F de l'abeille^F : ouvrière^F
äußere Merkmale^N einer Honigbiene^F: Arbeiterin^F
morfologia^F di un'ape^F: operaia

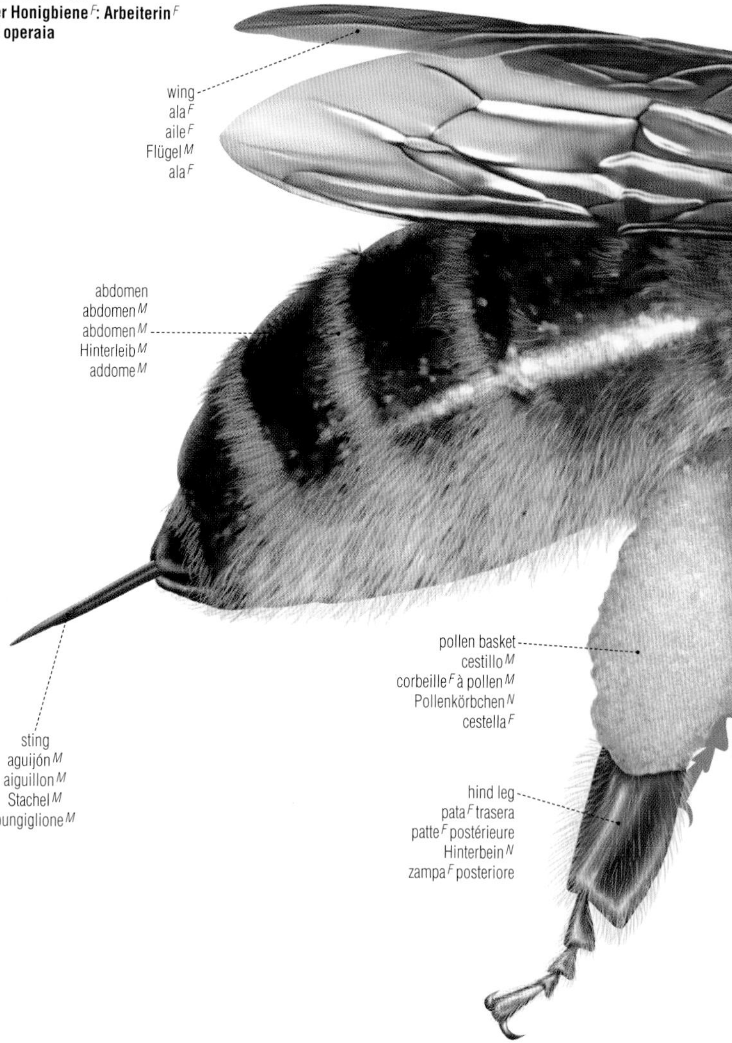
wing
ala F
aile F
Flügel M
ala F
abdomen
abdomen M
abdomen M
Hinterleib M
addome M
sting
aguijón M
aiguillon M
Stachel M
pungiglione M
pollen basket
cestillo M
corbeille F à pollen M
Pollenkörbchen N
cestella F
hind leg
pata F trasera
patte F postérieure
Hinterbein N
zampa F posteriore

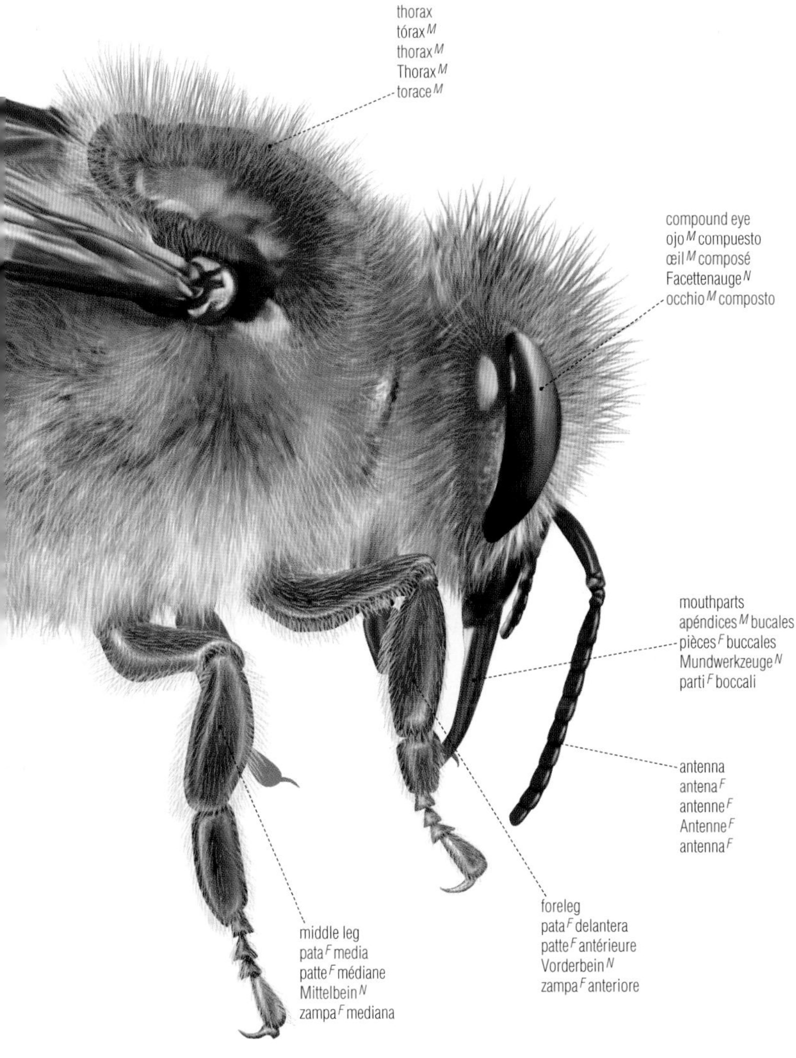
thorax
tórax M
thorax M
Thorax M
torace M
compound eye
ojo M compuesto
œil M composé
Facettenauge N
occhio M composto
mouthparts
apéndices M bucales
pièces F buccales
Mundwerkzeuge N
parti F boccali
antenna
antena F
antenne F
Antenne F
antenna F
foreleg
pata F delantera
patte F antérieure
Vorderbein N
zampa F anteriore
middle leg
pata F media
patte F médiane
Mittelbein N
zampa F mediana

honeybee

honeycomb section
corte M de un panal M
coupe F d'un rayon M de miel M
Wabenausschnitt M
sezione F del favo M

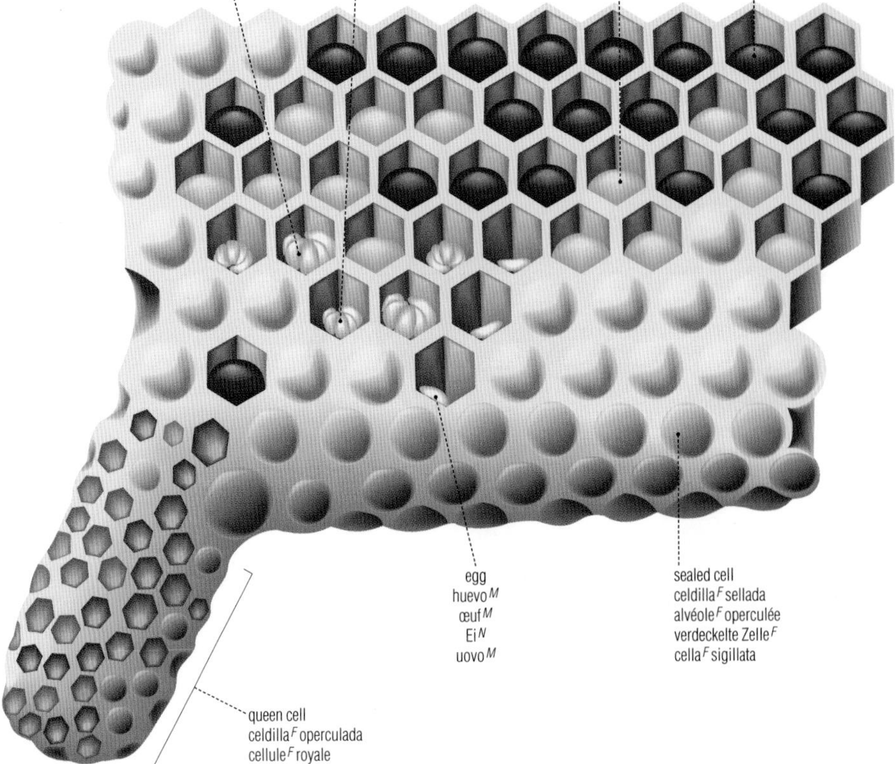

honey cell
celdilla F de la miel F
alvéole F à miel M
Honigzelle F
cella F da miele M
pupa
crisálida F
nymphe F
Puppe F
crisalide F
larva
larva F
larve F
Larve F
larva F
pollen cell
celdilla F del polen M
alvéole F à pollen M
Pollenzelle F
cella F da polline M
egg
huevo M
œuf M
Ei N
uovo M
sealed cell
celdilla F sellada
alvéole F operculée
verdeckelte Zelle F
cella F sigillata
queen cell
celdilla F operculada
cellule F royale
Weiselwiege F
cella F reale

examples of insects

ejemplos[M] de insectos[M] | exemples[M] d'insectes[M] | Beispiele[N] für Insekten[N] | esempi[M] di insetti[M]

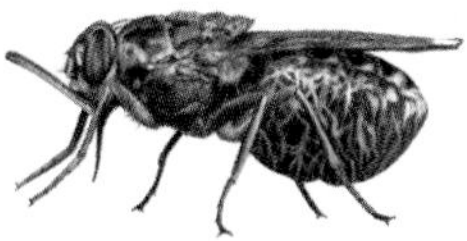

tsetse fly
mosca[F] tsetsé
mouche[F] tsé-tsé
Tsetsefliege[F]
mosca[F] tse-tse

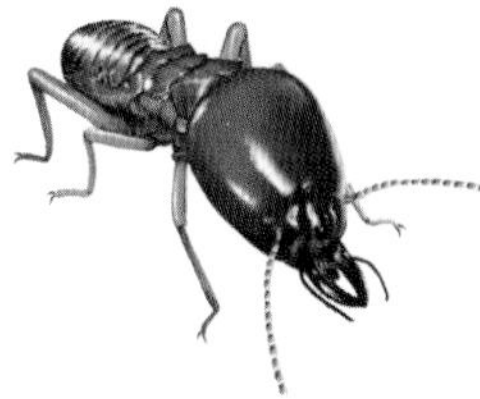

termite
termita[F]
termite[M]
Termite[F]
termite[F]

flea
pulga[F]
puce[F]
Floh[M]
pulce[F]

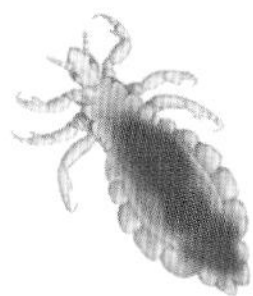

louse
piojo[M]
pou[M]
Laus[F]
pidocchio[M]

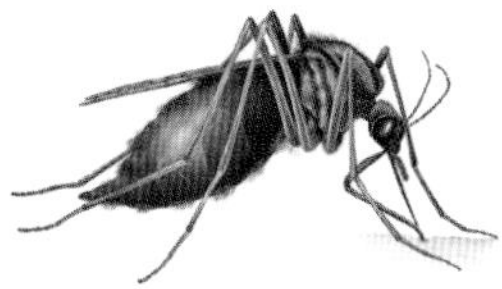

mosquito
mosquito[M]
moustique[M]
Moskito[M]
zanzara[F]

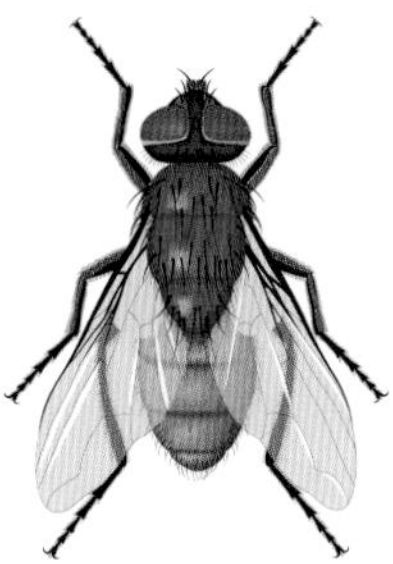

fly
mosca[F]
mouche[F]
Fliege[F]
mosca[F]

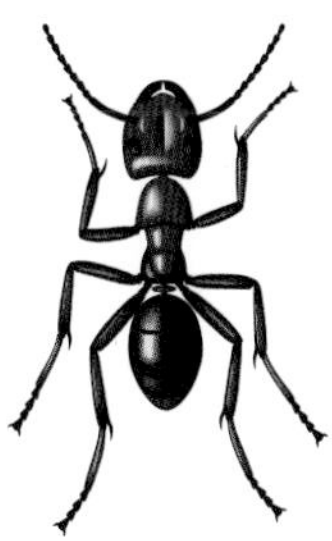

ant
hormiga[F]
fourmi[F]
Ameise[F]
formica[F]

furniture beetle
carcoma[F]
petite vrillette[F]
Bockkäfer[M]
tarlo[M]

examples of insects

burying beetle
escarabajo [M] necróforo
nécrophore [M]
Totengräber [M]
necroforo [M]

ladybug
mariquita [F]
coccinelle [F]
Marienkäfer [M]
coccinella [F]

shield bug
chinche [F] de campo [M]
punaise [F] rayée
Schildwanze [F]
cimice [F] rigata

horsefly
tábano [M]
taon [M]
Bremse [F]
tafano [M]

hornet
avispón [M]
frelon [M]
Hornisse [F]
calabrone [M]

yellowjacket
avispa [F]
guêpe [F]
Wespe [F]
vespa [F]

bumblebee
abejorro [M]
bourdon [M]
Hummel [F]
bombo [M]

oriental cockroach
cucaracha [F] oriental
blatte [F] orientale
orientalische Schabe [F]
blatta [F] orientale

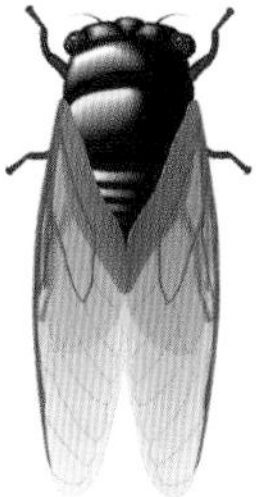

cicada
cigarra [F]
cigale [F]
Zikade [F]
cicala [F]

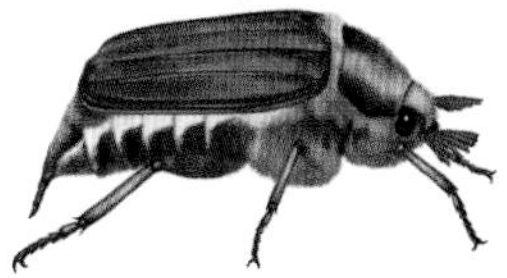

cockchafer
escarabajo [M]
hanneton [M]
Maikäfer [M]
maggiolino [M]

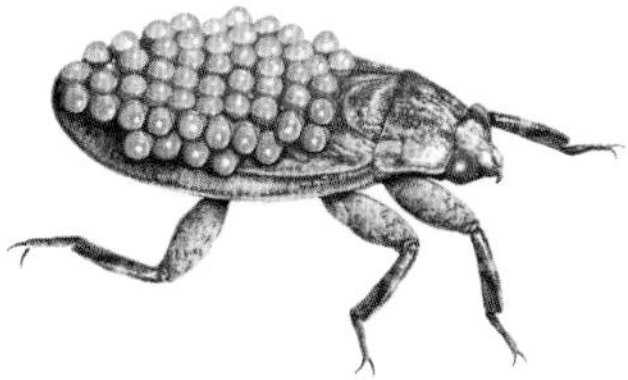

water bug
chinche [F] acuática
punaise [F] d'eau [F]
Wasserkäfer [M]
cimice [F] d'acqua [F]

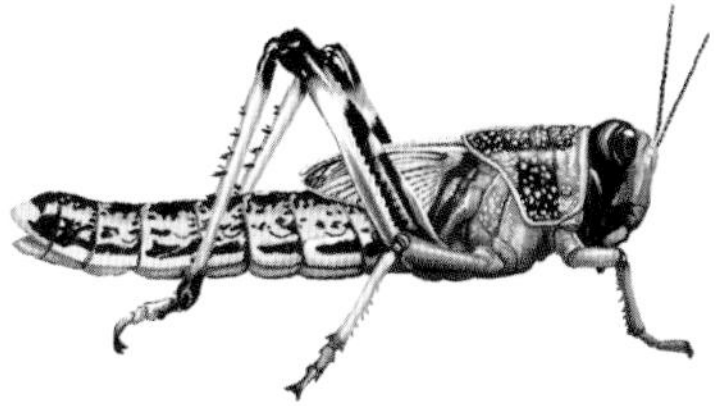

bow-winged grasshopper
grillo [M] campestre
criquet [M] mélodieux
Nachtigall [F]-Grashüpfer [M]
cavalletta [F]

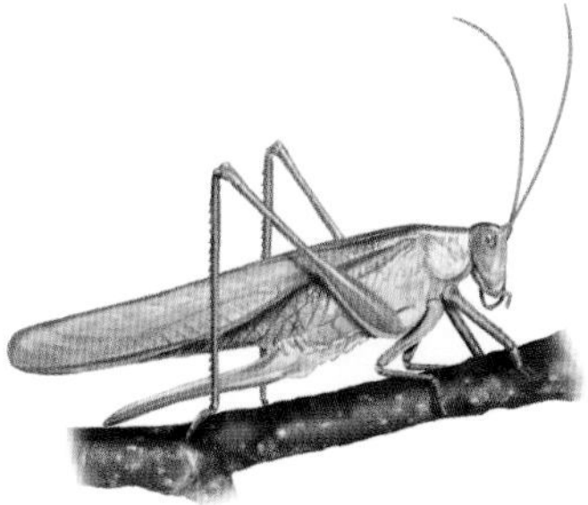

great green bush-cricket
saltamontes [M] verde
grande sauterelle [F] verte
Laubheuschrecke [F]
grillo [M] verde

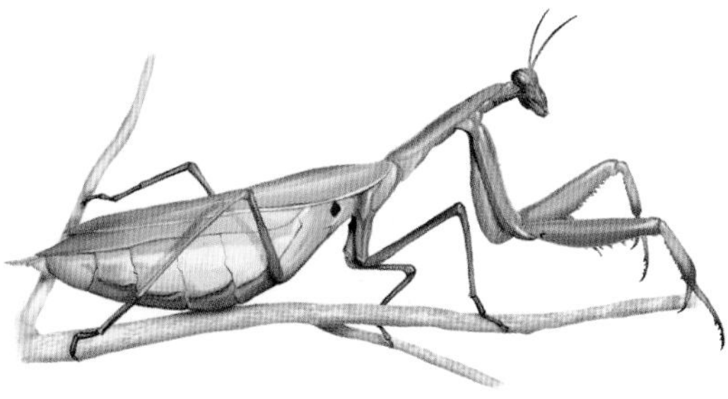

mantis
mantis [F] religiosa
mante [F] religieuse
Gottesanbeterin [F]
mantide [F] religiosa

examples of insects

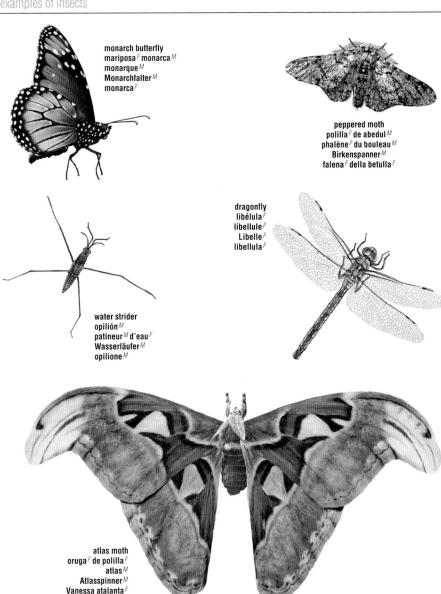

monarch butterfly
mariposa *F* **monarca** *M*
monarque *M*
Monarchfalter *M*
monarca *F*

peppered moth
polilla *F* **de abedul** *M*
phalène *F* **du bouleau** *M*
Birkenspanner *M*
falena *F* **della betulla** *F*

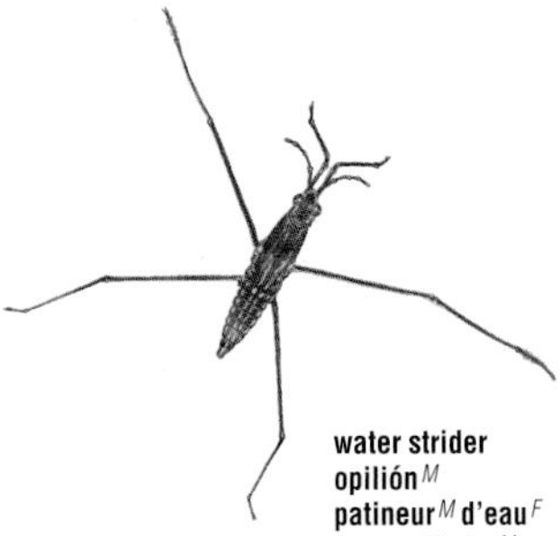

water strider
opilión *M*
patineur *M* **d'eau** *F*
Wasserläufer *M*
opilione *M*

dragonfly
libélula *F*
libellule *F*
Libelle *F*
libellula *F*

atlas moth
oruga *F* **de polilla** *F*
atlas *M*
Atlasspinner *M*
Vanessa atalanta *F*

examples of arachnids

ejemplos[M] de arácnidos[M] | exemples[M] d'arachnides[M] | Beispiele[N] für Spinnentiere[N] | esempi[M] di aracnidi[M]

garden spider
epeira[F]
épeire[F]
Gartenkreuzspinne[M]
epeira[F]

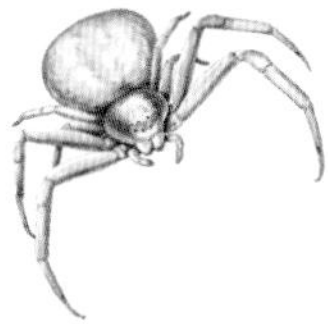

crab spider
araña[F] cangrejo
araignée[F]-crabe[M]
Krabbenspinne[F]
ragno[M]-granchio[M]

water spider
araña[F] de agua[F]
argyronète[F]
Wasserspinne[F]
ragno[M] acquatico

tick
garrapata[F]
tique[F]
Zecke[F]
zecca[F]

scorpion
escorpión[M]
scorpion[M]
Skorpion[M]
scorpione[M]

red-kneed tarantula
migala[F]
mygale[F] du Mexique[M]
Mexikanische Rotknievogelspinne[F]
migale[F] del Messico[M]

spider

araña F | araignée F | Spinne F | ragno M

morphology of a spider
morfología F de una araña F
morphologie F de l'araignée F
äußere Merkmale N einer Spinne F
morfologia F di un ragno M

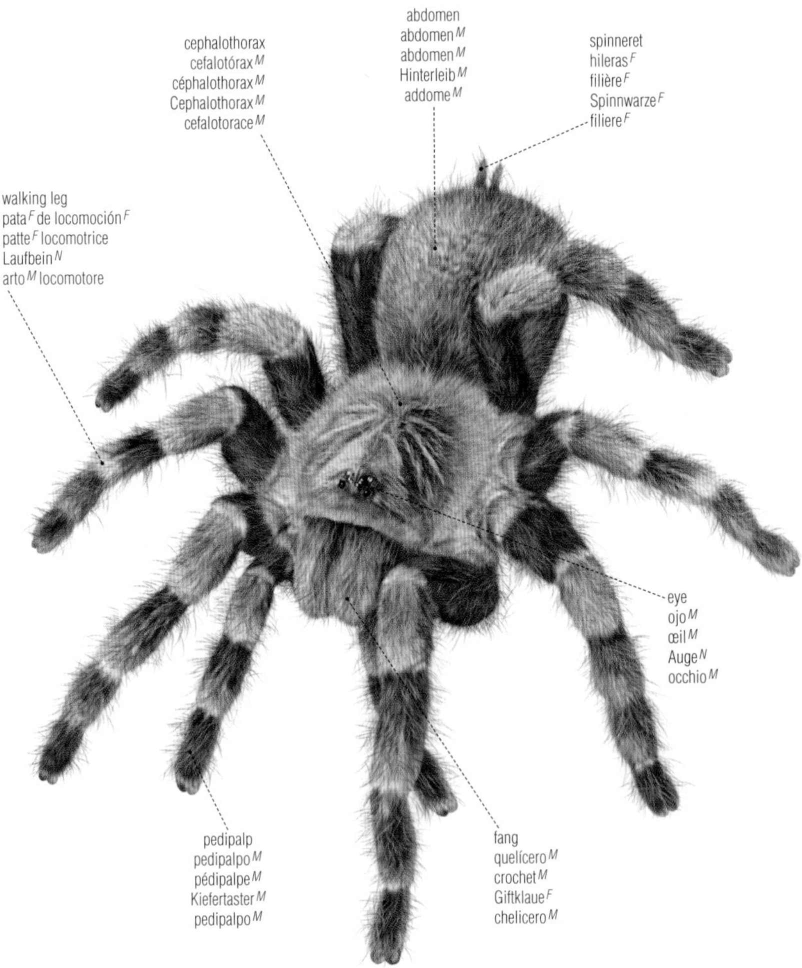
abdomen
abdomen M
abdomen M
Hinterleib M
addome M
cephalothorax
cefalotórax M
céphalothorax M
Cephalothorax M
cefalotorace M
spinneret
hileras F
filière F
Spinnwarze F
filiere F
walking leg
pata F de locomoción F
patte F locomotrice
Laufbein N
arto M locomotore
eye
ojo M
œil M
Auge N
occhio M
pedipalp
pedipalpo M
pédipalpe M
Kiefertaster M
pedipalpo M
fang
quelícero M
crochet M
Giftklaue F
chelicero M

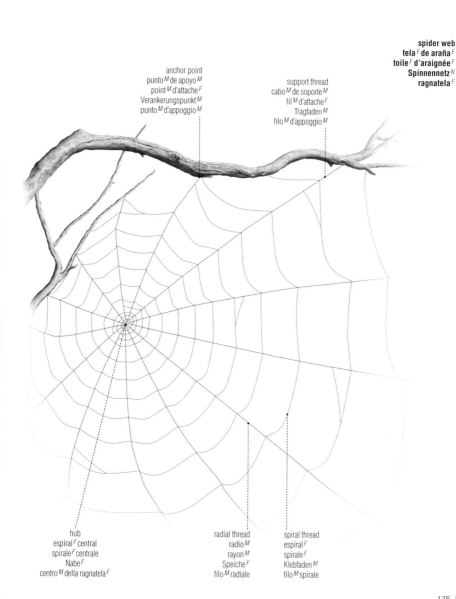

spider web
tela[F] de araña[F]
toile[F] d'araignée[F]
Spinnennetz[N]
ragnatela[F]

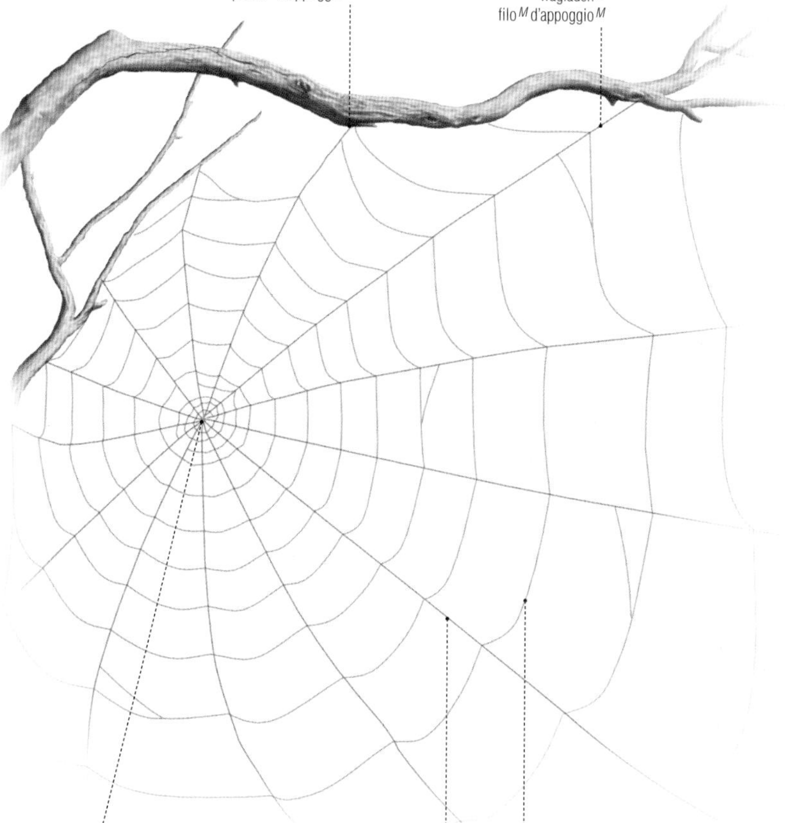
anchor point
punto[M] de apoyo[M]
point[M] d'attache[F]
Verankerungspunkt[M]
punto[M] d'appoggio[M]
support thread
cabo[M] de soporte[M]
fil[M] d'attache[F]
Tragfaden[M]
filo[M] d'appoggio[M]
hub
espiral[F] central
spirale[F] centrale
Nabe[F]
centro[M] della ragnatela[F]
radial thread
radio[M]
rayon[M]
Speiche[F]
filo[M] radiale
spiral thread
espiral[F]
spirale[F]
Klebfaden[M]
filo[M] spirale

octopus

pulpo[M] | pieuvre[F] | Tintenfisch[M] | polpo[M]

morphology of an octopus
morfología[F] de un pulpo[M]
morphologie[F] de la pieuvre[F]
äußere Merkmale[N] eines Tintenfischs[M]
morfologia[F] di un polpo[M]

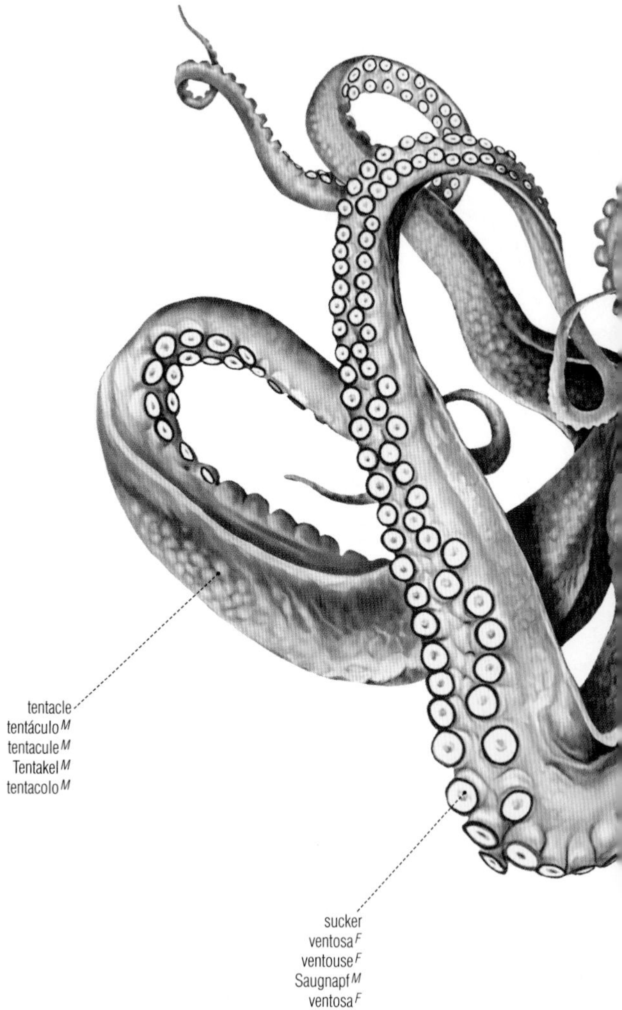
tentacle
tentáculo[M]
tentacule[M]
Tentakel[M]
tentacolo[M]
sucker
ventosa[F]
ventouse[F]
Saugnapf[M]
ventosa[F]

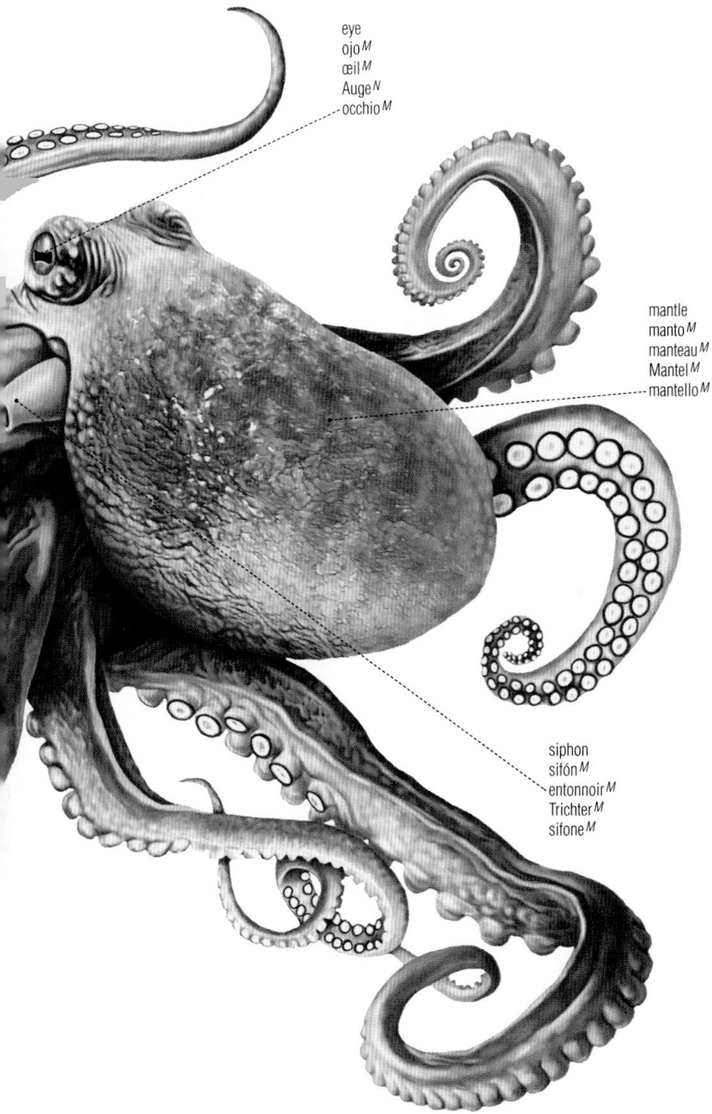
eye
ojo M
œil M
Auge N
occhio M
mantle
manto M
manteau M
Mantel M
mantello M
siphon
sifón M
entonnoir M
Trichter M
sifone M

lobster

bogavante^{M} | homard^{M} | Hummer^{M} | astice^{M}

morphology of a lobster
morfología^{F} de un bogavante^{M}
morphologie^{F} du homard^{M}
äußere Merkmale^{N} eines Hummers^{M}
morfologia^{F} di un astice^{M}

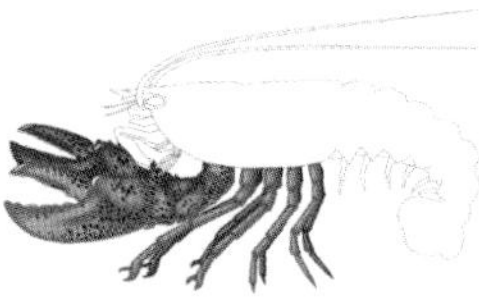

thoracic legs
apéndices^{M} torácicos
pattes^{F} thoraciques
Brustbeine^{N}
arti^{M} toracici

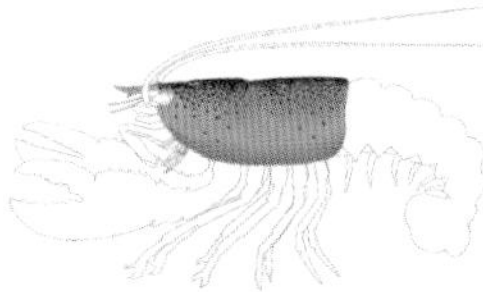

cephalothorax
cefalotórax^{M}
céphalothorax^{M}
Kopfbruststück^{N}
cefalotorace^{M}

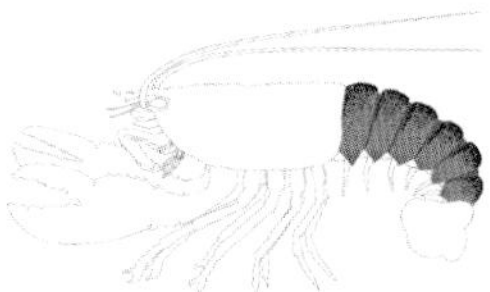

abdomen
abdomen^{M}
abdomen^{M}
Hinterleib^{N}
addome^{M}

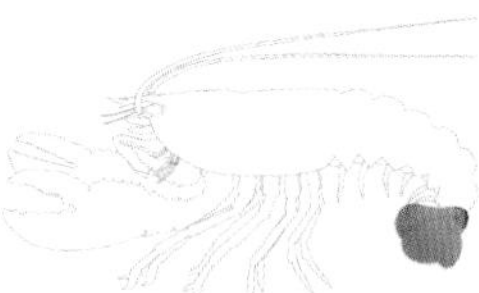

tail
cola^{F}
nageoire^{F} caudale
Schwanz^{M}
coda^{F}

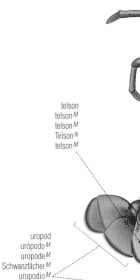

telson
telson M
telson M
Telson N
telson M
uropod
urópodo M
uropode M
Schwanzfächer M
uropodio M

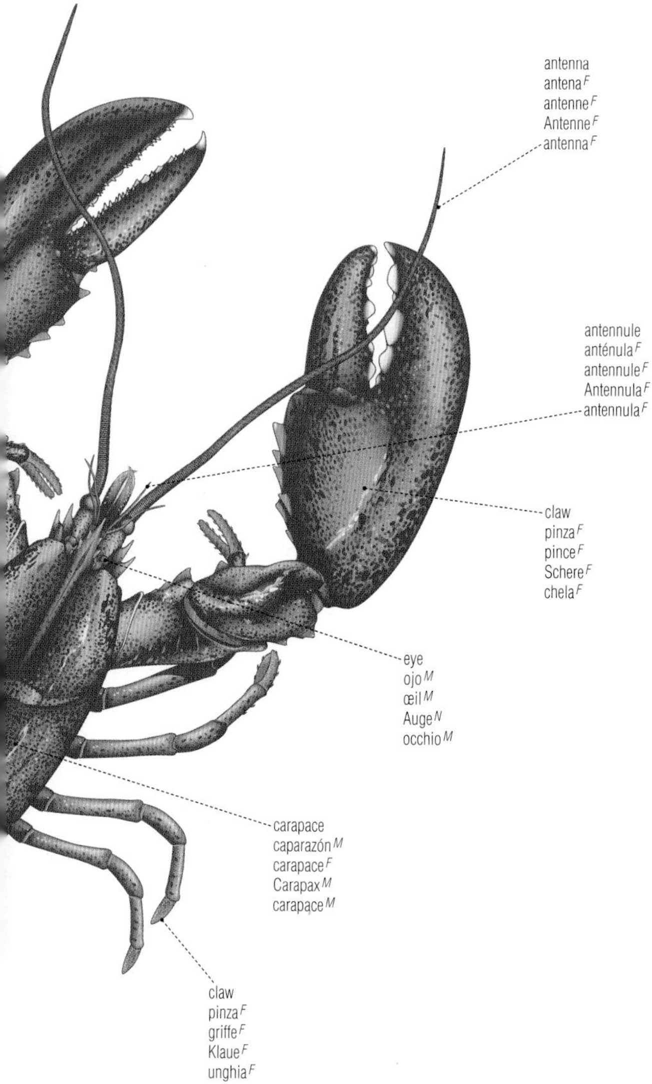
antenna
antena [F]
antenne [F]
Antenne [F]
antenna [F]
antennule
anténula [F]
antennule [F]
Antennula [F]
antennula [F]
claw
pinza [F]
pince [F]
Schere [F]
chela [F]
eye
ojo [M]
œil [M]
Auge [N]
occhio [M]
carapace
caparazón [M]
carapace [F]
Carapax [M]
carapace [M]
claw
pinza [F]
griffe [F]
Klaue [F]
unghia [F]

cartilaginous fish

pez[M] cartilaginoso | poisson[M] cartilagineux | Knorpelfisch[M] | pesce[M] cartilagineo

morphology of a shark
morfología[F] de un tiburón[M]
morphologie[F] du requin[M]
äußere Merkmale[N] eines Hais[M]
morfologia[F] di uno squalo[M]

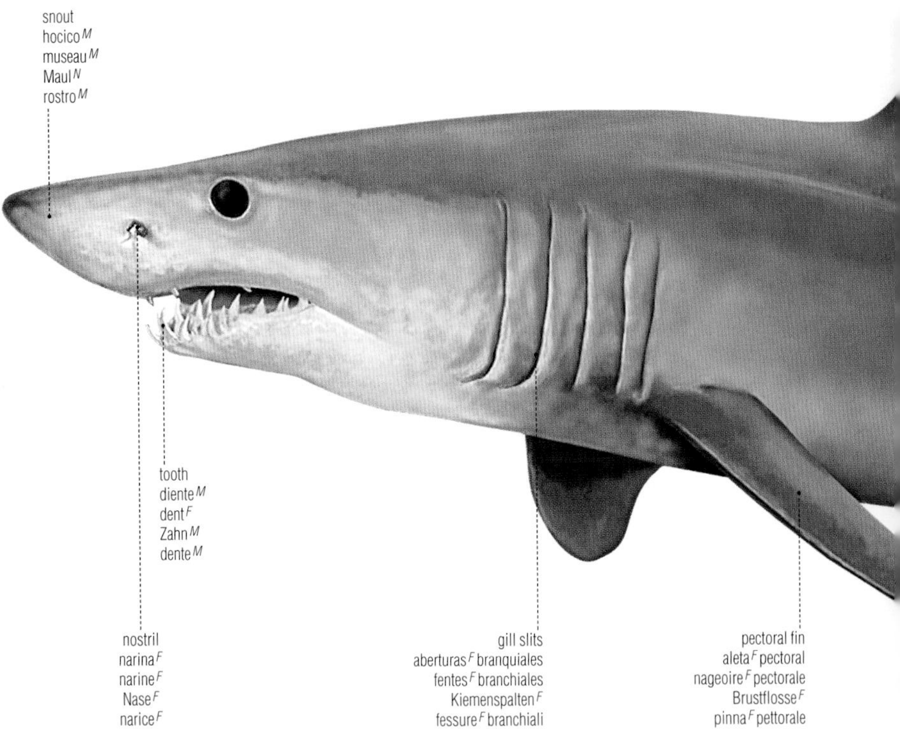
snout
hocico[M]
museau[M]
Maul[N]
rostro[M]
tooth
diente[M]
dent[F]
Zahn[M]
dente[M]
nostril
narina[F]
narine[F]
Nase[F]
narice[F]
gill slits
aberturas[F] branquiales
fentes[F] branchiales
Kiemenspalten[F]
fessure[F] branchiali
pectoral fin
aleta[F] pectoral
nageoire[F] pectorale
Brustflosse[F]
pinna[F] pettorale

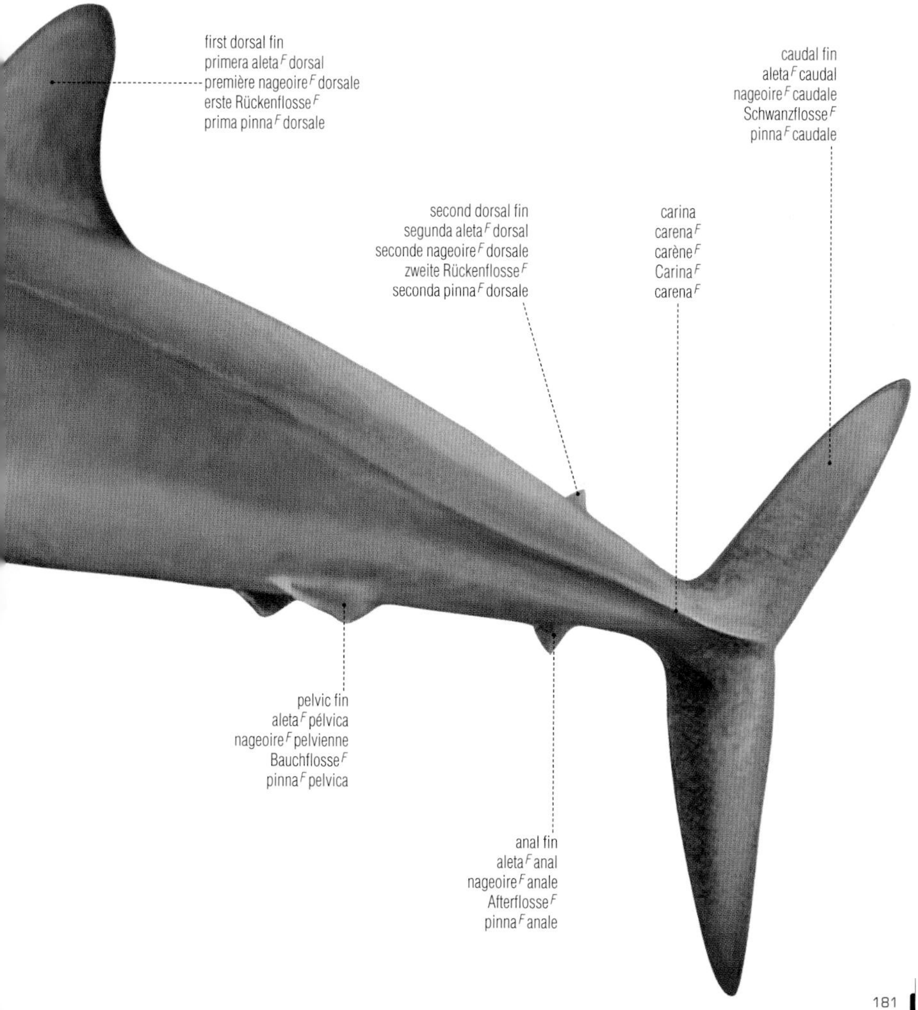
first dorsal fin
primera aleta[F] dorsal
première nageoire[F] dorsale
erste Rückenflosse[F]
prima pinna[F] dorsale
caudal fin
aleta[F] caudal
nageoire[F] caudale
Schwanzflosse[F]
pinna[F] caudale
second dorsal fin
segunda aleta[F] dorsal
seconde nageoire[F] dorsale
zweite Rückenflosse[F]
seconda pinna[F] dorsale
carina
carena[F]
carène[F]
Carina[F]
carena[F]
pelvic fin
aleta[F] pélvica
nageoire[F] pelvienne
Bauchflosse[F]
pinna[F] pelvica
anal fin
aleta[F] anal
nageoire[F] anale
Afterflosse[F]
pinna[F] anale

bony fish

pez^M óseo | poisson^M osseux | Knochenfisch^M | pesce^M osseo

morphology of a perch
morfología^F de una perca^F
morphologie^F de la perche^F
äußere Merkmale^N eines Flussbarschs^M
morfologia^F di un persico^M

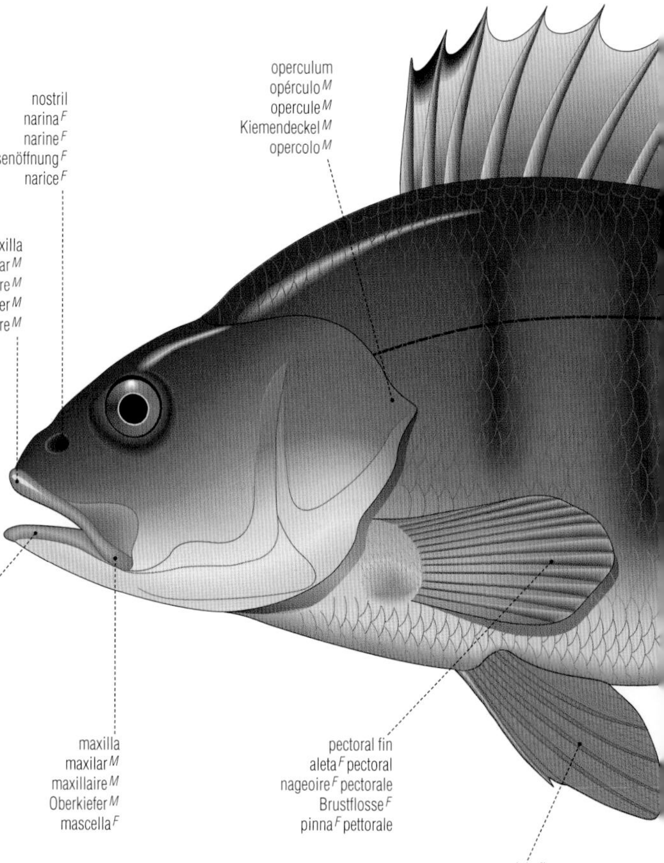

operculum
opérculo^M
opercule^M
Kiemendeckel^M
opercolo^M
nostril
narina^F
narine^F
Nasenöffnung^F
narice^F
premaxilla
premaxilar^M
prémaxillaire^M
vorderer Oberkiefer^M
premascellare^M
mandible
mandíbula^F
mandibule^F
Unterkiefer^M
mandibola^F
maxilla
maxilar^M
maxillaire^M
Oberkiefer^M
mascella^F
pectoral fin
aleta^F pectoral
nageoire^F pectorale
Brustflosse^F
pinna^F pettorale
pelvic fin
aleta^F abdominal
nageoire^F pelvienne
Bauchflosse^F
pinna^F pelvica

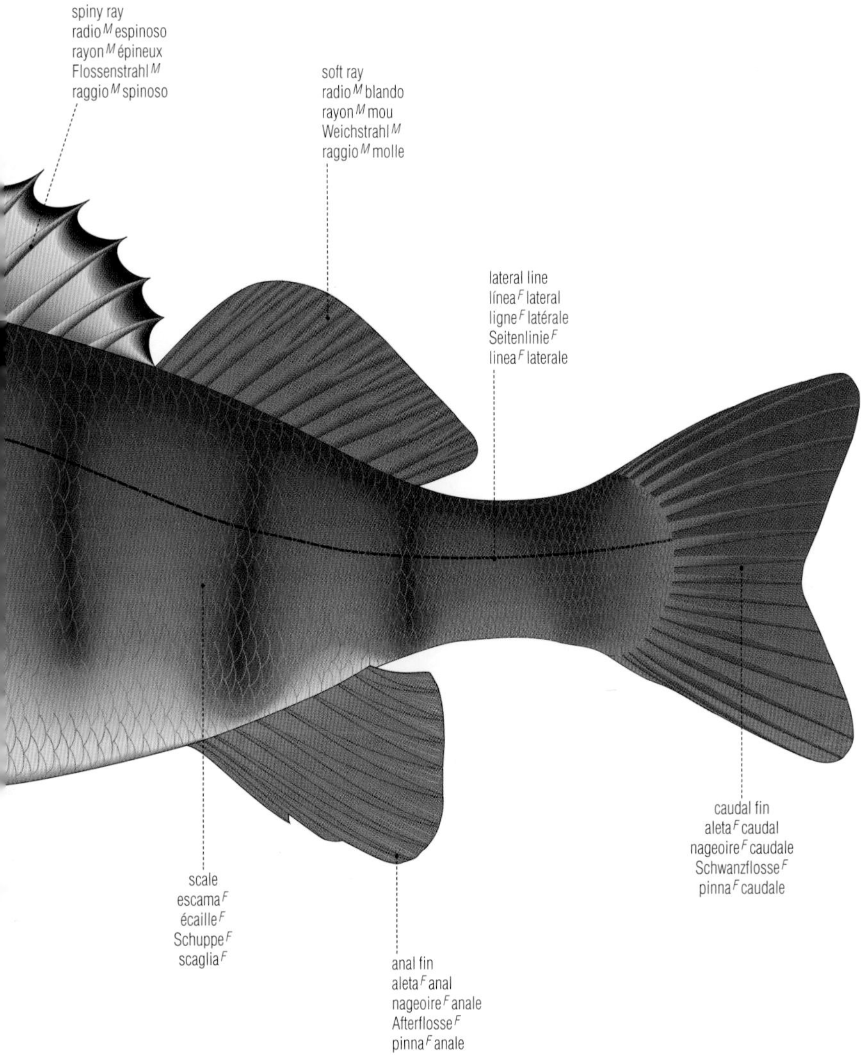
spiny ray
radio[M] espinoso
rayon[M] épineux
Flossenstrahl[M]
raggio[M] spinoso
soft ray
radio[M] blando
rayon[M] mou
Weichstrahl[M]
raggio[M] molle
lateral line
línea[F] lateral
ligne[F] latérale
Seitenlinie[F]
linea[F] laterale
caudal fin
aleta[F] caudal
nageoire[F] caudale
Schwanzflosse[F]
pinna[F] caudale
scale
escama[F]
écaille[F]
Schuppe[F]
scaglia[F]
anal fin
aleta[F] anal
nageoire[F] anale
Afterflosse[F]
pinna[F] anale

frog

rana^F | grenouille^F | Frosch^M | rana^F

morphology of a frog
morfología^F de una rana^F
morphologie^F de la grenouille^F
äußere Merkmale^N eines Froschs^M
morfologia^F di una rana^F

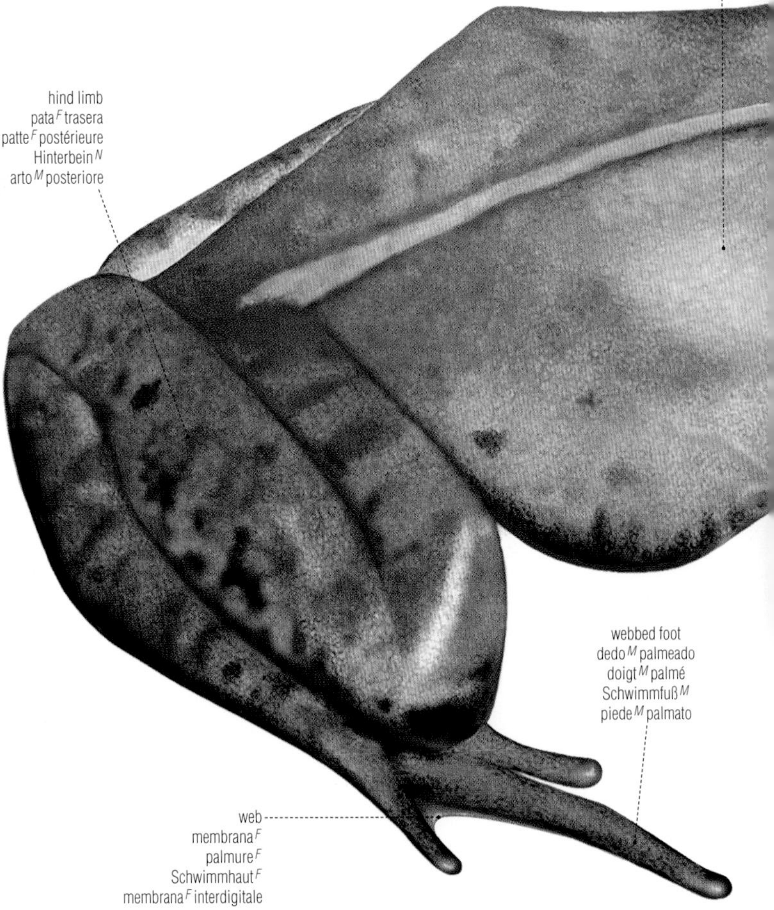
trunk
tronco^M
tronc^M
Rumpf^M
tronco^M
hind limb
pata^F trasera
patte^F postérieure
Hinterbein^N
arto^M posteriore
webbed foot
dedo^M palmeado
doigt^M palmé
Schwimmfuß^M
piede^M palmato
web
membrana^F
palmure^F
Schwimmhaut^F
membrana^F interdigitale

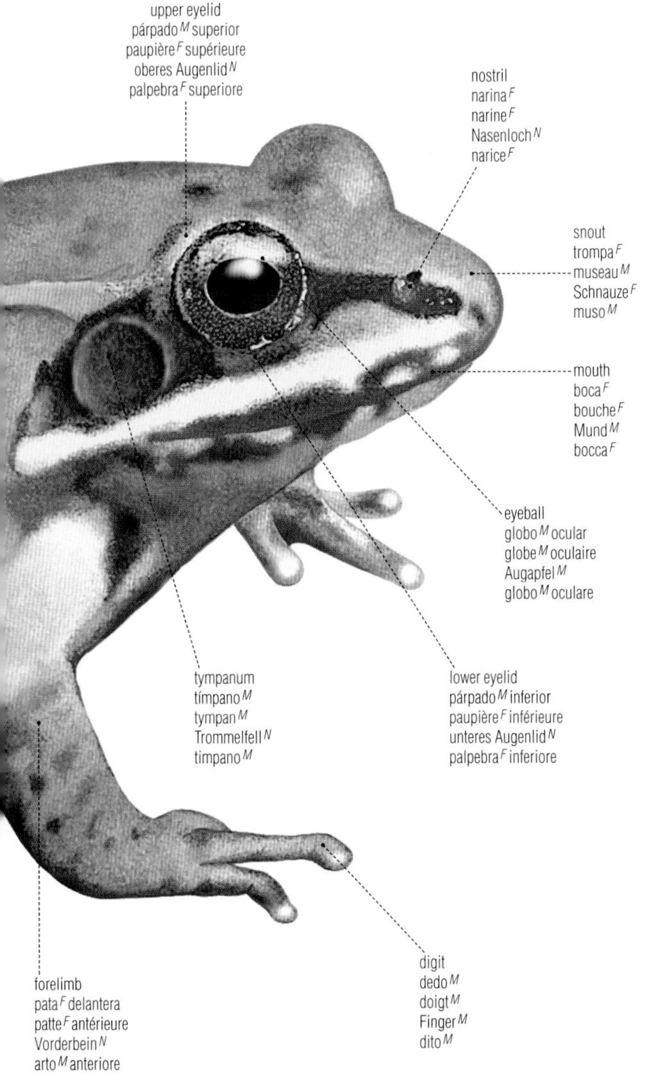
upper eyelid
párpado^M superior
paupière^F supérieure
oberes Augenlid^N
palpebra^F superiore
nostril
narina^F
narine^F
Nasenloch^N
narice^F
snout
trompa^F
museau^M
Schnauze^F
muso^M
mouth
boca^F
bouche^F
Mund^M
bocca^F
eyeball
globo^M ocular
globe^M oculaire
Augapfel^M
globo^M oculare
tympanum
tímpano^M
tympan^M
Trommelfell^N
timpano^M
lower eyelid
párpado^M inferior
paupière^F inférieure
unteres Augenlid^N
palpebra^F inferiore
forelimb
pata^F delantera
patte^F antérieure
Vorderbein^N
arto^M anteriore
digit
dedo^M
doigt^M
Finger^M
dito^M

life cycle of the frog
metamórfosis [F] de la rana [F]
métamorphose [F] de la grenouille [F]
Lebenszyklus [M] des Frosches [M]
ciclo [M] biologico della rana [F]

eggs
huevos [M]
œufs [M]
Eier [N]
uova [F]

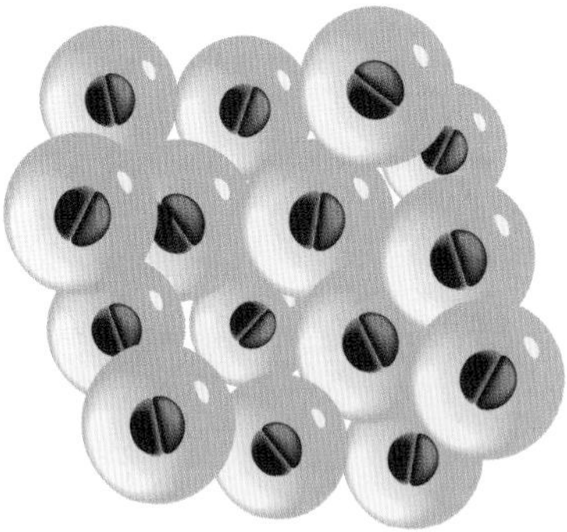

tadpole
renacuajo [M]
têtard [M]
Kaulquappe [F]
girino [M]

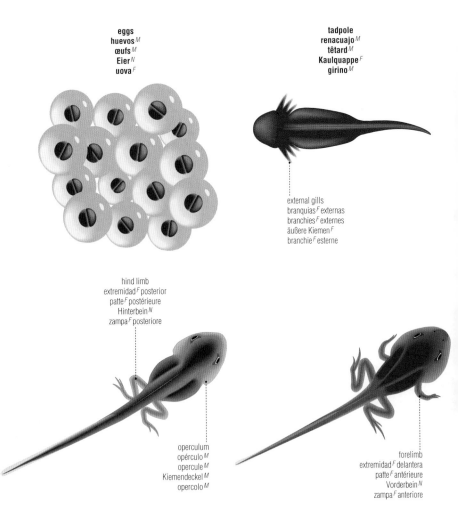

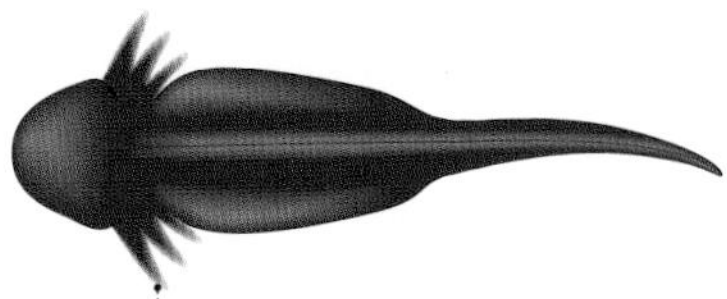
external gills
branquias [F] externas
branchies [F] externes
äußere Kiemen [F]
branchie [F] esterne

hind limb
extremidad [F] posterior
patte [F] postérieure
Hinterbein [N]
zampa [F] posteriore
operculum
opérculo [M]
opercule [M]
Kiemendeckel [M]
opercolo [M]

forelimb
extremidad [F] delantera
patte [F] antérieure
Vorderbein [N]
zampa [F] anteriore

examples of amphibians

ejemplos M de anfibios M | exemples M d'amphibiens M | Beispiele N für Amphibien F | esempi M di anfibi M

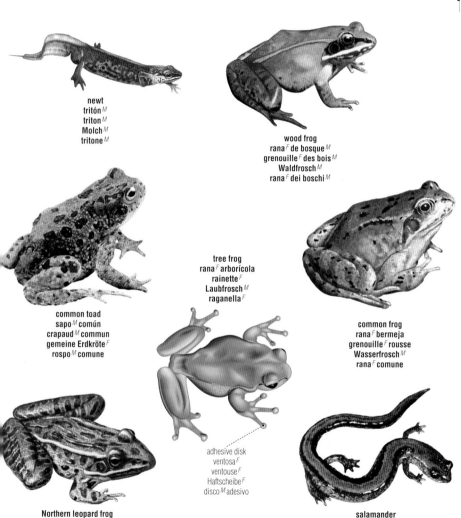

newt
tritón M
triton M
Molch M
tritone M

wood frog
rana F de bosque M
grenouille F des bois M
Waldfrosch M
rana F dei boschi M

common toad
sapo M común
crapaud M commun
gemeine Erdkröte F
rospo M comune

common frog
rana F bermeja
grenouille F rousse
Wasserfrosch M
rana F comune

tree frog
rana F arborícola
rainette F
Laubfrosch M
raganella F

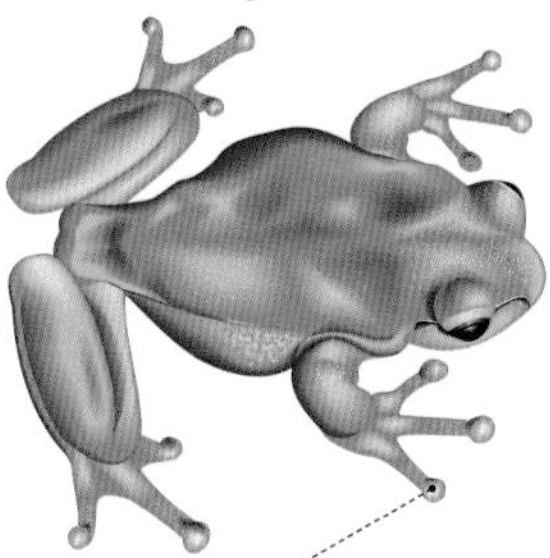

adhesive disk
ventosa F
ventouse F
Haftscheibe F
disco M adesivo

Northern leopard frog
rana F leopardo
grenouille F léopard M
Leopardfrosch M
rana F leopardo M

salamander
salamandra F
salamandre F
Salamander M
salamandra F

snake

serpiente F | serpent M | Schlange F | serpente M

anatomy of a venomous snake
anatomía F de una serpiente F venenosa
anatomie F du serpent M venimeux
Anatomie F einer Giftschlange F
anatomia F di un serpente M velenoso

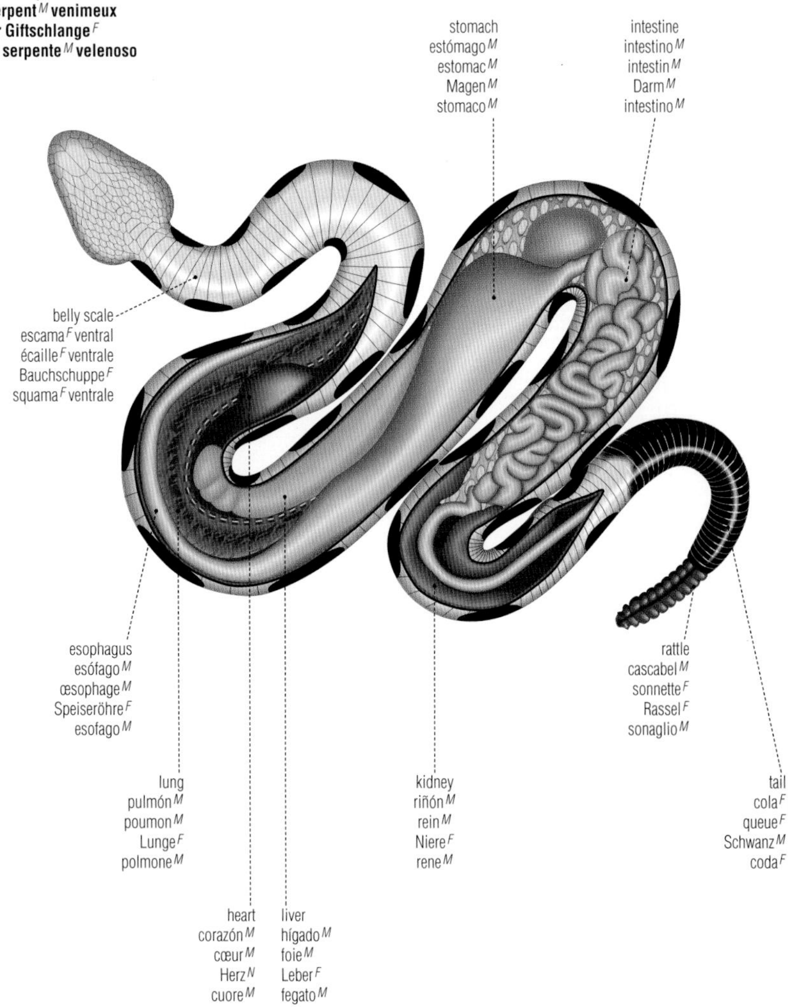

stomach
estómago M
estomac M
Magen M
stomaco M
intestine
intestino M
intestin M
Darm M
intestino M
belly scale
escama F ventral
écaille F ventrale
Bauchschuppe F
squama F ventrale
esophagus
esófago M
œsophage M
Speiseröhre F
esofago M
rattle
cascabel M
sonnette F
Rassel F
sonaglio M
lung
pulmón M
poumon M
Lunge F
polmone M
kidney
riñón M
rein M
Niere F
rene M
tail
cola F
queue F
Schwanz M
coda F
heart
corazón M
cœur M
Herz N
cuore M
liver
hígado M
foie M
Leber F
fegato M

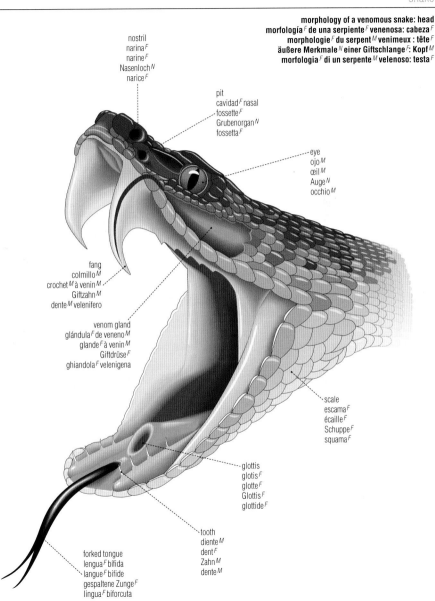

morphology of a venomous snake: head
morfología F de una serpiente F venenosa: cabeza F
morphologie F du serpent M venimeux : tête F
äußere Merkmale N einer Giftschlange F: Kopf M
morfologia F di un serpente M velenoso: testa F

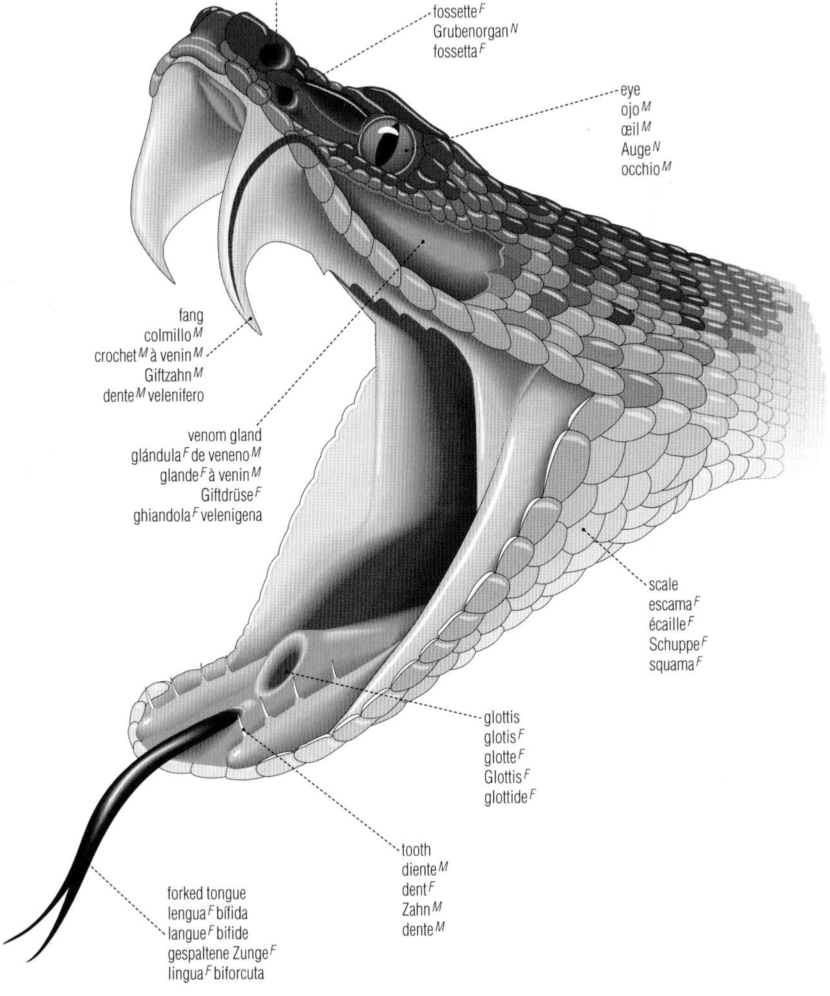
nostril
narina F
narine F
Nasenloch N
narice F
pit
cavidad F nasal
fossette F
Grubenorgan N
fossetta F
eye
ojo M
œil M
Auge N
occhio M
fang
colmillo M
crochet M à venin M
Giftzahn M
dente M velenifero
venom gland
glándula F de veneno M
glande F à venin M
Giftdrüse F
ghiandola F velenigena
scale
escama F
écaille F
Schuppe F
squama F
glottis
glotis F
glotte F
Glottis F
glottide F
tooth
diente M
dent F
Zahn M
dente M
forked tongue
lengua F bífida
langue F bifide
gespaltene Zunge F
lingua F biforcuta

turtle

tortuga^F | tortue^F | Schildkröte^F | tartaruga^F

morphology of a turtle
morfología^F de una tortuga^F
morphologie^F de la tortue^F
äußere Merkmale^N einer Schildkröte^F
morfologia^F di una tartaruga^F

vertebral shield
placa^F vertebral
plaque^F vertébrale
Vertebralschild^M
piastra^F neurale
eyelid
párpado^M
paupière^F
Augenlid^N
palpebra^F
eye
ojo^M
œil^M
Auge^N
occhio^M
horny beak
labio^M córneo
bec^M corné
Hornschnabel^M
becco^M corneo
neck
cuello^M
cou^M
Hals^M
collo^M
scale
escama^F
écaille^F
Schuppe^F
squama^F
claw
uña^F
griffe^F
Kralle^F
unghia^F

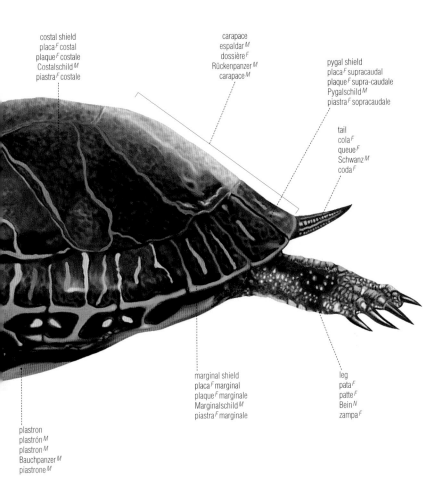

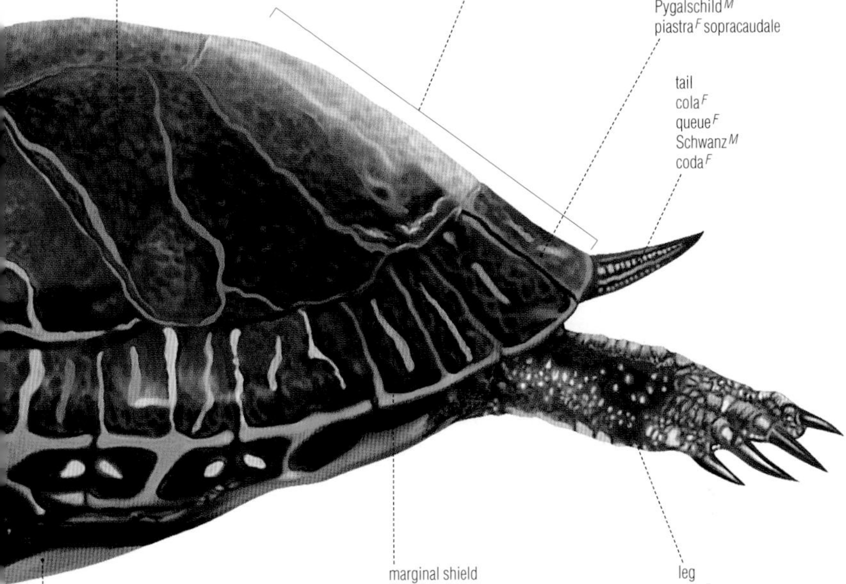
costal shield
placa F costal
plaque F costale
Costalschild M
piastra F costale
carapace
espaldar M
dossière F
Rückenpanzer M
carapace M
pygal shield
placa F supracaudal
plaque F supra-caudale
Pygalschild M
piastra F sopracaudale
tail
cola F
queue F
Schwanz M
coda F
marginal shield
placa F marginal
plaque F marginale
Marginalschild M
piastra F marginale
leg
pata F
patte F
Bein N
zampa F
plastron
plastrón M
plastron M
Bauchpanzer M
piastrone M

anatomy of a turtle
anatomía^F de una tortuga^F
anatomie^F de la tortue^F
Anatomie^F einer Schildkröte^F
anatomia^F di una tartaruga^F

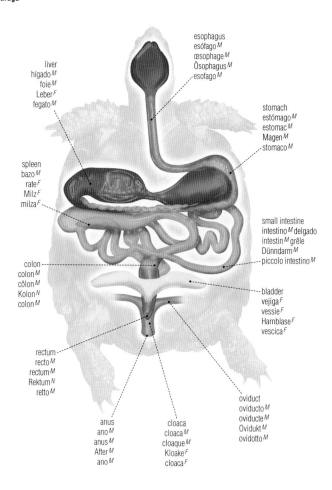

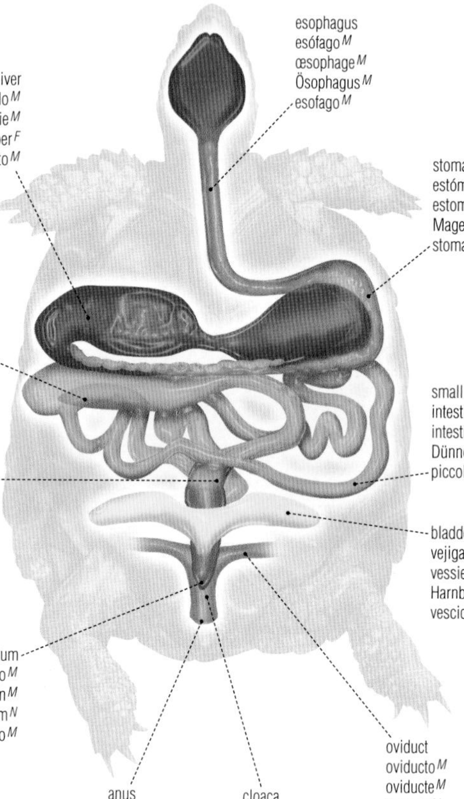
esophagus
esófago M
œsophage M
Ösophagus M
esofago M
liver
hígado M
foie M
Leber F
fegato M
stomach
estómago M
estomac M
Magen M
stomaco M
spleen
bazo M
rate F
Milz F
milza F
small intestine
intestino M delgado
intestin M grêle
Dünndarm M
piccolo intestino M
colon
colon M
côlon M
Kolon N
colon M
bladder
vejiga F
vessie F
Harnblase F
vescica F
rectum
recto M
rectum M
Rektum N
retto M
oviduct
oviducto M
oviducte M
Ovidukt M
ovidotto M
anus
ano M
anus M
After M
ano M
cloaca
cloaca M
cloaque M
Kloake F
cloaca F

examples of reptiles

ejemplos^M de reptiles^M | exemples^M de reptiles^M | Beispiele^N für Reptilien^N | esempi^M di rettili^M

viper
víbora F
vipère F
Viper F
vipera F

cobra
cobra F
cobra M
Kobra F
cobra M

garter snake
serpiente F **de jarretera** F
couleuvre F **rayée**
Ringelnatter F
serpente M **giarrettiera**

rattlesnake
serpiente F **de cascabel** M
serpent M **à sonnette** F
Klapperschlange F
serpente M **a sonagli** M

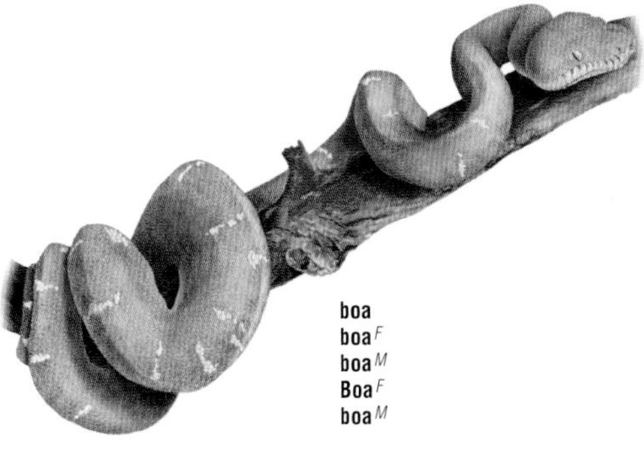

boa
boa F
boa M
Boa F
boa M

examples of reptiles

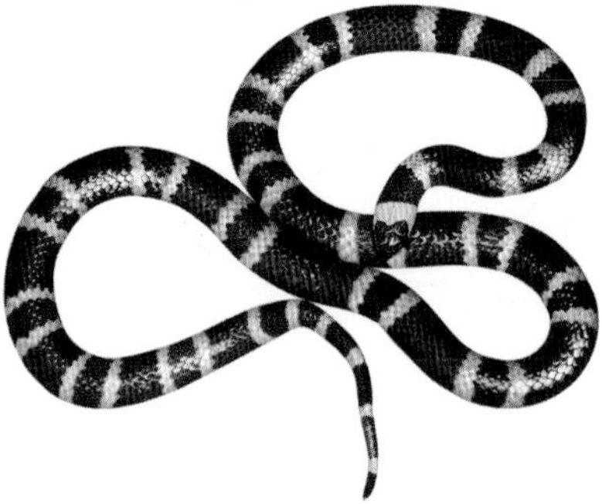

coral snake
serpiente F coral
serpent M corail M
Korallennatter F
serpente M corallo

python
pitón F
python M
Python M
pitone M

lizard
lagarto M
lézard M
Eidechse F
lucertola F

chameleon
camaleón M
caméléon M
Chamäleon N
camaleonte M

iguana
iguana F
iguane M
Leguan M
iguana F

monitor lizard
varano M
varan M
Waran M
varano M

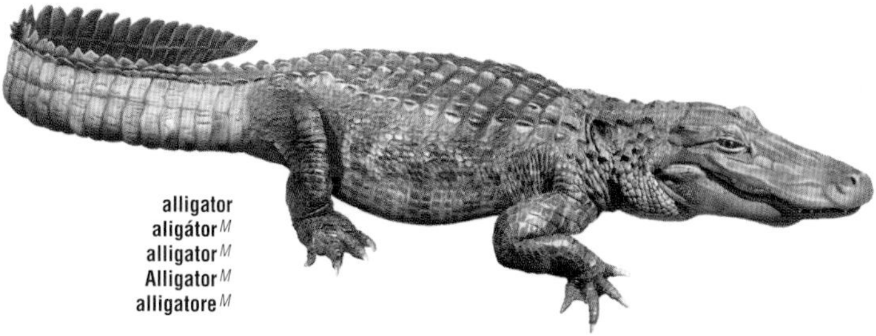

alligator
aligátor *M*
alligator *M*
Alligator *M*
alligatore *M*

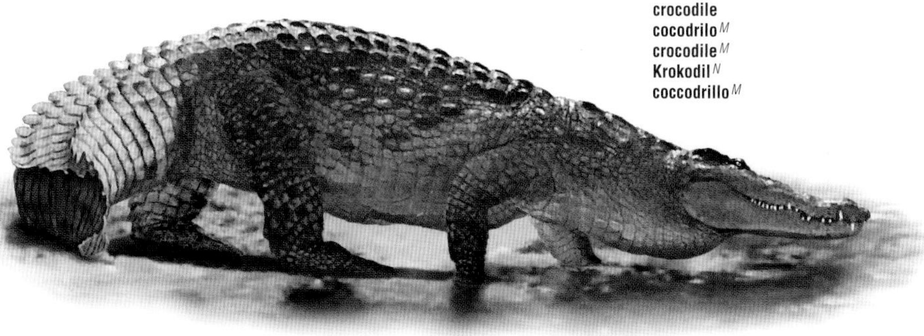

crocodile
cocodrilo *M*
crocodile *M*
Krokodil *N*
coccodrillo *M*

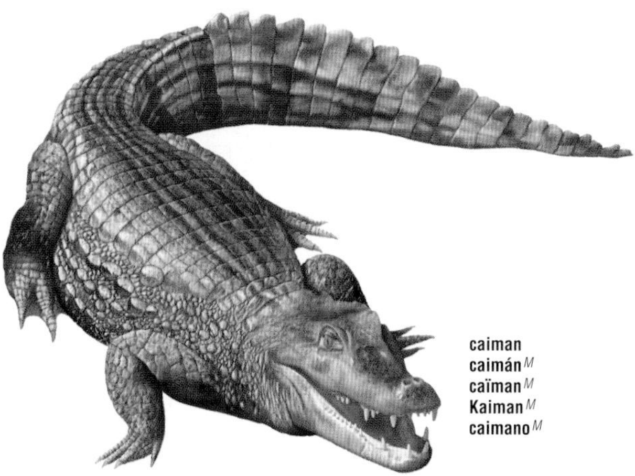

caiman
caimán *M*
caïman *M*
Kaiman *M*
caimano *M*

bird

ave[F] | oiseau[M] | Vogel[M] | uccello[M]

morphology of a bird
morfología[F] de un pájaro[M]
morphologie[F] de l'oiseau[M]
äußere Merkmale[N] eines Vogels[M]
morfologia[F] di un uccello[M]

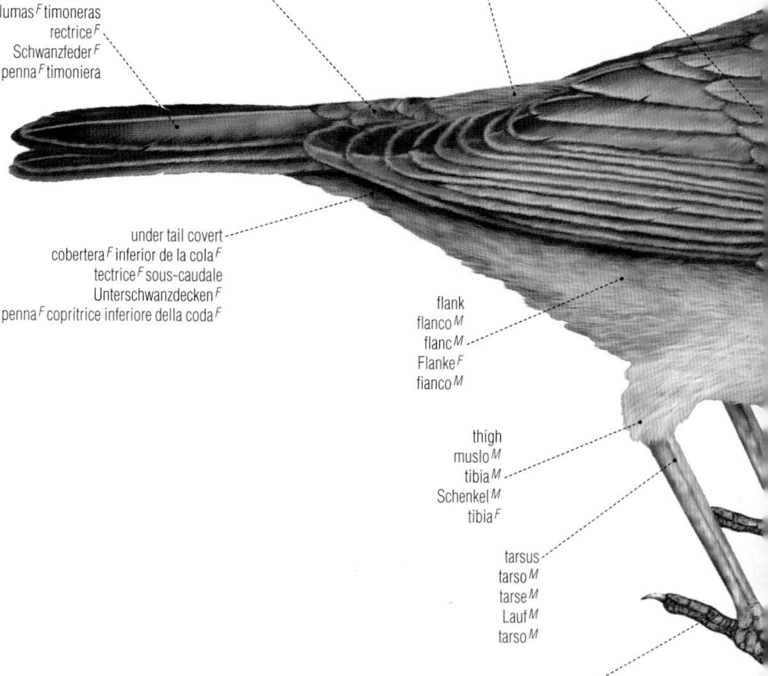
wing
ala[F]
aile[F]
Flügel[M]
ala[F]
back
lomo[M]
dos[M]
Rücken[M]
dorso[M]
upper tail covert
cobertera[F] superior de la cola[F]
tectrice[F] sus-caudale
Oberschwanzdecken[F]
penna[F] copritrice superiore della coda[F]
rump
obispillo[M]
croupion[M]
Bürzel[M]
codrione[M]
tail feather
plumas[F] timoneras
rectrice[F]
Schwanzfeder[F]
penna[F] timoniera
under tail covert
cobertera[F] inferior de la cola[F]
tectrice[F] sous-caudale
Unterschwanzdecken[F]
penna[F] copritrice inferiore della coda[F]
flank
flanco[M]
flanc[M]
Flanke[F]
fianco[M]
thigh
muslo[M]
tibia[M]
Schenkel[M]
tibia[F]
tarsus
tarso[M]
tarse[M]
Lauf[M]
tarso[M]
hind toe
dedo[M] posterior
doigt[M] postérieur
Hinterzehe[F]
dito[M] posteriore

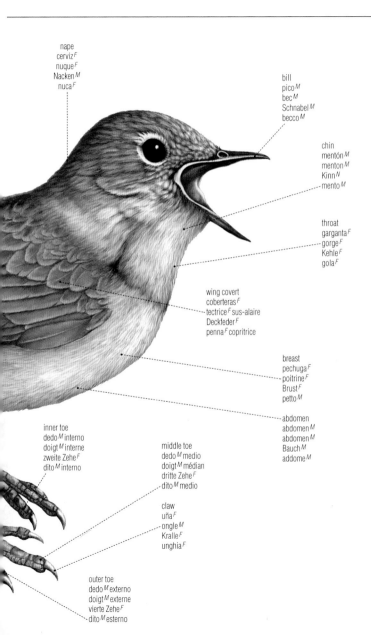

nape
cerviz[F]
nuque[F]
Nacken[M]
nuca[F]
bill
pico[M]
bec[M]
Schnabel[M]
becco[M]
chin
mentón[M]
menton[M]
Kinn[N]
mento[M]
throat
garganta[F]
gorge[F]
Kehle[F]
gola[F]
wing covert
coberteras[F]
tectrice[F] sus-alaire
Deckfeder[F]
penna[F] copritrice
breast
pechuga[F]
poitrine[F]
Brust[F]
petto[M]
abdomen
abdomen[M]
abdomen[M]
Bauch[M]
addome[M]
inner toe
dedo[M] interno
doigt[M] interne
zweite Zehe[F]
dito[M] interno
middle toe
dedo[M] medio
doigt[M] médian
dritte Zehe[F]
dito[M] medio
claw
uña[F]
ongle[M]
Kralle[F]
unghia[F]
outer toe
dedo[M] externo
doigt[M] externe
vierte Zehe[F]
dito[M] esterno

bird

wing
ala F
aile F
Flügel M
ala F

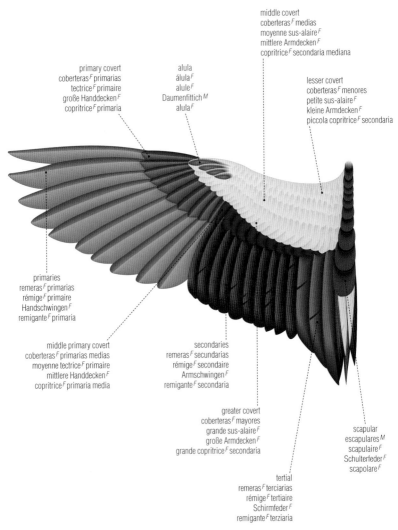

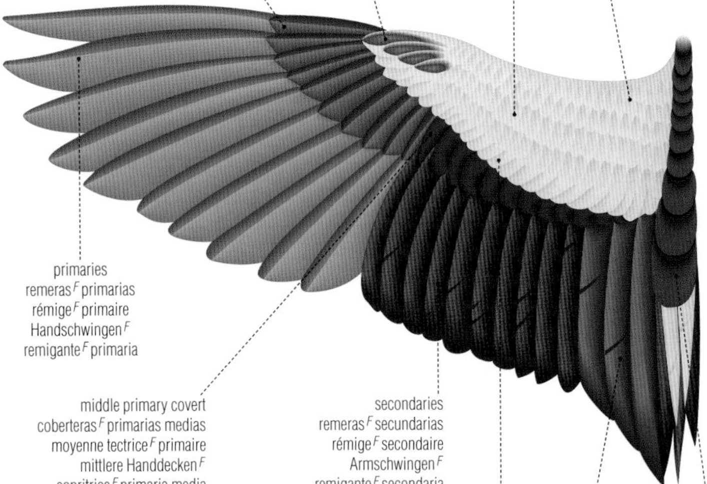
middle covert
coberteras F medias
moyenne sus-alaire F
mittlere Armdecken F
copritrice F secondaria mediana
primary covert
coberteras F primarias
tectrice F primaire
große Handdecken F
copritrice F primaria
alula
álula F
alule F
Daumenfittich M
alula F
lesser covert
coberteras F menores
petite sus-alaire F
kleine Armdecken F
piccola copritrice F secondaria
primaries
remeras F primarias
rémige F primaire
Handschwingen F
remigante F primaria
middle primary covert
coberteras F primarias medias
moyenne tectrice F primaire
mittlere Handdecken F
copritrice F primaria media
secondaries
remeras F secundarias
rémige F secondaire
Armschwingen F
remigante F secondaria
greater covert
coberteras F mayores
grande sus-alaire F
große Armdecken F
grande copritrice F secondaria
scapular
escapulares M
scapulaire F
Schulterfeder F
scapolare F
tertial
remeras F terciarias
rémige F tertiaire
Schirmfeder F
remigante F terziaria

contour feather
pluma *F*
penne *F*
Konturfeder *F*
penna *F* **del contorno** *M*

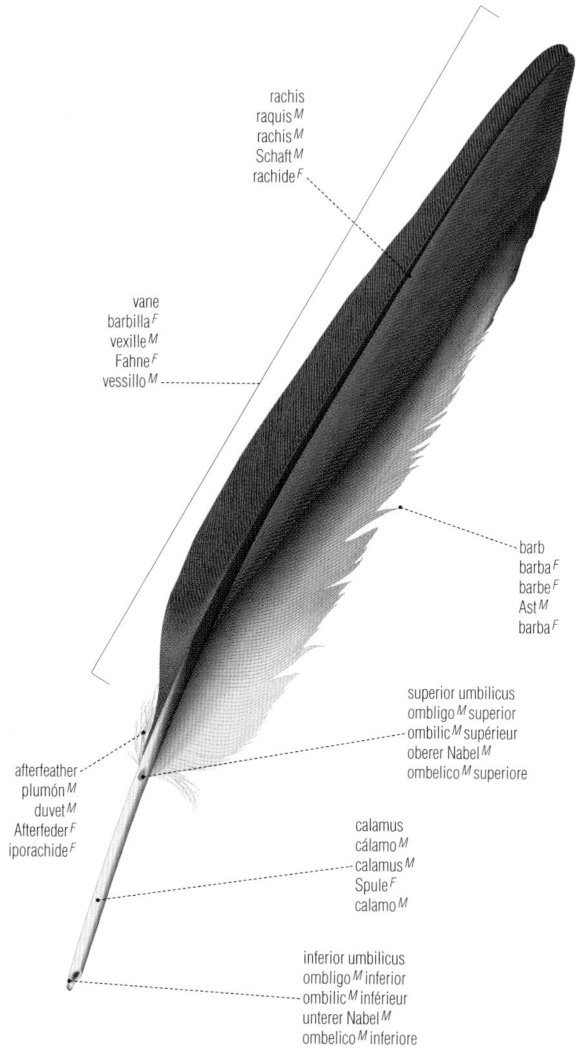

rachis
raquis M
rachis M
Schaft M
rachide F
vane
barbilla F
vexille M
Fahne F
vessillo M
barb
barba F
barbe F
Ast M
barba F
superior umbilicus
ombligo M superior
ombilic M supérieur
oberer Nabel M
ombelico M superiore
afterfeather
plumón M
duvet M
Afterfeder F
iporachide F
calamus
cálamo M
calamus M
Spule F
calamo M
inferior umbilicus
ombligo M inferior
ombilic M inférieur
unterer Nabel M
ombelico M inferiore

bird

skeleton of a bird
esqueleto^M de un pájaro^M
squelette^M de l'oiseau^M
Skelett^N eines Vogels^M
scheletro^M di un uccello^M

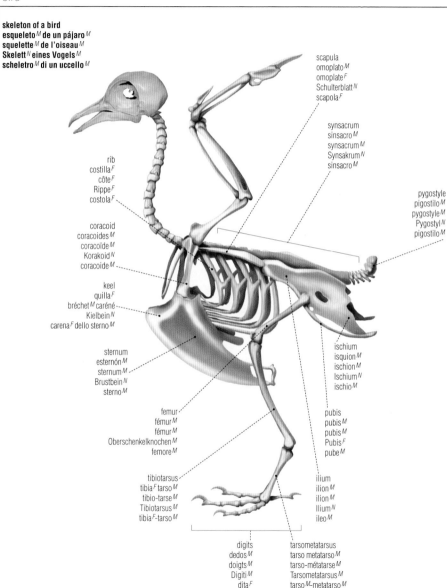

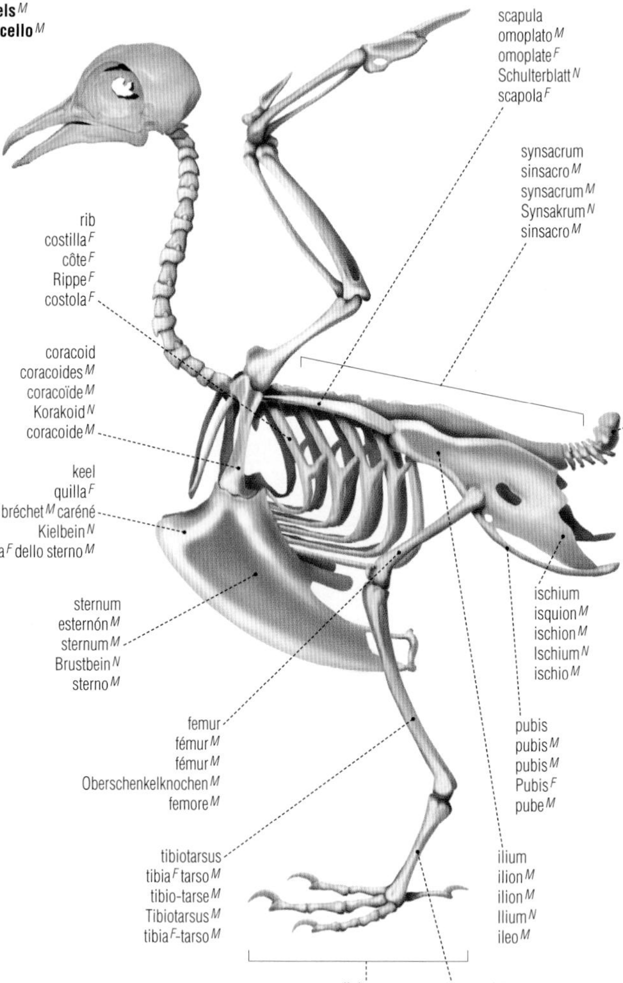
scapula
omoplato M
omoplate F
Schulterblatt N
scapola F
synsacrum
sinsacro M
synsacrum M
Synsakrum N
sinsacro M
rib
costilla F
côte F
Rippe F
costola F
pygostyle
pigostilo M
pygostyle M
Pygostyl N
pigostilo M
coracoid
coracoides M
coracoïde M
Korakoid N
coracoide M
keel
quilla F
bréchet M caréné
Kielbein N
carena F dello sterno M
sternum
esternón M
sternum M
Brustbein N
sterno M
ischium
isquion M
ischion M
Ischium N
ischio M
femur
fémur M
fémur M
Oberschenkelknochen M
femore M
pubis
pubis M
pubis M
Pubis F
pube M
tibiotarsus
tibia F tarso M
tibio-tarse M
Tibiotarsus M
tibia F-tarso M
ilium
ilion M
ilion M
Ilium N
ileo M
digits
dedos M
doigts M
Digiti M
dita F
tarsometatarsus
tarso metatarso M
tarso-métatarse M
Tarsometatarsus M
tarso M-metatarso M

head and wing
cabeza^F y ala^F
tête^F et aile^F
Kopf^M und Flügel^M
testa^F e ala^F

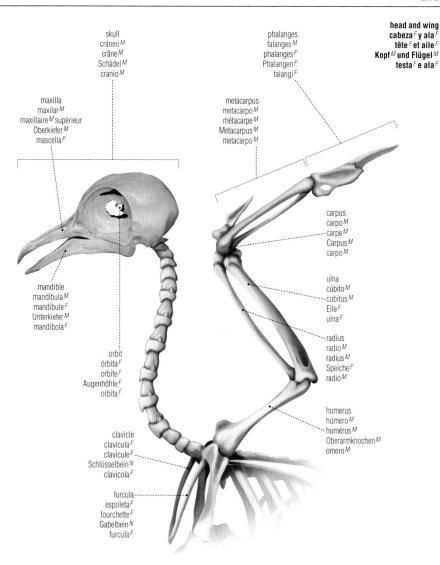

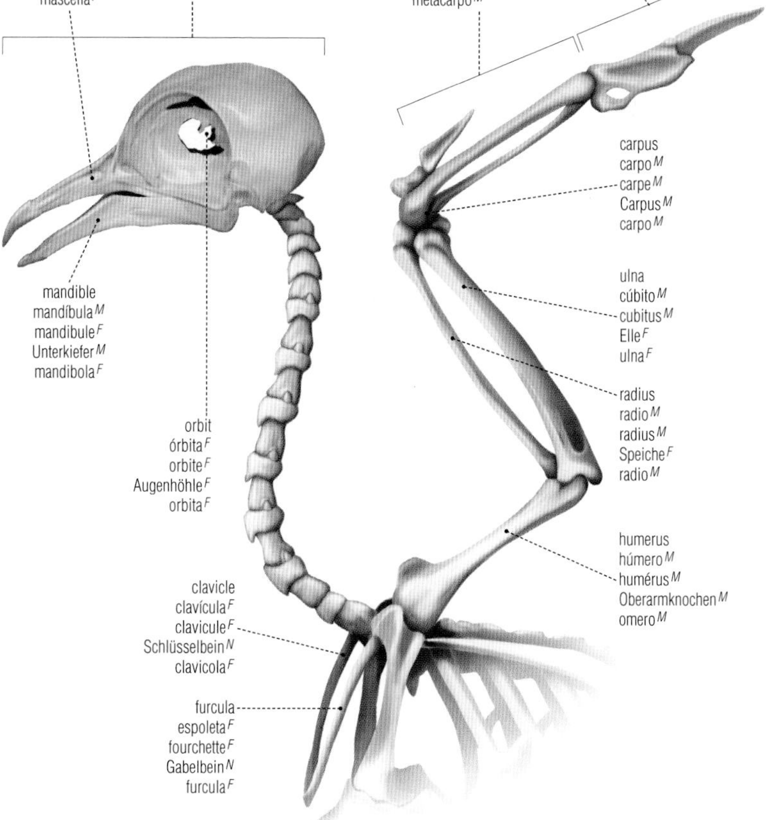
skull
cráneo M
crâne M
Schädel M
cranio M
phalanges
falanges M
phalanges F
Phalangen F
falangi F
maxilla
maxilar M
maxillaire M supérieur
Oberkiefer M
mascella F
metacarpus
metacarpo M
métacarpe M
Metacarpus M
metacarpo M
carpus
carpo M
carpe M
Carpus M
carpo M
mandible
mandíbula M
mandibule F
Unterkiefer M
mandibola F
ulna
cúbito M
cubitus M
Elle F
ulna F
radius
radio M
radius M
Speiche F
radio M
orbit
órbita F
orbite F
Augenhöhle F
orbita F
humerus
húmero M
humérus M
Oberarmknochen M
omero M
clavicle
clavícula F
clavicule F
Schlüsselbein N
clavicola F
furcula
espoleta F
fourchette F
Gabelbein N
furcula F

bird

examples of bills
ejemplos[M] de picos[M]
exemples[M] de becs[M]
Beispiele[N] für Vogelschnäbel[M]
esempi[M] di becchi[M]

bird of prey
ave[F] de rapiña[F]
oiseau[M] de proie[F]
Raubvogel[M]
uccello[M] predatore

granivorous bird
ave[F] granívora
oiseau[M] granivore
Körnerfresser[M]
uccello[M] granivoro

wading bird
ave[F] zancuda
oiseau[M] échassier
Watvogel[M]
uccello[M] trampoliere

aquatic bird
ave[F] acuática
oiseau[M] aquatique
Wasservogel[M]
uccello[M] acquatico

insectivorous bird
ave[F] insectívora
oiseau[M] insectivore
Insektenfresser[M]
uccello[M] insettivoro

examples of birds

ejemplos[M] de pájaros[M] | exemples[M] d'oiseaux[M] | unterschiedliche Vogeltypen[M] | esempi[M] di uccelli[M]

hummingbird
colibrí M
colibri M
Kolibri M
colibrì M

finch
pinzón M
pinson M
Fink M
fringuello M

sparrow
gorrión M
moineau M
Sperling M
passerotto M

European robin
petirrojo M
rouge-gorge M
Rotkehlchen N
pettirosso M

kingfisher
martín M **pescador**
martin-pêcheur M
Eisvogel M
martin pescatore M

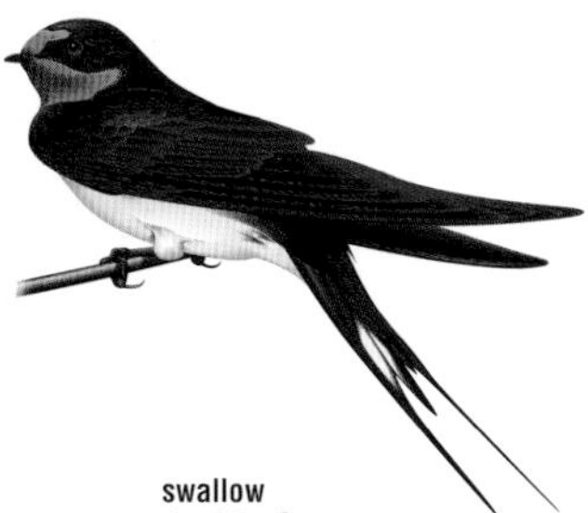

swallow
golondrina F
hirondelle F
Schwalbe F
rondine F

goldfinch
jilguero M
chardonneret M
Goldzeisig M
cardellino M

examples of birds

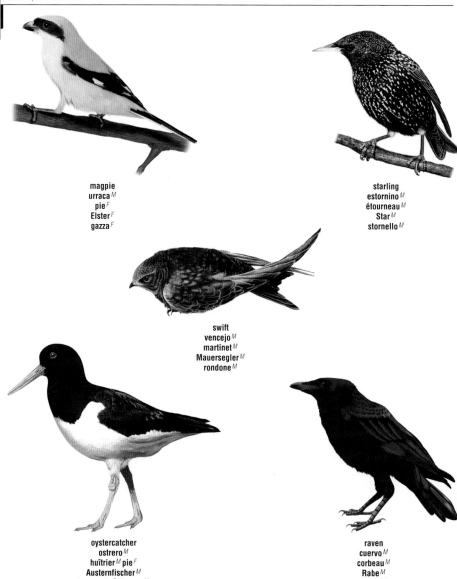

magpie
urraca *M*
pie *F*
Elster *F*
gazza *F*

starling
estornino *M*
étourneau *M*
Star *M*
stornello *M*

swift
vencejo *M*
martinet *M*
Mauersegler *M*
rondone *M*

oystercatcher
ostrero *M*
huîtrier *M* pie *F*
Austernfischer *M*
beccaccia *F* di mare *M*

raven
cuervo *M*
corbeau *M*
Rabe *M*
corvo *M*

nightingale
ruiseñor *M*
rossignol *M*
Nachtigall *F*
usignolo *M*

jay
arrendajo *M*
geai *M*
Eichelhäher *M*
ghiandaia *F*

northern saw-whet owl
lechuza *F* norteña
petite nyctale *F*
Sägekauz *M*
civetta *F* acadica

tern
golondrina *F* de mar
sterne *F*
Seeschwalbe *F*
rondine *F* di mare *M*

lapwing
avefría *F*
vanneau *M*
Kiebitz *M*
pavoncella *F*

examples of birds

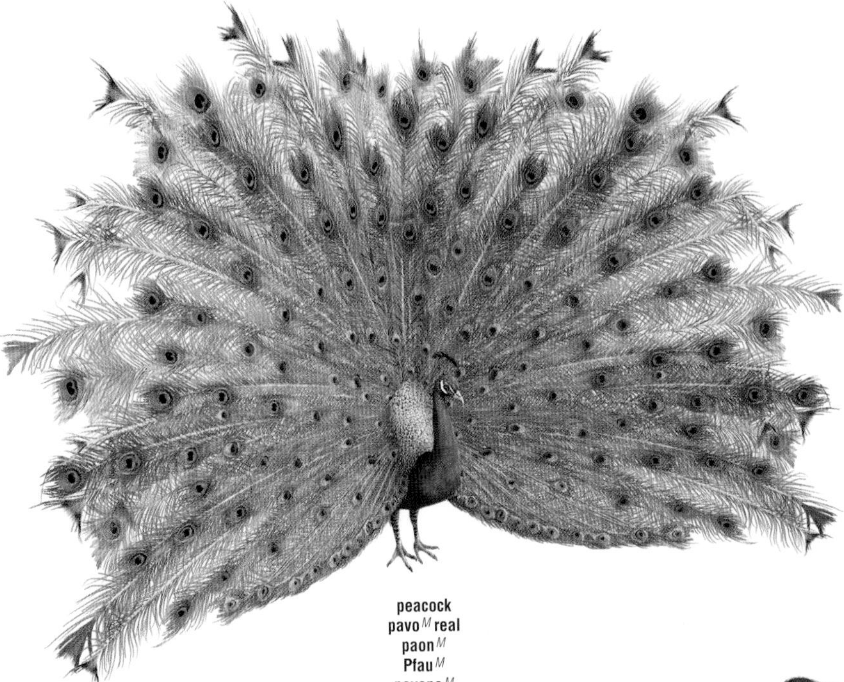

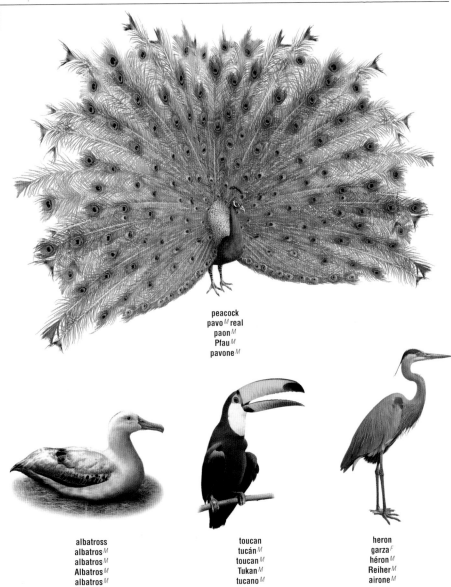

peacock
pavo *M* real
paon *M*
Pfau *M*
pavone *M*

albatross
albatros *M*
albatros *M*
Albatros *M*
albatros *M*

toucan
tucán *M*
toucan *M*
Tukan *M*
tucano *M*

heron
garza *F*
héron *M*
Reiher *M*
airone *M*

penguin
pingüino *M*
manchot *M*
Pinguin *M*
pinguino *M*

pelican
pelícano *M*
pélican *M*
Pelikan *M*
pellicano *M*

ostrich
avestruz *F*
autruche *F*
Strauß *M*
struzzo *M*

stork
cigüeña *F*
cigogne *F*
Storch *M*
cicogna *F*

flamingo
flamenco *M*
flamant *M*
Flamingo *M*
fenicottero *M*

examples of birds

condor
cóndor M
condor M
Kondor M
condor M

vulture
buitre M
vautour M
Geier M
avvoltoio M

eagle
águila F
aigle M
Adler M
aquila F

great horned owl
búho M real
grand duc M d'Amérique F
Uhu M
gufo M reale

falcon
halcón M
faucon M
Falke M
falco M

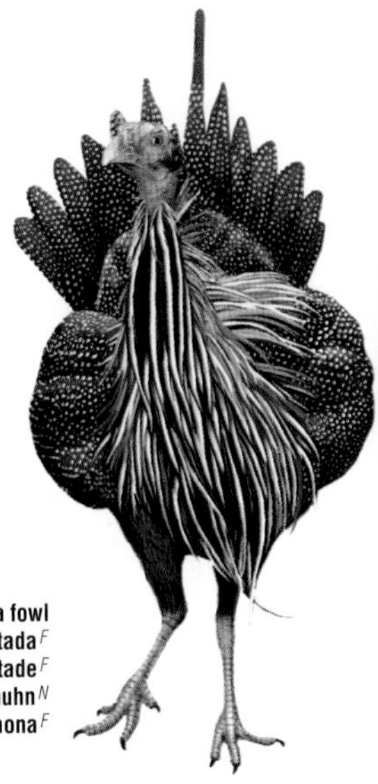

guinea fowl
pintada F
pintade F
Perlhuhn N
faraona F

rooster
gallo M
coq M
Hahn M
gallo M

chick
polluelo M
poussin M
Küken N
pulcino M

hen
gallina F
poule F
Huhn N
gallina F

turkey
pavo M
dindon M
Truthahn M
tacchino M

examples of birds

pheasant
faisán *M*
faisan *M*
Fasan *M*
fagiano *M*

pigeon
paloma *F*
pigeon *M*
Taube *F*
piccione *M*

quail
codorniz *F*
caille *F*
Wachtel *F*
quaglia *F*

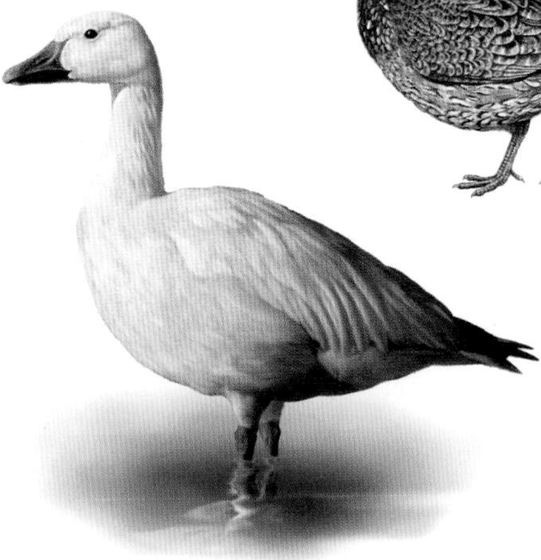

goose
oca *F*
oie *F*
Gans *F*
oca *F*

duck
pato *M*
canard *M*
Ente *F*
anatra *F*

bullfinch
pardillo *M*
bouvreuil *M*
Gimpel *M*
ciuffolotto *M*

cardinal
cardenal *M*
cardinal *M*
Kardinal *M*
cardinale *M*

partridge
perdiz *F*
perdrix *F*
Rebhuhn *N*
pernice *F*

cockatoo
cacatúa *F*
cacatoès *M*
Kakadu *M*
cacatua *M*

woodpecker
pájaro *M* carpintero
pic *M*
Specht *M*
picchio *M*

macaw
guacamayo *M*
ara *M*
Ara *M*
macao *M*

examples of rodents

ejemplos[M] de roedores[M] | exemples[M] de mammifères[M] rongeurs[M] | Beispiele[N] für Nagetiere[N] | esempi[M] di roditori[M]

hamster
hámster[M]
hamster[M]
Hamster[M]
criceto[M]

chipmunk
ardilla[F] **listada**
tamia[M]
Backenhörnchen[N]
tamia[M]

jerboa
jerbo[M]
gerboise[F]
Wüstenspringmaus[F]
gerboa[M]

guinea pig
cobaya[F]
cochon[M] **d'Inde**
Meerschweinchen[N]
cavia[F]

field mouse
ratón[M] **de campo**[M]
mulot[M]
Feldmaus[F]
topo[M] **campagnolo**

rat
rata [F]
rat [M]
Ratte [F]
ratto [M]

squirrel
ardilla [F]
écureuil [M]
Eichhörnchen [N]
scoiattolo [M]

woodchuck
marmota [F]
marmotte [F]
Waldmurmeltier [N]
marmotta [F]

beaver
castor [M]
castor [M]
Biber [M]
castoro [M]

porcupine
puerco [M] **espín**
porc-épic [M]
Stachelschwein [N]
porcospino [M]

examples of lagomorphs

ejemplos^M de lagomorfos^M | exemples^M de mammifères^M lagomorphes^M | Beispiele^N für Hasentiere^N | esempi^M di lagomorfi^M

pika
pica^F
pika^M
Pfeifhase^M
lepre^F **fischiante**

rabbit
conejo^M
lapin^M
Kaninchen^N
coniglio^M

hare
liebre^F
lièvre^M
Hase^M
lepre^F

examples of insectivorous mammals

ejemplos[M] de mamíferos [M] insectívoros | exemples[M] de mammifères[M] insectivores | Beispiele[N] für Insektenfresser[M] | esempi[M] di mammiferi[M] insettivori

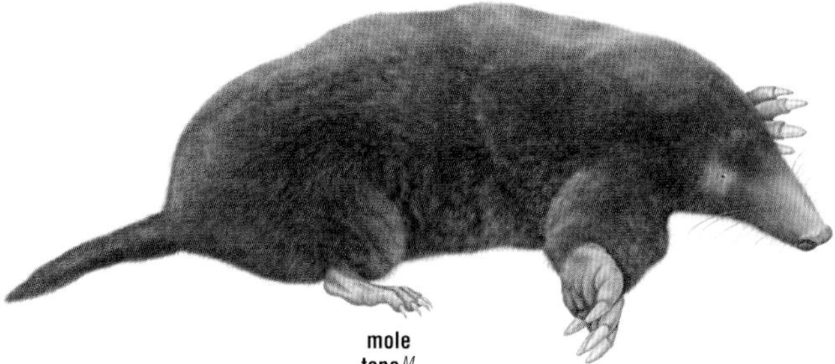

mole
topo[M]
taupe[F]
Maulwurf[M]
talpa[F]

hedgehog
erizo[M]
hérisson[M]
Igel[M]
riccio[M]

shrew
musaraña[F]
musaraigne[F]
Spitzmaus[F]
toporagno[M]

horse

caballo^M^ | cheval^M^ | Pferd^N^ | cavallo^M^

morphology of a horse
morfología^F^ de un caballo^M^
morphologie^F^ du cheval^M^
äußere Merkmale^N^ eines Pferdes^N^
morfologia^F^ di un cavallo^M^

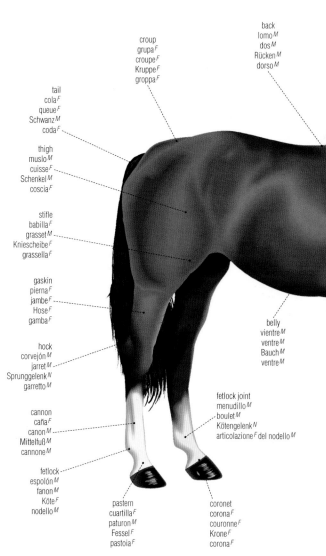

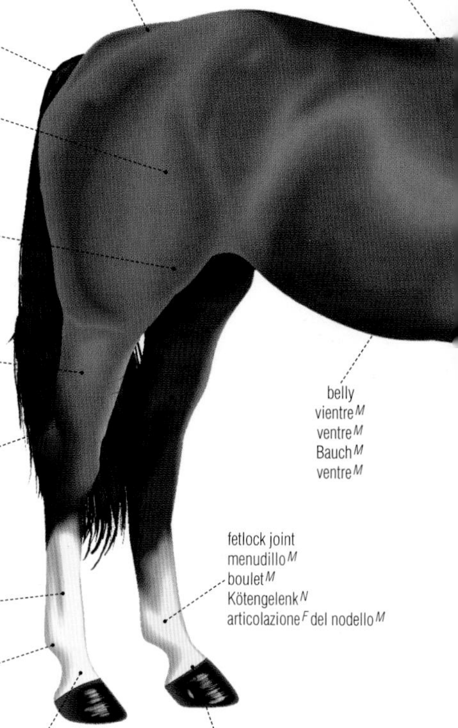
back
lomo M
dos M
Rücken M
dorso M
croup
grupa F
croupe F
Kruppe F
groppa F
tail
cola F
queue F
Schwanz M
coda F
thigh
muslo M
cuisse F
Schenkel M
coscia F
stifle
babilla F
grasset M
Kniescheibe F
grassella F
gaskin
pierna F
jambe F
Hose F
gamba F
belly
vientre M
ventre M
Bauch M
ventre M
hock
corvejón M
jarret M
Sprunggelenk N
garretto M
fetlock joint
menudillo M
boulet M
Kötengelenk N
articolazione F del nodello M
cannon
caña F
canon M
Mittelfuß M
cannone M
fetlock
espolón M
fanon M
Köte F
nodello M
pastern
cuartilla F
paturon M
Fessel F
pastoia F
coronet
corona F
couronne F
Krone F
corona F

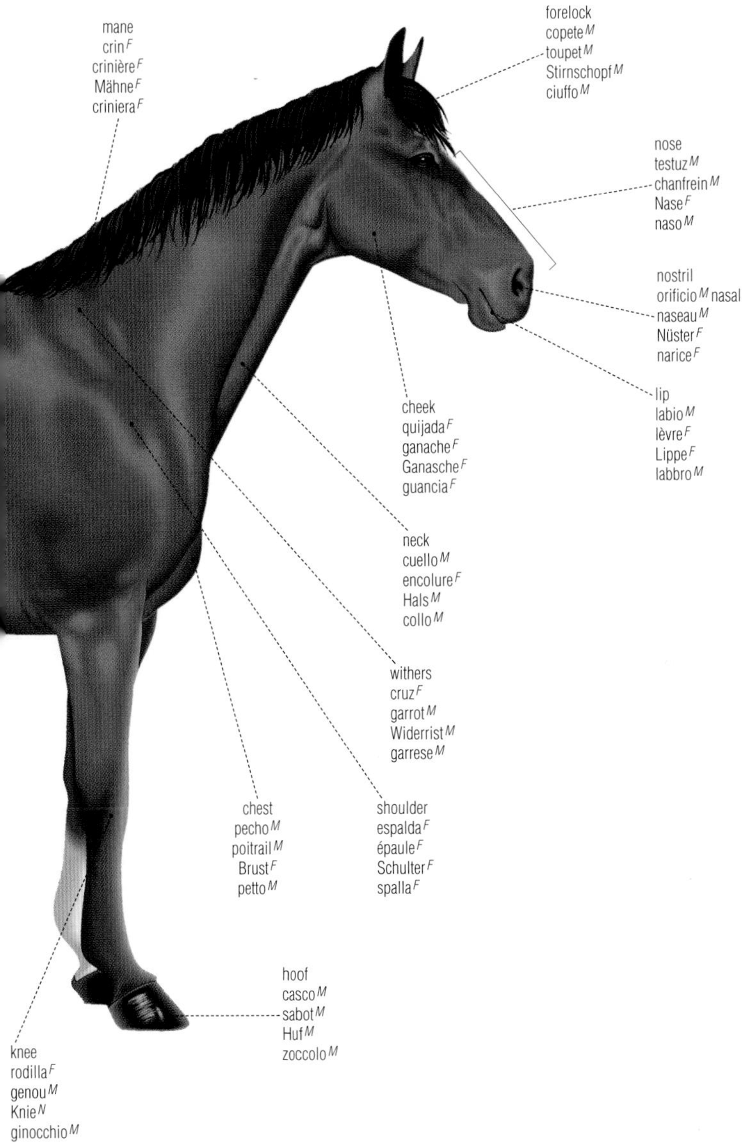
mane
crin F
crinière F
Mähne F
criniera F
forelock
copete M
toupet M
Stirnschopf M
ciuffo M
nose
testuz M
chanfrein M
Nase F
naso M
nostril
orificio M nasal
naseau M
Nüster F
narice F
lip
labio M
lèvre F
Lippe F
labbro M
cheek
quijada F
ganache F
Ganasche F
guancia F
neck
cuello M
encolure F
Hals M
collo M
withers
cruz F
garrot M
Widerrist M
garrese M
chest
pecho M
poitrail M
Brust F
petto M
shoulder
espalda F
épaule F
Schulter F
spalla F
hoof
casco M
sabot M
Huf M
zoccolo M
knee
rodilla F
genou M
Knie N
ginocchio M

examples of ungulate mammals

ejemplos[M] de mamíferos[M] ungulados | exemples[M] de mammifères[M] ongulés | Beispiele[N] für Huftiere[N] | esempi[M] di mammiferi[M] ungulati

peccary
pécari[M]
pécari[M]
Nabelschwein[N]
pecari[M]

wild boar
jabalí[M]
sanglier[M]
Wildschwein[N]
cinghiale[M]

pig
cerdo[M]
porc[M]
Schwein[N]
maiale[M]

sheep
oveja[F]
mouton[M]
Schaf[N]
pecora[F]

antelope
antílope[M]
antilope[F]
Antilope[F]
antilope[F]

mouflon
muflón[M]
mouflon[M]
Mufflon[M]
muflone[M]

ass
asno[M]
âne[M]
Esel[M]
asino[M]

mule
mula[F]
mulet[M]
Maultier[N]
mulo[M]

ox
buey *M*
bœuf *M*
Ochse *M*
bue *M*

cow
vaca *F*
vache *F*
Kuh *F*
mucca *F*

goat
cabra *F*
chèvre *F*
Ziege *F*
capra *F*

calf
ternero *M*
veau *M*
Kalb *N*
vitello *M*

zebra
cebra *F*
zèbre *M*
Zebra *N*
zebra *F*

horse
caballo *M*
cheval *M*
Pferd *N*
cavallo *M*

examples of ungulate mammals

caribou
reno[M]
renne[M]
Rentier[N]
renna[F]

white-tailed deer
ciervo[M] **de Virginia**[F]
cerf[M] **de Virginie**
Reh[N]
cervo[M] **dalla coda**[F] **bianca**

elk
uapití[M]
cerf[M] **du Canada**
Wapitihirsch[M]
wapiti[M]

buffalo
búfalo[M]
buffle[M]
Büffel[M]
bufalo[M]

llama
llama[F]
lama[M]
Lama[N]
lama[M]

okapi
okapi[M]
okapi[M]
Okapi[N]
okapi[M]

dromedary camel
dromedario *M*
dromadaire *M*
Dromedar *N*
dromedario *M*

bactrian camel
camello *M*
chameau *M*
Kamel *N*
cammello *M*

bison
bisonte *M*
bison *M*
Bison *M*
bisonte *M*

yak
yak *M*
yack *M*
Yak *M*
yak *M*

moose
alce *M*
élan *M*
Elch *M*
alce *F*

examples of ungulate mammals

rhinoceros
rinoceronte [M]
rhinocéros [M]
Nashorn [N]
rinoceronte [M]

giraffe
jirafa [F]
girafe [F]
Giraffe [F]
giraffa [F]

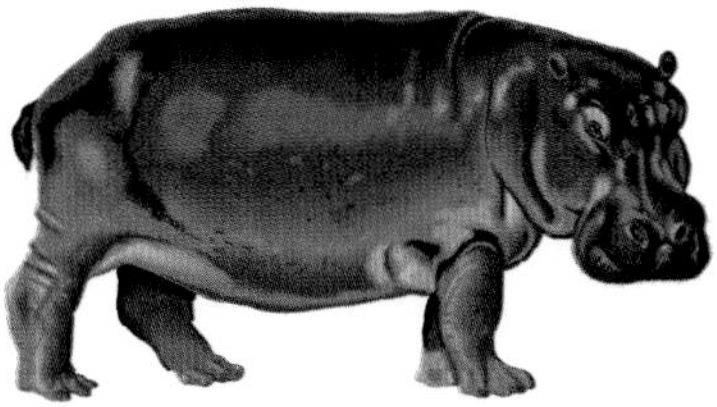

hippopotamus
hipopótamo [M]
hippopotame [M]
Nilpferd [N]
ippopotamo [M]

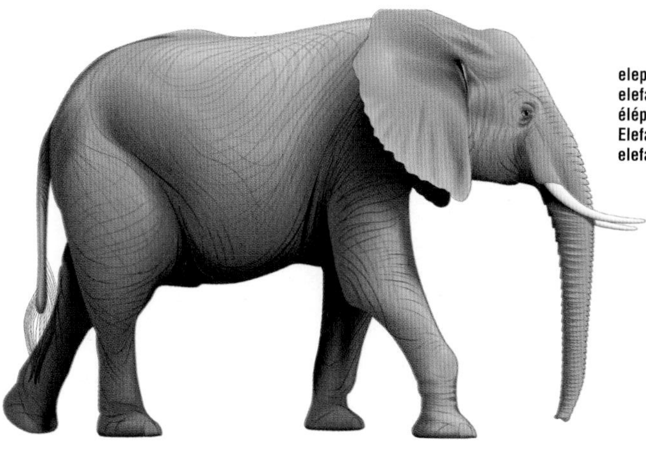

elephant
elefante [M]
éléphant [M]
Elefant [M]
elefante [M]

dog

perro^M | chien^M | Hund^M | cane^M

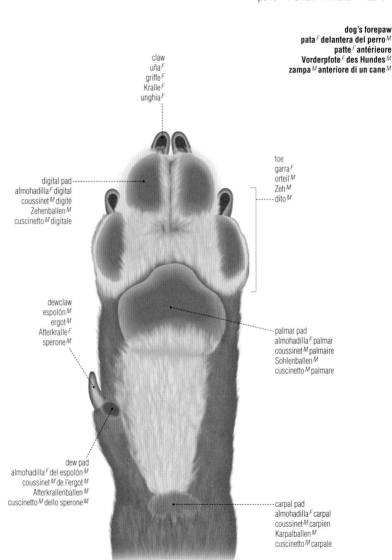

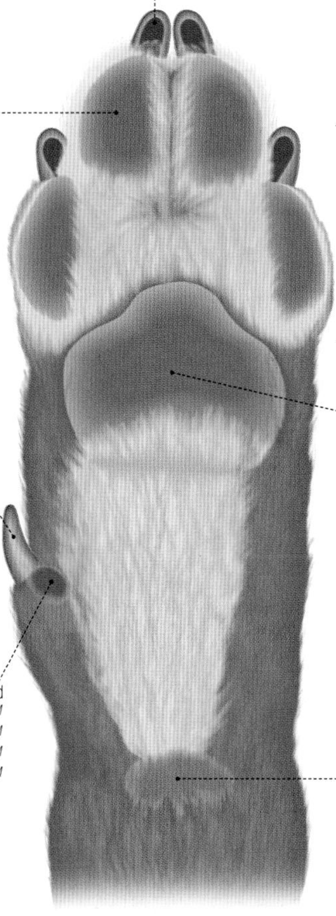
dog's forepaw
pata^F delantera del perro^M
patte^F antérieure
Vorderpfote^F des Hundes^M
zampa^M anteriore di un cane^M
claw
uña^F
griffe^F
Kralle^F
unghia^F
toe
garra^F
orteil^M
Zeh^M
dito^M
digital pad
almohadilla^F digital
coussinet^M digité
Zehenballen^M
cuscinetto^M digitale
dewclaw
espolón^M
ergot^M
Afterkralle^F
sperone^M
palmar pad
almohadilla^F palmar
coussinet^M palmaire
Sohlenballen^M
cuscinetto^M palmare
dew pad
almohadilla^F del espolón^M
coussinet^M de l'ergot^M
Afterkrallenballen^M
cuscinetto^M dello sperone^M
carpal pad
almohadilla^F carpal
coussinet^M carpien
Karpalballen^M
cuscinetto^M carpale

dog

morphology of a dog
morfología F de un perro M
morphologie F du chien M
äußere Merkmale N eines Hundes M
morfologia F di un cane M

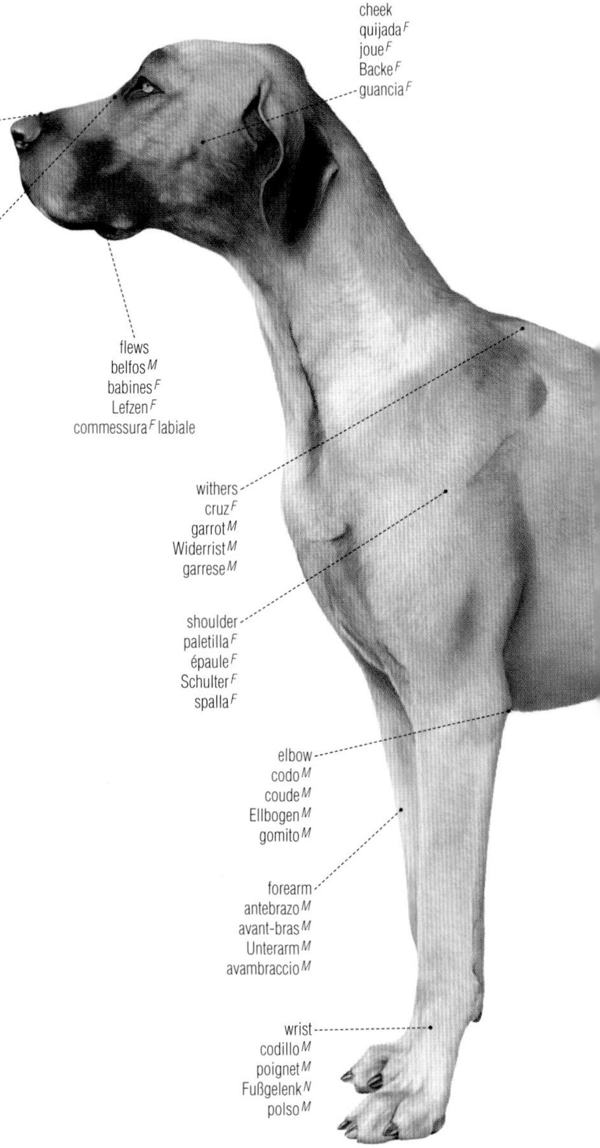
cheek
quijada F
joue F
Backe F
guancia F
muzzle
hocico M
museau M
Schnauze F
muso M
stop
entrecejo M
stop M
Stop M
stop M
flews
belfos M
babines F
Lefzen F
commessura F labiale
withers
cruz F
garrot M
Widerrist M
garrese M
shoulder
paletilla F
épaule F
Schulter F
spalla F
elbow
codo M
coude M
Ellbogen M
gomito M
forearm
antebrazo M
avant-bras M
Unterarm M
avambraccio M
wrist
codillo M
poignet M
Fußgelenk N
polso M

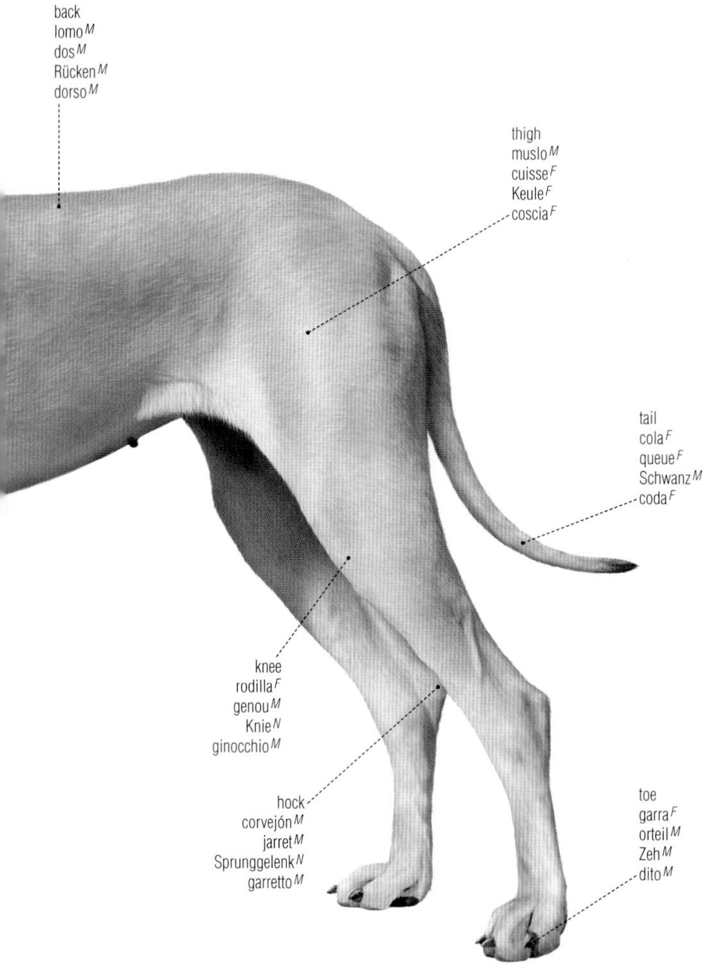
back
lomo M
dos M
Rücken M
dorso M
thigh
muslo M
cuisse F
Keule F
coscia F
tail
cola F
queue F
Schwanz M
coda F
knee
rodilla F
genou M
Knie N
ginocchio M
hock
corvejón M
jarret M
Sprunggelenk N
garretto M
toe
garra F
orteil M
Zeh M
dito M

cat

gato M doméstico | chat M | Katze F | gatto M

cat's head
cabeza F
tête F
Kopf M der Katze F
testa F di gatto M

pupil
pupila F
pupille F
Pupille F
pupilla F
eyelashes
pestañas F
cils M
Wimpern F
ciglia F
whiskers
bigotes M
sourcils M
Schnurrhaare N
vibrisse F
upper eyelid
párpado M superior
paupière F supérieure
oberes Augenlid N
palpebra F superiore
lower eyelid
párpado M inferior
paupière F inférieure
unteres Augenlid N
palpebra F inferiore
nictitating membrane
párpado M interno
paupière F interne
Nickhaut F
membrana F nittitante
whiskers
bigotes M
moustaches F
Schnurrhaare N
vibrisse F
nose leather
ala F de la nariz F
truffe F
Nasenspiegel M
rinario M
muzzle
hocico M
museau M
Schnauze F
muso M
lip
labio M
lèvre F
Lippe F
labbro M

morphology of a cat
morfología^F de un gato^M
morphologie^F du chat^M
äußere Merkmale^N einer Katze^F
morfologia^F di un gatto^M

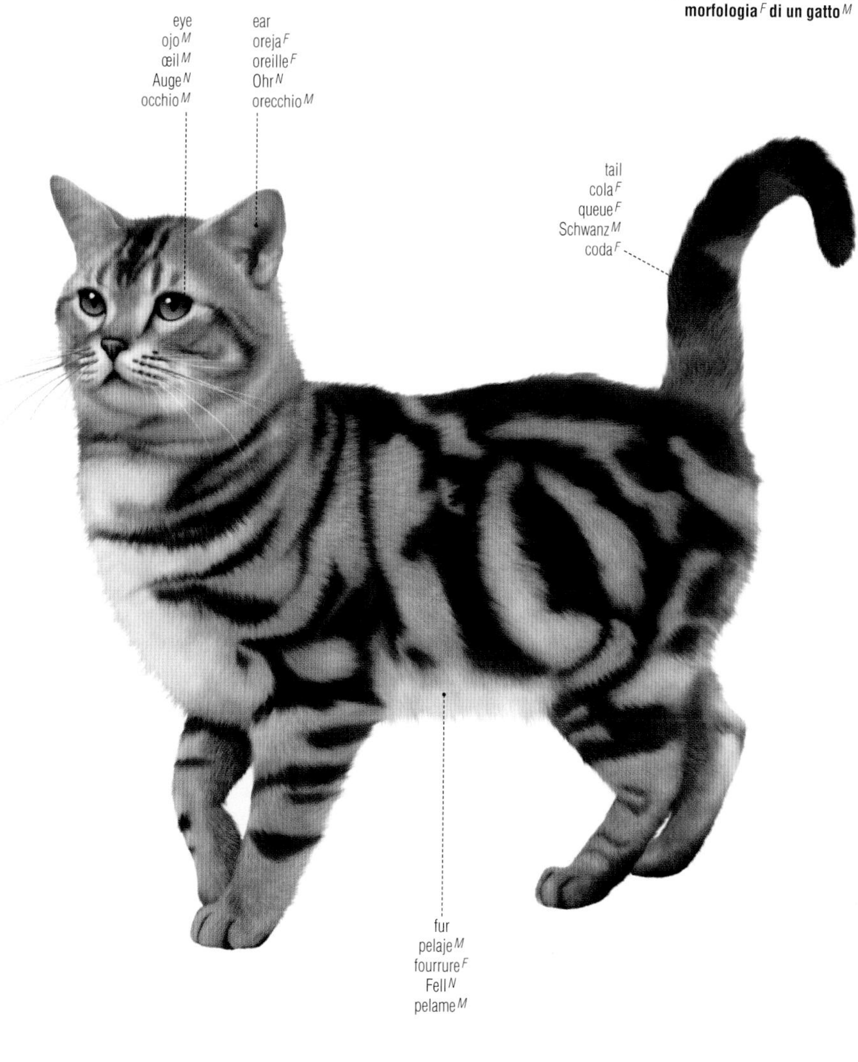
eye
ojo M
œil M
Auge N
occhio M
ear
oreja F
oreille F
Ohr N
orecchio M
tail
cola F
queue F
Schwanz M
coda F
fur
pelaje M
fourrure F
Fell N
pelame M

examples of carnivorous mammals

ejemplos[M] de mamíferos[M] carnívoros | exemples[M] de mammifères[M] carnivores | Beispiele[N] für Raubtiere[N] | esempi[M] di mammiferi[M] carnivori

weasel
comadreja[F]
belette[F]
Wiesel[N]
donnola[F]

mink
visón[M]
vison[M]
Nerz[M]
visone[M]

stone marten
garduña[F]
fouine[F]
Steinmarder[M]
faina[F]

fox
zorro[M]
renard[M]
Fuchs[M]
volpe[F]

fennec
fenec[M]
fennec[M]
Wüstenfuchs[M]
volpe[F] **del deserto**[M]

mongoose
mangosta[F]
mangouste[F]
Mungo[M]
mangusta[F]

badger
tejón[M]
blaireau[M]
Dachs[M]
tasso[M]

marten
marta[F]
martre[F]
Marder[M]
martora[F]

river otter
nutria[F] de río[M]
loutre[F] de rivière[F]
Seeotter[M]
lontra[F] comune

raccoon
mapache[M]
raton[M] laveur
Waschbär[M]
procione[M]

skunk
mofeta[F]
moufette[F]
Stinktier[N]
moffetta[F]

examples of carnivorous mammals

hyena
hiena F
hyène F
Hyäne F
iena F

lynx
lince M
lynx M
Luchs M
lince F

cougar
puma M
puma M
Puma M
puma M

lion
león M
lion M
Löwe M
leone M

examples of carnivorous mammals

cheetah
guepardo *M*
guépard *M*
Gepard *M*
ghepardo *M*

leopard
leopardo *M*
léopard *M*
Leopard *M*
leopardo *M*

jaguar
jaguar *M*
jaguar *M*
Jaguar *M*
giaguaro *M*

tiger
tigre *M*
tigre *M*
Tiger *M*
tigre *F*

examples of carnivorous mammals

wolf
lobo *M*
loup *M*
Wolf *M*
lupo *M*

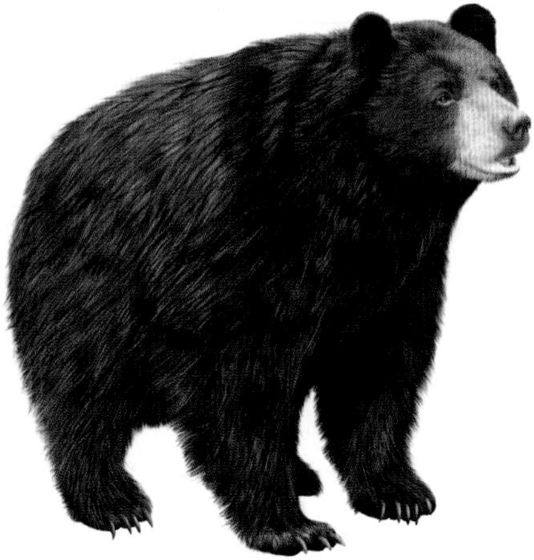

black bear
oso *M* **negro**
ours *M* **noir**
Schwarzbär *M*
orso *M* **bruno**

polar bear
oso *M* **polar**
ours *M* **polaire**
Eisbär *M*
orso *M* **polare**

examples of marine mammals

ejemplos^{M} de mamíferos^{M} marinos | exemples^{M} de mammifères^{M} marins | Beispiele^{N} für Meeressäugetiere^{N} | esempi^{M} di mammiferi^{M} marini

killer whale
orca^{F}
orque^{F}
Schwertwal^{M}
orca^{F}

northern right whale
ballena^{F}
baleine^{F}
Wal^{M}
balena^{F}

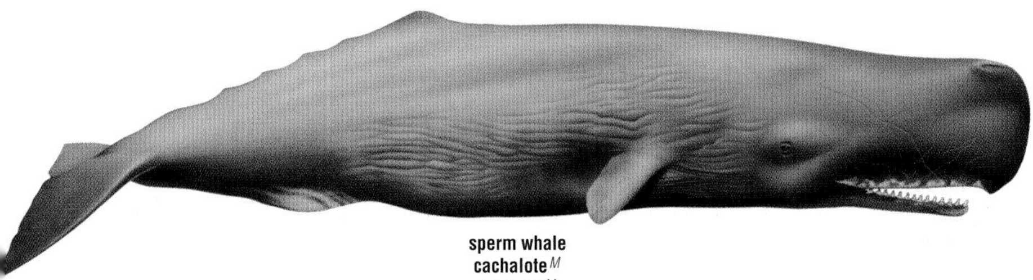

sperm whale
cachalote^{M}
cachalot^{M}
Pottwal^{M}
capodoglio^{M}

examples of marine mammals

sea lion
otaria *F*
otarie *F*
Seelöwe *M*
leone *M* **marino**

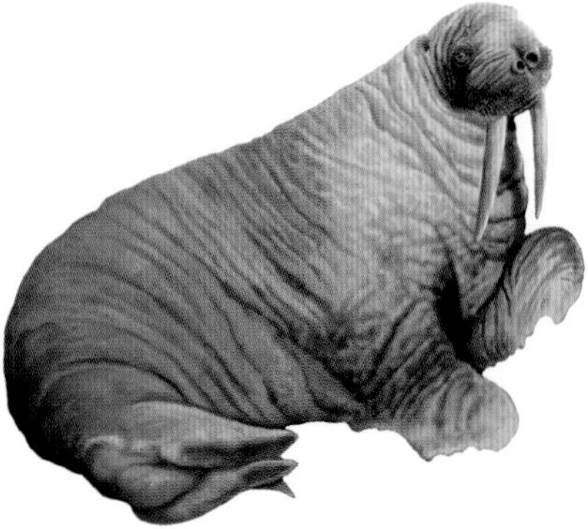

walrus
morsa *F*
morse *M*
Walross *N*
tricheco *M*

humpback whale
rorcual *M*
rorqual *M*
Buckelwal *M*
balenottera *F*

seal
foca *F*
phoque *M*
Seehund *M*
foca *F*

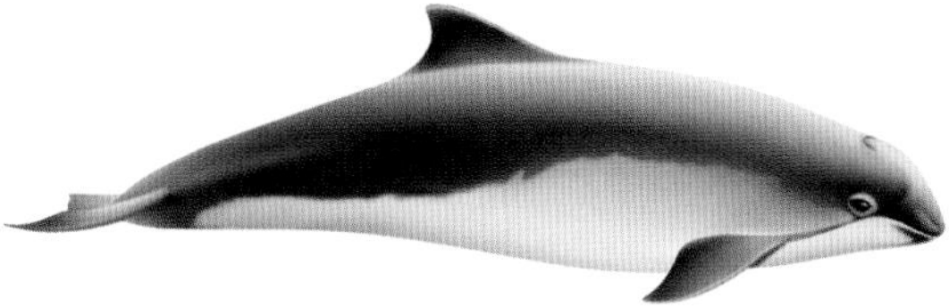

porpoise
marsopa *F*
marsouin *M*
Tümmler *M*
focena *F*

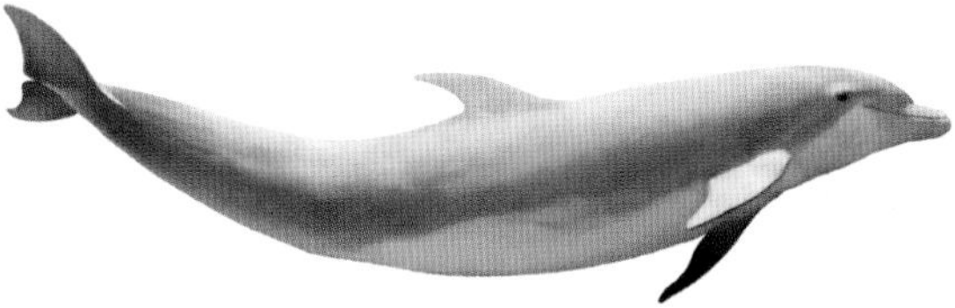

dolphin
delfín *M*
dauphin *M*
Delphin *M*
delfino *M*

narwhal
narval *M*
narval *M*
Narwal *M*
narvalo *M*

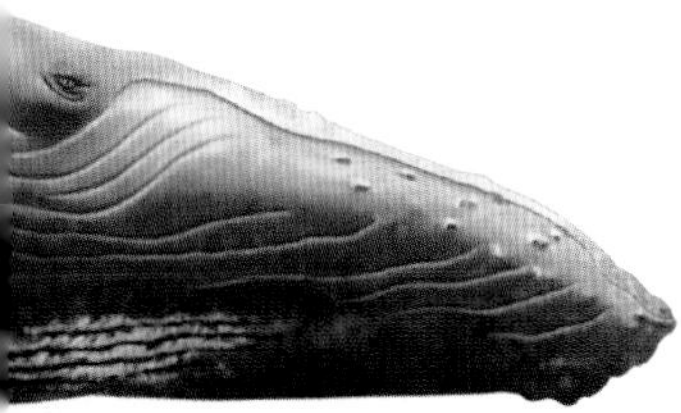

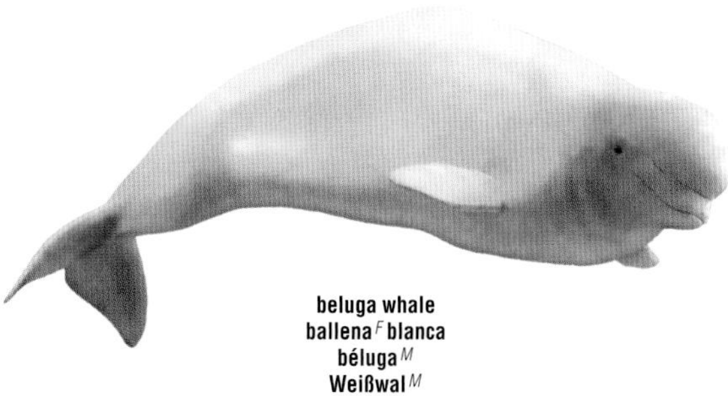

beluga whale
ballena *F* **blanca**
béluga *M*
Weißwal *M*
balena *F* **bianca**

examples of primates

ejemplos^M de primates^M | exemples^M de mammifères^M primates^M | Beispiele^N für Primaten^M | esempi^M di primati^M

tamarin
tamarino^M
tamarin^M
Tamarin^M
tamarino^M

baboon
babuino^M
babouin^M
Pavian^M
babbuino^M

orangutan
orangután^M
orang-outan^M
Orang-Utan^M
orangotango^M

macaque
macaco^M
macaque^M
Makak^M
macaco^M

marmoset
tití *M*
ouistiti *M*
Pinseläffchen *N*
uistitì *M*

lemur
lémur *M*
lémurien *M*
Lemure *M*
lemure *M*

gibbon
gibón *M*
gibbon *M*
Gibbon *M*
gibbone *M*

chimpanzee
chimpancé *M*
chimpanzé *M*
Schimpanse *M*
scimpanzé *M*

gorilla

gorila^{M} | gorille^{M} | Gorilla^{M} | gorilla^{M}

morphology of a gorilla
morfología^{F} de un gorila^{M}
morphologie^{F} du gorille^{M}
äußere Merkmale^{N} eines Gorillas^{M}
morfologia^{F} di un gorilla^{M}

face
cara F
face F
Gesicht N
muso M
arm
brazo M
bras M
Arm M
braccio M
fur
pelaje M
pelage M
Behaarung F
pelliccia F
opposable thumb
pulgar M oponible
pouce M opposable
opponierbarer Daumen M
pollice M opponibile
leg
pata F
jambe F
Bein N
gamba F
prehensile digit
dedos M prensiles
doigt M préhensile
Greiffinger M
dito M prensile
hand
mano F
main F
Hand F
mano F
foot
pie M
pied M
Fuß M
piede M

examples of marsupials

ejemplos[M] de marsupiales[M] | exemples[M] de marsupiaux[M] | Beispiele[N] für Beuteltiere[N] | esempi[M] di marsupiali[M]

Tasmanian devil
diablo[M] de Tasmania[F]
diable[M] de Tasmanie[F]
Tasmanischer Teufel[M]
diavolo[M] della Tasmania[F]

opossum
oposum[M]
opossum[M]
Opossum[N]
opossum[M]

wallaby
walaby[M]
wallaby[M]
Wallaby[N]
wallaby[M]

kangaroo
canguro[M]
kangourou[M]
Känguru[N]
canguro[M]

koala
koala[F]
koala[M]
Koala[M]
koala[M]

kangaroo

canguro M | kangourou M | Känguru N | canguro M

morphology of a kangaroo
morfología F de un canguro M
morphologie F du kangourou M
äußere Merkmale N eines Kängurus N
morfologia F di un canguro M

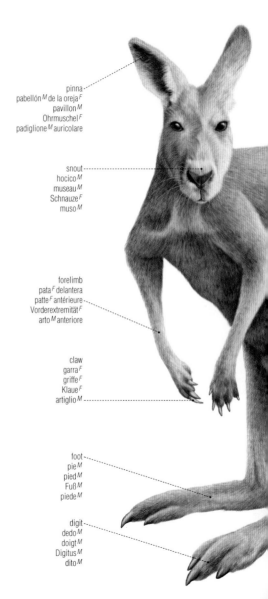

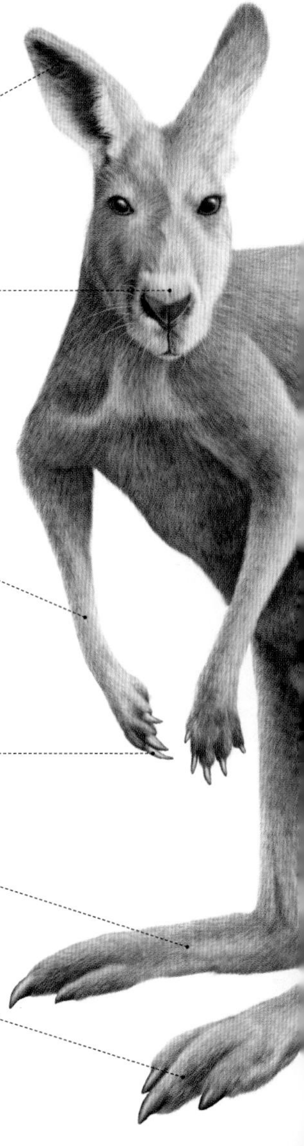
pinna
pabellón M de la oreja F
pavillon M
Ohrmuschel F
padiglione M auricolare
snout
hocico M
museau M
Schnauze F
muso M
forelimb
pata F delantera
patte F antérieure
Vorderextremität F
arto M anteriore
claw
garra F
griffe F
Klaue F
artiglio M
foot
pie M
pied M
Fuß M
piede M
digit
dedo M
doigt M
Digitus M
dito M

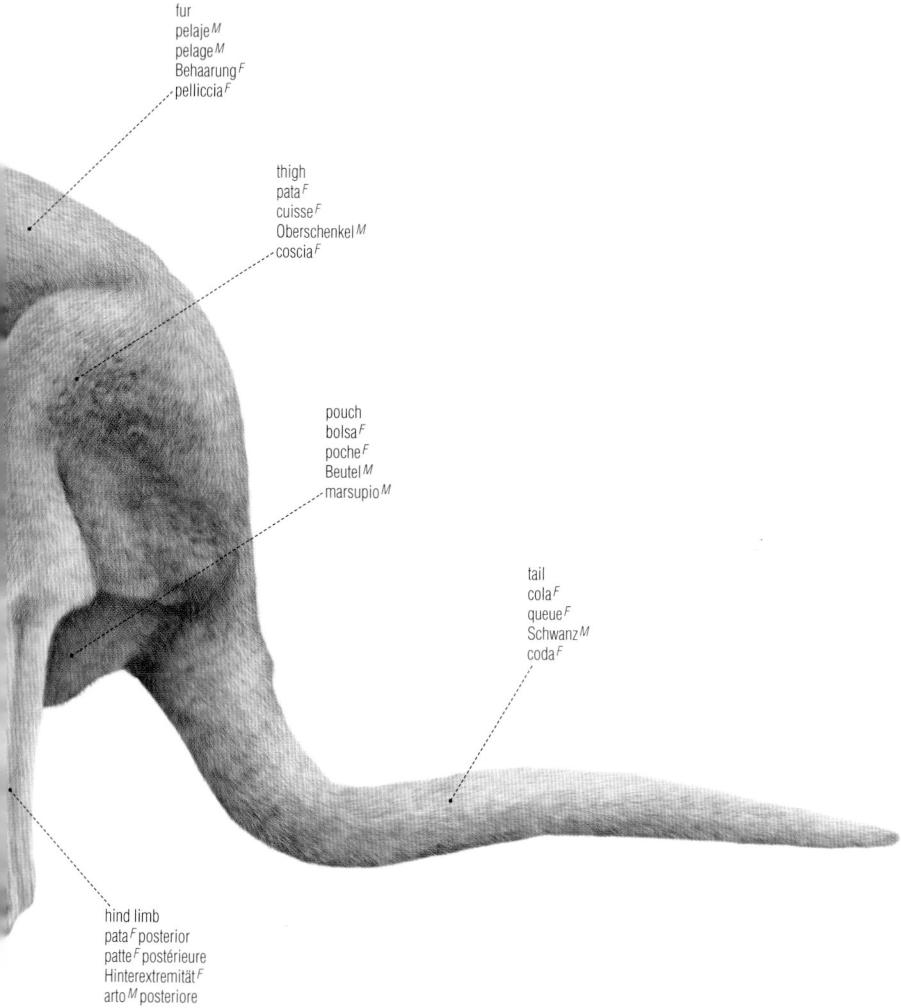
fur
pelaje M
pelage M
Behaarung F
pelliccia F
thigh
pata F
cuisse F
Oberschenkel M
coscia F
pouch
bolsa F
poche F
Beutel M
marsupio M
tail
cola F
queue F
Schwanz M
coda F
hind limb
pata F posterior
patte F postérieure
Hinterextremität F
arto M posteriore

bat

murciélago^{M} | chauve-souris^{F} | Fledermaus^{F} | pipistrello^{M}

morphology of a bat
morfología^{F} de un murciélago^{M}
morphologie^{F} de la chauve-souris^{F}
äußere Merkmale^{N} einer Fledermaus^{F}
morfologia^{F} di un pipistrello^{M}

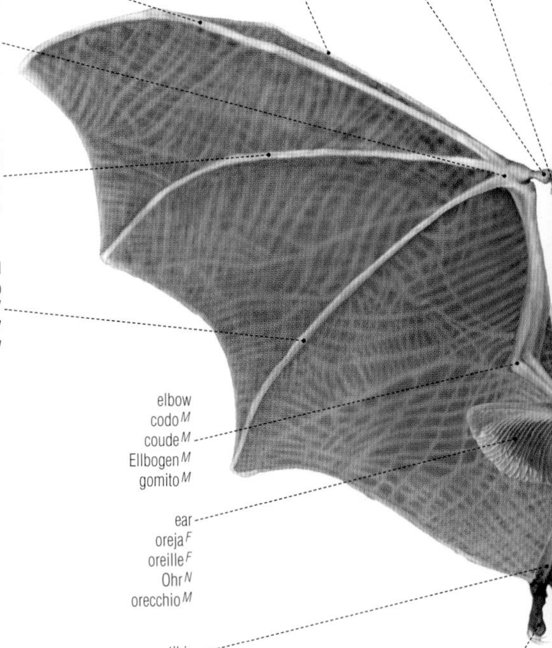

thumb
pulgar^{M}
pouce^{M}
Daumen^{M}
pollice^{M}

claw
uña^{F}
griffe^{F}
Klaue^{F}
unghia^{F}

2nd metacarpal
2° hueso^{M} metacarpiano
2e métacarpien^{M}
2. Finger^{M}
2° metacarpale^{M}

3rd metacarpal
3er hueso^{M} metacarpiano
3e métacarpien^{M}
3. Finger^{M}
3° metacarpale^{M}

wrist
muñeca^{F}
poignet^{M}
Handgelenk^{N}
polso^{M}

4th metacarpal
4° hueso^{M} metacarpiano
4e métacarpien^{M}
4. Finger^{M}
4° metacarpale^{M}

5th metacarpal
5° hueso^{M} metacarpiano
5e métacarpien^{M}
5. Finger^{M}
5° metacarpale^{M}

elbow
codo^{M}
coude^{M}
Ellbogen^{M}
gomito^{M}

ear
oreja^{F}
oreille^{F}
Ohr^{N}
orecchio^{M}

tibia
tibia^{F}
tibia^{M}
Unterschenkel^{M}
tibia^{F}

foot
pie^{M}
pied^{M}
Fuß^{M}
piede^{M}

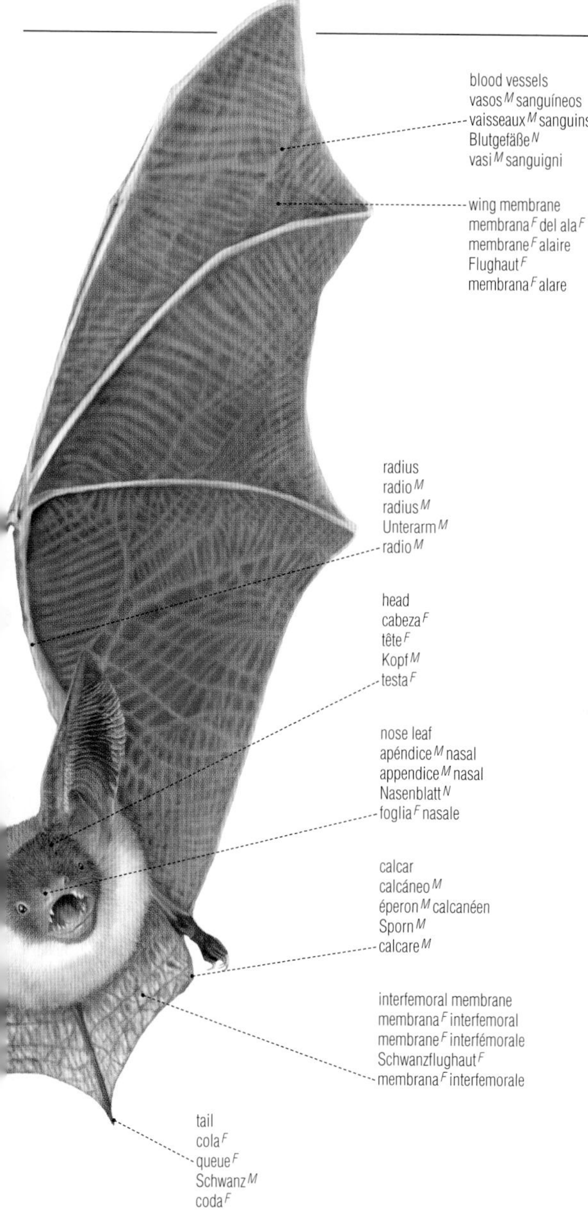
blood vessels
vasos M sanguíneos
vaisseaux M sanguins
Blutgefäße N
vasi M sanguigni
wing membrane
membrana F del ala F
membrane F alaire
Flughaut F
membrana F alare
radius
radio M
radius M
Unterarm M
radio M
head
cabeza F
tête F
Kopf M
testa F
nose leaf
apéndice M nasal
appendice M nasal
Nasenblatt N
foglia F nasale
calcar
calcáneo M
éperon M calcanéen
Sporn M
calcare M
interfemoral membrane
membrana F interfemoral
membrane F interfémorale
Schwanzflughaut F
membrana F interfemorale
tail
cola F
queue F
Schwanz M
coda F

wings
alas F
ailes F
Flügel M
ali F

man

hombre^{M} | homme^{M} | Mann^{M} | uomo^{M}

anterior view
vista^{F} anterior
face^{F} antérieure
Vorderansicht^{F}
vista^{F} anteriore

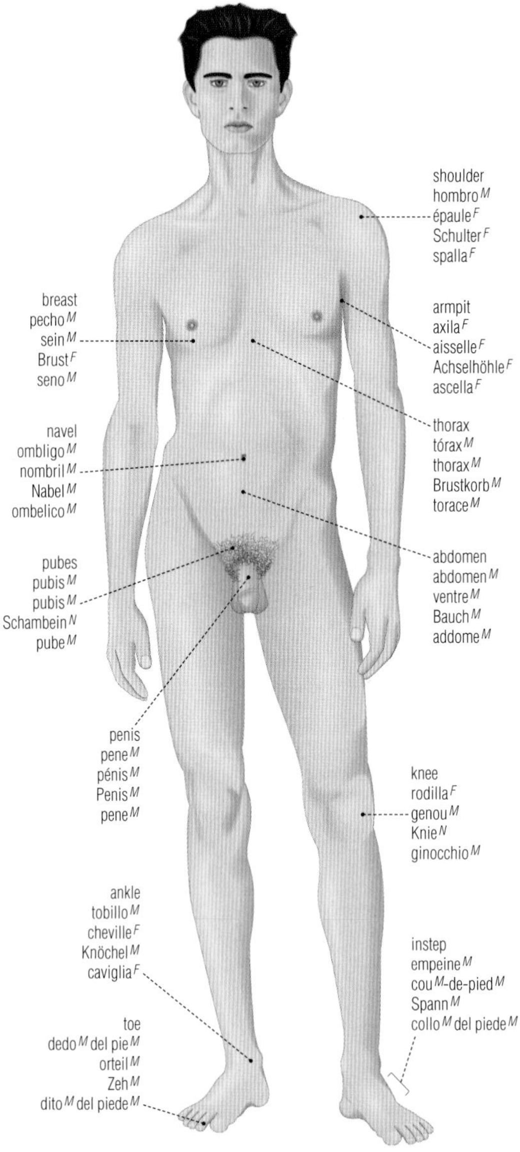
shoulder
hombro^{M}
épaule^{F}
Schulter^{F}
spalla^{F}
breast
pecho^{M}
sein^{M}
Brust^{F}
seno^{M}
armpit
axila^{F}
aisselle^{F}
Achselhöhle^{F}
ascella^{F}
thorax
tórax^{M}
thorax^{M}
Brustkorb^{M}
torace^{M}
navel
ombligo^{M}
nombril^{M}
Nabel^{M}
ombelico^{M}
abdomen
abdomen^{M}
ventre^{M}
Bauch^{M}
addome^{M}
pubes
pubis^{M}
pubis^{M}
Schambein^{N}
pube^{M}
penis
pene^{M}
pénis^{M}
Penis^{M}
pene^{M}
knee
rodilla^{F}
genou^{M}
Knie^{N}
ginocchio^{M}
ankle
tobillo^{M}
cheville^{F}
Knöchel^{M}
caviglia^{F}
instep
empeine^{M}
cou^{M}-de-pied^{M}
Spann^{M}
collo^{M} del piede^{M}
toe
dedo^{M} del pie^{M}
orteil^{M}
Zeh^{M}
dito^{M} del piede^{M}

face
cara *F*
visage *M*
Gesicht *N*
faccia *F*

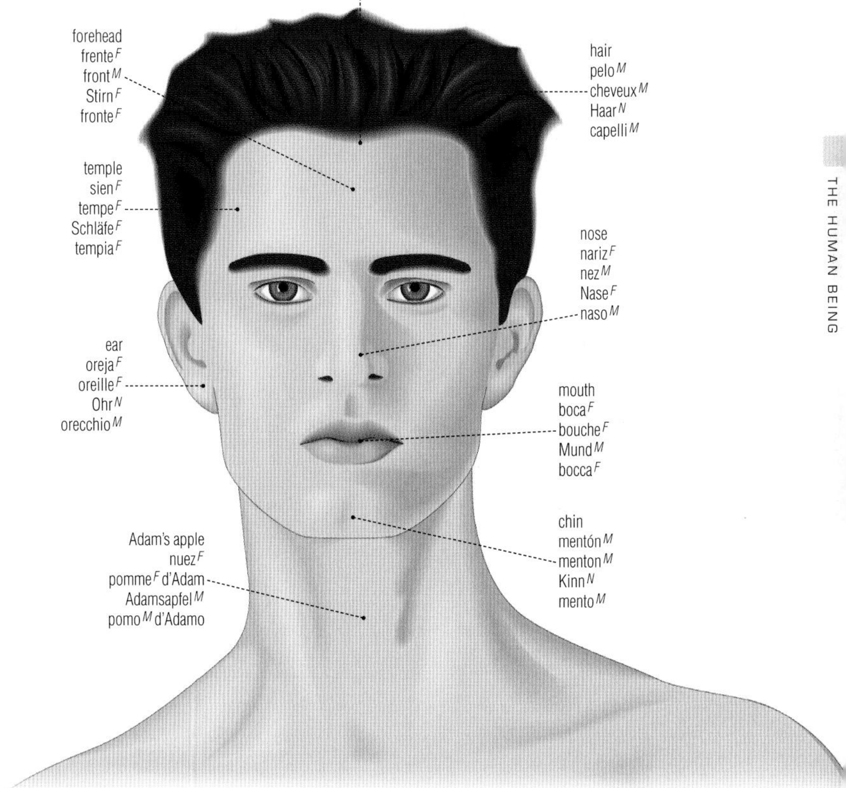
skull
cráneo M
crâne M
Schädel M
cranio M
forehead
frente F
front M
Stirn F
fronte F
hair
pelo M
cheveux M
Haar N
capelli M
temple
sien F
tempe F
Schläfe F
tempia F
nose
nariz F
nez M
Nase F
naso M
ear
oreja F
oreille F
Ohr N
orecchio M
mouth
boca F
bouche F
Mund M
bocca F
chin
mentón M
menton M
Kinn N
mento M
Adam's apple
nuez F
pomme F d'Adam
Adamsapfel M
pomo M d'Adamo

man

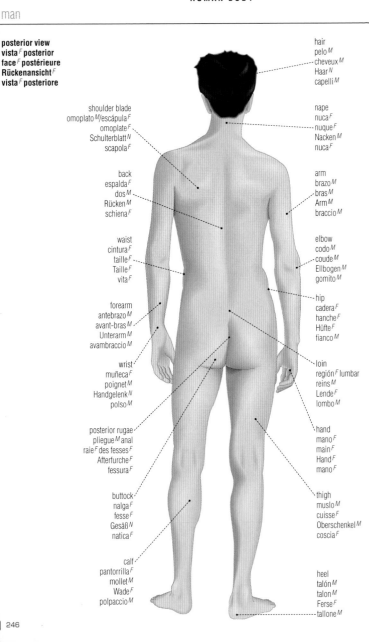

posterior view
vista[F] posterior
face[F] postérieure
Rückenansicht[F]
vista[F] posteriore

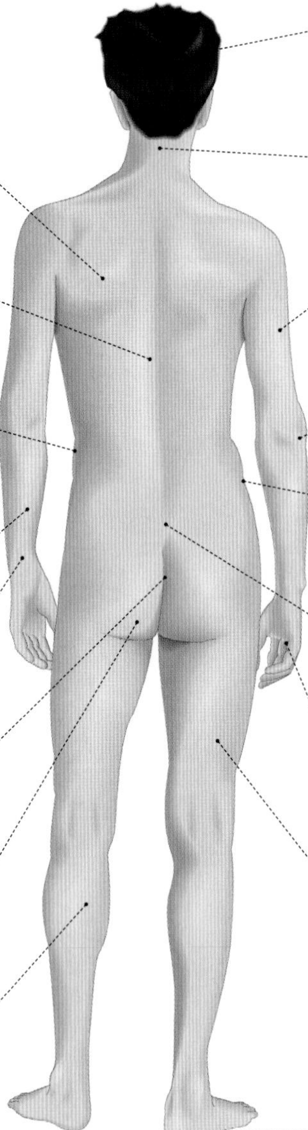
shoulder blade
omoplato[M]/escápula[F]
omoplate[F]
Schulterblatt[N]
scapola[F]
back
espalda[F]
dos[M]
Rücken[M]
schiena[F]
waist
cintura[F]
taille[F]
Taille[F]
vita[F]
forearm
antebrazo[M]
avant-bras[M]
Unterarm[M]
avambraccio[M]
wrist
muñeca[F]
poignet[M]
Handgelenk[N]
polso[M]
posterior rugae
pliegue[M] anal
raie[F] des fesses[F]
Afterfurche[F]
fessura[F]
buttock
nalga[F]
fesse[F]
Gesäß[N]
natica[F]
calf
pantorrilla[F]
mollet[M]
Wade[F]
polpaccio[M]
hair
pelo[M]
cheveux[M]
Haar[N]
capelli[M]
nape
nuca[F]
nuque[F]
Nacken[M]
nuca[F]
arm
brazo[M]
bras[M]
Arm[M]
braccio[M]
elbow
codo[M]
coude[M]
Ellbogen[M]
gomito[M]
hip
cadera[F]
hanche[F]
Hüfte[F]
fianco[M]
loin
región[F] lumbar
reins[M]
Lende[F]
lombo[M]
hand
mano[F]
main[F]
Hand[F]
mano[F]
thigh
muslo[M]
cuisse[F]
Oberschenkel[M]
coscia[F]
heel
talón[M]
talon[M]
Ferse[F]
tallone[M]

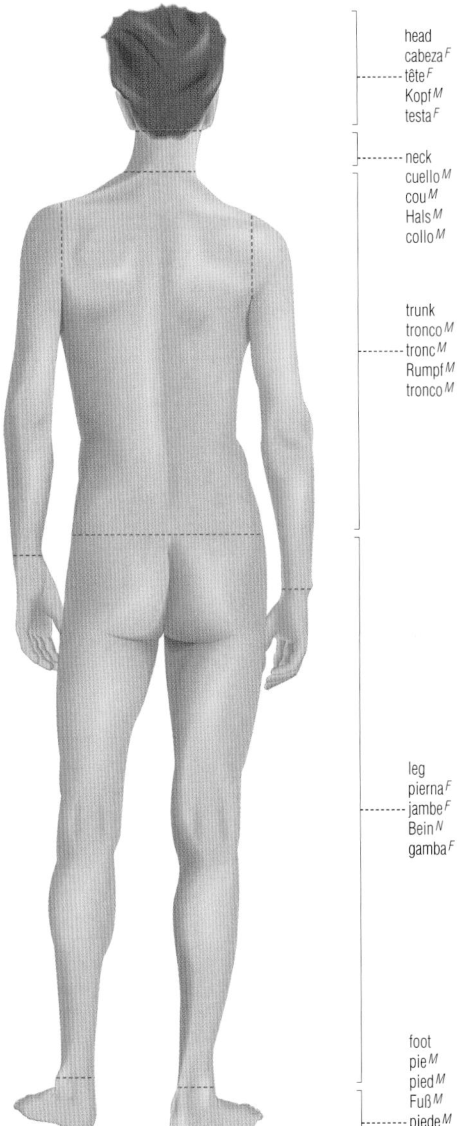
head
cabeza F
tête F
Kopf M
testa F
neck
cuello M
cou M
Hals M
collo M
trunk
tronco M
tronc M
Rumpf M
tronco M
leg
pierna F
jambe F
Bein N
gamba F
foot
pie M
pied M
Fuß M
piede M

woman

mujer^F | femme^F | Frau^F | donna^F

anterior view
vista^F anterior
face^F antérieure
Vorderansicht^F
vista^F anteriore

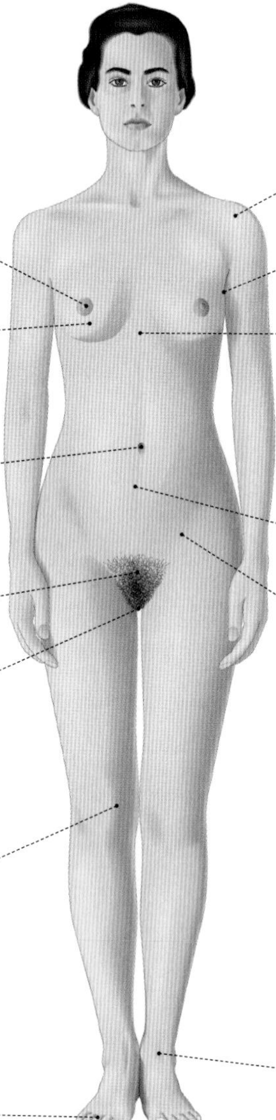

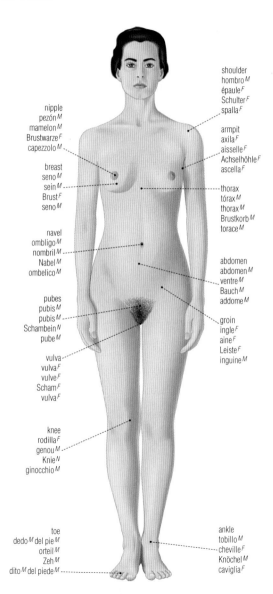

shoulder
hombro^M
épaule^F
Schulter^F
spalla^F
nipple
pezón^M
mamelon^M
Brustwarze^F
capezzolo^M
armpit
axila^F
aisselle^F
Achselhöhle^F
ascella^F
breast
seno^M
sein^M
Brust^F
seno^M
thorax
tórax^M
thorax^M
Brustkorb^M
torace^M
navel
ombligo^M
nombril^M
Nabel^M
ombelico^M
abdomen
abdomen^M
ventre^M
Bauch^M
addome^M
pubes
pubis^M
pubis^M
Schambein^N
pube^M
groin
ingle^F
aine^F
Leiste^F
inguine^M
vulva
vulva^F
vulve^F
Scham^F
vulva^F
knee
rodilla^F
genou^M
Knie^N
ginocchio^M
toe
dedo^M del pie^M
orteil^M
Zeh^M
dito^M del piede^M
ankle
tobillo^M
cheville^F
Knöchel^M
caviglia^F

face
cara F
visage M
Gesicht N
faccia F

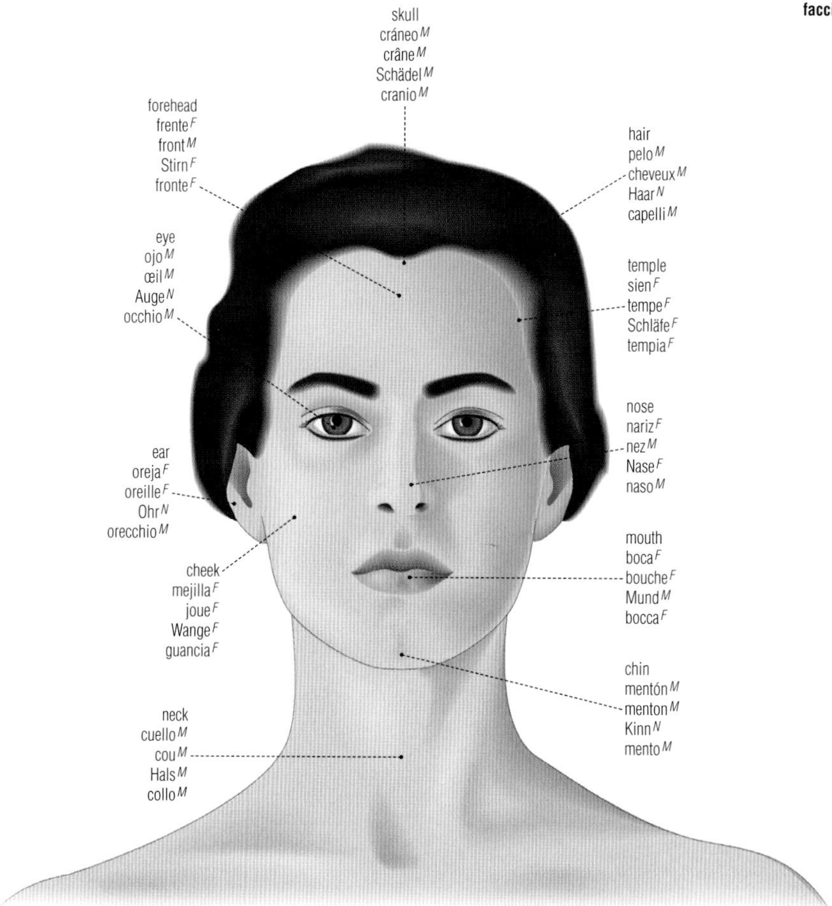
skull
cráneo M
crâne M
Schädel M
cranio M
forehead
frente F
front M
Stirn F
fronte F
hair
pelo M
cheveux M
Haar N
capelli M
eye
ojo M
œil M
Auge N
occhio M
temple
sien F
tempe F
Schläfe F
tempia F
nose
nariz F
nez M
Nase F
naso M
ear
oreja F
oreille F
Ohr N
orecchio M
mouth
boca F
bouche F
Mund M
bocca F
cheek
mejilla F
joue F
Wange F
guancia F
chin
mentón M
menton M
Kinn N
mento M
neck
cuello M
cou M
Hals M
collo M

woman

posterior view
vista[F] posterior
face[F] postérieure
Rückenansicht[F]
vista[F] posteriore

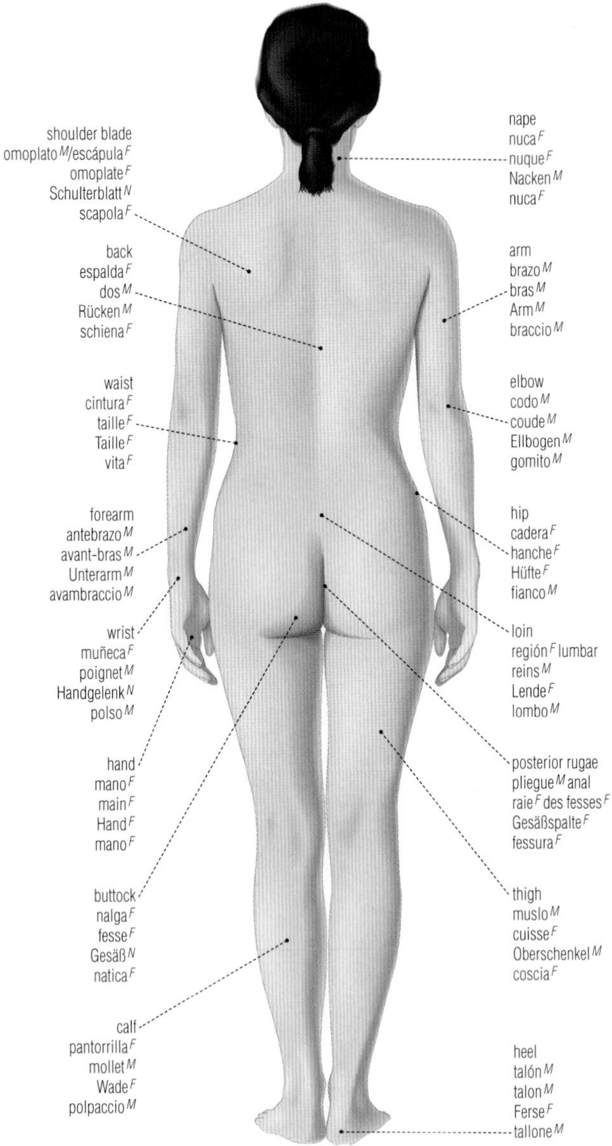

shoulder blade
omoplato[M]/escápula[F]
omoplate[F]
Schulterblatt[N]
scapola[F]
back
espalda[F]
dos[M]
Rücken[M]
schiena[F]
waist
cintura[F]
taille[F]
Taille[F]
vita[F]
forearm
antebrazo[M]
avant-bras[M]
Unterarm[M]
avambraccio[M]
wrist
muñeca[F]
poignet[M]
Handgelenk[N]
polso[M]
hand
mano[F]
main[F]
Hand[F]
mano[F]
buttock
nalga[F]
fesse[F]
Gesäß[N]
natica[F]
calf
pantorrilla[F]
mollet[M]
Wade[F]
polpaccio[M]
nape
nuca[F]
nuque[F]
Nacken[M]
nuca[F]
arm
brazo[M]
bras[M]
Arm[M]
braccio[M]
elbow
codo[M]
coude[M]
Ellbogen[M]
gomito[M]
hip
cadera[F]
hanche[F]
Hüfte[F]
fianco[M]
loin
región[F] lumbar
reins[M]
Lende[F]
lombo[M]
posterior rugae
pliegue[M] anal
raie[F] des fesses[F]
Gesäßspalte[F]
fessura[F]
thigh
muslo[M]
cuisse[F]
Oberschenkel[M]
coscia[F]
heel
talón[M]
talon[M]
Ferse[F]
tallone[M]

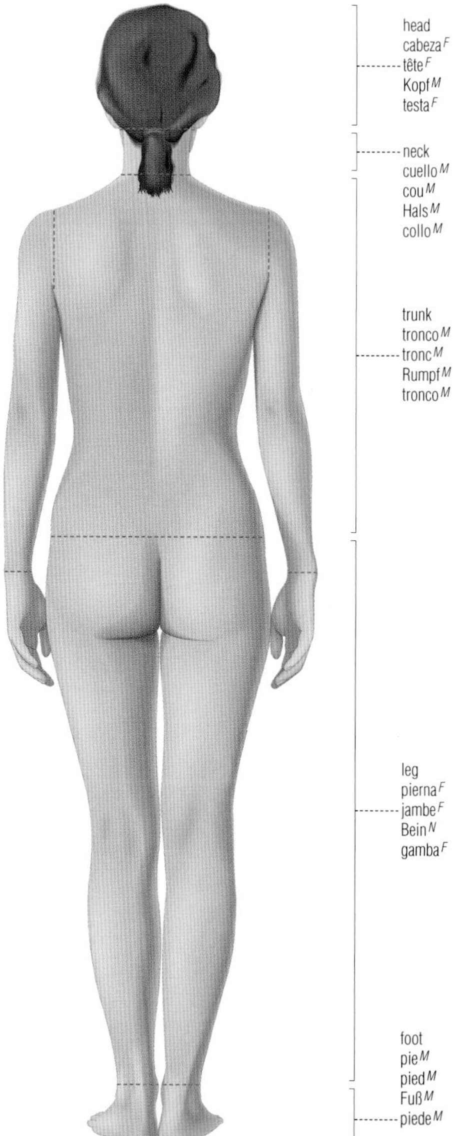
head
cabeza F
tête F
Kopf M
testa F
neck
cuello M
cou M
Hals M
collo M
trunk
tronco M
tronc M
Rumpf M
tronco M
leg
pierna F
jambe F
Bein N
gamba F
foot
pie M
pied M
Fuß M
piede M

muscles

músculos^M | muscles^M | Muskeln^M | muscoli^M

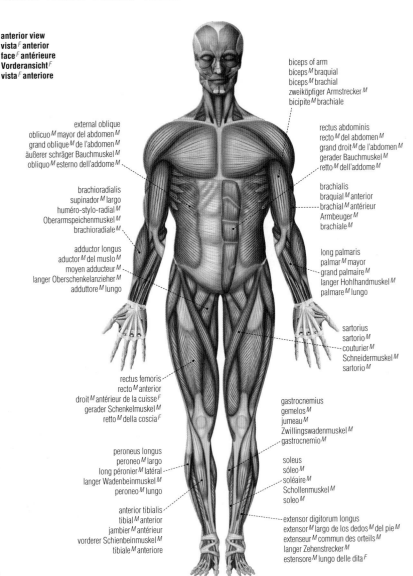

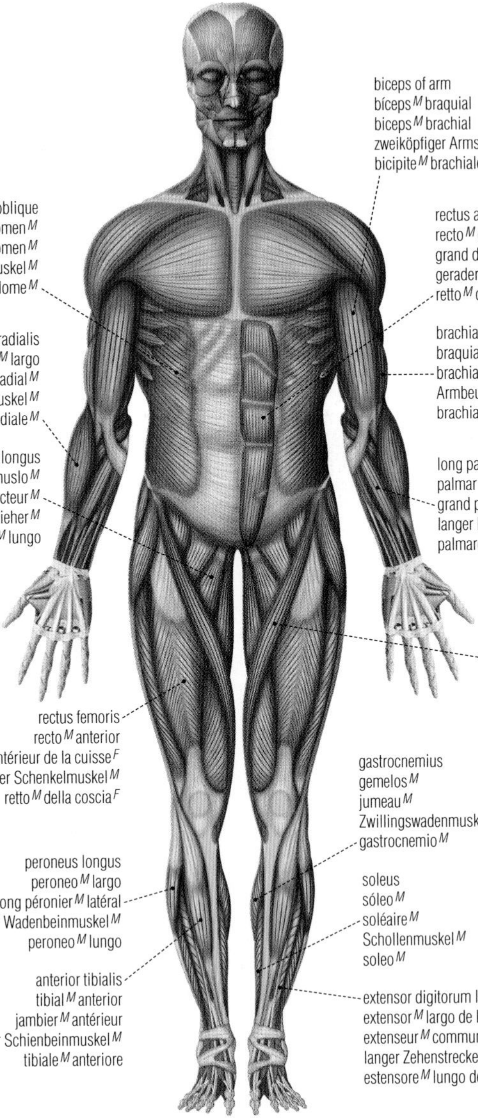
anterior view
vista^F anterior
face^F antérieure
Vorderansicht^F
vista^F anteriore
biceps of arm
bíceps^M braquial
biceps^M brachial
zweiköpfiger Armstrecker^M
bicipite^M brachiale
external oblique
oblicuo^M mayor del abdomen^M
grand oblique^M de l'abdomen^M
äußerer schräger Bauchmuskel^M
obliquo^M esterno dell'addome^M
rectus abdominis
recto^M del abdomen^M
grand droit^M de l'abdomen^M
gerader Bauchmuskel^M
retto^M dell'addome^M
brachioradialis
supinador^M largo
huméro-stylo-radial^M
Oberarmspeichenmuskel^M
brachioradiale^M
brachialis
braquial^M anterior
brachial^M antérieur
Armbeuger^M
brachiale^M
adductor longus
aductor^M del muslo^M
moyen adducteur^M
langer Oberschenkelanzieher^M
adduttore^M lungo
long palmaris
palmar^M mayor
grand palmaire^M
langer Hohlhandmuskel^M
palmare^M lungo
sartorius
sartorio^M
couturier^M
Schneidermuskel^M
sartorio^M
rectus femoris
recto^M anterior
droit^M antérieur de la cuisse^F
gerader Schenkelmuskel^M
retto^M della coscia^F
gastrocnemius
gemelos^M
jumeau^M
Zwillingswadenmuskel^M
gastrocnemio^M
peroneus longus
peroneo^M largo
long péronier^M latéral
langer Wadenbeinmuskel^M
peroneo^M lungo
soleus
sóleo^M
soléaire^M
Schollenmuskel^M
soleo^M
anterior tibialis
tibial^M anterior
jambier^M antérieur
vorderer Schienbeinmuskel^M
tibiale^M anteriore
extensor digitorum longus
extensor^M largo de los dedos^M del pie^M
extenseur^M commun des orteils^M
langer Zehenstrecker^M
estensore^M lungo delle dita^F

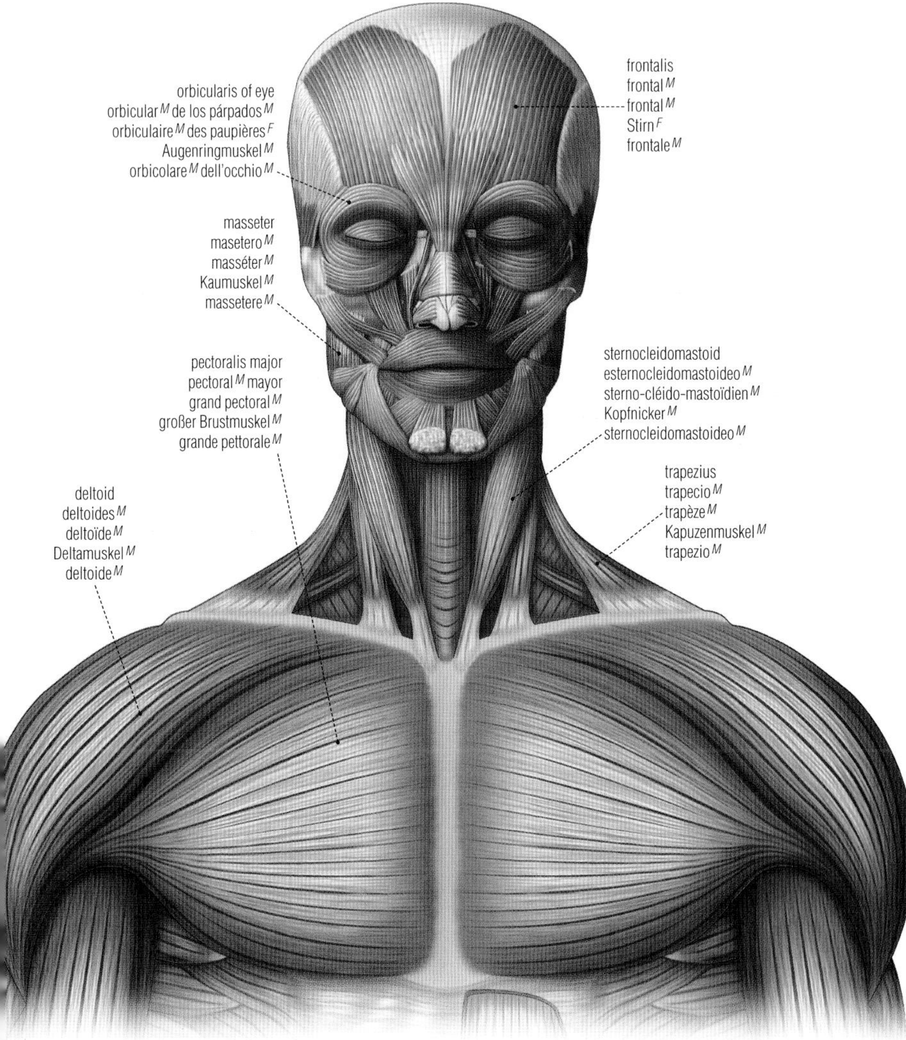
orbicularis of eye
orbicular M de los párpados M
orbiculaire M des paupières F
Augenringmuskel M
orbicolare M dell'occhio M
masseter
masetero M
masséter M
Kaumuskel M
massetere M
pectoralis major
pectoral M mayor
grand pectoral M
großer Brustmuskel M
grande pettorale M
deltoid
deltoides M
deltoïde M
Deltamuskel M
deltoide M
frontalis
frontal M
frontal M
Stirn F
frontale M
sternocleidomastoid
esternocleidomastoideo M
sterno-cléido-mastoïdien M
Kopfnicker M
sternocleidomastoideo M
trapezius
trapecio M
trapèze M
Kapuzenmuskel M
trapezio M

muscles

posterior view
vista[F] posterior
face[F] postérieure
Rückansicht[F]
vista[F] posteriore

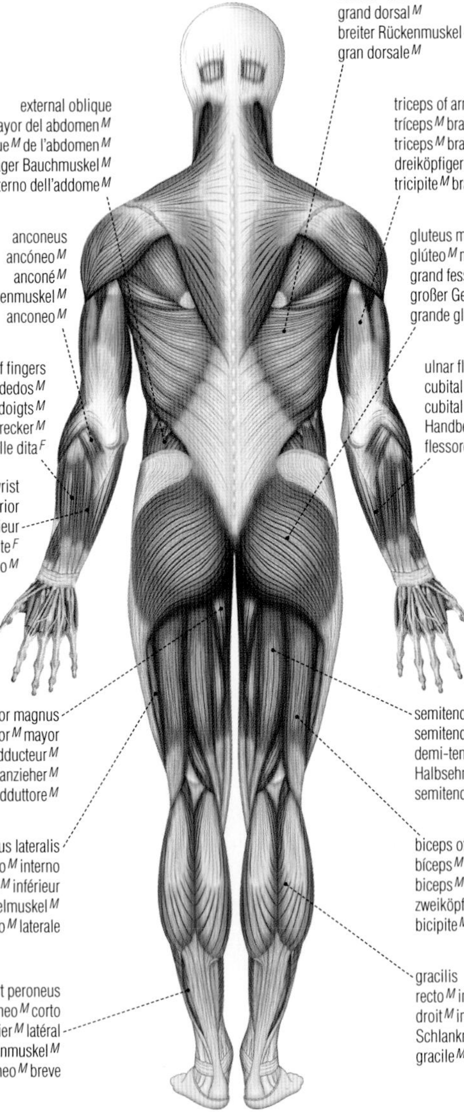

latissimus dorsi
dorsal[M] ancho
grand dorsal[M]
breiter Rückenmuskel[M]
gran dorsale[M]
external oblique
oblicuo[M] mayor del abdomen[M]
grand oblique[M] de l'abdomen[M]
äußerer schräger Bauchmuskel[M]
obliquo[M] esterno dell'addome[M]
triceps of arm
tríceps[M] braquial
triceps[M] brachial
dreiköpfiger Armstrecker[M]
tricipite[M] brachiale
anconeus
ancóneo[M]
anconé[M]
Knorrenmuskel[M]
anconeo[M]
gluteus maximus
glúteo[M] mayor
grand fessier[M]
großer Gesäßmuskel[M]
grande gluteo[M]
common extensor of fingers
extensor[M] común de los dedos[M]
extenseur[M] commun des doigts[M]
gemeinsamer Fingerstrecker[M]
estensore[M] comune delle dita[F]
ulnar flexor of wrist
cubital[M] anterior
cubital[M] antérieur
Handbeuger[M] der Ellenseite[F]
flessore[M] ulnare del carpo[M]
ulnar extensor of wrist
cubital[M] posterior
cubital[M] postérieur
Handstrecker[M] der Ellenseite[F]
estensore[M] ulnare del carpo[M]
adductor magnus
aductor[M] mayor
grand adducteur[M]
großer Oberschenkelanzieher[M]
grande adduttore[M]
semitendinosus
semitendinoso[M]
demi-tendineux[M]
Halbsehnenmuskel[M]
semitendinoso[M]
vastus lateralis
vasto[M] interno
vaste[M] externe du membre[M] inférieur
äußerer Schenkelmuskel[M]
vasto[M] laterale
biceps of thigh
bíceps[M] femoral
biceps[M] crural
zweiköpfiger Schenkelmuskel[M]
bicipite[M] femorale
short peroneus
peroneo[M] corto
court péronier[M] latéral
kurzer Wadenbeinmuskel[M]
peroneo[M] breve
gracilis
recto[M] interno del muslo[M]
droit[M] interne
Schlankmuskel[M]
gracile[M]

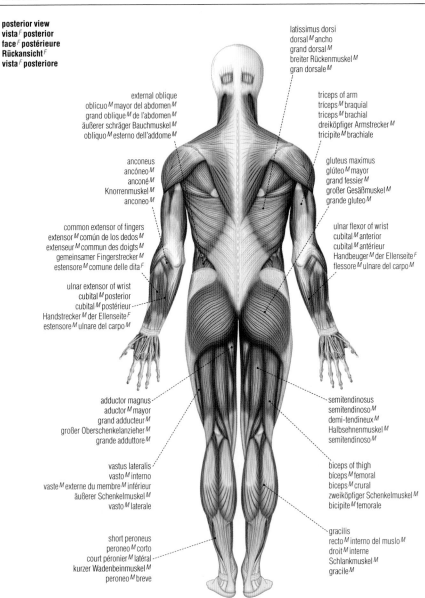

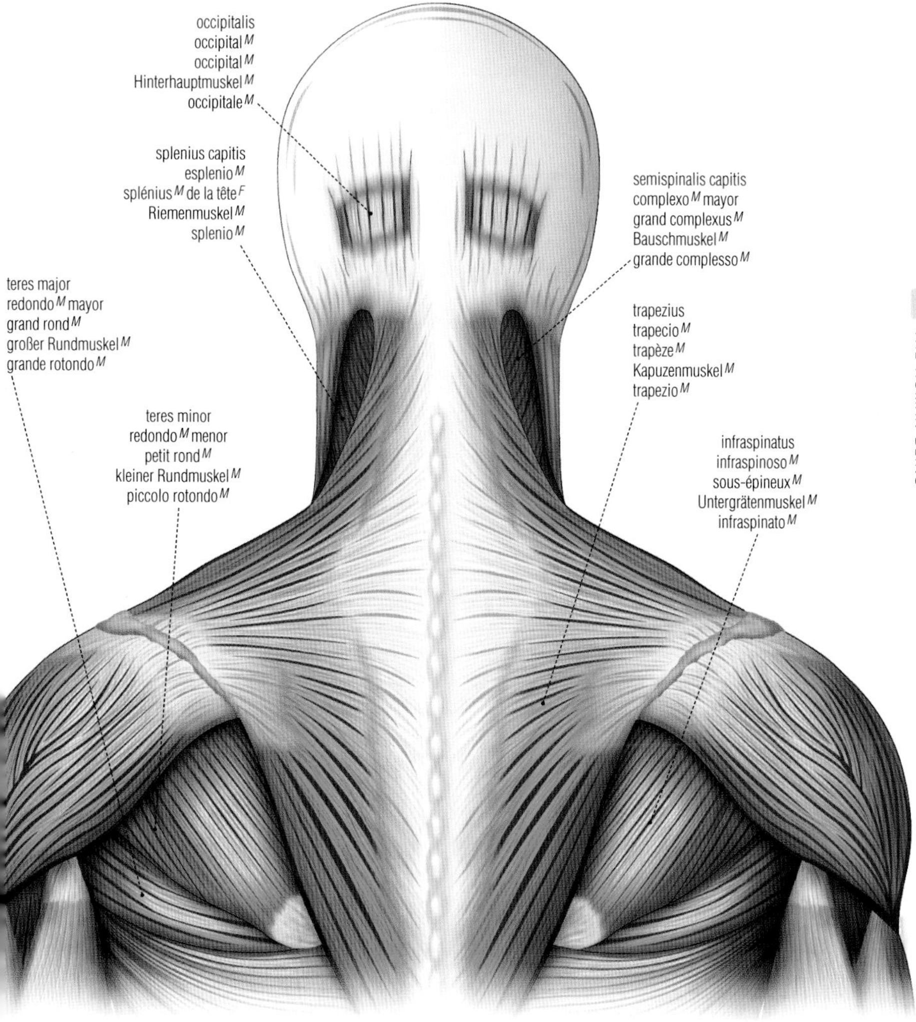
occipitalis
occipital M
occipital M
Hinterhauptmuskel M
occipitale M
splenius capitis
esplenio M
splénius M de la tête F
Riemenmuskel M
splenio M
semispinalis capitis
complexo M mayor
grand complexus M
Bauschmuskel M
grande complesso M
teres major
redondo M mayor
grand rond M
großer Rundmuskel M
grande rotondo M
trapezius
trapecio M
trapèze M
Kapuzenmuskel M
trapezio M
teres minor
redondo M menor
petit rond M
kleiner Rundmuskel M
piccolo rotondo M
infraspinatus
infraspinoso M
sous-épineux M
Untergrätenmuskel M
infraspinato M

skeleton

esqueleto[M] | squelette[M] | Skelett[N] | scheletro[M]

anterior view
vista[F] anterior
vue[F] antérieure
Vorderansicht[F]
vista[F] anteriore

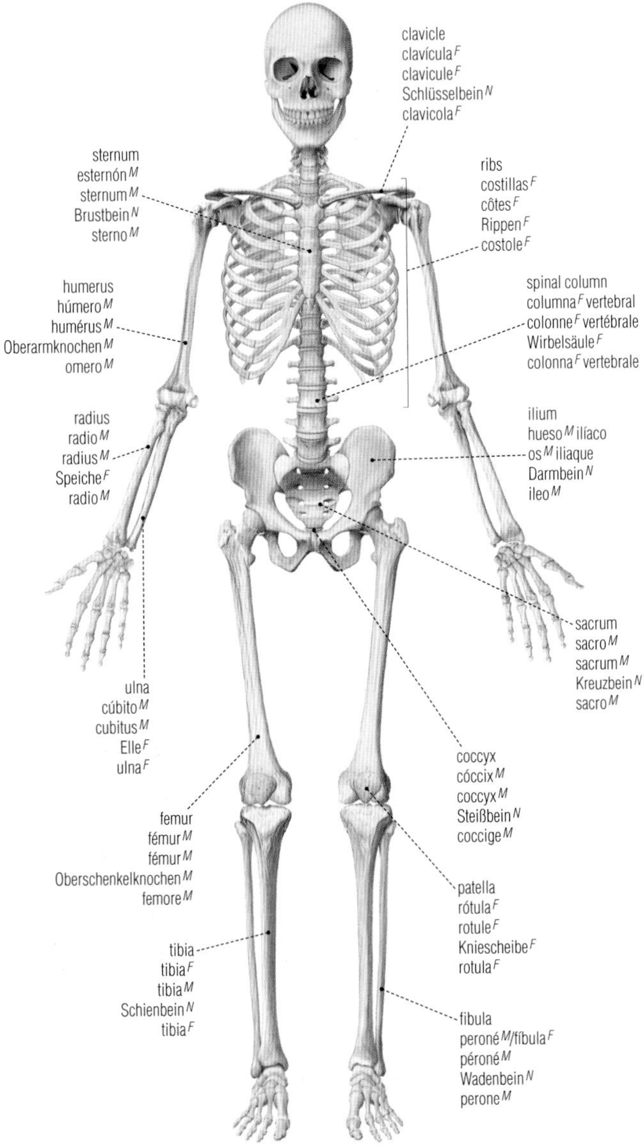
clavicle
clavícula F
clavicule F
Schlüsselbein N
clavicola F
sternum
esternón M
sternum M
Brustbein N
sterno M
ribs
costillas F
côtes F
Rippen F
costole F
humerus
húmero M
humérus M
Oberarmknochen M
omero M
spinal column
columna F vertebral
colonne F vertébrale
Wirbelsäule F
colonna F vertebrale
radius
radio M
radius M
Speiche F
radio M
ilium
hueso M ilíaco
os M iliaque
Darmbein N
ileo M
sacrum
sacro M
sacrum M
Kreuzbein N
sacro M
ulna
cúbito M
cubitus M
Elle F
ulna F
coccyx
cóccix M
coccyx M
Steißbein N
coccige M
femur
fémur M
fémur M
Oberschenkelknochen M
femore M
patella
rótula F
rotule F
Kniescheibe F
rotula F
tibia
tibia F
tibia M
Schienbein N
tibia F
fibula
peroné M/fíbula F
péroné M
Wadenbein N
perone M

skeleton

posterior view
vista^{F} posterior
vue^{F} postérieure
Rückansicht^{F}
vista^{F} posteriore

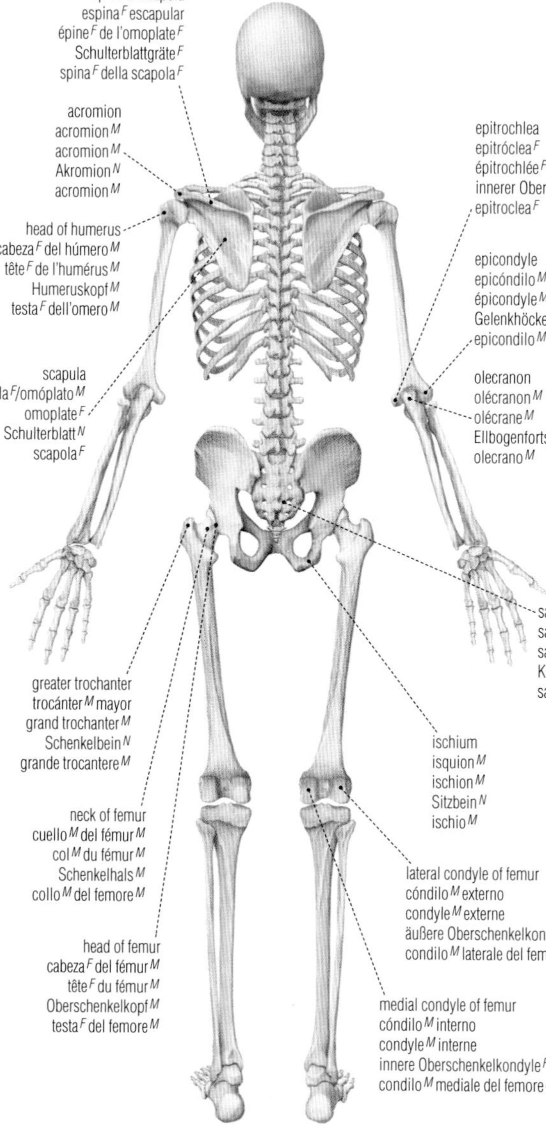
spine of scapula
espina^{F} escapular
épine^{F} de l'omoplate^{F}
Schulterblattgräte^{F}
spina^{F} della scapola^{F}
acromion
acromion^{M}
acromion^{M}
Akromion^{N}
acromion^{M}
head of humerus
cabeza^{F} del húmero^{M}
tête^{F} de l'humérus^{M}
Humeruskopf^{M}
testa^{F} dell'omero^{M}
scapula
escápula^{F}/omóplato^{M}
omoplate^{F}
Schulterblatt^{N}
scapola^{F}
greater trochanter
trocánter^{M} mayor
grand trochanter^{M}
Schenkelbein^{N}
grande trocantere^{M}
neck of femur
cuello^{M} del fémur^{M}
col^{M} du fémur^{M}
Schenkelhals^{M}
collo^{M} del femore^{M}
head of femur
cabeza^{F} del fémur^{M}
tête^{F} du fémur^{M}
Oberschenkelkopf^{M}
testa^{F} del femore^{M}
epitrochlea
epitróclea^{F}
épitrochlée^{F}
innerer Oberarmgelenkhöcker^{M}
epitroclea^{F}
epicondyle
epicóndilo^{M}
épicondyle^{M}
Gelenkhöcker^{M}
epicondilo^{M}
olecranon
olécranon^{M}
olécrane^{M}
Ellbogenfortsatz^{M}
olecrano^{M}
sacrum
sacro^{M}
sacrum^{M}
Kreuzbein^{N}
sacro^{M}
ischium
isquion^{M}
ischion^{M}
Sitzbein^{N}
ischio^{M}
lateral condyle of femur
cóndilo^{M} externo
condyle^{M} externe
äußere Oberschenkelkondyle^{F}
condilo^{M} laterale del femore^{M}
medial condyle of femur
cóndilo^{M} interno
condyle^{M} interne
innere Oberschenkelkondyle^{F}
condilo^{M} mediale del femore^{M}

THE HUMAN BEING

skeleton

hand
huesos *M* de la mano *F*
main *F*
Handknochen *M*
ossa *F* della mano *F*

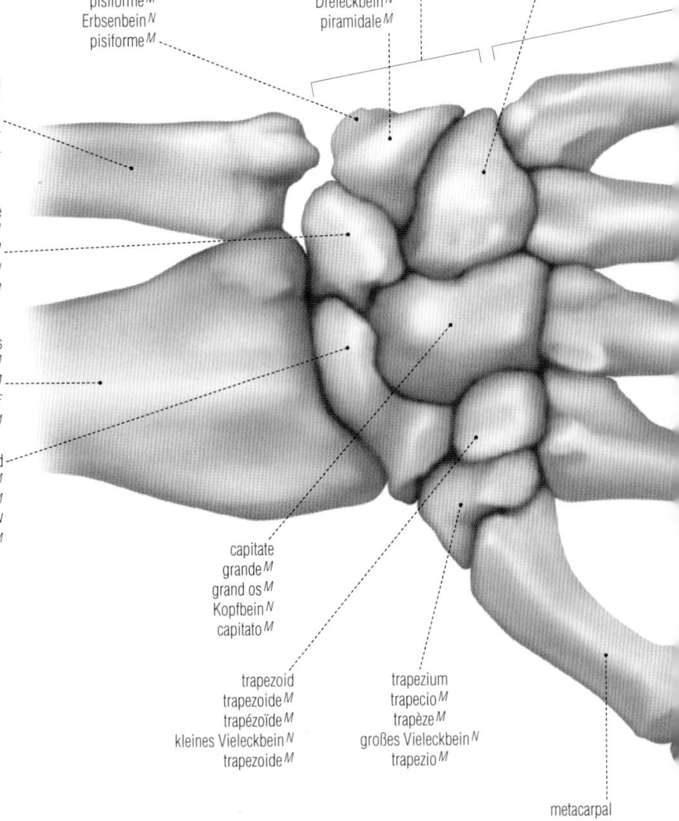
carpus
carpo *M*
carpe *M*
Handwurzel *F*
carpo *M*
hamate
ganchoso *M*
os *M* crochu
Hakenbein *N*
uncinato *M*
triquetral
piramidal *M*
pyramidal *M*
Dreieckbein *N*
piramidale *M*
pisiform
pisiforme *M*
pisiforme *M*
Erbsenbein *N*
pisiforme *M*
ulna
cúbito *M*
cubitus *M*
Elle *F*
ulna *F*
lunate
semilunar *M*
semi-lunaire *M*
Mondbein *N*
semilunare *M*
radius
radio *M*
radius *M*
Speiche *F*
radio *M*
scaphoid
escafoides *M*
scaphoïde *M*
Kahnbein *N*
scafoide *M*
capitate
grande *M*
grand os *M*
Kopfbein *N*
capitato *M*
trapezoid
trapezoide *M*
trapézoïde *M*
kleines Vieleckbein *N*
trapezoide *M*
trapezium
trapecio *M*
trapèze *M*
großes Vieleckbein *N*
trapezio *M*
metacarpal
metacarpiano *M*
métacarpien *M*
Mittelhandknochen *M*
metacarpale *M*

THE HUMAN BEING

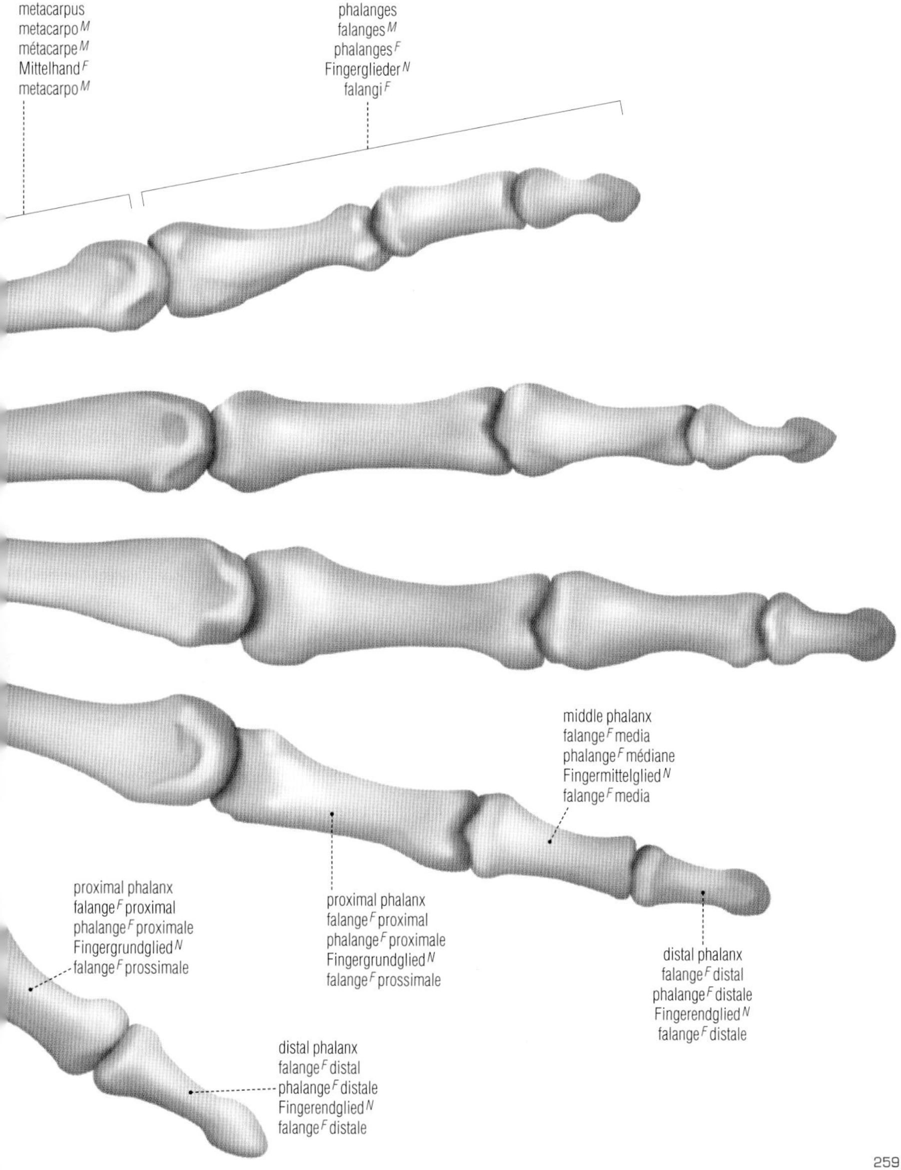
metacarpus
metacarpo M
métacarpe M
Mittelhand F
metacarpo M
phalanges
falanges M
phalanges F
Fingerglieder N
falangi F
middle phalanx
falange F media
phalange F médiane
Fingermittelglied N
falange F media
proximal phalanx
falange F proximal
phalange F proximale
Fingergrundglied N
falange F prossimale
proximal phalanx
falange F proximal
phalange F proximale
Fingergrundglied N
falange F prossimale
distal phalanx
falange F distal
phalange F distale
Fingerendglied N
falange F distale
distal phalanx
falange F distal
phalange F distale
Fingerendglied N
falange F distale

foot
huesos *M* **del pie**
pied *M*
Fußknochen *M*
ossa *F* **del piede** *M*

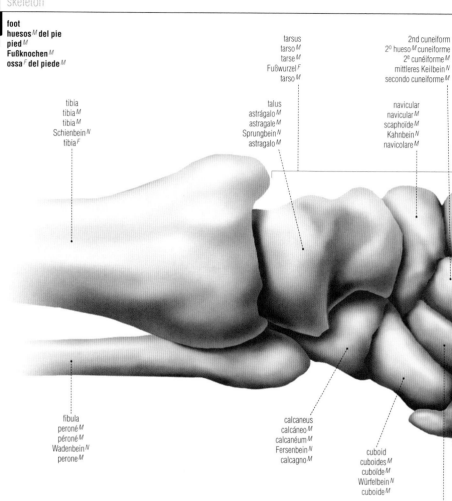

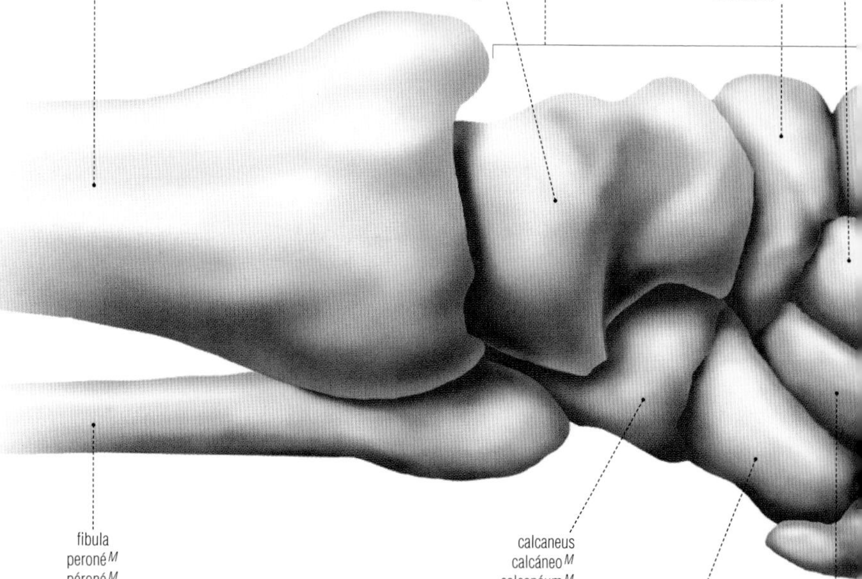
tarsus
tarso M
tarse M
Fußwurzel F
tarso M

2nd cuneiform
2º hueso M cuneiforme
2e cunéiforme M
mittleres Keilbein N
secondo cuneiforme M

tibia
tibia M
tibia M
Schienbein N
tibia F

talus
astrágalo M
astragale M
Sprungbein N
astragalo M

navicular
navicular M
scaphoïde M
Kahnbein N
navicolare M

fibula
peroné M
péroné M
Wadenbein N
perone M

calcaneus
calcáneo M
calcanéum M
Fersenbein N
calcagno M

cuboid
cuboides M
cuboïde M
Würfelbein N
cuboide M

lateral cuneiform
cuneiforme M lateral
3e cunéiforme M
inneres Keilbein N
cuneiforme M laterale

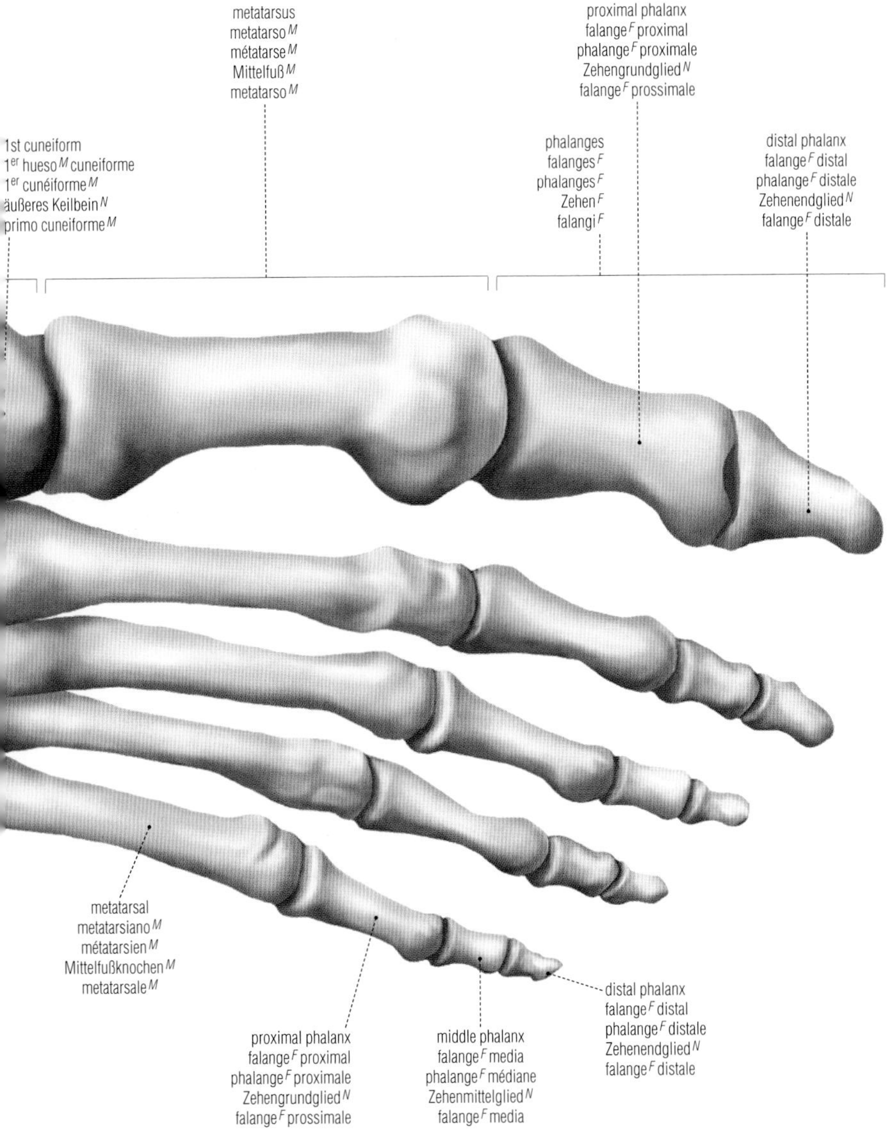
metatarsus
metatarso M
métatarse M
Mittelfuß M
metatarso M
proximal phalanx
falange F proximal
phalange F proximale
Zehengrundglied N
falange F prossimale
1st cuneiform
1er hueso M cuneiforme
1er cunéiforme M
äußeres Keilbein N
primo cuneiforme M
phalanges
falanges F
phalanges F
Zehen F
falangi F
distal phalanx
falange F distal
phalange F distale
Zehenendglied N
falange F distale
metatarsal
metatarsiano M
métatarsien M
Mittelfußknochen M
metatarsale M
distal phalanx
falange F distal
phalange F distale
Zehenendglied N
falange F distale
proximal phalanx
falange F proximal
phalange F proximale
Zehengrundglied N
falange F prossimale
middle phalanx
falange F media
phalange F médiane
Zehenmittelglied N
falange F media

lateral view of skull
vista *F* **lateral del cráneo** *M*
vue *F* **latérale du crâne** *M*
Seitenansicht *F* **eines Schädels** *M*
vista *F* **laterale del cranio** *M*

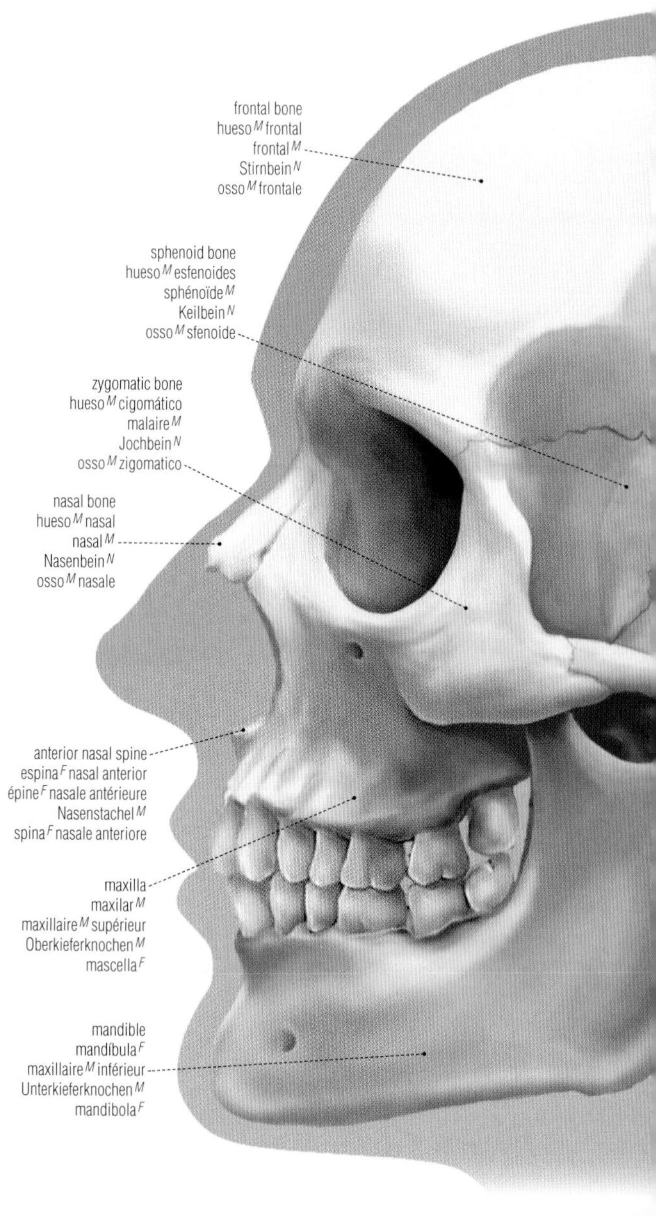

frontal bone
hueso M frontal
frontal M
Stirnbein N
osso M frontale
sphenoid bone
hueso M esfenoides
sphénoïde M
Keilbein N
osso M sfenoide
zygomatic bone
hueso M cigomático
malaire M
Jochbein N
osso M zigomatico
nasal bone
hueso M nasal
nasal M
Nasenbein N
osso M nasale
anterior nasal spine
espina F nasal anterior
épine F nasale antérieure
Nasenstachel M
spina F nasale anteriore
maxilla
maxilar M
maxillaire M supérieur
Oberkieferknochen M
mascella F
mandible
mandíbula F
maxillaire M inférieur
Unterkieferknochen M
mandibola F

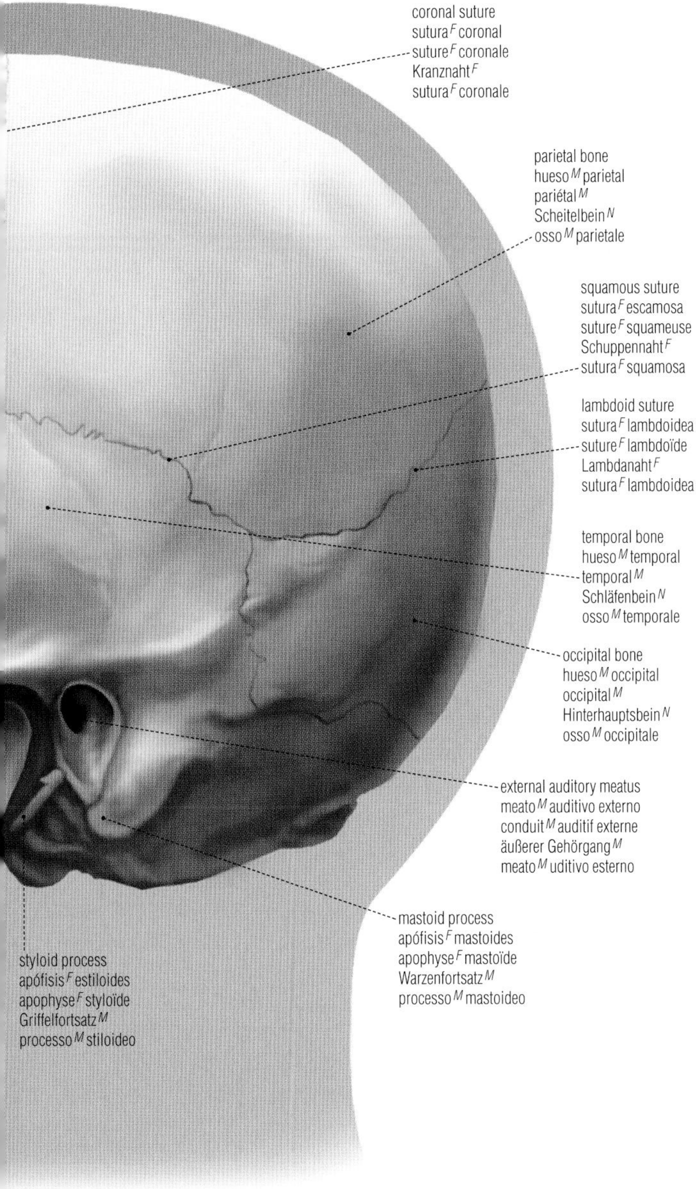
coronal suture
sutura F coronal
suture F coronale
Kranznaht F
sutura F coronale
parietal bone
hueso M parietal
pariétal M
Scheitelbein N
osso M parietale
squamous suture
sutura F escamosa
suture F squameuse
Schuppennaht F
sutura F squamosa
lambdoid suture
sutura F lambdoidea
suture F lambdoïde
Lambdanaht F
sutura F lambdoidea
temporal bone
hueso M temporal
temporal M
Schläfenbein N
osso M temporale
occipital bone
hueso M occipital
occipital M
Hinterhauptsbein N
osso M occipitale
external auditory meatus
meato M auditivo externo
conduit M auditif externe
äußerer Gehörgang M
meato M uditivo esterno
mastoid process
apófisis F mastoides
apophyse F mastoïde
Warzenfortsatz M
processo M mastoideo
styloid process
apófisis F estiloides
apophyse F styloïde
Griffelfortsatz M
processo M stiloideo

spinal column
columna[F] vertebral
os[M] de la colonne[F] vertébrale
Wirbelsäule[F]
colonna[F] vertebrale

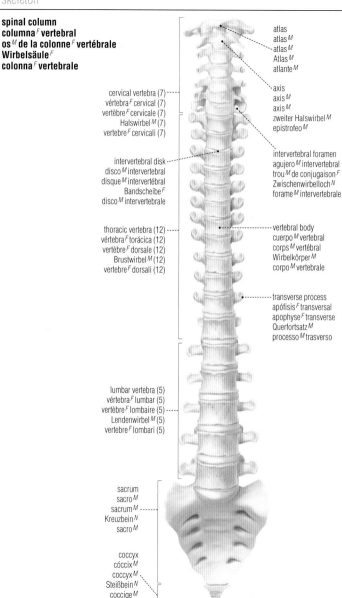

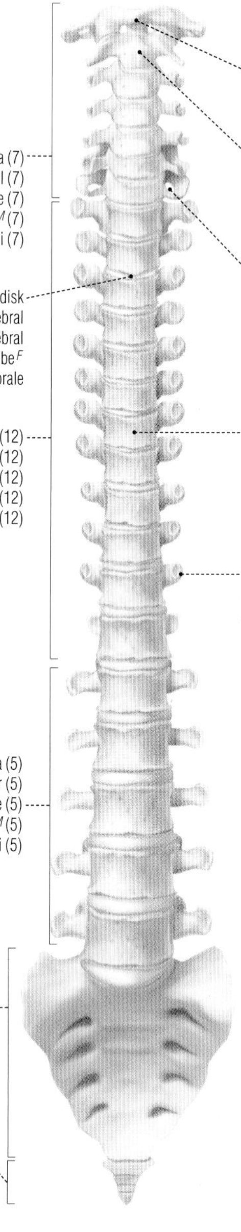
atlas
atlas[M]
atlas[M]
Atlas[M]
atlante[M]
axis
axis[M]
axis[M]
zweiter Halswirbel[M]
epistrofeo[M]
cervical vertebra (7)
vértebra[F] cervical (7)
vertèbre[F] cervicale (7)
Halswirbel[M] (7)
vertebre[F] cervicali (7)
intervertebral foramen
agujero[M] intervertebral
trou[M] de conjugaison[F]
Zwischenwirbelloch[N]
forame[M] intervertebrale
intervertebral disk
disco[M] intervertebral
disque[M] intervertébral
Bandscheibe[F]
disco[M] intervertebrale
thoracic vertebra (12)
vértebra[F] torácica (12)
vertèbre[F] dorsale (12)
Brustwirbel[M] (12)
vertebre[F] dorsali (12)
vertebral body
cuerpo[M] vertebral
corps[M] vertébral
Wirbelkörper[M]
corpo[M] vertebrale
transverse process
apófisis[F] transversal
apophyse[F] transverse
Querfortsatz[M]
processo[M] trasverso
lumbar vertebra (5)
vértebra[F] lumbar (5)
vertèbre[F] lombaire (5)
Lendenwirbel[M] (5)
vertebre[F] lombari (5)
sacrum
sacro[M]
sacrum[M]
Kreuzbein[N]
sacro[M]
coccyx
cóccix[M]
coccyx[M]
Steißbein[N]
coccige[M]

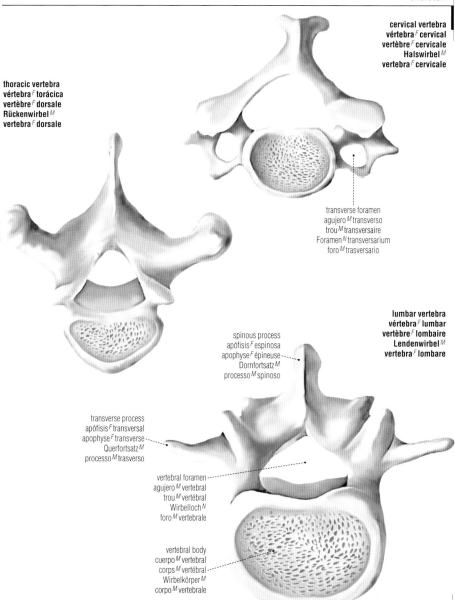

cervical vertebra
vértebra[F] cervical
vertèbre[F] cervicale
Halswirbel[M]
vertebra[F] cervicale

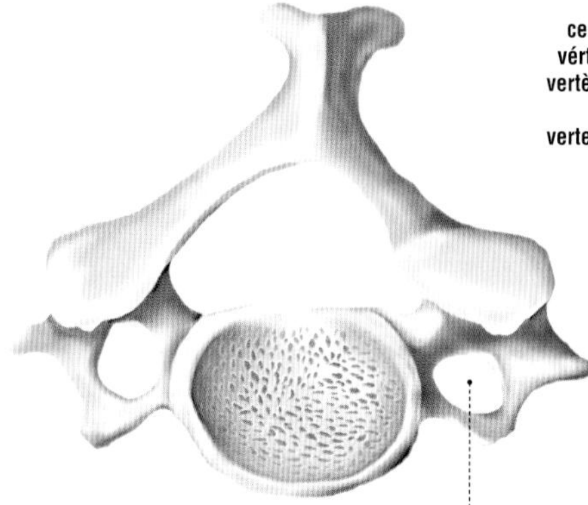
transverse foramen
agujero[M] transverso
trou[M] transversaire
Foramen[N] transversarium
foro[M] trasversario

thoracic vertebra
vértebra[F] torácica
vertèbre[F] dorsale
Rückenwirbel[M]
vertebra[F] dorsale

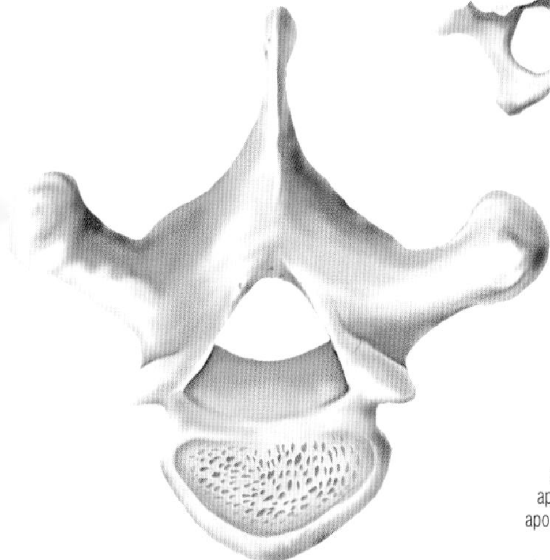

lumbar vertebra
vértebra[F] lumbar
vertèbre[F] lombaire
Lendenwirbel[M]
vertebra[F] lombare

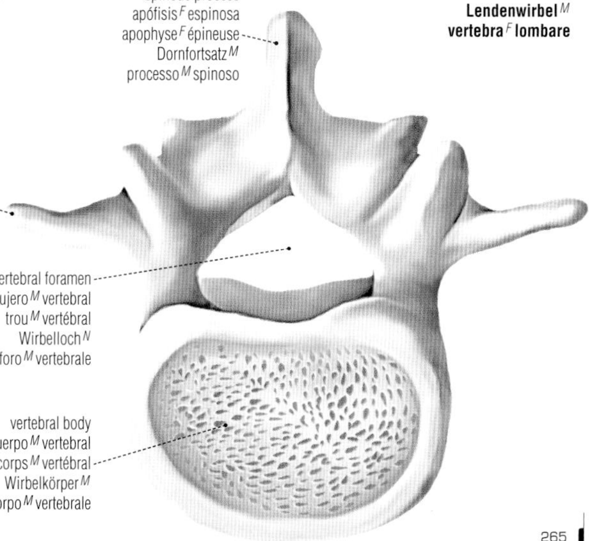
spinous process
apófisis[F] espinosa
apophyse[F] épineuse
Dornfortsatz[M]
processo[M] spinoso
transverse process
apófisis[F] transversal
apophyse[F] transverse
Querfortsatz[M]
processo[M] trasverso
vertebral foramen
agujero[M] vertebral
trou[M] vertébral
Wirbelloch[N]
foro[M] vertebrale
vertebral body
cuerpo[M] vertebral
corps[M] vertébral
Wirbelkörper[M]
corpo[M] vertebrale

teeth

dientes[M] | dents[F] | Zähne[M] | denti[M]

cross section of a molar
corte[M] transversal de un molar[M]
coupe[F] d'une molaire[F]
Backenzahn[M] im Längsschnitt[M]
sezione[F] trasversale di un molare[M]

crown
corona[F]
couronne[F]
Krone[F]
corona[F]

pulp
pulpa[F]
pulpe[F]
Pulpa[F]
polpa[F]

pulp chamber
cámara[F] pulpar
chambre[F] pulpaire
Kronenabschnitt[M] der Pulpahöhle[F]
camera[F] pulpare

neck
cuello[M]
collet[M]
Hals[M]
colletto[M]

root canal
conducto[M] radicular
canal[M] radiculaire
Wurzelkanal[M]
canale[M] della radice[F]

periodontal ligament
ligamento[M] alveolo-dentario
ligament[M] alvéolo-dentaire
Wurzelhaut[F]
legamento[M] periodontale

root
raíz[F]
racine[F]
Wurzel[F]
radice[F]

dental alveolus
alvéolo[M] dental
alvéole[F] dentaire
Zahnfach[N]
alveolo[M] dentario

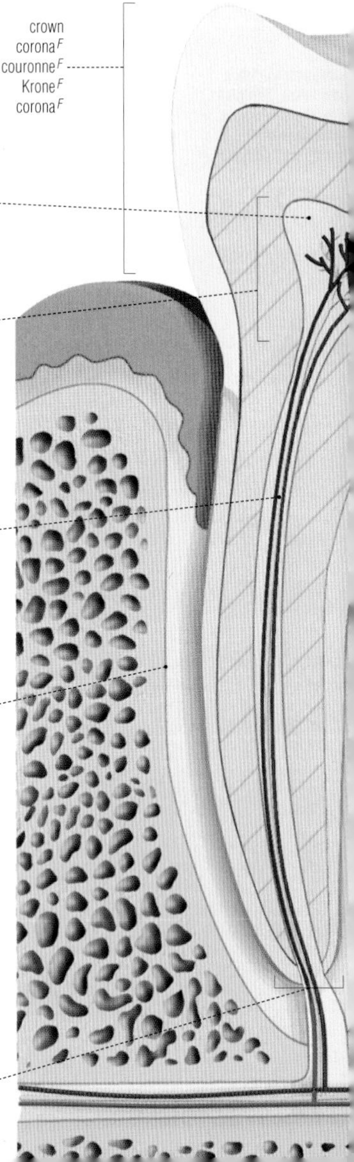

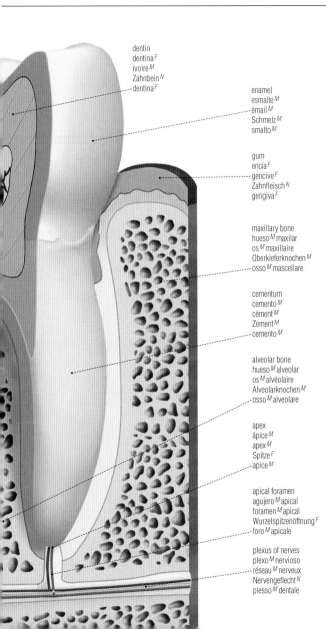

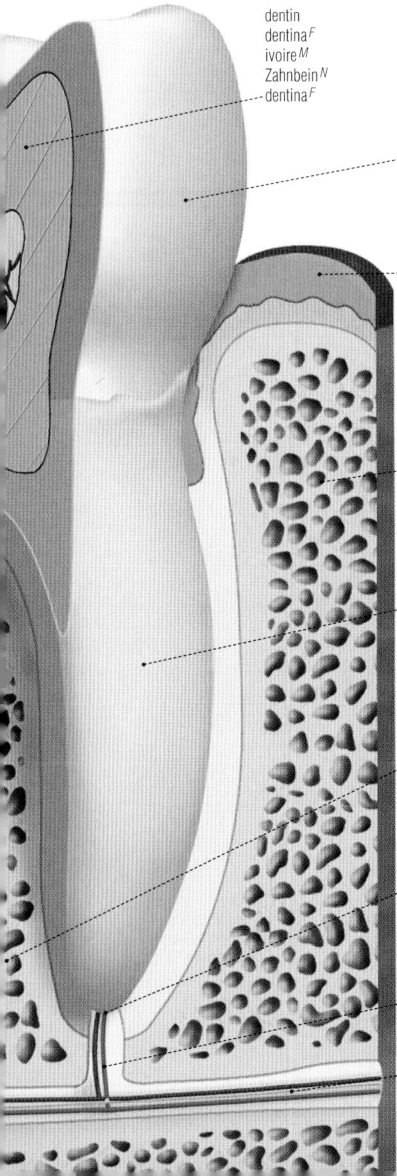
dentin
dentina *F*
ivoire *M*
Zahnbein *N*
dentina *F*
enamel
esmalte *M*
émail *M*
Schmelz *M*
smalto *M*
gum
encía *F*
gencive *F*
Zahnfleisch *N*
gengiva *F*
maxillary bone
hueso *M* maxilar
os *M* maxillaire
Oberkieferknochen *M*
osso *M* mascellare
cementum
cemento *M*
cément *M*
Zement *M*
cemento *M*
alveolar bone
hueso *M* alveolar
os *M* alvéolaire
Alveolarknochen *M*
osso *M* alveolare
apex
ápice *M*
apex *M*
Spitze *F*
apice *M*
apical foramen
agujero *M* apical
foramen *M* apical
Wurzelspitzenöffnung *F*
foro *M* apicale
plexus of nerves
plexo *M* nervioso
réseau *M* nerveux
Nervengeflecht *N*
plesso *M* dentale

human denture
dentadura^F humana
denture^F humaine
menschliches Gebiss^N
dentatura^F nell'uomo^M

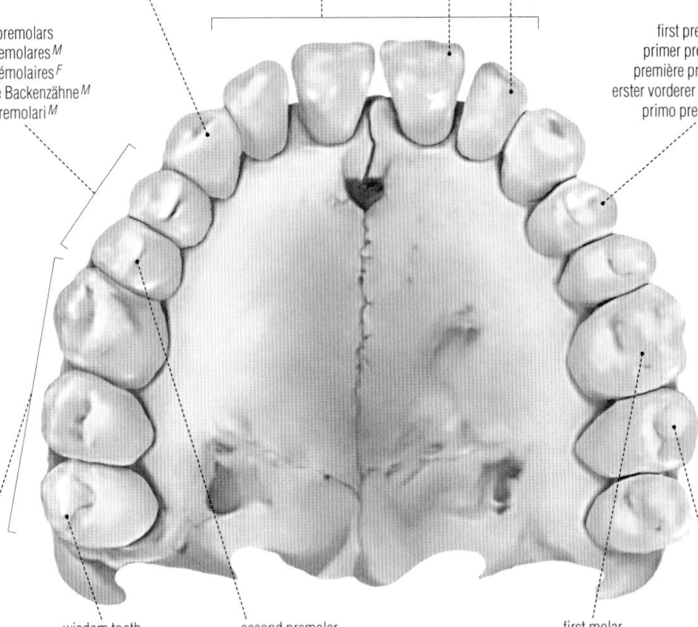

central incisor
incisivo^M central
incisive^F centrale
mittlerer Schneidezahn^M
incisivo^M centrale
canine
colmillo^M
canine^F
Eckzahn^M
canino^M
incisors
incisivos^M
incisives^F
Schneidezähne^M
incisivi^M
lateral incisor
incisivo^M lateral
incisive^F latérale
äußerer Schneidezahn^M
incisivo^M laterale
premolars
premolares^M
prémolaires^F
vordere Backenzähne^M
premolari^M
first premolar
primer premolar^M
première prémolaire^F
erster vorderer Backenzahn^M
primo premolare^M
wisdom tooth
muela^F del juicio^M
dent^F de sagesse^F
Weisheitszahn^M
dente^M del giudizio^M
second premolar
segundo premolar^M
deuxième prémolaire^F
zweiter vorderer Backenzahn^M
secondo premolare^M
first molar
primer molar^M
première molaire^F
erster Backenzahn^M
primo molare^M
molars
molares^M
molaires^F
Backenzähne^M
molari^M
second molar
segundo molar^M
deuxième molaire^F
zweiter Backenzahn^M
secondo molare^M

blood circulation

circulación[F] sanguínea | circulation[F] sanguine | Blutkreislauf[M] | circolazione[F] del sangue[M]

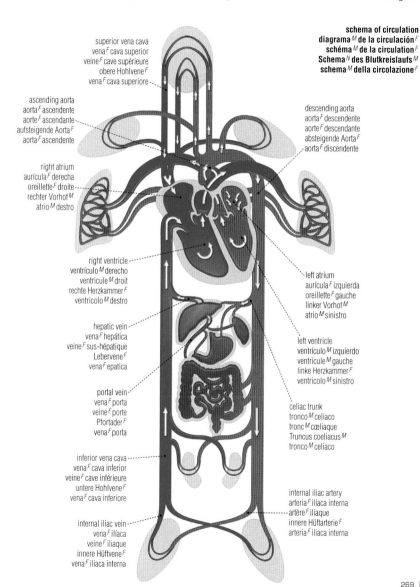

schema of circulation
diagrama[M] de la circulación[F]
schéma[M] de la circulation[F]
Schema[N] des Blutkreislaufs[M]
schema[M] della circolazione[F]

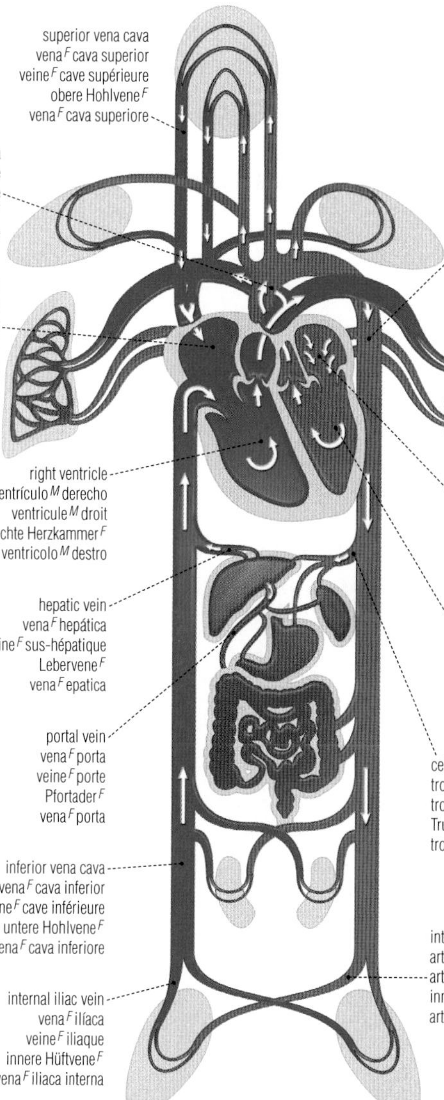

superior vena cava
vena[F] cava superior
veine[F] cave supérieure
obere Hohlvene[F]
vena[F] cava superiore
ascending aorta
aorta[F] ascendente
aorte[F] ascendante
aufsteigende Aorta[F]
aorta[F] ascendente
descending aorta
aorta[F] descendente
aorte[F] descendante
absteigende Aorta[F]
aorta[F] discendente
right atrium
aurícula[F] derecha
oreillette[F] droite
rechter Vorhof[M]
atrio[M] destro
right ventricle
ventrículo[M] derecho
ventricule[M] droit
rechte Herzkammer[F]
ventricolo[M] destro
left atrium
aurícula[F] izquierda
oreillette[F] gauche
linker Vorhof[M]
atrio[M] sinistro
hepatic vein
vena[F] hepática
veine[F] sus-hépatique
Lebervene[F]
vena[F] epatica
left ventricle
ventrículo[M] izquierdo
ventricule[M] gauche
linke Herzkammer[F]
ventricolo[M] sinistro
portal vein
vena[F] porta
veine[F] porte
Pfortader[F]
vena[F] porta
celiac trunk
tronco[M] celiaco
tronc[M] cœliaque
Truncus coeliacus[M]
tronco[M] celiaco
inferior vena cava
vena[F] cava inferior
veine[F] cave inférieure
untere Hohlvene[F]
vena[F] cava inferiore
internal iliac artery
arteria[F] ilíaca interna
artère[F] iliaque
innere Hüftarterie[F]
arteria[F] iliaca interna
internal iliac vein
vena[F] ilíaca
veine[F] iliaque
innere Hüftvene[F]
vena[F] iliaca interna

blood circulation

principal arteries
arterias[F] principales
principales artères[F]
Hauptschlagadern[F]
arterie[F] principali

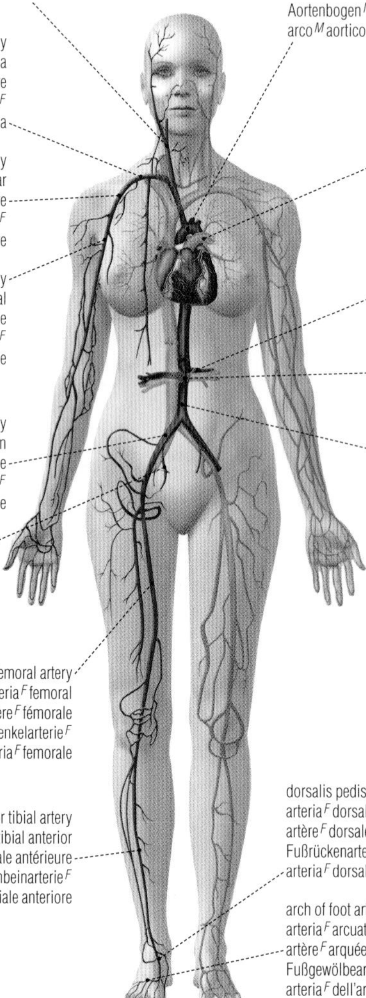
common carotid artery
arteria[F] carótida primitiva
artère[F] carotide primitive
Halsschlagader[F]
arteria[F] carotide comune
arch of aorta
cayado[M] de la aorta[F]
arc[M] de l'aorte[F]
Aortenbogen[M]
arco[M] aortico
subclavian artery
arteria[F] subclavia
artère[F] sous-clavière
Schlüsselbeinarterie[F]
arteria[F] succlavia
pulmonary artery
arteria[F] pulmonar
artère[F] pulmonaire
Lungenarterie[F]
arteria[F] polmonare
axillary artery
arteria[F] axilar
artère[F] axillaire
Achselarterie[F]
arteria[F] ascellare
renal artery
arteria[F] renal
artère[F] rénale
Nierenarterie[F]
arteria[F] renale
brachial artery
arteria[F] braquial
artère[F] brachiale
Oberarmarterie[F]
arteria[F] brachiale
superior mesenteric artery
arteria[F] mesentérica superior
artère[F] mésentérique supérieure
obere Mesenterialarterie[F]
arteria[F] mesenterica superiore
common iliac artery
arteria[F] ilíaca común
artère[F] iliaque commune
gemeinsame Hüftarterie[F]
arteria[F] iliaca comune
abdominal aorta
aorta[F] abdominal
aorte[F] abdominale
Bauchaorta[F]
aorta[F] addominale
internal iliac artery
arteria[F] ilíaca interna
artère[F] iliaque interne
innere Hüftarterie[F]
arteria[F] iliaca interna
femoral artery
arteria[F] femoral
artère[F] fémorale
Oberschenkelarterie[F]
arteria[F] femorale
dorsalis pedis artery
arteria[F] dorsal del pie[M]
artère[F] dorsale du pied[M]
Fußrückenarterie[F]
arteria[F] dorsale del piede[M]
anterior tibial artery
arteria[F] tibial anterior
artère[F] tibiale antérieure
vordere Schienbeinarterie[F]
arteria[F] tibiale anteriore
arch of foot artery
arteria[F] arcuata
artère[F] arquée
Fußgewölbearterie[F]
arteria[F] dell'arco[M] del piede[M]

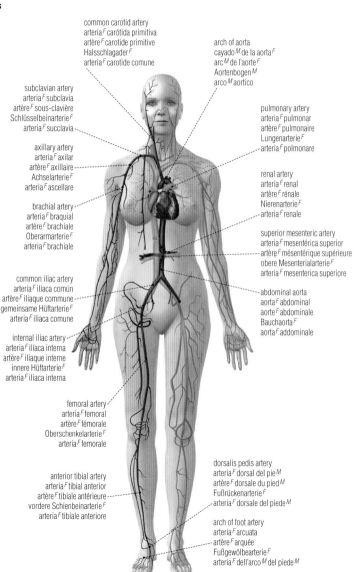

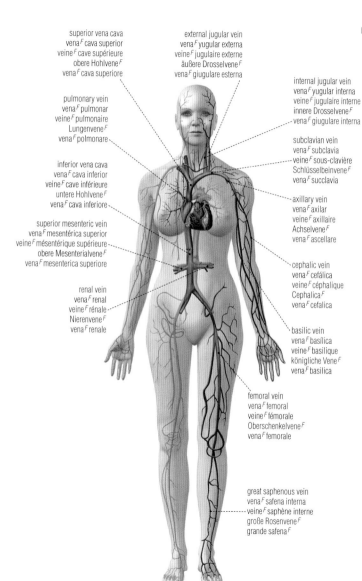

principal veins
venas[F] principales
principales veines[F]
Hauptvenen[F]
vene[F] principali

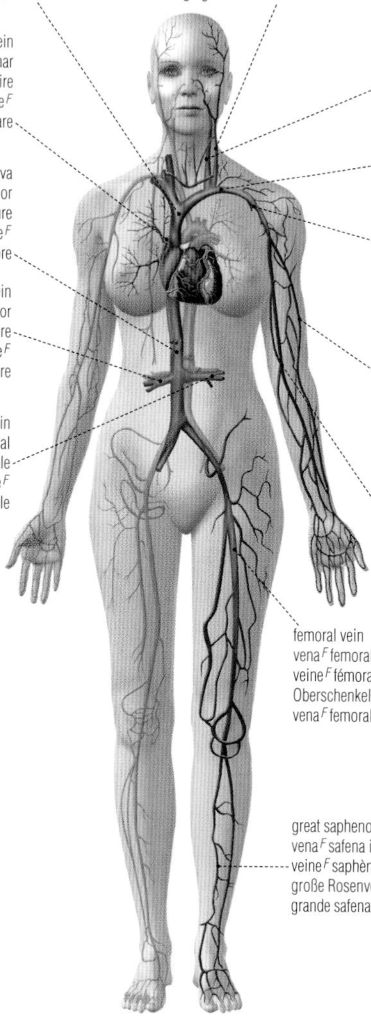
superior vena cava
vena[F] cava superior
veine[F] cave supérieure
obere Hohlvene[F]
vena[F] cava superiore
external jugular vein
vena[F] yugular externa
veine[F] jugulaire externe
äußere Drosselvene[F]
vena[F] giugulare esterna
internal jugular vein
vena[F] yugular interna
veine[F] jugulaire interne
innere Drosselvene[F]
vena[F] giugulare interna
pulmonary vein
vena[F] pulmonar
veine[F] pulmonaire
Lungenvene[F]
vena[F] polmonare
subclavian vein
vena[F] subclavia
veine[F] sous-clavière
Schlüsselbeinvene[F]
vena[F] succlavia
inferior vena cava
vena[F] cava inferior
veine[F] cave inférieure
untere Hohlvene[F]
vena[F] cava inferiore
axillary vein
vena[F] axilar
veine[F] axillaire
Achselvene[F]
vena[F] ascellare
superior mesenteric vein
vena[F] mesentérica superior
veine[F] mésentérique supérieure
obere Mesenterialvene[F]
vena[F] mesenterica superiore
cephalic vein
vena[F] cefálica
veine[F] céphalique
Cephalica[F]
vena[F] cefalica
renal vein
vena[F] renal
veine[F] rénale
Nierenvene[F]
vena[F] renale
basilic vein
vena[F] basílica
veine[F] basilique
königliche Vene[F]
vena[F] basilica
femoral vein
vena[F] femoral
veine[F] fémorale
Oberschenkelvene[F]
vena[F] femorale
great saphenous vein
vena[F] safena interna
veine[F] saphène interne
große Rosenvene[F]
grande safena[F]

blood circulation

heart
corazón *M*
cœur *M*
Herz *N*
cuore *M*

oxygenated blood
sangre *F* **oxigenada**
sang *M* **oxygéné**
sauerstoffreiches Blut *N*
sangue *M* **ossigenato**

deoxygenated blood
sangre *F* **desoxigenada**
sang *M* **désoxygéné**
sauerstoffarmes Blut *N*
sangue *M* **deossigenato**

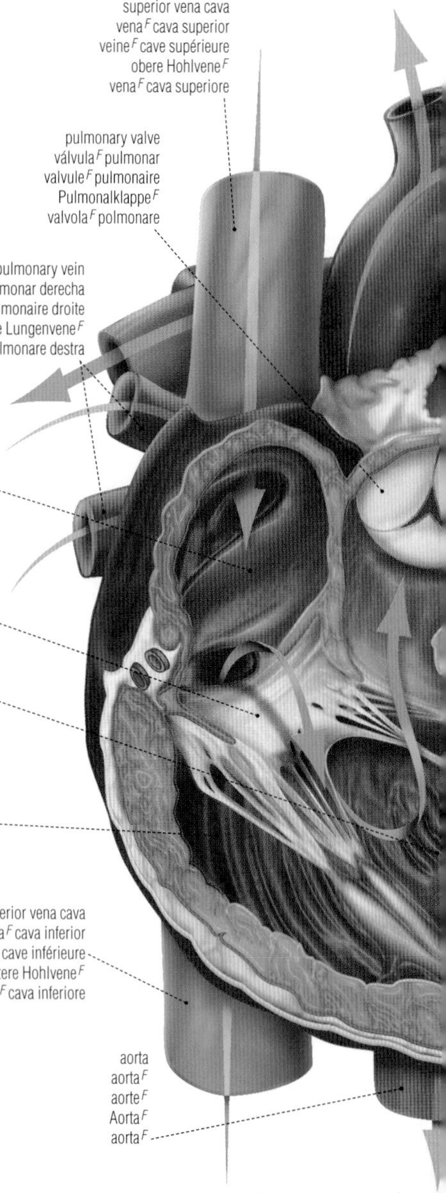
superior vena cava
vena F cava superior
veine F cave supérieure
obere Hohlvene F
vena F cava superiore
pulmonary valve
válvula F pulmonar
valvule F pulmonaire
Pulmonalklappe F
valvola F polmonare
right pulmonary vein
vena F pulmonar derecha
veine F pulmonaire droite
rechte Lungenvene F
vena F polmonare destra
right atrium
aurícula F derecha
oreillette F droite
rechter Vorhof M
atrio M destro
tricuspid valve
válvula F tricúspide
valvule F tricuspide
Trikuspidalklappe F
valvola F tricuspide
right ventricle
ventrículo M derecho
ventricule M droit
rechte Herzkammer F
ventricolo M destro
endocardium
endocardio M
endocarde M
Herzwandschicht F
endocardio M
inferior vena cava
vena F cava inferior
veine F cave inférieure
untere Hohlvene F
vena F cava inferiore
aorta
aorta F
aorte F
Aorta F
aorta F

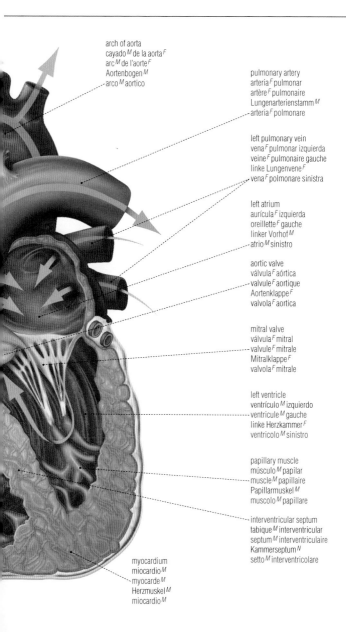

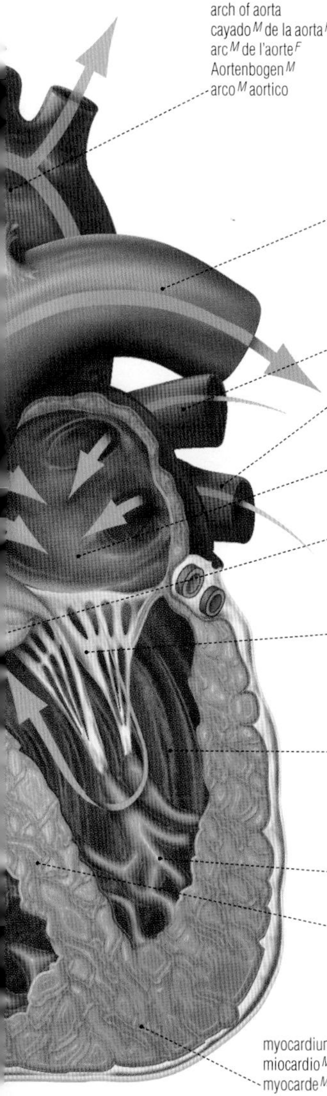

arch of aorta
cayado[M] de la aorta[F]
arc[M] de l'aorte[F]
Aortenbogen[M]
arco[M] aortico

pulmonary artery
arteria[F] pulmonar
artère[F] pulmonaire
Lungenarterienstamm[M]
arteria[F] polmonare

left pulmonary vein
vena[F] pulmonar izquierda
veine[F] pulmonaire gauche
linke Lungenvene[F]
vena[F] polmonare sinistra

left atrium
aurícula[F] izquierda
oreillette[F] gauche
linker Vorhof[M]
atrio[M] sinistro

aortic valve
válvula[F] aórtica
valvule[F] aortique
Aortenklappe[F]
valvola[F] aortica

mitral valve
válvula[F] mitral
valvule[F] mitrale
Mitralklappe[F]
valvola[F] mitrale

left ventricle
ventrículo[M] izquierdo
ventricule[M] gauche
linke Herzkammer[F]
ventricolo[M] sinistro

papillary muscle
músculo[M] papilar
muscle[M] papillaire
Papillarmuskel[M]
muscolo[M] papillare

interventricular septum
tabique[M] interventricular
septum[M] interventriculaire
Kammerseptum[N]
setto[M] interventricolare

myocardium
miocardio[M]
myocarde[M]
Herzmuskel[M]
miocardio[M]

respiratory system

aparato M respiratorio | appareil M respiratoire | Luftwege M | apparato M respiratorio

lungs
pulmones M
poumons M
Lungen F
polmoni M

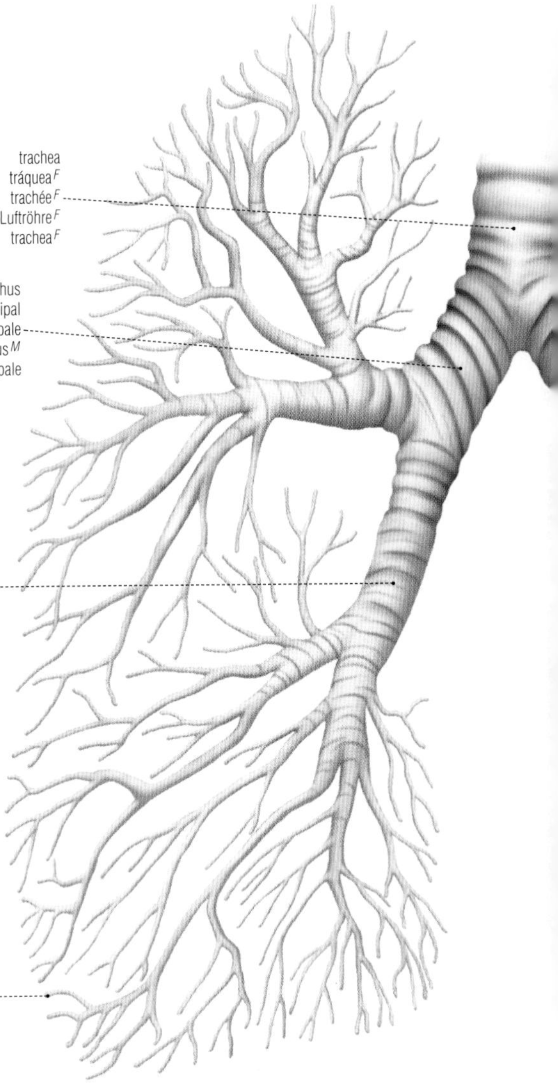
trachea
tráquea F
trachée F
Luftröhre F
trachea F
main bronchus
bronquio M principal
bronche F principale
Hauptbronchus M
bronco M principale
lobe bronchus
bronquio M lobular
bronche F lobaire
Lappenbronchus M
bronco M lobare
terminal bronchiole
bronquiolo M terminal
bronchiole F terminale
Terminalbronchiole F
bronchiolo M terminale

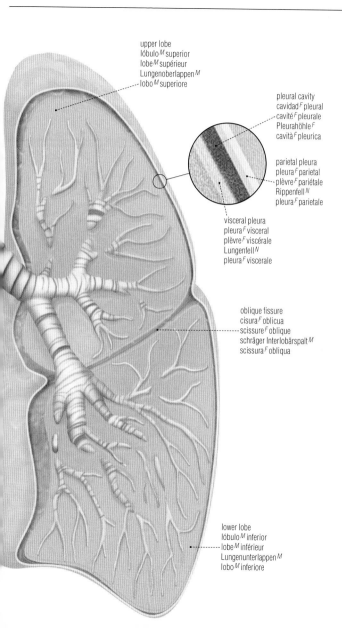

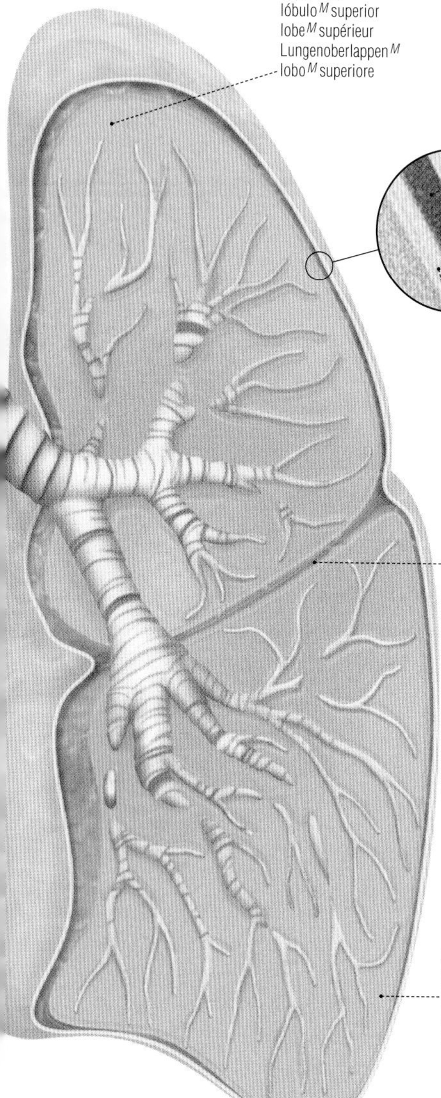
upper lobe
lóbulo M superior
lobe M supérieur
Lungenoberlappen M
lobo M superiore
pleural cavity
cavidad F pleural
cavité F pleurale
Pleurahöhle F
cavità F pleurica
parietal pleura
pleura F parietal
plèvre F pariétale
Rippenfell N
pleura F parietale
visceral pleura
pleura F visceral
plèvre F viscérale
Lungenfell N
pleura F viscerale
oblique fissure
cisura F oblicua
scissure F oblique
schräger Interlobärspalt M
scissura F obliqua
lower lobe
lóbulo M inferior
lobe M inférieur
Lungenunterlappen M
lobo M inferiore

main respiratory organs
órganos[M] principales del aparato[M] respiratorio
principaux organes[M] respiratoires
die wichtigsten Atemorgane[N]
organi[M] respiratori principali

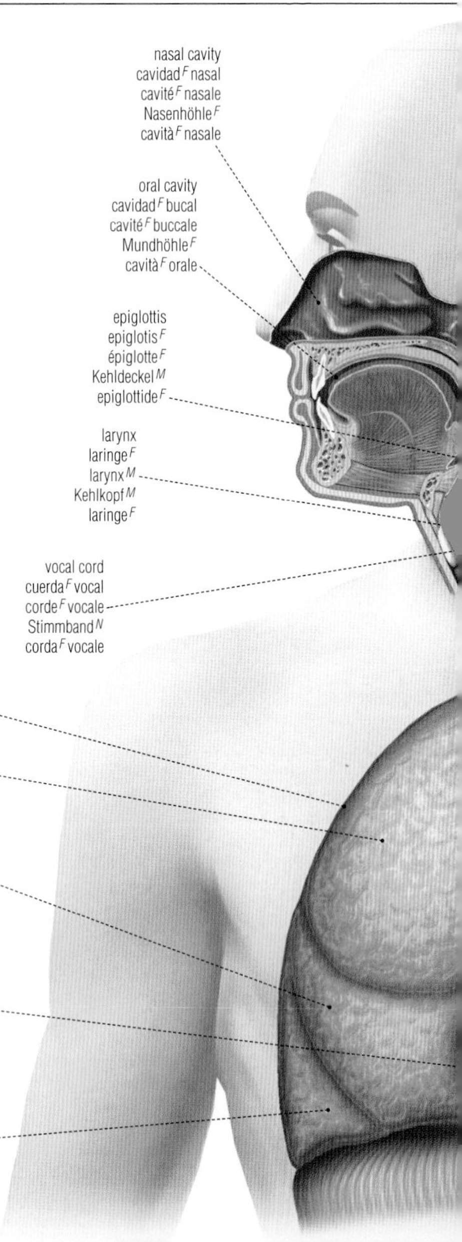

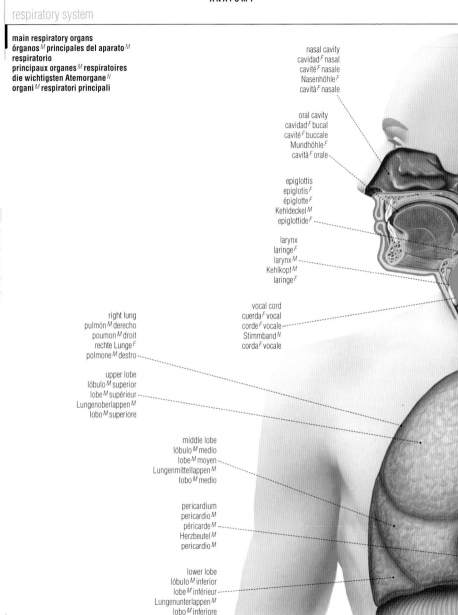

nasal cavity
cavidad[F] nasal
cavité[F] nasale
Nasenhöhle[F]
cavità[F] nasale

oral cavity
cavidad[F] bucal
cavité[F] buccale
Mundhöhle[F]
cavità[F] orale

epiglottis
epiglotis[F]
épiglotte[F]
Kehldeckel[M]
epiglottide[F]

larynx
laringe[F]
larynx[M]
Kehlkopf[M]
laringe[F]

vocal cord
cuerda[F] vocal
corde[F] vocale
Stimmband[N]
corda[F] vocale

right lung
pulmón[M] derecho
poumon[M] droit
rechte Lunge[F]
polmone[M] destro

upper lobe
lóbulo[M] superior
lobe[M] supérieur
Lungenoberlappen[M]
lobo[M] superiore

middle lobe
lóbulo[M] medio
lobe[M] moyen
Lungenmittellappen[M]
lobo[M] medio

pericardium
pericardio[M]
péricarde[M]
Herzbeutel[M]
pericardio[M]

lower lobe
lóbulo[M] inferior
lobe[M] inférieur
Lungenunterlappen[M]
lobo[M] inferiore

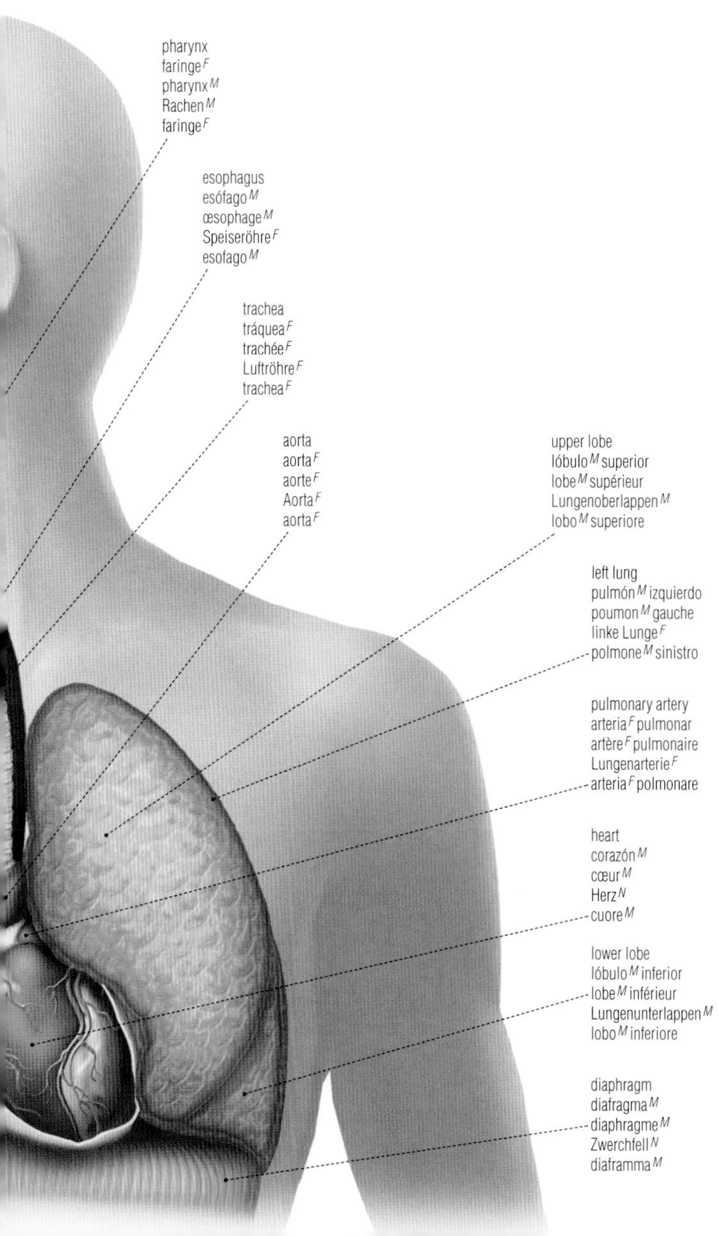
pharynx
faringe F
pharynx M
Rachen M
faringe F
esophagus
esófago M
œsophage M
Speiseröhre F
esofago M
trachea
tráquea F
trachée F
Luftröhre F
trachea F
aorta
aorta F
aorte F
Aorta F
aorta F
upper lobe
lóbulo M superior
lobe M supérieur
Lungenoberlappen M
lobo M superiore
left lung
pulmón M izquierdo
poumon M gauche
linke Lunge F
polmone M sinistro
pulmonary artery
arteria F pulmonar
artère F pulmonaire
Lungenarterie F
arteria F polmonare
heart
corazón M
cœur M
Herz N
cuore M
lower lobe
lóbulo M inferior
lobe M inférieur
Lungenunterlappen M
lobo M inferiore
diaphragm
diafragma M
diaphragme M
Zwerchfell N
diaframma M

digestive system

aparato^M digestivo | appareil^M digestif | Verdauungsapparat^M | apparato^M digerente

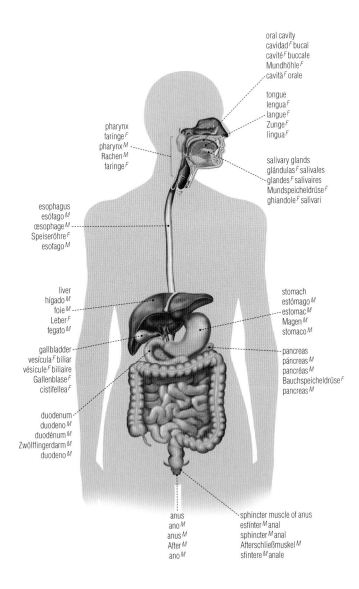

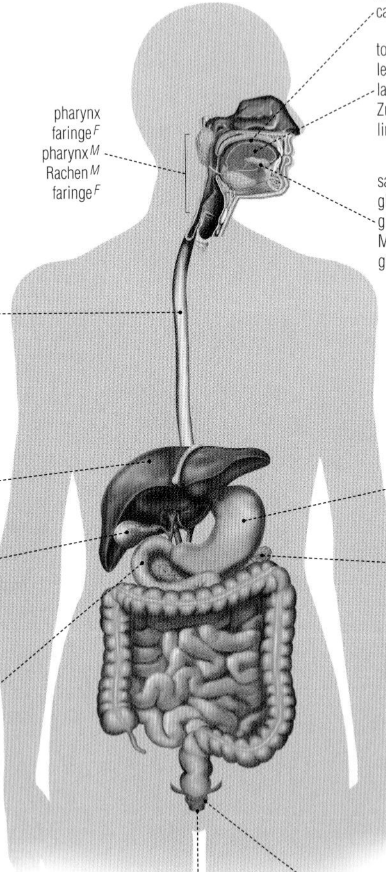
oral cavity
cavidad^F bucal
cavité^F buccale
Mundhöhle^F
cavità^F orale
tongue
lengua^F
langue^F
Zunge^F
lingua^F
pharynx
faringe^F
pharynx^M
Rachen^M
faringe^F
salivary glands
glándulas^F salivales
glandes^F salivaires
Mundspeicheldrüse^F
ghiandole^F salivari
esophagus
esófago^M
œsophage^M
Speiseröhre^F
esofago^M
liver
hígado^M
foie^M
Leber^F
fegato^M
stomach
estómago^M
estomac^M
Magen^M
stomaco^M
gallbladder
vesícula^F biliar
vésicule^F biliaire
Gallenblase^F
cistifellea^F
pancreas
páncreas^M
pancréas^M
Bauchspeicheldrüse^F
pancreas^M
duodenum
duodeno^M
duodénum^M
Zwölffingerdarm^M
duodeno^M
anus
ano^M
anus^M
After^M
ano^M
sphincter muscle of anus
esfínter^M anal
sphincter^M anal
Afterschließmuskel^M
sfintere^M anale

small intestine
intestino *M* **delgado**
intestin *M* **grêle**
Dünndarm *M*
intestino *M* **tenue**

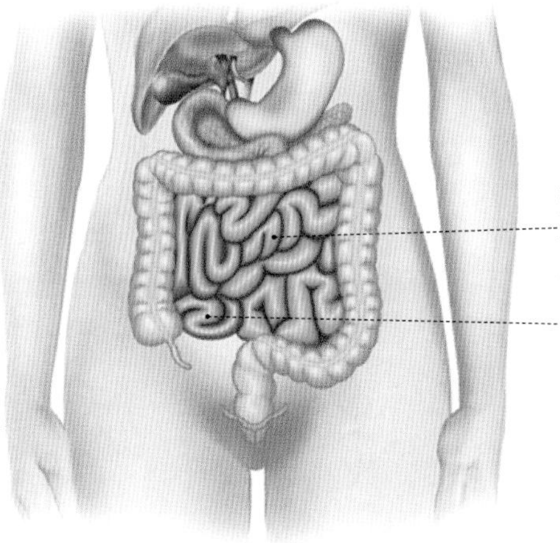
jejunum
yeyuno M
jéjunum M
Leerdarm M
digiuno M
ileum
íleon M
iléon M
Ileum N
ileo M

large intestine
intestino *M* **grueso**
gros intestin *M*
Dickdarm *M*
intestino *M* **crasso**

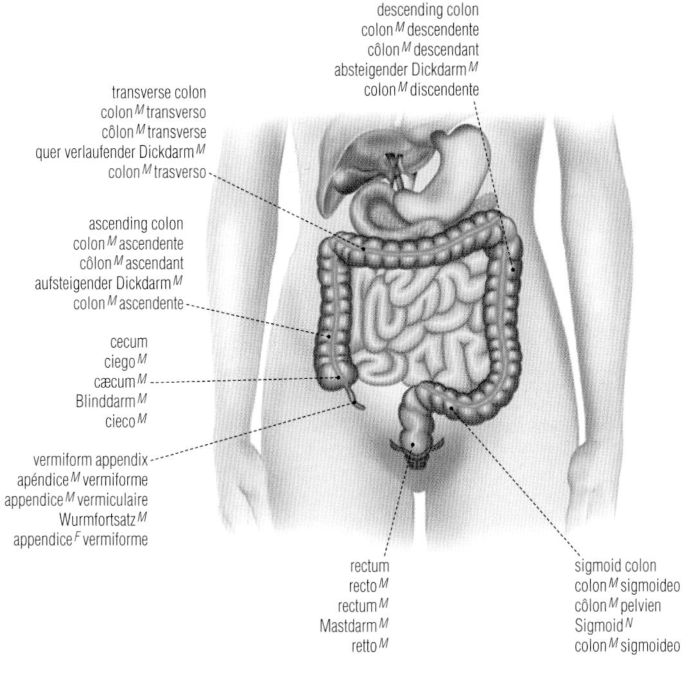
descending colon
colon M descendente
côlon M descendant
absteigender Dickdarm M
colon M discendente
transverse colon
colon M transverso
côlon M transverse
quer verlaufender Dickdarm M
colon M trasverso
ascending colon
colon M ascendente
côlon M ascendant
aufsteigender Dickdarm M
colon M ascendente
cecum
ciego M
cæcum M
Blinddarm M
cieco M
vermiform appendix
apéndice M vermiforme
appendice M vermiculaire
Wurmfortsatz M
appendice F vermiforme
rectum
recto M
rectum M
Mastdarm M
retto M
sigmoid colon
colon M sigmoideo
côlon M pelvien
Sigmoid N
colon M sigmoideo

urinary system

aparato^{M} urinario | appareil^{M} urinaire | Harnapparat^{M} | apparato^{M} urinario

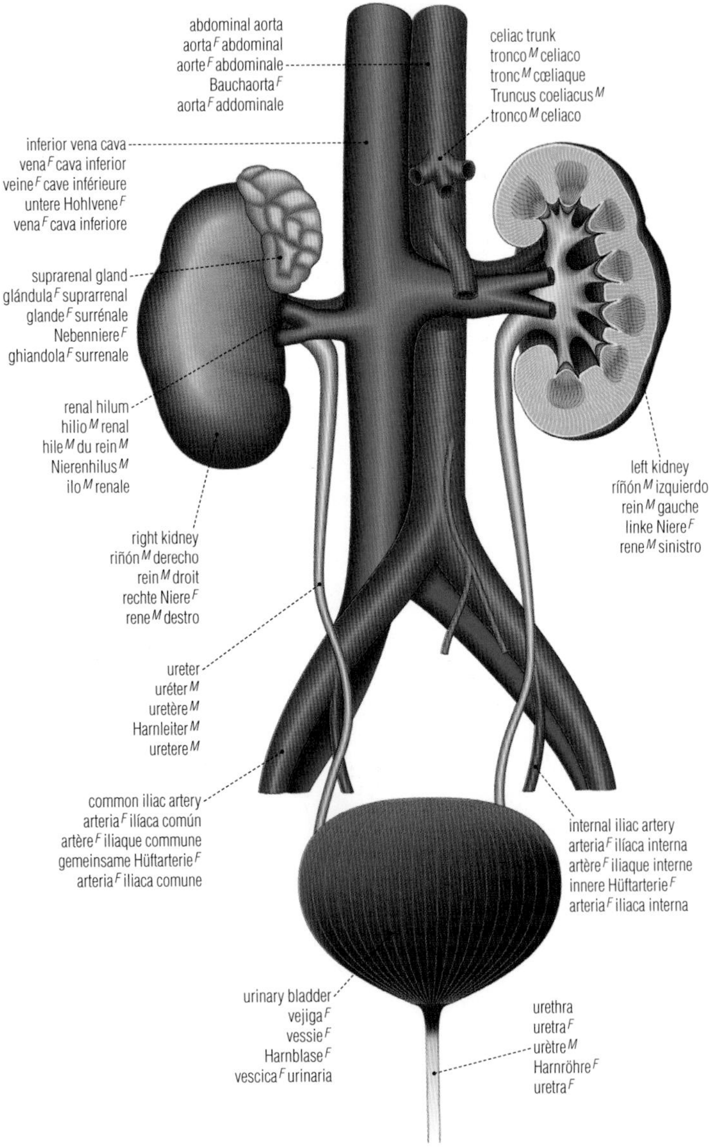
abdominal aorta
aorta F abdominal
aorte F abdominale
Bauchaorta F
aorta F addominale
celiac trunk
tronco M celiaco
tronc M cœliaque
Truncus coeliacus M
tronco M celiaco
inferior vena cava
vena F cava inferior
veine F cave inférieure
untere Hohlvene F
vena F cava inferiore
suprarenal gland
glándula F suprarrenal
glande F surrénale
Nebenniere F
ghiandola F surrenale
renal hilum
hilio M renal
hile M du rein M
Nierenhilus M
ilo M renale
left kidney
riñón M izquierdo
rein M gauche
linke Niere F
rene M sinistro
right kidney
riñón M derecho
rein M droit
rechte Niere F
rene M destro
ureter
uréter M
uretère M
Harnleiter M
uretere M
common iliac artery
arteria F ilíaca común
artère F iliaque commune
gemeinsame Hüftarterie F
arteria F iliaca comune
internal iliac artery
arteria F ilíaca interna
artère F iliaque interne
innere Hüftarterie F
arteria F iliaca interna
urinary bladder
vejiga F
vessie F
Harnblase F
vescica F urinaria
urethra
uretra F
urètre M
Harnröhre F
uretra F

urinary bladder
vejiga F
vessie F
Harnblase F
vescica F

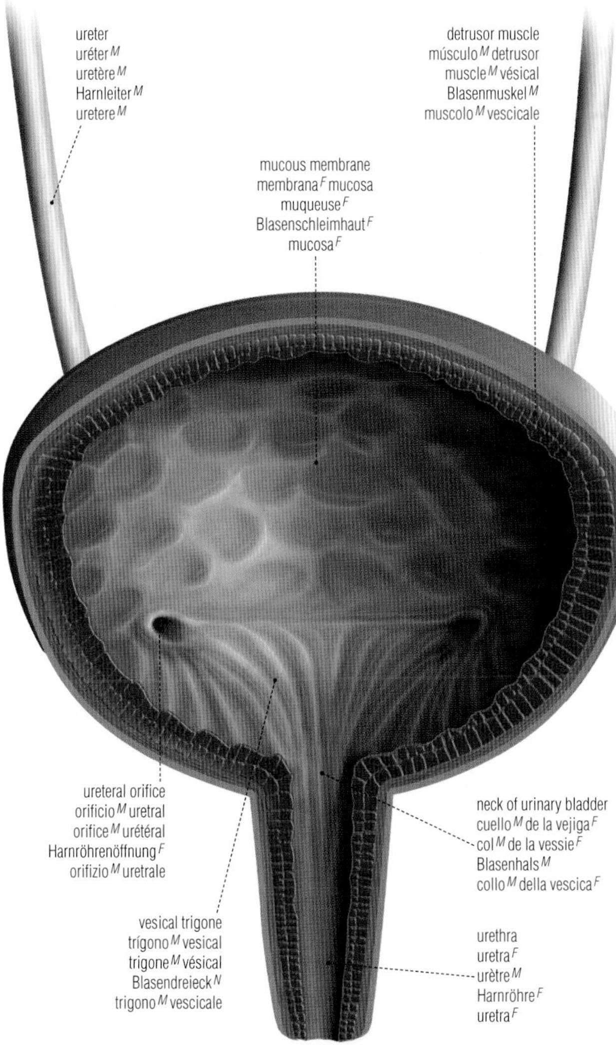
ureter
uréter M
uretère M
Harnleiter M
uretere M
detrusor muscle
músculo M detrusor
muscle M vésical
Blasenmuskel M
muscolo M vescicale
mucous membrane
membrana F mucosa
muqueuse F
Blasenschleimhaut F
mucosa F
ureteral orifice
orificio M uretral
orifice M urétéral
Harnröhrenöffnung F
orifizio M uretrale
neck of urinary bladder
cuello M de la vejiga F
col M de la vessie F
Blasenhals M
collo M della vescica F
vesical trigone
trígono M vesical
trigone M vésical
Blasendreieck N
trigono M vescicale
urethra
uretra F
urètre M
Harnröhre F
uretra F

nervous system

sistema[M] nervioso | système[M] nerveux | Nervensystem[N] | sistema[M] nervoso

peripheral nervous system
sistema[M] nervioso periférico
système[M] nerveux périphérique
peripheres Nervensystem[N]
sistema[M] nervoso periferico

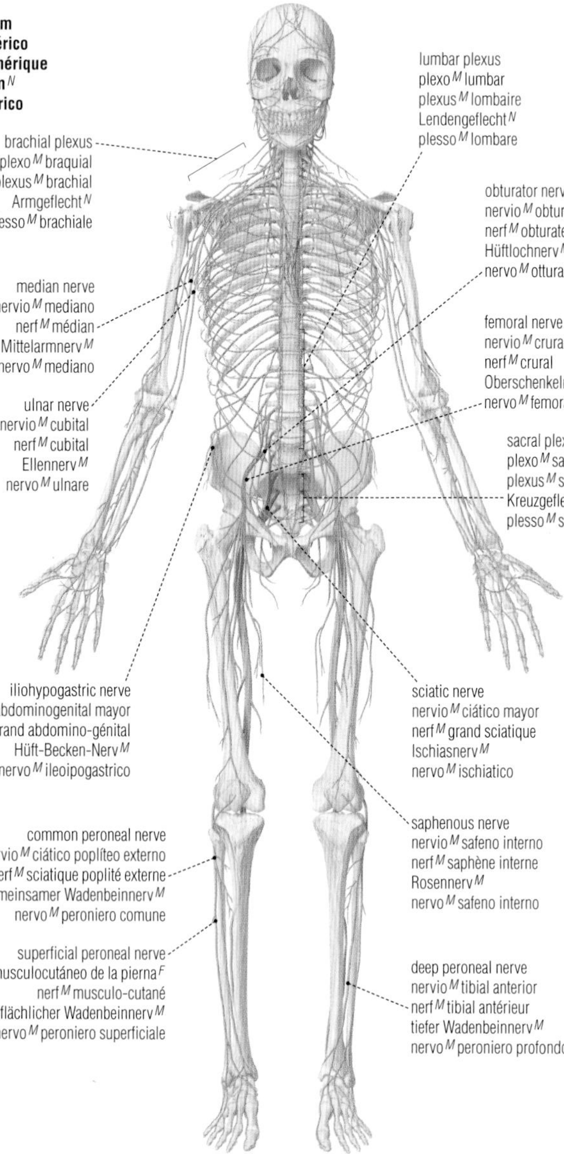

brachial plexus
plexo[M] braquial
plexus[M] brachial
Armgeflecht[N]
plesso[M] brachiale
median nerve
nervio[M] mediano
nerf[M] médian
Mittelarmnerv[M]
nervo[M] mediano
ulnar nerve
nervio[M] cubital
nerf[M] cubital
Ellennerv[M]
nervo[M] ulnare
iliohypogastric nerve
nervio[M] abdominogenital mayor
nerf[M] grand abdomino-génital
Hüft-Becken-Nerv[M]
nervo[M] ileoipogastrico
common peroneal nerve
nervio[M] ciático poplíteo externo
nerf[M] sciatique poplité externe
gemeinsamer Wadenbeinnerv[M]
nervo[M] peroniero comune
superficial peroneal nerve
nervio[M] musculocutáneo de la pierna[F]
nerf[M] musculo-cutané
oberflächlicher Wadenbeinnerv[M]
nervo[M] peroniero superficiale
lumbar plexus
plexo[M] lumbar
plexus[M] lombaire
Lendengeflecht[N]
plesso[M] lombare
obturator nerve
nervio[M] obturador
nerf[M] obturateur
Hüftlochnerv[M]
nervo[M] otturatorio
femoral nerve
nervio[M] crural
nerf[M] crural
Oberschenkelnerv[M]
nervo[M] femorale
sacral plexus
plexo[M] sacro
plexus[M] sacré
Kreuzgeflecht[N]
plesso[M] sacrale
sciatic nerve
nervio[M] ciático mayor
nerf[M] grand sciatique
Ischiasnerv[M]
nervo[M] ischiatico
saphenous nerve
nervio[M] safeno interno
nerf[M] saphène interne
Rosennerv[M]
nervo[M] safeno interno
deep peroneal nerve
nervio[M] tibial anterior
nerf[M] tibial antérieur
tiefer Wadenbeinnerv[M]
nervo[M] peroniero profondo

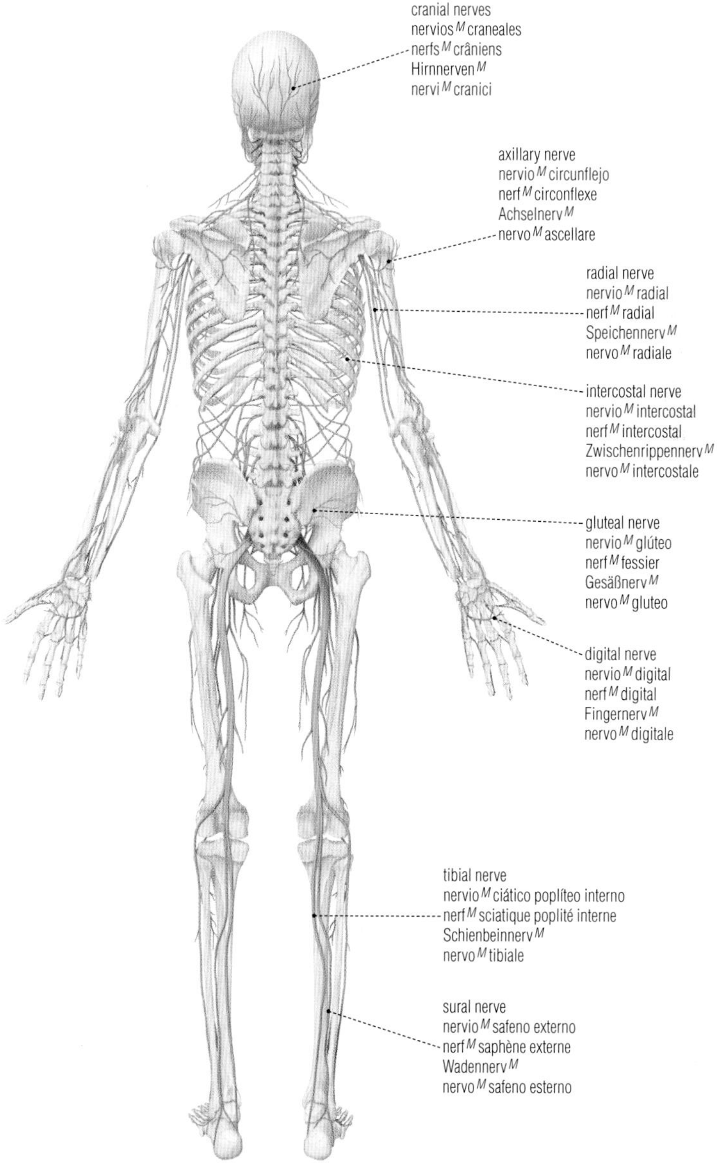
cranial nerves
nervios M craneales
nerfs M crâniens
Hirnnerven M
nervi M cranici
axillary nerve
nervio M circunflejo
nerf M circonflexe
Achselnerv M
nervo M ascellare
radial nerve
nervio M radial
nerf M radial
Speichennerv M
nervo M radiale
intercostal nerve
nervio M intercostal
nerf M intercostal
Zwischenrippennerv M
nervo M intercostale
gluteal nerve
nervio M glúteo
nerf M fessier
Gesäßnerv M
nervo M gluteo
digital nerve
nervio M digital
nerf M digital
Fingernerv M
nervo M digitale
tibial nerve
nervio M ciático poplíteo interno
nerf M sciatique poplité interne
Schienbeinnerv M
nervo M tibiale
sural nerve
nervio M safeno externo
nerf M saphène externe
Wadennerv M
nervo M safeno esterno

nervous system

central nervous system
sistema^{M} nervioso central
système^{M} nerveux central
Zentralnervensystem^{N}
sistema^{M} nervoso centrale

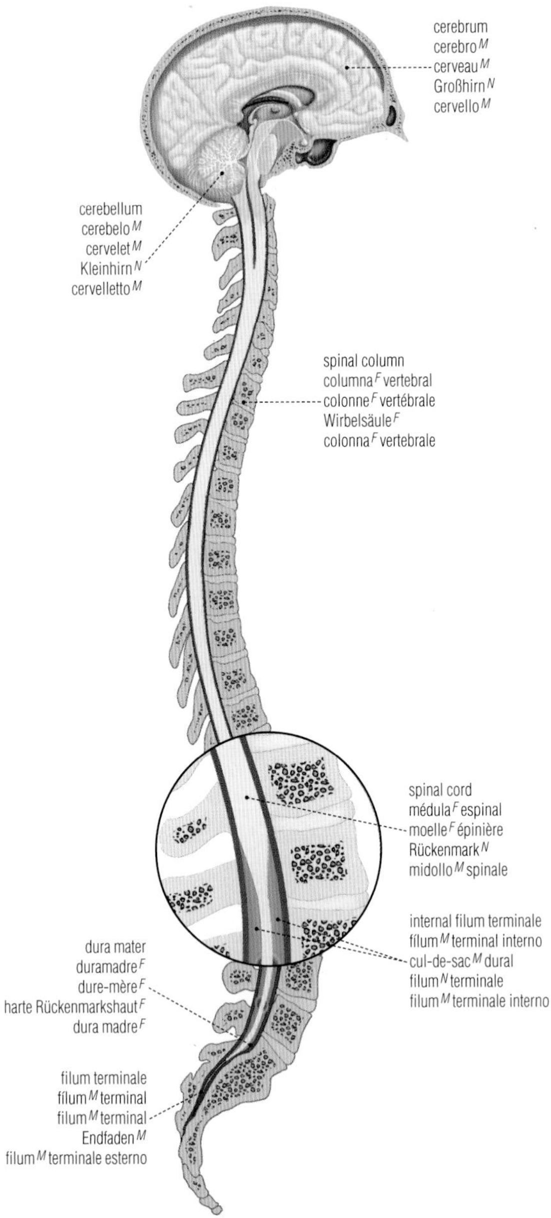
cerebrum
cerebro M
cerveau M
Großhirn N
cervello M
cerebellum
cerebelo M
cervelet M
Kleinhirn N
cervelletto M
spinal column
columna F vertebral
colonne F vertébrale
Wirbelsäule F
colonna F vertebrale
spinal cord
médula F espinal
moelle F épinière
Rückenmark N
midollo M spinale
internal filum terminale
fílum M terminal interno
cul-de-sac M dural
filum N terminale
filum M terminale interno
dura mater
duramadre F
dure-mère F
harte Rückenmarkshaut F
dura madre F
filum terminale
fílum M terminal
filum M terminal
Endfaden M
filum M terminale esterno

structure of the spinal cord
estructura[F] de la médula[F] espinal
structure[F] de la moelle[F] épinière
Aufbau[M] des Rückenmarks[N]
struttura[F] del midollo[M] spinale

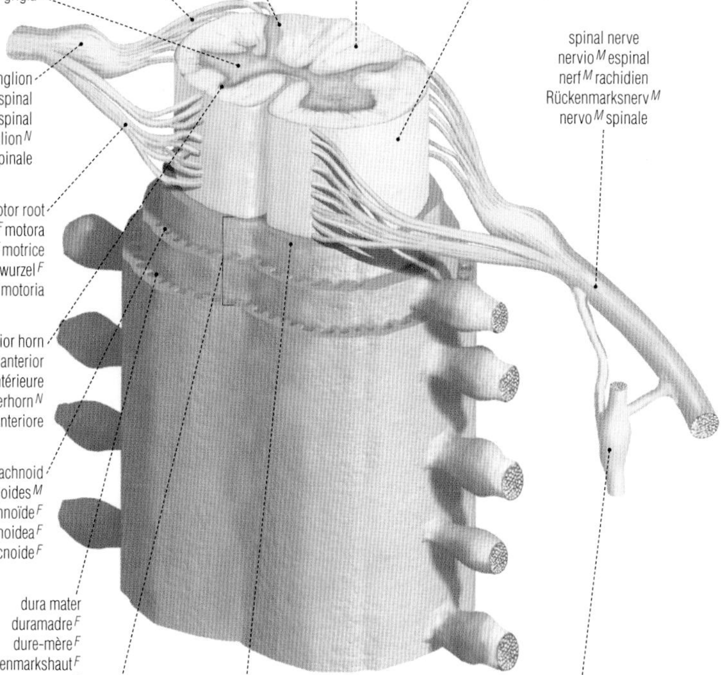
posterior horn
cuerno[M] posterior
corne[F] postérieure
Hinterhorn[N]
corno[M] posteriore
sensory root
raíz[F] sensitiva
racine[F] sensitive
hintere Nervenwurzel[F]
radice[F] sensoriale
white matter
sustancia[F] blanca
substance[F] blanche
weiße Substanz[F]
sostanza[F] bianca
spinal cord
médula[F] espinal
moelle[F] épinière
Rückenmark[N]
midollo[M] spinale
gray matter
sustancia[F] gris
substance[F] grise
graue Substanz[F]
sostanza[F] grigia
spinal nerve
nervio[M] espinal
nerf[M] rachidien
Rückenmarksnerv[M]
nervo[M] spinale
spinal ganglion
ganglio[M] espinal
ganglion[M] spinal
Spinalganglion[N]
ganglio[M] spinale
motor root
raíz[F] motora
racine[F] motrice
vordere Nervenwurzel[F]
radice[F] motoria
anterior horn
cuerno[M] anterior
corne[F] antérieure
Vorderhorn[N]
corno[M] anteriore
arachnoid
aracnoides[M]
arachnoïde[F]
Arachnoidea[F]
aracnoide[F]
dura mater
duramadre[F]
dure-mère[F]
harte Rückenmarkshaut[F]
dura madre[F]
sympathetic ganglion
ganglio[M] simpático
ganglion[M] du tronc[M] sympathique
symphatisches Ganglion[N]
ganglio[M] simpatico
meninges
meninges[F]
méninges[F]
Rückenmarkshaut[F]
meningi[F]
pia mater
piamadre[F]
pie-mère[F]
Pia Mater[F]
pia madre[F]

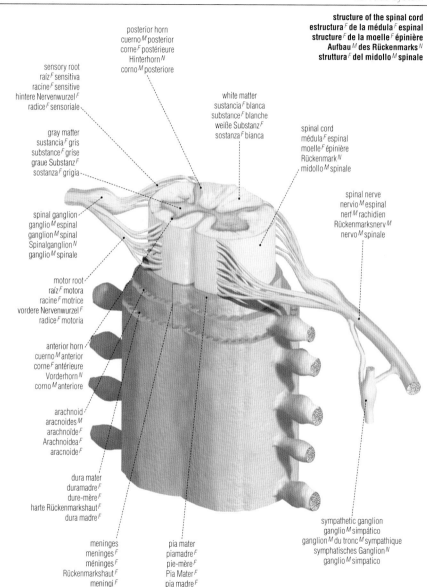

nervous system

brain
encéfalo *M*
encéphale *F*
Gehirn *N*
encefalo *M*

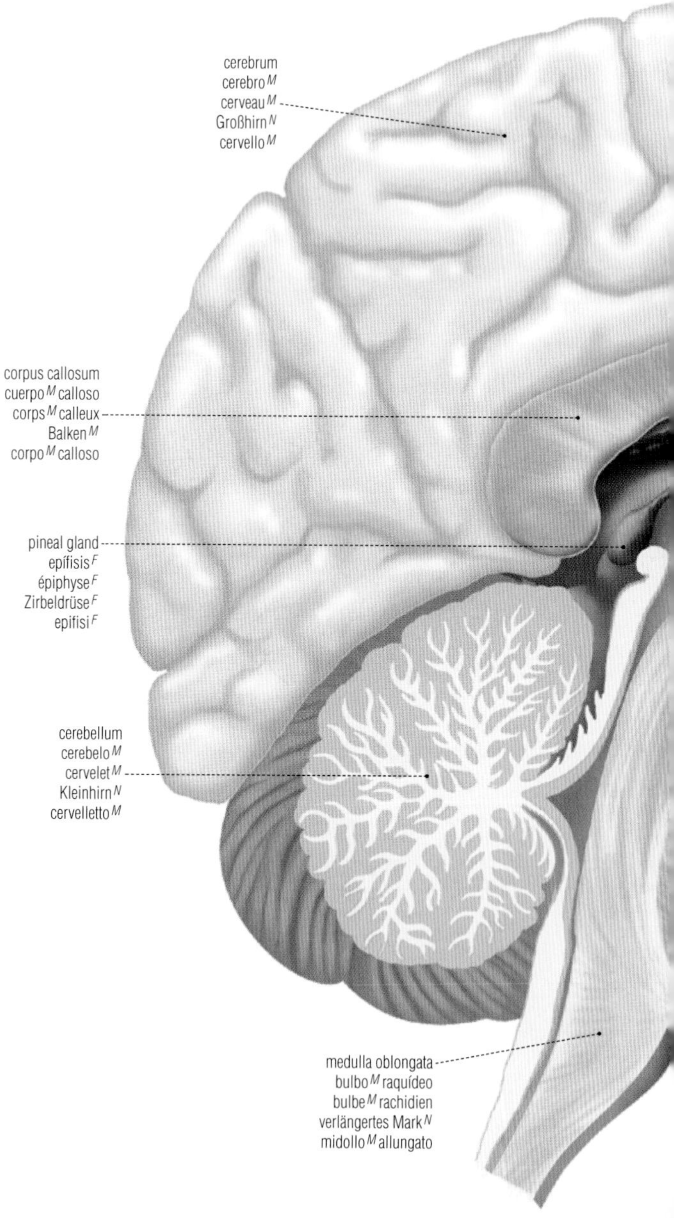
cerebrum
cerebro M
cerveau M
Großhirn N
cervello M
corpus callosum
cuerpo M calloso
corps M calleux
Balken M
corpo M calloso
pineal gland
epífisis F
épiphyse F
Zirbeldrüse F
epifisi F
cerebellum
cerebelo M
cervelet M
Kleinhirn N
cervelletto M
medulla oblongata
bulbo M raquídeo
bulbe M rachidien
verlängertes Mark N
midollo M allungato

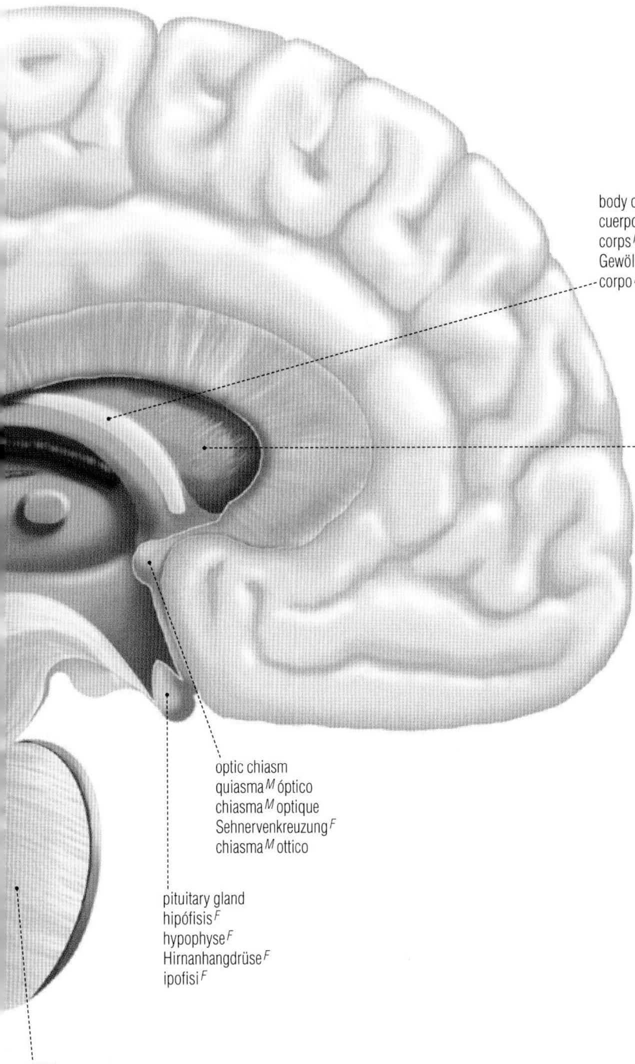
body of fornix
cuerpo[M] del fórnix[M]
corps[M] du fornix[M]
Gewölbekörper[M]
corpo[M] del fornice[M]
septum pellucidum
septum[M] pellucidum
septum[M] lucidum
Septum[N] pellucidum
setto[M] pellucido
optic chiasm
quiasma[M] óptico
chiasma[M] optique
Sehnervenkreuzung[F]
chiasma[M] ottico
pituitary gland
hipófisis[F]
hypophyse[F]
Hirnanhangdrüse[F]
ipofisi[F]
pons
puente[M] de Varolio
pont[M] de Varole
Brücke[F]
ponte[M] di Varolio

chain of neurons
cadena^F de neuronas^F
chaîne^F de neurones^M
Neuronenkette^F
catena^F di neuroni^M

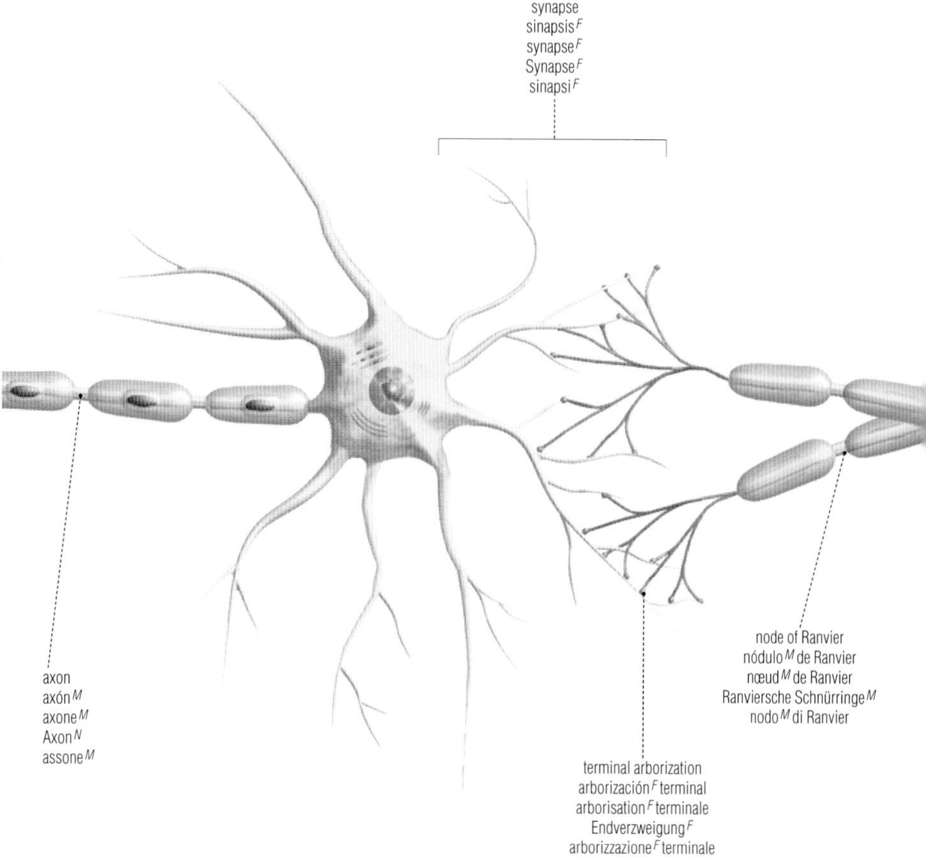
synapse
sinapsis^F
synapse^F
Synapse^F
sinapsi^F
axon
axón^M
axone^M
Axon^N
assone^M
node of Ranvier
nódulo^M de Ranvier
nœud^M de Ranvier
Ranviersche Schnürringe^M
nodo^M di Ranvier
terminal arborization
arborización^F terminal
arborisation^F terminale
Endverzweigung^F
arborizzazione^F terminale

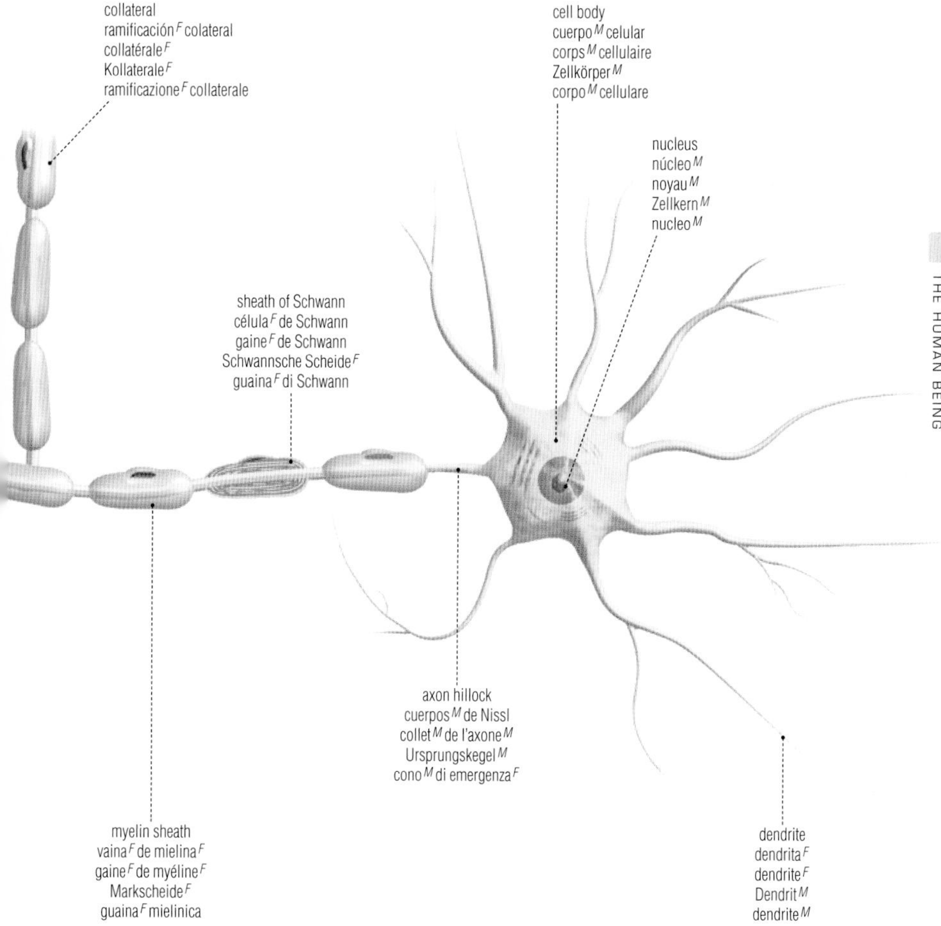
collateral
ramificación F colateral
collatérale F
Kollaterale F
ramificazione F collaterale
cell body
cuerpo M celular
corps M cellulaire
Zellkörper M
corpo M cellulare
nucleus
núcleo M
noyau M
Zellkern M
nucleo M
sheath of Schwann
célula F de Schwann
gaine F de Schwann
Schwannsche Scheide F
guaina F di Schwann
axon hillock
cuerpos M de Nissl
collet M de l'axone M
Ursprungskegel M
cono M di emergenza F
myelin sheath
vaina F de mielina F
gaine F de myéline F
Markscheide F
guaina F mielinica
dendrite
dendrita F
dendrite F
Dendrit M
dendrite M

cranial nerves
nervios^M craneales
nerfs^M crâniens
Hirnnerven^M
nervi^M cranici

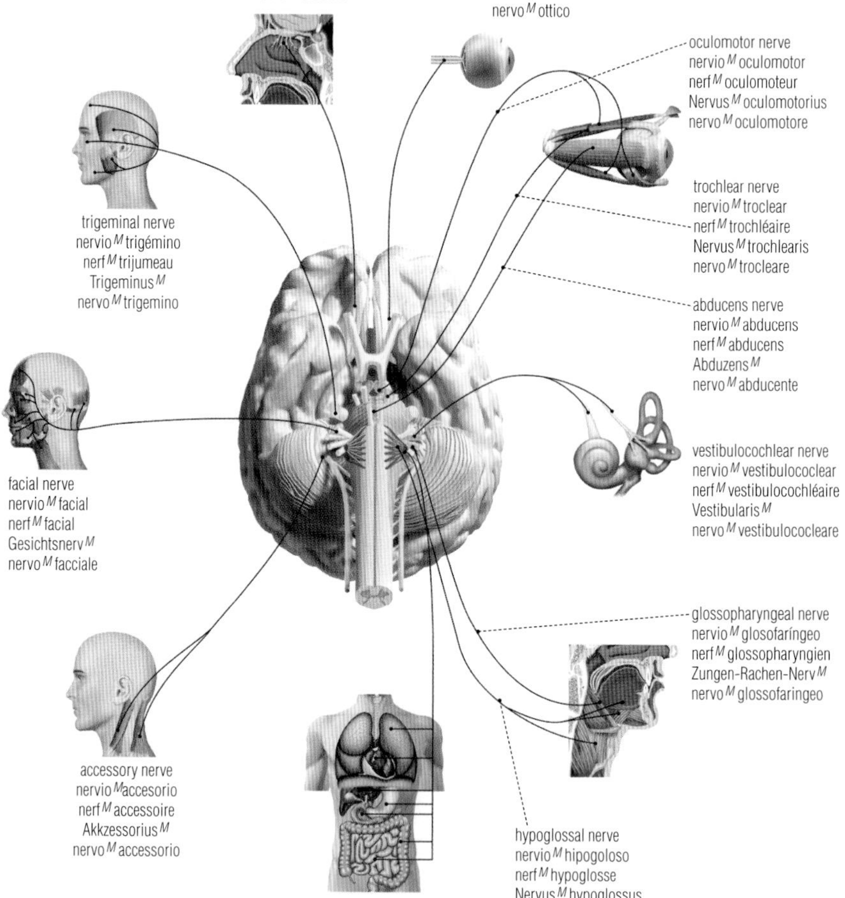

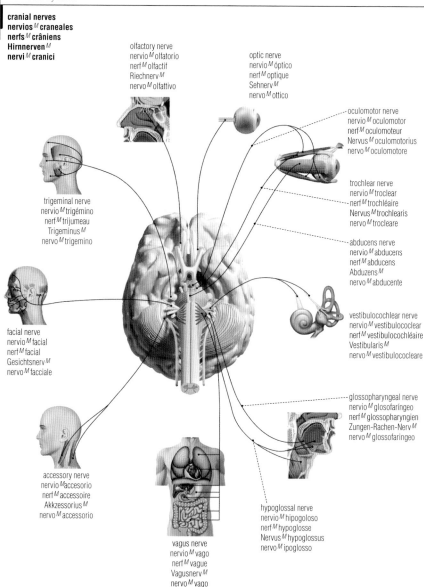

olfactory nerve
nervio^M olfatorio
nerf^M olfactif
Riechnerv^M
nervo^M olfattivo

optic nerve
nervio^M óptico
nerf^M optique
Sehnerv^M
nervo^M ottico

oculomotor nerve
nervio^M oculomotor
nerf^M oculomoteur
Nervus^M oculomotorius
nervo^M oculomotore

trochlear nerve
nervio^M troclear
nerf^M trochléaire
Nervus^M trochlearis
nervo^M trocleare

abducens nerve
nervio^M abducens
nerf^M abducens
Abduzens^M
nervo^M abducente

trigeminal nerve
nervio^M trigémino
nerf^M trijumeau
Trigeminus^M
nervo^M trigemino

facial nerve
nervio^M facial
nerf^M facial
Gesichtsnerv^M
nervo^M facciale

vestibulocochlear nerve
nervio^M vestibulococlear
nerf^M vestibulocochléaire
Vestibularis^M
nervo^M vestibulococleare

glossopharyngeal nerve
nervio^M glosofaríngeo
nerf^M glossopharyngien
Zungen-Rachen-Nerv^M
nervo^M glossofaringeo

accessory nerve
nervio^M accesorio
nerf^M accessoire
Akkzessorius^M
nervo^M accessorio

vagus nerve
nervio^M vago
nerf^M vague
Vagusnerv^M
nervo^M vago

hypoglossal nerve
nervio^M hipogoloso
nerf^M hypoglosse
Nervus^M hypoglossus
nervo^M ipoglosso

breast

seno^M | sein^M | Brust^F | seno^M

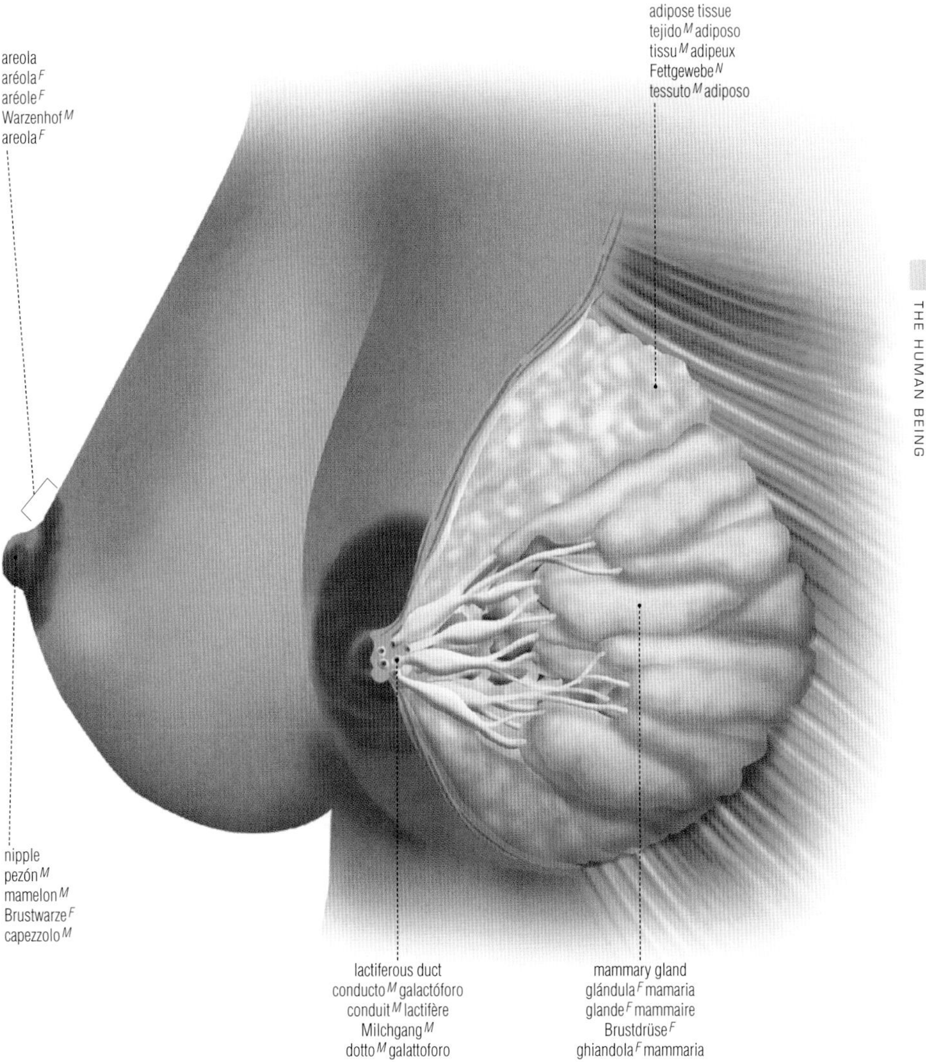
areola
aréola F
aréole F
Warzenhof M
areola F
adipose tissue
tejido M adiposo
tissu M adipeux
Fettgewebe N
tessuto M adiposo
nipple
pezón M
mamelon M
Brustwarze F
capezzolo M
lactiferous duct
conducto M galactóforo
conduit M lactifère
Milchgang M
dotto M galattoforo
mammary gland
glándula F mamaria
glande F mammaire
Brustdrüse F
ghiandola F mammaria

female reproductive organs

órganos^{M} genitales femeninos | organes^{M} génitaux féminins | weibliche Geschlechtsorgane^{N} | organi^{M} genitali femminili

sagittal section
sección^{F} sagital
coupe^{F} sagittale
Sagittalschnitt^{M}
sezione^{F} sagittale

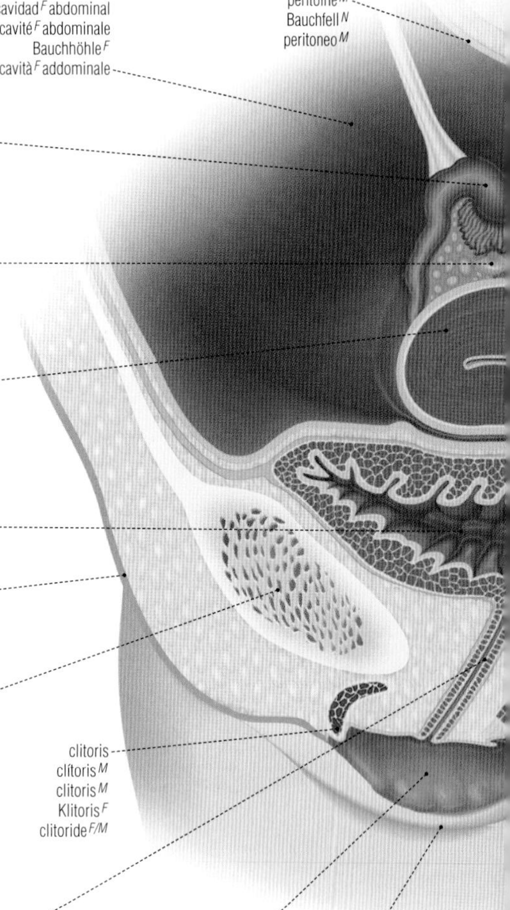

peritoneum
peritoneo^{M}
péritoine^{M}
Bauchfell^{N}
peritoneo^{M}

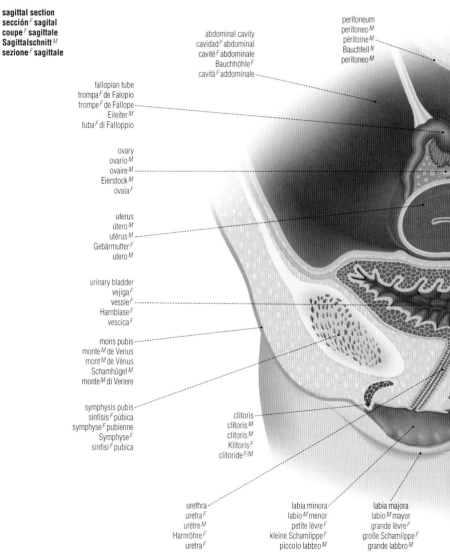

abdominal cavity
cavidad^{F} abdominal
cavité^{F} abdominale
Bauchhöhle^{F}
cavità^{F} addominale

fallopian tube
trompa^{F} de Falopio
trompe^{F} de Fallope
Eileiter^{M}
tuba^{F} di Falloppio

ovary
ovario^{M}
ovaire^{M}
Eierstock^{M}
ovaia^{F}

uterus
útero^{M}
utérus^{M}
Gebärmutter^{F}
utero^{M}

urinary bladder
vejiga^{F}
vessie^{F}
Harnblase^{F}
vescica^{F}

mons pubis
monte^{M} de Venus
mont^{M} de Vénus
Schamhügel^{M}
monte^{M} di Venere

symphysis pubis
sínfisis^{F} púbica
symphyse^{F} pubienne
Symphyse^{F}
sinfisi^{F} pubica

clitoris
clítoris^{M}
clitoris^{M}
Klitoris^{F}
clitoride$^{F/M}$

urethra
uretra^{F}
urètre^{M}
Harnröhre^{F}
uretra^{F}

labia minora
labio^{M} menor
petite lèvre^{F}
kleine Schamlippe^{F}
piccolo labbro^{M}

labia majora
labio^{M} mayor
grande lèvre^{F}
große Schamlippe^{F}
grande labbro^{M}

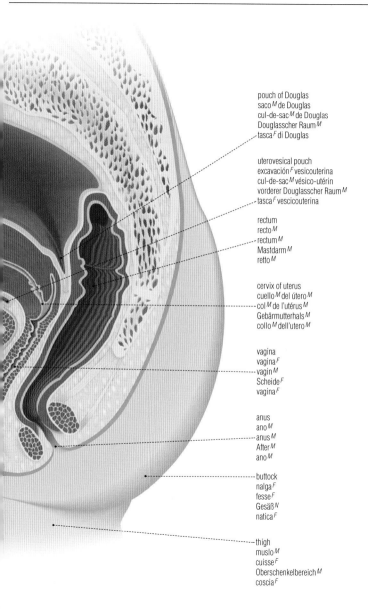

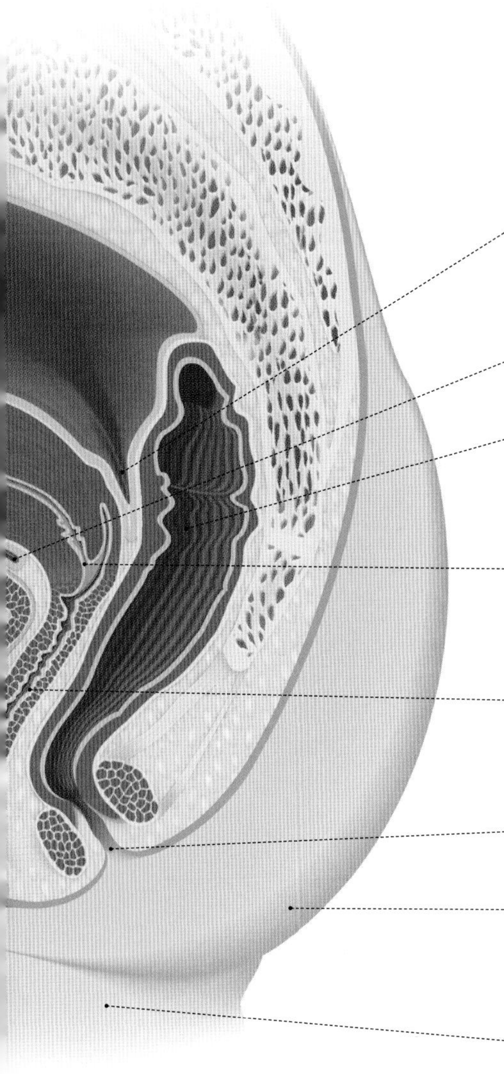
pouch of Douglas
saco[M] de Douglas
cul-de-sac[M] de Douglas
Douglasscher Raum[M]
tasca[F] di Douglas
uterovesical pouch
excavación[F] vesicouterina
cul-de-sac[M] vésico-utérin
vorderer Douglasscher Raum[M]
tasca[F] vescicouterina
rectum
recto[M]
rectum[M]
Mastdarm[M]
retto[M]
cervix of uterus
cuello[M] del útero[M]
col[M] de l'utérus[M]
Gebärmutterhals[M]
collo[M] dell'utero[M]
vagina
vagina[F]
vagin[M]
Scheide[F]
vagina[F]
anus
ano[M]
anus[M]
After[M]
ano[M]
buttock
nalga[F]
fesse[F]
Gesäß[N]
natica[F]
thigh
muslo[M]
cuisse[F]
Oberschenkelbereich[M]
coscia[F]

female reproductive organs

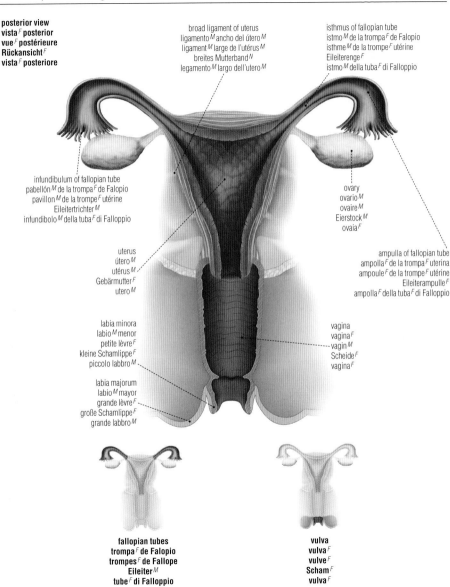

posterior view
vista[F] posterior
vue[F] postérieure
Rückansicht[F]
vista[F] posteriore

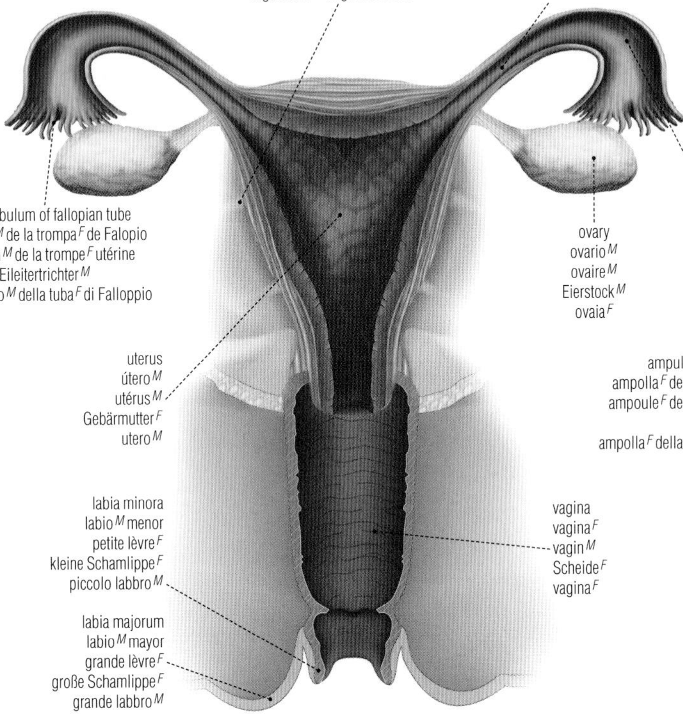

broad ligament of uterus
ligamento[M] ancho del útero[M]
ligament[M] large de l'utérus[M]
breites Mutterband[N]
legamento[M] largo dell'utero[M]
isthmus of fallopian tube
istmo[M] de la trompa[F] de Falopio
isthme[M] de la trompe[F] utérine
Eileiterenge[F]
istmo[M] della tuba[F] di Falloppio
infundibulum of fallopian tube
pabellón[M] de la trompa[F] de Falopio
pavillon[M] de la trompe[F] utérine
Eileitertrichter[M]
infundibolo[M] della tuba[F] di Falloppio
ovary
ovario[M]
ovaire[M]
Eierstock[M]
ovaia[F]
uterus
útero[M]
utérus[M]
Gebärmutter[F]
utero[M]
ampulla of fallopian tube
ampolla[F] de la trompa[F] uterina
ampoule[F] de la trompe[F] utérine
Eileiterampulle[F]
ampolla[F] della tuba[F] di Falloppio
labia minora
labio[M] menor
petite lèvre[F]
kleine Schamlippe[F]
piccolo labbro[M]
vagina
vagina[F]
vagin[M]
Scheide[F]
vagina[F]
labia majorum
labio[M] mayor
grande lèvre[F]
große Schamlippe[F]
grande labbro[M]

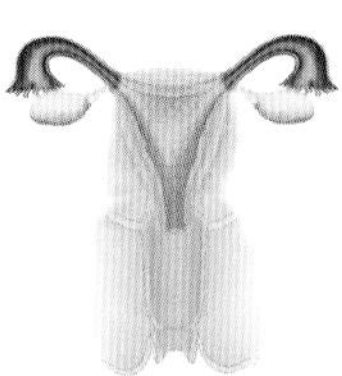

fallopian tubes
trompa[F] de Falopio
trompes[F] de Fallope
Eileiter[M]
tube[F] di Falloppio

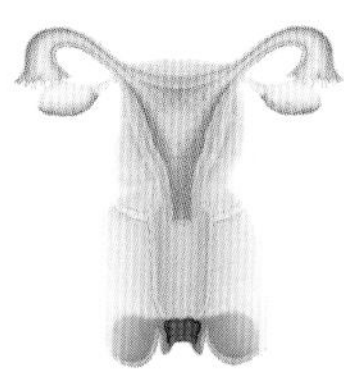

vulva
vulva[F]
vulve[F]
Scham[F]
vulva[F]

female reproductive organs

egg
óvulo *M*
ovule *M*
Eizelle *F*
ovulo *M*

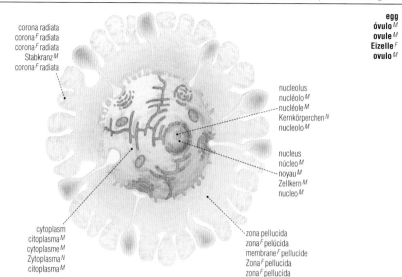

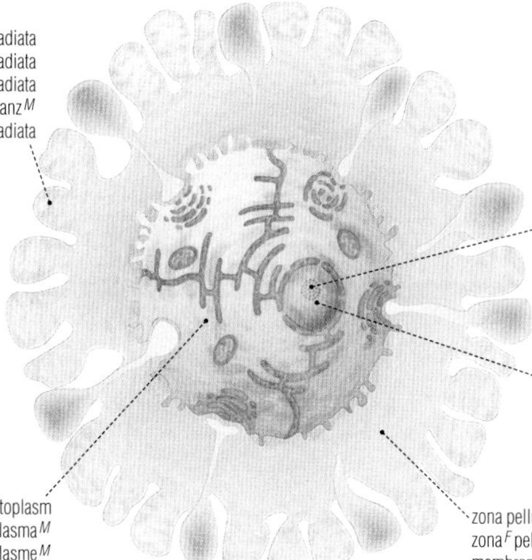
corona radiata
corona F radiata
corona F radiata
Stabkranz M
corona F radiata
nucleolus
nucléolo M
nucléole M
Kernkörperchen N
nucleolo M
nucleus
núcleo M
noyau M
Zellkern M
nucleo M
cytoplasm
citoplasma M
cytoplasme M
Zytoplasma N
citoplasma M
zona pellucida
zona F pelúcida
membrane F pellucide
Zona F pellucida
zona F pellucida

male reproductive organs

órganos *M* genitales masculinos | organes *M* génitaux masculins | männliche Geschlechtsorgane *N* | organi *M* genitali maschili

spermatozoon
espermatozoide *M*
spermatozoïde *M*
Spermium *N*
spermatozoo *M*

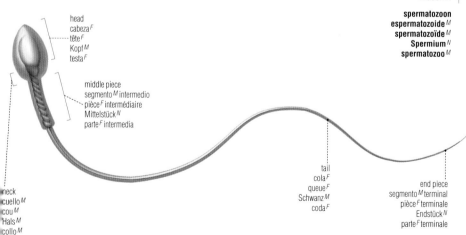

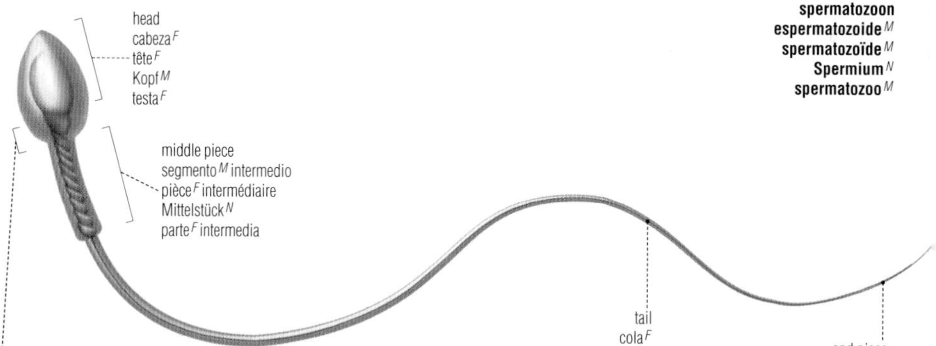
head
cabeza F
tête F
Kopf M
testa F
middle piece
segmento M intermedio
pièce F intermédiaire
Mittelstück N
parte F intermedia
tail
cola F
queue F
Schwanz M
coda F
end piece
segmento M terminal
pièce F terminale
Endstück N
parte F terminale
neck
cuello M
cou M
Hals M
collo M

sagittal section
sección^F sagital
coupe^F sagittale
Sagittalschnitt^M
sezione^F sagittale

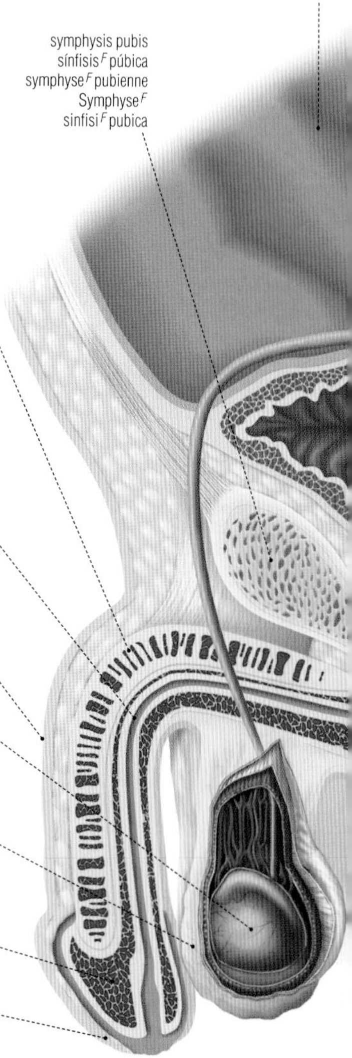

abdominal cavity
cavidad^F abdominal
cavité^F abdominale
Bauchhöhle^F
cavità^F addominale
symphysis pubis
sínfisis^F púbica
symphyse^F pubienne
Symphyse^F
sinfisi^F pubica
cavernous body
cuerpo^M cavernoso
corps^M caverneux
Rutenschwellkörper^M
corpo^M cavernoso
male urethra
uretra^F
urètre^M pénien
Harnröhre^F
uretra^F
penis
pene^M
verge^F
Penis^M
pene^M
testicle
testículo^M
testicule^M
Hoden^M
testicolo^M
scrotum
escroto^M
scrotum^M
Hodensack^M
scroto^M
glans penis
glande^M
gland^M
Eichel^F
glande^M
foreskin
prepucio^M
prépuce^M
Vorhaut^F
prepuzio^M

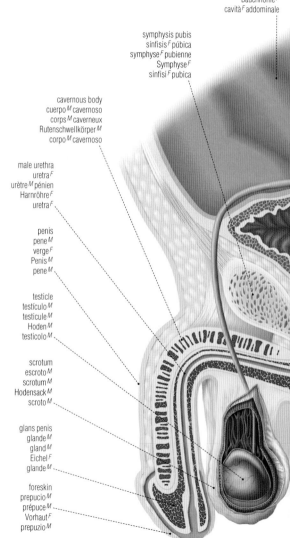

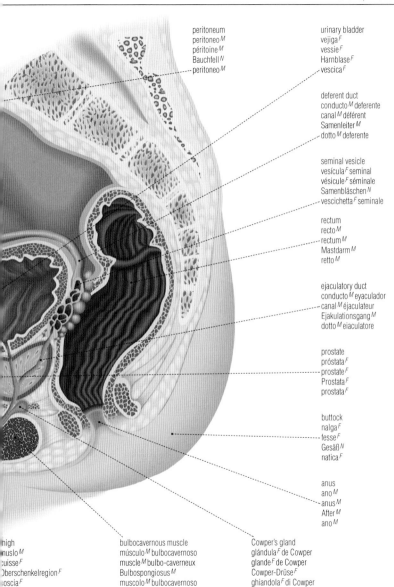

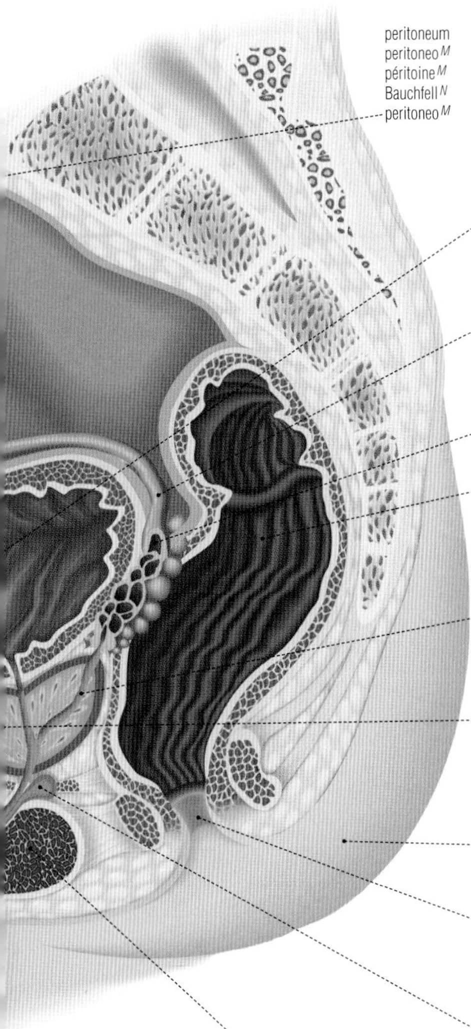
peritoneum
peritoneo M
péritoine M
Bauchfell N
peritoneo M
urinary bladder
vejiga F
vessie F
Harnblase F
vescica F
deferent duct
conducto M deferente
canal M déférent
Samenleiter M
dotto M deferente
seminal vesicle
vesícula F seminal
vésicule F séminale
Samenbläschen N
vescichetta F seminale
rectum
recto M
rectum M
Mastdarm M
retto M
ejaculatory duct
conducto M eyaculador
canal M éjaculateur
Ejakulationsgang M
dotto M eiaculatore
prostate
próstata F
prostate F
Prostata F
prostata F
buttock
nalga F
fesse F
Gesäß N
natica F
anus
ano M
anus M
After M
ano M
nigh
nuslo M
uisse F
berschenkelregion F
oscia F
bulbocavernous muscle
músculo M bulbocavernoso
muscle M bulbo-caverneux
Bulbospongiosus M
muscolo M bulbocavernoso
Cowper's gland
glándula F de Cowper
glande F de Cowper
Cowper-Drüse F
ghiandola F di Cowper

touch

tacto[M] | toucher[M] | Tastsinn[M] | tatto[M]

skin
piel[F]
peau[F]
Haut[F]
pelle[F]

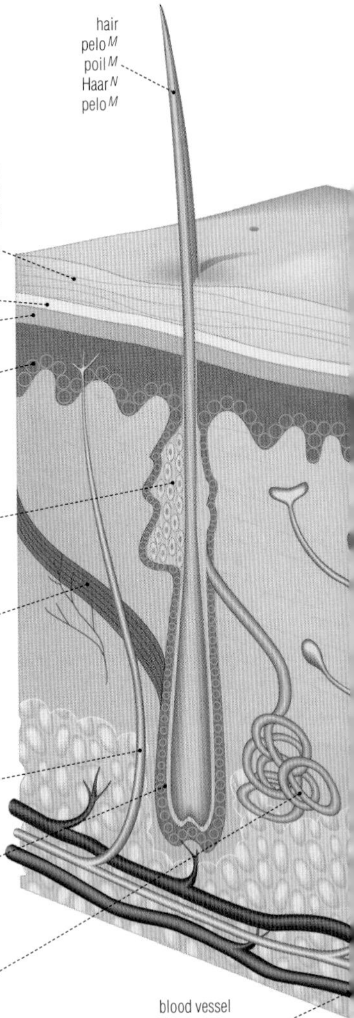
hair
pelo[M]
poil[M]
Haar[N]
pelo[M]
stratum corneum
estrato[M] córneo
couche[F] cornée
Hornschicht[F]
strato[M] corneo
stratum lucidum
estrato[M] lúcido
couche[F] claire
Glanzschicht[F]
strato[M] lucido
stratum granulosum
estrato[M] granuloso
couche[F] granuleuse
Körnerschicht[F]
strato[M] granulare
stratum basale
estrato[M] basal
couche[F] basale
Basalschicht[F]
strato[M] basale
sebaceous gland
glándula[F] sebácea
glande[F] sébacée
Talgdrüse[F]
ghiandola[F] sebacea
arrector pili muscle
músculo[M] erector del pelo[M]
muscle[M] arrecteur
Haaraufrichter[M]
muscolo[M] erettore del pelo[M]
nerve fiber
fibra[F] nerviosa
fibre[F] nerveuse
Nervenfaser[F]
fibra[F] nervosa
hair follicle
folículo[M] piloso
follicule[M]
Haarbalg[M]
follicolo[M] pilifero
apocrine sweat gland
glándula[F] sudorípara apocrina
glande[F] sudoripare apocrine
apokrine Schweißdrüse[F]
ghiandola[F] sudoripara apocrina
blood vessel
vaso[M] sanguíneo
vaisseau[M] sanguin
Blutgefäß[N]
vaso[M] sanguigno

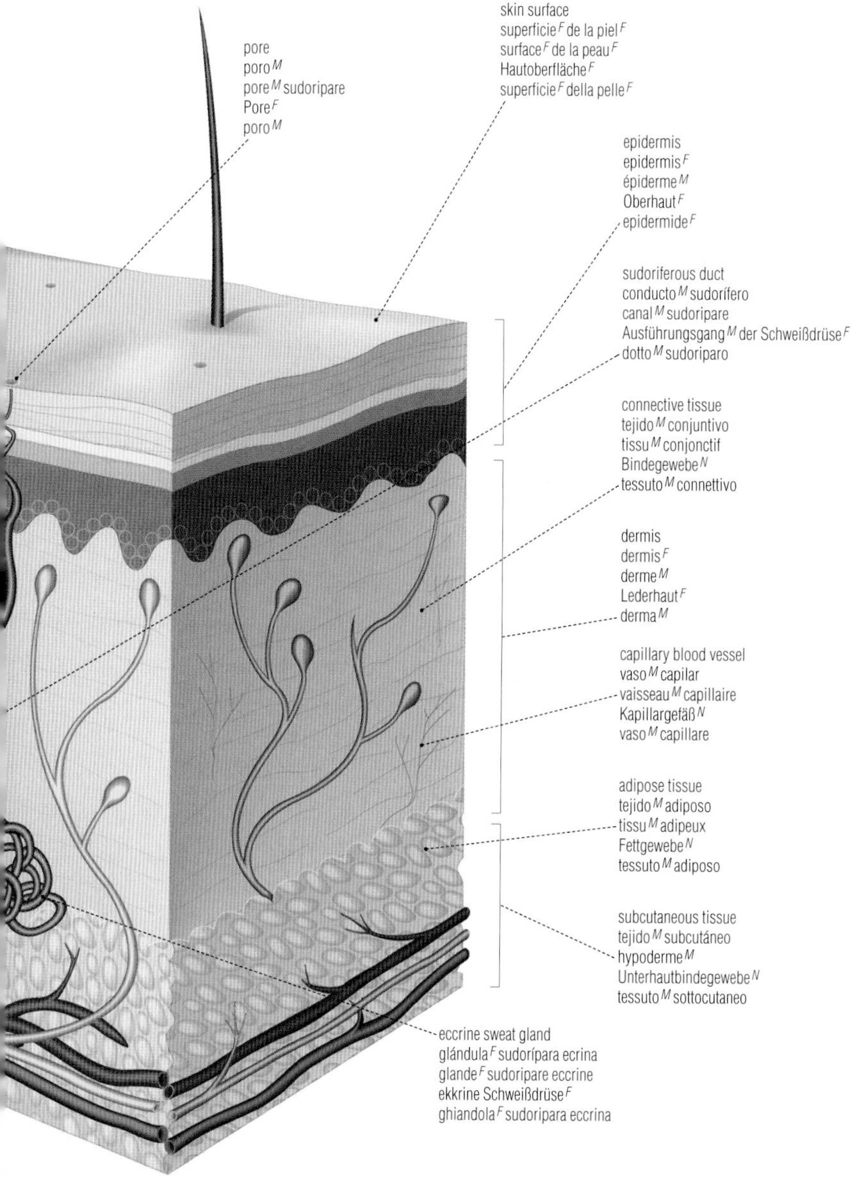
pore
poro M
pore M sudoripare
Pore F
poro M
skin surface
superficie F de la piel F
surface F de la peau F
Hautoberfläche F
superficie F della pelle F
epidermis
epidermis F
épiderme M
Oberhaut F
epidermide F
sudoriferous duct
conducto M sudorífero
canal M sudoripare
Ausführungsgang M der Schweißdrüse F
dotto M sudoriparo
connective tissue
tejido M conjuntivo
tissu M conjonctif
Bindegewebe N
tessuto M connettivo
dermis
dermis F
derme M
Lederhaut F
derma M
capillary blood vessel
vaso M capilar
vaisseau M capillaire
Kapillargefäß N
vaso M capillare
adipose tissue
tejido M adiposo
tissu M adipeux
Fettgewebe N
tessuto M adiposo
subcutaneous tissue
tejido M subcutáneo
hypoderme M
Unterhautbindegewebe N
tessuto M sottocutaneo
eccrine sweat gland
glándula F sudorípara ecrina
glande F sudoripare eccrine
ekkrine Schweißdrüse F
ghiandola F sudoripara eccrina

touch

finger
dedo[M]
doigt[M]
Finger[M]
dito[M]

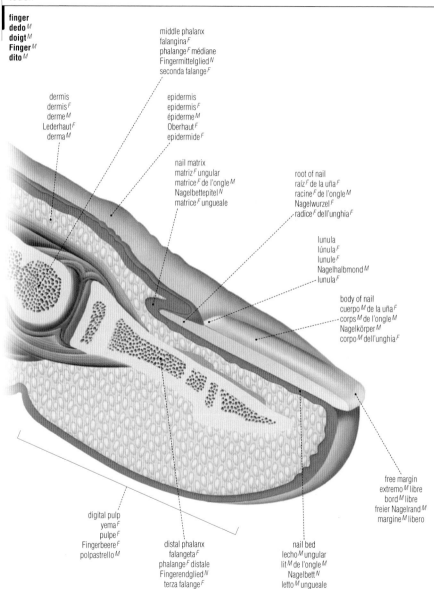

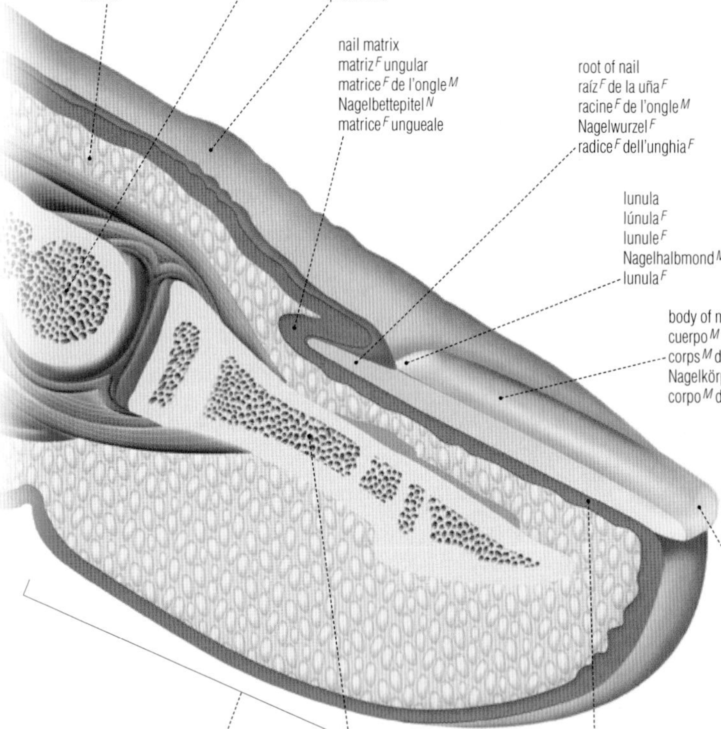
middle phalanx
falangina[F]
phalange[F] médiane
Fingermittelglied[N]
seconda falange[F]
dermis
dermis[F]
derme[M]
Lederhaut[F]
derma[M]
epidermis
epidermis[F]
épiderme[M]
Oberhaut[F]
epidermide[F]
nail matrix
matriz[F] ungular
matrice[F] de l'ongle[M]
Nagelbettepitel[N]
matrice[F] ungueale
root of nail
raíz[F] de la uña[F]
racine[F] de l'ongle[M]
Nagelwurzel[F]
radice[F] dell'unghia[F]
lunula
lúnula[F]
lunule[F]
Nagelhalbmond[M]
lunula[F]
body of nail
cuerpo[M] de la uña[F]
corps[M] de l'ongle[M]
Nagelkörper[M]
corpo[M] dell'unghia[F]
free margin
extremo[M] libre
bord[M] libre
freier Nagelrand[M]
margine[M] libero
digital pulp
yema[F]
pulpe[F]
Fingerbeere[F]
polpastrello[M]
distal phalanx
falangeta[F]
phalange[F] distale
Fingerendglied[N]
terza falange[F]
nail bed
lecho[M] ungular
lit[M] de l'ongle[M]
Nagelbett[N]
letto[M] ungueale

hearing

oído[M] | ouïe[F] | Gehör[N] | udito[M]

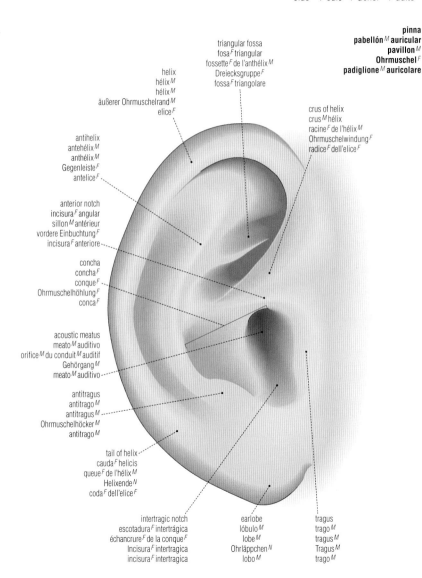

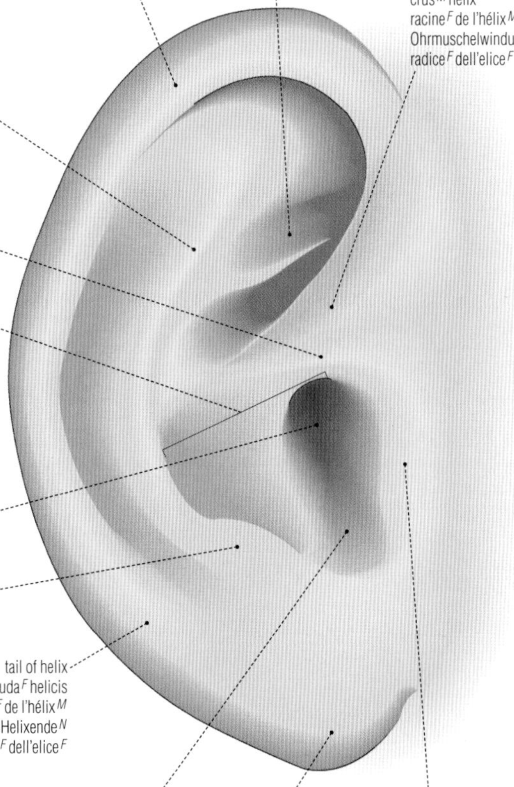
pinna
pabellón[M] auricular
pavillon[M]
Ohrmuschel[F]
padiglione[M] auricolare

triangular fossa
fosa[F] triangular
fossette[F] de l'anthélix[M]
Dreiecksgruppe[F]
fossa[F] triangolare

helix
hélix[M]
hélix[M]
äußerer Ohrmuschelrand[M]
elice[F]

crus of helix
crus[M] hélix
racine[F] de l'hélix[M]
Ohrmuschelwindung[F]
radice[F] dell'elice[F]

antihelix
antehélix[M]
anthélix[M]
Gegenleiste[F]
antelice[F]

anterior notch
incisura[F] angular
sillon[M] antérieur
vordere Einbuchtung[F]
incisura[F] anteriore

concha
concha[F]
conque[F]
Ohrmuschelhöhlung[F]
conca[F]

acoustic meatus
meato[M] auditivo
orifice[M] du conduit[M] auditif
Gehörgang[M]
meato[M] auditivo

antitragus
antitrago[M]
antitragus[M]
Ohrmuschelhöcker[M]
antitrago[M]

tail of helix
cauda[F] helicis
queue[F] de l'hélix[M]
Helixende[N]
coda[F] dell'elice[F]

intertragic notch
escotadura[F] intertrágica
échancrure[F] de la conque[F]
Incisura[F] intertragica
incisura[F] intertragica

earlobe
lóbulo[M]
lobe[M]
Ohrläppchen[N]
lobo[M]

tragus
trago[M]
tragus[M]
Tragus[M]
trago[M]

hearing

structure of the ear
estructura F del oído M
structure F de l'oreille F
Aufbau M des Ohres N
struttura F dell'orecchio M

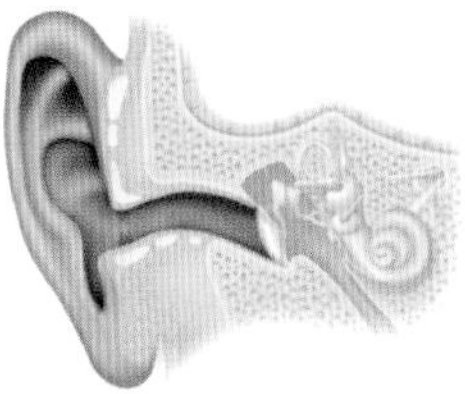

external ear
oreja F
oreille F externe
äußeres Ohr N
orecchio M esterno

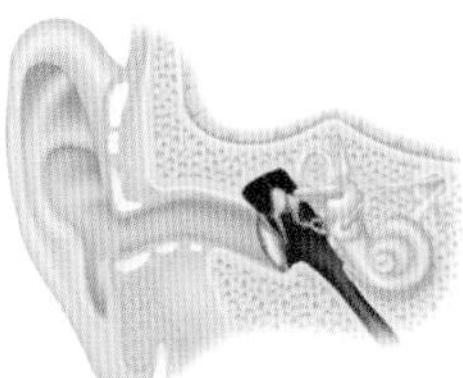

middle ear
oído M medio
oreille F moyenne
Mittelohr N
orecchio M medio

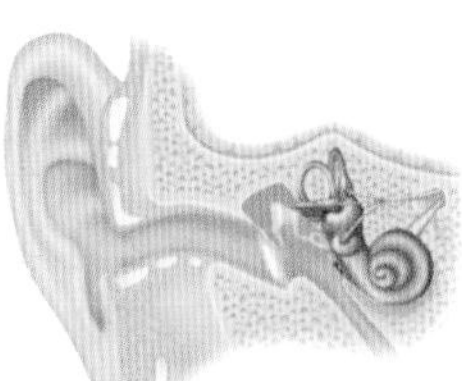

internal ear
oído M interno
oreille F interne
Innenohr N
orecchio M interno

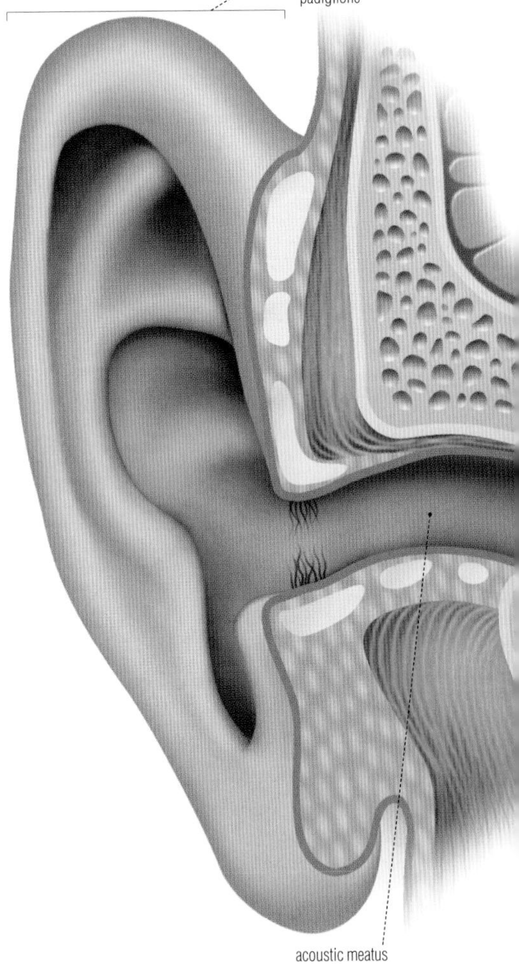
pinna
pabellón M auricular
pavillon M
Ohrmuschel F
padiglione M
acoustic meatus
meato M auditivo
conduit M auditif
Gehörgang M
meato M auditivo

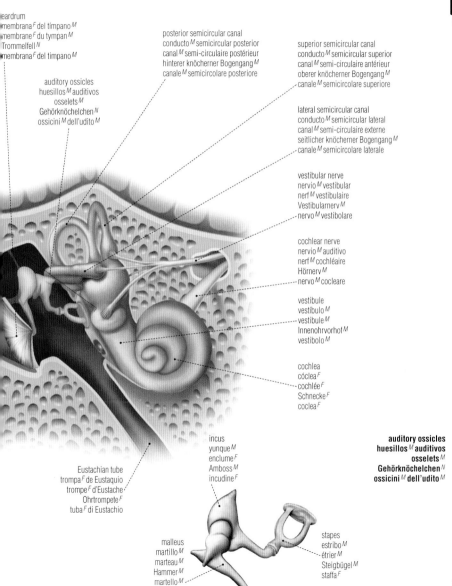

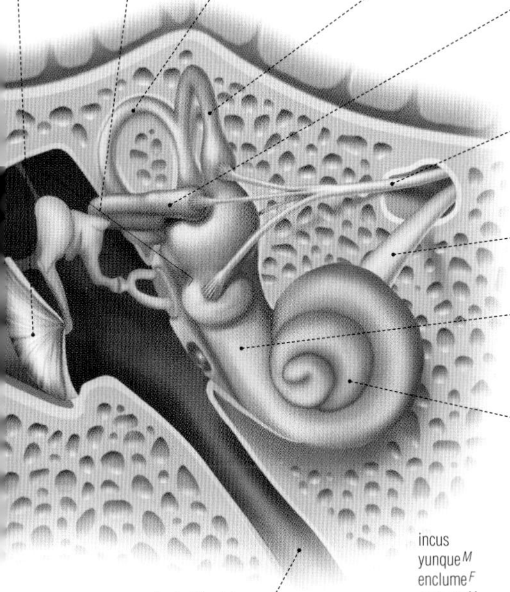
eardrum
membrana [F] del tímpano [M]
membrane [F] du tympan [M]
Trommelfell [N]
membrana [F] del timpano [M]
auditory ossicles
huesillos [M] auditivos
osselets [M]
Gehörknöchelchen [N]
ossicini [M] dell'udito [M]
posterior semicircular canal
conducto [M] semicircular posterior
canal [M] semi-circulaire postérieur
hinterer knöcherner Bogengang [M]
canale [M] semicircolare posteriore
superior semicircular canal
conducto [M] semicircular superior
canal [M] semi-circulaire antérieur
oberer knöcherner Bogengang [M]
canale [M] semicircolare superiore
lateral semicircular canal
conducto [M] semicircular lateral
canal [M] semi-circulaire externe
seitlicher knöcherner Bogengang [M]
canale [M] semicircolare laterale
vestibular nerve
nervio [M] vestibular
nerf [M] vestibulaire
Vestibularnerv [M]
nervo [M] vestibolare
cochlear nerve
nervio [M] auditivo
nerf [M] cochléaire
Hörnerv [M]
nervo [M] cocleare
vestibule
vestíbulo [M]
vestibule [M]
Innenohrvorhof [M]
vestibolo [M]
cochlea
cóclea [F]
cochlée [F]
Schnecke [F]
coclea [F]
Eustachian tube
trompa [F] de Eustaquio
trompe [F] d'Eustache
Ohrtrompete [F]
tuba [F] di Eustachio

auditory ossicles
huesillos [M] auditivos
osselets [M]
Gehörknöchelchen [N]
ossicini [M] dell'udito [M]

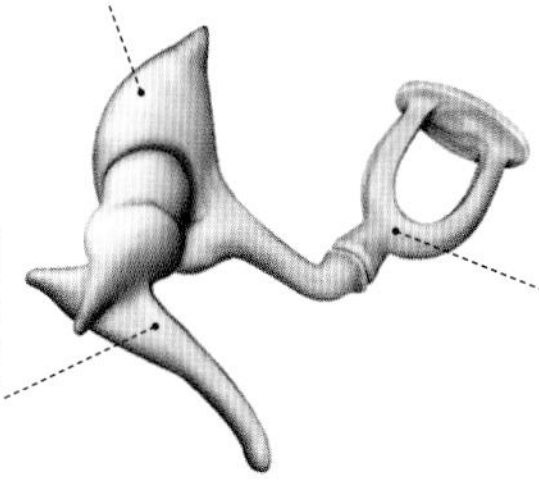
incus
yunque [M]
enclume [F]
Amboss [M]
incudine [F]
malleus
martillo [M]
marteau [M]
Hammer [M]
martello [M]
stapes
estribo [M]
étrier [M]
Steigbügel [M]
staffa [F]

smell and taste

olfato[M] y gusto[M] | odorat[M] et goût[M] | Geruchs-[M] und Geschmackssinn[M] | olfatto[M] e gusto[M]

mouth
boca[F]
bouche[F]
Mund[M]
bocca[F]

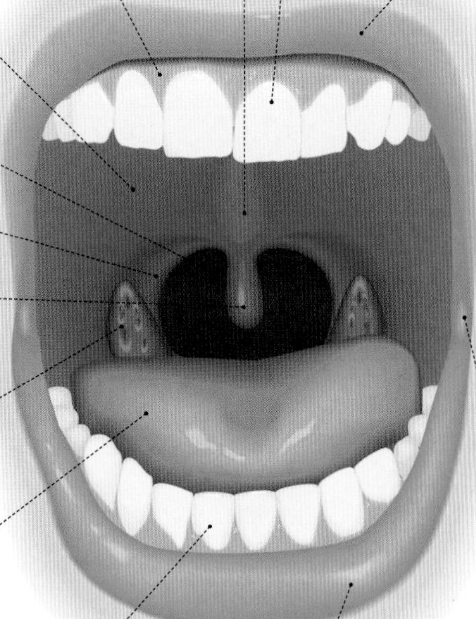
soft palate
velo[M] del paladar[M]
voile[M] du palais[M]
weicher Gaumen[M]
palato[M] molle
superior dental arch
arco[M] dentario superior
arcade[F] dentaire supérieure
obere Zahnreihe[F]
arcata[F] dentale superiore
gum
encía[F]
gencive[F]
Zahnfleisch[N]
gengiva[F]
upper lip
labio[M] superior
lèvre[F] supérieure
Oberlippe[F]
labbro[M] superiore
hard palate
bóveda[F] palatina
voûte[F] du palais[M]
harter Gaumen[M]
palato[M] duro
isthmus of fauces
istmo[M] de las fauces[F]
isthme[M] du gosier[M]
Rachenenge[F]
istmo[M] delle fauci[F]
palatoglossal arch
pilar[M] anterior del velo[M] del paladar[M]
pilier[M] du voile[M]
vorderer Gaumenbogen[M]
arco[M] palatoglosso
uvula
úvula[F]
luette[F]
Zäpfchen[N]
ugola[F]
tonsil
amígdala[F]
amygdale[F]
Mandel[F]
tonsilla[F]
tongue
lengua[F]
langue[F]
Zunge[F]
lingua[F]
inferior dental arch
arco[M] dentario inferior
arcade[F] dentaire inférieure
untere Zahnreihe[F]
arcata[F] dentale inferiore
lower lip
labio[M] inferior
lèvre[F] inférieure
Unterlippe[F]
labbro[M] inferiore
commissure of lips of mouth
comisura[F] labial
commissure[F] labiale
Mundwinkel[M]
commessura[F] labiale

external nose
nariz[F]
parties[F] externes du nez[M]
äußere Nase[F]
naso[M] esterno

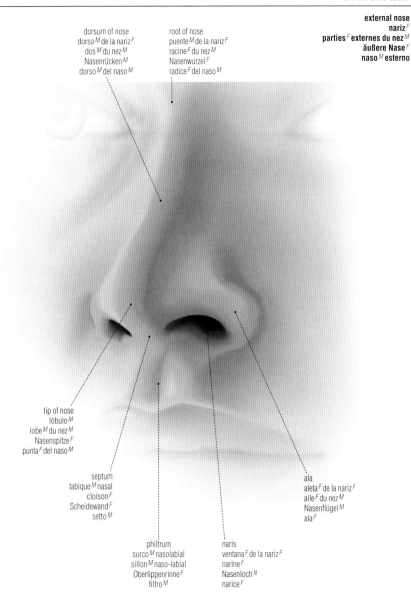

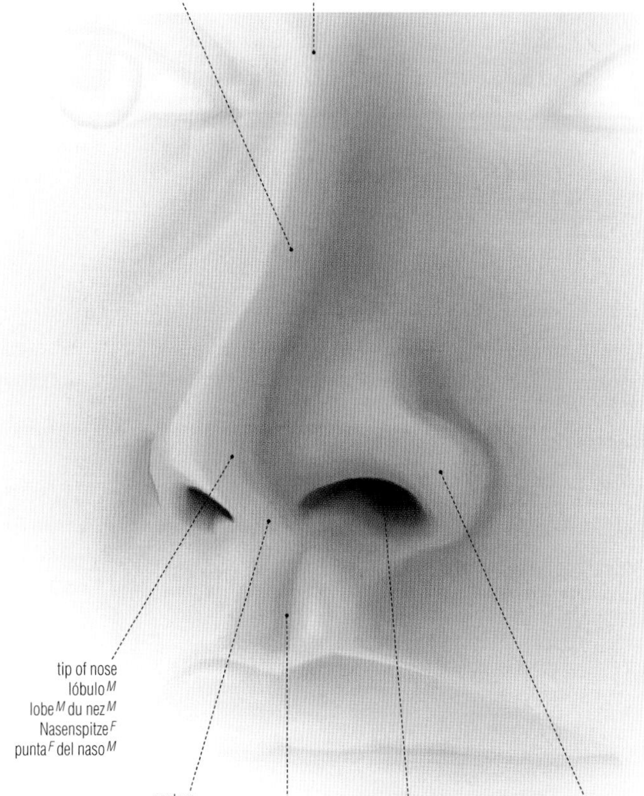
dorsum of nose
dorso[M] de la nariz[F]
dos[M] du nez[M]
Nasenrücken[M]
dorso[M] del naso[M]
root of nose
puente[M] de la nariz[F]
racine[F] du nez[M]
Nasenwurzel[F]
radice[F] del naso[M]
tip of nose
lóbulo[M]
lobe[M] du nez[M]
Nasenspitze[F]
punta[F] del naso[M]
septum
tabique[M] nasal
cloison[F]
Scheidewand[F]
setto[M]
ala
aleta[F] de la nariz[F]
aile[F] du nez[M]
Nasenflügel[M]
ala[F]
philtrum
surco[M] nasolabial
sillon[M] naso-labial
Oberlippenrinne[F]
filtro[M]
naris
ventana[F] de la nariz[F]
narine[F]
Nasenloch[N]
narice[F]

smell and taste

nasal fossae
fosas^F nasales
fosses^F nasales
Nasenhöhle^F
fosse^F nasali

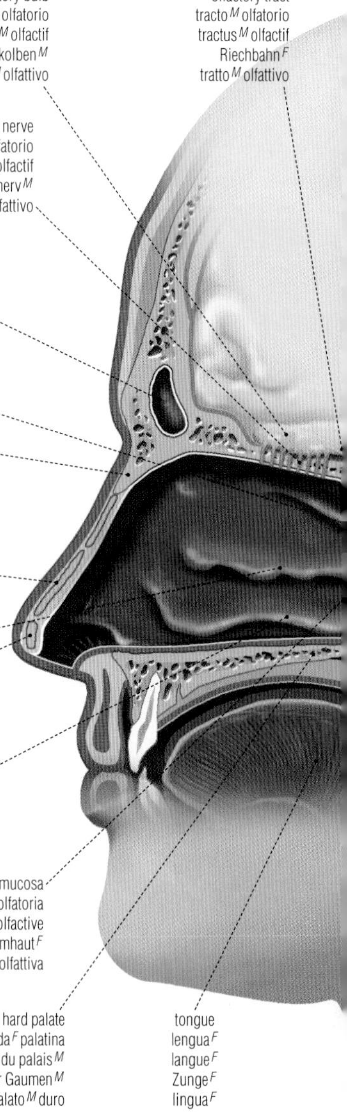
olfactory bulb
bulbo^M olfatorio
bulbe^M olfactif
Riechkolben^M
bulbo^M olfattivo
olfactory tract
tracto^M olfatorio
tractus^M olfactif
Riechbahn^F
tratto^M olfattivo
frontal sinus
seno^M frontal
sinus^M frontal
Stirnhöhle^F
seno^M frontale
olfactory nerve
nervio^M olfatorio
nerf^M olfactif
Riechnerv^M
nervo^M olfattivo
superior nasal concha
cornete^M superior
cornet^M supérieur
obere Nasenmuschel^F
conca^F nasale superiore
nasal bone
hueso^M nasal
os^M propre du nez^M
Nasenbein^N
osso^M nasale
septal cartilage of nose
cartílago^M nasal del tabique^M
cartilage^M de la cloison^F
Scheidewandknorpel^M
cartilagine^F del setto^M nasale
middle nasal concha
cornete^M medio
cornet^M moyen
mittlere Nasenmuschel^F
conca^F nasale media
greater alar cartilage
cartílago^M alar mayor
cartilage^M de l'aile^F du nez^M
großer Nasenflügelknorpel^M
cartilagine^F alare maggiore
inferior nasal concha
cornete^M inferior
cornet^M inférieur
untere Nasenmuschel^F
conca^F nasale inferiore
olfactory mucosa
mucosa^F olfatoria
muqueuse^F olfactive
Riechschleimhaut^F
mucosa^F olfattiva
hard palate
bóveda^F palatina
voûte^F du palais^M
harter Gaumen^M
palato^M duro
tongue
lengua^F
langue^F
Zunge^F
lingua^F

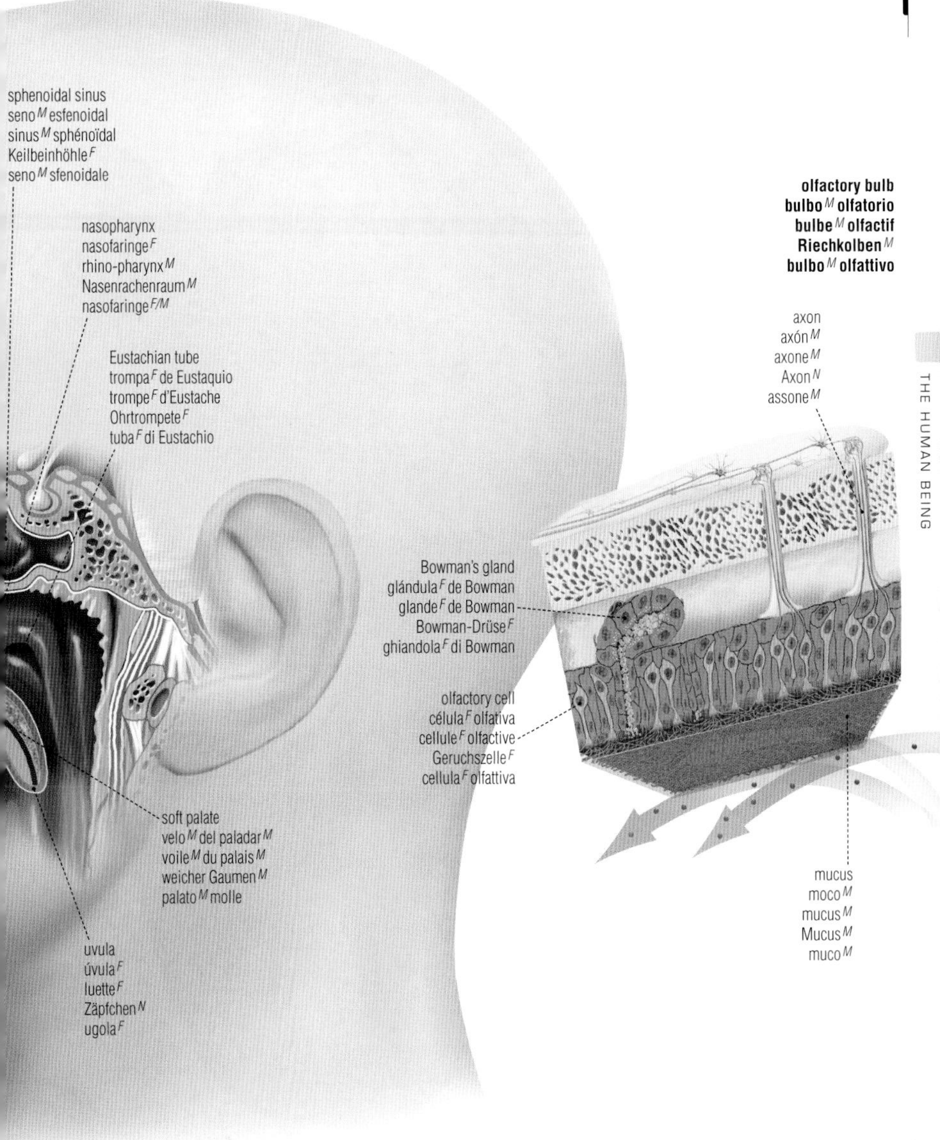
sphenoidal sinus
seno[M] esfenoidal
sinus[M] sphénoïdal
Keilbeinhöhle[F]
seno[M] sfenoidale
nasopharynx
nasofaringe[F]
rhino-pharynx[M]
Nasenrachenraum[M]
nasofaringe[F/M]
Eustachian tube
trompa[F] de Eustaquio
trompe[F] d'Eustache
Ohrtrompete[F]
tuba[F] di Eustachio
soft palate
velo[M] del paladar[M]
voile[M] du palais[M]
weicher Gaumen[M]
palato[M] molle
uvula
úvula[F]
luette[F]
Zäpfchen[N]
ugola[F]
olfactory bulb
bulbo[M] olfatorio
bulbe[M] olfactif
Riechkolben[M]
bulbo[M] olfattivo
axon
axón[M]
axone[M]
Axon[N]
assone[M]
Bowman's gland
glándula[F] de Bowman
glande[F] de Bowman
Bowman-Drüse[F]
ghiandola[F] di Bowman
olfactory cell
célula[F] olfativa
cellule[F] olfactive
Geruchszelle[F]
cellula[F] olfattiva
mucus
moco[M]
mucus[M]
Mucus[M]
muco[M]

dorsum of tongue
lengua *F*
dos *M* **de la langue** *F*
Zungenrücken *M*
dorso *M* **della lingua** *F*

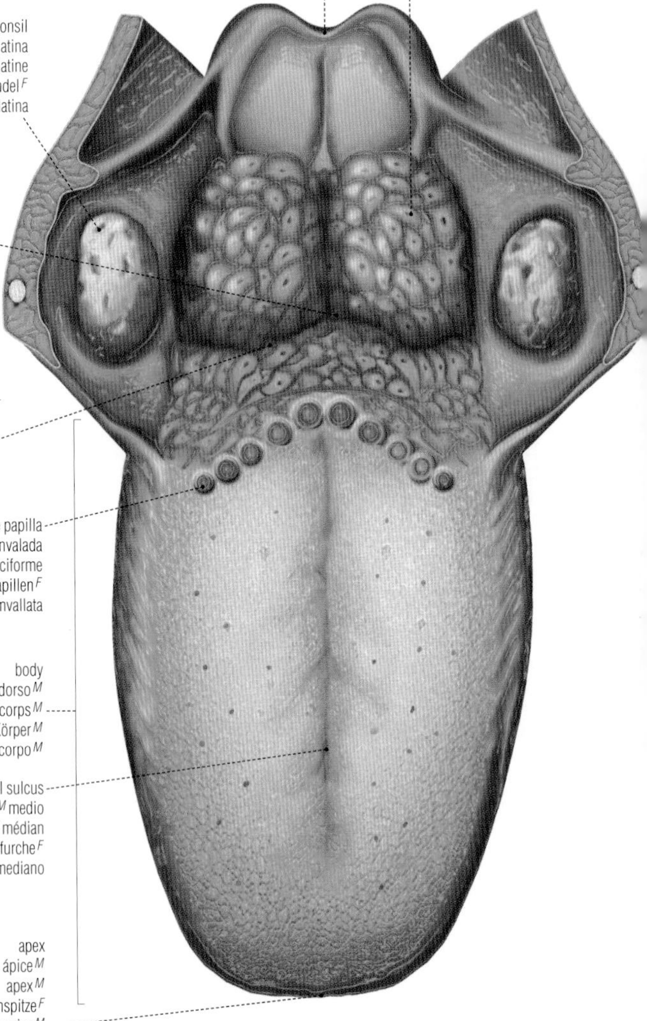

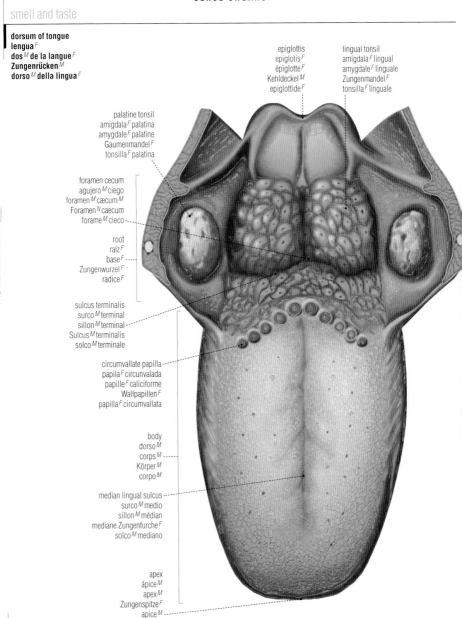

epiglottis
epiglotis F
épiglotte F
Kehldeckel M
epiglottide F
lingual tonsil
amígdala F lingual
amygdale F linguale
Zungenmandel F
tonsilla F linguale
palatine tonsil
amígdala F palatina
amygdale F palatine
Gaumenmandel F
tonsilla F palatina
foramen cecum
agujero M ciego
foramen M cæcum M
Foramen N caecum
forame M cieco
root
raíz F
base F
Zungenwurzel F
radice F
sulcus terminalis
surco M terminal
sillon M terminal
Sulcus M terminalis
solco M terminale
circumvallate papilla
papila F circunvalada
papille F caliciforme
Wallpapillen F
papilla F circumvallata
body
dorso M
corps M
Körper M
corpo M
median lingual sulcus
surco M medio
sillon M médian
mediane Zungenfurche F
solco M mediano
apex
ápice M
apex M
Zungenspitze F
apice M

taste receptors
receptores ^{M} gustativos
récepteurs ^{M} du goût ^{M}
Geschmacksrezeptoren ^{M}
recettori ^{M} gustativi

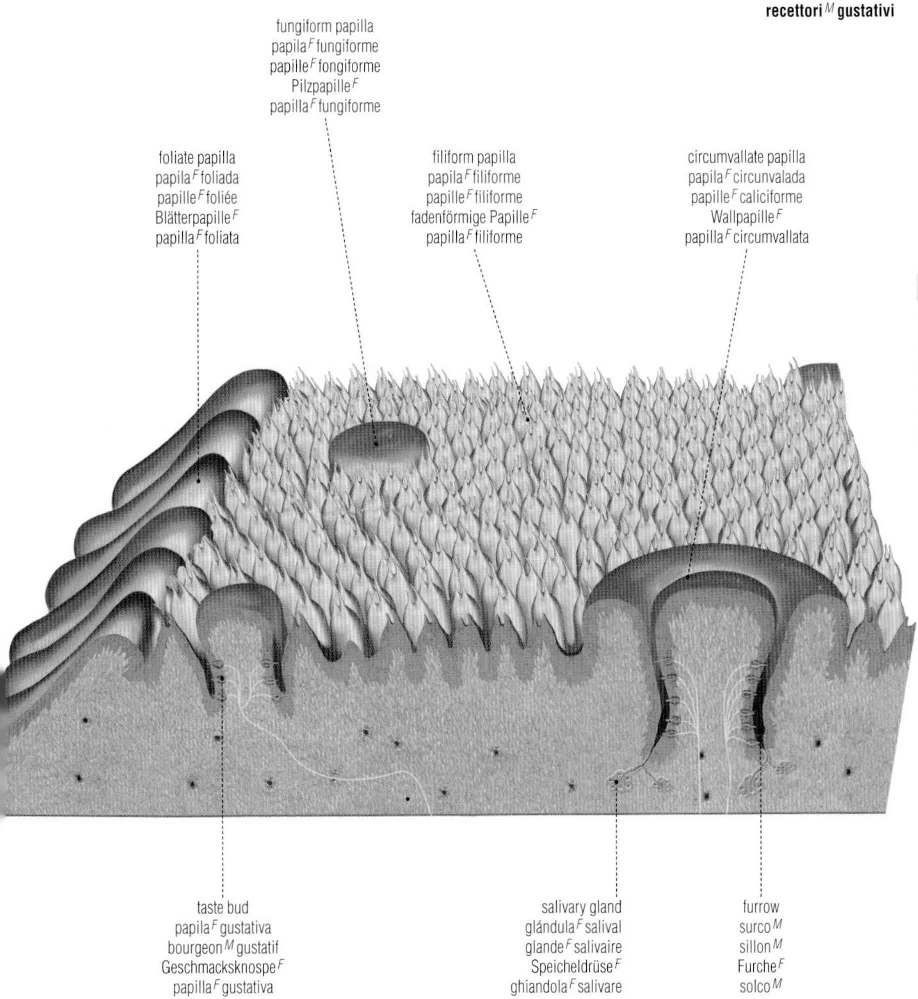
fungiform papilla
papila F fungiforme
papille F fongiforme
Pilzpapille F
papilla F fungiforme
foliate papilla
papila F foliada
papille F foliée
Blätterpapille F
papilla F foliata
filiform papilla
papila F filiforme
papille F filiforme
fadenförmige Papille F
papilla F filiforme
circumvallate papilla
papila F circunvalada
papille F caliciforme
Wallpapille F
papilla F circumvallata
taste bud
papila F gustativa
bourgeon M gustatif
Geschmacksknospe F
papilla F gustativa
salivary gland
glándula F salival
glande F salivaire
Speicheldrüse F
ghiandola F salivare
furrow
surco M
sillon M
Furche F
solco M

sight

vista^{F} | vue^{F} | Sehsinn^{N} | vista^{F}

eye
ojo^{M}
œil^{M}
Auge^{N}
occhio^{M}

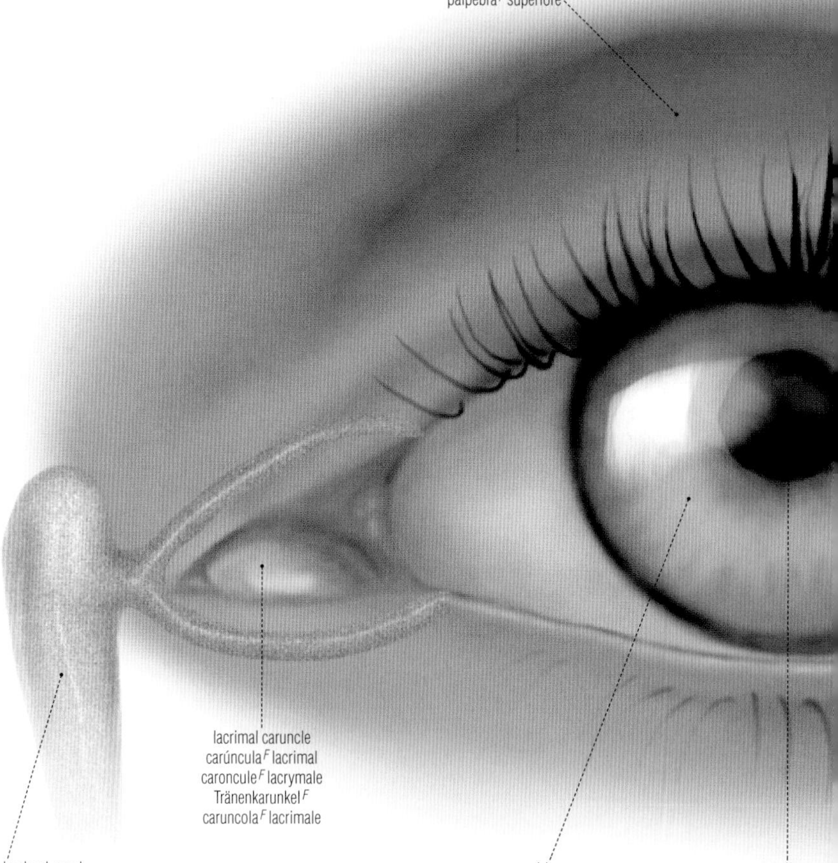
upper eyelid
párpado^{M} superior
paupière^{F} supérieure
Oberlid^{N}
palpebra^{F} superiore
lacrimal caruncle
carúncula^{F} lacrimal
caroncule^{F} lacrymale
Tränenkarunkel^{F}
caruncola^{F} lacrimale
lacrimal canal
canal^{M} lacrimal
canal^{M} lacrymal
Tränengang^{M}
canale^{M} lacrimale
iris
iris^{M}
iris^{M}
Iris^{F}
iride^{F}
pupil
pupila^{F}
pupille^{F}
Pupille^{F}
pupilla^{F}

lacrimal gland
glándula F lacrimal
glande F lacrymale
Tränendrüse F
ghiandola F lacrimale
eyelash
pestaña F
cil M
Wimper F
ciglio M
sclera
esclerótica F
sclérotique F
Lederhaut F
sclera F
lower eyelid
párpado M inferior
paupière F inférieure
Unterlid N
palpebra F inferiore

mushrooms

hongos M | champignons M | Pilze M | funghi M

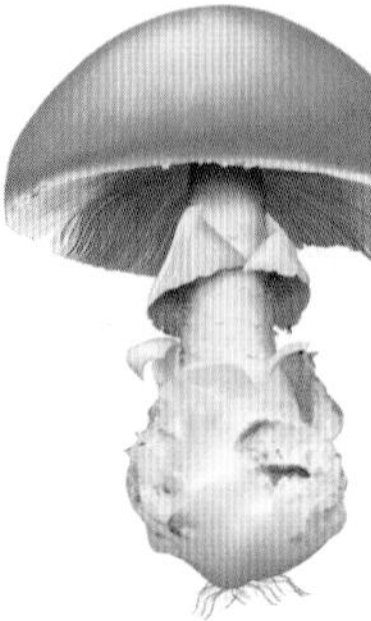

royal agaric
oronja F
oronge F vraie
Kaiserling M
ovolo M buono

delicious lactarius
mízcalo M
lactaire M délicieux
echter Reizker M
agarico M delizioso

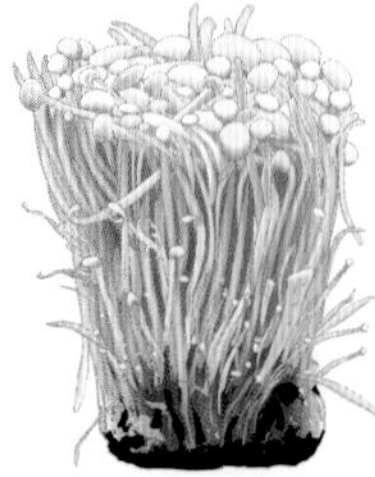

enoki mushroom
seta F enoki
collybie F à pied M velouté
Enoki M
collibia F

green russula
rusula F verde
russule F verdoyante
grasgrüner Täubling M
verdone M

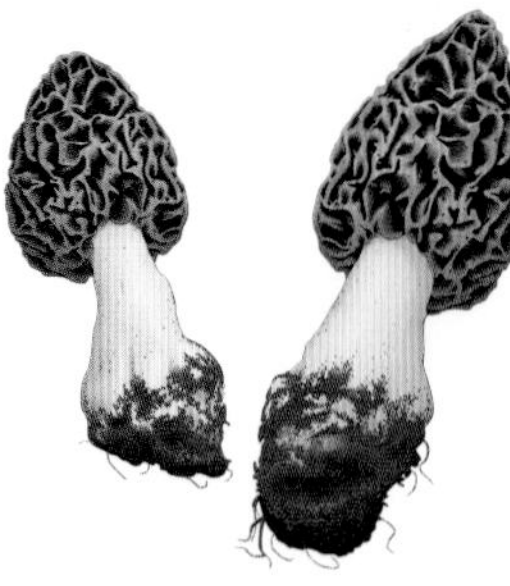

morel
morilla F
morille F
Morchel F
spugnola F

edible boletus
boleto M comestible
cèpe M
Steinpilz M
porcino M

truffle
trufa F
truffe F
Trüffel F
tartufo M

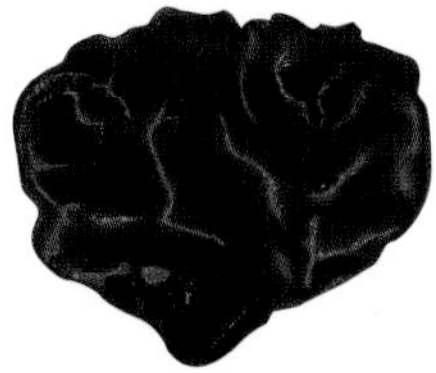

wood ear
oreja F de Judas
oreille-de-Judas F
Holzohr N
orecchio M di Giuda

oyster mushroom
orellana F
pleurote M en forme F d'huître F
Austernpilz M
gelone M

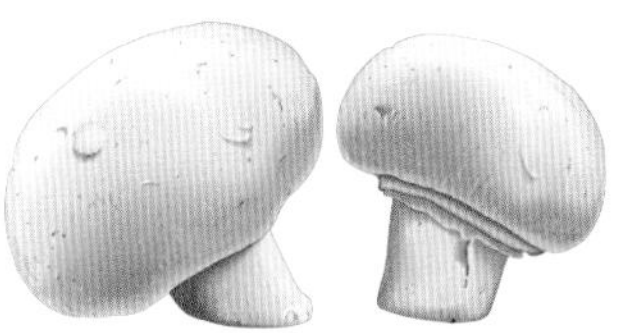

cultivated mushroom
champiñón M
champignon M de couche F
Champignon M
fungo M coltivato

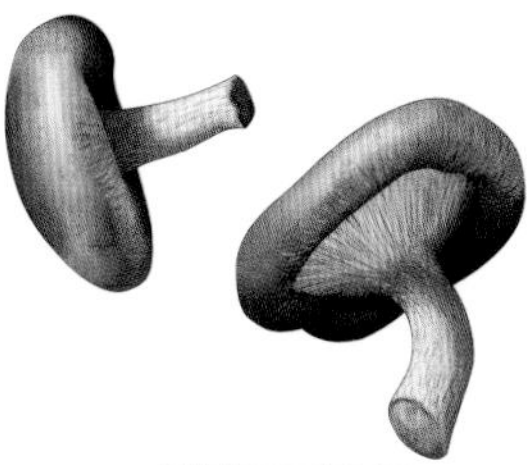

shiitake mushroom
shiitake M
shiitake M
Schiitakepilz M
shiitake M

chanterelle
rebozuelo M
chanterelle F commune
Pfifferling M
cantarello M

seaweed

algas[F] | algues[F] | Meeresalgen[F] | alga[F] marina

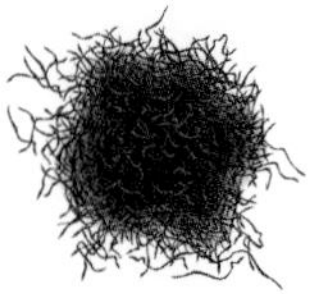

arame
arame[M]
aramé[M]
Arame[F]
arame[F]

wakame
wakame[M]
wakamé[M]
Wakame[F]
wakame[F]

spirulina
espirulina[F]
spiruline[F]
Spirulina[F]
spirulina[F]

Irish moss
Irish moss[M]
mousse[F] d'Irlande[F]
Irisch Moos[N]
muschio[M] d'Irlanda[F]

agar-agar
agar-agar[M]
agar-agar[M]
Agar-Agar[M/N]
agar-agar[M]

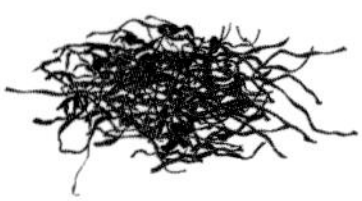

hijiki
hijiki[M]
hijiki[M]
Hijiki[F]
hijiki[F]

kombu
kombu[M]
kombu[M]
Kombu[F]
kombu[F]

sea lettuce
lechuga[F] marina
laitue[F] de mer[F]
Meersalat[M]
lattuga[F] marina

nori
nori[M]
nori[M]
Nori[N]
nori[F]

dulse
dulse[M]
rhodyménie[M] palmé
Dulse[F]
dulse[F]

vegetables

hortalizas F | légumes M | Gemüse N | ortaggi M

bulb vegetables
bulbos M
légumes M bulbes M
Zwiebelgemüse N
ortaggi M da bulbo M

leek
puerro M
poireau M
Lauch M
porro M

red onion
cebolla F roja
oignon M rouge
rote Zwiebel F
cipolla F rossa

yellow onion
cebolla F amarilla
oignon M jaune
Gemüsezwiebel F
cipolla F di Spagna F

pearl onion
cebolleta F
oignon M à mariner
Perlzwiebel F
cipollina F

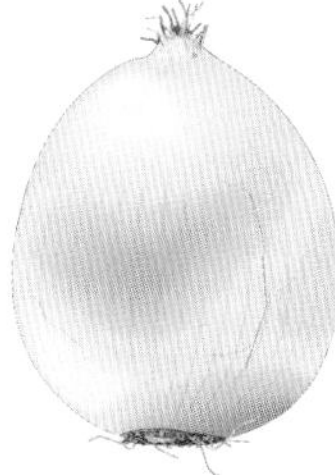

white onion
cebolla F blanca
oignon M blanc
weiße Zwiebel F
cipolla F bianca

vegetables

bulb vegetables

green onion
cebolla[F] tierna
oignon[M] vert
Frühlingszwiebel[F]
cipolla[F] verde

shallot
chalote[M]
échalote[F]
Schalotte[F]
scalogno[M]

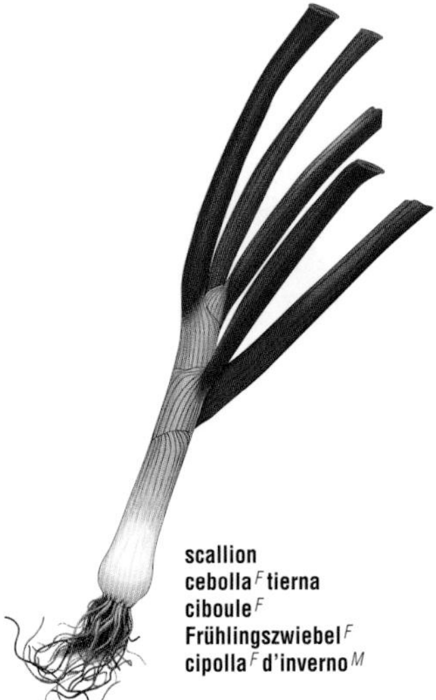

scallion
cebolla[F] tierna
ciboule[F]
Frühlingszwiebel[F]
cipolla[F] d'inverno[M]

water chestnut
castaña[F] de agua
châtaigne[F] d'eau[F]
Wasserkastanie[F]
castagna[F] d'acqua[F]

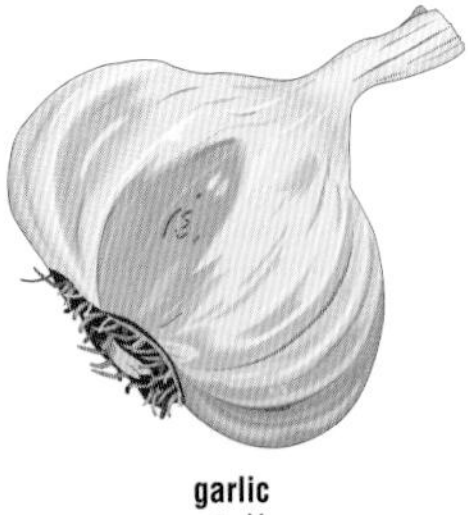

garlic
ajo[M]
ail[M]
Knoblauch[M]
aglio[M]

chive
cebollino[M]
ciboulette[F]
Schnittlauch[M]
erba[F] cipollina

tuber vegetables
tubérculos [M]
légumes [M] tubercules [M]
Knollengemüse [N]
ortaggi [M] da tubero [M]

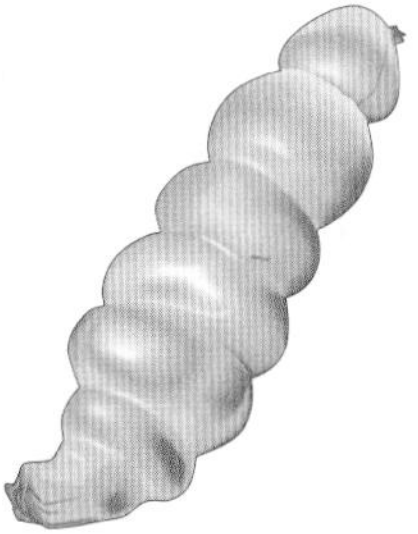

crosne
crosne [M]
crosne [M]
Knollenziest [M]
crosne [M]

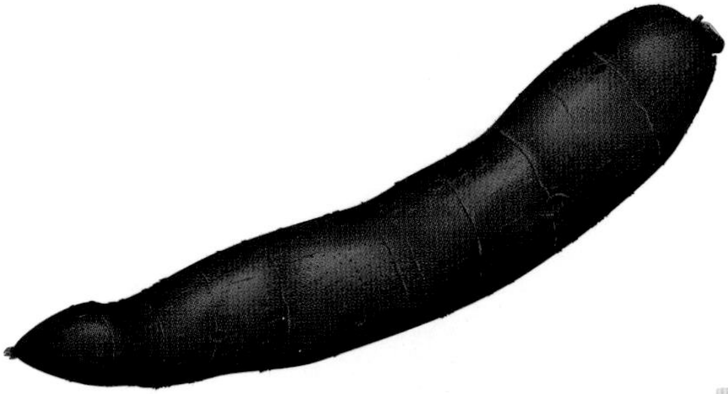

cassava
mandioca [F]
manioc [M]
Maniok [M]
manioca [F]

taro
taro [M]
taro [M]
Taro [M]
taro [M]

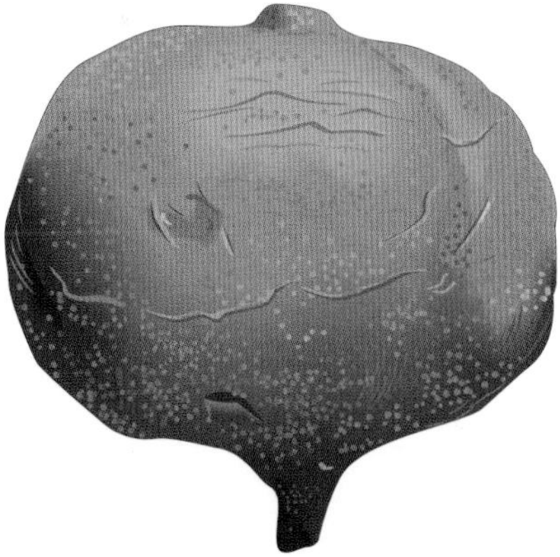

jicama
jícama [F]
jicama [M]
Jicama [F]
jicama [F]

vegetables

tuber vegetables

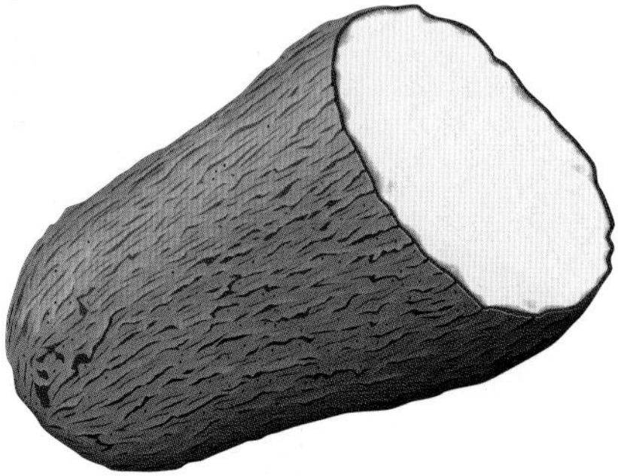

yam
batata F
igname F
Süßkartoffel F
igname M

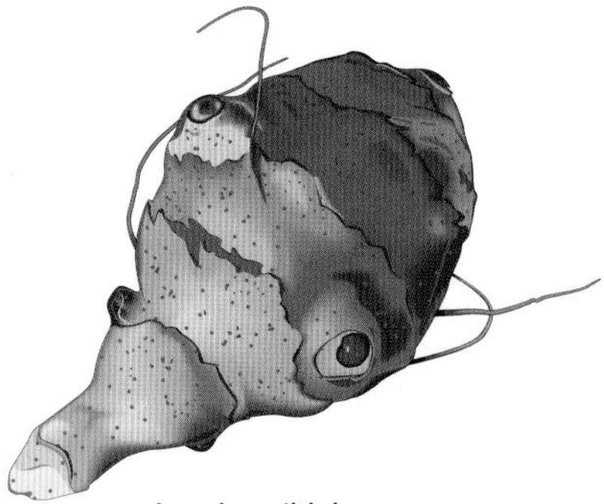

Jerusalem artichoke
aguaturma F
topinambour M
Topinambur M/F
topinambur M

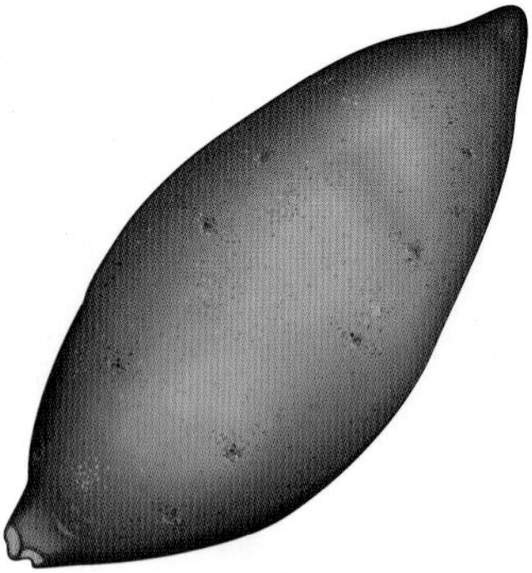

sweet potato
batata F
patate F
Süßkartoffel F
patata F americana

potato
patata F
pomme F de terre F
Kartoffel F
patata F

stalk vegetables
hortalizas^F de tallos^M
légumes^M tiges^F
Stängel- und Sprossengemüse^N
ortaggi^M da fusto^M

asparagus
espárrago^M
asperge^F
Spargel^M
asparago^M

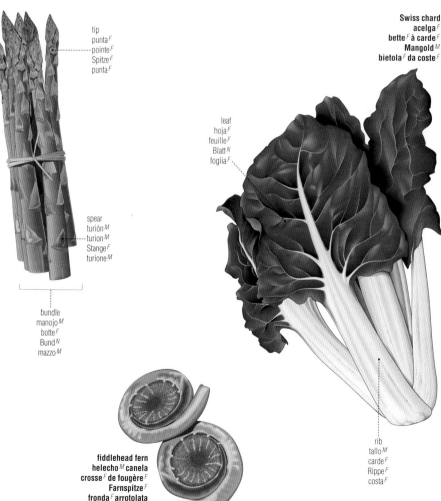

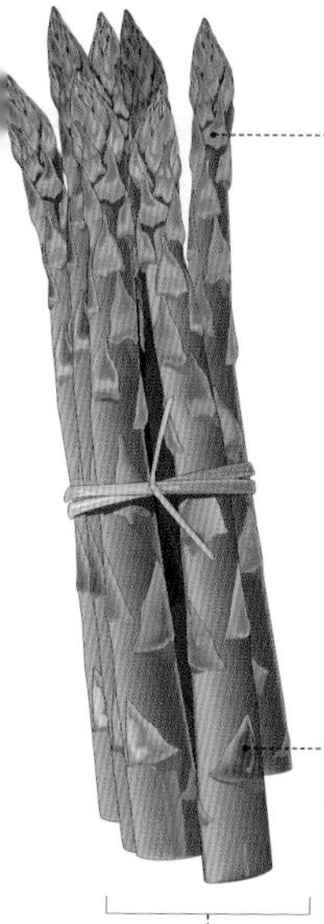
tip
punta^F
pointe^F
Spitze^F
punta^F
spear
turión^M
turion^M
Stange^F
turione^M
bundle
manojo^M
botte^F
Bund^N
mazzo^M

Swiss chard
acelga^F
bette^F **à carde**^F
Mangold^M
bietola^F **da coste**^F

leaf
hoja^F
feuille^F
Blatt^N
foglia^F
rib
tallo^M
carde^F
Rippe^F
costa^F

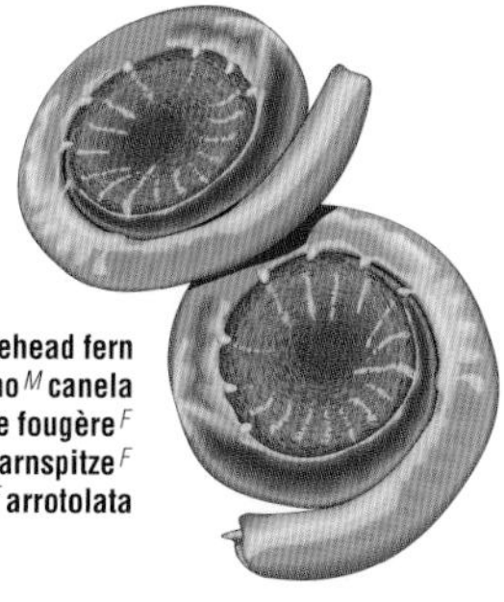

fiddlehead fern
helecho^M **canela**
crosse^F **de fougère**^F
Farnspitze^F
fronda^F **arrotolata**

vegetables

stalk vegetables

fennel
hinojo *M*
fenouil *M*
Fenchel *M*
finocchio *M*

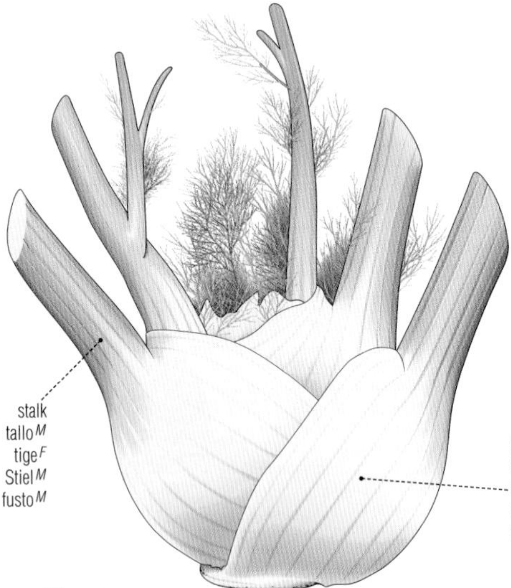
stalk
tallo M
tige F
Stiel M
fusto M
bulb
bulbo M
bulbe M
Knolle F
bulbo M

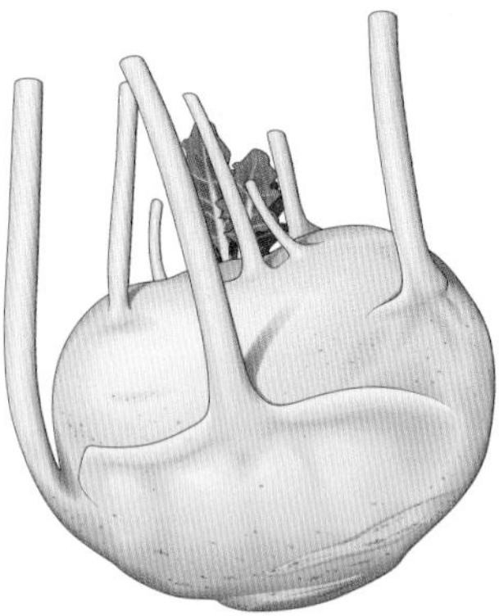

kohlrabi
colinabo *M*
chou *M*-**rave** *F*
Kohlrabi *M*
cavolo *M* **rapa** *F*

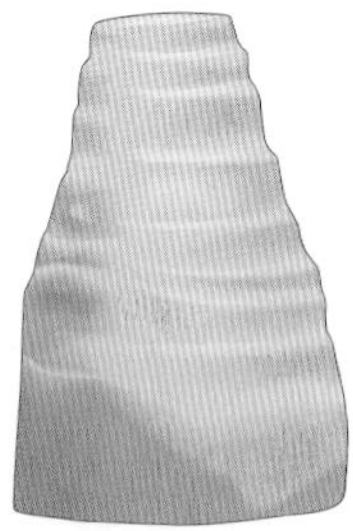

bamboo shoot
brote *M* **de bambú** *M*
pousse *F* **de bambou** *M*
Bambussprosse *F*
germoglio *M* **di bambù** *M*

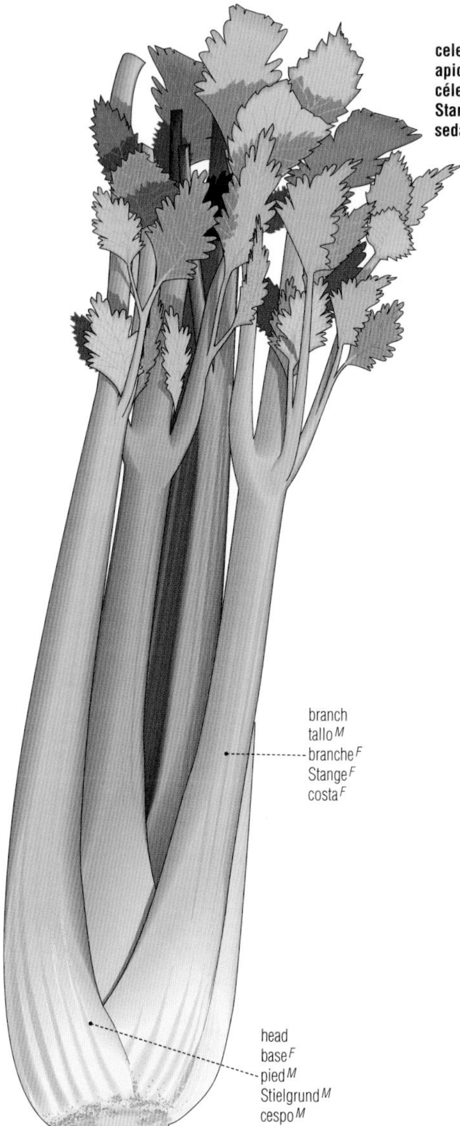
celery
apio M
céleri M
Stangensellerie M/F
sedano M
branch
tallo M
branche F
Stange F
costa F
head
base F
pied M
Stielgrund M
cespo M

cardoon
cardo M
cardon M
Kardone F
cardo M

leaf vegetables
verduras^{F} de hojas^{F}
légumes^{M} feuilles^{F}
Blattgemüse^{N}
ortaggi^{M} da foglia^{F}

leaf lettuce
lechuga^{F} rizada
laitue^{F} frisée
Friséesalat^{M}
insalata^{F} riccia

romaine lettuce
lechuga^{F} romana
romaine^{F}
Romagna-Salat^{M}
lattuga^{F} romana

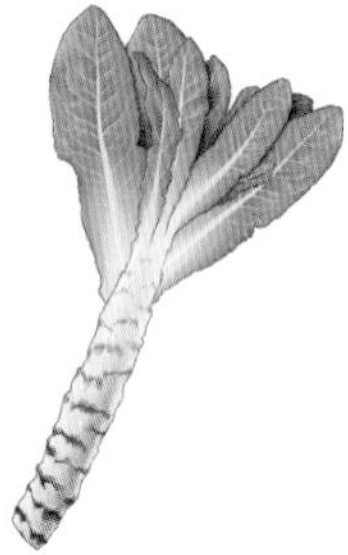

celtuce
lechuga^{F} de tallo^{M}
laitue^{F} asperge^{F}
Spargelsalat^{M}
lattuga^{F} asparago^{M}

escarole
escarola^{F}
scarole^{F}
Eskariol^{M}
scarola^{F}

butterhead lettuce
lechuga^{F} de cogollo^{M}
laitue^{F} pommée
Kopfsalat^{M}
lattuga^{F} cappuccina

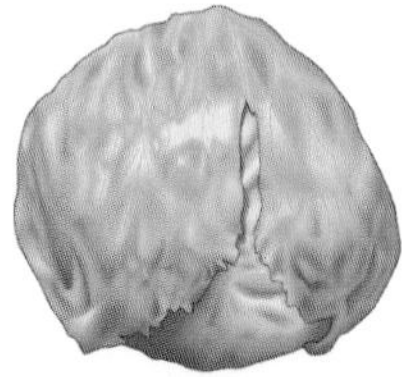

iceberg lettuce
lechuga^{F} iceberg
laitue^{F} iceberg^{M}
Eisbergsalat^{M}
lattuga^{F} iceberg^{M}

radicchio
achicoria^{F} de Treviso
chicorée^{F} de Trévise
Radicchio^{M}
radicchio^{M}

ornamental kale
col^{F} ornamental
chou^{M} laitue^{F}
Zierkohl^{M}
cavolo^{M} ornamentale

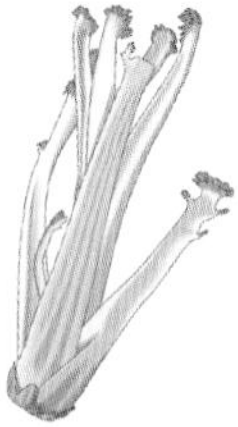

sea kale
col^{F} marina
chou^{M} marin
Meerkohl^{M}
cavolo^{M} marittimo

collards
berza^{F}
chou^{M} cavalier^{M}
Grünkohl^{M}; Blattkohl^{M}
gramigna^{F} crestata

curled kale
col^{F} rizada
chou^{M} frisé
Grünkohl^{M}
cavolo^{M} riccio

Brussels sprouts
coles^{F} de Bruselas
choux^{M} de Bruxelles
Rosenkohl^{M}
cavolini^{M} di Bruxelles

red cabbage
col^{F} lombarda
chou^{M} pommé rouge
Rotkohl^{M}
cavolo^{M} rosso

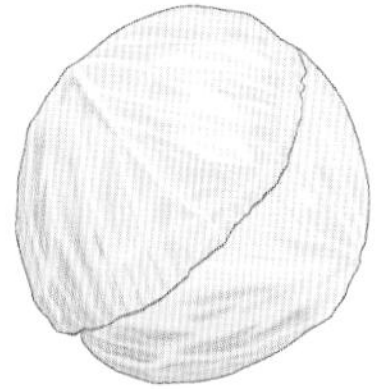

white cabbage
col^{F}/repollo^{M}
chou^{M} pommé blanc
Weißkohl^{M}
cavolo^{M} bianco

savoy cabbage
col^{F} rizada de otoño^{M}
chou^{M} de Milan
Wirsing^{M}
cavolo^{M} verzotto

green cabbage
col^{F} verde/repollo^{M} verde
chou^{M} pommé vert
Kohl^{M}
cavolo^{M} verza^{F}

vegetables

leaf vegetables

nettle
ortiga [F]
ortie [F]
Nessel [F]
ortica [F]

watercress
berro [M]
cresson [M] **de fontaine** [F]
Brunnenkresse [F]
crescione [M]

dandelion
diente [M] **de león**
pissenlit [M]
Löwenzahn [M]
dente [M] **di leone** [M]

purslane
verdolaga [F]
pourpier [M]
Portulak [M]
porcellana [F]

grape leaf
hoja [F] **de parra** [F]
feuille [F] **de vigne** [F]
Weinblatt [N]
pampino [M]

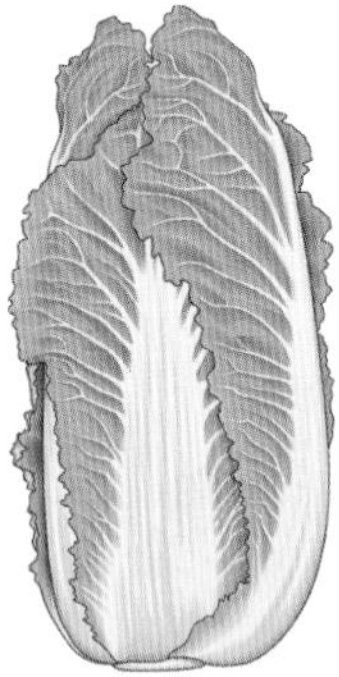

celery cabbage
col [F] **china**
pe-tsaï [M]
Chinakohl [M]
pe-tsai [M]

bok choy
pak-choi [M]
pak-choï [M]
Pak-Choi [M]
pak-choi [M]

corn salad
colleja [F]
mâche [F]
Feldsalat [M]
valerianella [F]

arugula
ruqueta [F]
roquette [F]
Rauke [F]
rucola [F]

garden sorrel
acedera [F]
oseille [F]
Garten-Sauerampfer [M]
acetosa [F]

spinach
espinaca [F]
épinard [M]
Spinat [M]
spinaci [M]

curled endive
escarola [F] rizada
chicorée [F] frisée
krause Endivie [F]
indivia [F] riccia

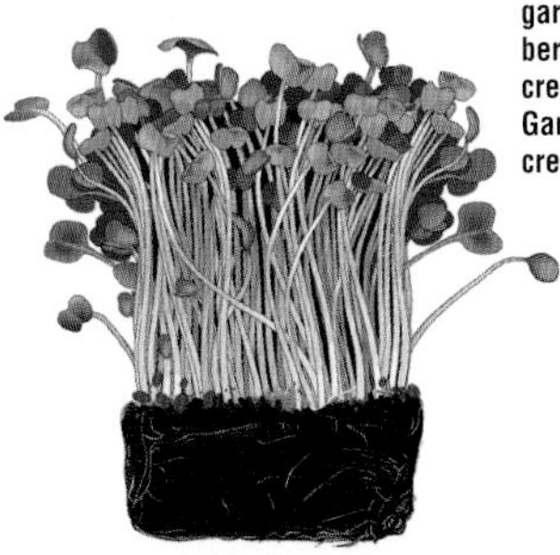

garden cress
berros [M] de jardín
cresson [M] alénois
Gartenkresse [F]
crescione [M] d'orto [M]

Belgian endive
endivia [F]
endive [F]
Chicorée [M/F]
insalata [F] belga

vegetables

inflorescent vegetables
inflorescencias F
légumes M fleurs F
Blütengemüse N
ortaggi M da infiorescenza F

Gai-lohn
brécol M chino
gai lon M
China-Broccoli M
Gai-lohn M

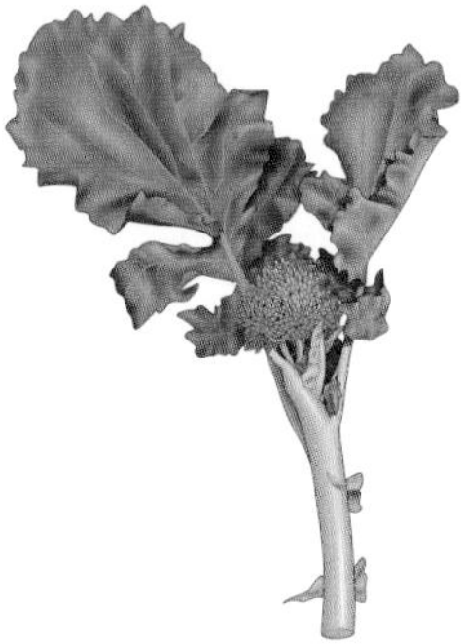

broccoli rabe
nabiza F
brocoli M italien
Rübenspross M
cime F di rapa F

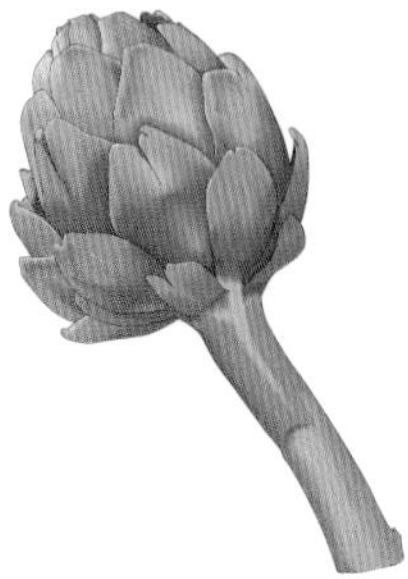

artichoke
alcachofa F
artichaut M
Artischocke F
carciofo M

cauliflower
coliflor F
chou M-fleur F
Blumenkohl M
cavolfiore M

broccoli
brécol M
brocoli M
Broccoli M
broccolo M

fruit vegetables
hortalizas [F] de fruto [M]
légumes [M] fruits [M]
Fruchtgemüse [N]
ortaggi [M] da frutto [M]

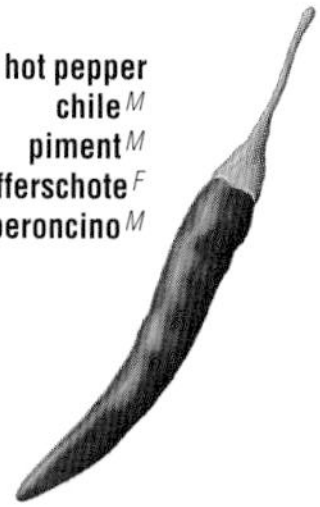

hot pepper
chile [M]
piment [M]
Pfefferschote [F]
peperoncino [M]

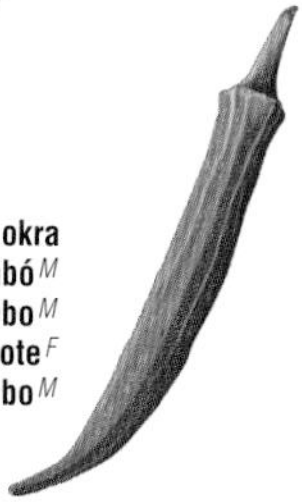

okra
gombo [M], quingombó [M]
gombo [M]
Okraschote [F]
gombo [M]

tomatillo
tomatillo [M]
tomatille [F]
Tomatillo [F]
tomatillo [M]

olive
aceituna [F]
olive [F]
Olive [F]
oliva [F]

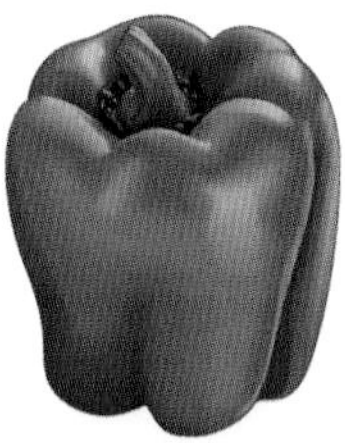

green sweet pepper
pimiento [M] dulce verde
poivron [M] vert
grüner Paprika [M]
peperone [M] verde

red sweet pepper
pimiento [M] dulce rojo
poivron [M] rouge
roter Paprika [M]
peperone [M] rosso

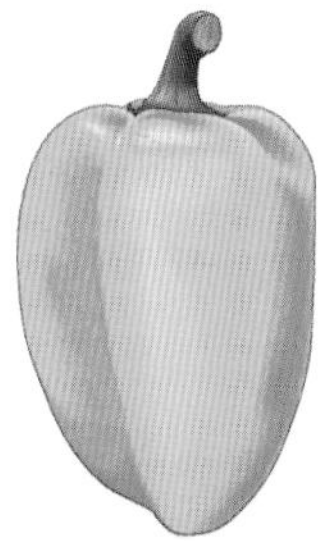

yellow sweet pepper
pimiento [M] dulce amarillo
poivron [M] jaune
gelber Paprika [M]
peperone [M] giallo

avocado
aguacate [M]
avocat [M]
Avocado [F]
avocado [M]

cherry tomato
tomate [M] en rama [F]
tomate [F] en grappe [F]
Kirschtomate [F]
pomodorini [M] a grappolo [M]

tomato
tomate [M]
tomate [F]
Tomate [F]
pomodoro [M]

fruit vegetables

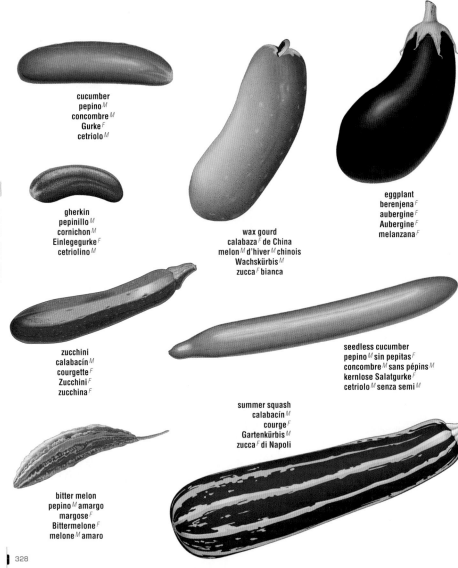

cucumber
pepino M
concombre M
Gurke F
cetriolo M

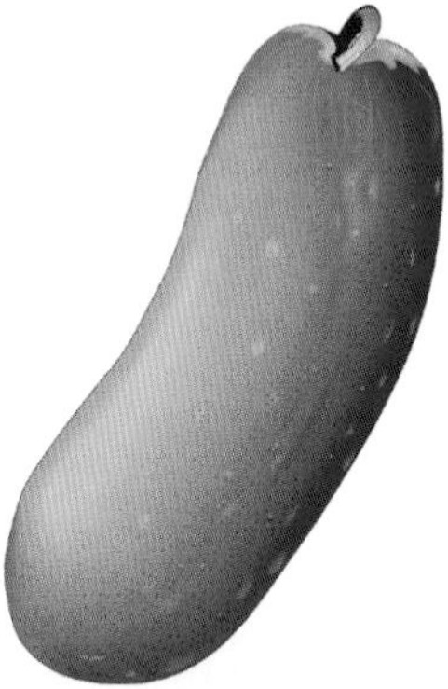

wax gourd
calabaza F de China
melon M d'hiver M chinois
Wachskürbis M
zucca F bianca

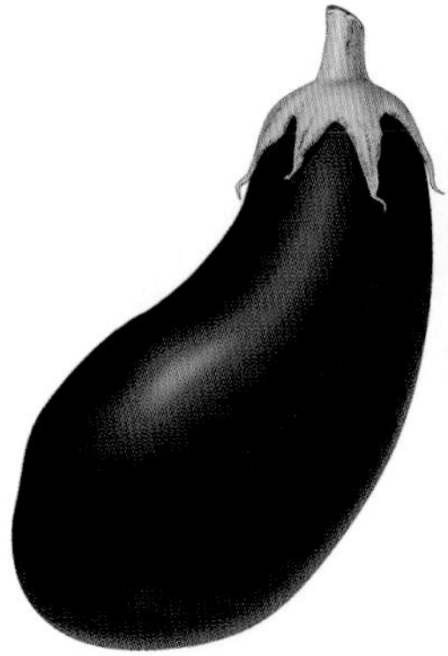

eggplant
berenjena F
aubergine F
Aubergine F
melanzana F

gherkin
pepinillo M
cornichon M
Einlegegurke F
cetriolino M

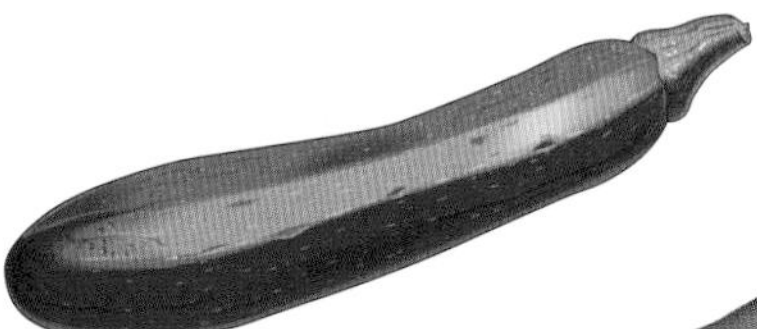

zucchini
calabacín M
courgette F
Zucchini F
zucchina F

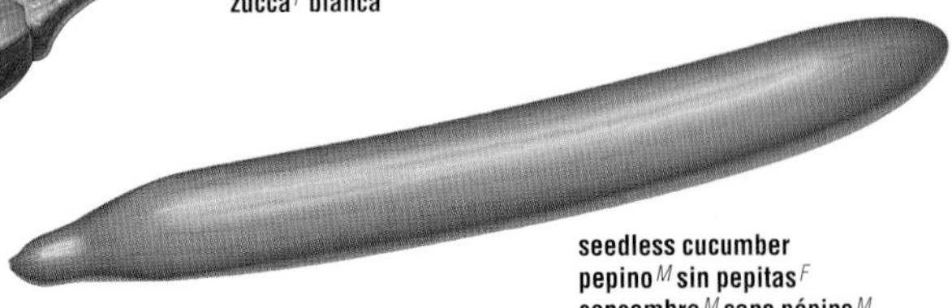

seedless cucumber
pepino M sin pepitas F
concombre M sans pépins M
kernlose Salatgurke F
cetriolo M senza semi M

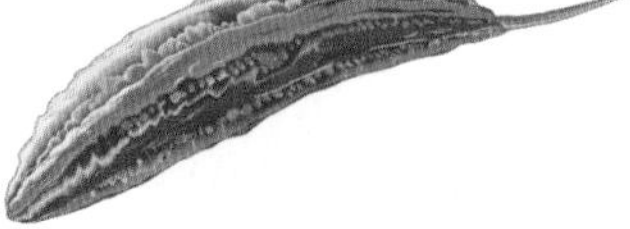

bitter melon
pepino M amargo
margose F
Bittermelone F
melone M amaro

summer squash
calabacín M
courge F
Gartenkürbis M
zucca F di Napoli

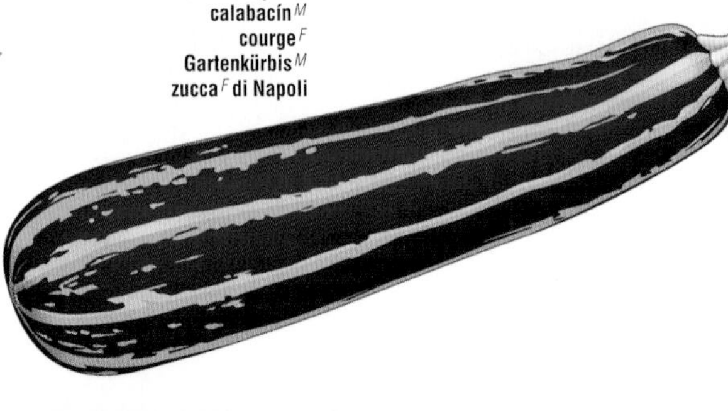

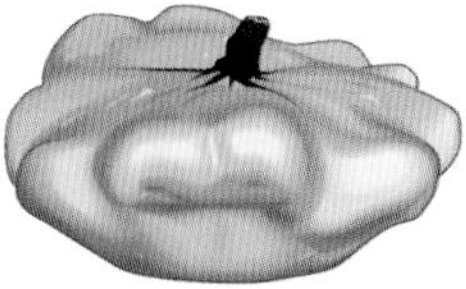

pattypan squash
calabaza [F] bonetera amarilla
pâtisson [M]
Patisson [M]
zucca [F] pasticcina

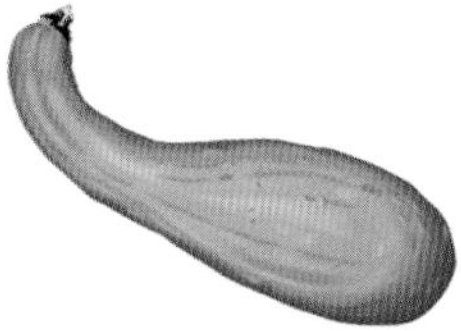

crookneck squash
calabaza [F] de cuello retorcido
courge [F] à cou [M] tors
Krummhalskürbis [M]
zucca [F] torta [F]

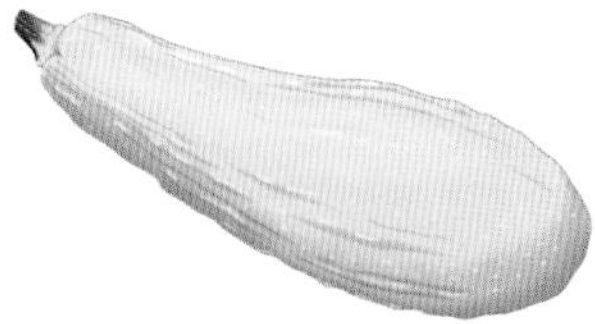

straightneck squash
calabaza [F] de cuello largo
courge [F] à cou [M] droit
gelbe Zucchini [F]
zucca [F] a collo [M] allungato

spaghetti squash
calabaza [F] romana
courge [F] spaghetti [M]
Spaghettikürbis [M]
zucca [F] spaghetti [M]

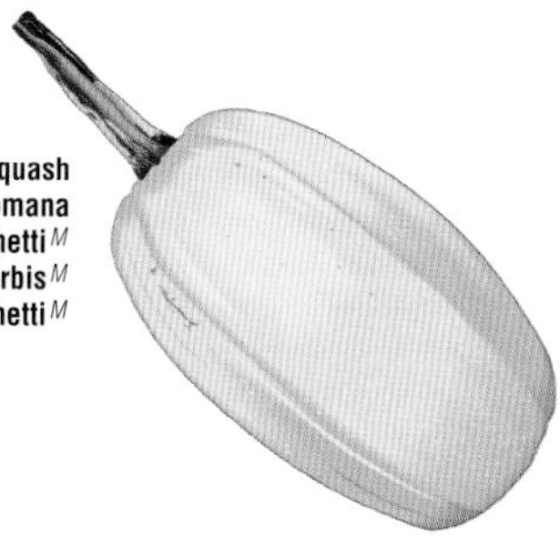

acorn squash
calabaza [F] bonetera
courgeron [M]
Eichelkürbis [M]
zucchetta [F]

pumpkin
calabaza [F] común
citrouille [F]
Kürbis [M]
zucca [F]

winter squash
cidra [F] cayote
potiron [M]
Patisson-Kürbis [M]
melone [M] invernale

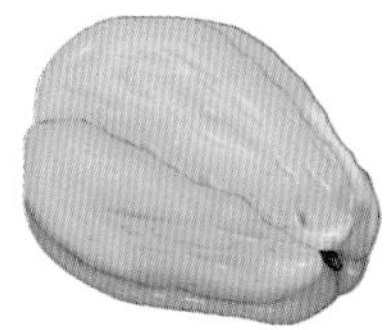

chayote
chayote [M]
chayote [F]
Chayote [F]
chayote [F]

root vegetables
raíces[F]
légumes[M] racines[F]
Wurzelgemüse[N]
ortaggi[M] da radice[F]

black radish
rábano[M] negro
radis[M] noir
Schwarzrettich[M]
ravanello[M] nero

radish
rábano[M]
radis[M]
Radieschen[N]
ravanello[M]

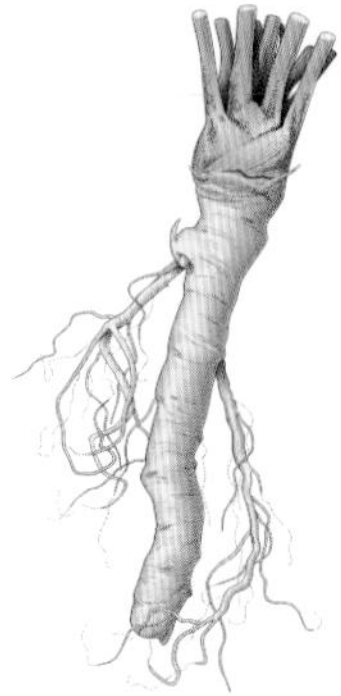

horseradish
rábano[M] blanco
raifort[M]
Meerrettich[M]
barbaforte[M]

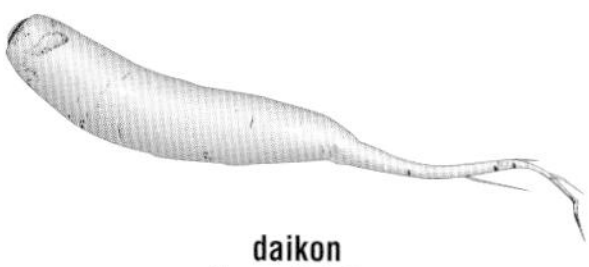

daikon
rábano[M] daikon
radis[M] oriental
Rettich[M]
rafano[M] giapponese

carrot
zanahoria[F]
carotte[F]
Karotte[F]
carota[F]

salsify
salsifí[M]
salsifis[M]
Haferwurz[F]
salsefica[F]

parsnip
chirivía[F]
panais[M]
Pastinake[F]
pastinaca[F]

black salsify
escorzonera [F]
scorsonère [F]
Schwarzwurzel [F]
scorzonera [F]

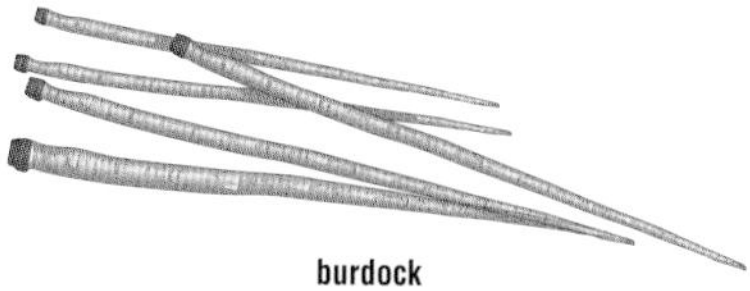

burdock
bardana [F]
bardane [F]
Klettenwurzel [F]
bardana [F]

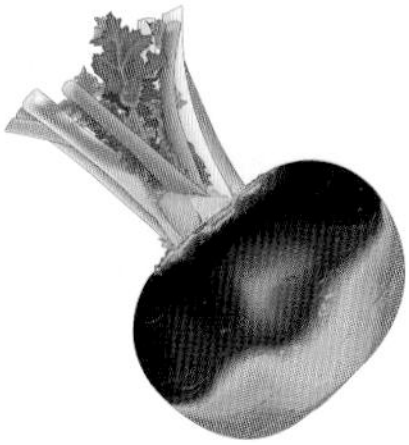

turnip
nabo [M]
navet [M]
Rübe [F]
rapa [F]

rutabaga
nabo [M] sueco
rutabaga [M]
Kohlrübe [F]
navone [M]

beet
remolacha [F]
betterave [F]
rote Beete [F]
barbabietola [F]

malanga
malanga [F]
malanga [M]
japanischer Rettich [M]
malanga [F]

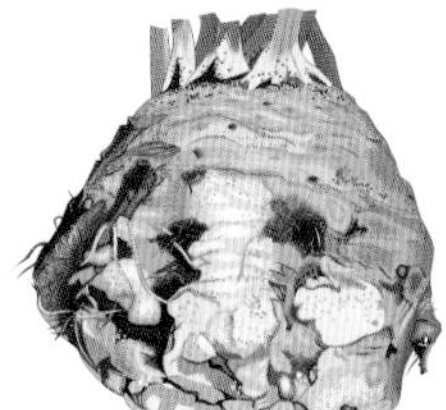

celeriac
apio [M] nabo
céleri [M]-rave [F]
Knollensellerie [F]
sedano [M] rapa [F]

legumes

legumbres F | légumineuses F | Hülsenfrüchte F | legumi M

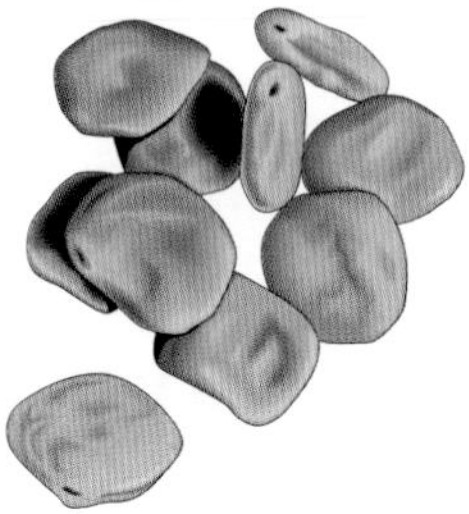

lupine
altramuz M
lupin M
Lupine F
lupino M

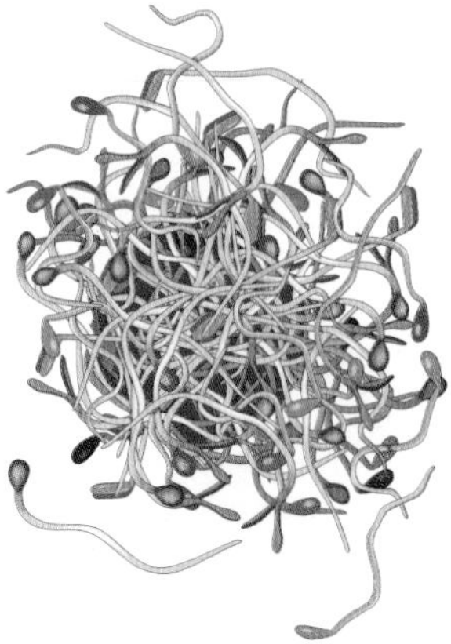

alfalfa
alfalfa F
luzerne F
blaue Luzerne F
erba F **medica**

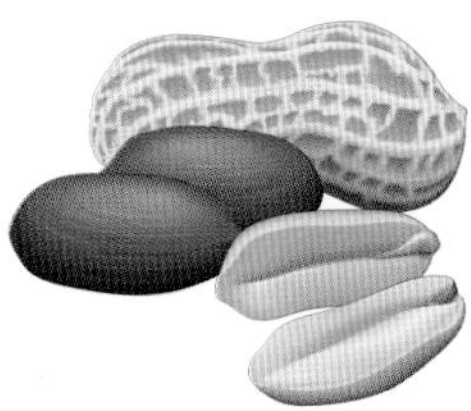

peanut
cacahuete M
arachide F
Erdnuss F
arachide F

lentils
lentejas F
lentilles F
Linsen F
lenticchie F

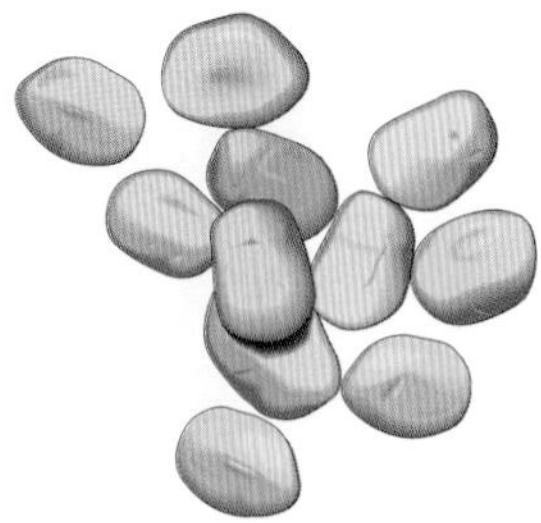

broad beans
habas F
fèves F
dicke Bohnen F
fave F

peas
guisantes[M]
pois[M]
Erbsen[F]
piselli[M]

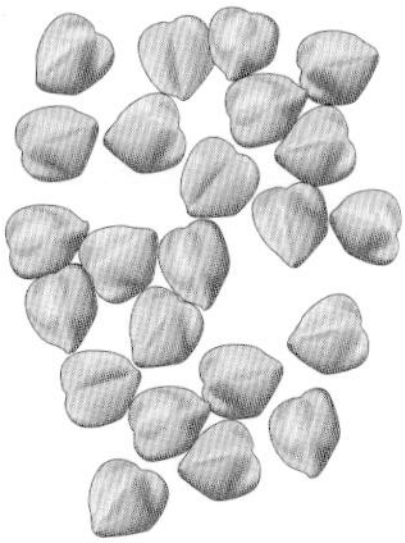

chick peas
garbanzos[M]
pois[M] chiches
Kichererbsen[F]
ceci[M]

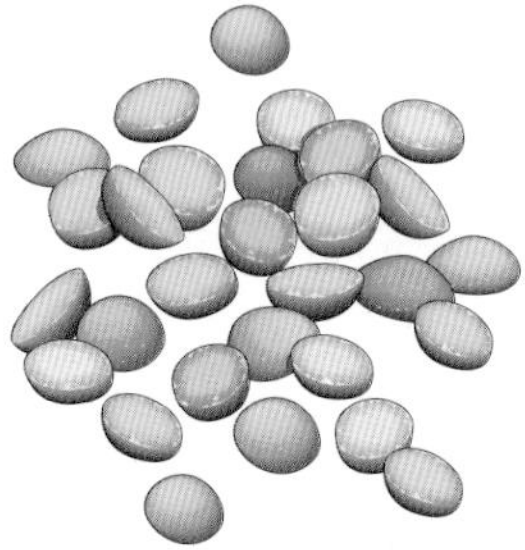

split peas
guisantes[M] partidos
pois[M] cassés
gespaltene Erbsen[F]
piselli[M] secchi spaccati

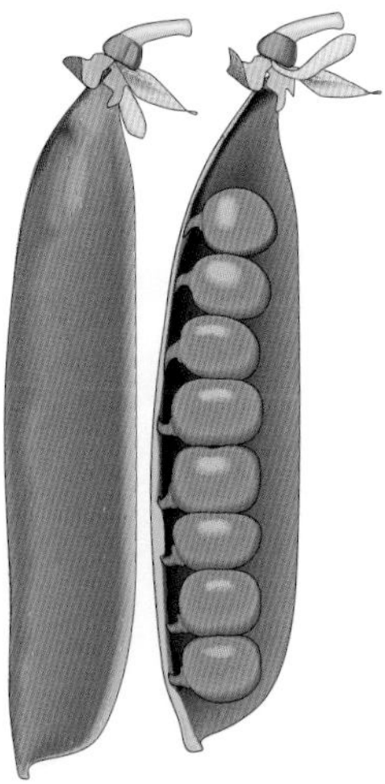

green peas
guisantes[M]
petits pois[M]
grüne Erbsen[F]
piselli[M]

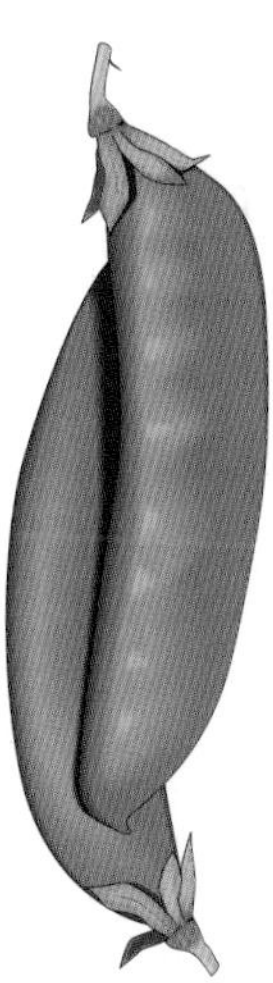

snow peas
guisantes[M] mollares
pois[M] mange-tout[M]
Zuckererbsen[F]
piselli[M] mangiatutto

legumes

dolichos beans
dolichos *M*
doliques *M*
Bohnen *F*
dolichi *M*

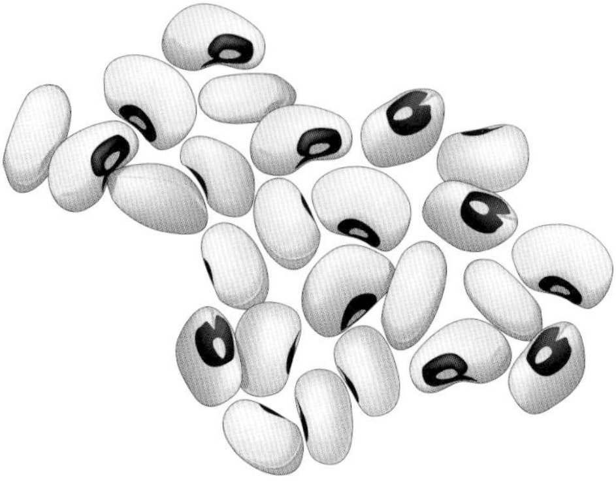

black-eyed pea
judía *F* de ojo
dolique *M* à œil *M* noir
schwarzäugige Bohne *F*
fagiolo *M* dall'occhio *M* nero

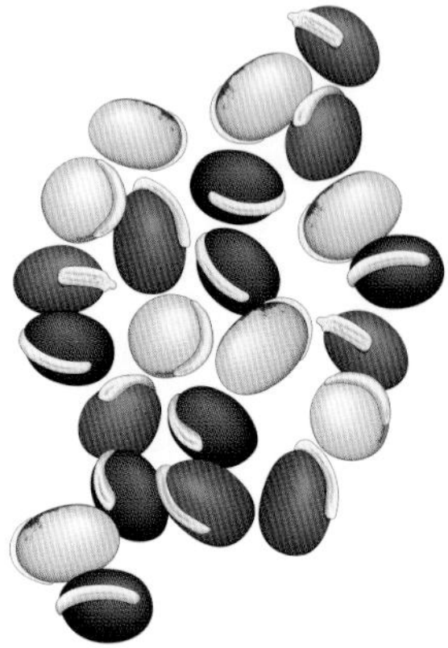

lablab bean
judía *F* de Egipto
dolique *M* d'Égypte *F*
Helmbohne *F*
fagiolo *M* egiziano

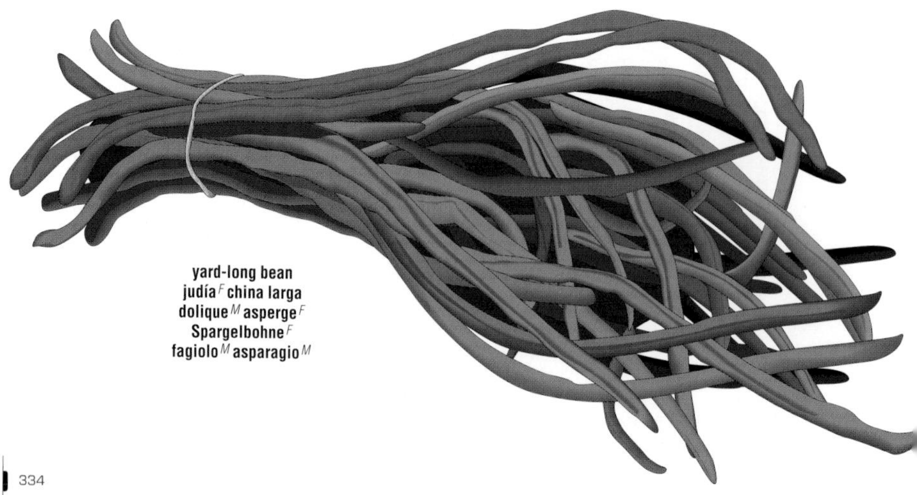

yard-long bean
judía *F* china larga
dolique *M* asperge *F*
Spargelbohne *F*
fagiolo *M* asparagio *M*

beans
judías F
haricots M
Bohnen F
fagioli M

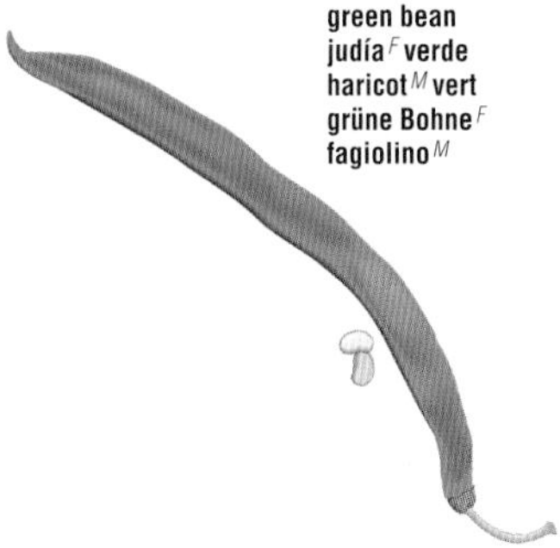

green bean
judía F verde
haricot M vert
grüne Bohne F
fagiolino M

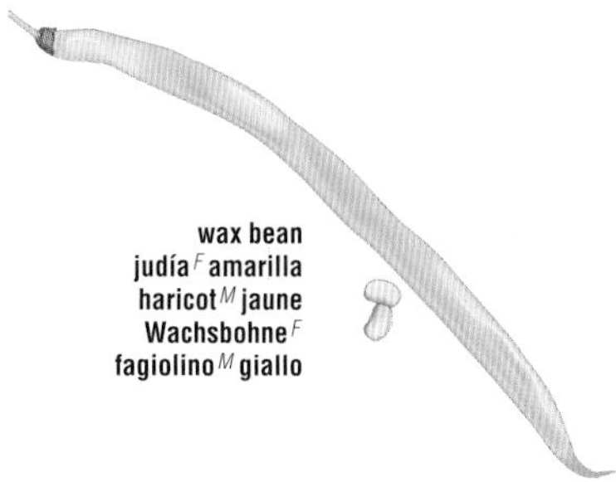

wax bean
judía F amarilla
haricot M jaune
Wachsbohne F
fagiolino M giallo

roman bean
judía F romana
haricot M romain
römische Bohne F
fagiolo M romano

adzuki bean
judía F adzuki
haricot M adzuki
Asukibohne F
fagiolo M adzuki

scarlet runner bean
judía F pinta
haricots M d'Espagne F
Feuerbohne F
fagiolo M da brodo M

mung bean
judía F mungo
haricot M mungo
Mungobohne F
fagiolo M mungo

lima bean
judía F de Lima
haricot M de Lima
Limabohne F
fagiolo M di Lima

pinto bean
judía F roja
haricot M pinto
Pintobohne F
fagiolo M pinto

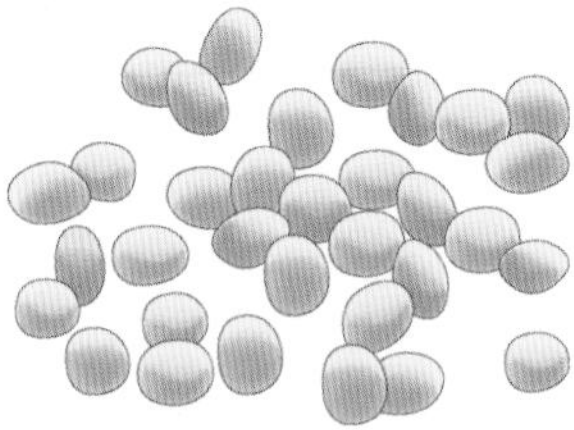

soybeans
semillas[F] de soja[F]
graine[F] de soja[M]
Sojabohnen[F]
semi[M] di soia[F]

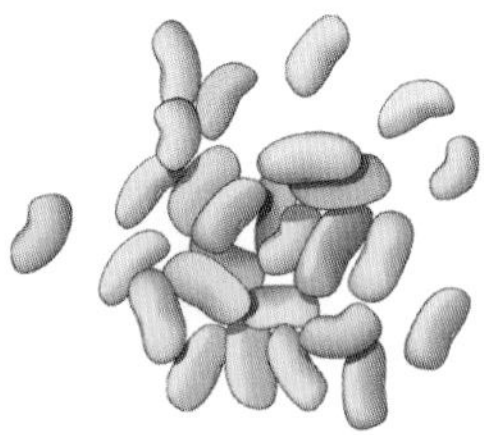

flageolet
frijol[M]
flageolet[M]
Flageolet-Bohne[F]
fagiolo[M] cannellino

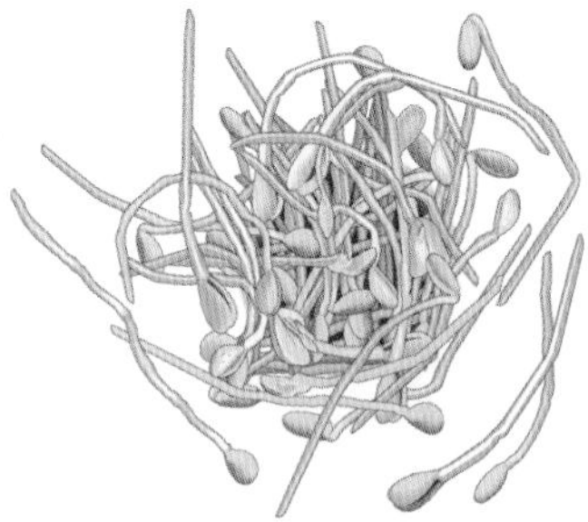

soybean sprouts
brotes[M] de soja[F]
germes[M] de soja[M]
Sojasprossen[F]
germogli[M] di soia[F]

red kidney bean
judia[F] roja
haricot[M] rouge
rote Kidneybohne[F]
fagiolo[M] borlotto

black gram
judía[F] mungo negra
haricot[M] mungo à grain[M] noir
schwarze Mungobohne[F]
fagiolo[M] mungo nero

black bean
judía[F] negra
haricot[M] noir
schwarze Bohne[F]
fagiolo[M] nero

fruits

frutas[F] | fruits[M] | Obst[N] | frutti[M]

stone fruits
drupas[F]
fruits[M] **à noyau**[M]
Steinfrüchte[F]
drupe[F]

date
dátil[M]
datte[F]
Dattel[F]
dattero[M]

plum
ciruela[F]
prune[F]
Pflaume[F]
prugna[F]

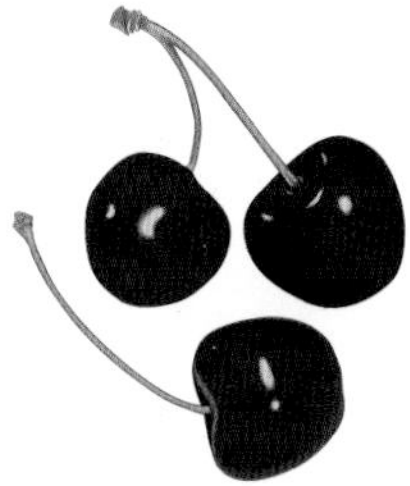

cherry
cereza[F]
cerise[F]
Kirsche[F]
ciliegia[F]

apricot
albaricoque[M]
abricot[M]
Aprikose[F]
albicocca[F]

peach
melocotón[M]
pêche[F]
Pfirsich[M]
pesca[F]

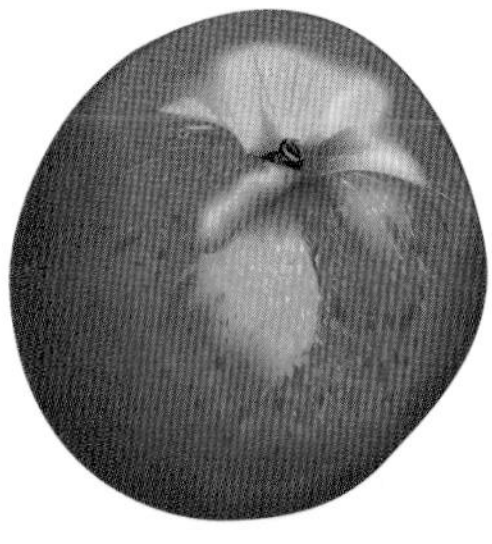

nectarine
nectarina[F]
nectarine[F]
Nektarine[F]
nettarina[F]

berries
bayas[F]
baies[F]
Beeren[F]
bacche[F]

black currant
grosella[F] negra
cassis[M]
schwarze Johannisbeere[F]
ribes[M] nero

currant
grosella[F]
groseille[F] à grappes[F]
rote Johannisbeere[F]
ribes[M]

gooseberry
grosella[F] espinosa
groseille[F] à maquereau[M]
Stachelbeere[F]
uvaspina[F]

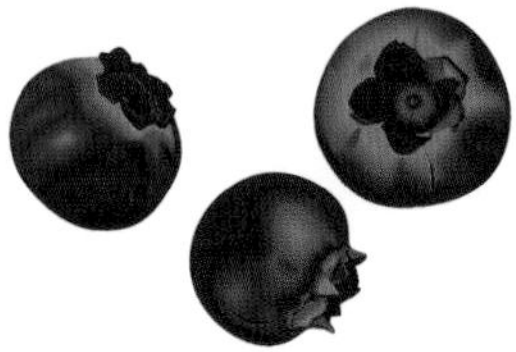

blueberry
arándano[M]
myrtille[F] d'Amérique[F]
Heidelbeere[F]
mirtillo[M]

bilberry
arándano[M] negro
myrtille[F]
Heidelbeere[F]
mirtillo[M]

red whortleberry
arándano[M] rojo
airelle[F]
rote Heidelbeere[F]
mirtillo[M] rosso

grape
uva [F]
raisin [M]
Weintraube [F]
uva [F]

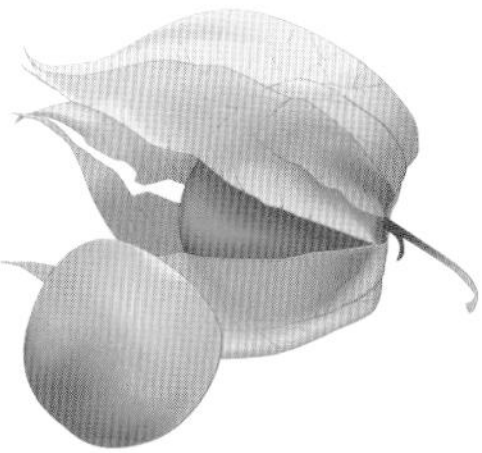

Chinese lantern plant
alquequenje [M]
alkékenge [M]
Physalis [F]
alchechengi [M]

cranberry
arándano [M] agrio
canneberge [F]
Preiselbeere [F]
mirtillo [M] palustre

strawberry
fresa [F]
fraise [F]
Erdbeere [F]
fragola [F]

blackberry
moras [F]
mûre [F]
Brombeere [F]
mora [F]

raspberry
frambuesa [F]
framboise [F]
Himbeere [F]
lampone [M]

dry fruits
frutas[F] secas
fruits[M] secs
Trockenfrüchte[F]
frutti[M] secchi

ginkgo nut
nuez[F] de ginkgo
noix[F] de ginkgo[M]
Ginkgonuss[F]
noce[F] di ginco[M]

pistachio nut
pistacho[M]
pistache[F]
Pistazie[F]
pistacchio[M]

macadamia nut
nuez[F] de macadamia[F]
noix[F] de macadamia[M]
Macadamianuss[F]
noce[F] di macadamia[F]

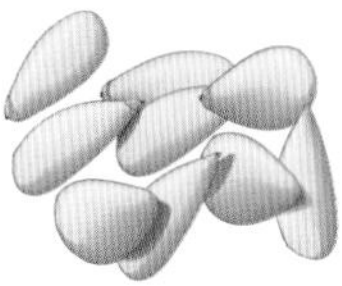

pine nut
piñón[M]
pignon[M]
Pinienkern[M]
pinolo[M]

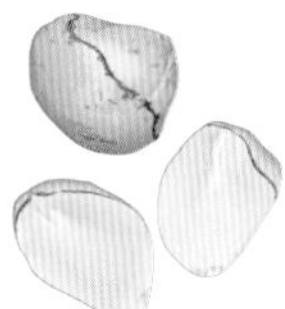

cola nut
nuez[F] de cola
noix[F] de cola[M]
Kolanuss[F]
noce[F] di cola[F]

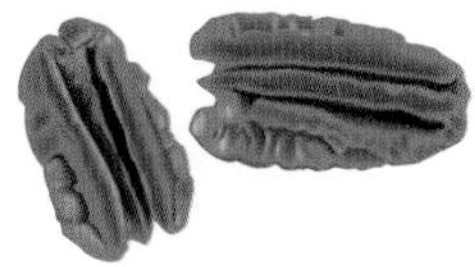

pecan nut
pacana[F]
noix[F] de pacane[F]
Pecannuss[F]
noce[F] di pecan[M]

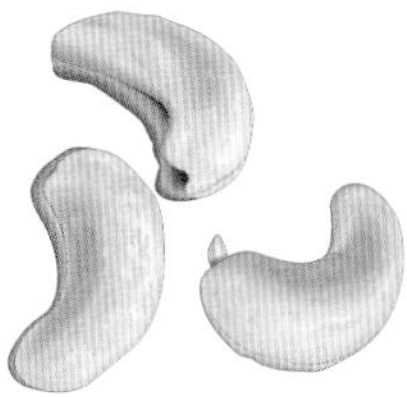

cashew
anacardo[M]
noix[F] de cajou[M]
Cashewkern[M]
noce[F] di acagiù[M]

almond
almendra[F]
amande[F]
Mandel[F]
mandorla[F]

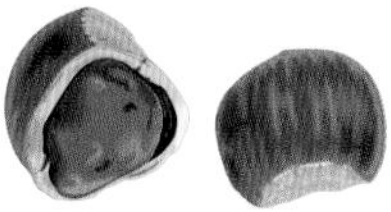

hazelnut
avellana [F]
noisette [F]
Haselnuss [F]
nocciola [F]

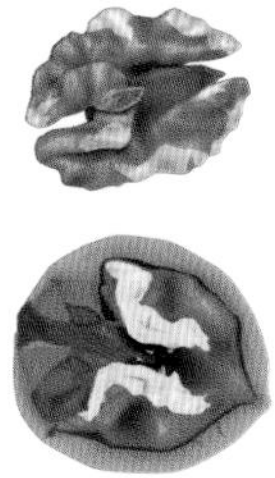

walnut
nuez [F]
noix [F]
Walnuss [F]
noce [F]

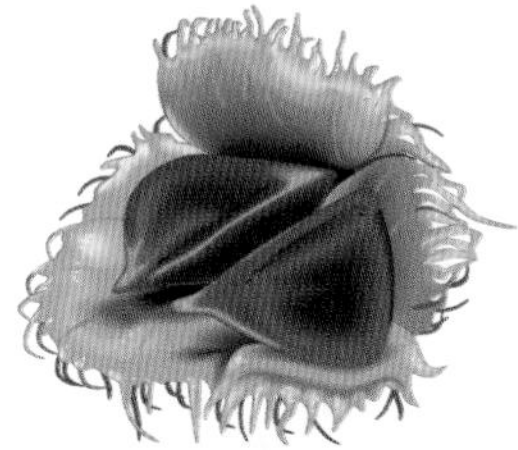

beechnut
hayuco [M]
faîne [F]
Buchecker [F]
faggiola [F]

chestnut
castaña [F]
marron [M]
Esskastanie [F]
castagna [F]

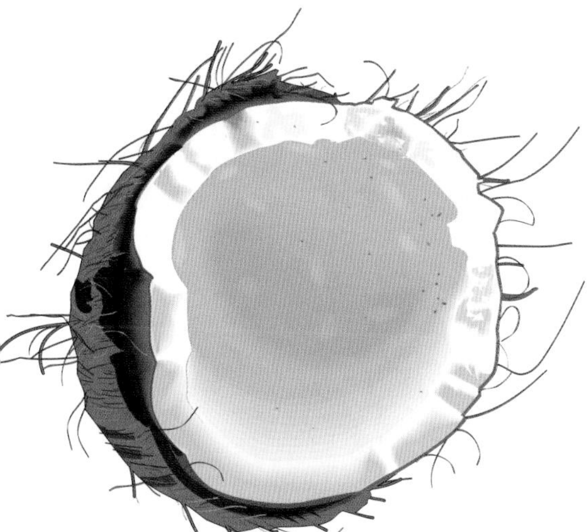

coconut
coco [M]
noix [F] **de coco** [M]
Kokosnuss [F]
noce [F] **di cocco** [M]

Brazil nut
nuez [F] **del Brasil** [M]
noix [F] **du Brésil** [M]
Paranuss [F]
noce [F] **del Brasile** [M]

fruits

citrus fruits
cítricos *M*
agrumes *M*
Zitrusfrüchte *F*
agrumi *M*

lime
lima *F*
lime *F*
Limette *F*
limetta *F*

kumquat
naranja *F* china
kumquat *M*
Kumquat *F*
kumquat *M*

mandarin
mandarina *F*
mandarine *F*
Mandarine *F*
mandarino *M*

bergamot
bergamota *F*
bergamote *F*
Bergamotte *F*
bergamotto *M*

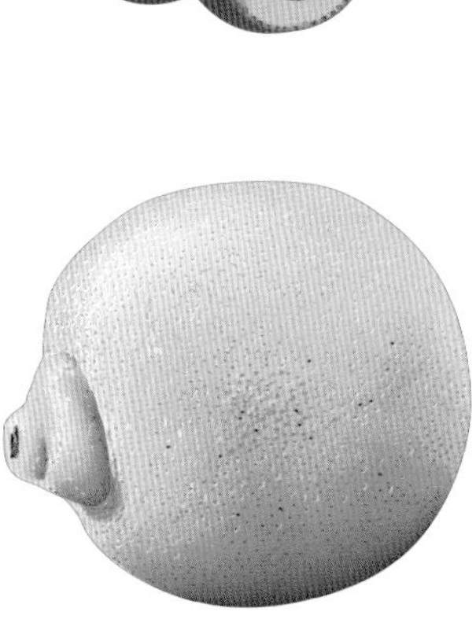

orange
naranja *F*
orange *F*
Orange *F*
arancia *F*

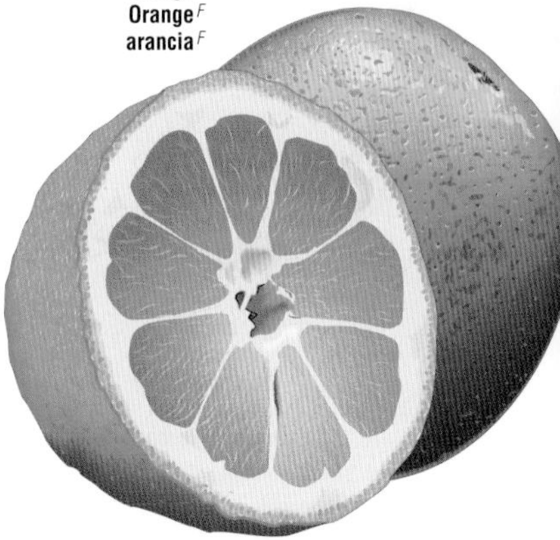

lemon
limón *M*
citron *M*
Zitrone *F*
limone *M*

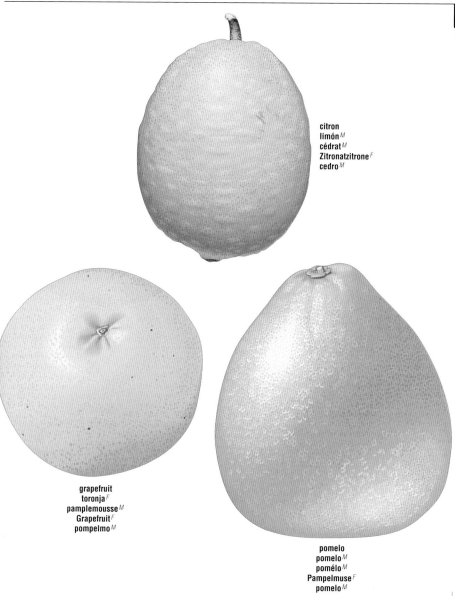

citron
limón *M*
cédrat *M*
Zitronatzitrone *F*
cedro *M*

grapefruit
toronja *F*
pamplemousse *M*
Grapefruit *F*
pompelmo *M*

pomelo
pomelo *M*
pomélo *M*
Pampelmuse *F*
pomelo *M*

melons
melones *M*
melons *M*
Melonen *F*
meloni *M*

casaba melon
melón *M* **invernal**
melon *M* **Casaba**
Casabamelone *F*
melone *M* **invernale**

honeydew melon
melón *M* **de miel**
melon *M* **miel** *M*
Honigmelone *F*
melone *M* **mieloso**

muskmelon
melón *M* **escrito**
melon *M* **brodé**
Zuckermelone *F*
melone *M* **retato**

cantaloupe
melón *M* **cantalupo**
cantaloup *M*
Honigmelone *F*
cantalupo *M*

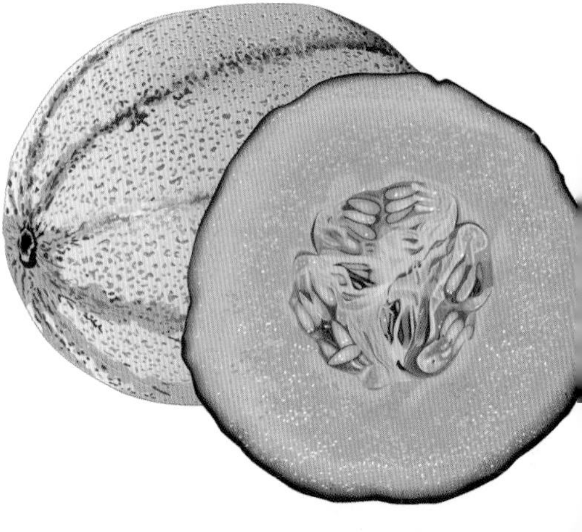

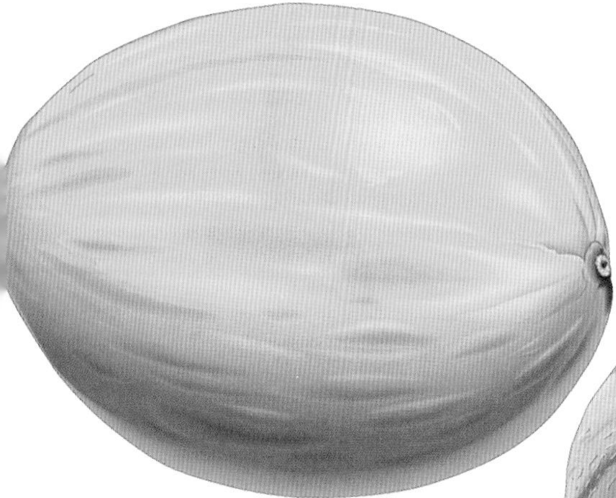

canary melon
melón[M] amarillo
melon[M] d'Espagne[F]
kanarische Melone[F]
melone[M] giallo canario

Ogen melon
melón[M] de Ogen
melon[M] d'Ogen
Ogenmelone[F]
melone[M] Ogen

watermelon
sandía[F]
pastèque[F]
Wassermelone[F]
cocomero[M]

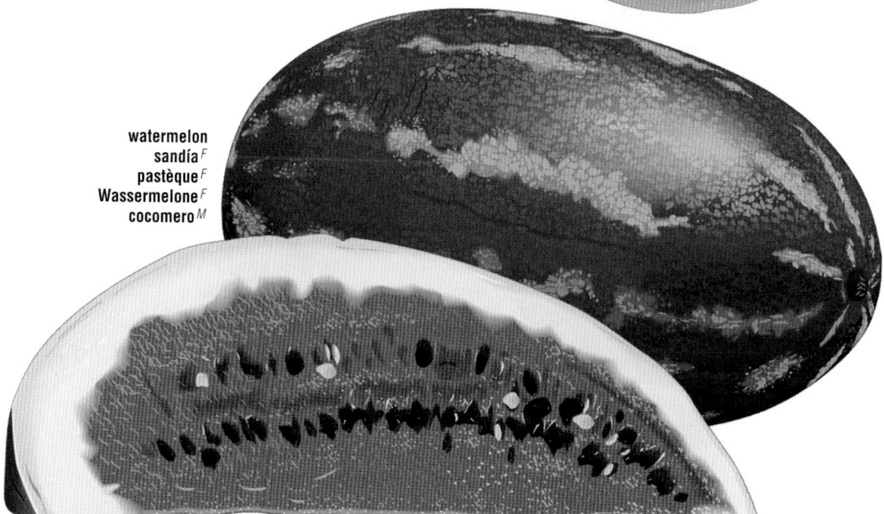

fruits

pome fruits
frutas^F pomo
fruits^M à pépins^M
Apfelfrüchte^F
pomi^M

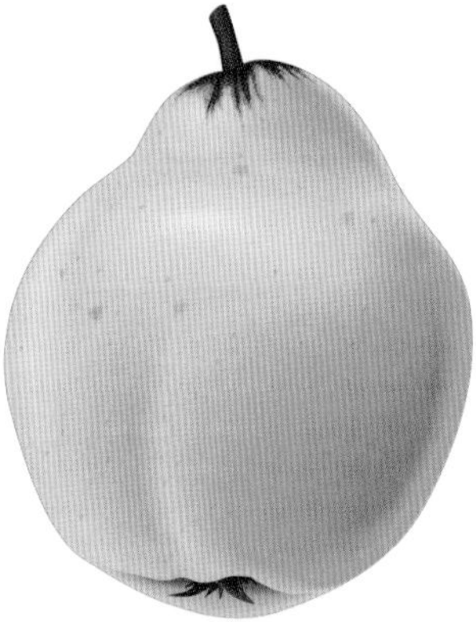

quince
membrillo^M
coing^M
Quitte^F
mela^F cotogna

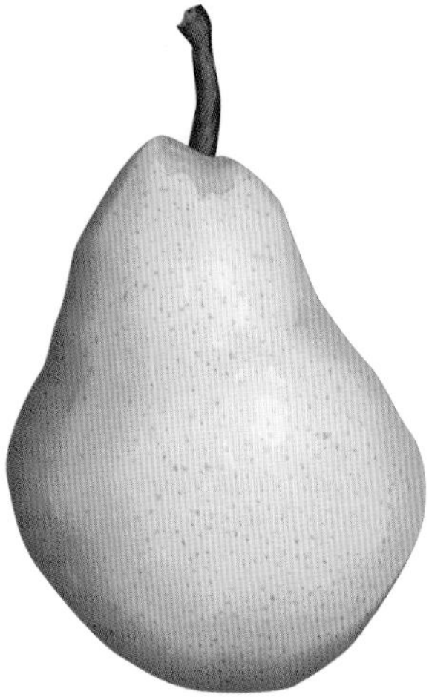

pear
pera^F
poire^F
Birne^F
pera^F

apple
manzana^F
pomme^F
Apfel^M
mela^F

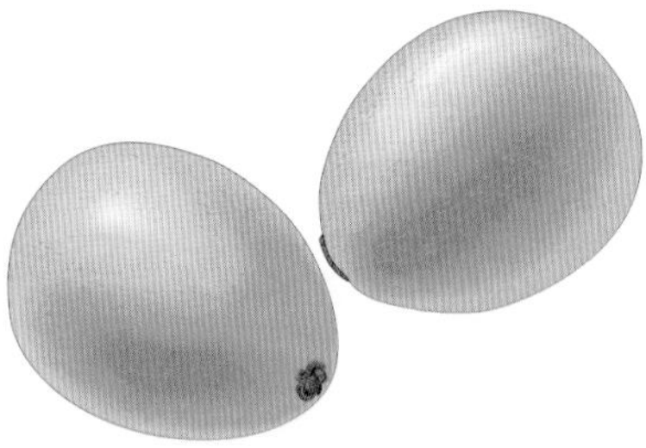

Japanese plum
níspero^M
nèfle^F du Japon^M
Mispel^F
nespola^F del Giappone^M

tropical fruits
frutas[F] tropicales
fruits[M] tropicaux
Südfrüchte[F]
frutti[M] tropicali

kiwi
kiwi[M]
kiwi[M]
Kiwi[F]
kiwi[M]

tamarillo
tamarillo[M]
tamarillo[M]
Baumtomate[F]
tamarillo[M]

longan
longan[M]
longane[M]
Longanfrucht[F]
longan[M]

horned melon
kiwano[M]
melon[M] à cornes[F]
Kiwano[F]
kiwano[M]

mangosteen
mangostán[M]
mangoustan[M]
Mangostane[F]
mangostano[M]

pineapple
piña[F]
ananas[M]
Ananas[F]
ananas[M]

banana
banana[F]
banane[F]
Banane[F]
banana[F]

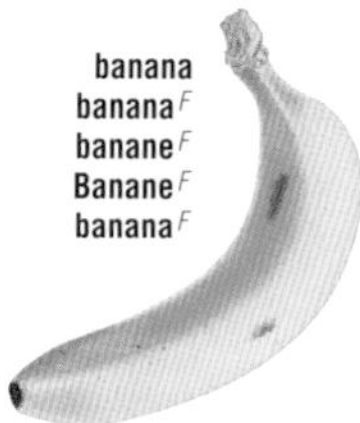

jackfruit
fruta[F] de jack
jaque[M]
Jackfrucht[F]
frutto[M] del jack

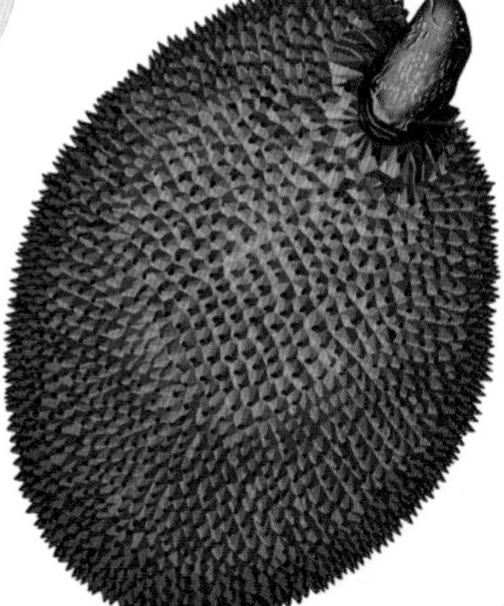

plantain
plátano[M]
banane[F] plantain[M]
Plantainbanane[F]
banana[F] plantain

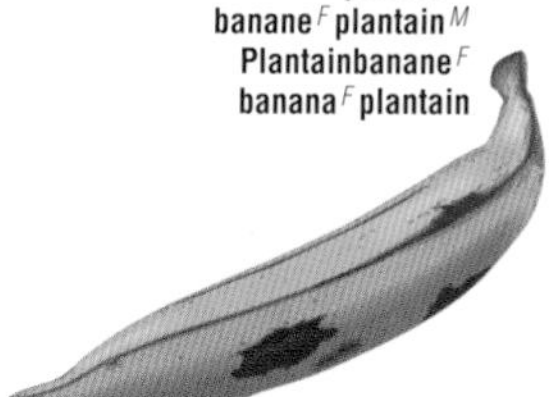

jujube
jojoba [F]
jujube [M]
chinesische Dattel [F]
giuggiola [F]

jaboticaba
jaboticaba [F]
jaboticaba [M]
Jaboticaba [F]
jaboticaba [F]

litchi
lichi [M]
litchi [M]
Litchi [F]
litchi [M]

sapodilla
zapote [M]
sapotille [F]
Breiapfel [M]
sapotiglia [F]

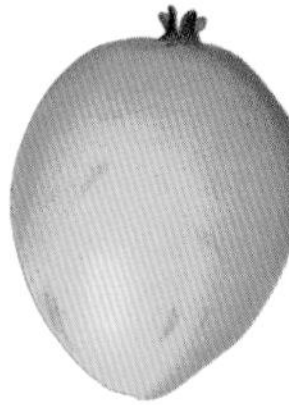

guava
guayaba [F]
goyave [F]
Guave [F]
guaiava [F]

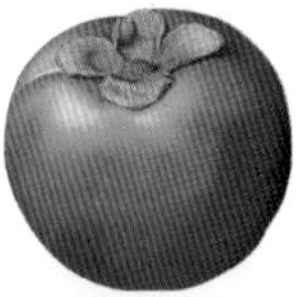

Japanese persimmon
caqui [M]
kaki [M]
Kaki [F]
cachi [M]

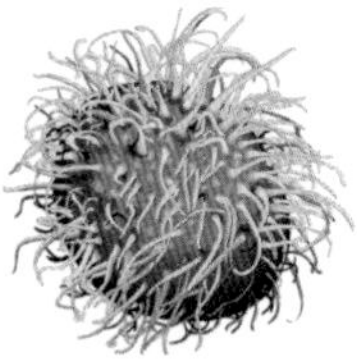

rambutan
rambután [M]
ramboutan [M]
Rambutan [F]
rambutan [M]

fig
higo [M]
figue [F]
Feige [F]
fico [M]

passion fruit
fruta [F] de la pasión [F]
fruit [M] de la Passion [F]
Passionsfrucht [F]
maracuja [F]

pomegranate
granada [F]
grenade [F]
Granatapfel [M]
melograno [M]

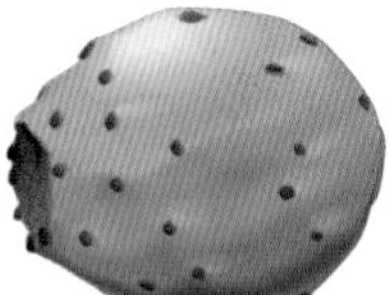

prickly pear
higo[M] chumbo
figue[F] de Barbarie
Kaktusfeige[F]
fico[M] d'India[F]

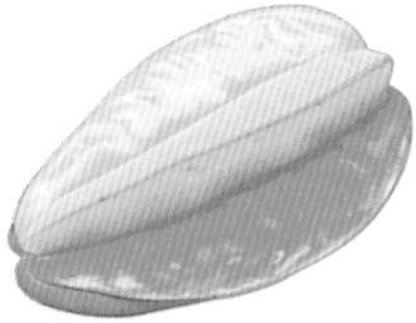

carambola
carambola[F]
carambole[F]
Sternfrucht[F]
carambola[F]

Asian pear
pera[F] asiática
pomme[F] poire[F]
asiatische Birne[F]
nashi[M]

mango
mango[M]
mangue[F]
Mango[F]
mango[M]

feijoa
feijoa[F]
feijoa[M]
Ananasguave[F]
feijoa[F]

cherimoya
chirimoya[F]
chérimole[F]
Chirimoya[F]
cerimolia[F]

papaya
papaya[F]
papaye[F]
Papaya[F]
papaia[F]

pepino
pepino[M] dulce
pepino[M]
Birnenmelone[F]
pepino[M]

durian
durión[M]
durian[M]
Durianfrucht[F]
durian[M]

herbs

hierbas[F] aromáticas | fines herbes[F] | Kräuter[N] | piante[F] aromatiche

dill
eneldo[M]
aneth[M]
Dill[M]
aneto[M]

anise
anís[M]
anis[M]
Anis[M]
anice[M]

sweet bay
laurel[M]
laurier[M]
Lorbeer[M]
alloro[M]

oregano
orégano[M]
origan[M]
Oregano[M]
origano[M]

basil
albahaca[F]
basilic[M]
Basilikum[N]
basilico[M]

sage
salvia[F]
sauge[F]
Salbei[M]
salvia[F]

tarragon
estragón[M]
estragon[M]
Estragon[M]
dragoncello[M]

thyme
tomillo[M]
thym[M]
Thymian[M]
timo[M]

mint
hierbabuena[F]
menthe[F]
Minze[F]
menta[F]

parsley
perejil [M]
persil [M]
Petersilie [F]
prezzemolo [M]

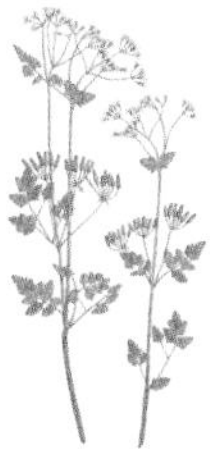

chervil
perifollo [M]
cerfeuil [M]
Kerbel [M]
cerfoglio [M]

savory
ajedrea [F]
sarriette [F]
Bohnenkraut [N]
santoreggia [F]

coriander
cilantro [M]
coriandre [F]
Koriander [M]
coriandolo [M]

hyssop
hisopo [M]
hysope [F]
Ysop [M]
issopo [M]

borage
borraja [F]
bourrache [F]
Boretsch [M]
borragine [F]

rosemary
romero [M]
romarin [M]
Rosmarin [M]
rosmarino [M]

lovage
alheña [F]
livèche [F]
Liebstöckel [M/N]
sedano [M] di monte [M]

lemon balm
melisa [F]
mélisse [F]
Zitronenmelisse [F]
melissa [F]

cereal products

cereales^{M} | produits^{M} céréaliers | Getreideprodukte^{N} | prodotti^{M} cerealicoli

bread
pan^{M}
pain^{M}
Brot^{N}
pane^{M}

bagel
rosquilla^{F}
bagel^{M}
Bagel^{M}
ciambella^{F}

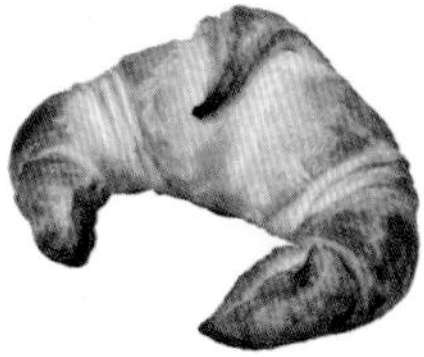

croissant
cruasán^{M}
croissant^{M}
Croissant^{N}
croissant^{M}

black rye bread
pan^{M} de centeno^{M} negro
pain^{M} de seigle^{M} noir
dunkles Roggenbrot^{N}
pane^{M} nero di segale^{F}

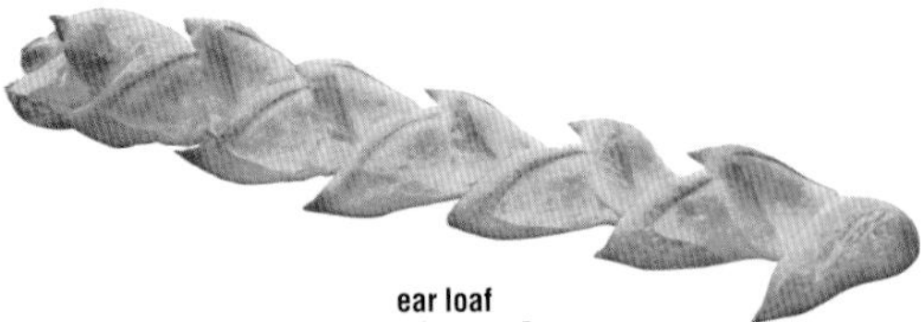

ear loaf
pan^{M} espiga^{F}
baguette^{F} épi^{M}
Ährenbrot^{N}
spiga^{F}

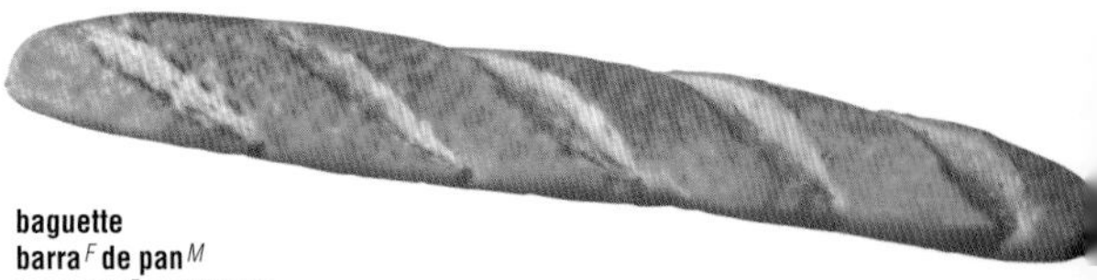

baguette
barra^{F} de pan^{M}
baguette^{F} parisienne
französisches Weißbrot^{N}
filone^{M} francese

Greek bread
pan^{M} griego
pain^{M} grec
griechisches Brot^{N}
pane^{F} greco

French bread
baguette^{F}
pain^{M} parisien
Baguette^{N}
baguette^{F}

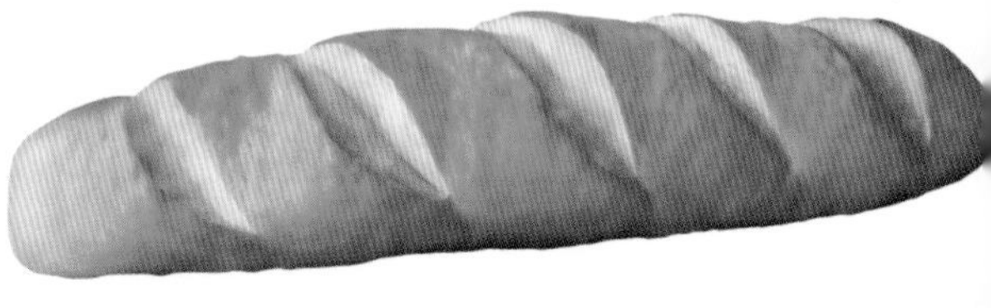

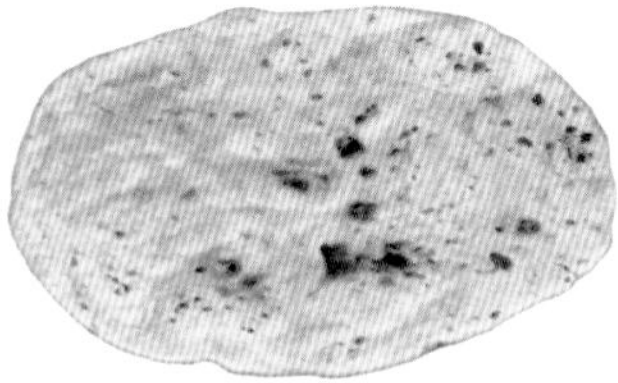

Indian chapati bread
pan[M] indio chapatí
pain[M] chapati indien
indisches Fladenbrot[N]
pane[M] chapati indiano

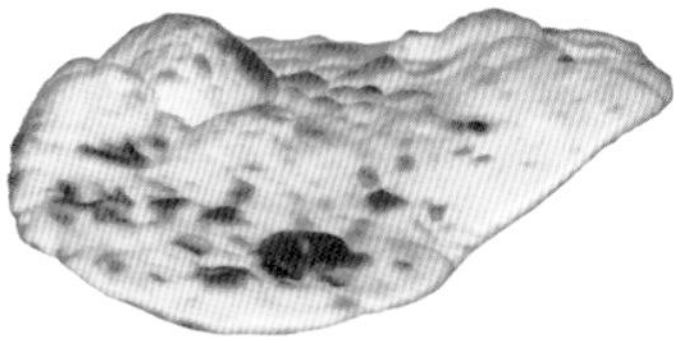

Indian naan bread
pan[M] indio naan
pain[M] naan indien
indisches Naanbrot[N]
pane[M] naan indiano

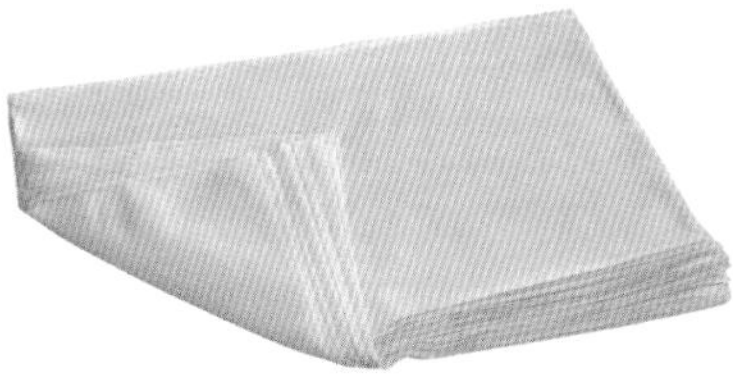

phyllo dough
pasta[F] de hojaldre[M]
pâte[F] phyllo[F]
Blätterteig[M]
pasta[F] sfoglia[F]

unleavened bread
pan[M] ácimo
pain[M] azyme
ungesäuertes Brot[N]
pane[M] azzimo

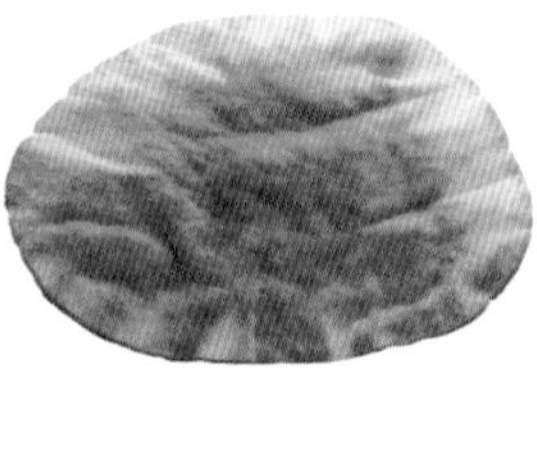

pita bread
pan[M] de pita[F]
pain[M] pita
Pittabrot[N]
pane[M] pita

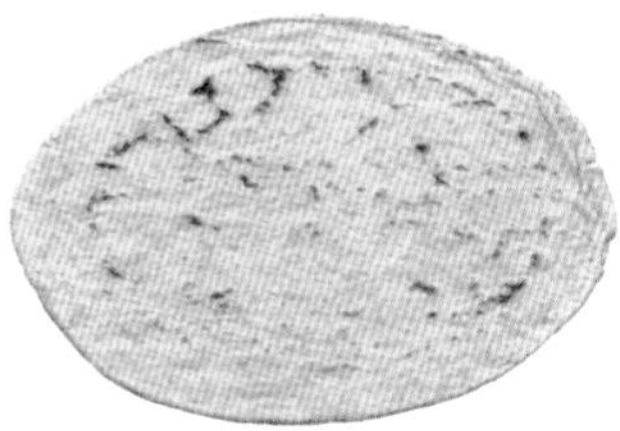

tortilla
tortilla[F]
tortilla[F]
Tortilla[F]
tortilla[F]

bread

Russian pumpernickel
pan^{M} negro ruso
pain^{M} noir russe
russischer Pumpernickel^{M}
Pumpernickel^{M} russo

German rye bread
pan^{M} alemán de centeno^{M}
pain^{M} de seigle^{M} allemand
deutsches Roggenbrot^{N}
pane^{M} di segale^{F} tedesco

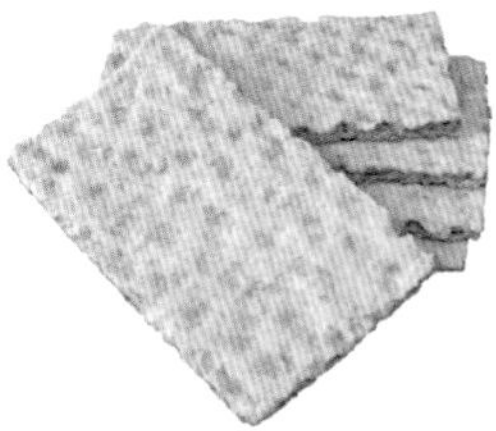

cracked rye bread
galleta^{F} de centeno^{M}
cracker^{M} de seigle^{M}
Roggenknäckebrot^{N}
galletta^{F} di segale^{F}

Danish rye bread
pan^{M} danés de centeno^{M}
pain^{M} de seigle^{M} danois
dänisches Roggenbrot^{N}
pane^{M} di segale^{F} danese

Jewish hallah
pan^{M} judío hallah
pain^{M} tchallah juif
Challa^{F}
pane^{M} ebraico

Scandinavian cracked bread
galleta^{F} escandinava
cracker^{M} scandinave
skandinavisches Knäckebrot^{N}
galletta^{F} scandinava

Irish bread
pan[M] irlandés
pain[M] irlandais
irisches Brot[N]
pane[M] irlandese

American corn bread
pan[M] americano de maíz[M]
pain[M] de maïs[M] américain
amerikanisches Maisbrot[N]
pane[M] di mais[M] americano

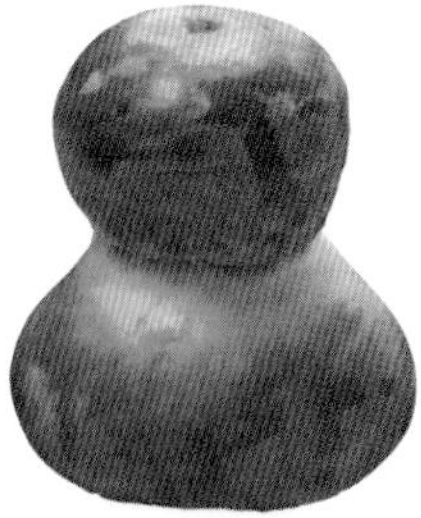

English loaf
pan[M] de flor[F]
pain[M] de mie[F]
englisches Weißbrot[N]
pagnottella[F] inglese

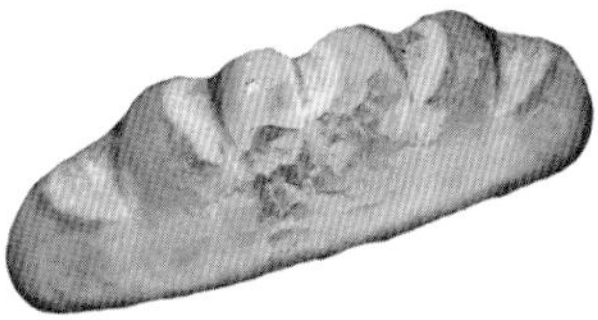

white bread
pan[M] blanco
pain[M] blanc
Weißbrot[N]
pane[M] bianco

multigrain bread
pan[M] multicereales
pain[M] multicéréales
Mehrkornbrot[N]
pane[M] multicereali

farmhouse bread
pan[M] campesino
pain[M] de campagne[F]
Bauernbrot[N]
pane[M] casereccio

whole wheat bread
pan[M] integral
pain[M] complet
Vollkornbrot[N]
pane[M] integrale

cereal products

pasta
pasta F
pâtes F alimentaires
Teigwaren F
pasta F

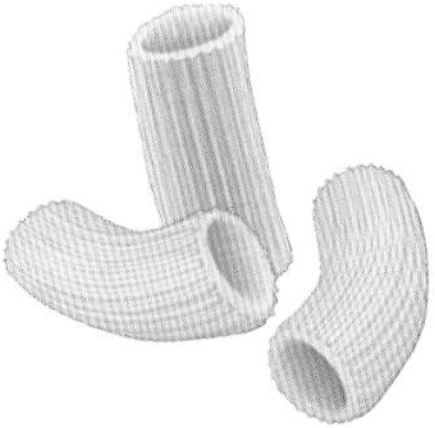

rigatoni
rigatoni M
rigatoni M
Rigatoni M
rigatoni M

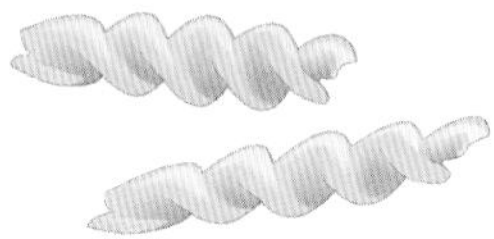

rotini
sacacorchos M
rotini M
Rotini M
eliche F

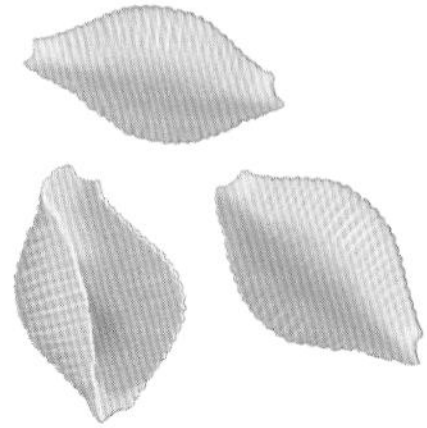

conchiglie
conchitas F
conchiglie F
Conchiglie F
conchiglie F

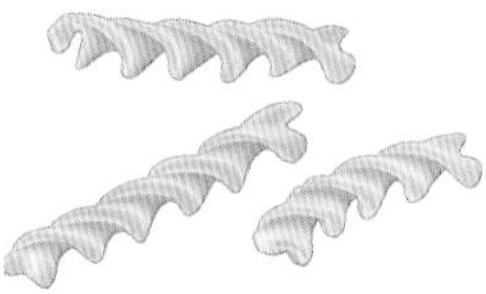

fusilli
fusilli M
fusilli M
Fusilli M
fusilli M

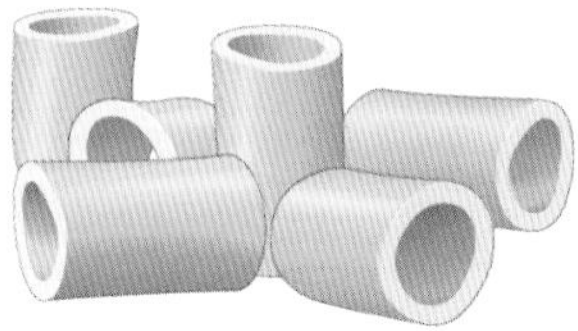

ditali
dedalitos M
ditali M
Ditali M
ditali M

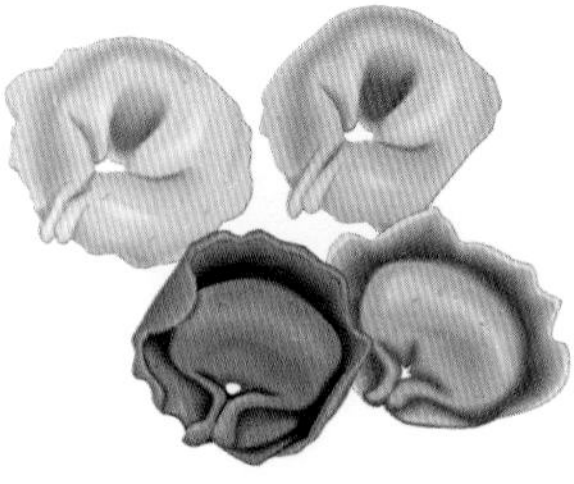

tortellini
tortellini M
tortellini M
Tortellini M
tortellini M

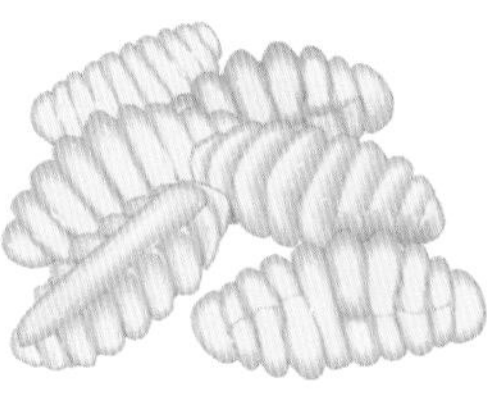

gnocchi
ñoquis M
gnocchi M
Gnocchi M
gnocchi M

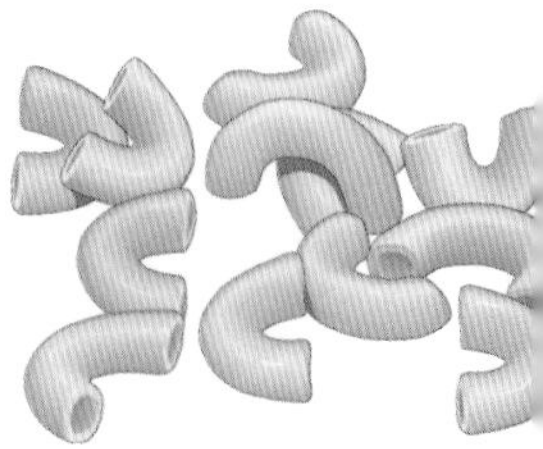

elbows
tiburones M
coudes M
Hörnchennudeln F
gomiti M

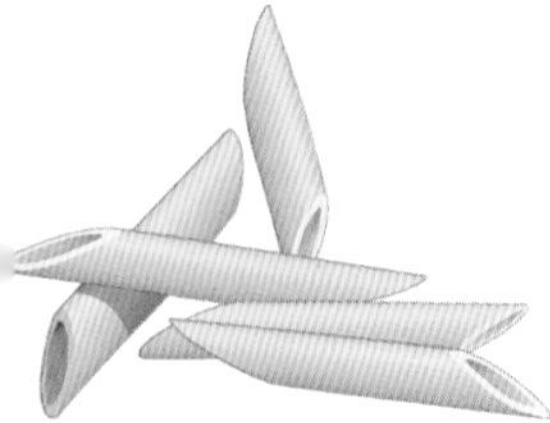

penne
macarrones *M*
penne *M*
Penne *F*
penne *F*

spaghetti
espagueti *M*
spaghetti *M*
Spaghetti *M*
spaghetti *M*

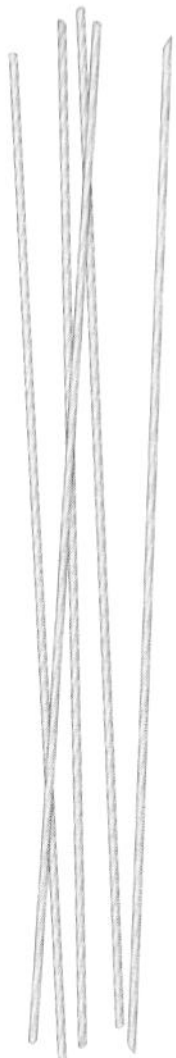

spaghettini
fideos *M*
spaghettini *M*
Spaghettini *M*
spaghettini *M*

fettucine
fetuchinas *F*
fettucine *M*
Fettuccine *F*
fettuccine *F*

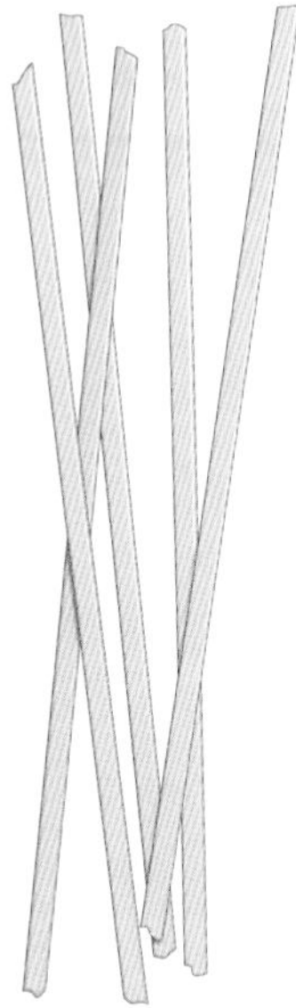

ravioli
raviolis *M*
ravioli *M*
Ravioli *M*
ravioli *M*

cannelloni
canelones *M*
cannelloni *M*
Cannelloni *M*
cannelloni *M*

spinach tagliatelle
tallarines *M* **de espinacas** *F*
tagliatelle *M* **aux épinards** *M*
grüne Tagliatelle *F*
tagliatelle *F* **verdi**

lasagna
lasañas *F*
lasagne *F*
Lasagne *F*
lasagne *F*

dairy products

productos^M lácteos | produits^M laitiers | Milchprodukte^N | prodotti^M caseari

soft cheeses
quesos^M blandos
fromages^M à pâte^F molle
Weichkäse^M
formaggi^M a pasta^F molle

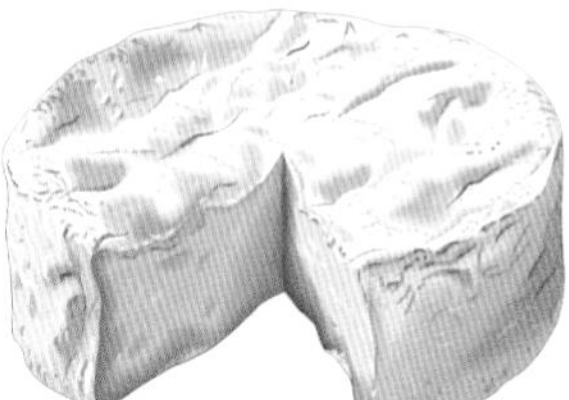

Camembert
camembert^M
camembert^M
Camembert^M
camembert^M

Coulommiers
coulommiers^M
coulommiers^M
Coulommiers^M
coulommiers^M

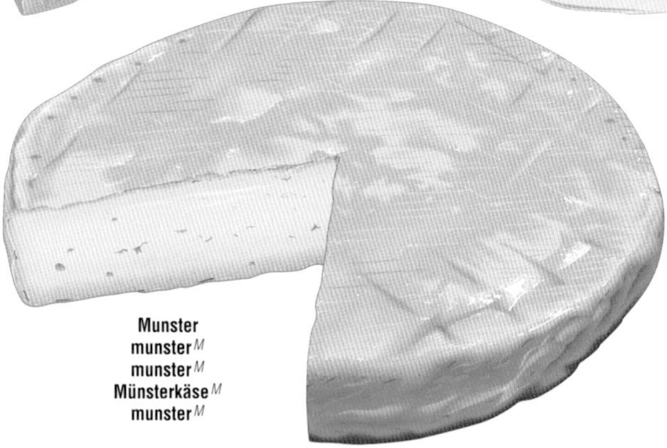

Munster
munster^M
munster^M
Münsterkäse^M
munster^M

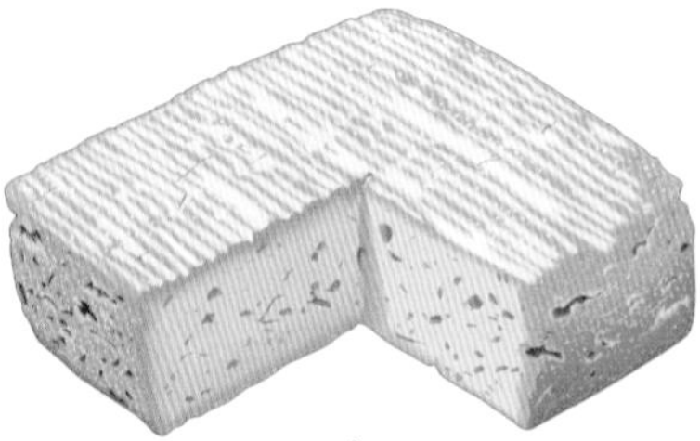

Pont-l'Évêque
Pont-l'Éveque^M
pont-l'évêque^M
Pont-l'Évêque^M
pont-l'évêque^M

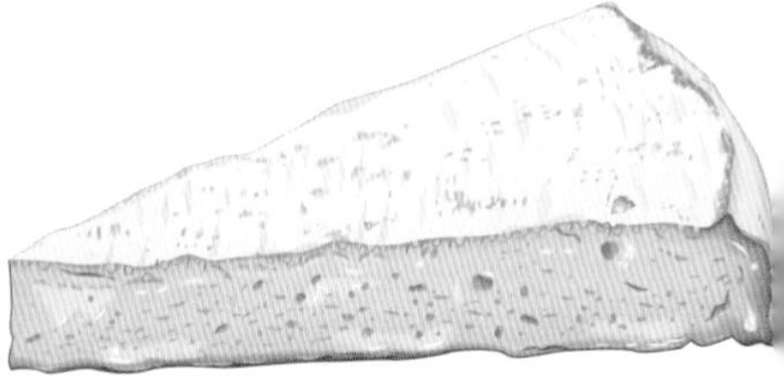

Brie
brie^M
brie^M
Brie^M
brie^M

goat's-milk cheeses
quesos[M] de cabra[F]
fromages[M] de chèvre[F]
Ziegenkäse[M]
formaggi[M] di capra[F]

Chèvre cheese
queso[M] chèvre
chèvre[M] frais
Ziegenfrischkäse[M]
formaggio[M] fresco di capra[F]

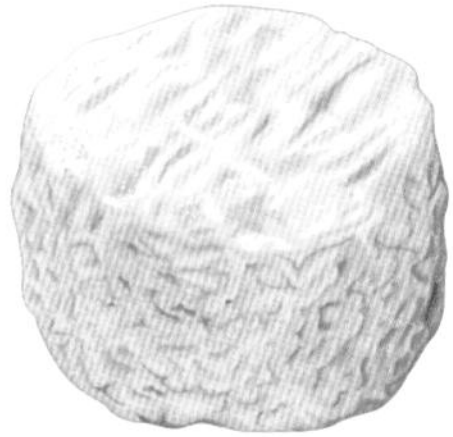

Crottin de Chavignol
Crottin[M] de Chavignol
crottin[M] de Chavignol
Crottin de Chavignol[M]
crottin[M] de chavignol

fresh cheeses
quesos[M] frescos
fromages[M] frais
Frischkäse[M]
formaggi[M] freschi

cottage cheese
queso[M] cottage
cottage[M]
Hüttenkäse[M]
cottage cheese[M]

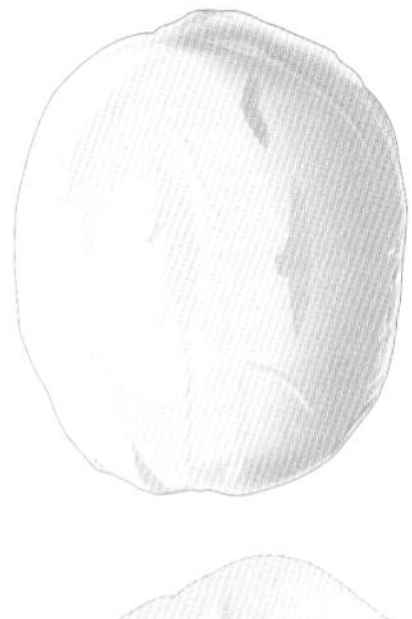

mozzarella
mozzarella[F]
mozzarella[F]
Mozzarella[M]
mozzarella[F]

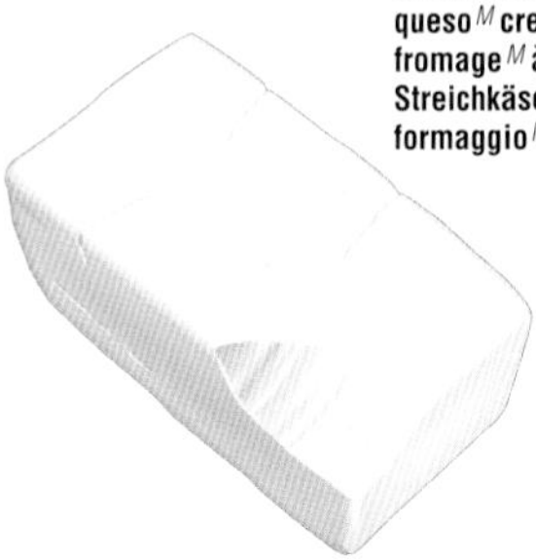

cream cheese
queso[M] cremoso
fromage[M] à la crème[F]
Streichkäse[M]
formaggio[M] cremoso

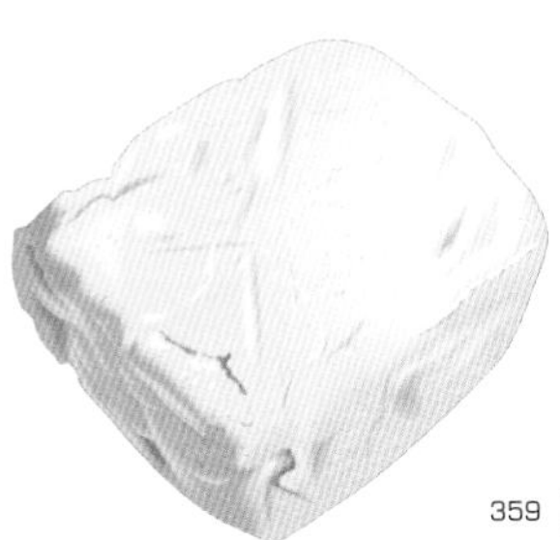

ricotta
ricotta[F]
ricotta[F]
Ricotta[M]
ricotta[F]

pressed cheeses
quesos M prensados
fromages M à pâte F pressée
Hartkäse M
formaggi M a pasta F dura

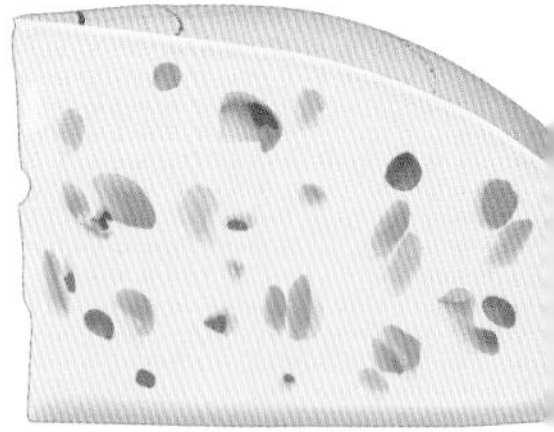

Emmenthal
emmenthal M
emmenthal M
Emmentaler M
emmental M

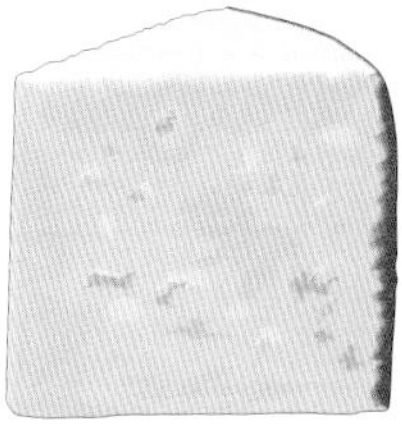

Romano
pecorino romano M
romano M
Pecorino Romano M
pecorino M romano

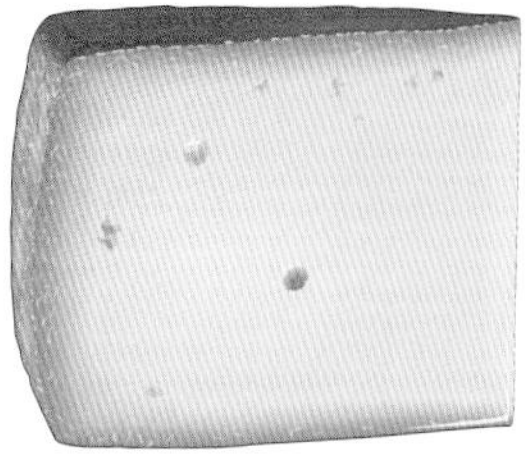

Raclette
raclette F
raclette F
Raclette M
raclette F

Gruyère
gruyère M
gruyère M
Gruyèrekäse M
groviera M/F

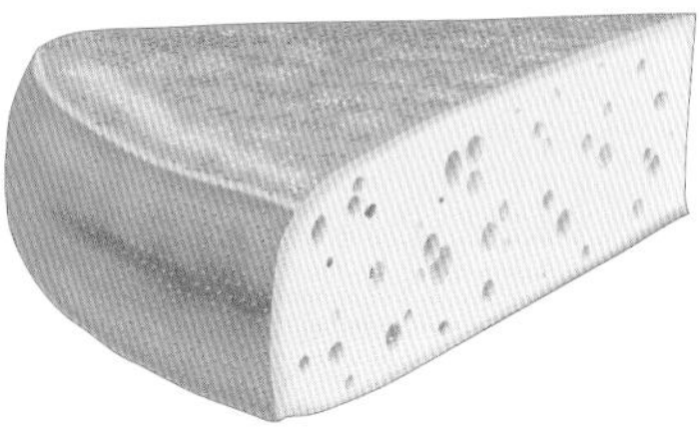

Jarlsberg
jarlsberg M
jarlsberg M
Jarlsberg M
jarlsberg M

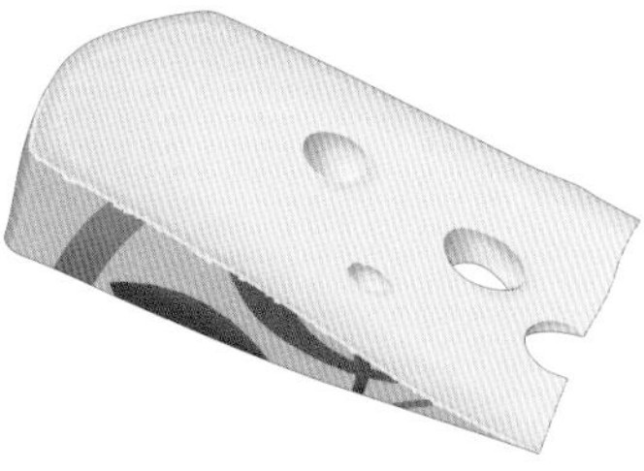

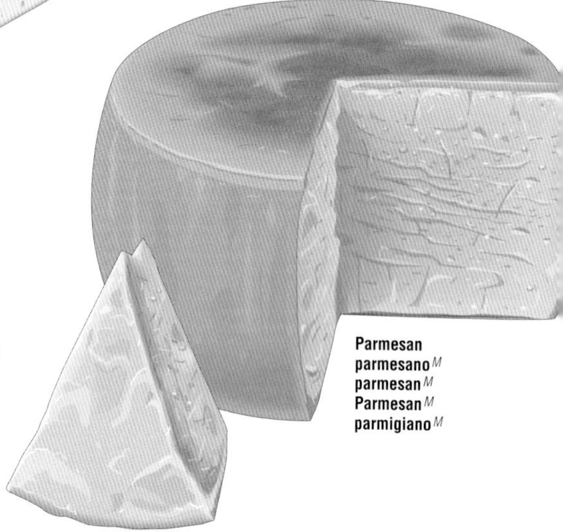

Parmesan
parmesano M
parmesan M
Parmesan M
parmigiano M

blue-veined cheeses
quesos^M azules
fromages^M à pâte^F persillée
Edelpilzkäse^M
formaggi^M erborinati

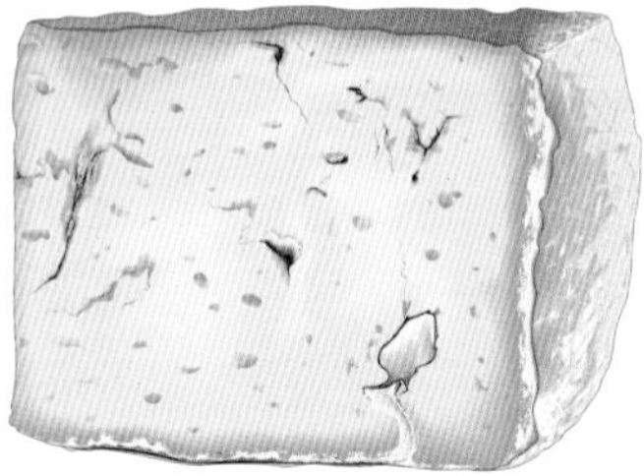

Gorgonzola
gorgonzola^M
gorgonzola^M
Gorgonzola^M
gorgonzola^M

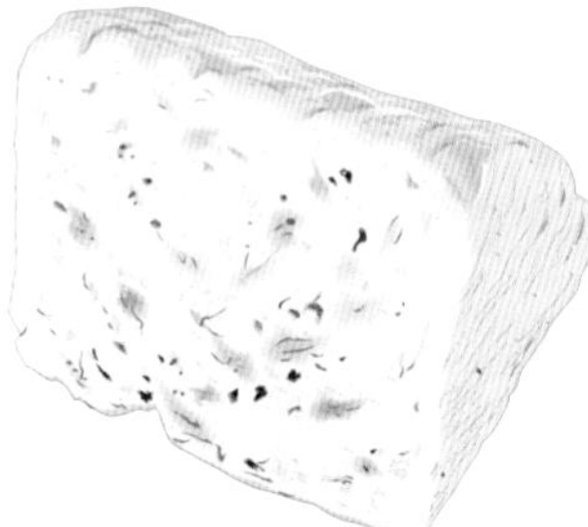

Danish Blue
azul danés^M
bleu^M **danois**
Danish Blue^M
danish blue^M

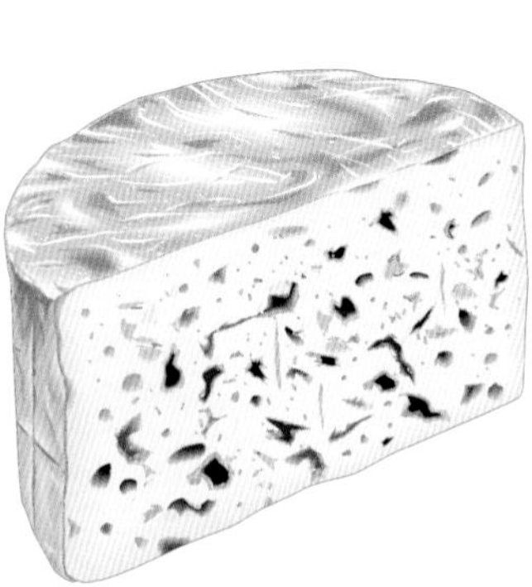

Roquefort
roquefort^M
roquefort^M
Roquefort^M
roquefort^M

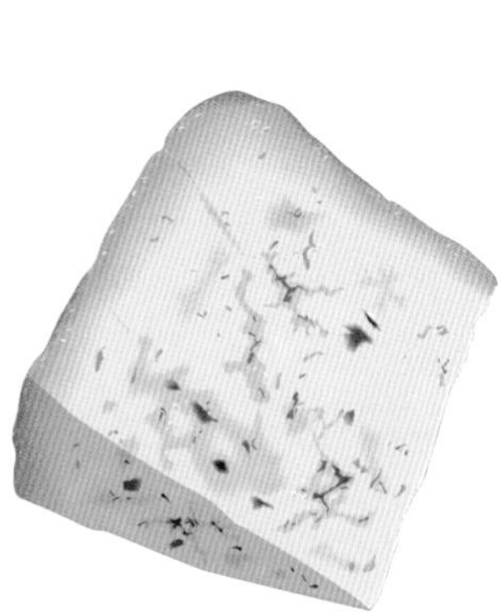

Stilton
stilton^M
stilton^M
Stilton^M
stilton^M

variety meat

despojos M | abats M | Innereien F | interiora F

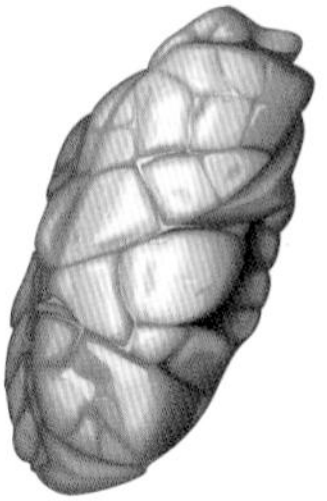

sweetbreads
mollejas F
ris M
Bries N
animelle F

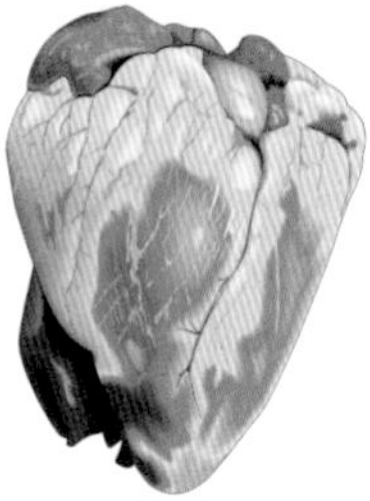

heart
corazón M
cœur M
Herz N
cuore M

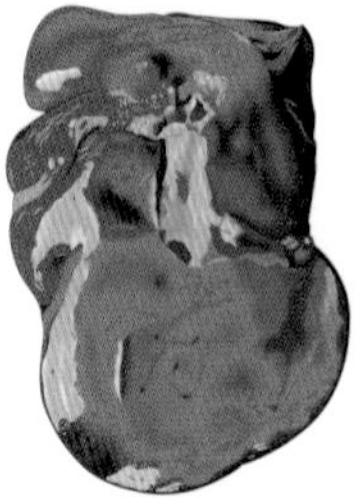

liver
hígado M
foie M
Leber F
fegato M

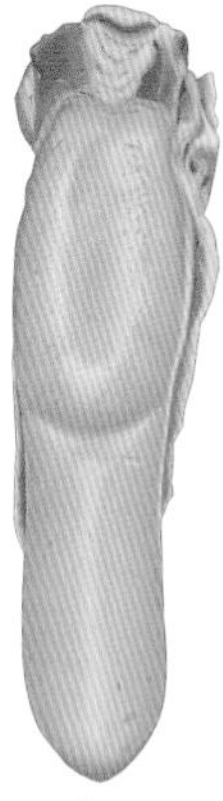

tongue
lengua F
langue F
Zunge F
lingua F

tripe
tripa F
tripes F
Kaldaune F
trippa F

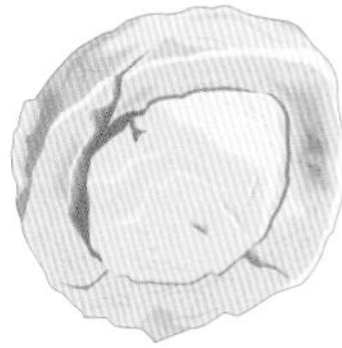

marrow
médula F
moelle F
Mark N
midollo M

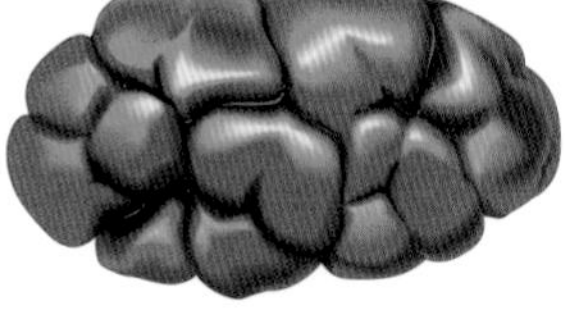

kidney
riñones M
rognons M
Niere F
rognone M

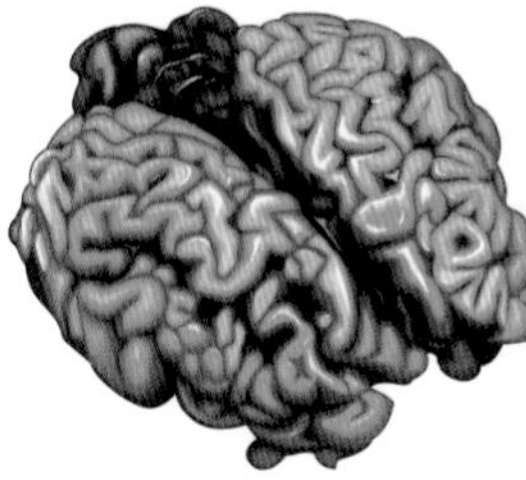

brains
sesos M
cervelle F
Hirn N
cervelli M

delicatessen

charcutería F | charcuterie F | Spezialitäten F | gastronomia F

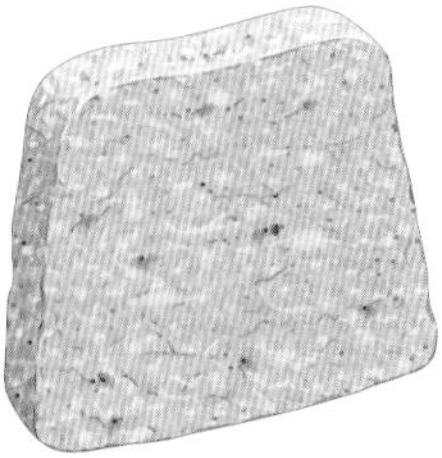

rillettes
rillettes F
rillettes F
Rillettes F
ciccioli M

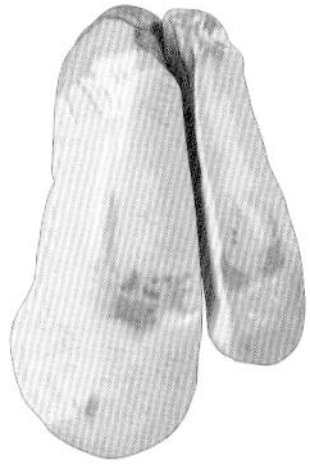

foie gras
foie gras M
foie M gras
Stopfleber F
foie-gras M

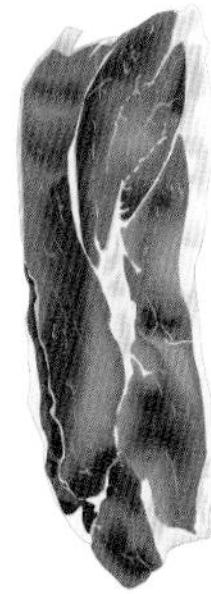

prosciutto
jamón M serrano
prosciutto M
roher Schinken M
prosciutto M

cooked ham
jamón M de York
jambon M cuit
gekochter Schinken M
prosciutto M cotto

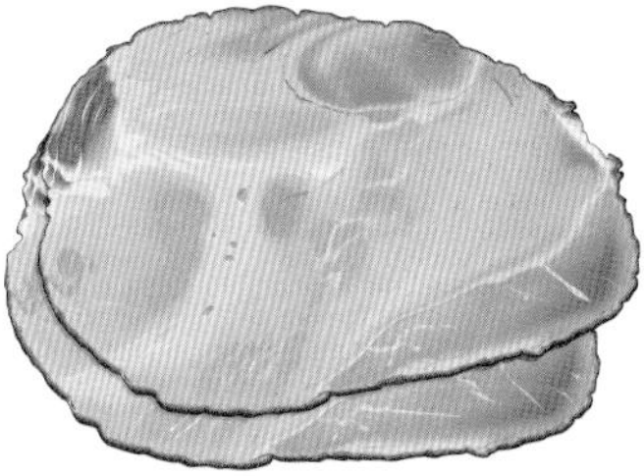

pancetta
panceta F
pancetta F
Bauchspeck M
pancetta F

American bacon
bacón M americano
bacon M américain
Frühstücksspeck M
bacon M americano

Canadian bacon
bacón M canadiense
bacon M canadien
kanadischer Bacon M
bacon M canadese

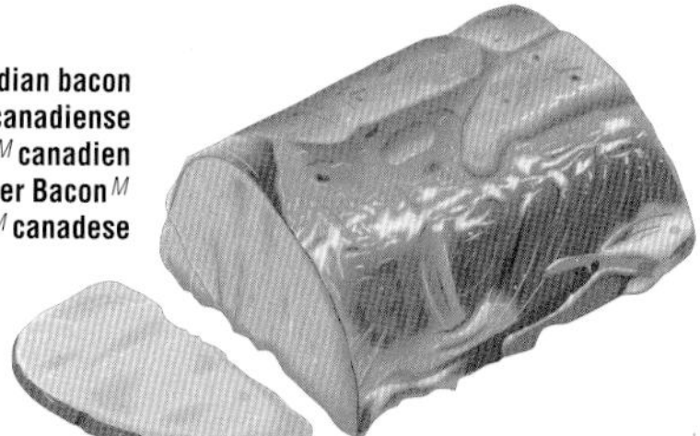

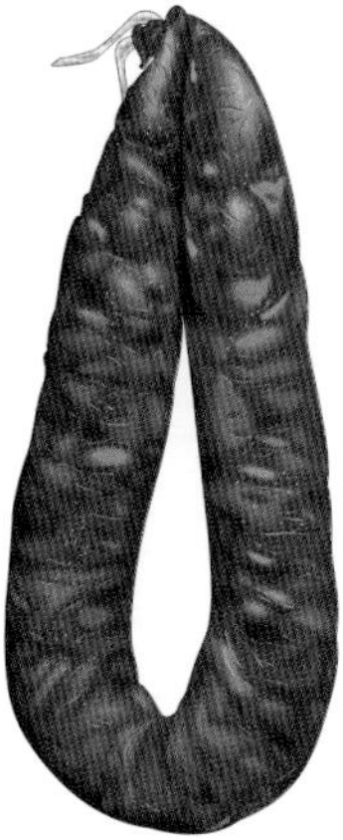

pepperoni
pepperoni[M]
pepperoni[M]
Pepperoniwurst[F]
salsiccia[F] piccante

chorizo
chorizo[M]
chorizo[M]
Chorizo-Wurst[F]
chorizo[M]

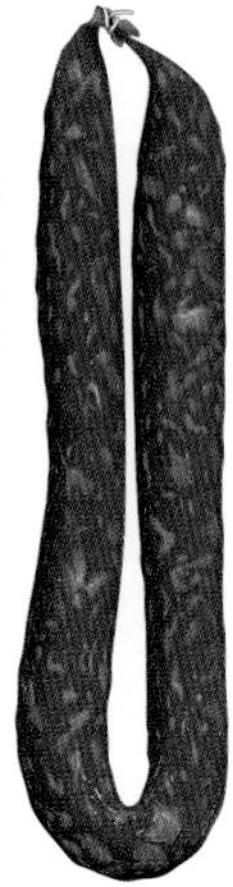

kielbasa sausage
salchicha[F] kielbasa
saucisson[M] kielbasa
Kielbasa-Wurst[F]
salsiccia[F] kielbasa

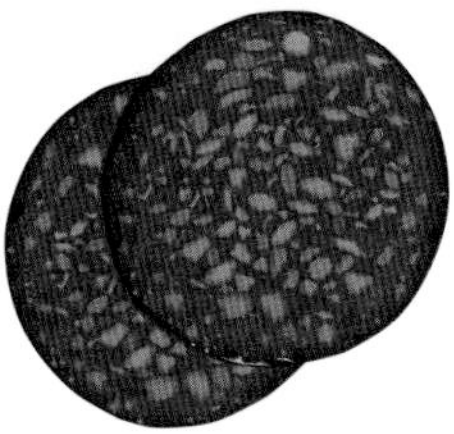

mortadella
mortadela[F]
mortadelle[F]
Mortadella[F]
mortadella[F]

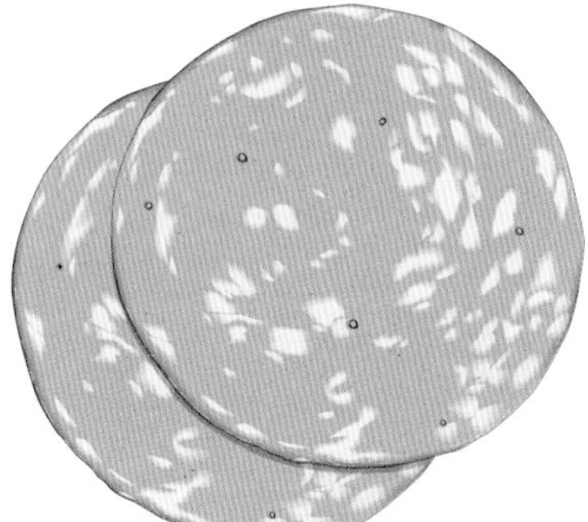

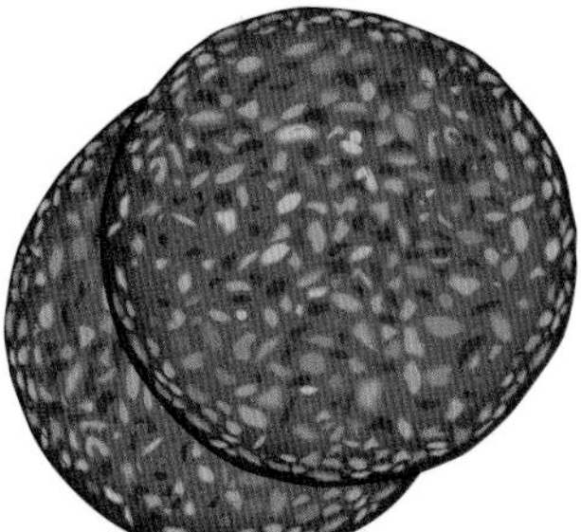

German salami
salami[M] alemán
salami[M] allemand
feine Salami[F]
salame[M] tedesco

Genoa salami
salami[M] de Génova
salami[M] de Gênes
grobe Salami[F]
salame[M] di Genova

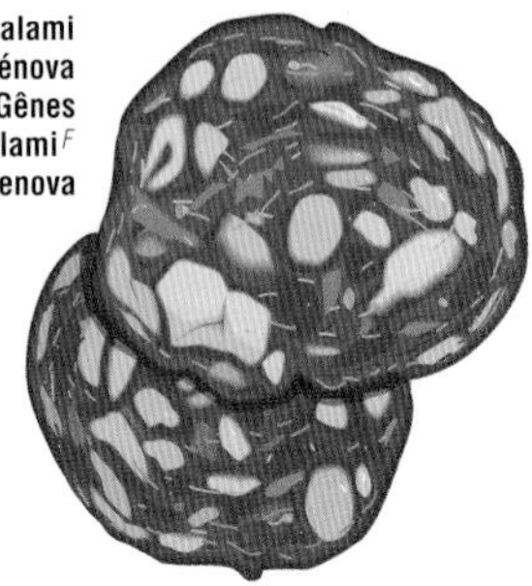

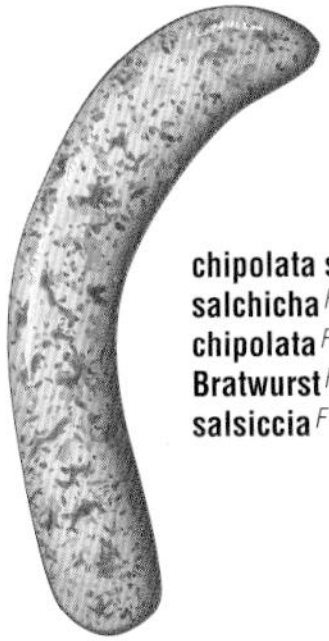

chipolata sausage
salchicha^{F} chipolata
chipolata^{F}
Bratwurst^{F}
salsiccia^{F} alle cipolle^{F}

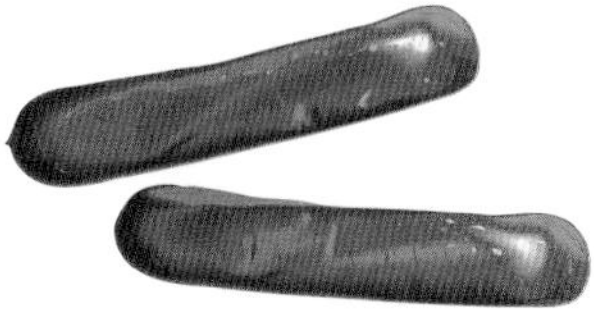

merguez sausage
salchicha^{F} merguez
merguez^{F}
Merguez-Wurst^{F}
merguez^{F}

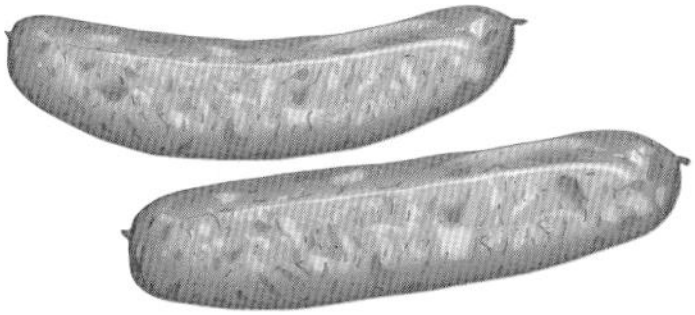

Toulouse sausage
salchicha^{F} de Toulouse
saucisse^{F} de Toulouse
Toulouser Wurst^{F}
salame^{M} di Tolosa

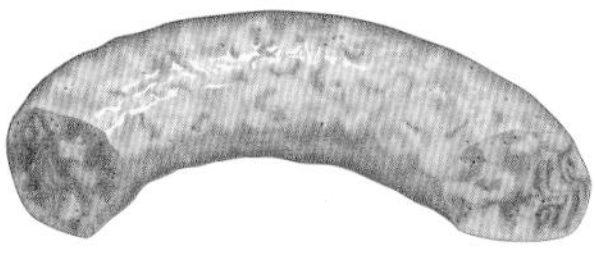

andouillette
andouillete^{F}
andouillette^{F}
Kuttelwurst^{F}
salsiccia^{F} di trippa^{F}

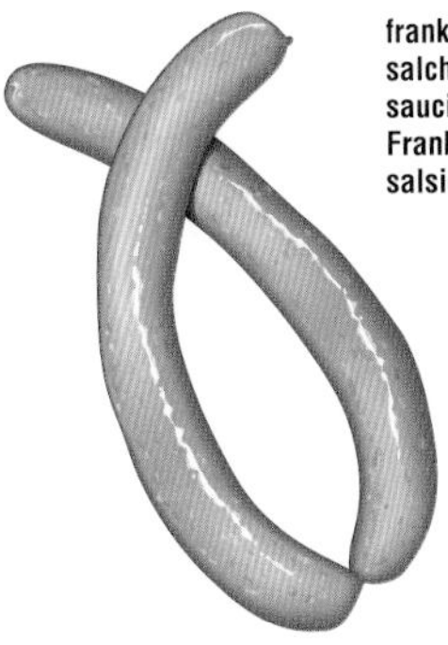

frankfurter
salchicha^{F} de Frankfurt
saucisse^{F} de Francfort
Frankfurter Würstchen^{N}
salsiccia^{F} di Francoforte

blood sausage
morcilla^{F}
boudin^{M}
Blutwurst^{F}
sanguinaccio^{M}

meat

carne[F] | viande[F] | Fleisch[N] | carne[F]

cuts of beef
cortes[M] de vacuno[M]
découpes[F] de bœuf[M]
Rindfleisch[N]
tagli[M] di manzo[M]

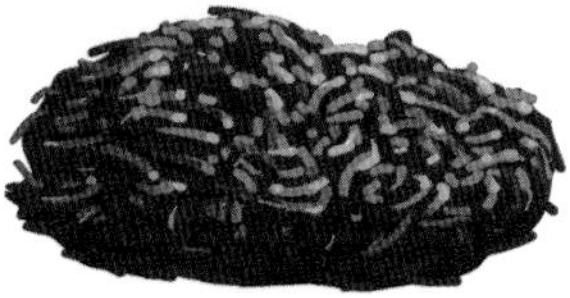

ground beef
carne[F] picada
bœuf[M] haché
Rinderhackfleisch[N]
macinato[M]

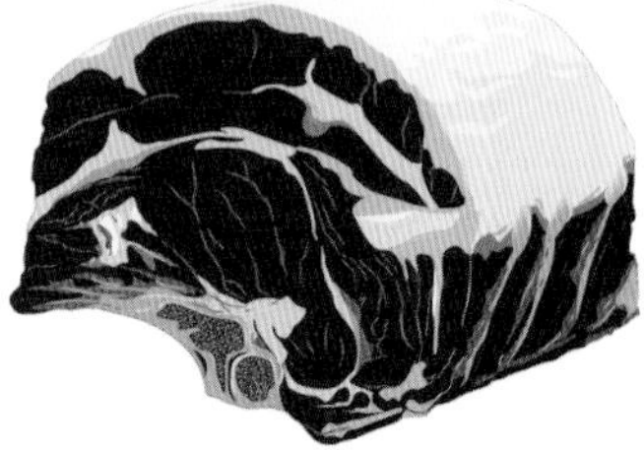

rib roast
chuletón[M]
rôti[M] de côtes[F]
hohe Rippe[F]
costate[F]

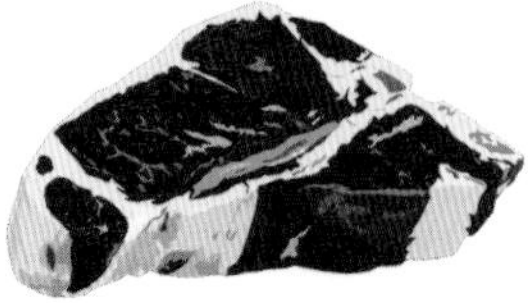

steak
bistec[M]
bifteck[M]
Steak[N]
bistecca[F]

beef cubes
carne[F] de vacuno[M] troceada
cubes[M] de bœuf[M]
Rindfleischwürfel[M]
spezzatino[M]

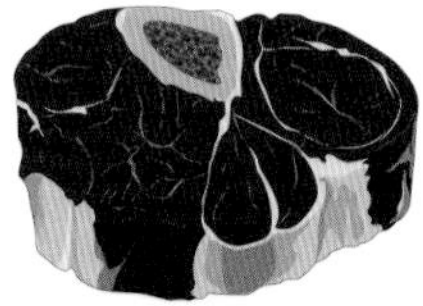

shank
morcillo[M]
jarret[M]
Hachse[F]
ossobuco[M]

tenderloin roast
lomo[M]
filet[M] de bœuf[M]
Rinderfilet[N]
filetto[M]

back ribs
costillar[M]
côtes[F] levées de dos[M]
Querrippe[F]
costine[F]

cuts of pork
cortes[M] de cerdo[M]
découpes[F] de porc[M]
Schweinefleisch[N]
tagli[M] di maiale[M]

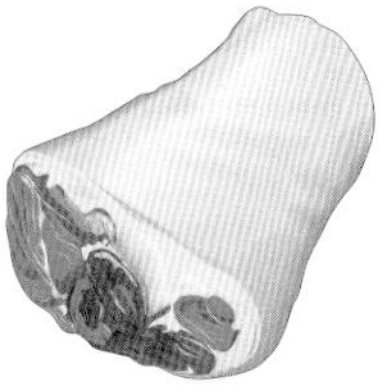

hock
codillo[M]
jarret[M]
Eisbein[N]
piedino[M]

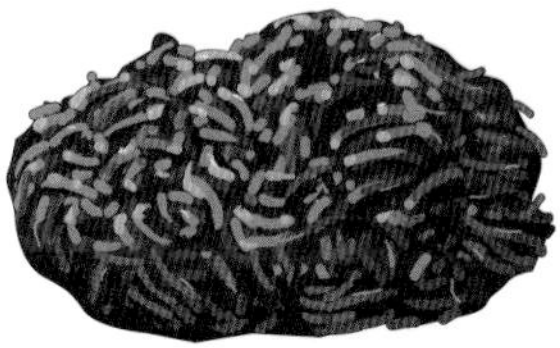

ground pork
carne[F] picada de cerdo[M]
porc[M] haché
Schweinehackfleisch[N]
macinato[M]

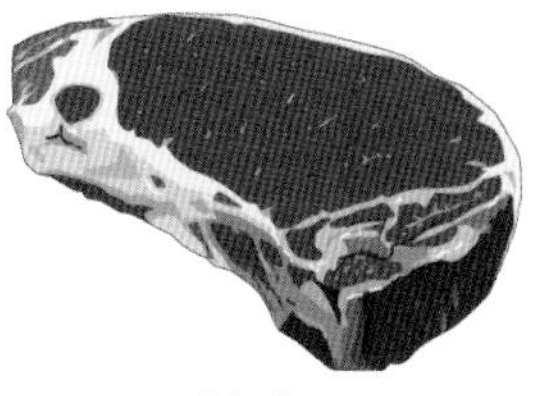

loin chop
chuleta[F]
côtelette[F]
Kotelett[N]
lonza[F]

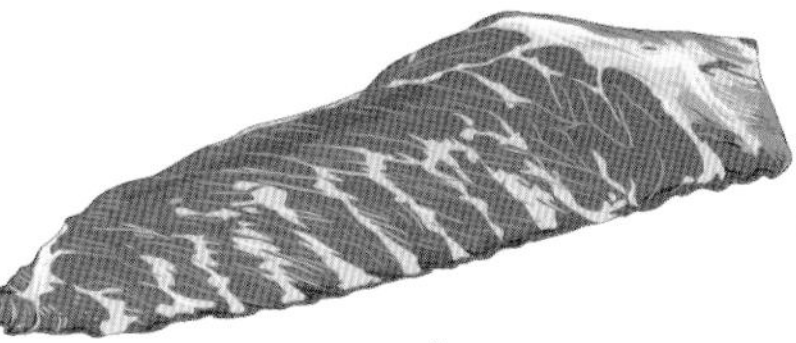

spareribs
costillar[M]
travers[M]
Spareribs/Schälrippchen[N]
costolette[F]

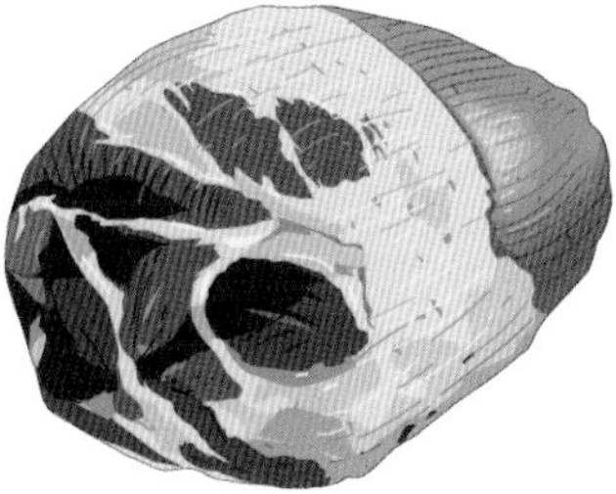

smoked ham
jamón[M] ahumado
jambon[M] fumé
Räucherschinken[M]
prosciutto[M] affumicato

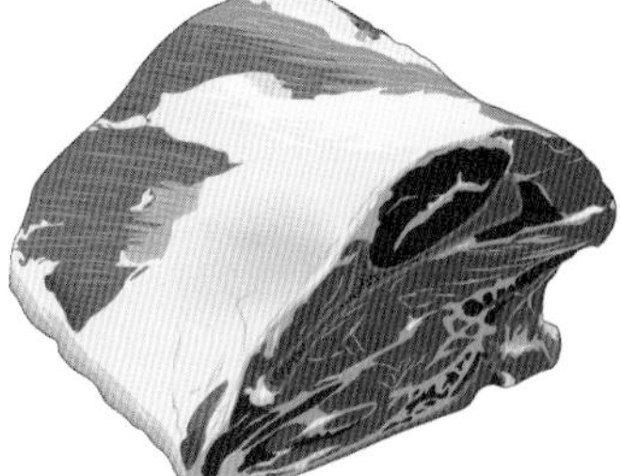

roast
asado[M] de cerdo[M]
rôti[M]
Braten[M]
arrosto[M]

mollusks

moluscos*M* | mollusques*M* | Mollusken*F* | molluschi*M*

octopus
pulpo*M*
pieuvre*F*
Krake*M*
polpo*M*

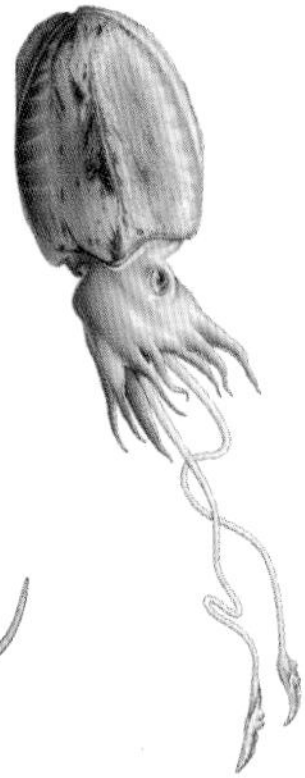

cuttlefish
sepia*F*
seiche*F*
Tintenfisch*M*
seppia*F*

squid
calamar*M*
calmar*M*
Kalmar*M*
calamaro*M*

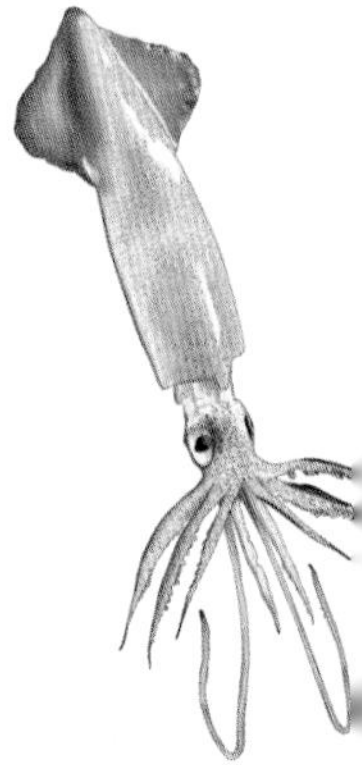

great scallop
vieira*F*
coquille*F* Saint-Jacques
Jakobsmuschel*F*
capasanta*F*

abalone
oreja*F* de mar*M*
ormeau*M*
Meerohr*N*
orecchia*F* di mare*M*

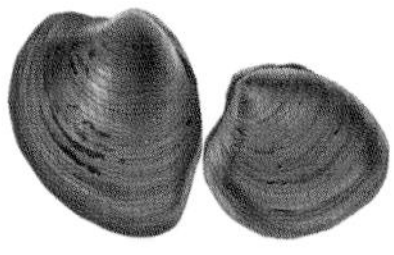

hard-shell clam
almeja*F*
palourde*F*
Kreuzmuster*N*-Teppichmuschel*F*
tartufo*M* di mare*M*

scallop
venera*F*
pétoncle*M*
Kammmuschel*F*
pettine*M*

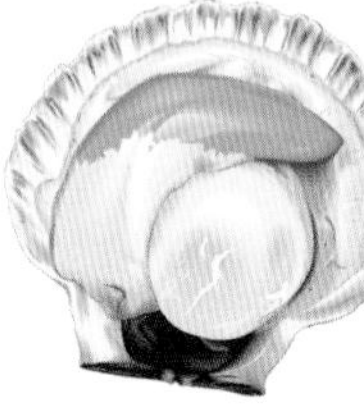

soft-shell clam
coquina*F*
mye*F*
Klaffmuschel*F*
vongola*F* molle

snail
caracol [M] terrestre
escargot [M]
Schnecke [F]
chiocciola [F]

limpet
lapa [F]
patelle [F]
Napfschnecke [F]
patella [F]

common periwinkle
bígaro [M]
bigorneau [M]
Strandschnecke [F]
littorina [F]

clam
almeja [F]
praire [F]
Venusmuschel [F]
vongola [F]

cockle
berberecho [M]
coque [F]
Herzmuschel [F]
cardio [M]

blue mussel
mejillón [M]
moule [F]
Miesmuschel [F]
mitilo [M]

whelk
buccino [M]
buccin [M]
Wellhornschnecke [F]
buccino [M]

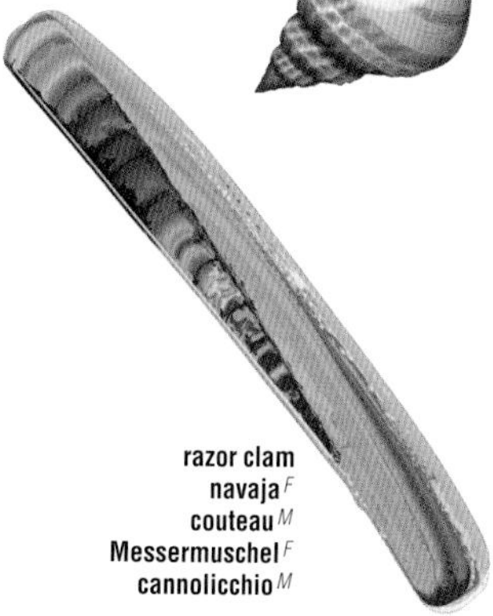

razor clam
navaja [F]
couteau [M]
Messermuschel [F]
cannolicchio [M]

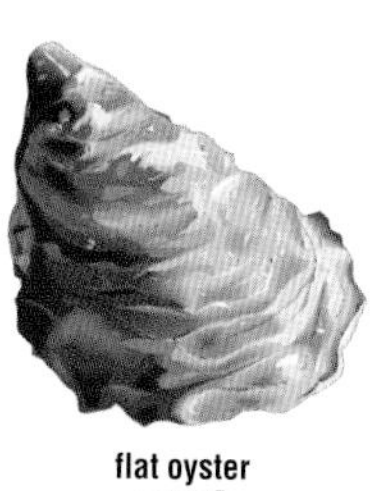

flat oyster
ostra [F]
huître [F] plate
Auster [F]
ostrica [F]

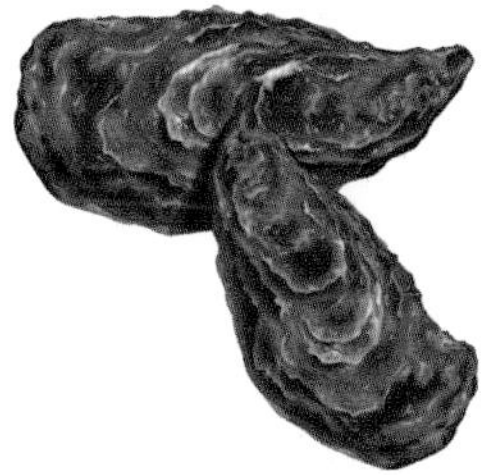

cupped Pacific oyster
ostra [F]
huître [F] creuse du Pacifique [M]
Auster [F]
ostrica [F]

crustaceans

crustáceos M | crustacés M | Krebstiere N | crostacei M

lobster
bogavante M
homard M
Hummer M
astice M

crayfish
cangrejo M de río M
écrevisse F
Flusskrebs M
gambero M di acqua F dolce

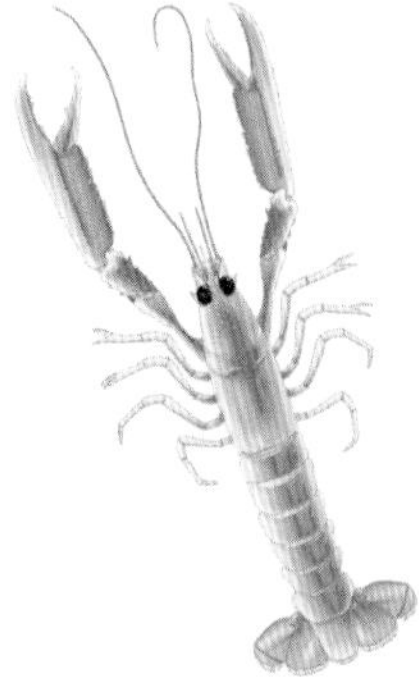

scampi
cigala F
langoustine F
Langustine F
scampo M

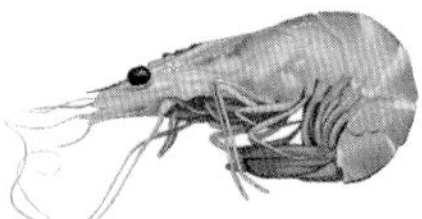

shrimp
gamba F
crevette F
Garnele F
gamberetto M

crab
cangrejo M de mar M
crabe M
Krabbe F
granchio M

spiny lobster
langosta F marina
langouste F
Languste F
aragosta F

cartilaginous fishes

peces[M] cartilaginosos | poissons[M] cartilagineux | Knorpelfische[M] | pesci[M] cartilaginei

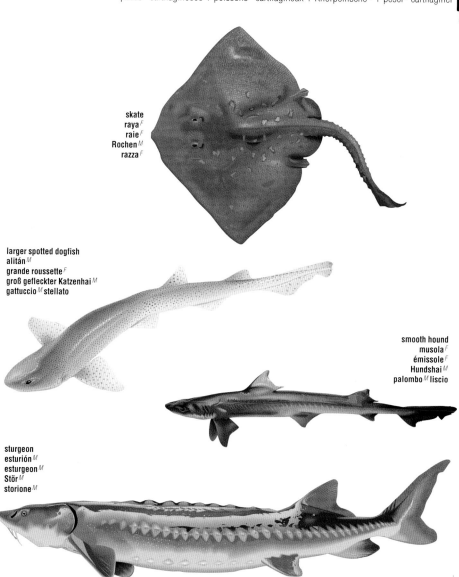

skate
raya[F]
raie[F]
Rochen[M]
razza[F]

larger spotted dogfish
alitán[M]
grande roussette[F]
groß gefleckter Katzenhai[M]
gattuccio[M] **stellato**

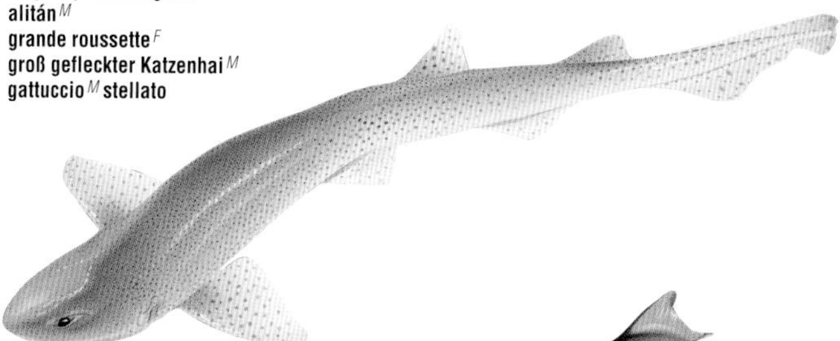

smooth hound
musola[F]
émissole[F]
Hundshai[M]
palombo[M] **liscio**

sturgeon
esturión[M]
esturgeon[M]
Stör[M]
storione[M]

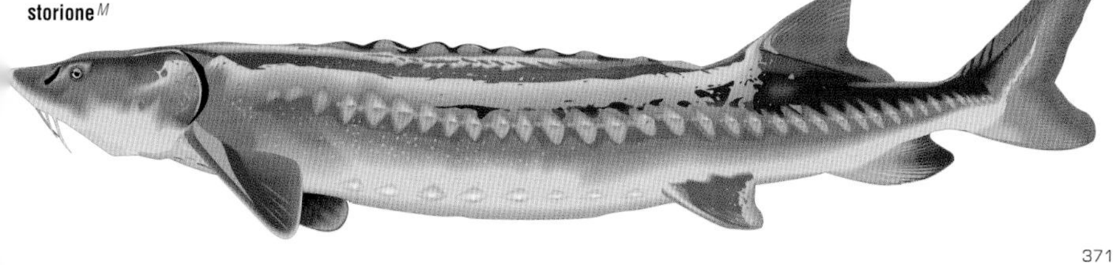

bony fishes

peces^M óseos | poissons^M osseux | Knochenfische^M | pesci^M ossei

sardine
sardina^F
sardine^F
Sardine^F
sardina^F

anchovy
boquerón^M
anchois^M
Sardelle^F
acciuga^F

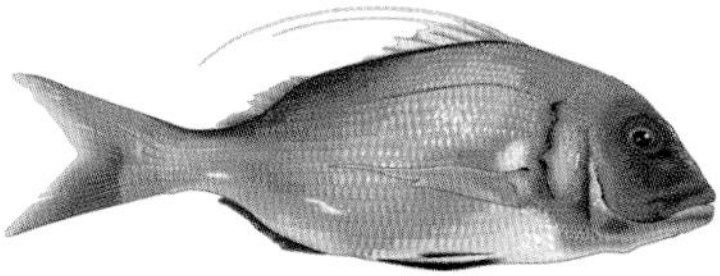

sea bream
dorada^F
dorade^F
Goldbrasse^F
orata^F

herring
arenque^M
hareng^M
Hering^M
aringa^F

goatfish
salmonete^M
rouget^M barbet^M
rote Meerbarbe^F
triglia^F

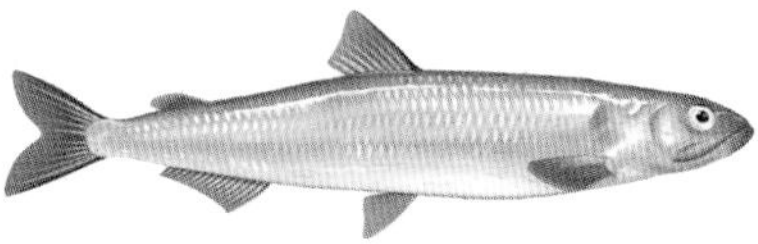

smelt
eperlano^M
éperlan^M
Stint^M
sperlano^M

swordfish
pez^M espada
espadon^M
Schwertfisch^M
pesce^M spada^F

eel
anguila[F]
anguille[F]
Aal[M]
anguilla[F]

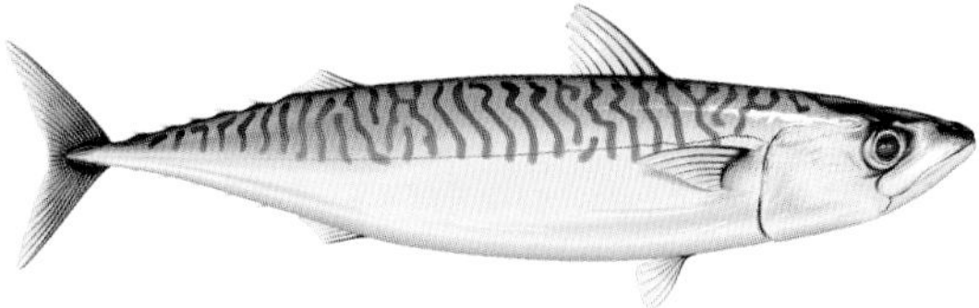

mackerel
caballa[F]
maquereau[M]
Makrele[F]
sgombro[M]

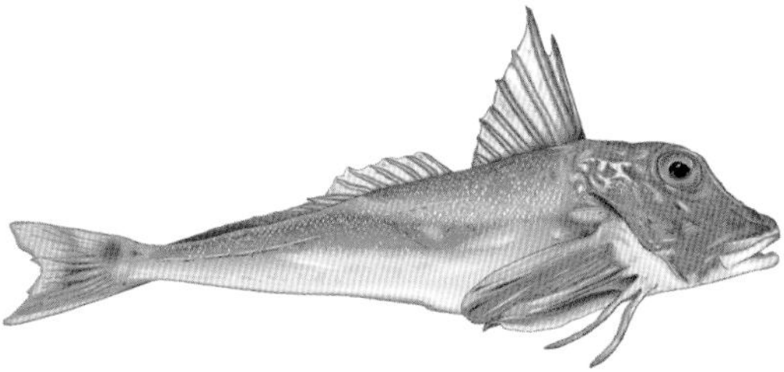

gurnard
rubio[M]
grondin[M]
Knurrhahn[M]
pesce[M] cappone[M]

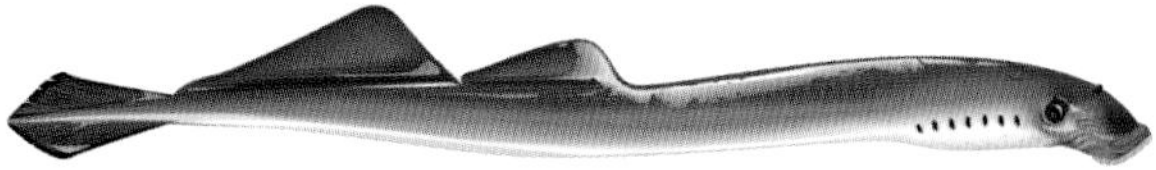

lamprey
lamprea[F]
lamproie[F]
Meerneunauge[N]
lampreda[F]

bony fishes

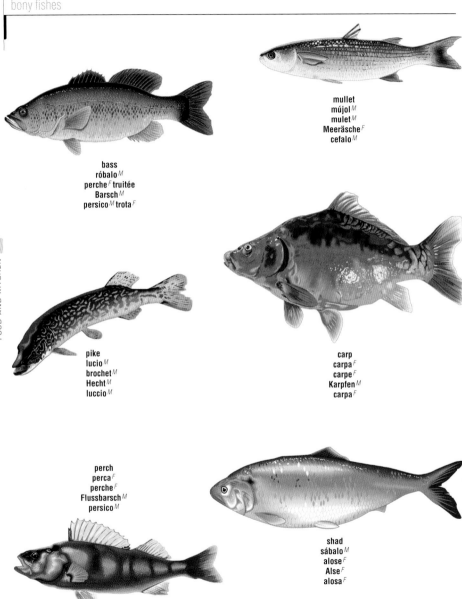

mullet
mújol [M]
mulet [M]
Meeräsche [F]
cefalo [M]

bass
róbalo [M]
perche [F] truitée
Barsch [M]
persico [M] trota [F]

carp
carpa [F]
carpe [F]
Karpfen [M]
carpa [F]

pike
lucio [M]
brochet [M]
Hecht [M]
luccio [M]

shad
sábalo [M]
alose [F]
Alse [F]
alosa [F]

perch
perca [F]
perche [F]
Flussbarsch [M]
persico [M]

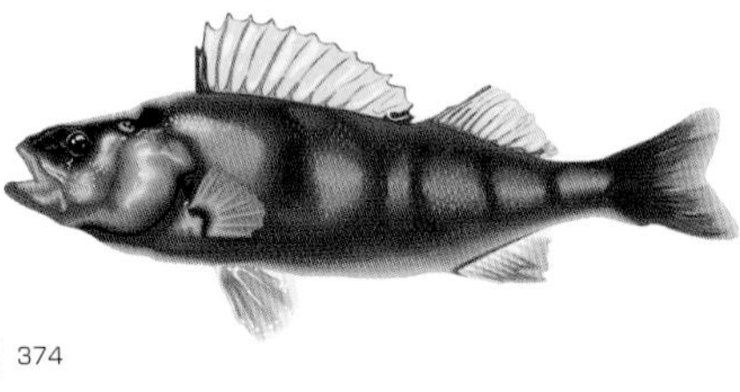

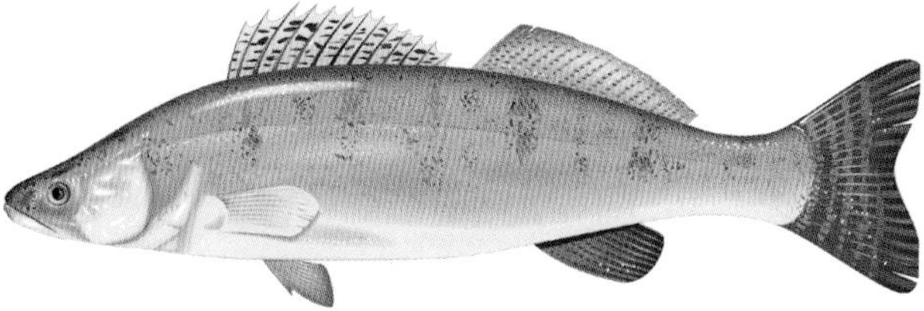

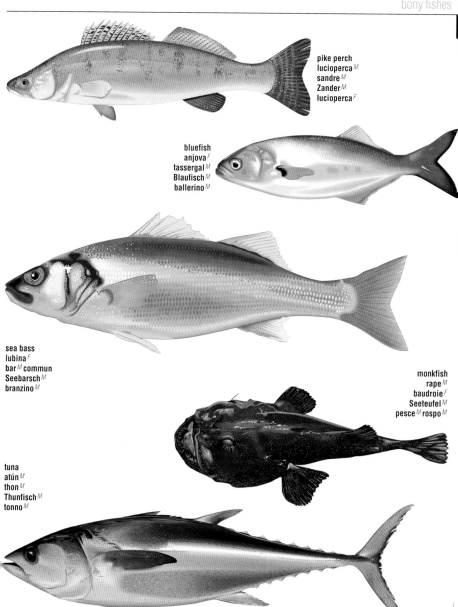

pike perch
lucioperca[M]
sandre[M]
Zander[M]
lucioperca[F]

bluefish
anjova[F]
tassergal[M]
Blaufisch[M]
ballerino[M]

sea bass
lubina[F]
bar[M] commun
Seebarsch[M]
branzino[M]

monkfish
rape[M]
baudroie[F]
Seeteufel[M]
pesce[M] rospo[M]

tuna
atún[M]
thon[M]
Thunfisch[M]
tonno[M]

bony fishes

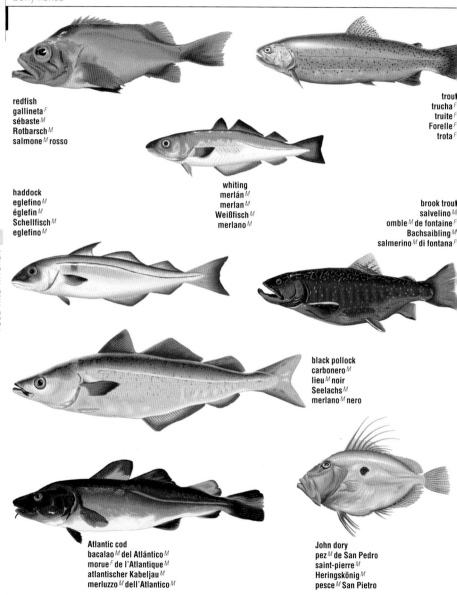

redfish
gallineta [F]
sébaste [M]
Rotbarsch [M]
salmone [M] rosso

trout
trucha [F]
truite [F]
Forelle [F]
trota [F]

whiting
merlán [M]
merlan [M]
Weißfisch [M]
merlano [M]

haddock
eglefino [M]
églefin [M]
Schellfisch [M]
eglefino [M]

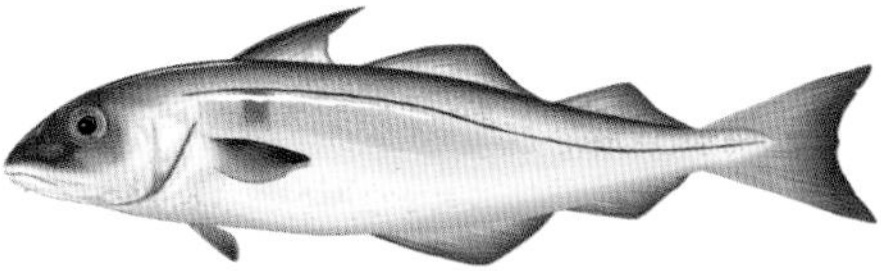

brook trout
salvelino [M]
omble [M] de fontaine [F]
Bachsaibling [M]
salmerino [M] di fontana [F]

black pollock
carbonero [M]
lieu [M] noir
Seelachs [M]
merlano [M] nero

Atlantic cod
bacalao [M] del Atlántico [M]
morue [F] de l'Atlantique [M]
atlantischer Kabeljau [M]
merluzzo [M] dell'Atlantico [M]

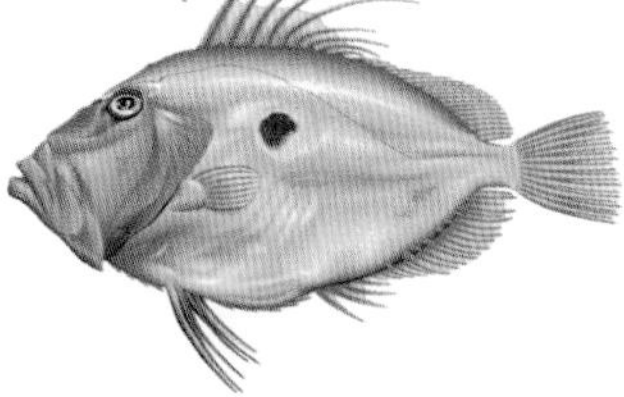

John dory
pez [M] de San Pedro
saint-pierre [M]
Heringskönig [M]
pesce [M] San Pietro

Pacific salmon
salmón[M] del Pacífico[M]
saumon[M] du Pacifique[M]
pazifischer Lachs[M]
salmone[M] del Pacifico[M]

Atlantic salmon
salmón[M] del Atlántico[M]
saumon[M] de l'Atlantique[M]
atlantischer Lachs[M]
salmone[M] dell'Atlantico[M]

turbot
rodaballo[M]
turbot[M]
Steinbutt[M]
rombo[M]

common plaice
platija[F]
plie[F] commune
Flunder[F]
passera[F] di mare[M]

halibut
halibut[M]
flétan[M]
Heilbutt[M]
ippoglosso[M]

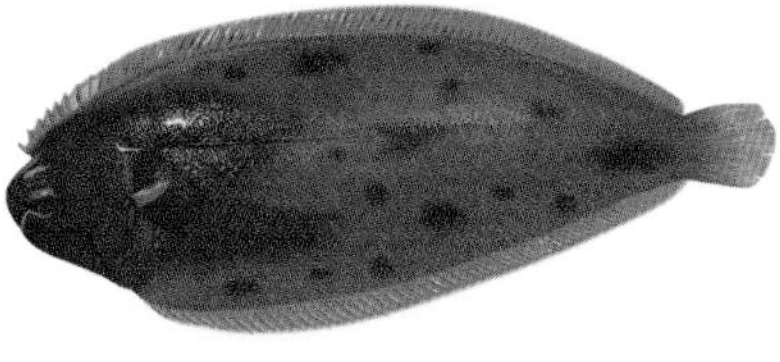

sole
lenguado[M]
sole[F]
Scholle[F]
sogliola[F]

kitchen

cocina^F | cuisine^F | Küche^F | cucina^F

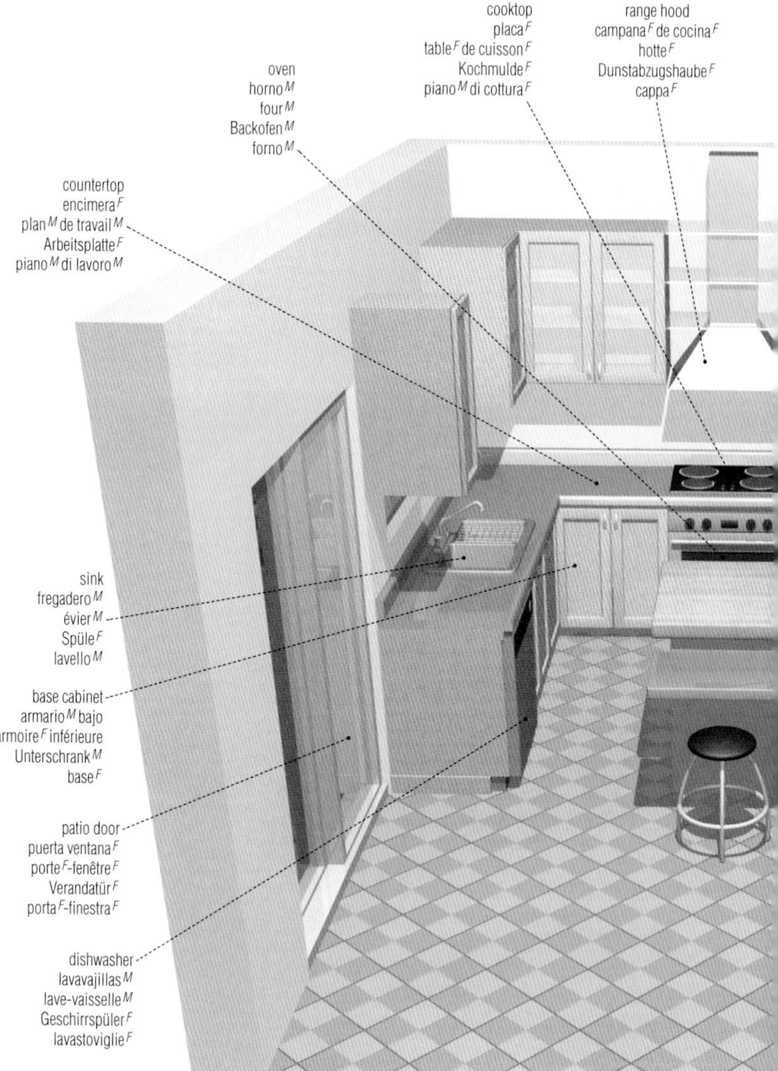
cooktop
placa F
table F de cuisson F
Kochmulde F
piano M di cottura F
range hood
campana F de cocina F
hotte F
Dunstabzugshaube F
cappa F
oven
horno M
four M
Backofen M
forno M
countertop
encimera F
plan M de travail M
Arbeitsplatte F
piano M di lavoro M
sink
fregadero M
évier M
Spüle F
lavello M
base cabinet
armario M bajo
armoire F inférieure
Unterschrank M
base F
patio door
puerta ventana F
porte F-fenêtre F
Verandatür F
porta F-finestra F
dishwasher
lavavajillas M
lave-vaisselle M
Geschirrspüler F
lavastoviglie F

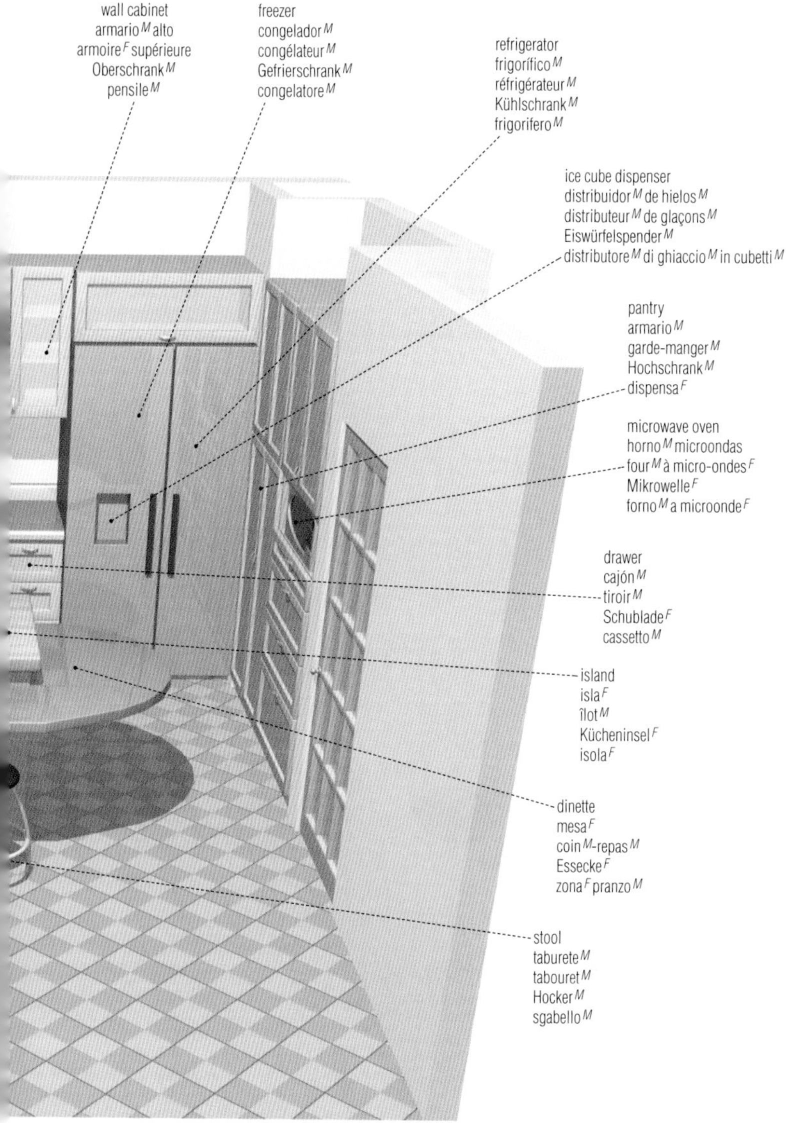
wall cabinet
armario[M] alto
armoire[F] supérieure
Oberschrank[M]
pensile[M]
freezer
congelador[M]
congélateur[M]
Gefrierschrank[M]
congelatore[M]
refrigerator
frigorífico[M]
réfrigérateur[M]
Kühlschrank[M]
frigorifero[M]
ice cube dispenser
distribuidor[M] de hielos[M]
distributeur[M] de glaçons[M]
Eiswürfelspender[M]
distributore[M] di ghiaccio[M] in cubetti[M]
pantry
armario[M]
garde-manger[M]
Hochschrank[M]
dispensa[F]
microwave oven
horno[M] microondas
four[M] à micro-ondes[F]
Mikrowelle[F]
forno[M] a microonde[F]
drawer
cajón[M]
tiroir[M]
Schublade[F]
cassetto[M]
island
isla[F]
îlot[M]
Kücheninsel[F]
isola[F]
dinette
mesa[F]
coin[M]-repas[M]
Essecke[F]
zona[F] pranzo[M]
stool
taburete[M]
tabouret[M]
Hocker[M]
sgabello[M]

glassware

cristalería^{F} | verres^{M} | Gläser^{N} | cristalleria^{F}

liqueur glass
copa^{F} para licores^{M}
verre^{M} à liqueur^{F}
Likörglas^{N}
bicchierino^{M} da liquore^{M}

port glass
copa^{F} para oporto^{M}
verre^{M} à porto^{M}
Portweinglas^{N}
bicchiere^{M} da porto^{M}

brandy snifter
copa^{F} para brandy^{M}
verre^{M} à cognac^{M}
Kognakschwenker^{M}
bicchiere^{M} da brandy^{M}

white wine glass
copa^{F} para vino^{M} blanco
verre^{M} à vin^{M} blanc
Weißweinglas^{N}
bicchiere^{M} da vino^{M} bianco

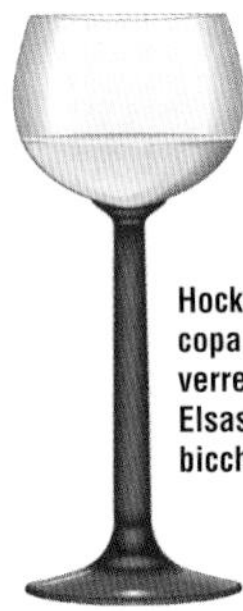

Hock glass
copa^{F} para vino^{M} de Alsacia
verre^{M} à vin^{M} d'Alsace^{F}
Elsassglas^{N}
bicchiere^{M} da vino^{M} alsaziano

sparkling wine glass
copa^{F} de champaña^{F}
coupe^{F} à mousseux^{M}
Sektschale^{F}
coppa^{F} da spumante^{M}

bordeaux glass
copa^{F} para vino^{M} de Burdeos
verre^{M} à bordeaux^{M}
Bordeauxglas^{N}
bicchiere^{M} da Bordeaux^{M}

burgundy glass
copa^{F} para vino^{M} de Borgoña
verre^{M} à bourgogne^{M}
Rotweinglas^{N}
bicchiere^{M} da Borgogna^{M}

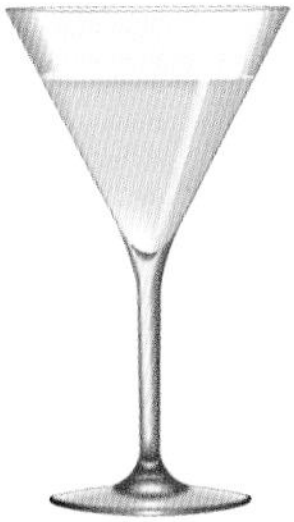

cocktail glass
copa [F] de cóctel [M]
verre [M] à cocktail [M]
Cocktailglas [N]
calice [M] da cocktail [M]

champagne flute
copa [F] de flauta [F]
flûte [F] à champagne [M]
Sektkelch [M]
flûte [M]

water goblet
copa [F] de agua [F]
verre [M] à eau [F]
Wasserglas [N]
bicchiere [M] da acqua [F]

highball glass
vaso [M] largo
verre [M] à gin [M]
Longdrinkglas [N]
bicchiere [M] da bibita [F]

old-fashioned glass
vaso [M] corto
verre [M] à whisky [M]
Whiskyglas [M]
tumbler [M]

beer mug
jarra [M] de cerveza [F]
chope [F] à bière [F]
Bierkrug [M]
boccale [M] da birra [F]

small decanter
decantador [M]
carafon [M]
kleine Karaffe [F]
caraffa [F]

decanter
garrafa [F]
carafe [F]
Karaffe [F]
bottiglia [F] da tavola [F]

dinnerware

vajilla^F y servicio^M de mesa^F | vaisselle^F | Geschirr^N | vasellame^M da tavola^F

demitasse
tacita^F de café^M
tasse^F à café^M
Mokkatasse^F
tazzina^F da caffè^M

coffee mug
jarra^F para café^M
chope^F à café^M
Becher^M
tazza^F alta da caffè^M

creamer
jarrita^F de leche^F
crémier^M
Milchkännchen^N
bricco^M del latte^M

cup
taza^F
tasse^F à thé^M
Tasse^F
tazza^F da tè^M

sugar bowl
azucarero^M
sucrier^M
Zuckerdose^F
zuccheriera^F

teapot
tetera^F
théière^F
Teekanne^F
teiera^F

bread and butter plate
platito [M] para el pan [M]
assiette [F] à dessert [M]
kleiner Teller [M]
piattino [M] per pane [M] e burro [M]

soup bowl
escudilla [F]
bol [M]
Suppenschale [F]
scodella [F]

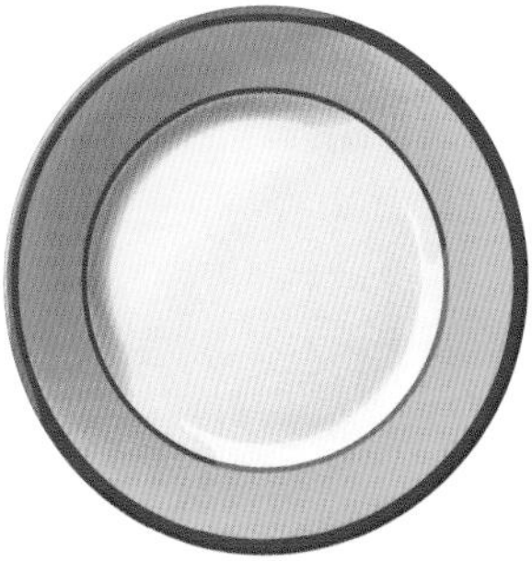

salad plate
plato [M] de postre [M]
assiette [F] à salade [F]
Salatteller [M]
piatto [M] frutta [F] / insalata [F]

rim soup bowl
plato [M] sopero
assiette [F] creuse
Suppenteller [M]
piatto [M] fondo

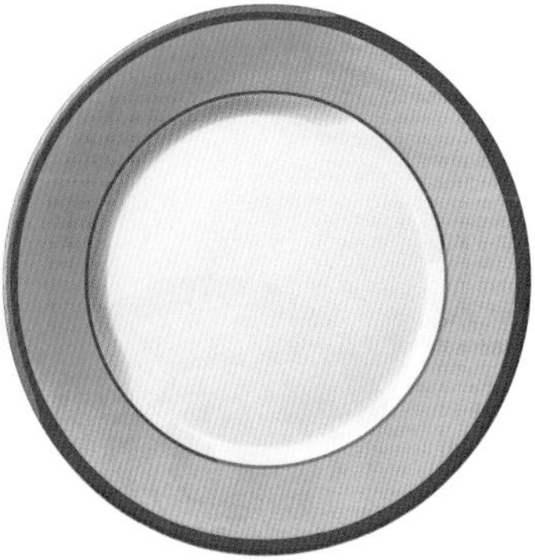

dinner plate
plato [M] llano
assiette [F] plate
flacher Teller [M]
piatto [M] piano

butter dish
mantequera [F]
beurrier [M]
Butterdose [F]
burriera [F]

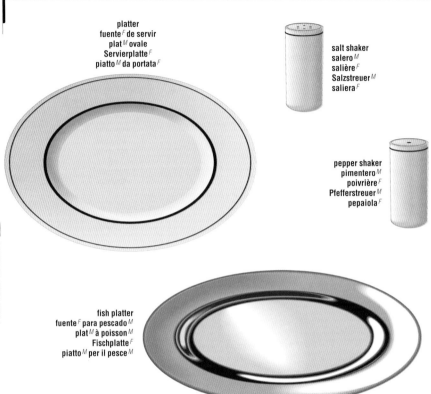

platter
fuente [F] de servir
plat [M] ovale
Servierplatte [F]
piatto [M] da portata [F]

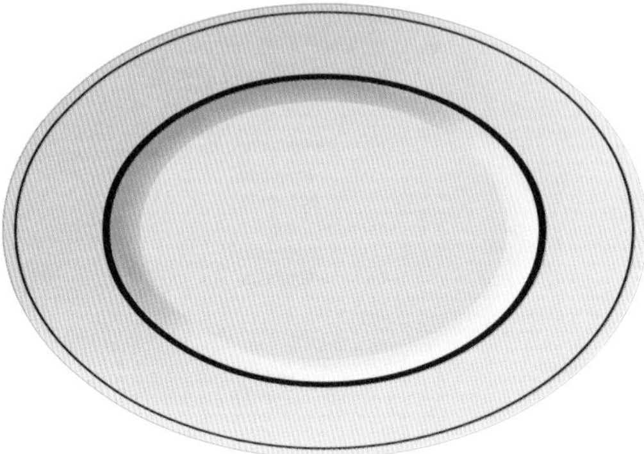

salt shaker
salero [M]
salière [F]
Salzstreuer [M]
saliera [F]

pepper shaker
pimentero [M]
poivrière [F]
Pfefferstreuer [M]
pepaiola [F]

fish platter
fuente [F] para pescado [M]
plat [M] à poisson [M]
Fischplatte [F]
piatto [M] per il pesce [M]

vegetable bowl
fuente [F] de verdura [F]
légumier [M]
Gemüseterrine [F]
legumiera [F]

hors d'oeuvre dish
bandeja [F] para los entremeses [M]
ravier [M]
Hors-d'Oeuvre-Schale [F]
antipastiera [F]

water pitcher
jarra F de agua F
pichet M
Wasserkrug M
caraffa F

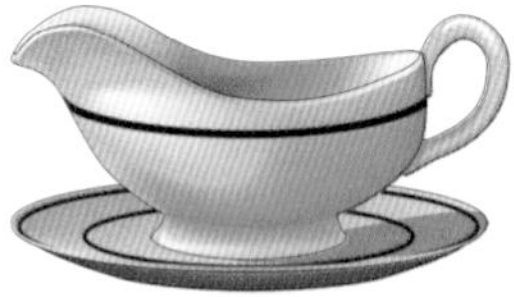

gravy boat
salsera F
saucière F
Sauciere F
salsiera F

soup tureen
sopera F
soupière F
Suppenterrine F
zuppiera F

ramekin
cuenco M de queso M blando
ramequin M
Auflaufförmchen N
formina F da forno M

salad dish
bol M para ensalada F
bol M à salade F
Salatschale F
coppetta F per l'insalata F

salad bowl
ensaladera F
saladier M
Salatschüssel F
insalatiera F

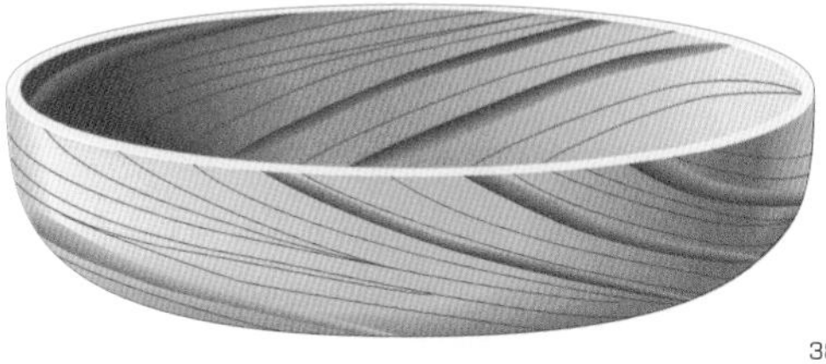

silverware

cubertería^F | couvert^M | Besteck^N | posateria^F

fork
tenedor^M
fourchette^F
Gabel^F
forchetta^F

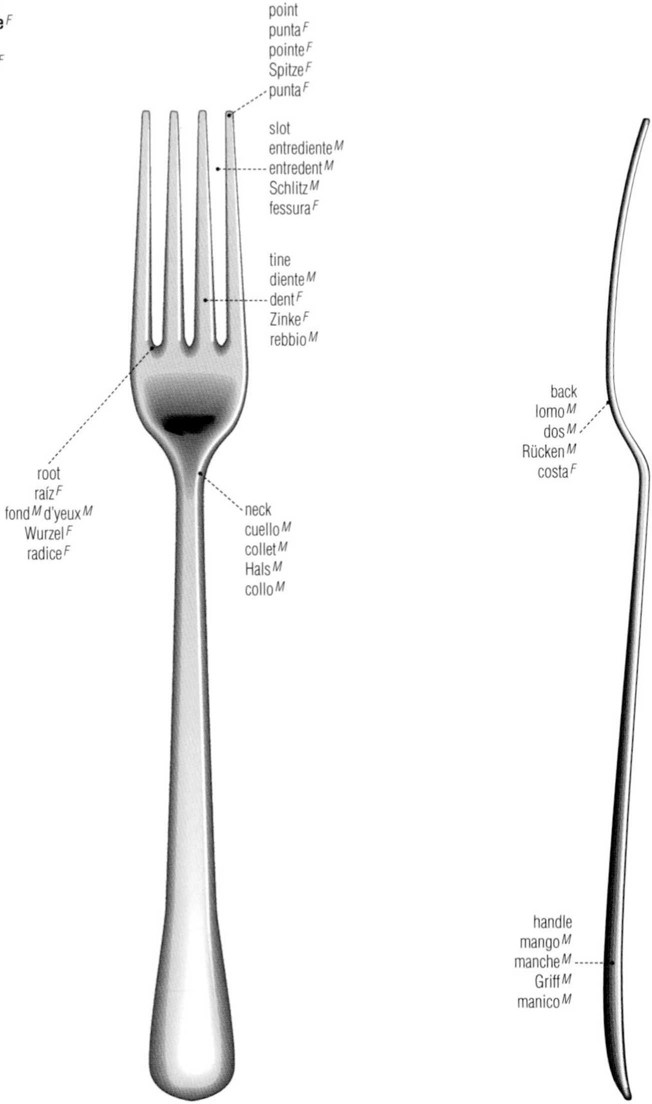
point
punta F
pointe F
Spitze F
punta F
slot
entrediente M
entredent M
Schlitz M
fessura F
tine
diente M
dent F
Zinke F
rebbio M
root
raíz F
fond M d'yeux M
Wurzel F
radice F
neck
cuello M
collet M
Hals M
collo M
back
lomo M
dos M
Rücken M
costa F
handle
mango M
manche M
Griff M
manico M

examples of forks
ejemplos[M] de tenedores[M]
exemples[M] de fourchettes[F]
Beispiele[N] für Gabeln[F]
esempi[M] di forchette[F]

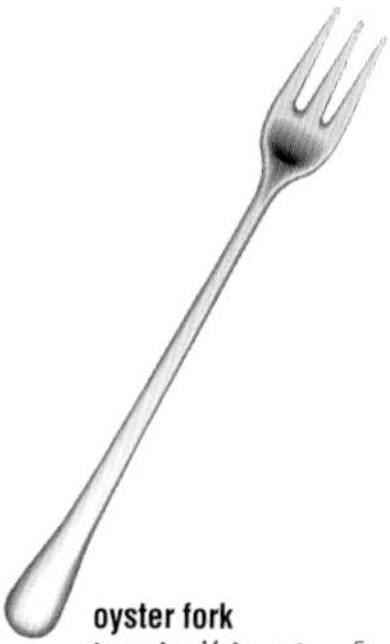

oyster fork
tenedor[M] de ostras[F]
fourchette[F] à huîtres[F]
Austerngabel[F]
forchetta[F] da ostriche[F]

dessert fork
tenedor[M] de postre[M]
fourchette[F] à dessert[M]
Dessertgabel[F]
forchetta[F] da dessert[M]

dinner fork
tenedor[M] de mesa[F]
fourchette[F] de table[F]
Menügabel[F]
forchetta[F] da tavola[F]

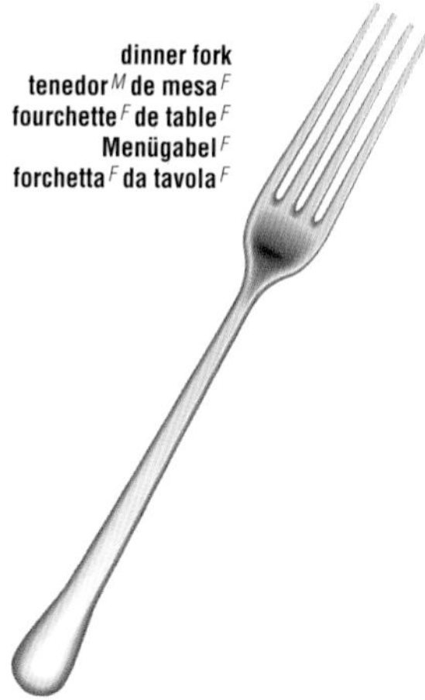

salad fork
tenedor[M] de ensalada[F]
fourchette[F] à salade[F]
Salatgabel[F]
forchetta[F] da insalata[F]

fish fork
tenedor[M] de pescado[M]
fourchette[F] à poisson[M]
Fischgabel[F]
forchetta[F] da pesce[M]

fondue fork
tenedor[M] de fondue[F]
fourchette[F] à fondue[F]
Fonduegabel[F]
forchetta[F] da fonduta[F]

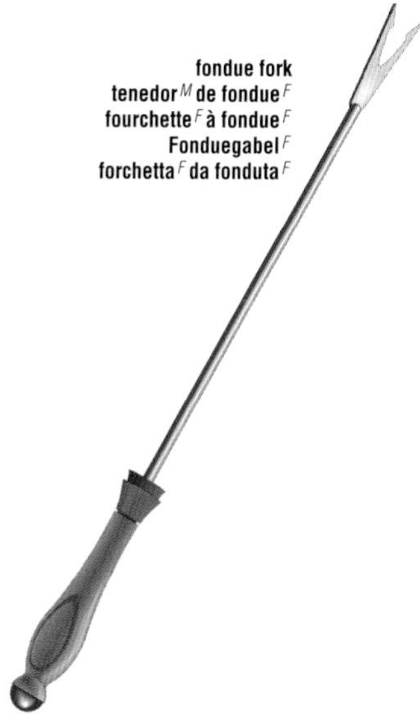

silverware

spoon
cuchara *F*
cuiller *F*
Löffel *M*
cucchiaio *M*

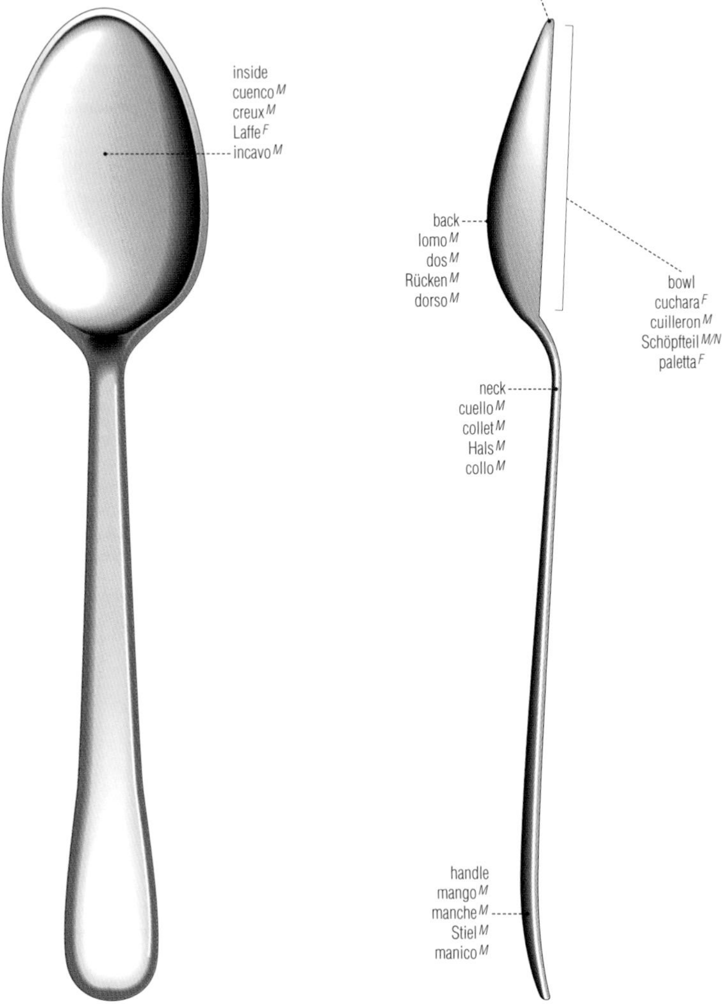
tip
punta F
bec M
Spitze F
punta F
inside
cuenco M
creux M
Laffe F
incavo M
back
lomo M
dos M
Rücken M
dorso M
bowl
cuchara F
cuilleron M
Schöpfteil M/N
paletta F
neck
cuello M
collet M
Hals M
collo M
handle
mango M
manche M
Stiel M
manico M

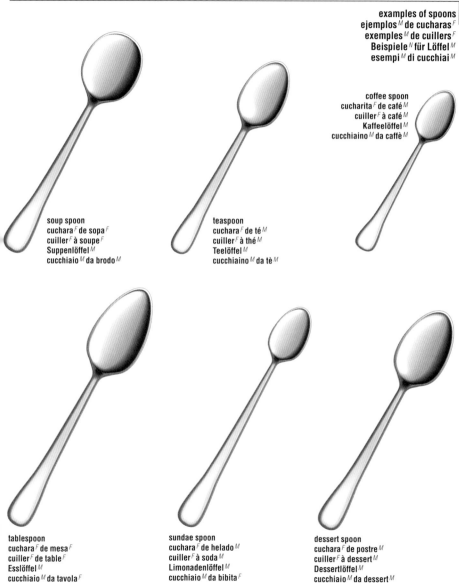

examples of spoons
ejemplos [M] de cucharas [F]
exemples [M] de cuillers [F]
Beispiele [N] für Löffel [M]
esempi [M] di cucchiai [M]

soup spoon
cuchara [F] de sopa [F]
cuiller [F] à soupe [F]
Suppenlöffel [M]
cucchiaio [M] da brodo [M]

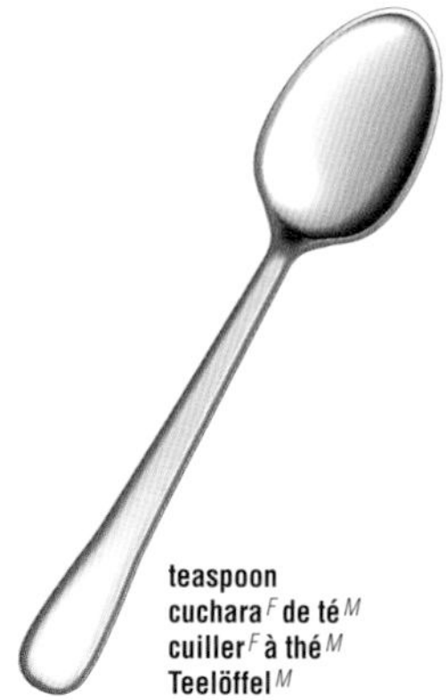

teaspoon
cuchara [F] de té [M]
cuiller [F] à thé [M]
Teelöffel [M]
cucchiaino [M] da tè [M]

coffee spoon
cucharita [F] de café [M]
cuiller [F] à café [M]
Kaffeelöffel [M]
cucchiaino [M] da caffè [M]

tablespoon
cuchara [F] de mesa [F]
cuiller [F] de table [F]
Esslöffel [M]
cucchiaio [M] da tavola [F]

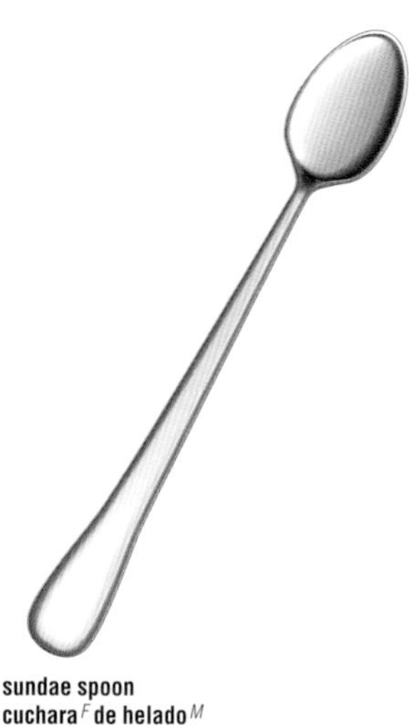

sundae spoon
cuchara [F] de helado [M]
cuiller [F] à soda [M]
Limonadenlöffel [M]
cucchiaio [M] da bibita [F]

dessert spoon
cuchara [F] de postre [M]
cuiller [F] à dessert [M]
Dessertlöffel [M]
cucchiaio [M] da dessert [M]

silverware

knife
cuchillo *M*
couteau *M*
Messer *N*
coltello *M*

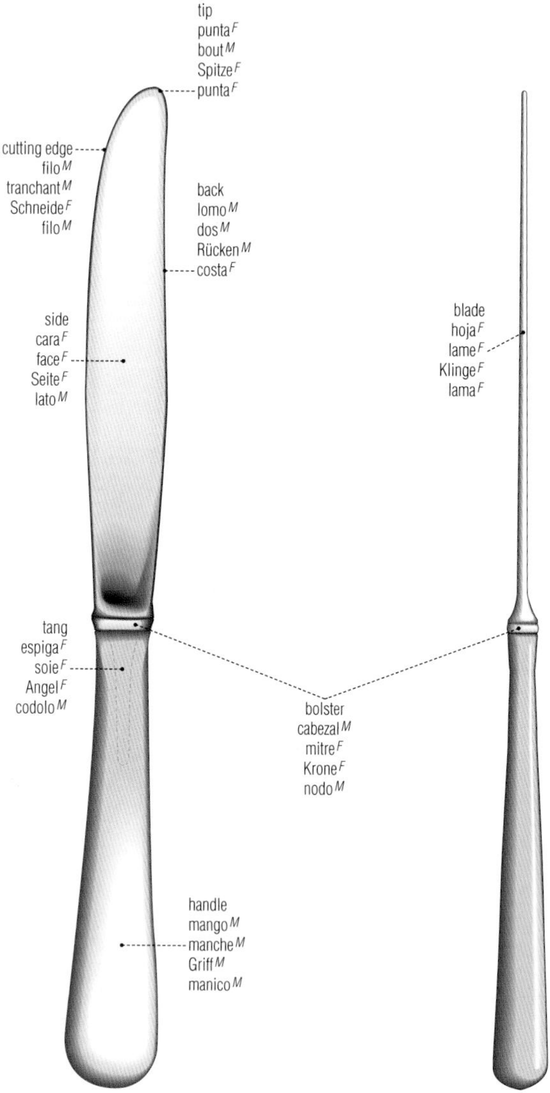
tip
punta F
bout M
Spitze F
punta F
cutting edge
filo M
tranchant M
Schneide F
filo M
back
lomo M
dos M
Rücken M
costa F
side
cara F
face F
Seite F
lato M
blade
hoja F
lame F
Klinge F
lama F
tang
espiga F
soie F
Angel F
codolo M
bolster
cabezal M
mitre F
Krone F
nodo M
handle
mango M
manche M
Griff M
manico M

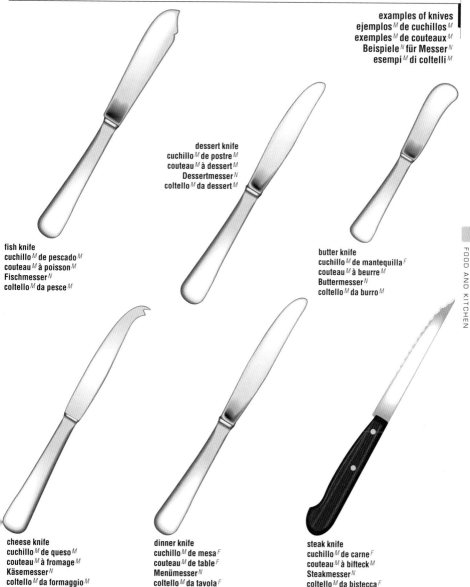

examples of knives
ejemplos[M] de cuchillos[M]
exemples[M] de couteaux[M]
Beispiele[N] für Messer[N]
esempi[M] di coltelli[M]

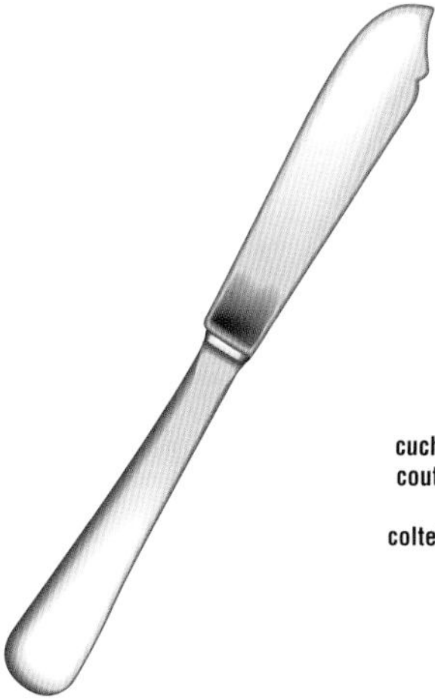

fish knife
cuchillo[M] de pescado[M]
couteau[M] à poisson[M]
Fischmesser[N]
coltello[M] da pesce[M]

dessert knife
cuchillo[M] de postre[M]
couteau[M] à dessert[M]
Dessertmesser[N]
coltello[M] da dessert[M]

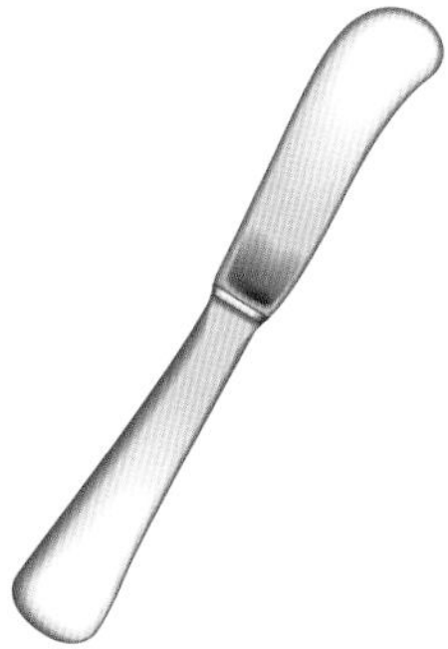

butter knife
cuchillo[M] de mantequilla[F]
couteau[M] à beurre[M]
Buttermesser[N]
coltello[M] da burro[M]

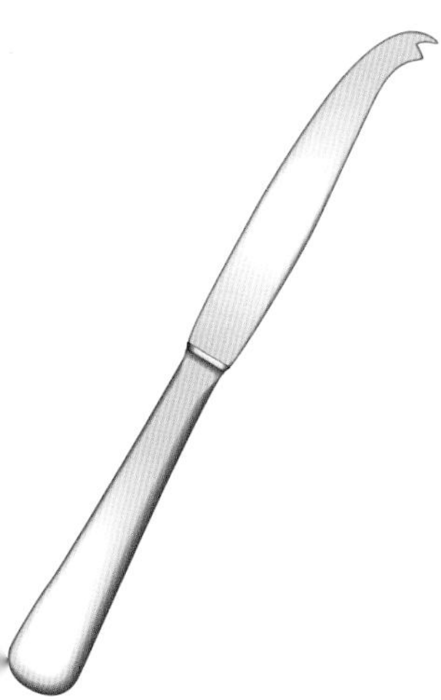

cheese knife
cuchillo[M] de queso[M]
couteau[M] à fromage[M]
Käsemesser[N]
coltello[M] da formaggio[M]

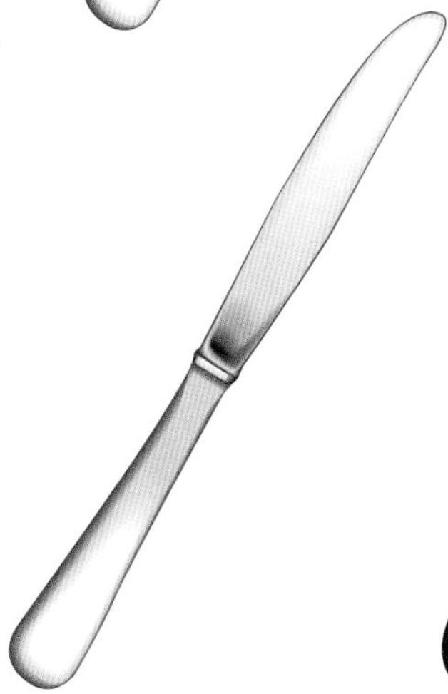

dinner knife
cuchillo[M] de mesa[F]
couteau[M] de table[F]
Menümesser[N]
coltello[M] da tavola[F]

steak knife
cuchillo[M] de carne[F]
couteau[M] à bifteck[M]
Steakmesser[N]
coltello[M] da bistecca[F]

kitchen utensils

utensilios^{M} de cocina^{F} | ustensiles^{M} de cuisine^{F} | Küchenutensilien^{N} | utensili^{M} da cucina^{F}

kitchen knife
cuchillo^{M} de cocina^{F}
couteau^{M} de cuisine^{F}
Küchenmesser^{N}
coltello^{M} da cucina^{F}

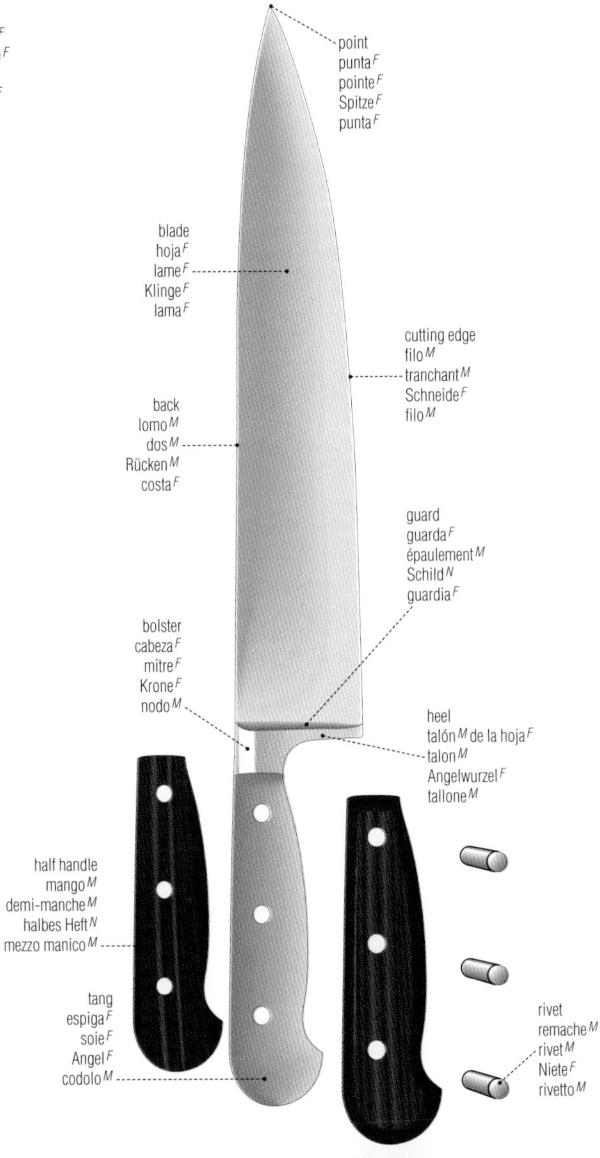
point
punta F
pointe F
Spitze F
punta F
blade
hoja F
lame F
Klinge F
lama F
cutting edge
filo M
tranchant M
Schneide F
filo M
back
lomo M
dos M
Rücken M
costa F
guard
guarda F
épaulement M
Schild N
guardia F
bolster
cabeza F
mitre F
Krone F
nodo M
heel
talón M de la hoja F
talon M
Angelwurzel F
tallone M
half handle
mango M
demi-manche M
halbes Heft N
mezzo manico M
tang
espiga F
soie F
Angel F
codolo M
rivet
remache M
rivet M
Niete F
rivetto M

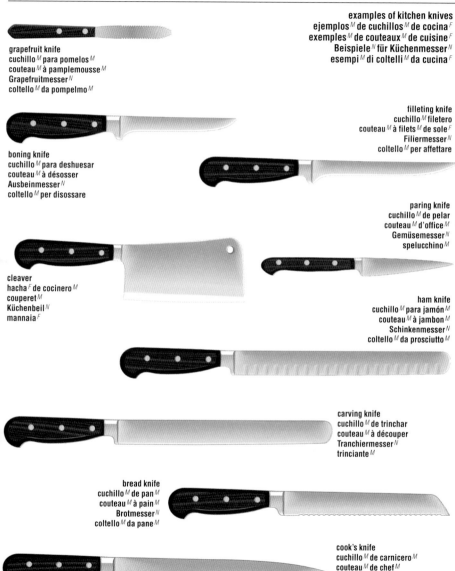

examples of kitchen knives
ejemplos[M] de cuchillos[M] de cocina[F]
exemples[M] de couteaux[M] de cuisine[F]
Beispiele[N] für Küchenmesser[N]
esempi[M] di coltelli[M] da cucina[F]

grapefruit knife
cuchillo[M] para pomelos[M]
couteau[M] à pamplemousse[M]
Grapefruitmesser[N]
coltello[M] da pompelmo[M]

boning knife
cuchillo[M] para deshuesar
couteau[M] à désosser
Ausbeinmesser[N]
coltello[M] per disossare

filleting knife
cuchillo[M] filetero
couteau[M] à filets[M] de sole[F]
Filiermesser[N]
coltello[M] per affettare

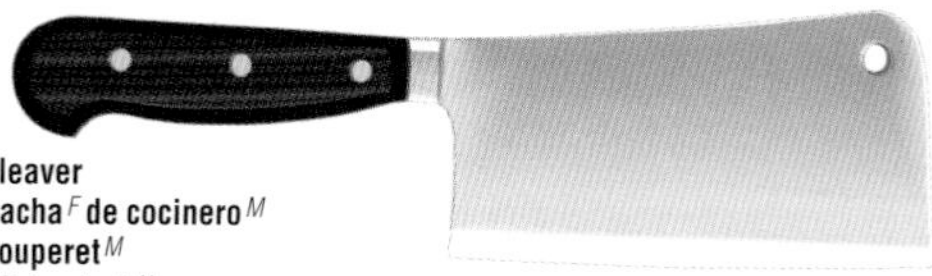

cleaver
hacha[F] de cocinero[M]
couperet[M]
Küchenbeil[N]
mannaia[F]

paring knife
cuchillo[M] de pelar
couteau[M] d'office[M]
Gemüsemesser[N]
spelucchino[M]

ham knife
cuchillo[M] para jamón[M]
couteau[M] à jambon[M]
Schinkenmesser[N]
coltello[M] da prosciutto[M]

carving knife
cuchillo[M] de trinchar
couteau[M] à découper
Tranchiermesser[N]
trinciante[M]

bread knife
cuchillo[M] de pan[M]
couteau[M] à pain[M]
Brotmesser[N]
coltello[M] da pane[M]

cook's knife
cuchillo[M] de carnicero[M]
couteau[M] de chef[M]
Kochmesser[N]
coltello[M] da cucina[F]

kitchen utensils

zester
rallador M
couteau M à zester
Zitronenschaber M
sbuccialimoni M

peeler
pelapatatas M
éplucheur M
Schäler M
sbucciatore M

carving fork
tenedor M de trinchar
fourchette F à découper
Tranchiergabel F
forchettone M

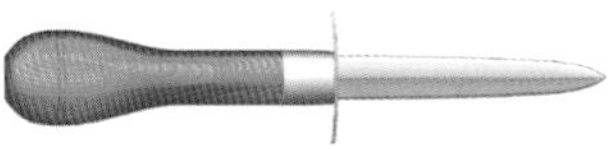

oyster knife
cuchillo M para ostras F
couteau M à huîtres F
Austernmesser N
coltello M da ostriche F

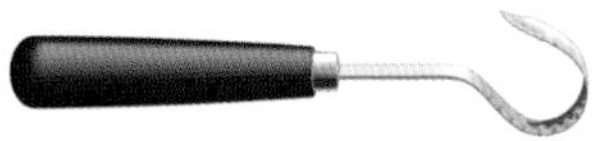

butter curler
rizador M de mantequilla F
coquilleur M à beurre M
Butterroller M
arricciaburro M

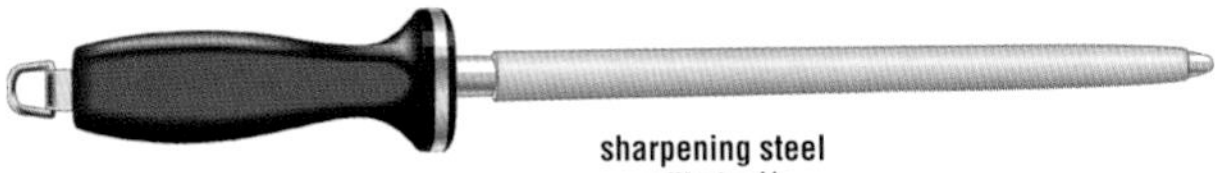

sharpening steel
afilador M
fusil M
Wetzstahl M
acciaiolo M

sharpening stone
piedra F de afilar
pierre F à affûter
Wetzstein M
pietra F affilacoltelli

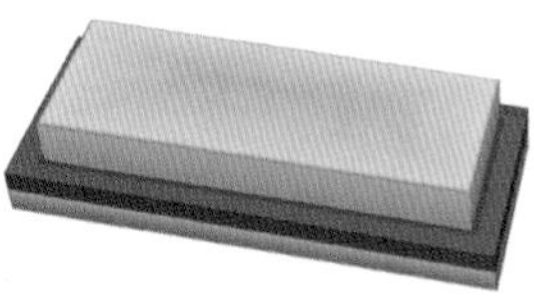

cutting board
tabla F de cortar
planche F à découper
Schneidbrett N
tagliere M

groove
ranura F
rainure F
Saftrinne F
scanalatura F

for opening
utensilios^M para abrir y descorchar
pour ouvrir
zum Öffnen^N
per aprire

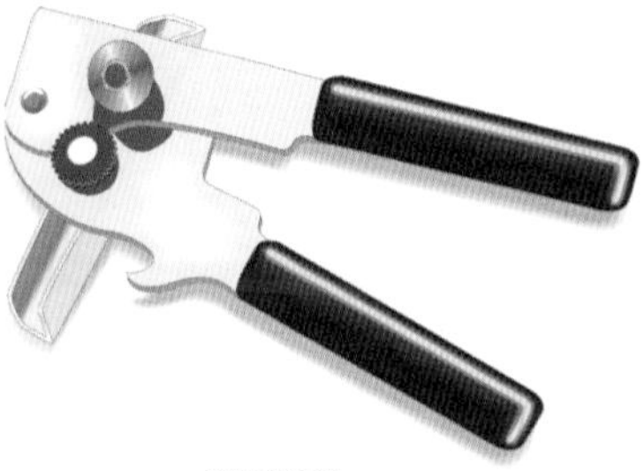

can opener
abrelatas M
ouvre-boîtes M
Büchsenöffner M
apriscatole M

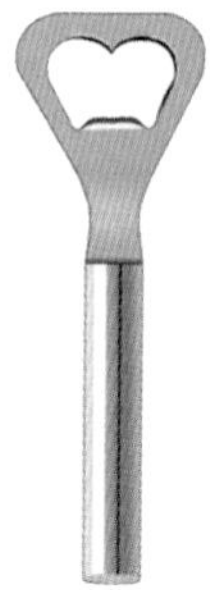

bottle opener
abrebotellas M
décapsuleur M
Flaschenöffner M
apribottiglie M

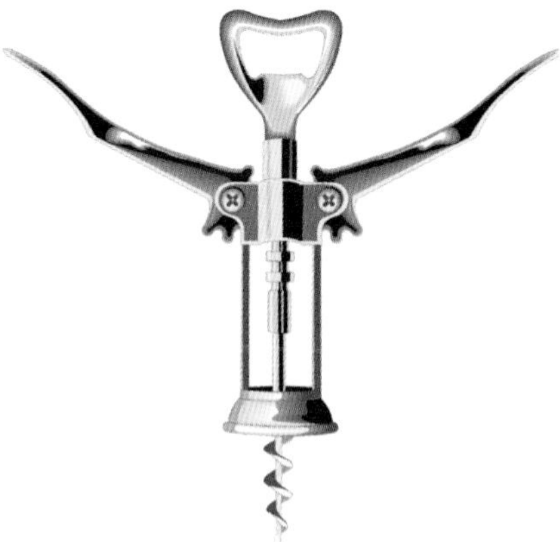

lever corkscrew
sacacorchos M con brazos M
tire-bouchon M à levier M
Hebel-Korkenzieher M
cavatappi M a leva F

wine waiter corkscrew
sacacorchos M
tire-bouchon M de sommelier M
Kellnerbesteck N
cavatappi M da cameriere M

kitchen utensils

for grinding and grating
para moler y rallar
pour broyer et râper
zum Zerkleinern[N] und Zerreiben[N]
per macinare e grattugiare

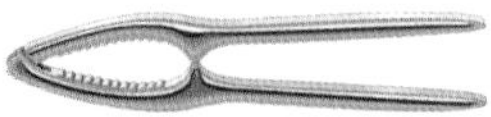

nutcracker
cascanueces[M]
casse-noix[M]
Nussknacker[M]
schiaccianoci[M]

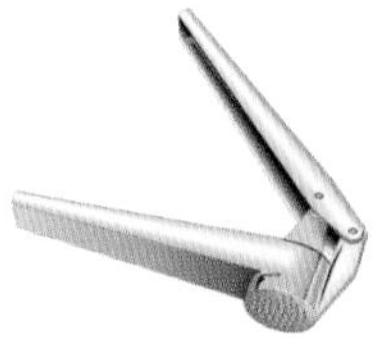

garlic press
triturador[M] **de ajos**[M]
presse-ail[M]
Knoblauchpresse[F]
spremiaglio[M]

nutmeg grater
rallador[M] **de nuez**[F] **moscada**
râpe[F] **à muscade**[F]
Muskatnussreibe[F]
grattugia[F] **per noce**[F] **moscata**

mortar
almirez[M]
mortier[M]
Mörser[M]
mortaio[M]

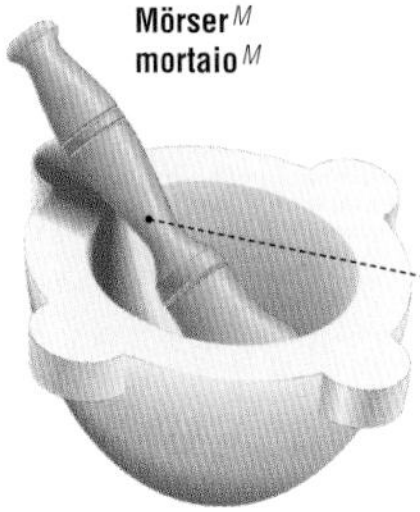

pestle
mano[F]
pilon[M]
Stößel[M]
pestello[M]

food mill
pasapurés[M]
moulin[M] **à légumes**[M]
Passiergerät[N]
passaverdure[M]

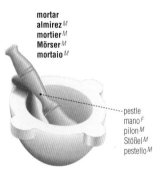

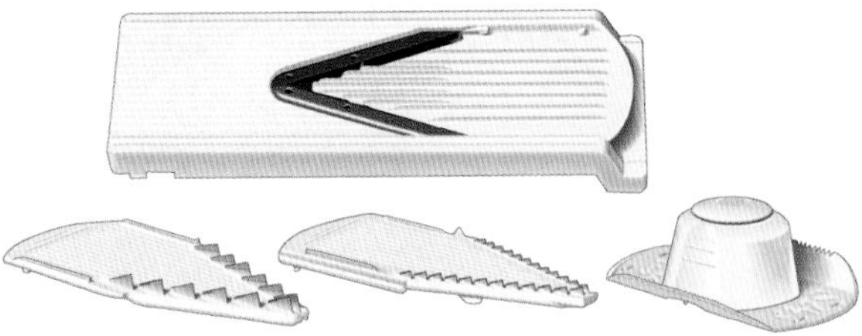

mandoline
mandolina[F]
mandoline[F]
Küchenreibe[F]
affettaverdure[M]

citrus juicer
exprimidor[M]
presse-agrumes[M]
Zitronenpresse[F]
spremiagrumi[M]

meat grinder
picadora F de carne F
hachoir M
Fleischwolf M
tritacarne M

rotary cheese grater
rallador M cilíndrico de queso M
râpe F à fromage M cylindrique
Käsereibe F
grattugiaformaggio M

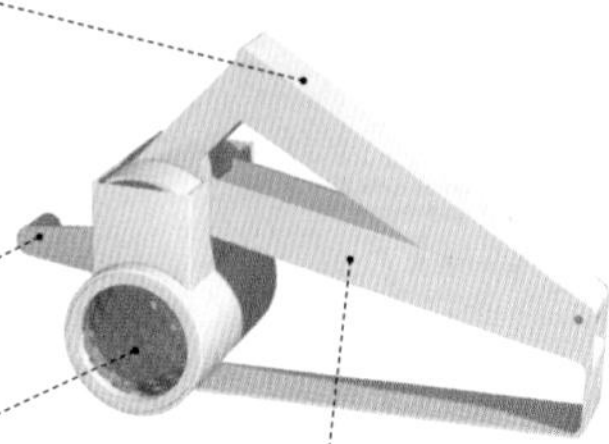
pusher
empujador M
poussoir M
Presshebel M
pigiatore M
crank
manivela F
manivelle F
Kurbel F
levetta F
drum
tambor M
tambour M
Trommel F
tamburo M
handle
mango M
poignée F
Griff M
impugnatura F

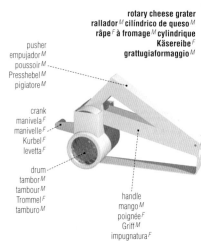

pasta maker
máquina F para hacer pasta F italiana
machine F à faire les pâtes F
Nudelmaschine F
macchina F per fare la pasta F

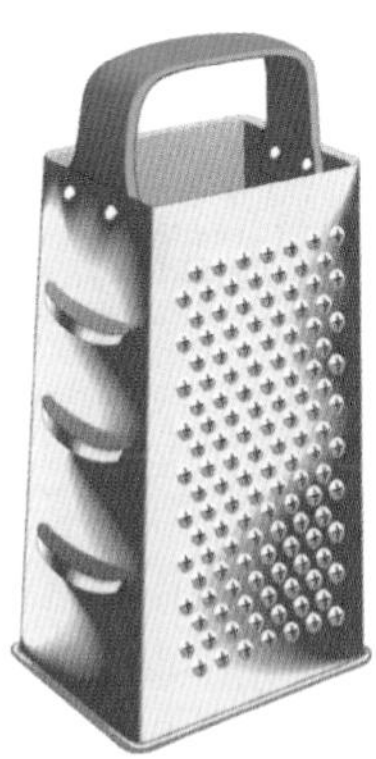

grater
rallador M
râpe F
Reibe F
grattugia F

kitchen utensils

for measuring
utensilios[M] para medir
pour mesurer
zum Messen[N]
per misurare

0
5
10
15
20
25
30
35
40
45
50
55

kitchen timer
minutero[M]
minuteur[M]
Küchenuhr[F]
contaminuti[M]

egg timer
reloj[M] de arena[F]
sablier[M]
Eieruhr[F]
clessidra[F] per uova[F] alla coque

measuring spoons
cucharas[F] dosificadoras
cuillers[F] doseuses
Messlöffel[M]
cucchiai[M] dosatori

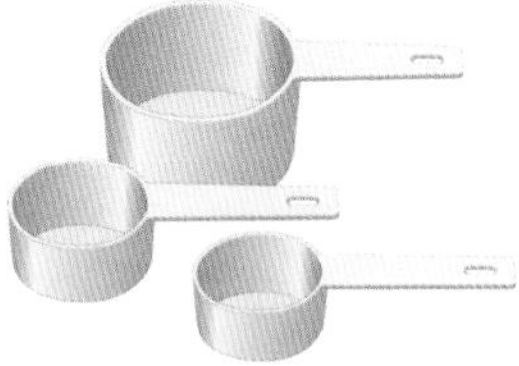

measuring cups
tazas[F] medidoras
mesures[F]
Messbecher[M]
misurini[M]

Tasse
Litre
1000
750
500
250

measuring cup
jarra[F] medidora
tasse[F] à mesurer
Maß[N]
tazza[F] graduata

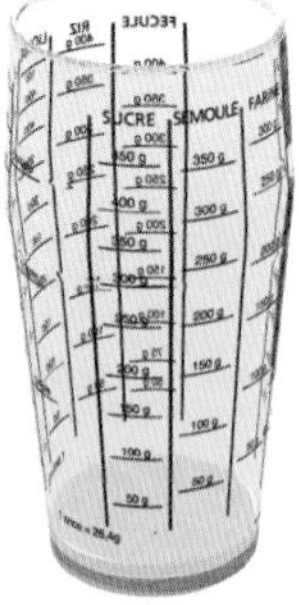

measuring beaker
vaso[M] medidor
verre[M] à mesurer
Messbecher[M]
recipiente[M] graduato

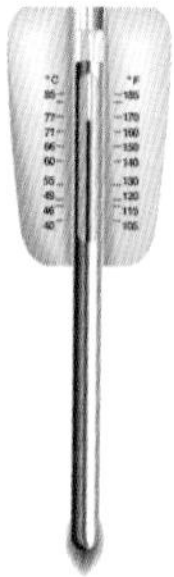

meat thermometer
termómetro[M] para carne[F]
thermomètre[M] à viande[F]
Fleischthermometer[N]
termometro[M] per carne[F]

candy thermometer
termómetro[M] de azúcar[M]
thermomètre[M] à sucre[M]
Einmachthermometer[N]
termometro[M] per zucchero[M]

200
250
300
350
400
450
500
100
150
200
250

oven thermometer
termómetro[M] de horno[M]
thermomètre[M] de four[M]
Backofenthermometer[N]
termometro[M] del forno[M]

ON OFF

instant-read thermometer
termómetro[M] de medida[F] instantánea
thermomètre[M] à mesure[F] instantanée
digitales Bratenthermometer[N]
termometro[M] a lettura[F] istantanea

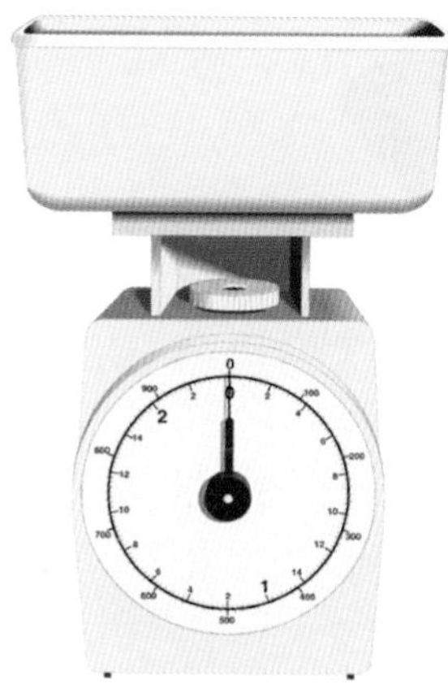

kitchen scale
báscula[F] de cocina[F]
balance[F] de cuisine[F]
Küchenwaage[F]
bilancia[F] da cucina[F]

kitchen utensils

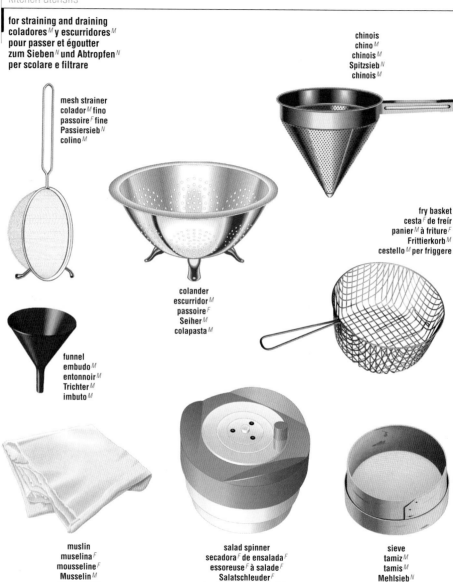

for straining and draining
coladores[M] y escurridores[M]
pour passer et égoutter
zum Sieben[N] und Abtropfen[N]
per scolare e filtrare

chinois
chino[M]
chinois[M]
Spitzsieb[N]
chinois[M]

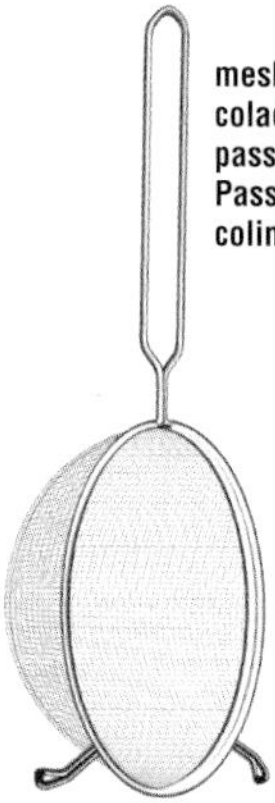

mesh strainer
colador[M] fino
passoire[F] fine
Passiersieb[N]
colino[M]

colander
escurridor[M]
passoire[F]
Seiher[M]
colapasta[M]

fry basket
cesta[F] de freír
panier[M] à friture[F]
Frittierkorb[M]
cestello[M] per friggere

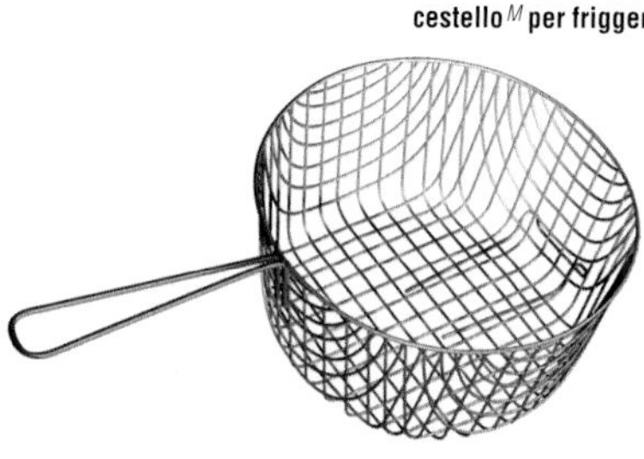

funnel
embudo[M]
entonnoir[M]
Trichter[M]
imbuto[M]

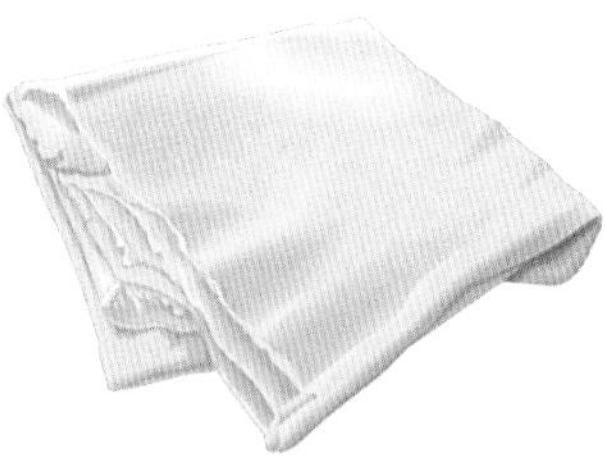

muslin
muselina[F]
mousseline[F]
Musselin[M]
mussolina[F]

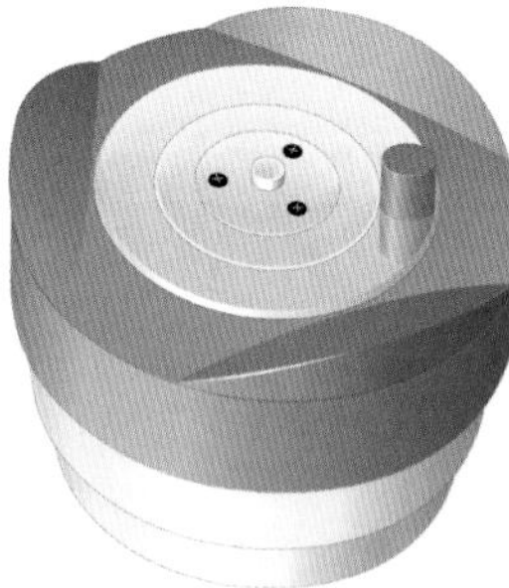

salad spinner
secadora[F] de ensalada[F]
essoreuse[F] à salade[F]
Salatschleuder[F]
centrifuga[F] scolainsalata

sieve
tamiz[M]
tamis[M]
Mehlsieb[N]
setaccio[M]

baking utensils
utensilios[M] para repostería[F]
pour la pâtisserie[F]
Backgeräte[N]
utensili[M] per dolci[M]

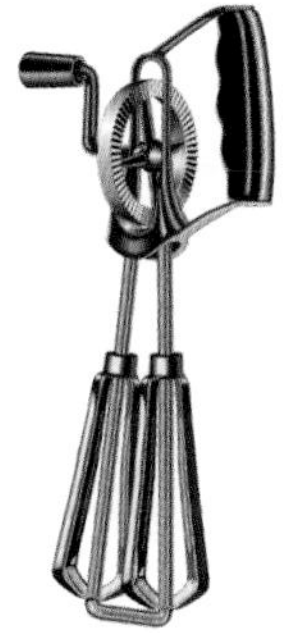

egg beater
batidor[M] mecánico
batteur[M] à œufs[M]
Rad-Schneeschläger[M]
frullino[M]

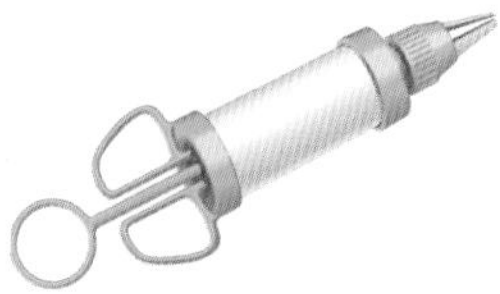

icing syringe
jeringa[F] de decoración[F]
piston[M] à décorer
Garnierspritze[F]
siringa[F] per decorazioni[F]

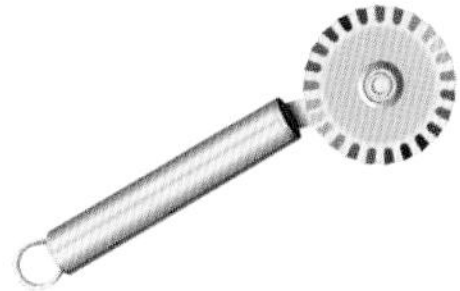

pastry cutting wheel
cortapastas[M]
roulette[F] de pâtissier[M]
Kuchenrad[N]
rotella[F] tagliapasta

cookie cutters
moldes[M] de pastas[F]
emporte-pièces[M]
Ausstechformen[F]
tagliabiscotti[M]

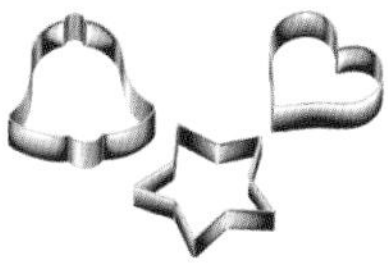

sifter
tamiz[M]
tamis[M] à farine[F]
Mehlsieb[N]
setaccio[M]

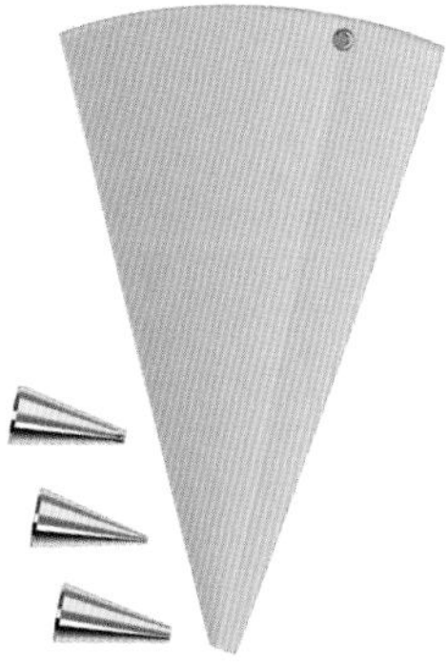

pastry bag and nozzles
manga[F] y boquillas[F]
poche[F] à douilles[F]
Spritzbeutel[M] mit Tüllen[F]
tasca[F] e bocchette[F]

whisk
batidor[M]
fouet[M]
Schneebesen[M]
frusta[F]

pastry brush
pincel[M] de repostería[F]
pinceau[M] à pâtisserie[F]
Kuchenpinsel[M]
pennello[M] per dolci[M]

baking sheet
bandeja [F] de pastelería [F]
plaque [F] à pâtisserie [F]
Backblech [N]
teglia [F] da forno [M]

dredger
espolvoreador [M]
saupoudreuse [F]
Streuer [M]
spolverino [M]

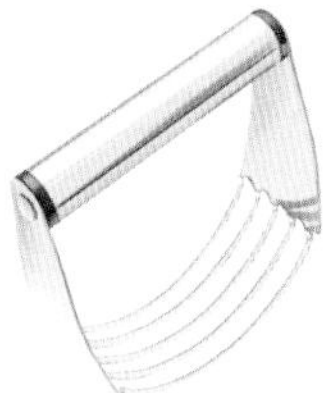

pastry blender
mezclador [M] de pastelería [F]
mélangeur [M] à pâtisserie [F]
Teigmischer [M]
miscelatore [M] per dolci [M]

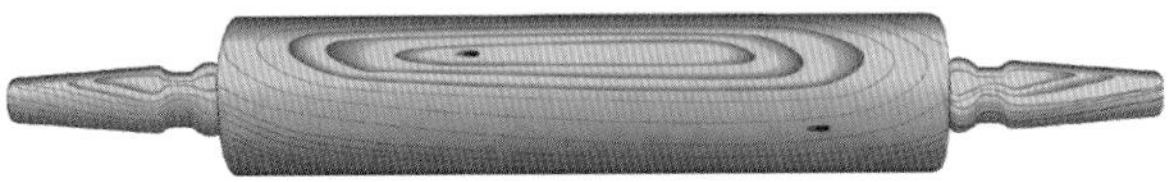

rolling pin
rodillo [M]
rouleau [M] à pâtisserie [F]
Nudelholz [N]
matterello [M]

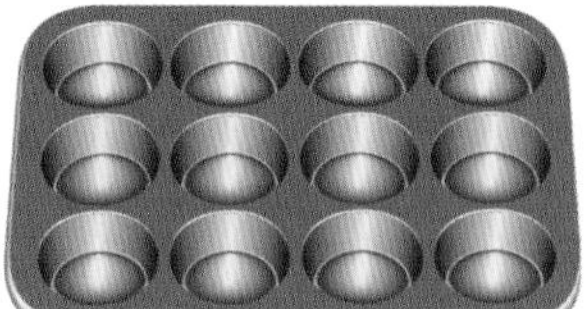

muffin pan
molde [M] para magdalenas [F]
moule [M] à muffins [M]
Muffinform [F]
stampini [M] per dolci [M]

mixing bowls
boles [M] para batir
bols [M] à mélanger
Rührschüsseln [F]
ciotole [F] per mescolare

cake pan
molde [M] para bizcocho [M]
moule [M] à gâteau [M]
Kuchenform [F]
tortiera [F]

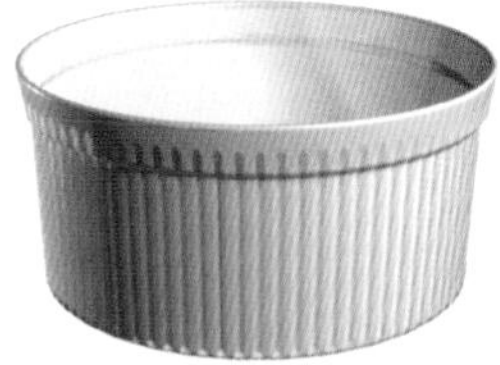

soufflé dish
molde [M] de soufflé [M]
moule [M] à soufflé [M]
Souffléform [F]
tegamino [M] per sufflè [M]

pie pan
molde [M] para tartas [F]
moule [M] à tarte [F]
flache Kuchenform [F]
teglia [F] per torta [F]

quiche plate
molde [M] acanalado
moule [M] à quiche [F]
Quicheform [F]
stampo [M] per crostata [F]

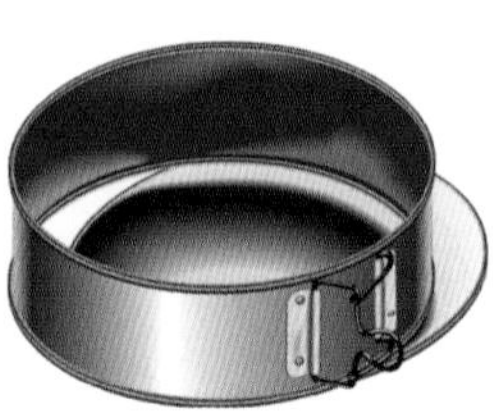

springform pan
molde [M] redondo con muelles [M]
moule [M] à fond [M] amovible
Springform [F]
teglia [F] con fondo [M] staccabile

charlotte mold
molde [M] de carlota [F]
moule [M] à charlotte [F]
Charlottenform [F]
stampo [M] per charlotte [F]

kitchen utensils

set of utensils
juego[M] de utensilios[M]
jeu[M] d'ustensiles[M]
Küchenset[N]
set[M] di utensili[M]

spatula
espátula[F]
spatule[F]
Palette[F]
spatola[F]

draining spoon
escurridera[F]
cuiller[F] à égoutter
Abseihlöffel[M]
cucchiaio[M] forato

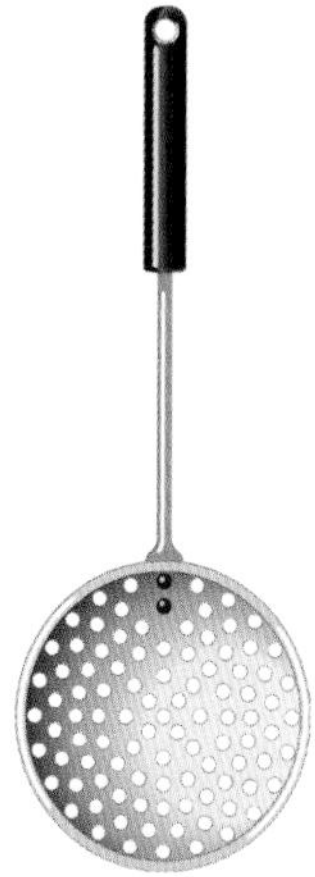

skimmer
espumadera[F]
écumoire[F]
Abseihkelle[F]
schiumaiola[F]

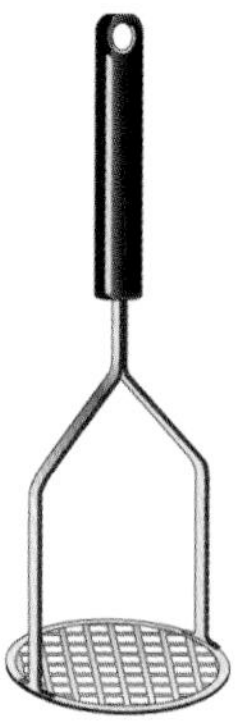

potato masher
pasapuré[M]
pilon[M]
Kartoffelstampfer[M]
schiacciapatate[M]

turner
paleta[F]
pelle[F]
Pfannenwender[M]
paletta[F]

ladle
cazo[M]
louche[F]
Schöpflöffel[M]
mestolo[M]

miscellaneous utensils
utensilios [M] diversos
ustensiles [M] divers
verschiedene Utensilien [N]
utensili [M] vari

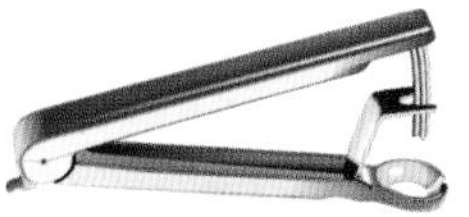

stoner
deshuesador [M]
dénoyauteur [M]
Entsteiner [M]
snocciolatore [M]

melon baller
vaciador [M]
cuiller [F] parisienne
Melonenlöffel [M]
scavamelone [M]

apple corer
descorazonador [M]
vide-pomme [M]
Kerngehäuseausstecher [M]
cavatorsoli [M]

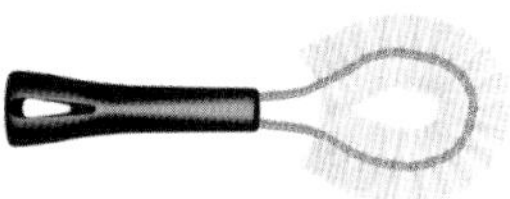

vegetable brush
cepillo [M] para verduras [F]
brosse [F] à légumes [M]
Gemüsebürste [F]
spazzola [F] per verdura [F]

trussing needle
aguja [F] de coser
aiguille [F] à brider
Dressiernadel [F]
ago [M] per legare

larding needle
aguja [F] picadora
aiguille [F] à piquer
Spicknadel [F]
lardatoio [M]

tasting spoon
cuchara [F] de degustación [F]
cuiller [F] à goûter
Probierlöffel [M]
cucchiaio [M] da assaggio [M]

ice cream scoop
cuchara [F] para servir helado [M]
cuiller [F] à glace [F]
Eisportionierer [M]
porzionatore [M] per gelato [M]

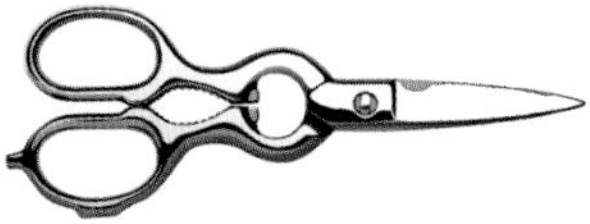

kitchen shears
tijeras[F] de cocina[F]
ciseaux[M] de cuisine[F]
Küchenschere[F]
forbici[F] da cucina[F]

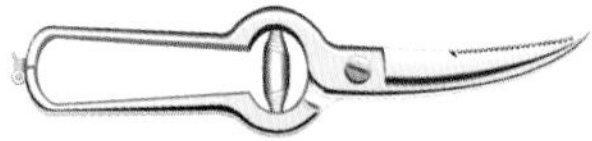

poultry shears
tijeras[F] para aves[F]
cisaille[F] à volaille[F]
Geflügelschere[F]
trinciapollo[M]

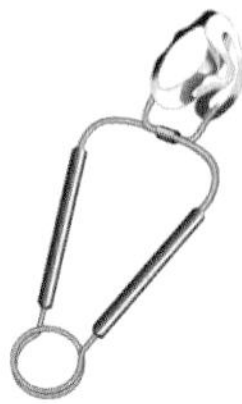

snail tongs
pinzas[F] para caracoles[M]
pince[F] à escargots[M]
Schneckenzange[F]
molle[F] per chiocciole[F]

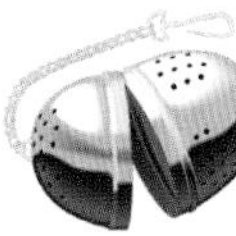

tea ball
esfera[F] de té[M]
boule[F] à thé[M]
Tee-Ei[N]
filtro[M] per il tè[M]

egg slicer
cortador[M] de huevos[M] duros
coupe-œuf[M]
Eierschneider[M]
affettauova[M]

baster
engrasador[M]
poire[F] à jus[M]
Fettgießer[M]
peretta[F] per ingrassare

tongs
pinzas[F]
pince[F]
Zange[F]
molle[F]

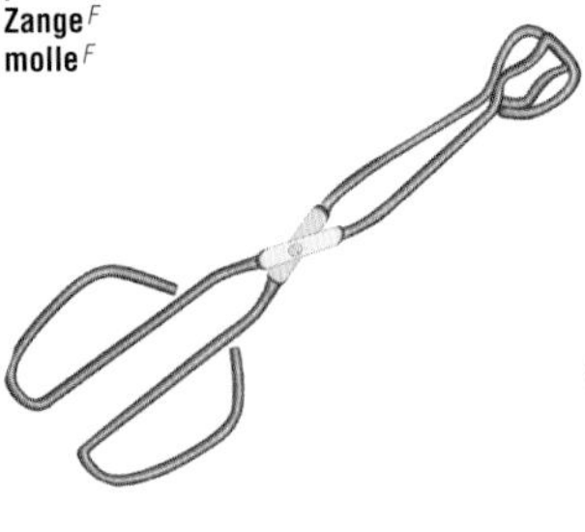

spaghetti tongs
pinzas[F] para espagueti[M]
pince[F] à spaghettis[M]
Spaghettizange[F]
molle[F] per spaghetti[M]

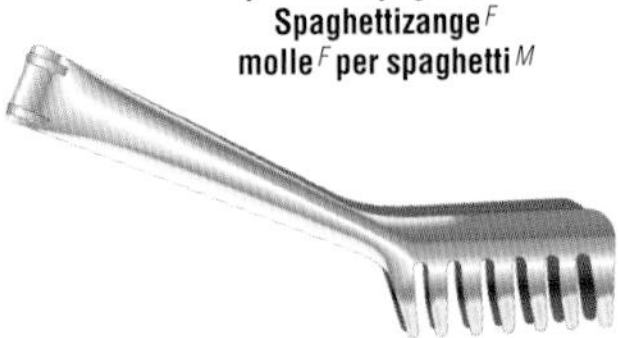

snail dish
plato[M] para caracoles[M]
plat[M] à escargots[M]
Schneckenpfännchen[N]
tegamino[M] per chiocciole[F]

cooking utensils

utensilios^{M} de cocina^{F} | batterie^{F} de cuisine^{F} | Kochgeräte^{N} | utensili^{M} per cucinare

fish poacher
besuguera^{F}
poissonnière^{F}
Fischkochtopf^{M}
pesciera^{F}

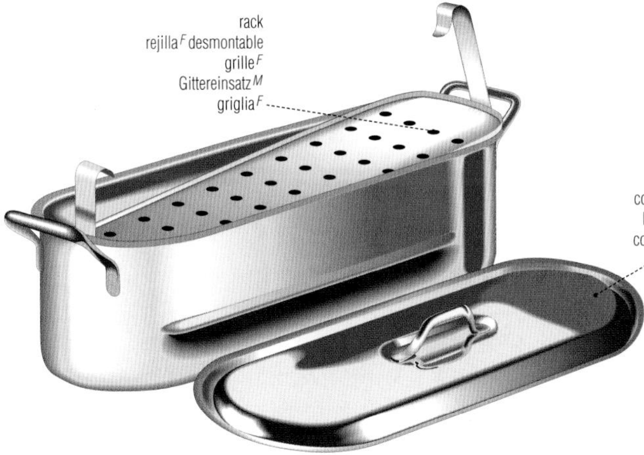
rack
rejilla^{F} desmontable
grille^{F}
Gittereinsatz^{M}
griglia^{F}
lid
tapa^{F}
couvercle^{M}
Deckel^{M}
coperchio^{M}

wok set
wok^{M}
wok^{M}
Wok-Set^{N}
servizio^{M} **da wok**^{M}

lid
tapa^{F}
couvercle^{M}
Deckel^{M}
coperchio^{M}
rack
rejilla^{F}
grille^{F}
Gittereinsatz^{M}
griglia^{F}
wok
wok^{M}
wok^{M}
Wok^{M}
wok^{M}
burner ring
quemador^{M}
collier^{M}
Aufsatz^{M}
bruciatore^{M} a corona^{F}

fondue set
servicio[M] para fondue[F]
service[M] à fondue[F]
Fondue-Set[N]
servizio[M] da fonduta[F]

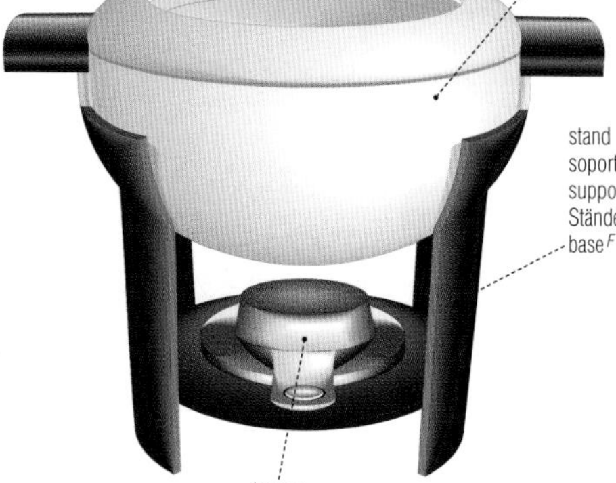
fondue pot
cacerola[F] para fondue[F]
caquelon[M]
Fonduetopf[M]
tegame[M] per fonduta[F]
stand
soporte[M]
support[M]
Ständer[M]
base[F]
burner
quemador[M]
réchaud[M]
Brenner[M]
fornellino[M]

tajine
tajina[F]
tajine[M]
Tajine[F]
tajina[F]

pressure cooker
olla[F] a presión[F]
autocuiseur[M]
Schnellkochtopf[M]
pentola[F] a pressione[F]

pressure regulator
regulador[M] de presión[F]
régulateur[M] de pression[F]
Überdruckventil[N]
regolatore[M] di pressione[F]
safety valve
válvula[F] de seguridad[F]
soupape[F]
Sicherheitsventil[N]
valvola[F] di sicurezza[F]

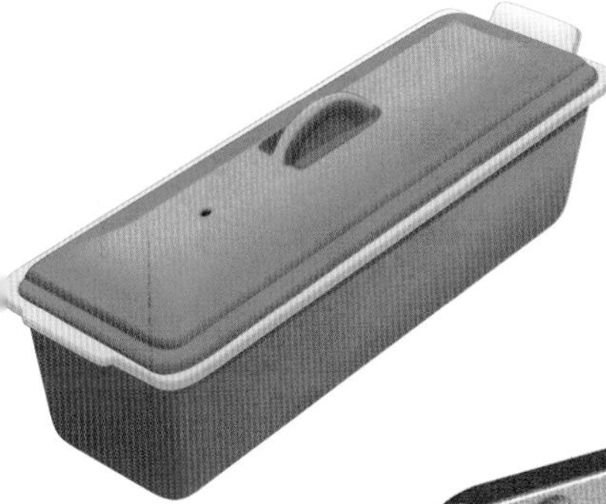

terrine
terrina [F]
terrine [F]
Terrine [F]
terrina [F]

dripping pan
grasera [F]
lèchefrite [F]
Fettpfanne [F]
leccarda [F]

roasting pans
asadores [M]
plats [M] à rôtir
Bräter [M]
teglie [F] da forno [M]

cooking utensils

Dutch oven
cacerola *F* refractaria
faitout *M*
Bradentopf *M*
casseruola *F*

stock pot
olla *F*
marmite *F*
Suppentopf *M*
pentola *F*

steamer
cazuela *F* vaporera
cuit-vapeur *M*
Dampfkochtopf *M*
pentola *F* a vapore *M*

couscous kettle
olla *F* para cuscús *M*
couscoussier *M*
Couscoustopf *M*
pentola *F* per cuscus *M*

steamer basket
cesto *M* de cocción *F* al vapor *M*
panier *M* cuit-vapeur *M*
Dämpfeinsatz *M*
cestello *M* per la cottura *F* a vapore *M*

egg poacher
escalfador *M* de huevos *M*
pocheuse *F*
Eipochierer *M*
tegame *M* per uova *F* in camicia *F*

frying pan
sartén [F]
poêle [F] à frire
Bratpfanne [F]
padella [F] per friggere

sauté pan
sartén [F] honda
sauteuse [F]
Schmorpfanne [F]
padella [F] per rosolare

pancake pan
sartén [F] para crepes [M]
poêle [F] à crêpes [F]
Crêpe-Pfanne [F]
padella [F] per crêpe [F]

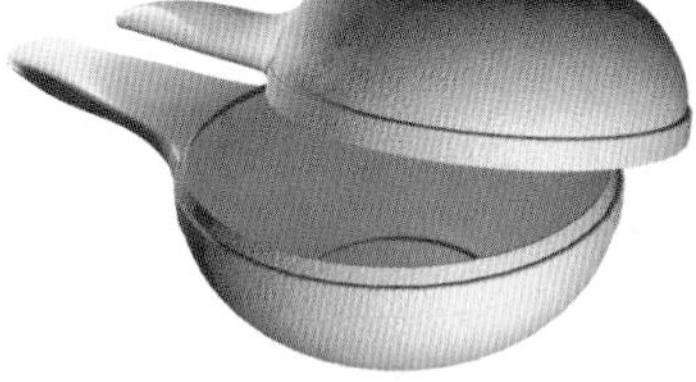

clay cooker
sartén [F] doble
diable [M]
Römertopf [M]
padella [F] doppia

saucepan
cacerola [F]
casserole [F]
Stielkasserolle [F]
tegame [M]

skillet
sartén [F] pequeña
poêlon [M]
Pfanne [F]
piccolo tegame [M]

double boiler
cacerola [F] para baño [M] María
bain-marie [M]
Wasserbadtopf [M]
pentola [F] per cucinare a bagnomaria

domestic appliances

aparatos^{M} electrodomésticos | appareils^{M} électroménagers | Haushaltsgeräte^{N} | elettrodomestici^{M}

for mixing and blending
para mezclar y batir
pour mélanger et battre
zum Mixen^{N} und Kneten^{N}
per frullare e miscelare

blender
batidora^{F} de vaso^{M}
mélangeur^{M}
Mixer^{M}
frullatore^{M}

cap
tapa^{F}
bouchon^{M}
Deckelknopf^{M}
tappo^{M}

container
vaso^{M} mezclador
récipient^{M}
Behälter^{M}
bicchiere^{M}

OZS 48 – 6 CUPS
40 – 5
32 – 4
24 – 3
16 – 2
OFF
Chop
Mix
Puree
Liquify
Pulse Mode
Crush Ice

cutting blade
cuchilla^{F}
couteau^{M}
Schneidmesser^{N}
coltello^{M}

motor unit
motor^{M}
bloc^{M}-moteur^{M}
Motorblock^{M}
blocco^{M} motore^{M}

control button
botón^{M} de control^{M}
touche^{F} de commande^{F}
Schalter^{M}
tasto^{M} di comando^{M}

table mixer
batidora F de mesa F
batteur M sur socle M
Tischrührgerät N
impastatrice F

tilt-back head
cabeza F móvil
tête F basculante
Schwenkarm M
testa F ribaltabile
beater ejector
eyector M de las varillas F
éjecteur M de fouets M
Auswurftaste F
espulsore M degli accessori M
beater
varilla F de batir
fouet M
Rührbesen M
frusta F
speed control
selector M de velocidades F
commande F de vitesse F
Geschwindigkeitsregelung F
regolatore M di velocità F
stand
pie M
socle M
Ständer M
base F
mixing bowl
bol M mezclador
bol M
Rührschüssel F
ciotola F
turntable
disco M giratorio
plateau M tournant
Drehscheibe F
piattaforma F girevole

hand mixer
batidora[F] de mano[F]
batteur[M] à main[F]
Handrührgerät[N]
frullatore[M] elettrico a mano[F]

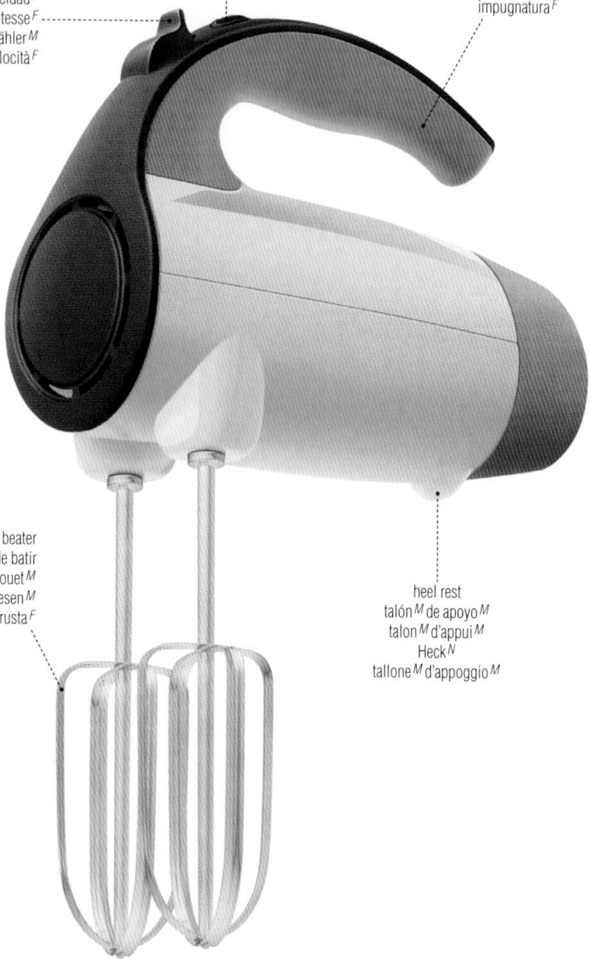
beater ejector
eyector[M] de las varillas[F]
éjecteur[M] de fouets[M]
Auswurftaste[F]
espulsore[M] degli accessori[M]
handle
asa[F]
poignée[F]
Griff[M]
impugnatura[F]
speed selector
selector[M] de velocidad[F]
sélecteur[M] de vitesse[F]
Geschwindigkeitswähler[M]
selettore[M] di velocità[F]
beater
varilla[F] de batir
fouet[M]
Rührbesen[M]
frusta[F]
heel rest
talón[M] de apoyo[M]
talon[M] d'appui[M]
Heck[N]
tallone[M] d'appoggio[M]

beaters
tipos [M] de varillas [F]
fouets [M]
Rührbesen [M]
fruste [F]

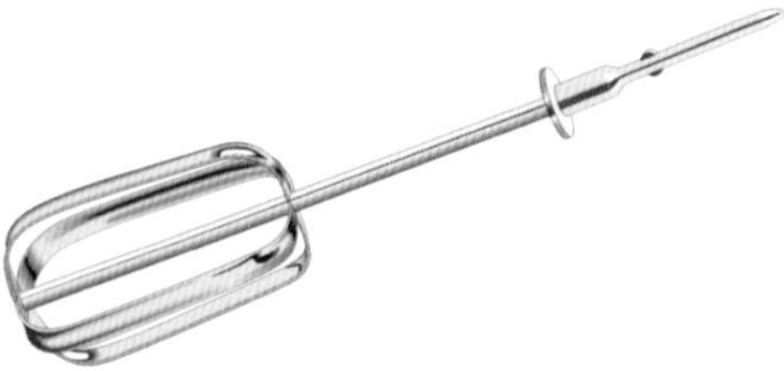

four blade beater
de aspas [F]
fouet [M] quatre pales [F]
Rührbesen [M]
frusta [F] a quattro bracci [M]

spiral beater
en espiral [F]
fouet [M] en spirale [F]
Spiralkneter [M]
frusta [F] a spirale [F]

wire beater
circular
fouet [M] à fil [M]
Drahtbesen [M]
frusta [F] ad anello [M]

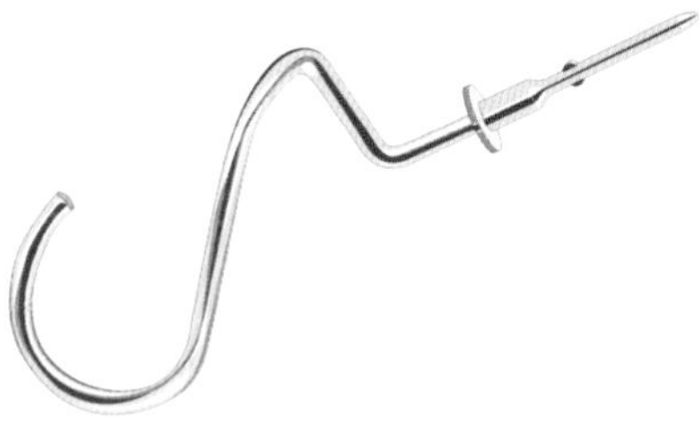

dough hook
de gancho [M]
crochet [M] pétrisseur
Knethaken [M]
gancio [M] per l'impasto [M]

domestic appliances

hand blender
batidora F de pie M
mélangeur M à main F
Stabmixer M
frullatore M a immersione F

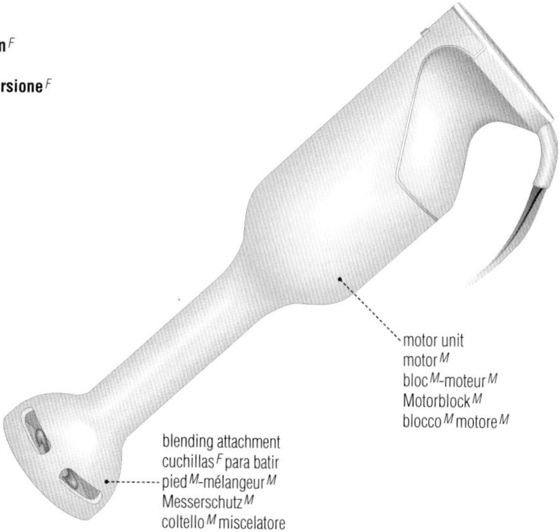
motor unit
motor M
bloc M-moteur M
Motorblock M
blocco M motore M
blending attachment
cuchillas F para batir
pied M-mélangeur M
Messerschutz M
coltello M miscelatore

for juicing
para exprimir
pour presser
zum Auspressen N
per spremere

citrus juicer
exprimidor M de cítricos M
presse-agrumes M
Zitruspresse F
spremiagrumi M elettrico

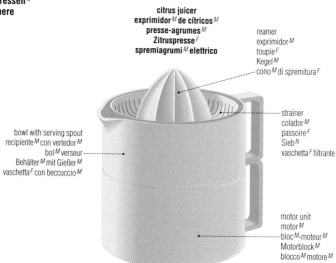

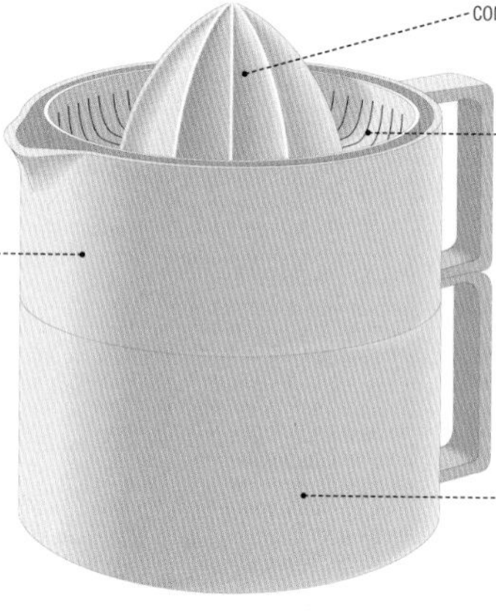
reamer
exprimidor M
toupie F
Kegel M
cono M di spremitura F
strainer
colador M
passoire F
Sieb N
vaschetta F filtrante
bowl with serving spout
recipiente M con vertedor M
bol M verseur
Behälter M mit Gießer M
vaschetta F con beccuccio M
motor unit
motor M
bloc M-moteur M
Motorblock M
blocco M motore M

for cutting
para cortar
pour couper
zum Schneiden[N]
per tagliare

food processor
robot[M] de cocina[F]
robot[M] de cuisine[F]
Küchenmaschine[F]
robot[M] da cucina[F]

feed tube
tubo[M] de entrada[F]
entonnoir[M]
Einfüllschacht[M]
bocchetta[F]
spindle
eje[M]
arbre[M]
Antriebswelle[F]
asse[M] di trasmissione[F] del motore[M]
lid
tapa[F]
couvercle[M]
Deckel[M]
coperchio[M]
bowl
bol[M]
bol[M]
Schüssel[F]
cestello[M]
handle
asa[F]
poignée[F]
Griff[M]
impugnatura[F]
blade
cuchilla[F]
couteau[M]
Schneidmesser[N]
lama[F]
motor unit
motor[M]
bloc[M]-moteur[M]
Motorblock[M]
blocco[M] motore[M]
Dough
Pulse

domestic appliances

for cooking
para cocinar
pour cuire
zum Kochen N
per cucinare

deep fryer
freidora F
friteuse F
Fritteuse F
friggitrice F

basket
canastilla F
panier M
Frittierkorb M
cestello M
lid
tapa F
couvercle M
Deckel M
coperchio M
handle
empuñadura F
poignée F
Griff M
maniglia F
thermostat
termostato M
thermostat M
Thermostat M
termostato M
signal lamp
piloto M
voyant M lumineux
Kontrollleuchte F
spia F luminosa
timer
reloj M
minuterie F
Zeituhr F
contaminuti M

microwave oven
horno^M microondas
four^M à micro-ondes^F
Mikrowellenherd^M
forno^M a microonde^F

door
puerta^F
porte^F
Tür^F
sportello^M
clock timer
reloj^M programador
horloge^F programmatrice
Zeitschalter^M
orologio^M contaminuti^M
control panel
panel^M de mandos^M
tableau^M de commande^F
Bedienblende^F
quadro^M di comando^M
latch
seguro^M
loquet^M
Riegel^M
chiusura^F a scatto^M
window
ventana^F
hublot^M
Sichtfenster^N
finestra^F di controllo^M
12:20
START
POWER LEVEL
Cook 1
Cook 2
Defrost
Reheat
1
2
3
4
5
6
7
8
9
Clock
0
Stop/Reset

raclette with grill
raclette-grill *M*
raclette *F*-**gril** *M*
Raclette *F*-**Grill** *M*
griglia *F* **per raclette** *F*

cooking plate
placa F de cocción F
surface F de cuisson F
Grillplatte F
piastra F di cottura F
dish
bandeja F
poêlon M
Pfännchen N
piatto M
base
base F
socle M
Unterteil M/N
base F

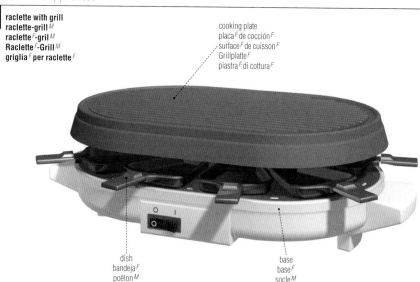

indoor electric grill
parrilla *F* **eléctrica**
gril *M* **barbecue** *M*
Elektrischer Tischgrill *M*
griglia *F* **elettrica per interni** *M*

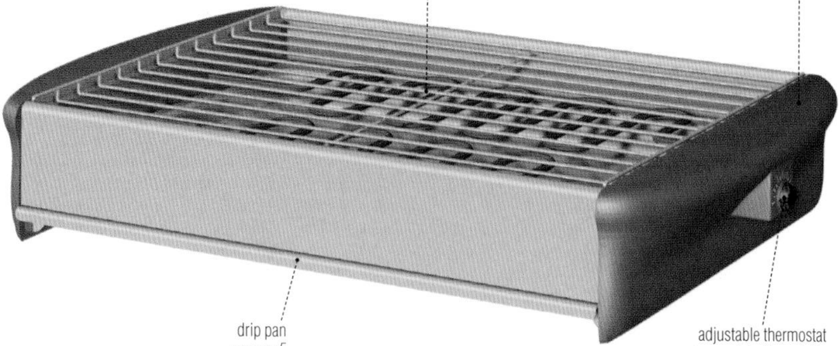
cooking surface
superficie F de cocción F
surface F de cuisson F
Grillfläche F
piano M di cottura F
insulated handle
asa F aislante
poignée F isolante
wärmeisolierter Griff M
maniglia F isolata
drip pan
grasera F
bac M ramasse-jus M
Fettpfanne F
leccarda F
adjustable thermostat
termostato M regulable
thermostat M réglable
regelbarer Thermostat M
termostato M regolabile

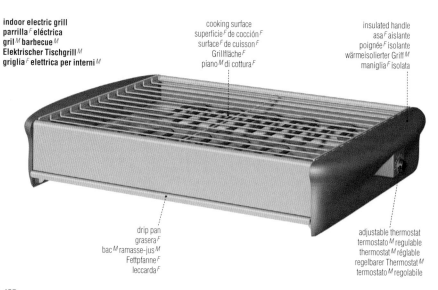

toaster
tostador [M]
grille-pain [M]
Toaster [M]
tostapane [M]

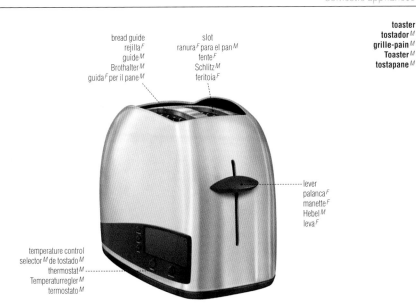

bread guide
rejilla [F]
guide [M]
Brothalter [M]
guida [F] per il pane [M]
slot
ranura [F] para el pan [M]
fente [F]
Schlitz [M]
feritoia [F]
lever
palanca [F]
manette [F]
Hebel [M]
leva [F]
temperature control
selector [M] de tostado [M]
thermostat [M]
Temperaturregler [M]
termostato [M]

griddle
plancha [F] **eléctrica**
gril [M] **électrique**
Grillplatte [F]
piastra [F] **elettrica**

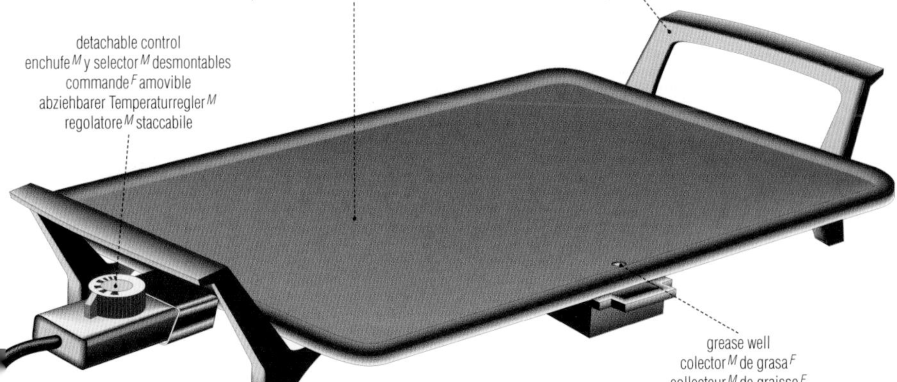
cooking surface
plancha [F]
surface [F] de cuisson [F]
Kochfeld [N]
piano [M] di cottura [F]
handle
asa [F]
poignée [F]
Griff [M]
maniglia [F]
detachable control
enchufe [M] y selector [M] desmontables
commande [F] amovible
abziehbarer Temperaturregler [M]
regolatore [M] staccabile
grease well
colector [M] de grasa [F]
collecteur [M] de graisse [F]
Fettauffangschale [F]
bacinella [F] raccogligrasso

waffle iron
gofrera F
gaufrier M**-gril** M
Waffeleisen N
griglia F **elettrica**

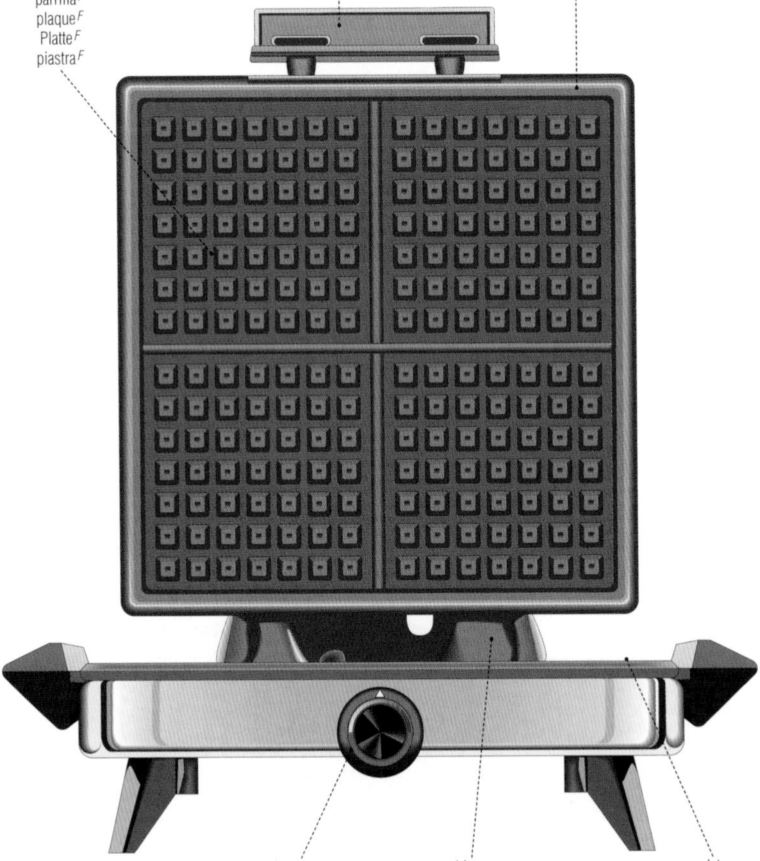

handle
asa F
poignée F
Griff M
maniglia F
lid
plancha F superior
couvercle M
Deckel M
coperchio M
plate
parrilla F
plaque F
Platte F
piastra F
temperature selector
selector M de temperatura F
sélecteur M de température F
Temperaturwähler M
selettore M della temperatura F
hinge
bisagra F
charnière F
Scharnier N
cerniera F
plate
parrilla F
plaque F
Platte F
piastra F

coffee makers

cafeteras[F] | cafetières[F] | Kaffeemaschinen[F] | macchine[F] da caffè[M]

automatic drip coffee maker
cafetera[F] de filtro[M] automática
cafetière[F] filtre[M]
Kaffeemaschine[F]
macchina[F] da caffè[M] a filtro[M]

reservoir
depósito[M] de agua[F]
réservoir[M]
Wasserbehälter[M]
serbatoio[M]

lid
tapa[F]
couvercle[M]
Deckel[M]
coperchio[M]

basket
filtro[M]
panier[M]
Filterhalter[M]
cassetta[F] filtro[M]

water level
nivel[M] de agua[F]
niveau[M] d'eau[F]
Wasserstand[M]
livello[M] dell'acqua[F]

warming plate
placa[F] térmica
plaque[F] chauffante
Warmhalteplatte[F]
piastra[F] riscaldante

carafe
cafetera[F]
verseuse[F]
Kanne[F]
caraffa[F]

signal lamp
piloto[M]
voyant[M] lumineux
Kontrollleuchte[F]
spia[F] luminosa

on-off switch
interruptor[M]
interrupteur[M]
Ein- und Ausschalter[M]
interruttore[M]

coffee makers

Neapolitan coffee maker
cafetera[F] napolitana
cafetière[F] napolitaine
Neapolitanische Tropfkanne[F]
caffettiera[F] napoletana

plunger
cafetera[F] de émbolo[M]
cafetière[F] à piston[M]
Pressfilterkanne[F]
caffettiera[F] a pistone[M]

espresso coffee maker
cafetera[F] italiana
cafetière[F] espresso[M]
Espressokocher[M]
caffettiera[F] per espresso[M]

espresso machine
máquina *F* de café *M* exprés
machine *F* à espresso *M*
Espressomaschine *F*
macchina *F* per espresso *M*

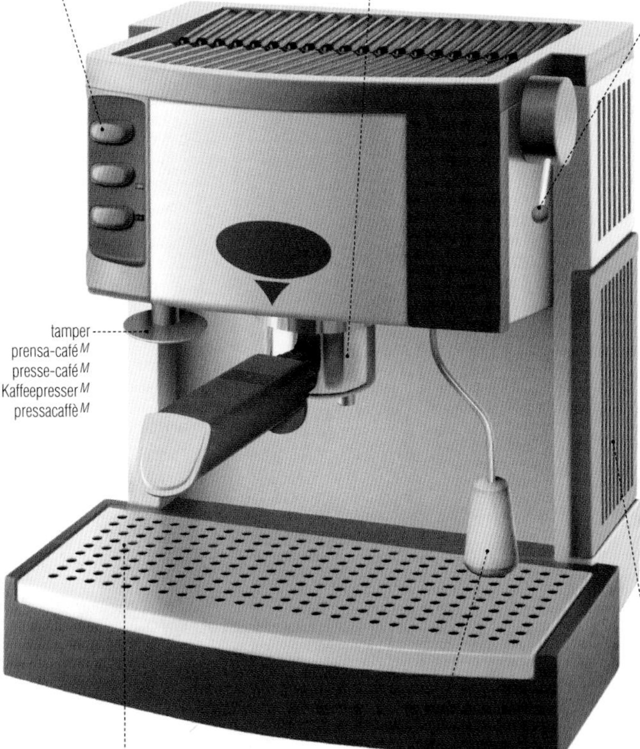
on-off switch
interruptor *M*
interrupteur *M*
Ein- und Ausschalter *M*
interruttore *M*
filter holder
porta-filtro *M*
porte-filtre *M*
Filterhalter *M*
portafiltro *M*
steam control knob
manecilla *F* de vapor *M*
manette *F* vapeur *F*
Dampfregler *M*
regolazione *F* del vapore *M*
tamper
prensa-café *M*
presse-café *M*
Kaffeepresser *M*
pressacaffè *M*
drip tray
cubeta *F* colectora de gotas *F*
cuvette *F* ramasse-gouttes *M*
Auffangschale *F*
vaschetta *F* di raccolta *F*
steam nozzle
tubo *M* de vapor *M*
buse *F* vapeur *F*
Aufschäumdüse *F*
ugello *M* vaporizzatore *M*
water tank
depósito *M* de agua *F*
réservoir *M* d'eau *F*
Wassertank *M*
serbatoio *M* dell'acqua *F*

coffee makers

vacuum coffee maker
cafetera[F] de infusión[F]
cafetière[F] à infusion[F]
Vakuum-Kaffeemaschine[F]
caffettiera[F] a infusione[F]

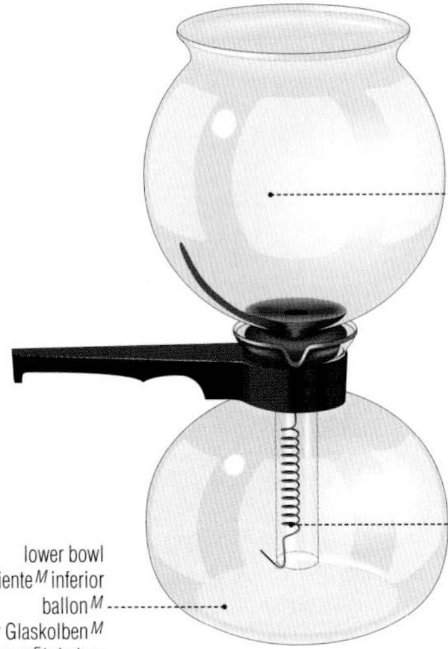
upper bowl
recipiente[M] superior
tulipe[F]
oberer Glaskolben[M]
coppa[F] superiore
stem
tubo[M] de subida[F] del agua[F]
tige[F]
Röhre[F]
gambo[M]
lower bowl
recipiente[M] inferior
ballon[M]
unterer Glaskolben[M]
coppa[F] inferiore

percolator
percoladora[F]
percolateur[M]
Kaffee-Filterkanne[M]
caffettiera[F] a filtro[M]

spout
pitorro[M]
bec[M] verseur
Tülle[F]
beccuccio[M]
signal lamp
piloto[M]
voyant[M] lumineux
Kontrollleuchte[F]
spia[F] luminosa

miscellaneous domestic appliances

varios aparatos[M] electrodomésticos | appareils[M] électroménagers divers | verschiedene Haushaltsgeräte[N] | elettrodomestici[M] vari

ice cream freezer
heladera[F]
sorbetière[F]
Eismaschine[F]
gelatiera[F]

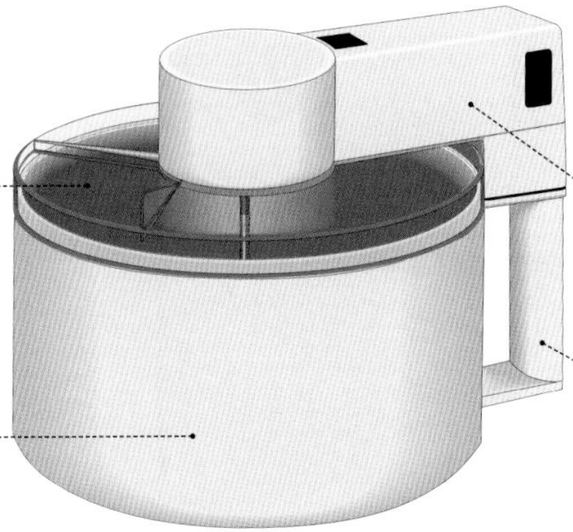
cover
cubierta[F]
couvercle[M]
Deckel[M]
coperchio[M]
freezer bucket
cubeta[F] congeladora
seau[M] isotherme
Eisbehälter[M]
cestello[M] di refrigerazione[F]
motor unit
motor[M]
bloc[M]-moteur[M]
Motorblock[M]
blocco[M] motore[M]
handle
asa[F]
poignée[F]
Griff[M]
impugnatura[F]

coffee mill
molinillo[M] de café[M]
moulin[M] à café[M]
Kaffeemühle[F]
macinacaffè[M]

lid
tapa[F]
couvercle[M]
Deckel[M]
coperchio[M]
blade
cuchilla[F]
couteau[M]
Messer[N]
lama[F]
on-off button
interruptor[M]
bouton[M] marche[F]/arrêt[M]
Ein- und Ausschalter[M]
interruttore[M]
motor unit
motor[M]
bloc[M]-moteur[M]
Motorblock[M]
blocco[M] motore[M]

miscellaneous domestic appliances

can opener
abrelatas *M*
ouvre-boîtes *M*
Dosenöffner *M*
apriscatole *M*

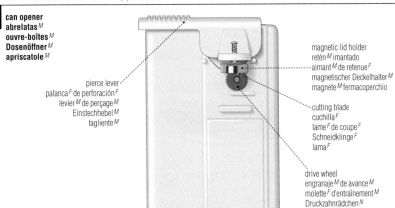

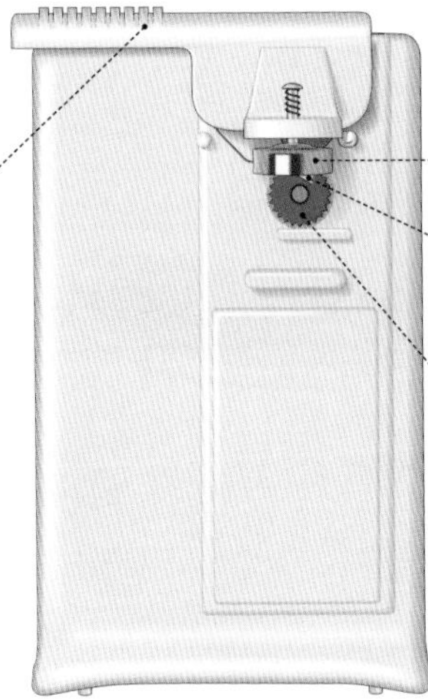
magnetic lid holder
retén M imantado
aimant M de retenue F
magnetischer Deckelhalter M
magnete M fermacoperchio
pierce lever
palanca F de perforación F
levier M de perçage M
Einstechhebel M
tagliente M
cutting blade
cuchilla F
lame F de coupe F
Schneidklinge F
lama F
drive wheel
engranaje M de avance M
molette F d'entraînement M
Druckzahnrädchen N
ingranaggio M di trascinamento M

kettle
hervidor *M*
bouilloire *F*
Wasserkessel *M*
bollitore *M*

handle
asa F
poignée F
Griff M
impugnatura F
spout
vertedor M
bec M verseur
Tülle F
beccuccio M
body
cuerpo M
corps M
Gehäuse N
corpo M
on-off switch
interruptor M
interrupteur M
Ein-/Ausschalter M
interruttore M
base
base F
socle M
Boden M
base F
signal lamp
piloto M
voyant M lumineux
Kontrollleuchte F
spia F luminosa

juicer
licuadora F
centrifugeuse F
Entsafter M
centrifuga F

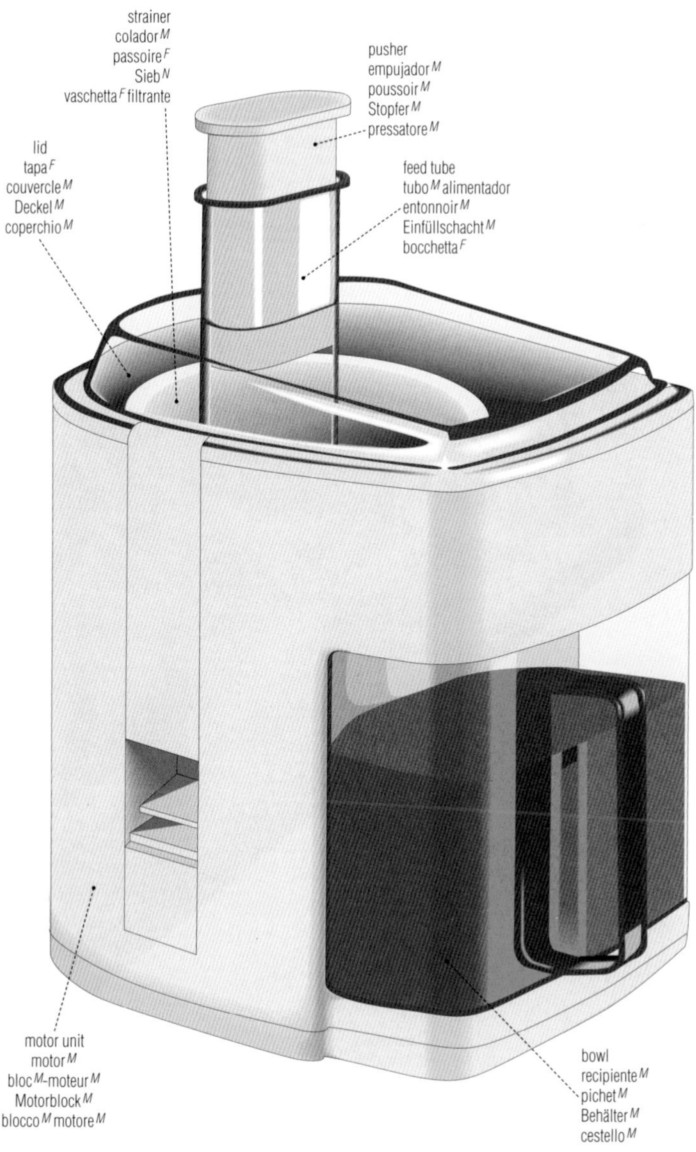
strainer
colador M
passoire F
Sieb N
vaschetta F filtrante
pusher
empujador M
poussoir M
Stopfer M
pressatore M
lid
tapa F
couvercle M
Deckel M
coperchio M
feed tube
tubo M alimentador
entonnoir M
Einfüllschacht M
bocchetta F
motor unit
motor M
bloc M-moteur M
Motorblock M
blocco M motore M
bowl
recipiente M
pichet M
Behälter M
cestello M

exterior of a house

exterior^{M} de una casa^{F} | extérieur^{M} d'une maison^{F} | Außenansicht^{F} eines Hauses^{N} | esterno^{M} di una casa^{F}

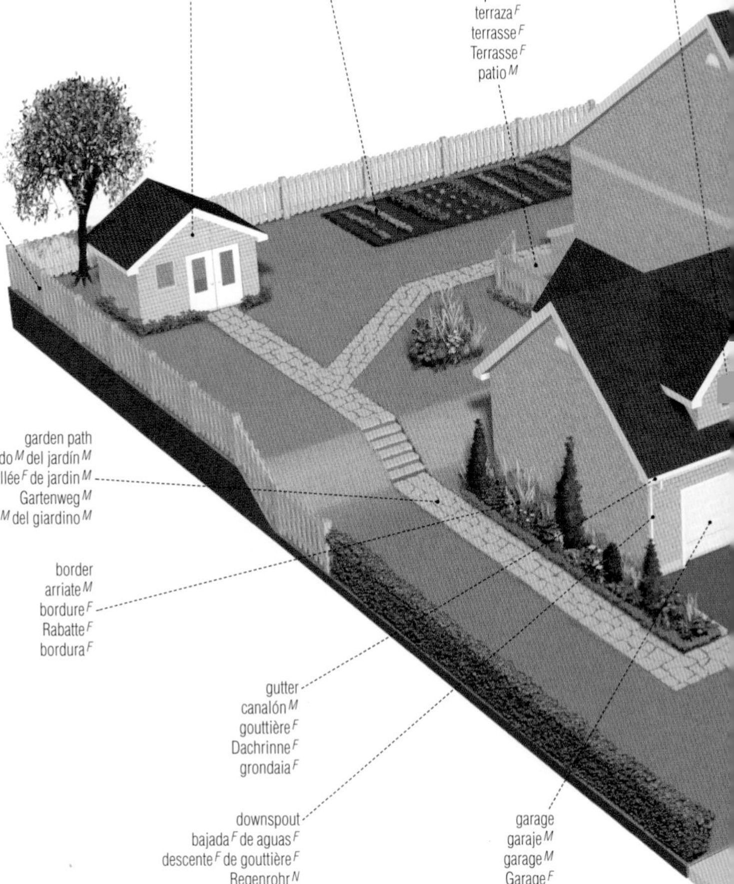
shed
cobertizo^{M}
remise^{F}
Schuppen^{M}
rimessa^{F}
vegetable garden
huerto^{M}
jardin^{M} potager
Gemüsegarten^{M}
orto^{M}
dormer window
tragaluz^{M}
lucarne^{F}
Mansardenfenster^{N}
abbaino^{M}
fence
vallado^{M}
clôture^{F}
Zaun^{M}
staccionata^{F}
patio
terraza^{F}
terrasse^{F}
Terrasse^{F}
patio^{M}
garden path
enlosado^{M} del jardín^{M}
allée^{F} de jardin^{M}
Gartenweg^{M}
vialetto^{M} del giardino^{M}
border
arriate^{M}
bordure^{F}
Rabatte^{F}
bordura^{F}
gutter
canalón^{M}
gouttière^{F}
Dachrinne^{F}
grondaia^{F}
downspout
bajada^{F} de aguas^{F}
descente^{F} de gouttière^{F}
Regenrohr^{N}
pluviale^{M}
garage
garaje^{M}
garage^{M}
Garage^{F}
garage^{M}

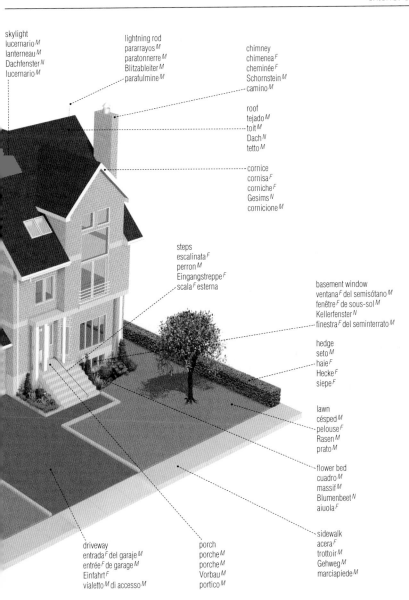

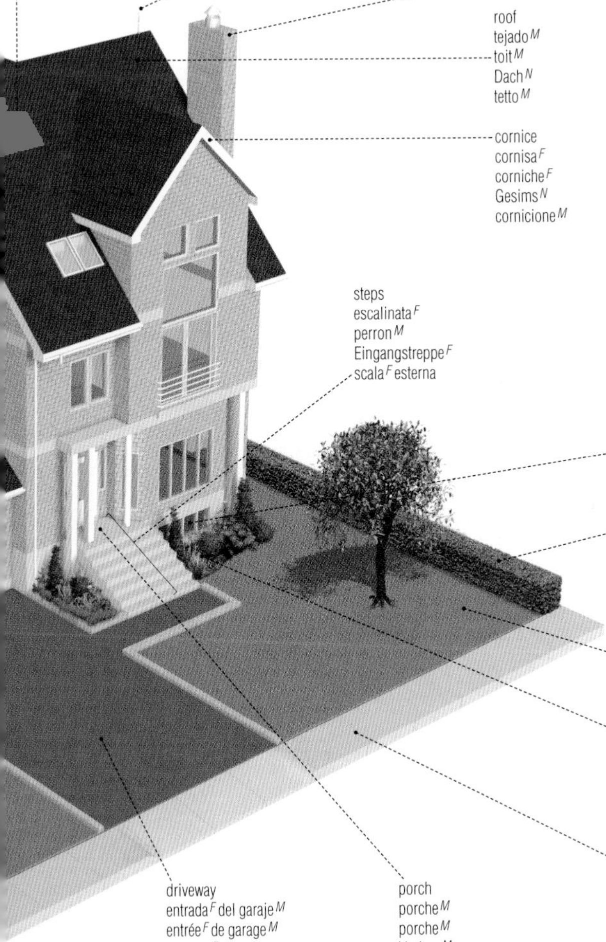
skylight
lucernario[M]
lanterneau[M]
Dachfenster[N]
lucernario[M]
lightning rod
pararrayos[M]
paratonnerre[M]
Blitzableiter[M]
parafulmine[M]
chimney
chimenea[F]
cheminée[F]
Schornstein[M]
camino[M]
roof
tejado[M]
toit[M]
Dach[N]
tetto[M]
cornice
cornisa[F]
corniche[F]
Gesims[N]
cornicione[M]
steps
escalinata[F]
perron[M]
Eingangstreppe[F]
scala[F] esterna
basement window
ventana[F] del semisótano[M]
fenêtre[F] de sous-sol[M]
Kellerfenster[N]
finestra[F] del seminterrato[M]
hedge
seto[M]
haie[F]
Hecke[F]
siepe[F]
lawn
césped[M]
pelouse[F]
Rasen[M]
prato[M]
flower bed
cuadro[M]
massif[M]
Blumenbeet[N]
aiuola[F]
sidewalk
acera[F]
trottoir[M]
Gehweg[M]
marciapiede[M]
driveway
entrada[F] del garaje[M]
entrée[F] de garage[M]
Einfahrt[F]
vialetto[M] di accesso[M]
porch
porche[M]
porche[M]
Vorbau[M]
portico[M]

main rooms

habitaciones^{F} principales | principales pièces^{F} d'une maison^{F} | Haupträume^{M} | stanze^{F} principali

elevation
alzado^{M}
élévation^{F}
Ansicht^{F}
prospetto^{M}

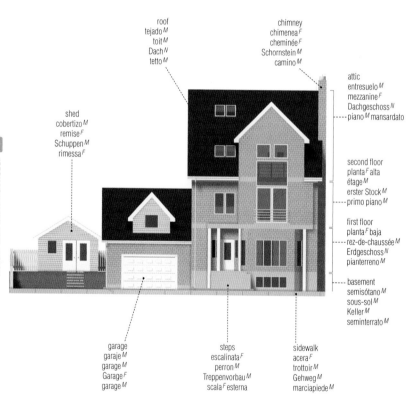

roof
tejado^{M}
toit^{M}
Dach^{N}
tetto^{M}
chimney
chimenea^{F}
cheminée^{F}
Schornstein^{M}
camino^{M}
attic
entresuelo^{M}
mezzanine^{F}
Dachgeschoss^{N}
piano^{M} mansardato
shed
cobertizo^{M}
remise^{F}
Schuppen^{M}
rimessa^{F}
second floor
planta^{F} alta
étage^{M}
erster Stock^{M}
primo piano^{M}
first floor
planta^{F} baja
rez-de-chaussée^{M}
Erdgeschoss^{N}
pianterreno^{M}
basement
semisótano^{M}
sous-sol^{M}
Keller^{M}
seminterrato^{M}
garage
garaje^{M}
garage^{M}
Garage^{F}
garage^{M}
steps
escalinata^{F}
perron^{M}
Treppenvorbau^{M}
scala^{F} esterna
sidewalk
acera^{F}
trottoir^{M}
Gehweg^{M}
marciapiede^{M}

loft
entresuelo M
mezzanine F
Zwischengeschoss N
piano M **mansardato**

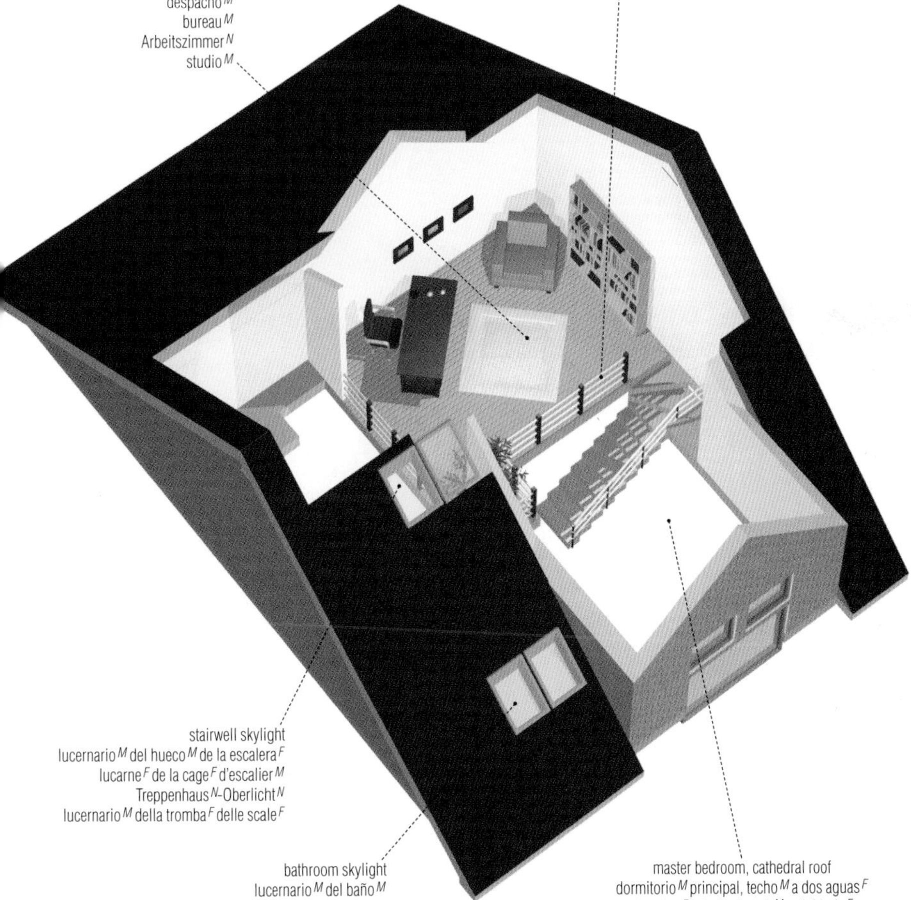
railing
barandilla F
garde-fou M
Geländer N
ringhiera F
study
despacho M
bureau M
Arbeitszimmer N
studio M
stairwell skylight
lucernario M del hueco M de la escalera F
lucarne F de la cage F d'escalier M
Treppenhaus N-Oberlicht N
lucernario M della tromba F delle scale F
bathroom skylight
lucernario M del baño M
lanterneau M de la salle F de bains M
Badezimmer N-Oberlicht N
lucernario M del bagno M
master bedroom, cathedral roof
dormitorio M principal, techo M a dos aguas F
chambre F principale, toit M cathédrale F
großes Schlafzimmer N, Giebeldach N
camera F da letto M principale, tetto M a due spioventi M

main rooms

second floor
planta[F] alta
étage[M]
erster Stock[M]
primo piano[M]

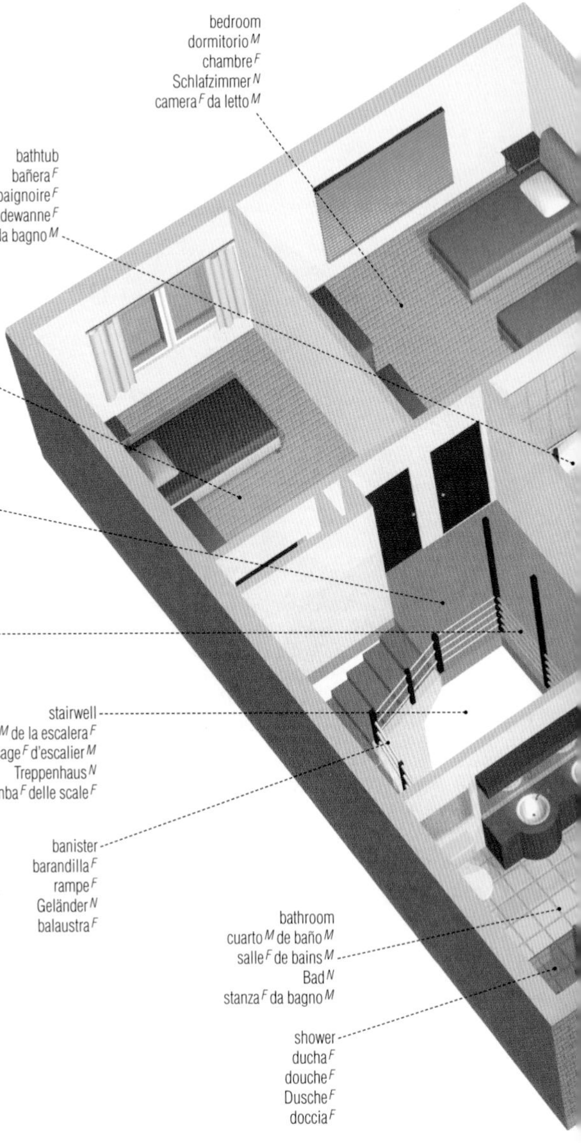

bedroom
dormitorio[M]
chambre[F]
Schlafzimmer[N]
camera[F] da letto[M]

bathtub
bañera[F]
baignoire[F]
Badewanne[F]
vasca[F] da bagno[M]

bedroom
dormitorio[M]
chambre[F]
Schlafzimmer[N]
camera[F] da letto[M]

landing
rellano[M] de la escalera[F]
palier[M]
Treppenabsatz[M]
pianerottolo[M]

railing
barandilla[F]
garde-fou[M]
Geländer[N]
ringhiera[F]

stairwell
hueco[M] de la escalera[F]
cage[F] d'escalier[M]
Treppenhaus[N]
tromba[F] delle scale[F]

banister
barandilla[F]
rampe[F]
Geländer[N]
balaustra[F]

bathroom
cuarto[M] de baño[M]
salle[F] de bains[M]
Bad[N]
stanza[F] da bagno[M]

shower
ducha[F]
douche[F]
Dusche[F]
doccia[F]

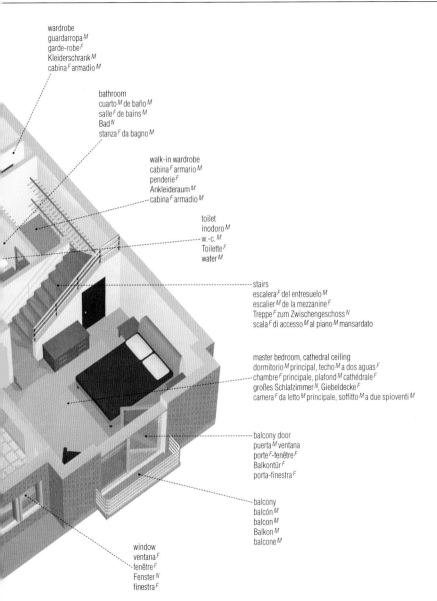

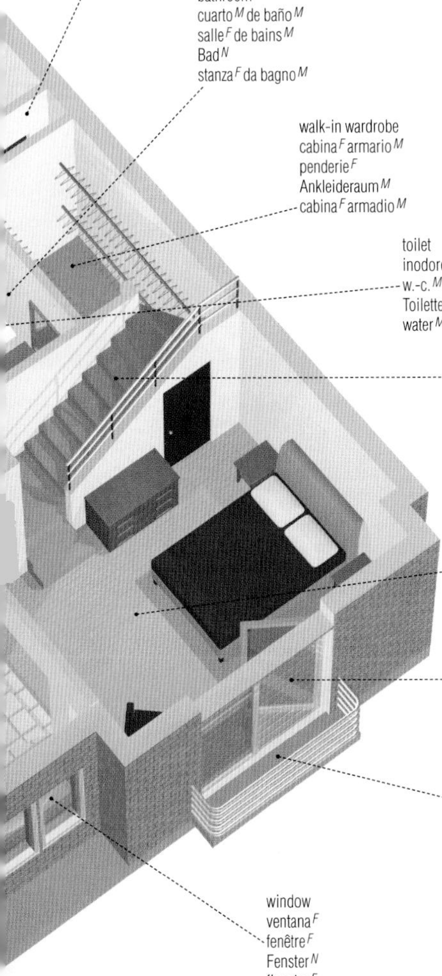
wardrobe
guardarropa[M]
garde-robe[F]
Kleiderschrank[M]
cabina[F] armadio[M]
bathroom
cuarto[M] de baño[M]
salle[F] de bains[M]
Bad[N]
stanza[F] da bagno[M]
walk-in wardrobe
cabina[F] armario[M]
penderie[F]
Ankleideraum[M]
cabina[F] armadio[M]
toilet
inodoro[M]
w.-c.[M]
Toilette[F]
water[M]
stairs
escalera[F] del entresuelo[M]
escalier[M] de la mezzanine[F]
Treppe[F] zum Zwischengeschoss[N]
scala[F] di accesso[M] al piano[M] mansardato
master bedroom, cathedral ceiling
dormitorio[M] principal, techo[M] a dos aguas[F]
chambre[F] principale, plafond[M] cathédrale[F]
großes Schlafzimmer[N], Giebeldecke[F]
camera[F] da letto[M] principale, soffitto[M] a due spioventi[M]
balcony door
puerta[M] ventana
porte[F]-fenêtre[F]
Balkontür[F]
porta-finestra[F]
balcony
balcón[M]
balcon[M]
Balkon[M]
balcone[M]
window
ventana[F]
fenêtre[F]
Fenster[N]
finestra[F]

first floor
planta^F baja
rez-de-chaussée^M
Erdgeschoss^N
pianterreno^M

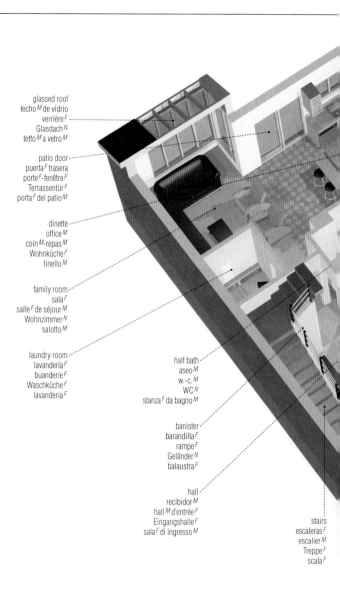

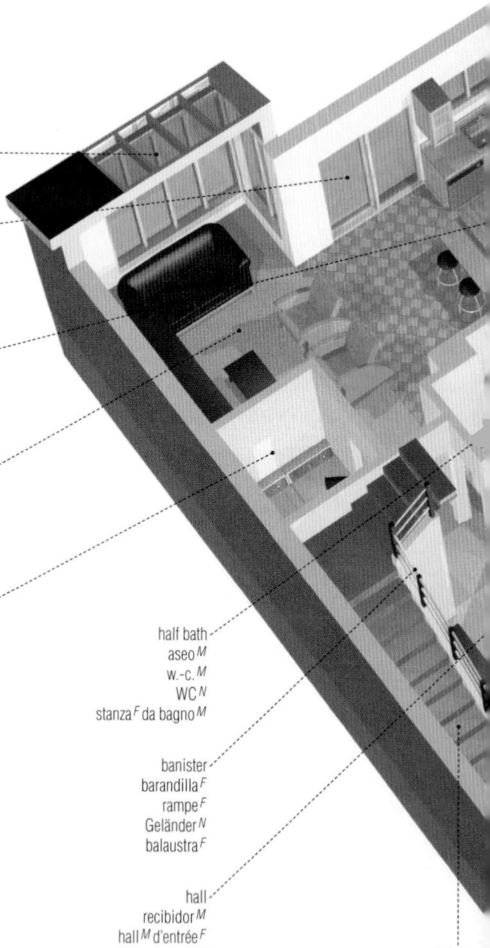
glassed roof
techo^M de vidrio
verrière^F
Glasdach^N
tetto^M a vetro^M
patio door
puerta^F trasera
porte^F-fenêtre^F
Terrassentür^F
porta^F del patio^M
dinette
office^M
coin^M-repas^M
Wohnküche^F
tinello^M
family room
sala^F
salle^F de séjour^M
Wohnzimmer^N
salotto^M
laundry room
lavandería^F
buanderie^F
Waschküche^F
lavanderia^F
half bath
aseo^M
w.-c.^M
WC^N
stanza^F da bagno^M
banister
barandilla^F
rampe^F
Geländer^N
balaustra^F
hall
recibidor^M
hall^M d'entrée^F
Eingangshalle^F
sala^F di ingresso^M
stairs
escaleras^F
escalier^M
Treppe^F
scala^F

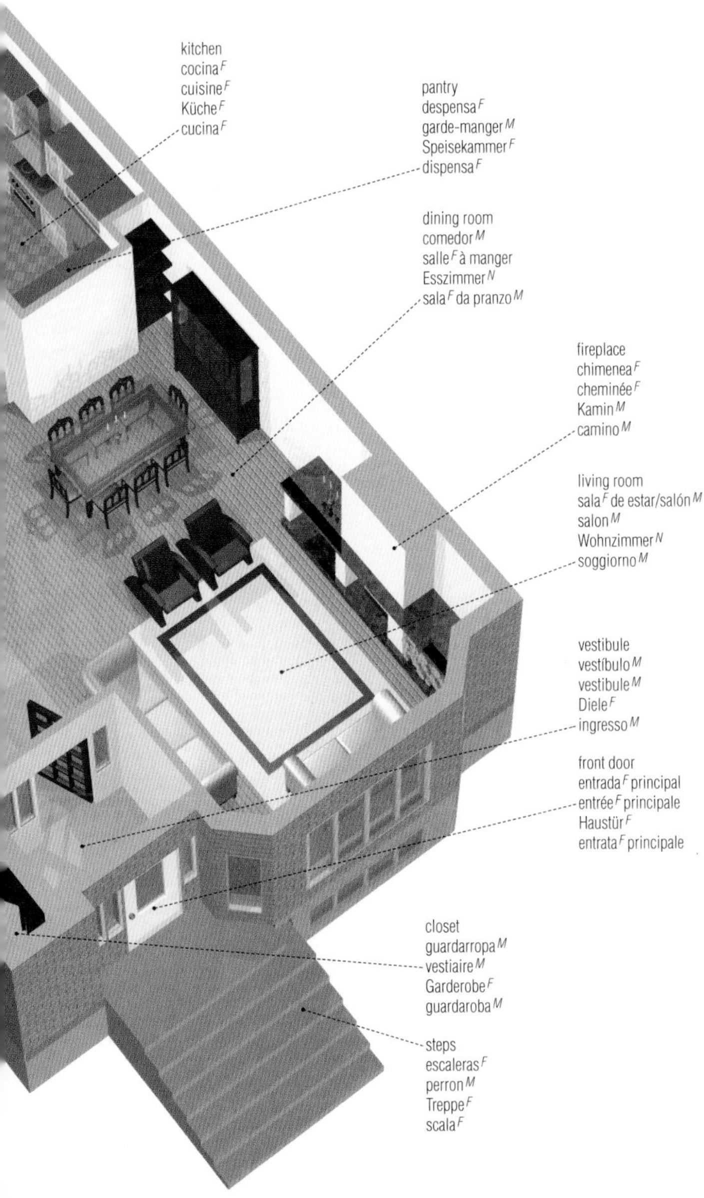
kitchen
cocina F
cuisine F
Küche F
cucina F
pantry
despensa F
garde-manger M
Speisekammer F
dispensa F
dining room
comedor M
salle F à manger
Esszimmer N
sala F da pranzo M
fireplace
chimenea F
cheminée F
Kamin M
camino M
living room
sala F de estar/salón M
salon M
Wohnzimmer N
soggiorno M
vestibule
vestíbulo M
vestibule M
Diele F
ingresso M
front door
entrada F principal
entrée F principale
Haustür F
entrata F principale
closet
guardarropa M
vestiaire M
Garderobe F
guardaroba M
steps
escaleras F
perron M
Treppe F
scala F

frame

armazón M | charpente F | Rahmen M | struttura F

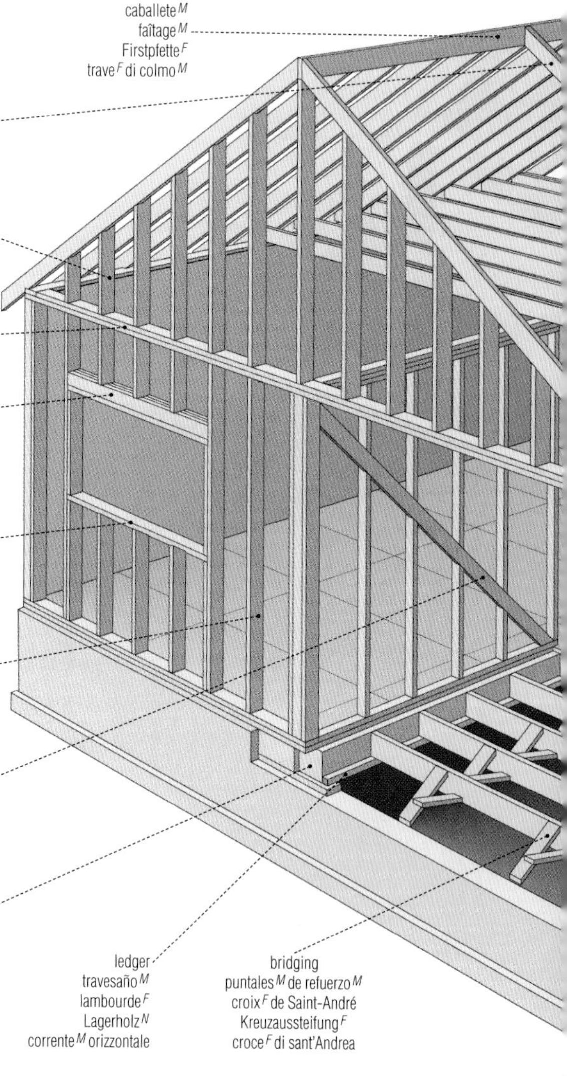
tie beam
caballete M
faîtage M
Firstpfette F
trave F di colmo M
rafter
cabrio M
chevron M
Sparren M
falso puntone M
gable stud
montante M
montant M
Giebelständer M
montante M del timpano M
double plate
solera F doble
sablière F double
Doppelriegel M
doppio corrente M
header
cabezal M
linteau M
Sturz M
traversa F superiore di finestra F
window sill
alféizar M
appui M de fenêtre F
Brüstungsriegel M
traversa F inferiore di finestra F
stud
pie M derecho
poteau M
Pfosten M
montante M
brace
tirante M
écharpe F
Strebe F
controvento M
girder
viga F maestra
poutre F
Träger M
trave F
ledger
travesaño M
lambourde F
Lagerholz N
corrente M orizzontale
bridging
puntales M de refuerzo M
croix F de Saint-André
Kreuzaussteifung F
croce F di sant'Andrea

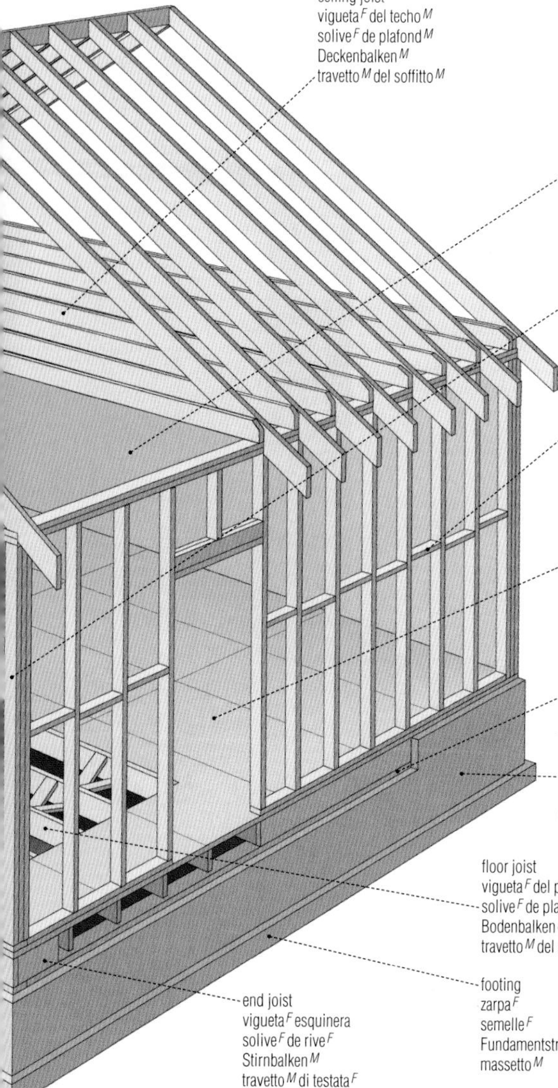
ceiling joist
vigueta F del techo M
solive F de plafond M
Deckenbalken M
travetto M del soffitto M
sheathing
entablado M
revêtement M
Verkleidung F
rivestimento M
corner stud
montante M esquinero
poteau M cornier
Eckpfosten M
montante M d'angolo M
strut
tornapunta F
étrésillon F
Strebe F
sbadacchio M
subfloor
contrapiso M
sous-plancher M
Unterboden M
sottofondo M
sill plate
solera F inferior
lisse F d'assise F
erste Holzlage F
corrente F di fondazione F
foundation
muro M de cimentación F
mur M de fondation F
Fundament N
muro M di fondazione F
floor joist
vigueta F del piso M
solive F de plancher M
Bodenbalken M
travetto M del solaio M
footing
zarpa F
semelle F
Fundamentstreifen M
massetto M
end joist
vigueta F esquinera
solive F de rive F
Stirnbalken M
travetto M di testata F

foundation

cimientos M | fondations F | Fundament N | fondazioni F

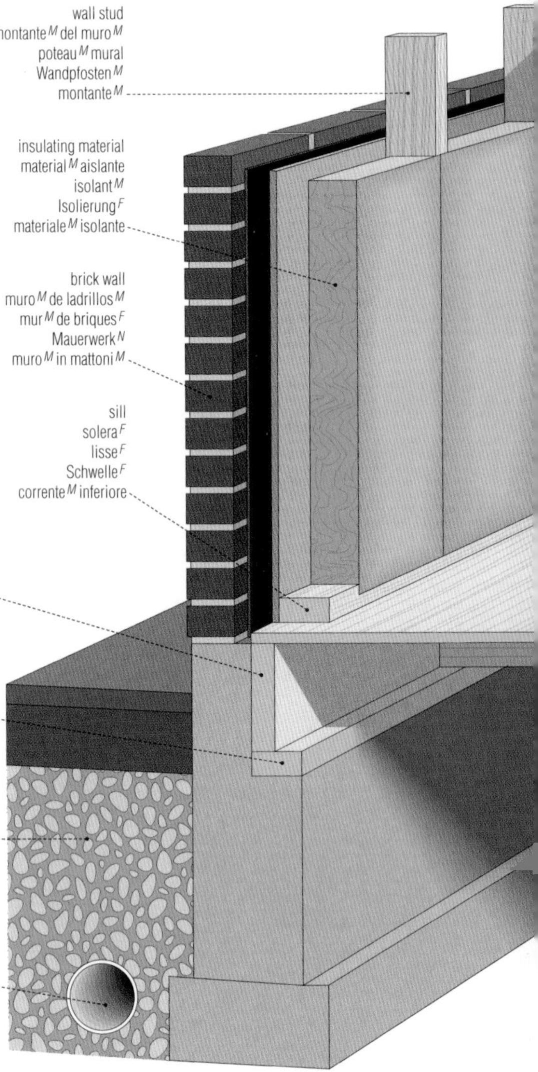
wall stud
montante M del muro M
poteau M mural
Wandpfosten M
montante M
insulating material
material M aislante
isolant M
Isolierung F
materiale M isolante
brick wall
muro M de ladrillos M
mur M de briques F
Mauerwerk N
muro M in mattoni M
sill
solera F
lisse F
Schwelle F
corrente M inferiore
end joist
vigueta F esquinera
solive F de rive F
Stirnbalken M
travetto M di testata F
sill plate
solera F interior
lisse F d'assise F
erste Holzlage F
corrente F di fondazione F
gravel
grava F
gravier M
Kies M
ghiaia F
drain tile
tubo M de drenaje M
drain M
Sickerrohr N
tubo M del drenaggio M

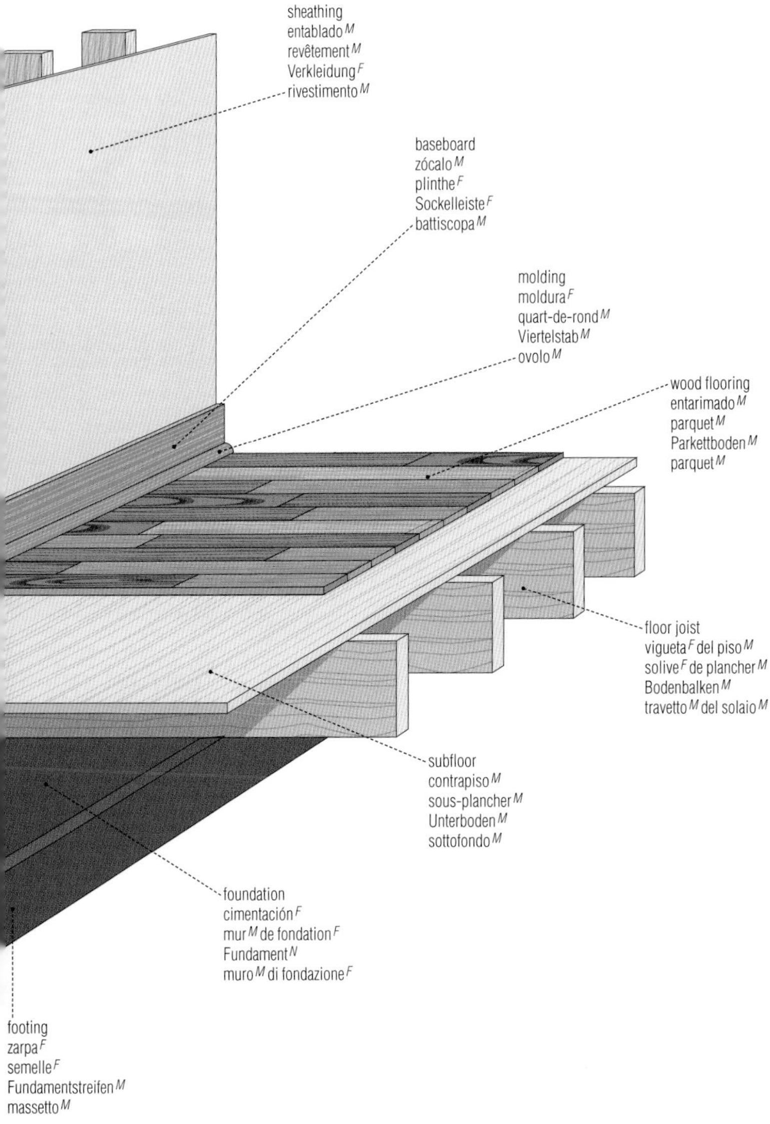
sheathing
entablado M
revêtement M
Verkleidung F
rivestimento M
baseboard
zócalo M
plinthe F
Sockelleiste F
battiscopa M
molding
moldura F
quart-de-rond M
Viertelstab M
ovolo M
wood flooring
entarimado M
parquet M
Parkettboden M
parquet M
floor joist
vigueta F del piso M
solive F de plancher M
Bodenbalken M
travetto M del solaio M
subfloor
contrapiso M
sous-plancher M
Unterboden M
sottofondo M
foundation
cimentación F
mur M de fondation F
Fundament N
muro M di fondazione F
footing
zarpa F
semelle F
Fundamentstreifen M
massetto M

stairs

escalera[F] | escalier[M] | Treppe[F] | scale[F]

cap
remate[M]
couronnement[M]
Kopfteil[M/N]
cappello[M]
banister
barandilla[F]
rampe[F]
Geländer[N]
parapetto[M]
landing
rellano[M]
palier[M]
Podest[N]
pianerottolo[M]
goose-neck
cuello[M] de cisne[M]
col[M]-de-cygne[M]
Krümmling[M]
collo[M] d'oca[F]
run
huella[F]
giron[M]
Stufe[F]
larghezza[F] del gradino[M]
baseboard
zócalo[M]
plinthe[F]
Sockelleiste[F]
zoccolo[M]
open stringe
zanca
limon[M] à crémaillère
Freiwange
fianco[M] intern

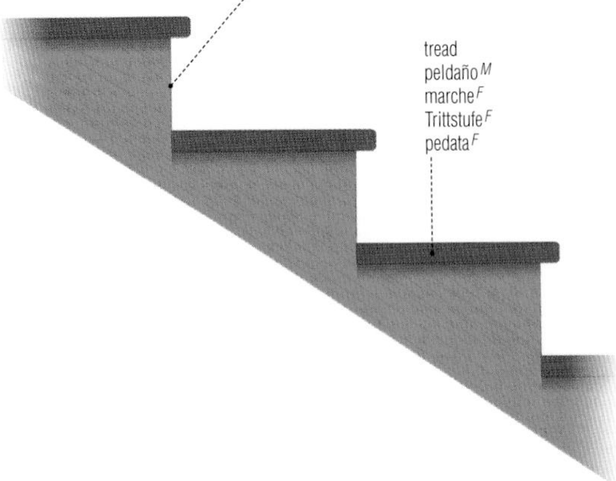
riser
contrahuella[F]
contremarche[F]
Setzstufe[F]
frontale[M]
tread
peldaño[M]
marche[F]
Trittstufe[F]
pedata[F]

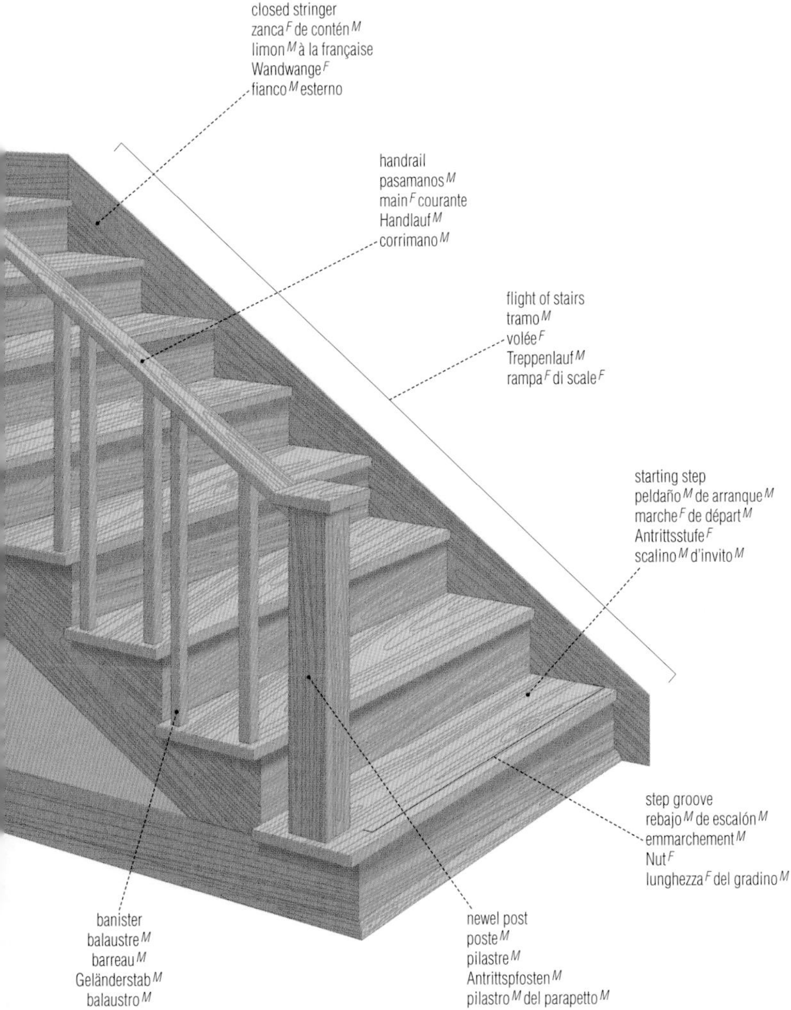
closed stringer
zanca F de contén M
limon M à la française
Wandwange F
fianco M esterno
handrail
pasamanos M
main F courante
Handlauf M
corrimano M
flight of stairs
tramo M
volée F
Treppenlauf M
rampa F di scale F
starting step
peldaño M de arranque M
marche F de départ M
Antrittsstufe F
scalino M d'invito M
step groove
rebajo M de escalón M
emmarchement M
Nut F
lunghezza F del gradino M
banister
balaustre M
barreau M
Geländerstab M
balaustro M
newel post
poste M
pilastre M
Antrittspfosten M
pilastro M del parapetto M

window

ventana^F | fenêtre^F | Fenster^N | finestra^F

structure
estructura ^F
structure ^F
Konstruktion ^F
struttura ^F

head of frame
travesaño M superior
tête F de dormant M
Blendrahmen M oben
parte F superiore dell'intelaiatura F
casing
marco M
chambranle M
Holzleibung F
chiambrana F
shutter
contraventana F
contrevent M
Fensterladen M
imposta F
stile tongue of sash
montante M central
montant M mouton M
Deckleiste F
giunzione F a linguetta F del telaio M
stile groove of sash
montante M embarbillado
montant M embrevé
Falz M
giunzione F scanalata del telaio M

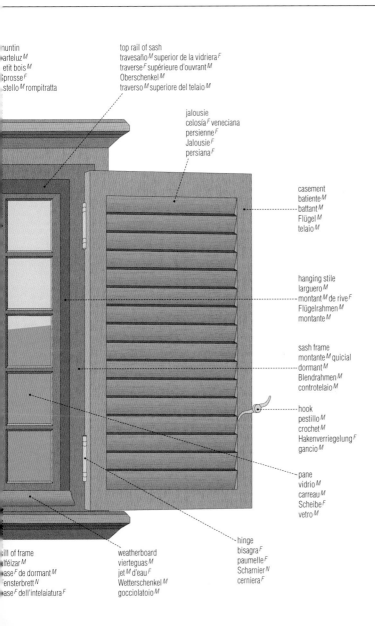

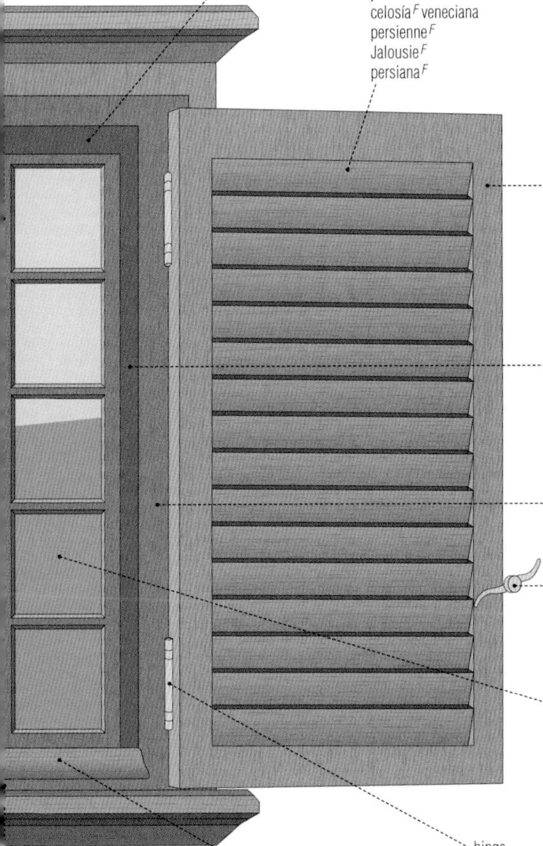
untin
arteluz^{M}
etit bois^{M}
prosse^{F}
stello^{M} rompitratta

top rail of sash
travesaño^{M} superior de la vidriera^{F}
traverse^{F} supérieure d'ouvrant^{M}
Oberschenkel^{M}
traverso^{M} superiore del telaio^{M}

jalousie
celosía^{F} veneciana
persienne^{F}
Jalousie^{F}
persiana^{F}

casement
batiente^{M}
battant^{M}
Flügel^{M}
telaio^{M}

hanging stile
larguero^{M}
montant^{M} de rive^{F}
Flügelrahmen^{M}
montante^{M}

sash frame
montante^{M} quicial
dormant^{M}
Blendrahmen^{M}
controtelaio^{M}

hook
pestillo^{M}
crochet^{M}
Hakenverriegelung^{F}
gancio^{M}

pane
vidrio^{M}
carreau^{M}
Scheibe^{F}
vetro^{M}

ill of frame
lféizar^{M}
ase^{F} de dormant^{M}
ensterbrett^{N}
ase^{F} dell'intelaiatura^{F}

weatherboard
vierteguas^{M}
jet^{M} d'eau^{F}
Wetterschenkel^{M}
gocciolatoio^{M}

hinge
bisagra^{F}
paumelle^{F}
Scharnier^{N}
cerniera^{F}

HOUSE AND DO-IT-YOURSELF

exterior door

puerta^F de entrada^F | porte^F extérieure | Haustür^F | porta^F esterna

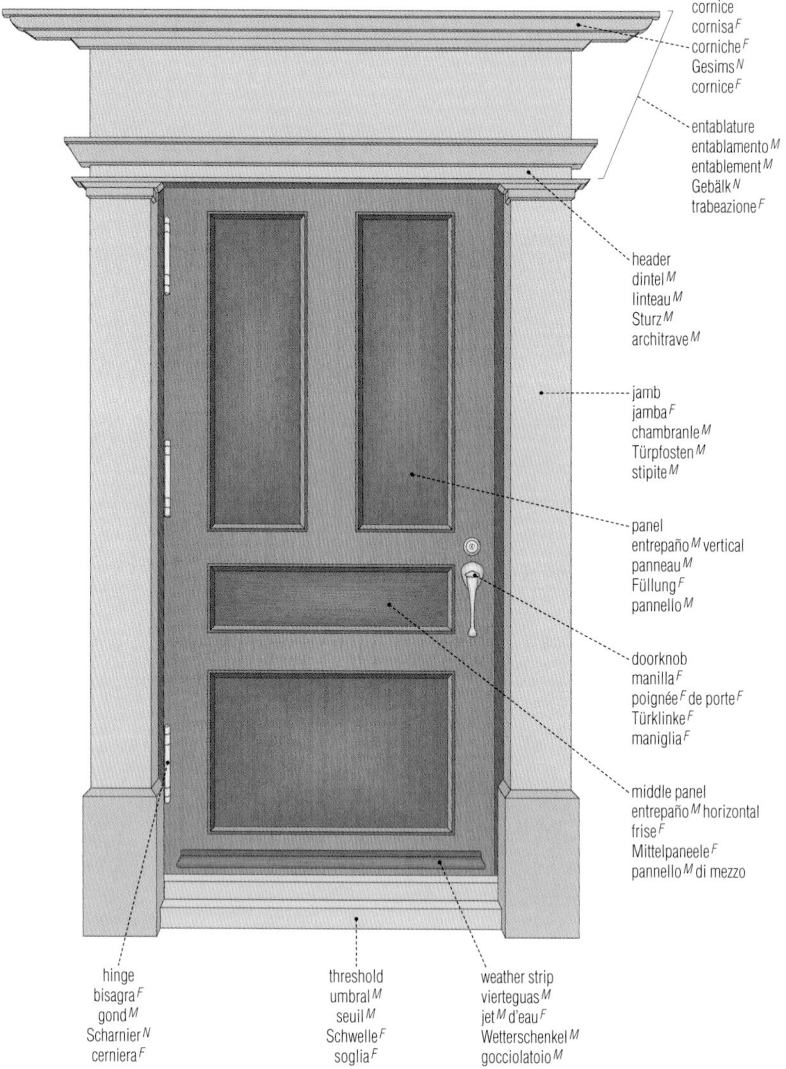
cornice
cornisa F
corniche F
Gesims N
cornice F
entablature
entablamento M
entablement M
Gebälk N
trabeazione F
header
dintel M
linteau M
Sturz M
architrave M
jamb
jamba F
chambranle M
Türpfosten M
stipite M
panel
entrepaño M vertical
panneau M
Füllung F
pannello M
doorknob
manilla F
poignée F de porte F
Türklinke F
maniglia F
middle panel
entrepaño M horizontal
frise F
Mittelpaneele F
pannello M di mezzo
hinge
bisagra F
gond M
Scharnier N
cerniera F
threshold
umbral M
seuil M
Schwelle F
soglia F
weather strip
vierteguas M
jet M d'eau F
Wetterschenkel M
gocciolatoio M

lock

cerrajería[F] | serrure[F] | Schloss[N] | serratura[F]

general view
vista[F] general
vue[F] d'ensemble[M]
Gesamtansicht[F]
visione[F] di insieme[M]

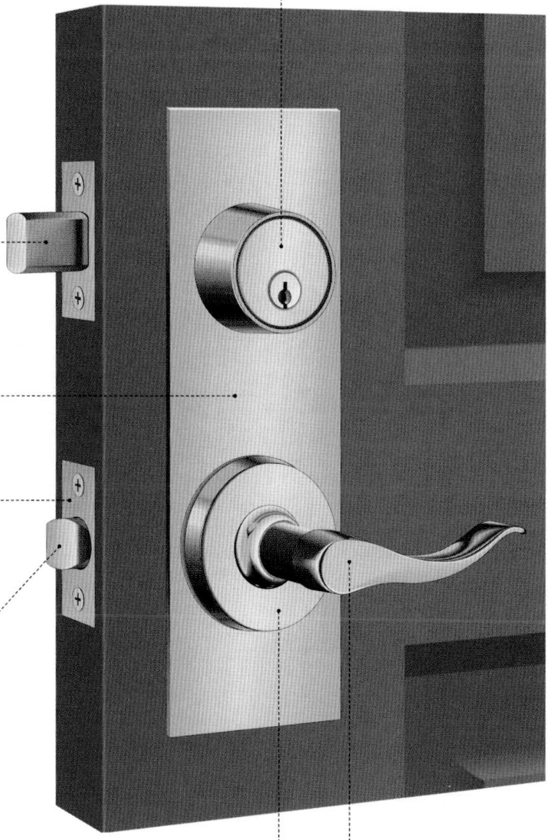
lock
cerradura[F]
serrure[F]
Schloss[N]
serratura[F]
dead bolt
pestillo[M]
pêne[M] dormant
Riegel[M]
chiavistello[M] senza scatto[M]
escutcheon
chapa[F]
écusson[M]
Schlüsselschild[N]
piastrina[F]
faceplate
tapa[F]
têtière[F]
Stulp[M]
bocchetta[F]
latch bolt
pasador[M]
pêne[M] demi-tour[M]
Falle[F]
chiavistello[M] a scatto[M]
rose
roseta[F]
rosette[F]
Rosette[F]
rosetta[F]
doorknob
manilla[F]
bec-de-cane[M]
Türklinke[F]
maniglia[F]

wood firing

calefacción[F] de leña[F] | chauffage[M] au bois[M] | Holzbeheizung[F] | riscaldamento[M] a legna[F]

fireplace
chimenea[F]
cheminée[F] à foyer[M] ouvert
Kamin[M]
camino[M]

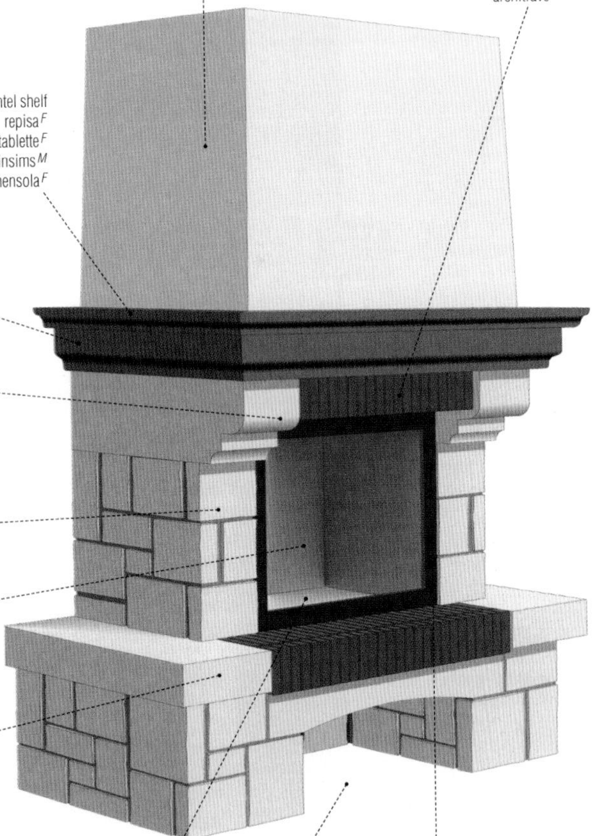
hood
campana[F]
hotte[F]
Rauchmantel[M]
cappa[F]
lintel
dintel[M]
linteau[M]
Sturz[M]
architrave[M]
mantel shelf
repisa[F]
tablette[F]
Kaminsims[M]
mensola[F]
mantel
manto[M]
manteau[M]
Kamineinfassung[F]
caminiera[F]
corbel piece
ménsula[F]
corbeau[M]
Kragstein[M]
mensolone[M]
jamb
jamba[F]
jambage[M]
seitliche Einfassung[F]
stipite[M]
firebrick back
ladrillos[M] refractarios
cœur[M]
Schamotteplatte[F]
fondo[M] refrattario
base
base[F] del hogar[M]
socle[M]
Sockel[M]
base[F]
inner hearth
hogar[M]
âtre[M]
Feuerstätte[F]
focolare[M]
woodbox
leñera[F]
bûcher[M]
Brennholzstauraum[M]
cassone[M] per legna[F] da ardere
frame
armazón[M]
encadrement[M]
Rahmen[M]
intelaiatura[F]

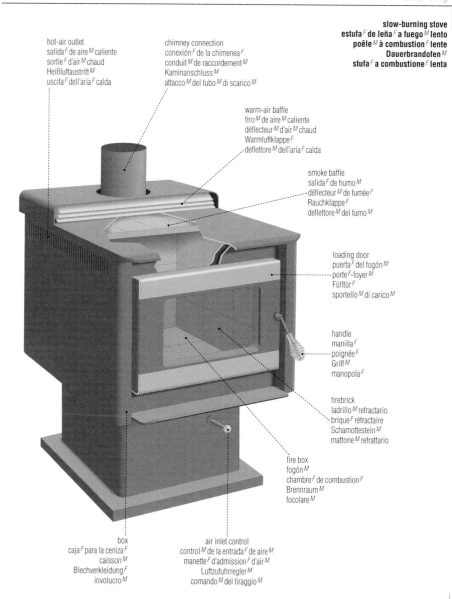

slow-burning stove
estufa^{F} de leña^{F} a fuego^{M} lento
poêle^{M} à combustion^{F} lente
Dauerbrandofen^{M}
stufa^{F} a combustione^{F} lenta

hot-air outlet
salida^{F} de aire^{M} caliente
sortie^{F} d'air^{M} chaud
Heißluftaustritt^{M}
uscita^{F} dell'aria^{F} calda

chimney connection
conexión^{F} de la chimenea^{F}
conduit^{M} de raccordement^{M}
Kaminanschluss^{M}
attacco^{M} del tubo^{M} di scarico^{M}

warm-air baffle
tiro^{M} de aire^{M} caliente
déflecteur^{M} d'air^{M} chaud
Warmluftklappe^{F}
deflettore^{M} dell'aria^{F} calda

smoke baffle
salida^{F} de humo^{M}
déflecteur^{M} de fumée^{F}
Rauchklappe^{F}
deflettore^{M} del fumo^{M}

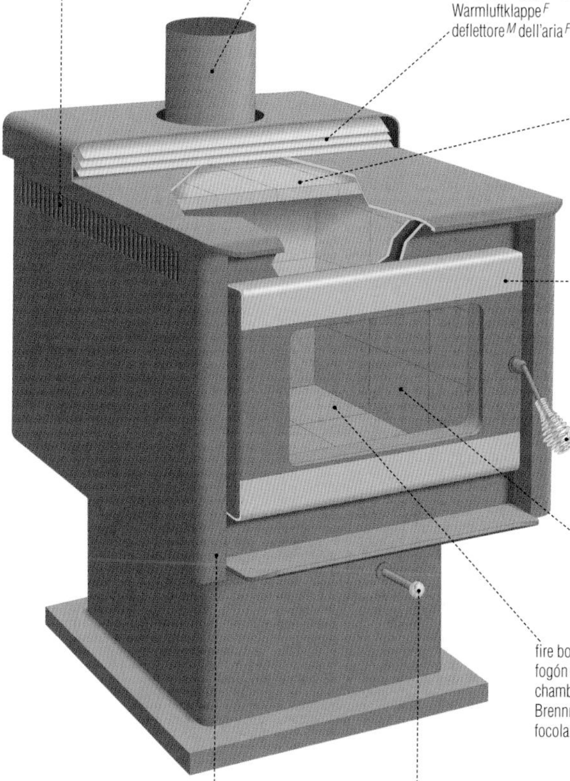

loading door
puerta^{F} del fogón^{M}
porte^{F}-foyer^{M}
Fülltür^{F}
sportello^{M} di carico^{M}

handle
manilla^{F}
poignée^{F}
Griff^{M}
manopola^{F}

firebrick
ladrillo^{M} refractario
brique^{F} réfractaire
Schamottestein^{M}
mattone^{M} refrattario

fire box
fogón^{M}
chambre^{F} de combustion^{F}
Brennraum^{M}
focolare^{M}

box
caja^{F} para la ceniza^{F}
caisson^{M}
Blechverkleidung^{F}
involucro^{M}

air inlet control
control^{M} de la entrada^{F} de aire^{M}
manette^{F} d'admission^{F} d'air^{M}
Luftzufuhrregler^{M}
comando^{M} del tiraggio^{M}

air-conditioning appliances

aparatos^M acondicionadores^M | appareils^M de conditionnement^M de l'air^M | Klimageräte^N | apparecchi^M per il condizionamento^M dell'aria^F

programmable thermostat
termostato^M programable
thermostat^M programmable
programmierbarer Thermostat^M
termostato^M programmabile

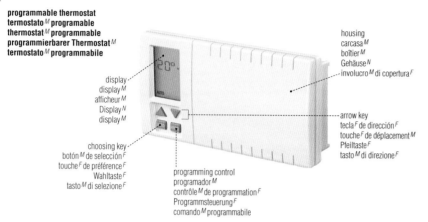

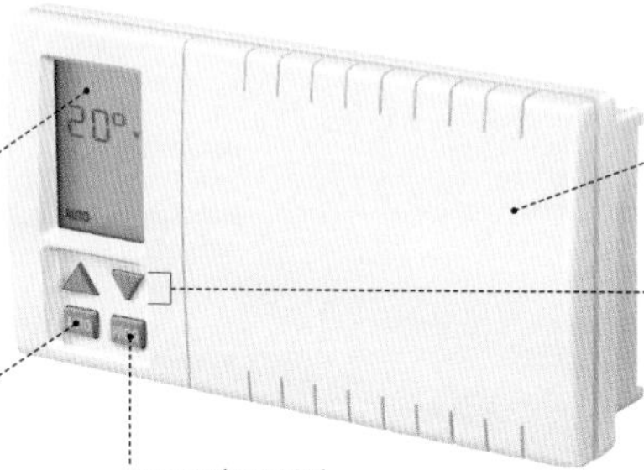
housing
carcasa^M
boîtier^M
Gehäuse^N
involucro^M di copertura^F
display
display^M
afficheur^M
Display^N
display^M
arrow key
tecla^F de dirección^F
touche^F de déplacement^M
Pfeiltaste^F
tasto^M di direzione^F
choosing key
botón^M de selección^F
touche^F de préférence^F
Wahltaste^F
tasto^M di selezione^F
programming control
programador^M
contrôle^M de programmation^F
Programmsteuerung^F
comando^M programmabile

hygrometer
higrómetro^M
hygromètre^M
Hygrometer^N
igrometro^M

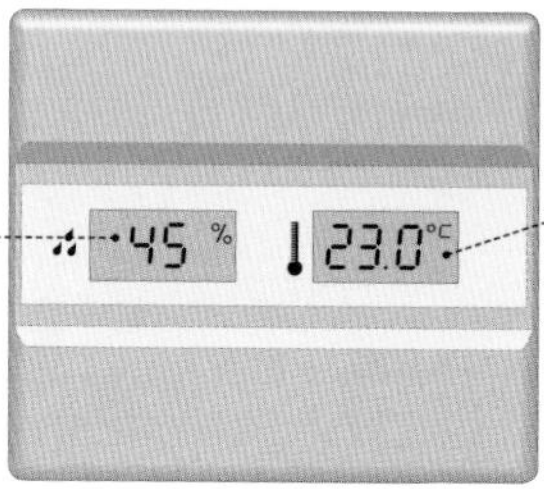
temperature
temperatura^F
température^F
Temperatur^F
temperatura^F
humidity
humedad^F del aire^M
humidité^F
Luftfeuchtigkeit^F
umidità^F

room thermostat
termostato^M
thermostat^M d'ambiance^F
Raumthermostat^M
termostato^M ambiente^M

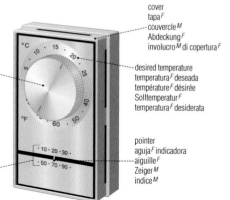

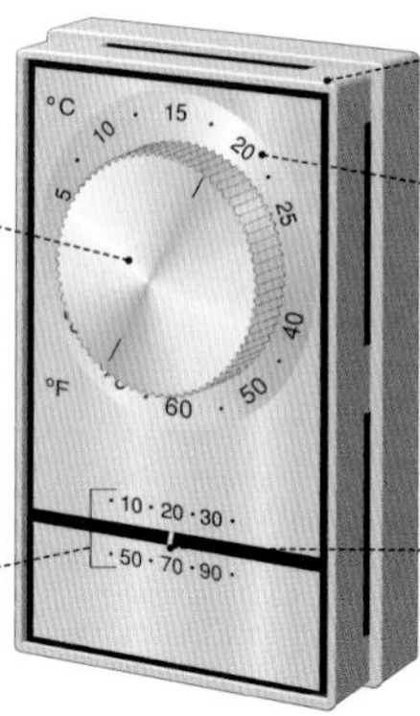
cover
tapa^F
couvercle^M
Abdeckung^F
involucro^M di copertura^F
desired temperature
temperatura^F deseada
température^F désirée
Solltemperatur^F
temperatura^F desiderata
temperature control
control^M de temperatura^F
réglage^M de la température^F
Temperaturregler^M
regolazione^F della temperatura^F
pointer
aguja^F indicadora
aiguille^F
Zeiger^M
indice^M
actual temperature
temperatura^F real
température^F ambiante
tatsächliche Temperatur^F
temperatura^F ambiente^M

air-conditioning appliances

room air conditioner
acondicionador M de aire M
climatiseur M de fenêtre F
Raumklimaanlage F
condizionatore M d'aria F da camera F

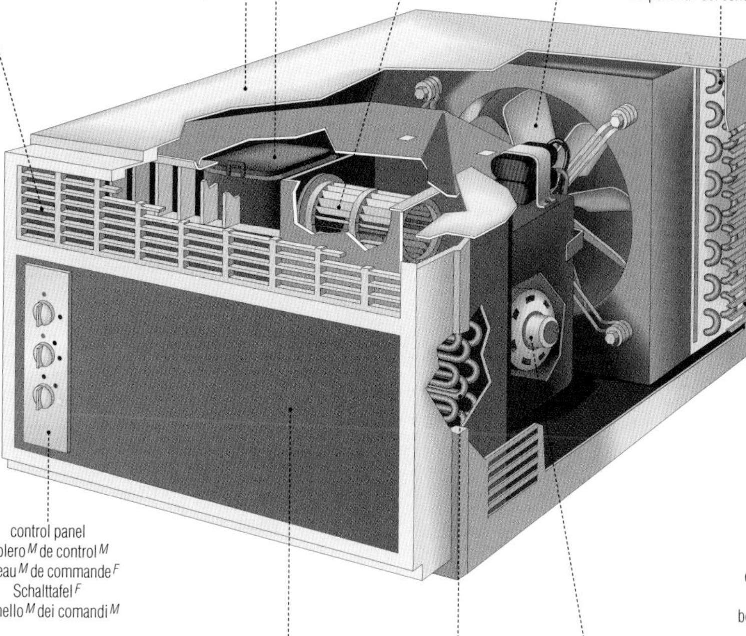
fan motor
motor M del ventilador M
moteur M du ventilateur M
Ventilatormotor M
motore M del ventilatore M
louver
rejilla F de ventilación F
déflecteur M
Lüftungsschlitz M mit Jalousieverschluss M
persiana F di ventilazione F
evaporator blower
ventilador M del evaporador M
ventilateur M de l'évaporateur M
Verdampfergebläse N
ventilatore M del vaporizzatore M
condenser fan
ventilador M del condensador M
ventilateur M du condenseur M
Kondensatorventilator M
ventilatore M del condensatore M
casing
cubierta F
boîtier M
Gehäuse N
involucro M di copertura F
condenser coil
serpentín M del condensador M
serpentin M du condenseur M
Wärmetauscher M
serpentina F del condensatore M
control panel
tablero M de control M
tableau M de commande F
Schalttafel F
pannello M dei comandi M
vent
respiradero M
évent M latéral
Entlüfter M
bocca F laterale
grille
rejilla F
grillage M
Gitter N
griglia F
evaporator coil
serpentín F del evaporador M
serpentin M de l'évaporateur M
Verdampferspirale F
serpentina F del vaporizzatore M
blower motor
motor M del ventilador M
moteur M du ventilateur M
Ventilatormotor M
motore M del ventilatore M

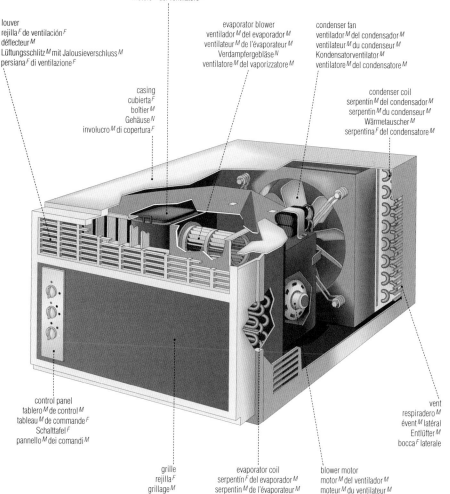

plumbing system

cañerías^{F} | circuit^{M} de plomberie^{F} | Sanitärinstallationssystem^{N} | impianto^{M} idraulico

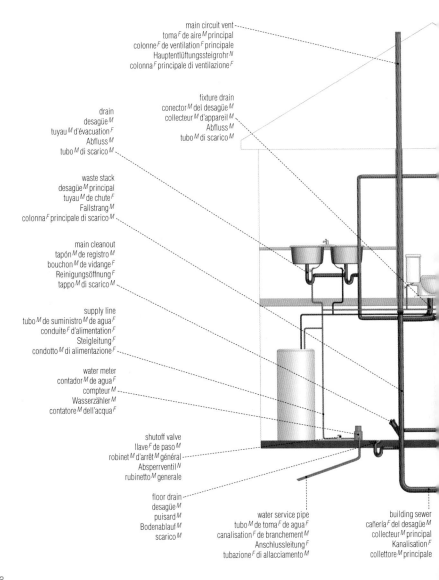

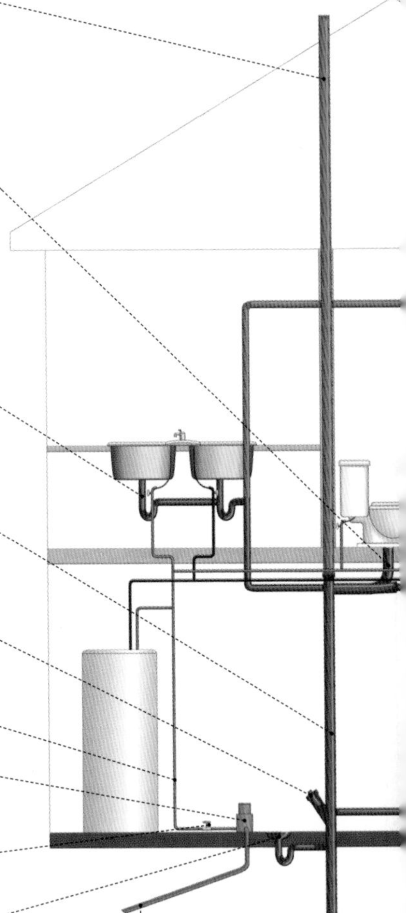

main circuit vent
toma^{F} de aire^{M} principal
colonne^{F} de ventilation^{F} principale
Hauptentlüftungssteigrohr^{N}
colonna^{F} principale di ventilazione^{F}

fixture drain
conector^{M} del desagüe^{M}
collecteur^{M} d'appareil^{M}
Abfluss^{M}
tubo^{M} di scarico^{M}

drain
desagüe^{M}
tuyau^{M} d'évacuation^{F}
Abfluss^{M}
tubo^{M} di scarico^{M}

waste stack
desagüe^{M} principal
tuyau^{M} de chute^{F}
Fallstrang^{M}
colonna^{F} principale di scarico^{M}

main cleanout
tapón^{M} de registro^{M}
bouchon^{M} de vidange^{F}
Reinigungsöffnung^{F}
tappo^{M} di scarico^{M}

supply line
tubo^{M} de suministro^{M} de agua^{F}
conduite^{F} d'alimentation^{F}
Steigleitung^{F}
condotto^{M} di alimentazione^{F}

water meter
contador^{M} de agua^{F}
compteur^{M}
Wasserzähler^{M}
contatore^{M} dell'acqua^{F}

shutoff valve
llave^{F} de paso^{M}
robinet^{M} d'arrêt^{M} général
Absperrventil^{N}
rubinetto^{M} generale

floor drain
desagüe^{M}
puisard^{M}
Bodenablauf^{M}
scarico^{M}

water service pipe
tubo^{M} de toma^{F} de agua^{F}
canalisation^{F} de branchement^{M}
Anschlussleitung^{F}
tubazione^{F} di allacciamento^{M}

building sewer
cañería^{F} del desagüe^{M}
collecteur^{M} principal
Kanalisation^{F}
collettore^{M} principale

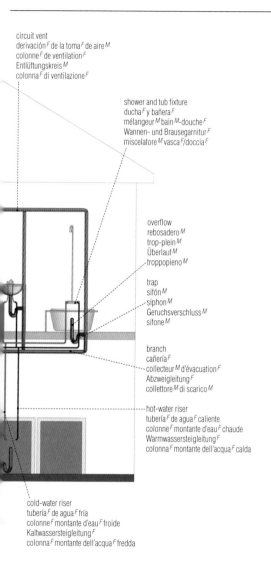

circuit vent
derivación[F] de la toma[F] de aire[M]
colonne[F] de ventilation[F]
Entlüftungskreis[M]
colonna[F] di ventilazione[F]

shower and tub fixture
ducha[F] y bañera[F]
mélangeur[M] bain[M]-douche[F]
Wannen- und Brausegarnitur[F]
miscelatore[M] vasca[F]/doccia[F]

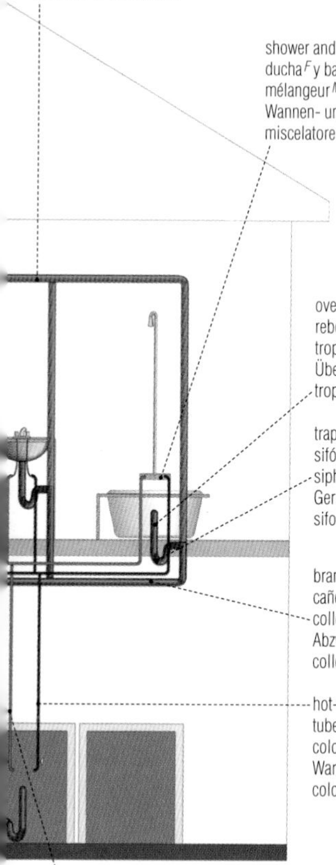

overflow
rebosadero[M]
trop-plein[M]
Überlauf[M]
troppopieno[M]

trap
sifón[M]
siphon[M]
Geruchsverschluss[M]
sifone[M]

branch
cañería[F]
collecteur[M] d'évacuation[F]
Abzweigleitung[F]
collettore[M] di scarico[M]

hot-water riser
tubería[F] de agua[F] caliente
colonne[F] montante d'eau[F] chaude
Warmwassersteigleitung[F]
colonna[F] montante dell'acqua[F] calda

cold-water riser
tubería[F] de agua[F] fría
colonne[F] montante d'eau[F] froide
Kaltwassersteigleitung[F]
colonna[F] montante dell'acqua[F] fredda

draining circuit
circuito[M] de desagüe[M]
circuit[M] d'évacuation[F]
Abflusskreislauf[M]
rete[F] di scarico[M]

hot-water circuit
circuito[M] de agua[F] caliente
circuit[M] d'eau[F] chaude
Warmwasserkreislauf[M]
rete[F] di distribuzione[F] dell'acqua[F] calda

ventilating circuit
circuito[M] de ventilación[F]
circuit[M] de ventilation[F]
Entlüftungskreislauf[M]
rete[F] di ventilazione[F]

cold-water circuit
circuito[M] de agua[F] fría
circuit[M] d'eau[F] froide
Kaltwasserkreislauf[M]
rete[F] di distribuzione[F] dell'acqua[F] fredda

pedestal-type sump pump

bomba^F tipo^M pedestal^M para sumidero^M | pompe^F de puisard^M | Schmutzwasserhebeanlage^F | pompa^F di spurgo^M

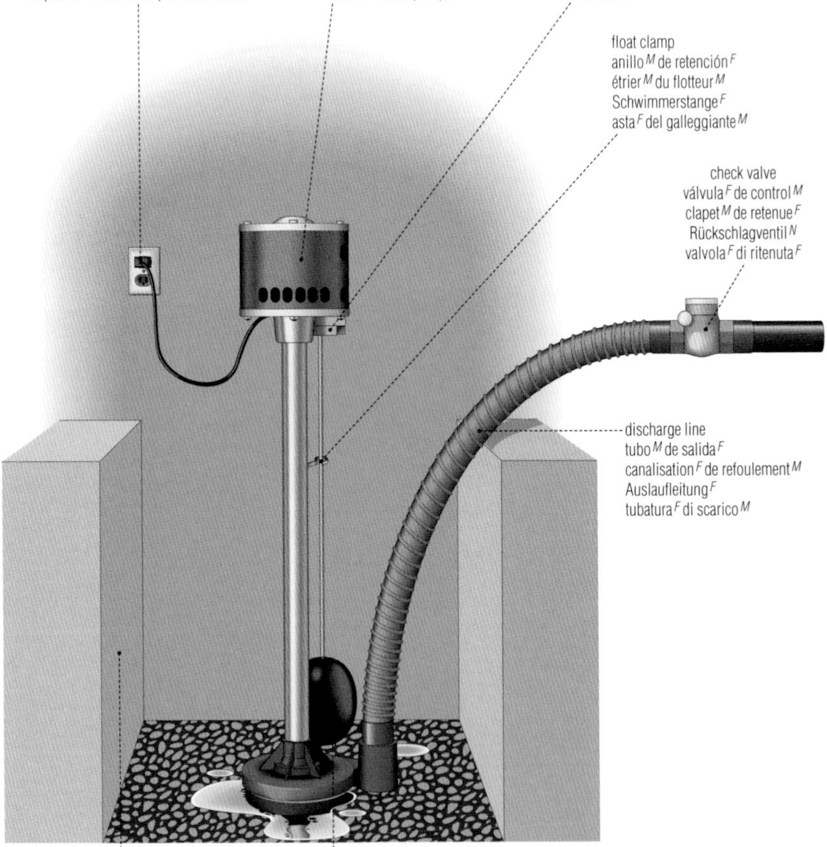
grounded receptacle
contacto^M con conexión^F de tierra^F
prise^F avec borne^F de terre^F
wasserdichter Stromanschluss^M
impianto^M elettrico impermeabilizzato
pump motor
motor^M de la bomba^F
moteur^M électrique
Pumpenmotor^M
motore^M della pompa^F
switch
interruptor^M de arranque^M automático
contacteur^M
Ein-/Ausschalter^M
interruttore^M
float clamp
anillo^M de retención^F
étrier^M du flotteur^M
Schwimmerstange^F
asta^F del galleggiante^M
check valve
válvula^F de control^M
clapet^M de retenue^F
Rückschlagventil^N
valvola^F di ritenuta^F
discharge line
tubo^M de salida^F
canalisation^F de refoulement^M
Auslaufleitung^F
tubatura^F di scarico^M
sump
sumidero^M
puisard^M
Pumpensumpf^M
pozzetto^M
float
flotador^M
flotteur^M
Schwimmer^M
galleggiante^M

septic tank

fosa*F* séptica | fosse*F* septique | Versitzgrube*F* | fossa*F* biologica

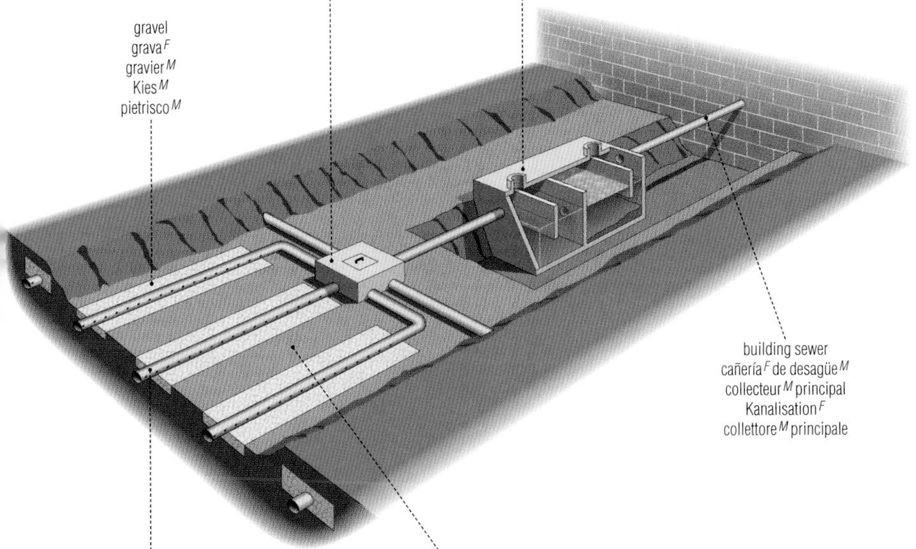
distribution box
caja F de distribución F
distributeur M
Zulaufverteiler M
vaschetta F di distribuzione F
tank
tanque M
réservoir M
Becken N
vasca F
gravel
grava F
gravier M
Kies M
pietrisco M
building sewer
cañería F de desagüe M
collecteur M principal
Kanalisation F
collettore M principale
perforated pipe
cañería F perforada
drain M
Lochrohr N
tubo M perdente
leach field
área F de lixiviación F
champ M d'épandage M
Sickeranlage F
campo M di dispersione F

bathroom

cuarto[M] de baño[M] | salle[F] de bains[M] | Badezimmer[N] | stanza[F] da bagno[M]

shower head
alcachofa[F] de la ducha[F]
pomme[F] de douche[F]
Brausenkopf[M]
doccia[F]

spray hose
manguera[F]
flexible[M]
Brauseschlauch[M]
tubo[M] flessibile

shower stall
cabina[F] de la ducha[F]
cabine[F] de douche[F]
Duschkabine[F]
box[M] doccia[F]

sliding door
puerta[F] plegable
porte[F] coulissante
Schiebetür[F]
porta[F] scorrevole

bidet
bidé[M]
bidet[M]
Bidet[N]
bidè[M]

tissue holder
portarrollos[M] de papel[M] higiénico
porte-rouleau[M]
Toilettenpapierhalter[M]
portarotolo[M]

toilet tank
cisterna[F] del inodoro[M]
réservoir[M] de chasse[F] d'eau[F]
Spülkasten[M]
sciacquone[M]

toilet
inodoro[M]
w.-c.[M]
Toilette[F]
water[M]

seat cover
asiento[M]
abattant[M]
Sitz[M]
sedile[M]

tub platform
zócalo[M] de la bañera[F]
banquette[F]
Podest[N]
piattaforma[F] della vasca[F]

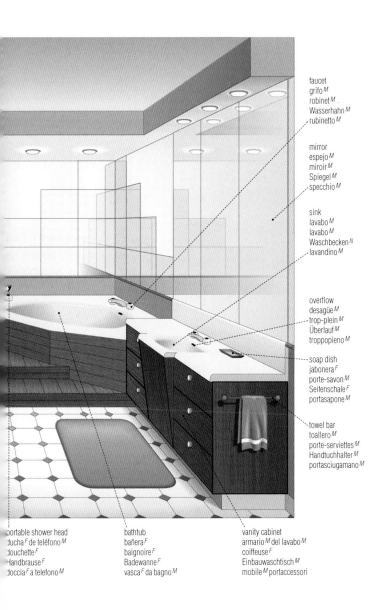

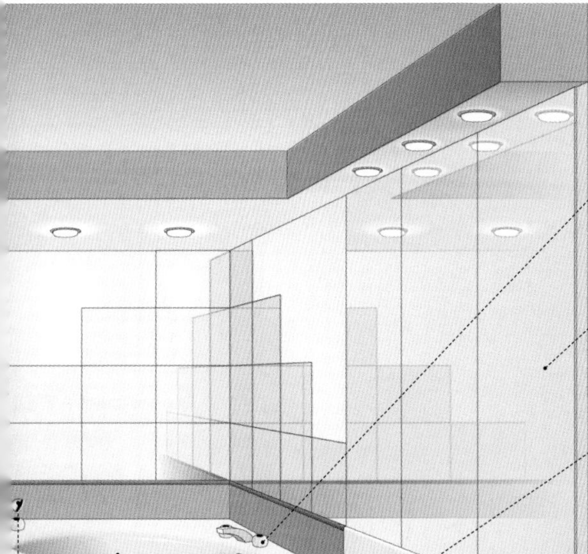
faucet
grifo [M]
robinet [M]
Wasserhahn [M]
rubinetto [M]

mirror
espejo [M]
miroir [M]
Spiegel [M]
specchio [M]

sink
lavabo [M]
lavabo [M]
Waschbecken [N]
lavandino [M]

overflow
desagüe [M]
trop-plein [M]
Überlauf [M]
troppopieno [M]

soap dish
jabonera [F]
porte-savon [M]
Seifenschale [F]
portasapone [M]

towel bar
toallero [M]
porte-serviettes [M]
Handtuchhalter [M]
portasciugamano [M]

portable shower head
ducha [F] de teléfono [M]
douchette [F]
Handbrause [F]
doccia [F] a telefono [M]

bathtub
bañera [F]
baignoire [F]
Badewanne [F]
vasca [F] da bagno [M]

vanity cabinet
armario [M] del lavabo [M]
coiffeuse [F]
Einbauwaschtisch [M]
mobile [M] portaccessori

toilet

inodoro[M] | w.-c.[M] | Toilette[F] | gabinetto[M]

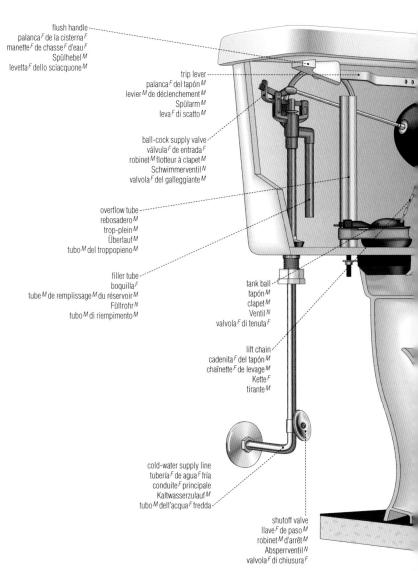

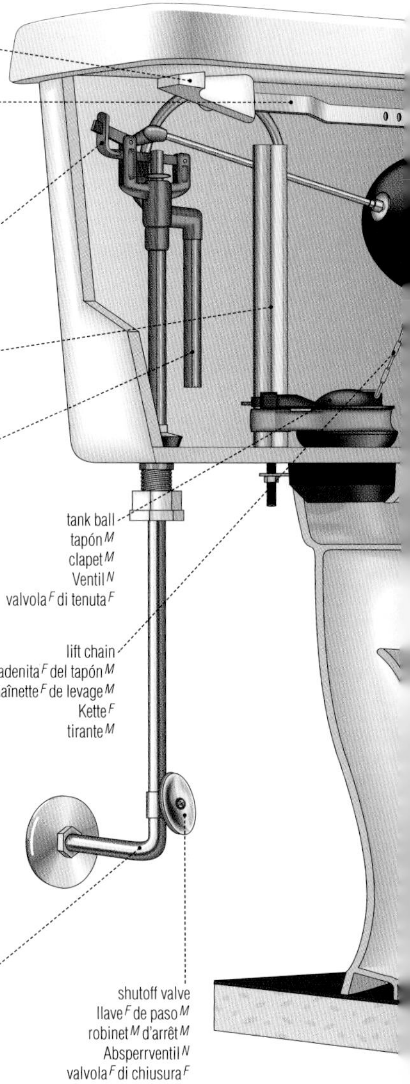
flush handle
palanca[F] de la cisterna[F]
manette[F] de chasse[F] d'eau[F]
Spülhebel[M]
levetta[F] dello sciacquone[M]
trip lever
palanca[F] del tapón[M]
levier[M] de déclenchement[M]
Spülarm[M]
leva[F] di scatto[M]
ball-cock supply valve
válvula[F] de entrada[F]
robinet[M] flotteur à clapet[M]
Schwimmerventil[N]
valvola[F] del galleggiante[M]
overflow tube
rebosadero[M]
trop-plein[M]
Überlauf[M]
tubo[M] del troppopieno[M]
filler tube
boquilla[F]
tube[M] de remplissage[M] du réservoir[M]
Füllrohr[N]
tubo[M] di riempimento[M]
tank ball
tapón[M]
clapet[M]
Ventil[N]
valvola[F] di tenuta[F]
lift chain
cadenita[F] del tapón[M]
chaînette[F] de levage[M]
Kette[F]
tirante[M]
cold-water supply line
tubería[F] de agua[F] fría
conduite[F] principale
Kaltwasserzulauf[M]
tubo[M] dell'acqua[F] fredda
shutoff valve
llave[F] de paso[M]
robinet[M] d'arrêt[M]
Absperrventil[N]
valvola[F] di chiusura[F]

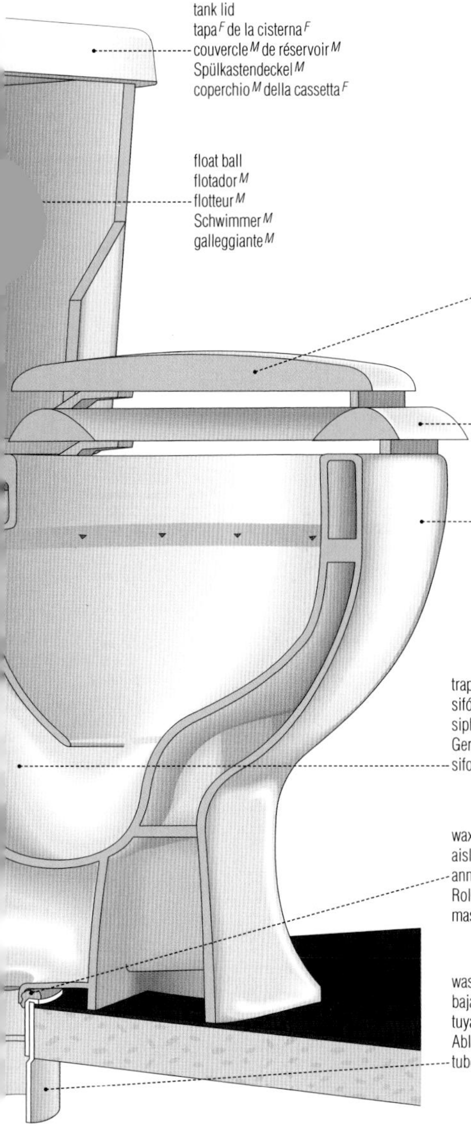
tank lid
tapa F de la cisterna F
couvercle M de réservoir M
Spülkastendeckel M
coperchio M della cassetta F
float ball
flotador M
flotteur M
Schwimmer M
galleggiante M
seat cover
tapa F del inodoro M
couvercle M
Klosettdeckel M
coperchio M del sedile M
seat
asiento M
abattant M
Sitz M
sedile M
toilet bowl
taza F
cuvette F
Klosettbecken N
vaso M
trap
sifón M
siphon M
Geruchsverschluss M
sifone M
wax seal
aislante M de cera F
anneau M d'étanchéité F en cire F
Rollring M
mastice M di tenuta F
waste pipe
bajante M
tuyau M de chute F
Ablaufrohr N
tubo M di scarico M

examples of branching

ejemplos^M de conexiones^F | exemples^M de branchement^M | Beispiele^N für Anschlüsse^M | esempi^M di allacciamento^M

garbage disposal sink
fregadero^M con triturador^M de basura^F
évier^M-broyeur^M
Spüle^F mit Müllschlucker^M
lavello^M con tritarifiuti^M

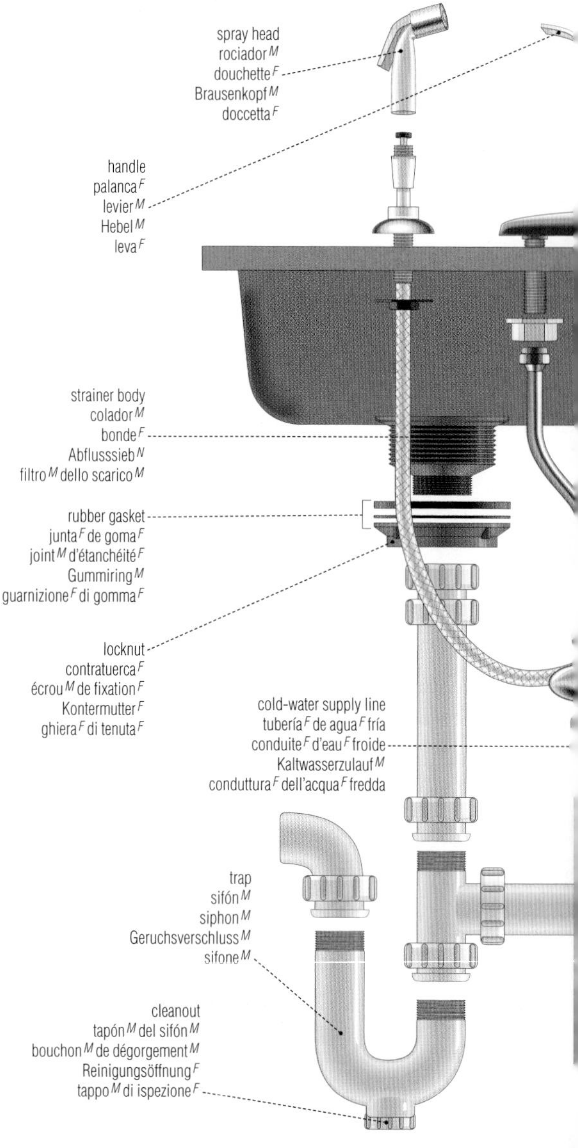
spray head
rociador M
douchette F
Brausenkopf M
doccetta F
handle
palanca F
levier M
Hebel M
leva F
strainer body
colador M
bonde F
Abflusssieb N
filtro M dello scarico M
rubber gasket
junta F de goma F
joint M d'étanchéité F
Gummiring M
guarnizione F di gomma F
locknut
contratuerca F
écrou M de fixation F
Kontermutter F
ghiera F di tenuta F
cold-water supply line
tubería F de agua F fría
conduite F d'eau F froide
Kaltwasserzulauf M
conduttura F dell'acqua F fredda
trap
sifón M
siphon M
Geruchsverschluss M
sifone M
cleanout
tapón M del sifón M
bouchon M de dégorgement M
Reinigungsöffnung F
tappo M di ispezione F

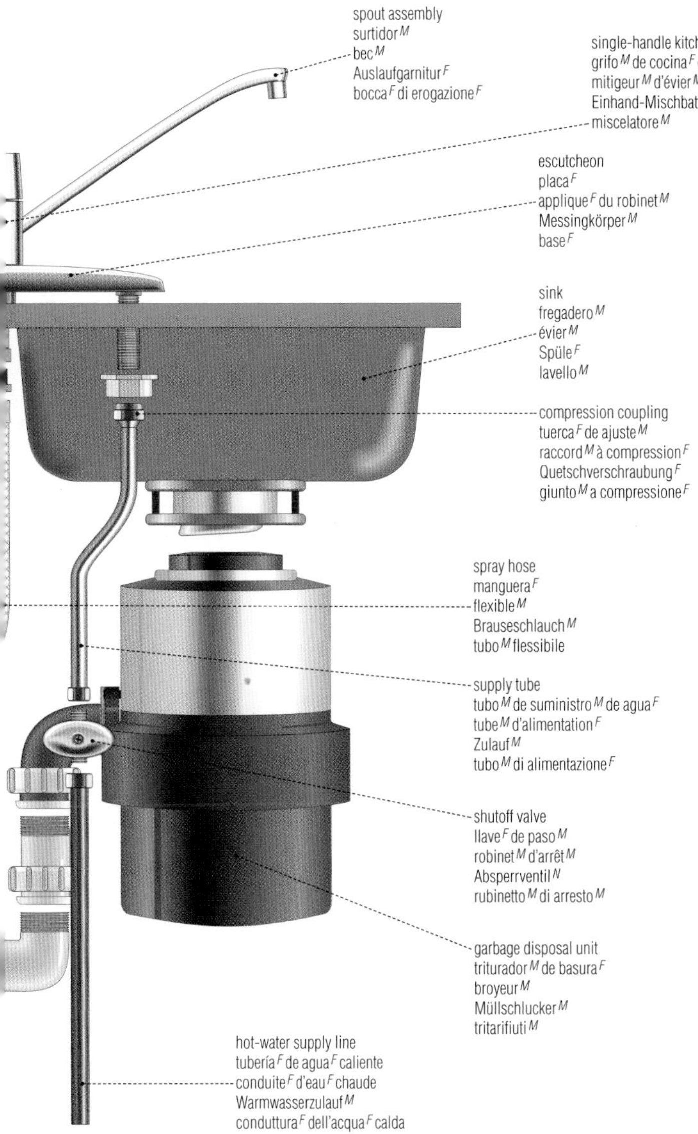
spout assembly
surtidor[M]
bec[M]
Auslaufgarnitur[F]
bocca[F] di erogazione[F]
single-handle kitchen faucet
grifo[M] de cocina[F] de tres vías[F]
mitigeur[M] d'évier[M]
Einhand-Mischbatterie[F]
miscelatore[M]
escutcheon
placa[F]
applique[F] du robinet[M]
Messingkörper[M]
base[F]
sink
fregadero[M]
évier[M]
Spüle[F]
lavello[M]
compression coupling
tuerca[F] de ajuste[M]
raccord[M] à compression[F]
Quetschverschraubung[F]
giunto[M] a compressione[F]
spray hose
manguera[F]
flexible[M]
Brauseschlauch[M]
tubo[M] flessibile
supply tube
tubo[M] de suministro[M] de agua[F]
tube[M] d'alimentation[F]
Zulauf[M]
tubo[M] di alimentazione[F]
shutoff valve
llave[F] de paso[M]
robinet[M] d'arrêt[M]
Absperrventil[N]
rubinetto[M] di arresto[M]
garbage disposal unit
triturador[M] de basura[F]
broyeur[M]
Müllschlucker[M]
tritarifiuti[M]
hot-water supply line
tubería[F] de agua[F] caliente
conduite[F] d'eau[F] chaude
Warmwasserzulauf[M]
conduttura[F] dell'acqua[F] calda

examples of branching

washer
lavadora F
lave-linge M
Waschmaschine F
lavatrice F

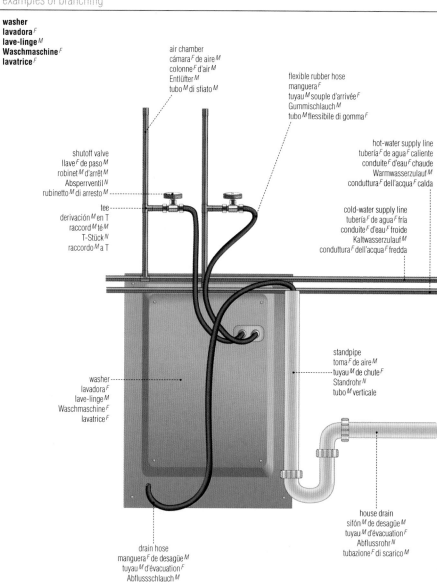

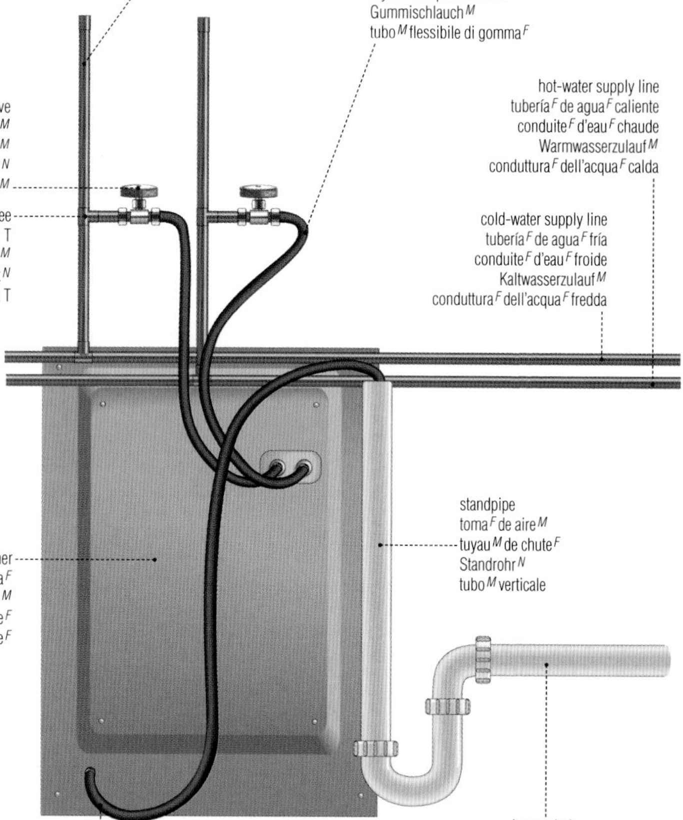
air chamber
cámara F de aire M
colonne F d'air M
Entlüfter M
tubo M di sfiato M
flexible rubber hose
manguera F
tuyau M souple d'arrivée F
Gummischlauch M
tubo M flessibile di gomma F
hot-water supply line
tubería F de agua F caliente
conduite F d'eau F chaude
Warmwasserzulauf M
conduttura F dell'acqua F calda
shutoff valve
llave F de paso M
robinet M d'arrêt M
Absperrventil N
rubinetto M di arresto M
tee
derivación M en T
raccord M té M
T-Stück N
raccordo M a T
cold-water supply line
tubería F de agua F fría
conduite F d'eau F froide
Kaltwasserzulauf M
conduttura F dell'acqua F fredda
standpipe
toma F de aire M
tuyau M de chute F
Standrohr N
tubo M verticale
washer
lavadora F
lave-linge M
Waschmaschine F
lavatrice F
house drain
sifón M de desagüe M
tuyau M d'évacuation F
Abflussrohr N
tubazione F di scarico M
drain hose
manguera F de desagüe M
tuyau M d'évacuation F
Abflussschlauch M
tubo M di scarico M

dishwasher
lavavajillas F
lave-vaisselle M
Geschirrspülmaschine F
lavastoviglie F

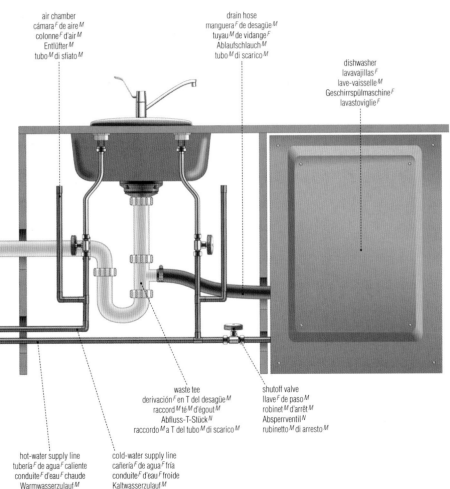

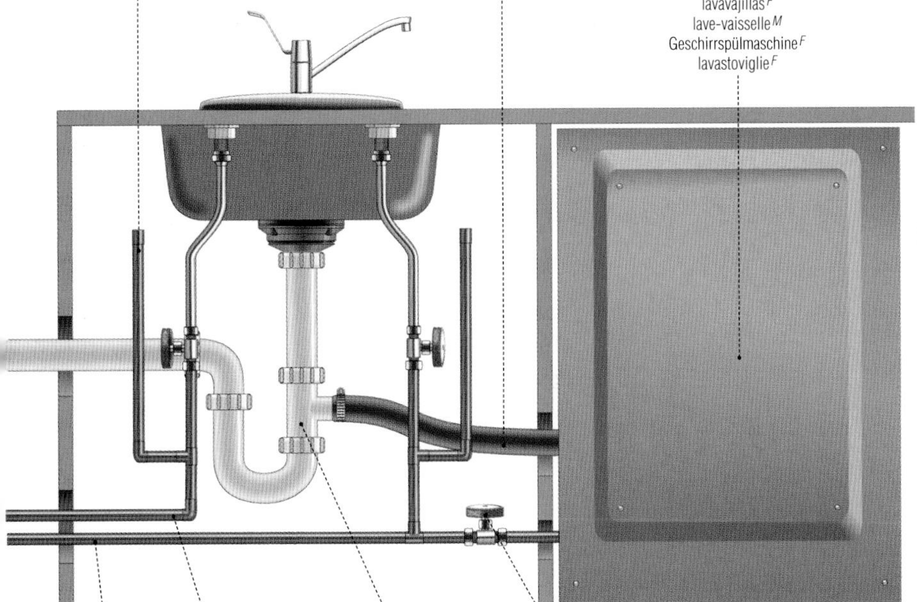
air chamber
cámara F de aire M
colonne F d'air M
Entlüfter M
tubo M di sfiato M
drain hose
manguera F de desagüe M
tuyau M de vidange F
Ablaufschlauch M
tubo M di scarico M
dishwasher
lavavajillas F
lave-vaisselle M
Geschirrspülmaschine F
lavastoviglie F
waste tee
derivación F en T del desagüe M
raccord M té M d'égout M
Abfluss-T-Stück N
raccordo M a T del tubo M di scarico M
shutoff valve
llave F de paso M
robinet M d'arrêt M
Absperrventil N
rubinetto M di arresto M
hot-water supply line
tubería F de agua F caliente
conduite F d'eau F chaude
Warmwasserzulauf M
conduttura F dell'acqua F calda
cold-water supply line
cañería F de agua F fría
conduite F d'eau F froide
Kaltwasserzulauf M
conduttura F dell'acqua F fredda

distribution panel

cuadro[M] de distribución[F] | panneau[M] de distribution[F] | Verteilerkasten[M] | pannello[M] di distribuzione[F]

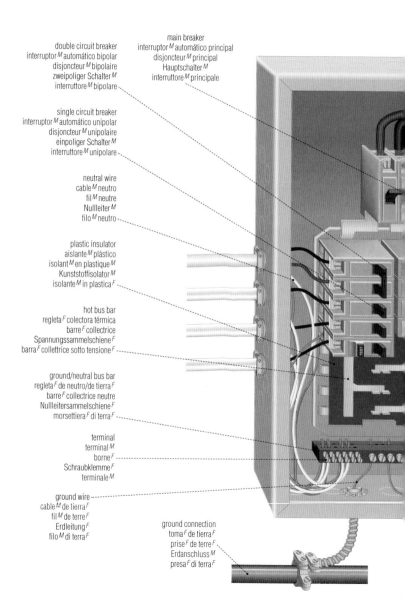

double circuit breaker
interruptor[M] automático bipolar
disjoncteur[M] bipolaire
zweipoliger Schalter[M]
interruttore[M] bipolare

main breaker
interruptor[M] automático principal
disjoncteur[M] principal
Hauptschalter[M]
interruttore[M] principale

single circuit breaker
interruptor[M] automático unipolar
disjoncteur[M] unipolaire
einpoliger Schalter[M]
interruttore[M] unipolare

neutral wire
cable[M] neutro
fil[M] neutre
Nullleiter[M]
filo[M] neutro

plastic insulator
aislante[M] plástico
isolant[M] en plastique[M]
Kunststoffisolator[M]
isolante[M] in plastica[F]

hot bus bar
regleta[F] colectora térmica
barre[F] collectrice
Spannungssammelschiene[F]
barra[F] collettrice sotto tensione[F]

ground/neutral bus bar
regleta[F] de neutro/de tierra[F]
barre[F] collectrice neutre
Nullleitersammelschiene[F]
morsettiera[F] di terra[F]

terminal
terminal[M]
borne[F]
Schraubklemme[F]
terminale[M]

ground wire
cable[M] de tierra[F]
fil[M] de terre[F]
Erdleitung[F]
filo[M] di terra[F]

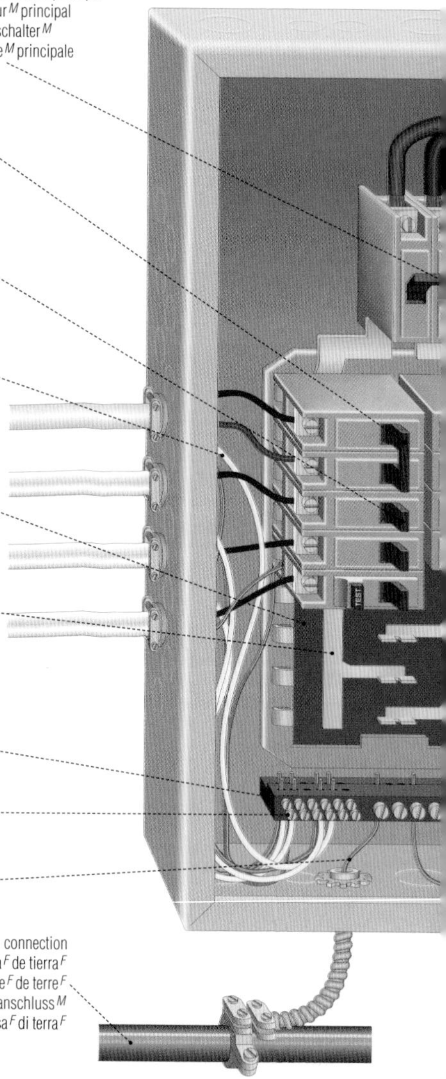
TEST

ground connection
toma[F] de tierra[F]
prise[F] de terre[F]
Erdanschluss[M]
presa[F] di terra[F]

HOUSE AND DO-IT-YOURSELF

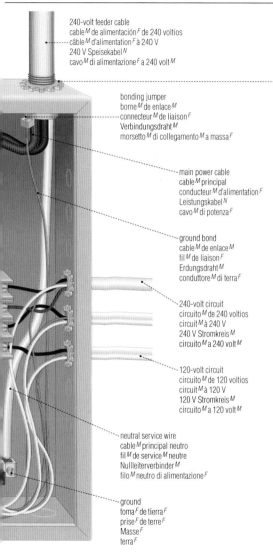

240-volt feeder cable
cable[M] de alimentación[F] de 240 voltios
câble[M] d'alimentation[F] à 240 V
240 V Speisekabel[N]
cavo[M] di alimentazione[F] a 240 volt[M]

connector
conector[M]
connecteur[M] de conduit[M] d'entrée[F]
Durchgangstülle[F]
connettore[M]

bonding jumper
borne[M] de enlace[M]
connecteur[M] de liaison[F]
Verbindungsdraht[M]
morsetto[M] di collegamento[M] a massa[F]

main power cable
cable[M] principal
conducteur[M] d'alimentation[F]
Leistungskabel[N]
cavo[M] di potenza[F]

ground bond
cable[M] de enlace[M]
fil[M] de liaison[F]
Erdungsdraht[M]
conduttore[M] di terra[F]

240-volt circuit
circuito[M] de 240 voltios
circuit[M] à 240 V
240 V Stromkreis[M]
circuito[M] a 240 volt[M]

120-volt circuit
circuito[M] de 120 voltios
circuit[M] à 120 V
120 V Stromkreis[M]
circuito[M] a 120 volt[M]

neutral service wire
cable[M] principal neutro
fil[M] de service[M] neutre
Nullleiterverbinder[M]
filo[M] neutro di alimentazione[F]

ground
toma[F] de tierra[F]
prise[F] de terre[F]
Masse[F]
terra[F]

contact devices

dispositivos^M de contacto^M | dispositifs^M de contact^M | Unterputzdose^F | dispositivi^M di contatto^M

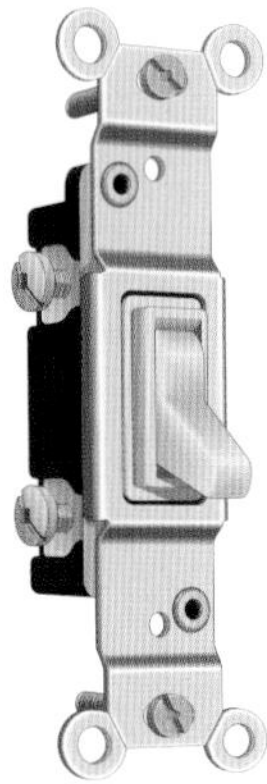

switch
interruptor ^M
interrupteur ^M
Schalter ^M
interruttore ^M

dimmer switch
conmutador ^M **de intensidad** ^F
gradateur ^M
Dimmerschalter ^M
reostato ^M

switch plate
placa ^F **del interruptor** ^M
plaque ^F **de commutateur** ^M
Schalterabdeckplatte ^F
placca ^F **dell'interruttore** ^M

electrical box
caja ^F **de conexiones** ^F
boîte ^F **d'encastrement** ^M
Buchsenhalter ^M
scatola ^F **da incasso** ^M

lighting

iluminación[F] | éclairage[M] | Beleuchtung[F] | illuminazione[F]

parts of a lamp socket
componentes[F] del portalámpara[M]
éléments[M] d'une douille[F] de lampe[F]
Teile[M/N] einer Lampenfassung[F]
componenti[M] del portalampada[M]

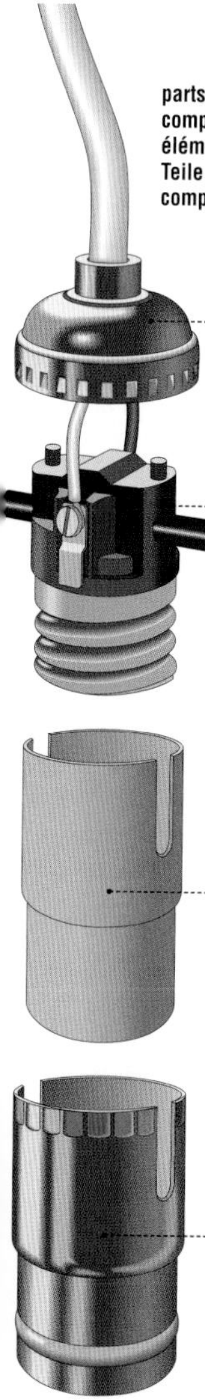
cap
tapa[F]
capuchon[M]
Kappe[F]
cappellotto[M]
socket
casquillo[M]
douille[F]
Fassung[F]
zoccolo[M]
insulating sleeve
manga[F] de aislamiento[M]
gaine[F] isolante
Isolierhülse[F]
manicotto[M] isolante
outer shell
cubierta[F]
enveloppe[F]
äußere Hülse[F]
protezione[F] esterna

bulb
ampolla[F] de vidrio[M]
ampoule[F]
Glaskolben[M]
bulbo[M]

tungsten-halogen lamp
lámpara[F] halógena
lampe[F] à halogène[M]
Glaskolben[M]
lampada[F] alogena al tungsteno[M]

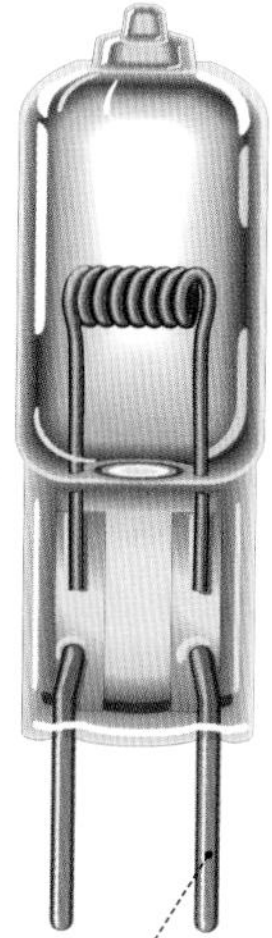
pin
contacto[M]
broche[F]
Stift[M]
spinotto[M]

bayonet base
bombilla[F] de bayoneta[F]
culot[M] à baïonnette[F]
Bajonettfassung[F]
attacco[M] a baionetta[F]

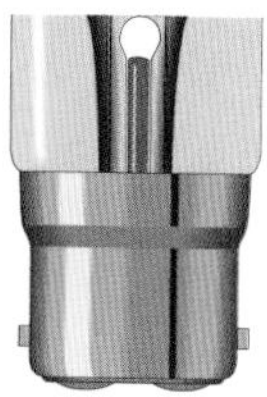

screw base
bombilla[F] de rosca[F]
culot[M] à vis[F]
Schraubfassung[F]
attacco[M] a vite[F]

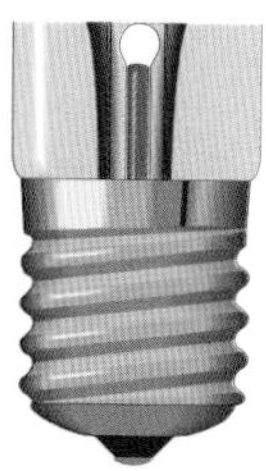

lighting

incandescent lamp
bombilla F incandescente
lampe F à incandescence F
Glühlampe F
lampadina F a incandescenza F

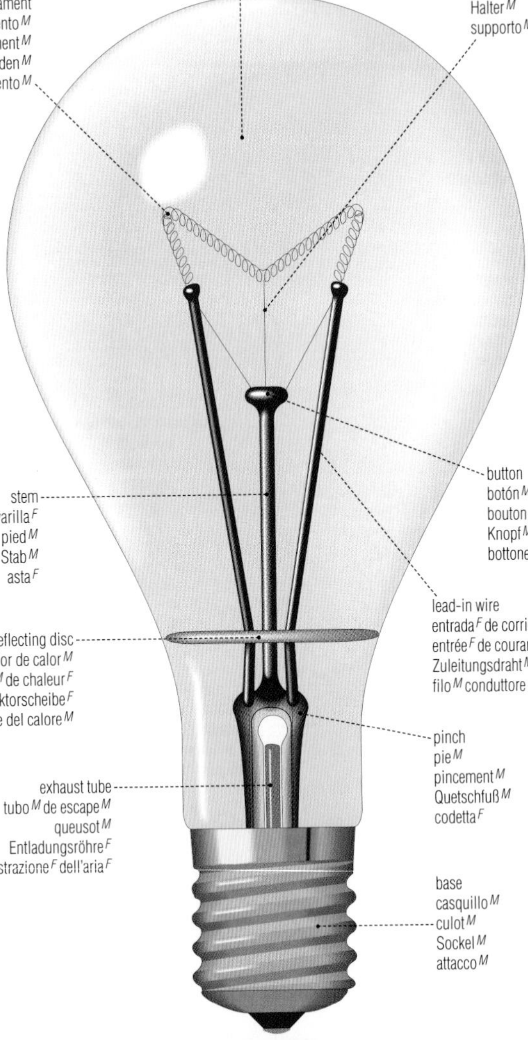
inert gas
gas M inerte
gaz M inerte
Edelgas N
gas M inerte
support
soporte M
support M
Halter M
supporto M
filament
filamento M
filament M
Glühfaden M
filamento M
button
botón M
bouton M
Knopf M
bottone M
stem
varilla F
pied M
Stab M
asta F
lead-in wire
entrada F de corriente F
entrée F de courant M
Zuleitungsdraht M
filo M conduttore
heat deflecting disc
disco M desviador de calor M
déflecteur M de chaleur F
Wärmedeflektorscheibe F
disco M deflettore del calore M
pinch
pie M
pincement M
Quetschfuß M
codetta F
exhaust tube
tubo M de escape M
queusot M
Entladungsröhre F
tubo M di estrazione F dell'aria F
base
casquillo M
culot M
Sockel M
attacco M

tungsten-halogen lamp
lámpara^F halógena
lampe^F à halogène^M
Wolfram-Halogenlampe^F
lampada^F alogena al tungsteno^M

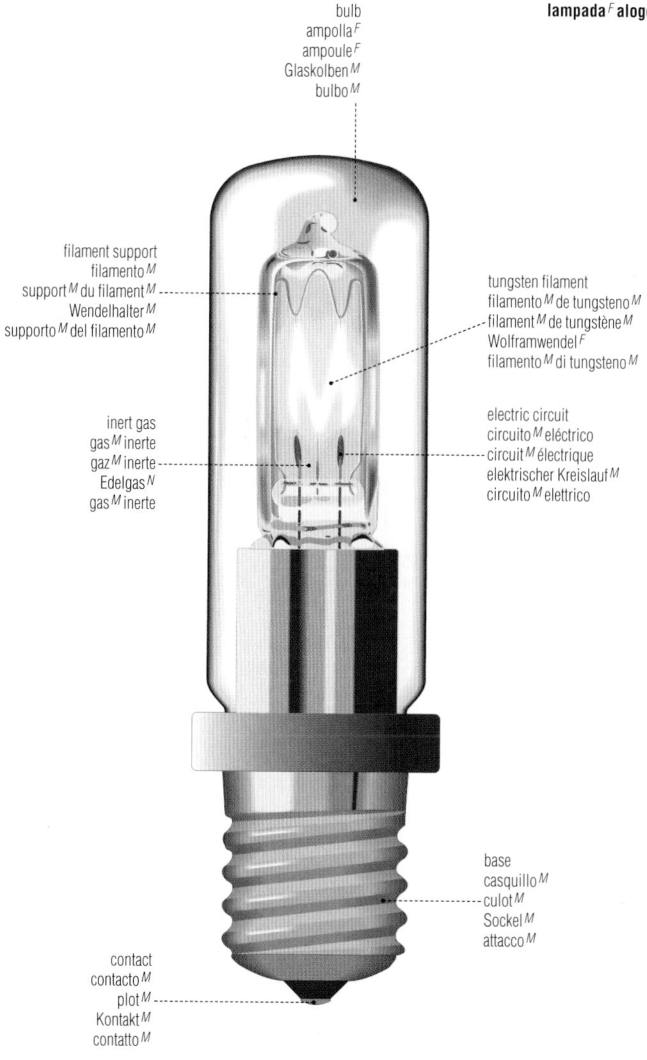
bulb
ampolla F
ampoule F
Glaskolben M
bulbo M
filament support
filamento M
support M du filament M
Wendelhalter M
supporto M del filamento M
tungsten filament
filamento M de tungsteno M
filament M de tungstène M
Wolframwendel F
filamento M di tungsteno M
inert gas
gas M inerte
gaz M inerte
Edelgas N
gas M inerte
electric circuit
circuito M eléctrico
circuit M électrique
elektrischer Kreislauf M
circuito M elettrico
base
casquillo M
culot M
Sockel M
attacco M
contact
contacto M
plot M
Kontakt M
contatto M

lighting

energy-saving bulb
bombilla [F] de bajo consumo [M]
lampe [F] à économie [F] d'énergie [F]
Cliphalterung [F]
lampadina [F] a risparmio [M] di energia [F]

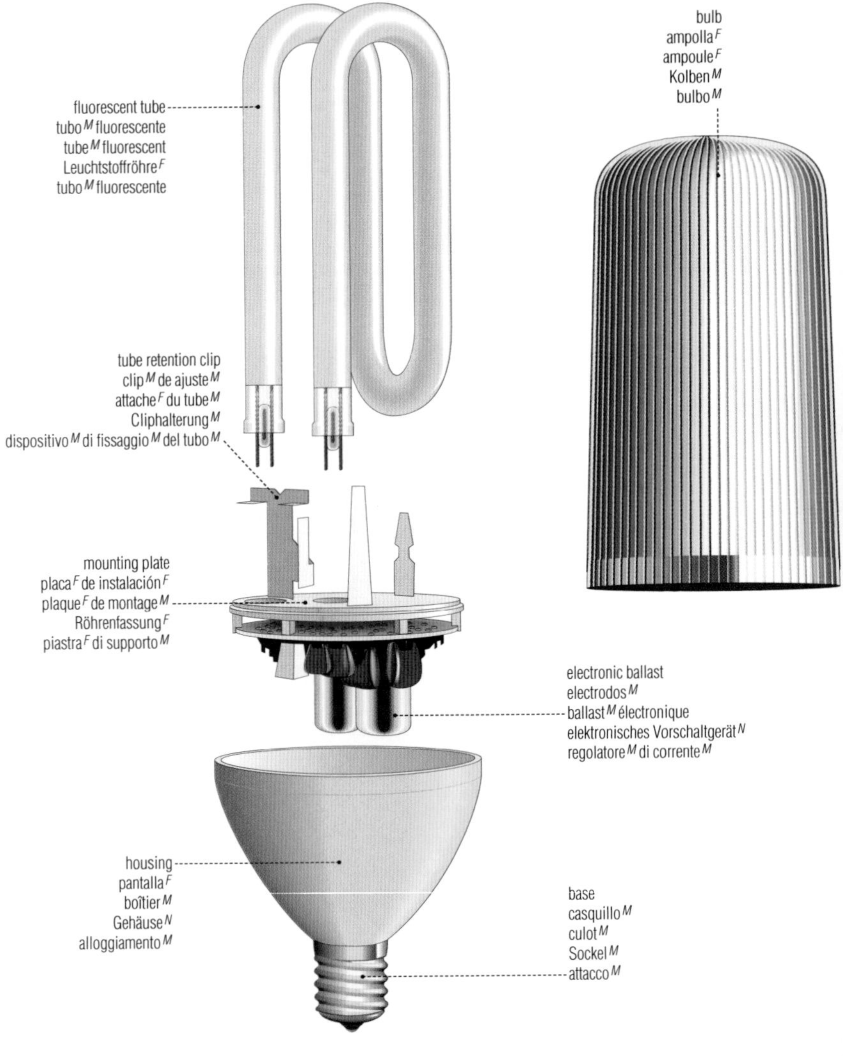

fluorescent tube
tubo M fluorescente
tube M fluorescent
Leuchtstoffröhre F
tubo M fluorescente
bulb
ampolla F
ampoule F
Kolben M
bulbo M
tube retention clip
clip M de ajuste M
attache F du tube M
Cliphalterung M
dispositivo M di fissaggio M del tubo M
mounting plate
placa F de instalación F
plaque F de montage M
Röhrenfassung F
piastra F di supporto M
electronic ballast
electrodos M
ballast M électronique
elektronisches Vorschaltgerät N
regolatore M di corrente M
housing
pantalla F
boîtier M
Gehäuse N
alloggiamento M
base
casquillo M
culot M
Sockel M
attacco M

fluorescent tube
tubo M fluorescente
tube M fluorescent
Leuchtstoffröhre F
tubo M fluorescente

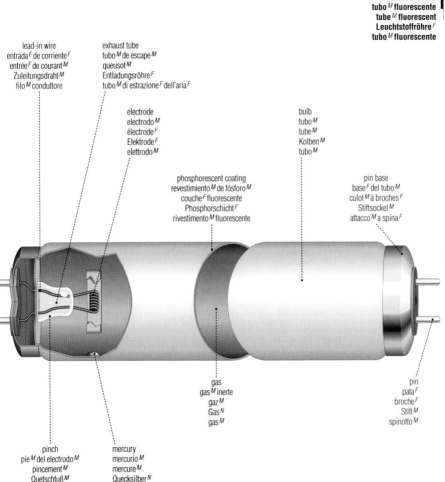

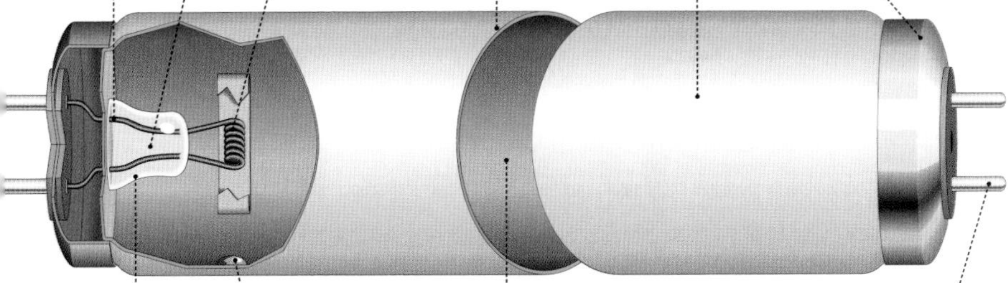
lead-in wire
entrada F de corriente F
entrée F de courant M
Zuleitungsdraht M
filo M conduttore
exhaust tube
tubo M de escape M
queusot M
Entladungsröhre F
tubo M di estrazione F dell'aria F
electrode
electrodo M
électrode F
Elektrode F
elettrodo M
bulb
tubo M
tube M
Kolben M
tubo M
phosphorescent coating
revestimiento M de fósforo M
couche F fluorescente
Phosphorschicht F
rivestimento M fluorescente
pin base
base F del tubo M
culot M à broches F
Stiftsockel M
attacco M a spina F
gas
gas M inerte
gaz M
Gas N
gas M
pin
pata F
broche F
Stift M
spinotto M
pinch
pie M del electrodo M
pincement M
Quetschfuß M
codetta F
mercury
mercurio M
mercure M
Quecksilber N
mercurio M

armchair

silla^{F} de brazos^{M} | fauteuil^{M} | Armlehnstuhl^{M} | poltrona^{F}

parts
partes^{F}
parties^{F}
Teile$^{M/N}$
parti^{F}

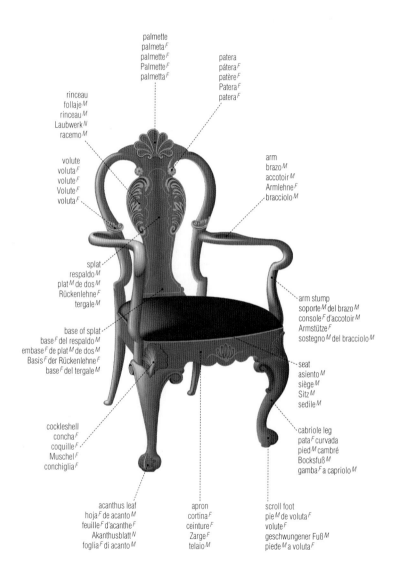

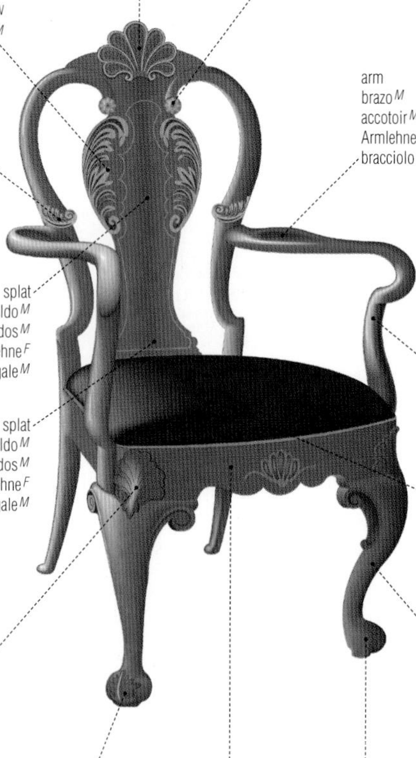
palmette
palmeta^{F}
palmette^{F}
Palmette^{F}
palmetta^{F}
patera
pátera^{F}
patère^{F}
Patera^{F}
patera^{F}
rinceau
follaje^{M}
rinceau^{M}
Laubwerk^{N}
racemo^{M}
volute
voluta^{F}
volute^{F}
Volute^{F}
voluta^{F}
arm
brazo^{M}
accotoir^{M}
Armlehne^{F}
bracciolo^{M}
splat
respaldo^{M}
plat^{M} de dos^{M}
Rückenlehne^{F}
tergale^{M}
arm stump
soporte^{M} del brazo^{M}
console^{F} d'accotoir^{M}
Armstütze^{F}
sostegno^{M} del bracciolo^{M}
base of splat
base^{F} del respaldo^{M}
embase^{F} de plat^{M} de dos^{M}
Basis^{F} der Rückenlehne^{F}
base^{F} del tergale^{M}
seat
asiento^{M}
siège^{M}
Sitz^{M}
sedile^{M}
cockleshell
concha^{F}
coquille^{F}
Muschel^{F}
conchiglia^{F}
cabriole leg
pata^{F} curvada
pied^{M} cambré
Bocksfuß^{M}
gamba^{F} a capriolo^{M}
acanthus leaf
hoja^{F} de acanto^{M}
feuille^{F} d'acanthe^{F}
Akanthusblatt^{N}
foglia^{F} di acanto^{M}
apron
cortina^{F}
ceinture^{F}
Zarge^{F}
telaio^{M}
scroll foot
pie^{M} de voluta^{F}
volute^{F}
geschwungener Fuß^{M}
piede^{M} a voluta^{F}

examples of armchairs
ejemplos^M de divanes^M y butacas^F
exemples^M de fauteuils^M
Beispiele^N für Armstühle^M
esempi^M di poltrone^F e divani^M

Wassily chair
silla^F Wassily
fauteuil^M Wassily
Wassily-Stuhl^M
poltrona^F Wassily

director's chair
silla^F plegable de lona^F
fauteuil^M metteur^M en scène^F
Regiestuhl^M
sedia^F da regista^M

rocking chair
mecedora^F
berceuse^F
Schaukelstuhl^M
sedia^F a dondolo^M

club chair
butaca^F
fauteuil^M club^M
Clubsessel^M
poltrona^F da salotto^M

bergère
silla^F poltrona
bergère^F
Bergère^F
bergère^F

cabriolet
silla^F cabriolé
cabriolet^M
kleiner Lehnstuhl^M
cabriolet^F

armchair

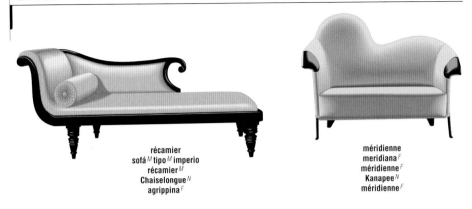

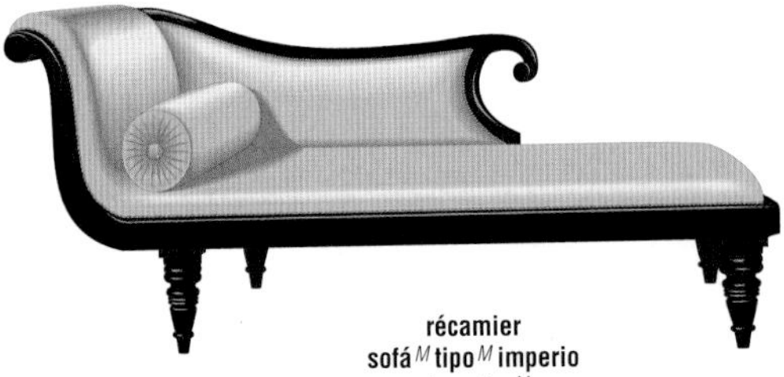

récamier
sofá M tipo M imperio
récamier M
Chaiselongue N
agrippina F

méridienne
meridiana F
méridienne F
Kanapee N
méridienne F

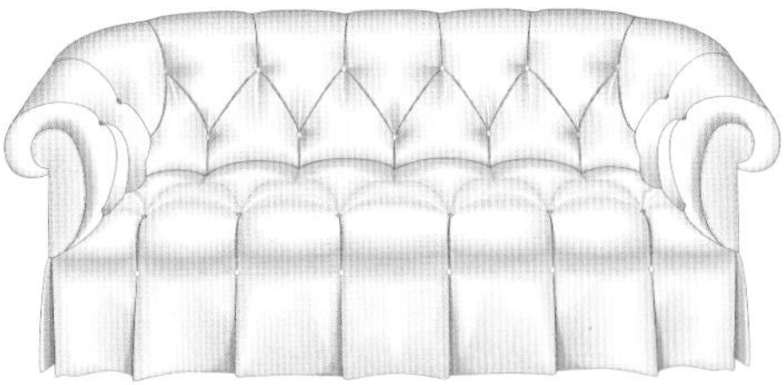

chesterfield
chesterfield M
canapé M capitonné
Chesterfieldsofa N
divano M Chesterfield

love seat
sofá M de dos plazas F
causeuse F
Zweisitzer M
divano M a due posti M

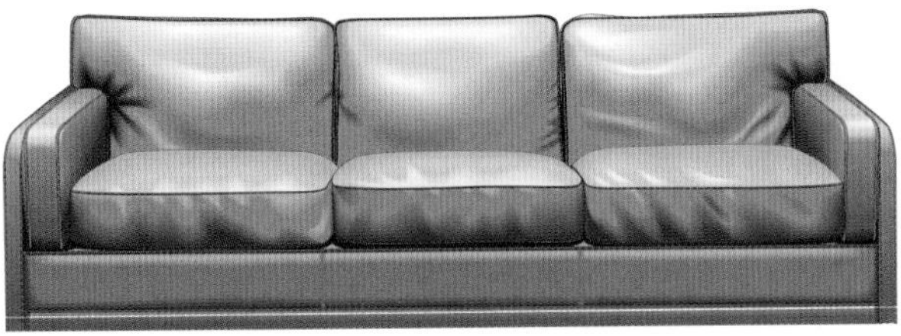

sofa
sofá M
canapé M
Sofa N
divano M

seats

asientos^M | sièges^M | Sitzmöbel^N | sedili^M

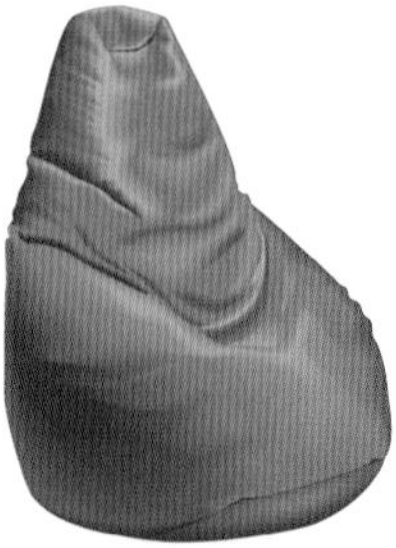

bean bag chair
silla^F cojín^M
fauteuil^M-sac^M
Sitzsack^M
poltrona^F sacco^M

ottoman
puf^M
pouf^M
Puff^M
pouf^M

step chair
silla^F escalera^F
chaise^F-escabeau^M
Tritthocker^M
sedia^F scala^F

stool
escabel^M
tabouret^M
Hocker^M
sgabello^M

bar stool
taburete^M
tabouret^M-bar^M
Barhocker^M
sgabello^M alto

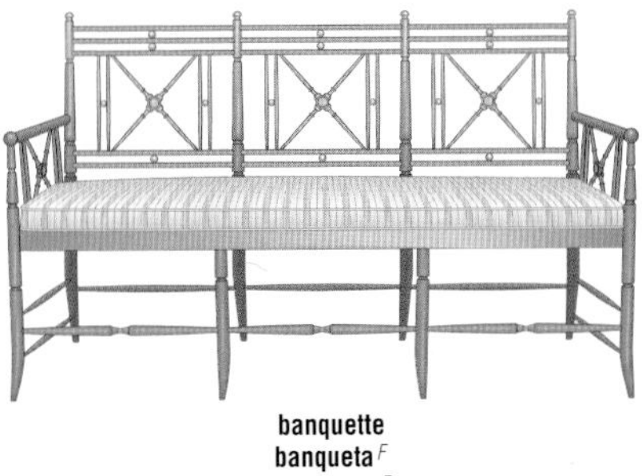

banquette
banqueta^F
banquette^F
Sitzbank^F
divanetto^M

bench
banco^M
banc^M
Bank^F
panchina^F

side chair

silla^{F} sin brazos^{M} | chaise^{F} | Stuhl^{M} | sedia^{F}

parts
partes^{F}
parties^{F}
Teile$^{M/N}$
parti^{F}

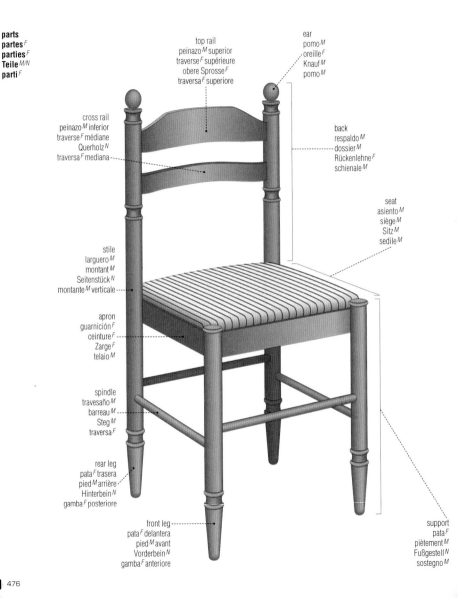

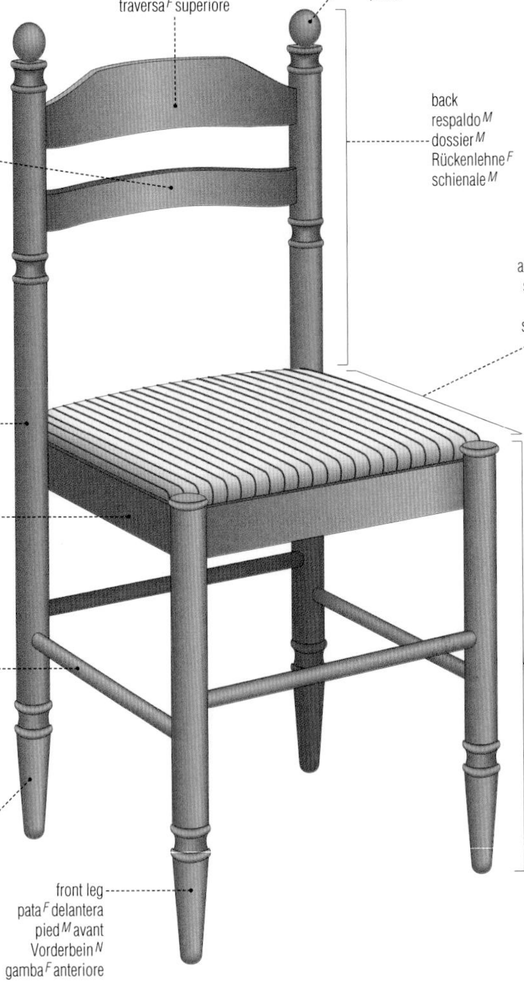
top rail
peinazo^{M} superior
traverse^{F} supérieure
obere Sprosse^{F}
traversa^{F} superiore
ear
pomo^{M}
oreille^{F}
Knauf^{M}
pomo^{M}
cross rail
peinazo^{M} inferior
traverse^{F} médiane
Querholz^{N}
traversa^{F} mediana
back
respaldo^{M}
dossier^{M}
Rückenlehne^{F}
schienale^{M}
seat
asiento^{M}
siège^{M}
Sitz^{M}
sedile^{M}
stile
larguero^{M}
montant^{M}
Seitenstück^{N}
montante^{M} verticale
apron
guarnición^{F}
ceinture^{F}
Zarge^{F}
telaio^{M}
spindle
travesaño^{M}
barreau^{M}
Steg^{M}
traversa^{F}
rear leg
pata^{F} trasera
pied^{M} arrière
Hinterbein^{N}
gamba^{F} posteriore
front leg
pata^{F} delantera
pied^{M} avant
Vorderbein^{N}
gamba^{F} anteriore
support
pata^{F}
piètement^{M}
Fußgestell^{N}
sostegno^{M}

table

mesa^F | table^F | Tisch^M | tavolo^M

gate-leg table
mesa^F de hojas^F abatibles
table^F à abattants^M
Klapptisch^M
tavolo^M a cancello^M

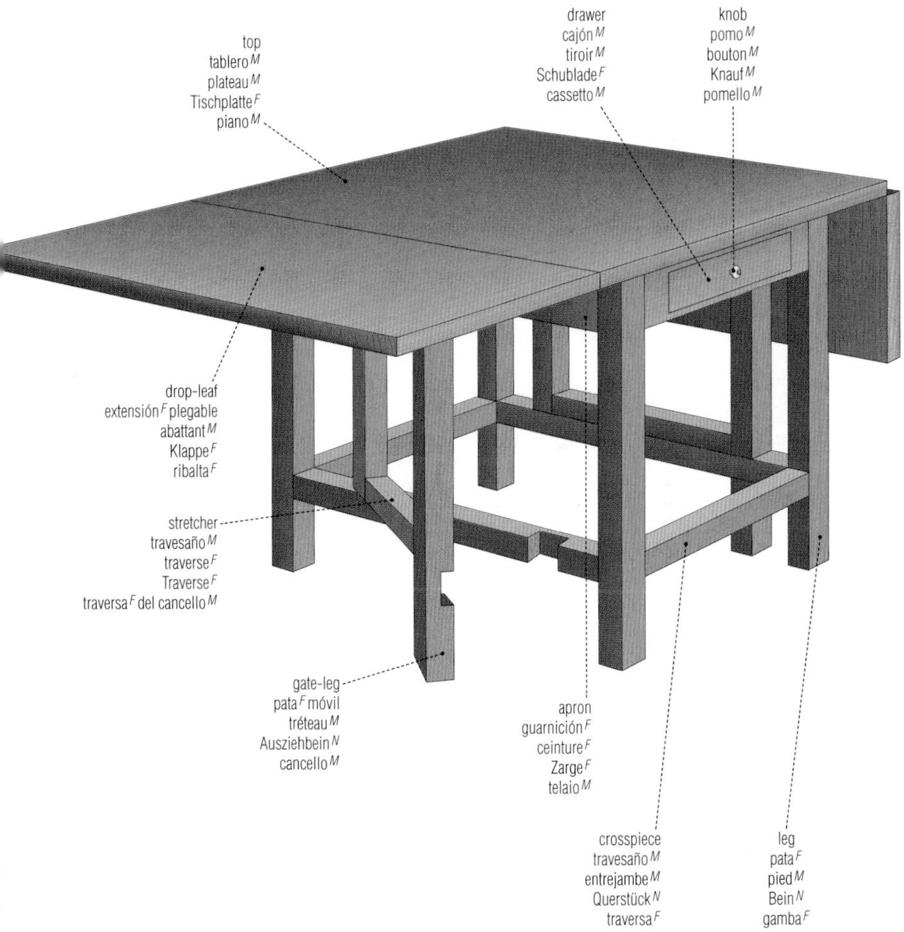
top
tablero^M
plateau^M
Tischplatte^F
piano^M
drawer
cajón^M
tiroir^M
Schublade^F
cassetto^M
knob
pomo^M
bouton^M
Knauf^M
pomello^M
drop-leaf
extensión^F plegable
abattant^M
Klappe^F
ribalta^F
stretcher
travesaño^M
traverse^F
Traverse^F
traversa^F del cancello^M
gate-leg
pata^F móvil
tréteau^M
Ausziehbein^N
cancello^M
apron
guarnición^F
ceinture^F
Zarge^F
telaio^M
crosspiece
travesaño^M
entrejambe^M
Querstück^N
traversa^F
leg
pata^F
pied^M
Bein^N
gamba^F

storage furniture

muebles M contenedores | meubles M de rangement M | Aufbewahrungsmöbel N | mobili M contenitori

armoire
armario M
armoire F
Kleiderschrank M
armadio M

frame
armazón M
bâti M
Rahmen M
telaio M

door
puerta F
vantail M
Tür F
porta F

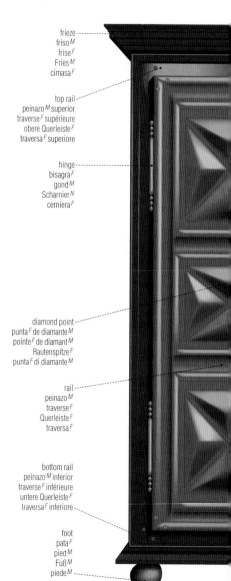

frieze
friso M
frise F
Fries M
cimasa F
top rail
peinazo M superior
traverse F supérieure
obere Querleiste F
traversa F superiore
hinge
bisagra F
gond M
Scharnier N
cerniera F
diamond point
punta F de diamante M
pointe F de diamant M
Rautenspitze F
punta F di diamante M
rail
peinazo M
traverse F
Querleiste F
traversa F
bottom rail
peinazo M inferior
traverse F inférieure
untere Querleiste F
traversa F inferiore
foot
pata F
pied M
Fuß M
piede M

cornice
cornisa [F]
corniche [F]
Kranzprofil [N]
cornice [F]
door panel
entrepaño [M]
panneau [M] de vantail [M]
Türfüllung [F]
pannello [M] dell'anta [F]
center post
montante [M] central
dormant [M]
Setzholz [N]
montante [M] centrale
hanging stile
larguero [M] de la bisagra [F]
montant [M] de ferrage [M]
Anschlagrahmen [M]
montante [M] verticale
lock
cerradura [F]
serrure [F]
Schloss [N]
serratura [F]
frame stile
larguero [M] del marco [M]
montant [M] de bâti [M]
Rahmenleiste [F]
montante [M] del telaio [M]
peg
espiga [F]
cheville [F]
Zapfen [M]
tassello [M]
bracket base
rodapié [M]
soubassement [M]
Sockelprofil [N]
base [F] di sostegno [M]

linen chest
baúl *M*
coffre *M*
Truhe *F*
cassapanca *F*

display cabinet
vitrina *F*
vitrine *F*
Vitrine *F*
vetrina *F*

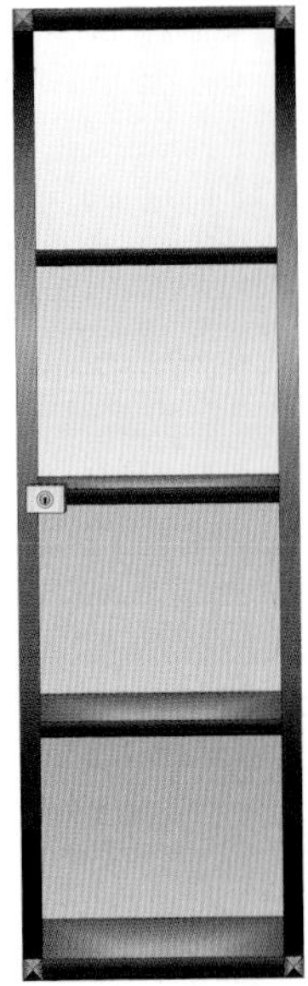

chiffonier
chifonier *M*
chiffonnier *M*
Chiffonière *F*
cassettiera *F*

drawer
cajón M
tiroir M
Schublade F
cassetto M

secretary
bufete *M*
secrétaire *M*
Sekretär *M*
secrétaire *M*

compartment
casillero M
casier M
Fach N
scomparto M
fall front
escritorio M
abattant M
herausklappbare Schreibplatte F
ribalta F

wardrobe
ropero *M*
armoire *F*-**penderie** *F*
Kleiderschrank *M*
guardaroba *M*

closet
guardarropa M
penderie F
Schrankteil M/N
armadio M appendiabiti
shelf
anaquel M
tablette F
Fach N
ripiano M

buffet
aparador *M*
buffet *M*
Büfett *N*
credenza *F*

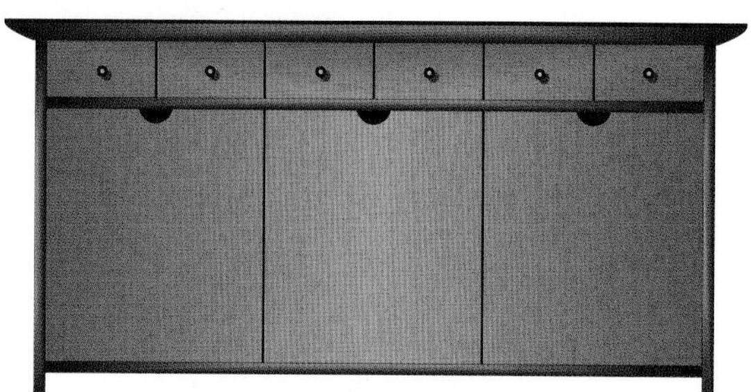

storage furniture

dresser
cómoda *F*
commode *F*
Kommode *F*
comò *M*

corner cupboard
rinconera *F*
encoignure *F*
Eckschrank *M*
angoliera *F*

glass-fronted display cabinet
aparador *M* **con vitrina** *F*
buffet *M*-**vaisselier** *M*
Vitrinenschrank *M*
credenza *F* **con vetrina** *F*

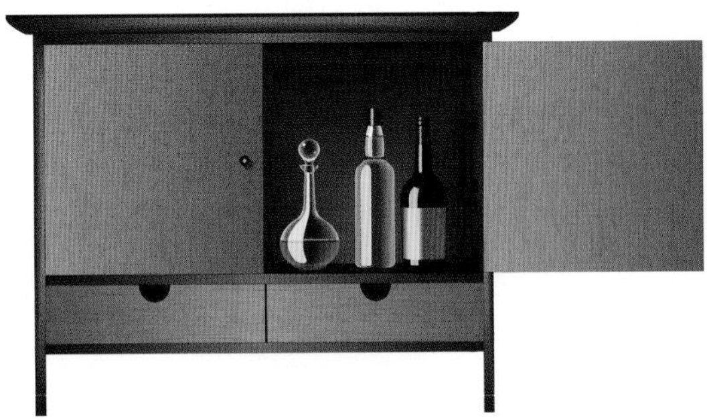

liquor cabinet
mueble *M* **bar** *M*
bar *M*
Barschrank *M*
mobile *M* **bar** *M*

bed

cama[F] | lit[M] | Bett[N] | letto[M]

sofa bed
sofá cama[M]
canapé[M] **convertible**
Schlafcouch[F]
divano-letto[M]

futon
futón M
futon M
Auflage F
futon M
frame
armazón M
cadre M
Rahmen M
telaio M

bed

parts
partes F
parties F
Teile M/N
parti F

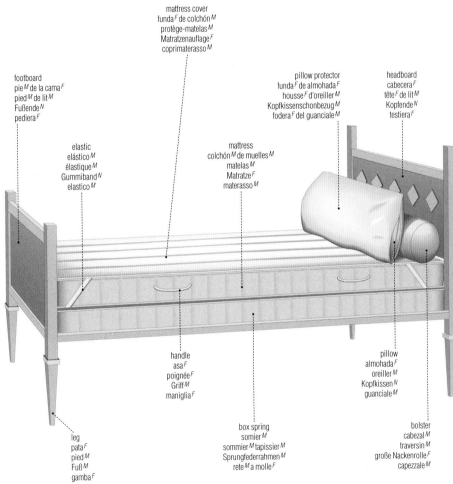

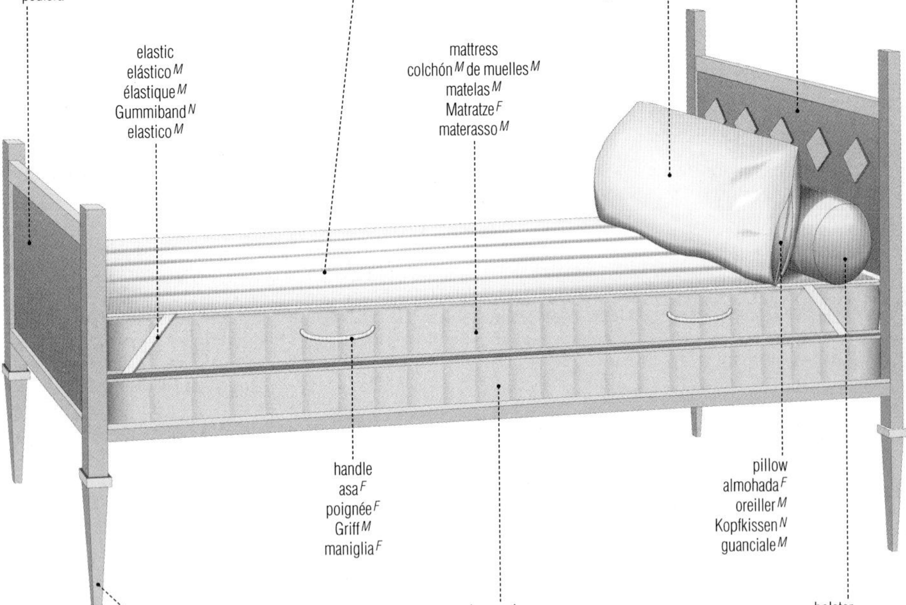
mattress cover
funda F de colchón M
protège-matelas M
Matratzenauflage F
coprimaterasso M
footboard
pie M de la cama F
pied M de lit M
Fußende N
pediera F
pillow protector
funda F de almohada F
housse F d'oreiller M
Kopfkissenschonbezug M
fodera F del guanciale M
headboard
cabecera F
tête F de lit M
Kopfende N
testiera F
elastic
elástico M
élastique M
Gummiband N
elastico M
mattress
colchón M de muelles M
matelas M
Matratze F
materasso M
handle
asa F
poignée F
Griff M
maniglia F
pillow
almohada F
oreiller M
Kopfkissen N
guanciale M
leg
pata F
pied M
Fuß M
gamba F
box spring
somier M
sommier M tapissier M
Sprungfederrahmen M
rete M a molle F
bolster
cabezal M
traversin M
große Nackenrolle F
capezzale M

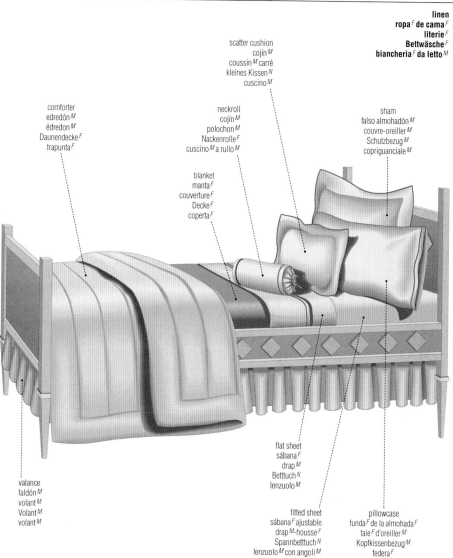

linen
ropa^F de cama^F
literie^F
Bettwäsche^F
biancheria^F da letto^M

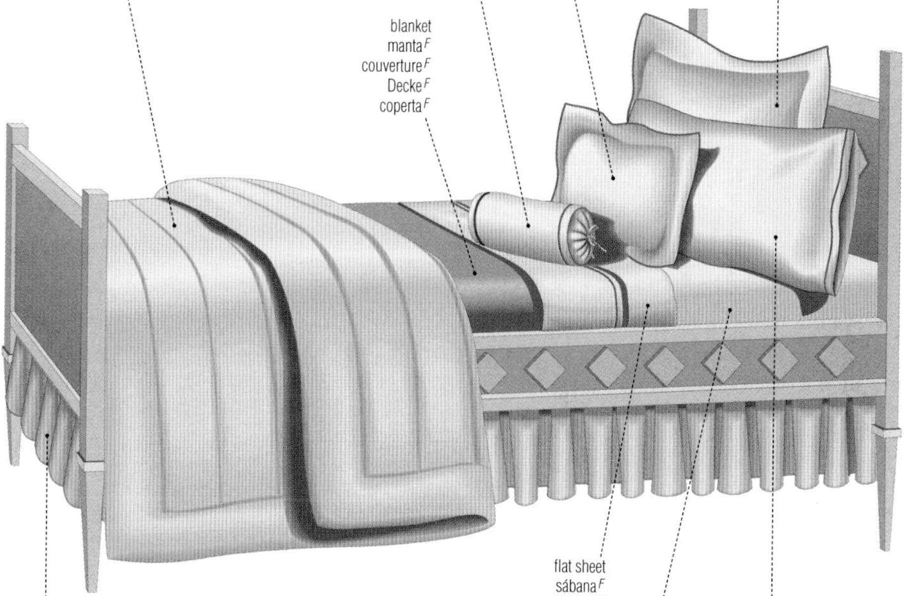
scatter cushion
cojín M
coussin M carré
kleines Kissen N
cuscino M
comforter
edredón M
édredon M
Daunendecke F
trapunta F
neckroll
cojín M
polochon M
Nackenrolle F
cuscino M a rullo M
sham
falso almohadón M
couvre-oreiller M
Schutzbezug M
copriguanciale M
blanket
manta F
couverture F
Decke F
coperta F
flat sheet
sábana F
drap M
Betttuch N
lenzuolo M
valance
faldón M
volant M
Volant M
volant M
fitted sheet
sábana F ajustable
drap M-housse F
Spannbetttuch N
lenzuolo M con angoli M
pillowcase
funda F de la almohada F
taie F d'oreiller M
Kopfkissenbezug M
federa F

children's furniture

muebles^{M} infantiles | meubles^{M} d'enfants^{M} | Kindermöbel^{N} | mobili^{M} per bambini^{M}

crib
cuna^{F}
lit^{M} à barreaux^{M}
Gitterbett^{N}
lettino^{M} a sponde^{F}

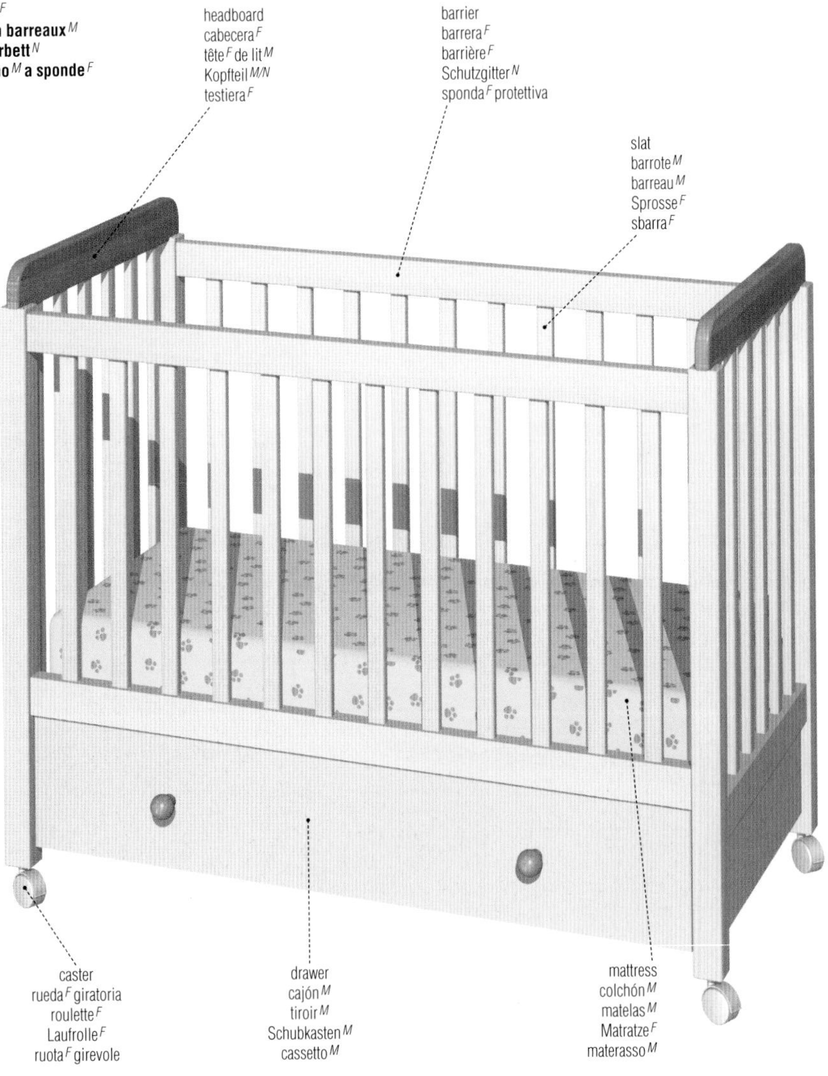
headboard
cabecera^{F}
tête^{F} de lit^{M}
Kopfteil$^{M/N}$
testiera^{F}
barrier
barrera^{F}
barrière^{F}
Schutzgitter^{N}
sponda^{F} protettiva
slat
barrote^{M}
barreau^{M}
Sprosse^{F}
sbarra^{F}
caster
rueda^{F} giratoria
roulette^{F}
Laufrolle^{F}
ruota^{F} girevole
drawer
cajón^{M}
tiroir^{M}
Schubkasten^{M}
cassetto^{M}
mattress
colchón^{M}
matelas^{M}
Matratze^{F}
materasso^{M}

changing table
cambiador *M*
table *F* **à langer**
Wickelkommode *F*
fasciatoio *M*

playpen
cuna *F* **plegable**
lit *M* **pliant**
Reisebett *N* **mit Wickelauflage** *F*
lettino *M* **pieghevole con fasciatoio** *M*

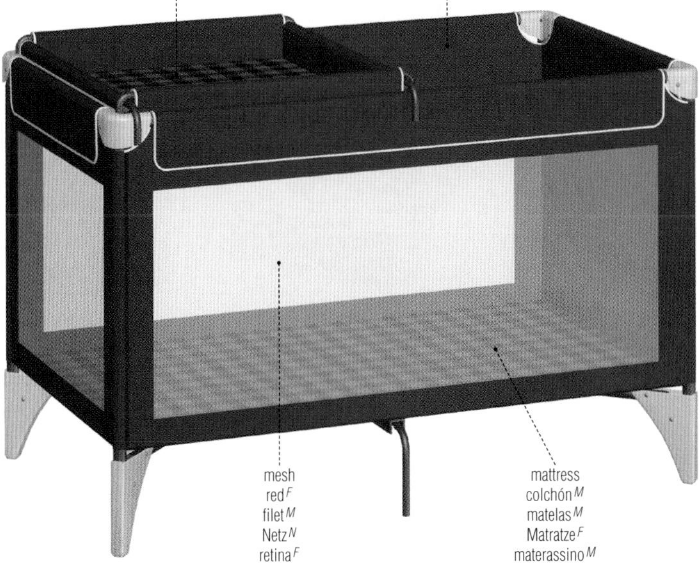
changing table
cambiador M
plan M à langer
Wickelauflage F
fasciatoio M
top rail
borde M
bordure F
oberer Abschluss M
bordo M
mesh
red F
filet M
Netz N
retina F
mattress
colchón M
matelas M
Matratze F
materassino M

children's furniture

booster seat
silla^F alzadora
rehausseur^M
Kindersessel^M
poltroncina^F per bambini^M

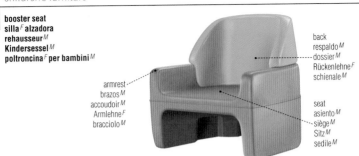

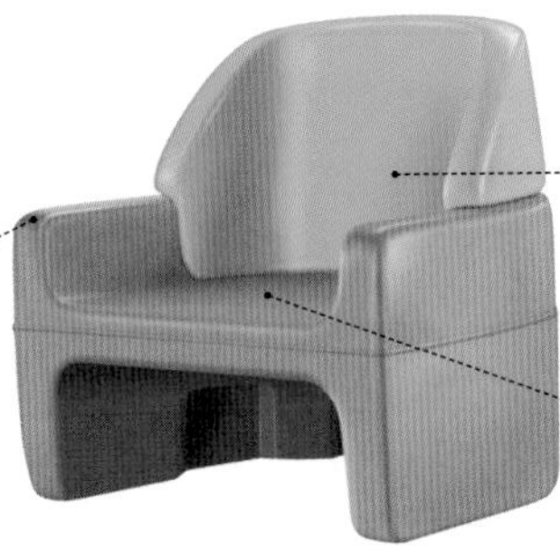

back
respaldo M
dossier M
Rückenlehne F
schienale M
armrest
brazos M
accoudoir M
Armlehne F
bracciolo M
seat
asiento M
siège M
Sitz M
sedile M

high chair
trona^F
chaise^F haute
Hochstuhl^M
seggiolone^M

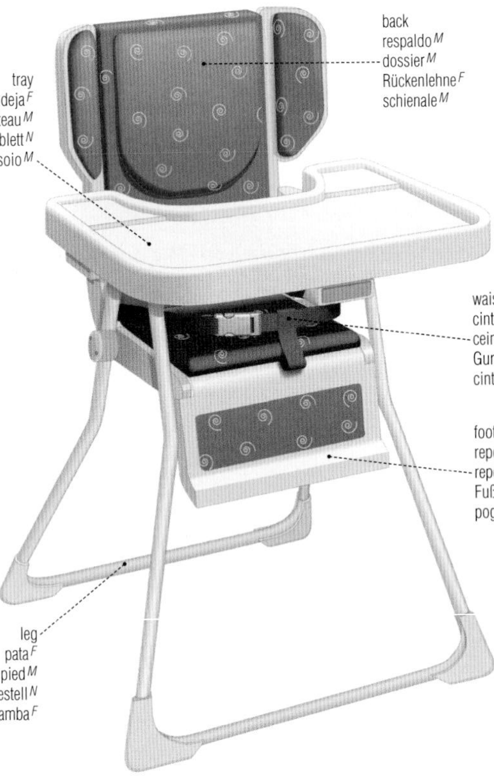

back
respaldo M
dossier M
Rückenlehne F
schienale M
tray
bandeja F
plateau M
Esstablett N
vassoio M
waist belt
cinturón M de seguridad F
ceinture F ventrale
Gurt M
cintura F di ritenuta F
footrest
reposapies M
repose-pieds M
Fußstütze F
poggiapiedi M
leg
pata F
pied M
Gestell N
gamba F

window accessories

accesorios M para las ventanas F | parures F de fenêtre F | Fensterdekorationen F | accessori M per finestre F

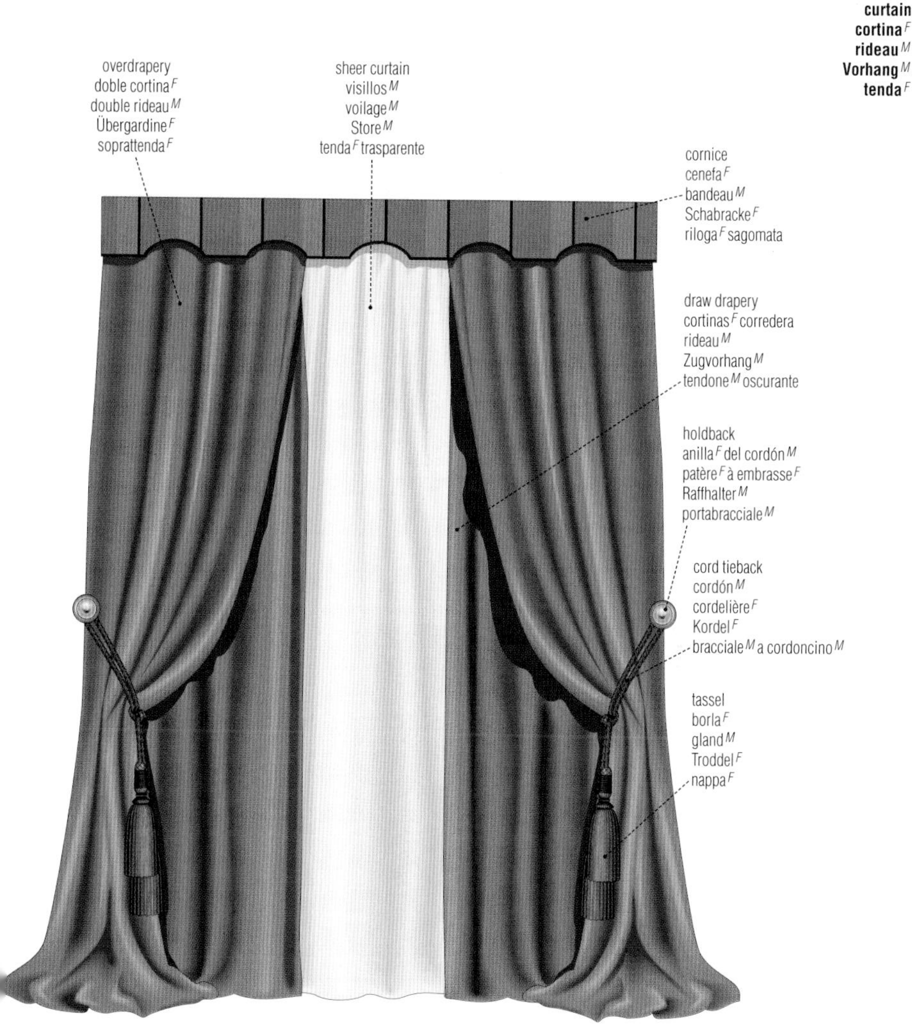
curtain
cortina F
rideau M
Vorhang M
tenda F
overdrapery
doble cortina F
double rideau M
Übergardine F
soprattenda F
sheer curtain
visillos M
voilage M
Store M
tenda F trasparente
cornice
cenefa F
bandeau M
Schabracke F
riloga F sagomata
draw drapery
cortinas F corredera
rideau M
Zugvorhang M
tendone M oscurante
holdback
anilla F del cordón M
patère F à embrasse F
Raffhalter M
portabracciale M
cord tieback
cordón M
cordelière F
Kordel F
bracciale M a cordoncino M
tassel
borla F
gland M
Troddel F
nappa F

examples of curtains
ejemplos M de cortinas F
exemples M de rideaux M
Beispiele N für Vorhänge M
esempi M di tende F

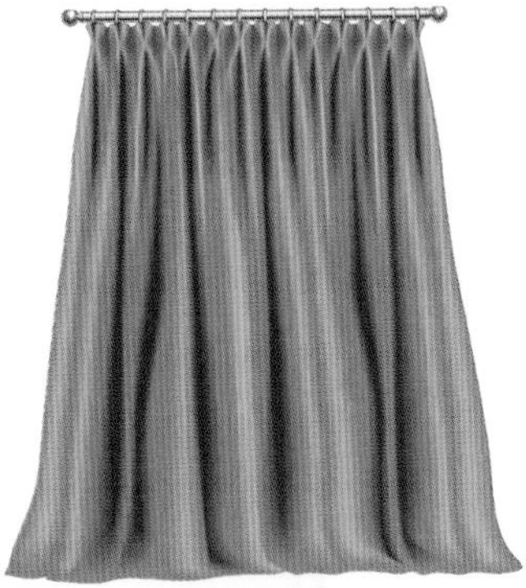

loose curtain
cortina F suelta corrediza
rideau M flottant
loser Vorhang M
tenda F a strappo M

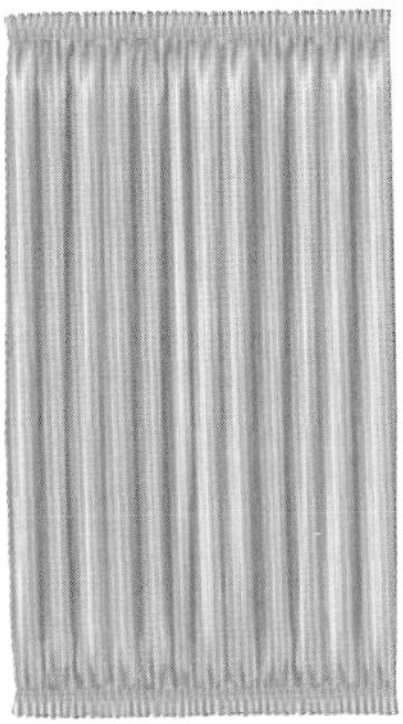

attached curtain
cortina F sujeta de doble barra F
rideau M coulissé
Spanngardine F
tenda F a vetro M

crisscross curtains
cortinas F cruzadas
rideaux M croisés
Raffgardine F
tende F con sormonto M totale

balloon curtain
cortina F abombada
rideau M ballon M
Wolkenstore M
tenda F a palloncino M

blinds
persianas^F enrollables
stores^M
Rollo^N und Jalousie^F
tende^F avvolgibili

Venetian blind
persiana^F veneciana
store^M vénitien
Jalousie^F
veneziana^F

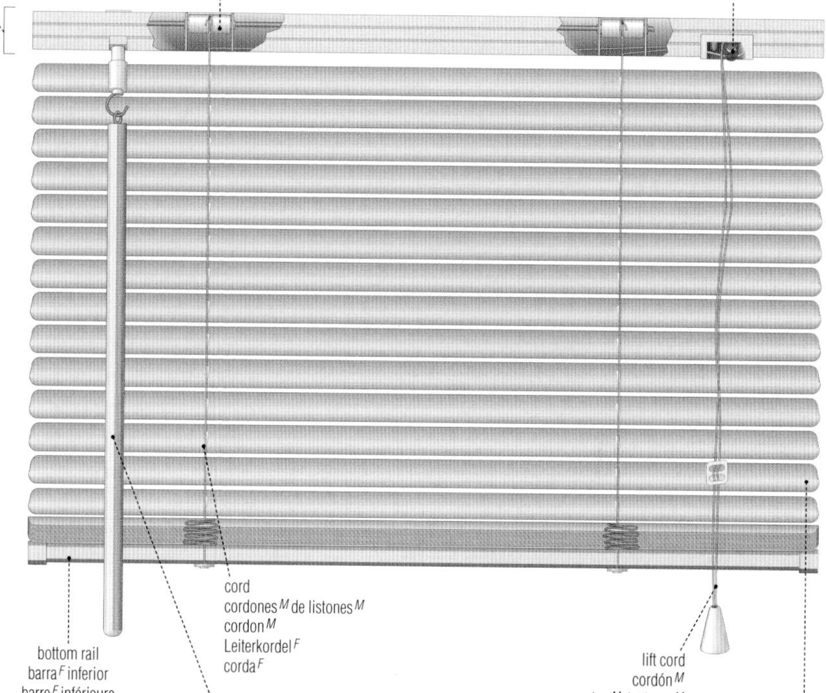
headrail
caja^F superior
boîtier^M
Kopfprofil^N
cassonetto^M
drum
tambor^M
tambour^M
Trommel^F
tamburo^M
lift cord lock
seguro^M del cordón^M
blocage^M du cordon^M de tirage^M
Schnurfeststeller^M
fermacorda^M
cord
cordones^M de listones^M
cordon^M
Leiterkordel^F
corda^F
bottom rail
barra^F inferior
barre^F inférieure
Abschlussprofil^N
barra^F inferiore
lift cord
cordón^M
cordon^M de tirage^M
Zugschnur^F
corda^F di sollevamento^M
lath tilt device
regulador^M de luminosidad^F
manivelle^F d'orientation^F des lames^F
Wendestab^M
asta^F di comando^M per l'orientamento^M delle lamelle^F
lath
listón^M
lame^F
Lamelle^F
lamella^F

roller shade
persiana^F enrollable automática
store^M à enroulement^M automatique
Rollo^N
tenda^F avvolgibile

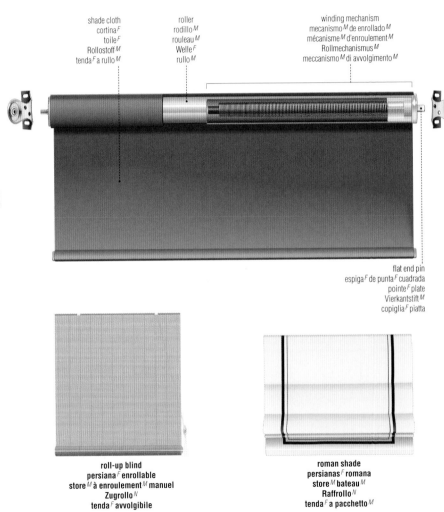

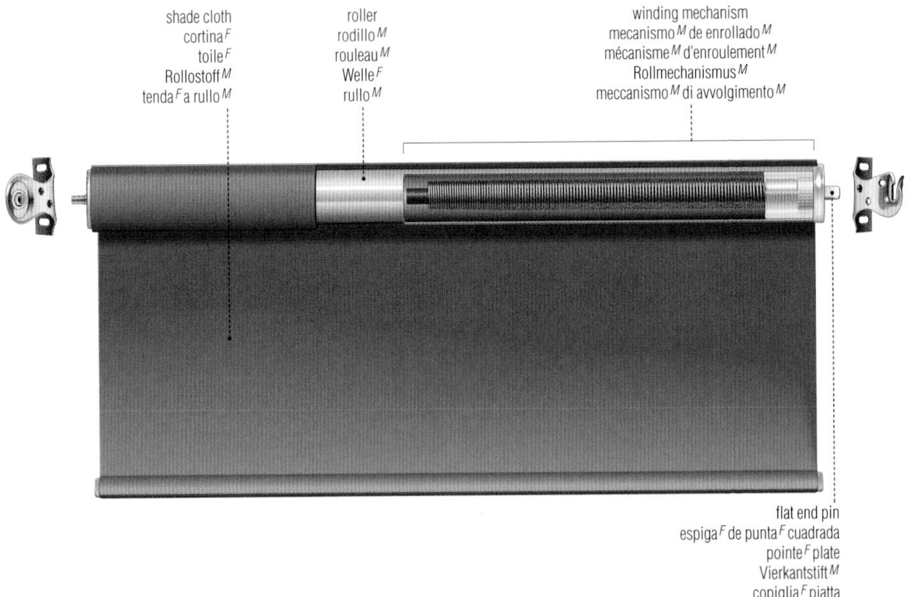
shade cloth
cortina F
toile F
Rollostoff M
tenda F a rullo M
roller
rodillo M
rouleau M
Welle F
rullo M
winding mechanism
mecanismo M de enrollado M
mécanisme M d'enroulement M
Rollmechanismus M
meccanismo M di avvolgimento M
flat end pin
espiga F de punta F cuadrada
pointe F plate
Vierkantstift M
copiglia F piatta

roll-up blind
persiana^F enrollable
store^M à enroulement^M manuel
Zugrollo^N
tenda^F avvolgibile

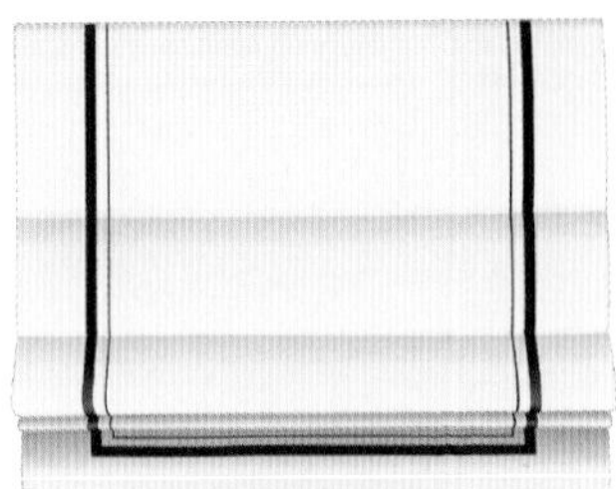

roman shade
persianas^F romana
store^M bateau^M
Raffrollo^N
tenda^F a pacchetto^M

lights

lámparas[F] | luminaires[M] | Lampen[F] | luci[F]

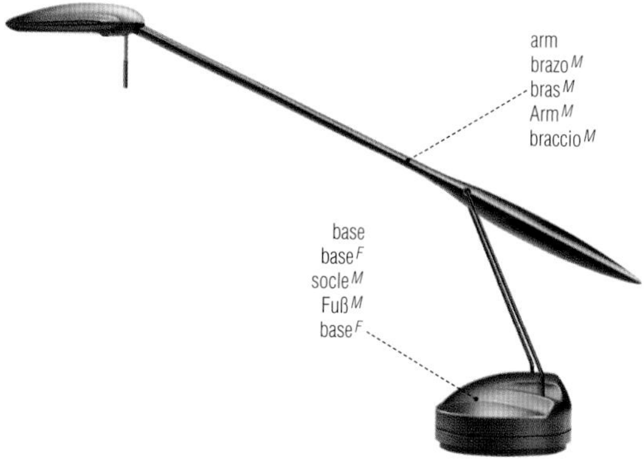
arm
brazo[M]
bras[M]
Arm[M]
braccio[M]
base
base[F]
socle[M]
Fuß[M]
base[F]

halogen desk lamp
lámpara[F] de despacho[M] halógena
lampe[F] de bureau[M] halogène
Halogen[N]-Tischleuchte[F]
lampada[F] alogena da tavolo[M]

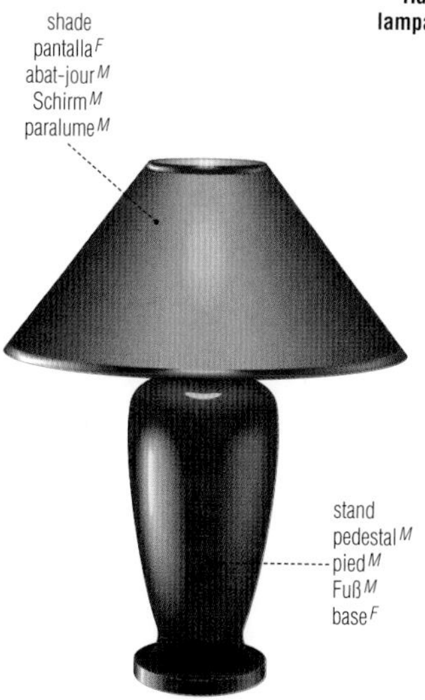
shade
pantalla[F]
abat-jour[M]
Schirm[M]
paralume[M]
stand
pedestal[M]
pied[M]
Fuß[M]
base[F]

table lamp
lámpara[F] de mesa[F]
lampe[F] de table[F]
Tischleuchte[F]
lampada[F] da tavolo[M]

desk lamp
lámpara[F] de escritorio[M]
lampe[F] de bureau[M]
Schreibtischleuchte[F]
lampada[F] da tavolo[M]

lights

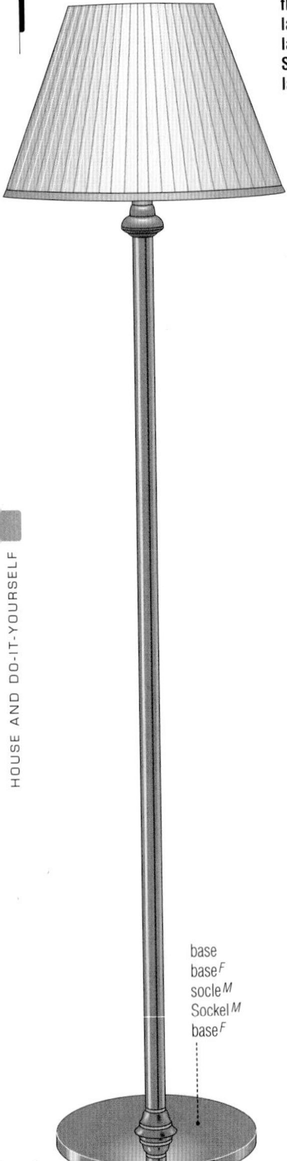
base
base[F]
socle[M]
Sockel[M]
base[F]

floor lamp
lámpara[F] de pie[M]
lampadaire[M]
Standleuchte[F]
lampada[F] a stelo[M]

clamp spotlight
lámpara[F] de pinza[F]
spot[M] à pince[F]
Klemmspot[M]
faretto[M] a pinza[F]

bed lamp
lámpara[F] de cabecera[F]
lampe[F] liseuse
Leseleuchte[F]
lampada[F] da lettura[F]

adjustable lamp
flexo[M]
lampe[F] d'architecte[M]
Arbeitsleuchte[F]
lampada[F] a braccio[M] regolabile

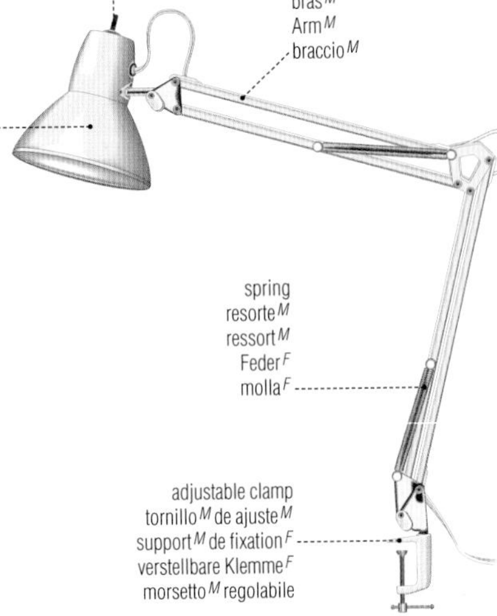
on-off switch
interruptor[M]
interrupteur[M]
Ein-/Ausschalter[M]
interruttore[M]
arm
brazo[M]
bras[M]
Arm[M]
braccio[M]
shade
pantalla[F]
abat-jour[M]
Schirm[M]
paralume[M]
spring
resorte[M]
ressort[M]
Feder[F]
molla[F]
adjustable clamp
tornillo[M] de ajuste[M]
support[M] de fixation[F]
verstellbare Klemme[F]
morsetto[M] regolabile

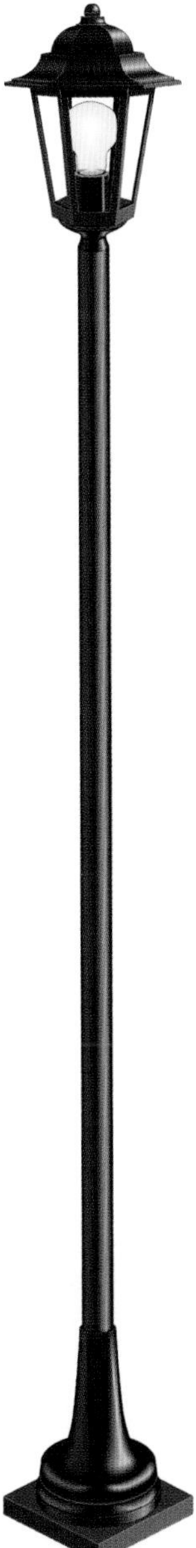

sconce
aplique *M*
applique *F*
Wandleuchte *F*
lampada *F* **da parete** *F*

wall lantern
farol *M*
lanterne *F* **murale**
Wandlaterne *F*
lampione *M* **da parete** *F*

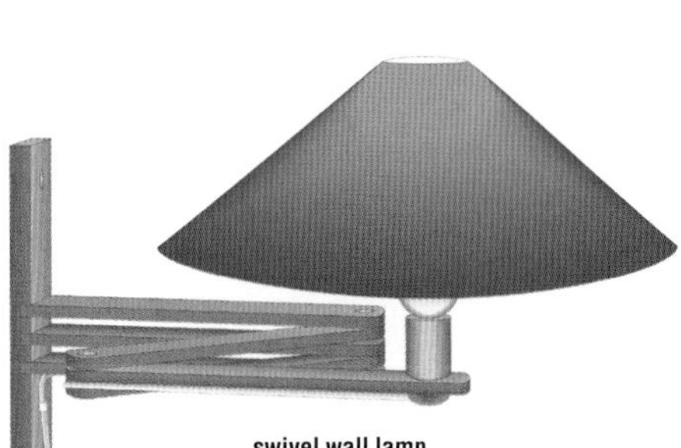

swivel wall lamp
lámpara *F* **orientable de pared** *F*
applique *F* **orientable**
Scherenleuchte *F*
lampada *F* **da parete** *F* **con braccio** *M* **estensibile**

post lantern
farola *F*
lanterne *F* **de pied** *M*
Straßenlaterne *F*
lampione *M*

track lighting
riel [M] de iluminación [F]
rail [M] d'éclairage [M]
Beleuchtungsschiene [F]
faretto [M] da binario [M]

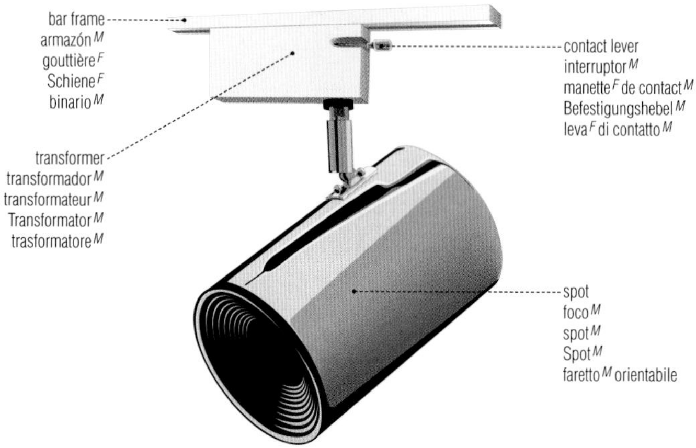
bar frame
armazón [M]
gouttière [F]
Schiene [F]
binario [M]
contact lever
interruptor [M]
manette [F] de contact [M]
Befestigungshebel [M]
leva [F] di contatto [M]
transformer
transformador [M]
transformateur [M]
Transformator [M]
trasformatore [M]
spot
foco [M]
spot [M]
Spot [M]
faretto [M] orientabile

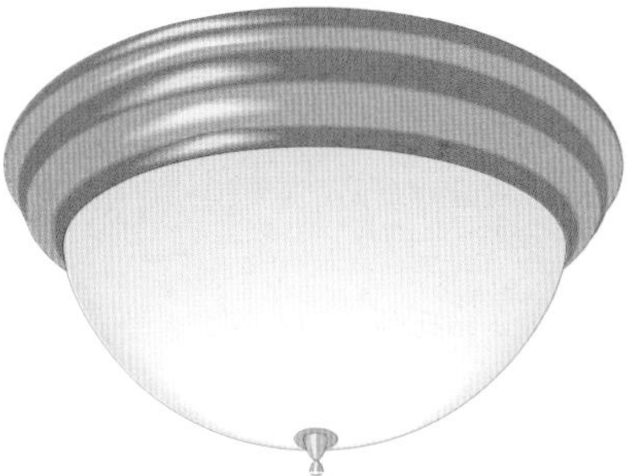

ceiling fitting
plafón [M]
plafonnier [M]
Deckenleuchte [F]
plafoniera [F]

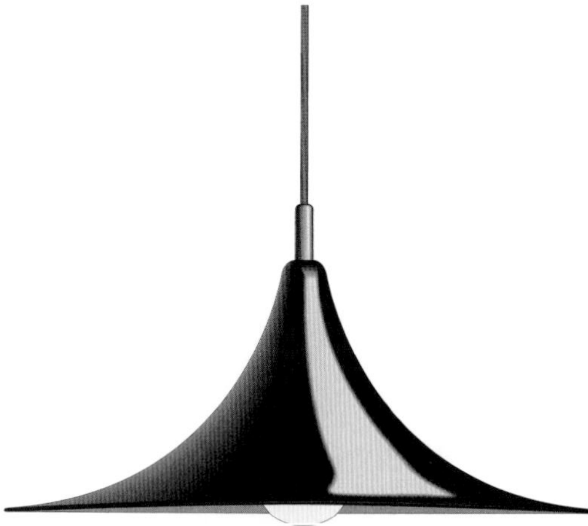

hanging pendant
lámpara [F] de techo [M]
suspension [F]
Hängeleuchte [F]
lampada [F] a sospensione [F]

chandelier
araña [F]
lustre [M]
Kronleuchter [M]
lampadario [M]

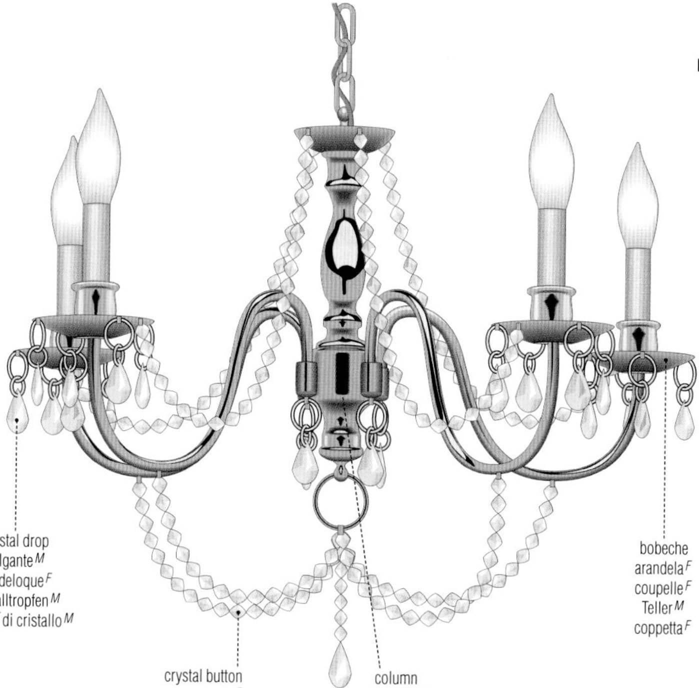
crystal drop
colgante [M]
pendeloque [F]
Kristalltropfen [M]
goccia [F] di cristallo [M]
crystal button
gota [F]
pampille [F]
Koppen [M]
perlina [F] di cristallo [M]
column
columna [F]
fût [M]
Mittelsäule [F]
colonna [F]
bobeche
arandela [F]
coupelle [F]
Teller [M]
coppetta [F]

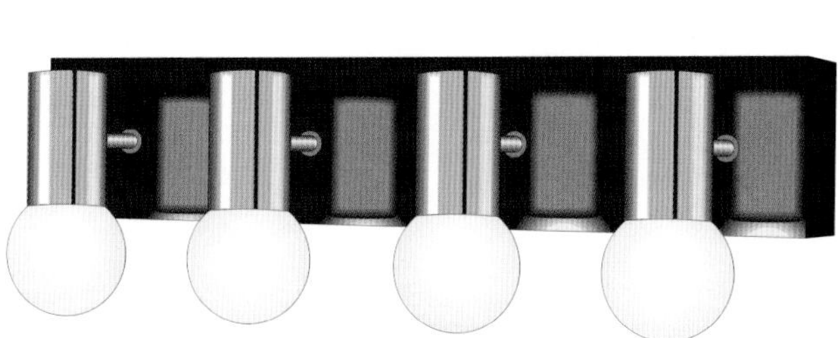

strip light
lámparas [F] **en serie** [F]
rampe [F] **d'éclairage** [M]
Lampenreihe [F]
lampade [F] **in serie** [F]

domestic appliances

aparatos^M electrodomésticos | appareils^M électroménagers | Haushaltsgeräte^N | elettrodomestici^M

steam iron
plancha^F de vapor^M
fer^M à vapeur^F
Dampfbügeleisen^N
ferro^M da stiro^M a vapore^M

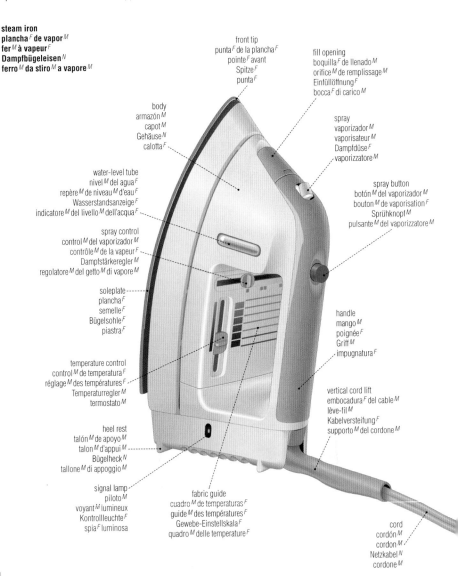

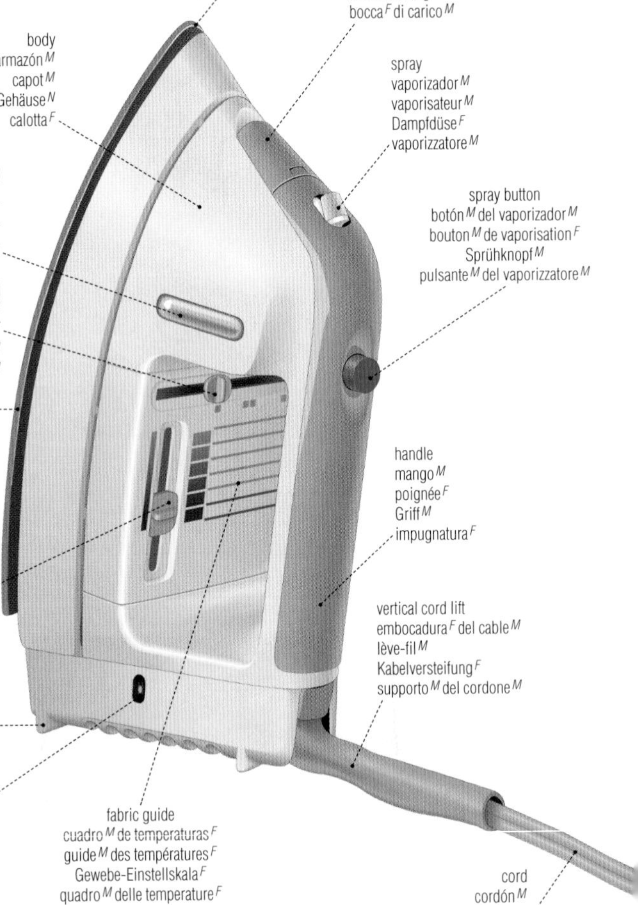
front tip
punta^F de la plancha^F
pointe^F avant
Spitze^F
punta^F
fill opening
boquilla^F de llenado^M
orifice^M de remplissage^M
Einfüllöffnung^F
bocca^F di carico^M
body
armazón^M
capot^M
Gehäuse^N
calotta^F
spray
vaporizador^M
vaporisateur^M
Dampfdüse^F
vaporizzatore^M
water-level tube
nivel^M del agua^F
repère^M de niveau^M d'eau^F
Wasserstandsanzeige^F
indicatore^M del livello^M dell'acqua^F
spray button
botón^M del vaporizador^M
bouton^M de vaporisation^F
Sprühknopf^M
pulsante^M del vaporizzatore^M
spray control
control^M del vaporizador^M
contrôle^M de la vapeur^F
Dampfstärkeregler^M
regolatore^M del getto^M di vapore^M
soleplate
plancha^F
semelle^F
Bügelsohle^F
piastra^F
handle
mango^M
poignée^F
Griff^M
impugnatura^F
temperature control
control^M de temperatura^F
réglage^M des températures^F
Temperaturregler^M
termostato^M
vertical cord lift
embocadura^F del cable^M
lève-fil^M
Kabelversteifung^F
supporto^M del cordone^M
heel rest
talón^M de apoyo^M
talon^M d'appui^M
Bügelheck^N
tallone^M di appoggio^M
signal lamp
piloto^M
voyant^M lumineux
Kontrollleuchte^F
spia^F luminosa
fabric guide
cuadro^M de temperaturas^F
guide^M des températures^F
Gewebe-Einstellskala^F
quadro^M delle temperature^F
cord
cordón^M
cordon^M
Netzkabel^N
cordone^M

upright vacuum cleaner
escoba^F eléctrica
aspirateur^M-balai^M
Handstaubsauger^M
aspirapolvere^M verticale

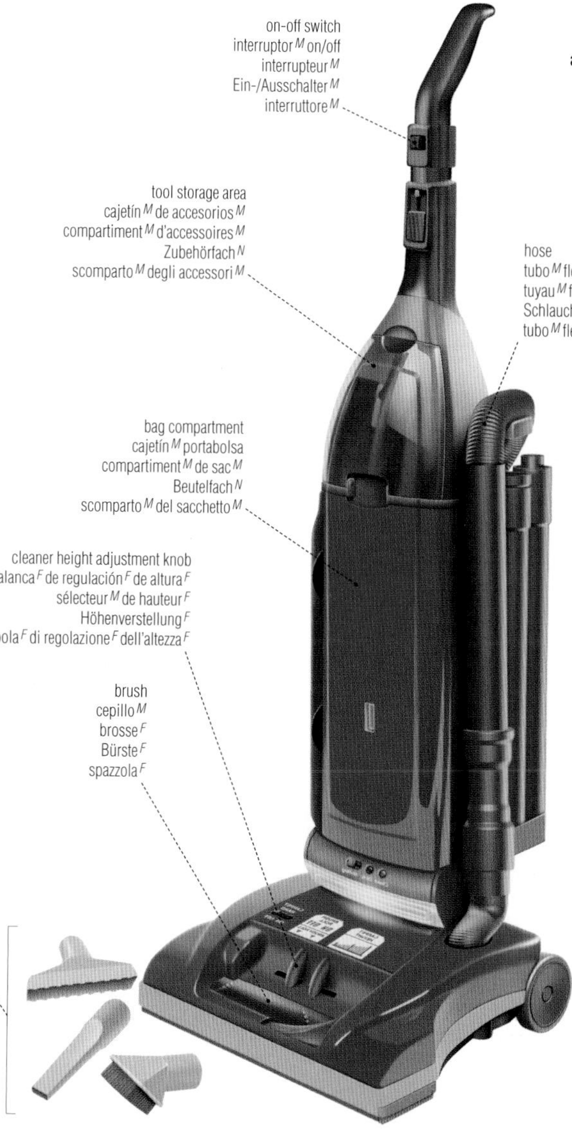
on-off switch
interruptor M on/off
interrupteur M
Ein-/Ausschalter M
interruttore M
tool storage area
cajetín M de accesorios M
compartiment M d'accessoires M
Zubehörfach N
scomparto M degli accessori M
hose
tubo M flexible
tuyau M flexible
Schlauch M
tubo M flessibile
bag compartment
cajetín M portabolsa
compartiment M de sac M
Beutelfach N
scomparto M del sacchetto M
cleaner height adjustment knob
palanca F de regulación F de altura F
sélecteur M de hauteur F
Höhenverstellung F
manopola F di regolazione F dell'altezza F
brush
cepillo M
brosse F
Bürste F
spazzola F
tools
accesorios M
accessoires M
Zubehör N
accessori M

domestic appliances

canister vacuum cleaner
aspirador [M]
aspirateur [M]-traîneau [M]
Bodenstaubsauger [M]
aspirapolvere [M]

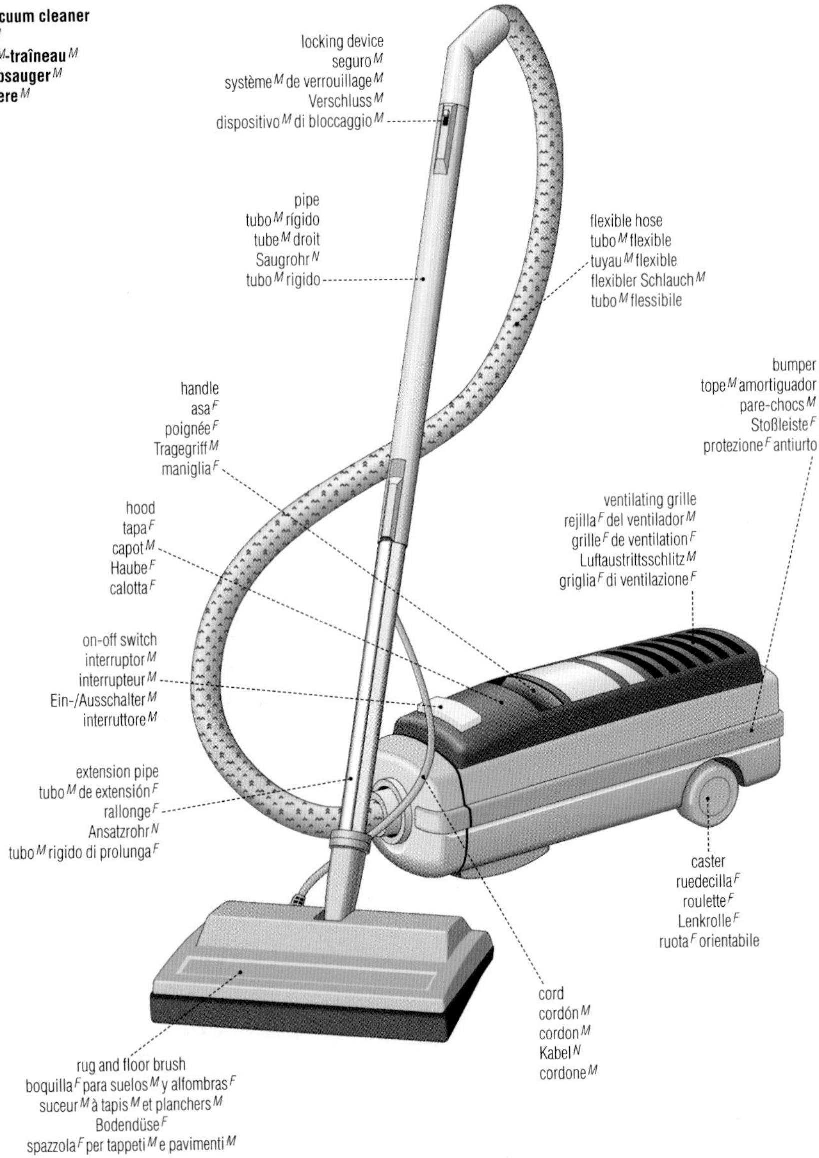
locking device
seguro [M]
système [M] de verrouillage [M]
Verschluss [M]
dispositivo [M] di bloccaggio [M]
pipe
tubo [M] rígido
tube [M] droit
Saugrohr [N]
tubo [M] rigido
flexible hose
tubo [M] flexible
tuyau [M] flexible
flexibler Schlauch [M]
tubo [M] flessibile
handle
asa [F]
poignée [F]
Tragegriff [M]
maniglia [F]
bumper
tope [M] amortiguador
pare-chocs [M]
Stoßleiste [F]
protezione [F] antiurto
hood
tapa [F]
capot [M]
Haube [F]
calotta [F]
ventilating grille
rejilla [F] del ventilador [M]
grille [F] de ventilation [F]
Luftaustrittsschlitz [M]
griglia [F] di ventilazione [F]
on-off switch
interruptor [M]
interrupteur [M]
Ein-/Ausschalter [M]
interruttore [M]
extension pipe
tubo [M] de extensión [F]
rallonge [F]
Ansatzrohr [N]
tubo [M] rigido di prolunga [F]
caster
ruedecilla [F]
roulette [F]
Lenkrolle [F]
ruota [F] orientabile
cord
cordón [M]
cordon [M]
Kabel [N]
cordone [M]
rug and floor brush
boquilla [F] para suelos [M] y alfombras [F]
suceur [M] à tapis [M] et planchers [M]
Bodendüse [F]
spazzola [F] per tappeti [M] e pavimenti [M]

cleaning tools
accesorios [M]
accessoires [M]
Saugzubehör [N]
accessori [M] di pulitura [F]

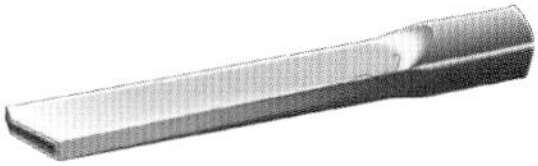

crevice tool
boquilla [F] rinconera
suceur [M] plat
Fugendüse [F]
bocchetta [F] per fessure [F]

dusting brush
cepillo [M]-plumero [M]
brosse [F] à épousseter
Saugbürste [F]
spazzola [F] a pennello [M]

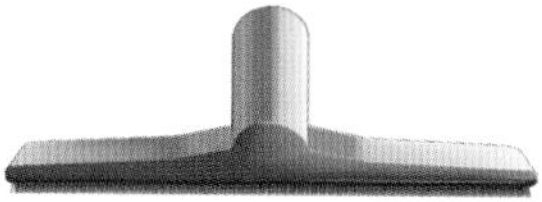

floor brush
cepillo [M] para suelos [M]
brosse [F] à planchers [M]
Bürste [F]
spazzola [F] per pavimenti [M]

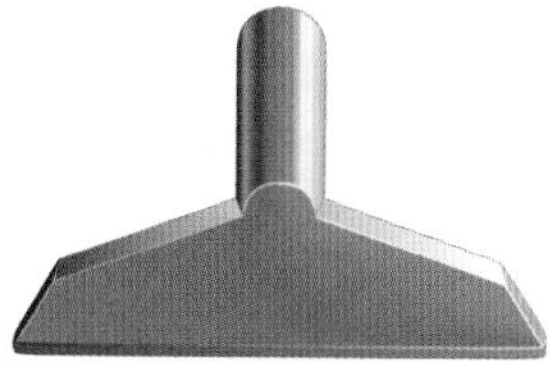

upholstery nozzle
boquilla [F] para tapicería [F]
suceur [M] triangulaire à tissus [M]
Polsterdüse [F]
bocchetta [F] per tappezzeria [F]

hand vacuum cleaner
aspirador [M] manual
aspirateur [M] à main [F]
Akku-Mini-Staubsauger [M]
miniaspiratutto [M]

locking button
botón [M] de cierre [M]
verrouillage [M]
Entriegelungstaste [F]
pulsante [M] di bloccaggio [M]

dust receiver
depósito [M] de polvo [M]
godet [M] à poussière [F]
Staubbehälter [M]
vano [M] raccoglipolvere

on-off switch
interruptor [M]
interrupteur [M]
Ein-/Ausschalter [M]
interruttore [M]

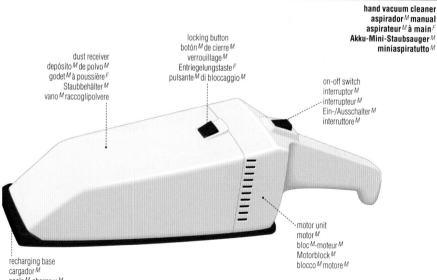

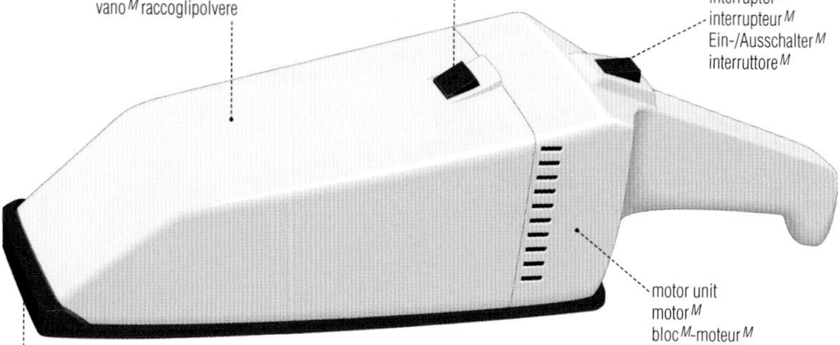

motor unit
motor [M]
bloc [M]-moteur [M]
Motorblock [M]
blocco [M] motore [M]

recharging base
cargador [M]
socle [M]-chargeur [M]
Lade-Anschlussbuchse [F]
presa [F] per ricarica [F]

domestic appliances

gas range
cocina *F* **de gas** *M*
cuisinière *F* **à gaz** *M*
Gasherd *M*
cucina *F* **a gas** *M*

grate
rejilla F
grille F
Rost M
griglia F
burner control knobs
mandos M de los quemadores M
robinets M
Regelschalter M
manopole F di comando M dei bruciatori M
burner
quemador M
brûleur M
Brenner M
bruciatore M
cooktop
encimera F
table F de travail M
Kochmulde F
piano M di cottura F
control panel
panel M de mandos M
tableau M de commande F
Bedienleiste F
quadro M di comando M
oven
horno M
four M
Backofen M
forno M
window
visor M
hublot M
Frontscheibe F
finestra F di controllo M
rack
parrilla F
grille F
Back-/Grillrost M
griglia F
door
puerta F
porte F
Backofentür F
sportello M

chest freezer
arcón M **congelador**
congélateur M **coffre** M
Gefriertruhe F
congelatore M **orizzontale**

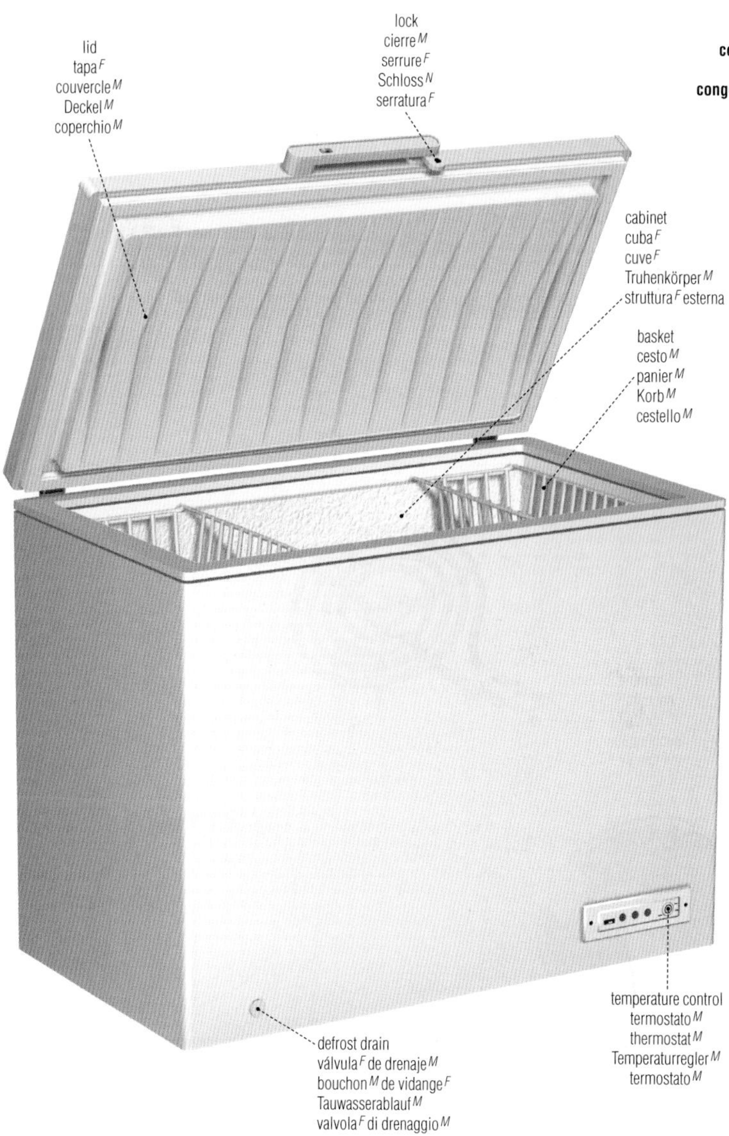
lid
tapa F
couvercle M
Deckel M
coperchio M
lock
cierre M
serrure F
Schloss N
serratura F
cabinet
cuba F
cuve F
Truhenkörper M
struttura F esterna
basket
cesto M
panier M
Korb M
cestello M
temperature control
termostato M
thermostat M
Temperaturregler M
termostato M
defrost drain
válvula F de drenaje M
bouchon M de vidange F
Tauwasserablauf M
valvola F di drenaggio M

domestic appliances

range hood
campana [F]
hotte [F]
Dunstabzugshaube [F]
cappa [F]

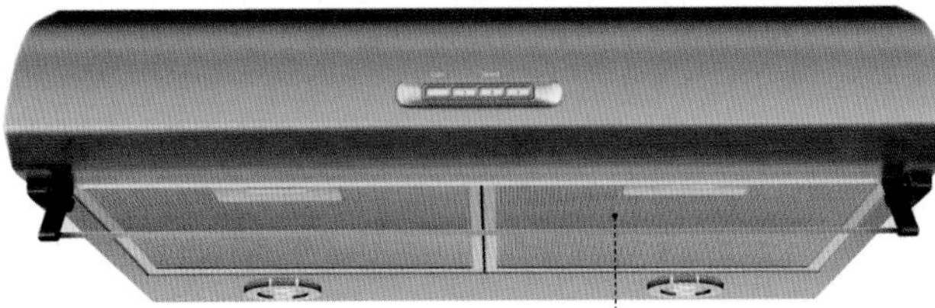
filter
filtro [M]
filtre [M]
Filter [M]
filtro [M]

surface element
placa [F] **eléctrica**
serpentin [M]
Kochplatte [F]
piastra [F] **elettrica**

tubular element
resistencia [F]
élément [M] tubulaire
Heizspirale [F]
serpentina [F]
terminal
enchufe [M]
borne [F]
Anschluss [M]
terminale [M]

drip bowl
protector [M]
cuvette [F]
Auffangschüssel [F]
bacinella [F] **raccogligocce**

trim ring
arandela [F]
anneau [M]
Schutzring [M]
anello [M] **di chiusura** [F]

electric range
cocina^F eléctrica
cuisinière^F électrique
Elektroherd^M
cucina^F elettrica

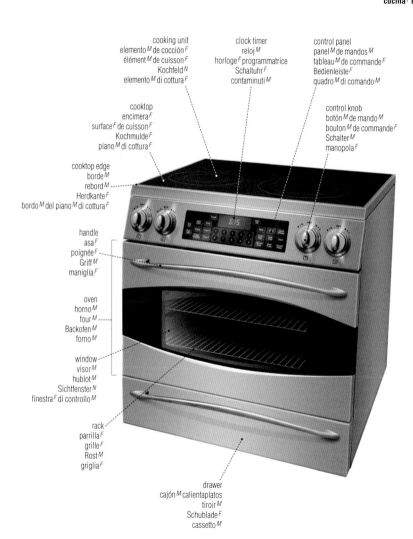

cooking unit
elemento^M de cocción^F
élément^M de cuisson^F
Kochfeld^N
elemento^M di cottura^F
clock timer
reloj^M
horloge^F programmatrice
Schaltuhr^F
contaminuti^M
control panel
panel^M de mandos^M
tableau^M de commande^F
Bedienleiste^F
quadro^M di comando^M
cooktop
encimera^F
surface^F de cuisson^F
Kochmulde^F
piano^M di cottura^F
control knob
botón^M de mando^M
bouton^M de commande^F
Schalter^M
manopola^F
cooktop edge
borde^M
rebord^M
Herdkante^F
bordo^M del piano^M di cottura^F
handle
asa^F
poignée^F
Griff^M
maniglia^F
oven
horno^M
four^M
Backofen^M
forno^M
window
visor^M
hublot^M
Sichtfenster^N
finestra^F di controllo^M
rack
parrilla^F
grille^F
Rost^M
griglia^F
drawer
cajón^M calientaplatos
tiroir^M
Schublade^F
cassetto^M

refrigerator
frigorífico *M*
réfrigérateur *M*
Kühlschrank *M*
frigorifero *M*

switch
interruptor M
interrupteur M
Schalter M
interruttore M
shelf
rejilla F
clayette F
Abstellrost N
ripiano M
handle
manilla F
poignée F
Griff M
maniglia F
water dispenser
dispensador M de agua F
distributeur M d'eau F
Wasserautomat M
distributore M automatico d'acqua F
refrigerator compartment
espacio M interior
réfrigérateur M
Kühlfach N
scomparto M del frigorifero M
freezer compartment
congelador M incorporado
congélateur M
Gefrierfach N
scomparto M del congelatore M
crisper
cesto M para verdura F
bac M à légumes M
Obst- und Gemüseschale F
cassetto M per la verdura F

door stop
tope[M] de la puerta[F]
butée[F] de porte[F]
Türstopper[M]
fermaporta[M]

magnetic gasket
imán[M]
joint[M] magnétique
magnetische Dichtung[F]
guarnizione[F] magnetica

butter compartment
compartimiento[M] para mantequilla[F]
casier[M] à beurre[M]
Butterfach[N]
scomparto[M] per il burro[M]

meat keeper
cajón[M] para carnes[F]
bac[M] à viande[F]
Fleisch- und Wurstfach[N]
cassetto[M] per la carne[F]

shelf channel
riel[M] para las rejillas[F]
crémaillère[F]
Rasterleiste[F]
griglia[F] dei ripiani[M]

storage door
puerta[F] del refrigerador[M]
porte[F] étagère[F]
Innentür[F]
controporta[F] attrezzata

guard rail
listón[M]
barre[F] de retenue[F]
Sicherheitsleiste[F]
listarella[F]

dairy compartment
compartimiento[M] para lácteos[M]
casier[M] laitier
Fach[N] für Molkereiprodukte[N]
scomparto[M] per i latticini[M]

domestic appliances

top-loading washer
lavadora F de carga F vertical
lave-linge M à chargement M vertical
Toplader M
lavatrice F a carica F verticale

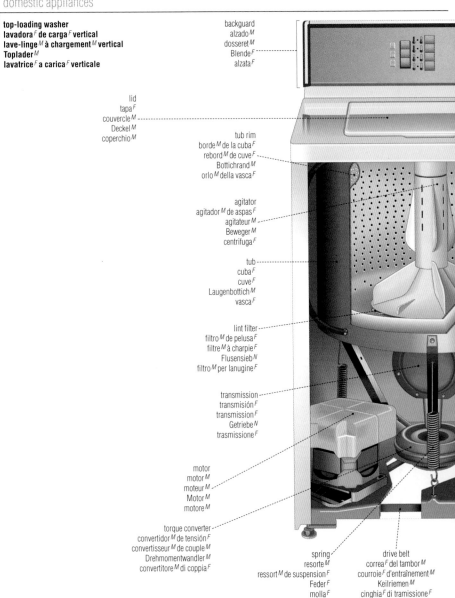

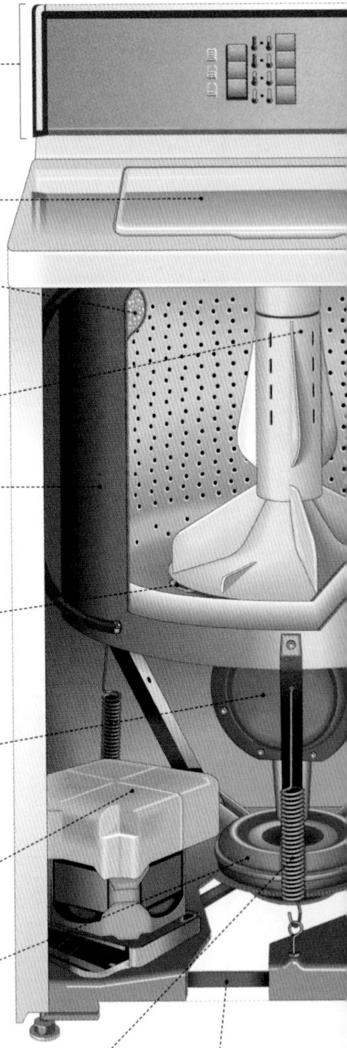
backguard
alzado M
dosseret M
Blende F
alzata F
lid
tapa F
couvercle M
Deckel M
coperchio M
tub rim
borde M de la cuba F
rebord M de cuve F
Bottichrand M
orlo M della vasca F
agitator
agitador M de aspas F
agitateur M
Beweger M
centrifuga F
tub
cuba F
cuve F
Laugenbottich M
vasca F
lint filter
filtro M de pelusa F
filtre M à charpie F
Flusensieb N
filtro M per lanugine F
transmission
transmisión F
transmission F
Getriebe N
trasmissione F
motor
motor M
moteur M
Motor M
motore M
torque converter
convertidor M de tensión F
convertisseur M de couple M
Drehmomentwandler M
convertitore M di coppia F
spring
resorte M
ressort M de suspension F
Feder F
molla F
drive belt
correa F del tambor M
courroie F d'entraînement M
Keilriemen M
cinghia F di tramissione F

basket
tambor^{M}
panier^{M} de lavage^{M}
Trommel^{F}
cestello^{M}

cabinet
armazón^{M}
carrosserie^{F}
Gehäuse^{N}
struttura^{F} esterna

suspension arm
brazo^{M} de suspensión^{F}
bras^{M} de suspension^{F}
Schwingungsdämpfer^{M}
braccio^{M} di sospensione^{F}

drain hose
manguera^{F} de desagüe^{M}
tuyau^{M} d'évacuation^{F}
Ablaufschlauch^{M}
tubo^{M} di drenaggio^{M}

emptying hose
manguera^{F} de vaciado^{M}
tuyau^{M} de vidange^{F}
Entleerungsschlauch^{M}
tubo^{M} di scarico^{M}

leveling foot
pie^{M} ajustable
pied^{M} de nivellement^{M}
Nivellierfuß^{M}
piedino^{M} regolabile

pump
bomba^{F}
pompe^{F}
Pumpe^{F}
pompa^{F}

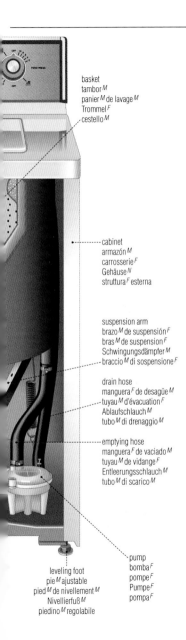

front-loading washer
lavadora^{F} de carga^{F} frontal
lave-linge^{M} à chargement^{M} frontal
Waschmaschine^{F} (Frontlader^{M})
lavatrice^{F} a carica^{F} frontale

temperature selector
selector^{M} de temperatura^{F}
sélecteur^{M} de température^{F}
Temperaturwähler^{M}
termostato^{M}

water-level selector
selector^{M} de nivel^{M} de agua^{F}
sélecteur^{M} de niveau^{M} d'eau^{F}
Wasserstandsregler^{M}
selettore^{M} del livello^{M} dell'acqua^{F}

control knob
programador^{M}
programmateur^{M}
Programmwähler^{M}
programmatore^{M}

control panel
panel^{M} de control^{M}
tableau^{M} de commande^{F}
Bedienleiste^{F}
quadro^{M} di comando^{M}

door
puerta^{F}
porte^{F}
Tür^{F}
portello^{M}

electric dryer
secadora[F] de ropa[F]
sèche-linge[M] électrique
Wäschetrockner[M]
asciugatrice[F]

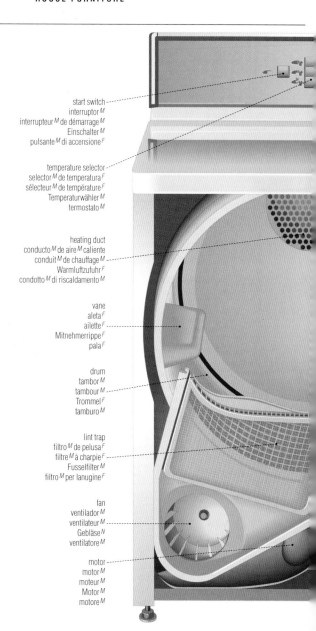

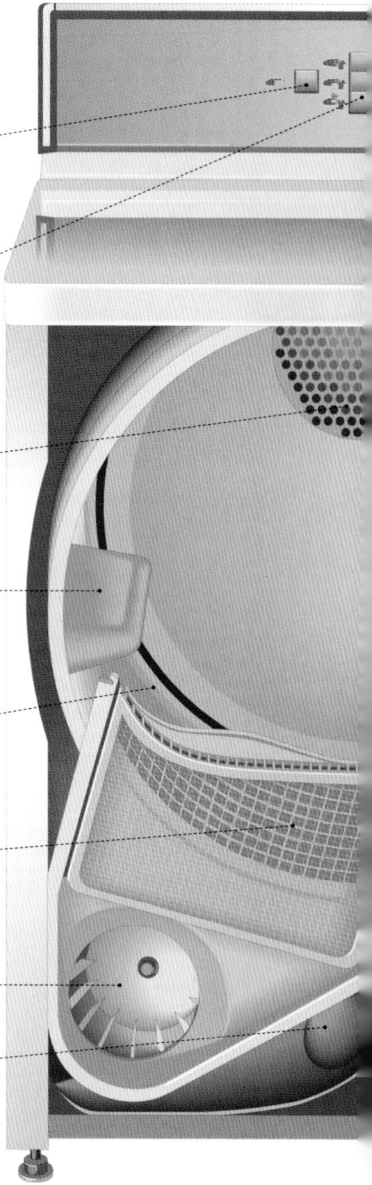
start switch
interruptor[M]
interrupteur[M] de démarrage[M]
Einschalter[M]
pulsante[M] di accensione[F]
temperature selector
selector[M] de temperatura[F]
sélecteur[M] de température[F]
Temperaturwähler[M]
termostato[M]
heating duct
conducto[M] de aire[M] caliente
conduit[M] de chauffage[M]
Warmluftzufuhr[F]
condotto[M] di riscaldamento[M]
vane
aleta[F]
ailette[F]
Mitnehmerrippe[F]
pala[F]
drum
tambor[M]
tambour[M]
Trommel[F]
tamburo[M]
lint trap
filtro[M] de pelusa[F]
filtre[M] à charpie[F]
Fusselfilter[M]
filtro[M] per lanugine[F]
fan
ventilador[M]
ventilateur[M]
Gebläse[N]
ventilatore[M]
motor
motor[M]
moteur[M]
Motor[M]
motore[M]

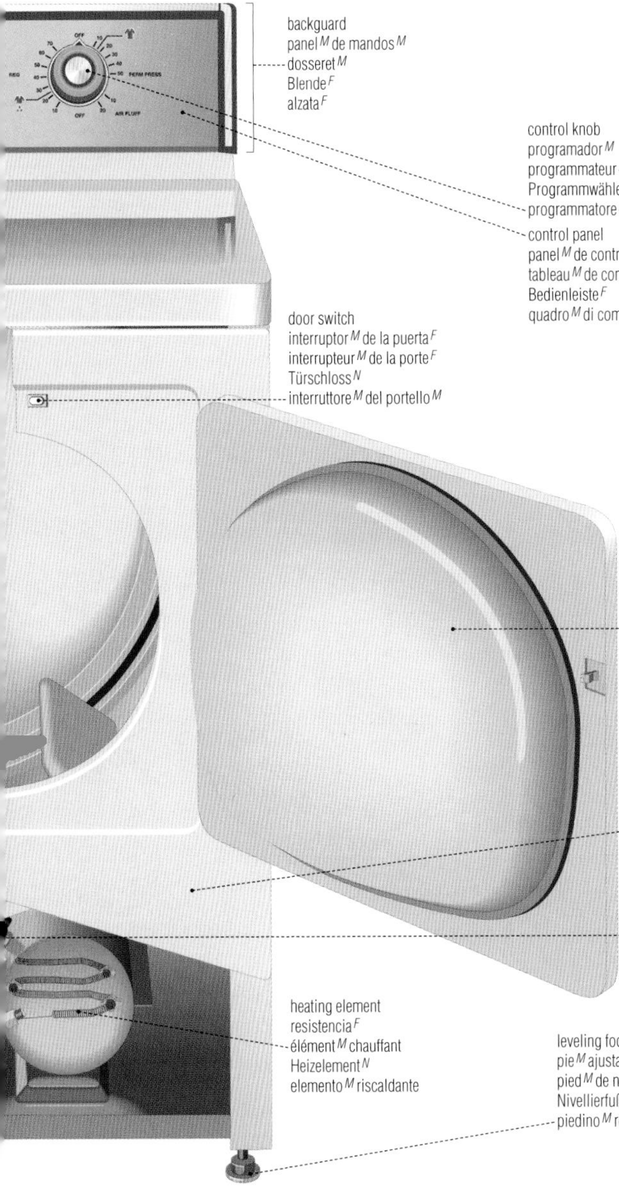
OFF
REG
PERM PRESS
AIR FLUFF
backguard
panel[M] de mandos[M]
dosseret[M]
Blende[F]
alzata[F]
control knob
programador[M]
programmateur[M]
Programmwähler[M]
programmatore[M]
control panel
panel[M] de control[M]
tableau[M] de commande[F]
Bedienleiste[F]
quadro[M] di comando[M]
door switch
interruptor[M] de la puerta[F]
interrupteur[M] de la porte[F]
Türschloss[N]
interruttore[M] del portello[M]
door
puerta[F]
porte[F]
Tür[F]
portello[M]
cabinet
armazón[M]
carrosserie[F]
Gehäuse[N]
armadio[M]
safety thermostat
termostato[M] de seguridad[F]
limiteur[M] de surchauffe[F]
Sicherheitsthermostat[M]
termostato[M] di sicurezza[F]
heating element
resistencia[F]
élément[M] chauffant
Heizelement[N]
elemento[M] riscaldante
leveling foot
pie[M] ajustable
pied[M] de nivellement[M]
Nivellierfuß[M]
piedino[M] regolabile

dishwasher
lavavajillas *M*
lave-vaisselle *M*
Geschirrspülmaschine *F*
lavastoviglie *F*

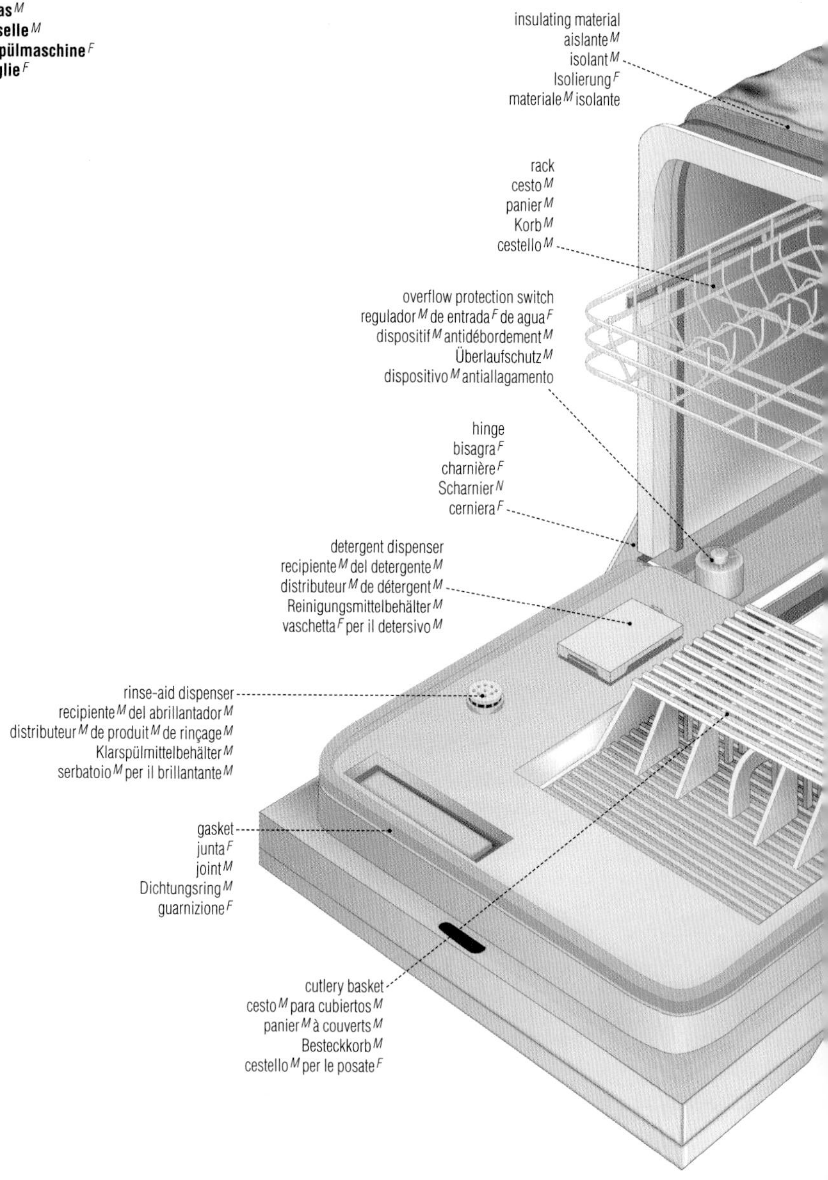
insulating material
aislante M
isolant M
Isolierung F
materiale M isolante
rack
cesto M
panier M
Korb M
cestello M
overflow protection switch
regulador M de entrada F de agua F
dispositif M antidébordement M
Überlaufschutz M
dispositivo M antiallagamento
hinge
bisagra F
charnière F
Scharnier N
cerniera F
detergent dispenser
recipiente M del detergente M
distributeur M de détergent M
Reinigungsmittelbehälter M
vaschetta F per il detersivo M
rinse-aid dispenser
recipiente M del abrillantador M
distributeur M de produit M de rinçage M
Klarspülmittelbehälter M
serbatoio M per il brillantante M
gasket
junta F
joint M
Dichtungsring M
guarnizione F
cutlery basket
cesto M para cubiertos M
panier M à couverts M
Besteckkorb M
cestello M per le posate F

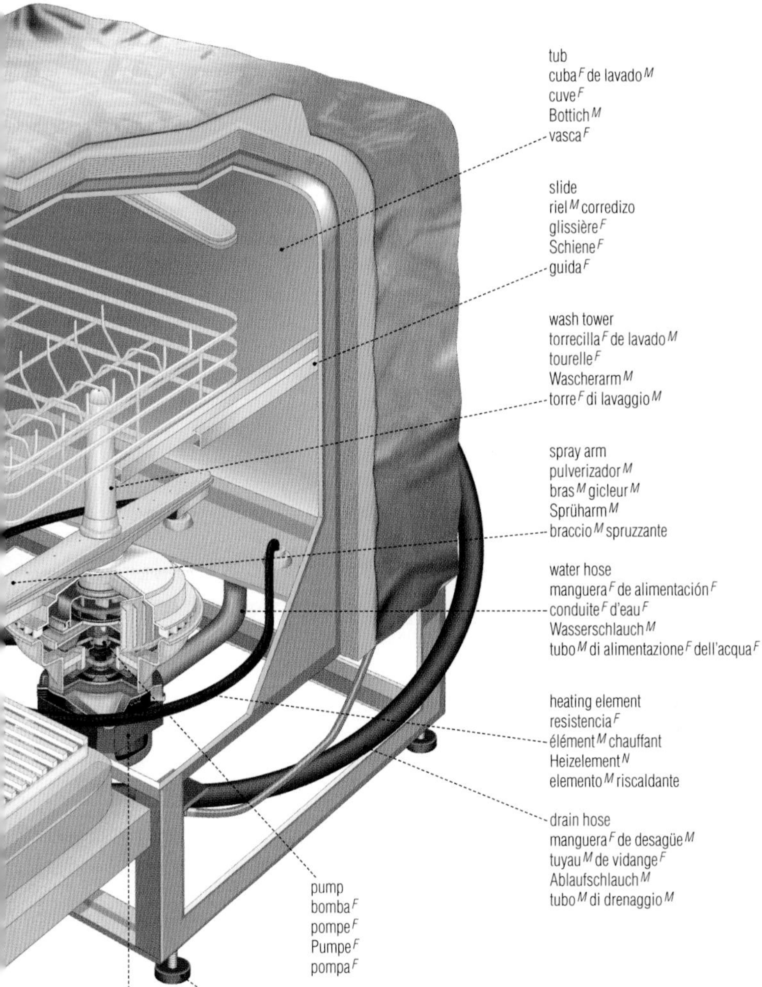
tub
cuba^F de lavado^M
cuve^F
Bottich^M
vasca^F
slide
riel^M corredizo
glissière^F
Schiene^F
guida^F
wash tower
torrecilla^F de lavado^M
tourelle^F
Wascherarm^M
torre^F di lavaggio^M
spray arm
pulverizador^M
bras^M gicleur^M
Sprüharm^M
braccio^M spruzzante
water hose
manguera^F de alimentación^F
conduite^F d'eau^F
Wasserschlauch^M
tubo^M di alimentazione^F dell'acqua^F
heating element
resistencia^F
élément^M chauffant
Heizelement^N
elemento^M riscaldante
drain hose
manguera^F de desagüe^M
tuyau^M de vidange^F
Ablaufschlauch^M
tubo^M di drenaggio^M
pump
bomba^F
pompe^F
Pumpe^F
pompa^F
leveling foot
pie^M ajustable
pied^M de nivellement^M
Nivellierfuß^M
piedino^M regolabile
motor
motor^M
moteur^M
Motor^M
motore^M

carpentry: nailing tools

carpintería[F]: herramientas[F] para clavar | menuiserie[F]: outils[M] pour clouer | Bautischlerei[F]: Nagelwerkzeuge[N] | carpenteria[F]: attrezzi[M] per chiodare

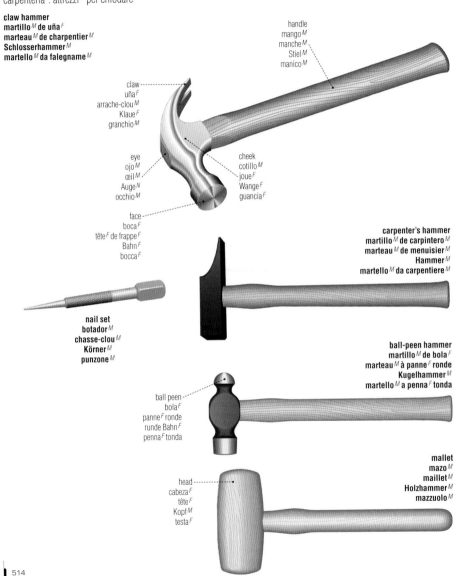

claw hammer
martillo[M] de uña[F]
marteau[M] de charpentier[M]
Schlosserhammer[M]
martello[M] da falegname[M]

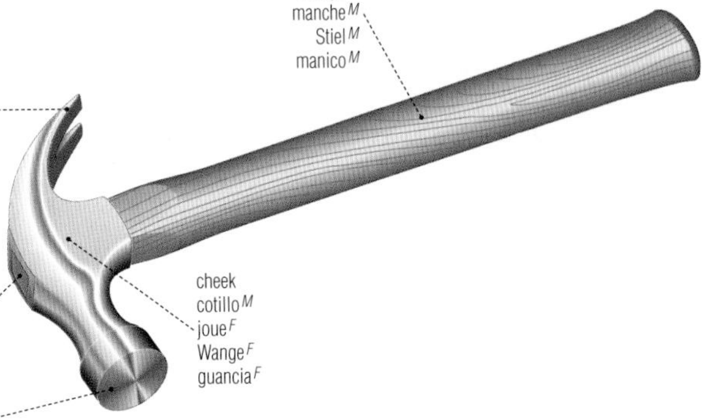
handle
mango[M]
manche[M]
Stiel[M]
manico[M]
claw
uña[F]
arrache-clou[M]
Klaue[F]
granchio[M]
eye
ojo[M]
œil[M]
Auge[N]
occhio[M]
cheek
cotillo[M]
joue[F]
Wange[F]
guancia[F]
face
boca[F]
tête[F] de frappe[F]
Bahn[F]
bocca[F]

carpenter's hammer
martillo[M] de carpintero[M]
marteau[M] de menuisier[M]
Hammer[M]
martello[M] da carpentiere[M]

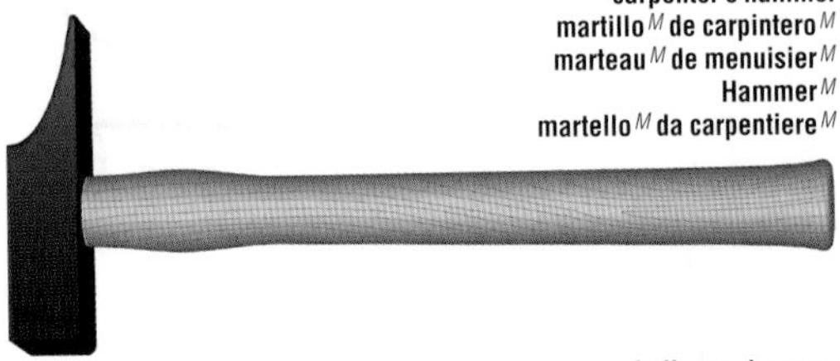

nail set
botador[M]
chasse-clou[M]
Körner[M]
punzone[M]

ball-peen hammer
martillo[M] de bola[F]
marteau[M] à panne[F] ronde
Kugelhammer[M]
martello[M] a penna[F] tonda

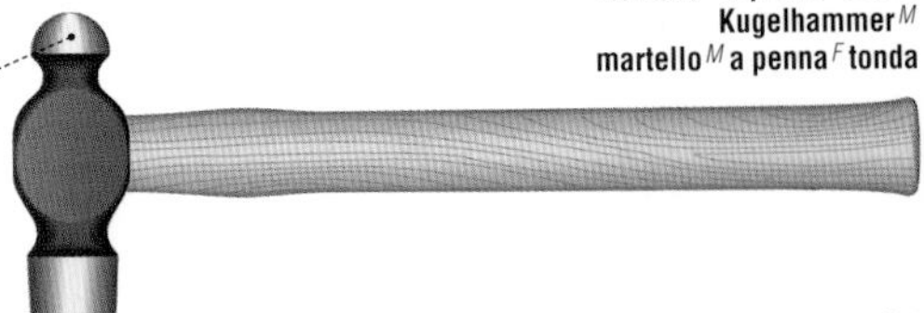
ball peen
bola[F]
panne[F] ronde
runde Bahn[F]
penna[F] tonda

mallet
mazo[M]
maillet[M]
Holzhammer[M]
mazzuolo[M]

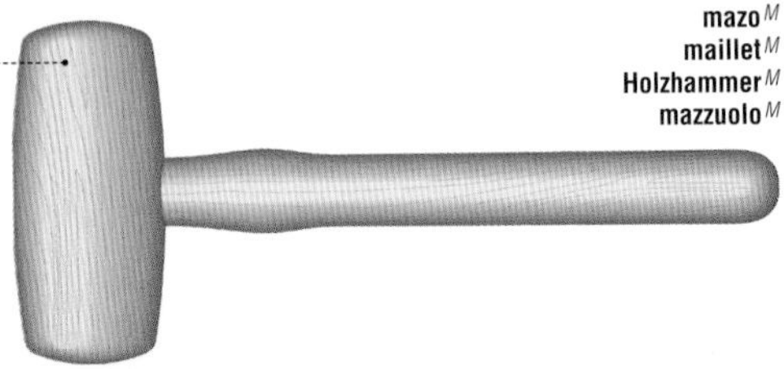
head
cabeza[F]
tête[F]
Kopf[M]
testa[F]

nail
clavo *M*
clou *M*
Nagel *M*
chiodo *M*

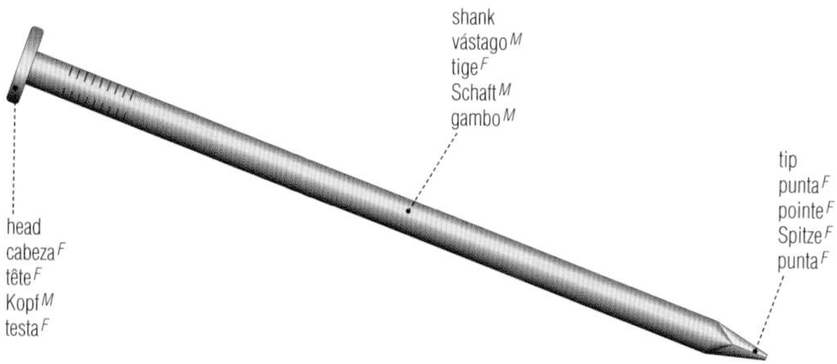
shank
vástago M
tige F
Schaft M
gambo M
tip
punta F
pointe F
Spitze F
punta F
head
cabeza F
tête F
Kopf M
testa F

examples of nails
ejemplos *M* **de clavos** *M*
exemples *M* **de clous** *M*
Beispiele *N* **für Nägel** *M*
esempi *M* **di chiodi** *M*

tack
tachuela *F*
semence *F*
Zwecke *F*
bulletta *F*

common nail
clavo *M* **común**
clou *M* **commun**
gewöhnlicher Nagel *M*
chiodo *M* **comune**

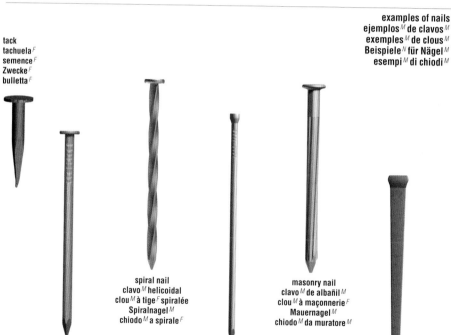

spiral nail
clavo *M* **helicoidal**
clou *M* **à tige** *F* **spiralée**
Spiralnagel *M*
chiodo *M* **a spirale** *F*

finishing nail
clavo *M* **sin cabeza** *F*
clou *M* **à tête** *F* **homme** *M*
Versenknagel *M*
chiodo *M* **di finitura** *F*

masonry nail
clavo *M* **de albañil** *M*
clou *M* **à maçonnerie** *F*
Mauernagel *M*
chiodo *M* **da muratore** *M*

cut nail
clavo *M* **cortado**
clou *M* **coupé**
geschnittener Nagel *M*
chiodo *M* **troncato**

carpentry: screwing tools

carpintería[F]: herramientas[F] para atornillar | menuiserie[F]: outils[M] pour visser | Bautischlerei[F]: Schraubwerkzeuge[N] | carpenteria[F]: utensili [M] per avvitare

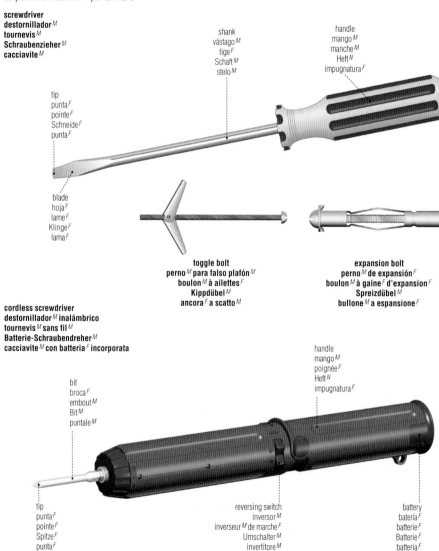

screwdriver
destornillador[M]
tournevis[M]
Schraubenzieher[M]
cacciavite[M]

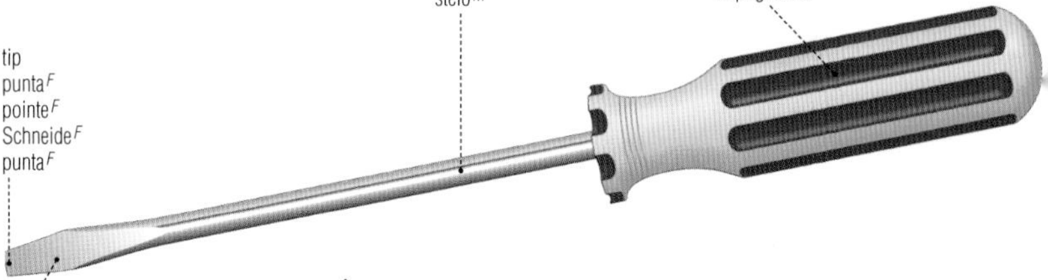
shank
vástago[M]
tige[F]
Schaft[M]
stelo[M]
handle
mango[M]
manche[M]
Heft[N]
impugnatura[F]
tip
punta[F]
pointe[F]
Schneide[F]
punta[F]
blade
hoja[F]
lame[F]
Klinge[F]
lama[F]

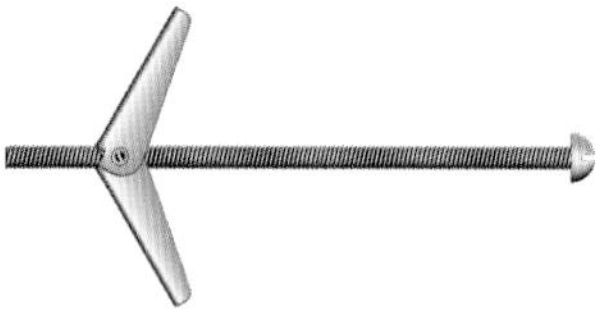

toggle bolt
perno[M] para falso plafón[M]
boulon[M] à ailettes[F]
Kippdübel[M]
ancora[F] a scatto[M]

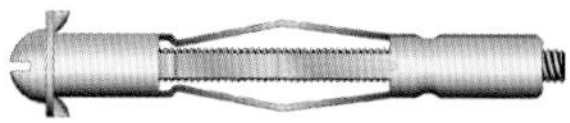

expansion bolt
perno[M] de expansión[F]
boulon[M] à gaine[F] d'expansion[F]
Spreizdübel[M]
bullone[M] a espansione[F]

cordless screwdriver
destornillador[M] inalámbrico
tournevis[M] sans fil[M]
Batterie-Schraubendreher[M]
cacciavite[M] con batteria[F] incorporata

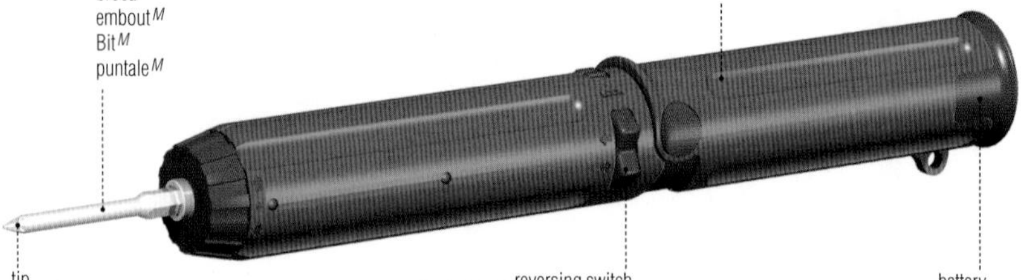
handle
mango[M]
poignée[F]
Heft[N]
impugnatura[F]
bit
broca[F]
embout[M]
Bit[M]
puntale[M]
tip
punta[F]
pointe[F]
Spitze[F]
punta[F]
reversing switch
inversor[M]
inverseur[M] de marche[F]
Umschalter[M]
invertitore[M]
battery
batería[F]
batterie[F]
Batterie[F]
batteria[F]

spiral screwdriver
destornillador[M] de trinquete[M]
tournevis[M] à spirale[F]
Drillschraubenzieher[M]
cacciavite[M] automatico

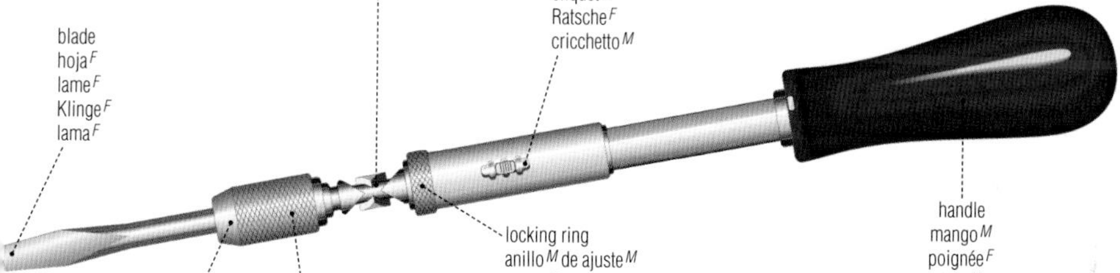
spiral
espiral F
spirale F
Spiralspindel F
spirale F
ratchet
trinquete M
cliquet M
Ratsche F
cricchetto M
blade
hoja F
lame F
Klinge F
lama F
locking ring
anillo M de ajuste M
bague F de blocage M
Feststellring M
ghiera F di bloccaggio M
handle
mango M
poignée F
Heft N
impugnatura F
jaw
mordaza F
mors M
Backen F
griffa F
chuck
mandril M
mandrin M
Bohrfutter N
morsetto M

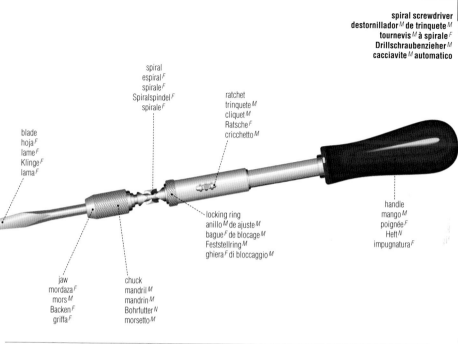

examples of tips
tipos[M] de puntas[F]
exemples[M] de pointes[F]
Klingenarten[F]
tipi[M] di punte[F]

square-headed tip
punta[F] de caja[F] cuadrada
pointe[F] carrée
Einsatz[M] für Imbusschrauben[F]
punta[F] a testa[F] quadra

flat tip
punta[F] de hoja[F] plana
pointe[F] plate
Einsatz[M] für Schlitzschrauben[F]
punta[F] piana

cross-headed tip
punta[F] cruciforme
pointe[F] cruciforme
Einsatz[M] für Kreuzschlitzschrauben[F]
punta[F] a croce[F]

carpentry: screwing tools

screw
tornillo^{M}
vis^{F}
Schraube^{F}
vite^{F}

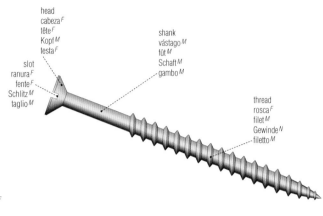

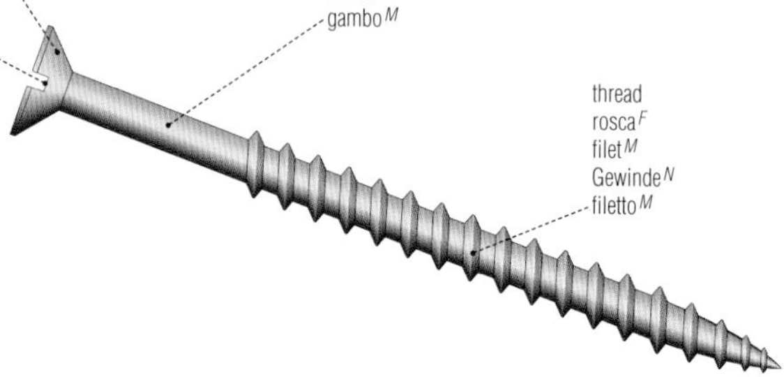
head
cabeza^{F}
tête^{F}
Kopf^{M}
testa^{F}
shank
vástago^{M}
fût^{M}
Schaft^{M}
gambo^{M}
slot
ranura^{F}
fente^{F}
Schlitz^{M}
taglio^{M}
thread
rosca^{F}
filet^{M}
Gewinde^{N}
filetto^{M}

examples of heads
tipos^{M} de cabeza^{F}
exemples^{M} de têtes^{F}
Kopfarten^{F}
tipi^{M} di teste^{F}

flat head
tornillo^{M} de cabeza^{F} avellanada
tête^{F} plate
Senkkopf^{M} mit Schlitz^{M}
testa^{F} piatta

one-way head
tornillo^{M} de un solo sentido^{M}
tête^{F} à sens^{M} unique
Sicherungskopf^{M}
testa^{F} non svitabile

round head
tornillo^{M} de cabeza^{F} redonda
tête^{F} ronde
Rundkopf^{M} mit Schlitz^{M}
testa^{F} tonda

oval head
tornillo^{M} de cabeza^{F} achaflanada
tête^{F} bombée
Linsenkopf^{M} mit Schlitz^{M}
testa^{F} bombata

Phillips
tornillo^{M} cruciforme (Phillips)
tête^{F} cruciforme
Senkkopf^{M} mit Kreuzschlitz^{M}
testa^{F} a croce^{F}

socket head
tornillo^{M} de caja^{F} cuadrada
tête^{F} creuse
Senkkopf^{M} mit Imbus^{M}
testa^{F} concava

carpentry: sawing tools

carpintería^{F}: herramientas^{F} para serrar | menuiserie^{F}: outils^{M} pour scier | Bautischlerei^{F}: Sägewerkzeuge^{N} | carpenteria^{F}: utensili^{M} per segare

hacksaw
sierra^{F} para metales^{M}
scie^{F} à métaux^{M}
Bügelsäge^{F}
seghetto^{M}

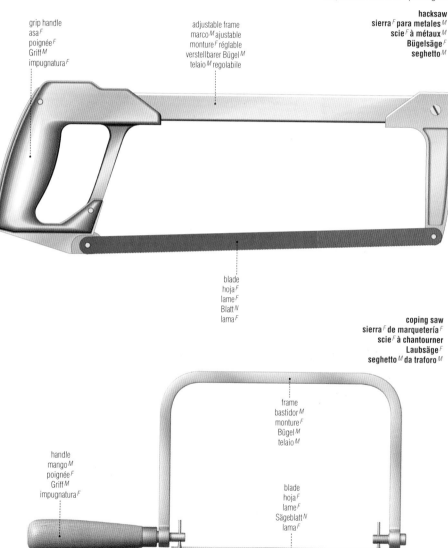

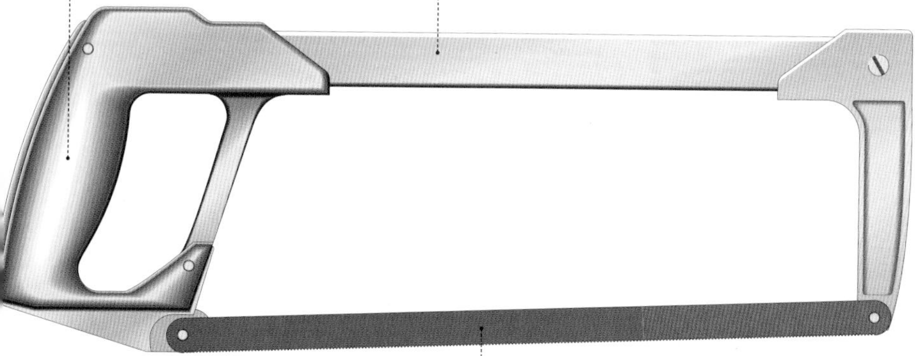
grip handle
asa^{F}
poignée^{F}
Griff^{M}
impugnatura^{F}
adjustable frame
marco^{M} ajustable
monture^{F} réglable
verstellbarer Bügel^{M}
telaio^{M} regolabile
blade
hoja^{F}
lame^{F}
Blatt^{N}
lama^{F}

coping saw
sierra^{F} de marquetería^{F}
scie^{F} à chantourner
Laubsäge^{F}
seghetto^{M} da traforo^{M}

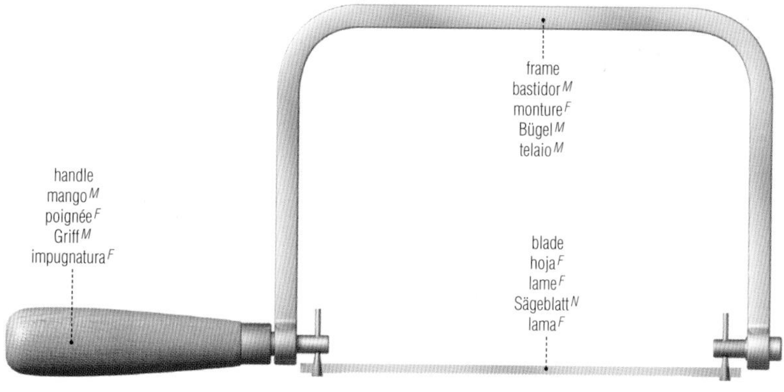
frame
bastidor^{M}
monture^{F}
Bügel^{M}
telaio^{M}
handle
mango^{M}
poignée^{F}
Griff^{M}
impugnatura^{F}
blade
hoja^{F}
lame^{F}
Sägeblatt^{N}
lama^{F}

carpentry: sawing tools

compass saw
serrucho *M* **de punta** *F*
scie *F* **à guichet** *M*
Stichsäge *F*
gattuccio *M*

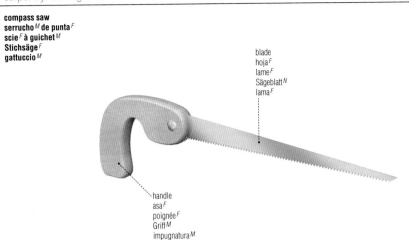

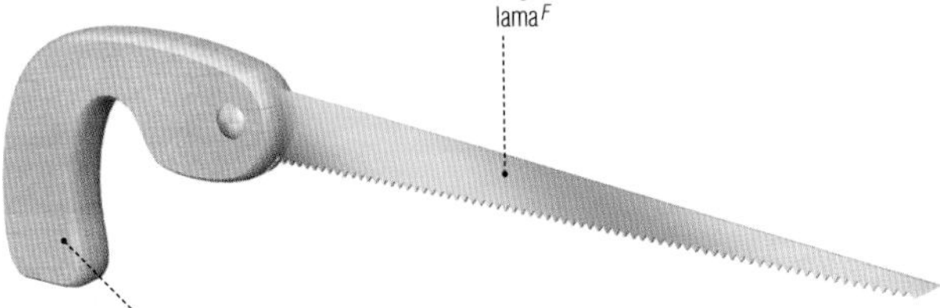
blade
hoja F
lame F
Sägeblatt N
lama F
handle
asa F
poignée F
Griff M
impugnatura M

handsaw
serrucho *M*
scie *F* **égoïne**
Fuchsschwanz *M*
saracco *M*

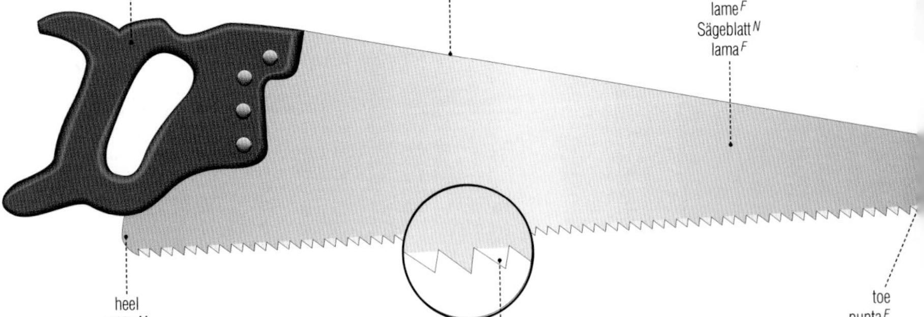
handle
asa F
poignée F
Griff M
impugnatura F
back
canto M
dos M
Rücken M
dorso M
blade
hoja F
lame F
Sägeblatt N
lama F
heel
talón M
talon M
hinteres Ende N
tallone M
tooth
diente M
dent F
Zahn M
dente M
toe
punta F
pointe F
Spitze F
punta F

hand miter saw
sierra F de ingletes M
scie F à onglet M manuelle
Hand-Gehrungssäge F
sega F per augnatura F manuale

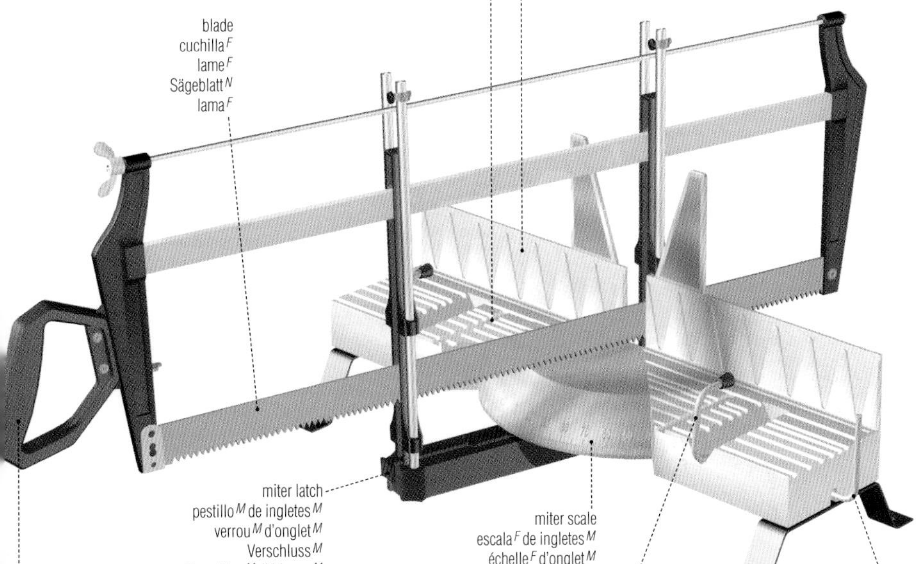
miter box
caja F de ingletes M
boîte F à onglets M
Gehrungsschneidlade F
cassetta F ad augnatura F
fence
guía F
guide M
Anschlag M
guida F di appoggio M
blade
cuchilla F
lame F
Sägeblatt N
lama F
miter latch
pestillo M de ingletes M
verrou M d'onglet M
Verschluss M
dispositivo M di blocco M
miter scale
escala F de ingletes M
échelle F d'onglet M
Gehrmaß N
scala F graduata
handle
mango M
poignée F
Griff M
impugnatura F
clamp
mordaza F
serre-joint M
Werkstückspanner M
morsetto M
end stop
final M de carrera F
butée F
Endanschlag M
finecorsa M

carpentry: sawing tools

circular saw
sierra F circular de mano F
scie F circulaire
Handkreissäge F
sega F circolare

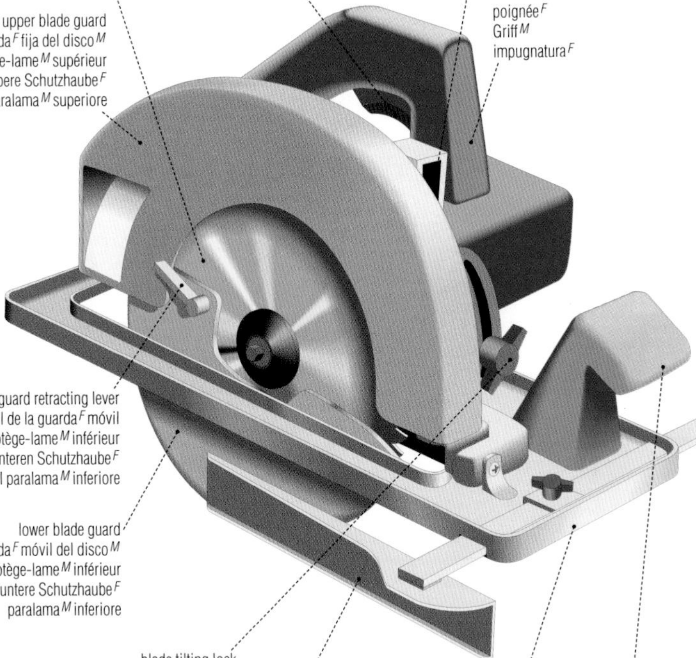
height adjustment scale
escala F de altura F
échelle F de profondeur F
Höhenverstellskala F
indice M di regolazione F dell'altezza F
blade
disco M
lame F
Blatt N
lama F
trigger switch
interruptor M de gatillo M
interrupteur M à gâchette F
Druckschalter M
interruttore M a grilletto M
handle
asa F
poignée F
Griff M
impugnatura F
upper blade guard
guarda F fija del disco M
protège-lame M supérieur
obere Schutzhaube F
paralama M superiore
lower guard retracting lever
palanca F retráctil de la guarda F móvil
levier M du protège-lame M inférieur
Hebeleiste F der unteren Schutzhaube F
leva F per togliere il paralama M inferiore
lower blade guard
guarda F móvil del disco M
protège-lame M inférieur
untere Schutzhaube F
paralama M inferiore
blade tilting lock
seguro M de inclinación F del disco M
blocage M de l'inclinaison F
Feststellschraube F für Schrägstellung F
dispositivo M di blocco M dell'inclinazione F della lama F
rip fence
guía F de corte M
guide M parallèle
Parallelanschlag M
guida F parallela
base plate
soporte M
semelle F
Gleitschuh M
piastra F di base F
knob handle
perilla F
bouton M-guide M
Führungsgriff M
poggiamano M

jig saw
sierra[F] de calar
scie[F] sauteuse
elektrische Stichsäge[F]
seghetto[M] alternativo

speed selector switch
interruptor[M] selector[M] de velocidad[F]
sélecteur[M] de vitesse[F]
Hubzahlvorwahl[F]
selettore[M] di velocità[F]

lock-on button
botón[M] de bloqueo[M]
bouton[M] de verrouillage[M] de l'interrupteur[M]
Feststellknopf[M]
pulsante[F] di aggancio[M]

trigger switch
interruptor[M] de gatillo[M]
interrupteur[M] à gâchette[F]
Druckschalter[M]
interruttore[M] a grilletto[M]

handle
empuñadura[F]
poignée[F]
Griff[M]
impugnatura[F]

orbital-action selector
selector[M] de movimiento[M] orbital
sélecteur[M] d'inclinaison[F] de la lame[F]
Pendelhub-Einstellung[F]
selettore[M] del movimento[M] orbitale

chip cover
protector[M] contra virutas[F]
déflecteur[M] de copeaux[M]
Späneschutz[M]
paratrucioli[M]

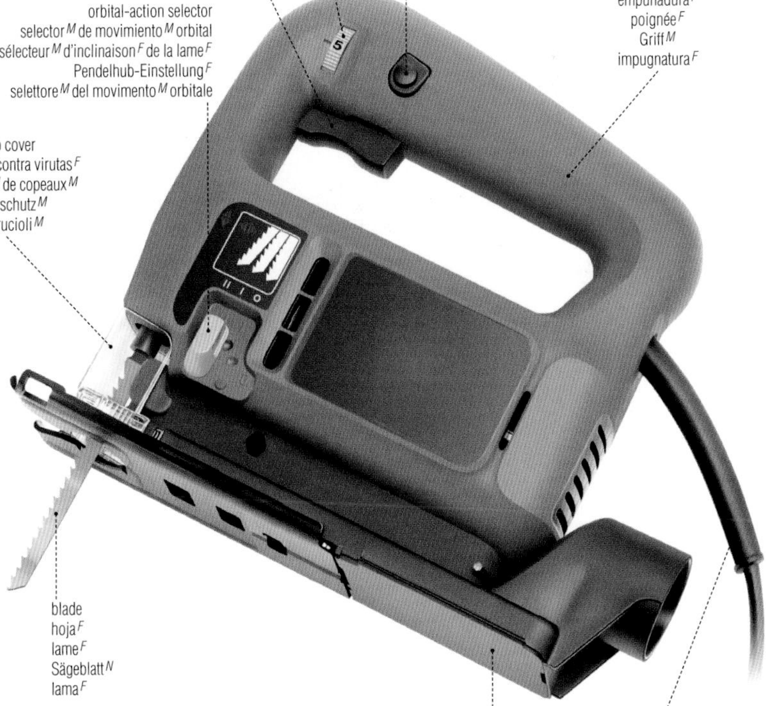
5
II I O

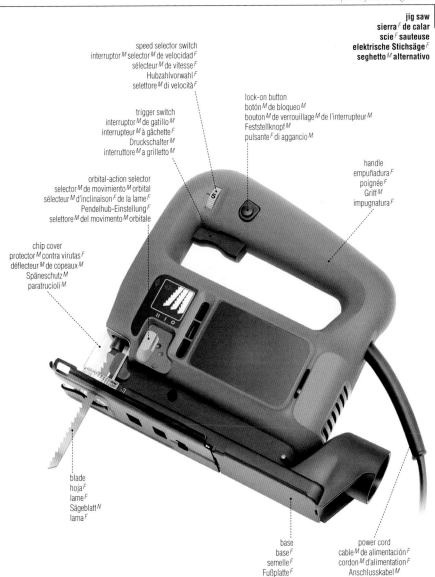

blade
hoja[F]
lame[F]
Sägeblatt[N]
lama[F]

base
base[F]
semelle[F]
Fußplatte[F]
basamento[M]

power cord
cable[M] de alimentación[F]
cordon[M] d'alimentation[F]
Anschlusskabel[M]
cavo[M] di alimentazione[F]

carpentry: drilling tools

carpintería^F: herramientas^F percutoras | menuiserie^F: outils^M pour percer | Bautischlerei^F: Bohrwerkzeuge^N | carpenteria^F: attrezzi^M per trapanare

electric drill
taladro^M eléctrico
perceuse^F électrique
elektrische Bohrmaschine^F
trapano^M elettrico

switch lock
seguro^M del interruptor^M
blocage^M de l'interrupteur^M
Feststellknopf^M
dispositivo^M di blocco^M dell'interruttore^M
pistol grip handle
mango^M
poignée^F-pistolet^M
Pistolengriff^M
impugnatura^F a pistola^F
nameplate
placa^F de especificaciones^F
plaque^F signalétique
Typenschild^N
targhetta^F del costruttore^M
trigger switch
interruptor^M de gatillo^M
interrupteur^M à gâchette^F
Druckschalter^M
interruttore^M a grilletto^M
chuck
mandril^M
mandrin^M
Bohrfutter^N
mandrino^M
jaw
mordaza^F
mors^M
Backen^F
griffa^F
auxiliary handle
mango^M auxiliar
poignée^F auxiliaire
zusätzlicher Griff^M
impugnatura^F laterale
plug
enchufe^M
fiche^F
Stecker^M
spina^F
cable
cable^M
câble^M
Kabel^N
cavo^M
cable sleeve
protector^M del cable^M
manchon^M de câble^M
Kabelmuffe^F
manicotto^M del cavo^M

brace
berbiquí M
vilebrequin M
Bohrwinde F
girabecchino M

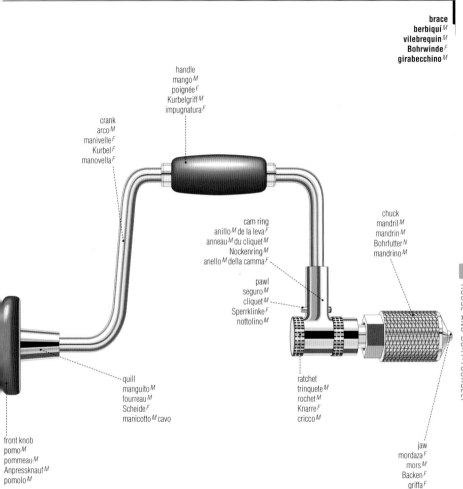

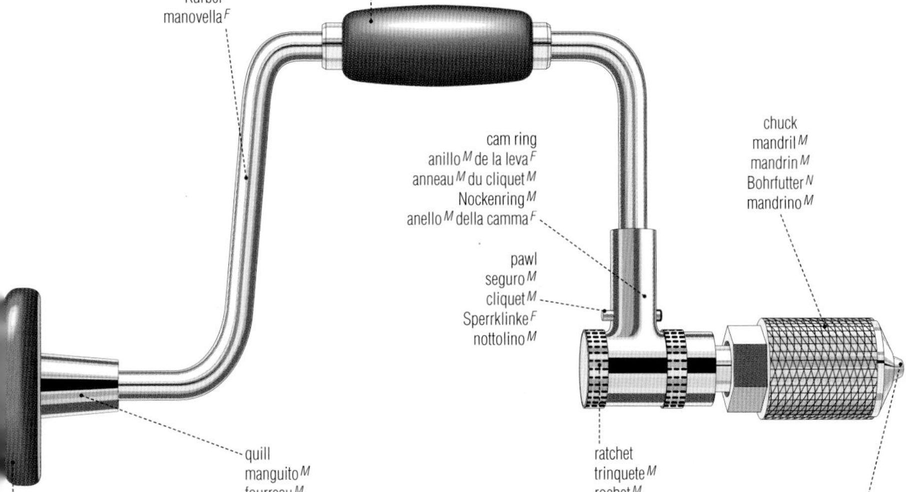
handle
mango M
poignée F
Kurbelgriff M
impugnatura F
crank
arco M
manivelle F
Kurbel F
manovella F
cam ring
anillo M de la leva F
anneau M du cliquet M
Nockenring M
anello M della camma F
chuck
mandril M
mandrin M
Bohrfutter N
mandrino M
pawl
seguro M
cliquet M
Sperrklinke F
nottolino M
quill
manguito M
fourreau M
Scheide F
manicotto M cavo
ratchet
trinquete M
rochet M
Knarre F
cricco M
front knob
pomo M
pommeau M
Anpressknauf M
pomolo M
jaw
mordaza F
mors M
Backen F
griffa F

examples of bits and drills
ejemplos[M] de brocas[F] y barrenas[F]
exemples[M] de mèches[F] et de forets[M]
Beispiele[N] für Bits[M] und Bohrer[M]
esempi[M] di mecchie[F] e punte[F] da trapano[M]

twist bit
broca[F] helicoidal
mèche[F] hélicoïdale
Spiralbohrer[M]
mecchia[F] elicoidale

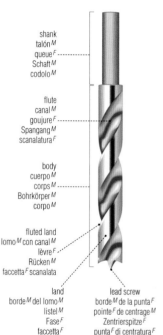

shank
talón[M]
queue[F]
Schaft[M]
codolo[M]
flute
canal[M]
goujure[F]
Spangang[M]
scanalatura[F]
body
cuerpo[M]
corps[M]
Bohrkörper[M]
corpo[M]
fluted land
lomo[M] con canal[M]
lèvre[F]
Rücken[M]
faccetta[F] scanalata
land
borde[M] del lomo[M]
listel[M]
Fase[F]
faccetta[F]
lead screw
borde[M] de la punta[F]
pointe[F] de centrage[M]
Zentrierspitze[F]
punta[F] di centratura[F]

solid center auger bit
broca[F] helicoidal central
mèche[F] hélicoïdale à âme[F] centrale
Schneckenbohrer[M]
mecchia[F] a tortiglione[M]

shank
talón[M]
queue[F]
Schaft[M]
codolo[M]
twist
torsión[F]
torsade[F]
Spirale[F]
elica[F]
spur
espolón[M]
traçoir[M]
Vorschneider[M]
tagliente[M]
lead screw
tornillo[M] guía
pointe[F] de centrage[M]
Zentrierspitze[F]
punta[F] di centratura[F]

twist drill
broca[F] helicoidal
foret[M] hélicoïdal
Spiralbohrer[M]
punta[F] elicoidale

masonry drill
barrena[F] de muro[M]
foret[M] de maçonnerie[F]
Steinbohrer[M]
punta[F] da muro[M]

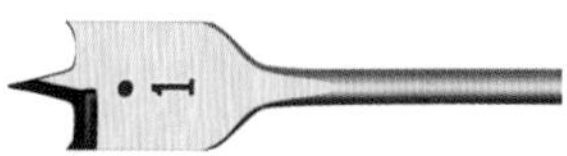

spade bit
broca[F] de pala[F]
mèche[F] à centre[M] plat
Flachfräsbohrer[M]
mecchia[F] a lancia[F]

double-twist auger bit
broca[F] salomónica de canal[M] angosto
mèche[F] hélicoïdale à double torsade[F]
Schlangenbohrer[M] mit doppeltem Gewindegang
mecchia[F] a doppia elica[F]

carpentry: shaping tools

carpintería[F]: herramientas[F] de perfilado[M] | menuiserie[F]: outils[M] pour façonner | Bautischlerei[F]: Formwerkzeuge[N] | carpenteria[F]: attrezzi[M] per sagomare

random orbit sander
lijadora[F] excéntrica
ponceuse[F] excentrique
Exzenterschleifer[M]
smerigliatrice[F] eccentrica

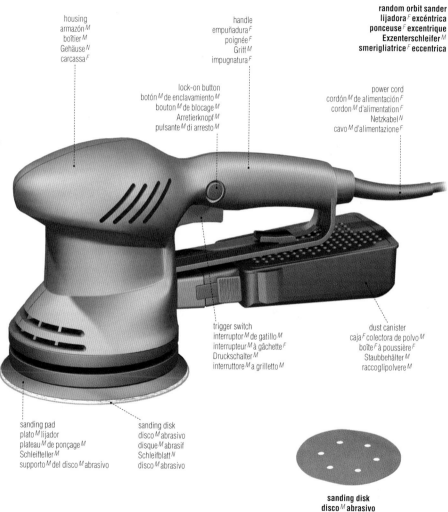

housing
armazón[M]
boîtier[M]
Gehäuse[N]
carcassa[F]
handle
empuñadura[F]
poignée[F]
Griff[M]
impugnatura[F]
lock-on button
botón[M] de enclavamiento[M]
bouton[M] de blocage[M]
Arretierknopf[M]
pulsante[M] di arresto[M]
power cord
cordón[M] de alimentación[F]
cordon[M] d'alimentation[F]
Netzkabel[N]
cavo[M] d'alimentazione[F]
trigger switch
interruptor[M] de gatillo[M]
interrupteur[M] à gâchette[F]
Druckschalter[M]
interruttore[M] a grilletto[M]
dust canister
caja[F] colectora de polvo[M]
boîte[F] à poussière[F]
Staubbehälter[M]
raccoglipolvere[M]
sanding pad
plato[M] lijador
plateau[M] de ponçage[M]
Schleifteller[M]
supporto[M] del disco[M] abrasivo
sanding disk
disco[M] abrasivo
disque[M] abrasif
Schleifblatt[N]
disco[M] abrasivo

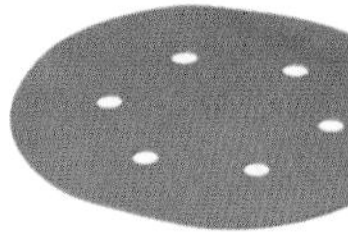

sanding disk
disco[M] abrasivo
disque[M] abrasif
Schleifblatt[N]
disco[M] abrasivo

carpentry: shaping tools

router
fresadora *F*
défonceuse *F*
Oberfräse *F*
fresatrice *F* **verticale**

head
cabeza F
tête F
Kopf M
testa F
motor
motor M
moteur M
Motor M
motore M
depth adjustment
ajuste M de profundidad F
réglage M de profondeur F
Tiefeneinstellung F
regolatore M di profondità F
switch
interruptor M
interrupteur M
Schalter M
interruttore M
cord sleeve
protector M del cable M
manchon M du cordon M
Kabelmantel M
manicotto M del cordone M
guide handle
asa F
poignée F de guidage M
Führungsgriff M
impugnatura F
base
base F
semelle F
Fuß M
base F
collet
collarín M
écrou M du porte-outil M
Anlaufhülse F
collare M
tool holder
mordaza F
porte-outil M
Werkzeugfutter N
portautensili M

examples of bits
ejemplos^{F} de fresas^{F}
exemples^{M} de fraises^{F}
Beispiele^{N} für Fräser^{M}
esempi^{M} di frese^{F}

rounding-over bit
fresa^{F} de pecho^{M} de paloma^{F}
fraise^{F} à quart^{M} de rond^{M}
Viertelstabfräser^{M}
fresa^{F} a quarto^{M} di anello^{M}

core box bit
fresa^{F} de enrasar
fraise^{F} à gorge^{F}
Hohlkehlfräser^{M}
fresa^{F} a corona^{F}

dovetail bit
fresa^{F} de cola^{F} de milano^{M}
fraise^{F} à queue^{F} d'aronde^{F}
Zinkenfräser^{M}
fresa^{F} a coda^{F} di rondine^{F}

cove bit
fresa^{F} de caveto^{M}
fraise^{F} à congé^{M}
Hohlkehlfräser^{M} mit Anlaufzapfen^{N}
fresa^{F} di raccordo^{M}

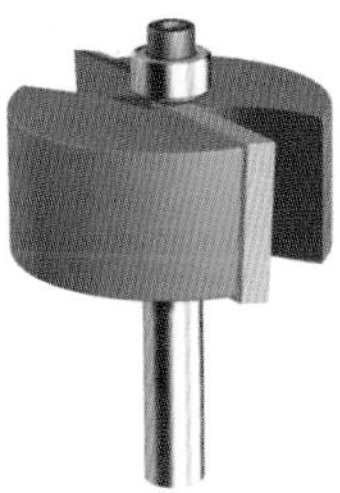

rabbet bit
fresa^{F} de acanalar
fraise^{F} à feuillure^{F}
Falzfräser^{M}
fresa^{F} per scanalare

chamfer bit
fresa^{F} de biselar
fraise^{F} à chanfrein^{M}
Faserfräser^{M}
fresa^{F} per smussare

plane
cepillo M
rabot M
Hobel M
pialla F

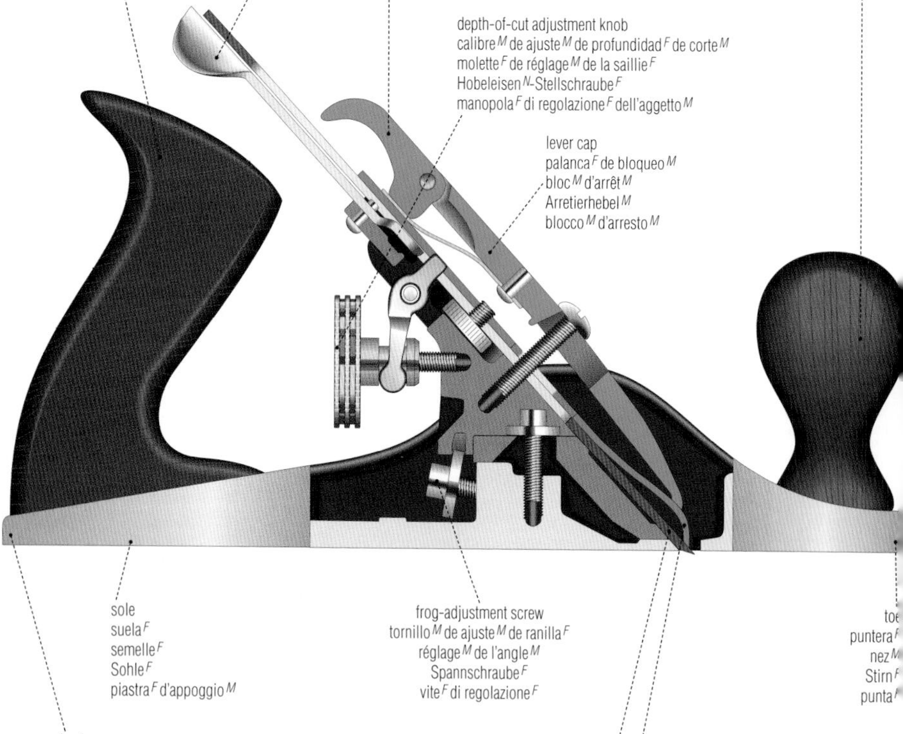
lateral-adjustment lever
nivelador M
levier M de réglage M latéral
Seitenverstellhebel M
leva F di regolazione F laterale
handle
empuñadura F
poignée F
Griff M
impugnatura F
wedge lever
palanca F de la cuña F
levier M du bloc M
Keilhebel M
leva F di serraggio M
knob
pomo M
pommeau M
Handgriff M
pomolo M
depth-of-cut adjustment knob
calibre M de ajuste M de profundidad F de corte M
molette F de réglage M de la saillie F
Hobeleisen N-Stellschraube F
manopola F di regolazione F dell'aggetto M
lever cap
palanca F de bloqueo M
bloc M d'arrêt M
Arretierhebel M
blocco M d'arresto M
sole
suela F
semelle F
Sohle F
piastra F d'appoggio M
frog-adjustment screw
tornillo M de ajuste M de ranilla F
réglage M de l'angle M
Spannschraube F
vite F di regolazione F
heel
talón M
talon M
hinteres Ende N
tallone M
blade
hoja F
fer M
Hobeleisen N
ferro M
cap iron
contrahoja F
contre-fer M
Klappe F
controferro M

file
lima[F]
lime[F]
Flachfeile[F]
lima[F]

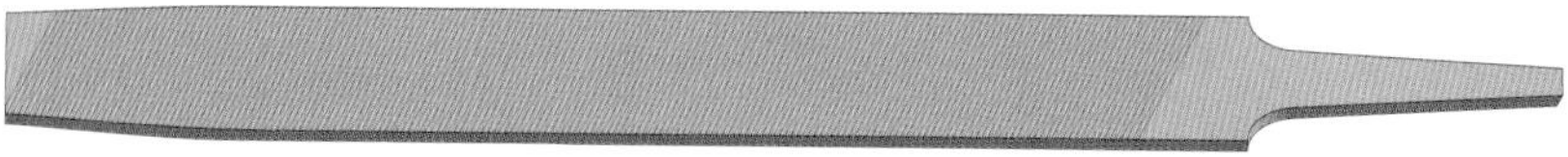

wood chisel
escoplo[M]
ciseau[M] **à bois**[M]
Stemmeisen[N]
scalpello[M] **da falegname**[M]

rasp
escofina[F]
râpe[F]
Raspel[F]
raspa[F]

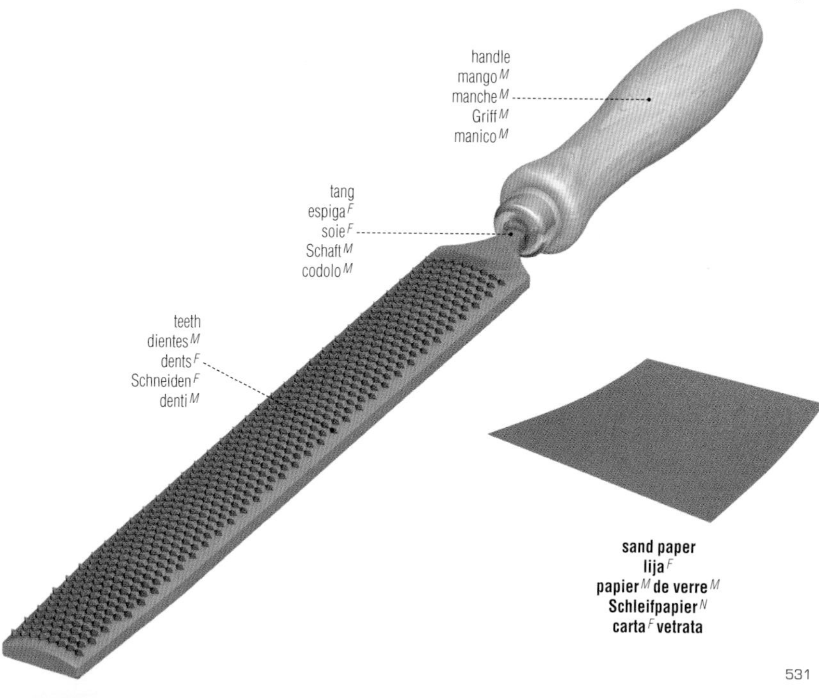
handle
mango[M]
manche[M]
Griff[M]
manico[M]
tang
espiga[F]
soie[F]
Schaft[M]
codolo[M]
teeth
dientes[M]
dents[F]
Schneiden[F]
denti[M]

sand paper
lija[F]
papier[M] **de verre**[M]
Schleifpapier[N]
carta[F] **vetrata**

carpentry: gripping and tightening tools

carpintería^F: herramientas^F para apretar | menuiserie^F: outils^M pour serrer | Bautischlerei^F: Greif- und Spannwerkzeuge^N | carpenteria^F: attrezzi^M di serraggio^M

pliers
alicates^M
pinces^F
Zangen^F
pinze^F

slip joint pliers
pinzas^F universales
pince^F à joint^M coulissant
Kombizange^F
pinza^F a giunto^M scorrevole

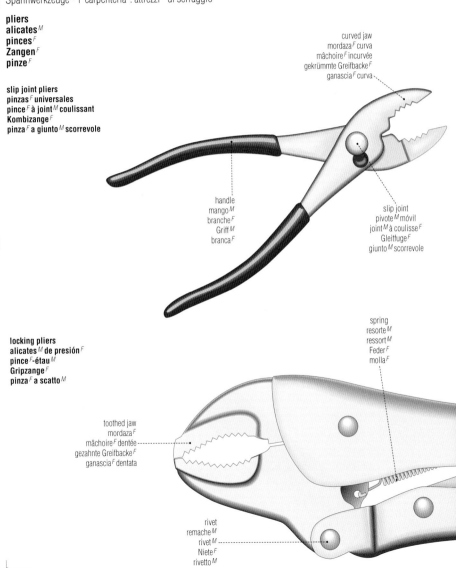

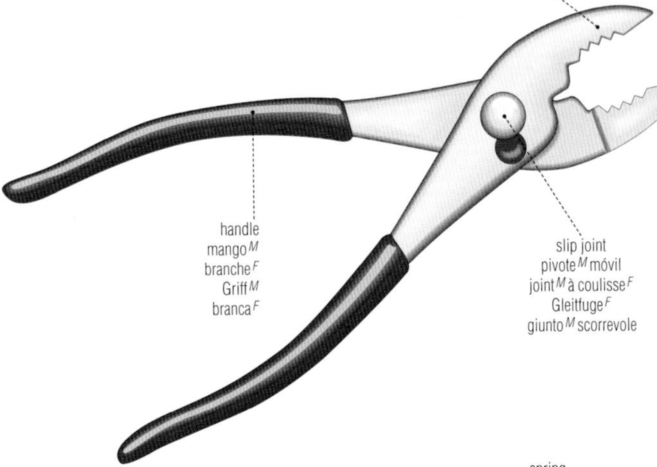
curved jaw
mordaza^F curva
mâchoire^F incurvée
gekrümmte Greifbacke^F
ganascia^F curva
handle
mango^M
branche^F
Griff^M
branca^F
slip joint
pivote^M móvil
joint^M à coulisse^F
Gleitfuge^F
giunto^M scorrevole

locking pliers
alicates^M de presión^F
pince^F-étau^M
Gripzange^F
pinza^F a scatto^M

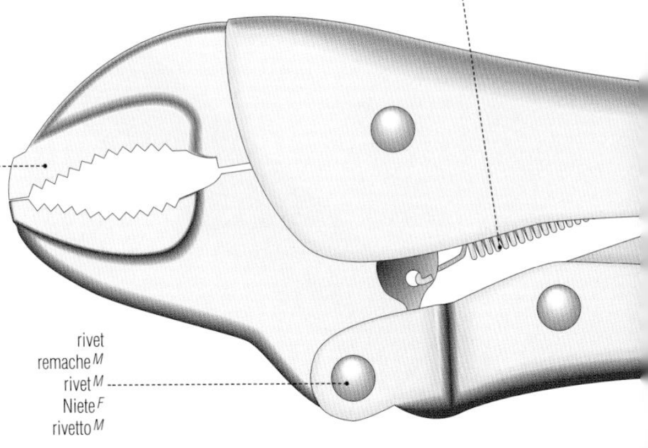
spring
resorte^M
ressort^M
Feder^F
molla^F
toothed jaw
mordaza^F
mâchoire^F dentée
gezahnte Greifbacke^F
ganascia^F dentata
rivet
remache^M
rivet^M
Niete^F
rivetto^M

carpentry: gripping and tightening tools

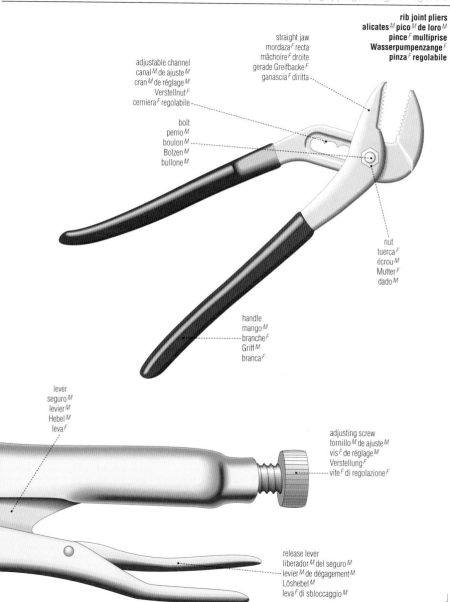

rib joint pliers
alicates[M] pico[M] de loro[M]
pince[F] multiprise
Wasserpumpenzange[F]
pinza[F] regolabile

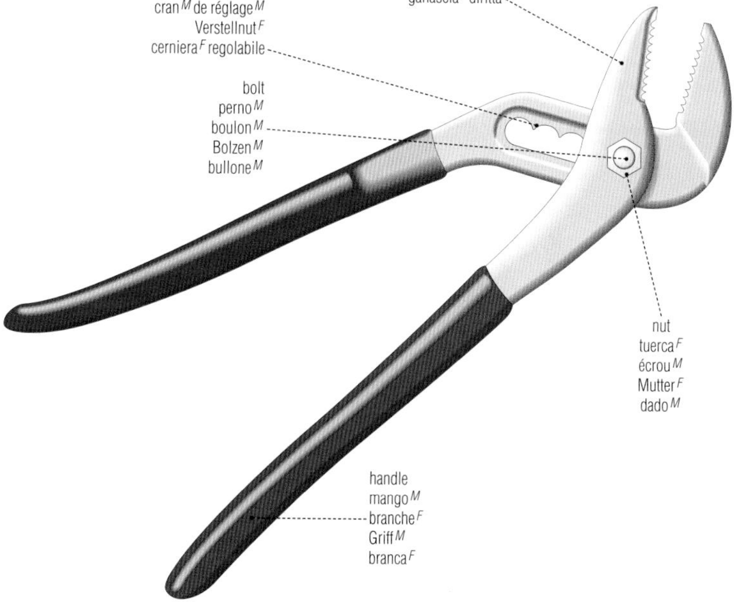
straight jaw
mordaza[F] recta
mâchoire[F] droite
gerade Greifbacke[F]
ganascia[F] diritta
adjustable channel
canal[M] de ajuste[M]
cran[M] de réglage[M]
Verstellnut[F]
cerniera[F] regolabile
bolt
perno[M]
boulon[M]
Bolzen[M]
bullone[M]
nut
tuerca[F]
écrou[M]
Mutter[F]
dado[M]
handle
mango[M]
branche[F]
Griff[M]
branca[F]

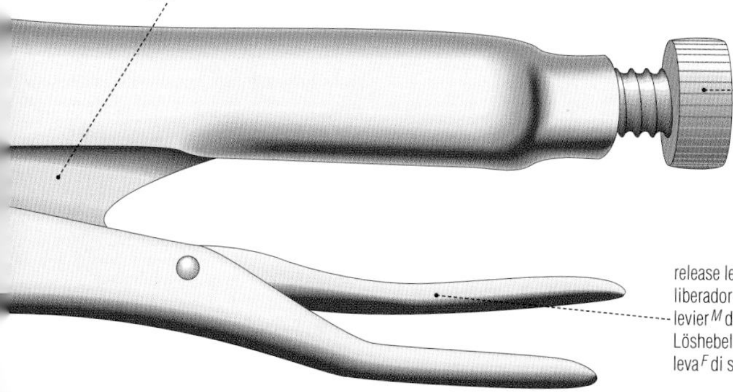
lever
seguro[M]
levier[M]
Hebel[M]
leva[F]
adjusting screw
tornillo[M] de ajuste[M]
vis[F] de réglage[M]
Verstellung[F]
vite[F] di regolazione[F]
release lever
liberador[M] del seguro[M]
levier[M] de dégagement[M]
Löshebel[M]
leva[F] di sbloccaggio[M]

carpentry: gripping and tightening tools

wrenches
llaves F
clés F
Schlüssel M
chiavi F

socket set
juego M de casquillos M
jeu M de douilles F
Steckschlüsselsatz M
set M di bussole F

ratchet socket wrench
llave F de carraca F
clé F à douille F à cliquet M
Knarre F
chiave F a bussola F a cricchetto M

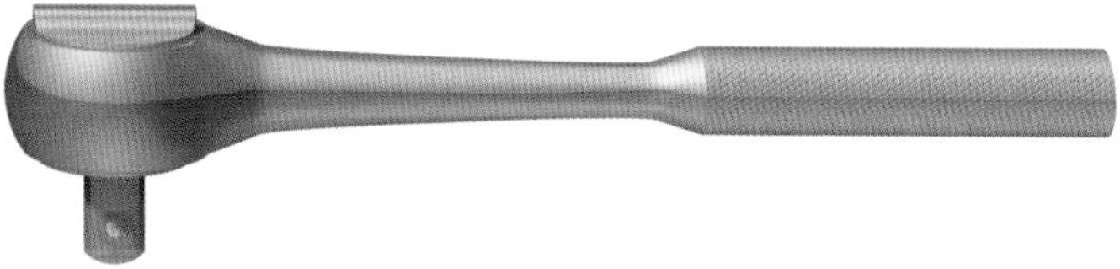

open end wrench
llave F de tuercas F española
clé F à fourches F
Doppelmaulschlüssel M
chiave F a forchetta F doppia

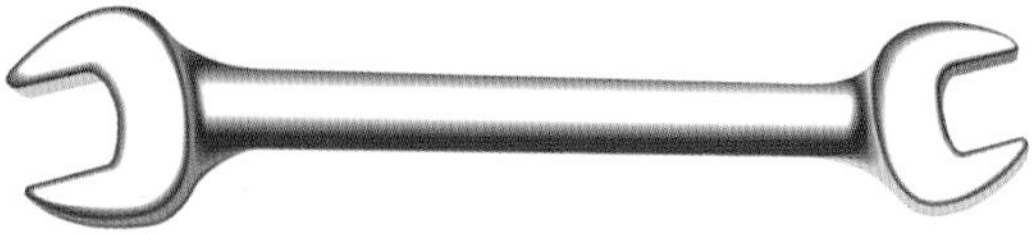

box end wrench
llave F de estrella F común
clé F polygonale
Doppelringschlüssel M
chiave F poligonale doppia

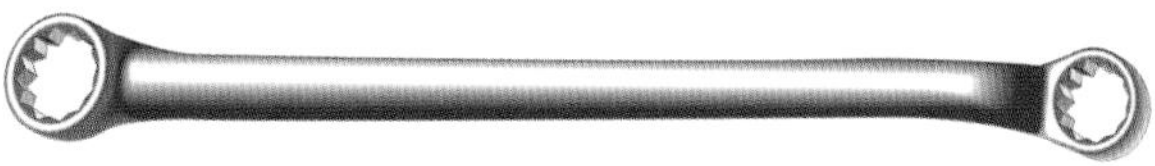

crescent wrench
llave F inglesa
clé F à molette F
Rollgabelschlüssel M
chiave F a rullino M

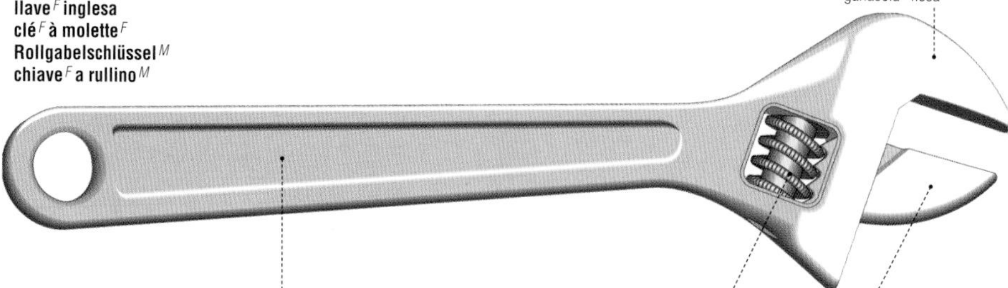
fixed jaw
mordaza F fija
mâchoire F fixe
feste Backe F
ganascia F fissa
handle
mango M
manche M
Griff M
manico M
thumbscrew
tornillo M
molette F
Rädelung F
rullino M
movable jaw
mordaza F móvil
mâchoire F mobile
bewegliche Backe F
ganascia F mobile

nuts
tuercas[F]
écrous[M]
Muttern[F]
dadi[M]

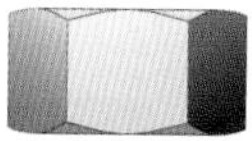

hexagon nut
tuerca[F] hexagonal
écrou[M] hexagonal
Sechskantmutter[F]
dado[M] esagonale

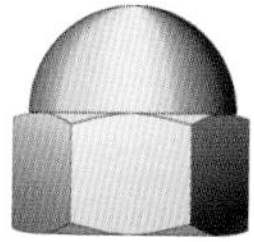

acorn nut
tuerca[F] cerrada
écrou[M] borgne
Hutmutter[F]
dado[M] cieco

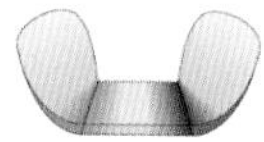

wing nut
tuerca[F] de mariposa[F]
écrou[M] à oreilles[F]
Flügelmutter[F]
galletto[M]

bolts
pernos[M]
boulons[M]
Schrauben[F]
bulloni[M]

bolt
perno[M]
boulon[M]
Schraubenbolzen[M]
bullone[M]

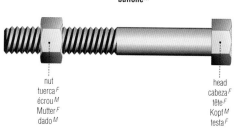

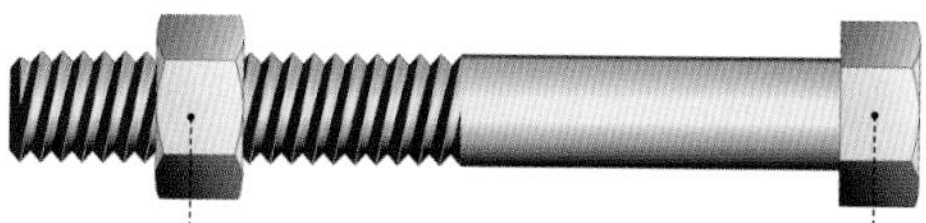
nut
tuerca[F]
écrou[M]
Mutter[F]
dado[M]
head
cabeza[F]
tête[F]
Kopf[M]
testa[F]

shoulder bolt
perno[M] con collarín[M]
boulon[M] à épaulement[M]
Schraubenbolzen[M] mit Ansatz[M]
bullone[M] di spallamento[M]

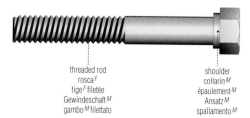

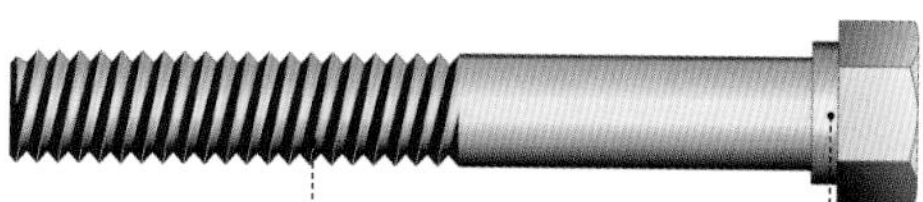
threaded rod
rosca[F]
tige[F] filetée
Gewindeschaft[M]
gambo[M] filettato
shoulder
collarín[M]
épaulement[M]
Ansatz[M]
spallamento[M]

carpentry: gripping and tightening tools

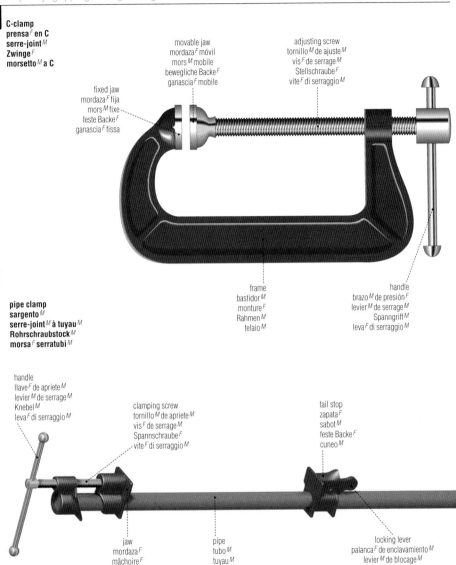

C-clamp
prensa F en C
serre-joint M
Zwinge F
morsetto M a C

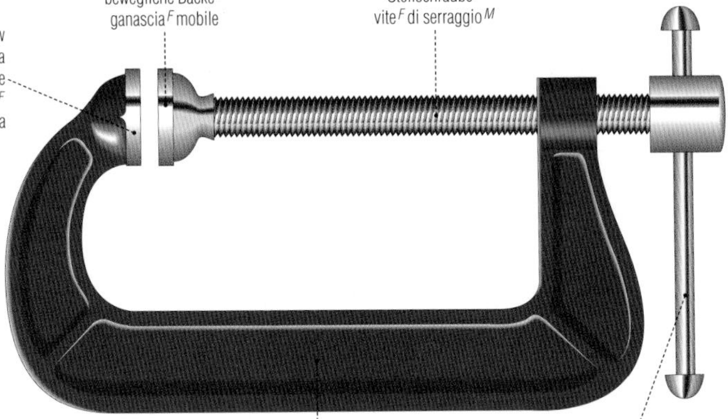
movable jaw
mordaza F móvil
mors M mobile
bewegliche Backe F
ganascia F mobile
adjusting screw
tornillo M de ajuste M
vis F de serrage M
Stellschraube F
vite F di serraggio M
fixed jaw
mordaza F fija
mors M fixe
feste Backe F
ganascia F fissa
frame
bastidor M
monture F
Rahmen M
telaio M
handle
brazo M de presión F
levier M de serrage M
Spanngriff M
leva F di serraggio M

pipe clamp
sargento M
serre-joint M à tuyau M
Rohrschraubstock M
morsa F serratubi M

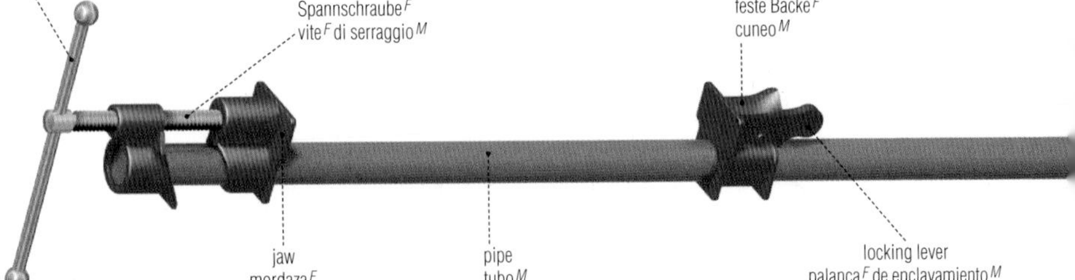
handle
llave F de apriete M
levier M de serrage M
Knebel M
leva F di serraggio M
clamping screw
tornillo M de apriete M
vis F de serrage M
Spannschraube F
vite F di serraggio M
tail stop
zapata F
sabot M
feste Backe F
cuneo M
jaw
mordaza F
mâchoire F
bewegliche Backe F
ganascia F
pipe
tubo M
tuyau M
Rohr N
tubo M
locking lever
palanca F de enclavamiento M
levier M de blocage M
Arretierhebel M
leva F di bloccaggio M

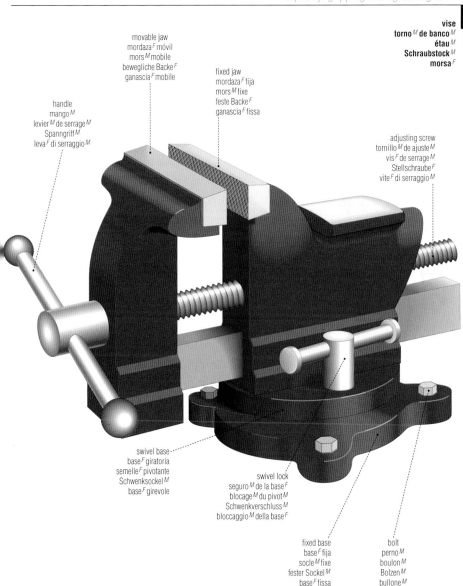

vise
torno M **de banco** M
étau M
Schraubstock M
morsa F

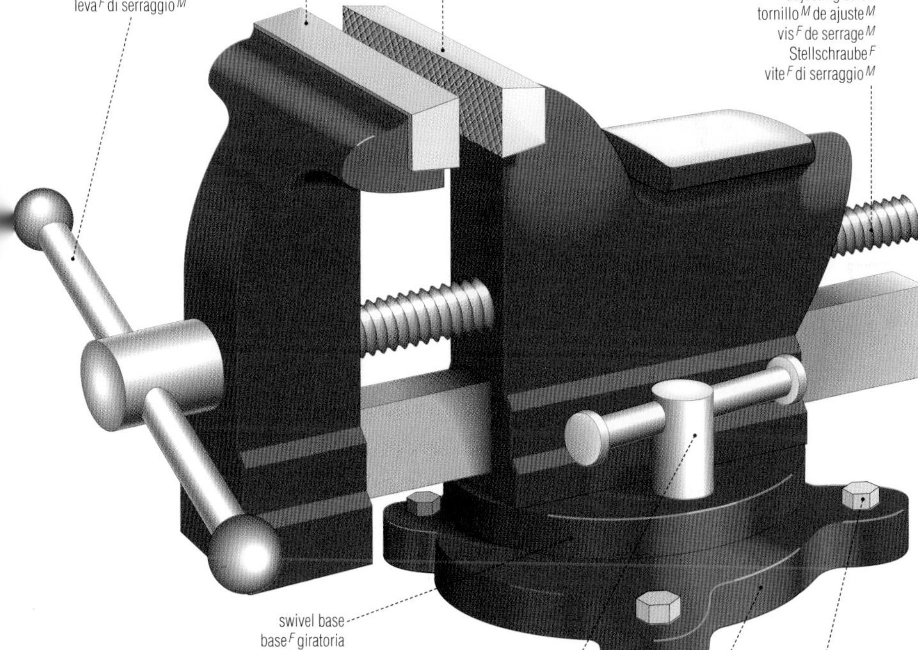
movable jaw
mordaza F móvil
mors M mobile
bewegliche Backe F
ganascia F mobile
fixed jaw
mordaza F fija
mors M fixe
feste Backe F
ganascia F fissa
handle
mango M
levier M de serrage M
Spanngriff M
leva F di serraggio M
adjusting screw
tornillo M de ajuste M
vis F de serrage M
Stellschraube F
vite F di serraggio M
swivel base
base F giratoria
semelle F pivotante
Schwenksockel M
base F girevole
swivel lock
seguro M de la base F
blocage M du pivot M
Schwenkverschluss M
bloccaggio M della base F
fixed base
base F fija
socle M fixe
fester Sockel M
base F fissa
bolt
perno M
boulon M
Bolzen M
bullone M

carpentry: measuring and marking tools

carpintería[F]: instrumentos[M] de trazado[M] y de medición[F] | menuiserie[F]: instruments[M] de traçage[M] et de mesure[F] | Bautischlerei[F]: Mess- und Markierinstrumente[N] | carpenteria[F]: strumenti[M] di misurazione[F] e tracciamento[M]

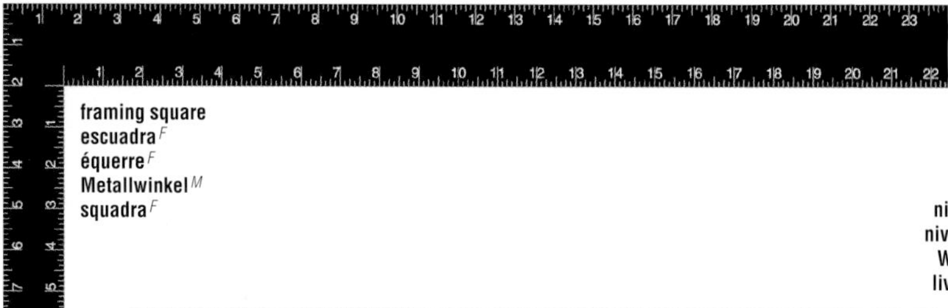

framing square
escuadra[F]
équerre[F]
Metallwinkel[M]
squadra[F]

spirit level
nivel[M] de aire[M]
niveau[M] à bulle[F]
Wasserwaage[F]
livella[F] a bolla[F]

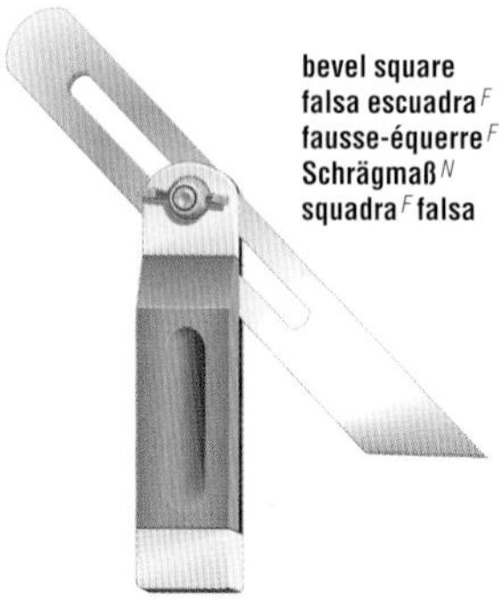

bevel square
falsa escuadra[F]
fausse-équerre[F]
Schrägmaß[N]
squadra[F] falsa

tape measure
cinta[F] métrica
mètre[M] à ruban[M]
Messband[N]
flessometro[M]

chalk line
cordón[M] de trazar
cordeau[M] à tracer
Markierschnur[F]
filo[M] di tracciamento[M]

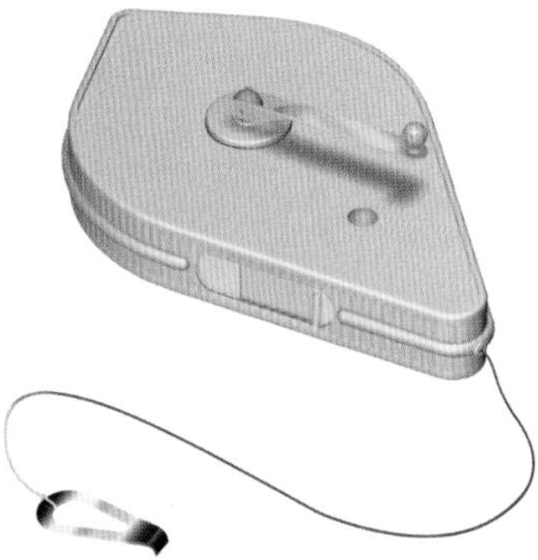

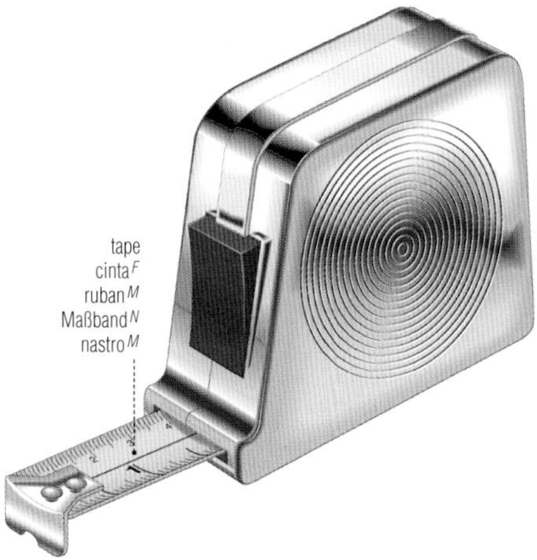
tape
cinta[F]
ruban[M]
Maßband[N]
nastro[M]

carpentry: miscellaneous material

carpintería F : materiales M varios | menuiserie F : matériel M divers | Bautischlerei F: Verschiedenes NPL | carpenteria F: materiale M vario

tool belt
cinturón M de herramientas F
ceinture F porte-outils M
Werkzeuggürtel M
cintura F portautensili

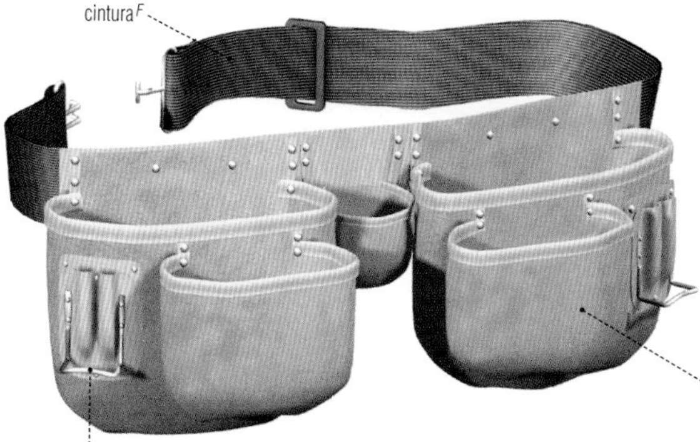
belt
cinturón M
ceinture F
Riemen M
cintura F
pocket
bolsillo M
poche F
Tasche F
tasca F
hammer loop
porta martillo M
porte-marteau M
Hammerhalter M
portamartello M

tool box
caja F de herramientas F
boîte F à outils M
Werkzeugkasten M
cassetta F degli attrezzi M

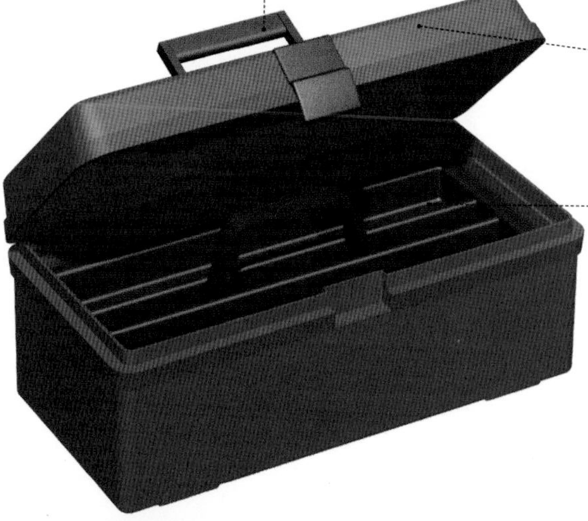
handle
asa F
poignée F
Griff M
maniglia F
lid
tapa F
couvercle M
Deckel M
coperchio M
tray
bandeja F
plateau M
Einlage F
piano M a scomparti M

plumbing tools

fontanería[F]: herramientas[F] | plomberie[F]: outils[M] | Klempnerwerkzeuge[N] | attrezzi[M] idraulici

pipe wrench
llave[F] inglesa
clé[F] à tuyau[M]
Einhand-Rohrzange[F]
giratubi[M]

Teflon® tape
cinta[F] de teflón®[M]
ruban[M] de Téflon®[M]
Teflonband[N]
nastro[M] di Teflon®[M]

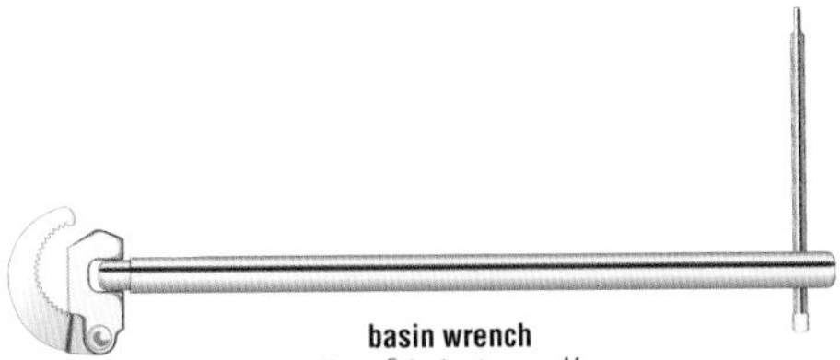

basin wrench
llave[F] de fontanero[M]
clé[F] coudée à tuyau[M]
Standhahn-Mutternschlüssel[M]
chiave[F] regolabile da lavandino[M]

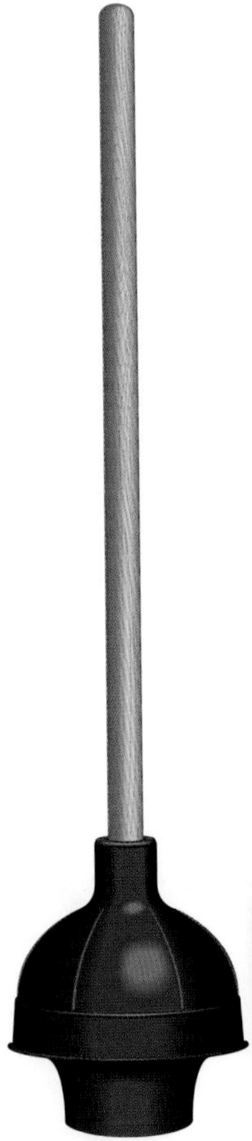

plunger
desatascador[M]
ventouse[F]
Ausgussreiniger[M]
sturalavandini[M]

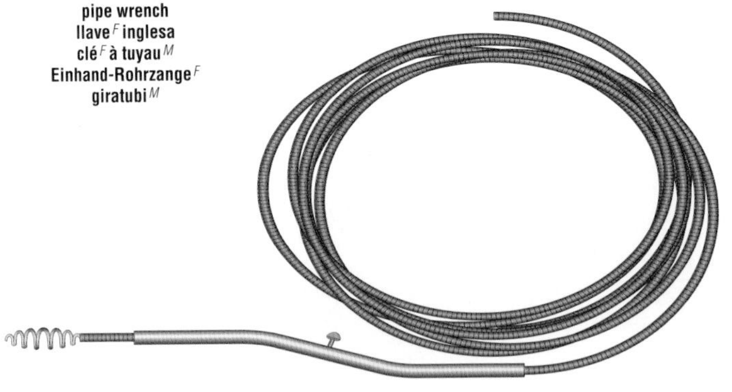

plumber's snake
sonda[F] destapacaños[M]
furet[M] de dégorgement[M]
Reinigungswelle[F]
molla[F] sturatrice per scarichi[M]

masonry tools

albañilería[F]: herramientas[F] | maçonnerie[F]: outils[M] | Maurerwerkzeuge[N] | attrezzi[M] da muratore[M]

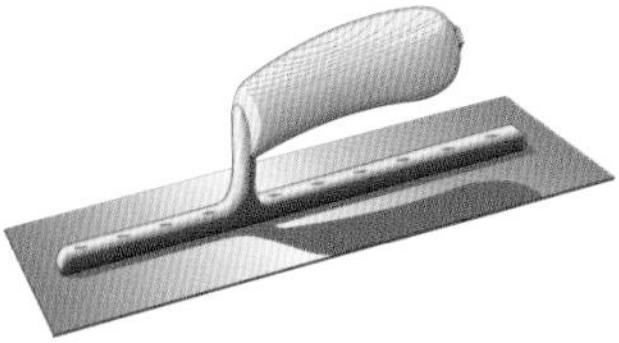

square trowel
llana[F]
truelle[F] de plâtrier[M]
Putzkelle[F]
frattazzo[M]

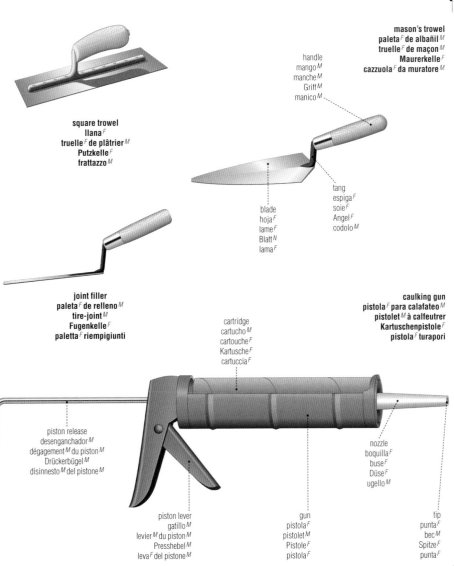

mason's trowel
paleta[F] de albañil[M]
truelle[F] de maçon[M]
Maurerkelle[F]
cazzuola[F] da muratore[M]

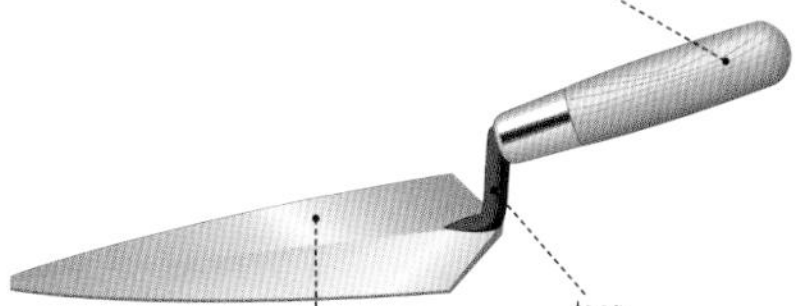
handle
mango[M]
manche[M]
Griff[M]
manico[M]
blade
hoja[F]
lame[F]
Blatt[N]
lama[F]
tang
espiga[F]
soie[F]
Angel[F]
codolo[M]

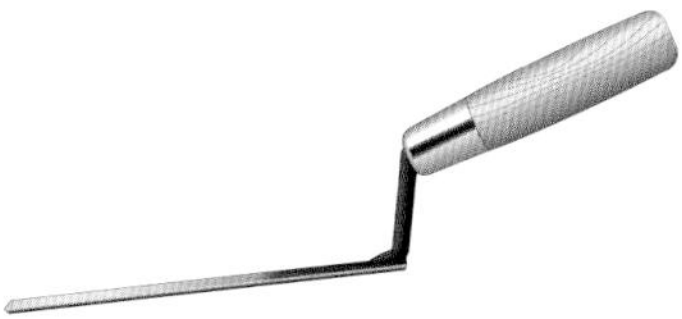

joint filler
paleta[F] de relleno[M]
tire-joint[M]
Fugenkelle[F]
paletta[F] riempigiunti

caulking gun
pistola[F] para calafateo[M]
pistolet[M] à calfeutrer
Kartuschenpistole[F]
pistola[F] turapori

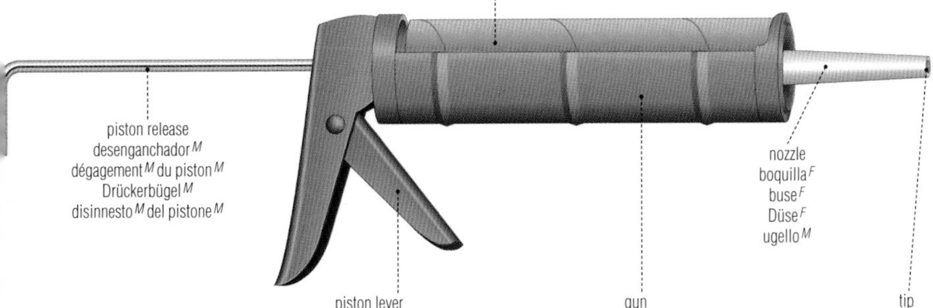
cartridge
cartucho[M]
cartouche[F]
Kartusche[F]
cartuccia[F]
piston release
desenganchador[M]
dégagement[M] du piston[M]
Drückerbügel[M]
disinnesto[M] del pistone[M]
nozzle
boquilla[F]
buse[F]
Düse[F]
ugello[M]
piston lever
gatillo[M]
levier[M] du piston[M]
Presshebel[M]
leva[F] del pistone[M]
gun
pistola[F]
pistolet[M]
Pistole[F]
pistola[F]
tip
punta[F]
bec[M]
Spitze[F]
punta[F]

electrical tools

electricidad^{F}: herramientas^{F} | électricité^{F}: outils^{M} | Elektroinstallateurwerkzeuge^{N} | attrezzatura^{F} elettrica

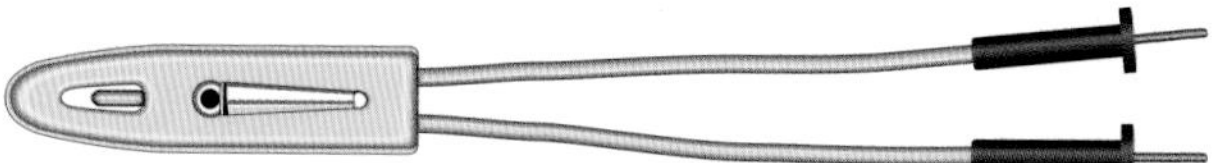

neon tester
lámpara^{F} de prueba^{F} de neón^{M}
vérificateur^{M} de circuit^{M}
Prüflampe^{F}
lampada^{F} provacircuiti

multipurpose tool
pinzas^{F} multiuso
pince^{F} universelle
Mehrzweckzange^{F}
pinza^{F} multiuso

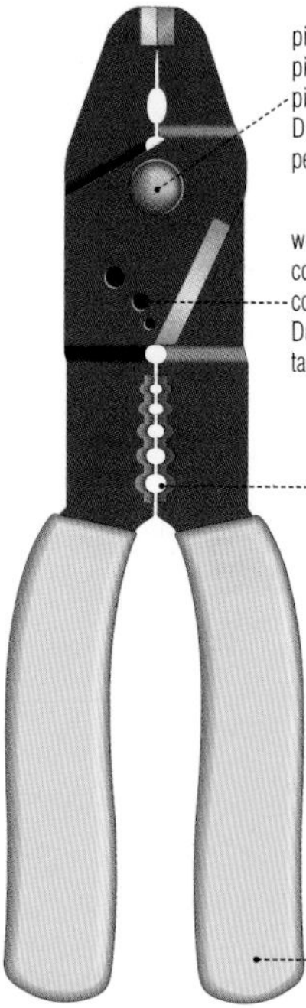
pivot
pivote M
pivot M
Drehzapfen M
perno M
wire cutter
cortador M de alambre M
coupe-fil M
Drahtschneider M
tagliafili M
wire stripper
pinzas F pelacables
dénude-fil M
Abisolierzange M
spelafili M
insulated handle
mango M aislante
manche M isolant
isolierter Griff M
manico M isolato

lineman's pliers
alicates^{M} de electricista^{M}
pince^{F} d'électricien^{M}
Kombizange^{F}
pinza^{F} universale

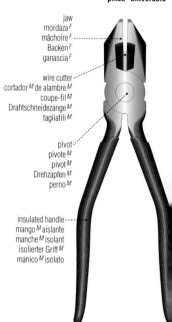

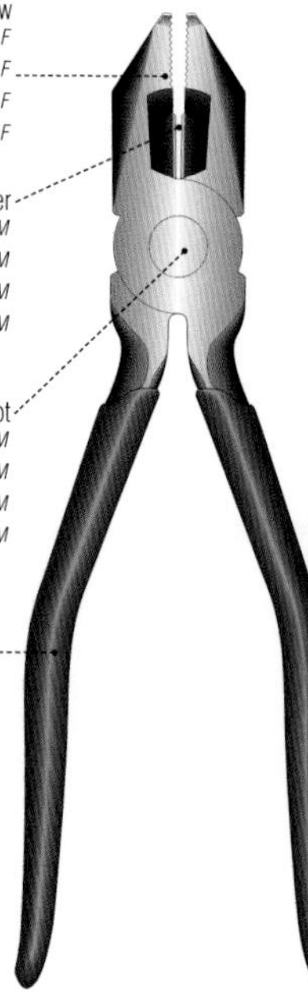
jaw
mordaza F
mâchoire F
Backen F
ganascia F
wire cutter
cortador M de alambre M
coupe-fil M
Drahtschneidezange M
tagliafili M
pivot
pivote M
pivot M
Drehzapfen M
perno M
insulated handle
mango M aislante
manche M isolant
isolierter Griff M
manico M isolato

receptacle analyzer
probador M de contactos M con tierra F
vérificateur M de prise F de courant M
Steckdosenprüfer M
tester M di presa F

voltage tester
detector M de tensión F
vérificateur M de tension F
Spannungsprüfer M
cercafase M

insulated blade
vástago M aislado
lame F isolée
isolierte Klinge F
lama F isolata
insulated handle
mango M aislado
manche M isolé
isolierter Griff M
manico M isolato
neon lamp
lámpara F de neón M
lampe F au néon M
Glimmlampe F
lampada F al neon M

drop light
linterna F movible
baladeuse F
Handlampe F
lampada F portatile a gabbia F

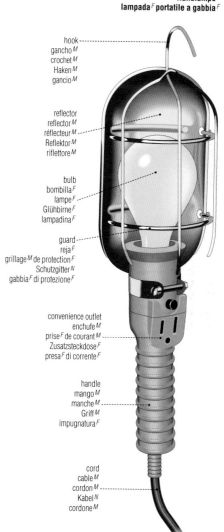

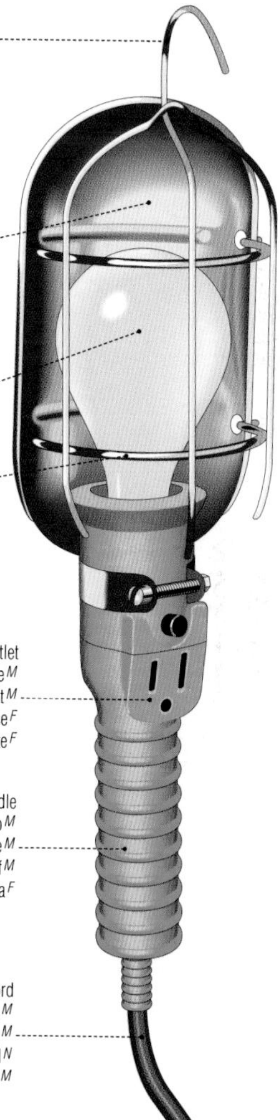
hook
gancho M
crochet M
Haken M
gancio M
reflector
reflector M
réflecteur M
Reflektor M
riflettore M
bulb
bombilla F
lampe F
Glühbirne F
lampadina F
guard
reja F
grillage M de protection F
Schutzgitter N
gabbia F di protezione F
convenience outlet
enchufe M
prise F de courant M
Zusatzsteckdose F
presa F di corrente F
handle
mango M
manche M
Griff M
impugnatura F
cord
cable M
cordon M
Kabel N
cordone M

headgear

sombreros [M] | coiffure [F] | Kopfbedeckungen [F] | copricapi [M]

unisex headgear
sombreros [M] unisex
coiffures [F] unisexes
Unisex-Kopfbedeckungen [F]
copricapi [M] unisex

beret
boina [F]
béret [M]
Baskenmütze [F]
basco [M]

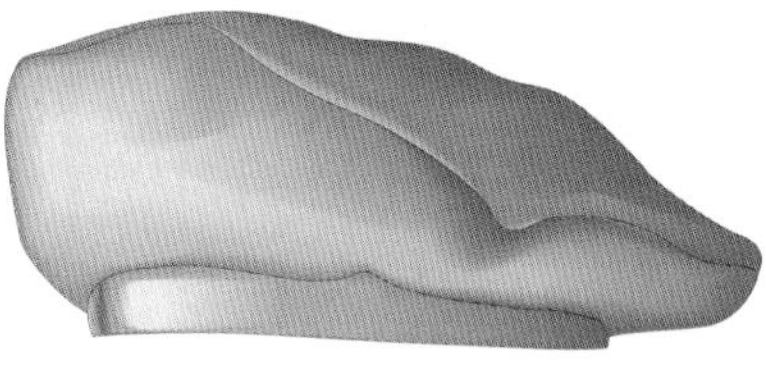

stocking cap
gorro [M] de punto [M] con borla [F]
bonnet [M] pompon [M]
Pudelmütze [F]
berretto [M] con pompon [M]

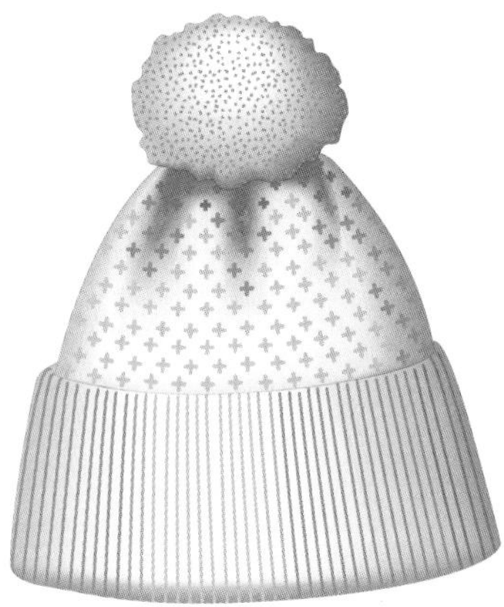

balaclava
pasamontañas [M]
cagoule [F]
Kapuzenmütze [F]
passamontagna [M]

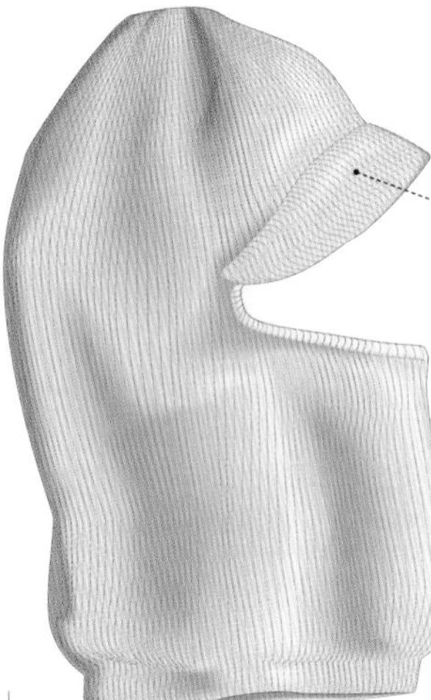
peak
visera [F]
visière [F]
Mützenschirm [M]
visiera [F]

fedora
sombrero [M] de fieltro [M]
chapeau [M] de feutre [M]
Filzhut [M]
cappello [M] di feltro [M]

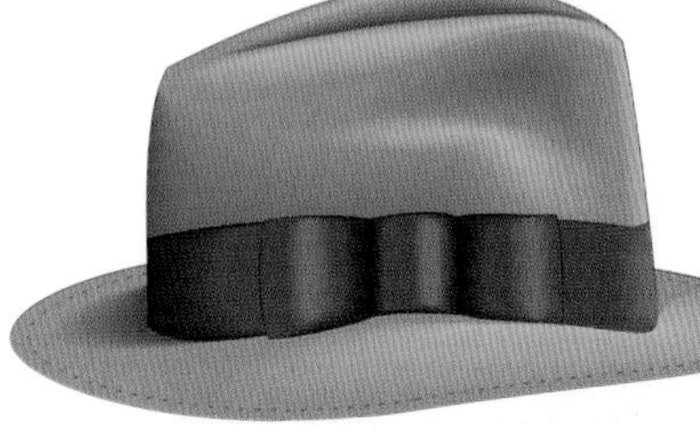

women's headgear
sombreros[M] de mujer[F]
coiffures[F] de femme[F]
Damenkopfbedeckungen[F]
copricapi[M] femminili

sailor's hat
gorro[M] de marinero[M]
bob[M]
Matrosenmütze[F]
cappello[M] da marinaio[M]

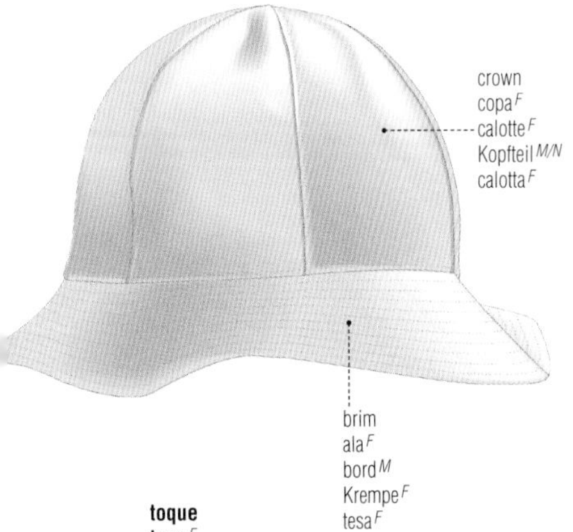
crown
copa[F]
calotte[F]
Kopfteil[M/N]
calotta[F]
brim
ala[F]
bord[M]
Krempe[F]
tesa[F]

southwester
sueste[M]
suroît[M]
Südwester[M]
berretto[M] impermeabile

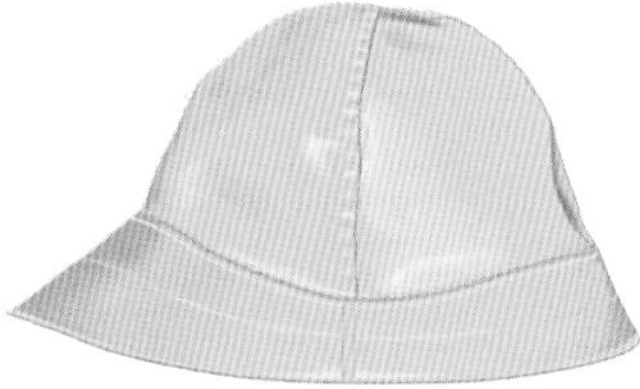

toque
toca[F]
toque[F]
Toque[F]
toque[F]

pillbox hat
sombrero[M] sin alas[F]
tambourin[M]
Pillbox[F]
tocco[M]

turban
turbante[M]
turban[M]
Turban[M]
turbante[M]

cartwheel hat
pamela[F]
capeline[F]
Wagenradhut[M]
cappello[M] a falda[F] larga

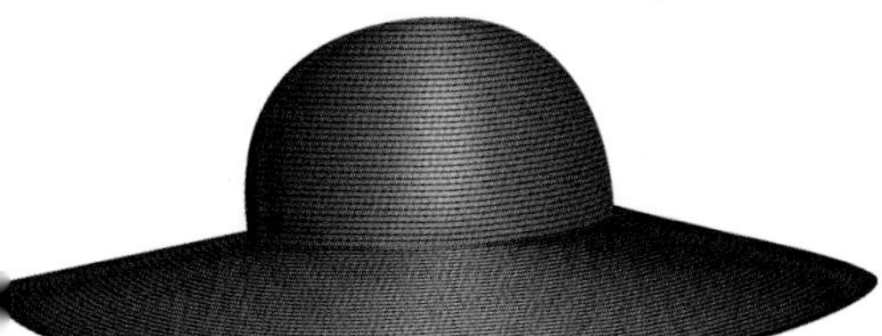

cloche
sombrero[M] de campana[F]
cloche[F]
Topfhut[M]
cloche[F]

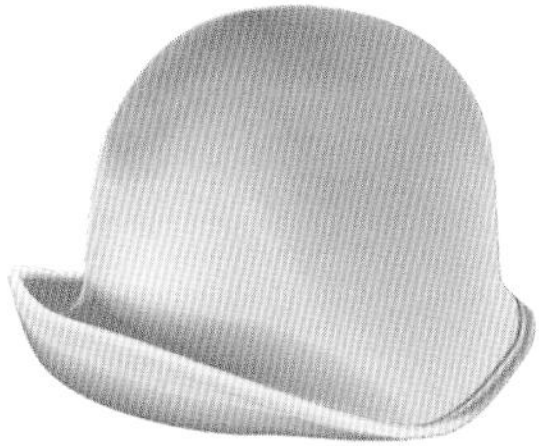

men's headgear
sombreros^{M} de hombre^{M}
coiffures^{F} d'homme^{M}
Herrenkopfbedeckungen^{F}
copricapi^{M} maschili

fedora
sombrero^{M} de fieltro^{M}
chapeau^{M} de feutre^{M}
Filzhut^{M}
cappello^{M} di feltro^{M}

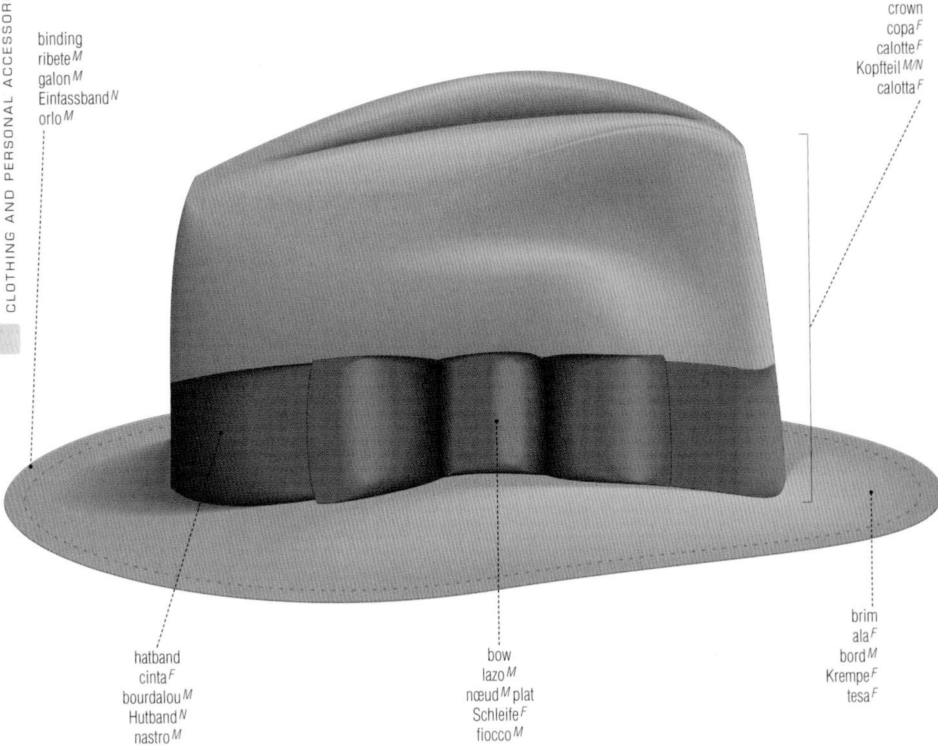
binding
ribete M
galon M
Einfassband N
orlo M
crown
copa F
calotte F
Kopfteil M/N
calotta F
hatband
cinta F
bourdalou M
Hutband N
nastro M
bow
lazo M
nœud M plat
Schleife F
fiocco M
brim
ala F
bord M
Krempe F
tesa F

boater
canotier *M*
canotier *M*
Strohhut *M*
paglietta *F*

skullcap
solideo *M*
calotte *F*
Käppchen *N*
papalina *F*

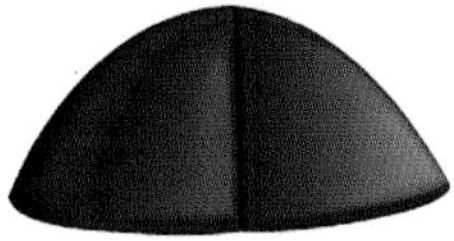

derby
sombrero *M* **de hongo** *M*
melon *M*
Melone *F*
bombetta *F*

garrison cap
gorra *F* **de cuartel** *M*
calot *M*
Fellmütze *F*
bustina *F*

top hat
chistera *F*
haut-de-forme *M*
Zylinder *M*
cilindro *M*

shapka
chapka *F*
chapska *M*
Kosakenmütze *F*
colbacco *M*

cap
gorra *F*
casquette *F*
Schirmmütze *F*
berretto *M*

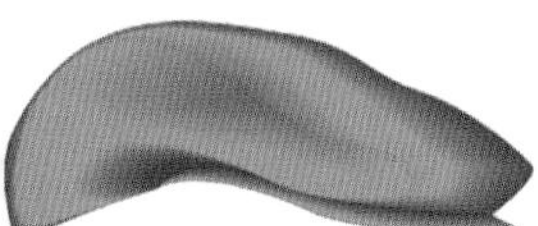

hunting cap
gorra *F* **noruega**
casquette *F* **norvégienne**
Jagdkappe *F*
berretto *M* **da cacciatore** *M*

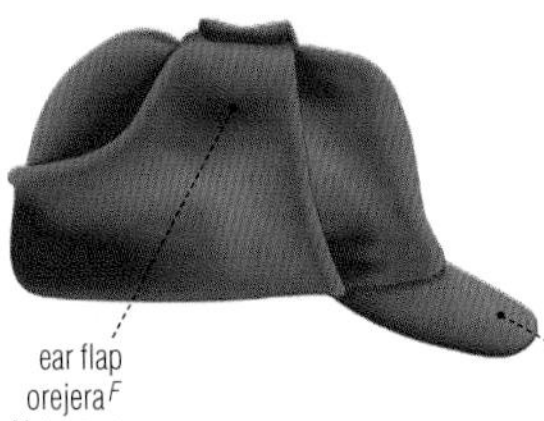

ear flap
orejera *F*
cache-oreilles *M* abattant
Ohrenschützer *M*
paraorecchi *M*

peak
visera *F*
visière *F*
Mützenschirm *M*
visiera *F*

panama
panamá *M*
panama *M*
Panamahut *M*
panama *M*

shoes

calzado[M] | chaussures[F] | Schuhe[M] | scarpe[F]

unisex shoes
calzado[M] unisex
chaussures[F] unisexes
Unisex-Schuhe[M]
scarpe[F] unisex

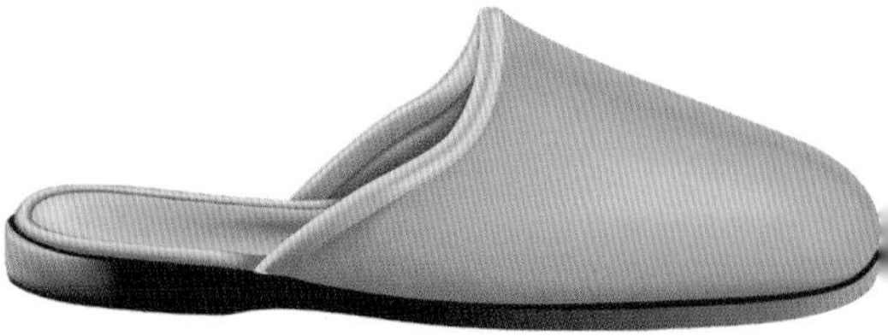

mule
pantufla[F]
mule[F]
Pantoffel[M]
pianella[F]

tennis shoe
zapatilla[F] de tenis[M]
tennis[M]
Tennisschuh[M]
scarpa[F] da tennis[M]

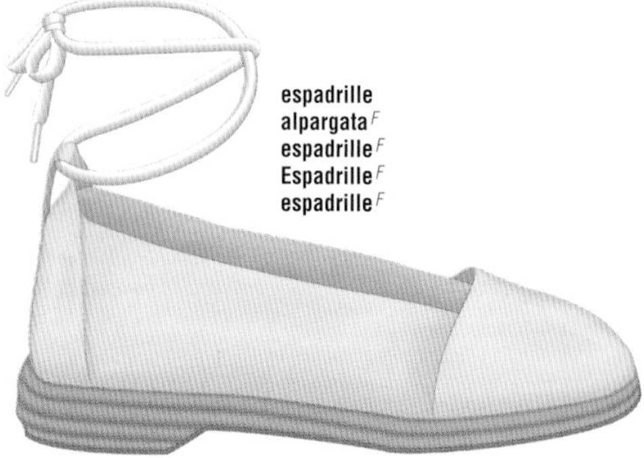

espadrille
alpargata[F]
espadrille[F]
Espadrille[F]
espadrille[F]

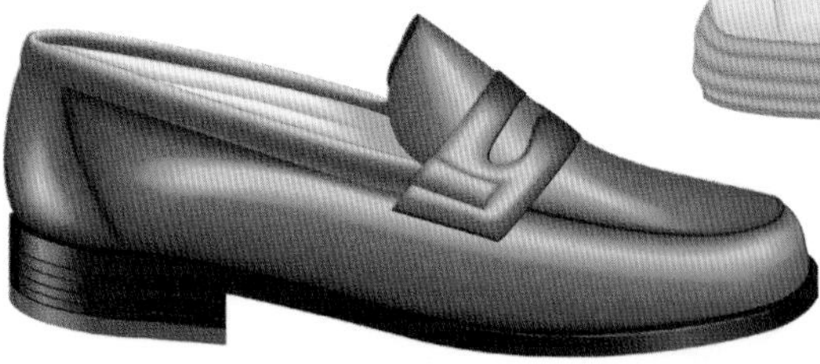

loafer
mocasín[M]
loafer[M]
Slipper[M]
mocassino[M] classico

moccasin
mocasín[M]
mocassin[M]
Mokassin[M]
mocassino[M]

sandal
sandalia [F]
nu-pied [M]
Sandale [F] mit Zehenriemchen [N]
sandalo [M] indiano

thong
chancleta [F] playera
tong [M]
Römerpantolette [F]
infradito [M]

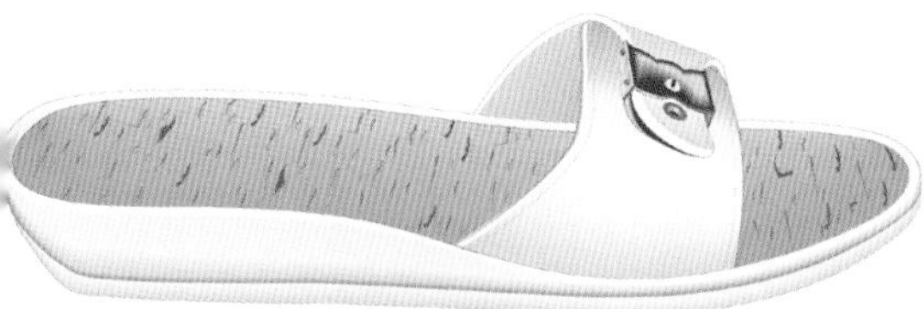

clog
chancleta [F]
socque [M]
Pantolette [F]
zoccolo [M]

sandal
sandalia [F]
sandalette [F]
Sandale [F]
sandalo [M]

hiking boot
bota [F] de montaña [F]
brodequin [M] de randonnée [F]
Wanderschuh [M]
pedula [F]

shoes

women's shoes
zapatos[M] de mujer[F]
chaussures[F] de femme[F]
Damenschuhe[M]
scarpe[F] da donna[F]

ballerina
bailarina[F]
ballerine[F]
Ballerinaschuh[M]
ballerina[F]

sandal
sandalia[F]
sandale[F]
Sandalette[F] mit Fersenriemen[M]
sandalo[M]

pump
zapato[M] de salón[M]
escarpin[M]
Pumps[M]
scarpa[F] décolleté[M]

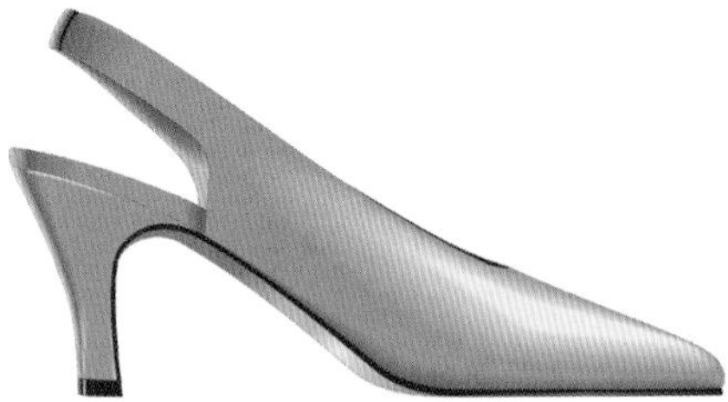

sling back shoe
zapato[M] de talón[M] abierto
escarpin[M]-sandale[F]
Slingpumps[M]
scarpa[F] chanel

one-bar shoe
zapato[M] de tacón[M] con correa[F]
Charles IX[M]
Einspangenschuh[M]
scarpa[F] con cinturino[M]

T-strap shoe
zapato[M] de correa[F]
salomé[M]
Stegspangenschuh[M]
scarpa[F] con cinturino[M] a T

casual shoe
zapato [M] con cordones [M]
trotteur [M]
Straßenschuh [M]
francesina [F]

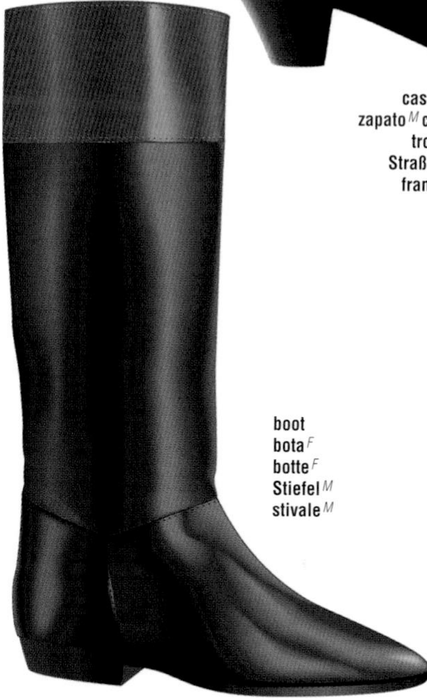

boot
bota [F]
botte [F]
Stiefel [M]
stivale [M]

thigh-boot
bota [F] de medio muslo [M]
cuissarde [F]
Schaftstiefel [M]
stivale [M] alla moschettiera

ankle boot
botín [M]
bottine [F]
Stiefelette [F]
polacchina [F]

men's shoes
zapatos M de hombre M
chaussures F d'homme M
Herrenschuhe M
scarpe F da uomo M

parts of a shoe
partes F de un zapato M
parties F d'une chaussure F
Teile M/N des Schuhs M
parti F di una scarpa F

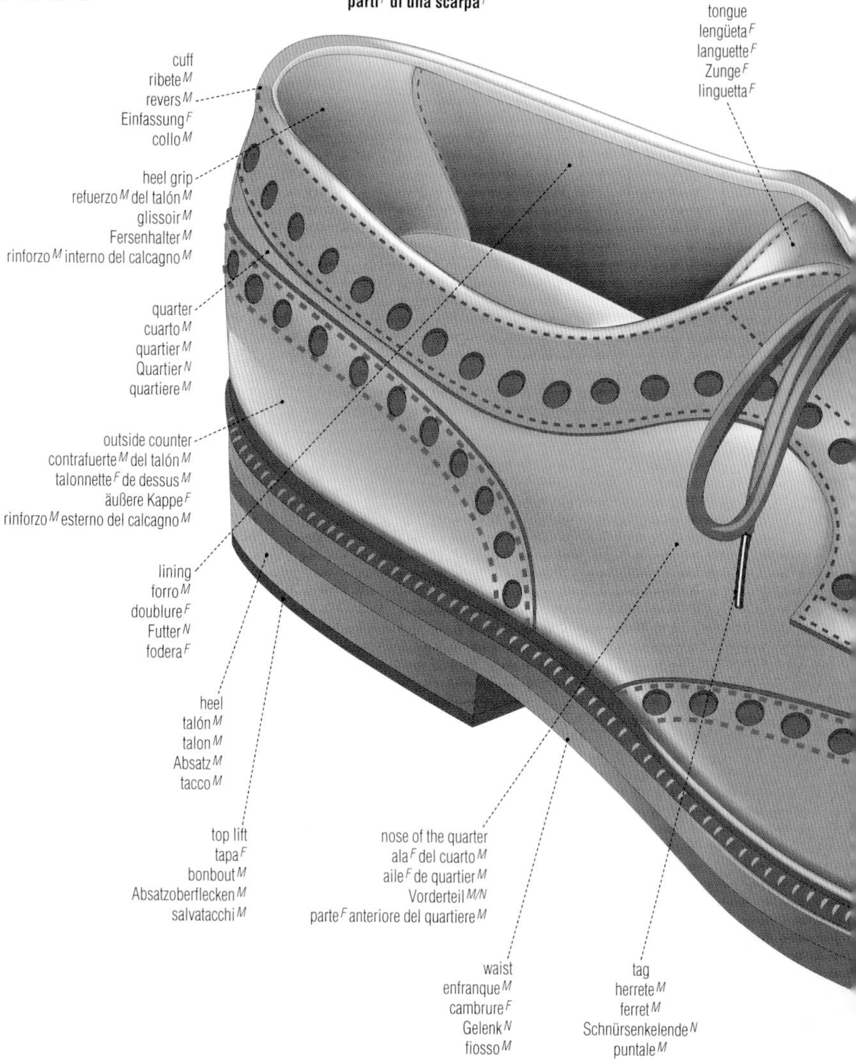
tongue
lengüeta F
languette F
Zunge F
linguetta F
cuff
ribete M
revers M
Einfassung F
collo M
heel grip
refuerzo M del talón M
glissoir M
Fersenhalter M
rinforzo M interno del calcagno M
quarter
cuarto M
quartier M
Quartier N
quartiere M
outside counter
contrafuerte M del talón M
talonnette F de dessus M
äußere Kappe F
rinforzo M esterno del calcagno M
lining
forro M
doublure F
Futter N
fodera F
heel
talón M
talon M
Absatz M
tacco M
top lift
tapa F
bonbout M
Absatzoberflecken M
salvatacchi M
nose of the quarter
ala F del cuarto M
aile F de quartier M
Vorderteil M/N
parte F anteriore del quartiere M
waist
enfranque M
cambrure F
Gelenk N
fiosso M
tag
herrete M
ferret M
Schnürsenkelende N
puntale M

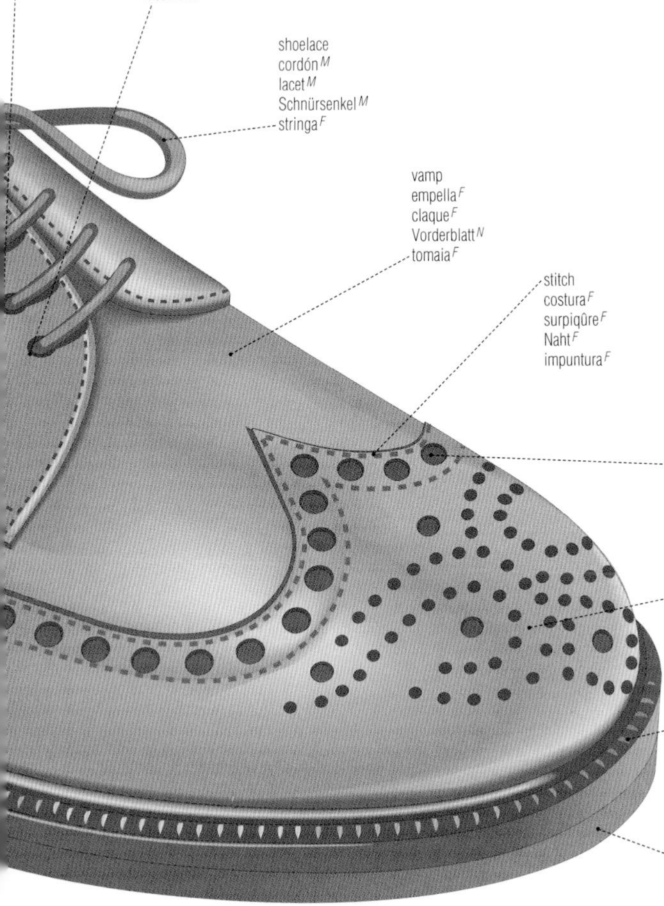
eyelet tab
oreja F
garant M
Schnürlochteil M/N
lunetta F
eyelet
ojete M
œillet M
Schnürloch N
occhiello M
shoelace
cordón M
lacet M
Schnürsenkel M
stringa F
vamp
empella F
claque F
Vorderblatt N
tomaia F
stitch
costura F
surpiqûre F
Naht F
impuntura F
punch hole
perforaciones F
perforation F
gestanztes Loch N
foro M
perforated toe cap
puntera F perforada
bout M fleuri
perforierte Vorderkappe F
mascherina F perforata
welt
vira F
trépointe F
Rahmen M
guardolo M
outsole
suela F
semelle F d'usure F
Laufsohle F
suola F

oxford shoe
zapato[M] oxford
richelieu[M]
Herrenhalbschuh[M]
scarpa[F] oxford

blucher oxford
zapato[M] de cordones[M]
derby[M]
Schnürschuh[M]
scarpa[F] stringata

chukka
media bota[F]
chukka[M]
Boot[M]
scarpa[F] a collo[M] alto

bootee
botín[M]
bottillon[M]
Halbstiefel[M]
scarponcino[M]

heavy duty boot
bota[F] de trabajo[M]
brodequin[M] de travail[M]
Arbeitsstiefel[M]
scarpone[M]

rubber
chanclo[M] de goma[F]
claque[F]
Überschuh[M]
galoscia[F]

accessories
accesorios[M]
accessoires[M]
Zubehör[N]
accessori[M]

shoe polisher
enceradora[F]
cireur[M]
Schuhbürste[F]
lucidascarpe[M] a batteria[F]

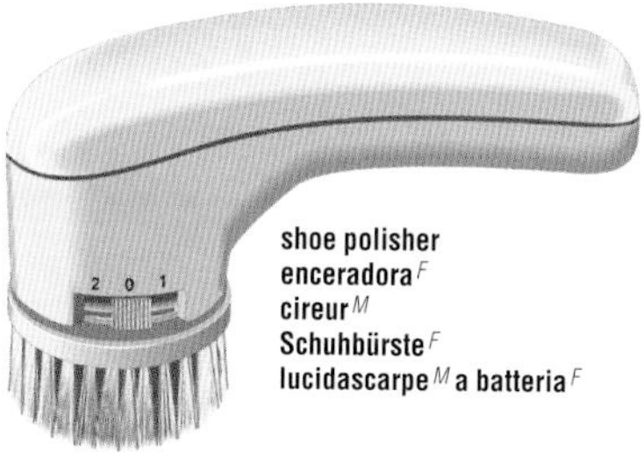

shoeshine kit
juego[M] limpiabotas[M]
nécessaire[M] à chaussures[F]
Schuhputzzeug[N]
kit[M] per la pulizia[F] delle scarpe[F]

chamois leather
gamuza[F]
peau[F] de chamois[M]
Ledertuch[N]
pelle[F] di camoscio[M]

case
estuche[M]
étui[M]
Tasche[F]
astuccio[M]

shoebrush
cepillo[M]
brosse[F] à chaussure[F]
Schuhbürste[F]
spazzola[F]

shoe polish
betún[M]
boîte[F] de cirage[M]
Schuhcreme[F]
lucido[M]

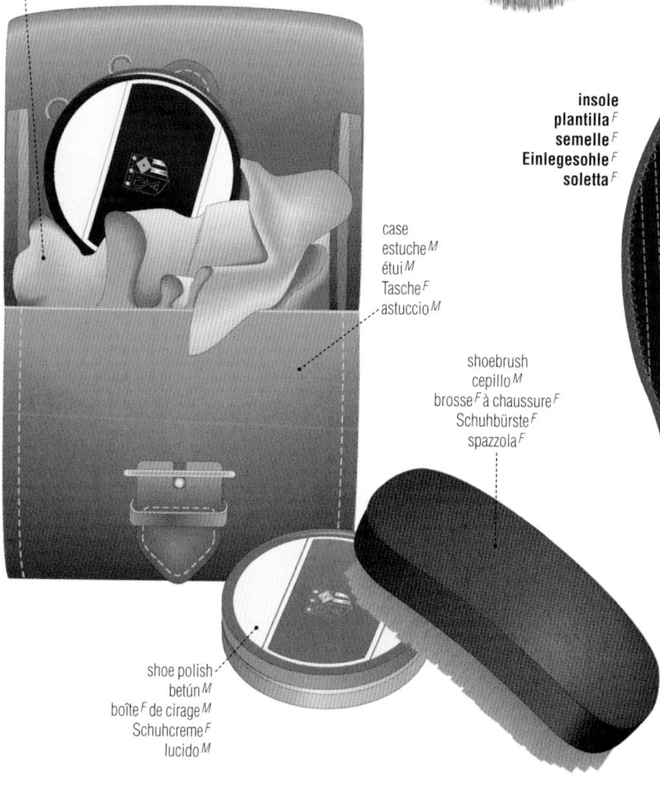

insole
plantilla[F]
semelle[F]
Einlegesohle[F]
soletta[F]

gloves

guantes^{M} | gants^{M} | Handschuhe^{M} | guanti^{M}

women's gloves
guantes^{M} de mujer^{F}
gants^{M} de femme^{F}
Damenhandschuhe^{M}
guanti^{M} da donna^{F}

gauntlet
manopla^{F}
gant^{M} à crispin^{M}
Stulpenhandschuh^{M}
guanto^{M} alla scudiera

short glove
guante^{M} corto
gant^{M} court
Kurzhandschuh^{M}
guanto^{M} corto

evening glove
guante^{M} largo
gant^{M} long
langer Abendhandschuh^{M}
guanto^{M} da sera^{F}

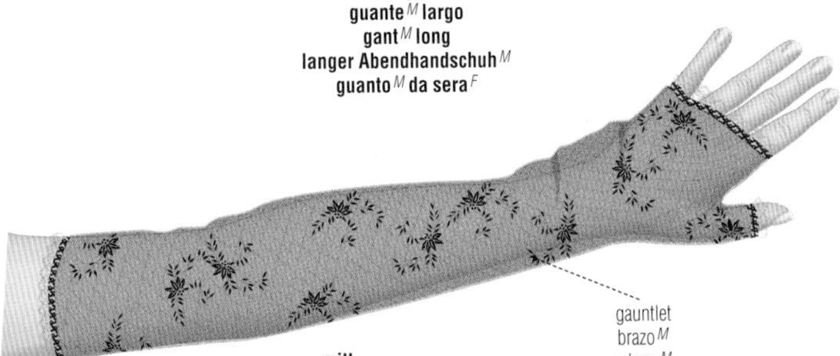

gauntlet
brazo^{M}
rebras^{M}
Stulpe^{F}
manopola^{F}

mitt
mitón^{M} largo
mitaine^{F}
fingerloser Spitzenhandschuh^{M}
mezzoguanto^{M}

wrist-length glove
guante^{M} a la muñeca^{F}
gant^{M} saxe
Langhandschuh^{M}
guanto^{M} lungo

men's gloves
guantes [M] de hombre [M]
gants [M] d'homme [M]
Herrenhandschuhe [M]
guanti [M] da uomo [M]

back of a glove
dorso [M] de un guante [M]
dos [M] d'un gant [M]
Handschuh [M]-Außenseite [F]
dorso [M] del guanto [M]

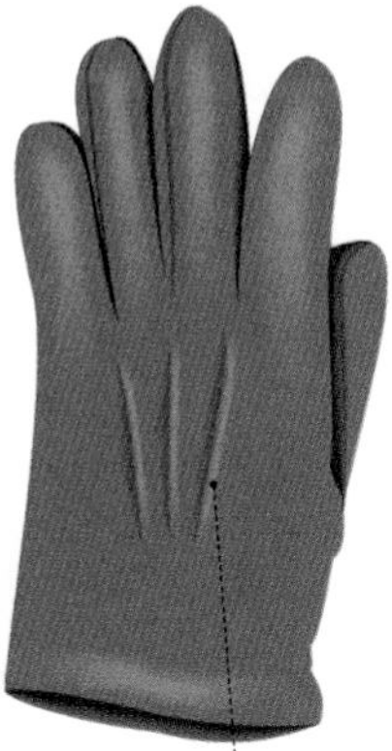

stitching
pespunte [M]
baguette [F]
Ziernaht [F]
impuntura [F]

palm of a glove
palma [F] de un guante [M]
paume [F] d'un gant [M]
Handschuh [M]-Innenseite [F]
palmo [M] del guanto [M]

fourchette
horquilla [F]
fourchette [F]
Keil [M]
linguella [F]

glove finger
dedo [M]
doigt [M]
Finger [M]
dito [M] del guanto [M]

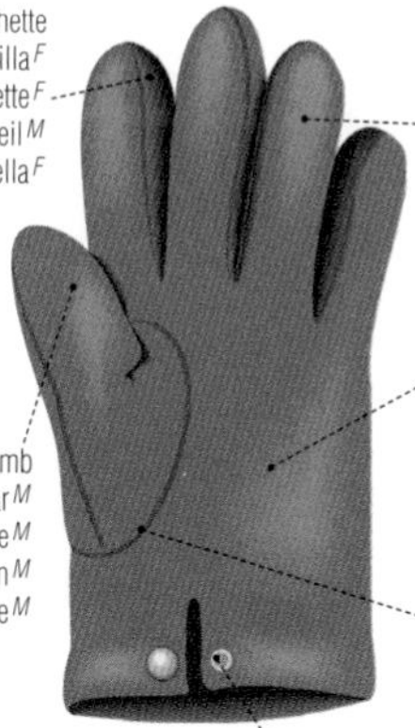

palm
palma [F]
paume [F]
Innenfläche [F]
palmo [M]

thumb
pulgar [M]
pouce [M]
Daumen [M]
pollice [M]

seam
costura [F]
couture [F] d'assemblage [M]
Naht [F]
cucitura [F]

snap fastener
botón [M] de presión [F]
bouton [M]-pression [F]
Druckknopf [M]
bottone [M] a pressione [F]

mitten
manopla [F]
moufle [F]
Fäustling [M]
muffola [F]

perforation
perforaciones [F]
perforation [F]
Perforierung [F]
foro [M]

opening
aberturas [F] para los nudillos [M]
fenêtre [F]
Öffnung [F]
apertura [F]

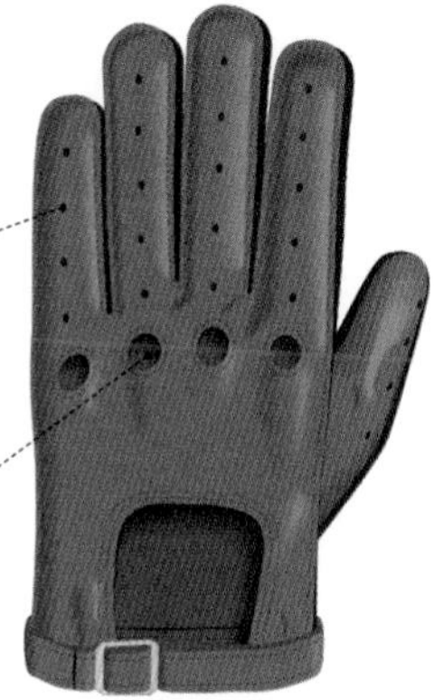

driving glove
guante [M] para conducir
gant [M] de conduite [F]
Autohandschuh [M]
guanto [M] da guida [F]

men's clothing

ropa[F] de hombre[M] | vêtements[M] d'homme[M] | Herrenbekleidung[F] | abbigliamento[M] maschile

double-breasted jacket
chaqueta[F] cruzada
veston[M] croisé
Zweireiher[M]
giacca[F] a doppiopetto[M]

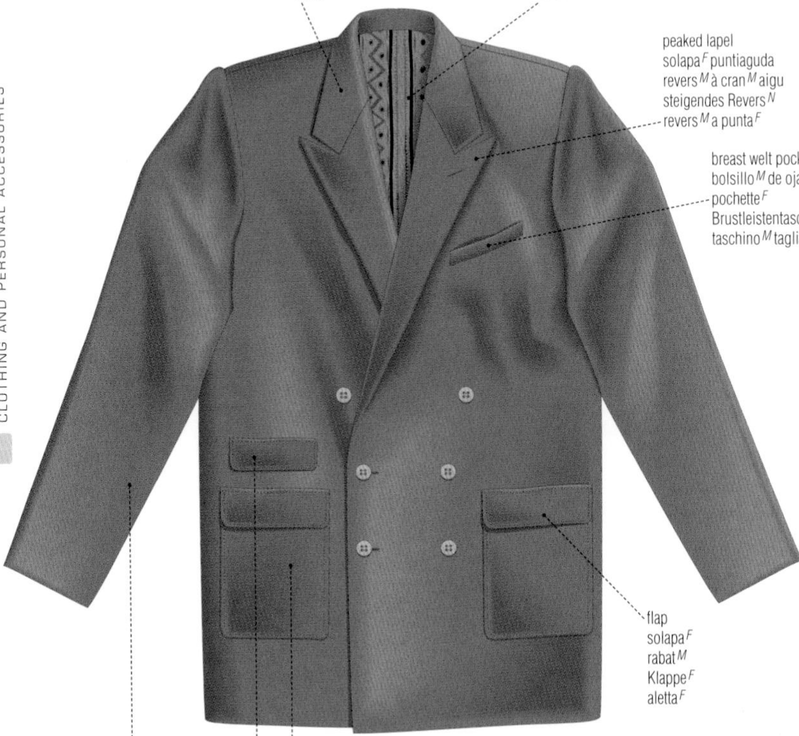
collar
cuello[M]
col[M]
Kragen[M]
collo[M]
lining
forro[M]
doublure[F]
Futter[N]
fodera[F]
peaked lapel
solapa[F] puntiaguda
revers[M] à cran[M] aigu
steigendes Revers[N]
revers[M] a punta[F]
breast welt pocket
bolsillo[M] de ojal[M]
pochette[F]
Brustleistentasche[F]
taschino[M] tagliato con aletta[F]
flap
solapa[F]
rabat[M]
Klappe[F]
aletta[F]
sleeve
manga[F]
manche[F]
Ärmel[M]
manica[F]
patch pocket
bolsillo[M] de parche[M]
poche[F] plaquée
aufgesetzte Tasche[F]
tasca[F] applicata
outside ticket pocket
bolsillo[M] del cambio[M]
poche[F]-ticket[M]
Billettasche[F]
taschino[M] con aletta[F]

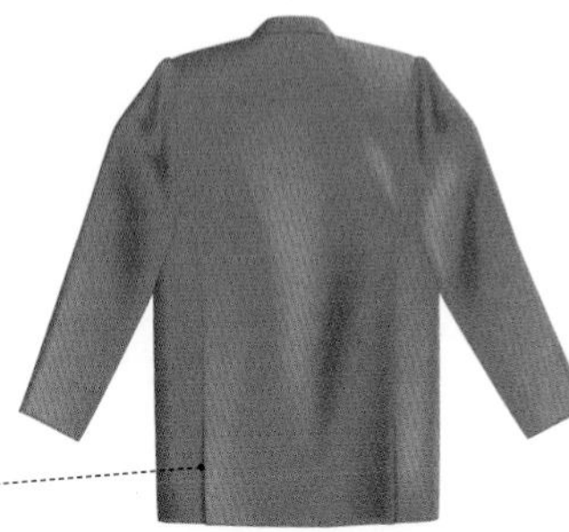
side back vent
abertura[F] trasera lateral
fente[F] latérale
seitlicher Rückenschlitz[M]
spacco[M] laterale

single-breasted jacket
chaqueta[F] recta
veste[F] droite
Einreiher[M]
giacca[F] a un petto[M]

notch
muesca[F]
cran[M]
Crochetwinkel[M]
dente[M]
lining
forro[M]
doublure[F]
Futter[N]
fodera[F]
pocket handkerchief
pañuelo[M] de bolsillo[M]
pochette[F]
Einstecktuch[N]
fazzoletto[M] da taschino[M]
lapel
solapa[F]
revers[M]
Revers[N]
revers[M]
front
delantero[M]
devant[M]
Vorderseite[F]
davanti[M]
flap pocket
bolsillo[M] con cartera[F]
poche[F] tiroir[M]
Klappentasche[F]
tasca[F] profilata con aletta[F]

back
espalda[F]
dos[M]
Rücken[M]
dietro[M]
sleeve
manga[F]
manche[F]
Ärmel[M]
manica[F]
center back vent
abertura[F] trasera central
fente[F] médiane
Rückenmittelschlitz[M]
spacco[M] centrale

men's clothing

shirt
camisa[F]
chemise[F]
Hemd[N]
camicia[F]

collar
cuello[M]
col[M]
Kragen[M]
colletto[M]
yoke
canesú[M]
empiècement[M]
Sattel[M]
sprone[M]
set-in sleeve
manga[F] empotrada
manche[F] montée
eingesetzter Ärmel[M]
manica[F] a giro[M]
collar point
punta[F] del cuello[M]
pointe[F] de col[M]
Kragenspitze[F]
punta[F] del colletto[M]
breast pocket
bolsillo[M] superior
poche[F] poitrine[F]
Brusttasche[F]
tasca[F] applicata con aletta[F]
front
delantero[M]
devant[M]
Vorderseite[F]
davanti[M]
pointed tab end
abertura[F] con tirilla[F]
patte[F] capucin[M]
Ärmelschlitz[M]
profilo[M] dello spacco[M]
button
botón[M]
bouton[M]
Knopf[M]
bottone[M]
cuff
puño[M]
poignet[M]
Manschette[F]
polsino[M]
buttoned placket
tirilla[F]
patte[F] de boutonnage[M]
Knopfleiste[F]
cannoncino[M]
shirttail
faldón[M] de la camisa[F]
pan[M]
Schoß[M]
lembo[M] della camicia[F]

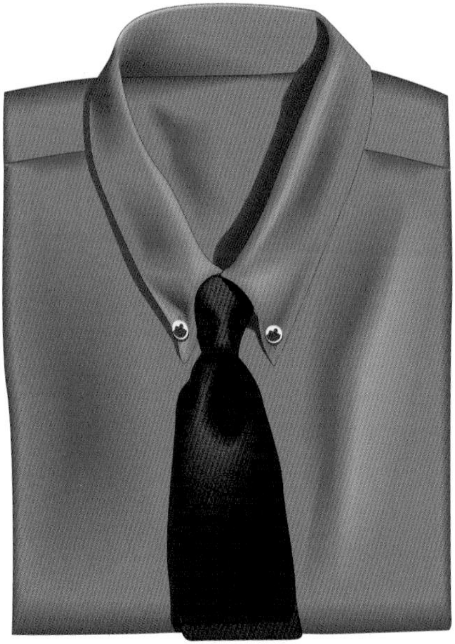

buttondown collar
cuello [M] con botones [M]
col [M] pointes [F] boutonnées
Button-Down-Kragen [M]
collo [M] button-down

spread collar
cuello [M] italiano
col [M] italien
gespreizter Kragen [M]
collo [M] a camicia [F]

collar stay
ballena [F]
baleine [F] de col [M]
Kragenstäbchen [N]
tendicollo [M]

necktie
corbata F
cravate F
Krawatte F
cravatta F

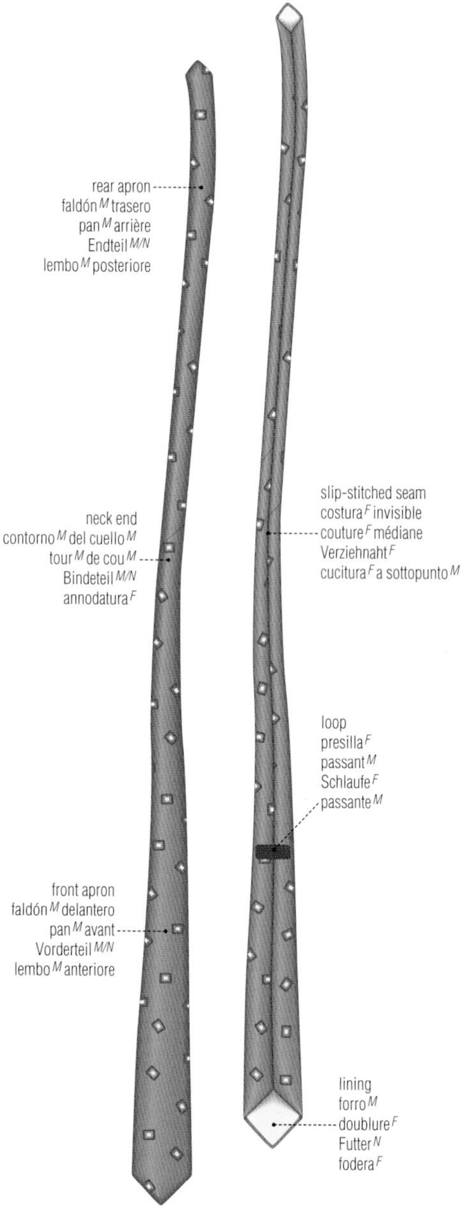
rear apron
faldón M trasero
pan M arrière
Endteil M/N
lembo M posteriore
neck end
contorno M del cuello M
tour M de cou M
Bindeteil M/N
annodatura F
front apron
faldón M delantero
pan M avant
Vorderteil M/N
lembo M anteriore
slip-stitched seam
costura F invisible
couture F médiane
Verziehnaht F
cucitura F a sottopunto M
loop
presilla F
passant M
Schlaufe F
passante M
lining
forro M
doublure F
Futter N
fodera F

ascot tie
corbata F **inglesa**
ascot F
Krawattenschal M
lavallière F

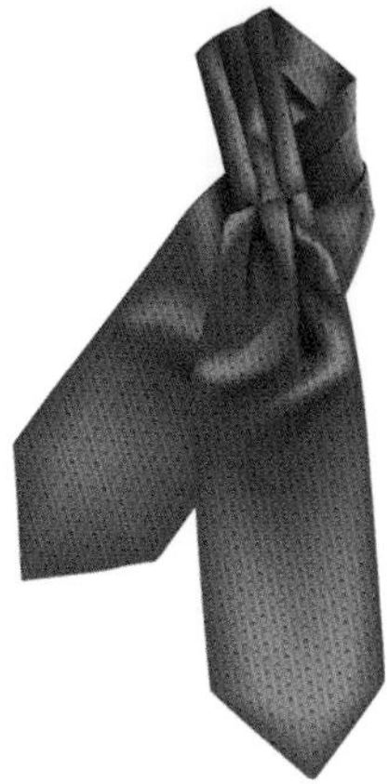

bow tie
pajarita F
nœud M **papillon** M
Fliege F
papillon M

pants
pantalones [M]
pantalon [M]
Hose [F]
pantaloni [M]

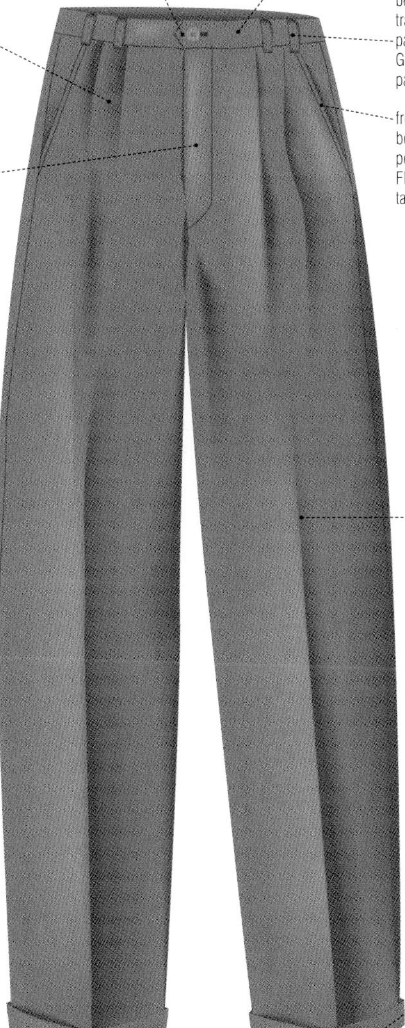
waistband extension
trabilla [F] de la pretina [F]
patte [F] boutonnée
Bundverlängerung [F]
abbottonatura [F] della cintura [F]
waistband
pretina [F]
ceinture [F] montée
Hosenbund [M]
cintura [F]
knife pleat
pinza [F]
pli [M] plat
einfache Falte [F]
piega [F] piatta
belt loop
trabilla [F]
passant [M]
Gürtelschlaufe [F]
passante [M]
front top pocket
bolsillo [M] delantero
poche [F] cavalière
Flügeltasche [F]
tasca [F] anteriore
fly
bragueta [F]
braguette [F]
Hosenschlitz [M]
patta [F]
crease
raya [F]
pli [M]
Bügelfalte [F]
piega [F]
cuff
vuelta [F]
revers [M]
Aufschlag [M]
risvolto [M]

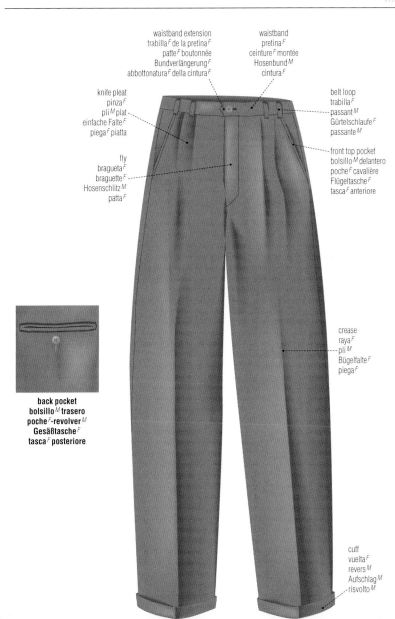

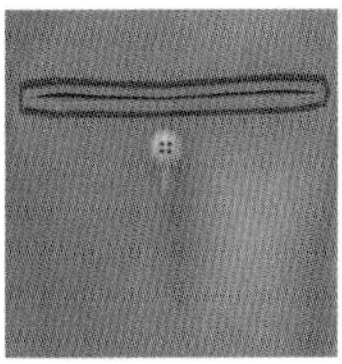

back pocket
bolsillo [M] trasero
poche [F]-revolver [M]
Gesäßtasche [F]
tasca [F] posteriore

men's clothing

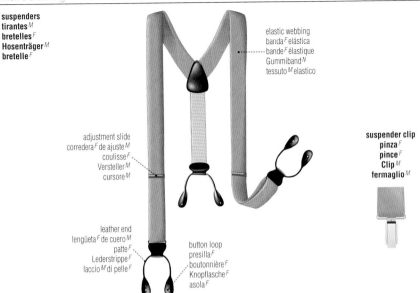

suspenders
tirantes M
bretelles F
Hosenträger M
bretelle F

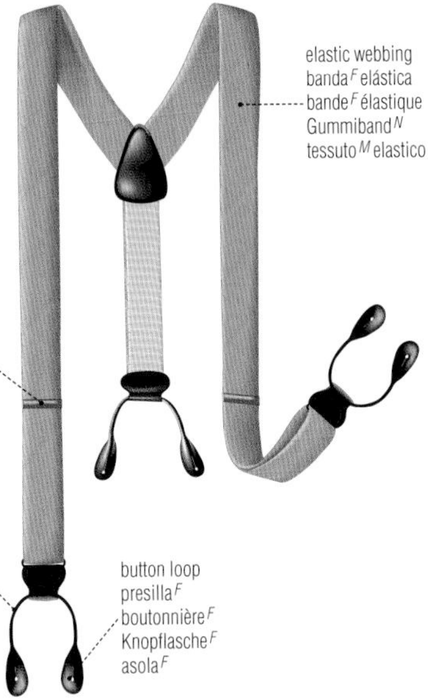
elastic webbing
banda F elástica
bande F élastique
Gummiband N
tessuto M elastico
adjustment slide
corredera F de ajuste M
coulisse F
Versteller M
cursore M
leather end
lengüeta F de cuero M
patte F
Lederstrippe F
laccio M di pelle F
button loop
presilla F
boutonnière F
Knopflasche F
asola F

suspender clip
pinza F
pince F
Clip M
fermaglio M

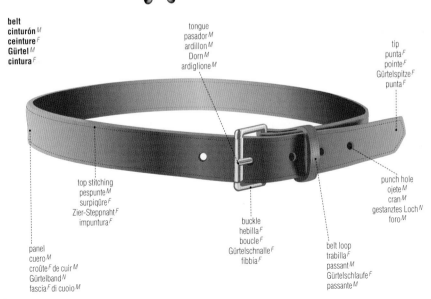

belt
cinturón M
ceinture F
Gürtel M
cintura F

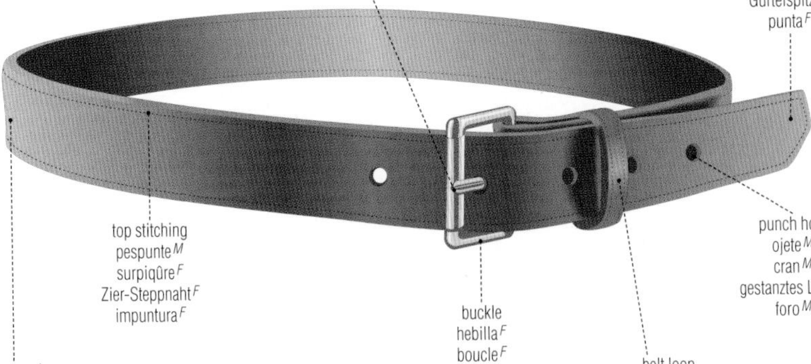
tongue
pasador M
ardillon M
Dorn M
ardiglione M
tip
punta F
pointe F
Gürtelspitze F
punta F
top stitching
pespunte M
surpiqûre F
Zier-Steppnaht F
impuntura F
buckle
hebilla F
boucle F
Gürtelschnalle F
fibbia F
punch hole
ojete M
cran M
gestanztes Loch N
foro M
panel
cuero M
croûte F de cuir M
Gürtelband N
fascia F di cuoio M
belt loop
trabilla F
passant M
Gürtelschlaufe F
passante M

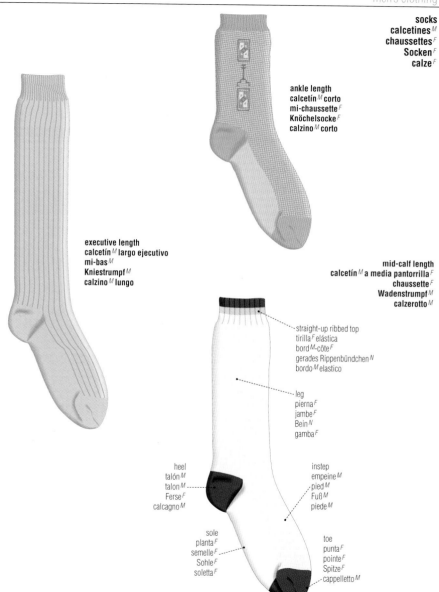

socks
calcetines *M*
chaussettes *F*
Socken *F*
calze *F*

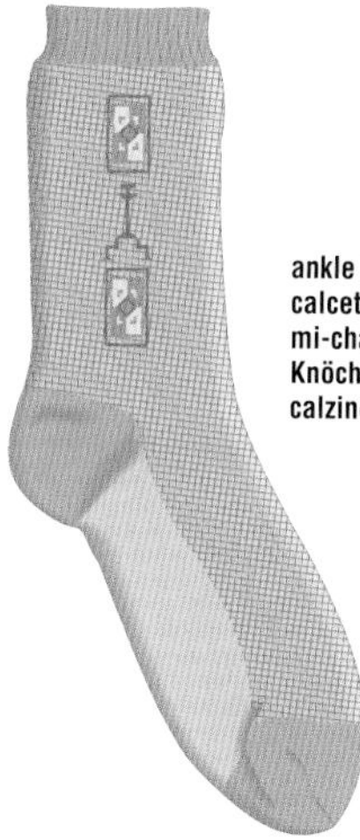

ankle length
calcetín *M* corto
mi-chaussette *F*
Knöchelsocke *F*
calzino *M* corto

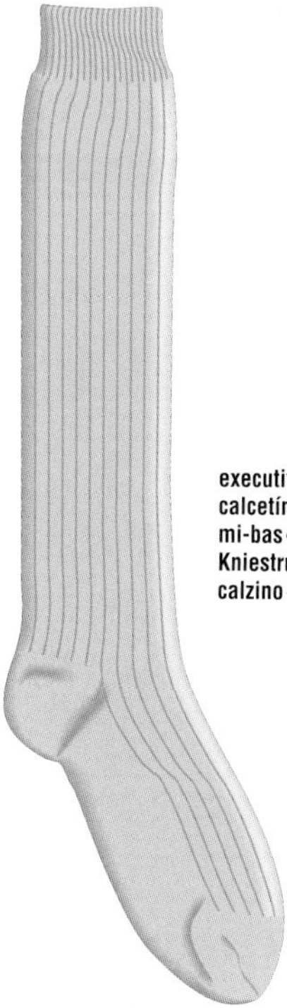

executive length
calcetín *M* largo ejecutivo
mi-bas *M*
Kniestrumpf *M*
calzino *M* lungo

mid-calf length
calcetín *M* a media pantorrilla *F*
chaussette *F*
Wadenstrumpf *M*
calzerotto *M*

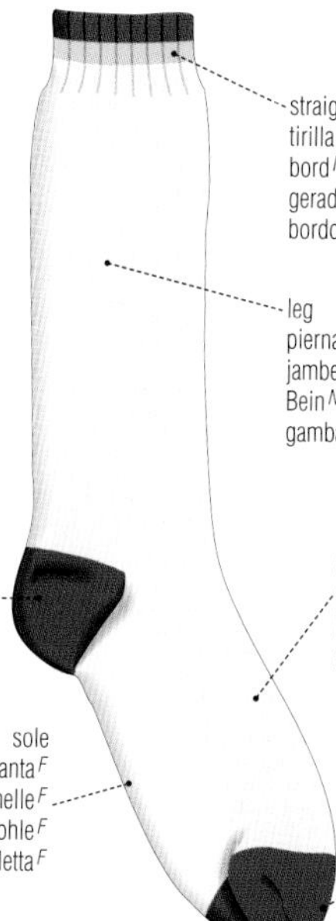
straight-up ribbed top
tirilla *F* elástica
bord *M*-côte *F*
gerades Rippenbündchen *N*
bordo *M* elastico
leg
pierna *F*
jambe *F*
Bein *N*
gamba *F*
heel
talón *M*
talon *M*
Ferse *F*
calcagno *M*
instep
empeine *M*
pied *M*
Fuß *M*
piede *M*
sole
planta *F*
semelle *F*
Sohle *F*
soletta *F*
toe
punta *F*
pointe *F*
Spitze *F*
cappelletto *M*

underwear
ropa[F] interior
sous-vêtements[M]
Unterwäsche[F]
biancheria[F] intima

athletic shirt
camiseta[F]
maillot[M] de corps[M]
Trägerhemd[N]
canottiera[F]

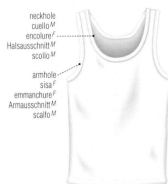

neckhole
cuello[M]
encolure[F]
Halsausschnitt[M]
scollo[M]

armhole
sisa[F]
emmanchure[F]
Armausschnitt[M]
scalfo[M]

union suit
pijama[M] de una pieza[F]
combinaison[F]
Hemdhose[F]
combinazione[F]

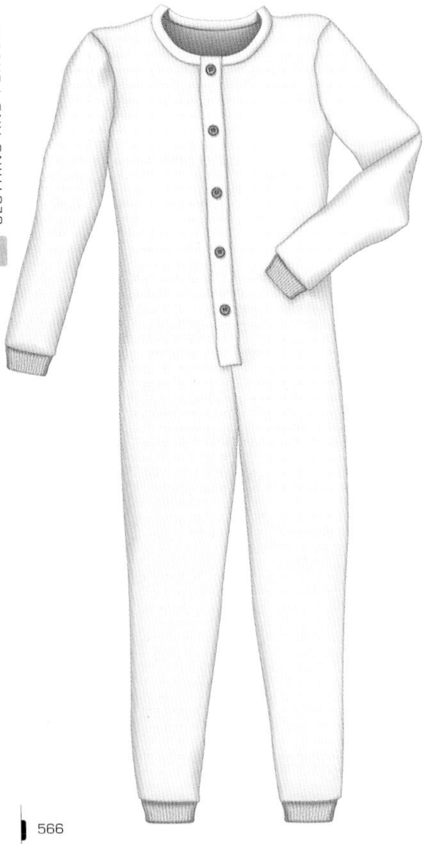

drawers
calzoncillos[M] largos
caleçon[M] long
lange Unterhose[F]
mutandoni[M]

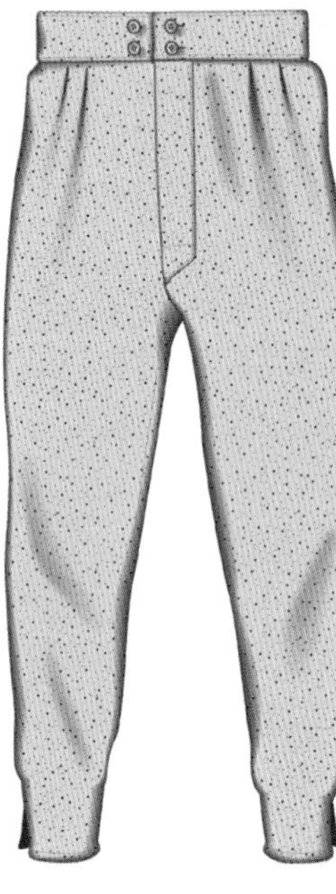

briefs
calzoncillos *M*
slip *M*
Slip *M*
mutande *F*

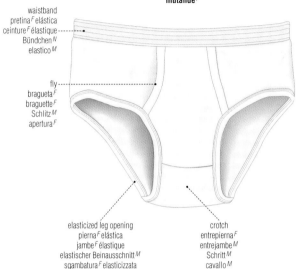

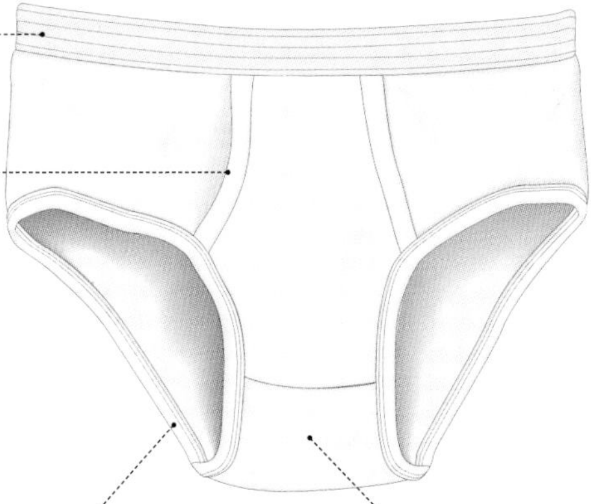
waistband
pretina *F* elástica
ceinture *F* élastique
Bündchen *N*
elastico *M*
fly
bragueta *F*
braguette *F*
Schlitz *M*
apertura *F*
elasticized leg opening
pierna *F* elástica
jambe *F* élastique
elastischer Beinausschnitt *M*
sgambatura *F* elasticizzata
crotch
entrepierna *F*
entrejambe *M*
Schritt *M*
cavallo *M*

bikini briefs
slip *M*
minislip *M*
Minislip *M*
slip *M*

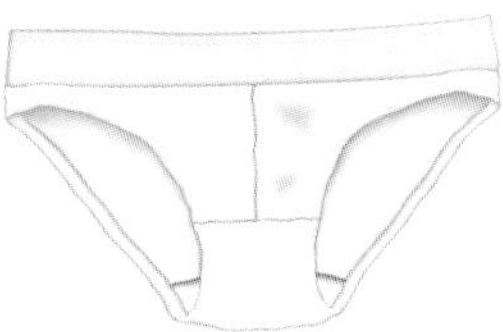

boxer shorts
calzoncillos *M*
caleçon *M*
Boxershorts *F*
boxer *M*

coats
abrigos^M e impermeables^F
manteaux^M et blousons^M
Mäntel^M und Jacken^F
esempi^M di giacconi^M e cappotti^M

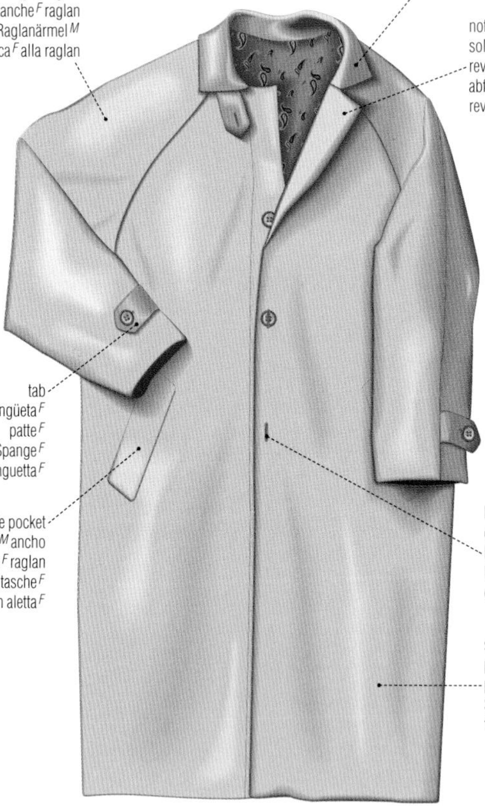
raincoat
impermeable M
imperméable M
Regenmantel M
impermeabile M
collar
cuello M
col M
Kragen M
collo M
raglan sleeve
manga F raglán
manche F raglan
Raglanärmel M
manica F alla raglan
notched lapel
solapa F con ojal M
revers M cranté
abfallendes Revers N
revers M
tab
lengüeta F
patte F
Spange F
linguetta F
broad welt side pocket
bolsillo M de ribete M ancho
poche F raglan
schräge Pattentasche F
tasca F interna con aletta F
buttonhole
ojal M
boutonnière F
Knopfloch N
occhiello M
side panel
paño M lateral
pan M
Seitenteil M/N
falda F

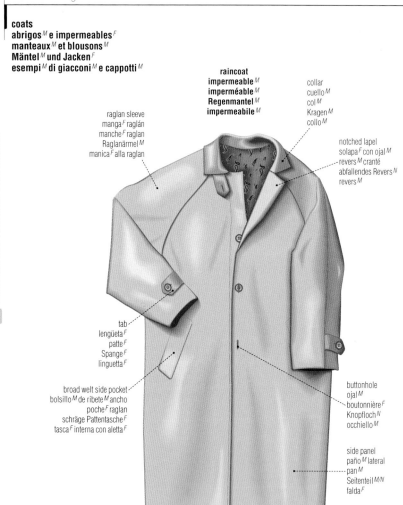

overcoat
abrigo *M*
pardessus *M*
Mantel *M*
cappotto *M*
notched lapel
solapa *F* con ojal *M*
revers *M* cranté
abfallendes Revers *N*
revers *M*
breast pocket
bolsillo *M* superior
poche *F* poitrine *F*
Brusttasche *F*
taschino *M*
breast dart
pinza *F*
pince *F* de taille *F*
Taillenabnäher *M*
ripresa *F*
flap pocket
bolsillo *M* con cartera *F*
poche *F* à rabat *M*
Klappentasche *F*
tasca *F* profilata con aletta *F*

three-quarter coat
abrigo *M* **de tres cuartos**
paletot *M*
dreiviertellanger Mantel *M*
trequarti *M*

men's clothing

trench coat
trincheraF
trenchM
doppelreihige KnöpfungF
trenchM

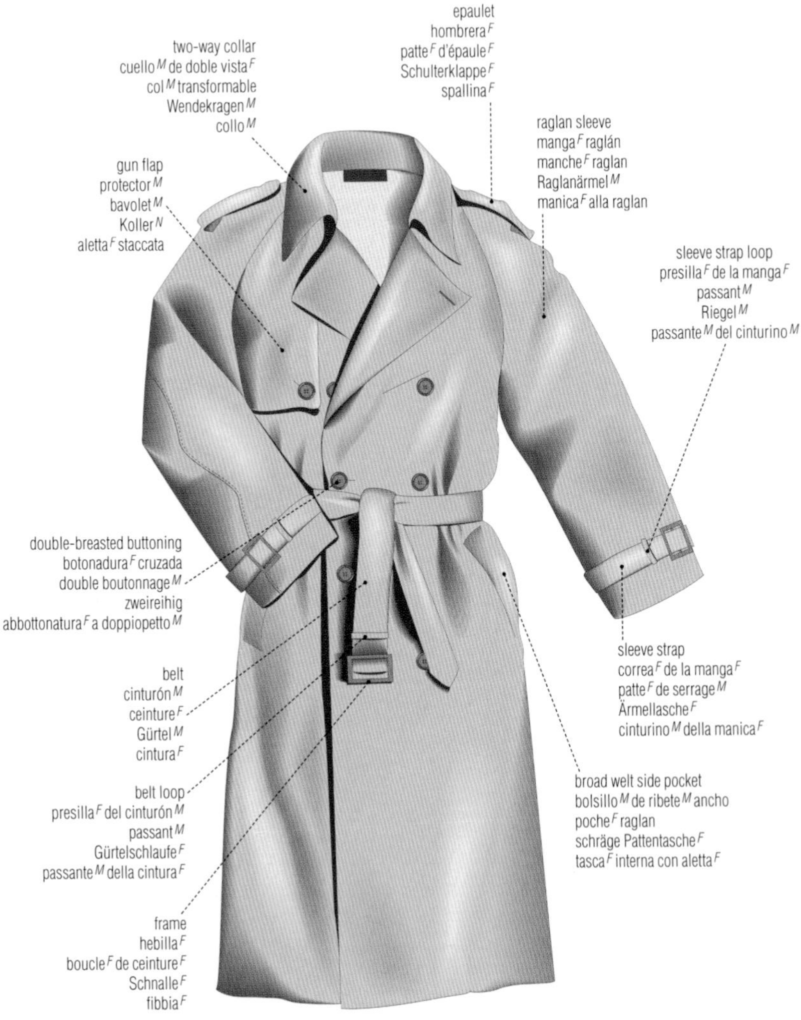

two-way collar
cuello M de doble vista F
col M transformable
Wendekragen M
collo M
epaulet
hombrera F
patte F d'épaule F
Schulterklappe F
spallina F
raglan sleeve
manga F raglán
manche F raglan
Raglanärmel M
manica F alla raglan
gun flap
protector M
bavolet M
Koller N
aletta F staccata
sleeve strap loop
presilla F de la manga F
passant M
Riegel M
passante M del cinturino M
double-breasted buttoning
botonadura F cruzada
double boutonnage M
zweireihig
abbottonatura F a doppiopetto M
sleeve strap
correa F de la manga F
patte F de serrage M
Ärmellasche F
cinturino M della manica F
belt
cinturón M
ceinture F
Gürtel M
cintura F
broad welt side pocket
bolsillo M de ribete M ancho
poche F raglan
schräge Pattentasche F
tasca F interna con aletta F
belt loop
presilla F del cinturón M
passant M
Gürtelschlaufe F
passante M della cintura F
frame
hebilla F
boucle F de ceinture F
Schnalle F
fibbia F

parka
parka^{F}
parka^{F}
Parka^{M}
parka^{M}

snap-fastening tab
botón^{M} de presión^{F}
patte^{F} à boutons^{M}-pression^{F}
Druckknopfleiste^{F}
allacciatura^{F} con bottoni^{M} a pressione^{F}

zipper
cremallera^{F}
fermeture^{F} à glissière^{F}
Reißverschluss^{M}
chiusura^{F} lampo

jacket
cazadora^{F}
blouson^{M} **court**
Blouson^{M}
giacca^{F} **a vento**^{M}

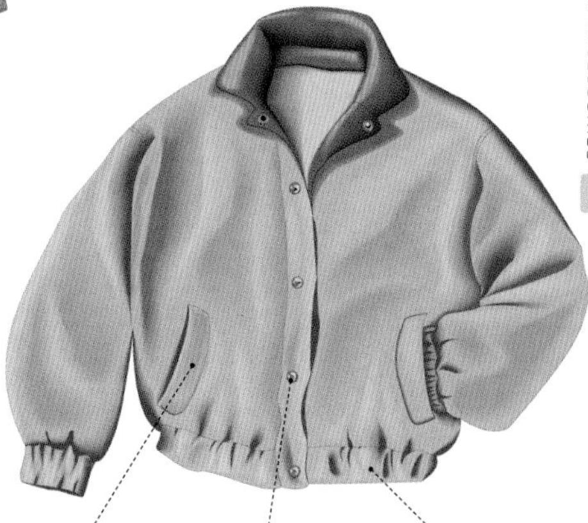

hand-warmer pocket
bolsillo^{M} de ojal^{M}
poche^{F} repose-bras^{M}
Mufftasche^{F}
tasca^{F} interna con aletta^{F}

elastic waistband
pretina^{F} elástica
ceinture^{F} élastique
elastischer Bund^{M}
fascia^{F} elastica

snap fastener
botón^{M} de presión^{F}
bouton^{M}-pression^{F}
Druckknopf^{M}
bottone^{M} a pressione^{F}

sheepskin jacket
zamarra^{F}
canadienne^{F}
Lammfelljacke^{F}
montone^{M}

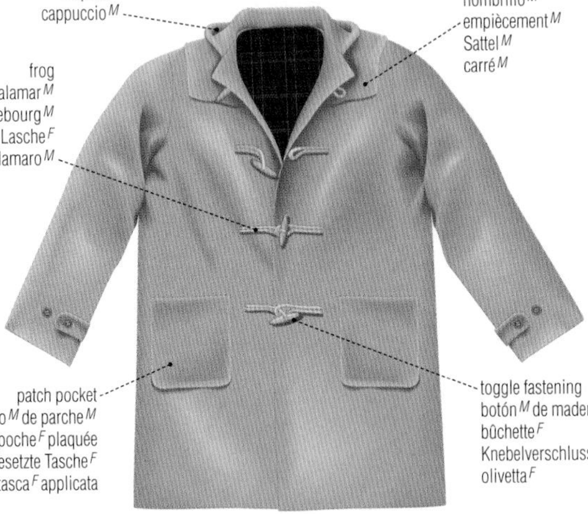
duffle coat
trenca F
duffle-coat M
Dufflecoat M
montgomery M
hood
capucha F
capuchon M
Kapuze F
cappuccio M
yoke
hombrillo M
empiècement M
Sattel M
carré M
frog
alamar M
brandebourg M
Lasche F
alamaro M
patch pocket
bolsillo M de parche M
poche F plaquée
aufgesetzte Tasche F
tasca F applicata
toggle fastening
botón M de madera F
bûchette F
Knebelverschluss M
olivetta F

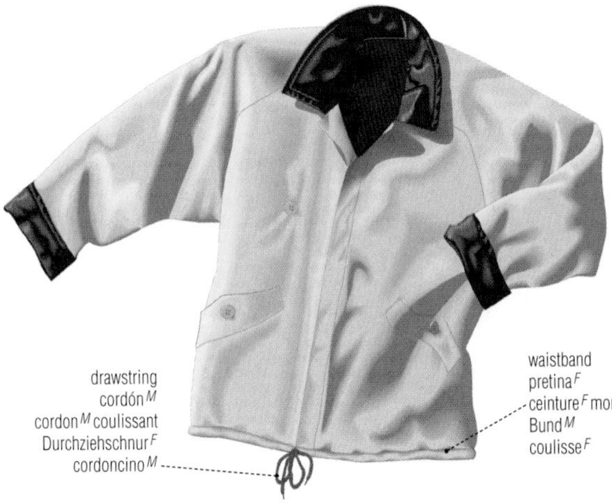
windbreaker
cazadora F
blouson M **long**
Windjacke F
giacca F **a vento** M
drawstring
cordón M
cordon M coulissant
Durchziehschnur F
cordoncino M
waistband
pretina F
ceinture F montée
Bund M
coulisse F

women's clothing

ropa[F] de mujer[F] | vêtements[M] de femme[F] | Damenbekleidung[F] | abbigliamento[M] femminile

suit
traje[M] de chaqueta[F]
tailleur[M]
Kostüm[N]
tailleur[M]

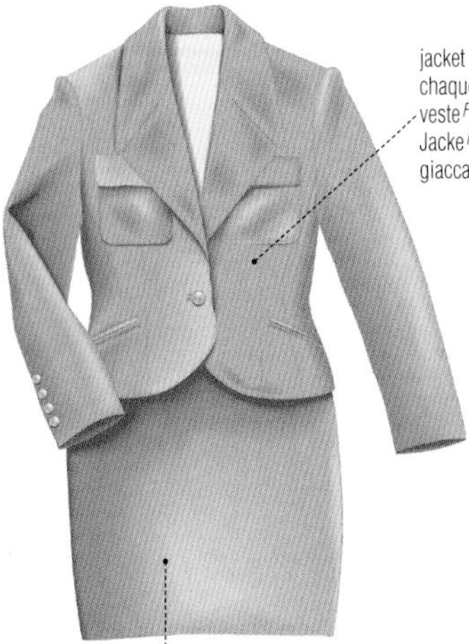
jacket
chaqueta[F]
veste[F]
Jacke[F]
giacca[F]
skirt
falda[F]
jupe[F]
Rock[M]
gonna[F]

coats
chaquetones[M] y abrigos[M]
manteaux[M]
Mäntel[M] und Jacken[F]
esempi[M] di giacche[F] e cappotti[M]

cape
capa[F]
cape[F]
Cape[N]
mantella[F]

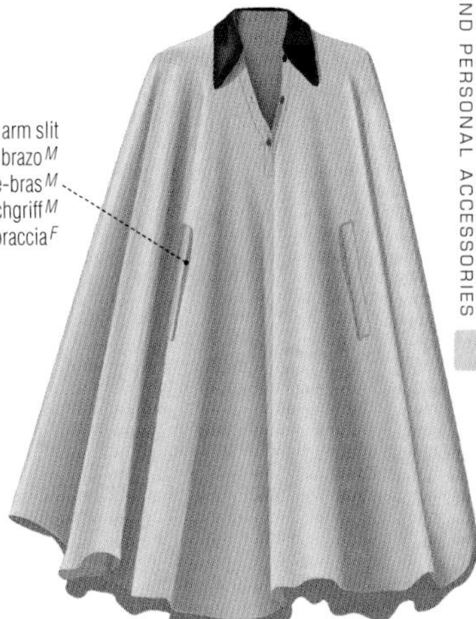
arm slit
abertura[F] para el brazo[M]
passe-bras[M]
Armdurchgriff[M]
apertura[F] per le braccia[F]

pea jacket
chaquetón[M] marinero
caban[M]
Cabanjacke[F]
giacca[F] alla marinara

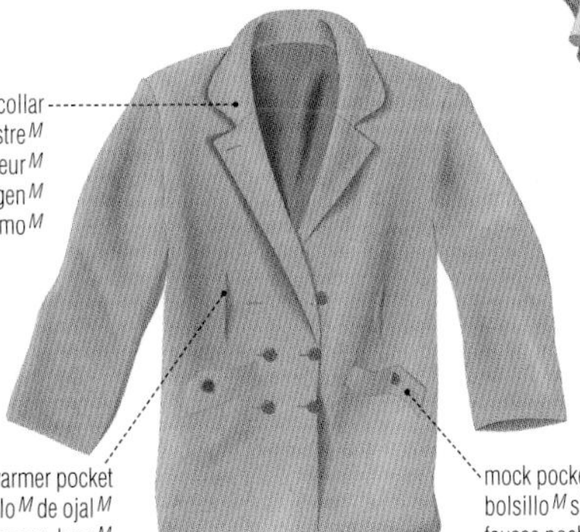
tailored collar
cuello[M] hechura[F] sastre[M]
col[M] tailleur[M]
Schneiderkragen[M]
collo[M] a uomo[M]
hand-warmer pocket
bolsillo[M] de ojal[M]
poche[F] repose-bras[M]
Mufftasche[F]
tasca[F] tagliata in verticale
mock pocket
bolsillo[M] simulado
fausse poche[F]
blinde Tasche[F]
tasca[F] finta

raglan
abrigo [M] raglán
raglan [M]
Raglanmantel [M]
cappotto [M] alla raglan

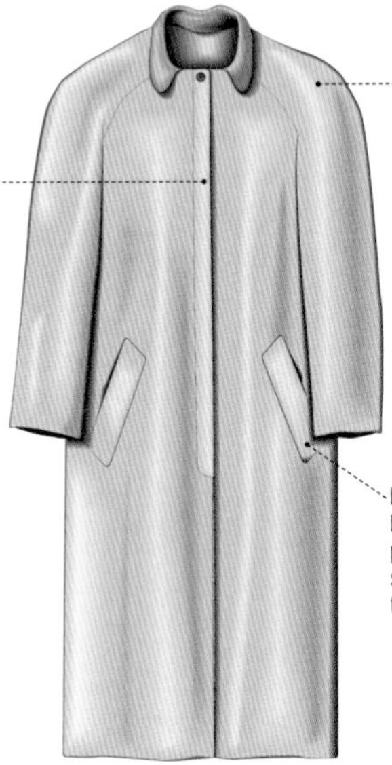
raglan sleeve
manga [F] raglán
manche [F] raglan
Raglanärmel [M]
manica [F] alla raglan
fly front closing
pestaña [F]
boutonnage [M] sous patte [F]
verdeckte Knopfleiste [F]
finta [F]
broad welt side pocket
bolsillo [M] de ribete [M] ancho
poche [F] raglan
schräge Pattentasche [F]
tasca [F] interna con aletta [F]

overcoat
abrigo [M]
manteau [M]
Mantel [M]
cappotto [M]

top coat
abrigo [M] redingote
redingote [F]
Redingote [F]
redingote [F]

pelerine
abrigo[M] con esclavina[F]
pèlerine[F]
Pelerine[F]
cappotto[M] con pellegrina[F]

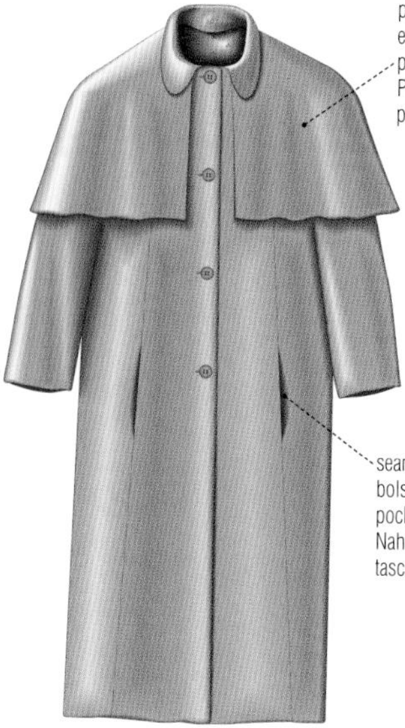
pelerine
esclavina[F]
pèlerine[F]
Pelerine[F]
pellegrina[F]
seam pocket
bolsillo[M] disimulado
poche[F] prise dans une couture[F]
Nahttasche[F]
tasca[F] inserita nella cucitura[F]

car coat
chaquetón[M] de tres cuartos
paletot[M]
Autocoat[M]
giaccone[M]

jacket
chaquetón[M]
veste[F]
Blazer[M]
giacca[F]

poncho
poncho[M]
poncho[M]
Poncho[M]
poncho[M]

women's clothing

examples of dresses
ejemplos[M] de vestidos[M]
exemples[M] de robes[F]
Beispiele[N] für Kleider[N]
esempi[M] di abiti[M]

sheath dress
recto[M] entallado
robe[F] fourreau[M]
Schlauchkleid[N]
tubino[M]

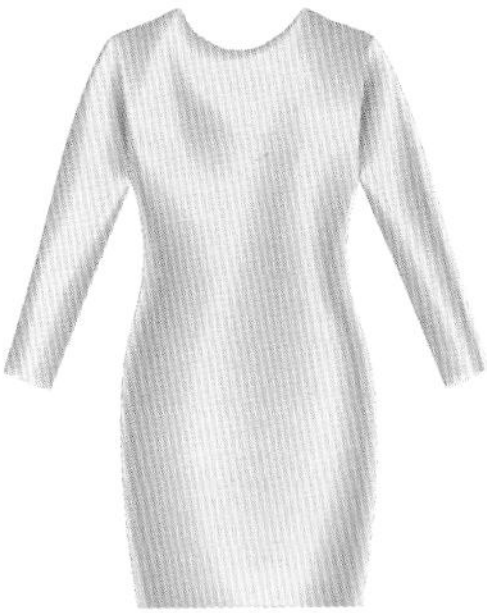

princess dress
corte[M] princesa[F]
robe[F] princesse[F]
Prinzesskleid[N]
princesse[F]

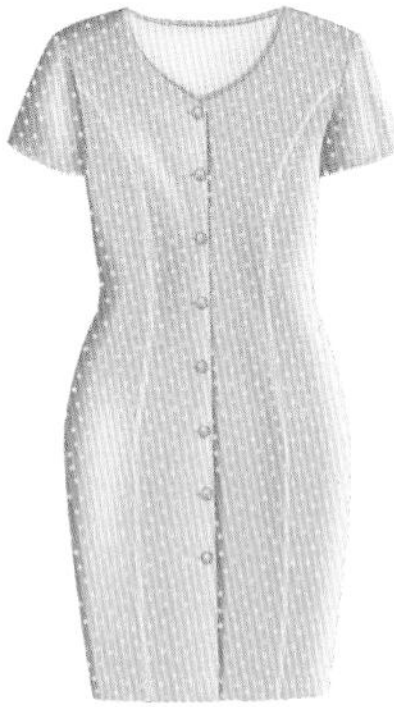

coat dress
traje[M] cruzado
robe[F]-manteau[M]
Mantelkleid[N]
robe-manteau[F/M]

polo dress
vestido[M] de camiseta[F]
robe[F]-polo[M]
Polokleid[N]
abito[M] a polo[F]

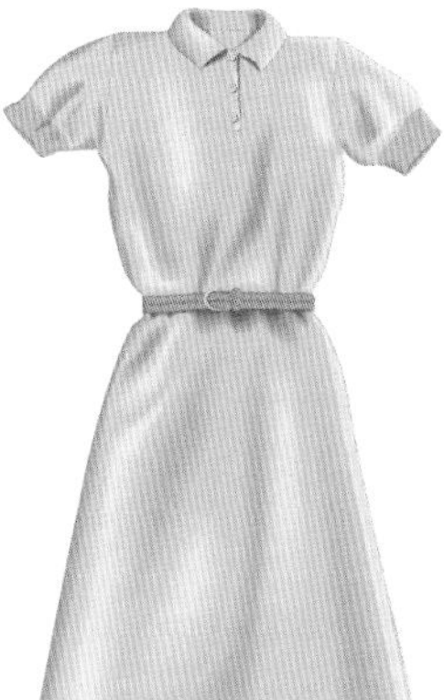

house dress
vestido[M] camisero sin mangas[F]
robe[F] d'intérieur[M]
Hauskleid[N]
abito[M] da casa[F]

shirtwaist dress
vestido[M] camisero
robe[F] chemisier[M]
Hemdblusenkleid[N]
chemisier[M]

wraparound dress
vestido[M] cruzado
robe[F] enveloppe[F]
Wickelkleid[N]
abito[M] a vestaglia[F]

tunic dress
túnica[F]
robe[F] tunique[F]
Tunikakleid[N]
abito[M] a tunica[F]

jumper
pichi[M]
chasuble[F]
Trägerrock[M]
scamiciato[M]

drop waist dress
vestido[M] de talle[M] bajo
robe[F] taille[F] basse
Kleid[N] mit angesetztem Schoß[M]
abito[M] a vita[F] bassa

trapeze dress
vestido[M] acampanado
robe[F] trapèze[M]
Kleid[N] in Trapez-Form[F]
abito[M] a trapezio[M]

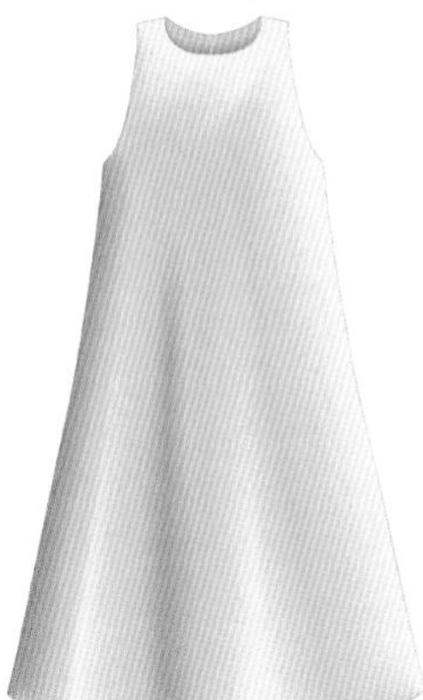

sundress
vestido[M] de tirantes[M]
robe[F] bain[M]-de-soleil[M]
leichtes Sonnenkleid[N]
prendisole[M]

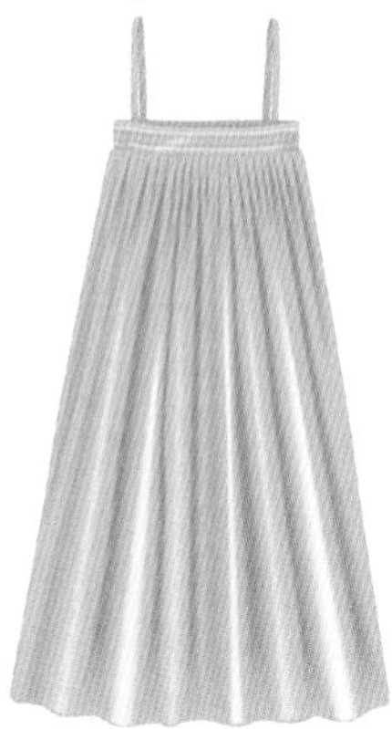

examples of skirts
ejemplos[M] de faldas[F]
exemples[M] de jupes[F]
Beispiele[N] für Röcke[M]
esempi[M] di gonne[F]

kilt
falda[F] escocesa
kilt[M]
Schottenrock[M]
kilt[M]

gored skirt
falda[F] de piezas[F]
jupe[F] à lés[M]
Bahnenrock[M]
gonna[F] a teli[M]

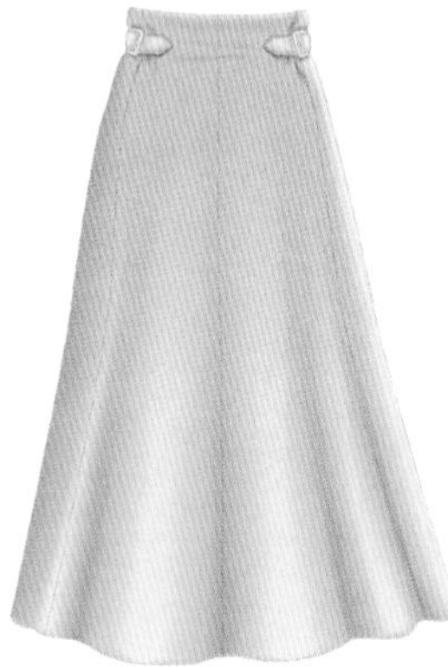

sarong
falda[F] sarong[M]
paréo[M]
Sarong[M]
sarong[M]

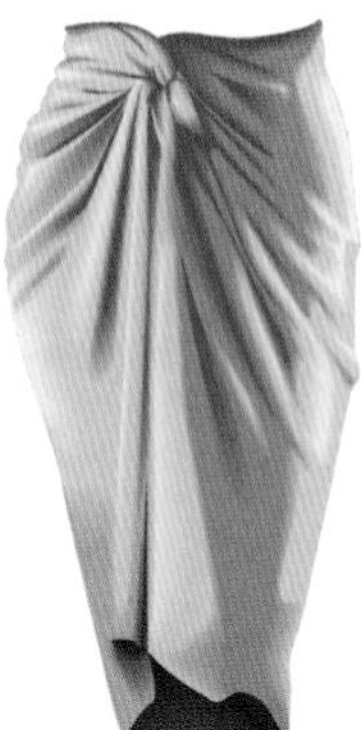

wraparound skirt
falda[F] cruzada
jupe[F] portefeuille[M]
Wickelrock[M]
gonna[F] a portafoglio[M]

sheath skirt
falda[F] de tubo[M]
jupe[F] fourreau[M]
Etuirock[M]
gonna[F] ad anfora[F]

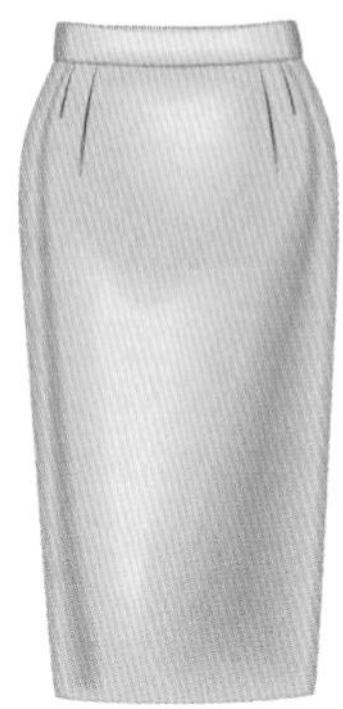

ruffled skirt
falda ^{F} de volantes ^{M}
jupe ^{F} à volants ^{M} étagés
Stufenrock ^{M}
gonna ^{F} a balze ^{F}

straight skirt
falda ^{F} recta
jupe ^{F} droite
gerader Rock ^{M}
gonna ^{F} diritta

gather skirt
falda ^{F} fruncida
jupe ^{F} froncée
Kräuselrock ^{M}
gonna ^{F} arricciata

yoke skirt
falda ^{F} acampanada
jupe ^{F} à empiècement ^{M}
Sattelrock ^{M}
gonna ^{F} con baschina ^{F}

culottes
falda ^{F} pantalón ^{M}
jupe ^{F}-culotte ^{F}
Hosenrock ^{M}
gonna ^{F} pantalone ^{M}

examples of pleats
ejemplos[M] de tablas[F]
exemples[M] de plis[M]
Beispiele[N] für Falten[F]
esempi[M] di pieghe[F]

inverted pleat
tabla[F] delantera
pli[M] creux
Kellerfalte[F]
piega[F] invertita

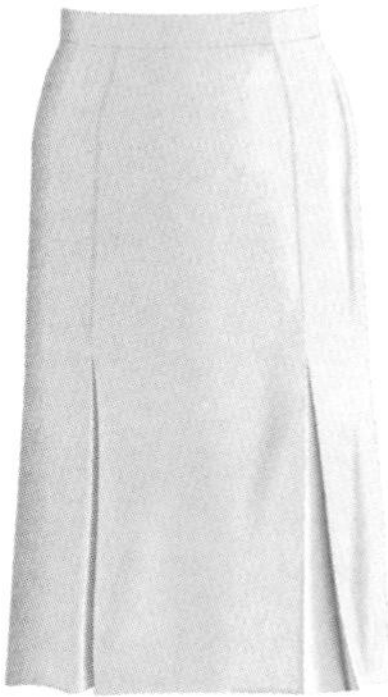

kick pleat
tabla[F] abierta
pli[M] d'aisance[F]
Gehfalte[F]
piega[F] sovrapposta

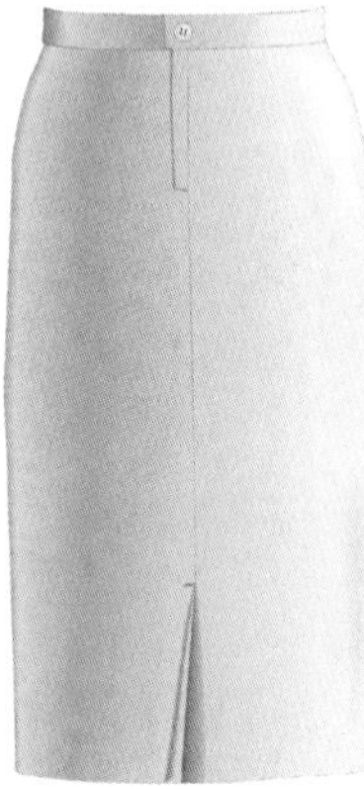

accordion pleat
plisada
plissé[M] accordéon[M]
Bahnenplissee[N]
plissé[M]

top stitched pleat
pespunteada
pli[M] surpiqué
abgesteppte Falte[F]
piega[F] impunturata

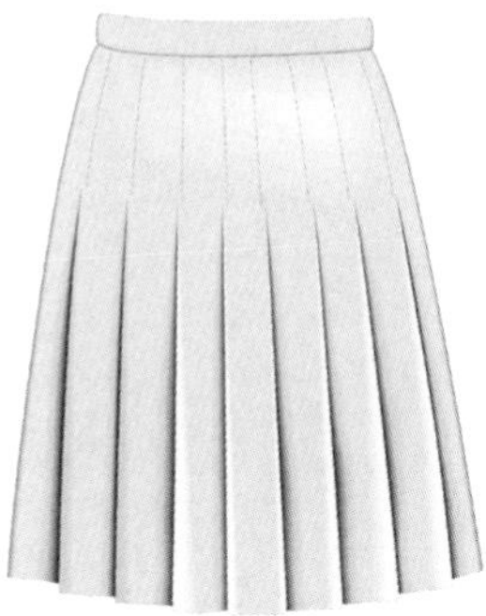

knife pleat
tablas[F]
pli[M] plat
einfache Falte[F]
piega[F] a coltello[M]

jackets, vest and sweaters
chalecos[M], jerseys[M] y chaquetas[F]
vestes[F] et pulls[M]
Westen[F] und Jacken[F]
esempi[M] di giacche[F] e pullover[M]

twin-set
jerseys[M] combinados
tandem[M]
Twinset[N]
twin-set[M]

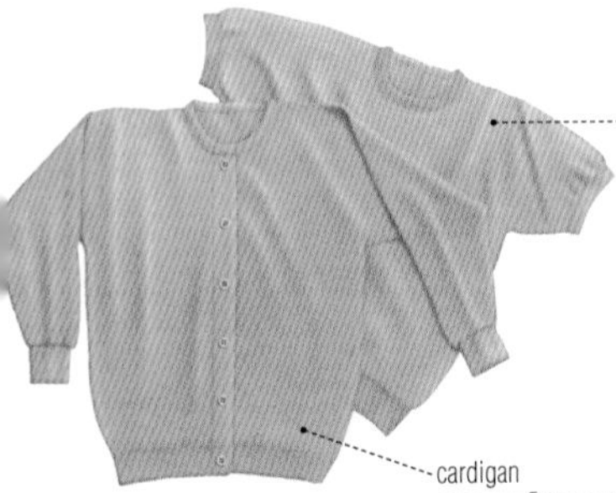
crew neck sweater
jersey[M] de cuello[M] redondo
ras-de-cou[M]
Pullover[M] mit Rundhalsausschnitt[M]
maglia[F] girocollo[M]
cardigan
chaqueta[F] de punto[M]
cardigan[M]
Cardigan[M]
cardigan[M]

vest
chaleco[M]
gilet[M]
Weste[F]
gilè[M]

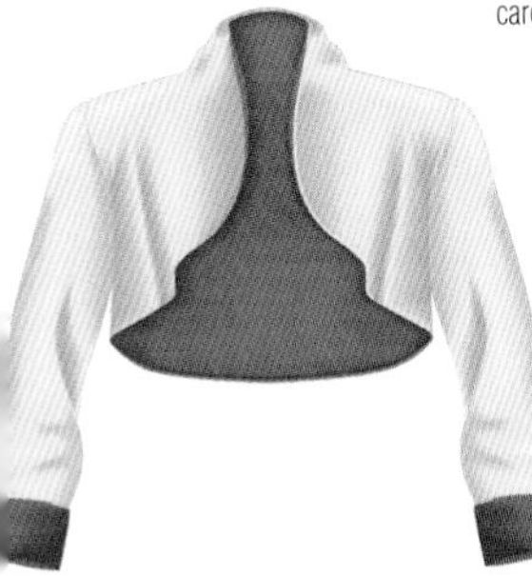

bolero
bolero[M]
boléro[M]
Bolero[M]
bolero[M]

spencer
bolero[M] con botones[M]
spencer[M]
Spenzer[M]
spencer[M]

blazer
americana[F]
blazer[M]
Blazer[M]
blazer[M]

safari jacket
sahariana[F]
saharienne[F]
Safarijacke[F]
sahariana[F]

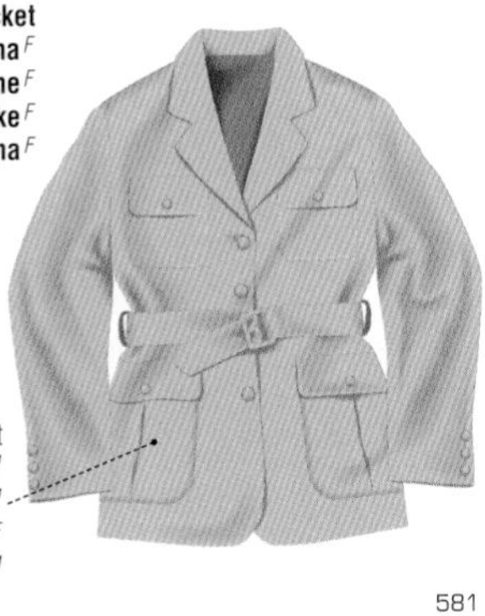
gusset pocket
bolsillo[M] de fuelle[M]
poche[F] soufflet[M]
Blasebalgtasche[F]
tasca[F] applicata a soffietto[M]

examples of pants
ejemplos M de pantalones M
exemples M de pantalons M
Beispiele N für Hosen F
esempi M di pantaloni M

shorts
pantalón M corto
short M
kurze Hose F
shorts M

Bermuda shorts
bermudas M
bermuda M
Bermudashorts F
bermuda M

bell bottoms
pantalones M acampanados
pantalon M pattes F d'éléphant M
Schlaghose F
pantaloni M a zampa F di elefante M

ski pants
pantalones M de tubo M
fuseau M
Steghose F
fuseau M

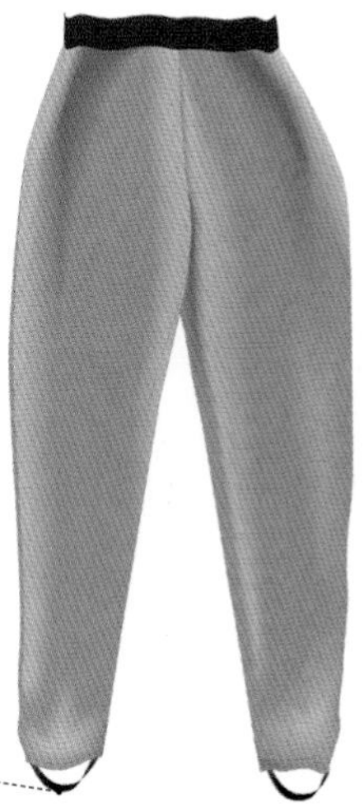
footstrap
trabilla F
sous-pied M
Steg M
staffa F

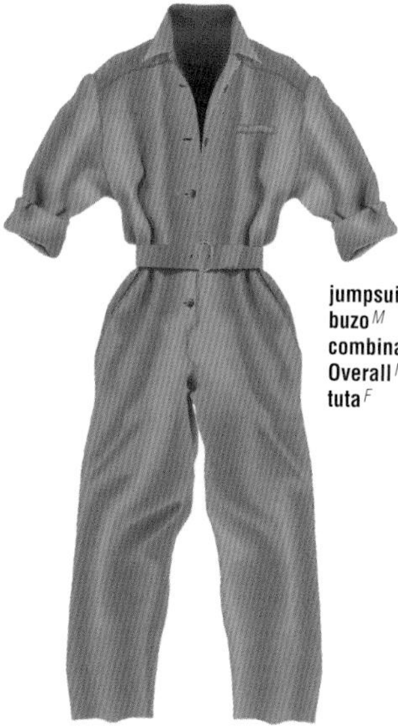

jumpsuit
buzo[M]
combinaison[F]**-pantalon**[M]
Overall[M]
tuta[F]

overalls
pantalón[M] **peto**[M]
salopette[F]
Latzhose[F]
salopette[F]

knickers
bombachos[M]
knicker[M]
Kniebundhose[F]
pantaloni[M] **alla zuava**

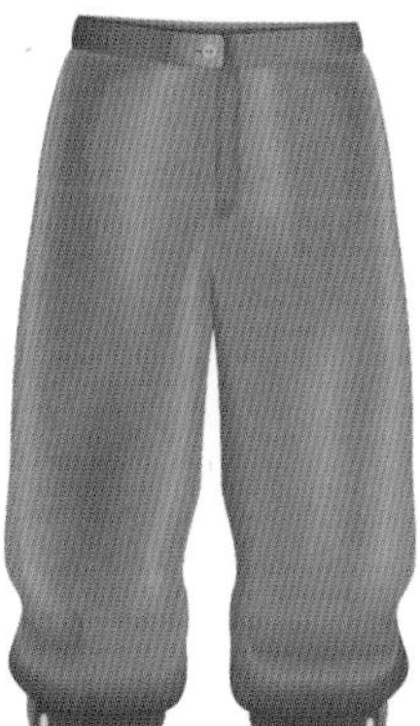

jeans
vaqueros[M]
jean[M]
Jeans[F]
jeans[M]

pedal pushers
pirata[M]
corsaire[M]
Caprihose[F]
pantaloni[M] **alla pescatora**

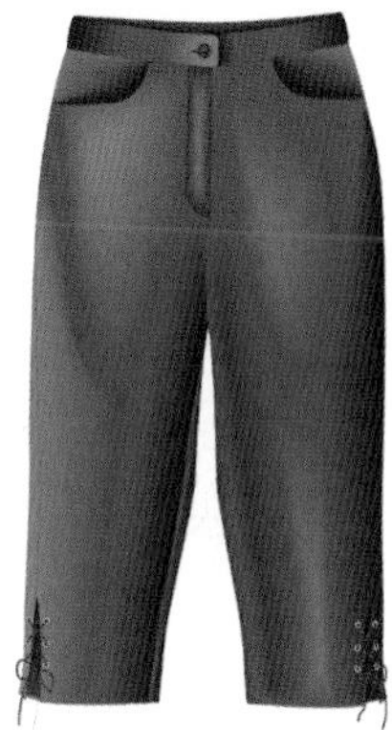

examples of blouses
ejemplos^M de blusas^F
exemples^M de corsages^M
Beispiele^N für Blusen^F und Hemden^N
esempi^M di camicette^F

classic blouse
camisera^F clásica
chemisier^M classique
klassische Bluse^F
camicetta^F classica

shirttail
faldón M
pan M
Schoß M
lembo M

mini shirtdress
camisa^F
liquette^F
Hosenbluse^F
camicione^M

crotch piece
entrepierna F
patte F d'entrejambe M
Schritt M
cavallo M

body shirt
body^M
corsage^M-culotte^F
Bodyshirt^N
body^M

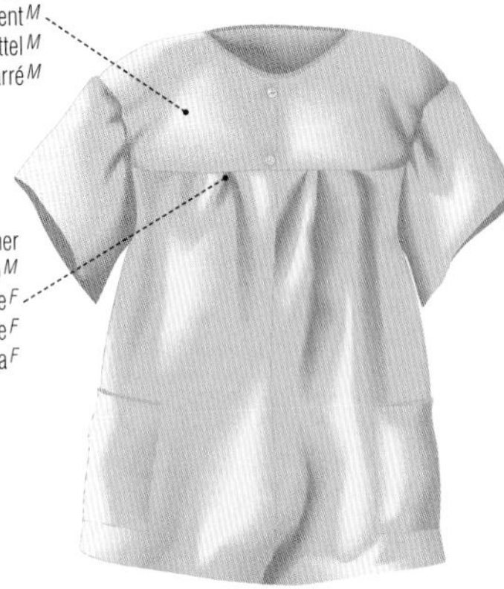
yoke
canesú M
empiècement M
Sattel M
carré M
gather
fruncido M
fronce F
Kräuselfalte F
arricciatura F

smock
blusón^M
tablier^M-blouse^F
Kittelbluse^F
sopravveste^F a grembiule^M

wrapover top
chaqueta [F] cruzada
cache-cœur [M]
Wickelbluse [F]
camicetta [F] incrociata

over-blouse
casaca [F]
casaque [F]
Tunika [F]
casacca [F]

middy
camisa [F] marinera
marinière [F]
Matrosenbluse [F]
maglietta [F] alla marinara

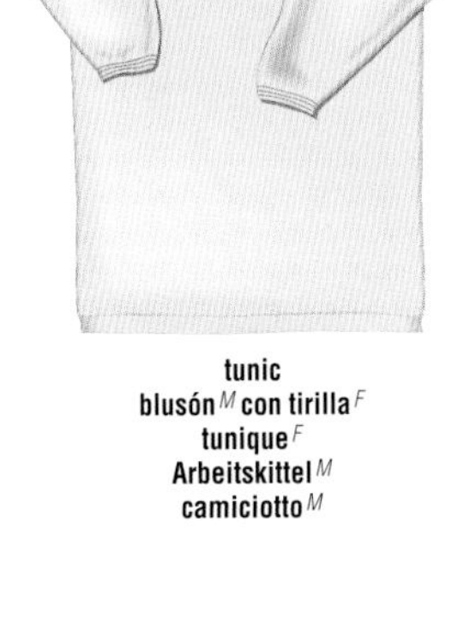

tunic
blusón [M] con tirilla [F]
tunique [F]
Arbeitskittel [M]
camiciotto [M]

polo shirt
polo [M]
polo [M]
Polohemd [N]
polo [F]

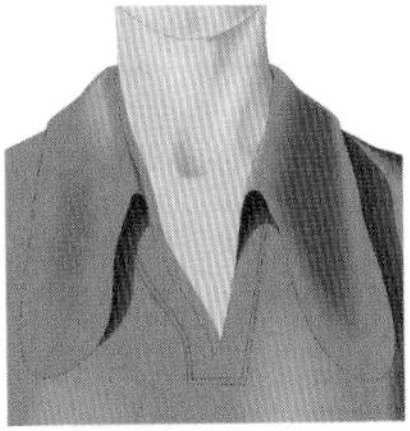

dog ear collar
cuello [M] plano con orejas [F]
col [M] banane [F]
Dackelohrkragen [M]
collo [M] a orecchie [F] di cane [M]

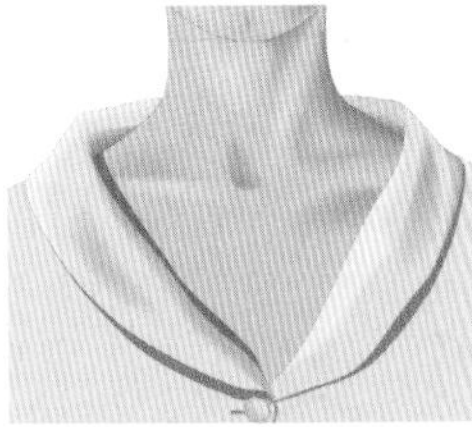

shawl collar
cuello [M] de chal [M]
col [M] châle [M]
Schalkragen [M]
collo [M] a scialle [M]

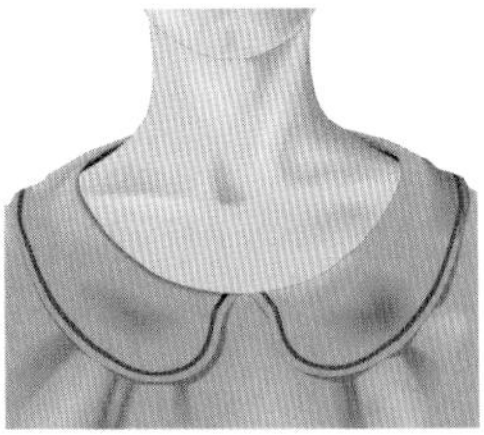

Peter Pan collar
cuello [M] plano tipo [M] Peter Pan
col [M] Claudine
Bubikragen [M]
collo [M] alla Peter Pan

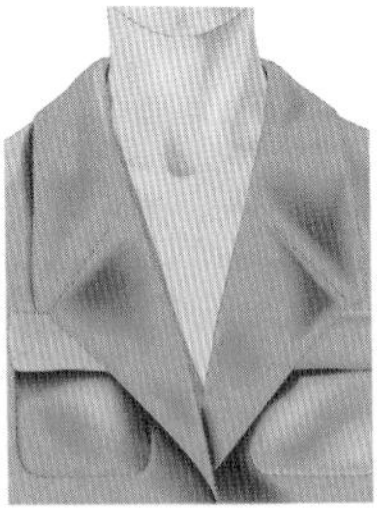

tailored collar
cuello [M] de hechura [F] de sastre [M]
col [M] tailleur [M]
Schneiderkragen [M]
collo [M] a uomo [M]

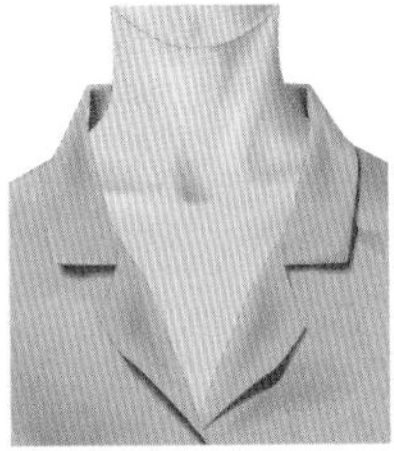

shirt collar
cuello [M] camisero
col [M] chemisier [M]
Hemdblusenkragen [M]
collo [M] a camicia [F]

bow collar
cuello [M] de lazo [M]
col [M] cravate [F]
Schleifenkragen [M]
collo [M] con sciarpa [F]

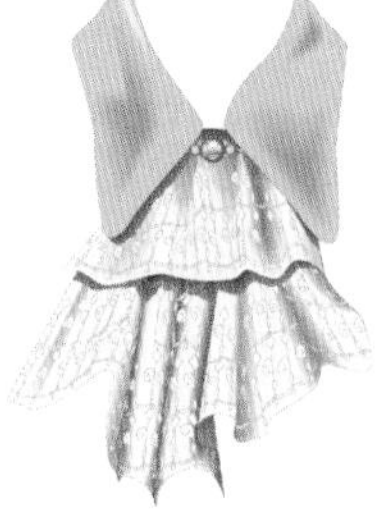

jabot
chorrera [F]
jabot [M]
Jabot [N]
jabot [M]

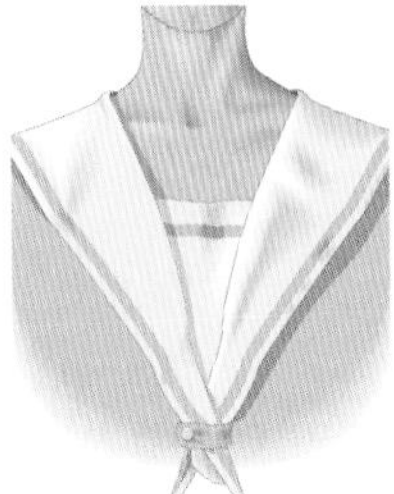

sailor collar
cuello [M] marinero
col [M] marin [M]
Matrosenkragen [M]
collo [M] alla marinara

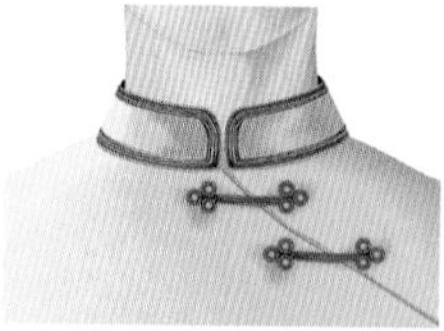

mandarin collar
cuello *M* chino
col *M* chinois
Chinesenkragen *M*
collo *M* alla coreana *F*

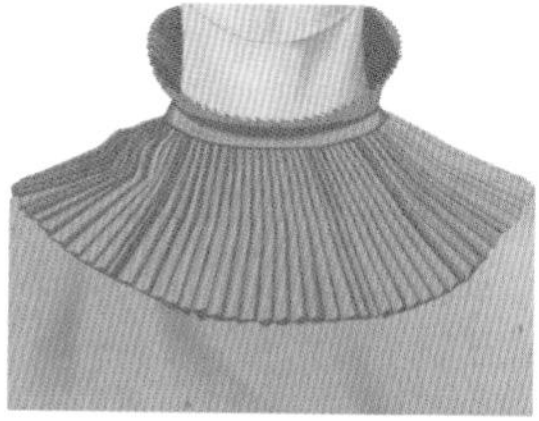

collaret
cuello *M* de volantes *M*
collerette *F*
Halskrause *F*
collaretto *M*

bertha collar
cuello *M* Berta
col *M* berthe *F*
Berthe *F*
berta *F*

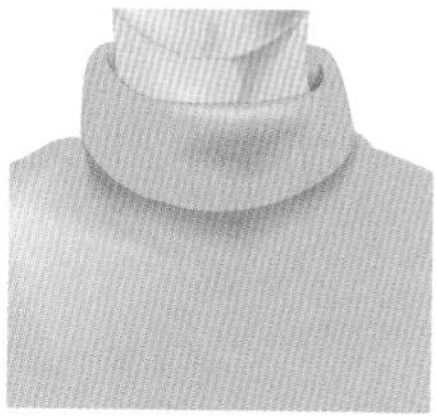

turtleneck
cuello *M* de tortuga *F*
col *M* roulé
Rollkragen *M*
dolcevita *M*

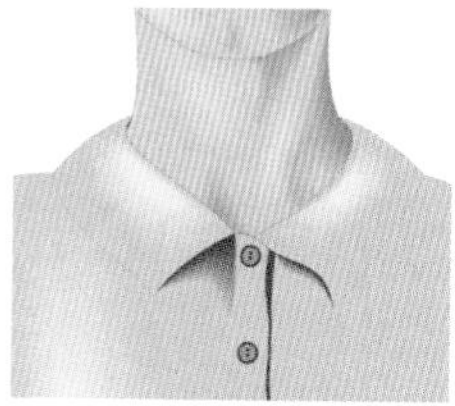

polo collar
cuello *M* de polo *M*
col *M* polo *M*
Polokragen *M*
collo *M* a polo *F*

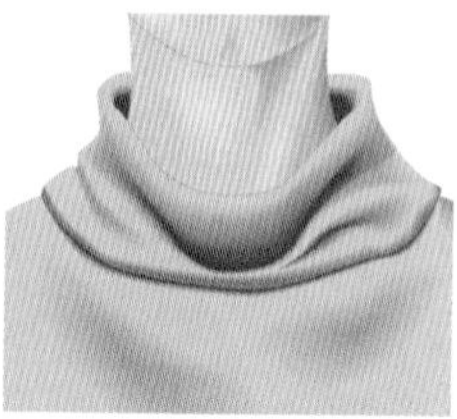

cowl neck
cuello *M* tipo cogulla *F*
col *M* cagoule *F*
Kuttenkragen *M*
collo *M* a cappuccio *M*

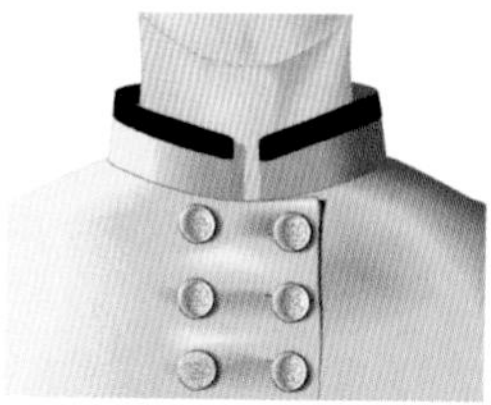

stand-up collar
cuello *M* Mao
col *M* officier *M*
Stehbundkragen *M*
collo *M* a listino *M*

women's clothing

underwear
ropa[F] interior
sous-vêtements[M]
Unterwäsche[F]
biancheria[F] intima

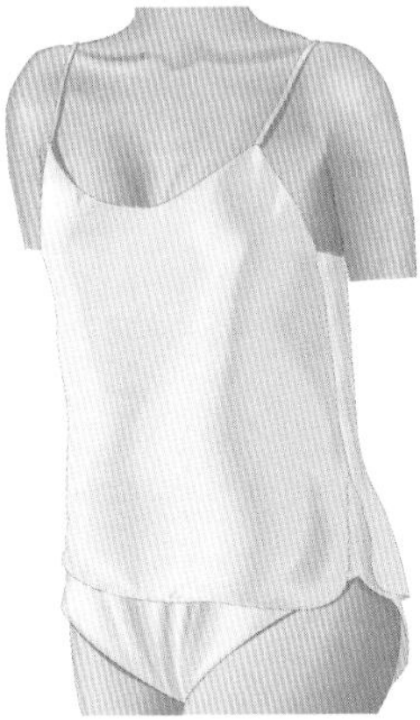

camisole
camisola[F]
caraco[M]
Camisol[N]
top[M]

corselette
faja[F] con sostén[M]
combiné[M]
Korselett[N]
modellatore[M] aperto

teddy
canesú[M]
teddy[M]
Teddy[M]
pagliaccetto[M]

body suit
body[M]
body[M]
Bodysuit[M]
body[M]

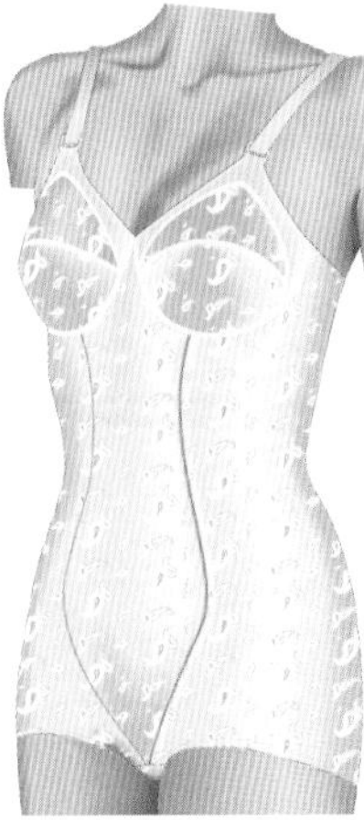

panty corselette
faja[F] corsé[M]
combiné[M]-culotte[F]
Panty-Korselett[N]
modellatore[M] sgambato

princess seaming
costura[F] de corte[M] princesa[F]
découpe[F] princesse[F]
Prinzessnaht[F]
cucitura[F] a princesse[F]

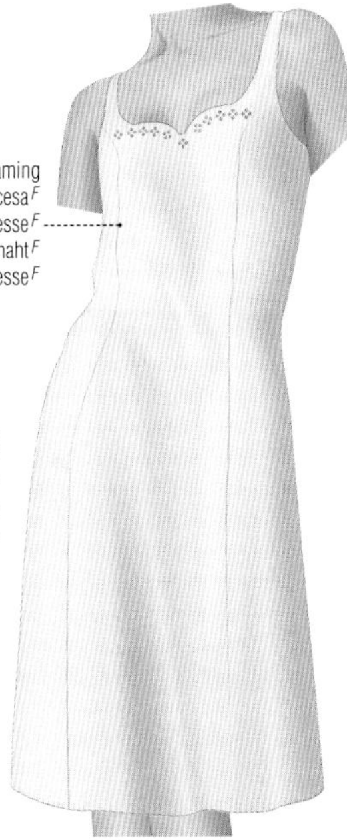

foundation slip
combinación[F]
fond[M] de robe[F]
Vollachsel-Unterkleid[N]
sottoveste[F]

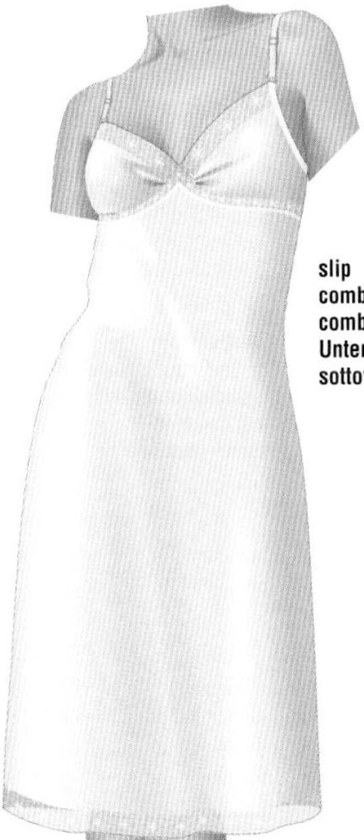

slip
combinación[F] con sujetador[M]
combinaison[F]-jupon[M]
Unterkleid[N]
sottoveste[F] con reggiseno[M]

half-slip
falda[F] combinación[F]
jupon[M]
Unterrock[M]
sottogonna[F]

wasp-waisted corset
corsé M de cintura F de avispa F
guêpière F
Torselett N
guepière F

underwire
varilla F
armature F
Unterbruststäbchen N
ferretto M
bikini
braga F
slip M
Slip M
slip M
garter
liga F
jarretelle F
Strumpfhalter M
giarrettiera F
hose
medias F
bas M
Strumpf M
calza F

strapless bra
sujetador M sin tirantes M
bustier M
trägerloser Büstenhalter M
reggiseno M a bustino M

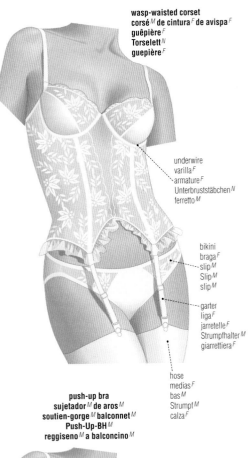

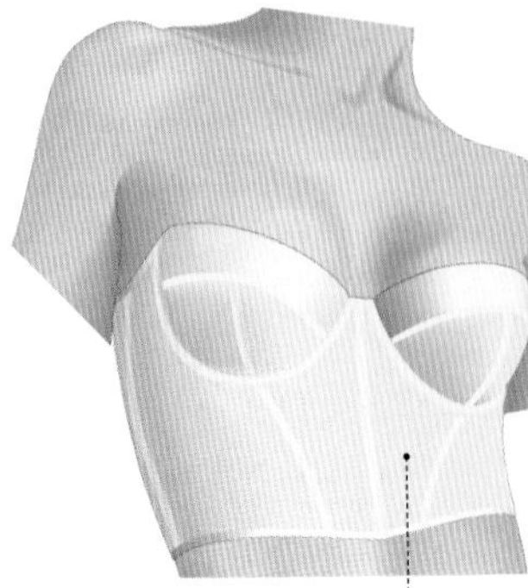
steel
varilla F
baleine F
Stab M
stecca F

push-up bra
sujetador M de aros M
soutien-gorge M balconnet M
Push-Up-BH M
reggiseno M a balconcino M

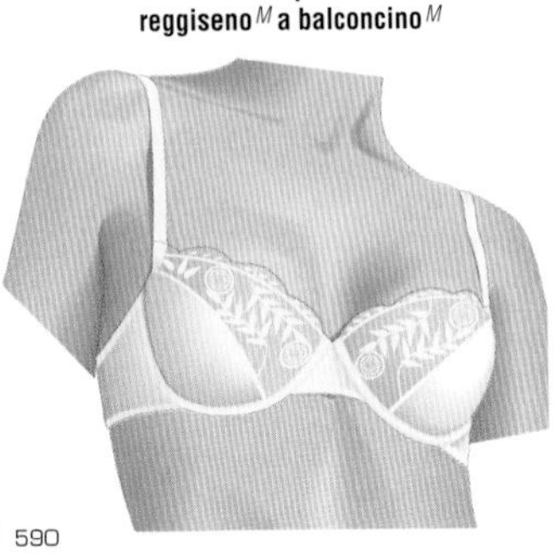

décolleté bra
sujetador M de escote M bajo
soutien-gorge M corbeille F
Halbschalen-BH M
reggiseno M décolleté M

bra
sujetador^{M}
soutien-gorge^{M}
BH^{M}
reggiseno^{M}

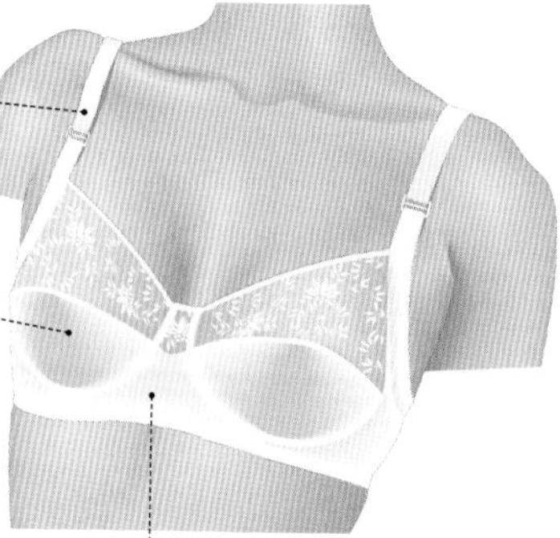

shoulder strap
tirante^{M}
bretelle^{F}
Träger^{M}
spallina^{F}

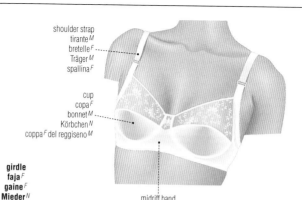

cup
copa^{F}
bonnet^{M}
Körbchen^{N}
coppa^{F} del reggiseno^{M}

midriff band
talle^{M} corto
basque^{F}
Mittelsteg^{M}
triangolo^{M} divisorio

girdle
faja^{F}
gaine^{F}
Mieder^{N}
panciera^{F}

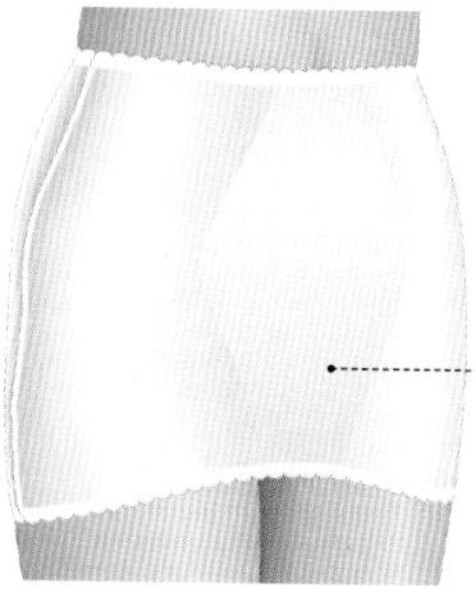

panel
refuerzo^{M}
plastron^{M}
Magenstütze^{F}
pannello^{M}

briefs
braga^{F}
culotte^{F}
Slip^{M}
mutandina^{F}

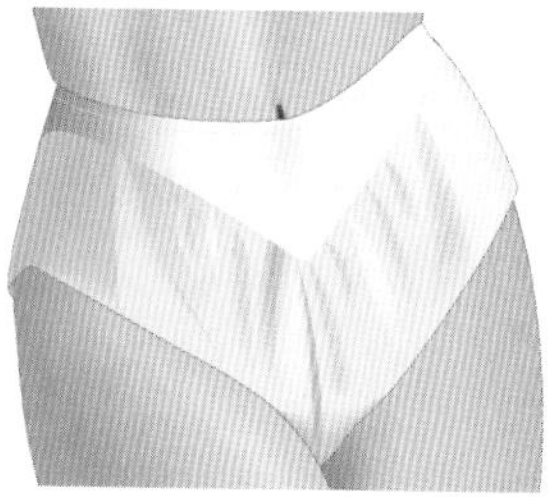

garter belt
liguero^{M}
porte-jarretelles^{M}
Strumpfhaltergürtel^{M}
reggicalze^{M}

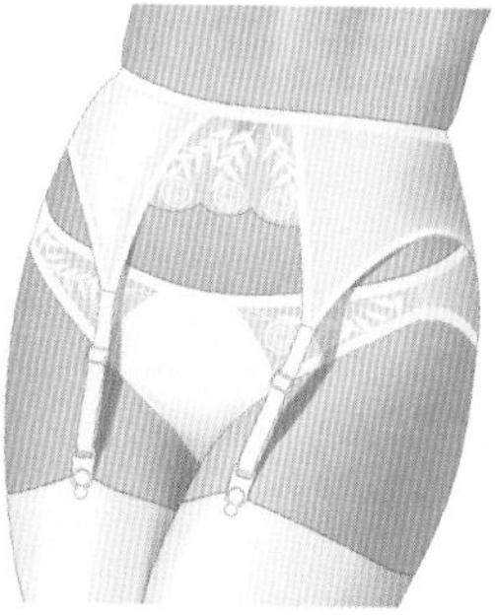

panty girdle
faja^{F} **braga**
gaine^{F}**-culotte**^{F}
Miederhose^{F}
mutandina^{F} **elastica**

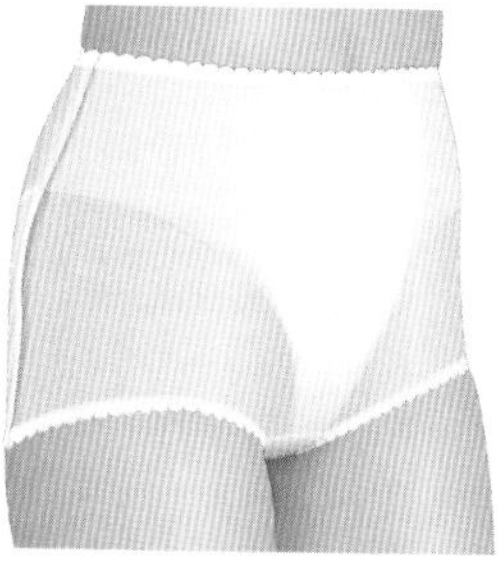

corset
faja^{F} **con liguero**^{M}
corset^{M}
Korsett^{N}
corsetto^{M}

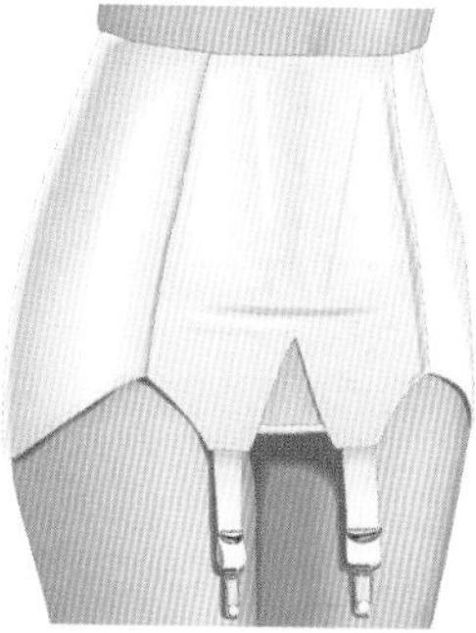

women's clothing

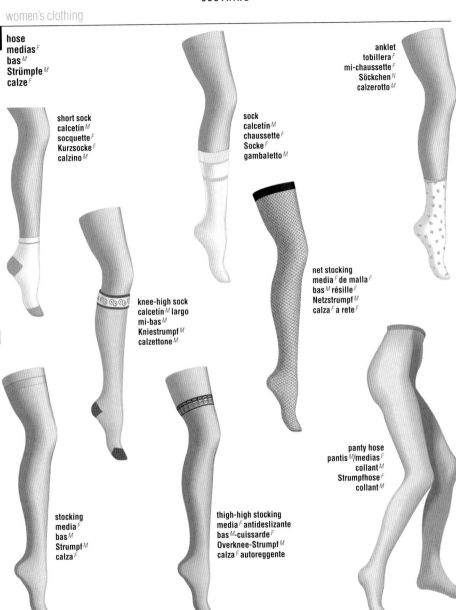

hose
medias [F]
bas [M]
Strümpfe [M]
calze [F]

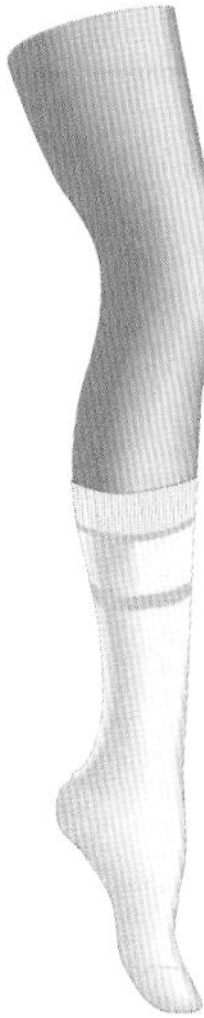

sock
calcetín [M]
chaussette [F]
Socke [F]
gambaletto [M]

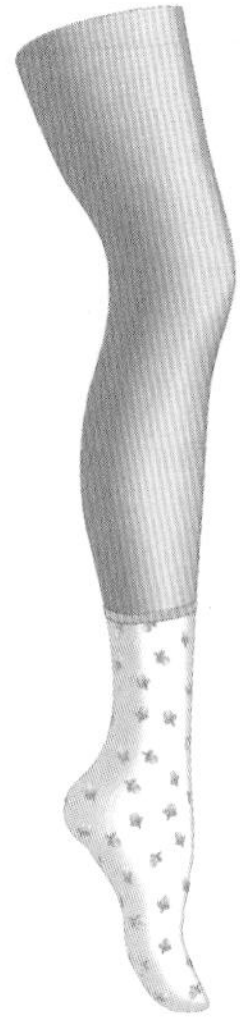

anklet
tobillera [F]
mi-chaussette [F]
Söckchen [N]
calzerotto [M]

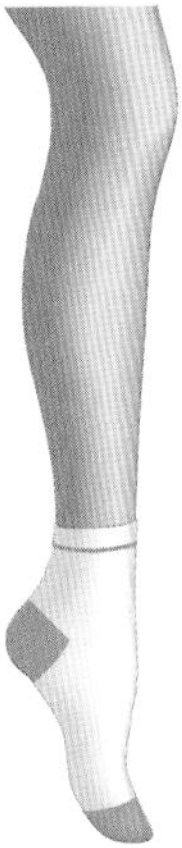

short sock
calcetín [M]
socquette [F]
Kurzsocke [F]
calzino [M]

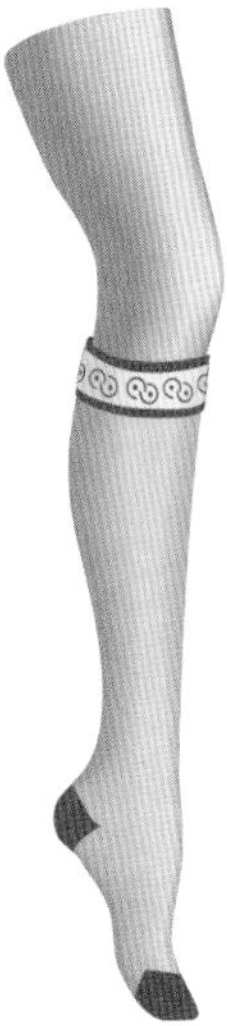

knee-high sock
calcetín [M] **largo**
mi-bas [M]
Kniestrumpf [M]
calzettone [M]

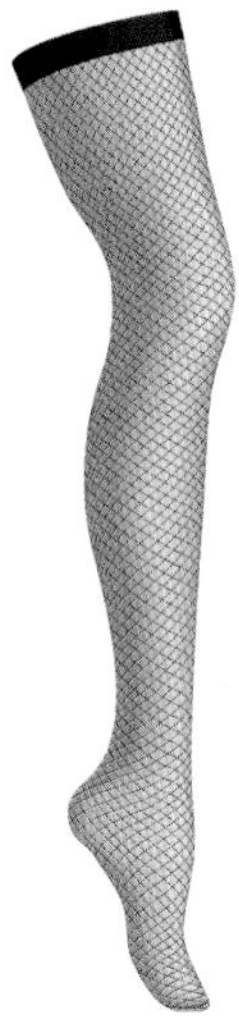

net stocking
media [F] **de malla** [F]
bas [M] **résille** [F]
Netzstrumpf [M]
calza [F] **a rete** [F]

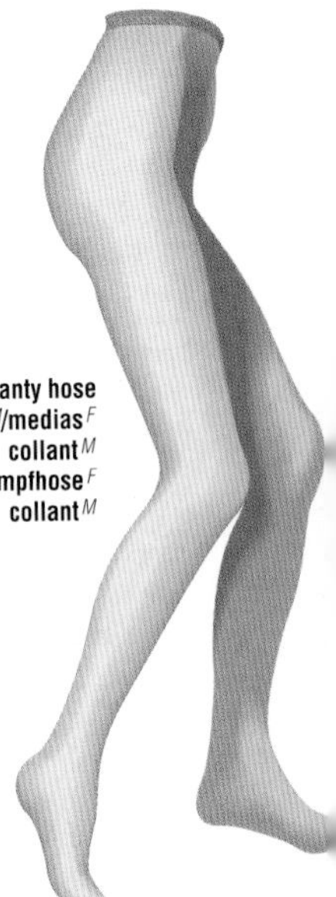

panty hose
pantis [M]**/medias** [F]
collant [M]
Strumpfhose [F]
collant [M]

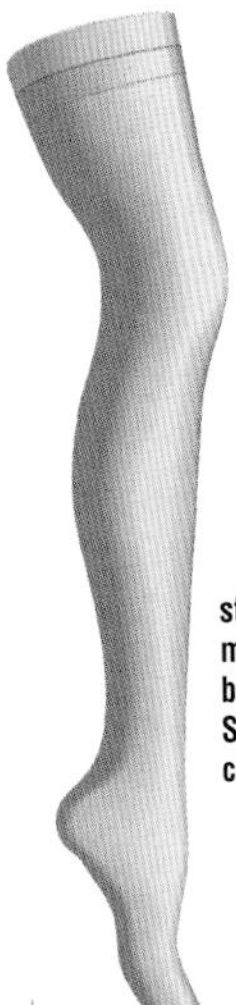

stocking
media [F]
bas [M]
Strumpf [M]
calza [F]

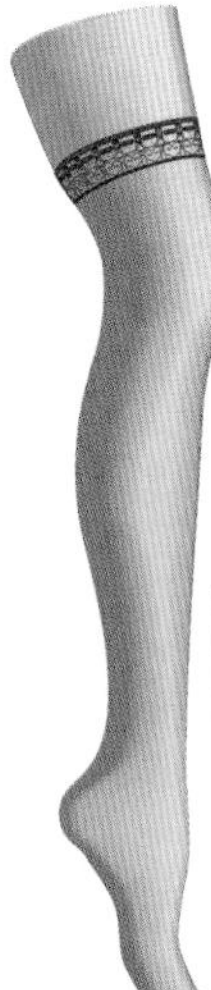

thigh-high stocking
media [F] **antideslizante**
bas [M]**-cuissarde** [F]
Overknee-Strumpf [M]
calza [F] **autoreggente**

bathing wrap
toalla F con capuchón M
cape F de bain M
Badetuch N mit Kapuze F
telo M di spugna F con cappuccio M

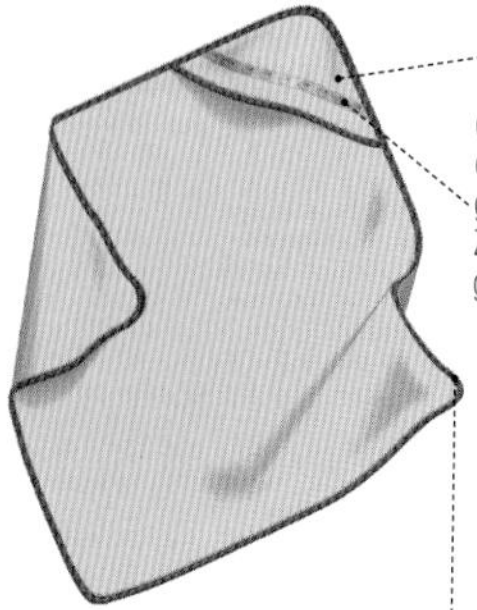
hood
capuchón M
capuche F
Kapuze F
cappuccio M
decorative braid
orla F decorativa
galon M d'ornement M
Zierborte F
guarnizione F
false tuck
falsa doblez F
biais M
Paspel F
profilo M sbieco

ruffled rumba pants
braga F de volantes M
culotte F à ruchés M
Rüschenhöschen N
mutandina F con ruches F

ruching
volantes M
ruché M
Rüschen F
ruches F

shirt
camiseta F
brassière F
Hemdchen N
maglietta F intima

bodysuit
body M
body M
Body M
body M

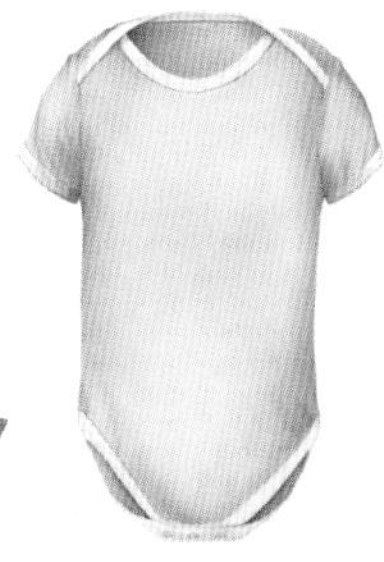

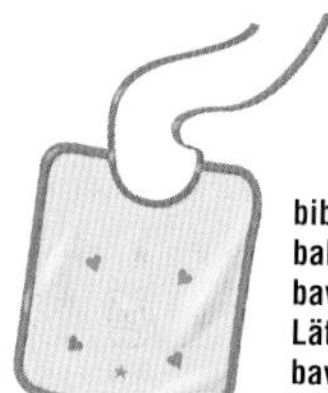

bib
babero M
bavoir M
Lätzchen N
bavaglino M

bunting bag
saco M portabebé M
nid M d'ange M
Schneesack M
tutina F a sacco M

jumpsuit
pantalón M de peto M
grenouillère F
Strampelhöschen N
salopette F a tutina F

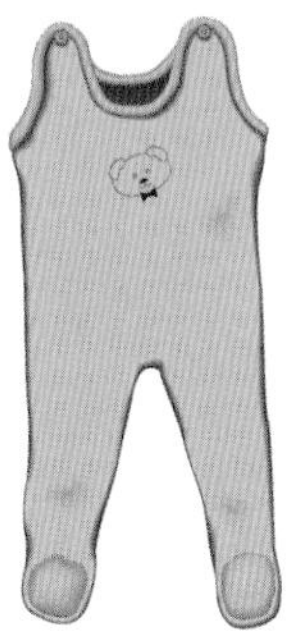

mittens
manoplas F
moufles F
Fäustlinge M
muffole F

bootees
botín M
chaussons M
Babyschuhe M
scarponcino M

newborn children's clothing

high-back overalls
pantalón[M] de peto[M]
salopette[F] à dos[M] montant
Latzhose[F] mit hohem Rückenteil[M/N]
salopette[F]

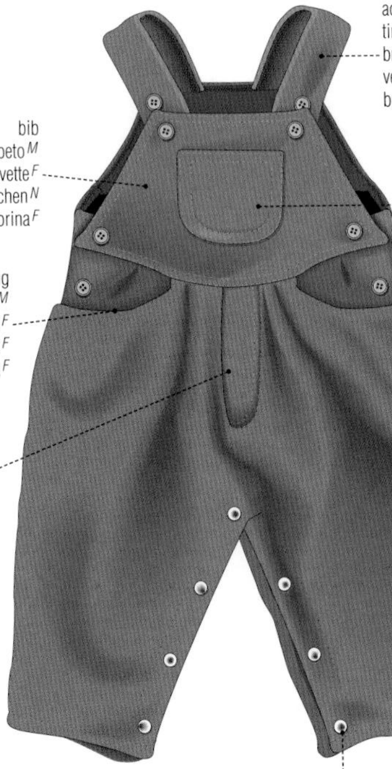
adjustable strap
tirante[M] ajustable
bretelle[F] réglable
verstellbarer Träger[M]
bretella[F] regolabile
bib
peto[M]
bavette[F]
Lätzchen[N]
pettorina[F]
patch pocket
bolsillo[M] de parche[M]
poche[F] plaquée
aufgesetzte Tasche[F]
tasca[F] applicata
top stitching
pespunte[M]
surpiqûre[F]
Zier-Steppnaht[F]
impuntura[F]
fly
bragueta[F]
braguette[F]
Schlitz[M]
patta[F]
inside-leg snap-fastening
botón[M] de presión[F]
entrejambe[M] pressionné
Druckknopfleiste[F] an der Beininnenseite[F]
interno[M] gamba[F] con abbottonatura[F] a pressione[F]

diaper
pañal[M]
couche[F]
Windel[F]
pannolino[M]

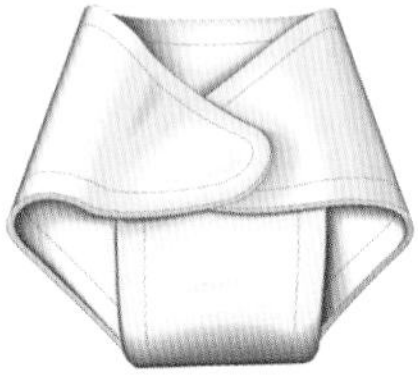

disposable diaper
pañal[M] desechable
couche[F]-culotte[F]
Einwegwindel[F]
pannolino[F] usa e getta

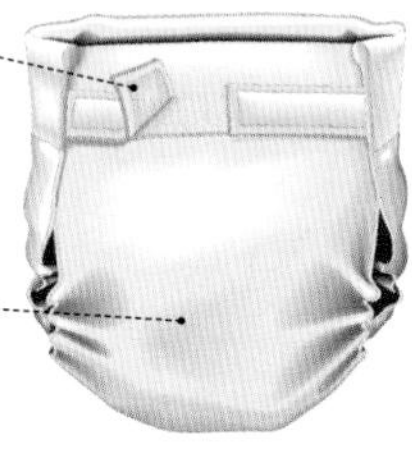
Velcro® closure
tirita[F] Velcro®
fermeture[F] Velcro®[M]
Haftgurtband[N]
velcro®[M]
waterproof pants
material[M] impermeable
poche[F] intérieure isolante
dichtes Windelhöschen[N]
mutandina[F] impermeabile

sleepers
pelele[M]
combinaison[F] de nuit[F]
Schlafanzug[M]
pigiamino[M]

raglan sleeve
manga[F] raglán
manche[F] raglan
Raglanärmel[M]
manica[F] alla raglan

snap-fastening front
botones[M] de presión[F] delanteros
pression[F] devant
vordere Druckknopfleiste[F]
abbottonatura[F] anteriore a pressione[F]

inside-leg snap-fastening
botones[M] de presión[F] de la pierna[F]
entrejambe[M] pressionné
Druckknopfleiste[F] an der Beininnenseite[F]
interno[M] gamba[F] con abbottonatura[F] a pressione[F]

blanket sleepers
pelele[M]
dormeuse[F]-couverture[F]
Wagenanzug[M]
pigiamino[M]

ribbing
tirilla[F] elástica
bord[M]-côte[F]
Rippenbündchen[N]
bordo[M] a coste[F]

zipper
cremallera[F]
fermeture[F] à glissière[F]
Reißverschluss[M]
chiusura[F] lampo

vinyl grip sole
suela[F] antiderrapante
semelle[F] antidérapante
rutschfeste Laufsohle[F]
soletta[F] antiscivolo

grow sleepers
pelele[M] de dos piezas[F]
dormeuse[F] de croissance[F]
zweiteiliger Schlafanzug[M]
pigiamino[M] a due pezzi[M]

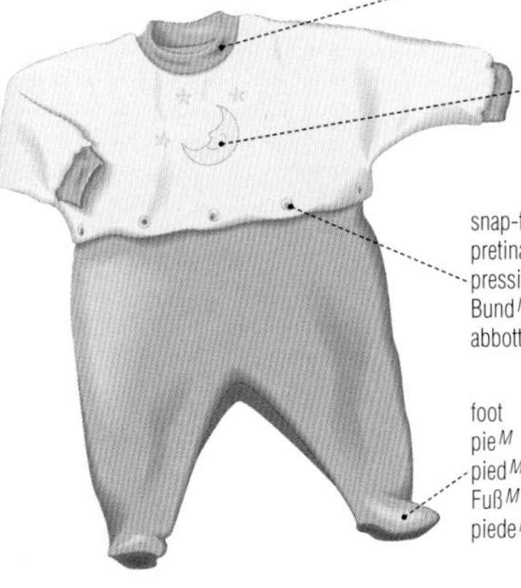

crew neck
cuello[M] redondo
encolure[F] ras-de-cou[M]
halsnaher Ausschnitt[M]
girocollo[M]

screen print
dibujo[M]
motif[M]
Aufdruck[M]
disegno[M] stampato

snap-fastening waist
pretina[F] con botones[M] de presión[F]
pression[F] à la taille[F]
Bund[M] mit Druckknöpfen[M]
abbottonatura[F] a pressione[F]

foot
pie[M]
pied[M]
Fuß[M]
piede[M]

sweaters

jerseys M | tricots M | Pullover M | maglioni M

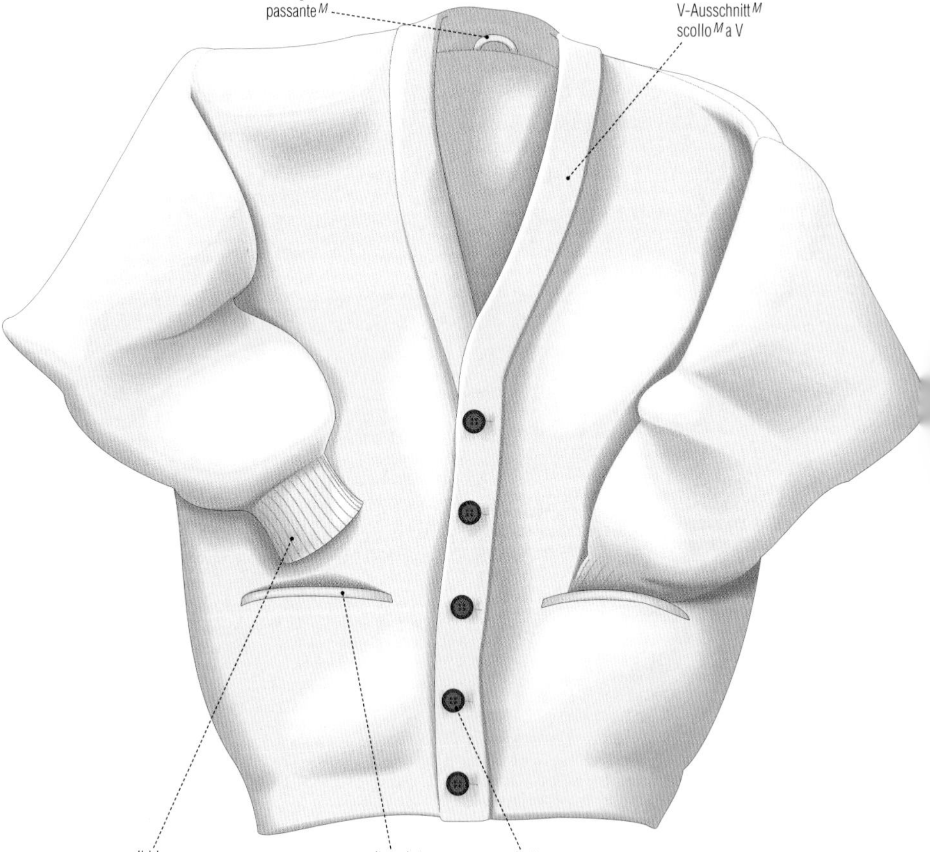
V-neck cardigan
cárdigan M
gilet M de laine F
Strickjacke F mit V-Ausschnitt M
cardigan M con scollo M a V
hanger loop
trabilla F de suspensión F
bride F de suspension F
Aufhänger M
passante M
V-neck
cuello M de pico M
encolure F en V
V-Ausschnitt M
scollo M a V
ribbing
tirilla F elástica
bord M-côte F
Patent-Strickbündchen N
bordo M a coste F
welt pocket
bolsillo M
poche F passepoilée
Paspeltasche F
tasca F profilata
button
botón M
bouton M
Knopf M
bottone M

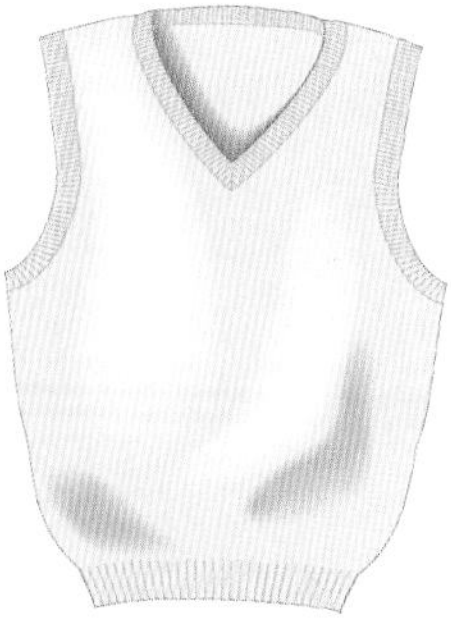

sweater vest
chaleco[M] de punto[M]
débardeur[M]
Pullunder[M]
gilè[M]

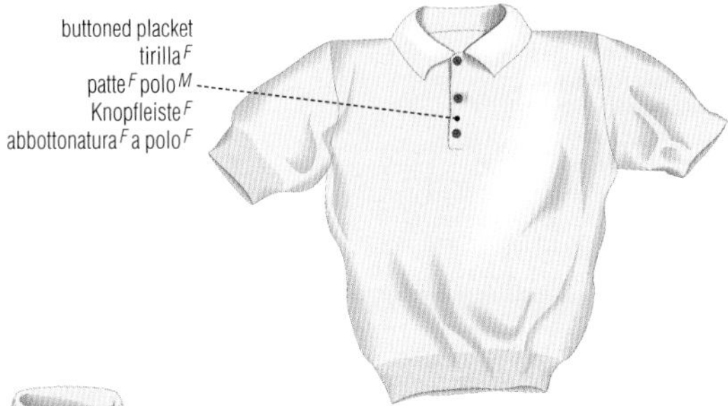
buttoned placket
tirilla[F]
patte[F] polo[M]
Knopfleiste[F]
abbottonatura[F] a polo[F]

knit shirt
polo[M]
polo[M]
Poloshirt[N]
polo[F]

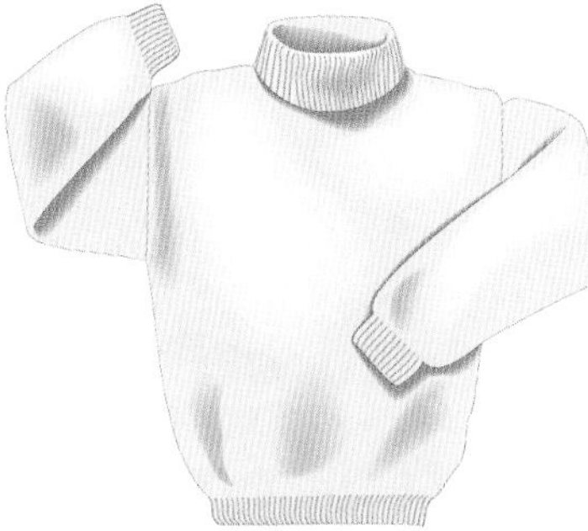

turtleneck
jersey[M] de cuello[M] de tortuga[F]
col[M] roulé
Rollkragenpullover[M]
maglione[M] dolcevita[M]

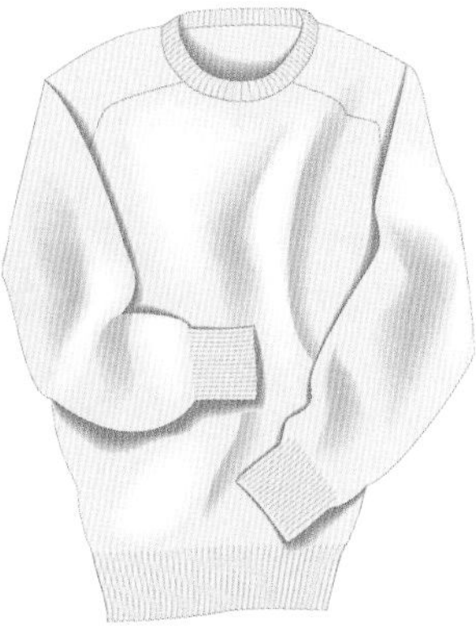

crew neck sweater
jersey[M] de cuello[M] redondo
ras-de-cou[M]
Pullover[M] mit Rundhalsausschnitt[M]
maglione[M] girocollo[M]

cardigan
chaqueta[F] de punto[M]
cardigan[M]
Strickjacke[F]
cardigan[M]

sportswear

ropa^F deportiva | tenue^F d'exercice^M | Sportkleidung^F | abbigliamento^M sportivo

running shoe
zapatilla^F deportiva
chaussure^F de sport^M
Joggingschuh^M
scarpa^F da corsa^F

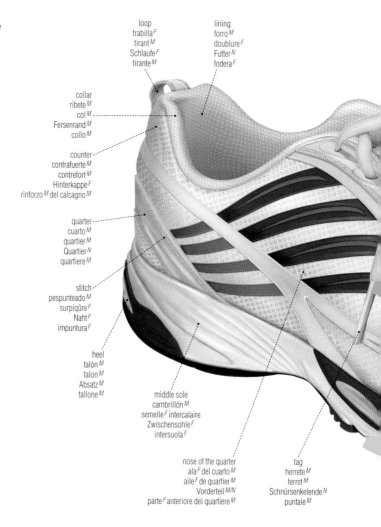

loop
trabilla^F
tirant^M
Schlaufe^F
tirante^M
lining
forro^M
doublure^F
Futter^N
fodera^F
collar
ribete^M
col^M
Fersenrand^M
collo^M
counter
contrafuerte^M
contrefort^M
Hinterkappe^F
rinforzo^M del calcagno^M
quarter
cuarto^M
quartier^M
Quartier^N
quartiere^M
stitch
pespunteado^M
surpiqûre^F
Naht^F
impuntura^F
heel
talón^M
talon^M
Absatz^M
tallone^M
middle sole
cambrillón^M
semelle^F intercalaire
Zwischensohle^F
intersuola^F
nose of the quarter
ala^F del cuarto^M
aile^F de quartier^M
Vorderteil^M/N
parte^F anteriore del quartiere^M
tag
herrete^M
ferret^M
Schnürsenkelende^N
puntale^M

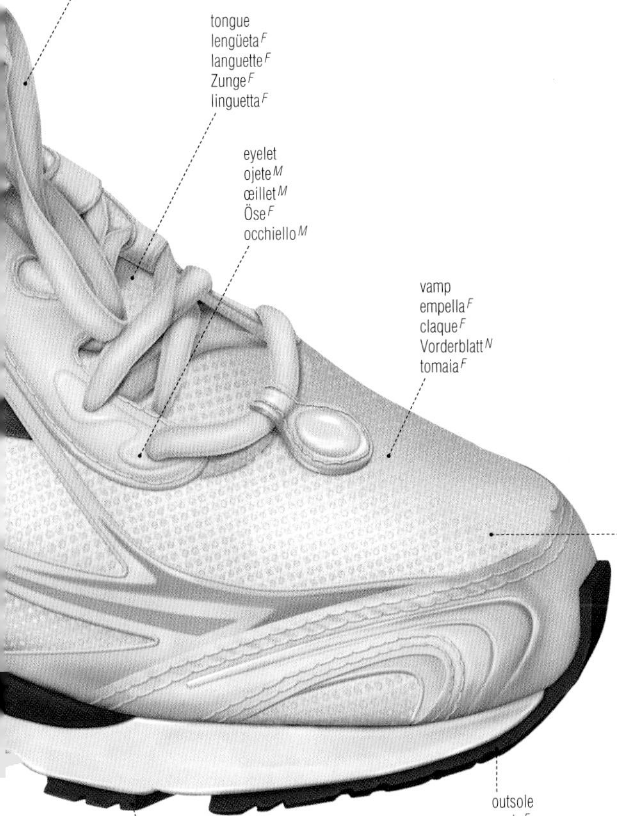
shoelace
cordón [M]
lacet [M]
Schnürsenkel [M]
laccio [M]
tongue
lengüeta [F]
languette [F]
Zunge [F]
linguetta [F]
eyelet
ojete [M]
œillet [M]
Öse [F]
occhiello [M]
vamp
empella [F]
claque [F]
Vorderblatt [N]
tomaia [F]
punch hole
perforación [F]
perforation [F]
gestanztes Loch [N]
foro [M]
stud
montante [M]
crampon [M]
Stollen [M]
tacchetto [M]
outsole
suela [F]
semelle [F] d'usure [F]
Laufsohle [F]
suola [F]

sportswear

exercise wear
ropa *F* **para ejercicio** *M*
vêtements *M* **d'exercice** *M*
Sportkleidung *F*
abbigliamento *M* **da ginnastica** *F*

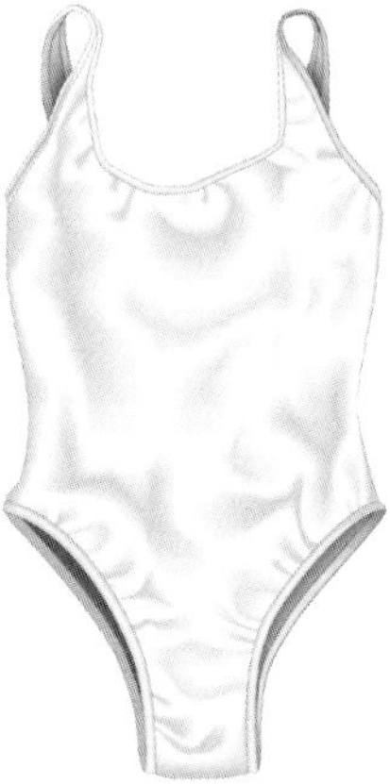

swimsuit
traje *M* de baño *M*
maillot *M* de bain *M*
Badeanzug *M*
costume *M* da bagno *M*

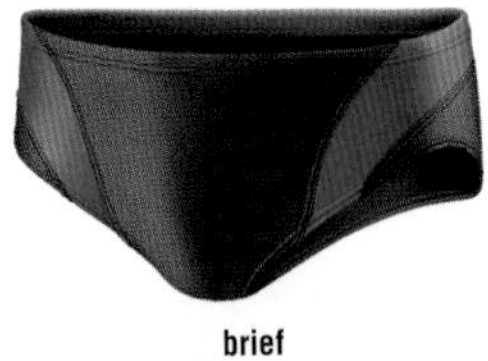

brief
traje *M* de baño *M*
slip *M* de bain *M*
Badehose *F*
slip *M* da bagno *M*

leotard
body *M*
justaucorps *M*
Trikot *N*
body *M*

leg-warmer
calentador *M* de pierna *F*
jambière *F*
Legwarmer *M*
scaldamuscoli *M*

footless tights
mallas *F*
collant *M* sans pieds *M*
Leggins *F*
pantacollant *M*

fleece jacket
chaqueta[F] polar
veste[F] polaire
Fleece-Jacke[F]
giacca[F] in pile[M]

T-shirt
camiseta[F]
T-shirt[M]
T-Shirt[N]
T-shirt[F]

tank top
camiseta[F]
débardeur[M]
Trägerhemd[N]
canottiera[F]

bicycle pants
pantalón[M] ciclista[M]
cuissard[M]
Radhose[F]
pantaloncini[M] da ciclista[F]

anorak
anorak[M]
anorak[M]
Anorak[M]
k-way[M]

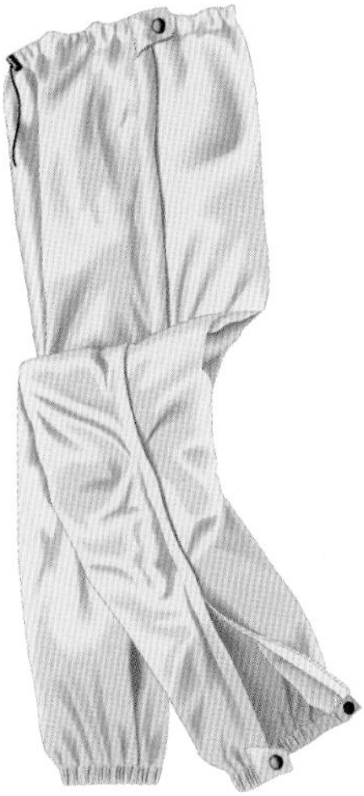

pants
pantalones[M]
pantalon[M]
Hose[F]
pantaloni[M]

boxer shorts
pantalón[M] de boxeo[M]
short[M] boxeur[M]
Shorts[F]
pantaloncini[M] da corsa[F]

jewelry

joyería[F] | bijouterie[F] | Schmuck[M] | gioielli[M]

earrings
pendientes[M]
boucles[F] d'oreille[F]
Ohrringe[M]
orecchini[M]

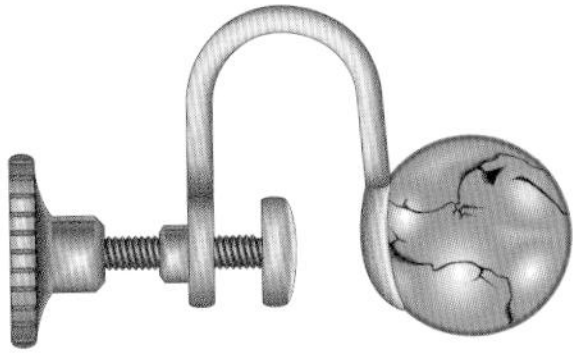

screw earrings
pendientes[M] de tornillo[M]
boucles[F] d'oreille[F] à vis[F]
Ohrringe[M] mit Schraubverschluss[M]
orecchini[M] a vite[F]

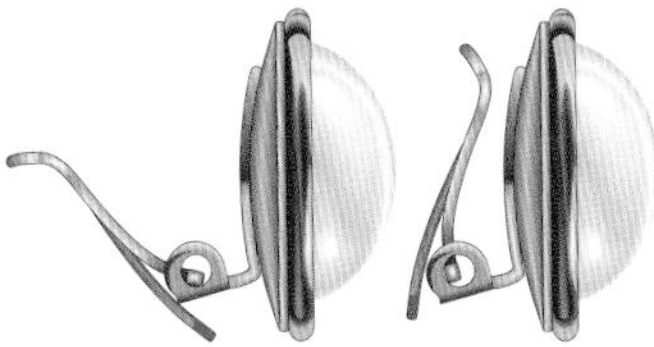

clip earrings
pendientes[M] de clip[M]
boucles[F] d'oreille[F] à pince[F]
Klips[M]
orecchini[M] a clip[F]

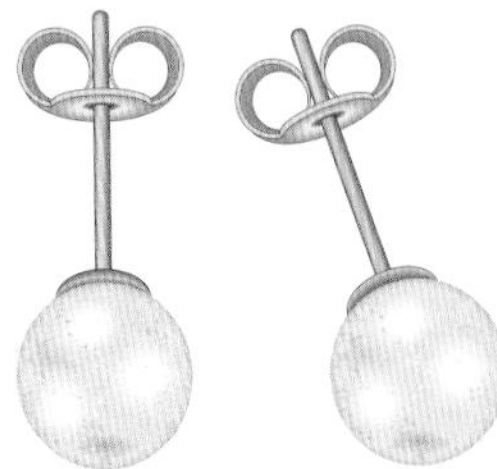

pierced earrings
pendientes[M] de espiga[F]
boucles[F] d'oreille[F] à tige[F]
Ohrstecker[M]
orecchini[M] a perno[M]

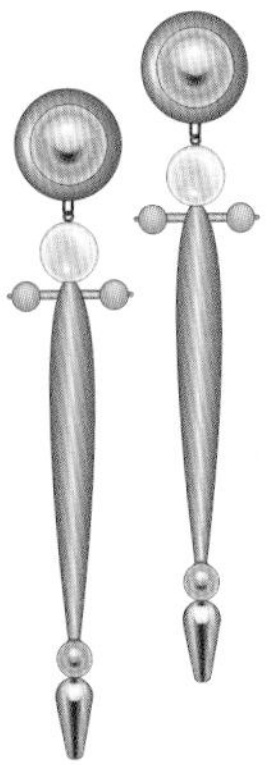

drop earrings
pendientes[M]
pendants[M] d'oreille[F]
Ohrgehänge[N]
orecchini[M] pendenti

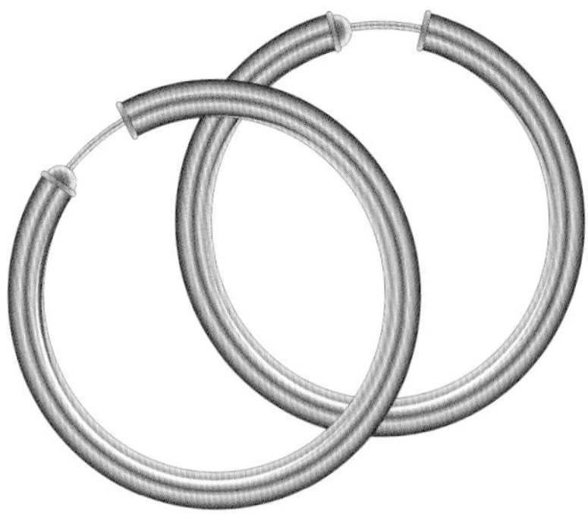

hoop earrings
pendientes[M] de aro[M]
anneaux[M]
Creolen[F]
orecchini[M] ad anello[M]

necklaces
collares [M]
colliers [M]
Halsketten [F]
collane [F]

pendant
pendiente [M]
pendentif [M]
Anhänger [M]
pendenti [M]

locket
medallón [M]
médaillon [M]
Medaillon [N]
medaglione [M]

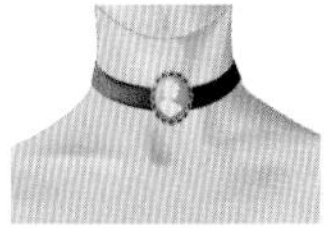

velvet-band choker
gargantilla [F] de terciopelo [M]
collier [M]-de-chien [M]
Samtkropfband [N]
collarino [M] di velluto [M]

rope
lazo [M]
sautoir [M]
Endlosperlenkette [F]
collana [F] lunga alla vita [F]

opera-length necklace
collar [M] de una vuelta [F], ópera [F]
sautoir [M], longueur [F] opéra [M]
Halskette [F] in Opernlänge [F]
collana [F] lunga

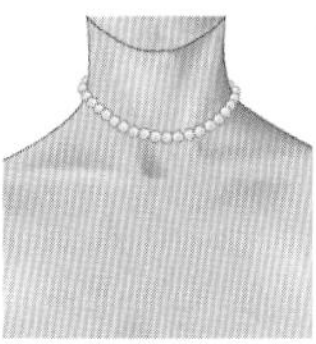

choker
gargantilla [F]
ras-de-cou [M]
Chokerkette [F]
girocollo [M]

bib necklace
collar [M] de 5 vueltas [F], peto [M]
collier [M] de soirée [F]
mehrreihige Halskette [F]
collana [F] a cinque giri [M]

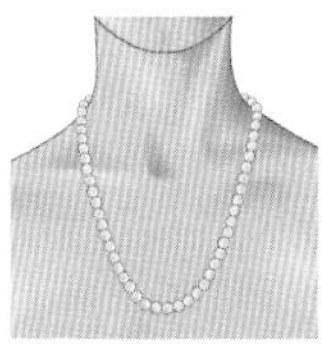

matinee-length necklace
collar [M] de una vuelta [F], matinée [F]
collier [M] de perles [F], longueur [F] matinée [F]
Halskette [F] in Matineelänge [F]
collana [F]

jewelry

semiprecious stones
piedras [F] semipreciosas
pierres [F] fines
Halbedelsteine [M]
pietre [F] semipreziose

amethyst
amatista [F]
améthyste [F]
Amethyst [M]
ametista [F]

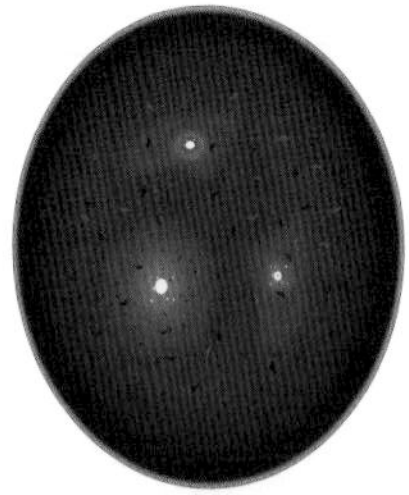

lapis lazuli
lapislázuli [M]
lapis-lazuli [M]
Lapislazuli [M]
lapislazzuli [M]

tourmaline
turmalina [F]
tourmaline [F]
Turmalin [M]
tormalina [F]

aquamarine
aguamarina [F]
aigue-marine [F]
Aquamarin [M]
acquamarina [F]

topaz
topacio [M]
topaze [F]
Topas [M]
topazio [M]

opal
ópalo [M]
opale [F]
Opal [M]
opale [M]

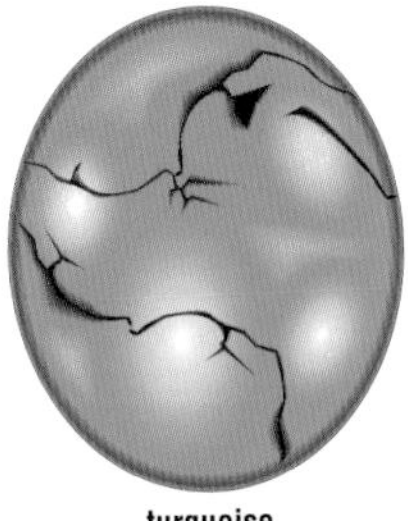

turquoise
turquesa [F]
turquoise [F]
Türkis [M]
turchese [M]

garnet
granate [M]
grenat [M]
Granat [M]
granato [M]

precious stones
piedras^F preciosas
pierres^F précieuses
Edelsteine^M
pietre^F preziose

diamond
diamante *M*
diamant *M*
Diamant *M*
diamante *M*

ruby
rubí *M*
rubis *M*
Rubin *M*
rubino *M*

sapphire
zafiro *M*
saphir *M*
Saphir *M*
zaffiro *M*

emerald
esmeralda *F*
émeraude *F*
Smaragd *M*
smeraldo *M*

rings
anillos *M*
bagues *F*
Ringe *M*
anelli *M*

parts of a ring
partes *M* **de un anillo** *M*
parties *F* **d'une bague** *F*
Teile *M/N* **eines Rings** *M*
componenti *M* **di un anello** *M*

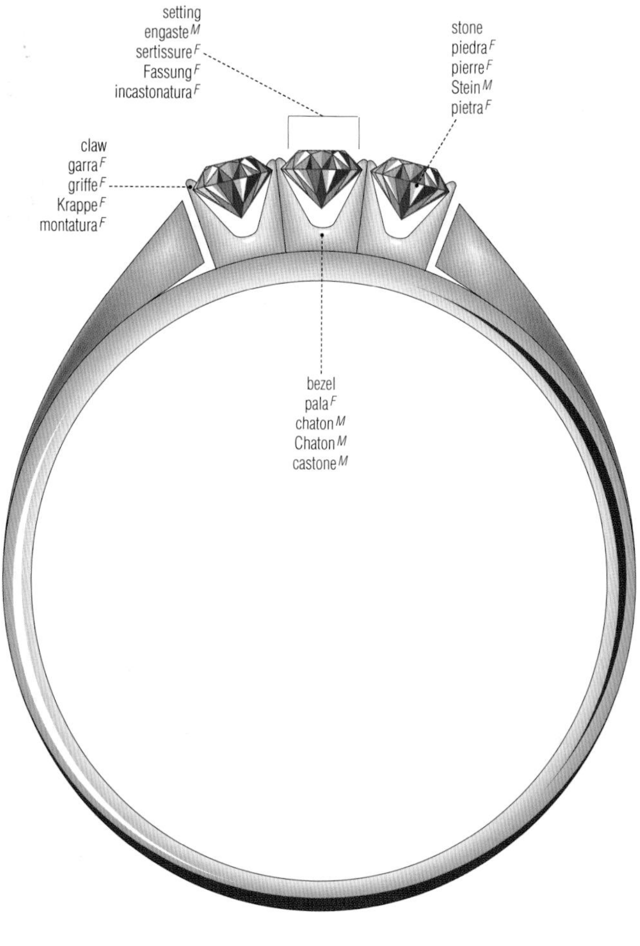
setting
engaste M
sertissure F
Fassung F
incastonatura F
stone
piedra F
pierre F
Stein M
pietra F
claw
garra F
griffe F
Krappe F
montatura F
bezel
pala F
chaton M
Chaton M
castone M

COLLÈGE
1992

class ring
anillo M de graduación F
bague F de finissant M
Collegering M
anello M studentesco

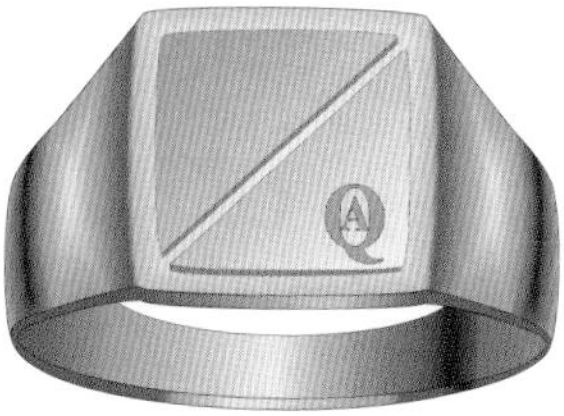
AQ

signet ring
sortija F de sello M
chevalière F
Herrenring M
anello M con sigillo M

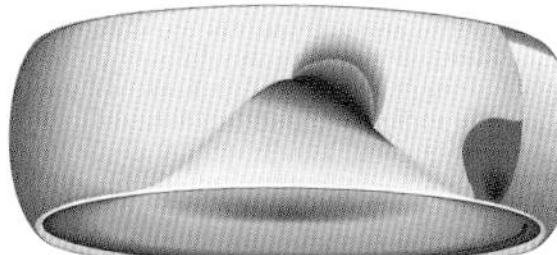

band ring
alianza F
jonc M
Bandring M
anello M a fascia F

wedding ring
alianza F
alliance F
Ehering M
fede F nuziale

engagement ring
anillo M de compromiso M
bague F de fiançailles F
Verlobungsring M
anello M di fidanzamento M

solitaire ring
solitario M
bague F solitaire M
Solitärring M
solitario M

jewelry

charms
dijes [M]
breloques [F]
Anhänger [M]
ciondoli [M]

nameplate
placa [F] de identificación [F]
plaque [F] d'identité [F]
Gravurplatte [F]
piastrina [F] d'identità [F]

horseshoe
herradura [F]
fer [M] à cheval [M]
Hufeisen [N]
ferro [M] di cavallo [M]

horn
cuerno [M]
corne [F]
Horn [N]
corno [M]

bracelets
brazaletes [M]
bracelets [M]
Armbänder [N]
bracciali [M]

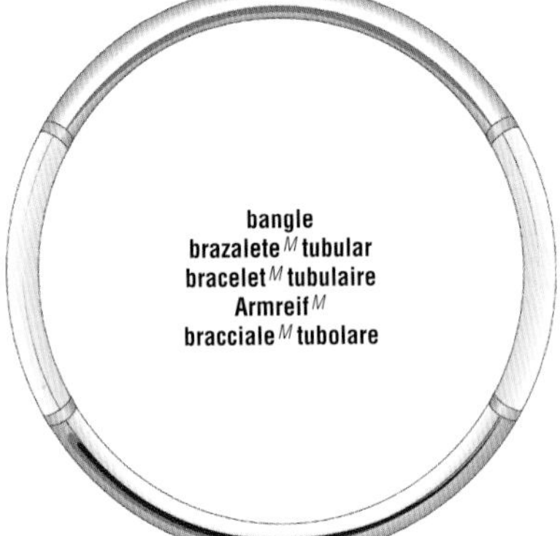

bangle
brazalete [M] tubular
bracelet [M] tubulaire
Armreif [M]
bracciale [M] tubolare

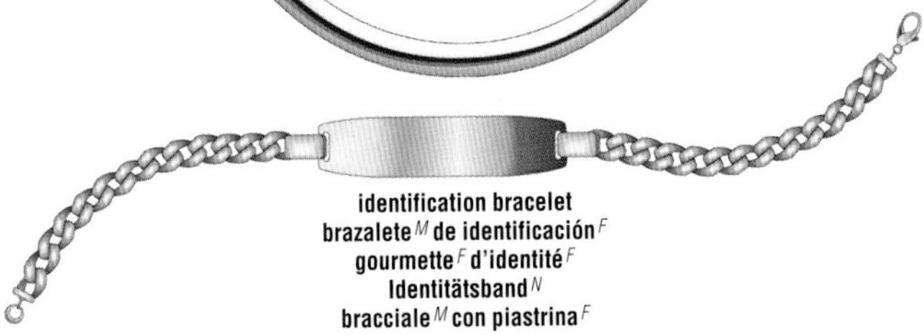

identification bracelet
brazalete [M] de identificación [F]
gourmette [F] d'identité [F]
Identitätsband [N]
bracciale [M] con piastrina [F]

charm bracelet
pulsera [F] de dijes [M]
gourmette [F]
Armband [N]
bracciale [M] con ciondoli [M]

pins
alfileres[M]
épingles[F]
Anstecknadeln[F]
spille[F]

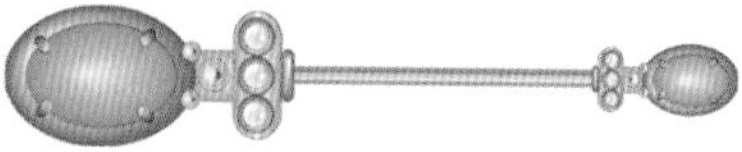

stickpin
alfiler[M] de corbata[F]
broche[F] épingle[F]
Sticker[M]
spillone[M]

brooch
broche[M]
broche[F]
Brosche[F]
spilla[F]

tie bar
pisacorbatas[M]
pince[F] à cravate[F]
Krawattenklemme[F]
fermacravatta[M]

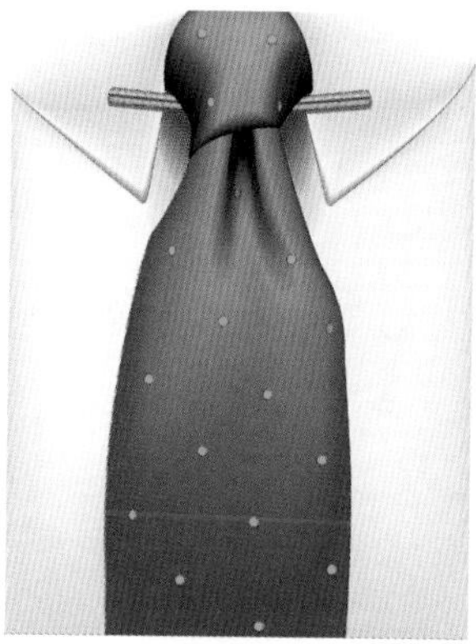

collar bar
yugo[M]
tige[F] pour col[M]
Kragenklammer[F]
fermacolletto[M]

tiepin
alfiler[M] de corbata[F]
épingle[F] à cravate[F]
Krawattennadel[F]
spillo[M] fermacravatta[M]

nail care

manicura[F] | manucure[F] | Maniküre[F] | manicure[F]

manicure set
estuche[M] de manicura[F]
trousse[F] de manucure[F]
Nagelnecessaire[N]
set[M] per manicure[F]

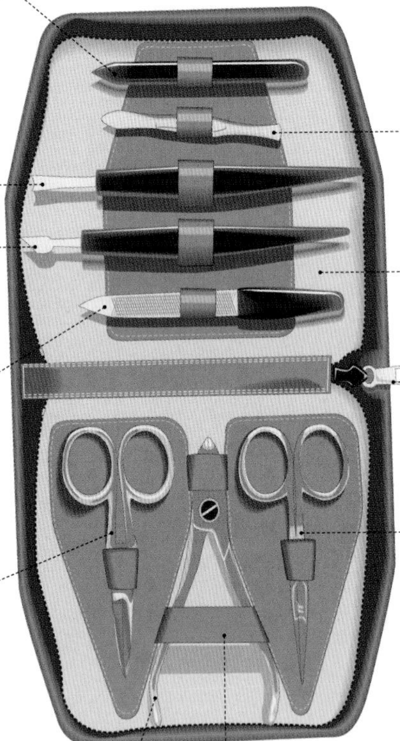
cuticle pusher
retiracutículas[M]
repousse-chair[M]
Nagelhautschieber[M]
spingicuticole[M]
cuticle trimmer
cortacutículas[M]
coupe-cuticules[M]
Nagelhautentferner[M]
tagliacuticole[M]
nail shaper
moldeador[M] de cutículas[F]
gratte-ongles[M]
Nagelhautschaber[M]
sollevacuticole[M]
nail file
lima[F] de uñas[F]
lime[F] à ongles[M]
Nagelfeile[F]
limetta[F]
nail scissors
tijeras[F] de uñas[F]
ciseaux[M] à ongles[M]
Nagelschere[F]
forbicine[F] per unghie[F]
eyebrow tweezers
pinzas[F] para depilar cejas[F]
pince[F] à épiler
Augenbrauenpinzette[F]
pinzette[F] per sopracciglia[F]
case
estuche[M]
étui[M]
Etui[N]
astuccio[M]
zipper
cremallera[F]
fermeture[F] à glissière[F]
Reißverschluss[M]
cerniera[F] lampo
cuticle scissors
tijeras[F] para cutículas[F]
ciseaux[M] à cuticules[F]
Nagelhautschere[F]
forbicine[F] per cuticole[F]
cuticle nippers
alicates[M] para cutículas[F]
pince[F] à cuticules[F]
Nagelzange[F]
tronchesina[F] per cuticole[F]
strap
correa[F]
bride[F]
Schlaufe[F]
fascetta[F]

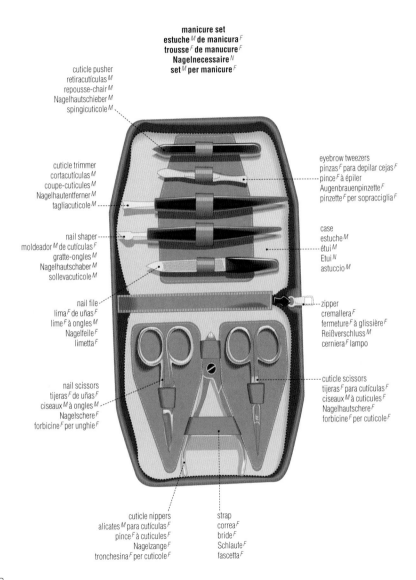

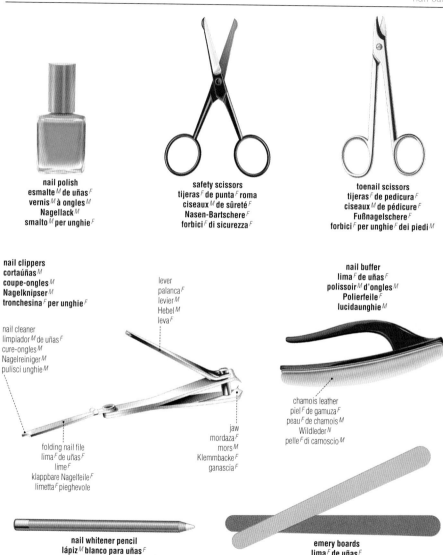

nail polish
esmalte[M] **de uñas**[F]
vernis[M] **à ongles**[M]
Nagellack[M]
smalto[M] **per unghie**[F]

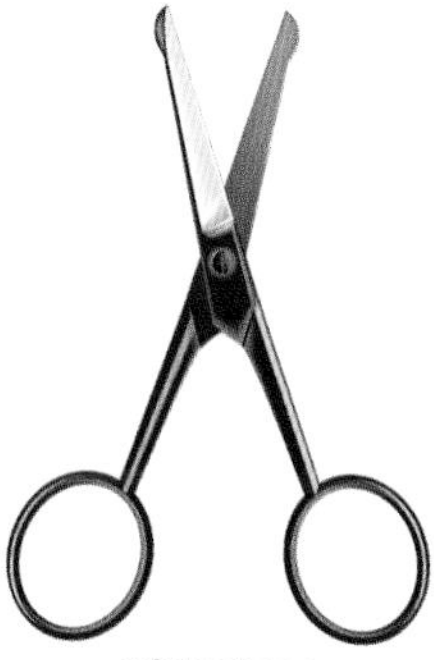

safety scissors
tijeras[F] **de punta**[F] **roma**
ciseaux[M] **de sûreté**[F]
Nasen-Bartschere[F]
forbici[F] **di sicurezza**[F]

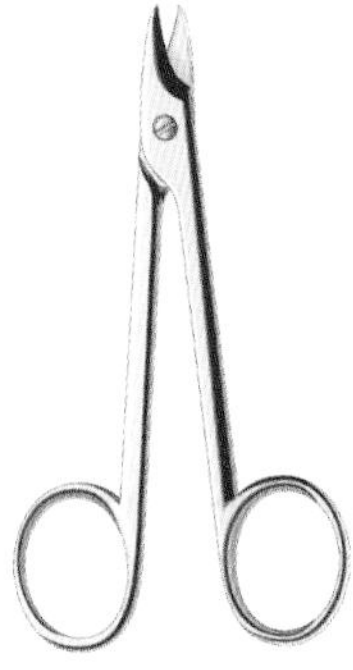

toenail scissors
tijeras[F] **de pedicura**[F]
ciseaux[M] **de pédicure**[F]
Fußnagelschere[F]
forbici[F] **per unghie**[F] **dei piedi**[M]

nail clippers
cortaúñas[M]
coupe-ongles[M]
Nagelknipser[M]
tronchesina[F] **per unghie**[F]

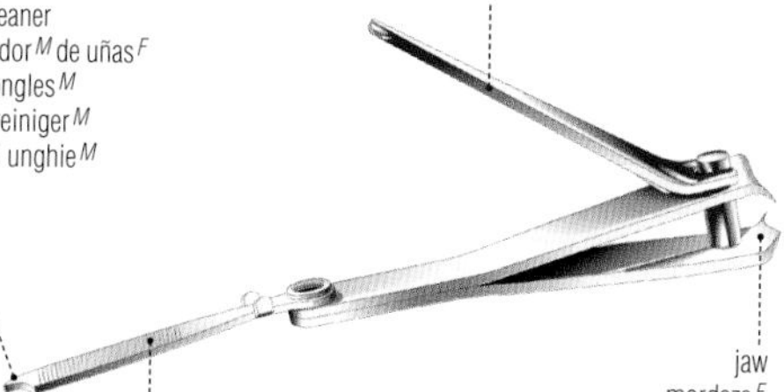
lever
palanca[F]
levier[M]
Hebel[M]
leva[F]
nail cleaner
limpiador[M] de uñas[F]
cure-ongles[M]
Nagelreiniger[M]
pulisci unghie[M]
folding nail file
lima[F] de uñas[F]
lime[F]
klappbare Nagelfeile[F]
limetta[F] pieghevole
jaw
mordaza[F]
mors[M]
Klemmbacke[F]
ganascia[F]

nail buffer
lima[F] **de uñas**[F]
polissoir[M] **d'ongles**[M]
Polierfeile[F]
lucidaunghie[M]

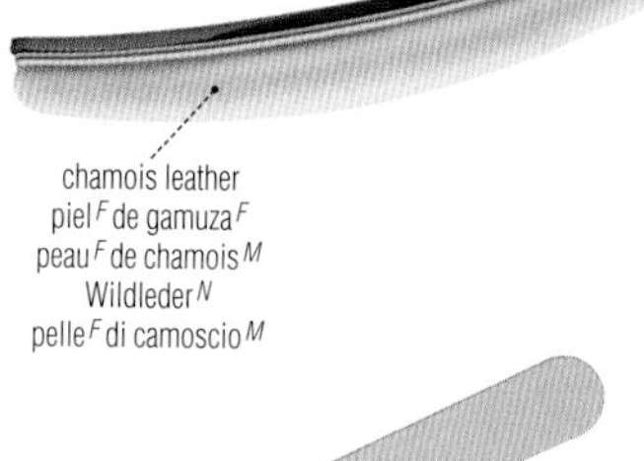
chamois leather
piel[F] de gamuza[F]
peau[F] de chamois[M]
Wildleder[N]
pelle[F] di camoscio[M]

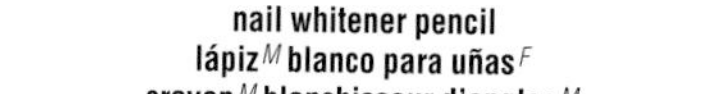

nail whitener pencil
lápiz[M] **blanco para uñas**[F]
crayon[M] **blanchisseur d'ongles**[M]
Nagelweißstift[M]
matita[F] **sbiancante per unghie**[F]

emery boards
lima[F] **de uñas**[F]
limes[F]**-émeri**[M]
Nagelfeilen[F]
limetta[F] **di cartoncino**[M] **vetrato**

makeup

maquillaje^{M} | maquillage^{M} | Make-up^{N} | trucco^{M}

facial makeup
maquillaje^{M} facial
maquillage^{M}
Make-up^{N}
trucco^{M} per il viso^{M}

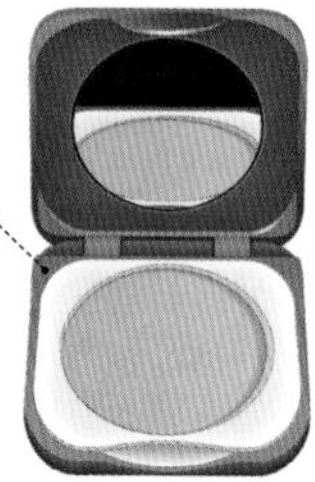
compact
polvera^{F}
poudrier^{M}
Puderdose^{F}
portacipria^{M}

pressed powder
polvo^{M} compacto
poudre^{F} pressée
Kompaktpuder^{M}
cipria^{F} compatta

fan brush
brocha^{F} en forma^{F} de abanico^{M}
pinceau^{M} éventail^{M}
Fächerpinsel^{M}
pennello^{M} a ventaglio^{M}

loose powder brush
brocha^{F}
pinceau^{M} pour poudre^{F} libre
Puderpinsel^{M}
pennello^{M} da cipria^{F} in polvere^{F}

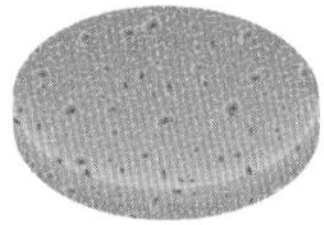

synthetic sponge
esponja^{F} sintética
éponge^{F} synthétique
Kunstschwamm^{M}
spugna^{F} sintetica

powder puff
borla^{F}
houppette^{F}
Puderkissen^{N}
piumino^{M} da cipria^{F}

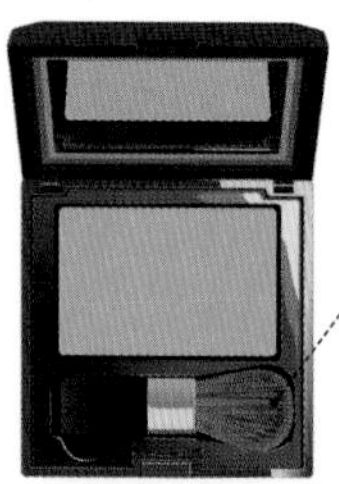
blusher brush
brocha^{F} aplicadora de colorete^{M}
pinceau^{M} pour fard^{M} à joues^{F}
Rougepinsel^{M}
pennello^{M} da fard^{M}

powder blusher
colorete^{M} en polvo^{M}
fard^{M} à joues^{F} en poudre^{F}
Puderrouge^{N}
fard^{M} in polvere^{F}

liquid foundation
base^{F} líquida
fond^{M} de teint^{M} liquide
flüssige Grundierung^{F}
fondotinta^{M} fluido

loose powder
polvos^{M} sueltos
poudre^{F} libre
loser Puder^{M}
cipria^{F} in polvere^{F}

eye makeup
maquillaje M para ojos M
maquillage M des yeux M
Augen-Make-up N
trucco M per gli occhi M

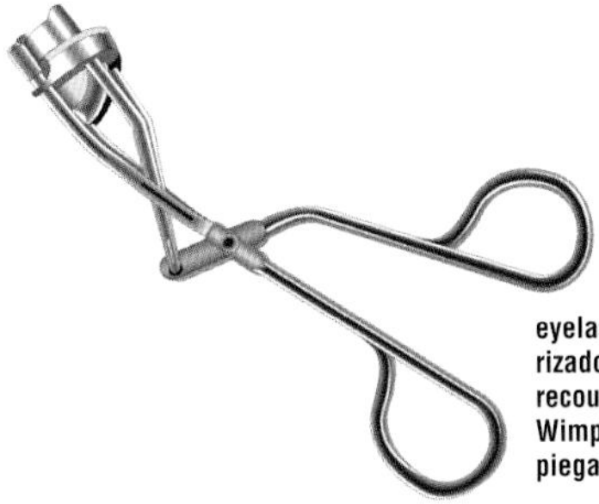

eyelash curler
rizador M de pestañas F
recourbe-cils M
Wimpernzange F
piegaciglia M

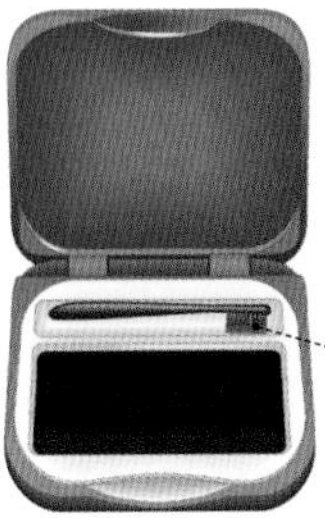
mascara brush
cepillo M aplicador de rímel M
brosse F à mascara M
Mascarabürstchen N
spazzolino M per mascara M

cake mascara
rímel M en pasta F
mascara M en pain M
Mascarastein M
mascara M compatto

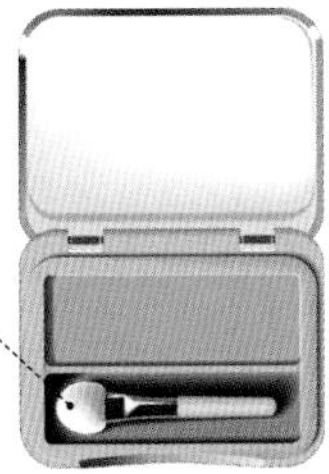
sponge-tipped applicator
aplicador M de esponja F
applicateur M-mousse F
Schwammstäbchen N
applicatore M a spugnetta F

eyeshadow
sombra F de ojos M
ombre F à paupières F
Lidschatten M
ombretto M

eyebrow pencil
lápiz M de cejas F
crayon M à sourcils M
Augenbrauenstift M
matita F per sopracciglia F

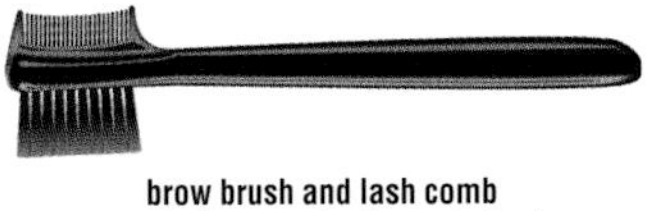

brow brush and lash comb
cepillo M para cejas F y pestañas F
brosse F-peigne M pour cils M et sourcils M
Brauenbürstchen N und Wimpernkämmchen N
pettinino M per ciglia F e spazzolino M per sopracciglia F

liquid eyeliner
delineador M
eye-liner M liquide
flüssiger Eyeliner M
eye-liner M

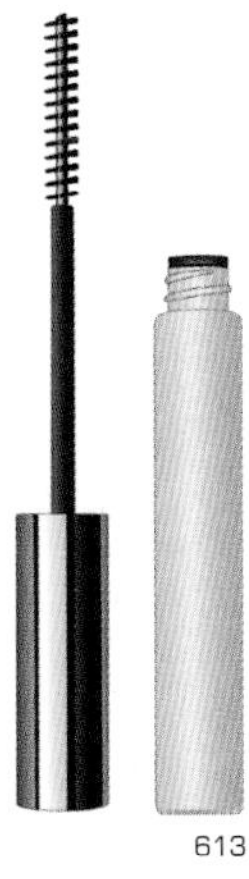

liquid mascara
rímel M líquido
mascara M liquide
flüssiges Mascara N
mascara M liquido

lip makeup
maquillaje[M] labial
maquillage[M] des lèvres[F]
Lippen-Make-up[N]
trucco[M] per le labbra[F]

lipbrush
pincel[M] para labios[M]
pinceau[M] à lèvres[F]
Lippenpinsel[M]
pennellino[M] per labbra[F]

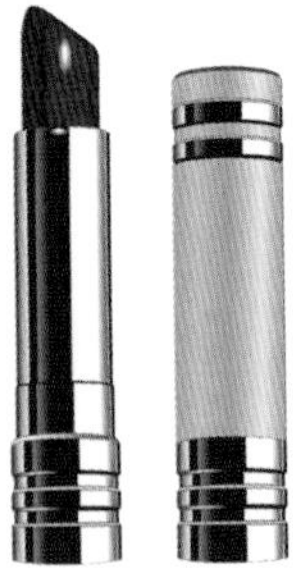

lipstick
pintalabios[M]
rouge[M] à lèvres[F]
Lippenstift[M]
rossetto[M]

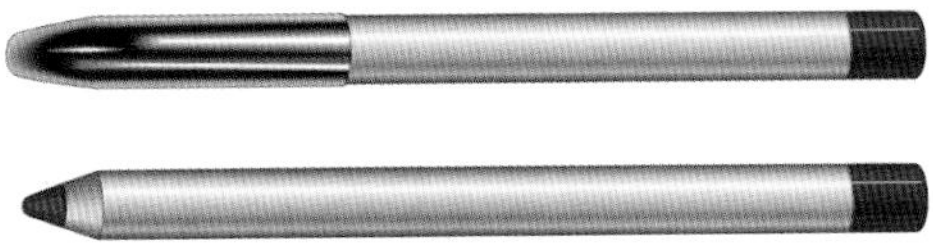

lipliner
delineador[M] de labios[M]
crayon[M] contour[M] des lèvres[F]
Lippenkonturenstift[M]
matite[F] per il contorno[M] delle labbra[F]

hygiene

higiene[F] | hygiène[F] | Hygiene[F] | igiene[F]

tissues
pañuelos[M]
papiers[M]-mouchoirs[M]
Kosmetiktücher[NPL]
fazzoletti[M] di carta[F]

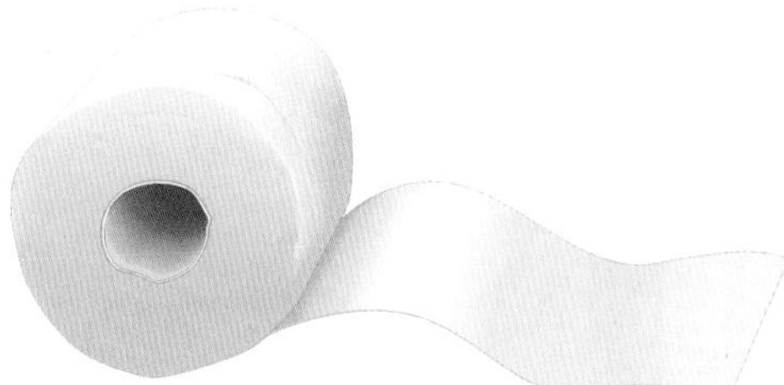

toilet paper
papel[M] higiénico
papier[M] hygiénique
Toilettenpapier[N]
carta[F] igienica

hairdressing

peinado[M] | coiffure[F] | Haarpflege[F] | articoli[M] per acconciatura[F]

hairbrushes
cepillos[M]
brosses[F] à cheveux[M]
Haarbürsten[F]
spazzole[F] per capelli[M]

flat-back brush
cepillo[M] con base[F] de goma[F]
brosse[F] pneumatique
flache Frisierbürste[F]
spazzola[F] a dorso[M] piatto

round brush
cepillo[M] redondo
brosse[F] ronde
Rundbürste[F]
spazzola[F] rotonda

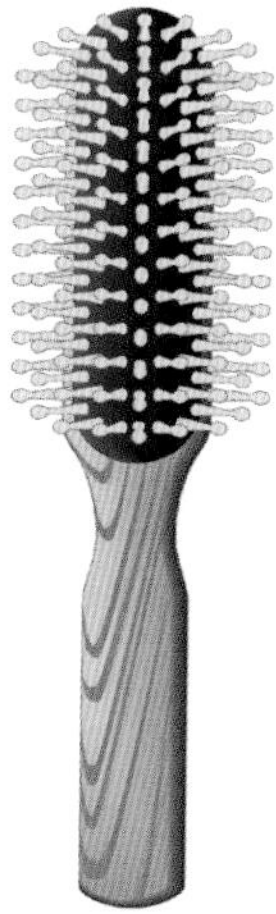

quill brush
cepillo[M] de púas[F]
brosse[F] anglaise
Drahtbürste[F]
spazzola[F] antistatica

vent brush
cepillo[M] de esqueleto[M]
brosse[F]-araignée[F]
Skelettbürste[F]
spazzola[F] ragno

hairdressing

combs
peines [M]
peignes [M]
Kämme [M]
pettini [M]

tail comb
peine [M] de mango [M]
peigne [M] à tige [F]
Stielkamm [M]
pettine [M] a coda [F]

pitchfork comb
peine [M] combinado
combiné [M] 2 dans 1
Haarliftkamm [M]
pettine [M] a forchetta [F]

barber comb
peine [M] de peluquero [M]
peigne [M] de coiffeur [M]
Haarschneidekamm [M]
pettine [M] da barbiere [M]

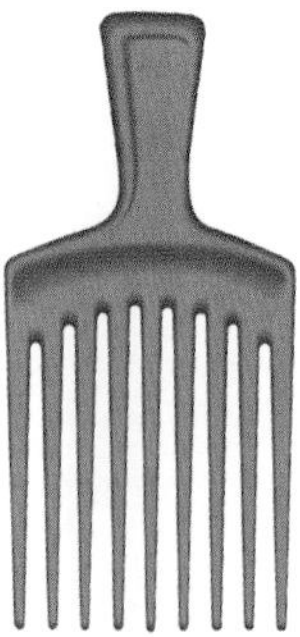

Afro pick
peine [M] afro
peigne [M] afro
Strähnenkamm [M]
pettine [M] afro

teaser comb
peine [M] de cardar
peigne [M] à crêper
Toupierkamm [M]
pettine [M] per cotonare

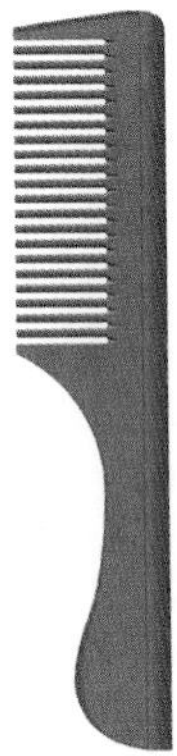

rake comb
peine [M] para desenredar
démêloir [M]
Griffkamm [M]
pettine [M] rado

hair roller
rulo[M] para el cabello[M]
bigoudi[M]
Lockenwickler[M]
bigodino[M]

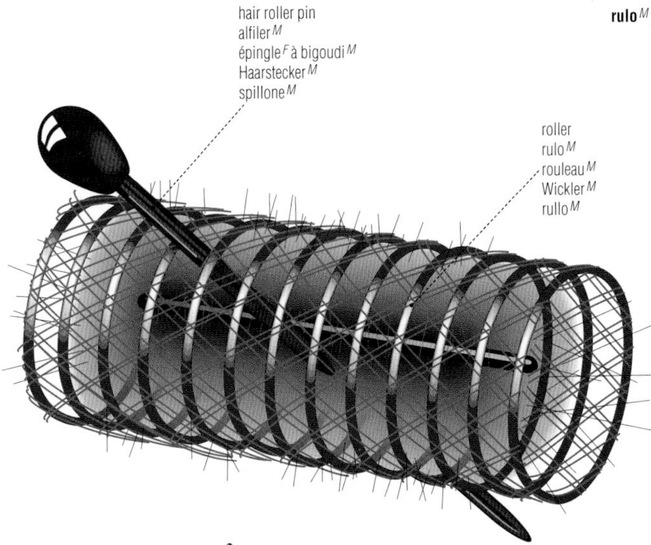
hair roller pin
alfiler[M]
épingle[F] à bigoudi[M]
Haarstecker[M]
spillone[M]
roller
rulo[M]
rouleau[M]
Wickler[M]
rullo[M]

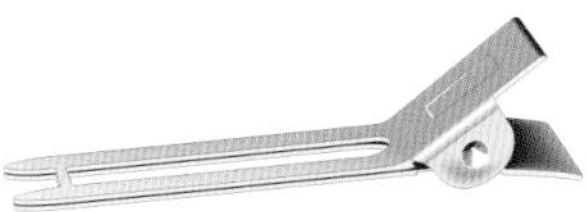

hair clip
pinza[F] para el cabello[M]
pince[F] de mise[F] en plis[M]
Haarclip[M]
beccuccio[M]

bobby pin
horquilla[F]
pince[F] à cheveux[M]
Haarklemme[F]
molletta[F]

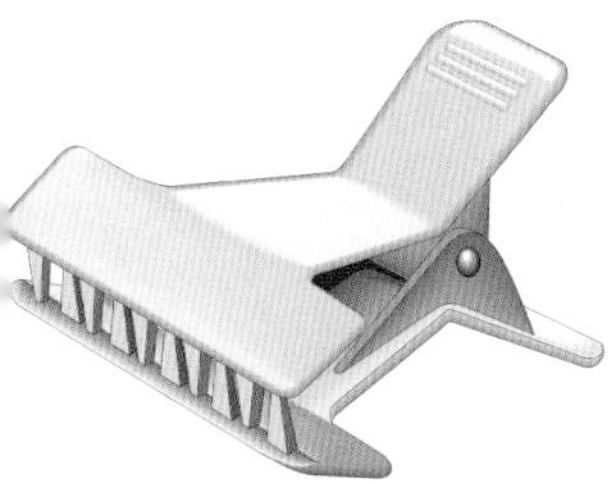

wave clip
pinza[F] para rizar
pince[F] à boucles[F] de cheveux[M]
Abteilklammer[F]
pinza[F] per capelli[M]

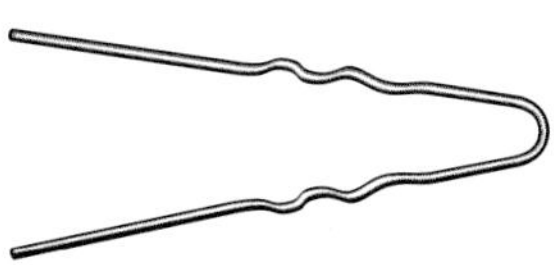

hairpin
horquilla[F] de moño[M]
épingle[F] à cheveux[M]
Lockennadel[F]
forcina[F]

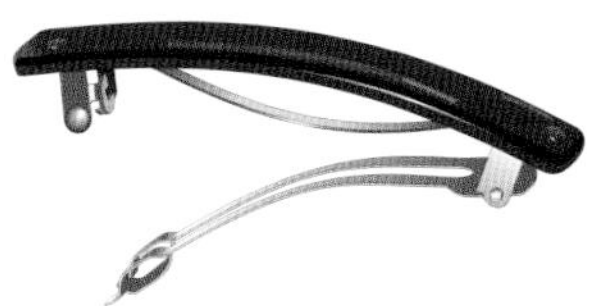

barrette
pasador[M]
barrette[F]
Haarspange[F]
fermacapelli[M]

curling iron
tenacillas[F]
fer[M] à friser
Lockenstab[M]
arricciacapelli[M]

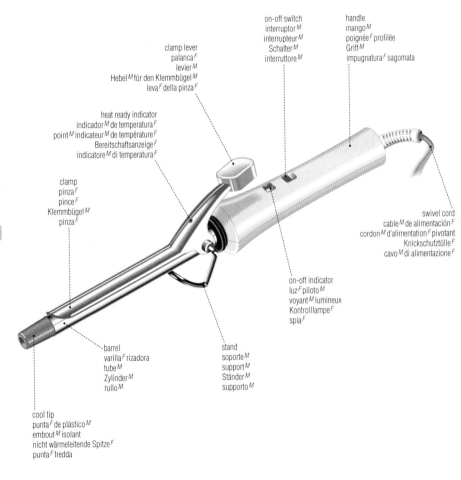

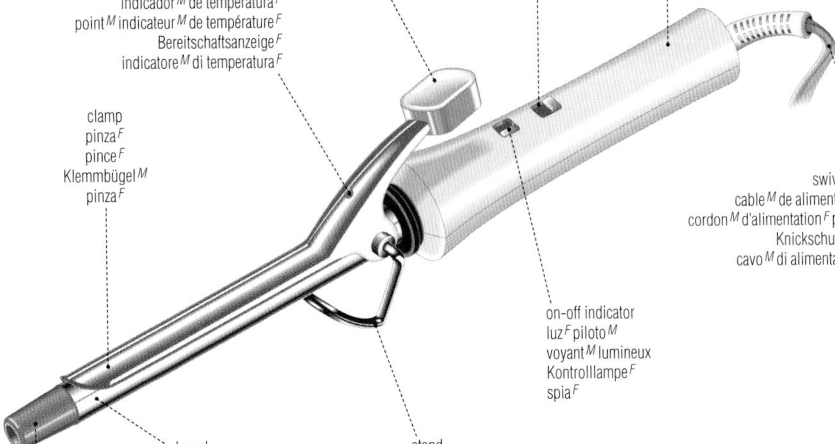

on-off switch
interruptor[M]
interrupteur[M]
Schalter[M]
interruttore[M]
handle
mango[M]
poignée[F] profilée
Griff[M]
impugnatura[F] sagomata
clamp lever
palanca[F]
levier[M]
Hebel[M] für den Klemmbügel[M]
leva[F] della pinza[F]
heat ready indicator
indicador[M] de temperatura[F]
point[M] indicateur[M] de température[F]
Bereitschaftsanzeige[F]
indicatore[M] di temperatura[F]
clamp
pinza[F]
pince[F]
Klemmbügel[M]
pinza[F]
swivel cord
cable[M] de alimentación[F]
cordon[M] d'alimentation[F] pivotant
Knickschutztülle[F]
cavo[M] di alimentazione[F]
on-off indicator
luz[F] piloto[M]
voyant[M] lumineux
Kontrolllampe[F]
spia[F]
barrel
varilla[F] rizadora
tube[M]
Zylinder[M]
rullo[M]
stand
soporte[M]
support[M]
Ständer[M]
supporto[M]
cool tip
punta[F] de plástico[M]
embout[M] isolant
nicht wärmeleitende Spitze[F]
punta[F] fredda

hair dryer
secador[M] de mano[F]
sèche-cheveux[M]
Fön[M]
asciugacapelli[M]

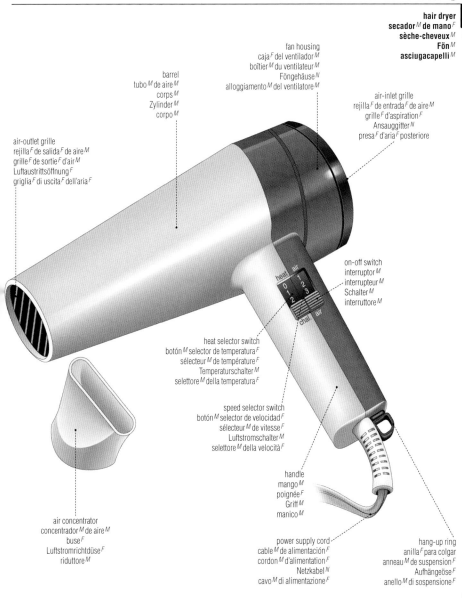

fan housing
caja[F] del ventilador[M]
boîtier[M] du ventilateur[M]
Föngehäuse[N]
alloggiamento[M] del ventilatore[M]
barrel
tubo[M] de aire[M]
corps[M]
Zylinder[M]
corpo[M]
air-inlet grille
rejilla[F] de entrada[F] de aire[M]
grille[F] d'aspiration[F]
Ansauggitter[N]
presa[F] d'aria[F] posteriore
air-outlet grille
rejilla[F] de salida[F] de aire[M]
grille[F] de sortie[F] d'air[M]
Luftaustrittsöffnung[F]
griglia[F] di uscita[F] dell'aria[F]
heat
air
0
1
2
1
2
3
chal.
air
on-off switch
interruptor[M]
interrupteur[M]
Schalter[M]
interruttore[M]
heat selector switch
botón[M] selector de temperatura[F]
sélecteur[M] de température[F]
Temperaturschalter[M]
selettore[M] della temperatura[F]
speed selector switch
botón[M] selector de velocidad[F]
sélecteur[M] de vitesse[F]
Luftstromschalter[M]
selettore[M] della velocità[F]
handle
mango[M]
poignée[F]
Griff[M]
manico[M]
air concentrator
concentrador[M] de aire[M]
buse[F]
Luftstromrichtdüse[F]
riduttore[M]
power supply cord
cable[M] de alimentación[F]
cordon[M] d'alimentation[F]
Netzkabel[N]
cavo[M] di alimentazione[F]
hang-up ring
anilla[F] para colgar
anneau[M] de suspension[F]
Aufhängeöse[F]
anello[M] di sospensione[F]

body care

cuidado[M] personal | soins[M] du corps[M] | Körperpflege[F] | cura[F] del corpo[M]

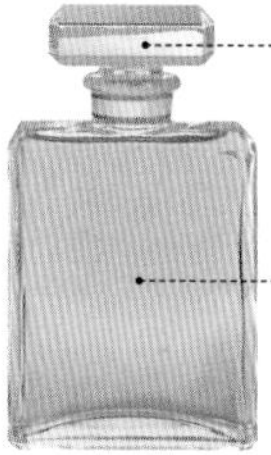
stopper
tapón[M]
bouchon[M]
Stopfen[M]
tappo[M]
bottle
botella[F]
flacon[M]
Flasche[F]
bottiglia[F]

eau de parfum
agua[F] de perfume[M]
eau[F] de parfum[M]
Eau de parfum[N]
profumo[M]

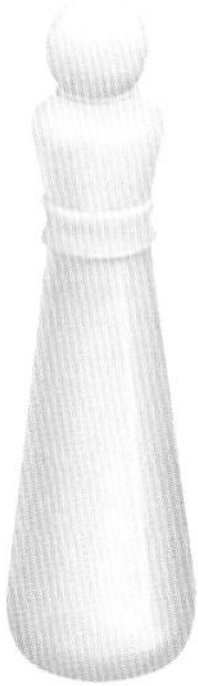

bubble bath
gel[M] de baño[M]
bain[M] moussant
Schaumbad[N]
bagnoschiuma[M]

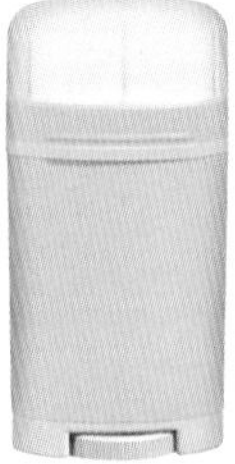

deodorant
desodorante[M]
déodorant[M]
Deodorant[N]
deodorante[M]

eau de toilette
agua[F] de colonia[F]
eau[F] de toilette[F]
Eau de toilette[N]
eau de toilette[F]

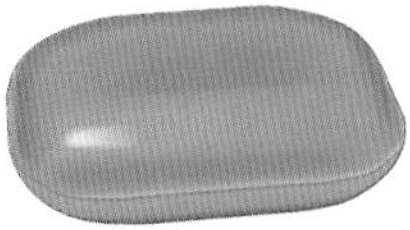

toilet soap
jabón[M] de tocador[M]
savon[M] de toilette[F]
Toilettenseife[F]
saponetta[F]

hair conditioner
acondicionador[M]
revitalisant[M] capillaire
Haarspülung[F]
balsamo[M] per capelli[M]

haircolor
tinte[M] para el cabello[M]
colorant[M] capillaire
Haarfärbemittel[N]
tintura[F] per capelli[M]

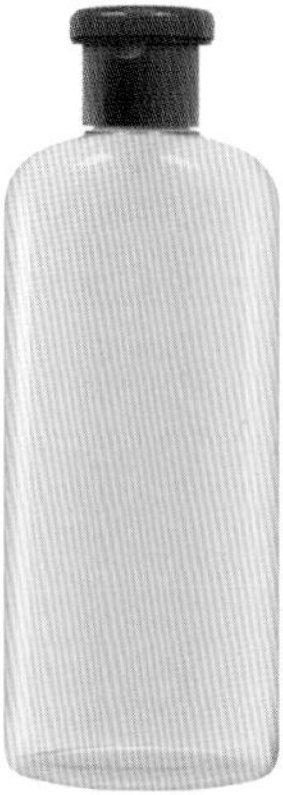

shampoo
champú[M]
shampooing[M]
Shampoo[N]
shampoo[M]

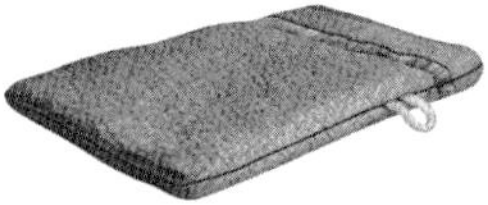

washcloth
manopla *F* de baño *M*
gant *M* de toilette *F*
Waschhandschuh *M*
manopola *F*

bath towel
toalla *F* de lavabo *M*
serviette *F* de toilette *F*
Handtuch *N*
asciugamano *M*

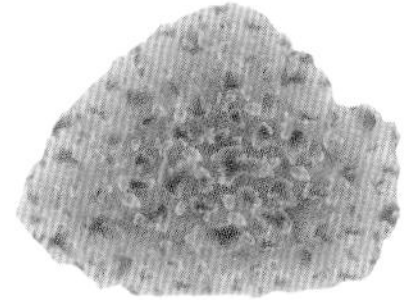

natural sponge
esponja *F* natural
éponge *F* de mer *F*
Naturschwamm *M*
spugna *F* naturale

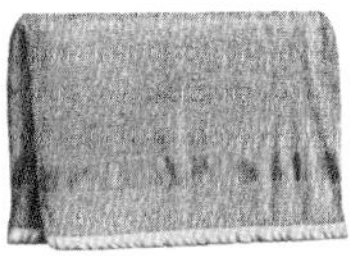

washcloth
toalla *F* para la cara *F*
débarbouillette *F*
Waschlappen *M*
ospite *M*

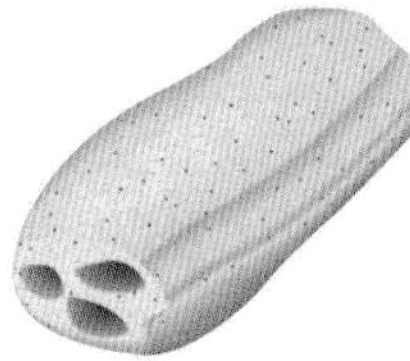

loofah
esponja *F* vegetal
éponge *F* végétale
Luffaschwamm *M*
spugna *F* vegetale

massage glove
guante *M* de crin *M*
gant *M* de crin *M*
Massagehandschuh *M*
guanto *M* di crine *M*

bath sheet
toalla *F* de baño *M*
drap *M* de bain *M*
Badetuch *N*
asciugamano *M* da bagno *M*

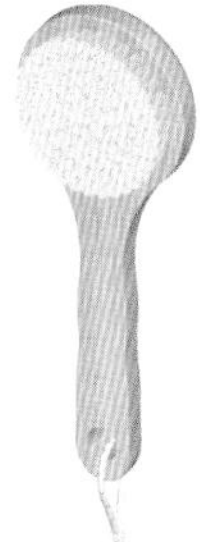

bath brush
cepillo *M* de baño *M*
brosse *F* pour le bain *M*
Badebürste *F*
spazzola *F* da bagno *M*

back brush
cepillo *M* de espalda *F*
brosse *F* pour le dos *M*
Massagebürste *F*
spazzola *F* per la schiena *F*

shaving

afeitado^{M} | rasage^{M} | Rasur^{F} | rasatura^{F}

electric razor
máquina^{F} de afeitar eléctrica
rasoir^{M} électrique
Elektrorasierer^{M}
rasoio^{M} elettrico

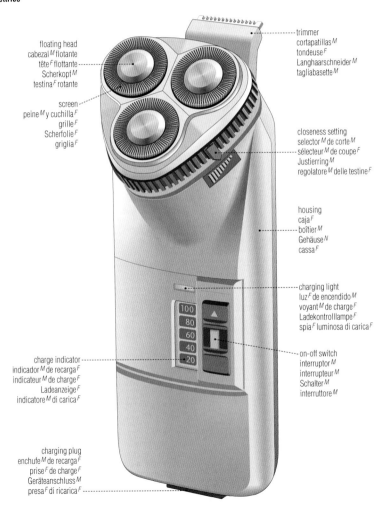

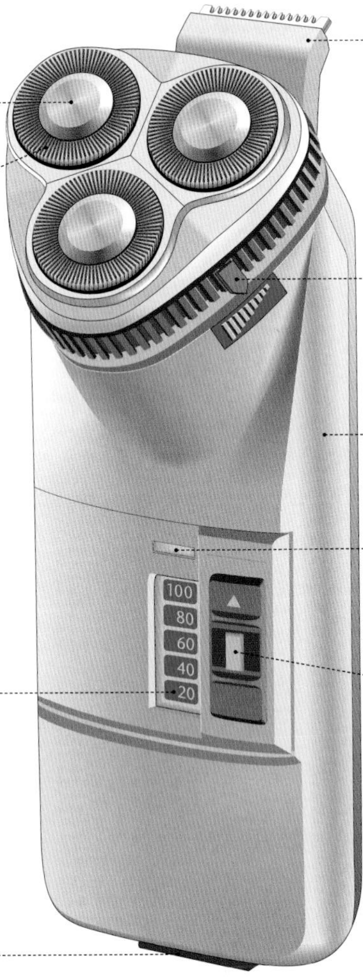
floating head
cabezal^{M} flotante
tête^{F} flottante
Scherkopf^{M}
testina^{F} rotante
screen
peine^{M} y cuchilla^{F}
grille^{F}
Scherfolie^{F}
griglia^{F}
trimmer
cortapatillas^{M}
tondeuse^{F}
Langhaarschneider^{M}
tagliabasette^{M}
closeness setting
selector^{M} de corte^{M}
sélecteur^{M} de coupe^{F}
Justierring^{M}
regolatore^{M} delle testine^{F}
housing
caja^{F}
boîtier^{M}
Gehäuse^{N}
cassa^{F}
charging light
luz^{F} de encendido^{M}
voyant^{M} de charge^{F}
Ladekontrolllampe^{F}
spia^{F} luminosa di carica^{F}
100
80
60
40
20
on-off switch
interruptor^{M}
interrupteur^{M}
Schalter^{M}
interruttore^{M}
charge indicator
indicador^{M} de recarga^{F}
indicateur^{M} de charge^{F}
Ladeanzeige^{F}
indicatore^{M} di carica^{F}
charging plug
enchufe^{M} de recarga^{F}
prise^{F} de charge^{F}
Geräteanschluss^{M}
presa^{F} di ricarica^{F}

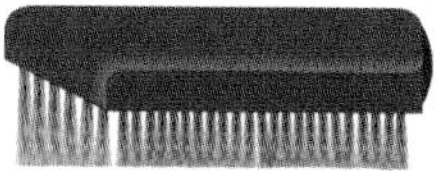

cleaning brush
escobilla *F* limpiadora
brosse *F* de nettoyage *M*
Reinigungsbürste *F*
spazzolino *M* di pulizia *F*

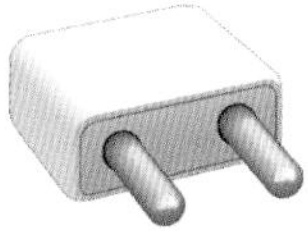

plug adapter
adaptador *M*
adaptateur *M* de fiche *F*
Adapter *M*
adattatore *M*

shaving cream
espuma *F* de afeitar
mousse *F* à raser
Rasierschaum *M*
schiuma *F* da barba *F*

shaving brush
brocha *F* de afeitar
blaireau *M*
Rasierpinsel *M*
pennello *M* da barba *F*

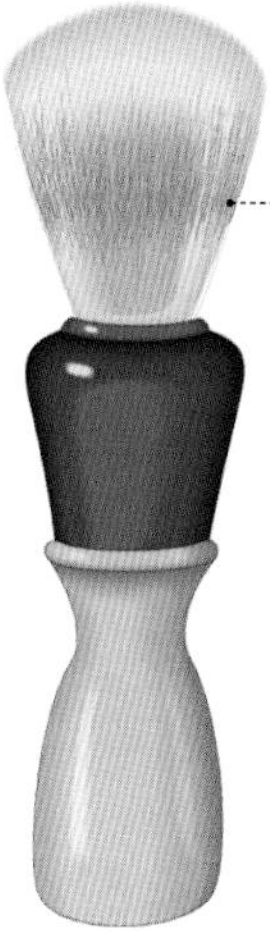
bristle
cerdas F
soie F
Borste F
setola F

power cord
cable *M* de alimentación *F*
cordon *M* d'alimentation *F*
Netzkabel *N*
cordone *M* dell'alimentazione *F*

after shave
loción *F* para después del afeitado *M*
après-rasage *M*
Rasierwasser *N*
dopobarba *M*

shaving mug
jabonera *F*
bol *M* à raser
Seifenbecher *M*
tazza *F* per sapone *M* da barba *F*

shaving

disposable razor
maquinilla[F] desechable
rasoir[M] jetable
Einwegrasierer[M]
rasoio[M] usa e getta

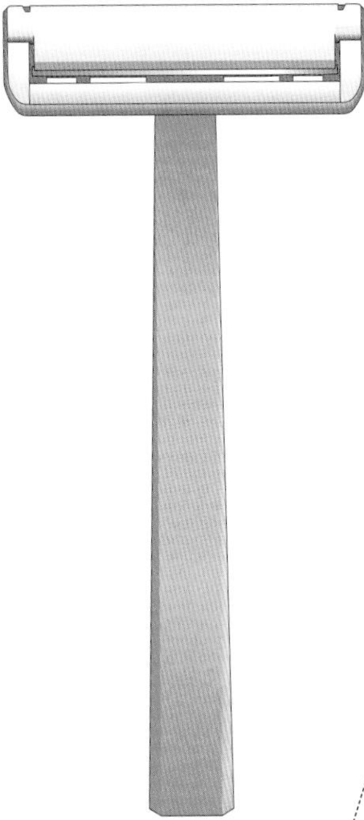

straight razor
navaja[F] de barbero[M]
rasoir[M] à manche[M]
Rasiermesser[N]
rasoio[M] a mano[F] libera

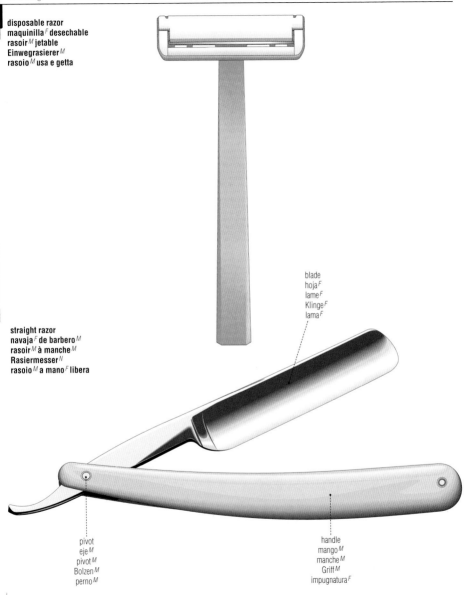

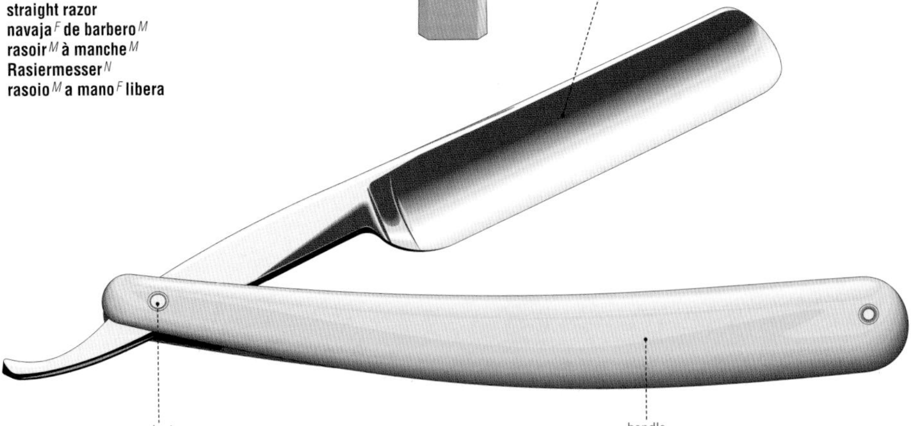
blade
hoja[F]
lame[F]
Klinge[F]
lama[F]
pivot
eje[M]
pivot[M]
Bolzen[M]
perno[M]
handle
mango[M]
manche[M]
Griff[M]
impugnatura[F]

safety razor
maquinilla[F] de afeitar
rasoir[M] à double tranchant[M]
Nassrasierer[M]
rasoio[M] di sicurezza[F]

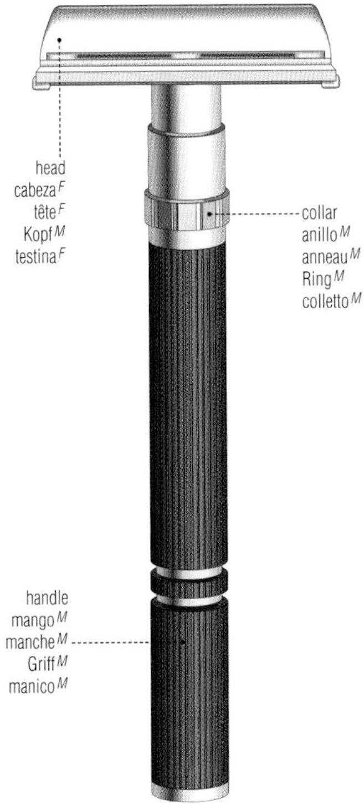
head
cabeza[F]
tête[F]
Kopf[M]
testina[F]
collar
anillo[M]
anneau[M]
Ring[M]
colletto[M]
handle
mango[M]
manche[M]
Griff[M]
manico[M]

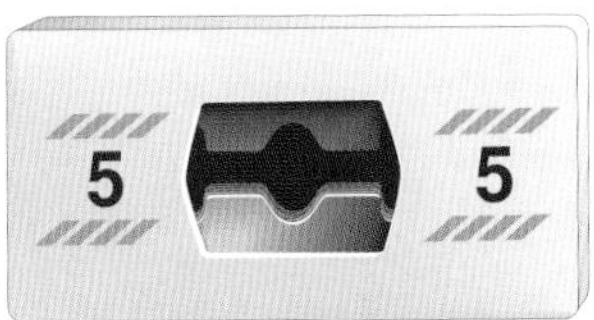
5
5

razor blade dispenser
distribuidor[M] de hojas[F] de afeitar
distributeur[M] de lames[F]
Klingendose[F]
caricatore[M] di lamette[F]

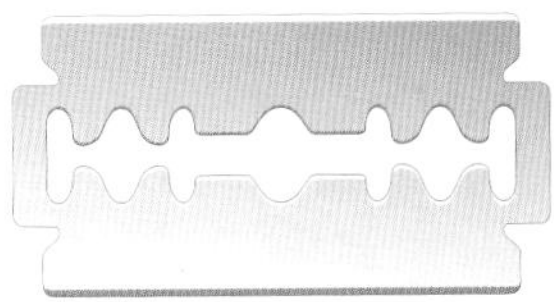

double-edged blade
hoja[F] de afeitar
lame[F] à double tranchant[M]
zweischneidige Klinge[F]
lametta[F] a due tagli[M]

dental care

higiene^F dental | hygiène^F dentaire | Zahnpflege^F | igiene^F orale

toothbrush
cepillo^M de dientes^M
brosse^F à dents^F
Zahnbürste^F
spazzolino^M da denti^M

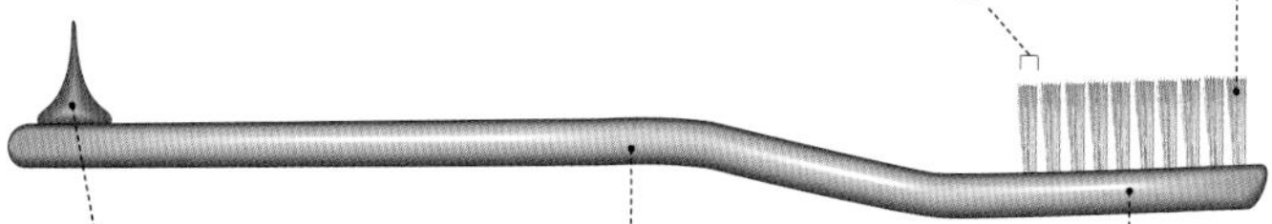
row
hilera^F
rang^M
Reihe^F
fila^F
bristle
cerda^F
poil^M
Borste^F
setola^F
stimulator tip
estimulador^M de encías^F
stimulateur^M de gencives^F
Massagespitze^F
stimolatore^M gengivale
handle
mango^M
manche^M
Griff^M
manico^M
head
cabeza^F hexagonal
tête^F
Kopf^M
testa^F

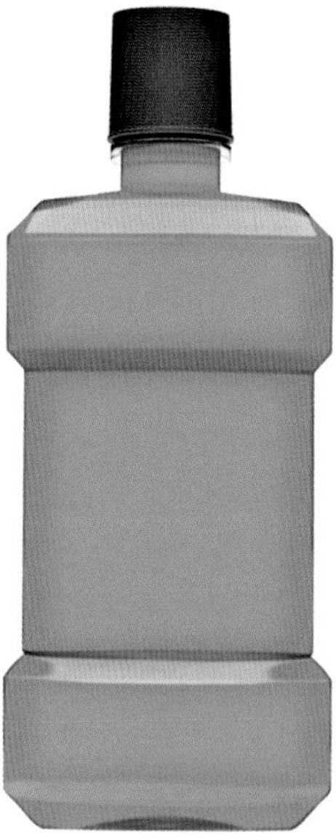

mouthwash
colutorio^M
eau^F dentifrice^M
Mundwasser^N
collutorio^M

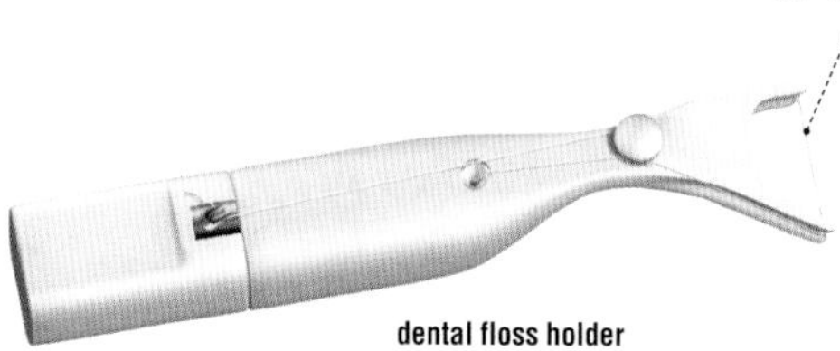
dental floss
hilo^M dental
fil^M dentaire
Zahnseide^F
filo^M interdentale

dental floss holder
estuche^M de hilo^M dental
porte-fil^M dentaire
Zahnseidenhalter^M
contenitore^M per filo^M interdentale

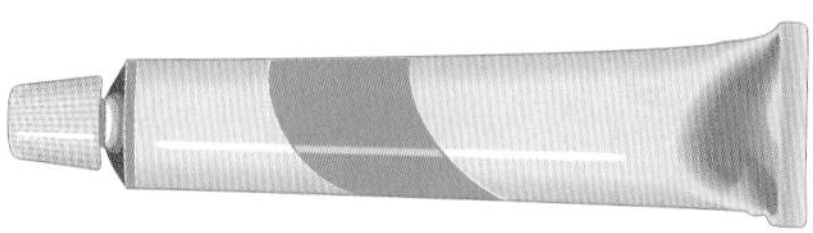

toothpaste
dentífrico^M
dentifrice^M
Zahnpasta^F
dentifricio^M

dental floss
hilo^M dental
fil^M dentaire
Zahnseide^F
filo^M interdentale

oral hygiene center
cepillo[M] de dientes[M] eléctrico
combiné[M] bucco-dentaire
elektrische Zahnbürste[F]
spazzolino[M] da denti[M] elettrico

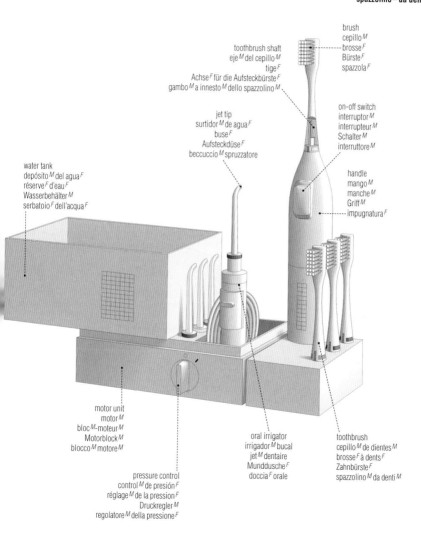

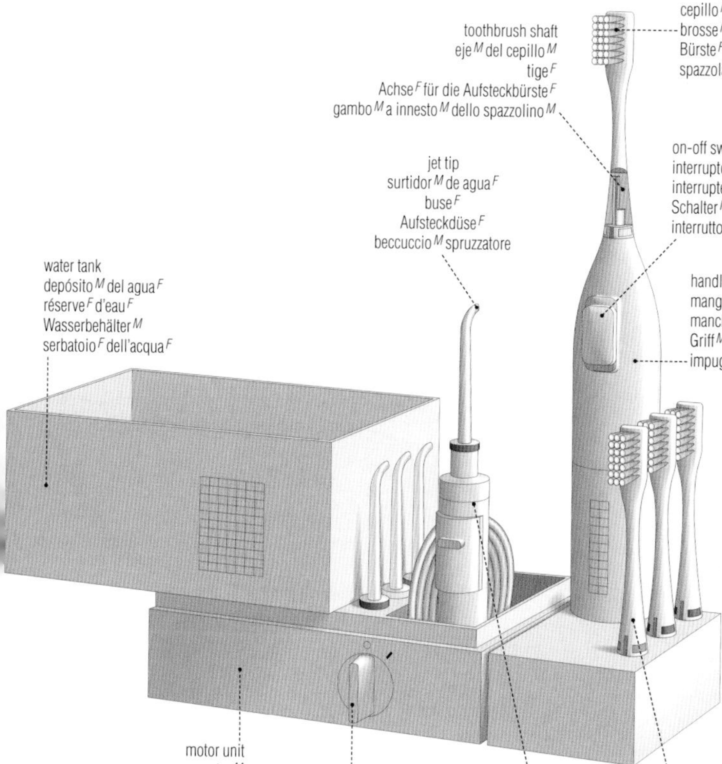
brush
cepillo[M]
brosse[F]
Bürste[F]
spazzola[F]
toothbrush shaft
eje[M] del cepillo[M]
tige[F]
Achse[F] für die Aufsteckbürste[F]
gambo[M] a innesto[M] dello spazzolino[M]
on-off switch
interruptor[M]
interrupteur[M]
Schalter[M]
interruttore[M]
jet tip
surtidor[M] de agua[F]
buse[F]
Aufsteckdüse[F]
beccuccio[M] spruzzatore
water tank
depósito[M] del agua[F]
réserve[F] d'eau[F]
Wasserbehälter[M]
serbatoio[F] dell'acqua[F]
handle
mango[M]
manche[M]
Griff[M]
impugnatura[F]
motor unit
motor[M]
bloc[M]-moteur[M]
Motorblock[M]
blocco[M] motore[M]
oral irrigator
irrigador[M] bucal
jet[M] dentaire
Mundddusche[F]
doccia[F] orale
toothbrush
cepillo[M] de dientes[M]
brosse[F] à dents[F]
Zahnbürste[F]
spazzolino[M] da denti[M]
pressure control
control[M] de presión[F]
réglage[M] de la pression[F]
Druckregler[M]
regolatore[M] della pressione[F]

eyeglasses

gafas^{F} | lunettes^{F} | Brille^{F} | occhiali^{M}

eyeglasses parts
gafas^{F}: partes^{F}
parties^{F} des lunettes^{F}
Teile$^{M/N}$ der Brille^{F}
parti^{F} degli occhiali^{M}

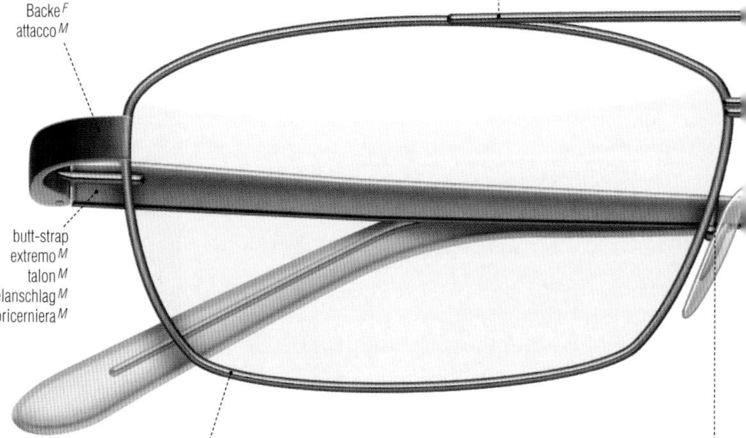
bar
barra F
barre F
Steg M
barretta F
endpiece
espiga F
tenon M
Backe F
attacco M
butt-strap
extremo M
talon M
Bügelanschlag M
copricerniera M
rim
aro M
cercle M
Rand M
montatura F
pad plate
soporte M de la plaqueta F
support M de plaquette F
Stegplättchen N
placchetta F del portanasello M

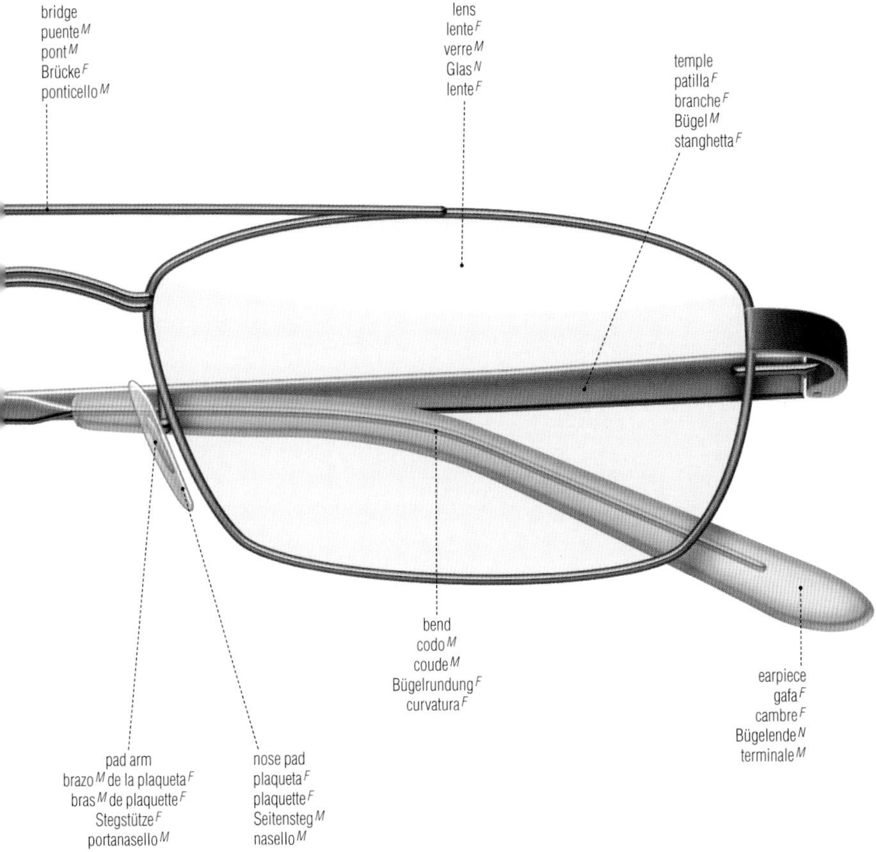
bridge
puente M
pont M
Brücke F
ponticello M
lens
lente F
verre M
Glas N
lente F
temple
patilla F
branche F
Bügel M
stanghetta F
bend
codo M
coude M
Bügelrundung F
curvatura F
earpiece
gafa F
cambre F
Bügelende N
terminale M
pad arm
brazo M de la plaqueta F
bras M de plaquette F
Stegstütze F
portanasello M
nose pad
plaqueta F
plaquette F
Seitensteg M
nasello M

eyeglasses

frames
montura F
monture F
Fassungen F
montatura F

rim
aro M
cercle M
Rand M
montatura F

examples of eyeglasses
ejemplos M de gafas F
exemples M de lunettes F
Beispiele N für Sehhilfen F
esempi M di occhiali M

pince-nez
quevedos M
bésicles F à pont M élastique
Kneifer M
pince-nez M

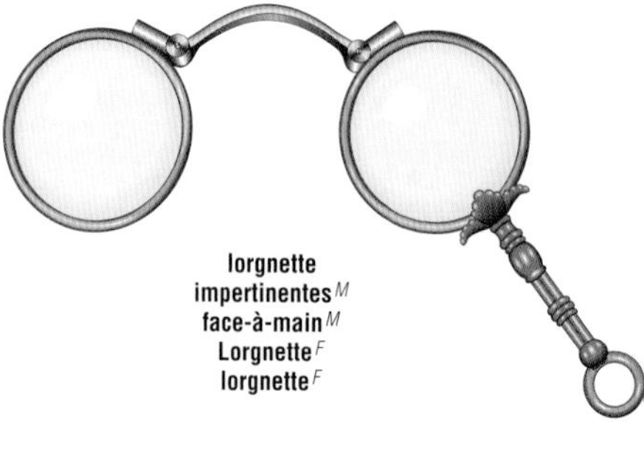
lorgnette
impertinentes M
face-à-main M
Lorgnette F
lorgnette F

monocle
monóculo M
monocle M
Monokel N
monocolo M

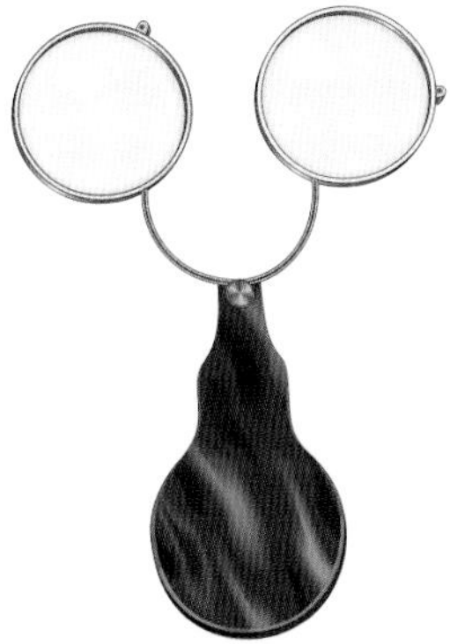

scissors-glasses
binóculos M de tijera F
binocle M
Scherenbrille F
occhiali M a forbice F

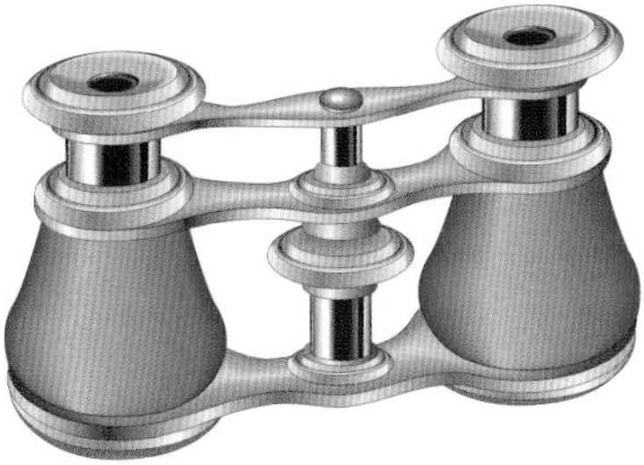

opera glasses
gemelos M de teatro M
lorgnette F
Opernglas N
binocolo M da teatro M

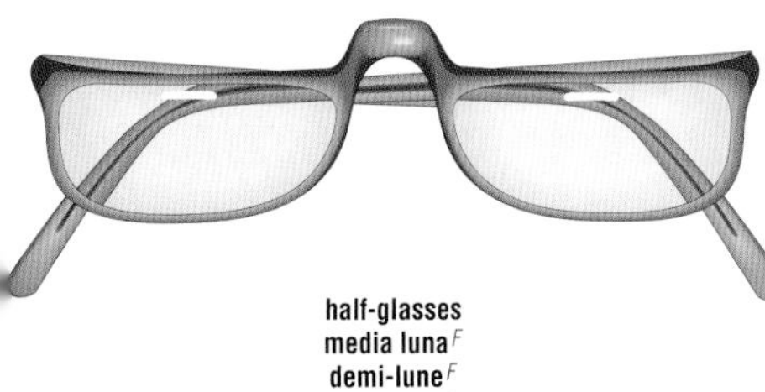

half-glasses
media luna F
demi-lune F
Halbbrille F
mezzi occhiali M

sunglasses
gafas F de sol M
lunettes F de soleil M
Sonnenbrille F
occhiali M da sole M

contact lenses

lentes^{F} de contacto^{M} | lentilles^{F} de contact^{M} | Kontaktlinsen^{F} | lenti^{F} a contatto^{M}

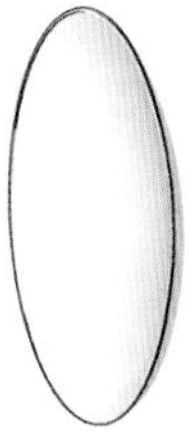

disposable contact lens
lentes^{F} de contacto^{M} desechables
lentille^{F} jetable
Einwegkontaktlinse^{F}
lente^{F} a contatto^{M} monouso

soft contact lens
lentes^{F} de contacto^{M} blandas
lentille^{F} souple
weiche Kontaktlinse^{F}
lente^{F} a contatto^{M} morbida

hard contact lens
lentes^{F} de contacto^{M} duras
lentille^{F} rigide
harte Kontaktlinse^{F}
lente^{F} a contatto^{M} rigida

multipurpose solution
solución^{F} multipropósito
solution^{F} multifonctions
Kombi-Pflegelösung^{F}
soluzione^{F} multiuso

left side
lado^{M} izquierdo
logement^{M} gauche
linke Seite^{F}
lato^{M} sinistro

right side
lado^{M} derecho
logement^{M} droit
rechte Seite^{F}
lato^{M} destro

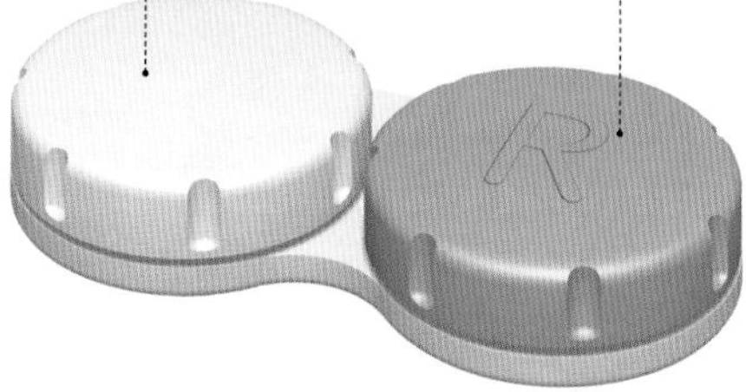
R

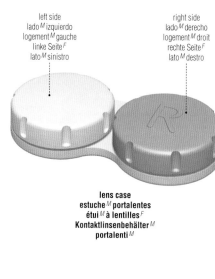

lens case
estuche^{M} portalentes
étui^{M} à lentilles^{F}
Kontaktlinsenbehälter^{M}
portalenti^{M}

lubricant eye drops
gotas^{F} oftalmológicas lubricantes
gouttes^{F} ophtalmiques lubrifiantes
Tropfen^{M} für trockene Augen^{N}
gocce^{F} oftalmiche lubrificanti

leather goods

artículos^M de marroquinería^F | articles^M de maroquinerie^F | Lederwaren^F | articoli^M di pelletteria^F

attaché case
maletín M
mallette F **porte-documents** M
Aktenkoffer M
ventiquattrore F

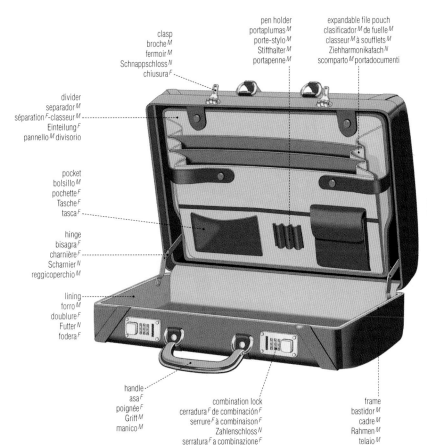

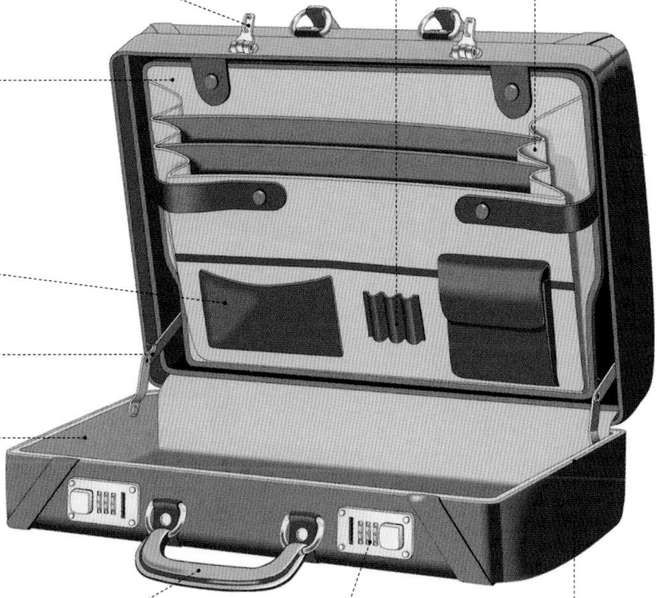

clasp
broche M
fermoir M
Schnappschloss N
chiusura F
pen holder
portaplumas M
porte-stylo M
Stifthalter M
portapenne M
expandable file pouch
clasificador M de fuelle M
classeur M à soufflets M
Ziehharmonikafach N
scomparto M portadocumenti
divider
separador M
séparation F-classeur M
Einteilung F
pannello M divisorio
pocket
bolsillo M
pochette F
Tasche F
tasca F
hinge
bisagra F
charnière F
Scharnier N
reggicoperchio M
lining
forro M
doublure F
Futter N
fodera F
handle
asa F
poignée F
Griff M
manico M
combination lock
cerradura F de combinación F
serrure F à combinaison F
Zahlenschloss N
serratura F a combinazione F
frame
bastidor M
cadre M
Rahmen M
telaio M

leather goods

bottom-fold portfolio
cartera F de fondo M plegable
porte-documents M à soufflet M
Kollegmappe F mit Griff M
portacarte M a soffietto M

retractable handle
asa F extensible
poignée F rentrante
ausziehbarer Griff M
manico M a scomparsa F
exterior pocket
bolsillo M delantero
poche F extérieure
Außentasche F
tasca F esterna

briefcase
cartera F
serviette F
Aktentasche F
borsa F a soffietto M

tab
lengüeta F
patte F
Lasche F
linguetta F
key lock
cerradura F
serrure F à clé F
Schlüsselschloss N
serratura F a chiave F
gusset
fuelle M
soufflet M
Keil M
soffietto M

checkbook/secretary clutch
chequera[F] con calculadora[F]
portefeuille[M] chéquier[M]
Etui[N] für Taschenrechner[M] und Scheckheft[N]
portassegni[M]/portacalcolatrice[M]

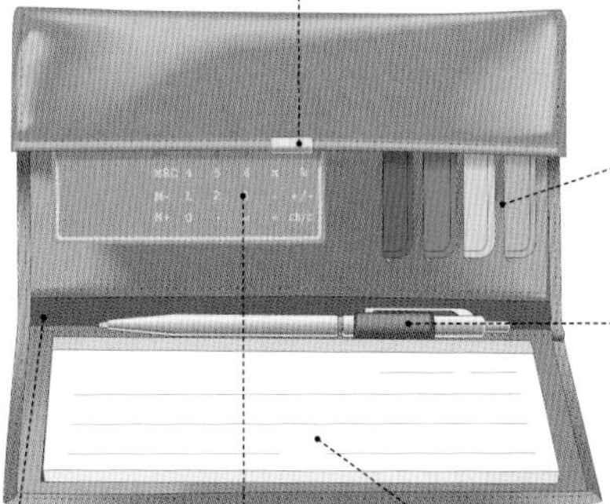
trimming
broche[M] automático
grébiche[F]
Druckverschluss[M]
chiusura[F] metallica a pressione[F]
card case
tarjetero[M]
porte-cartes[M]
Kreditkartenfach[N]
scomparto[M] per carte[F] di credito[M]
pen holder
portaplumas[M]
porte-stylo[M]
Stifthalter[M]
portapenne[M]
hidden pocket
bolsillo[M] secreto
poche[F] secrète
Unterfach[N]
tasca[F] nascosta
calculator
calculadora[F]
calculette[F]
Taschenrechner[M]
calcolatrice[F]
checkbook
talonario[M] de cheques[M]
chéquier[M]
Scheckheft[N]
libretto[M] degli assegni[M]

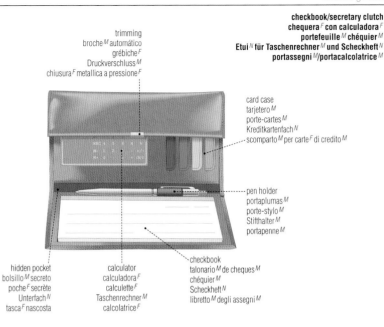

card case
tarjetero[M]
porte-cartes[M]
Kreditkartenetui[N]
portafoglio[M] per carte[F] di credito[M]

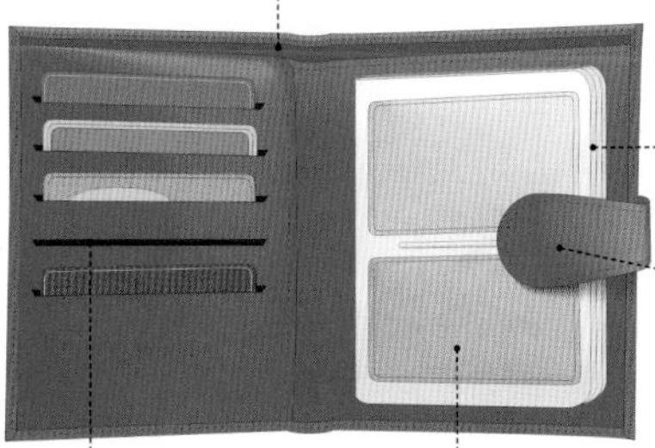
bill compartment
billetera[F]
poche[F] américaine
Geldscheinfach[N]
scomparto[M] per banconote[F]
windows
plásticos[M] transparentes
feuillets[M]
Klarsichthüllen[F]
bustine[F] trasparenti
tab
lengüeta[F]
patte[F]
Lasche[F]
linguetta[F]
slot
ranura[F]
fente[F]
Fach[N]
fessura[F]
ID window
plástico[M] transparente
volet[M] transparent
Klarsichtfenster[N]
riquadro[M]

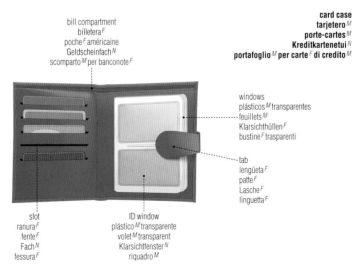

leather goods

purse
monedero *M*
bourse *F* à monnaie *F*
Geldbeutel *M*
borsellino *M*

billfold
billetera *F*
porte-coupures *M*
Brieftasche *F*
portafoglio *M*

coin purse
portamonedas *M*
porte-monnaie *M*
Geldbeutel *M* für Münzen *F*
portamonete *M*

Notes

checkbook case
talonario *M* de cheques *M*
porte-chéquier *M*
Scheckhülle *F*
portassegni *M*

underarm portfolio
cartera *F* portadocumentos *M*
porte-documents *M* plat
Unterarmmappe *F*
busta *F* portadocumenti

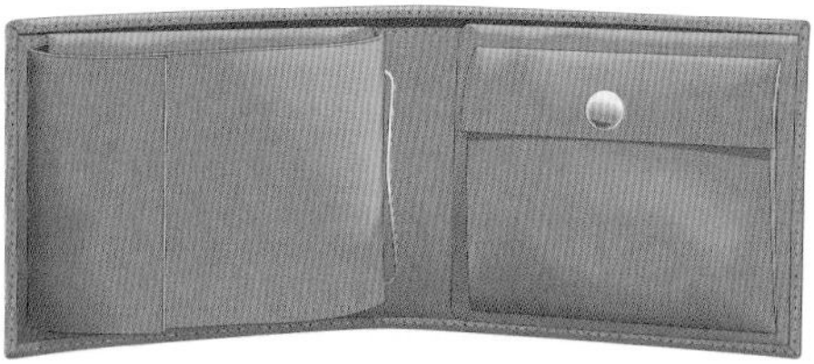

wallet
billetero *M*
portefeuille *M*
Brieftasche *F*
portafoglio *M*

passport case
porta pasaportes *M*
porte-passeport *M*
Brieftasche *F*
portapassaporto *M*

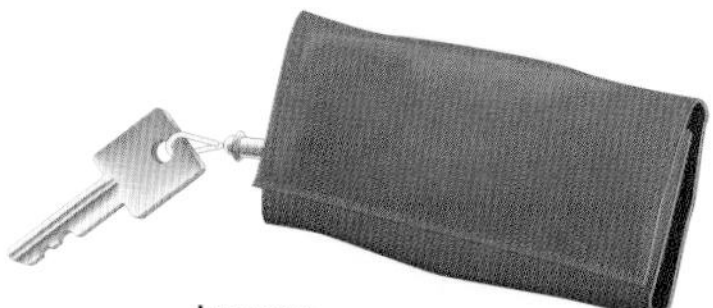

key case
llavero *M*
porte-clés *M*
Schlüsseletui *N*
portachiavi *M*

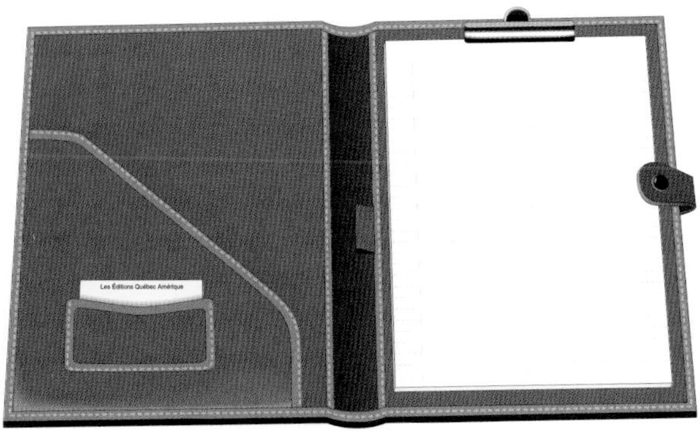
Les Éditions Québec Amérique

writing case
agenda *F*
écritoire *F*
Schreibmappe *F*
portablocco *M*

eyeglasses case
funda *F* de gafas *F*
étui *M* à lunettes *F*
Brillenetui *N*
astuccio *M* per occhiali *M*

handbags

bolsos M | sacs M à main F | Handtaschen F | borse F

satchel bag
bolso M clásico
sac M cartable M
Aktentasche F
cartella F

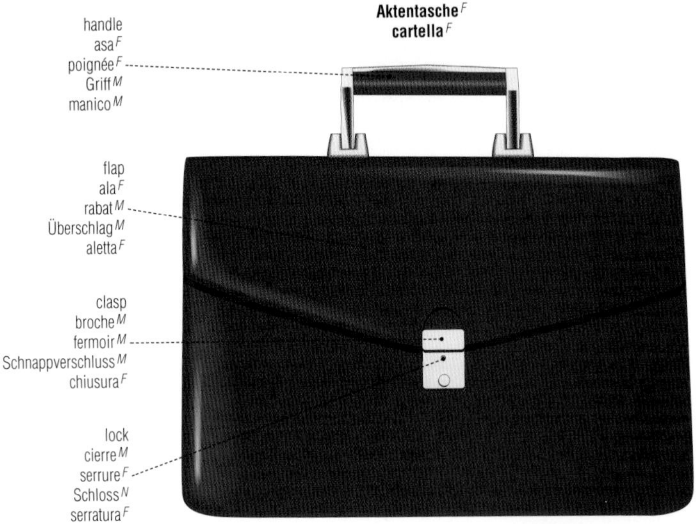
handle
asa F
poignée F
Griff M
manico M
flap
ala F
rabat M
Überschlag M
aletta F
clasp
broche M
fermoir M
Schnappverschluss M
chiusura F
lock
cierre M
serrure F
Schloss N
serratura F

carrier bag
bolso M de la compra F
sac M à provisions F
Einkaufstasche F
borsa F della spesa F

shopping bag
capazo M
cabas M
große Einkaufstasche F
borsa F della spesa F

box bag
bolso [M] de vestir
sac [M] boîte [F]
Boxtasche [F]
borsa [F] a telaio [M] rigido

hobo bag
morral [M]
sac [M] besace [F]
Umhängetasche [F] mit Reißverschluss [M]
sacca [F] a tracolla [F]

drawstring bag
bolso [M] saco
balluchon [M]
kleine Beuteltasche [F]
secchiello [M] piccolo con cordoncino [M]

drawstring bag
bolso [M] tipo cubo [M]
sac [M] seau [M]
Beuteltasche [F]
secchiello [M] con cordoncino [M]

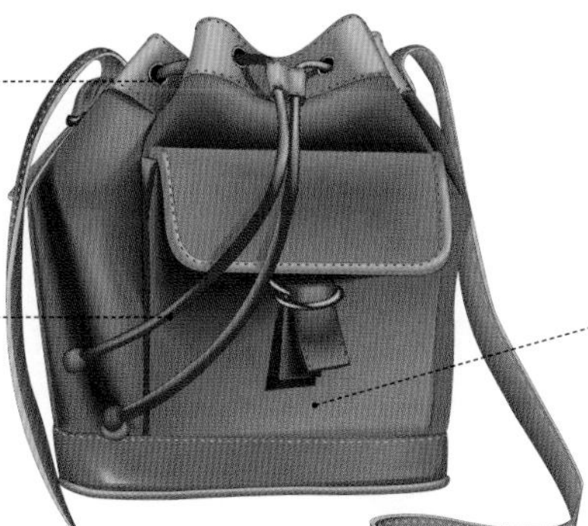
eyelet
ojal [M]
œillet [M]
Öse [F]
occhiello [M]
drawstring
cordón [M]
lacet [M] de serrage [M]
Zugschnur [F]
cordoncino [M] di chiusura [F]
front pocket
bolsillo [M] exterior
poche [F] frontale
Vortasche [F]
tasca [F] frontale

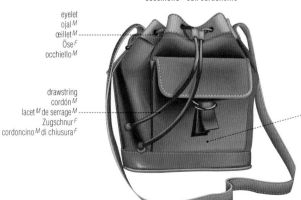

handbags

tote bag
bolsa *F* **de lona** *F*
sac *M* **fourre-tout** *M*
Einkaufstasche *F*
sporta *F*

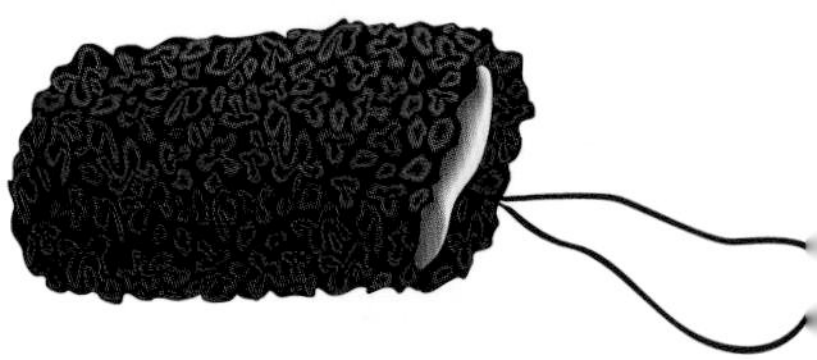

muff
bolso *M* **manguito** *M*
manchon *M*
Mufftasche *F*
borsa *F* **a manicotto** *M*

duffel bag
bolso *M* **de viaje** *M*
sac *M* **polochon** *M*
Reisetasche *F*
borsone *M* **da viaggio** *M*

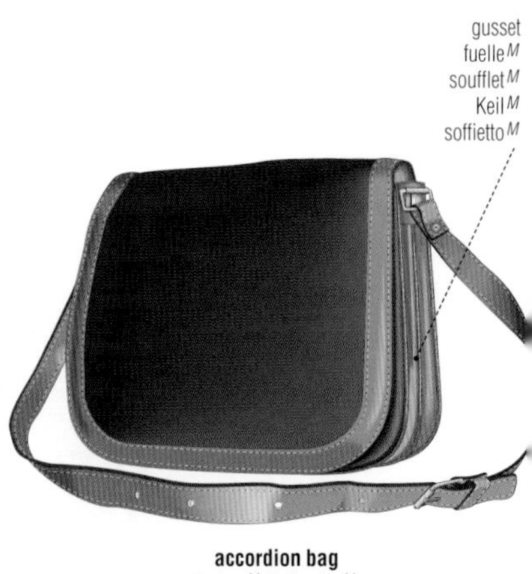
gusset
fuelle M
soufflet M
Keil M
soffietto M

accordion bag
bolso *M* **de fuelle** *M*
sac *M* **accordéon** *M*
Umhängetasche *F* **mit Dehnfalte** *F*
borsa *F* **da postino** *M*

men's bag
bolso *M* **de hombre**
pochette *F* **d'homme** *M*
Herrentasche *F*
borsello *M*

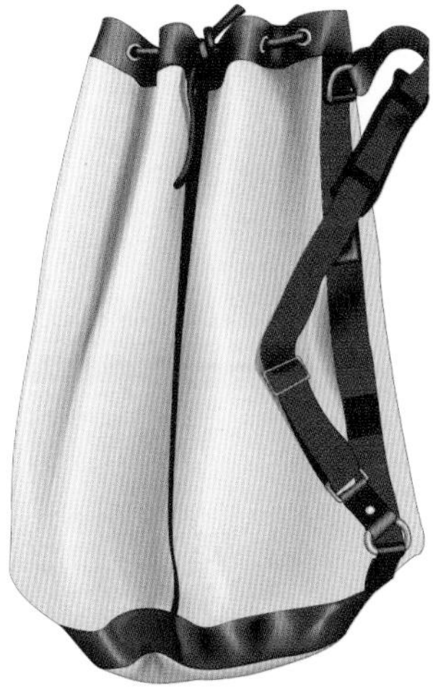

sea bag
saco *M* **de marinero** *M*
sac *M* **marin** *M*
Matchbeutel *M*
sacca *F* **da marinaio** *M*

shoulder bag
bolso *M* **de bandolera** *F*
sac *M* **à bandoulière** *F*
Schultertasche *F*
borsa *F* **a tracolla** *F*

buckle
hebilla *F*
boucle *F*
Schnalle *F*
fibbia *F*

shoulder strap
bandolera *F*
bandoulière *F*
Schulterriemen *M*
tracolla *F*

luggage

equipaje^M | bagages^M | Gepäck^N | bagagli^M

tote bag
maletín M
sac M **fourre-tout** M
Flugtasche F
bagaglio M **a mano** F

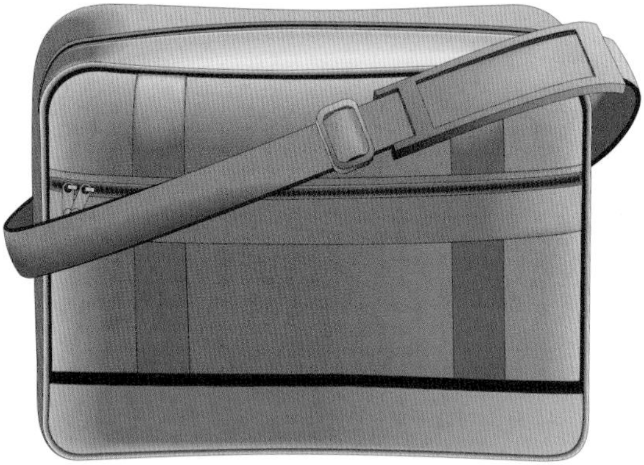

carry-on bag
bolso M **de viaje** M
bagage M **à main** F
Flugumhänger M
borsa F **da viaggio** M

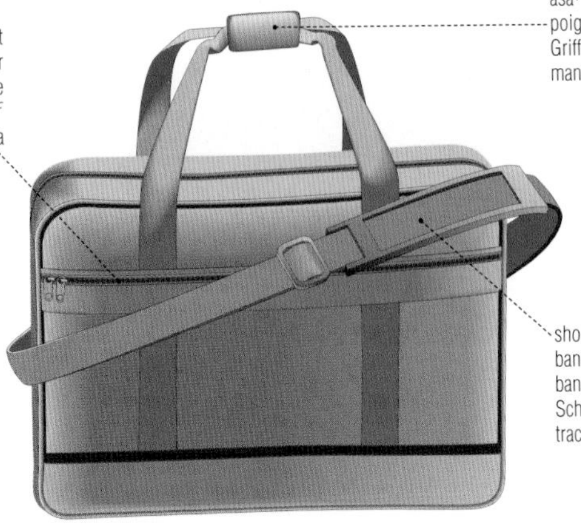
exterior pocket
bolsillo M exterior
poche F extérieure
Außentasche F
tasca F esterna
handle
asa F
poignée F
Griff M
manico M
shoulder strap
bandolera F
bandoulière F
Schulterriemen M
tracolla F

suitcase
maleta[F] clásica
valise[F] pullman[M]
Koffer[M]
valigia[F]

frame
bastidor[M]
cadre[M]
Rahmen[M]
telaio[M]
handle
asa[F]
poignée[F]
Griff[M]
manico[M]
pull strap
correa[F]
dragonne[F]
Zugriemen[M]
maniglia[F] di traino[M]
identification tag
etiqueta[F] de identificación[F]
porte-adresse[M]
Gepäckanhänger[M]
etichetta[F] portaindirizzo
wheel
ruedecilla[F]
roulette[F]
Rolle[F]
ruota[F]
trim
guarnición[F]
garniture[F]
Blende[F]
bordo[M] di rifinitura[F]

painting and drawing

pintura[F] y dibujo[M] | peinture[F] et dessin[M] | Malen[N] und Zeichnen[N] | disegno[M] e pittura[F]

equipment
equipo[M]
matériel[M]
Ausstattung[F]
attrezzatura[F]

watercolor/gouache tube
tubo[M] de acuarela[F]/de guache[M]
tube[M] d'aquarelle[F]/ gouache[F]
Tube[F] mit Aquarellfarbe[F]/Gouachefarbe[F]
tubo[M] d'acquerello[M]/guazzo[M]

watercolor/gouache cakes
pastillas[F] de acuarela[F]/de guaches[M]
pastilles[F] d'aquarelle[F]/ gouache[F]
Näpfchen[N] mit Aquarellfarbe[F]/Gouachefarbe[F]
pastiglie[F] d'acquerello[M]/guazzo[M]

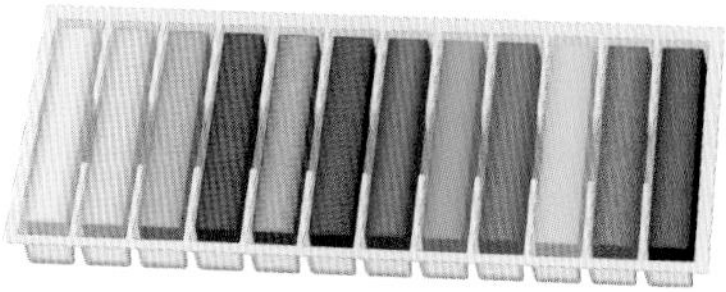

dry pastel
pastel[M]
pastels[M] secs
Pastell[N]
pastelli[M] morbidi

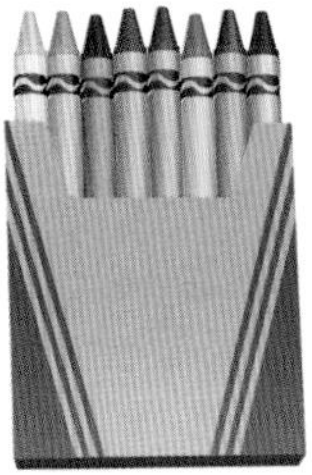

wax crayons
ceras[F]
crayons[M] de cire[F]
Wachsfarbstifte[M]
pastelli[M] a cera[F]

oil pastel
pastel[M] al óleo[M]
pastels[M] gras
Ölpastell[N]
pastelli[M] a olio[M]

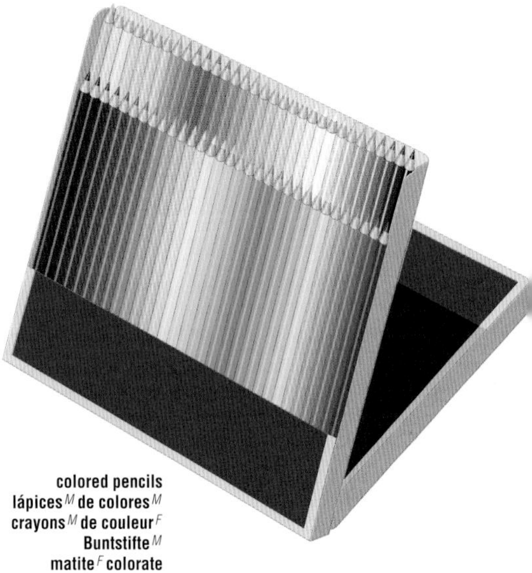

colored pencils
lápices[M] de colores[M]
crayons[M] de couleur[F]
Buntstifte[M]
matite[F] colorate

marker
marcador [M]
marqueur [M]
Marker [M]
evidenziatore [M]

oil/acrylic paint
óleo [M]
couleur [F] à l'huile [F]
Ölfarbe [F]
colore [M] a olio [M]

felt tip pen
rotulador [M]
feutre [M]
Filzstift [M]
pennarello [M]

ink
tinta [F] china
encre [F]
Tinte [F]
inchiostro [M]

fan brush
brocha [F]
brosse [F] éventail [M]
Fächerpinsel [M]
pennello [M] a ventaglio [M]

brush
pincel [M]
pinceau [M]
Pinsel [M]
pennello [M]

palette knife
cuchillo [M] paleta [F]
couteau [M] à peindre
Malspachtel [M]
mestichino [M]

reservoir-nib pen
pluma [F]
plume [F]
Graphosfeder [F]
pennino [M]

charcoal
carboncillo [M]
fusain [M]
Kohle [F]
carboncino [M]

spatula
espátula [F]
spatule [F]
Palettmesser [N]
spatola [F]

flat brush
pincel [M] plano
brosse [F]
Flachpinsel [M]
pennello [M] piatto [M]

sumi-e brush
sumie [M]
pinceau [M] à sumie [M]
Japanpinsel [M]
penna [F] sumi

movie set

plató^{M} de rodaje^{M} | plateau^{M} de tournage^{M} | Aufnahmebühne^{F} | set^{M} delle riprese^{F}

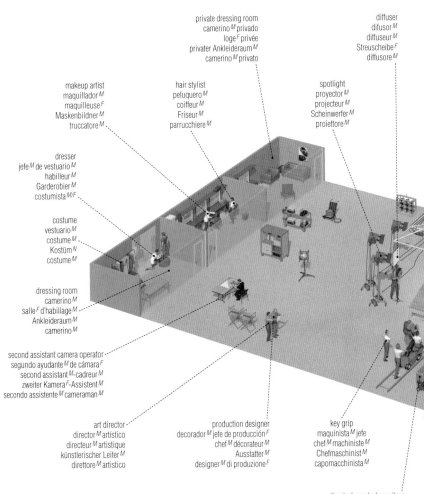

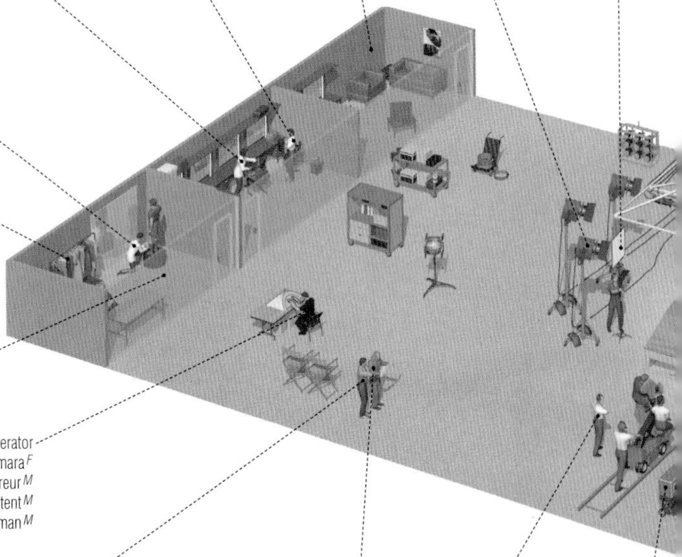
private dressing room
camerino^{M} privado
loge^{F} privée
privater Ankleideraum^{M}
camerino^{M} privato
diffuser
difusor^{M}
diffuseur^{M}
Streuscheibe^{F}
diffusore^{M}
makeup artist
maquillador^{M}
maquilleuse^{F}
Maskenbildner^{M}
truccatore^{M}
hair stylist
peluquero^{M}
coiffeur^{M}
Friseur^{M}
parrucchiere^{M}
spotlight
proyector^{M}
projecteur^{M}
Scheinwerfer^{M}
proiettore^{M}
dresser
jefe^{M} de vestuario^{M}
habilleur^{M}
Garderobier^{M}
costumista$^{M/F}$
costume
vestuario^{M}
costume^{M}
Kostüm^{N}
costume^{M}
dressing room
camerino^{M}
salle^{F} d'habillage^{M}
Ankleideraum^{M}
camerino^{M}
second assistant camera operator
segundo ayudante^{M} de cámara^{F}
second assistant^{M}-cadreur^{M}
zweiter Kamera^{F}-Assistent^{M}
secondo assistente^{M} cameraman^{M}
art director
director^{M} artístico
directeur^{M} artistique
künstlerischer Leiter^{M}
direttore^{M} artistico
production designer
decorador^{M} jefe de producción^{F}
chef^{M} décorateur^{M}
Ausstatter^{M}
designer^{M} di produzione^{F}
key grip
maquinista^{M} jefe
chef^{M} machiniste^{M}
Chefmaschinist^{M}
capomacchinista^{M}
director's control monitors
monitor^{M} de control^{M} del director^{M}
moniteurs^{M} de contrôle^{M} du réalisateur^{M}
Regie^{F}-Kontrollmonitore^{M}
monitor^{M} di controllo^{M} del regista^{M}

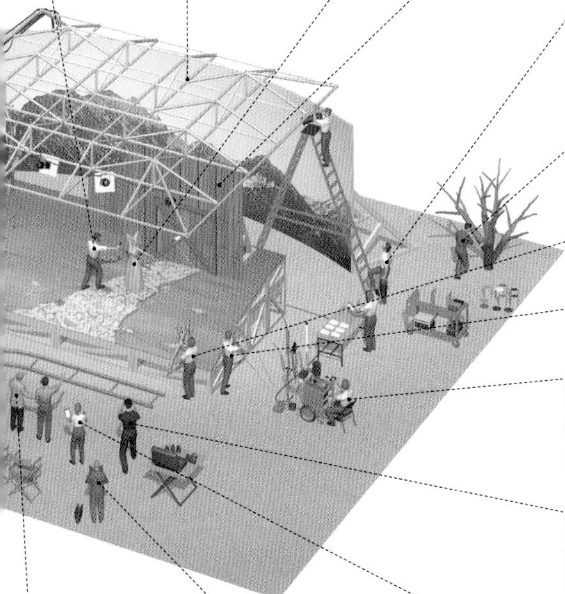
director of photography
director[M] de fotografía[F]
directeur[M] de la photographie[F]
Chef[M]-Kameramann[M]
direttore[M] della fotografia[F]

actress
actriz[F]
actrice[F]
Schauspielerin[F]
attrice[F]

set
set[M]
décor[M]
Filmset[N]
set[M]

gaffer
jefe[M] de luminotecnia[F]
chef[M] électricien[M]
Oberbeleuchter[M]
caposquadra[M]

lighting grid
peine[M] de iluminación[F]
grille[F] d'éclairage[M]
Beleuchtungsgitter[N]
griglia[F] di illuminazione[F]

set dresser
decorador[M]
décorateur[M]
Dekorateur[M]
decoratore[M] scenico

property man
atrecista[M]
accessoiriste[M]
Requisiteur[M]
attrezzista[M]

boom operator
operador[M] de jirafa[F]
perchiste[M]
Tonassistent[M]
giraffista[M]

sound engineer
ingeniero[M] de sonido[M]
chef[M] opérateur[M] du son[M]
Tonmeister[M]
ingegnere[M] del suono[M]

stills photographer
fotógrafo[M] de plató[M]
photographe[M] de plateau[M]
Standfotograf[M]
fotografo[M] di scena[F]

director
director[M]
réalisateur[M]
Regisseur[M]
regista[M]

producer
productor[M]
producteur[M]
Produzent[M]
produttore[M]

continuity person
secretario/a[M/F] de producción[F]
scripte[F]
Scriptgirl[N]
segretaria[F] di produzione[F]

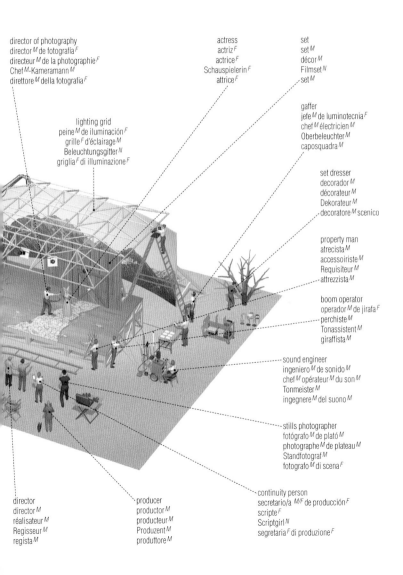

theater

teatro [M] | salle [F] de spectacle [M] | Theater [N] | teatro [M]

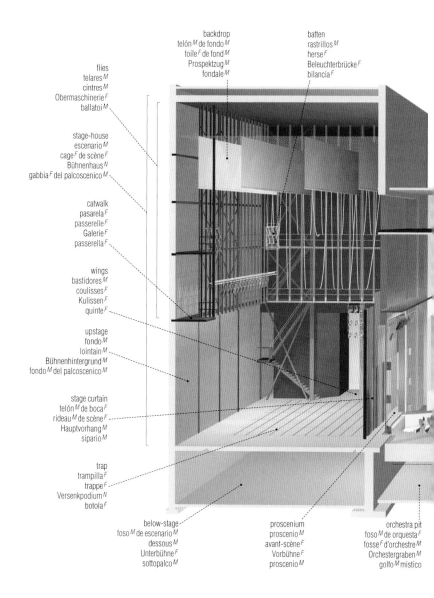

backdrop
telón [M] de fondo [M]
toile [F] de fond [M]
Prospektzug [M]
fondale [M]
batten
rastrillos [M]
herse [F]
Beleuchterbrücke [F]
bilancia [F]
flies
telares [M]
cintres [M]
Obermaschinerie [F]
ballatoi [M]
stage-house
escenario [M]
cage [F] de scène [F]
Bühnenhaus [N]
gabbia [F] del palcoscenico [M]
catwalk
pasarela [F]
passerelle [F]
Galerie [F]
passerella [F]
wings
bastidores [M]
coulisses [F]
Kulissen [F]
quinte [F]
upstage
fondo [M]
lointain [M]
Bühnenhintergrund [M]
fondo [M] del palcoscenico [M]
stage curtain
telón [M] de boca [F]
rideau [M] de scène [F]
Hauptvorhang [M]
sipario [M]
trap
trampilla [F]
trappe [F]
Versenkpodium [N]
botola [F]
below-stage
foso [M] de escenario [M]
dessous [M]
Unterbühne [F]
sottopalco [M]
proscenium
proscenio [M]
avant-scène [F]
Vorbühne [F]
proscenio [M]
orchestra pit
foso [M] de orquesta [F]
fosse [F] d'orchestre [M]
Orchestergraben [M]
golfo [M] mistico

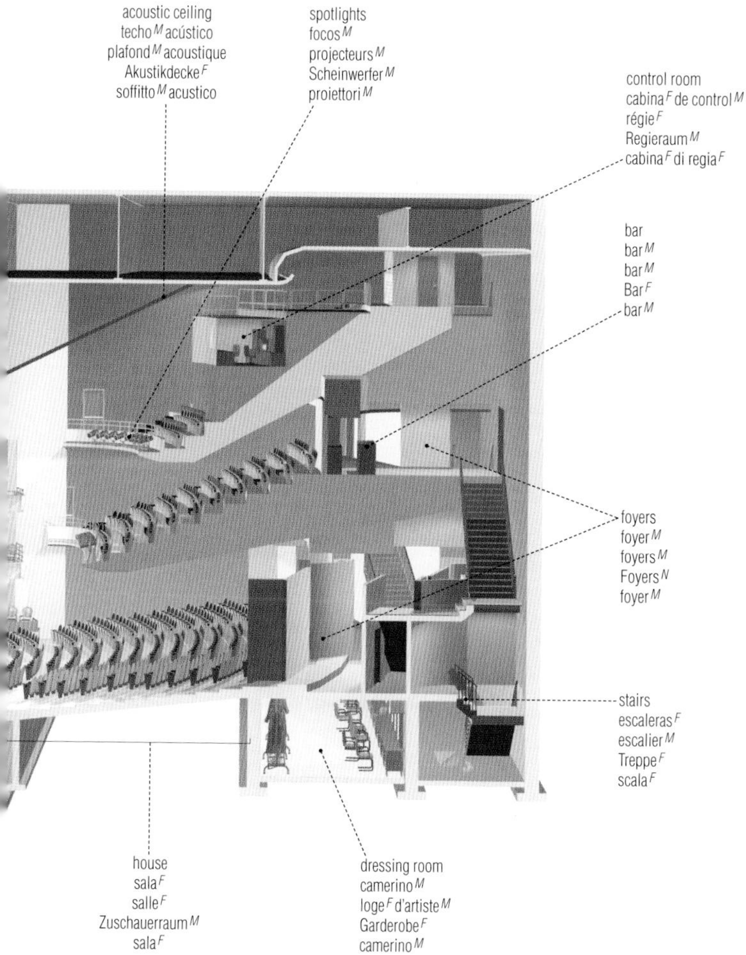
acoustic ceiling
techo M acústico
plafond M acoustique
Akustikdecke F
soffitto M acustico
spotlights
focos M
projecteurs M
Scheinwerfer M
proiettori M
control room
cabina F de control M
régie F
Regieraum M
cabina F di regia F
bar
bar M
bar M
Bar F
bar M
foyers
foyer M
foyers M
Foyers N
foyer M
stairs
escaleras F
escalier M
Treppe F
scala F
house
sala F
salle F
Zuschauerraum M
sala F
dressing room
camerino M
loge F d'artiste M
Garderobe F
camerino M

photography

fotografía[F] | photographie[F] | Fotografie[F] | fotografia[F]

single-lens reflex (SLR) camera: front view
cámara[F] réflex monocular: vista[F] frontal
appareil[M] à visée[F] reflex mono-objectif[M] : vue avant
einäugige Spiegelreflexkamera[F]/SLR-Kamera[F]: Vorderansicht[F]
macchina[F] fotografica reflex monoculare: vista[F] frontale

accessory shoe
patín[M] de los accesorios[M]
griffe[F] porte-accessoires[M]
Zubehörschuh[M]
slitta[F] per accessori[M]
exposure adjustment knob
botón[M] de compensación[M] de la exposición[F]
correction[F] d'exposition[F]
Belichtungskorrekturknopf[M]
pulsante[M] di compensazione[F] dell'esposizione[F]
film advance mode
modo[M] dispositivo[M]
mode[M] d'acquisition[F]
Aufnahmemodus[M]
modo[M] di acquisizione[F]
command control dial
selector[M] de programa[M]
sélecteur[M] de fonctions[F]
Programmwählscheibe[F]
selettore[M] dei programmi[M]
exposure mode
modalidad[F] de exposición[F]
mode[M] d'exposition[F]
Belichtungseinstellung[F]
tasto[M] per il modo[M] di esposizione[F]
multiple exposure mode
modalidad[F] de exposición[F] múltiple
surimpression[F]
Belichtungsmesser[M]
tasto[M] per le esposizioni[F] multiple
film speed
sensibilidad[F]
sensibilité[F]
Empfindlichkeit[F]
sensibilità[F]
depth-of-field preview button
botón[M] de previsionado de profundidad[F] de campo[M]
vérification[F] de la profondeur[F] de champ[M]
Schärfentiefenknopf[M]
pulsante[M] di controllo[M] della profondità[F] di campo[M]
camera body
caja[F]
boîtier[M]
Kameragehäuse[N]
corpo[M] della macchina[F] fotografica
focus mode selector
selector[M] de focalización[F]
mode[M] de mise[F] au point[M]
Autofocus-Umschalter[M]
selettore[M] della messa[F] a fuoco[M]
shutter release button
disparador[M]
déclencheur[M]
Auslöser[M]
pulsante[M] di scatto[M]
objective lens
objetivo[M]
objectif[M]
Objektiv[N]
obiettivo[M]

single-lens reflex (SLR) camera: camera back
cámara[F] réflex analógica: vista[F] posterior
appareil[M] à visée[F] reflex argentique : dos[M]
analoge Spiegelreflexkamera[F]: Rückseite[F]
macchina[F] fotografica reflex a pellicola[F]: dorso[M]

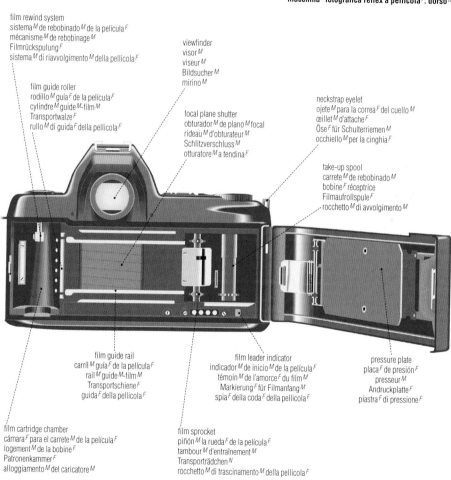

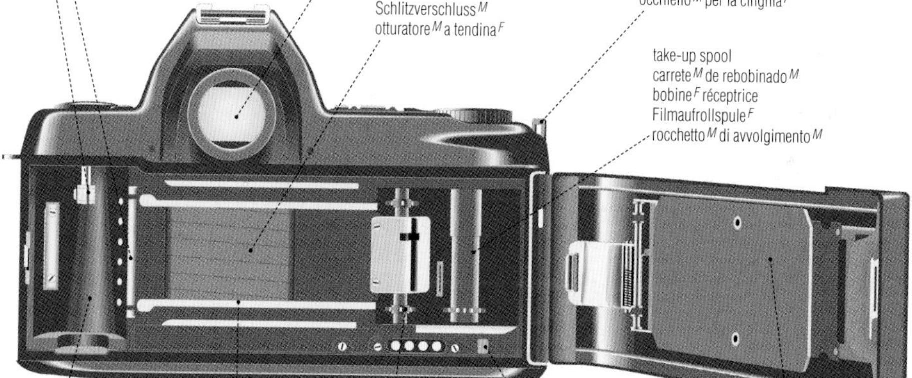
film rewind system
sistema[M] de rebobinado[M] de la película[F]
mécanisme[M] de rebobinage[M]
Filmrückspulung[F]
sistema[M] di riavvolgimento[M] della pellicola[F]
viewfinder
visor[M]
viseur[M]
Bildsucher[M]
mirino[M]
film guide roller
rodillo[M] guía[F] de la película[F]
cylindre[M] guide[M]-film[M]
Transportwalze[F]
rullo[M] di guida[F] della pellicola[F]
focal plane shutter
obturador[M] de plano[M] focal
rideau[M] d'obturateur[M]
Schlitzverschluss[M]
otturatore[M] a tendina[F]
neckstrap eyelet
ojete[M] para la correa[F] del cuello[M]
œillet[M] d'attache[F]
Öse[F] für Schulterriemen[M]
occhiello[M] per la cinghia[F]
take-up spool
carrete[M] de rebobinado[M]
bobine[F] réceptrice
Filmaufrollspule[F]
rocchetto[M] di avvolgimento[M]
film guide rail
carríl[M] guía[F] de la película[F]
rail[M] guide[M]-film[M]
Transportschiene[F]
guida[F] della pellicola[F]
film leader indicator
indicador[M] de inicio[M] de la película[F]
témoin[M] de l'amorce[F] du film[M]
Markierung[F] für Filmanfang[M]
spia[F] della coda[F] della pellicola[F]
pressure plate
placa[F] de presión[F]
presseur[M]
Andruckplatte[F]
piastra[F] di pressione[F]
film cartridge chamber
cámara[F] para el carrete[M] de la película[F]
logement[M] de la bobine[F]
Patronenkammer[F]
alloggiamento[M] del caricatore[M]
film sprocket
piñón[M] la rueda[F] de la película[F]
tambour[M] d'entraînement[M]
Transporträdchen[N]
rocchetto[M] di trascinamento[M] della pellicola[F]

digital reflex camera: control panel
cámara[F] réflex digital: pantalla[F] de control[M]
appareil[M] à visée[F] reflex numérique : écran[M] de contrôle[M]
digitale Spiegelreflexkamera[F]: Kontrollanzeige[F]
macchina[F] fotografica reflex digitale: monitor[M] di controllo[M]

sensitivity
sensibilidad[F]
sensibilité[F]
Empfindlichkeit[F]
sensibilità[F]

metering mode
modo[M] de medición[F]
mode[M] de mesure[F]
Messmodus[M]
modalità[F] di misurazione[F]

aperture
apertura[F]
ouverture[F]
Blendeneinstellung[F]
apertura[F]

frames remaining/timer
contador[M] de fotos[F]/contador[M] de tiempo[M]
compteur[M] de vues[F]/retardateur[M]
verbleibende Aufnahmen[F]/Selbstauslöser-Vorlaufzeit[F]
contascatti[M]/timer[M]

shutter speed
velocidad[F] de obturación[F]
vitesse[F] d'obturation[F]
Verschlusszeit[F]
velocità[F] di otturazione[F]

white balance
balance[M] de blancos[M]
balance[F] des blancs[M]
Weißabgleich[M]
bilanciamento[M] del bianco[M]

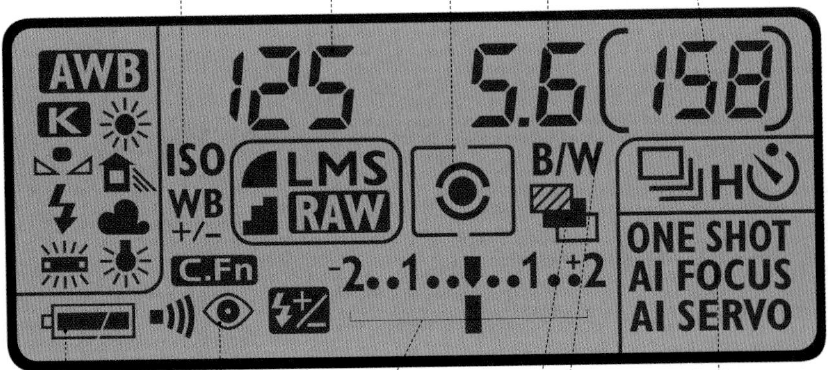
AWB
K
125
5.6
158
ISO
WB
+/–
LMS
RAW
C.Fn
B/W
H
ONE SHOT
AI FOCUS
AI SERVO
-2..1..|..1..+2

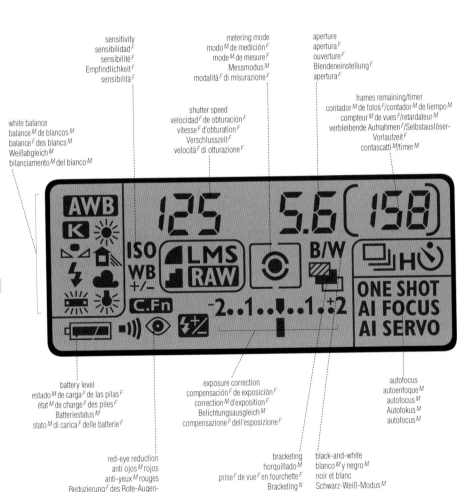

battery level
estado[M] de carga[F] de las pilas[F]
état[M] de charge[F] des piles[F]
Batteriestatus[M]
stato[M] di carica[F] delle batterie[F]

exposure correction
compensación[F] de exposición[F]
correction[M] d'exposition[F]
Belichtungsausgleich[M]
compensazione[F] dell'esposizione[F]

autofocus
autoenfoque[M]
autofocus[M]
Autofokus[M]
autofocus[M]

red-eye reduction
anti ojos[M] rojos
anti-yeux[M] rouges
Reduzierung[F] des Rote-Augen-Effekts[M]
riduzione[F] occhi[M] rossi

bracketing
horquillado[M]
prise[F] de vue[F] en fourchette[F]
Bracketing[N]
bracketing[M]

black-and-white
blanco[M] y negro[M]
noir et blanc
Schwarz-Weiß-Modus[M]
bianco e nero

digital reflex camera: camera back
cámara[F] réflex digital: vista[F] posterior
appareil[M] à visée[F] reflex numérique : dos[M]
digitale Spiegelreflexkamera[F]: Rückansicht[F]
macchina[F] fotografica reflex digitale: dorso[M]

liquid crystal display
pantalla[F] de cristal[M] líquido
écran[M] à cristaux[M] liquides
Flüssigkristallanzeige[F]
display[M] a cristalli[M] liquidi

viewfinder
visor[M]
viseur[M]
Sucherokular[N]
mirino[M]

power switch
conmutador[M] de alimentación[F]
commutateur[M] d'alimentation[F]
Hauptschalter[M]
interruttore[M] di accensione[F]

compact memory card
tarjeta[F] de memoria[F]
carte[F] de mémoire[F]
Speicherkarte[F]
scheda[F] di memoria[F]

ON
OFF
MENU
INFO.
JUMP
64 MB

image review button
botón[M] de visualización[F] de imágenes[F]
touche[F] de visualisation[F] des images[F]
Bildanzeige[F]
pulsante[M] di visualizzazione[F] delle immagini[F]

erase button
botón[M] de cancelación[F]
touche[F] d'effacement[M]
Löschtaste[F]
pulsante[M] di cancellazione[F]

four-way selector
selector[M] cuadro-direccional
sélecteur[M] quadridirectionnel
Vierwegeregler[M]
selettore[M] quadridirezionale

video and digital terminals
tomas[F] vídeo y digital
prises[F] vidéo et numérique
Anschlussbuchsen[F] für Video- und Digitalübertragung[F]
prese[F] video e digitali

photography

cross section of a reflex camera
sección^F transversal de una cámara^F reflex analógica
coupe^F d'un appareil^M reflex argentique
analoge Spiegelreflexkamera^F im Querschnitt^M
macchina^F fotografica reflex a pellicola^F: sezione^F

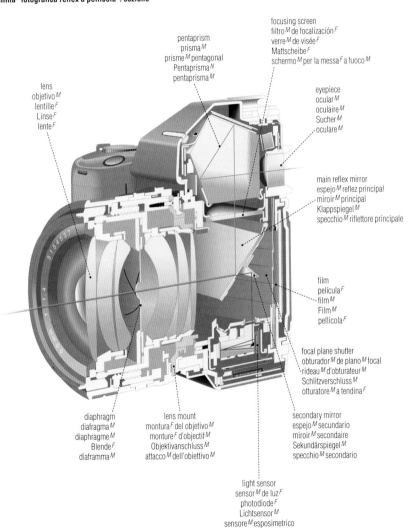

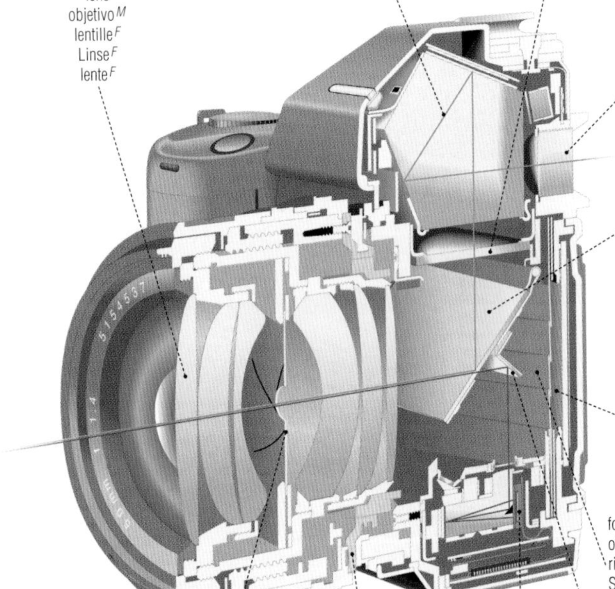
focusing screen
filtro^M de focalización^F
verre^M de visée^F
Mattscheibe^F
schermo^M per la messa^F a fuoco^M
pentaprism
prisma^M
prisme^M pentagonal
Pentaprisma^N
pentaprisma^M
lens
objetivo^M
lentille^F
Linse^F
lente^F
eyepiece
ocular^M
oculaire^M
Sucher^M
oculare^M
main reflex mirror
espejo^M reflez principal
miroir^M principal
Klappspiegel^M
specchio^M riflettore principale
film
película^F
film^M
Film^M
pellicola^F
focal plane shutter
obturador^M de plano^M focal
rideau^M d'obturateur^M
Schlitzverschluss^M
otturatore^M a tendina^F
diaphragm
diafragma^M
diaphragme^M
Blende^F
diaframma^M
lens mount
montura^F del objetivo^M
monture^F d'objectif^M
Objektivanschluss^M
attacco^M dell'obiettivo^M
secondary mirror
espejo^M secundario
miroir^M secondaire
Sekundärspiegel^M
specchio^M secondario
light sensor
sensor^M de luz^F
photodiode^F
Lichtsensor^M
sensore^M esposimetrico

films
películas F
pellicules F
Filme M
pellicole F

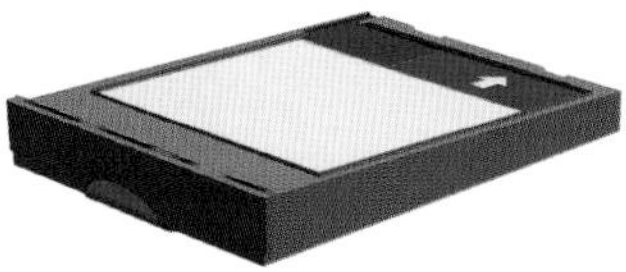

film pack
paquete M de placas F fotográficas
film M-pack M
Filmkassette F
filmpack M

roll film
rollo M de película F
rouleau M de pellicule F
Rollfilm M
pellicola F in rotolo M

cartridge film
cartucho M de la película F
cassette F de pellicule F
Kassettenfilm M
caricatore M

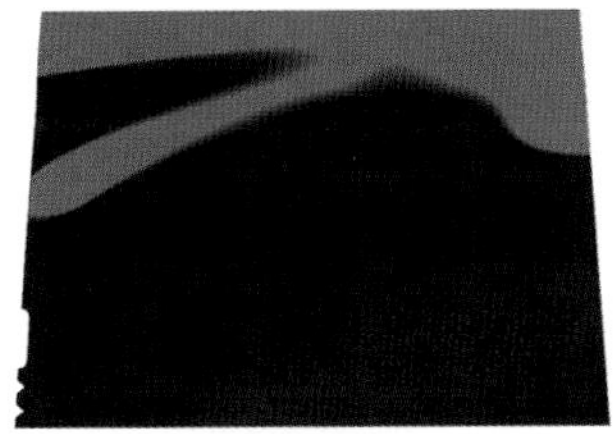

sheet film
hoja F de la película F
pellicule F en feuille F
Planfilm M
pellicola F piana

memory cards
tarjetas F de memoria F
cartes F de mémoire F
Speicherkarten F
schede F di memoria

xD-Picture card
tarjeta F xD Picture
carte F xD Picture
xD-Karte F
scheda F xD Picture

xD
1GB

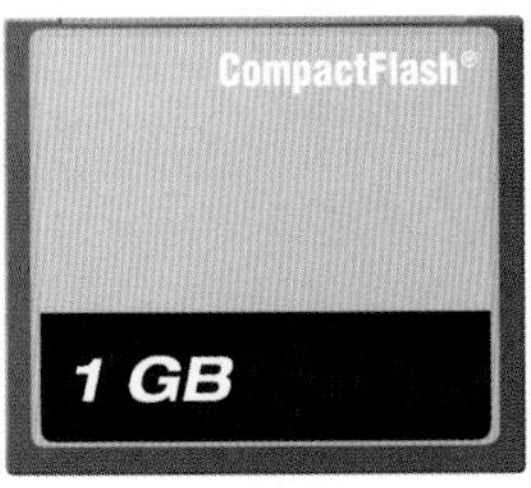
CompactFlash®
1 GB

compact flash card
tarjeta F flash compacta
carte F flash compacte
Compact-Flash-Karte F
scheda F compact flash

1 GB

Secure Digital card
tarjeta F Digital Segura
carte F Secure Digital
SD-Karte F
scheda F Secure Digital

MEMORY STICK
1GB

Memory Stick
tarjeta F Memory Stick
carte F Memory Stick
Memory-Stick-Karte F
scheda F Memory Stick

still cameras
cámaras[F] fijas
appareils[M] photographiques
Fotoapparate[M]
macchine[F] fotografiche

disposable camera
cámara[F] desechable
appareil[M] jetable
Einwegkamera[F]
macchina[F] fotografica usa e getta

compact camera
aparato[M] compacto
appareil[M] compact
Kompaktkamera[F]
macchina[F] compatta

ultracompact camera
aparato[M] ultracompacto
appareil[M] ultracompact
Ultrakompaktkamera[F]
macchina[F] ultracompatta

single-lens reflex (SLR) camera
cámara[F] reflex de un solo objetivo[M]
appareil[M] à visée[F] reflex mono-objectif[M]
einäugige Spiegelreflexkamera[F]
macchina[F] fotografica reflex

underwater camera
cámara[F] submarina
appareil[M] de plongée[F]
Unterwasserkamera[F]
macchina[F] fotografica subacquea

Polaroid® camera
cámara *F* Polaroid® Land
Polaroid® *M*
Sofortbildkamera *F*
Polaroid® *F*

medium format SLR (6 x 6)
cámara *F* reflex de formato *M* medio SLR (6x6)
appareil *M* reflex 6 X 6 mono-objectif *M*
Mittelformatkamera *F* SLR (6 x 6)
macchina *F* fotografica reflex (6x6)

twin-lens reflex camera
cámara *F* réflex con dos objetivos *M*
appareil *M* reflex à deux objectifs *M*
Zweiäugige Spiegelreflexkamera *F*
macchina *F* fotografica reflex biottica

view camera
cámara *F* de fuelle *M*
chambre *F* photographique
Großformatkamera *F*
macchina *F* fotografica a banco *M* ottico

traditional musical instruments

instrumentos^M musicales tradicionales | instruments^M traditionnels | traditionelle Musikinstrumente^N | strumenti^M musicali tradizionali

accordion
acordeón M
accordéon M
Akkordeon N
fisarmonica F

harmonica
armónica F
harmonica M
Mundharmonika F
armonica F **a bocca** F

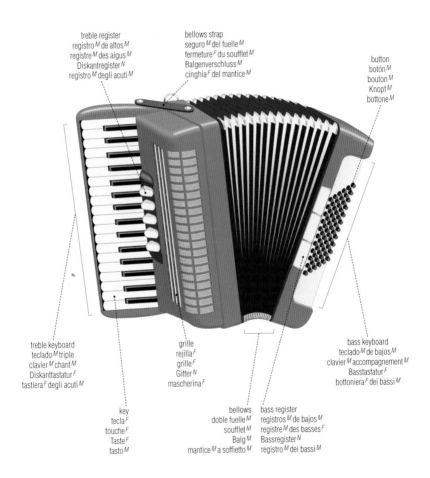

treble register
registro M de altos M
registre M des aigus M
Diskantregister N
registro M degli acuti M
bellows strap
seguro M del fuelle M
fermeture F du soufflet M
Balgenverschluss M
cinghia F del mantice M
button
botón M
bouton M
Knopf M
bottone M
treble keyboard
teclado M triple
clavier M chant M
Diskanttastatur F
tastiera F degli acuti M
grille
rejilla F
grille F
Gitter N
mascherina F
bass keyboard
teclado M de bajos M
clavier M accompagnement M
Basstastatur F
bottoniera F dei bassi M
key
tecla F
touche F
Taste F
tasto M
bellows
doble fuelle M
soufflet M
Balg M
mantice M a soffietto M
bass register
registros M de bajos M
registre M des basses F
Bassregister N
registro M dei bassi M

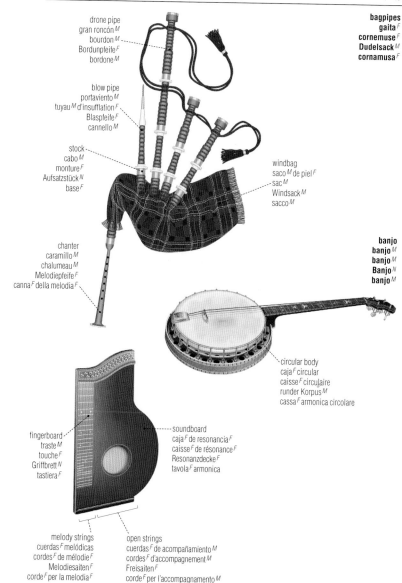

bagpipes
gaita F
cornemuse F
Dudelsack M
cornamusa F

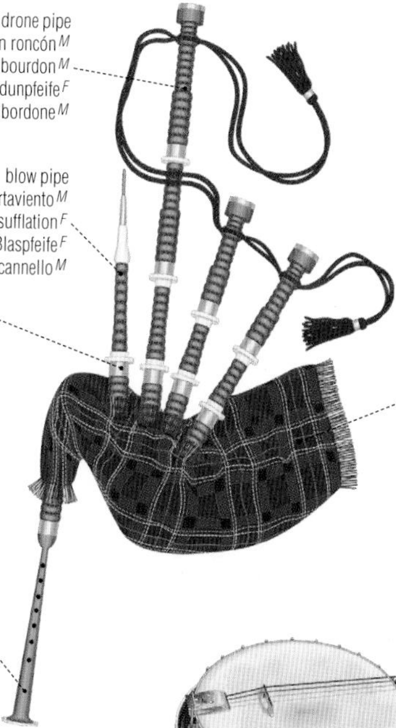
drone pipe
gran roncón M
bourdon M
Bordunpfeife F
bordone M
blow pipe
portaviento M
tuyau M d'insufflation F
Blaspfeife F
cannello M
stock
cabo M
monture F
Aufsatzstück N
base F
windbag
saco M de piel F
sac M
Windsack M
sacco M
chanter
caramillo M
chalumeau M
Melodiepfeife F
canna F della melodia F

banjo
banjo M
banjo M
Banjo N
banjo M

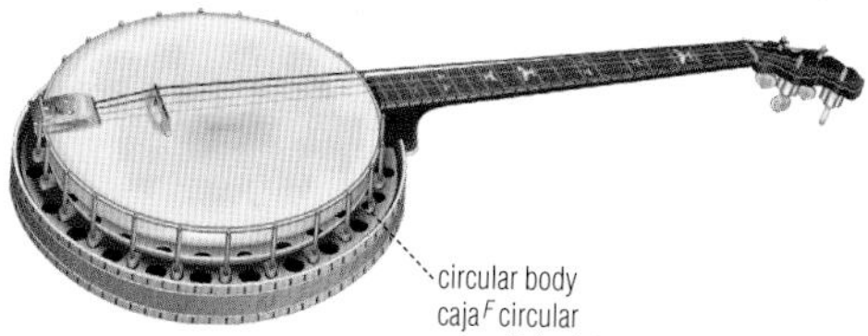
circular body
caja F circular
caisse F circulaire
runder Korpus M
cassa F armonica circolare

zither
cítara F
cithare F
Zither F
zither M

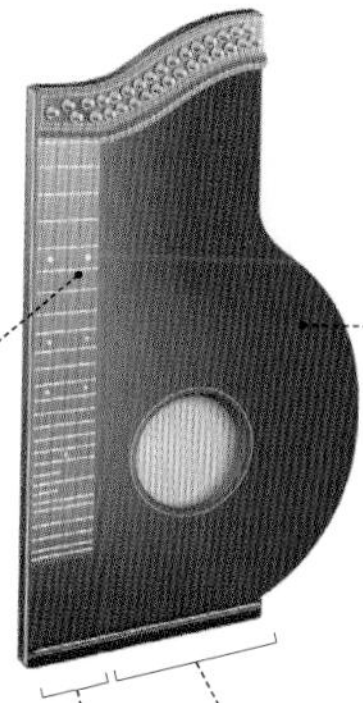
fingerboard
traste M
touche F
Griffbrett N
tastiera F
soundboard
caja F de resonancia F
caisse F de résonance F
Resonanzdecke F
tavola F armonica
melody strings
cuerdas F melódicas
cordes F de mélodie F
Melodiesaiten F
corde F per la melodia F
open strings
cuerdas F de acompañamiento M
cordes F d'accompagnement M
Freisaiten F
corde F per l'accompagnamento M

symphony orchestra

orquesta^F sinfónica | orchestre^M symphonique | Sinfonieorchester^N | orchestra^F sinfonica

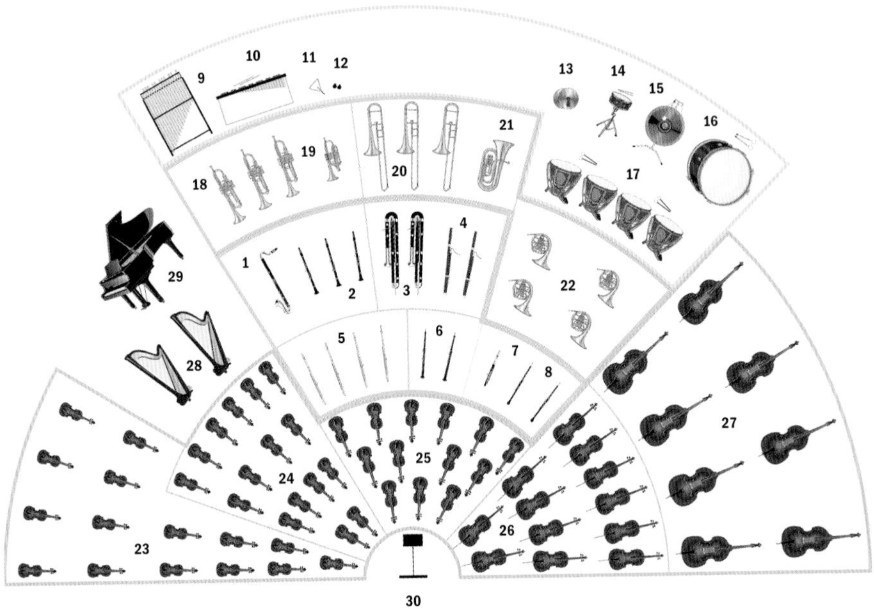

1
2
3
4
5
6
7
8
9
10
11
12
13
14
15
16
17
18
19
20
21
22
23
24
25
26
27
28
29
30

woodwind family
familia^F de instrumentos^M de madera^F
famille^F des bois^M
Familie^F der Holzblasinstrumente^N
famiglia^F dei legni^M

1 bass clarinet
clarinete^M bajo
clarinette^F basse
Bassklarinette^F
clarinetto^M basso

2 clarinets
clarinetes^M
clarinettes^F
Klarinetten^F
clarinetti^M

3 contrabassoons
contrafagots^M
contrebassons^M
Kontrafagotte^N
controfagotti^M

4 bassoons
fagotes^M
bassons^M
Fagotte^N
fagotti^M

5 flutes
flautas^F traveseras
flûtes^F
Querflöten^F
flauti^M

6 oboes
oboes^M
hautbois^M
Oboen^F
oboi^M

7 piccolo
píccolo^M
piccolo^M
Pikkoloflöte^F
ottavino^M

8 English horns
cornos^M ingleses
cors^M anglais
Englischhörner^N
corni^M inglesi

percussion instruments
instrumentos^M **de percusión**^F
instruments^M **à percussion**^F
Schlaginstrumente^N
strumenti^M **a percussione**^F

9
tubular bells
campanas^F tubulares
carillon^M tubulaire
Röhrenglocken^F
campane^F tubolari

10
xylophone
xilófono^M
xylophone^M
Xylophon^N
xilofono^M

11
triangle
triángulo^M
triangle^M
Triangel^M
triangolo^M

12
castanets
castañuelas^F
castagnettes^F
Kastagnetten^F
nacchere^F

13
cymbals
platillos^M
cymbales^F
Becken^N
piatti^M

14
snare drum
caja^F clara
caisse^F claire
kleine Trommel^F
cassa^F chiara

15
gong
gong^M
gong^M
Gong^M
gong^M

16
bass drum
bombo^M
grosse caisse^F
Basstrommel^F
grancassa^F

17
timpani
timbales^M
timbales^F
Pauken^F
timpani^M

brass family
familia^F **de los metales**^M
famille^F **des cuivres**^M
Familie^F **der Blechbläser**^M
famiglia^F **degli ottoni**^M

18
trumpets
trompetas^F
trompettes^F
Trompeten^F
trombe^F

19
cornet
cornetín^M
cornet^M à pistons^M
Kornett^N
cornetta^F

20
trombones
trombones^M
trombones^M
Posaunen^F
tromboni^M

21
tuba
tuba^F
tuba^M
Tuba^F
tuba^F

22
French horns
cornos^M franceses/trompas^F
cors^M d'harmonie^F
Waldhörner^N
corni^M

violin family
familia^F **de los violines**^M
famille^F **du violon**^M
Geigenfamilie^F
famiglia^F **degli archi**^M

23
first violins
primeros violines^M
premiers violons^M
erste Violinen^F
primi violini^M

24
second violins
segundos violines^M
seconds violons^M
zweite Violinen^F
secondi violini^M

25
violas
violas^F
altos^M
Bratschen^F
viole^F

26
cellos
violoncelos^M
violoncelles^M
Celli^N
violoncelli^M

27
double basses
contrabajos^M
contrebasses^F
Kontrabasse^M
contrabbassi^M

28
harps
arpas^F
harpes^F
Harfen^F
arpe^F

29
piano
piano^M
piano^M
Flügel^M
pianoforte^M

30
conductor's podium
estrado^M del director^M
pupitre^M du chef^M d'orchestre^M
Dirigentenpult^N
podio^M del direttore^M d'orchestra^F

stringed instruments

instrumentos^M de cuerda^F | instruments^M à cordes^F | Saiteninstrumente^N | strumenti^M a corde^F

violin
violín^M
violon^M
Violine^F
violino^M

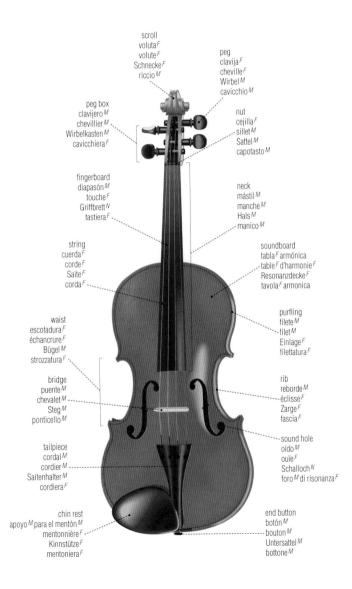

scroll
voluta^F
volute^F
Schnecke^F
riccio^M
peg
clavija^F
cheville^F
Wirbel^M
cavicchio^M
peg box
clavijero^M
chevillier^M
Wirbelkasten^M
cavicchiera^F
nut
cejilla^F
sillet^M
Sattel^M
capotasto^M
fingerboard
diapasón^M
touche^F
Griffbrett^N
tastiera^F
neck
mástil^M
manche^M
Hals^M
manico^M
string
cuerda^F
corde^F
Saite^F
corda^F
soundboard
tabla^F armónica
table^F d'harmonie^F
Resonanzdecke^F
tavola^F armonica
purfling
filete^M
filet^M
Einlage^F
filettatura^F
waist
escotadura^F
échancrure^F
Bügel^M
strozzatura^F
bridge
puente^M
chevalet^M
Steg^M
ponticello^M
rib
reborde^M
éclisse^F
Zarge^F
fascia^F
sound hole
oído^M
ouïe^F
Schalloch^N
foro^M di risonanza^F
tailpiece
cordal^M
cordier^M
Saitenhalter^M
cordiera^F
chin rest
apoyo^M para el mentón^M
mentonnière^F
Kinnstütze^F
mentoniera^F
end button
botón^M
bouton^M
Untersattel^M
bottone^M

bow
arco [M]
archet [M]
Bogen [M]
archetto [M]

head
cabeza [F]
tête [F]
Kopf [M]
testina [F]
point
punta [F]
pointe [F]
Spitze [F]
punta [F]
stick
vara [F]
baguette [F]
Stange [F]
bacchetta [F]
hair
crin [F]
mèche [F]
Haar [N]
crine [M]
handle
mango [M]
poignée [F]
Griff [M]
impugnatura [F]
heel
talón [M]
talon [M]
Bogenansatz [M]
tallone [M]
frog
alza [F]
hausse [F]
Frosch [M]
bietta [F]
screw
tornillo [M]
vis [F]
Schraube [F]
vite [F]

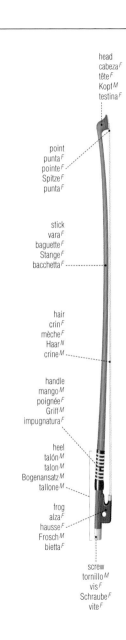

violin family
familia [F] de los violines [M]
famille [F] du violon [M]
Violinfamilie [F]
famiglia [F] degli archi [M]

viola
viola [F]
alto [M]
Bratsche [F]
viola [F]

violin
violín [M]
violon [M]
Violine [F]
violino [M]

cello
violoncelo [M]
violoncelle [M]
Cello [N]
violoncello [M]

double bass
contrabajo [M]
contrebasse [F]
Kontrabass [M]
contrabbasso [M]

stringed instruments

harp
arpa F
harpe F
Harfe F
arpa F

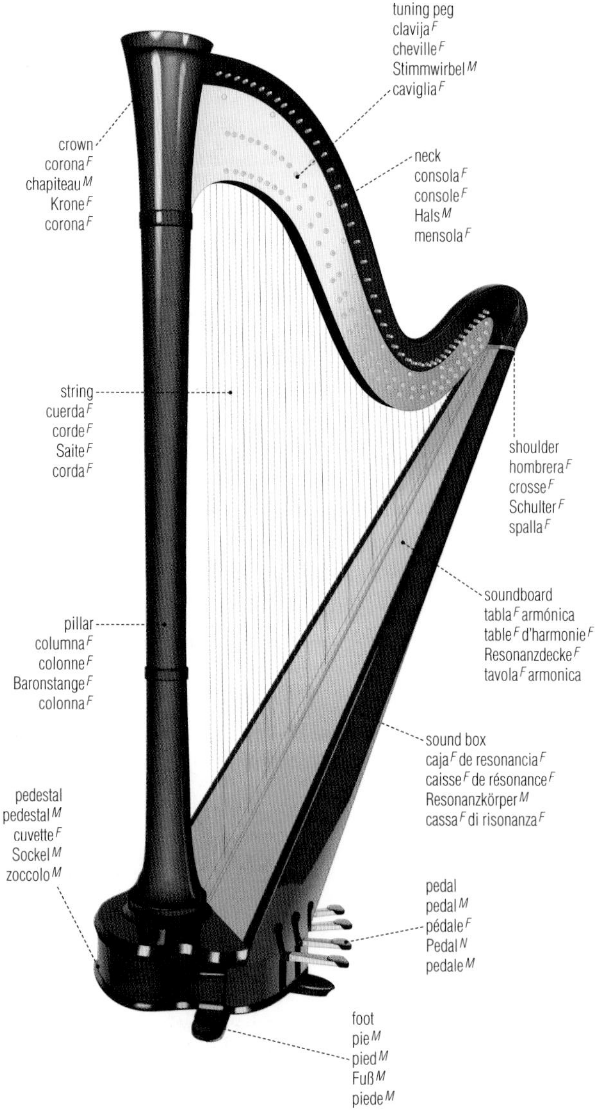
tuning peg
clavija F
cheville F
Stimmwirbel M
caviglia F
crown
corona F
chapiteau M
Krone F
corona F
neck
consola F
console F
Hals M
mensola F
string
cuerda F
corde F
Saite F
corda F
shoulder
hombrera F
crosse F
Schulter F
spalla F
soundboard
tabla F armónica
table F d'harmonie F
Resonanzdecke F
tavola F armonica
pillar
columna F
colonne F
Baronstange F
colonna F
sound box
caja F de resonancia F
caisse F de résonance F
Resonanzkörper M
cassa F di risonanza F
pedestal
pedestal M
cuvette F
Sockel M
zoccolo M
pedal
pedal M
pédale F
Pedal N
pedale M
foot
pie M
pied M
Fuß M
piede M

acoustic guitar
guitarra^{F} clásica
guitare^{F} acoustique
akustische Gitarre^{F}
chitarra^{F} acustica

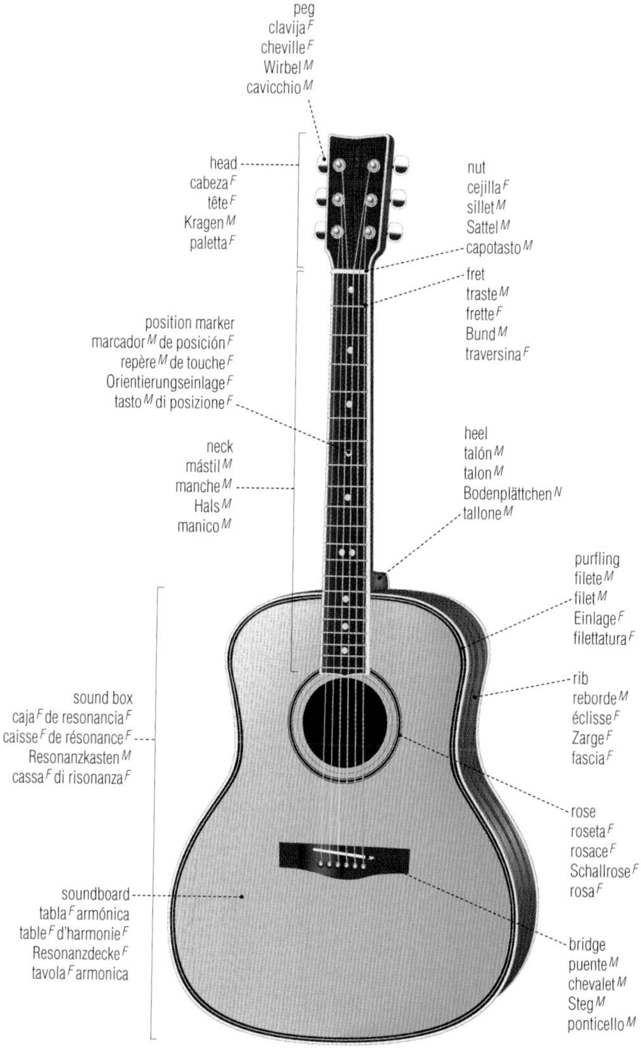
peg
clavija F
cheville F
Wirbel M
cavicchio M
head
cabeza F
tête F
Kragen M
paletta F
nut
cejilla F
sillet M
Sattel M
capotasto M
fret
traste M
frette F
Bund M
traversina F
position marker
marcador M de posición F
repère M de touche F
Orientierungseinlage F
tasto M di posizione F
neck
mástil M
manche M
Hals M
manico M
heel
talón M
talon M
Bodenplättchen N
tallone M
purfling
filete M
filet M
Einlage F
filettatura F
sound box
caja F de resonancia F
caisse F de résonance F
Resonanzkasten M
cassa F di risonanza F
rib
reborde M
éclisse F
Zarge F
fascia F
rose
roseta F
rosace F
Schallrose F
rosa F
soundboard
tabla F armónica
table F d'harmonie F
Resonanzdecke F
tavola F armonica
bridge
puente M
chevalet M
Steg M
ponticello M

electric guitar
guitarra[F] eléctrica
guitare[F] électrique
elektrische Gitarre[F]
chitarra[F] elettrica

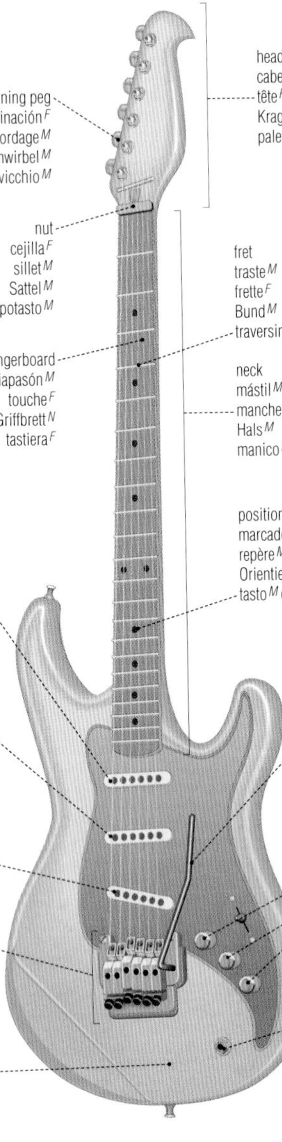
head
cabeza[F]
tête[F]
Kragen[M]
paletta[F]
tuning peg
clavija[F] de afinación[F]
mécanique[F] d'accordage[M]
Stimmwirbel[M]
cavicchio[M]
nut
cejilla[F]
sillet[M]
Sattel[M]
capotasto[M]
fret
traste[M]
frette[F]
Bund[M]
traversina[F]
fingerboard
diapasón[M]
touche[F]
Griffbrett[N]
tastiera[F]
neck
mástil[M]
manche[M]
Hals[M]
manico[M]
bass pickup
receptor[M] de los bajos[M]
micro[M] de fréquences[F] graves
Bass-Tonabnehmer[M]
pick-up[M] per basse frequenze[F]
position marker
marcador[M] de posición[F]
repère[M] de touche[F]
Orientierungseinlage[F]
tasto[M] di posizione[F]
midrange pickup
receptor[M] de los intermedios[M]
micro[M] de fréquences[F] moyennes
Mittellage-Tonabnehmer[M]
pick-up[M] per medie frequenze[F]
vibrato arm
palanca[F] de vibración[F]
levier[M] de vibrato[M]
Vibratohebel[M]
braccio[M] del tremolo[M]
treble pickup
receptor[M] triple
micro[M] de fréquences[F] aiguës
Höhen-Tonabnehmer[M]
pick-up[M] per alte frequenze[F]
volume control
control[M] de volumen[M]
réglage[M] du volume[M]
Lautstärkeregler[M]
regolazione[F] del volume[M]
bridge assembly
puente[M] de ensamblaje[M]
ensemble[M] du chevalet[M]
Saitenaufhängung[F]
blocco[M] del ponticello[M]
tone control
control[M] del sonido[M]
réglage[M] de la tonalité[F]
Klangfarbenregler[M]
regolazione[F] dei toni[M]
body
cuerpo[M] sólido
caisse[F]
massiver Korpus[M]
cassa[F] piena
output jack
conector[M] de salida[F]
jack[M] de sortie[F]
Anschlussbuchse[F]
presa[F] d'uscita[F]

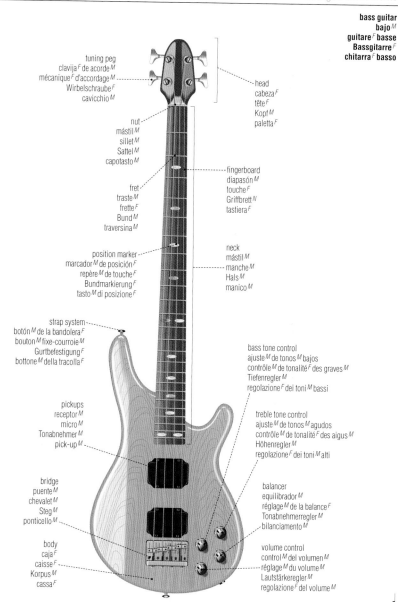

bass guitar
bajo [M]
guitare [F] basse
Bassgitarre [F]
chitarra [F] basso

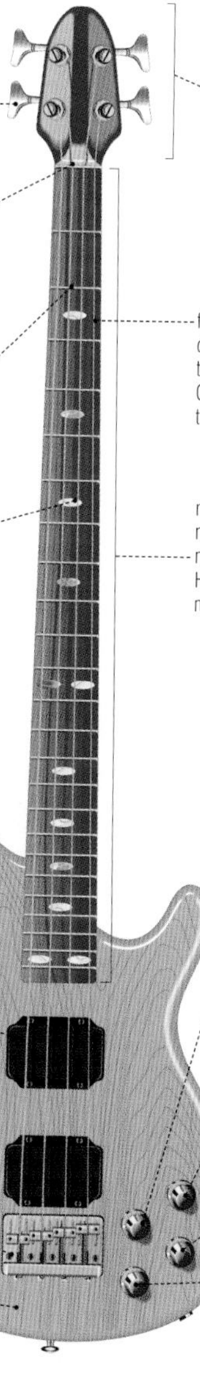
tuning peg
clavija [F] de acorde [M]
mécanique [F] d'accordage [M]
Wirbelschraube [F]
cavicchio [M]
head
cabeza [F]
tête [F]
Kopf [M]
paletta [F]
nut
mástil [M]
sillet [M]
Sattel [M]
capotasto [M]
fingerboard
diapasón [M]
touche [F]
Griffbrett [N]
tastiera [F]
fret
traste [M]
frette [F]
Bund [M]
traversina [M]
neck
mástil [M]
manche [M]
Hals [M]
manico [M]
position marker
marcador [M] de posición [F]
repère [M] de touche [F]
Bundmarkierung [F]
tasto [M] di posizione [F]
strap system
botón [M] de la bandolera [F]
bouton [M] fixe-courroie [M]
Gurtbefestigung [F]
bottone [M] della tracolla [F]
bass tone control
ajuste [M] de tonos [M] bajos
contrôle [M] de tonalité [F] des graves [M]
Tiefenregler [M]
regolazione [F] dei toni [M] bassi
pickups
receptor [M]
micro [M]
Tonabnehmer [M]
pick-up [M]
treble tone control
ajuste [M] de tonos [M] agudos
contrôle [M] de tonalité [F] des aigus [M]
Höhenregler [M]
regolazione [F] dei toni [M] alti
bridge
puente [M]
chevalet [M]
Steg [M]
ponticello [M]
balancer
equilibrador [M]
réglage [M] de la balance [F]
Tonabnehmerregler [M]
bilanciamento [M]
body
caja [F]
caisse [F]
Korpus [M]
cassa [F]
volume control
control [M] del volumen [M]
réglage [M] du volume [M]
Lautstärkeregler [M]
regolazione [F] del volume [M]

keyboard instruments

instrumentos^M de teclado^M | instruments^M à clavier^M | Tasteninstrumente^N | strumenti^M a tastiera^F

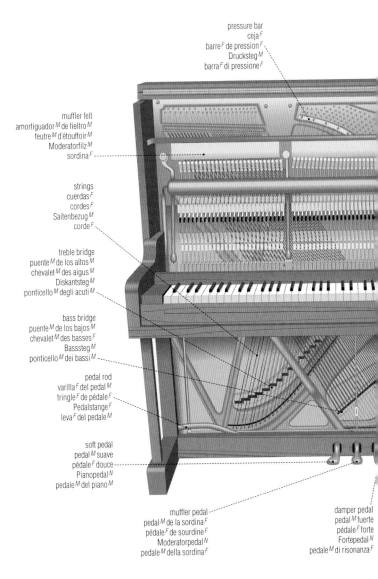

upright piano
piano^M vertical
piano^M droit
Klavier^N
pianoforte^M verticale

pressure bar
ceja^F
barre^F de pression^F
Drucksteg^M
barra^F di pressione^F
muffler felt
amortiguador^M de fieltro^M
feutre^M d'étouffoir^M
Moderatorfilz^M
sordina^F
strings
cuerdas^F
cordes^F
Saitenbezug^M
corde^F
treble bridge
puente^M de los altos^M
chevalet^M des aigus^M
Diskantsteg^M
ponticello^M degli acuti^M
bass bridge
puente^M de los bajos^M
chevalet^M des basses^F
Basssteg^M
ponticello^M dei bassi^M
pedal rod
varilla^F del pedal^M
tringle^F de pédale^F
Pedalstange^F
leva^F del pedale^M
soft pedal
pedal^M suave
pédale^F douce
Pianopedal^N
pedale^M del piano^M
muffler pedal
pedal^M de la sordina^F
pédale^F de sourdine^F
Moderatorpedal^N
pedale^M della sordina^F
damper pedal
pedal^M fuerte
pédale^F forte
Fortepedal^N
pedale^M di risonanza^F

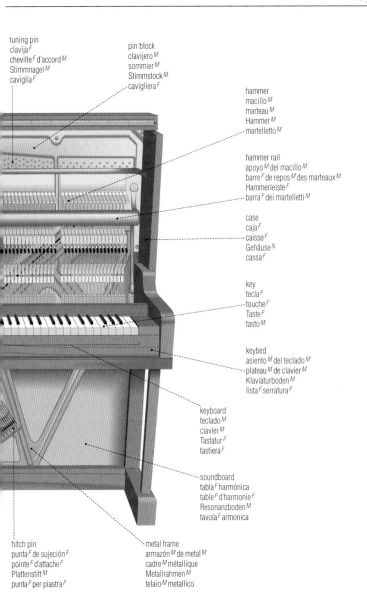

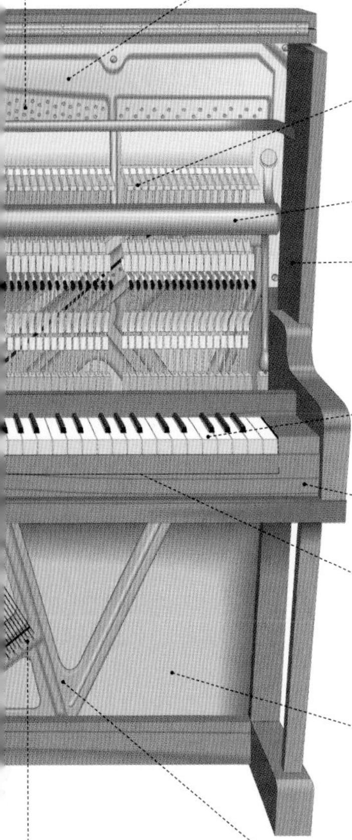

tuning pin
clavija[F]
cheville[F] d'accord[M]
Stimmnagel[M]
caviglia[F]

pin block
clavijero[M]
sommier[M]
Stimmstock[M]
cavigliera[F]

hammer
macillo[M]
marteau[M]
Hammer[M]
martelletto[M]

hammer rail
apoyo[M] del macillo[M]
barre[F] de repos[M] des marteaux[M]
Hammerleiste[F]
barra[F] dei martelletti[M]

case
caja[F]
caisse[F]
Gehäuse[N]
cassa[F]

key
tecla[F]
touche[F]
Taste[F]
tasto[M]

keybed
asiento[M] del teclado[M]
plateau[M] de clavier[M]
Klaviaturboden[M]
lista[F] serratura[F]

keyboard
teclado[M]
clavier[M]
Tastatur[F]
tastiera[F]

soundboard
tabla[F] harmónica
table[F] d'harmonie[F]
Resonanzboden[M]
tavola[F] armonica

hitch pin
punta[F] de sujeción[F]
pointe[F] d'attache[F]
Plattenstift[M]
punta[F] per piastra[F]

metal frame
armazón[M] de metal[M]
cadre[M] métallique
Metallrahmen[M]
telaio[M] metallico

upright piano action
mecanismo^M del piano^M vertical
mécanique^F du piano^M droit
Klaviermechanik^F
meccanica^F del pianoforte^M verticale

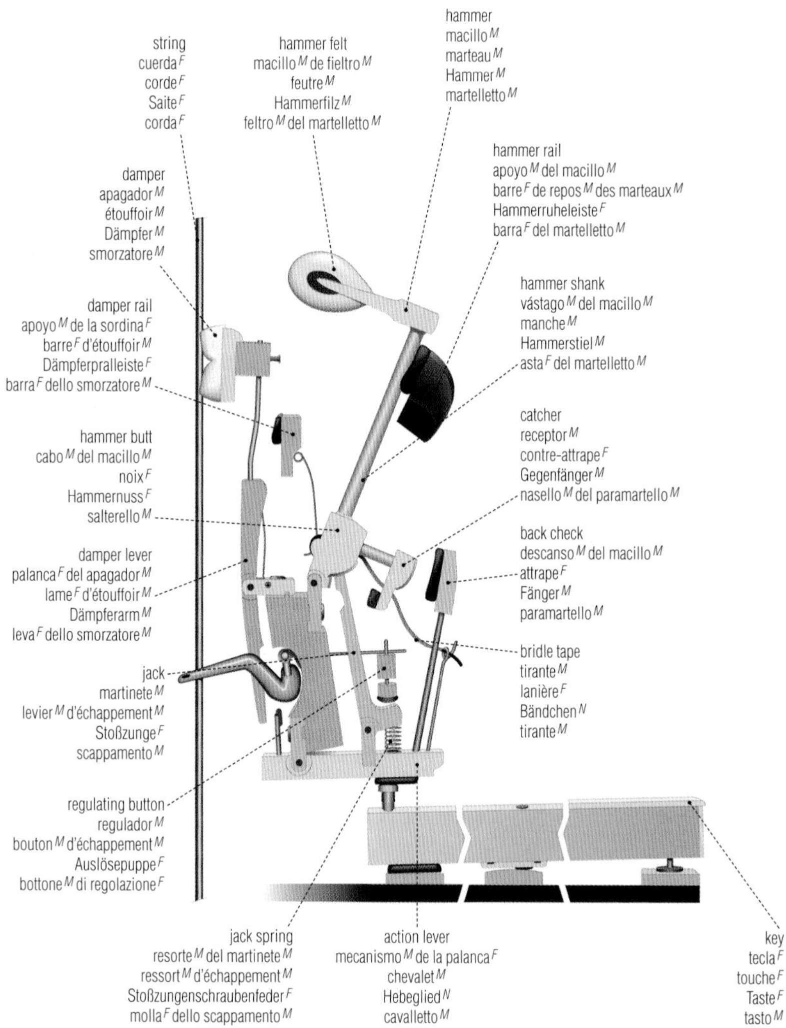
string
cuerda F
corde F
Saite F
corda F
hammer felt
macillo M de fieltro M
feutre M
Hammerfilz M
feltro M del martelletto M
hammer
macillo M
marteau M
Hammer M
martelletto M
hammer rail
apoyo M del macillo M
barre F de repos M des marteaux M
Hammerruheleiste F
barra F del martelletto M
damper
apagador M
étouffoir M
Dämpfer M
smorzatore M
hammer shank
vástago M del macillo M
manche M
Hammerstiel M
asta F del martelletto M
damper rail
apoyo M de la sordina F
barre F d'étouffoir M
Dämpferpralleiste F
barra F dello smorzatore M
catcher
receptor M
contre-attrape F
Gegenfänger M
nasello M del paramartello M
hammer butt
cabo M del macillo M
noix F
Hammernuss F
salterello M
back check
descanso M del macillo M
attrape F
Fänger M
paramartello M
damper lever
palanca F del apagador M
lame F d'étouffoir M
Dämpferarm M
leva F dello smorzatore M
bridle tape
tirante M
lanière F
Bändchen N
tirante M
jack
martinete M
levier M d'échappement M
Stoßzunge F
scappamento M
regulating button
regulador M
bouton M d'échappement M
Auslösepuppe F
bottone M di regolazione F
jack spring
resorte M del martinete M
ressort M d'échappement M
Stoßzungenschraubenfeder F
molla F dello scappamento M
action lever
mecanismo M de la palanca F
chevalet M
Hebeglied N
cavalletto M
key
tecla F
touche F
Taste F
tasto M

examples of keyboard instruments
ejemplos [M] de instrumentos [M] de teclado [M]
exemples [M] d'instruments [M] à clavier [M]
Beispiele [N] für Tasteninstrumente [N]
esempi [M] di strumenti [M] a tastiera [F]

concert grand
piano [M] de cola [F] de concierto [M]
piano [M] à queue [F] de concert [M]
Konzertflügel [M]
pianoforte [M] a coda [F] da concerto [M]

baby grand
piano [M] cuarto de cola [M]
piano [M] quart-de-queue [M]
Kleinflügel [M]
pianoforte [M] a un quarto [M] di coda [F]

boudoir grand
piano [M] de media cola [F]
piano [M] demi-queue [M]
Salonflügel [M]
pianoforte [M] a mezza coda [F]

harpsichord
clavecín [M]
clavecin [M]
Cembalo [N]
clavicembalo [M]

wind instruments

instrumentos[M] de viento[M] | instruments[M] à vent[M] | Blasinstrumente[N] | strumenti[M] a fiato[M]

saxophone
saxofón[M]
saxophone[M]
Saxophon[N]
sassofono[M]

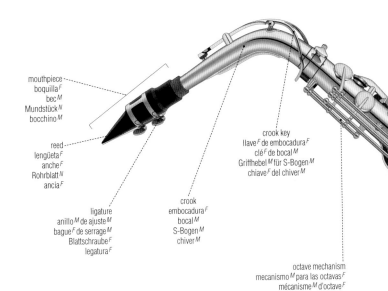

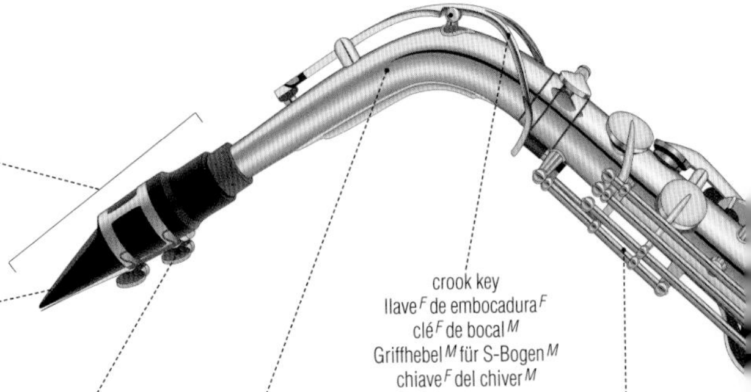

mouthpiece
boquilla[F]
bec[M]
Mundstück[N]
bocchino[M]
reed
lengüeta[F]
anche[F]
Rohrblatt[N]
ancia[F]
ligature
anillo[M] de ajuste[M]
bague[F] de serrage[M]
Blattschraube[F]
legatura[F]
crook
embocadura[F]
bocal[M]
S-Bogen[M]
chiver[M]
crook key
llave[F] de embocadura[F]
clé[F] de bocal[M]
Griffhebel[M] für S-Bogen[M]
chiave[F] del chiver[M]
octave mechanism
mecanismo[M] para las octavas[F]
mécanisme[M] d'octave[F]
Oktavmechanik[F]
meccanismo[M] dell'ottava[F]

double reed
doble caña[F]
anche[F] double
Doppelblatt[N]
ancia[F] doppia

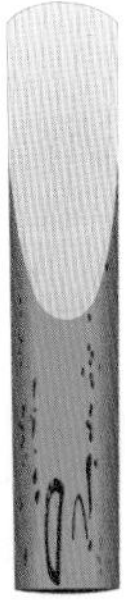

single reed
caña[F] simple
anche[F] simple
Rohrblatt[N]
ancia[F] semplice

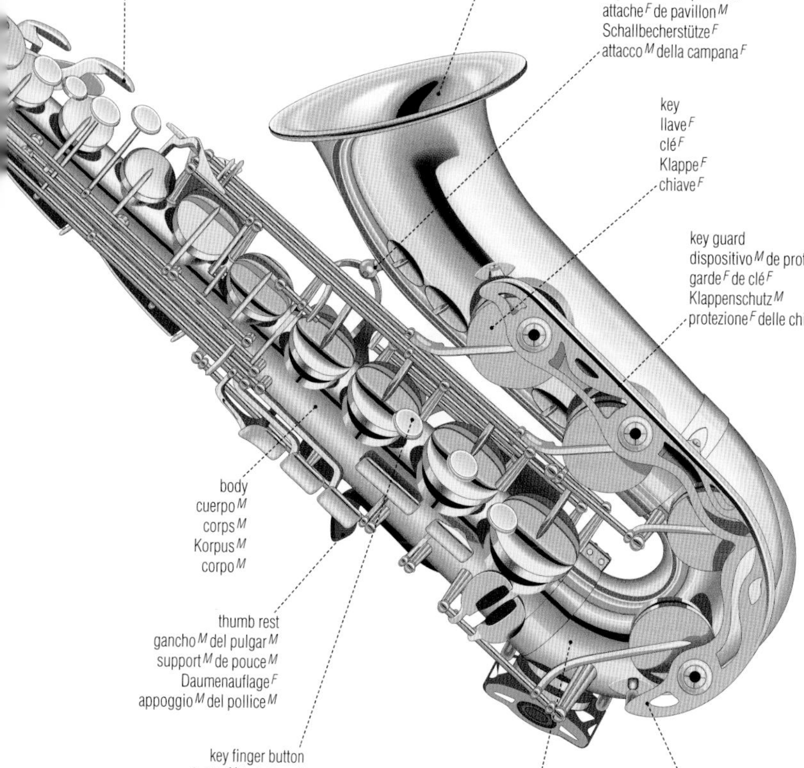
key lever
palanca F
levier M de clé F
Klappenstiel M
leva F della chiave F
bell
pabellón M
pavillon M
Trichter M
campana F
bell brace
sujetador M del pabellón M
attache F de pavillon M
Schallbecherstütze F
attacco M della campana F
key
llave F
clé F
Klappe F
chiave F
key guard
dispositivo M de protección F
garde F de clé F
Klappenschutz M
protezione F delle chiavi F
body
cuerpo M
corps M
Korpus M
corpo M
thumb rest
gancho M del pulgar M
support M de pouce M
Daumenauflage F
appoggio M del pollice M
key finger button
botón M de la llave F
bouton M de clé F
Klappendrücker M
tasto M
breech
culata F
culasse F
Bogen M
curva F
breech guard
protector M de la culata F
garde F de culasse F
Bogenschutz M
rinforzo M della curva F

wind instruments

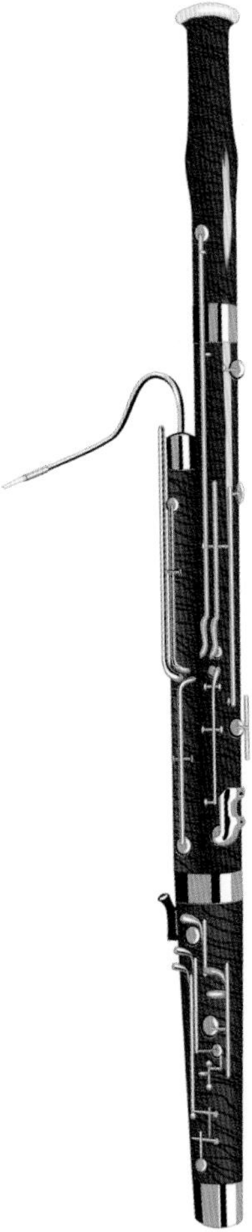

bassoon
fagot *M*
basson *M*
Fagott *N*
fagotto *M*

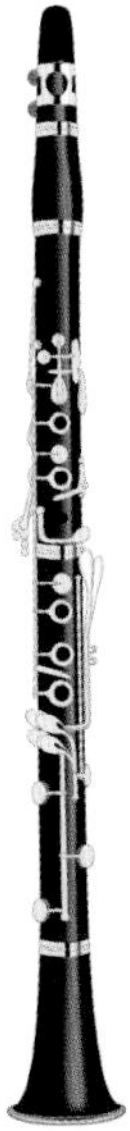

clarinet
clarinete *M*
clarinette *F*
Klarinette *F*
clarinetto *M*

piccolo
píccolo *M*
piccolo *M*
Pikkoloflöte *F*
ottavino *M*

oboe
oboe *M*
hautbois *M*
Oboe *F*
oboe *M*

transverse flute
flauta *F* travesera
flûte *F* traversière
Querflöte *F*
flauto *M* traverso

English horn
corno *M* inglés
cor *M* anglais
Englischhorn *N*
corno *M* inglese

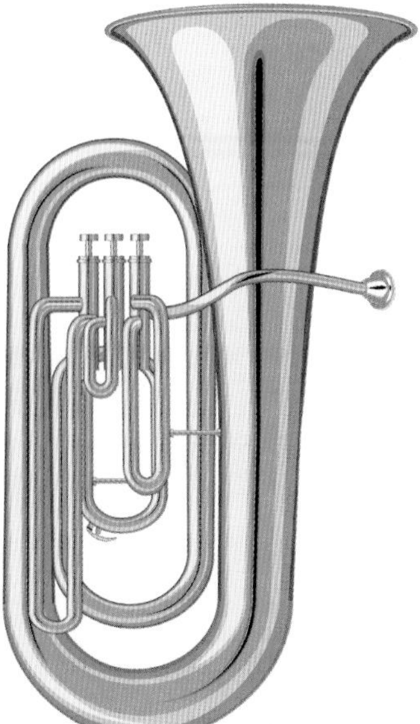

tuba
tuba *F*
tuba *M*
Tuba *F*
tuba *F*

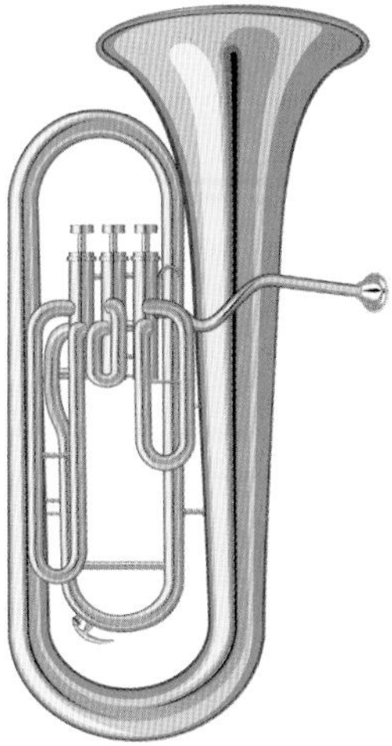

saxhorn
bombardino *M*
saxhorn *M*
Saxhorn *N*
saxhorn *M*

French horn
corno *M* francés/trompa *F*
cor *M* d'harmonie *F*
Waldhorn *N*
corno *M*

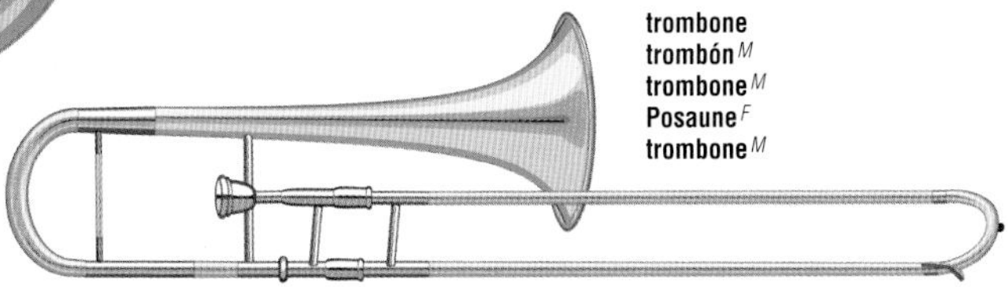

trombone
trombón *M*
trombone *M*
Posaune *F*
trombone *M*

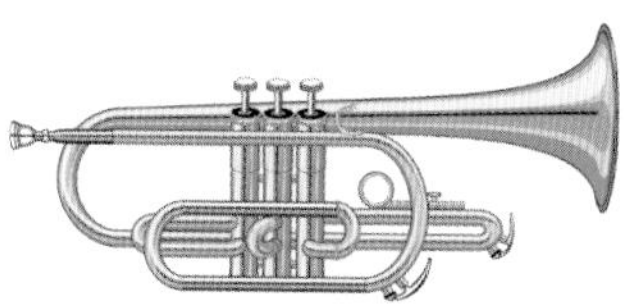

cornet
cornetín *M*
cornet *M* à pistons *M*
Kornett *N*
cornetta *F*

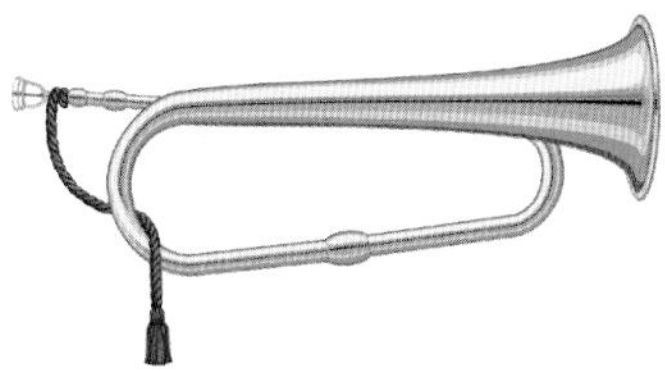

bugle
clarín *M*
clairon *M*
Bügelhorn *N*
tromba *F* militare

trumpet
trompeta [F]
trompette [F]
Trompete [F]
tromba [F]

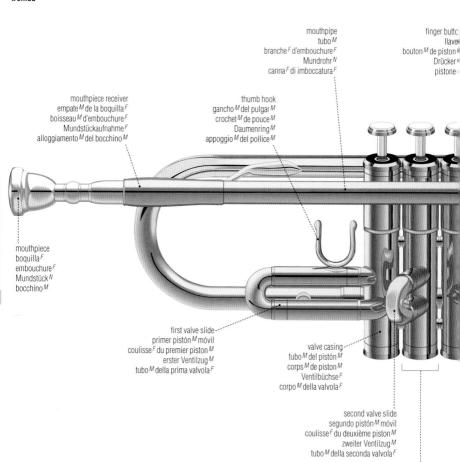

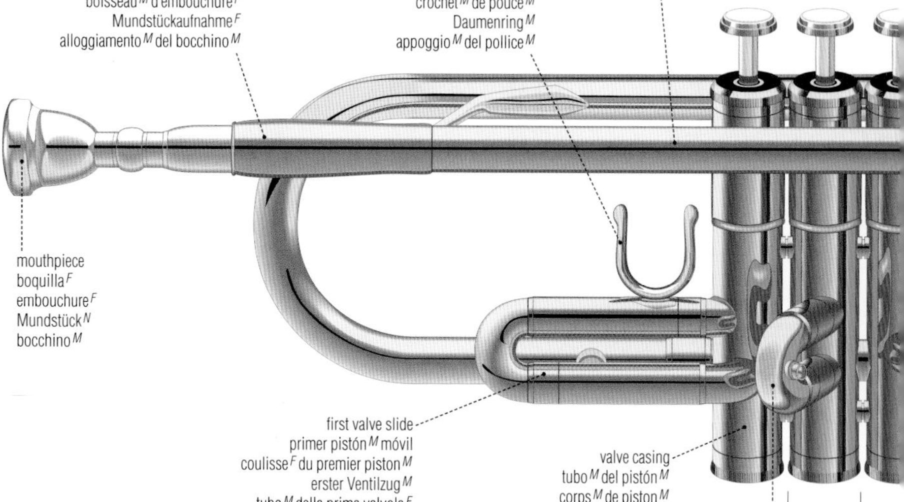
mouthpipe
tubo [M]
branche [F] d'embouchure [F]
Mundrohr [N]
canna [F] di imboccatura [F]
llave
bouton [M] de piston
pistone
mouthpiece receiver
empate [M] de la boquilla [F]
boisseau [M] d'embouchure [F]
Mundstückaufnahme [F]
alloggiamento [M] del bocchino [M]
thumb hook
gancho [M] del pulgar [M]
crochet [M] de pouce [M]
Daumenring [M]
appoggio [M] del pollice [M]
mouthpiece
boquilla [F]
embouchure [F]
Mundstück [N]
bocchino [M]
first valve slide
primer pistón [M] móvil
coulisse [F] du premier piston [M]
erster Ventilzug [M]
tubo [M] della prima valvola [F]
valve casing
tubo [M] del pistón [M]
corps [M] de piston [M]
Ventilbüchse [F]
corpo [M] della valvola [F]
second valve slide
segundo pistón [M] móvil
coulisse [F] du deuxième piston [M]
zweiter Ventilzug [M]
tubo [M] della seconda valvola [F]
valve
pistón [M]
piston [M]
Ventil [N]
valvola [F]

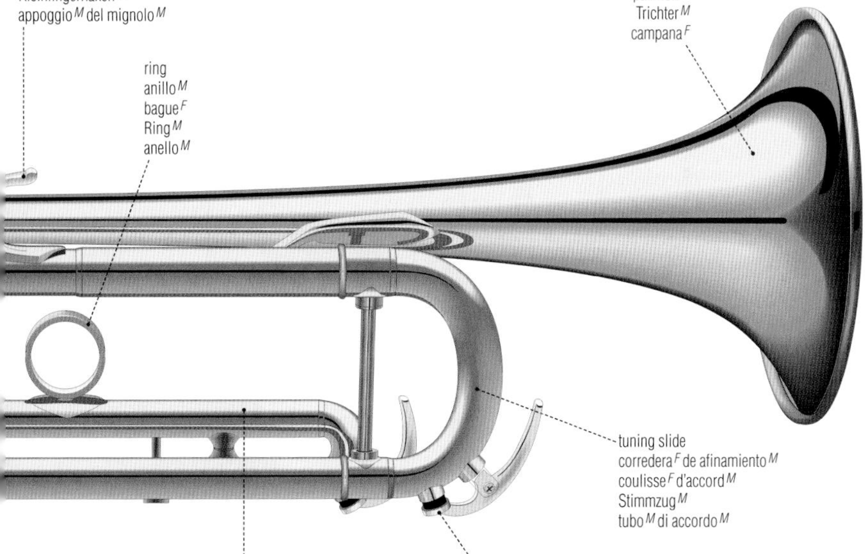
little finger hook
gancho M del meñique M
crochet M de petit doigt M
Kleinfingerhaken M
appoggio M del mignolo M
ring
anillo M
bague F
Ring M
anello M
bell
pabellón M
pavillon M
Trichter M
campana F
tuning slide
corredera F de afinamiento M
coulisse F d'accord M
Stimmzug M
tubo M di accordo M
third valve slide
tercer pistón M móvil
coulisse F du troisième piston M
dritter Ventilzug M
tubo M della terza valvola F
water key
llave F para agua F
soupape F d'évacuation F
Wasserklappe F
chiave F dell'acqua F

mute
sordina F
sourdine F
Dämpfer M
sordina F

percussion instruments

instrumentos[M] de percusión[F] | instruments[M] à percussion[F] | Schlaginstrumente[N] | strumenti[M] a percussione[F]

drums
batería[F]
batterie[F]
Trommeln[F]
batteria[F]

cymbal
platillo[M] suspendido
cymbale[F] suspendue
Becken[N]
piatto[M]
tom-tom
tam-tam[M]
tam-tam[M]
Tomtom[N]
tom tom[M]
high-hat cymbal
platillo[M] high hat
cymbale[F] charleston
Charlestonmaschine[F]
charleston[M]
batter head
parche[M] superior
peau[F] de batterie[F]
Trommelfell[N]
battitoia[F]
snare drum
caja[F] clara
caisse[F] claire
kleine Trommel[F]
cassa[F] chiara
bass drum
bombo[M]
grosse caisse[F]
Basstrommel[F]
grancassa[F]
tension screw
clavija[F] de tensión[F]
vis[F] de tension[F]
Stellschraube[F]
tirante[M] a vite[F]
tenor drum
tamboril[M]
caisse[F] roulante
Standtom[N]
tamburo[M] tenore[M]
mallet
palillo[M]
mailloche[F]
Schlägel[M]
mazza[F]
pedal
pedal[M]
pédale[F]
Pedal[N]
pedale[M]
spur
espolón[M]
éperon[M]
Feststellspitze[F]
piedino[M]

kettledrum
timbal M
timbale F
Kesselpauke F
timpano M

batter head
parche M superior
peau F de batterie F
Trommelfell N
battitoia F
shell
concha F
fût M
Kessel M
caldaia F
tie rod
barra F sujetadora
tirant M
Spannschraube F
tirante M a vite F
metal counterhoop
arco M tensor
cercle M de serrage M
Metallspannreifen M
cerchio M di serraggio M
tuning gauge
afinación F
manomètre M d'accord M
Stimmanzeiger M
chiavi F di tensione F
strut
puntal M
châssis M
Strebe F
gabbia F
tension rod
varilla F de tensión F
tringle F de tension F
Stimmeinrichtung F
tirante M
crown
corona F
couronne F
Aufhängung F
corona F
caster
ruedecilla F
roulette F
Rolle F
rotella F orientabile
foot
pata F
pied M
Bodenplatte F
base F
pedal
pedal M
pédale F
Pedal N
pedale M

percussion instruments

snare drum
caja [F] clara
caisse [F] claire
kleine Trommel [F]
cassa [F] chiara

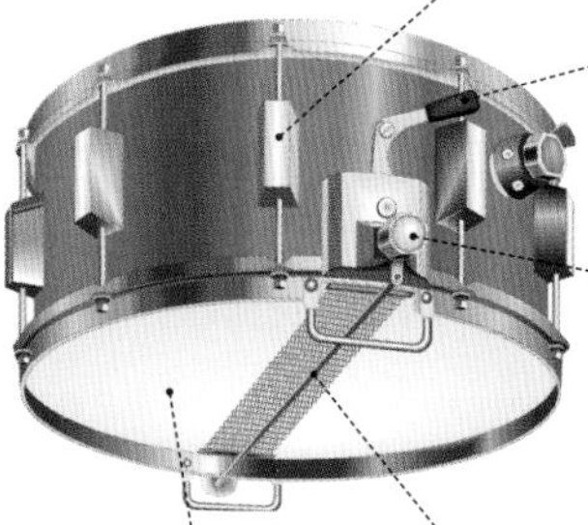

lug
sujetador [M]
attache [F]
Böckchen [N]
blocchetto [M]

tension rod
varilla [F] de tensión [F]
tringle [F] de tension [F]
Stimmeinrichtung [F]
tirante [M]

snare strainer
tensor [M] de las cuerdas [F]
tendeur [M] de timbre [M]
Schnarrsaitenspanner [M]
tirante [M] della cordiera [F]

snare head
parche [M] inferior
peau [F] de timbre [M]
Resonanzfell [N]
bordoniera [F]

snare
cuerdas [F]
cordes [F] de timbre [M]
Schnarrsaite [F]
cordiera [F]

tambourine
pandereta [F]
tambour [M] de basque [M]
Tamburin [N]
tamburello [M]

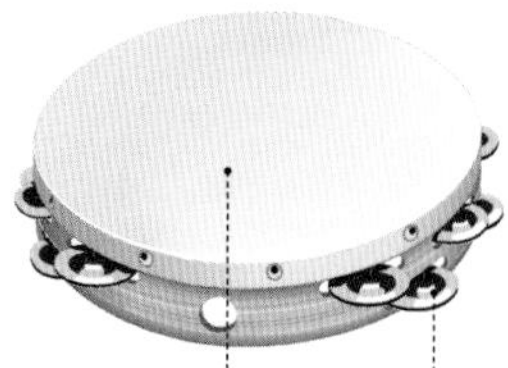

head
parche [M]
peau [F]
Fell [N]
membrana [F]

jingle
cascabel [M]
cymbalette [F]
Schelle [F]
sonagli [M]

bongos
bongos [M]
bongo [M]
Bongos [N]
bongos [M]

wire brush
escobilla [F] metálica
balai [M] métallique
Jazzbesen [M]
spazzola [F] metallica

sticks
baquetas [F]
baguettes [F]
Stöcke [M]
bacchette [F]

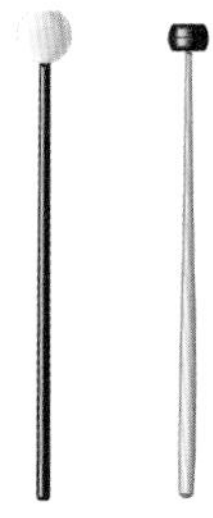

mallets
maza [F]
mailloches [F]
Schlägel [M]
mazze [F]

sleigh bells
cascabeles[M]
grelots[M]
Schellen[F]
sonagli[M]

set of bells
campanillas[F]
clochettes[F]
Glockenband[N]
campanelle[F]

castanets
castañuelas[F]
castagnettes[F]
Kastagnetten[F]
nacchere[F]

gong
gong[M]
gong[M]
Gong[M]
gong[M]

triangle
triángulo[M]
triangle[M]
Triangel[M]
triangolo[M]

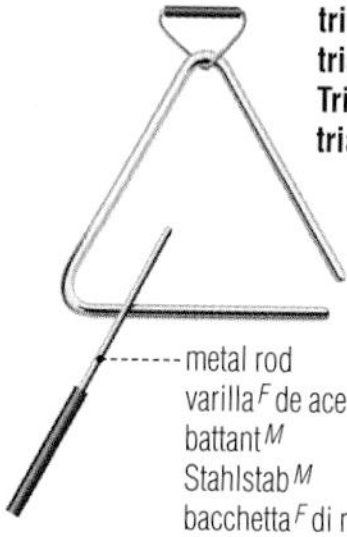

metal rod
varilla[F] de acero[M]
battant[M]
Stahlstab[M]
bacchetta[F] di metallo[M]

sistrum
sistro[M]
sistre[M]
Sistrum[N]
sistro[M]

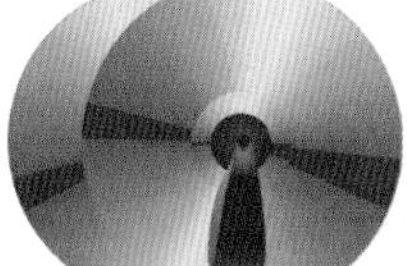

cymbals
platillos[M]
cymbales[F]
Becken[N]
piatti[M]

xylophone
xilófono[M]
xylophone[M]
Xylophon[N]
xilofono[M]

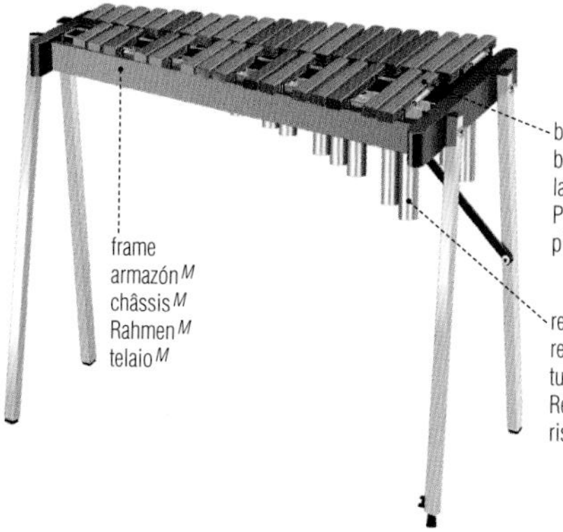

bar
barra[F]
lame[F]
Platte[F]
piastra[F]

frame
armazón[M]
châssis[M]
Rahmen[M]
telaio[M]

resonator
resonador[M]
tube[M] de résonance[F]
Resonanzröhren[F]
risonatore[M]

tubular bells
campanas[F] **tubulares**
carillon[M] **tubulaire**
Röhrenglocken[F]
campane[F] **tubolari**

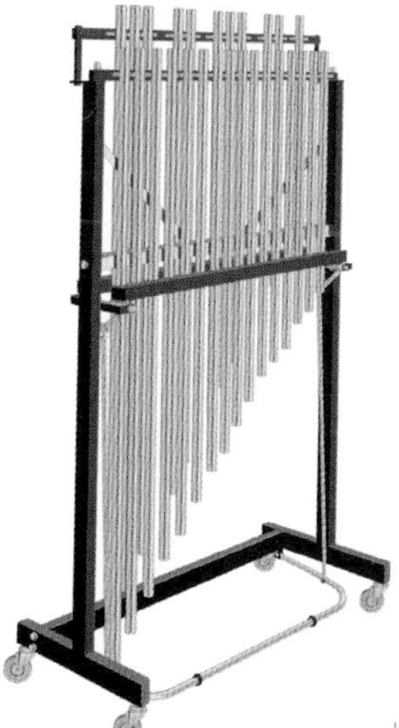

Greek temple

templo[M] griego | temple[M] grec | griechischer Tempel[M] | tempio[M] greco

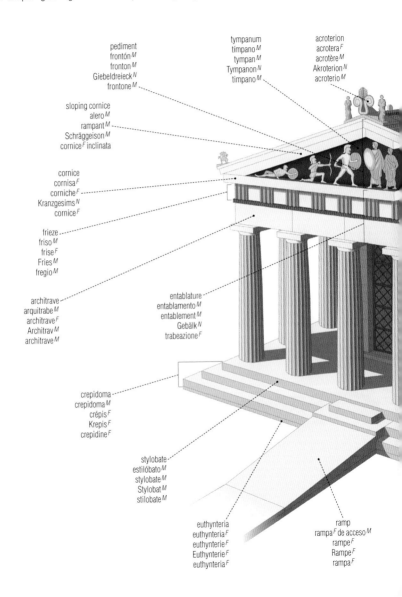

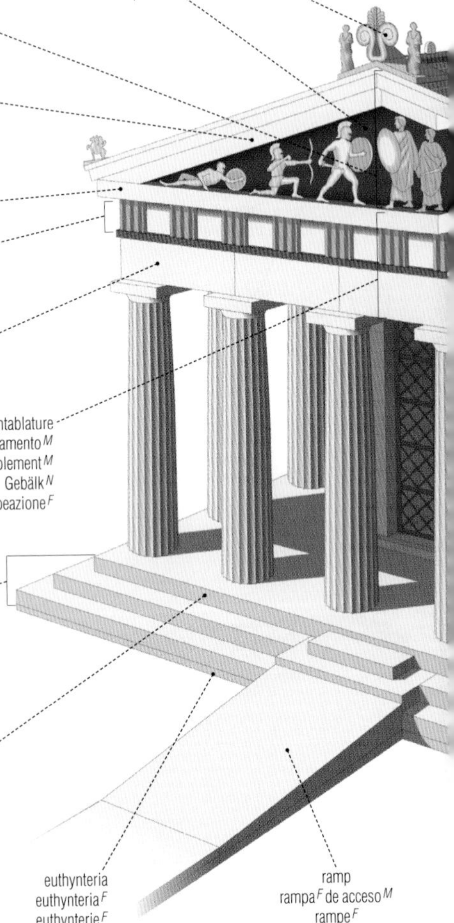
pediment
frontón M
fronton M
Giebeldreieck N
frontone M
tympanum
tímpano M
tympan M
Tympanon N
timpano M
acroterion
acrotera F
acrotère M
Akroterion N
acroterio M
sloping cornice
alero M
rampant M
Schräggeison M
cornice F inclinata
cornice
cornisa F
corniche F
Kranzgesims N
cornice F
frieze
friso M
frise F
Fries M
fregio M
architrave
arquitrabe M
architrave F
Architrav M
architrave M
entablature
entablamento M
entablement M
Gebälk N
trabeazione F
crepidoma
crepidoma M
crépis F
Krepis F
crepidine F
stylobate
estilóbato M
stylobate M
Stylobat M
stilobate M
euthynteria
euthynteria F
euthynterie F
Euthynterie F
euthynteria F
ramp
rampa F de acceso M
rampe F
Rampe F
rampa F

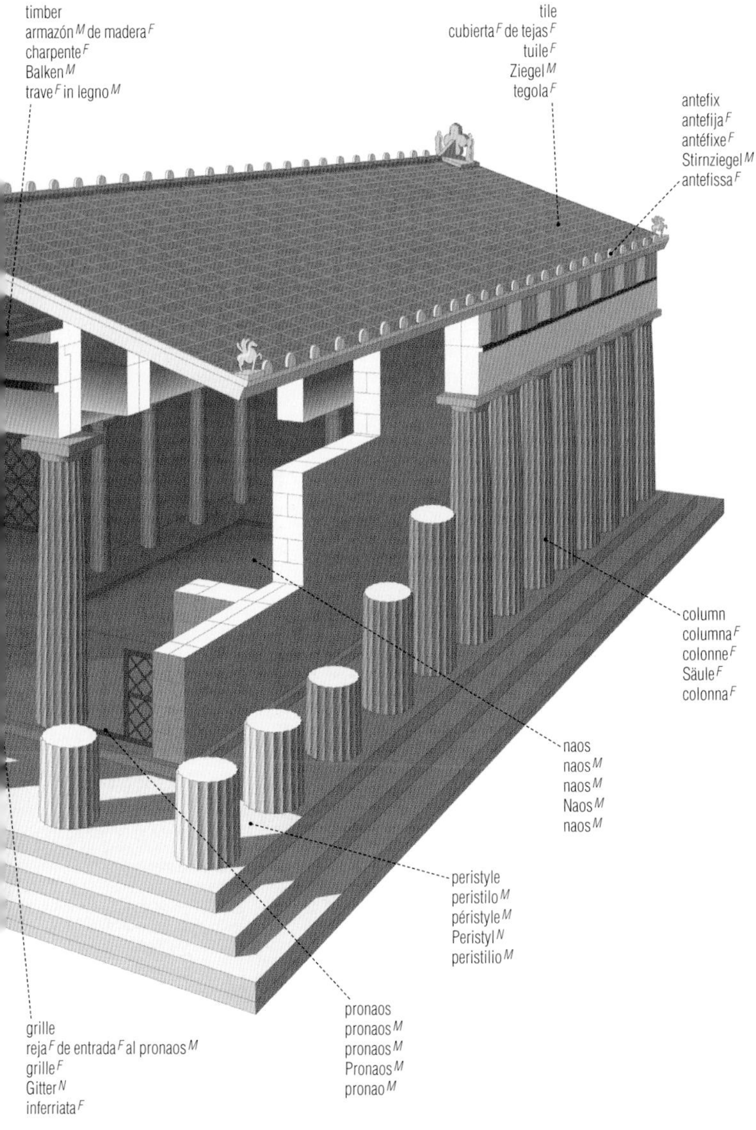
timber
armazón M de madera F
charpente F
Balken M
trave F in legno M
tile
cubierta F de tejas F
tuile F
Ziegel M
tegola F
antefix
antefija F
antéfixe F
Stirnziegel M
antefissa F
column
columna F
colonne F
Säule F
colonna F
naos
naos M
naos M
Naos M
naos M
peristyle
peristilo M
péristyle M
Peristyl N
peristilio M
grille
reja F de entrada F al pronaos M
grille F
Gitter N
inferriata F
pronaos
pronaos M
pronaos M
Pronaos M
pronao M

pyramid

pirámide[F] | pyramide[F] | Pyramide[F] | piramide[F]

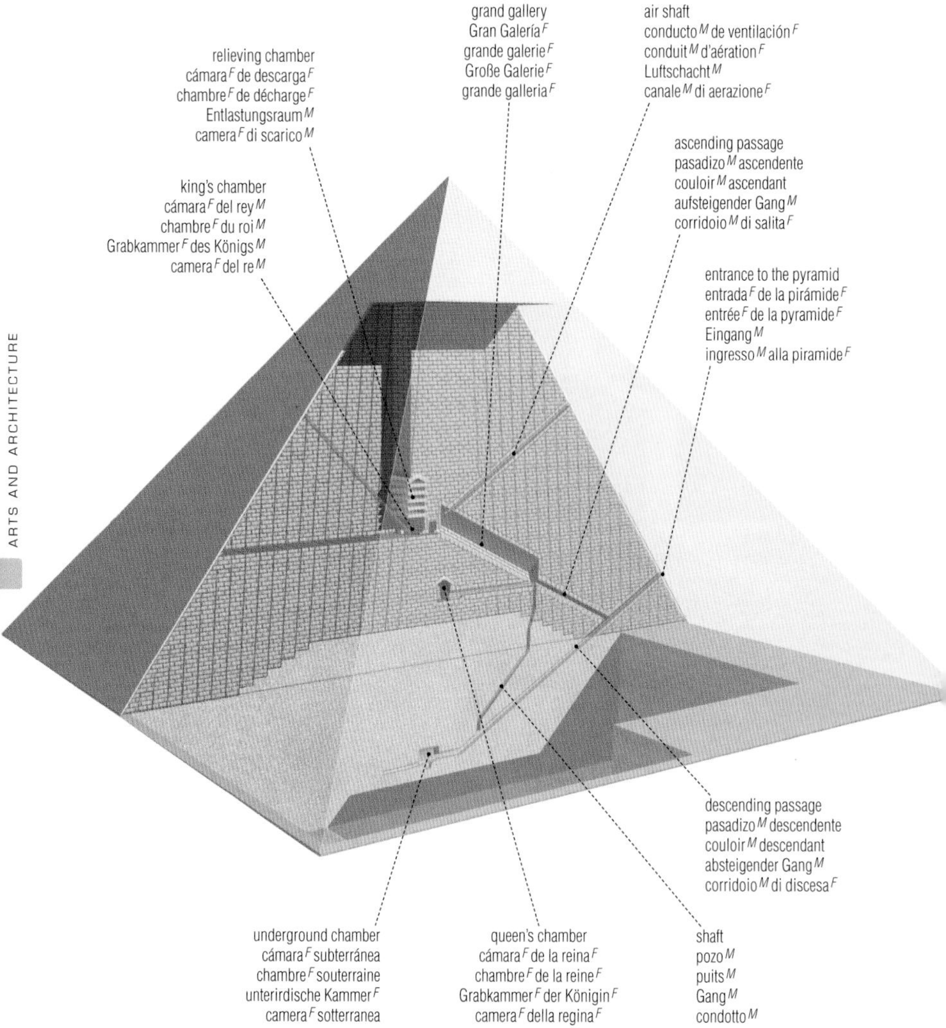
grand gallery
Gran Galería[F]
grande galerie[F]
Große Galerie[F]
grande galleria[F]
air shaft
conducto[M] de ventilación[F]
conduit[M] d'aération[F]
Luftschacht[M]
canale[M] di aerazione[F]
relieving chamber
cámara[F] de descarga[F]
chambre[F] de décharge[F]
Entlastungsraum[M]
camera[F] di scarico[M]
ascending passage
pasadizo[M] ascendente
couloir[M] ascendant
aufsteigender Gang[M]
corridoio[M] di salita[F]
king's chamber
cámara[F] del rey[M]
chambre[F] du roi[M]
Grabkammer[F] des Königs[M]
camera[F] del re[M]
entrance to the pyramid
entrada[F] de la pirámide[F]
entrée[F] de la pyramide[F]
Eingang[M]
ingresso[M] alla piramide[F]
descending passage
pasadizo[M] descendente
couloir[M] descendant
absteigender Gang[M]
corridoio[M] di discesa[F]
underground chamber
cámara[F] subterránea
chambre[F] souterraine
unterirdische Kammer[F]
camera[F] sotterranea
queen's chamber
cámara[F] de la reina[F]
chambre[F] de la reine[F]
Grabkammer[F] der Königin[F]
camera[F] della regina[F]
shaft
pozo[M]
puits[M]
Gang[M]
condotto[M]

architectural styles

estilos[M] arquitectónicos | styles[M] d'architecture[F] | Baustile[M] | stili[M] architettonici

Doric order
orden[M] dórico
ordre[M] dorique
dorische Säulenordnung[F]
ordine[M] dorico

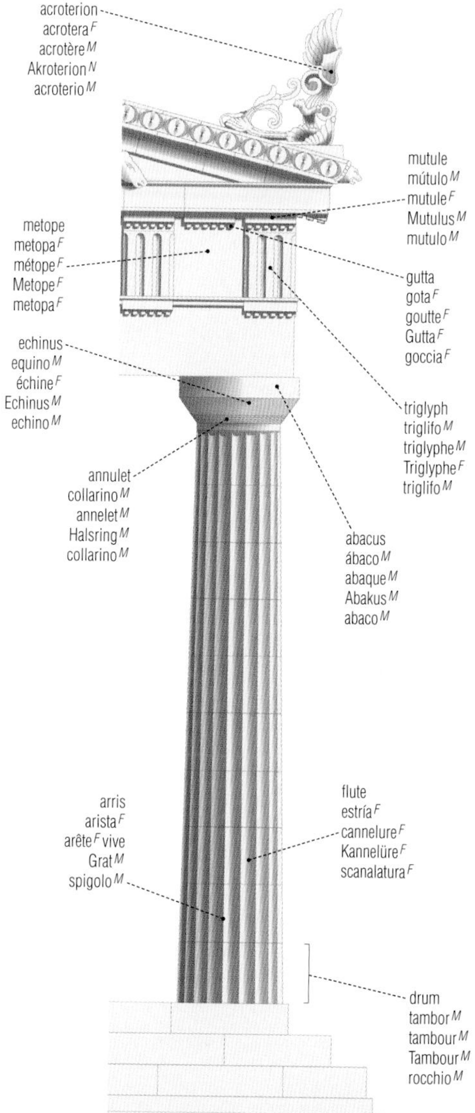
acroterion
acrotera F
acrotère M
Akroterion N
acroterio M
mutule
mútulo M
mutule F
Mutulus M
mutulo M
metope
metopa F
métope F
Metope F
metopa F
gutta
gota F
goutte F
Gutta F
goccia F
echinus
equino M
échine F
Echinus M
echino M
triglyph
triglifo M
triglyphe M
Triglyphe F
triglifo M
annulet
collarino M
annelet M
Halsring M
collarino M
abacus
ábaco M
abaque M
Abakus M
abaco M
flute
estría F
cannelure F
Kannelüre F
scanalatura F
arris
arista F
arête F vive
Grat M
spigolo M
drum
tambor M
tambour M
Tambour M
rocchio M

architectural styles

Ionic order
orden [M] jónico
ordre [M] ionique
ionische Säulenordnung [F]
ordine [M] ionico

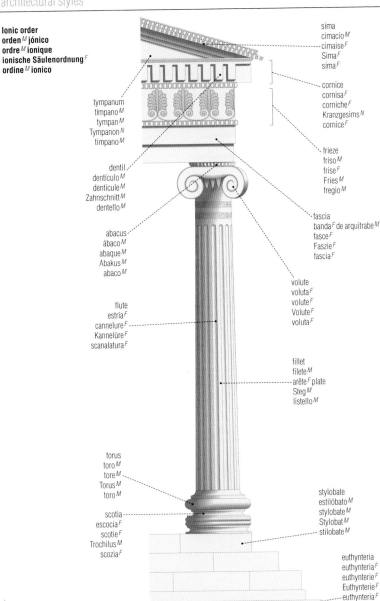

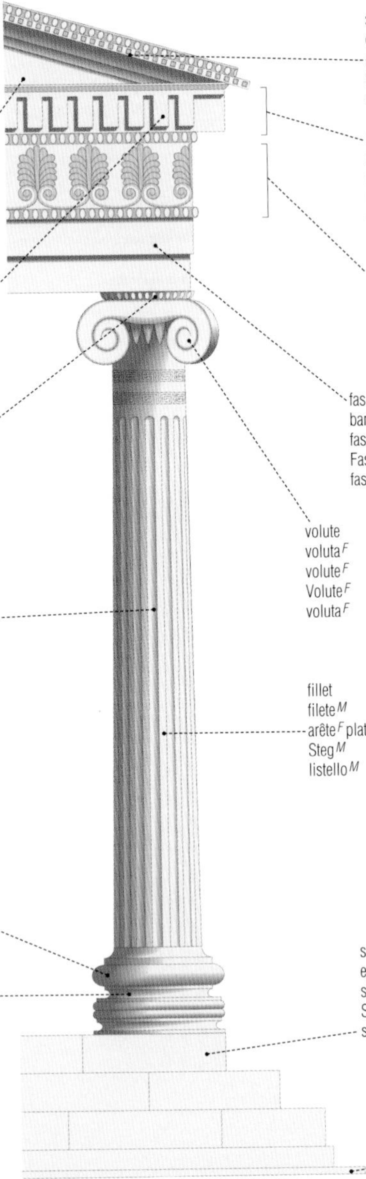

sima
cimacio [M]
cimaise [F]
Sima [F]
sima [F]

cornice
cornisa [F]
corniche [F]
Kranzgesims [N]
cornice [F]

tympanum
tímpano [M]
tympan [M]
Tympanon [N]
timpano [M]

frieze
friso [M]
frise [F]
Fries [M]
fregio [M]

dentil
dentículo [M]
denticule [M]
Zahnschnitt [M]
dentello [M]

fascia
banda [F] de arquitrabe [M]
fasce [F]
Faszie [F]
fascia [F]

abacus
ábaco [M]
abaque [M]
Abakus [M]
abaco [M]

volute
voluta [F]
volute [F]
Volute [F]
voluta [F]

flute
estría [F]
cannelure [F]
Kannelüre [F]
scanalatura [F]

fillet
filete [M]
arête [F] plate
Steg [M]
listello [M]

torus
toro [M]
tore [M]
Torus [M]
toro [M]

stylobate
estilóbato [M]
stylobate [M]
Stylobat [M]
stilobate [M]

scotia
escocia [F]
scotie [F]
Trochilus [M]
scozia [F]

euthynteria
euthynteria [F]
euthynterie [F]
Euthynterie [F]
euthynteria [F]

Corinthian order
orden^M corintio
ordre^M corinthien
korinthische Säulenordnung^F
ordine^M corinzio

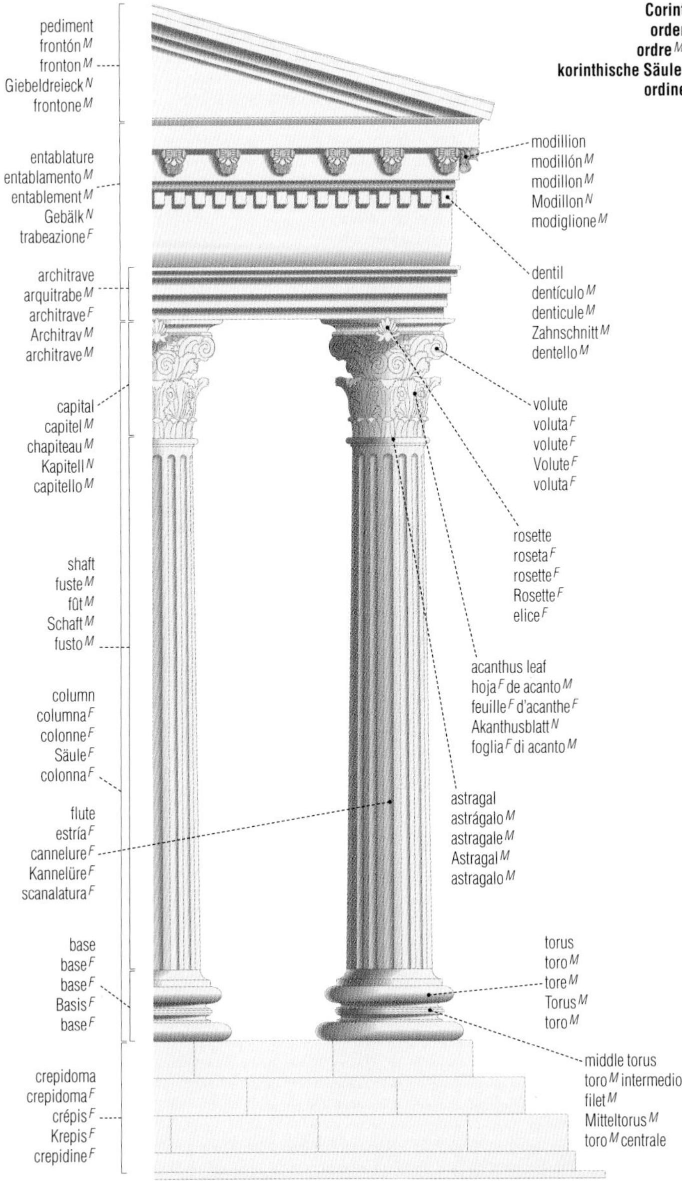
pediment
frontón M
fronton M
Giebeldreieck N
frontone M
entablature
entablamento M
entablement M
Gebälk N
trabeazione F
architrave
arquitrabe M
architrave F
Architrav M
architrave M
capital
capitel M
chapiteau M
Kapitell N
capitello M
shaft
fuste M
fût M
Schaft M
fusto M
column
columna F
colonne F
Säule F
colonna F
flute
estría F
cannelure F
Kannelüre F
scanalatura F
base
base F
base F
Basis F
base F
crepidoma
crepidoma F
crépis F
Krepis F
crepidine F
modillion
modillón M
modillon M
Modillon N
modiglione M
dentil
dentículo M
denticule M
Zahnschnitt M
dentello M
volute
voluta F
volute F
Volute F
voluta F
rosette
roseta F
rosette F
Rosette F
elice F
acanthus leaf
hoja F de acanto M
feuille F d'acanthe F
Akanthusblatt N
foglia F di acanto M
astragal
astrágalo M
astragale M
Astragal M
astragalo M
torus
toro M
tore M
Torus M
toro M
middle torus
toro M intermedio
filet M
Mitteltorus M
toro M centrale

Roman house

casa^F romana | maison^F romaine | römisches Wohnhaus^N | casa^F romana

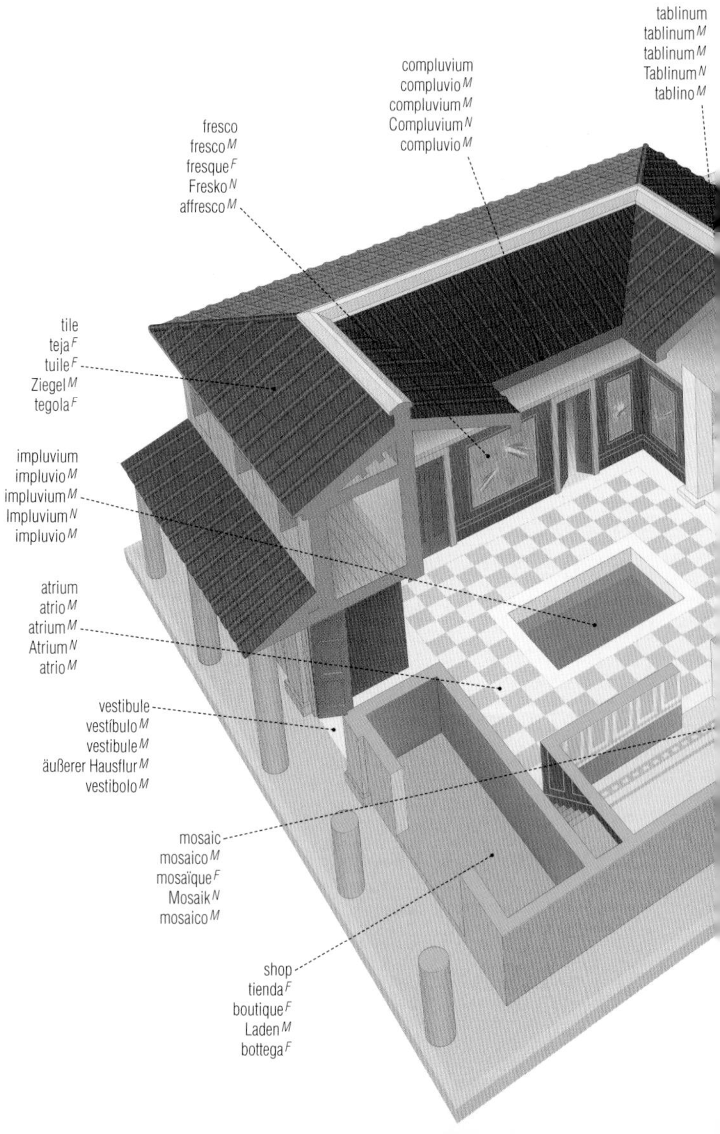
tablinum
tablinum M
tablinum M
Tablinum N
tablino M
compluvium
compluvio M
compluvium M
Compluvium N
compluvio M
fresco
fresco M
fresque F
Fresko N
affresco M
tile
teja F
tuile F
Ziegel M
tegola F
impluvium
impluvio M
impluvium M
Impluvium N
impluvio M
atrium
atrio M
atrium M
Atrium N
atrio M
vestibule
vestíbulo M
vestibule M
äußerer Hausflur M
vestibolo M
mosaic
mosaico M
mosaïque F
Mosaik N
mosaico M
shop
tienda F
boutique F
Laden M
bottega F

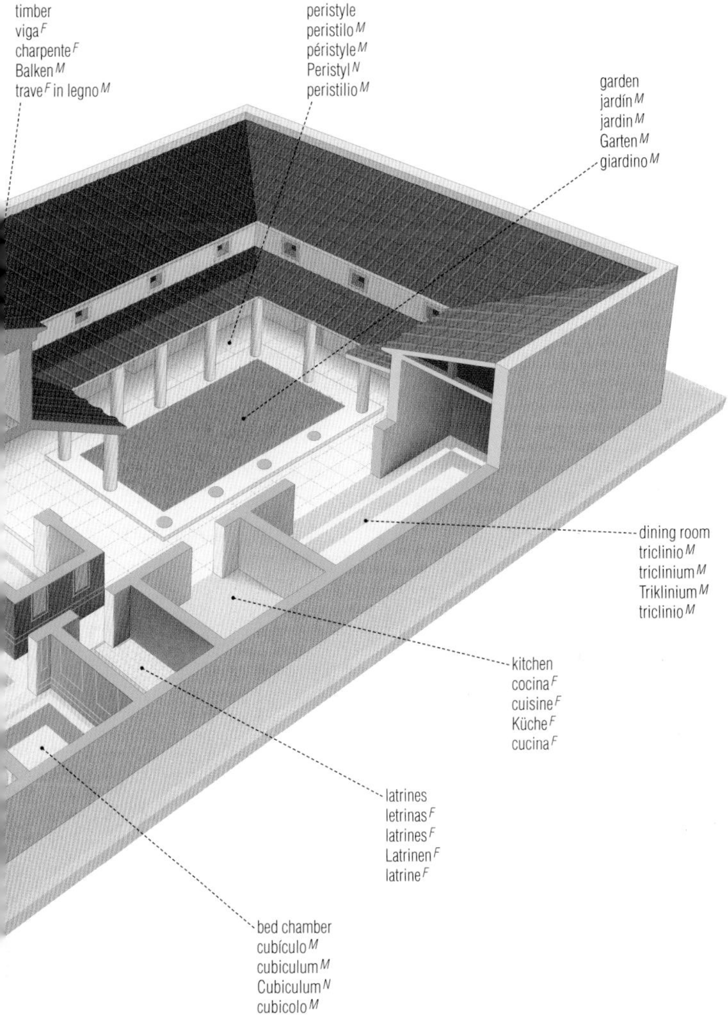
timber
viga F
charpente F
Balken M
trave F in legno M
peristyle
peristilo M
péristyle M
Peristyl N
peristilio M
garden
jardín M
jardin M
Garten M
giardino M
dining room
triclinio M
triclinium M
Triklinium M
triclinio M
kitchen
cocina F
cuisine F
Küche F
cucina F
latrines
letrinas F
latrines F
Latrinen F
latrine F
bed chamber
cubículo M
cubiculum M
Cubiculum N
cubicolo M

Roman amphitheater

anfiteatro^M romano | amphithéâtre^M romain | römisches Amphitheater^N | anfiteatro^M romano

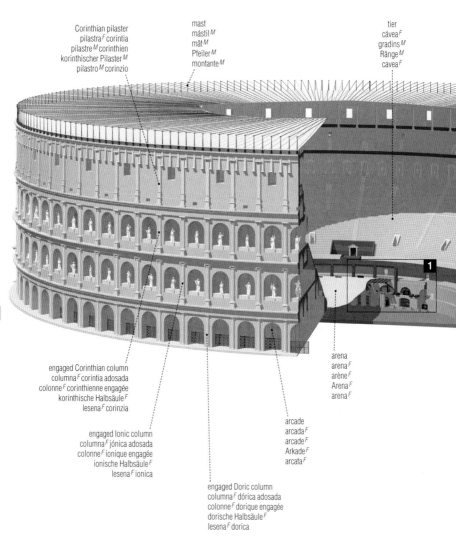

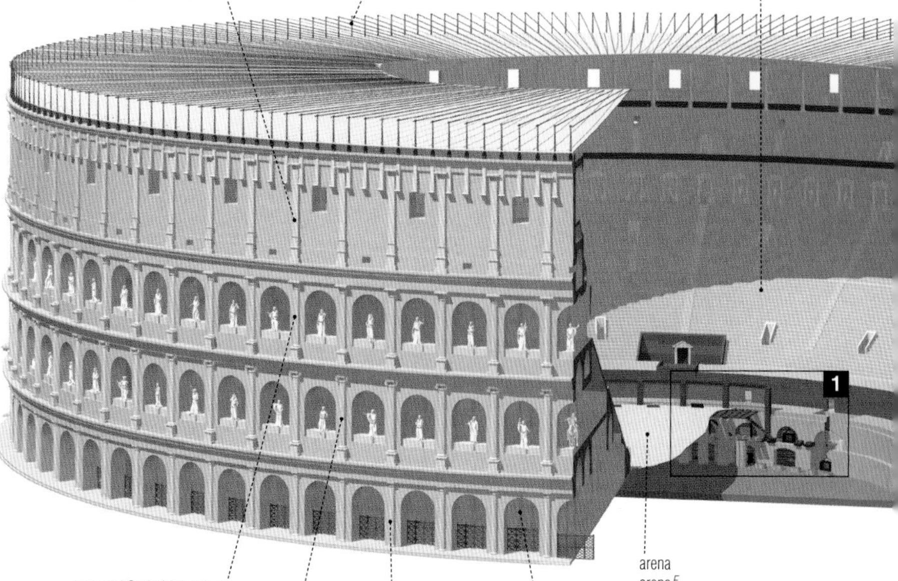
Corinthian pilaster
pilastra^F corintia
pilastre^M corinthien
korinthischer Pilaster^M
pilastro^M corinzio
mast
mástil^M
mât^M
Pfeiler^M
montante^M
tier
cávea^F
gradins^M
Ränge^M
cavea^F
1
arena
arena^F
arène^F
Arena^F
arena^F
engaged Corinthian column
columna^F corintia adosada
colonne^F corinthienne engagée
korinthische Halbsäule^F
lesena^F corinzia
arcade
arcada^F
arcade^F
Arkade^F
arcata^F
engaged Ionic column
columna^F jónica adosada
colonne^F ionique engagée
ionische Halbsäule^F
lesena^F ionica
engaged Doric column
columna^F dórica adosada
colonne^F dorique engagée
dorische Halbsäule^F
lesena^F dorica

velarium
velarium M
velarium M
Velarium N
velario M
barrel vault
bóveda F de cañón M
voûte F en berceau M
Tonnengewölbe N
volta F a botte F

underground
subterráneo M
sous-sol M
unterirdische Anlagen F
sotterraneo M

1
elevator
elevador M
ascenseur M
Aufzug M
ascensore M
cage
jaula F
cage F
Käfig M
gabbia F
trapdoor
trampilla F
trappe F
Falltür F
botola F
arena
arena F
arène F
Arena F
arena F
ramp
rampa F
rampe F
Rampe F
rampa F
cell
celda F
cellule F
Zelle F
cella F

castle

castillo[M] | château[M] fort | Burg[F] | castello[M]

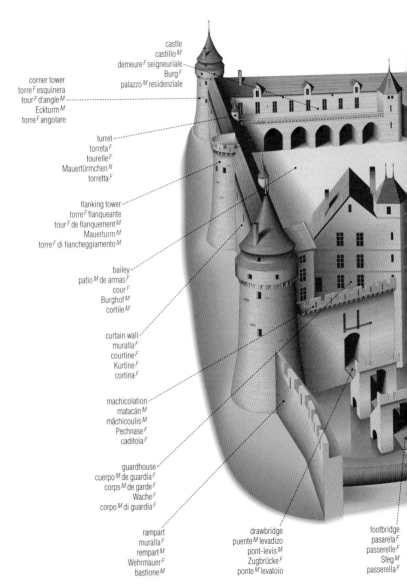

castle
castillo[M]
demeure[F] seigneuriale
Burg[F]
palazzo[M] residenziale
corner tower
torre[F] esquinera
tour[F] d'angle[M]
Eckturm[M]
torre[F] angolare
turret
torreta[F]
tourelle[F]
Mauertürmchen[N]
torretta[F]
flanking tower
torre[F] flanqueante
tour[F] de flanquement[M]
Mauerturm[M]
torre[F] di fiancheggiamento[M]
bailey
patio[M] de armas[F]
cour[F]
Burghof[M]
cortile[M]
curtain wall
muralla[F]
courtine[F]
Kurtine[F]
cortina[F]
machicolation
matacán[M]
mâchicoulis[M]
Pechnase[F]
caditoia[F]
guardhouse
cuerpo[M] de guardia[F]
corps[M] de garde[F]
Wache[F]
corpo[M] di guardia[F]
rampart
muralla[F]
rempart[M]
Wehrmauer[F]
bastione[M]
drawbridge
puente[M] levadizo
pont-levis[M]
Zugbrücke[F]
ponte[M] levatoio
footbridge
pasarela[F]
passerelle[F]
Steg[M]
passerella[F]

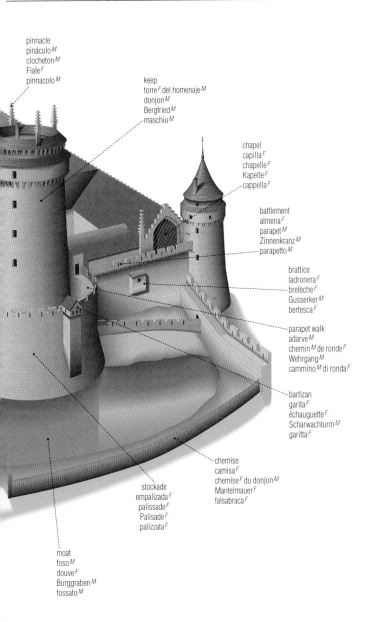

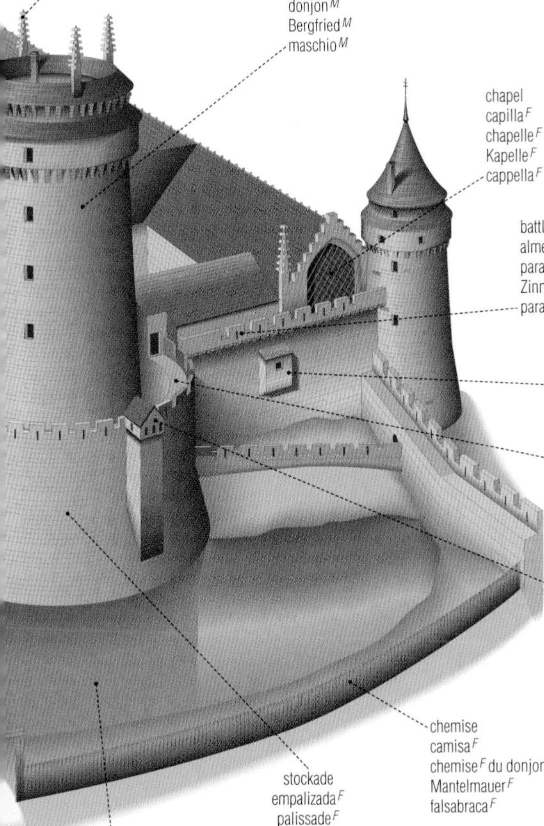
pinnacle
pináculo M
clocheton M
Fiale F
pinnacolo M
keep
torre F del homenaje M
donjon M
Bergfried M
maschio M
chapel
capilla F
chapelle F
Kapelle F
cappella F
battlement
almena F
parapet M
Zinnenkranz M
parapetto M
brattice
ladronera F
bretèche F
Gusserker M
bertesca F
parapet walk
adarve M
chemin M de ronde F
Wehrgang M
cammino M di ronda F
bartizan
garita F
échauguette F
Scharwachturm M
garitta F
chemise
camisa F
chemise F du donjon M
Mantelmauer F
falsabraca F
stockade
empalizada F
palissade F
Palisade F
palizzata F
moat
foso M
douve F
Burggraben M
fossato M

cathedral

catedral^{F} | cathédrale^{F} | Dom^{M} | cattedrale^{F}

Gothic cathedral
catedral^{F} gótica
cathédrale^{F} gothique
gotischer Dom^{M}
cattedrale^{F} gotica

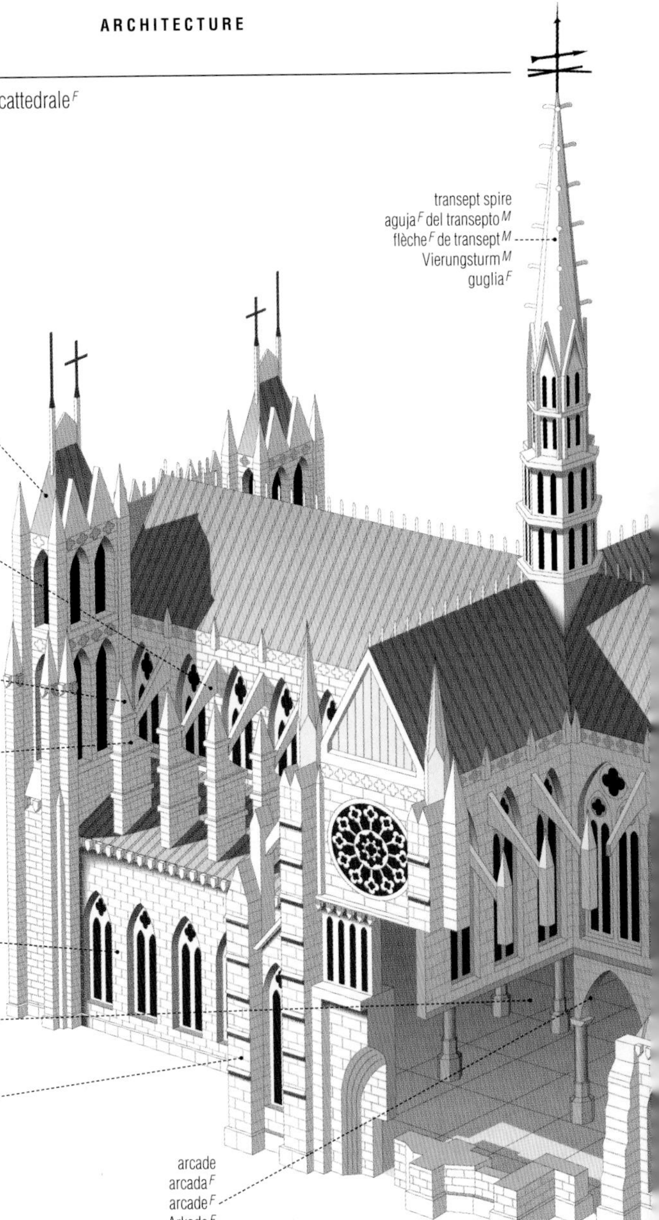

transept spire
aguja^{F} del transepto^{M}
flèche^{F} de transept^{M}
Vierungsturm^{M}
guglia^{F}
tower
torre^{F}
tour^{F}
Turm^{M}
torre^{F}
flying buttress
arbotante^{M}
arc^{M}-boutant
Strebebogen^{M}
arco^{M} rampante
pinnacle
pináculo^{M}
pinacle^{M}
Fiale^{F}
pinnacolo^{M}
abutment
estribo^{M}
culée^{F}
Widerlager^{M}
spalla^{F}
side chapel
capilla^{F} lateral
chapelle^{F} latérale
Seitenkapelle^{F}
cappella^{F} laterale
crossing
crucero^{M}
croisée^{F}
Vierung^{F}
crociera^{F}
buttress
contrafuerte^{M}
contrefort^{M}
Strebepfeiler^{M}
contrafforte^{M}
arcade
arcada^{F}
arcade^{F}
Arkade^{F}
arcata^{F}

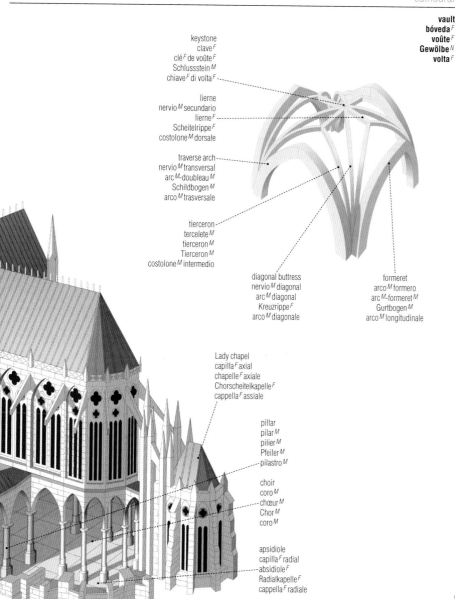

vault
bóveda[F]
voûte[F]
Gewölbe[N]
volta[F]

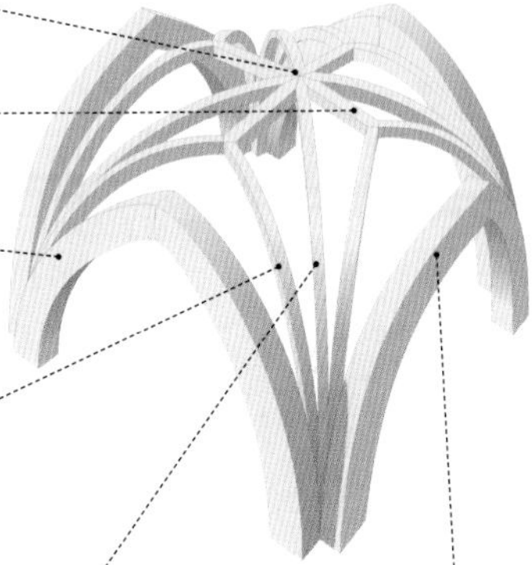
keystone
clave[F]
clé[F] de voûte[F]
Schlussstein[M]
chiave[F] di volta[F]
lierne
nervio[M] secundario
lierne[F]
Scheitelrippe[F]
costolone[M] dorsale
traverse arch
nervio[M] transversal
arc[M]-doubleau[M]
Schildbogen[M]
arco[M] trasversale
tierceron
tercelete[M]
tierceron[M]
Tierceron[M]
costolone[M] intermedio
diagonal buttress
nervio[M] diagonal
arc[M] diagonal
Kreuzrippe[F]
arco[M] diagonale
formeret
arco[M] formero
arc[M]-formeret[M]
Gurtbogen[M]
arco[M] longitudinale

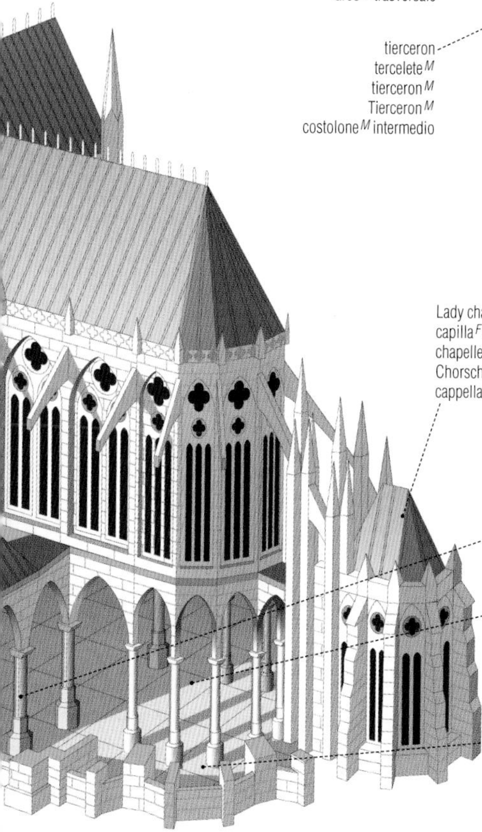
Lady chapel
capilla[F] axial
chapelle[F] axiale
Chorscheitelkapelle[F]
cappella[F] assiale
pillar
pilar[M]
pilier[M]
Pfeiler[M]
pilastro[M]
choir
coro[M]
chœur[M]
Chor[M]
coro[M]
apsidiole
capilla[F] radial
absidiole[F]
Radialkapelle[F]
cappella[F] radiale

newspaper

periódico*M* | journal*M* | Zeitung*F* | giornale*M*

front page
primera plana*F*
une*F*
Titelseite*F*
prima pagina*F*

FFM > nonummy nibh euismod tincidunt ut laoreet dolore magna
INTERNATIONAL
VOL. CLII No. 51,948
SUNDAY, NOVEMBER 25, 2002
luptatum zril delenit
Normand de Bellefeuille
Ut wisi enim ad minim veniam, quis nostrud
Lorem ipsum dolor sit amet
François Fortin
Dolor in hendrerit in vulputate
Michel Joubert
Suscipit lobortis nisl ut aliquip ex ea commodo consequat
Wisi enim ad minim veniam
Nostrud exerci tation ullamcorper
Nathalie Frechette
Nonummy nibh

nameplate
nombre*M* del periódico*M*
titre*M* du journal*M*
Zeitungsname*M*
nome*M* del giornale*M*

banner
grandes titulares*M*
tribune*F*
Schlagzeile*F*
titolo*M* a caratteri*M* cubitali

heading
cabecera*F*
manchette*F*
Zeitungskopf*M*
testata*F*

front picture
foto*F* de primera plana*F*
photographie*F* à la une*F*
Titelfoto*N*
foto*F* in prima pagina*F*

article
artículo*M*
article*M*
Artikel*M*
articolo*M*

caption
pie*M* de foto*F*
légende*F*
Bildunterschrift*F*
didascalia*F*

kicker
ladillo*M*
surtitre*M*
Vortitel*M*
occhiello*M*

headline
titular*M*
titre*M*
Titelzeile*F*
titolo*M*

deck
subtítulo*M*
sous-titre*M*
Untertitel*M*
sottotitolo*M*

index
sumario*M*
sommaire*M*
Inhalt*M*
indice*M*

subhead
intertítulo*M*
intertitre*M*
Zwischentitel*M*
testatina*F*

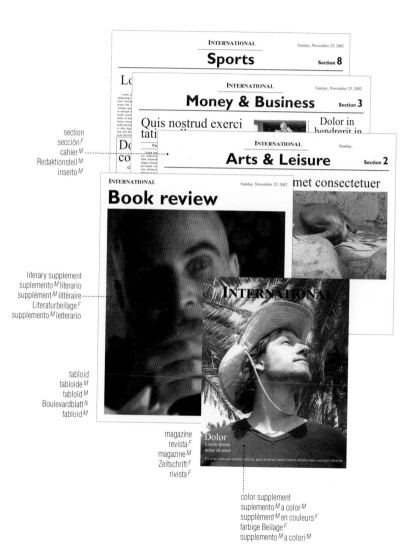

INTERNATIONAL
Sunday, November 25, 2002
Sports
Section 8
INTERNATIONAL
Sunday, November 25, 2002
Money & Business
Section 3
Quis nostrud exerci
Dolor in
INTERNATIONAL
Sunday,
Arts & Leisure
Section 2
met consectetuer
INTERNATIONAL
Sunday, November 25, 2002
Book review
INTERNATIONAL
Dolor
Lorem ipsum
dolor sit amet
Ut wisi enim ad minim veniam, quis nostrud exerci tation ullamcorper suscipit lobortis.

section
sección *F*
cahier *M*
Redaktionsteil *M*
inserto *M*

literary supplement
suplemento *M* literario
supplément *M* littéraire
Literaturbeilage *F*
supplemento *M* letterario

tabloid
tabloide *M*
tabloïd *M*
Boulevardblatt *N*
tabloid *M*

magazine
revista *F*
magazine *M*
Zeitschrift *F*
rivista *F*

color supplement
suplemento *M* a color *M*
supplément *M* en couleurs *F*
farbige Beilage *F*
supplemento *M* a colori *M*

cartoon
caricatura F
caricature F
Karikatur F
vignetta F

editorial
editorial M
éditorial M
redaktioneller Beitrag M
editoriale M

lead
entradilla F
chapeau M
Zusammenfassung F
cappello M

letters to the editor
cartas F al editor M
courrier M des lecteurs M
Leserbriefe M
lettere F al direttore M

rule
filete M
filet M
Trennlinie F
filetto M

Op-Ed article
entrevista F
interview F
Kommentar N
intervista F

column
columna F
colonne F
Spalte F
colonna F

advertisement
anuncio M
annonce F publicitaire
Anzeige F
inserzione F pubblicitaria

A2
INTERNATIONAL SUNDAY, NOVEMBER 25, 2002
Editorial
Ullamcorper suscipit lobortis
Lorem ipsum dolor sit amet, consectetuer adipiscing elit, sed diam nonummy nibh euismod tincidunt ut laoreet dolore magna aliquam erat volutpat.
Luc Roberge
Aliquam
Dolor in hendrerit in vulputate
Paul-Émile Tremblay
Ut wisi enim ad minim veniam
Andrew Eastman
Consequat
Serge D'Amico commodo consequa
Marie-Nicole Cimon
Euismod

masthead
cabecera F
ours M
Impressum N
testata F

column
columna *F*
chronique *F*
Kolumne *F*
articolo *M* di spalla *F*

INTERNATIONAL SUNDAY, NOVEMBER 25, 2002
A3
News
Dolor in hendrerit in vulputate
Nonummy
Anne Tremblay
Wisi enim ad minim
Le Titanic sed diam nonummy
Theo Diamantis
Fortino
Lobortis
Commodo

news items
sucesos *M*
faits *M* divers
Nachrichten *F*
notizie *F*

shorts
noticias *F* breves
brèves *F*
Kurzmeldungen *F*
notizie *F* in breve

television program schedule
horario *M* de la programación *F* televisiva
grille *F* des programmes *M* de télévision *F*
Fernsehprogramm *N*
programmi *M* televisivi

restaurant review
reseña *F* gastronómica
critique *F* gastronomique
Restaurantkritik *F*
recensione *F* gastronomica

photo credit line
fuente *F* de servicio *M*
crédit *M* photographique
Quellenangabe *F*
fonte *F* del servizio *M*

classified advertisements
anuncios *M* por palabras *F*
petites annonces *F*
Kleinanzeigen *F*
piccoli annunci *M*

obituaries
necrológica *F*
nécrologie *F*
Todesanzeigen *F*
necrologia *F*

broadcast satellite communication

comunicación^{F} vía satélite^{M} | télédiffusion^{F} par satellite^{M} | Satellitenübertragungstechnik^{F} | trasmissione^{F} via satellite^{M}

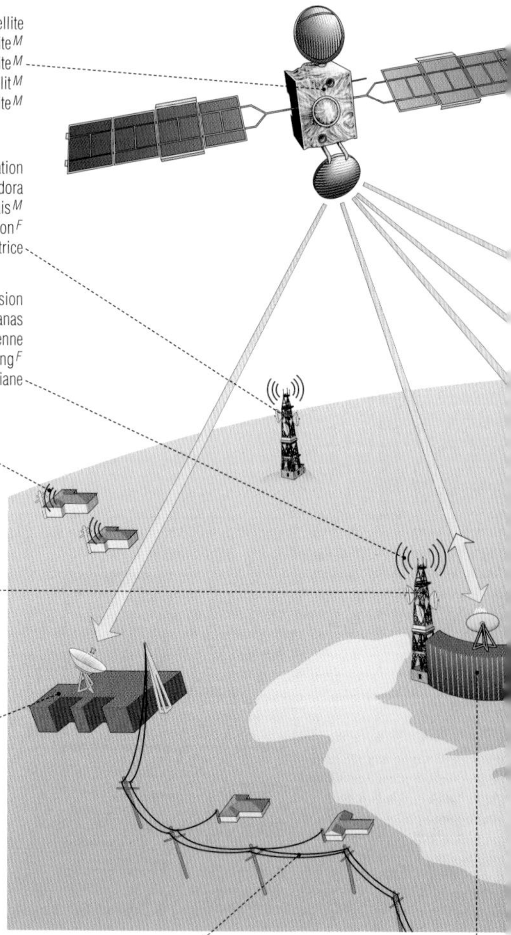

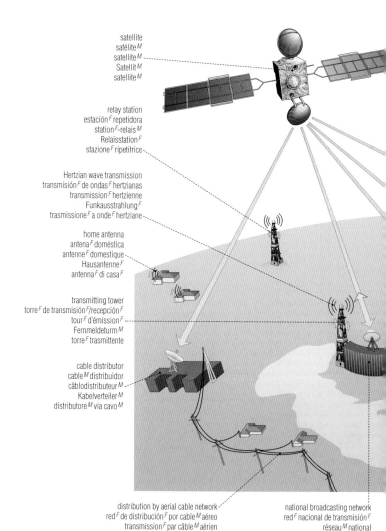

satellite
satélite^{M}
satellite^{M}
Satellit^{M}
satellite^{M}

relay station
estación^{F} repetidora
station^{F}-relais^{M}
Relaisstation^{F}
stazione^{F} ripetitrice

Hertzian wave transmission
transmisión^{F} de ondas^{F} hertzianas
transmission^{F} hertzienne
Funkausstrahlung^{F}
trasmissione^{F} a onde^{F} hertziane

home antenna
antena^{F} doméstica
antenne^{F} domestique
Hausantenne^{F}
antenna^{F} di casa^{F}

transmitting tower
torre^{F} de transmisión^{F}/recepción^{F}
tour^{F} d'émission^{F}
Fernmeldeturm^{M}
torre^{F} trasmittente

cable distributor
cable^{M} distribuidor
câblodistributeur^{M}
Kabelverteiler^{M}
distributore^{M} via cavo^{M}

distribution by aerial cable network
red^{F} de distribución^{F} por cable^{M} aéreo
transmission^{F} par câble^{M} aérien
Verteilung^{F} über Freileitungen^{F}
trasmissione^{F} via cavo^{M} aereo

national broadcasting network
red^{F} nacional de transmisión^{F}
réseau^{M} national
öffentliches Übertragungsnetz^{N}
rete^{F} trasmittente nazionale

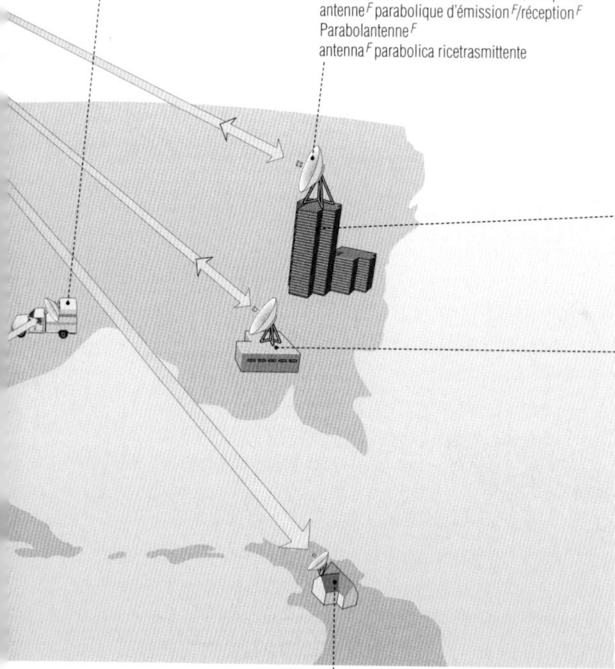
mobile unit
unidad^F móvil
car^M de reportage^M
mobile Einheit^F
unità^F mobile
transceiving parabolic antenna
antena^F parabólica de transmisión^F/recepción^F
antenne^F parabolique d'émission^F/réception^F
Parabolantenne^F
antenna^F parabolica ricetrasmittente
private broadcasting network
red^F de transmisión^F privada
réseau^M privé
privates Rundfunknetz^N
rete^F trasmittente privata
local station
estación^F local
station^F locale
Lokale Station^F
stazione^F locale
direct home reception
recepción^F directa en la casa^F
réception^F directe
Satelliten-Direktempfang^M
ricezione^F privata diretta

telecommunications by satellite

telecomunicaciones[F] vía satélite[M] | télécommunications[F] par satellite[M] | Telekommunikation[F] über Nachrichtensatellit[M] | telecomunicazioni[F] via satellite[M]

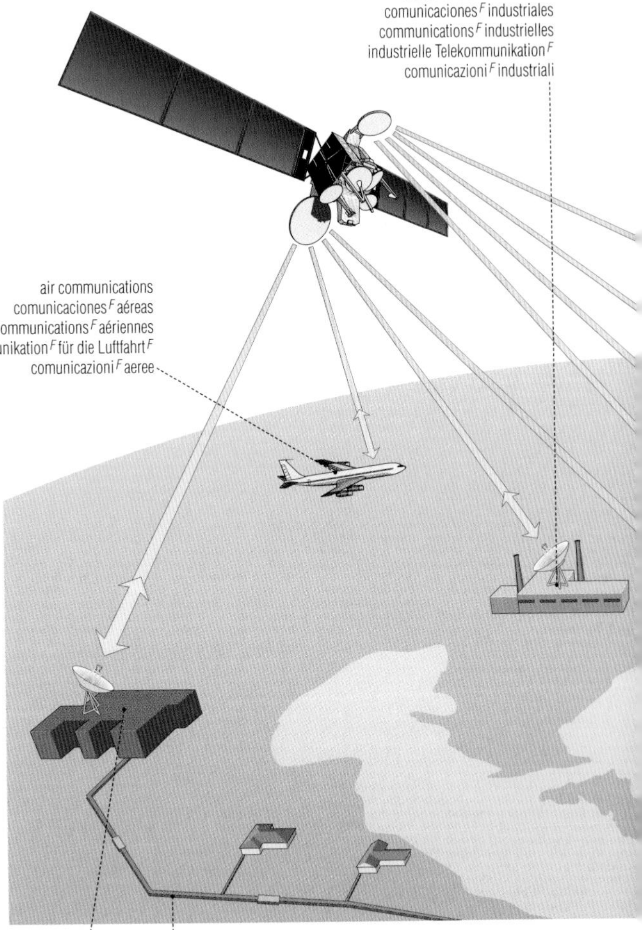
industrial communications
comunicaciones[F] industriales
communications[F] industrielles
industrielle Telekommunikation[F]
comunicazioni[F] industriali
air communications
comunicaciones[F] aéreas
communications[F] aériennes
Telekommunikation[F] für die Luftfahrt[F]
comunicazioni[F] aeree
telephone network
red[F] telefónica
réseau[M] téléphonique
Telefonnetz[N]
rete[F] telefonica
distribution by underground cable network
red[F] de transmisión[F] por cable[M] subterráneo
transmission[F] par câble[M] souterrain
Verteilung[F] über unterirdisches Kabelnetz[N]
trasmissione[F] via cavo[M] sotterraneo

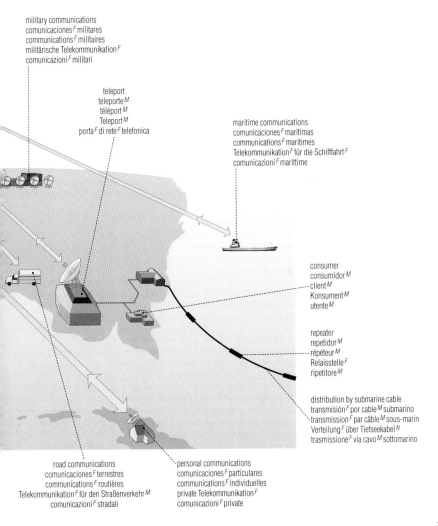

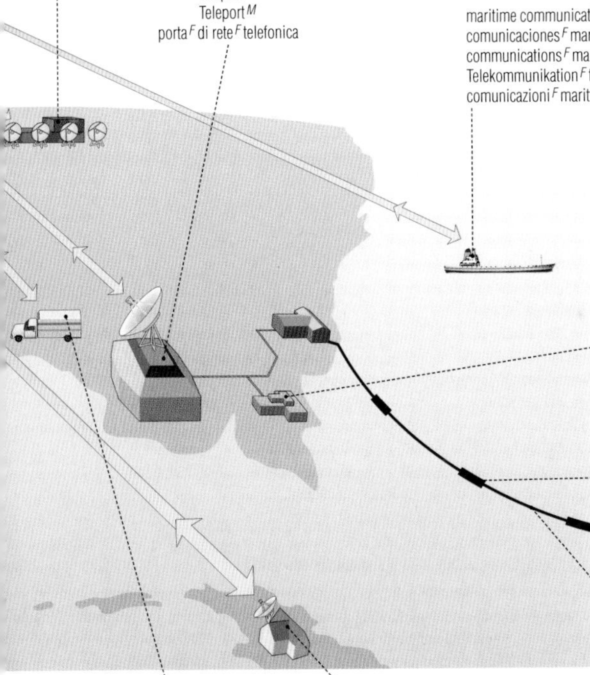
military communications
comunicaciones F militares
communications F militaires
militärische Telekommunikation F
comunicazioni F militari
teleport
teleporte M
téléport M
Teleport M
porta F di rete F telefonica
maritime communications
comunicaciones F marítimas
communications F maritimes
Telekommunikation F für die Schifffahrt F
comunicazioni F marittime
consumer
consumidor M
client M
Konsument M
utente M
repeater
repetidor M
répéteur M
Relaisstelle F
ripetitore M
distribution by submarine cable
transmisión F por cable M submarino
transmission F par câble M sous-marin
Verteilung F über Tiefseekabel N
trasmissione F via cavo M sottomarino
road communications
comunicaciones F terrestres
communications F routières
Telekommunikation F für den Straßenverkehr M
comunicazioni F stradali
personal communications
comunicaciones F particulares
communications F individuelles
private Telekommunikation F
comunicazioni F private

television

televisión F | télévision F | Fernsehen N | televisione F

studio and control rooms
estudio M de televisión F y cabinas F de control M
plateau M et régies F
Sprecher- und Regieräume M
studio M e cabine F di regia F

studio floor
estudio M
plateau M
Studioebene F
studio M televisivo

lighting/camera control area
sala F de control M de luces F/de cámara F
régie F image F/éclairage M
Beleuchtung F/Bildregie F
area F di controllo M luci F/video M

audio control room
control M de sonido M
régie F du son M
Tonregieraum M
cabina F di controllo M audio M

production control room
sala F de producción F y control M
régie F de production F
Regieraum M
cabina F di regia F

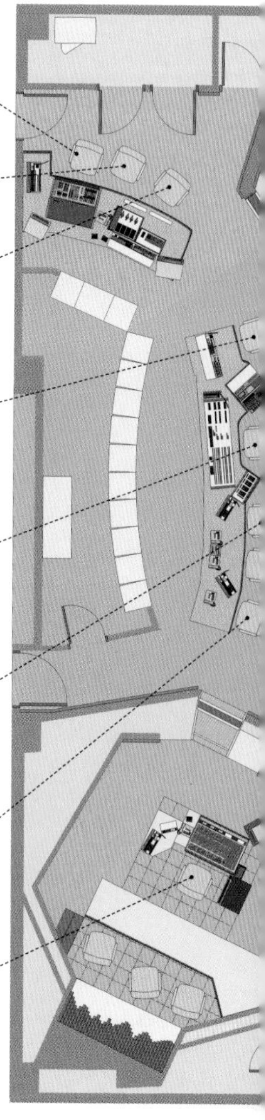

lighting board operator
operador M del tablero M de luces F
opérateur M de régie F d'éclairage M
Oberbeleuchtungstechniker M
operatore M del pannello M delle luci F
lighting technician
técnico M de luces F
éclairagiste M
Beleuchtungstechniker M
tecnico M delle luci F
camera control technician
técnico M de control M de cámaras F
contrôleur M d'images F
Bildtechniker M
tecnico M video M
technical producer
productor M técnico
directeur M technique
Aufsichtsingenieur M
direttore M tecnico
video switcher technician
operador M técnico de video M
technicien M aiguilleur M
Video-Switch-Techniker M
tecnico M di commutazione F video M
producer
productor M
réalisateur M
Sendeleiter M
regista M
production adviser
consejero M de producción F
conseiller M de production F
Regieassistent M
assistente M alla regia F
audio technician
técnico M de sonido M
preneur M de son M
Tontechniker M
tecnico M audio M

lighting grid access
puerta[F] de acceso[M] a la rejilla[F] de las luces[F]
accès[M] à la grille[F] d'éclairage[M]
Zugang[M] zur Beleuchtungsanlage[F]
accesso[M] alla griglia[F] di illuminazione[F]

auxiliary facilities room
sala[F] de instalaciones[F] auxiliares
salle[F] polyvalente
allgemeiner Geräteraum[M]
sala[F] delle strutture[F] ausiliarie

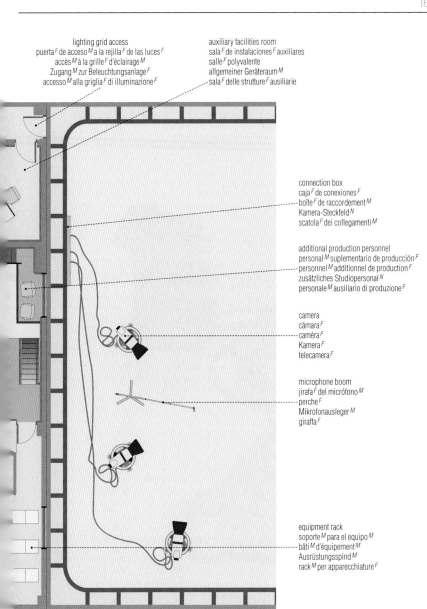

connection box
caja[F] de conexiones[F]
boîte[F] de raccordement[M]
Kamera-Steckfeld[N]
scatola[F] dei collegamenti[M]

additional production personnel
personal[M] suplementario de producción[F]
personnel[M] additionnel de production[F]
zusätzliches Studiopersonal[N]
personale[M] ausiliario di produzione[F]

camera
cámara[F]
caméra[F]
Kamera[F]
telecamera[F]

microphone boom
jirafa[F] del micrófono[M]
perche[F]
Mikrofonausleger[M]
giraffa[F]

equipment rack
soporte[M] para el equipo[M]
bâti[M] d'équipement[M]
Ausrüstungsspind[M]
rack[M] per apparecchiature[F]

camera
cámara F
caméra F
Kamera F
telecamera F

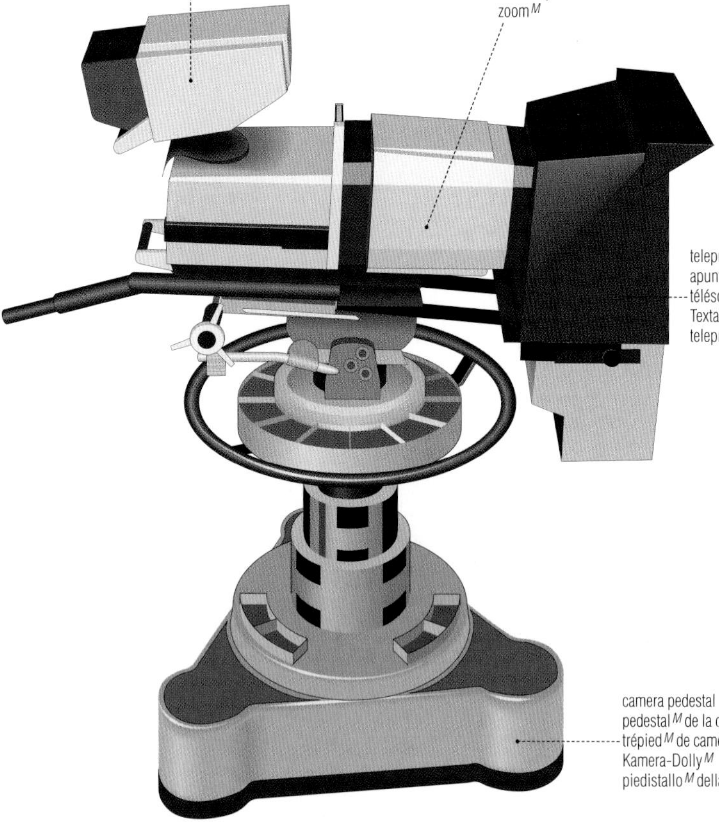
camera viewfinder
visor M
viseur M de caméra F
Bildsucher M
mirino M
zoom lens
zoom M
zoom M
Zoomobjektiv N
zoom M
teleprompter
apuntador M electrónico
télésouffleur M
Textablesetafel F
teleprompter M
camera pedestal
pedestal M de la cámara F
trépied M de caméra F
Kamera-Dolly M
piedistallo M della telecamera F

liquid crystal display (LCD) television
televisor M de cristal M líquido
téléviseur M à cristaux M liquides
LCD-Fernseher M (Liquid-Crystal-Display-Fernseher M)
televisore M a cristalli M liquidi

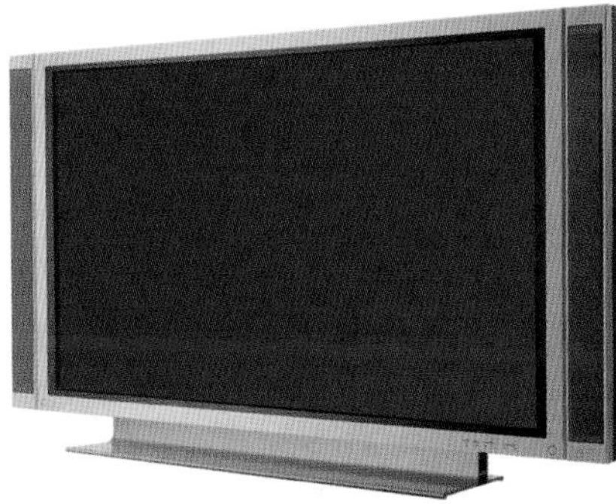

plasma television
televisor M plasma M
téléviseur M à plasma M
Plasmafernseher M
televisore M al plasma M

cathod ray tube (CRT) television
televisor M con pantalla F catódica
téléviseur M à écran M cathodique
CRT-Fernseher M
(Kathodenstrahlröhren-Fernseher M)
televisore M a tubo M catodico

cabinet
caja F
coffret M
Gehäuse N
mobile M

screen
pantalla F
écran M
Bildschirm M
schermo M

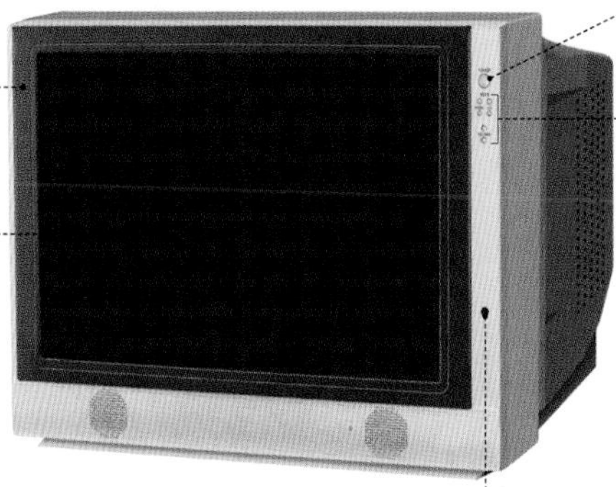

power button
botón M de encendido
interrupteur M d'alimentation F
Netzschalter M
interruttore M di accensione F

tuning controls
controles M de sintonización F
boutons M de réglage M
Bedientasten F
comandi M di sintonia F

remote control sensor
sensor M del mando M a distancia F
capteur M de télécommande F
Sensor M für Fernbedienung F
sensore M del telecomando M

videocassette
cinta *F* de vídeo *M*
cassette *F* vidéo
Videokassette *F*
videocassetta *F*

reel
bobina *F*
bobine *F*
Spule *F*
bobina *F*

recording tape
cinta *F* magnética
bande *F* magnétique
Magnetband *N*
nastro *M* magnetico

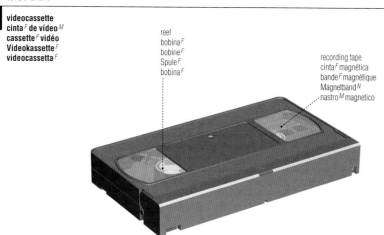

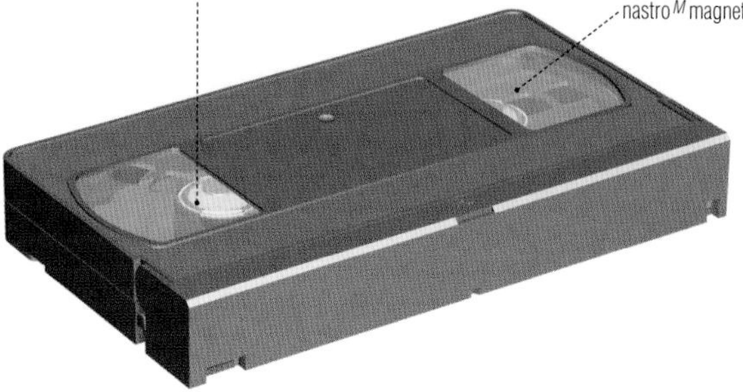

videocassette recorder (VCR)
reproductor/grabador de video *M*
VCR
magnétoscope *M*
Videorecorder *M*
videoregistratore *M*

cassette compartment
alojamiento *M* para la cinta *F*
logement *M* de la cassette *F*
Kassettenschacht *M*
vano *M* cassetta *F*

POWER
VIDEO (MONO)L-AUDIO-R
C.RESET
DISPLAY
18-34
CH
RE-VIEW
PLAY
REW
FF

power button
interruptor *M*
interrupteur *M* d'alimentation *F*
Ein-/Ausschalter *M*
interruttore *M* generale

display
indicador *M*
afficheur *M*
Display *N*
display *M*

digital versatile disc (DVD)
disco^M versátil digital (DVD)
disque^M numérique polyvalent (DVD)
DVD^F
disco^M versatile digitale (DVD)

DVD recorder
grabadora^F DVD
enregistreur^M de DVD^M vidéo
DVD-Recorder^M
registratore^M DVD^M

power button
interruptor^M de alimentación^F
interrupteur^M d'alimentation^F
Ein-/Ausschalter^M
pulsante^M di alimentazione^F

channel select
selección^F de canales^M
sélection^F des canaux^M
Kanalauswahl^F
selezione^F dei canali^M

record button
tecla^F para grabar
touche^F d'enregistrement^M
Aufnahmetaste^F
tasto^M di registrazione^F

disc compartment control
control^M de la bandeja^F de carga^F
contrôle^M du plateau^M
Auswurftaste^F
apertura^M/chiusura^F vassoio del disco^M

stop button
tecla^F de parada^F
touche^F d'arrêt^M
Stopptaste^F
tasto^M stop^M

play button
tecla^F de lectura^F
touche^F de lecture^F
Playtaste^F
tasto^M play^M

disc tray
bandeja^F de carga^F
plateau^M de chargement^M
DVD-Lade^F
vassoio^M del disco^M

display
pantalla^F
afficheur^M
Display^N
display^M

pause/still button
pausa^F/imagen^F fija
pause^F/arrêt^M sur l'image^F
Pausetaste^F
tasto^M di pausa^F/fermo^M immagine^F

track search/fast operation buttons
cambio^M de pista^F/lectura^F rápida
changement^M de piste^F/lecture^F rapide
Kapitelsuche^F/Schnellvorlauf^M
ricerca^F traccia^F/riproduzione^F rapida

remote control
mando[M] a distancia[F]
télécommande[F]
Fernbedienung[F]
telecomando[M]

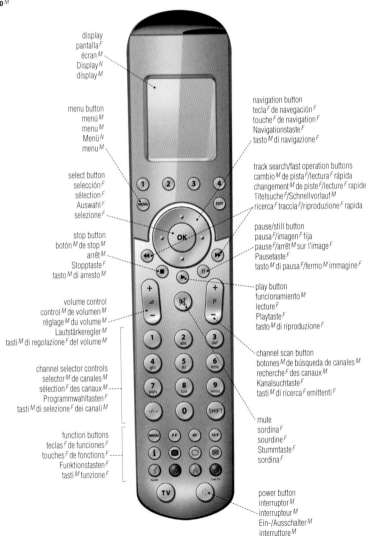

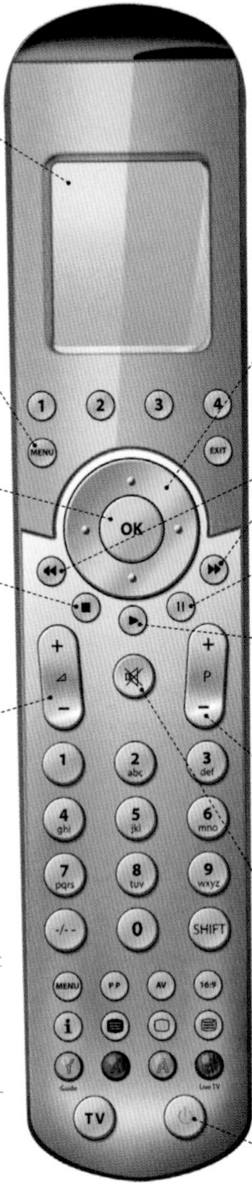
display
pantalla[F]
écran[M]
Display[N]
display[M]
menu button
menú[M]
menu[M]
Menü[N]
menu[M]
select button
selección[F]
sélection[F]
Auswahl[F]
selezione[F]
stop button
botón[M] de stop[M]
arrêt[M]
Stopptaste[F]
tasto[M] di arresto[M]
volume control
control[M] de volumen[M]
réglage[M] du volume[M]
Lautstärkeregler[M]
tasti[M] di regolazione[F] del volume[M]
channel selector controls
selector[M] de canales[M]
sélection[F] des canaux[M]
Programmwahltasten[F]
tasti[M] di selezione[F] dei canali[M]
function buttons
teclas[F] de funciones[F]
touches[F] de fonctions[F]
Funktionstasten[F]
tasti[M] funzione[F]
navigation button
tecla[F] de navegación[F]
touche[F] de navigation[F]
Navigationstaste[F]
tasto[M] di navigazione[F]
track search/fast operation buttons
cambio[M] de pista[F]/lectura[F] rápida
changement[M] de piste[F]/lecture[F] rapide
Titelsuche[F]/Schnellvorlauf[M]
ricerca[F] traccia[F]/riproduzione[F] rapida
pause/still button
pausa[F]/imagen[F] fija
pause[F]/arrêt[M] sur l'image[F]
Pausetaste[F]
tasto[M] di pausa[F]/fermo[M] immagine[F]
play button
funcionamiento[M]
lecture[F]
Playtaste[F]
tasto[M] di riproduzione[F]
channel scan button
botones[M] de búsqueda de canales[M]
recherche[F] des canaux[M]
Kanalsuchtaste[F]
tasti[M] di ricerca[F] emittenti[F]
mute
sordina[F]
sourdine[F]
Stummtaste[F]
sordina[F]
power button
interruptor[M]
interrupteur[M]
Ein-/Ausschalter[M]
interruttore[M]

compact videocassette adapter
adaptador M de cinta F de vídeo M compacto
adaptateur M de cassette F vidéo compacte
Videokassettenadapter M
adattatore M per videocassette F compatte

cassette compartment
alojamiento M de la cinta F
logement M de la cassette F
Videokassettenschacht M
vano M della videocassetta F

DV 60

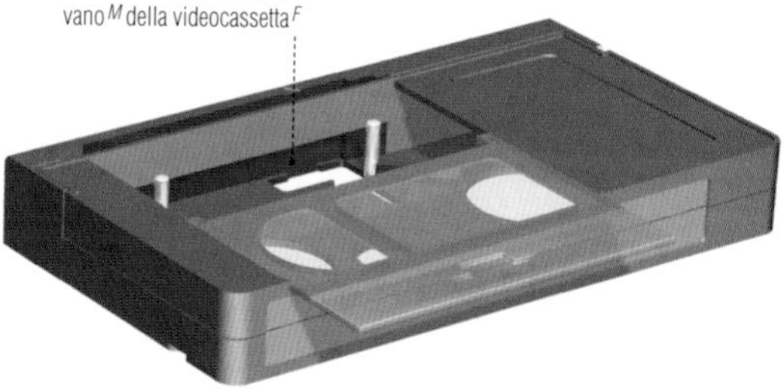

miniDV cassette
cassette F mini DV
cassette F mini-DV
Mini-DV-Kassette F
cassetta F mini-DV

HDD

hard disk drive camcorder
videocámara F con disco M duro
caméscope M à disque M dur
Camcorder M mit Festplatte F
videocamera F con disco M fisso

120x
DVD

DVD camcorder
videocámara F DVD M
caméscope M DVD M
DVD-Camcorder M
videocamera F DVD

mini-DV camcorder: front view
videocámara[F] mini DV : vista[F] de frente
caméscope[M] mini-DV : vue[F] avant
Mini-DV-Camcorder[M]: Vorderansicht[F]
videocamera[F] mini-DV: vista[F] frontale

photoshot button
tecla[F] foto[F]
touche[F] photo[F]
Fototaste[F]
tasto[M] foto[F]

electronic viewfinder
visor[M] electrónico
viseur[M] électronique
elektronischer Sucher[M]
mirino[M] elettronico

zoom button
tecla[F] de zoom[M]
commande[F] du zoom[M]
Zoomtaste[F]
comando[M] zoom[M]

recording mode
modo[M] grabación[F]
mode[M] d'enregistrement[M]
Aufnahmemodus[M]
modo[M] di registrazione[F]

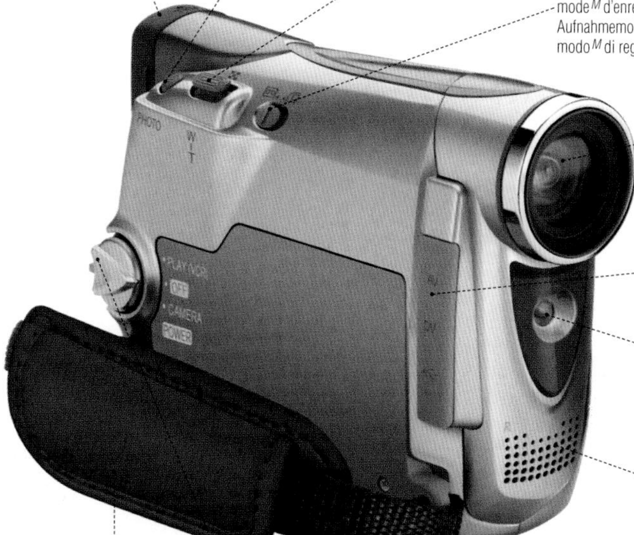

zoom lens
objetivo[M] zoom
objectif[M] zoom[M]
Zoomobjektiv[N]
zoom[M]

terminal cover
tapa[F] de conexión[F]
couvre-prises[M]
Anschlussabdeckung[F]
copriprese[M]

lamp
lámpara[F]
lampe[F]
Lampe[F]
lampada[F]

microphone
micrófono[M]
microphone[M]
Mikrofon[N]
microfono[M]

hand strap
correa[F] para la mano[F]
dragonne[F]
Faustriemen[M]
tracolla[F]

power/functions switch
interruptor[M] alimentación[F]/funciones[F]
commutateur[M] alimentation[F]/fonctions[F]
Haupt-/Funktionsschalter[M]
interruttore[M] di accensione[F]/funzioni[F]

mini-DV camcorder: rear view
videocámara[F] mini DV : vista[F] posterior
caméscope[M] mini-DV : vue[F] arrière
Mini-DV-Camcorder[M]: Rückansicht[F]
videocamera[F] mini-DV: vista[F] posteriore

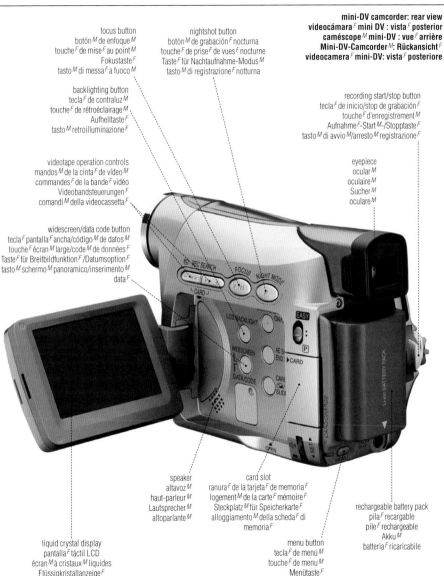

focus button
botón[M] de enfoque[M]
touche[F] de mise[F] au point[M]
Fokustaste[F]
tasto[M] di messa[F] a fuoco[M]

nightshot button
botón[M] de grabación[F] nocturna
touche[F] de prise[F] de vues[F] nocturne
Taste[F] für Nachtaufnahme-Modus[M]
tasto[M] di registrazione[F] notturna

backlighting button
tecla[F] de contraluz[M]
touche[F] de rétroéclairage[M]
Aufhelltaste[F]
tasto[M] retroilluminazione[F]

recording start/stop button
tecla[F] de inicio/stop de grabación[F]
touche[F] d'enregistrement[M]
Aufnahme[F]-Start[M]-/Stopptaste[F]
tasto[M] di avvio[M]/arresto[M] registrazione[F]

videotape operation controls
mandos[M] de la cinta[F] de vídeo[M]
commandes[F] de la bande[F] vidéo
Videobandsteuerungen[F]
comandi[M] della videocassetta[F]

eyepiece
ocular[M]
oculaire[M]
Sucher[M]
oculare[M]

widescreen/data code button
tecla[F] pantalla[F] ancha/código[M] de datos[M]
touche[F] écran[M] large/code[M] de données[F]
Taste[F] für Breitbildfunktion[F]/Datumsoption[F]
tasto[M] schermo[M] panoramico/inserimento[M] data[F]

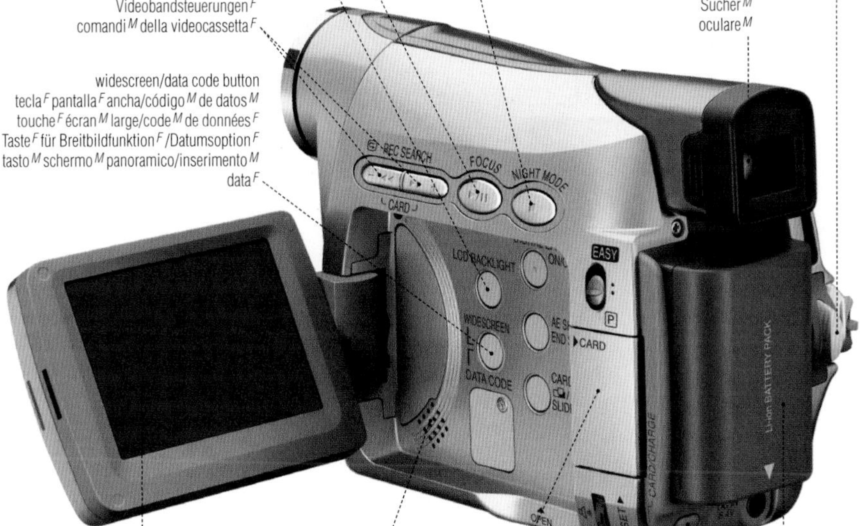
REC SEARCH
FOCUS
NIGHT MODE
CARD
LCD BACKLIGHT
EASY
WIDESCREEN
DATA CODE
CARD
P
Li-ion BATTERY PACK
CARD CHARGE
OPEN
SET
MENU

speaker
altavoz[M]
haut-parleur[M]
Lautsprecher[M]
altoparlante[M]

card slot
ranura[F] de la tarjeta[F] de memoria[F]
logement[M] de la carte[F] mémoire[F]
Steckplatz[M] für Speicherkarte[F]
alloggiamento[M] della scheda[F] di memoria[F]

rechargeable battery pack
pila[F] recargable
pile[F] rechargeable
Akku[M]
batteria[F] ricaricabile

liquid crystal display
pantalla[F] táctil LCD
écran[M] à cristaux[M] liquides
Flüssigkristallanzeige[F]
display[M] a cristalli[M] liquidi

menu button
tecla[F] de menú[M]
touche[F] de menu[M]
Menütaste[F]
tasto[M] menu

sound reproducing system

equipo[M] de alta fidelidad[F] | chaîne[F] stéréo | Tonwiedergabesystem[N] | impianto[M] hi-fi di riproduzione[F] del suono[M]

system components
componentes[M] del sistema[M]
composantes[F] d'un système[M]
Teile[N] des System[N]
elementi[M] del sistema[M]

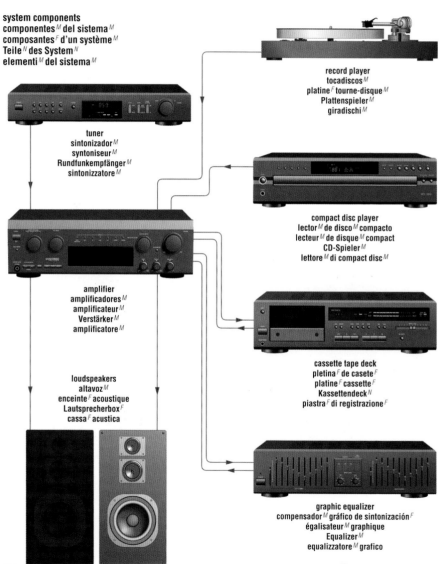

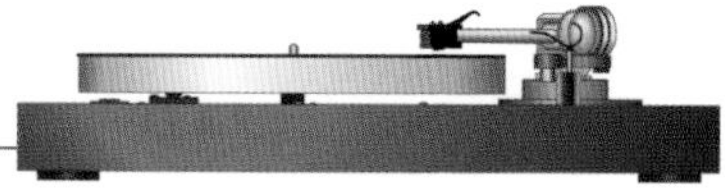

record player
tocadiscos[M]
platine[F] tourne-disque[M]
Plattenspieler[M]
giradischi[M]

tuner
sintonizador[M]
syntoniseur[M]
Rundfunkempfänger[M]
sintonizzatore[M]

compact disc player
lector[M] de disco[M] compacto
lecteur[M] de disque[M] compact
CD-Spieler[M]
lettore[M] di compact disc[M]

amplifier
amplificadores[M]
amplificateur[M]
Verstärker[M]
amplificatore[M]

cassette tape deck
pletina[F] de casete[F]
platine[F] cassette[F]
Kassettendeck[N]
piastra[F] di registrazione[F]

loudspeakers
altavoz[M]
enceinte[F] acoustique
Lautsprecherbox[F]
cassa[F] acustica

graphic equalizer
compensador[M] gráfico de sintonización[F]
égalisateur[M] graphique
Equalizer[M]
equalizzatore[M] grafico

tuner
sintonizador^{M}
syntoniseur^{M}
Rundfunkempfänger^{M}
sintonizzatore^{M}

tuning mode
modalidad^{F} sintonizador^{M}
mode^{M} de sélection^{F} des stations^{F}
Modus-Taste^{F}
modo^{M} della sintonia^{F}

band selector
selector^{M} de banda^{F}
touche^{F} de modulation^{F}
Wellenbereichseinstellung^{F}
selettore^{M} di banda^{F}

mode selector
selector^{M} mono/estéreo
commutateur^{M} mono^{F}/stéréo^{F}
Mono-Stereo-Taste^{F}
commutatore^{M} mono/stereo

tuning control
control^{M} del sintonizador^{M}
sélecteur^{M} de stations^{F}
Sendereinstellung^{F}
manopola^{F} di ricerca^{F} delle stazioni^{F}

preset tuning button
selector^{M} de emisoras^{F} memorizadas
touche^{F} de présélection^{F}
Stationsspeichertaste^{F}
pulsante^{M} di preselezione^{F} della sintonia^{F}

digital frequency display
indicador^{M} digital de frecuencia^{F}
affichage^{M} numérique des stations^{F}
digitale Frequenzanzeige^{F}
indicatore^{M} digitale di frequenza^{F}

active tracking
búsqueda^{F} automática de canales^{M}
balayage^{M} automatique des stations^{F}
automatischer Sendersuchlauf^{M}
ricerca^{F} automatica

graphic equalizer
compensador^{M} **gráfico de sintonización**^{F}
égalisateur^{M} **graphique**
Equalizer^{M}
equalizzatore^{M} **grafico**

frequency bands
bandas^{F} de frecuencia^{F}
bandes^{F} de fréquences^{F}
Frequenzbänder^{N}
bande^{F} di frequenza^{F}

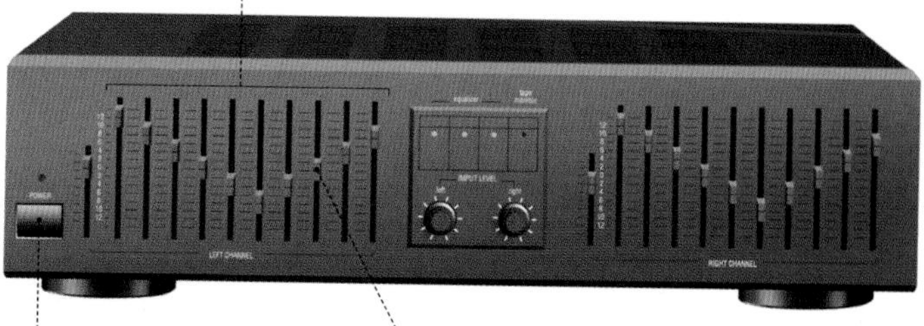

power button
interruptor^{M} de alimentación^{F}
interrupteur^{M} d'alimentation^{F}
Ein-/Ausschalter^{M}
interruttore^{M} di accensione^{F}

frequency setting slide control
cursor^{M} de ajuste^{M} de la frecuencia^{F}
curseur^{M} de réglage^{M} de la fréquence^{F}
Frequenzregler^{M}
cursore^{M} di regolazione^{F} della frequenza^{F}

ampli-tuner: front view
amplificador[M]/sintonizador[M]: vista[F] frontal
ampli[M]-syntoniseur[M]: vue[F] avant
Receiver[M]: Vorderansicht[F]
sintoamplificatore[M]: vista[F] frontale

input lights
indicadores[M] de entrada[F]
voyants[M] d'entrée[F]
Kontrollleuchten[F] für Tonsignalquellen[F]
luci[F] delle sorgenti[F]

volume control
control[M] del volumen[M]
réglage[M] du volume[M]
Lautstärkeregler[M]
regolatore[M] di volume[M]

power button
botón[M] de encendido
interrupteur[M] d'alimentation[F]
Ein-/Ausschalter[M]
interruttore[M] di accensione[F]

treble tone control
control[M] de agudos[M]
contrôle[M] de tonalité[F] des aigus[M]
Höhenregler[M]
regolatore[M] degli alti[M]

band select button
tecla[F] de selección[F] de banda
touche[F] de modulation[F]
Bandwahltaste[F]
tasto[M] di selezione[F] della banda[F]

input selector
selector[M] de entrada[F]
sélecteur[M] d'entrée[F]
Eingangsschalter[M]
selettore[M] di ingresso[M]

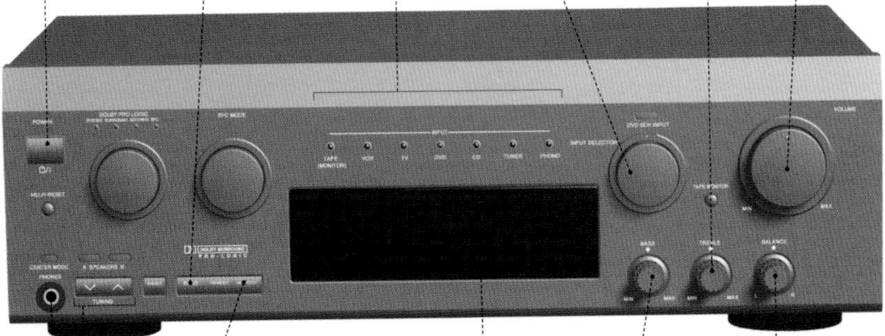

memory button
tecla[M] memoria
touche[F] mémoire[F]
Speichertaste[F]
tasto[M] di memorizzazione[F]

display
display[M]
afficheur[M]
Display[N]
display[M]

tuning buttons
teclas[F] de selección[F] de la sintonía[F]
touches[F] de sélection[F] des stations[F]
Sendersuchlauftasten[F]
tasti[M] di selezione[F] della sintonia[F]

bass tone control
control[M] de graves[M]
contrôle[M] de tonalité[F] des graves[M]
Bassregler[M]
regolatore[M] dei bassi[M]

headphone jack
toma[F] para los auriculares[M]
prise[F] casque[M]
Kopfhörerbuchse[F]
presa[F] per cuffia[F]

balance control
control[M] de balance[M]
équilibrage[M] des haut-parleurs[M]
Balanceregler[M]
bilanciamento[M] degli altoparlanti[M]

ampli-tuner: back view
amplificador^{M}/sintonizador^{M} : vista^{F} posterior
ampli^{M}-syntoniseur^{M} : vue^{F} arrière
Amplituner^{M}: Rückansicht^{F}
sintoamplificatore^{M}: dorso^{M}

power cord
cable^{M} de alimentación^{F}
cordon^{M} d'alimentation^{F}
Netzkabel^{N}
cavo^{M} di alimentazione^{F}

antenna terminals
conectores^{M} de antenas^{F}
bornes^{F} de raccordement^{M} des antennes^{F}
Antennenbuchsen^{F}
terminali^{M} di collegamento^{M} delle antenne^{F}

cooling fan
ventilador^{M}
ventilateur^{M}
Lüfter^{M}
ventola^{F}

switched outlet
conmutador^{M} de corriente^{F}
prise^{F} de courant^{M} commutée
geschaltete Steckdose^{F}
presa^{F} di corrente^{F} commutata

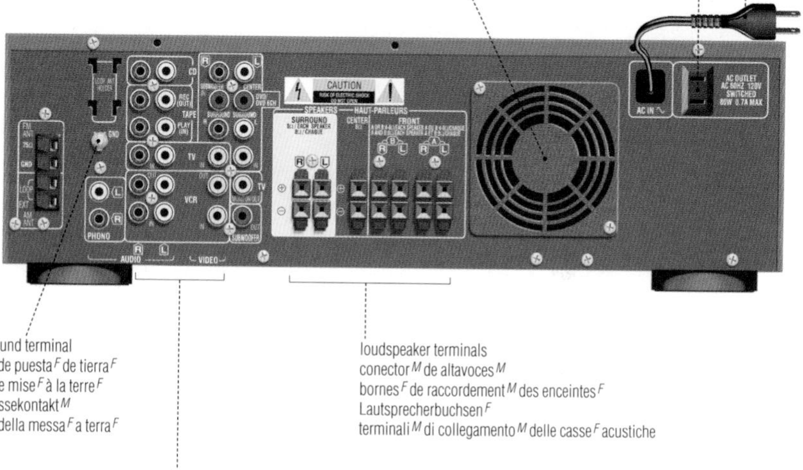
CD
TAPE
TV
VCR
PHONO
AUDIO
VIDEO
CAUTION
SPEAKERS
HAUT-PARLEURS
SURROUND
CENTER
FRONT
SUBWOOFER
AC IN
AC OUTLET
AC 60HZ 120V
SWITCHED
80W 0.7A MAX

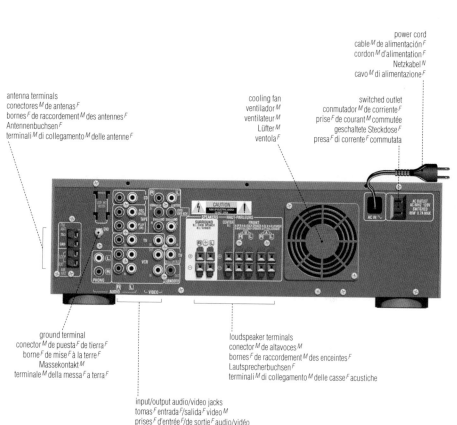

ground terminal
conector^{M} de puesta^{F} de tierra^{F}
borne^{F} de mise^{F} à la terre^{F}
Massekontakt^{M}
terminale^{M} della messa^{F} a terra^{F}

loudspeaker terminals
conector^{M} de altavoces^{M}
bornes^{F} de raccordement^{M} des enceintes^{F}
Lautsprecherbuchsen^{F}
terminali^{M} di collegamento^{M} delle casse^{F} acustiche

input/output audio/video jacks
tomas^{F} entrada^{F}/salida^{F} video^{M}
prises^{F} d'entrée^{F}/de sortie^{F} audio/vidéo
Video-Ein- und -Ausgänge^{M}
ingressi^{M} uscite^{F} audio^{M}/video^{M}

cassette
casete [F]
cassette [F]
Kassette [F]
cassetta [F]

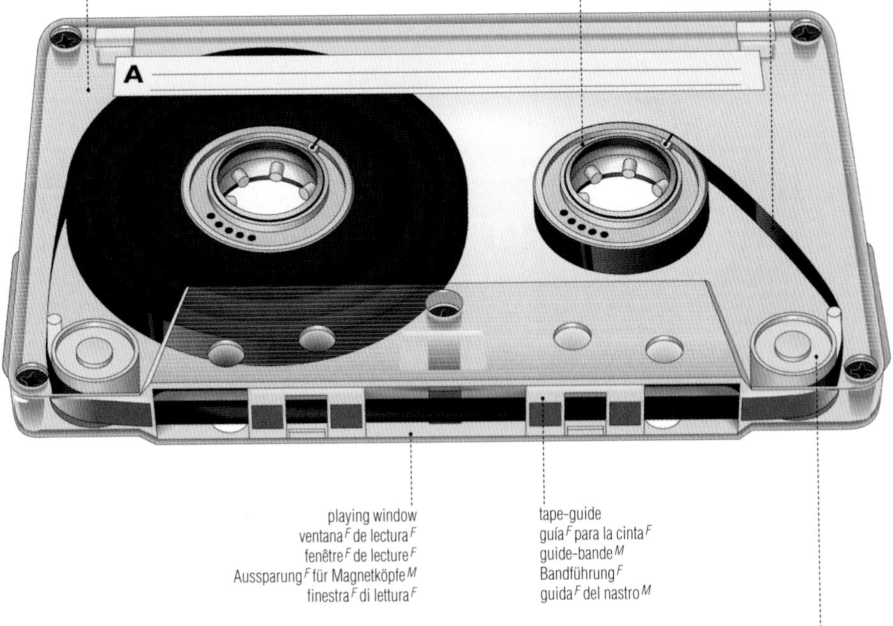
housing
cubierta [F]
boîtier [M]
Gehäuse [N]
caricatore [M]
take-up reel
carrete [M] receptor de la cinta [F]
bobine [F] réceptrice
Aufwickelkern [M]
bobina [F] di avvolgimento [M]
recording tape
cinta [F] de grabación [F]
bande [F] magnétique
Kassettenband [N]
nastro [M] di registrazione [F]
A
playing window
ventana [F] de lectura [F]
fenêtre [F] de lecture [F]
Aussparung [F] für Magnetköpfe [M]
finestra [F] di lettura [F]
tape-guide
guía [F] para la cinta [F]
guide-bande [M]
Bandführung [F]
guida [F] del nastro [M]
guide roller
rodillo [M] guía [F]
galet [M]
Führungsrolle [F]
rullo [M] di guida [F]

cassette tape deck
pletina[F] de casete[F]
platine[F] cassette[F]
Kassettendeck[N]
piastra[F] di registrazione[F]

counter reset button
botón[M] de ajuste[M] a cero[M] del contador[M]
bouton[M] de remise[F] à zéro[M]
Rückstelltaste[F]
tasto[M] di azzeramento[M] del contatore[M]

tape counter
contador[M]
compteur[M]
Zählwerk[N]
contatore[M]

peak level meter
medidor[M] de altos niveles[M] de frecuencia[F]
indicateur[M] de niveau[M]
LED-Pegelanzeige[F]
LED[M] indicatore[M] del livello[M] di picco[M]

eject button
botón[M] de expulsión[F]
bouton[M] d'éjection[F]
Auswurftaste[F]
tasto[M] di espulsione[F]

tape selector
selector[M] de tipo[M] de cinta[F]
sélecteur[M] de bandes[F]
Bandsortenschalter[M]
selettore[M] del nastro[M]

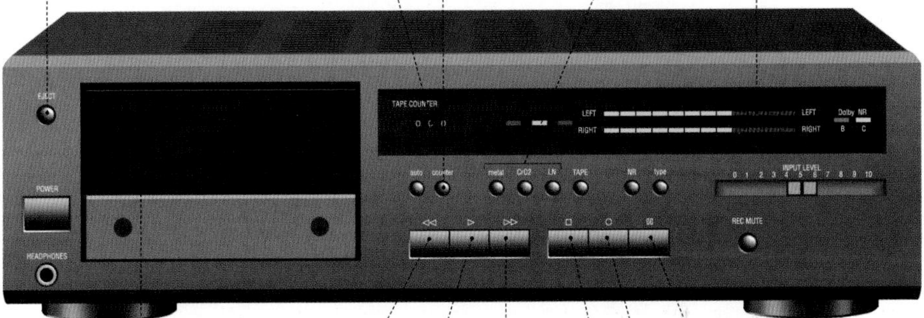
EJECT
TAPE COUNTER
LEFT
RIGHT
LEFT
RIGHT
Dolby NR
B C
POWER
auto
counter
metal
CrO2
LN
TAPE
NR
type
INPUT LEVEL
0 1 2 3 4 5 6 7 8 9 10
REC MUTE
HEADPHONES

cassette holder
alojamiento[M] de la casete[F]
logement[M] de cassette[F]
Kassettenfach[N]
vano[M] della cassetta[F]

pause button
botón[M] de pausa[F]
pause[F]
Pausetaste[F]
tasto[M] di pausa[F]

rewind button
botón[M] de rebobinado[M]
rebobinage[M]
Rücklauftaste[F]
tasto[M] di riavvolgimento[M]

record button
botón[M] de inicio[M] de grabación[F]
enregistrement[M]
Aufnahmetaste[F]
tasto[M] di registrazione[F]

play button
botón[M] de reproducción[F]
lecture[F]
Playtaste[F]
tasto[M] di riproduzione[F]

fast-forward button
botón[M] de avance[M] rápido
avance[F] rapide
Schnellvorlauftaste[F]
tasto[M] di avanzamento[M] rapido

stop button
botón[M] de stop[M]
arrêt[M]
Stopptaste
tasto[M] di arresto[M]

record
disco *M*
disque *M*
Schallplatte *F*
disco *M*

spiral
espiral M de separación F
plage F de séparation F
Schallrille F
solco M di separazione F
center hole
orificio M central
trou M central
Mittelloch N
foro M centrale
spiral-in groove
surco M en espiral M
sillon M de départ M
Einlaufrille F
solco M iniziale
tail-out groove
surco M de salida F
sillon M de sortie F
Auslaufrille F
solco M finale
band
banda F grabada
surface F gravée
Track M
banda F
locked groove
surco M concéntrico
sillon M concentrique
Ausschaltrille F
solco M concentrico
label
etiqueta F
étiquette F
Label N
etichetta F

record player
tocadiscos [M]
platine [F] tourne-disque [M]
Plattenspieler [M]
giradischi [M]

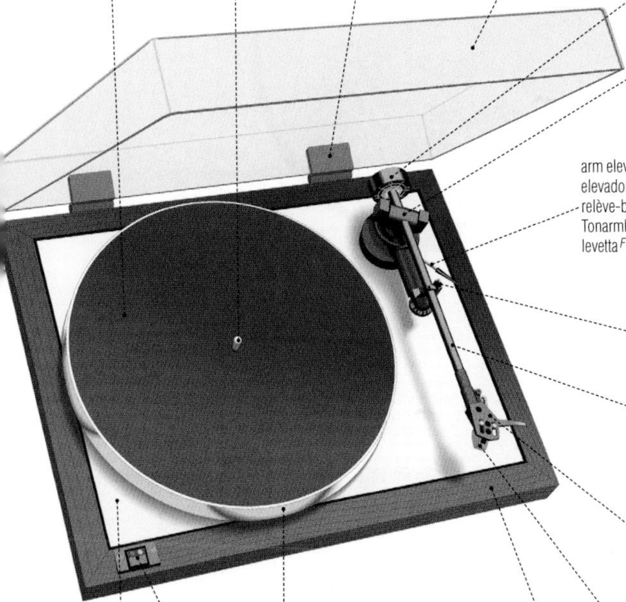
rubber mat
disco [M] de caucho [M]
couvre-plateau [M]
Gummimatte [F]
tappetino [M] di gomma [F]
hinge
bisagra [F]
charnière [F]
Scharnier [N]
cerniera [F]
spindle
pivote [M]
axe [M]
Plattenstift [M]
perno [M] centrale
dust cover
tapa [M] guardapolvo
couvercle [M]
Abdeckhaube [F]
coperchio [M]
counterweight
contrapeso [M]
contrepoids [M]
Balancegewicht [N]
contrappeso [M]
antiskating device
dispositivo [M] antideslizante
compensateur [M] de poussée [F] latérale
Antiskating-Vorrichtung [F]
controllo [M] antiskating
arm elevator
elevador [M] del brazo [M]
relève-bras [M]
Tonarmheber [M]
levetta [F] per il sollevamento [M] del braccio [M]
arm rest
soporte [M] del brazo [M]
repose-bras [M]
Tonarmstütze [F]
supporto [M] del braccio [M]
tone arm
brazo [M] fonocaptor
bras [M] de lecture [F]
Tonarm [M]
braccio [M]
stylus cartridge
cubierta [F] de la aguja [F]
tête [F] de lecture [F]
Tonabnehmersystem [N]
conchiglia [F] portatestina
cartridge
cartucho [M]
cartouche [F]
Tonabnehmer [M]
testina [F]
turntable
plato [M]
plateau [M]
Plattenteller [M]
piatto [M]
base plate
base [F] del plato [M]
contre-platine [F]
Grundplatte [F]
piastra [F] di base [F]
speed selector
selector [M] de velocidad [F]
sélecteur [M] de vitesse [F]
Drehzahl-Einstellung [F]
selettore [M] di velocità [F]
base
base [F]
socle [M]
Sockel [M]
base [F]

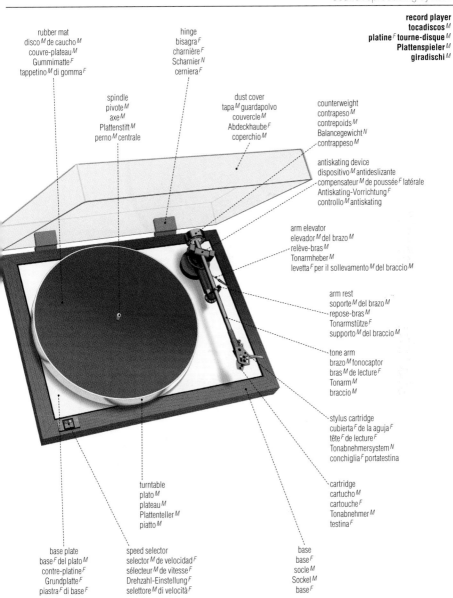

sound reproducing system

compact disc
disco[M] compacto
disque[M] compact
CD[F]
compact disc[M]

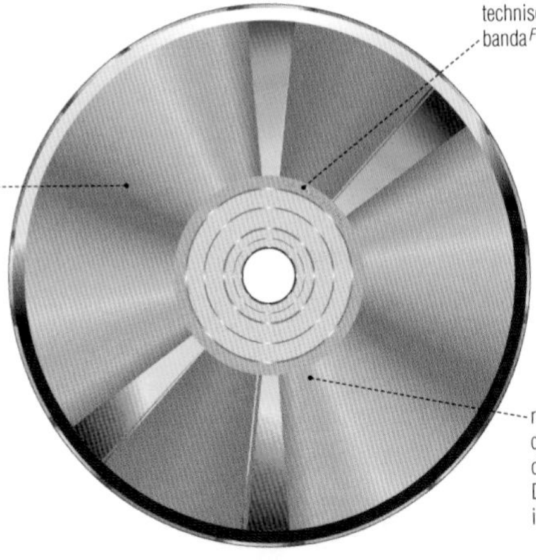

technical identification band
banda[F] de identificación[F] técnica
bande[F] d'identification[F] technique
technische Identifikationsnummer[F]
banda[F] di identificazione[F] tecnica

pressed area
área[F] grabada
surface[F] pressée
Programmbereich[M]
area[F] registrata

reading start
comienzo[M] de lectura[F]
début[M] de lecture[F]
Datenanfang[M]
inizio[M] lettura[F]

compact disc reading
lectura[M] de disco[M] compacto
lecture[F] du disque[M] compact
Lesen[N] von Compact Discs[F]
lettura[F] di compact disc[M]

asperity
pit[M]
aspérité[F]
Pit[N]
pit[M]

resin surface
superficie[F] de resina[F]
surface[F] de résine[F]
transparentes Akrylharz[N]
superficie[F] trasparente in resina[F]

objective lens
objetivo[M]
objectif[M]
Objektivlinse[F]
lente[F]

laser beam
rayo[M] láser
faisceau[M] laser[M]
Laserstrahl[M]
raggio[M] laser[M]

aluminum layer
capa[F] de aluminio[M]
couche[F] d'aluminium[M]
reflektierende Aluminiumschicht[F]
strato[M] riflettente in alluminio[M]

compact disc player
lector[M] de disco[M] compacto
lecteur[M] de disque[M] compact
CD-Spieler[M]
lettore[M] di compact disc[M]

stop button
parada[F]
arrêt[M]
Stopptaste[F]
stop[M]

play button
lectura[F]
lecture[F]
Playtaste[F]
riproduzione[F]

display
indicador[M]
afficheur[M]
Display[N]
display[M]

track search/fast operation buttons
cambio[M] de pista[F]/lectura[F] rápida
changement[M] de piste[F]/lecture[F] rapide
Titelsuche[F]/Schnellvorlauf[M]
ricerca[F] traccia[F]/riproduzione[F] rapida

direct disc access buttons
teclas[F] numéricas
touches[F] numériques
Direktwahltasten[F]
tasti[M] di accesso[M] diretto

shuffle play
lectura[F] aleatoria
lecture[F] aléatoire
Zufallswiedergabe[F]
riproduzione[F] casuale

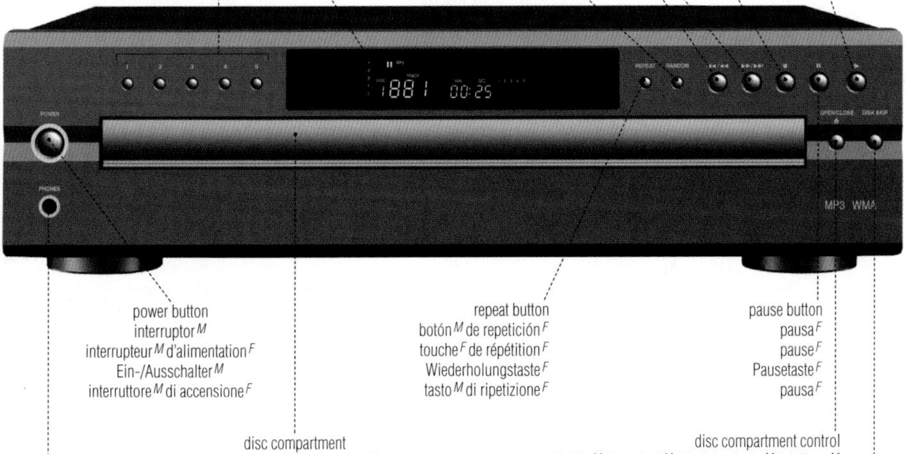
MP3 WMA

power button
interruptor[M]
interrupteur[M] d'alimentation[F]
Ein-/Ausschalter[M]
interruttore[M] di accensione[F]

repeat button
botón[M] de repetición[F]
touche[F] de répétition[F]
Wiederholungstaste[F]
tasto[M] di ripetizione[F]

pause button
pausa[F]
pause[F]
Pausetaste[F]
pausa[F]

disc compartment
alojamiento[M] para el disco[M]
logement[M] du plateau[M]
CD-Fach[N]
vano[M] del disco[M]

disc compartment control
botón[M] de control[M] del alojamiento[M] del disco[M]
contrôle[M] du plateau[M]
Auswurftaste[F]
tasto[M] di espulsione[F]

headphone jack
toma[F] para los auriculares[M]
prise[F] casque[M]
Kopfhöreranschluss[M]
presa[F] cuffie

disc skip
cambio[M] de disco[M]
changement[M] de disque[M]
CD[F] wechseln
cambio[M] disco[M]

mini stereo sound system

mini-cadena^{F} estéreo | minichaîne^{F} stéréo | Mini-HiFi^{F}-System^{N} | mini impianto^{M} hi-fi

compact disc recorder
reproductor^{M} de disco^{M} compacto
graveur^{M} de disque^{M} compact
CD^{F}-Rekorder^{M}
registratore^{M} di compact disc^{M}

compact disc player
lector de disco^{M} compacto
lecteur^{M} de disque^{M} compact
CD^{F}-Spieler^{M}
lettore^{M} di compact disc^{M}

ampli-tuner
amplificador^{M}-sintonizador^{M}
ampli^{M}-syntoniseur^{M}
Receiver^{M}
sintoamplificatore^{M}

CD TEXT EDITING
CD RECORDER
TAPE 1
TAPE 2

loudspeaker
altavoz^{M}
enceinte^{F} acoustique
Lautsprecher^{M}
cassa^{F} acustica

dual cassette deck
doble pletina^{F} de casete^{F}
double platine^{F} cassette^{F}
Doppel-Kassettendeck^{N}
doppia piastra^{F} di registrazione^{F}

portable sound systems

sistemas[M] de sonido[M] portátiles | appareils[M] de son[M] portatifs | tragbare Tonwiedergabesysteme[N] | riproduttori[M] portatili

portable radio
radio[F] portátil
radio[F] portable
Kofferradio[N]
radio[F] portatile

handle
mango[M]
poignée[F]
Tragebügel[M]
maniglia[F]
telescoping antenna
antena[F] telescópica
antenne[F] télescopique
Teleskopantenne[F]
antenna[F] telescopica
frequency display
display[M] de frecuencia
affichage[M] des stations[F]
Frequenzanzeige[F]
display[M] delle frequenze[F]
tuning control
selector[M] de sintonización[F]
sélecteur[M] de stations[F]
Frequenzwähler[M]
manopola[F] di sintonizzazione[F]
treble tone control
control[M] de tonos[M] de graves[M]
contrôle[M] de tonalité[F] des aigus[M]
Höhenregler[M]
regolatore[M] dei toni[M] alti
bass tone control
control[M] de tonos[M] de bajos
contrôle[M] de tonalité[F] des graves[M]
Bassregler[M]
regolatore[M] dei toni[M] bassi
volume control
selector[M] de volumen[M]
réglage[M] du volume[M]
Lautstärkeregler[M]
manopola[F] del volume[M]

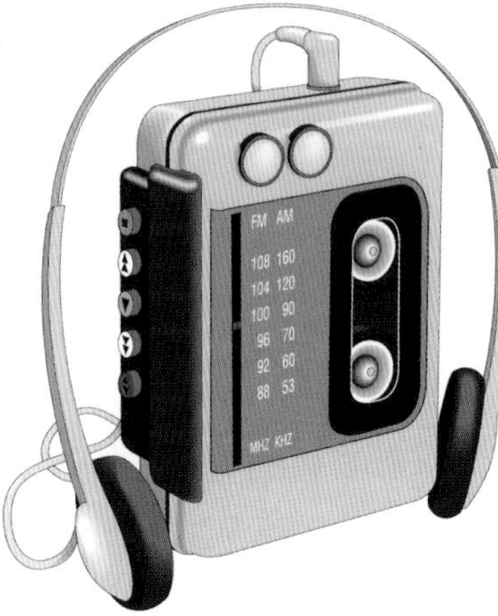

personal radio cassette player
Walkman® *M*
baladeur *M*
Walkman® *M* mit Radioteil *N*
Walkman® *M*

clock radio
radio *M* despertador
radio *F*-réveil *M*
Uhrenradio *N*
radiosveglia *F*

portable compact disc player
reproductor *M* de CD portátil
baladeur *M* pour disque *M* compact
tragbarer CD *F*-Spieler *M*
lettore *M* CD *M* portatile

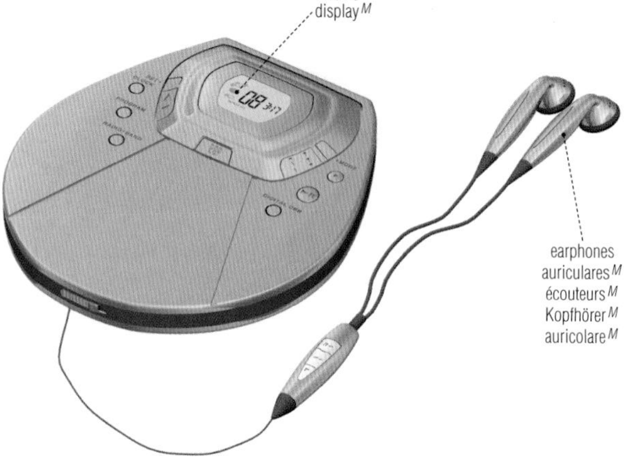
display
display M
afficheur M
Display N
display M
earphones
auriculares M
écouteurs M
Kopfhörer M
auricolare M

portable digital audio player
audio M player portátil digital
baladeur M numérique
MP3-Spieler M
lettore M audio digitale portatile

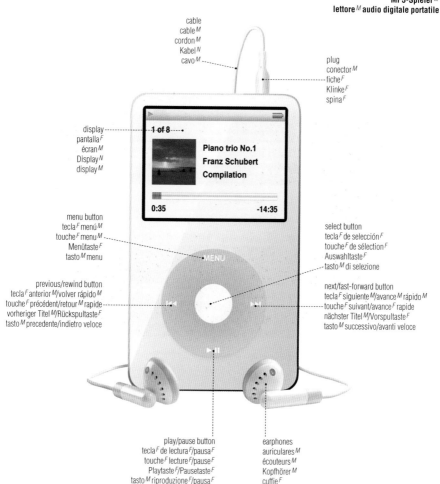

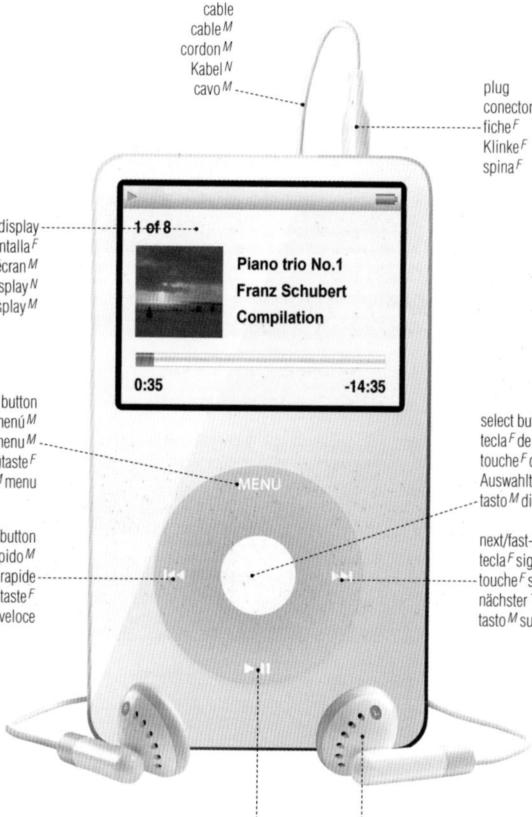
cable
cable M
cordon M
Kabel N
cavo M
plug
conector M
fiche F
Klinke F
spina F
display
pantalla F
écran M
Display N
display M
1 of 8
Piano trio No.1
Franz Schubert
Compilation
0:35
-14:35
menu button
tecla F menú M
touche F menu M
Menütaste F
tasto M menu
MENU
select button
tecla F de selección F
touche F de sélection F
Auswahltaste F
tasto M di selezione
previous/rewind button
tecla F anterior M/volver rápido M
touche F précédent/retour M rapide
vorheriger Titel M/Rückspultaste F
tasto M precedente/indietro veloce
next/fast-forward button
tecla F siguiente M/avance M rápido M
touche F suivant/avance F rapide
nächster Titel M/Vorspultaste F
tasto M successivo/avanti veloce
play/pause button
tecla F de lectura F/pausa F
touche F lecture F/pause F
Playtaste F/Pausetaste F
tasto M riproduzione F/pausa F
earphones
auriculares M
écouteurs M
Kopfhörer M
cuffie F

satellite radio receiver
receptor^{M} de radio^{F} vía satélite^{M}
récepteur^{M} de radio^{F} par satellite^{M}
Satellitenradioempfänger^{M}
ricevitore^{M} radio^{F} satellitare

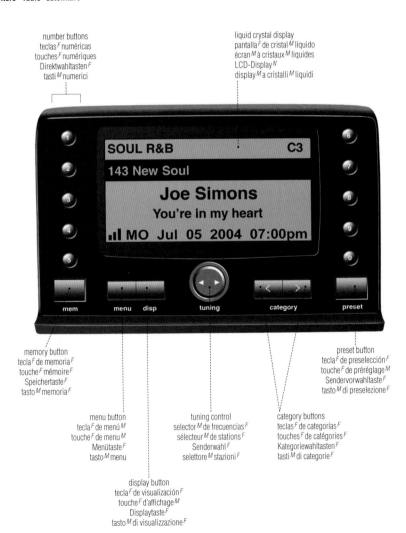

number buttons
teclas^{F} numéricas
touches^{F} numériques
Direktwahltasten^{F}
tasti^{M} numerici

liquid crystal display
pantalla^{F} de cristal^{M} líquido
écran^{M} à cristaux^{M} liquides
LCD-Display^{N}
display^{M} a cristalli^{M} liquidi

SOUL R&B
C3
143 New Soul
Joe Simons
You're in my heart
MO Jul 05 2004 07:00pm
1
2
3
4
5
6
7
8
9
0
mem
menu
disp
tuning
category
preset

memory button
tecla^{F} de memoria^{F}
touche^{F} mémoire^{F}
Speichertaste^{F}
tasto^{M} memoria^{F}

preset button
tecla^{F} de preselección^{F}
touche^{F} de préréglage^{M}
Sendervorwahltaste^{F}
tasto^{M} di preselezione^{F}

menu button
tecla^{F} de menú^{M}
touche^{F} de menu^{M}
Menütaste^{F}
tasto^{M} menu

tuning control
selector^{M} de frecuencias^{F}
sélecteur^{M} de stations^{F}
Senderwahl^{F}
selettore^{M} stazioni^{F}

category buttons
teclas^{F} de categorías^{F}
touches^{F} de catégories^{F}
Kategoriewahltasten^{F}
tasti^{M} di categorie^{F}

display button
tecla^{F} de visualización^{F}
touche^{F} d'affichage^{M}
Displaytaste^{F}
tasto^{M} di visualizzazione^{F}

wireless communication

comunicación^M sin hilos^M | communication^F sans fil^M | drahtlose Kommunikation^F | comunicazione^F senza fili^M

walkie-talkie
walkie-talkie^M
talkie-walkie^M
Walkie-Talkie^N
walkie-talkie^M

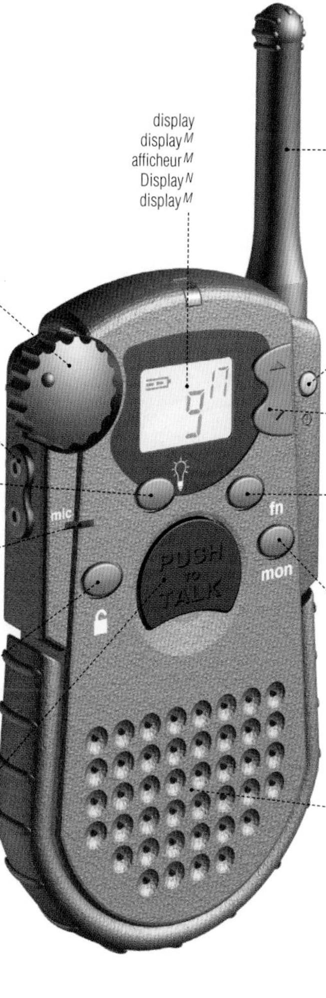

PUSH to TALK
mic
fn
mon

display
display^M
afficheur^M
Display^N
display^M

antenna
antena^F
antenne^F
Antenne^F
antenna^F

volume control
ajuste^M de volumen^M
réglage^M du volume^M
Lautstärkeregler^M
manopola^F del volume^M

power button
interruptor^M
interrupteur^M
Ein-/Ausschalter^M
interruttore^M di accensione^F

call button
tecla^F de llamada^F
touche^F d'appel^M
Ruftaste^F
tasto^M di chiamata^F

scroll button
tecla^F de desplazamiento^M
touche^F de défilement^M
Scrolltaste^F
tasto^M di scorrimento^M

light button
tecla^F de luminosidad^F
touche^F de luminosité^F
Helligkeitstaste^F
tasto^M di luminosità^F

menu button
tecla^M del menú^M
touche^F de menu^M
Menütaste^F
tasto^M del menu^M

microphone
micrófono^M
microphone^M
Mikrofon^N
microfono^M

monitor button
tecla^F de menú^M
touche^F de contrôle^M
Kontrolltaste^F
tasto^M di controllo^M

lock button
tecla^F de bloqueo^M
touche^F de verrouillage^M
Feststelltaste^F
tasto^M di blocco^M

speaker
altavoz^M
haut-parleur^M
Lautsprecher^M
altoparlante^M

push-to-talk switch
interruptor^M de emisión^F
interrupteur^M d'émission^F
Wechselsprechschalter^M
interruttore^M di trasmissione^F

wireless communication

numeric pager
buscapersonas *M*
téléavertisseur *M* **numérique**
Pager *M*
cercapersone *M*

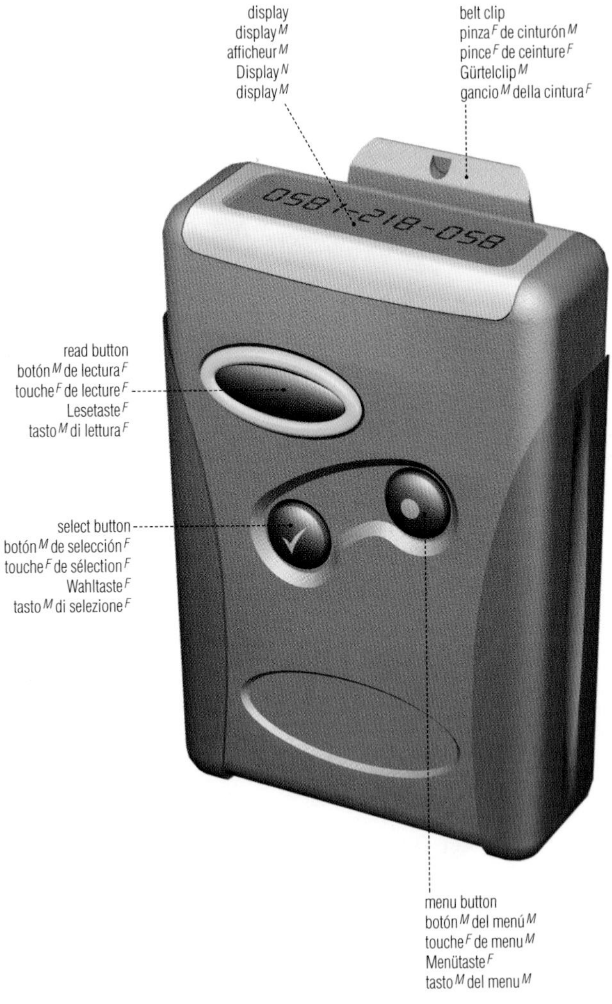
display
display M
afficheur M
Display N
display M
belt clip
pinza F de cinturón M
pince F de ceinture F
Gürtelclip M
gancio M della cintura F
read button
botón M de lectura F
touche F de lecture F
Lesetaste F
tasto M di lettura F
select button
botón M de selección F
touche F de sélection F
Wahltaste F
tasto M di selezione F
menu button
botón M del menú M
touche F de menu M
Menütaste F
tasto M del menu M

CB radio
radio^M CB
poste^M CB^F
CB-Funkanlage^F
radio^F CB

push-to-talk switch
interruptor^M de transmisión^F
interrupteur^M d'émission^F
Wechselsprechschalter^M
interruttore^M di trasmissione^F
microphone
micrófono^M
microphone^M
Mikrofon^N
microfono^M
cord
cordón^M
cordon^M
Kabel^N
cavo^M
display
display^M
afficheur^M
Display^N
display^M
microphone jack
toma^F del micrófono^M
prise^F microphone^M
Mikrofonanschlussbuchse^F
presa^F del microfono^M
channel selector
selector^M de canales^M
sélecteur^M de canaux^M
Kanalwahlschalter^M
selettore^M dei canali^M

communication by telephone

comunicación^F por teléfono^M | communication^F par téléphone^M | Telefonieren^N | comunicazione^F via telefono^M

portable cellular telephone
teléfono^M celular
téléphone^M portable
Handy^N
telefono^M cellulare

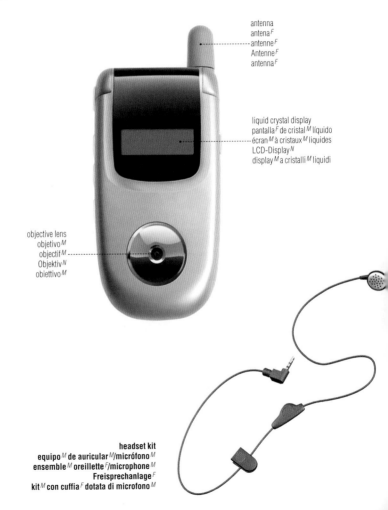

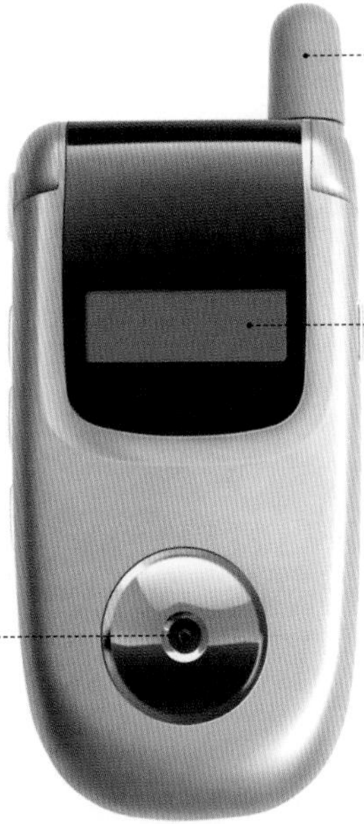

antenna
antena^F
antenne^F
Antenne^F
antenna^F

liquid crystal display
pantalla^F de cristal^M líquido
écran^M à cristaux^M liquides
LCD-Display^N
display^M a cristalli^M liquidi

objective lens
objetivo^M
objectif^M
Objektiv^N
obiettivo^M

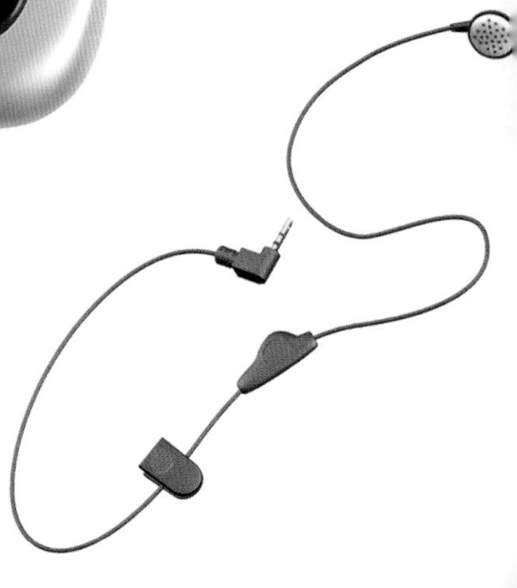

headset kit
equipo^M de auricular^M/micrófono^M
ensemble^M oreillette^F/microphone^M
Freisprechanlage^F
kit^M con cuffia^F dotata di microfono^M

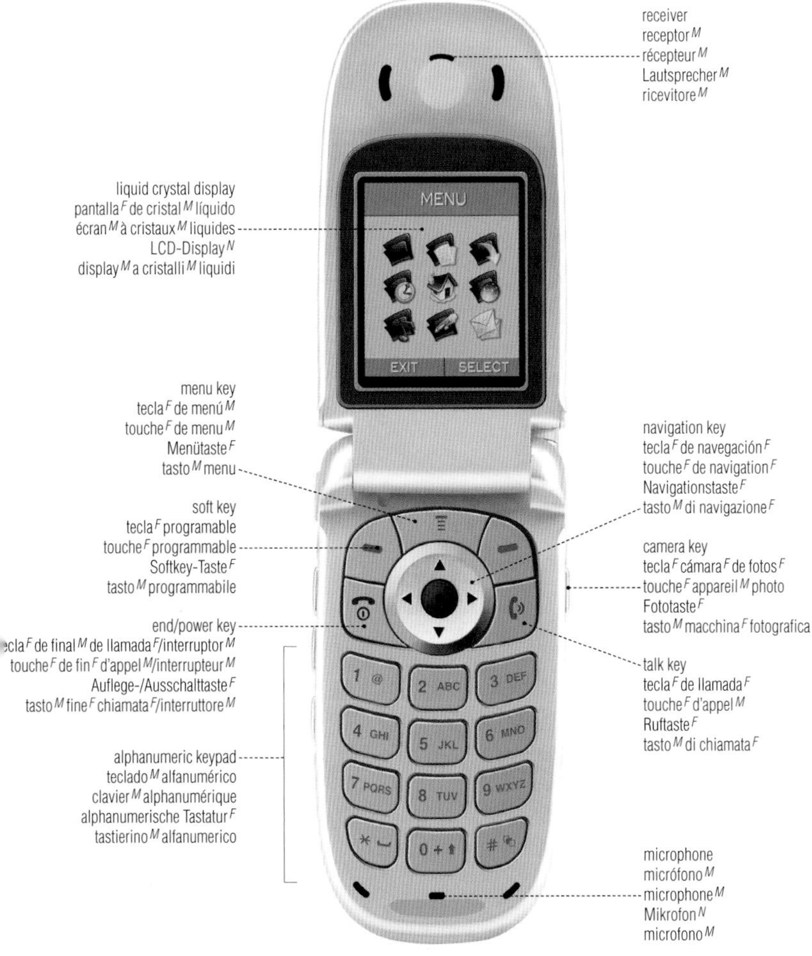
receiver
receptor M
récepteur M
Lautsprecher M
ricevitore M
liquid crystal display
pantalla F de cristal M líquido
écran M à cristaux M liquides
LCD-Display N
display M a cristalli M liquidi
menu key
tecla F de menú M
touche F de menu M
Menütaste F
tasto M menu
soft key
tecla F programable
touche F programmable
Softkey-Taste F
tasto M programmabile
end/power key
ecla F de final M de llamada F/interruptor M
touche F de fin F d'appel M/interrupteur M
Auflege-/Ausschalttaste F
tasto M fine F chiamata F/interruttore M
alphanumeric keypad
teclado M alfanumérico
clavier M alphanumérique
alphanumerische Tastatur F
tastierino M alfanumerico
navigation key
tecla F de navegación F
touche F de navigation F
Navigationstaste F
tasto M di navigazione F
camera key
tecla F cámara F de fotos F
touche F appareil M photo
Fototaste F
tasto M macchina F fotografica
talk key
tecla F de llamada F
touche F d'appel M
Ruftaste F
tasto M di chiamata F
microphone
micrófono M
microphone M
Mikrofon N
microfono M
MENU
EXIT
SELECT

communication by telephone

telephone set
teléfono *M*
poste *M* **téléphonique**
Telefonapparat *M*
apparecchio *M* **telefonico**

handset
auricular M
combiné M
Hörer M
microtelefono M
receiver volume control
control M de volumen M del auricular M
commande F de volume M du récepteur M
Lautstärkeregler M für den Hörer M
regolatore M del volume M di ricezione F
transmitter
transmisor M
microphone M
Sprechmuschel F
microfono M
handset cord
cable M del auricular M
cordon M de combiné M
Schnur F
cordone M del microtelefono M
push buttons
teclado M
clavier M
Tasten F
tastiera F
telephone index
agenda F telefónica
répertoire M téléphonique
Rufnummernregister N
rubrica F telefonica

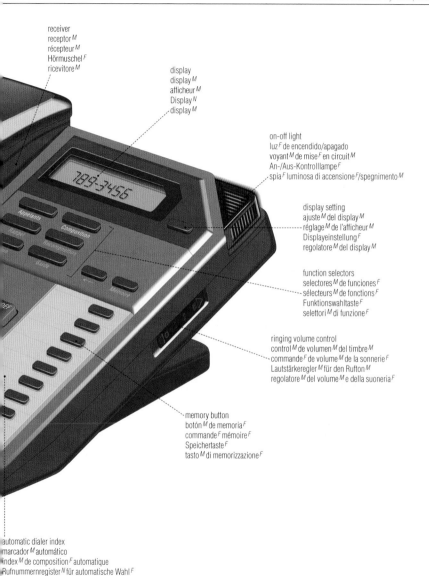

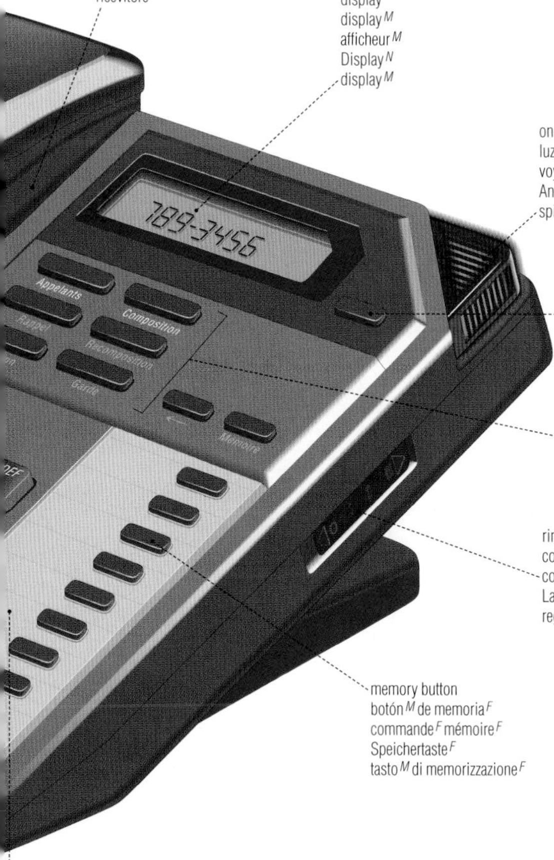
receiver
receptor [M]
récepteur [M]
Hörmuschel [F]
ricevitore [M]
display
display [M]
afficheur [M]
Display [N]
display [M]
on-off light
luz [F] de encendido/apagado
voyant [M] de mise [F] en circuit [M]
An-/Aus-Kontrolllampe [F]
spia [F] luminosa di accensione [F]/spegnimento [M]
display setting
ajuste [M] del display [M]
réglage [M] de l'afficheur [M]
Displayeinstellung [F]
regolatore [M] del display [M]
function selectors
selectores [M] de funciones [F]
sélecteurs [M] de fonctions [F]
Funktionswahltaste [F]
selettori [M] di funzione [F]
ringing volume control
control [M] de volumen [M] del timbre [M]
commande [F] de volume [M] de la sonnerie [F]
Lautstärkeregler [M] für den Rufton [M]
regolatore [M] del volume [M] e della suoneria [F]
memory button
botón [M] de memoria [F]
commande [F] mémoire [F]
Speichertaste [F]
tasto [M] di memorizzazione [F]
automatic dialer index
marcador [M] automático
index [M] de composition [F] automatique
Rufnummernregister [N] für automatische Wahl [F]
tasti [M] di chiamata [F] automatica
789-3456
Appelants
Composition
Rappel
Recomposition
Garde
Mémoire

communication by telephone

pay phone
teléfono[M] público
téléphone[M] public
öffentlicher Fernsprecher[M]
apparecchio[M] telefonico a gettoni[M]

coin slot
ranura[F] para monedas[F]
fente[F] à monnaie[F]
Münzeinwurf[M]
fessura[F] per gettoni[M]

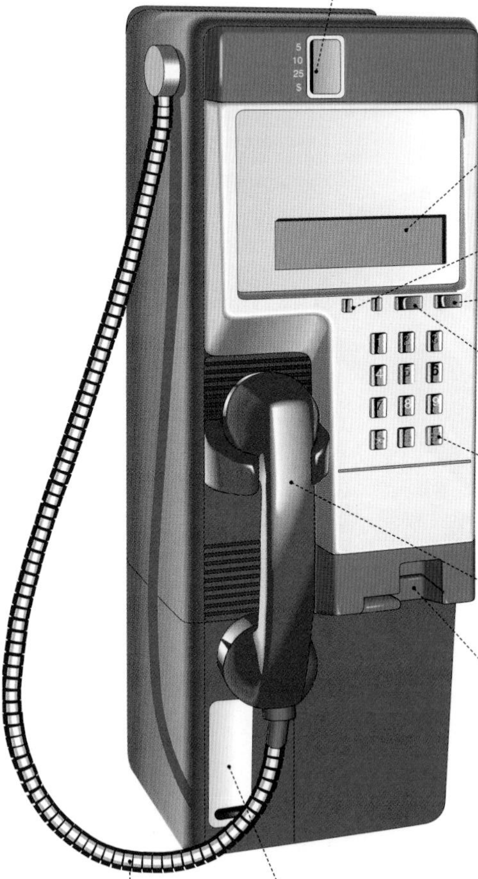

display
visualización[F]
écran[M]
Display[N]
display[M]

volume control
control[M] de volumen[M]
contrôle[M] du volume[M]
Lautstärkeregler[M]
regolatore[M] del volume[M]

next call
próxima llamada[F]
appel[M] suivant
nächster Ruf[M]
tasto[M] di chiamata[F] successiva

language display button
botón[M] de selección[F] de idioma[M]
choix[M] de la langue[F] d'affichage[M]
Sprachanzeigetaste[F]
tasto[M] di selezione[F] della lingua[F] del display[M]

push button
teclado[M]
clavier[M]
Taste[F]
tastiera[F]

handset
auricular[M]
combiné[M]
Hörer[M]
microtelefono[M]

card reader
lector[M] de tarjetas[F]
lecteur[M] de carte[F]
Kartenschlitz[M]
lettore[M] di schede[F]

armored cord
cable[M] con funda[F] metálica
cordon[M] à gaine[F] métallique
Panzerschnur[F]
cavo[M] armato

coin return bucket
devolución[F] de monedas[F]
sébile[F] de remboursement[M]
Geldrückgabefach[F]
finestrella[F] per la restituzione[F] dei gettoni[M]

push-button telephone
teléfono M de teclado M
poste M à clavier M
Tastentelefon N
telefono M a tastiera F

smartphone
asistente M numérico comunicante
assistant M numérique communiquant
Smartphone N
palmare M

display
pantalla F
écran M
Display N
display M
function keys
teclas F de función F
touches F de fonctions F
Funktionstasten F
tasti M funzione
keypad
teclado M
clavier M
Tastatur F
tastiera F

cordless telephone
teléfono M inalámbrico
poste M sans cordon M
schnurloses Telefon N
telefono M senza fili M

call director telephone
centralita F
pupitre M dirigeur
Telefonzentrale F
centralina F

facsimile (fax) machine
fax *M*
télécopieur *M*
Telefaxgerät *N*
telefax *M*

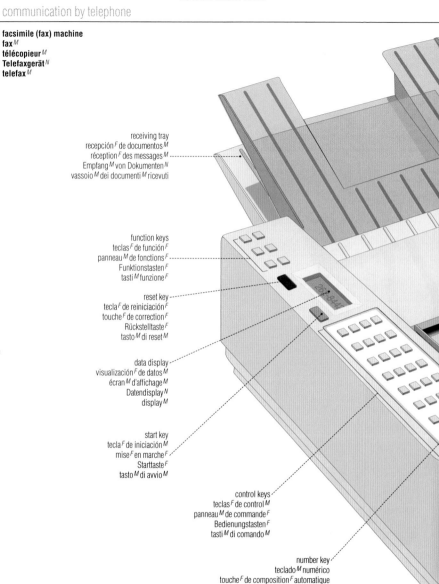

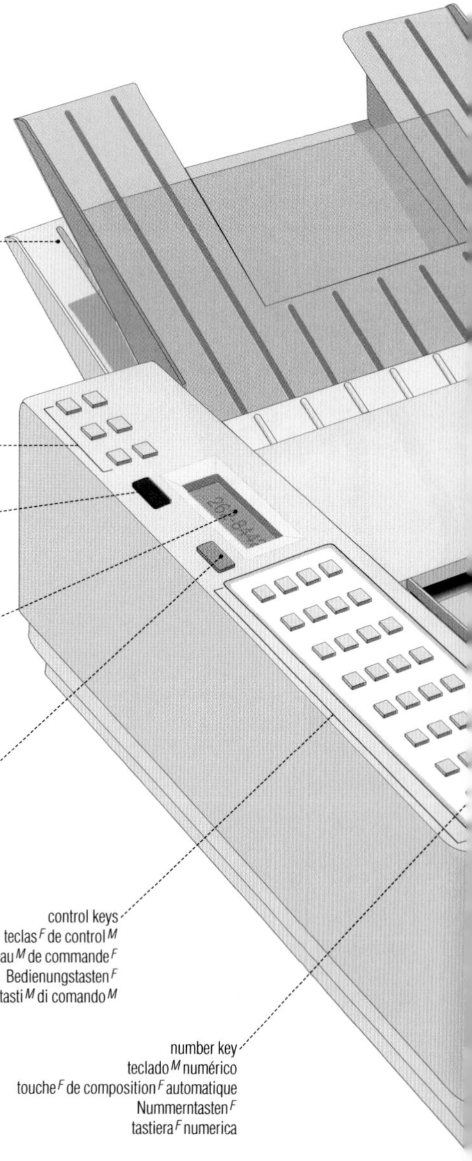

receiving tray
recepción *F* de documentos *M*
réception *F* des messages *M*
Empfang *M* von Dokumenten *N*
vassoio *M* dei documenti *M* ricevuti
function keys
teclas *F* de función *F*
panneau *M* de fonctions *F*
Funktionstasten *F*
tasti *M* funzione *F*
reset key
tecla *F* de reiniciación *F*
touche *F* de correction *F*
Rückstelltaste *F*
tasto *M* di reset *M*
data display
visualización *F* de datos *M*
écran *M* d'affichage *M*
Datendisplay *N*
display *M*
start key
tecla *F* de iniciación *M*
mise *F* en marche *F*
Starttaste *F*
tasto *M* di avvio *M*
control keys
teclas *F* de control *M*
panneau *M* de commande *F*
Bedienungstasten *F*
tasti *M* di comando *M*
number key
teclado *M* numérico
touche *F* de composition *F* automatique
Nummerntasten *F*
tastiera *F* numerica

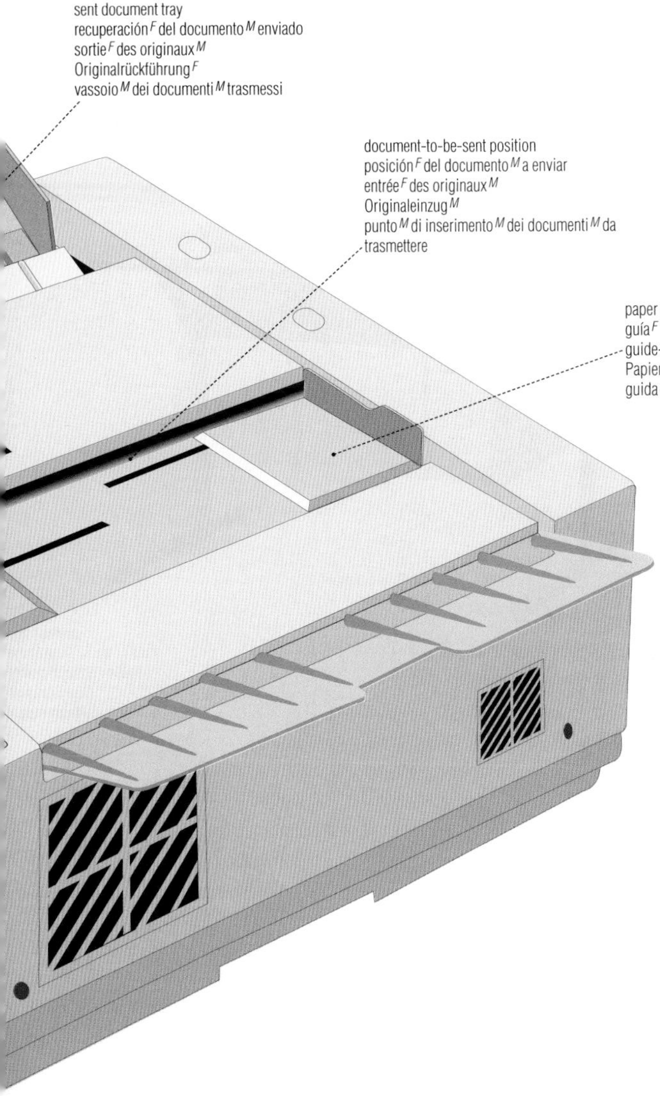
sent document tray
recuperación F del documento M enviado
sortie F des originaux M
Originalrückführung F
vassoio M dei documenti M trasmessi
document-to-be-sent position
posición F del documento M a enviar
entrée F des originaux M
Originaleinzug M
punto M di inserimento M dei documenti M da trasmettere
paper guide
guía F del papel M
guide-papier M
Papierführung F
guida F della carta F

office furniture

muebles[M] de oficina[F] | mobilier[M] de bureau[M] | Büromöbel[N] | mobili[M] per ufficio[M]

work furniture
muebles[M] de trabajo[M]
meubles[M] de travail[M]
Arbeitsmöbel[N]
mobili[M] da lavoro[M]

computer table
mesa[F] del ordenador[M]
table[F] d'ordinateur[M]
Computertisch[M]
tavolo[M] portacomputer

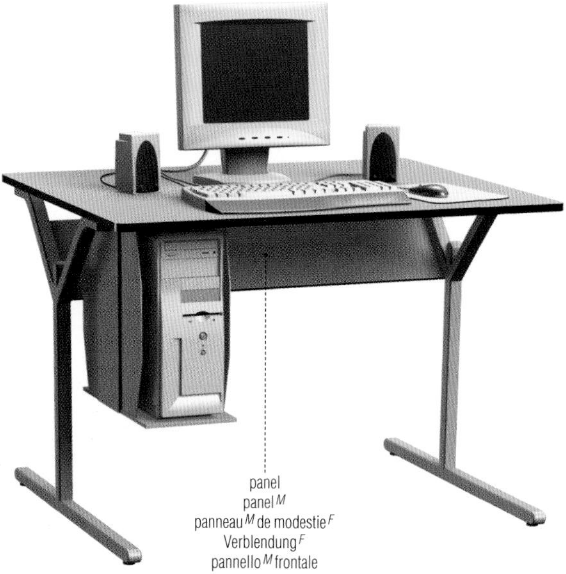
panel
panel[M]
panneau[M] de modestie[F]
Verblendung[F]
pannello[M] frontale

printer tabl
mesa[F] de la impresora
table[F] d'imprimante
Druckertisch
tavolo[M] portastampant

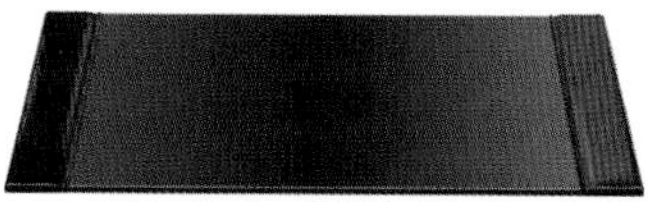

desk mat
vade[M]
sous-main[M]
Schreibunterlage[F]
sottomano[M]

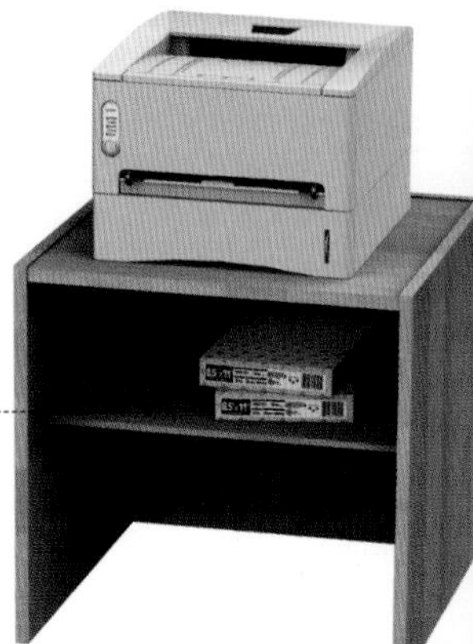
shelf
tablilla[F]
tablette[F]
Ablage[F]
ripiano[M]

swivel-tilter armchair
sillón M giratorio
fauteuil M pivotant à bascule F
Drehsessel M
poltrona F girevole reclinabile

typist's chair
silla F de secretaria F
chaise F dactylo M
Bürodrehstuhl M
sedia F dattilo

executive desk
escritorio M de ejecutivo M
bureau M de direction F
Chefschreibtisch M
scrivania F direzionale

secretarial desk
escritorio M de secretaria F
bureau M secrétaire M
Arbeitsplatz M
scrivania F operativa

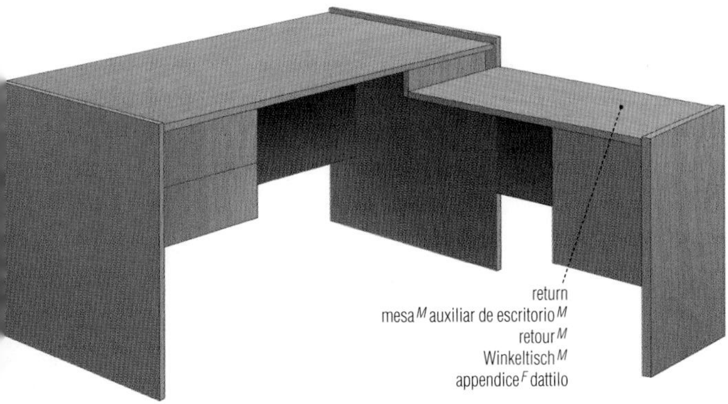
return
mesa M auxiliar de escritorio M
retour M
Winkeltisch M
appendice F dattilo

filing furniture
archivadores^M
meubles^M de classement^M
Archivmöbel^N
mobili^M di archivio^M

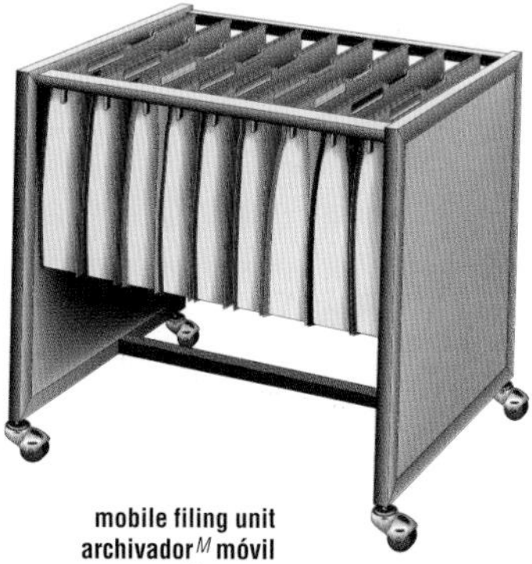

mobile filing unit
archivador^M móvil
classeur^M mobile
fahrbare Aktenablage^F
schedario^M mobile

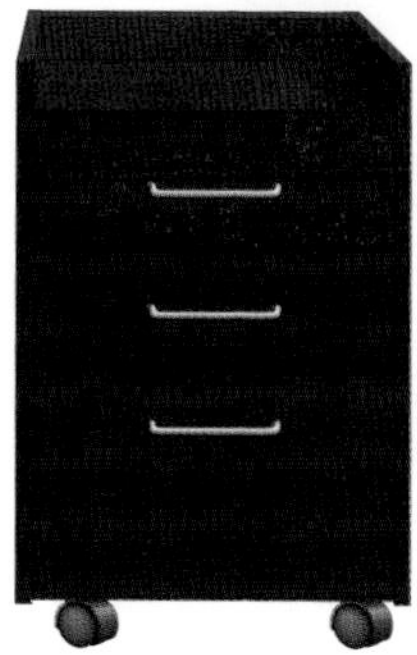

mobile drawer unit
cajonera^F móvil
caisson^M
fahrbares Schubladenelement^N
cassettiera^F mobile

lateral filing cabinet
archivador^M lateral
classeur^M à clapets^M
Hängekartei^F
schedario^M a visibilità^F laterale

photocopier
fotocopiadora *F*
photocopieur *M*
Fotokopierer *M*
fotocopiatrice *F*

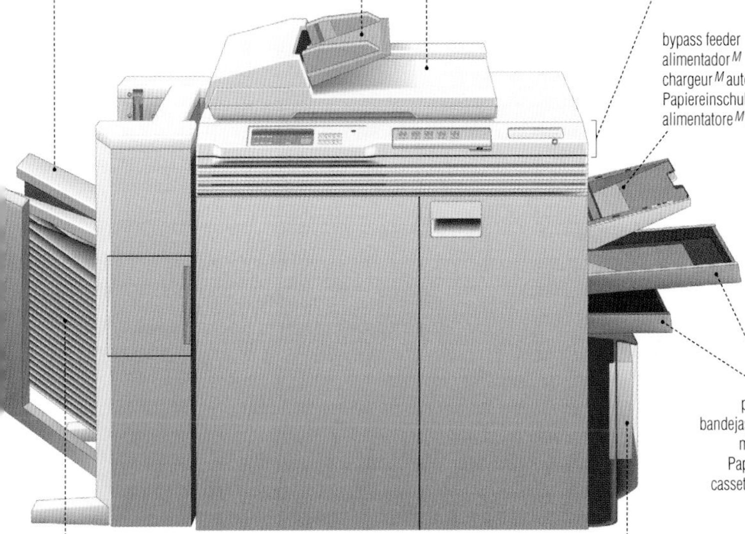
document handler
cargador M de documentos M
chargeur M manuel
Vorlageneinzug M
alimentatore M automatico

feeder output tray
bandeja F de recepción F de copias F
plateau M récepteur
Kopienablage F
vassoio M di uscita F della carta F

cover
tapa F
couvercle M
Abdeckung F
coperchio M

control panel
tablero M de controles M
tableau M de commande F
Bedienungskonsole F
pannello M di comando M

bypass feeder
alimentador M
chargeur M automatique
Papiereinschubfach N
alimentatore M manuale

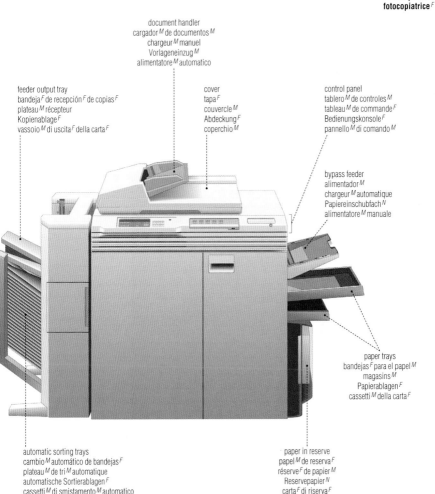

paper trays
bandejas F para el papel M
magasins M
Papierablagen F
cassetti M della carta F

automatic sorting trays
cambio M automático de bandejas F
plateau M de tri M automatique
automatische Sortierablagen F
cassetti M di smistamento M automatico

paper in reserve
papel M de reserva F
réserve F de papier M
Reservepapier N
carta F di riserva F

personal computer

ordenador^M personal | micro-ordinateur^M | Personalcomputer^M | personal computer^M

tower case: front view
ordenador^M: vista^F frontal
boîtier^M tour^F: vue^F avant
Towergehäuse^N: Vorderansicht^F
châssis^M: vista^F frontale

CD/DVD-ROM drive
unidad^F de CD/DVD-ROM
lecteur^M de CD/DVD-ROM^M
CD^F-/DVD^F-Laufwerk^N
lettore^M CD^M/DVD-ROM^M
CD/DVD-ROM eject button
botón^M de expulsión de CD/DVD-ROM
bouton^M d'éjection^F du CD/DVD-ROM^M
CD^F-/DVD^F-Auswurftaste^F
pulsante^M di espulsione^F del CD^M/DVD-ROM^M
bay filler panel
panel^M de cierre^M
obturateur^M de baie^F
Schutzdeckel^M
otturatore^M
reset button
botón^M de reiniciación^F
bouton^M de réinitialisation^F
Resettaste^F
pulsante^M di reset^M
memory card reader
lector^M de tarjeta^F de memoria^F
lecteur^M de carte^F mémoire^F
Speicherkartenleser^M
lettore^M di scheda^F di memoria^F
power button
interruptor^M de encendido
bouton^M de démarrage^M
Ein-/Ausschalter^M
interruttore^M di accensione^F
USB port
puerto^M USB
port^M USB
USB-Schnittstelle^F
porta^F USB

tower case: back view
ordenador[M]: vista[F] posterior
boîtier[M] tour[F]: vue[F] arrière
Towergehäuse[N]: Rückansicht[F]
châssis[M]: dorso[M]

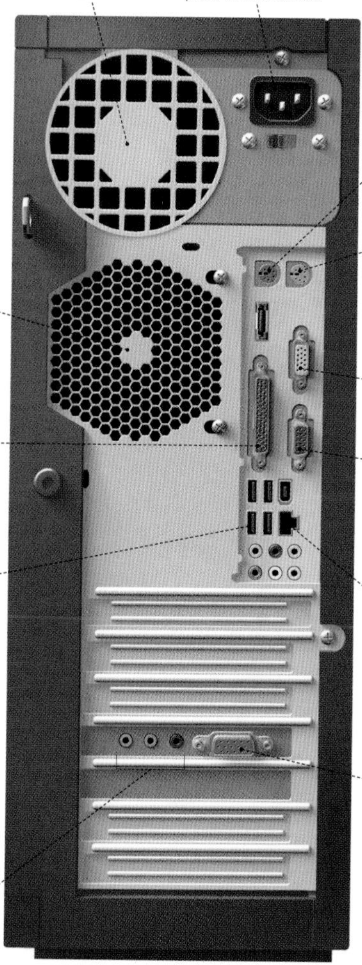
power supply fan
ventilador[M] del equipo[M] de alimentación[F]
ventilateur[M] du bloc[M] d'alimentation[F]
Netzteillüfter[M]
ventola[F] dell'alimentatore[M]
power cable plug
toma[F] de alimentación[F]
prise[F] d'alimentation[F]
Netzanschlussbuchse[F]
presa[F] di alimentazione[F]
keyboard port
puerto[M] teclado
port[M] clavier[M]
Tastaturschnittstelle[F]
porta[F] della tastiera[F]
mouse port
puerto[M] ratón
port[M] souris[F]
Mausschnittstelle[F]
porta[F] del mouse[M]
case fan
ventilador[M] de la carcasa[F]
ventilateur[M] du boîtier[M]
Gehäuselüfter[M]
ventola[F] dello châssis[M]
serial port
puerto[M] serial
port[M] série[F]
serielle Schnittstelle[F]
porta[F] seriale
parallel port
puerto[M] paralelo
port[M] parallèle
Parallelschnittstelle[F]
porta[F] parallela
video port
puerto[M] de vídeo[M]
port[M] vidéo
Videoschnittstelle[F]
porta[F] video[M]
USB port
puerto[M] USB
port[M] USB
USB-Schnittstelle[F]
porta[F] USB
network port
puerto[M] de red[F]
port[M] réseau[M]
Netzwerkschnittstelle[F]
porta[F] di rete[F]
game/MIDI port
puerto[M] juego[M]/puerto[M] MIDI
port[M] jeux[M]/MIDI
Spiele[N]-/MIDI-Schnittstelle[F]
porta[F] giochi[M]/ porta[F] MIDI
audio jack
toma[F] audio
prise[F] audio
Audiobuchse[F]
presa[F] audio[M]

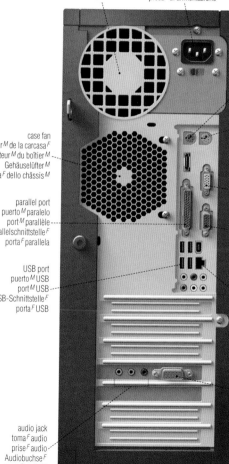

personal computer

tower case: interior view
ordenador M : vista F interna
boîtier M tour F : vue F intérieure
Towergehäuse N: Innenansicht F
châssis M: interno M

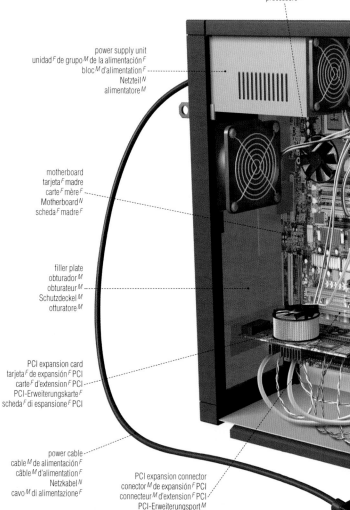

processor
procesador M
processeur M
Prozessor M
processore M
power supply unit
unidad F de grupo M de la alimentación F
bloc M d'alimentation F
Netzteil N
alimentatore M
motherboard
tarjeta F madre
carte F mère F
Motherboard N
scheda F madre F
filler plate
obturador M
obturateur M
Schutzdeckel M
otturatore M
PCI expansion card
tarjeta F de expansión F PCI
carte F d'extension F PCI
PCI-Erweiterungskarte F
scheda F di espansione F PCI
power cable
cable M de alimentación F
câble M d'alimentation F
Netzkabel N
cavo M di alimentazione F
PCI expansion connector
conector M de expansión F PCI
connecteur M d'extension F PCI
PCI-Erweiterungsport M
connettore M per espansioni F PCI

D/DVD-ROM drive
nidad[F] CD/DVD-ROM
ecteur[M] de CD/DVD-ROM[M]
D[F]-/DVD[F]-Laufwerk[N]
ettore[M] CD[M]/DVD-ROM[M]
battery
batería[F]
pile[F]
Akku[M]
pila[F]
random access memory (RAM) module
unidad[F] de memoria[F] de acceso[M] aleatorio (RAM)
barrette[F] de mémoire[F] vive (RAM)
Schreib-Lese-Speicher[M] (RAM[M])
modulo[M] RAM[F]
chipset
chipset[M]
jeu[M] de puces[F]
Chipset[N]
chipset[M]
AGP expansion connector
conector[M] de expansión[F] AGP
connecteur[M] d'extension[F] AGP
AGP-Erweiterungsport[M]
connettore[M] per espansioni[F] AGP
secondary hard disk drive
unidad[F] secundaria de disco[M] duro
lecteur[M] de disque[M] dur secondaire
zusätzliches Festplattenlaufwerk[N]
unità[F] hard disk[M] secondaria
primary hard disk drive
unidad[F] de disco[M] duro primario
lecteur[M] de disque[M] dur primaire
Hauptfestplattenlaufwerk[N]
unità[F] hard disk[M] principale

input devices

unidades[F] de entrada[F] de información[F] | périphériques[M] d'entrée[F] | Eingabegeräte[N] | dispositivi[M] di entrata[F]

keyboard and pictograms
teclado[M] y pictogramas[M]
clavier[M] et pictogrammes[M]
Tastatur[F] und Piktogramme[N]
tastiera[F] e pittogrammi[M]

escape key
tecla[F] escape
touche[F] d'échappement[M]
Escapetaste[F]
tasto[M] Esc

function keys
teclas[F] de funciones[F]
touches[F] de fonction[F]
Funktionstasten[F]
tasti[M] funzione[F]

tabulation key
tecla[F] tabulación
touche[F] de tabulation[F]
Tabulatortaste[F]
tasto[M] di tabulazione[F]

capitals lock key
tecla[F] de bloqueo[M] de mayúsculas
touche[F] de verrouillage[M] des majuscules[F]
Großschriftfeststellungstaste[F]
tasto[M] di blocco[M] delle maiuscole[F]

shift key
tecla[F] de mayúsculas[F]
touche[F] majuscule
Umschalttasten[F]
tasto[M] delle maiuscole[F]

control key
tecla[F] de servicio[M]
touche[F] de contrôle[M]
Steuerungstaste[F]
tasto[M] Control

start key
tecla[F] inicio
touche[F] de démarrage[M]
Startmenütaste[F]
tasto[M] Avvio[M]

alternate key
tecla[F] alternativa
touche[F] alternative
Alt-Taste[F]
tasto[M] Alt

Back
Forward
Stop
Mail
Search
Esc
F1 Help
F2
F3
F4
F5
F6
F7
Tab
CapsLock
Shift
Ctrl
Alt

detachable palm rest
reposamanos[M]
repose-poignets[M] détachable
abnehmbare Handballenauflage[F]
poggiamano[M] amovibile

space bar
barra[F] espaciadora
barre[F] d'espacement[M]
Leertaste[F]
barra[F] spaziatrice

alphanumeric keypa
teclado[M] alfanuméric
pavé[M] alphanumériqu
alphanumerische Tastatur
tastiera[F] alfanumeric

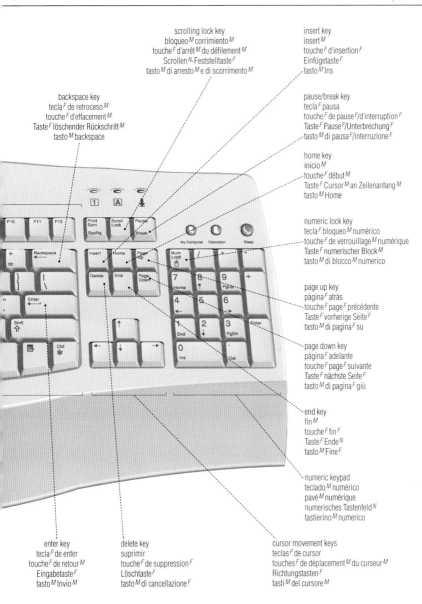

scrolling lock key
bloqueo^{M} corrimiento^{M}
touche^{F} d'arrêt^{M} du défilement^{M}
Scrollen^{N}-Feststelltaste^{F}
tasto^{M} di arresto^{M} e di scorrimento^{M}

insert key
insert^{M}
touche^{F} d'insertion^{F}
Einfügetaste^{F}
tasto^{M} Ins

backspace key
tecla^{F} de retroceso^{M}
touche^{F} d'effacement^{M}
Taste^{F} löschender Rückschritt^{M}
tasto^{M} backspace

pause/break key
tecla^{F} pausa
touche^{F} de pause^{F}/d'interruption^{F}
Taste^{F} Pause^{F}/Unterbrechung^{F}
tasto^{M} di pausa^{F}/interruzione^{F}

home key
inicio^{M}
touche^{F} début^{M}
Taste^{F} Cursor^{M} an Zeilenanfang^{M}
tasto^{M} Home

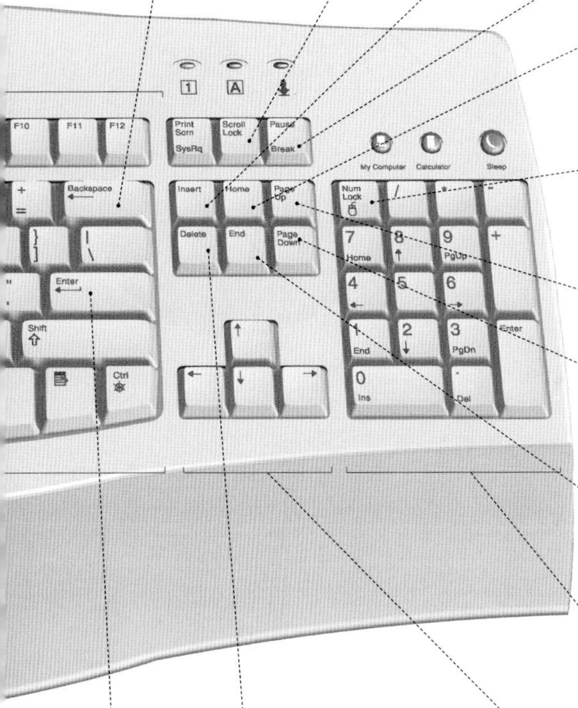
F10
F11
F12
Print Scrn SysRq
Scroll Lock
Pause Break
My Computer
Calculator
Sleep
Backspace
Insert
Home
Page Up
Delete
End
Page Down
Num Lock
Enter
Shift
Ctrl
7 Home
8
9 PgUp
4
5
6
1 End
2
3 PgDn
0 Ins
. Del
Enter

numeric lock key
tecla^{F} bloqueo^{M} numérico
touche^{F} de verrouillage^{M} numérique
Taste^{F} numerischer Block^{M}
tasto^{M} di blocco^{M} numerico

page up key
página^{F} atrás
touche^{F} page^{F} précédente
Taste^{F} vorherige Seite^{F}
tasto^{M} di pagina^{F} su

page down key
página^{F} adelante
touche^{F} page^{F} suivante
Taste^{F} nächste Seite^{F}
tasto^{M} di pagina^{F} giù

end key
fin^{M}
touche^{F} fin^{F}
Taste^{F} Ende^{N}
tasto^{M} Fine^{F}

numeric keypad
teclado^{M} numérico
pavé^{M} numérique
numerisches Tastenfeld^{N}
tastierino^{M} numerico

enter key
tecla^{F} de enter
touche^{F} de retour^{M}
Eingabetaste^{F}
tasto^{M} Invio^{M}

delete key
suprimir
touche^{F} de suppression^{F}
Löschtaste^{F}
tasto^{M} di cancellazione^{F}

cursor movement keys
teclas^{F} de cursor
touches^{F} de déplacement^{M} du curseur^{M}
Richtungstasten^{F}
tasti^{M} del cursore^{M}

input devices

wheel mouse
ratón[M] de rueda[F]
souris[F] à roulette[F]
Kugelmaus[F]
mouse[M] a rotella[F]

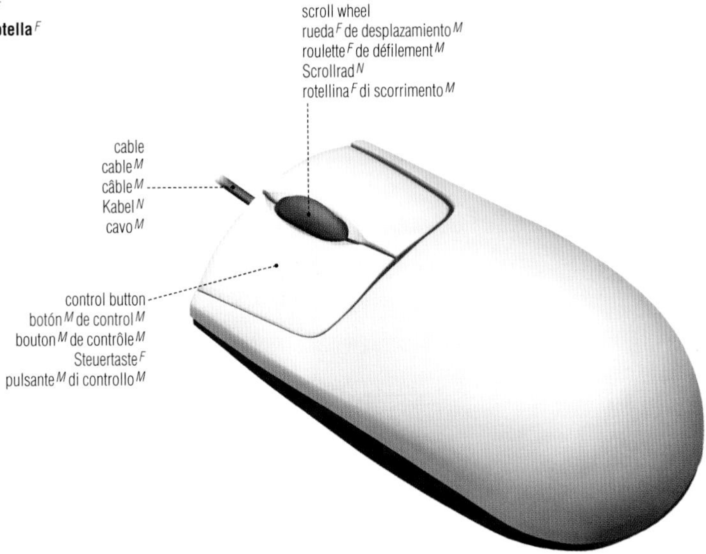
scroll wheel
rueda[F] de desplazamiento[M]
roulette[F] de défilement[M]
Scrollrad[N]
rotellina[F] di scorrimento[M]
cable
cable[M]
câble[M]
Kabel[N]
cavo[M]
control button
botón[M] de control[M]
bouton[M] de contrôle[M]
Steuertaste[F]
pulsante[M] di controllo[M]

cordless mouse
ratón[M] inalámbrico
souris[F] sans fil[M]
Funkmaus[F]
mouse[M] senza fili[M]

mechanical mouse
ratón *M* **mecánico**
souris *F* **mécanique**
mechanische Maus *F*
mouse *M* **meccanico**

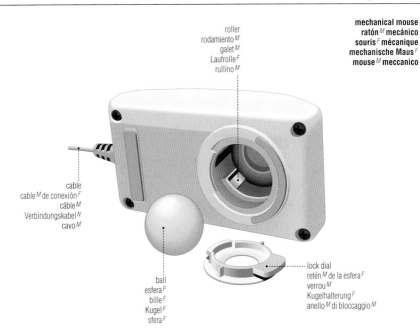

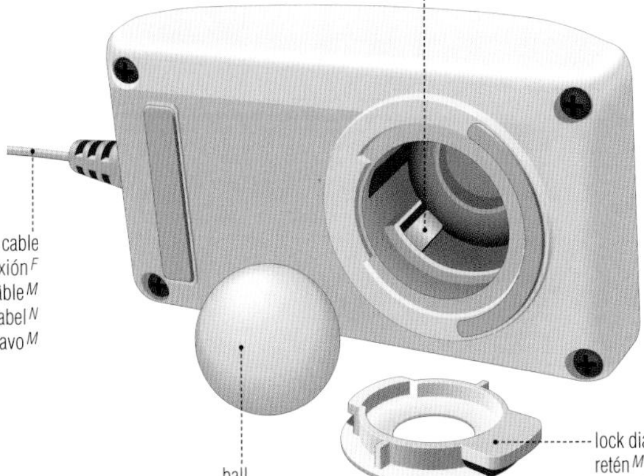
roller
rodamiento M
galet M
Laufrolle F
rullino M
cable
cable M de conexión F
câble M
Verbindungskabel N
cavo M
ball
esfera F
bille F
Kugel F
sfera F
lock dial
retén M de la esfera F
verrou M
Kugelhalterung F
anello M di bloccaggio M

optical mouse
ratón *M* **óptico**
souris *F* **optique**
optische Maus *F*
mouse *M* **ottico**

optical sensor
sensor M óptico
capteur M optique
optischer Sensor M
sensore M ottico

input devices

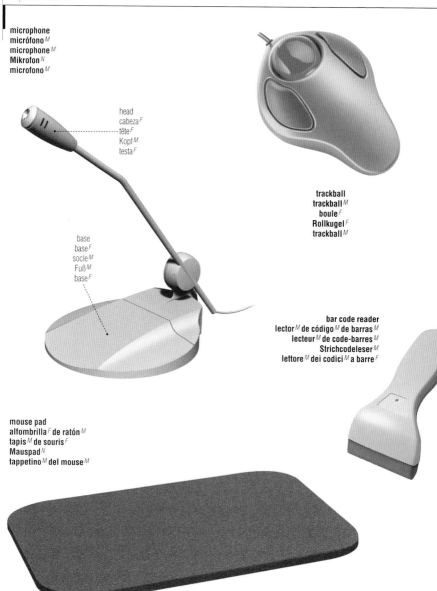

microphone
micrófono *M*
microphone *M*
Mikrofon *N*
microfono *M*

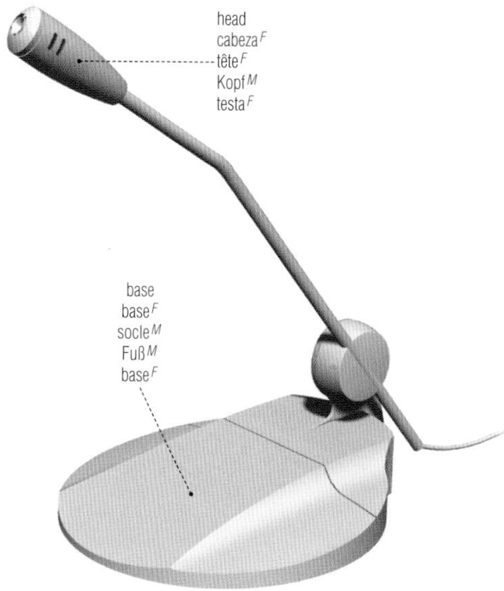
head
cabeza *F*
tête *F*
Kopf *M*
testa *F*
base
base *F*
socle *M*
Fuß *M*
base *F*

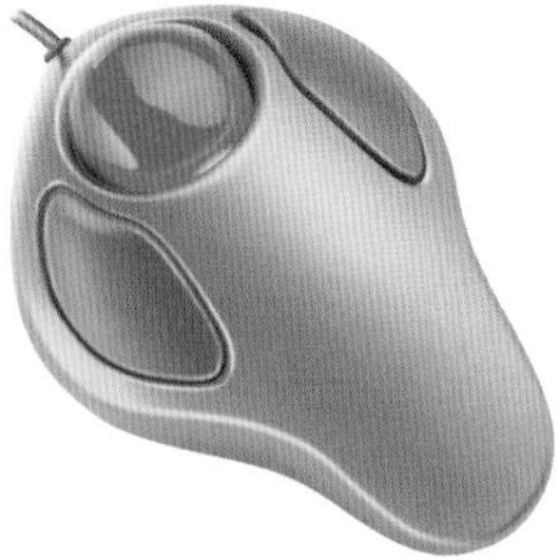

trackball
trackball *M*
boule *F*
Rollkugel *F*
trackball *M*

bar code reader
lector *M* **de código** *M* **de barras** *M*
lecteur *M* **de code-barres** *M*
Strichcodeleser *M*
lettore *M* **dei codici** *M* **a barre** *F*

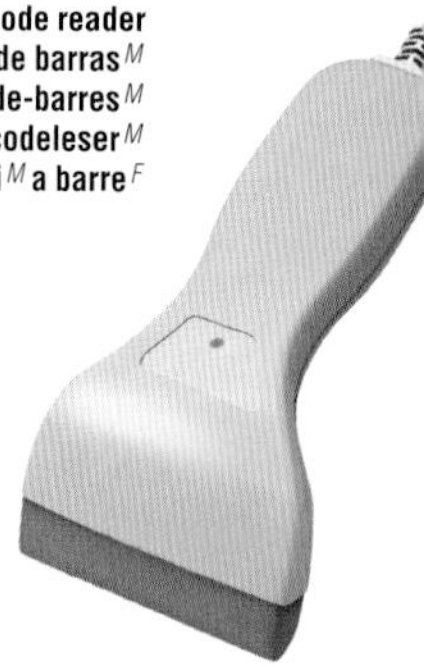

mouse pad
alfombrilla *F* **de ratón** *M*
tapis *M* **de souris** *F*
Mauspad *N*
tappetino *M* **del mouse** *M*

joystick
joystick M
manche M **à balai** M
Joystick M
joystick M

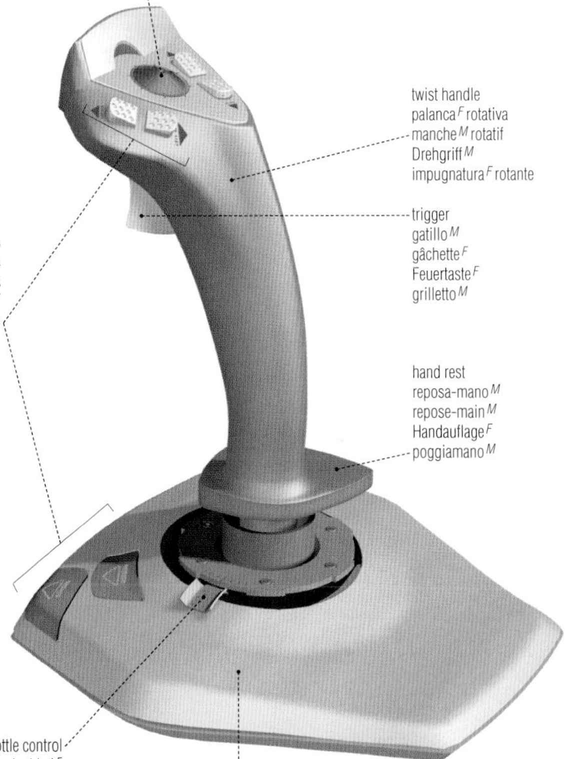
hat switch
botón M de seta F
bouton M champignon M
Hat-Switch M
hat switch M
twist handle
palanca F rotativa
manche M rotatif
Drehgriff M
impugnatura F rotante
trigger
gatillo M
gâchette F
Feuertaste F
grilletto M
programmable buttons
botones M programables
boutons M programmables
programmierbare Tasten F
pulsanti M programmabili
hand rest
reposa-mano M
repose-main M
Handauflage F
poggiamano M
throttle control
control M de velocidad F
manette F des gaz M
Schubkontrolle F
controllo M dell'accelerazione F
base
base F
socle M
Fuß M
base F

Webcam
cámara^F web
webcaméra^F
Webcam^F
webcam^F

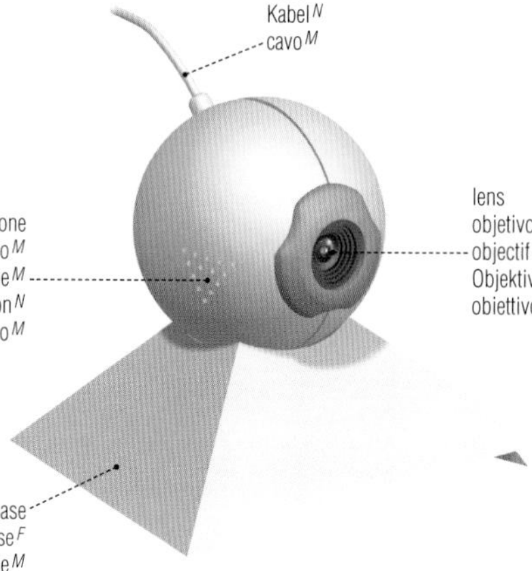
cable
cable^M
câble^M
Kabel^N
cavo^M
lens
objetivo^M
objectif^M
Objektiv^N
obiettivo^M
microphone
micrófono^M
microphone^M
Mikrofon^N
microfono^M
base
base^F
socle^M
Fuß^M
base^F

digital camera
cámara^F digital
appareil^M numérique
Digitalkamera^F
macchina^F fotografica digitale

digital camcorde
camcorder^F digit
caméscope^M numériqu
Digital-Camcorder
videocamera^F digita

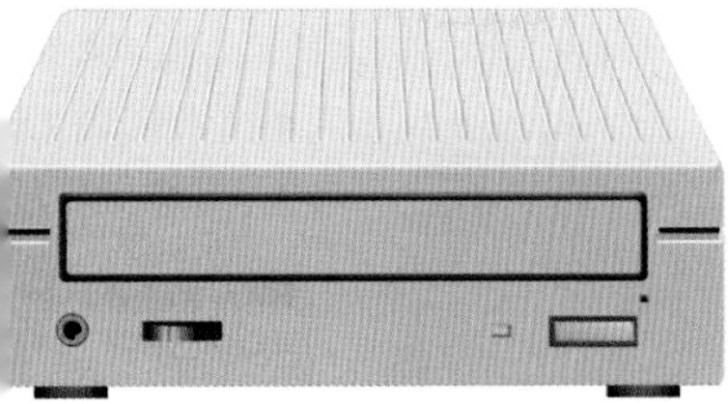

CD-ROM drive
lector[M] de CD-ROM
lecteur[M] de disque[M] compact
CD-ROM-Laufwerk[N]
lettore[M] di compact disc[M]

digitizing pad
tableta[F] digitalizada
tablette[F] graphique
Digitalisierungsunterlage[F]
tavoletta[F] grafica

stylus holder
porta stilus[M]
porte-stylet[M]
Stifthalter[M]
portastilo[M]

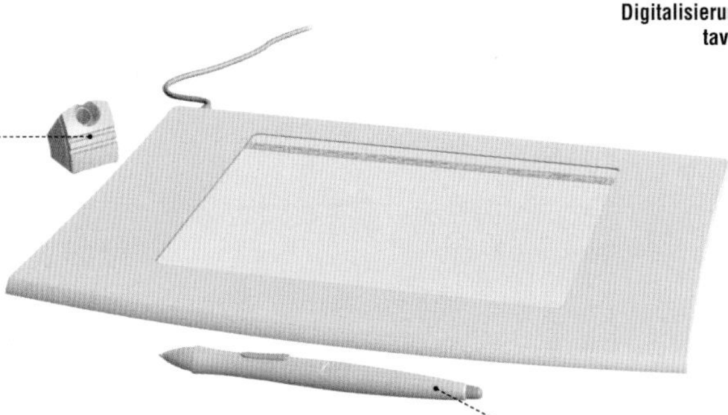

stylus
stylus
stylet[M]
Stift[M]
stilo[F]

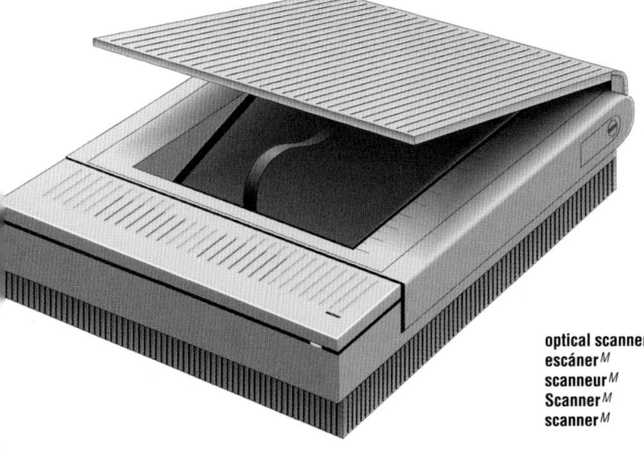

optical scanner
escáner[M]
scanneur[M]
Scanner[M]
scanner[M]

output devices

unidades^F de salida^F de información^F | périphériques^M de sortie^F | Ausgabegeräte^N | dispositivi^M di uscita^F

flat screen monitor
pantalla^F plana
écran^M plat
Flachbildschirm^M
monitor^M a schermo^M piatto

video monitor
monitor^M de vídeo^M
écran^M
Bildschirm^M
monitor^M

menu button
botón^M de menú^M
bouton^M de menu^M
Menütaste^F
tasto^M del menu^M
adjust buttons
boutones^M de ajuste^M
boutons^M de réglage^M
Einstellungstasten^F
tasti^M di regolazione^F
select button
botón^M de selección^F
bouton^M de sélection^F
Optionstaste^F
tasto^M di selezione
power switch
interruptor^M
interrupteur^M
Netzschalter^M
interruttore^M di accensione^F
power indicator
indicador^M de encendido
témoin^M d'alimentation^F
Leuchtanzeige^F
spia^F di alimentazione^F

projector
proyector M
vidéoprojecteur M
Beamer M
proiettore M

power switch
interruptor M de encendido
interrupteur M d'alimentation F
Ein-/Ausschalter M
interruttore M di accensione F
connector panel
panel M de conexión F
panneau M de connexions F
Anschlussfeld N
pannello M di connessione F
control panel
panel M de control M
panneau M de contrôle M
Bedienfeld N
pannello M di controllo M
computer connector
conector M del ordenador M
entrée F informatique
Computeranschlussbuchse F
ingresso M per il computer M
mouse port
conector M del ratón M
port M souris F
Mausschnittstelle F
porta F del mouse M
lens
objetivo M
objectif M
Objektiv N
obiettivo M
remote sensor
sensor infrarrojos
capteur M infrarouge M
Infrarotsensor M
telesensore M

output devices

inkjet printer
impresora[F] de líneas[F]
imprimante[F] à jet[M] d'encre[F]
Tintenstrahldrucker[M]
stampante[F] a getto[M] di inchiostro[M]

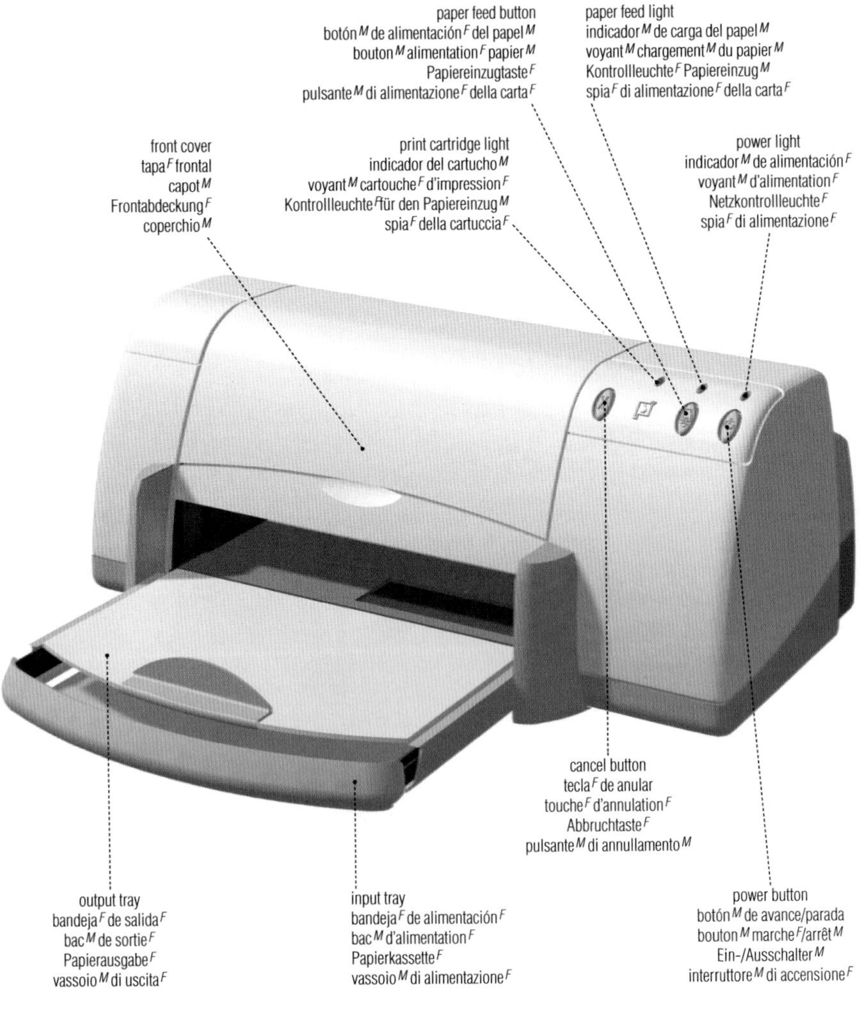
paper feed button
botón[M] de alimentación[F] del papel[M]
bouton[M] alimentation[F] papier[M]
Papiereinzugtaste[F]
pulsante[M] di alimentazione[F] della carta[F]
paper feed light
indicador[M] de carga del papel[M]
voyant[M] chargement[M] du papier[M]
Kontrollleuchte[F] Papiereinzug[M]
spia[F] di alimentazione[F] della carta[F]
front cover
tapa[F] frontal
capot[M]
Frontabdeckung[F]
coperchio[M]
print cartridge light
indicador del cartucho[M]
voyant[M] cartouche[F] d'impression[F]
Kontrollleuchte[F] für den Papiereinzug[M]
spia[F] della cartuccia[F]
power light
indicador[M] de alimentación[F]
voyant[M] d'alimentation[F]
Netzkontrollleuchte[F]
spia[F] di alimentazione[F]
cancel button
tecla[F] de anular
touche[F] d'annulation[F]
Abbruchtaste[F]
pulsante[M] di annullamento[M]
output tray
bandeja[F] de salida[F]
bac[M] de sortie[F]
Papierausgabe[F]
vassoio[M] di uscita[F]
input tray
bandeja[F] de alimentación[F]
bac[M] d'alimentation[F]
Papierkassette[F]
vassoio[M] di alimentazione[F]
power button
botón[M] de avance/parada
bouton[M] marche[F]/arrêt[M]
Ein-/Ausschalter[M]
interruttore[M] di accensione[F]

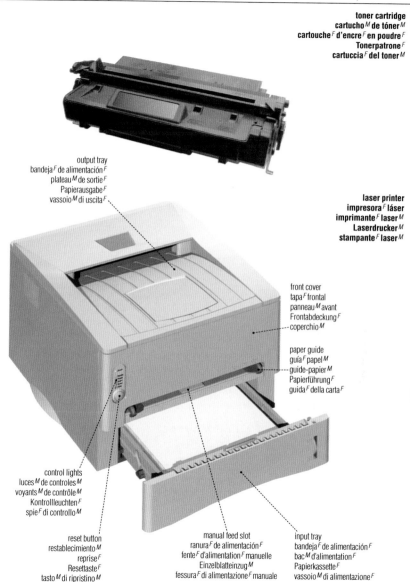

toner cartridge
cartucho M de tóner M
cartouche F d'encre F en poudre F
Tonerpatrone F
cartuccia F del toner M

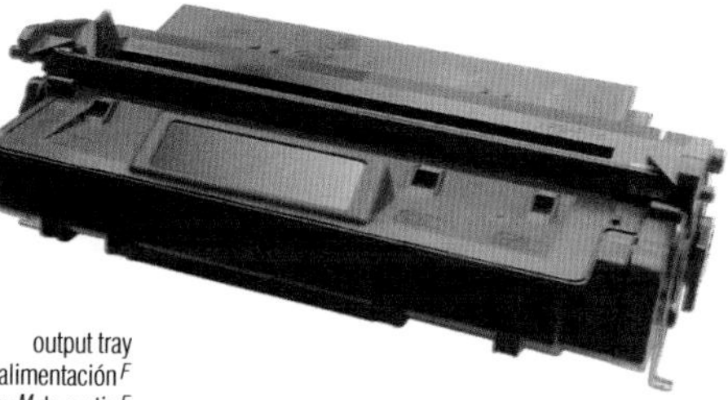

laser printer
impresora F láser
imprimante F laser M
Laserdrucker M
stampante F laser M

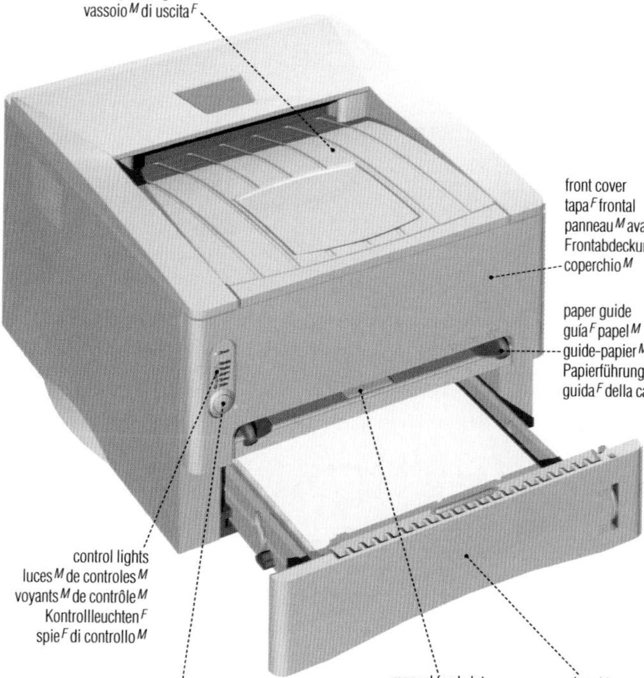
output tray
bandeja F de alimentación F
plateau M de sortie F
Papierausgabe F
vassoio M di uscita F
front cover
tapa F frontal
panneau M avant
Frontabdeckung F
coperchio M
paper guide
guía F papel M
guide-papier M
Papierführung F
guida F della carta F
control lights
luces M de controles M
voyants M de contrôle M
Kontrollleuchten F
spie F di controllo M
reset button
restablecimiento M
reprise F
Resettaste F
tasto M di ripristino M
manual feed slot
ranura F de alimentación F
fente F d'alimentation F manuelle
Einzelblatteinzug M
fessura F di alimentazione F manuale
input tray
bandeja F de alimentación F
bac M d'alimentation F
Papierkassette F
vassoio M di alimentazione F

data storage devices

unidades^F de almacenamiento^M de información^F | périphériques^M de stockage^M | Speichergeräte^N | dispositivi^M di memorizzazione^F dei dati^M

hard disk drive
unidad^F del disco^M duro
lecteur^M de disque^M dur
Festplattenlaufwerk^N
unità^F hard disk^M

disk
disco^M
disque^M
Platte^F
disco^M
disk motor
motor^M del disco^M
moteur^M de disques^M
Laufwerksantrieb^M
motore^M del disco^M
actuator arm motor
motor^M del brazo^M actuador
moteur^M de guides^M
Führungsschienenantrieb^M
motore^M del braccio^M
read/write head
cabeza^F de lectura^F/escritura^F
tête^F de lecture^F/écriture^F
Schreib-/Lesekopf^M
testina^F di lettura^F/scrittura^F
actuator arm
brazo^M actuador
guide^M
Sucharm^M
braccio^M

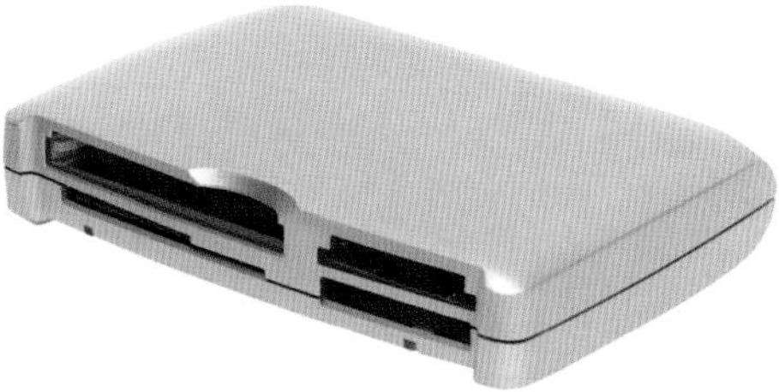

memory card reader
lector^{M} de tarjeta^{F} de memoria^{F}
lecteur^{M} de carte^{F} mémoire^{F}
Speicherkartenlesegerät^{N}
lettore^{M} di scheda^{F} di memoria^{F}

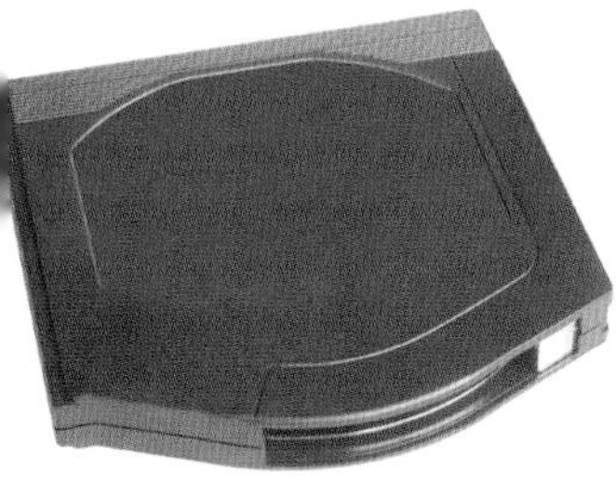

removable hard disk
disco^{M} duro extraíble
disque^{M} dur amovible
herausnehmbare Festplatte^{F}
hard disk^{M} estraibile

removable hard disk drive
unidad^{F} de disco^{M} duro extraíble
lecteur^{M} de disque^{M} dur amovible
externes Festplattenlaufwerk^{N}
unità^{F} hard disk^{M} estraibile

disk eject button
botón^{M} de expulsión^{F} del disco^{F}
bouton^{M} d'éjection^{F} du disque^{M}
Diskettenauswurftaste^{F}
pulsante^{M} di espulsione^{F} del disco^{M}

data storage devices

external floppy disk drive
unidad^F de disquete^M externo
lecteur^M de disquette^F externe
externes Diskettenlaufwerk^N
unità^F floppy disk^M esterna

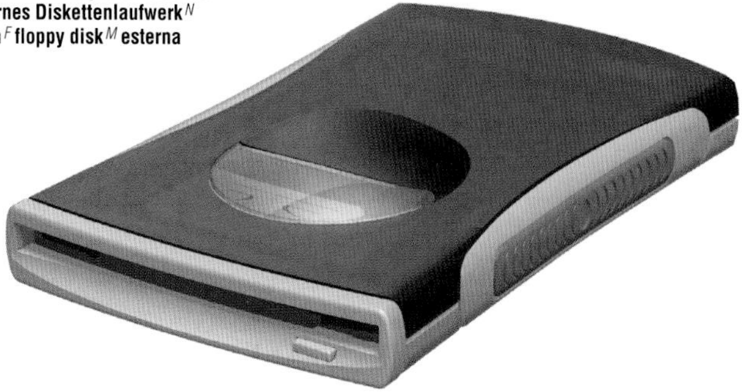

USB flash drive
dispositivo^M USB
clé^F USB
USB-Stick^M
chiave^F USB

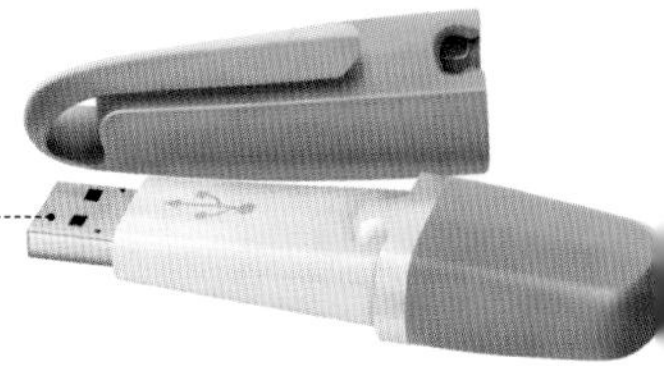
USB connector
conector^M USB
connecteur^M USB
USB-Stecker^M
connettore^M USB

diskette
disquete^M
disquette^F
Diskette^F
floppy disk^M

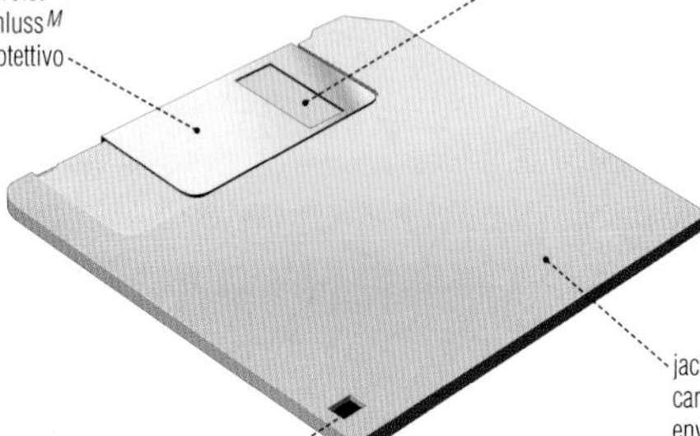
access window
ventana^F de acceso^M
fenêtre^F de lecture^F
Zugriffsöffnung^F
finestra^F di accesso^M
shutter
obturador^M
volet^M
Verschluss^M
coperchio^M protettivo
jacket
carcasa^F
enveloppe^F
Hülle^F
involucro^M
protect tab
lengüeta^F protectora
taquet^M de verrouillage^M
Schreibschutz^M
linguetta^F di protezione^F

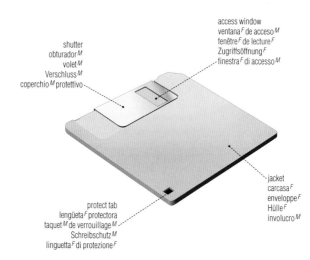

cassette
casete F
cassette F
Kassette F
cassetta F

EJECT
BUSY
TAPE
STATUS

cassette drive
unidad F de casetes F
lecteur M de cassette F
Kassettenlaufwerk N
drive M per cassette F

DVD burner
grabadora F de DVD M
graveur M de DVD M
DVD-Brenner M
registratore M di DVD M

DVD-RW
DVD REWRITABLE
disc tray
alojamiento F de disco M
plateau M de chargement M
CD F-Lade F
vassoio M portadischi
rewritable DVD disc
DVD M regrabable
DVD M réinscriptible
wiederbeschreibbare DVD F
DVD M riscrivibile

Internet

Internet[M] | Internet[M] | Internet[N] | Internet[F]

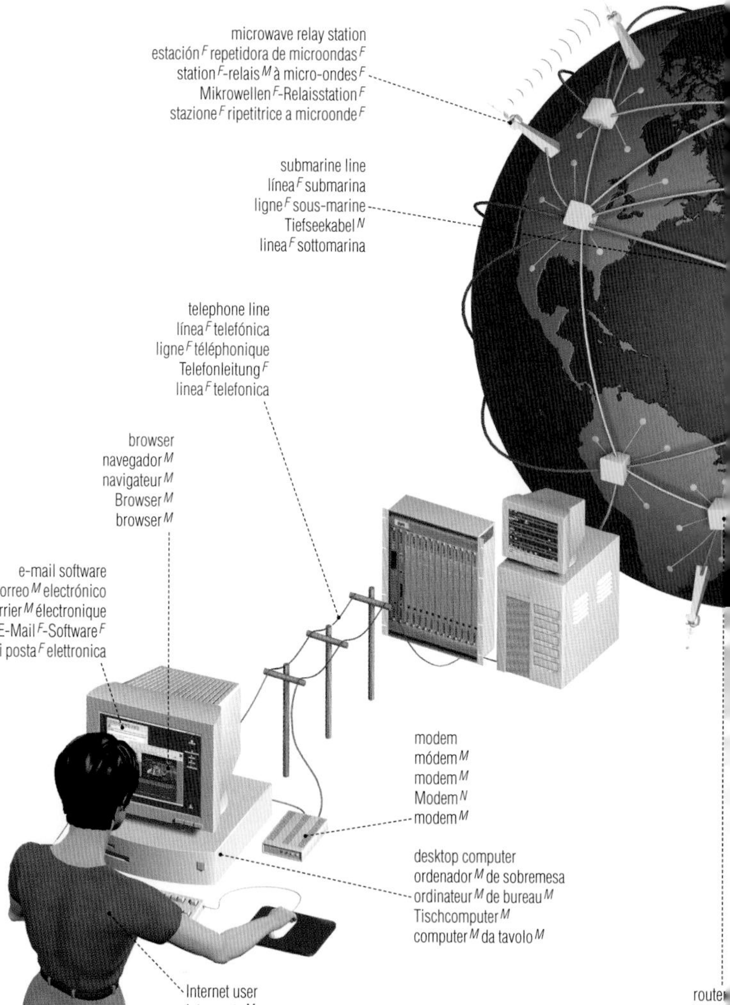
microwave relay station
estación[F] repetidora de microondas[F]
station[F]-relais[M] à micro-ondes[F]
Mikrowellen[F]-Relaisstation[F]
stazione[F] ripetitrice a microonde[F]
submarine line
línea[F] submarina
ligne[F] sous-marine
Tiefseekabel[N]
linea[F] sottomarina
telephone line
línea[F] telefónica
ligne[F] téléphonique
Telefonleitung[F]
linea[F] telefonica
browser
navegador[M]
navigateur[M]
Browser[M]
browser[M]
e-mail software
programa[M] de correo[M] electrónico
logiciel[M] de courrier[M] électronique
E-Mail[F]-Software[F]
software[M] di posta[F] elettronica
modem
módem[M]
modem[M]
Modem[N]
modem[M]
desktop computer
ordenador[M] de sobremesa
ordinateur[M] de bureau[M]
Tischcomputer[M]
computer[M] da tavolo[M]
Internet user
internauta[M]
internaute[F]
Internet[N]-Nutzer[M]
utente[M] di Internet[F]
route
router[M]
routeur[M]
Router[M]
router[M]

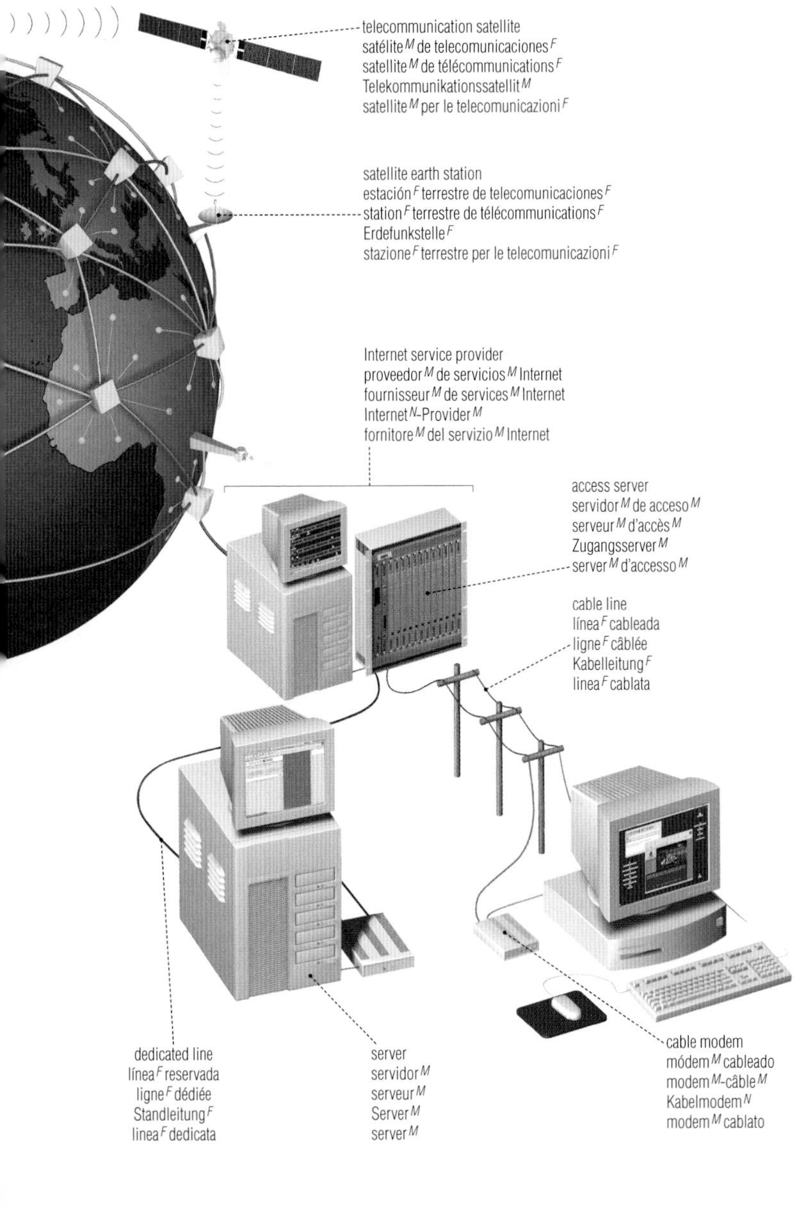
telecommunication satellite
satélite[M] de telecomunicaciones[F]
satellite[M] de télécommunications[F]
Telekommunikationssatellit[M]
satellite[M] per le telecomunicazioni[F]
satellite earth station
estación[F] terrestre de telecomunicaciones[F]
station[F] terrestre de télécommunications[F]
Erdefunkstelle[F]
stazione[F] terrestre per le telecomunicazioni[F]
Internet service provider
proveedor[M] de servicios[M] Internet
fournisseur[M] de services[M] Internet
Internet[N]-Provider[M]
fornitore[M] del servizio[M] Internet
access server
servidor[M] de acceso[M]
serveur[M] d'accès[M]
Zugangsserver[M]
server[M] d'accesso[M]
cable line
línea[F] cableada
ligne[F] câblée
Kabelleitung[F]
linea[F] cablata
dedicated line
línea[F] reservada
ligne[F] dédiée
Standleitung[F]
linea[F] dedicata
server
servidor[M]
serveur[M]
Server[M]
server[M]
cable modem
módem[M] cableado
modem[M]-câble[M]
Kabelmodem[N]
modem[M] cablato

Internet uses

usos^{M} de Internet^{M} | utilisations^{F} d'Internet^{M} | Internet^{N}-Nutzungen^{F} | impieghi^{M} di Internet^{F}

government organization
organización^{F} gubernamental
organisation^{F} gouvernementale
Regierungsorganisation^{F}
organizzazione^{F} governativa

home user
usuario^{M} particular
usager^{M} domestique
privater Nutzer^{M}
utente^{M} privato

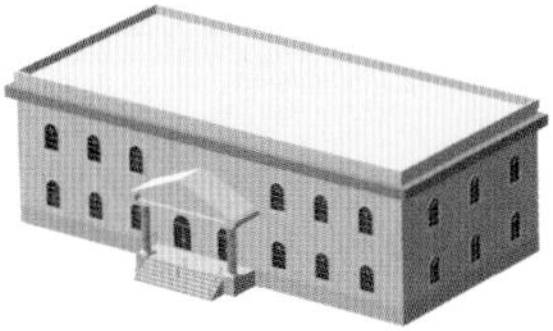

cultural organization
organismo^{M} cultural
organisme^{M} culturel
Kulturorganisation^{F}
organizzazione^{F} culturale

educational institution
institución^{F} educativa
établissement^{M} d'enseignement^{M}
Bildungseinrichtung^{F}
istituzioni^{F} educative

enterprise
empresa^{F}
entreprise^{F}
Unternehmen^{N}
azienda^{F}

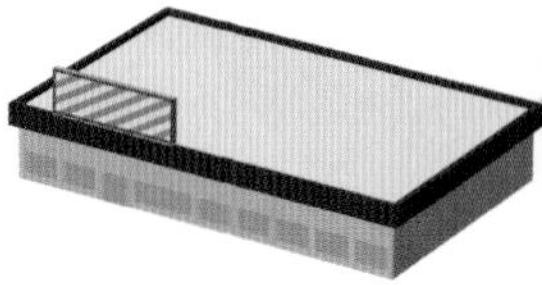

commercial concern
empresas^{F} distribución^{F}/venta^{F}
entreprise^{F} de distribution^{F}/vente^{F}
Handelsunternehmen^{N}
azienda^{F} commerciale

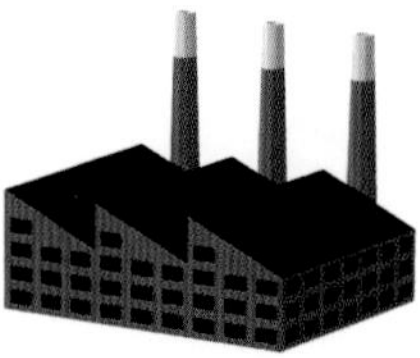

industry
industria^{F}
industrie^{F}
Industrie^{F}
industria^{F}

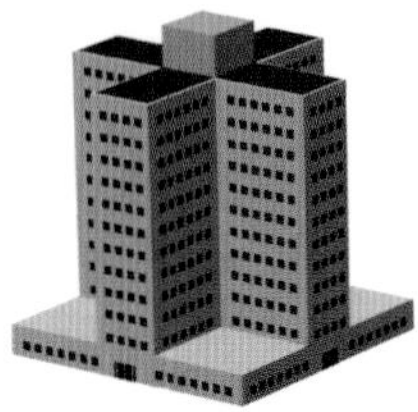

health organization
organismo^{M} de salud^{F}
organisme^{M} de santé^{F}
Gesundheitsorganisation^{F}
enti^{M} sanitari

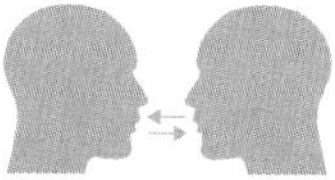

chat room
chat room [M]
clavardage [M]
Chatroom [M]
chat room [F]

e-commerce
comercio [M] electrónico
commerce [M] électronique
E-Commerce [M]
e-commerce [M]

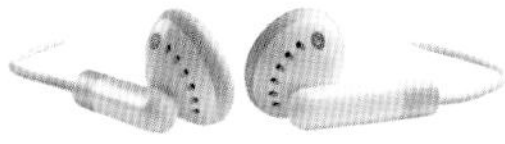

podcasting
creación [F] y distribución [F] de archivos [M] de sonido [M] digital
baladodiffusion [F]
Podcasting [N]
podcasting [M]

e-mail
correo [M] electrónico
courrier [M] électronique
elektronische Post [F]
posta [F] elettronica

information spreading
difusión [F] de información [F]
diffusion [F] d'information [F]
Informationsverbreitung [F]
diffusione [F] di informazioni [F]

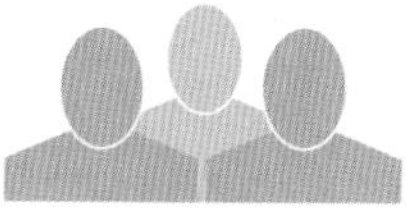

newsgroup
foro [M]
forum [M]
Forum [N]
forum [M]

database
base [F] de datos [M]
banque [F] de données [F]
Datenbank [F]
data base [M]

blog
blog [M]
blogue [M]
Blog [M]
blog [M]

search
búsqueda [F]
recherche [F]
Suche [F]
ricerca [F]

online game
juego [M] en línea [F]
jeux [M] en ligne [F]
Online-Spiel [N]
gioco [M] online

videophony
videotelefonía [F]
visiophonie [F]
Bildfernsprechen [N]
videotelefonia [F]

telephony
telefonía [F]
téléphonie [F]
Fernsprechwesen [N]
telefonia [F]

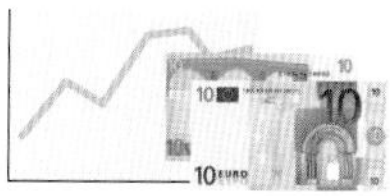

business transactions
transacciones [F] financieras
transactions [F] financières
Warengeschäfte [N]
transazioni [F] commerciali

laptop computer

ordenador^M portátil | ordinateur^M portable | Laptop^M | computer^M portatile

laptop computer: front view
ordenador^M portátil: vista^F frontal
ordinateur^M portable : vue^F avant
Laptop^M: Vorderansicht^F
computer^M portatile: vista^F frontale

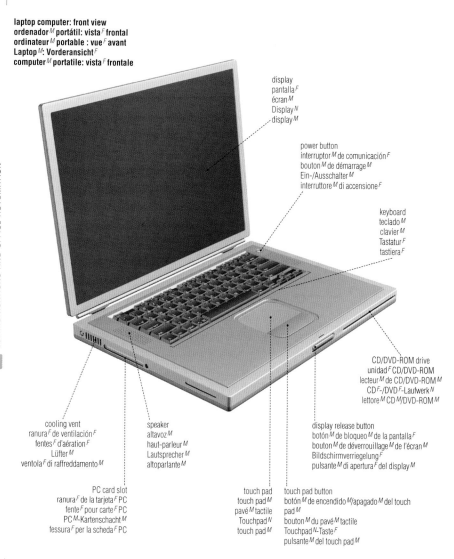

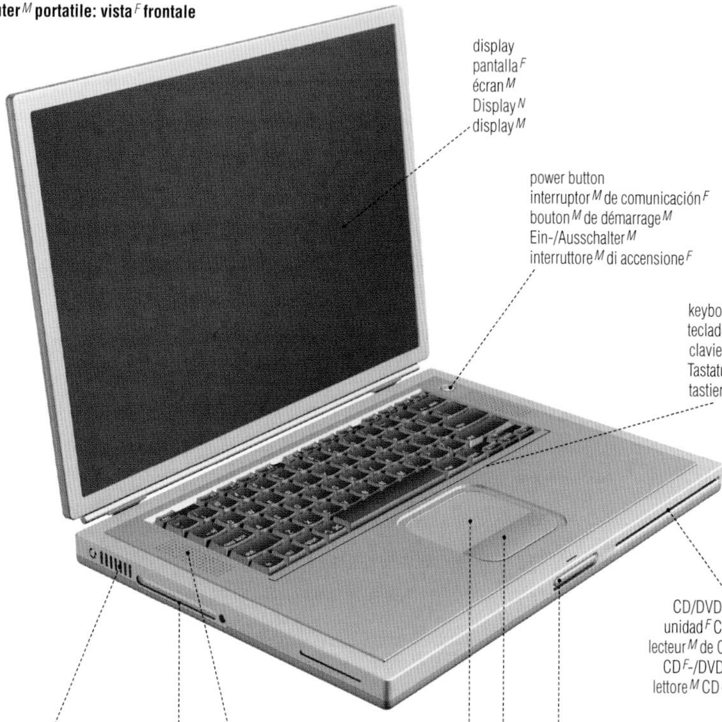
display
pantalla^F
écran^M
Display^N
display^M
power button
interruptor^M de comunicación^F
bouton^M de démarrage^M
Ein-/Ausschalter^M
interruttore^M di accensione^F
keyboard
teclado^M
clavier^M
Tastatur^F
tastiera^F
CD/DVD-ROM drive
unidad^F CD/DVD-ROM
lecteur^M de CD/DVD-ROM^M
CD^F-/DVD^F-Laufwerk^N
lettore^M CD^M/DVD-ROM^M
display release button
botón^M de bloqueo^M de la pantalla^F
bouton^M de déverrouillage^M de l'écran^M
Bildschirmverriegelung^F
pulsante^M di apertura^F del display^M
cooling vent
ranura^F de ventilación^F
fentes^F d'aération^F
Lüfter^M
ventola^F di raffreddamento^M
speaker
altavoz^M
haut-parleur^M
Lautsprecher^M
altoparlante^M
PC card slot
ranura^F de la tarjeta^F PC
fente^F pour carte^F PC
PC^M-Kartenschacht^M
fessura^F per la scheda^F PC
touch pad
touch pad^M
pavé^M tactile
Touchpad^N
touch pad^M
touch pad button
botón^M de encendido^M/apagado^M del touch pad^M
bouton^M du pavé^M tactile
Touchpad^N-Taste^F
pulsante^M del touch pad^M

laptop computer: rear view
ordenador^M portátil: vista^F posterior
ordinateur^M portable : vue^F arrière
Laptop^M: Rückansicht^F
computer^M portatile: dorso^M

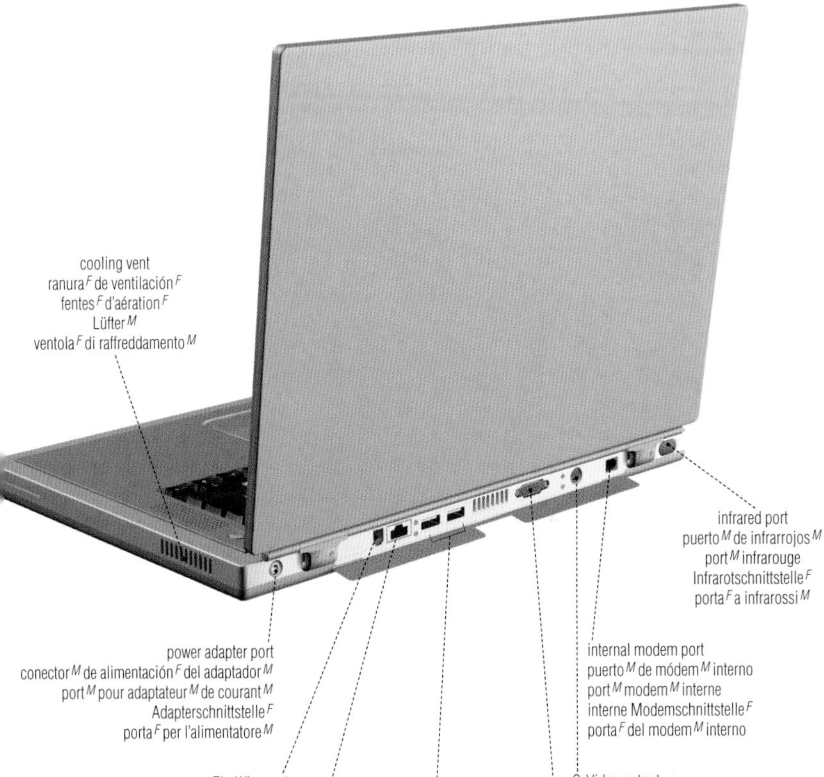

cooling vent
ranura^F de ventilación^F
fentes^F d'aération^F
Lüfter^M
ventola^F di raffreddamento^M
infrared port
puerto^M de infrarrojos^M
port^M infrarouge
Infrarotschnittstelle^F
porta^F a infrarossi^M
power adapter port
conector^M de alimentación^F del adaptador^M
port^M pour adaptateur^M de courant^M
Adapterschnittstelle^F
porta^F per l'alimentatore^M
internal modem port
puerto^M de módem^M interno
port^M modem^M interne
interne Modemschnittstelle^F
porta^F del modem^M interno
FireWire port
puerto^M FireWire
port^M FireWire
FireWire-Schnittstelle^F
porta^F FireWire
S-Video output
puerto^M de salida^F de S-video
sortie^F S-Video
S-Video-Ausgang^M
uscita^F S-Video
Ethernet port
puerto^M de Ethernet^M
port^M Ethernet^M
Wechselfestplatte^F
porta^F Ethernet
USB port
puerto^M USB
port^M USB
USB-Schnittstelle^F
porta^F USB
video port
puerto^M de salida^F de TV
port^M vidéo
Videoschnittstelle^F
porta^F video^M

handheld computer

ordenador[M] de bolsillo[M] | ordinateur[M] de poche[F] | Handheld-Computer[M] | computer[M] tascabile

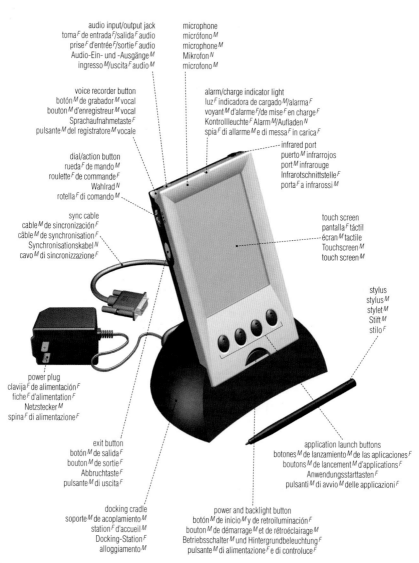

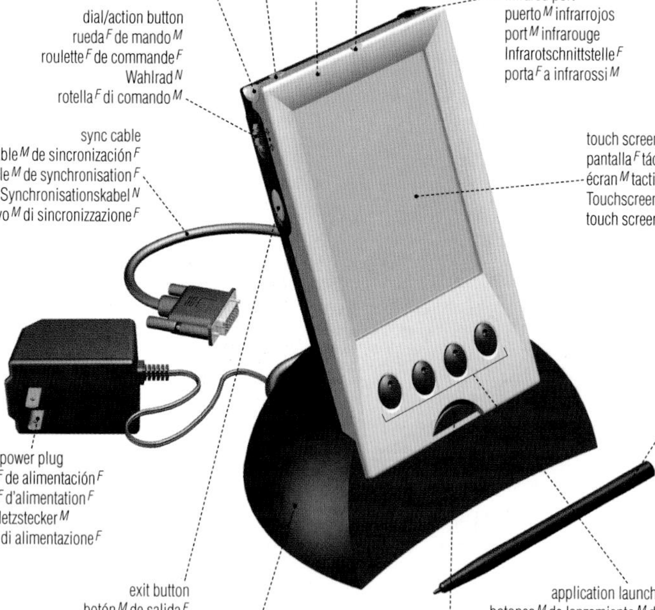
audio input/output jack
toma[F] de entrada[F]/salida[F] audio
prise[F] d'entrée[F]/sortie[F] audio
Audio-Ein- und -Ausgänge[M]
ingresso[M]/uscita[F] audio[M]
microphone
micrófono[M]
microphone[M]
Mikrofon[N]
microfono[M]
voice recorder button
botón[M] de grabador[M] vocal
bouton[M] d'enregistreur[M] vocal
Sprachaufnahmetaste[F]
pulsante[M] del registratore[M] vocale
alarm/charge indicator light
luz[F] indicadora de cargado[M]/alarma[F]
voyant[M] d'alarme[F]/de mise[F] en charge[F]
Kontrollleuchte[F] Alarm[M]/Aufladen[N]
spia[F] di allarme[M] e di messa[F] in carica[F]
infrared port
puerto[M] infrarrojos
port[M] infrarouge
Infrarotschnittstelle[F]
porta[F] a infrarossi[M]
dial/action button
rueda[F] de mando[M]
roulette[F] de commande[F]
Wahlrad[N]
rotella[F] di comando[M]
sync cable
cable[M] de sincronización[F]
câble[M] de synchronisation[F]
Synchronisationskabel[N]
cavo[M] di sincronizzazione[F]
touch screen
pantalla[F] táctil
écran[M] tactile
Touchscreen[M]
touch screen[M]
stylus
stylus[M]
stylet[M]
Stift[M]
stilo[F]
power plug
clavija[F] de alimentación[F]
fiche[F] d'alimentation[F]
Netzstecker[M]
spina[F] di alimentazione[F]
exit button
botón[M] de salida[F]
bouton[M] de sortie[F]
Abbruchtaste[F]
pulsante[M] di uscita[F]
application launch buttons
botones[M] de lanzamiento[M] de las aplicaciones[F]
boutons[M] de lancement[M] d'applications[F]
Anwendungsstarttasten[F]
pulsanti[M] di avvio[M] delle applicazioni[F]
docking cradle
soporte[M] de acoplamiento[M]
station[F] d'accueil[M]
Docking-Station[F]
alloggiamento[M]
power and backlight button
botón[M] de inicio[M] y de retroiluminación[F]
bouton[M] de démarrage[M] et de rétroéclairage[M]
Betriebsschalter[M] und Hintergrundbeleuchtung[F]
pulsante[M] di alimentazione[F] e di controluce[F]

stationery

artículos^{M} de escritorio^{M} | articles^{M} de bureau^{M} | Schreibwaren^{F} | articoli^{M} di cancelleria^{F}

pocket calculator
calculadora^{F} de bolsillo^{M}
calculette^{F}
Taschenrechner^{M}
calcolatrice^{F} tascabile

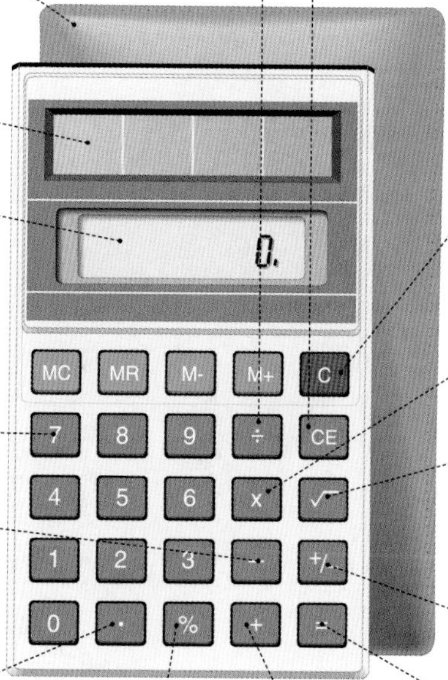
MC
MR
M-
M+
C
7
8
9
÷
CE
4
5
6
x
1
2
3
+/-
0
%
+
0.

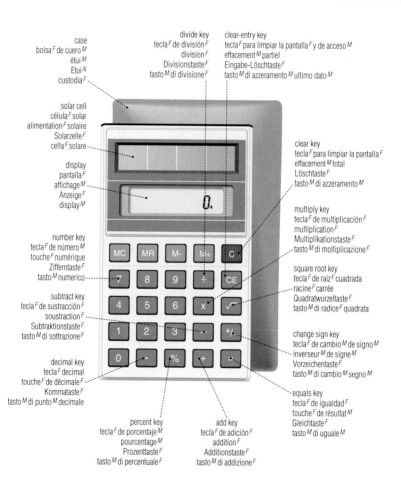

case
bolsa^{F} de cuero^{M}
étui^{M}
Etui^{N}
custodia^{F}

divide key
tecla^{F} de división^{F}
division^{F}
Divisionstaste^{F}
tasto^{M} di divisione^{F}

clear-entry key
tecla^{F} para limpiar la pantalla^{F} y de acceso^{M}
effacement^{M} partiel
Eingabe-Löschtaste^{F}
tasto^{M} di azzeramento^{M} ultimo dato^{M}

solar cell
célula^{F} solar
alimentation^{F} solaire
Solarzelle^{F}
cella^{F} solare

clear key
tecla^{F} para limpiar la pantalla^{F}
effacement^{M} total
Löschtaste^{F}
tasto^{M} di azzeramento^{M}

display
pantalla^{F}
affichage^{M}
Anzeige^{F}
display^{M}

multiply key
tecla^{F} de multiplicación^{F}
multiplication^{F}
Multiplikationstaste^{F}
tasto^{M} di moltiplicazione^{F}

number key
tecla^{F} de número^{M}
touche^{F} numérique
Zifferntaste^{F}
tasto^{M} numerico

square root key
tecla^{F} de raíz^{F} cuadrada
racine^{F} carrée
Quadratwurzeltaste^{F}
tasto^{M} di radice^{F} quadrata

subtract key
tecla^{F} de sustracción^{F}
soustraction^{F}
Subtraktionstaste^{F}
tasto^{M} di sottrazione^{F}

change sign key
tecla^{F} de cambio^{M} de signo^{M}
inverseur^{M} de signe^{M}
Vorzeichentaste^{F}
tasto^{M} di cambio^{M} segno^{M}

decimal key
tecla^{F} decimal
touche^{F} de décimale^{F}
Kommataste^{F}
tasto^{M} di punto^{M} decimale

equals key
tecla^{F} de igualdad^{F}
touche^{F} de résultat^{M}
Gleichtaste^{F}
tasto^{M} di uguale^{M}

percent key
tecla^{F} de porcentaje^{M}
pourcentage^{M}
Prozenttaste^{F}
tasto^{M} di percentuale^{F}

add key
tecla^{F} de adición^{F}
addition^{F}
Additionstaste^{F}
tasto^{M} di addizione^{F}

scientific calculator
calculadora^F científica
calculatrice^F scientifique
wissenschaftlicher Taschenrechner^M
calcolatrice^F scientifica

access to the second level of operations
acceso^M al segundo nivel^M de operaciones^F
accès^M au second niveau^M d'opérations^F
Zugang^M zur zweiten Funktionsebene^F
accesso^M al secondo livello^M di operazioni^F

result line
línea^F del resultado^M
affichage^M du résultat^M
Ergebniszeile^F
riga^F dei risultati^M

entries line
línea^F de datos^M introducidos
affichage^M des données^F
Eingabezeile^F
riga^F dei dati^M immessi

cursor movement keys
teclas^F de desplazamiento^M del cursor^M
touches^F de déplacement^M du curseur^M
Cursortasten^F
tasti^M di posizionamento^M del cursore^M

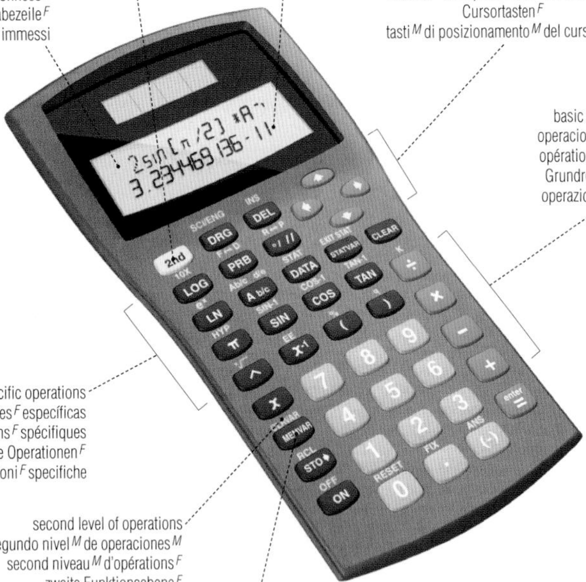
DEL
DRG
2nd
PRB
LOG
LN
SIN
COS
TAN
DATA
CLEAR
ON
enter

basic operations
operaciones^M básicas
opérations^F de base^F
Grundrechenarten^F
operazioni^F di base^F

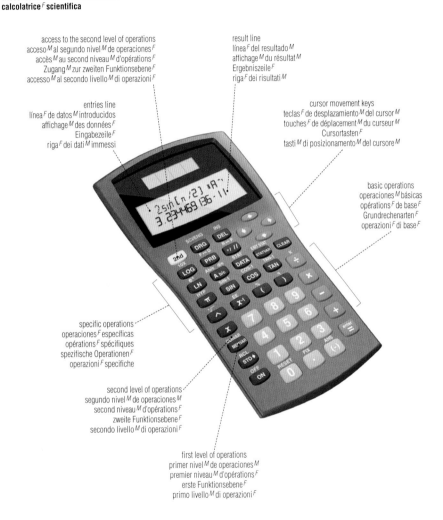

specific operations
operaciones^F específicas
opérations^F spécifiques
spezifische Operationen^F
operazioni^F specifiche

second level of operations
segundo nivel^M de operaciones^M
second niveau^M d'opérations^F
zweite Funktionsebene^F
secondo livello^M di operazioni^F

first level of operations
primer nivel^M de operaciones^M
premier niveau^M d'opérations^F
erste Funktionsebene^F
primo livello^M di operazioni^F

printing calculator
calculadora[F] con impresora[F]
calculatrice[F] à imprimante[F]
Tischrechner[M] mit Druckerteil[N]
calcolatrice[F] da tavolo[M]

multiple use key
tecla[F] de utilización[F] múltiple
touche[F] multifonctionnelle
Multifunktionstaste[F]
tasto[M] multifunzionale

printer
impresora[F]
imprimante[F]
Druckerteil[N]
stampante[F]

non-add/subtotal
subtotal[M]/sin adición[F]
non-addition[F]/total[M] partiel
Zwischensummentaste[F]
tasto[M] di subtotale[M]/non-addizione[F]

add/equals key
tecla[F] de más/igual
touche[F] plus[M]-égalité[F]
Addiertaste[F]
tasto[M] di più-uguale[M]

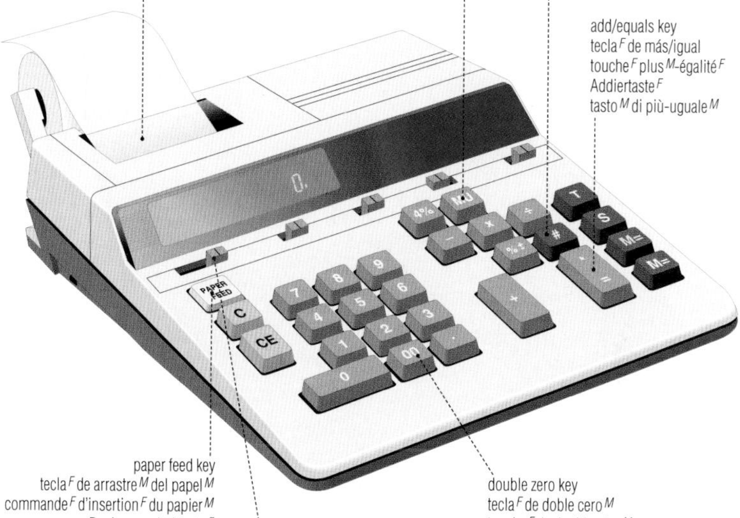
PAPER FEED
C
CE
M=
T
S

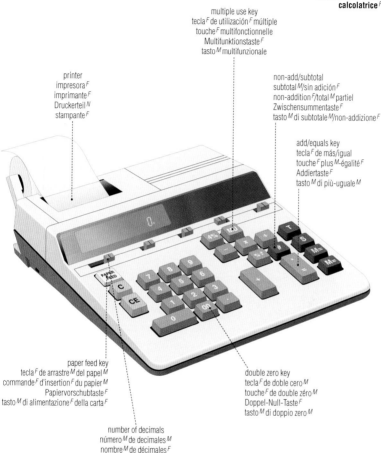

paper feed key
tecla[F] de arrastre[M] del papel[M]
commande[F] d'insertion[F] du papier[M]
Papiervorschubtaste[F]
tasto[M] di alimentazione[F] della carta[F]

double zero key
tecla[F] de doble cero[M]
touche[F] de double zéro[M]
Doppel-Null-Taste[F]
tasto[M] di doppio zero[M]

number of decimals
número[M] de decimales[M]
nombre[M] de décimales[F]
Anzahl[F] der Kommastellen[F]
selettore[M] del numero[M] dei decimali[M]

stationery

for time management
para el empleo^{M} del tiempo^{M}
pour l'emploi^{M} du temps^{M}
für die Terminplanung^{F}
per la gestione^{F} del tempo^{M}

personal digital assistant
agenda^{F} electrónica
organiseur^{M}
Organizer^{M}
organizer^{M}

SUN MON TUE WED THU FRI SAT
ESC
Q
W
E
R
T
Y
U
I
O
P
A
S
D
F
G
H
J
K
L
Z
X
C
V
B
N
M
SHIFT
CAPS
SEARCH
SYMBOL
SPACE
SET
NEXT
DEL
7
8
9
4
5
6
1
2
3
0

display
pantalla^{F}
écran^{M}
Display^{N}
display^{M}

alphabetical keypad
teclado^{M} alfabético
pavé^{M} alphabétique
alphabetische Tastatur^{F}
tastierino^{M} alfabetico

numeric keypad
teclado^{M} numérico
pavé^{M} numérique
numerische Tastatur^{F}
tastierino^{M} numerico

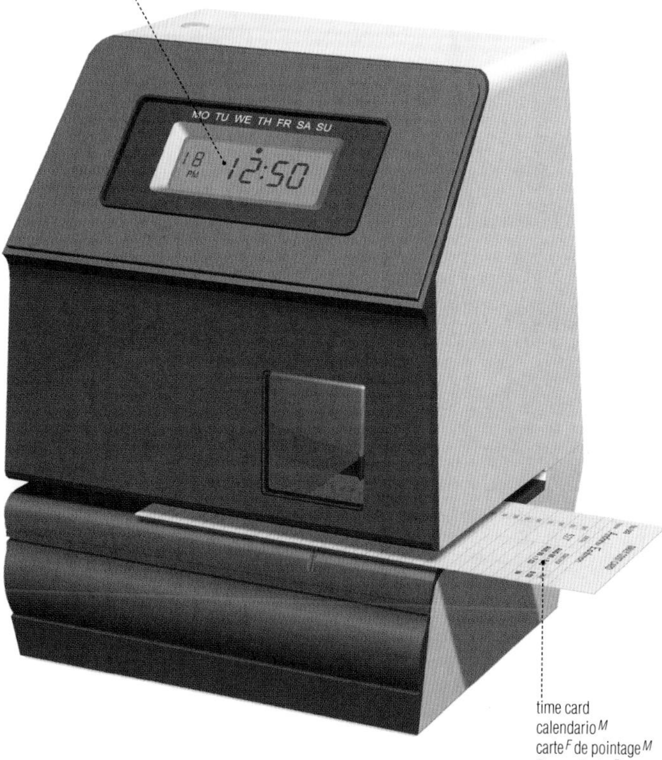
time clock
timbradora F
pointeuse F
Stempeluhr F
orologio M per la timbratura F dei cartellini M
display
pantalla F
écran M
Display N
display M
MO TU WE TH FR SA SU
18
PM
12:50
time card
calendario M
carte F de pointage M
Stempelkarte F
cartellino M orario

self-stick note
lámina F adhesiva
feuillet M adhésif
Haftnotiz F
post-it M

MERCREDI
WEDNESDAY
24
JUIN
JUNE

tear-off calendar
calendario *M* **de sobremesa**
calendrier *M*-**mémorandum** *M*
Abreißkalender *M*
calendario *M* **a fogli** *M* **staccabili**

23
24

calendar pad
calendario *M* **de sobremesa**
bloc *M*-**éphéméride** *F*
Ringbuchkalender *M*
calendario *M* **da tavolo** *M*

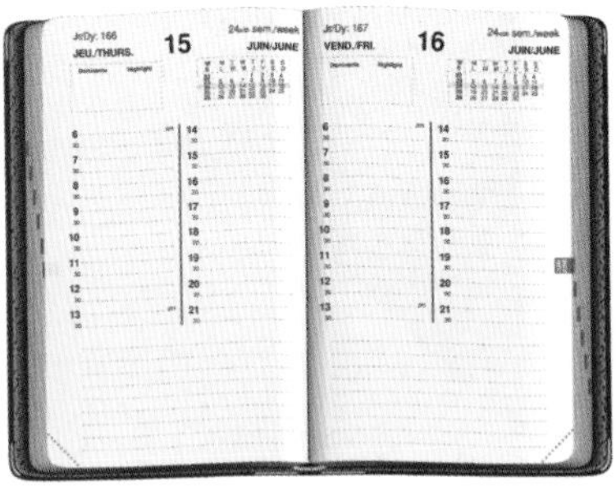
15
JEU./THURS.
JUIN/JUNE
16
VEND./FRI.
JUIN/JUNE

appointment book
agenda *F*
agenda *M*
Terminkalender *M*
agenda *F*

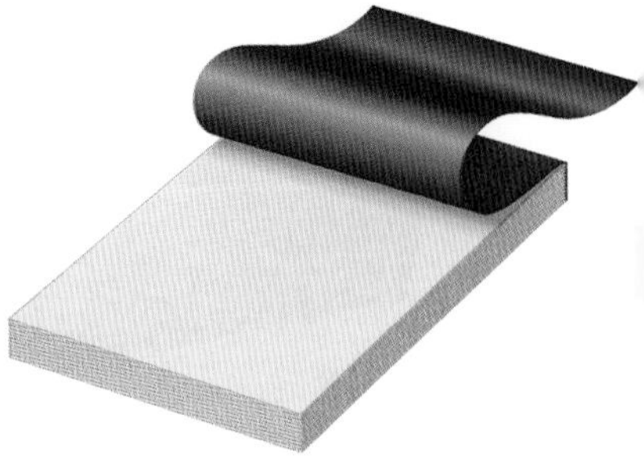

memo pad
libreta *F*
bloc *M*-**notes** *F*
Notizblock *M*
bloc-notes *M*

for correspondence
para la correspondencia[F]
pour la correspondance[F]
für die Korrespondenz[F]
per la corrispondenza[F]

postage meter
máquina[F] franqueadora
machine[F] à affranchir
Frankiermaschine[F]
affrancatrice[F]

feed deck
plataforma[F] de alimentación[F]
plateau[M] d'alimentation[F]
Einzugsablage[F]
piano[M] di alimentazione[F]

postmarking module
módulo[M] de franqueado[M]
module[M] d'affranchissement[M]
Frankiermodul[N]
modulo[M] di affrancamento[M]

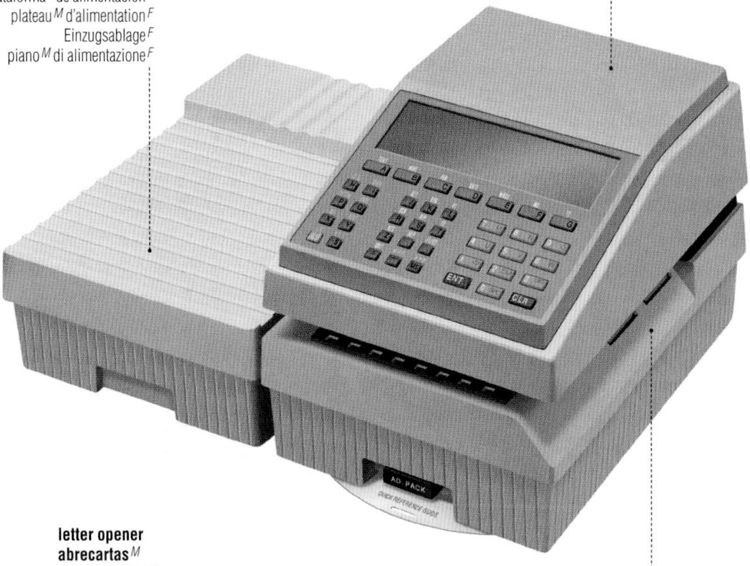
AD. PACK
ENT
CLR

base
base[F]
base[F]
Unterteil[M/N]
base[F]

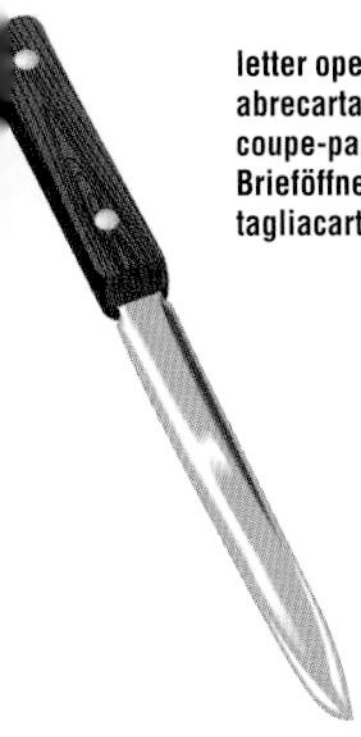

letter opener
abrecartas[M]
coupe-papier[M]
Brieföffner[M]
tagliacarte[M]

finger tip
dedil[M]
doigtier[M]
elastischer Fingerhut[M]
ditale[M] in gomma[F]

rotary file
fichero *M* giratorio
fichier *M* rotatif
Drehkartei *F*
schedario *M* rotativo

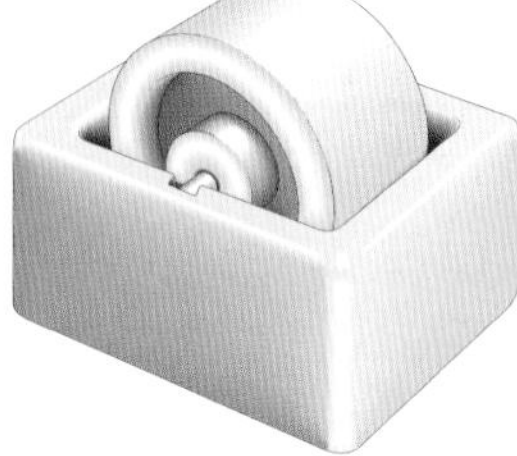

moistener
rueda *F* humedecedora
mouilleur *M*
Befeuchter *M*
spugnetta *F*

letter scale
balanza *F* para cartas *F*
pèse-lettres *M*
Briefwaage *F*
pesalettere *M*

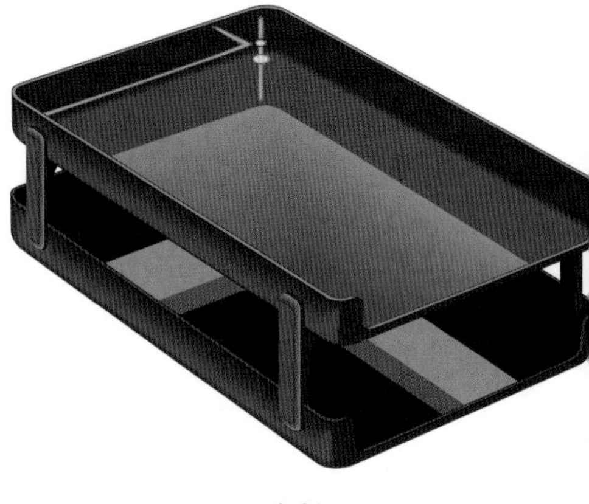

desk tray
bandeja *F* de correspondencia *F*
boîte *F* à courrier *M*
Dokumentenablage *F*
vaschetta *F* portacorrispondenza

ABCDEFGHIJKLMNOPQRSTUWY
VXZ

telephone index
agenda *F* **telefónica**
répertoire *M* **téléphonique**
Telefonverzeichnis *N*
rubrica *F* **telefonica**

padded envelope
sobre *M* **almohadillado**
enveloppe *F* **matelassée**
Luftpolsterumschlag *M*
busta *F* **imbottita**

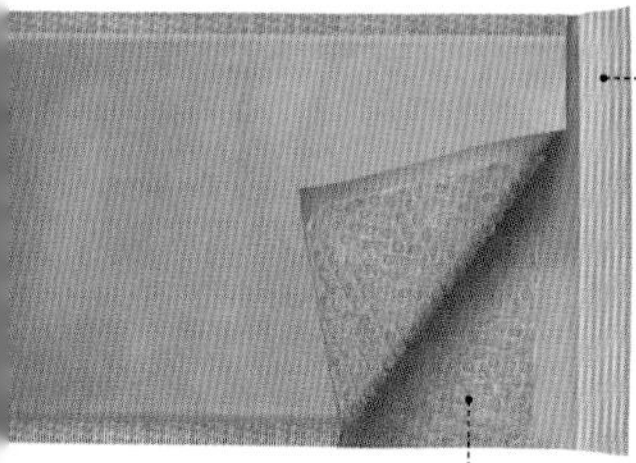

self-sealing flap
solapa *F* autoadhesiva
patte *F* autocollante
selbstklebende Lasche *F*
aletta *F* autoadesiva

air bubbles
burbujas *F* de aire *M*
bulles *F* d'air *M*
Luftpolster *N*
bolle *F* d'aria *F*

signature book
libro *M* **de firmas** *M*
parapheur *M*
Unterschriftenmappe *F*
libro *M* **delle firme** *F*

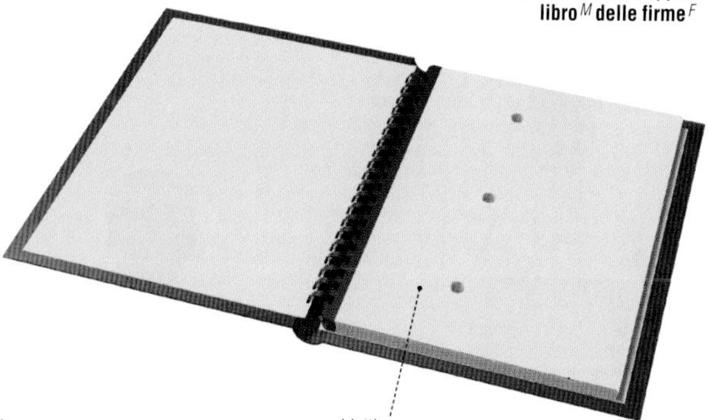

blotting paper
papel *M* secante
papier *M* buvard *M*
Löschpapier *N*
carta *F* assorbente

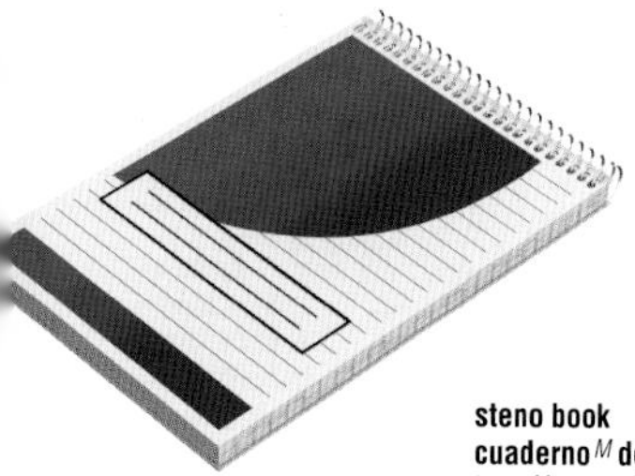

steno book
cuaderno *M* **de taquigrafía** *F*
bloc *M*-**sténo** *F*
Stenografieblock *M*
blocchetto *M* **per stenografia** *F*

stamp rack
portasellos *M*
porte-timbres *M*
Stempelrad *N*
portatimbri *M*

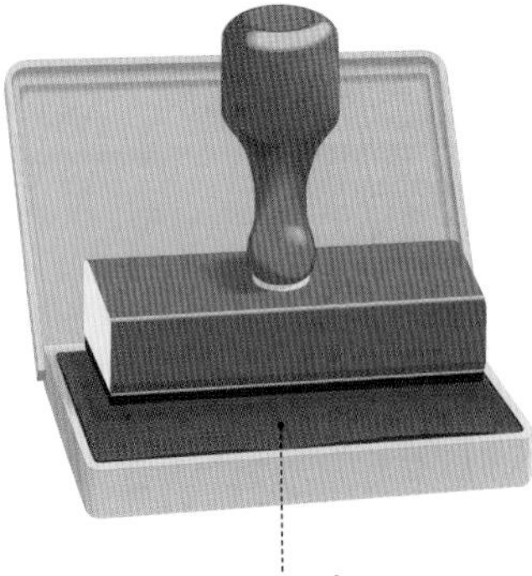

stamp pad
cojín *M* para sellos *M*
tampon *M* encreur
Stempelkissen *N*
tampone *M*

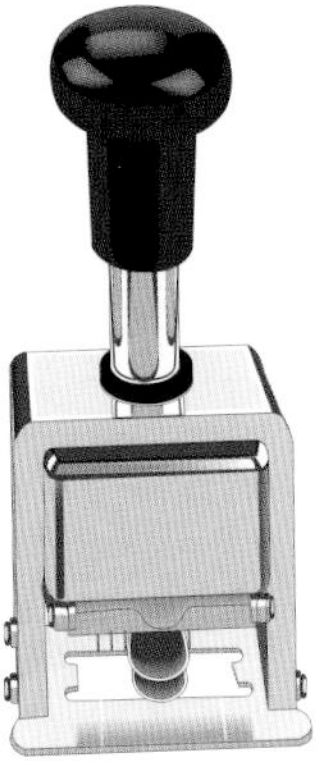

numbering machine
foliador *M*
numéroteur *M*
Nummerierstempel *M*
numeratore *M*

rubber stamp
sello *M* de goma *F*
timbre *M* caoutchouc *M*
Stempel *M*
timbro *M* di gomma *F*

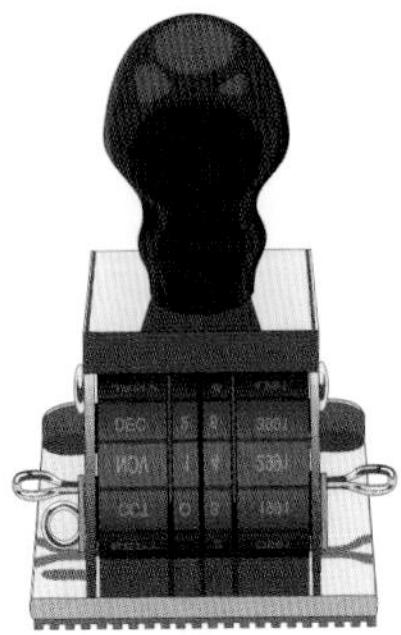

dater
fechador *M*
timbre *M* dateur
Datumstempel *M*
datario *M*

for filing
para archivar
pour le classement [M]
für die Ablage [F]
per l'archiviazione [F]

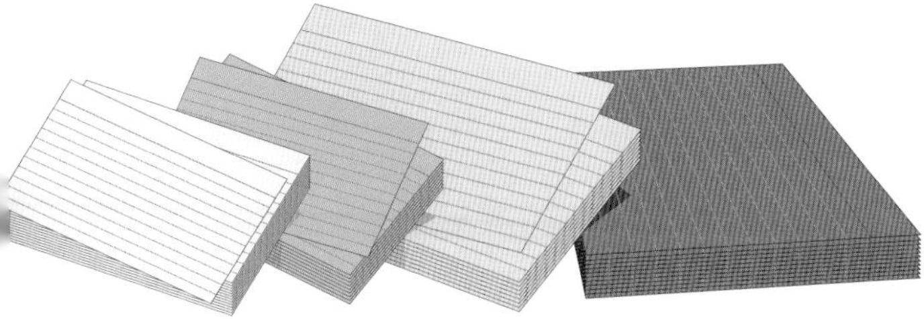

index cards
fichas [F]
fiches [F]
Karteikarten [F]
schede [F]

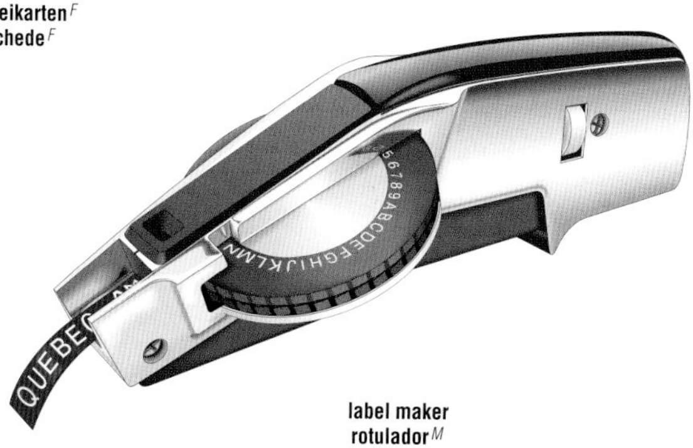

label maker
rotulador [M]
pince [F] à étiqueter
Präger [M]
etichettatrice [F]

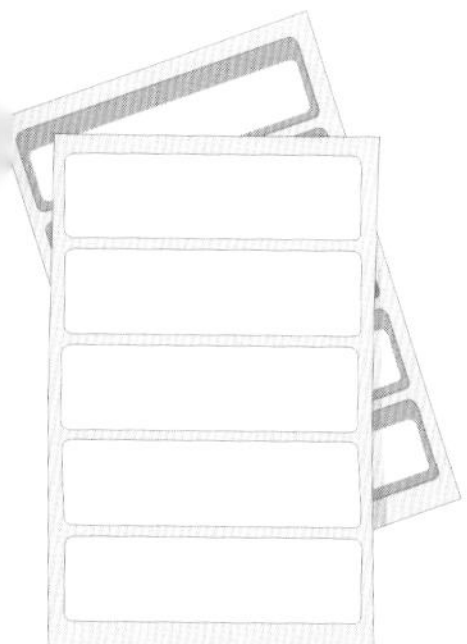

self-adhesive labels
etiquetas [F] adhesivas
étiquettes [F] autocollantes
Selbstklebeetiketten [N]
etichette [F] autoadesive

tab
indicador [M]
onglet [M]
Reiter [M]
linguetta [F]

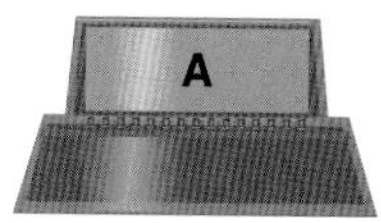
A

window tab
indicador [M] transparente
onglet [M] à fenêtre [F]
durchsichtiger Reiter [M]
linguetta [F] con finestra [F]

dividers
divisores[M]
feuillets[M] intercalaires
Registriereinlagen[F]
divisori[M]

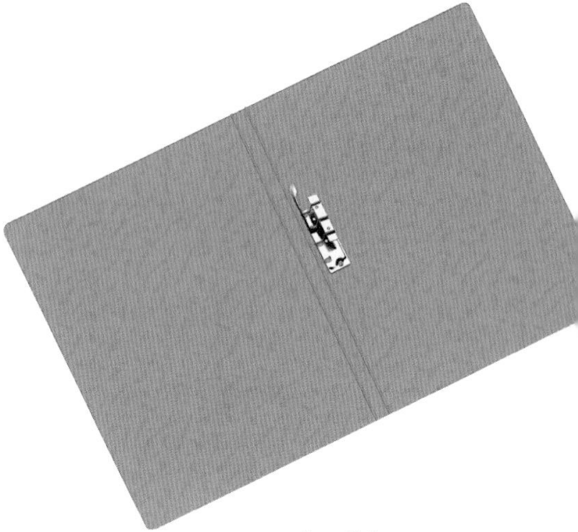

clamp binder
carpeta[F] con mecanismo[M] de presión[F]
reliure[F] à pince[F]
Aktenordner[M]
cartella[F] con pressino[M]

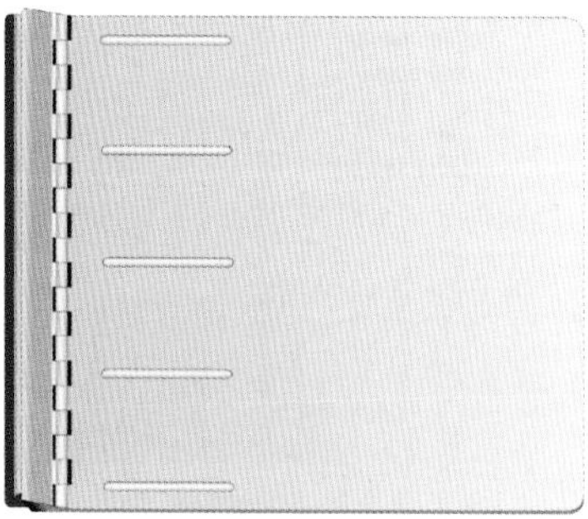

spring binder
carpeta[F] de costilla[F] de resorte[M]
reliure[F] à ressort[M]
Klemmhefter[M]
raccoglitore[M] a molla[F]

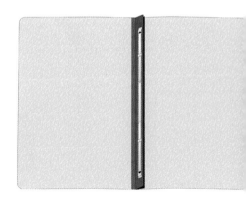

fastener binder
carpeta[F] de broches[M]
reliure[F] à glissière[F]
Schnellhefter[M]
cartella[F] con linguetta[F]

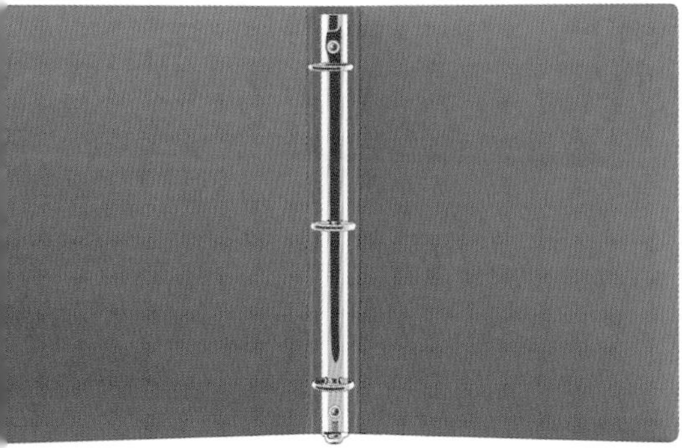

ring binder
carpeta[F] de argollas[F]
classeur[M]
Ringbuch[N]
raccoglitore[M] ad anelli[M]

spiral binder
carpeta[F] de espiral[F]
reliure[F] spirale[F]
Spiralringbuch[N]
rilegatura[F] con spirale[F]

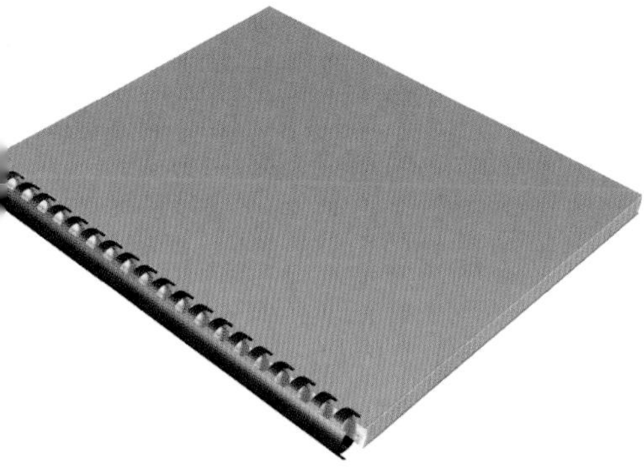

comb binding
encuadernación[F] de anillas[F]
reliure[F] à anneaux[M] plastiques
Spiralheftung[F]
rilegatura[F] con spirale[F]

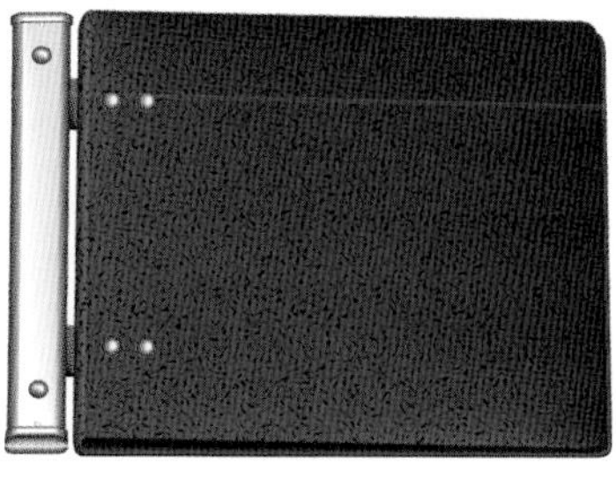

post binder
carpeta[F] de tornillos[M]
reliure[F] à vis[F]
Hefter[M]
portatabulati[M]

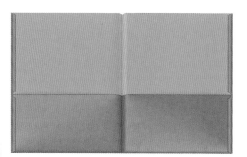

document folder
carpeta F con guardas F
pochette F d'information F
Dokumentenmappe F
cartella F per documenti M

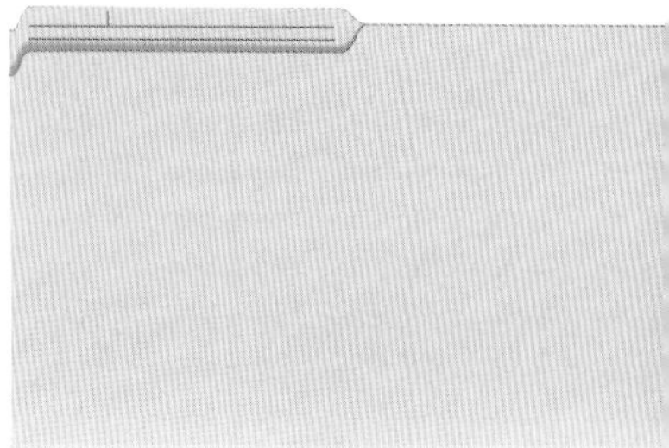

folder
carpeta F de archivo M
chemise F
Aktenmappe F
cartelletta F

A
B
C
D
E

file guides
guías F de archivo M
guides M de classement M
Karteiregister N
divisori M alfabetici per schedario M

hanging file
archivador M colgante
dossier M suspendu
Hängemappe F
cartella F sospesa

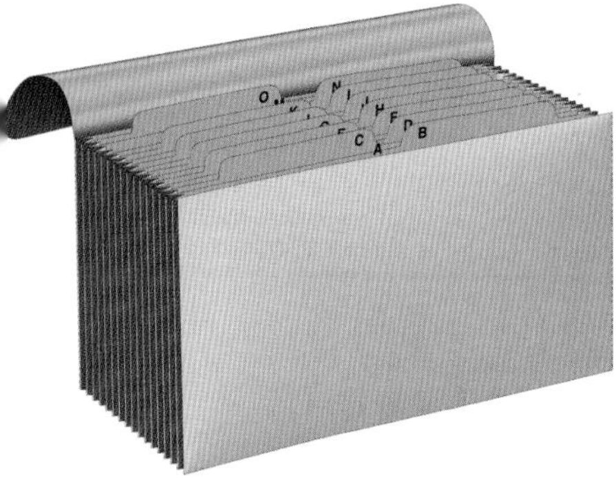
O
N
I
H
F
D
B
C
A

expanding file
archivador^{M} de fuelle^{M}
pochette^{F} de classement^{M}
Erweiterungskartei^{F}
classificatore^{M} a soffietto^{M}

paper punch
perforadora^{F}
perforatrice^{F}
Locher^{M}
perforatore^{M}

filing box
caja^{F} archivo^{M}
boîte^{F}-classeur^{M}
Aktenbox^{F}
scatola^{F} per archivio^{M}

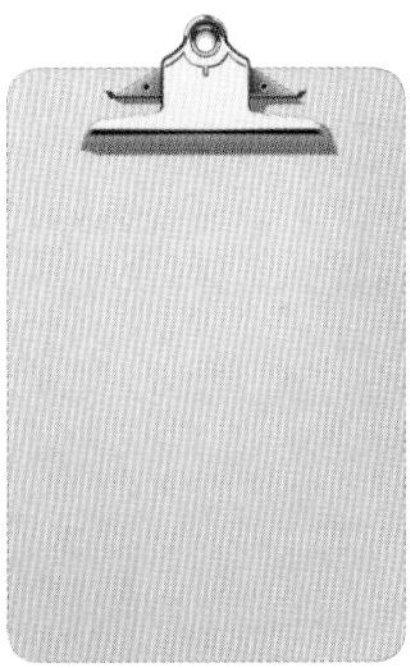

clipboard
tabla^{F} con pinza^{F}
planchette^{F} à pince^{F}
Klemmbrett^{N}
tavoletta^{F} portablocco^{M}

archboard
tabla^{F} con argollas^{F}
planchette^{F} à arches^{F}
Ringablage^{F}
portablocco^{M}

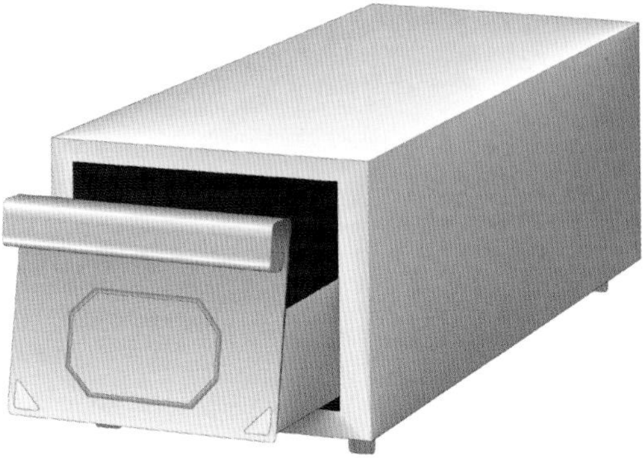

index card cabinet
archivador[M] de fichas[F]
fichier[M]
Karteikasten[M]
schedario[M]

index card drawer
gaveta[F] de archivador[M]
tiroir[M] de fichier[M]
Karteischubfach[N]
cassetto[M] di schedario[M]

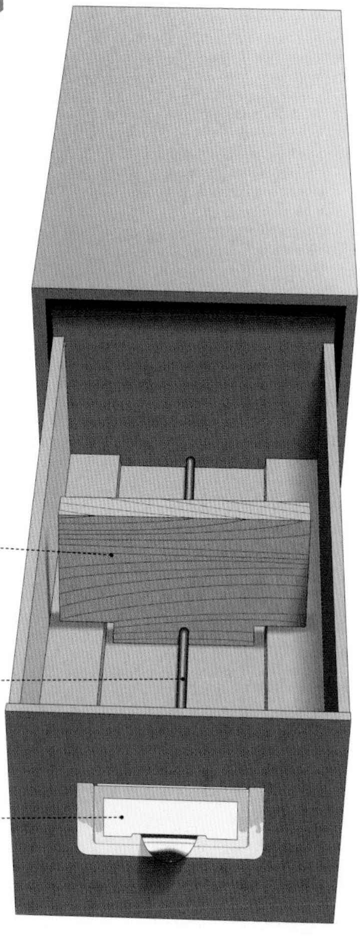
compressor
compresor[M]
compresseur[M]
Begrenzungseinsatz[M]
pressore[M]
metal rail
riel[M] metálico
tringle[F] métallique
Führungsschiene[F]
guida[F] metallica
label holder
soporte[M] del rótulo[M]
porte-étiquette[M]
Etikettenfenster[N]
portaetichetta[M]

miscellaneous articles
artículos^{M} varios
articles^{M} divers
Verschiedenes^{N}
articoli^{M} vari

box sealing tape dispenser
porta-cinta^{M} adhesiva
dévidoir^{M} pistolet^{M}
Klebebandabroller^{M}
nastratrice^{F}

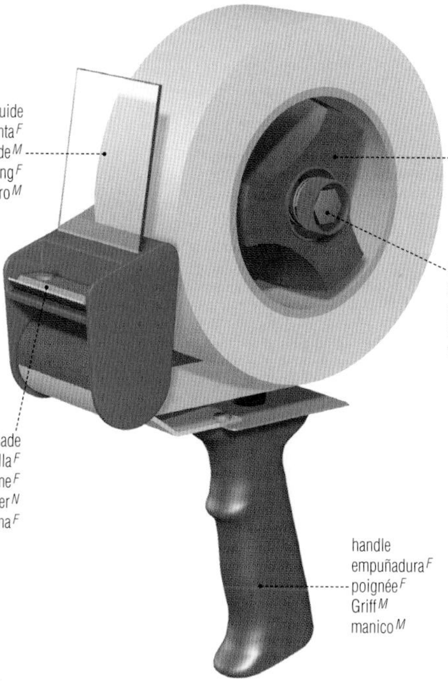
tape guide
guía^{F} de cinta^{F}
guide-bande^{M}
Bandführung^{F}
guida^{F} del nastro^{M}
hub
cubo^{M}
moyeu^{M}
Nabe^{F}
mozzo^{M}
tension adjusting screw
tornillo^{M} de ajuste^{M} de tensión^{F}
vis^{F} de réglage^{M} de tension^{F}
Feststellschraube^{F}
vite^{F} di regolazione^{F} della tensione^{F}
cutting blade
cuchilla^{F}
lame^{F}
Messer^{N}
lama^{F}
handle
empuñadura^{F}
poignée^{F}
Griff^{M}
manico^{M}

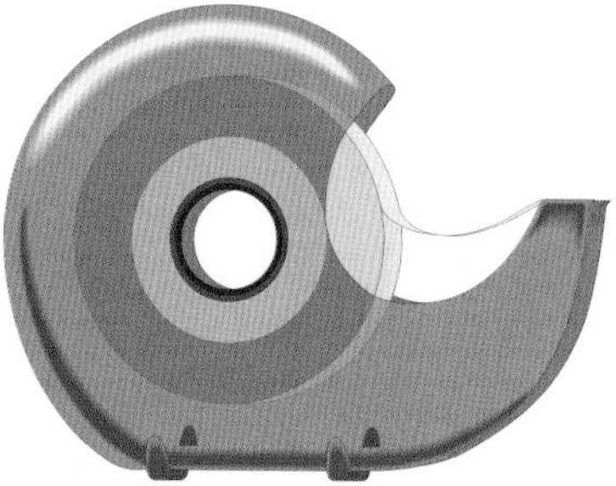

tape dispenser
porta-celo^{M}
dévidoir^{M} de ruban^{M} adhésif
Klebebandspender^{M}
chiocciola^{F} per nastro^{M} adesivo

eraser holder
porta goma F
porte-gomme M
Radiergummihalter M
portagomma M

clip
pinza F
pince-notes M
Papierclip M
fermaglio M a molla F

eraser stick
lápiz M borrador M
crayon M gomme F
Bleistift M mit Radiergummi M
matita F con gomma F

eraser
goma F
gomme F
Radiergummi M
gomma F

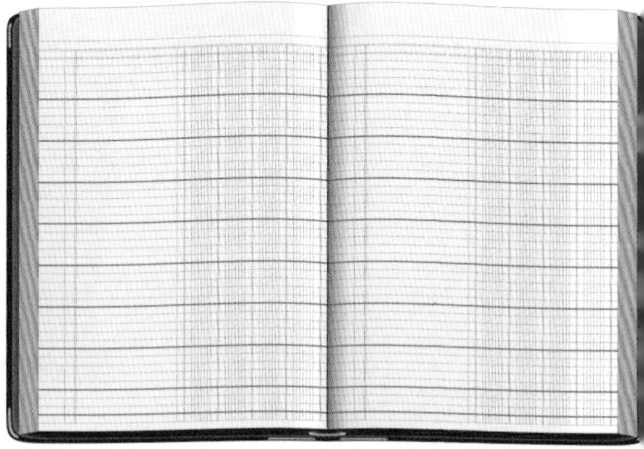

account book
agenda F de caja F
registre M de comptabilité F
Geschäftsbuch N, Journal N
libro M contabile

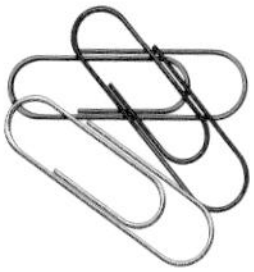

paper clips
clip [M]
trombones [M]
Büroklammern [F]
fermagli [M]

thumb tacks
chinchetas [F]
punaises [F]
Reißnägel [M]
puntine [F] **da disegno** [M]

paper fasteners
tachuelas [F] **para papel** [M]
attaches [F] **parisiennes**
Beutelklammern [F]
fermacampioni [M]

paper clip holder
distribuidor [M] **de clips** [M]
distributeur [M] **de trombones** [M]
Büroklammerhalter [M]
portafermagli [M]

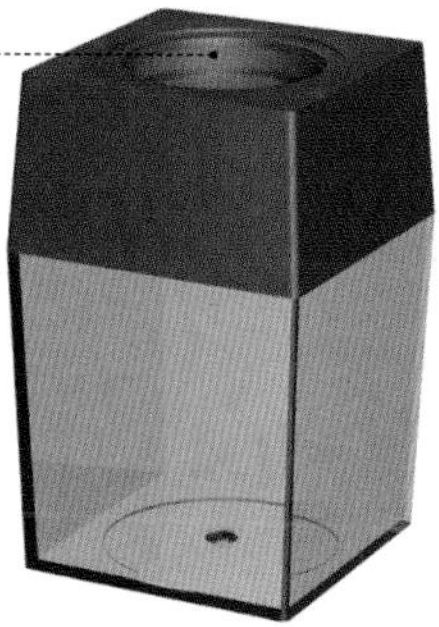
magnet
imán [M]
aimant [M]
Magnet [M]
calamita [F]

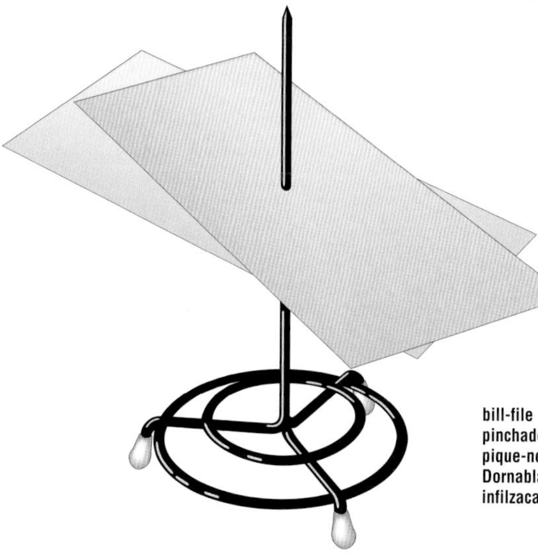

bill-file
pinchador [M]
pique-notes [M]
Dornablage [F]
infilzacarte [M]

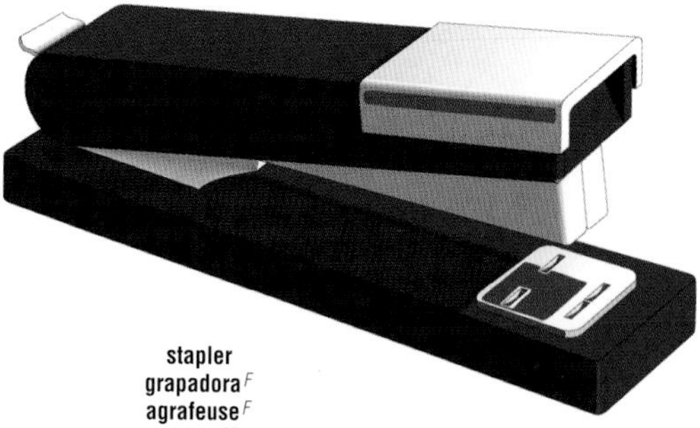

stapler
grapadora F
agrafeuse F
Hefter M
cucitrice F

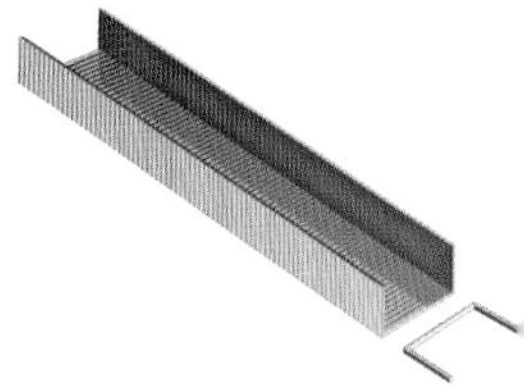

staples
grapas F
agrafes F
Heftklammern F
punti M metallici

staple remover
quitagrapas M
dégrafeuse F
Entklammerer M
levapunti M

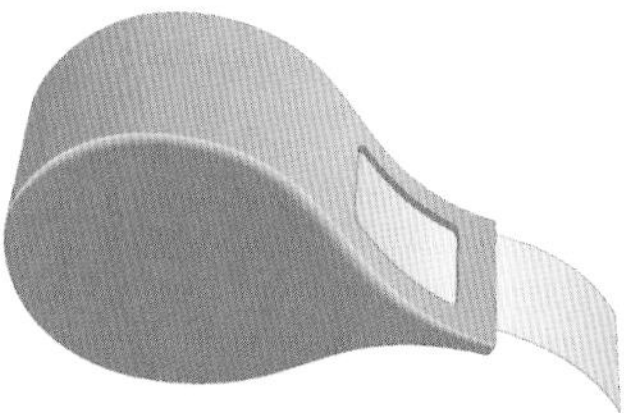

correction paper
papel M corrector
ruban M correcteur
Korrekturstreifen M
nastro M per correzioni F

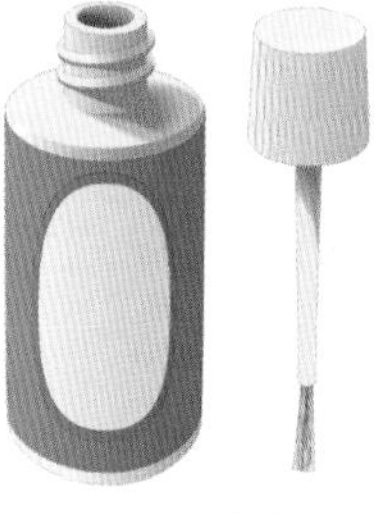

correction fluid
liquido M corrector
correcteur M liquide
Korrekturflüssigkeit F
correttore M liquido

pencil sharpener
sacapuntas M
taille-crayon M
Bleistiftspitzer M
temperamatite M

pencil sharpener
sacapuntas M
taille-crayon M
Bleistiftspitzer M
temperamatite M

overhead projector
proyector
rétroprojecteur *M*
Tageslichtprojektor *M*
proiettore *M*

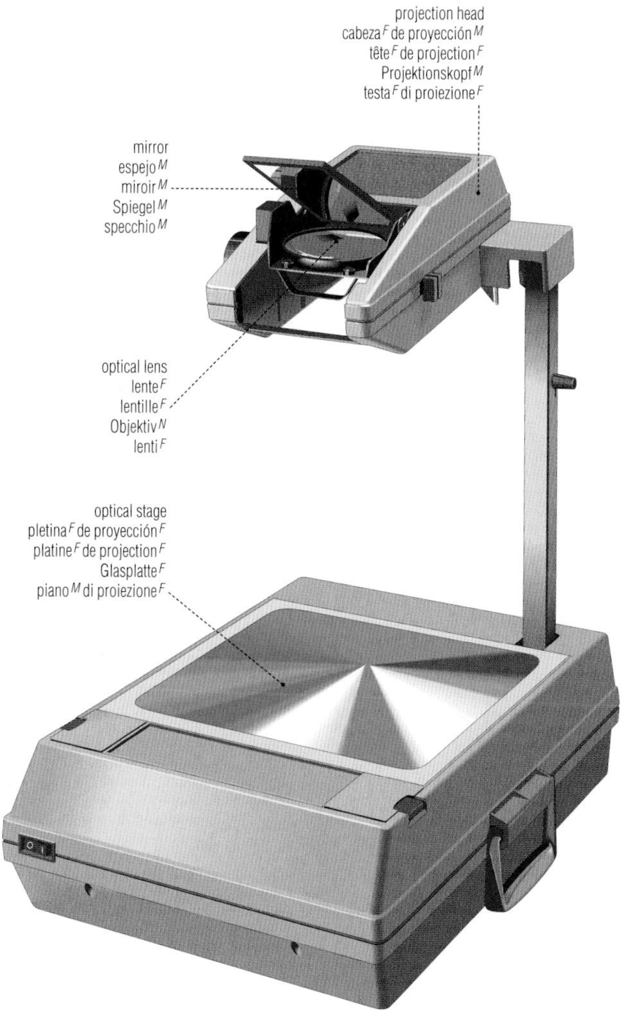
projection head
cabeza F de proyección M
tête F de projection F
Projektionskopf M
testa F di proiezione F
mirror
espejo M
miroir M
Spiegel M
specchio M
optical lens
lente F
lentille F
Objektiv N
lenti F
optical stage
pletina F de proyección F
platine F de projection F
Glasplatte F
piano M di proiezione F

road system

sistema^M de carreteras^F | système^M routier | Straßenbau^M | sistema^M stradale

cross section of a road
sección^F transversal de una carretera^F
coupe^F d'une route^F
Straße^F im Querschnitt^M
sezione^F trasversale di una strada^F

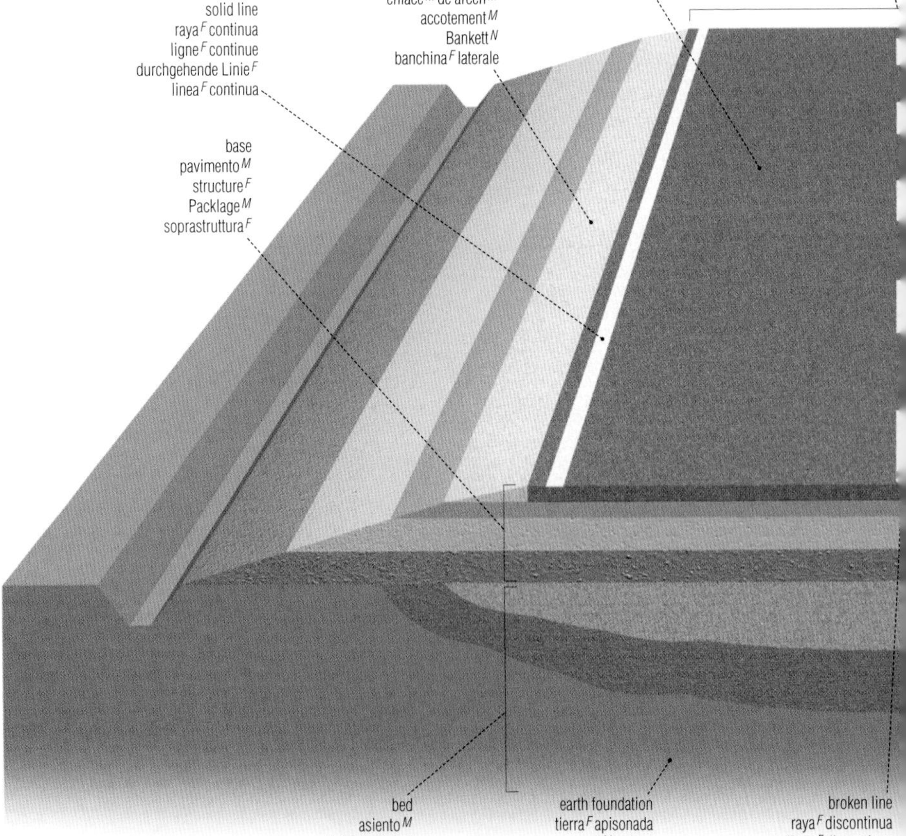
surface course
capa^F de rodadura^F
couche^F de surface^F
Decke^F
manto^M di usura^F
roadway
calzada^F
chaussée^F
Fahrbahn^F
piano^M stradale
shoulder
enlace^M de arcén^M
accotement^M
Bankett^N
banchina^F laterale
solid line
raya^F continua
ligne^F continue
durchgehende Linie^F
linea^F continua
base
pavimento^M
structure^F
Packlage^M
soprastruttura^F
bed
asiento^M
infrastructure^F
Untergrund^M
corpo^M stradale
earth foundation
tierra^F apisonada
sol^M naturel
gewachsener Boden^M
fondazione^F naturale
broken line
raya^F discontinua
ligne^F discontinue
unterbrochene Linie^F
linea^F tratteggiata

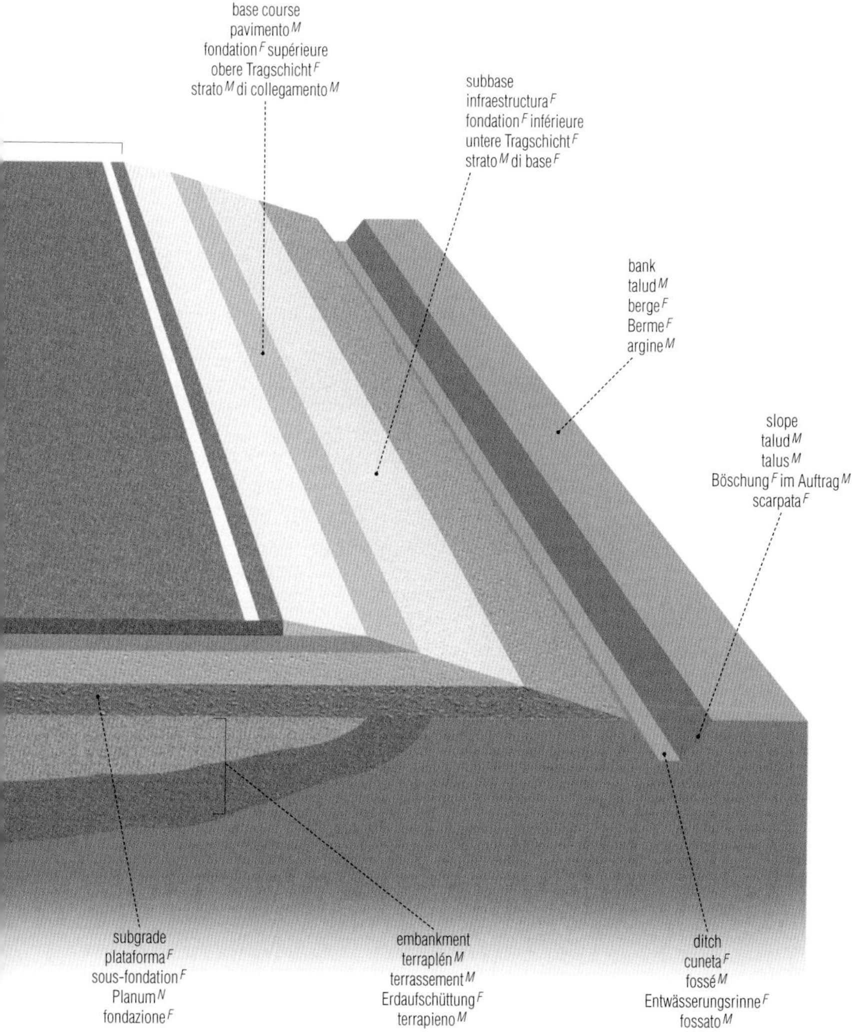
base course
pavimento M
fondation F supérieure
obere Tragschicht F
strato M di collegamento M
subbase
infraestructura F
fondation F inférieure
untere Tragschicht F
strato M di base F
bank
talud M
berge F
Berme F
argine M
slope
talud M
talus M
Böschung F im Auftrag M
scarpata F
subgrade
plataforma F
sous-fondation F
Planum N
fondazione F
embankment
terraplén M
terrassement M
Erdaufschüttung F
terrapieno M
ditch
cuneta F
fossé M
Entwässerungsrinne F
fossato M

road system

cloverleaf
enlace[M] de trébol[M]
échangeur[M] en trèfle[M]
Kleeblatt[N]
raccordo[M] a quadrifoglio[M]

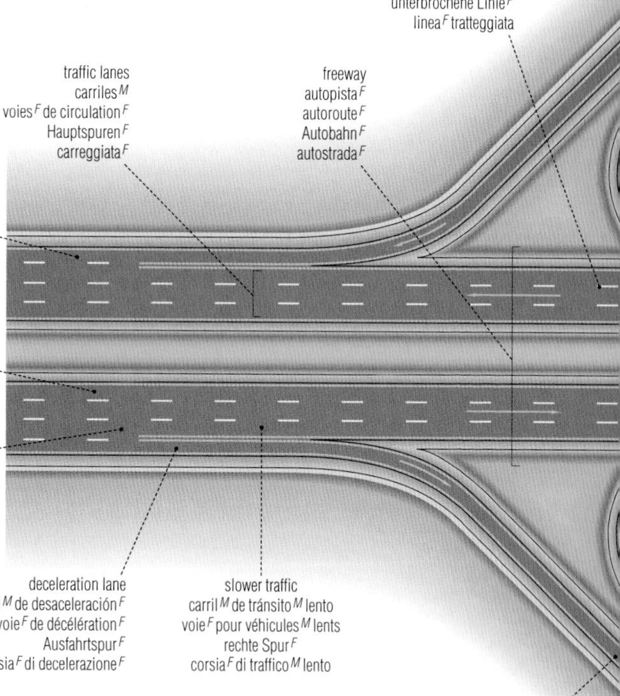
loo
curva
boucle
Schlaufe
rampa[F] ad anello
broken line
raya[F] discontinua
ligne[F] discontinue
unterbrochene Linie[F]
linea[F] tratteggiata
traffic lanes
carriles[M]
voies[F] de circulation[F]
Hauptspuren[F]
carreggiata[F]
freeway
autopista[F]
autoroute[F]
Autobahn[F]
autostrada[F]
acceleration lane
carril[M] de aceleración[F]
voie[F] d'accélération[F]
Beschleunigungsspur[F]
corsia[F] di accelerazione[F]
passing lane
carril[M] de adelantamiento[M]
voie[F] de dépassement[M]
Überholspur[F]
corsia[F] di sorpasso[M]
traffic lane
carril[M] de tránsito[M]
voie[F] de circulation[F]
Mittelspur[F]
corsia[F] di marcia[F] normale
deceleration lane
carril[M] de desaceleración[F]
voie[F] de décélération[F]
Ausfahrtspur[F]
corsia[F] di decelerazione[F]
slower traffic
carril[M] de tránsito[M] lento
voie[F] pour véhicules[M] lents
rechte Spur[F]
corsia[F] di traffico[M] lento
ramp
rampa[F]
bretelle[F]
Rampe[F]
rampa[F]

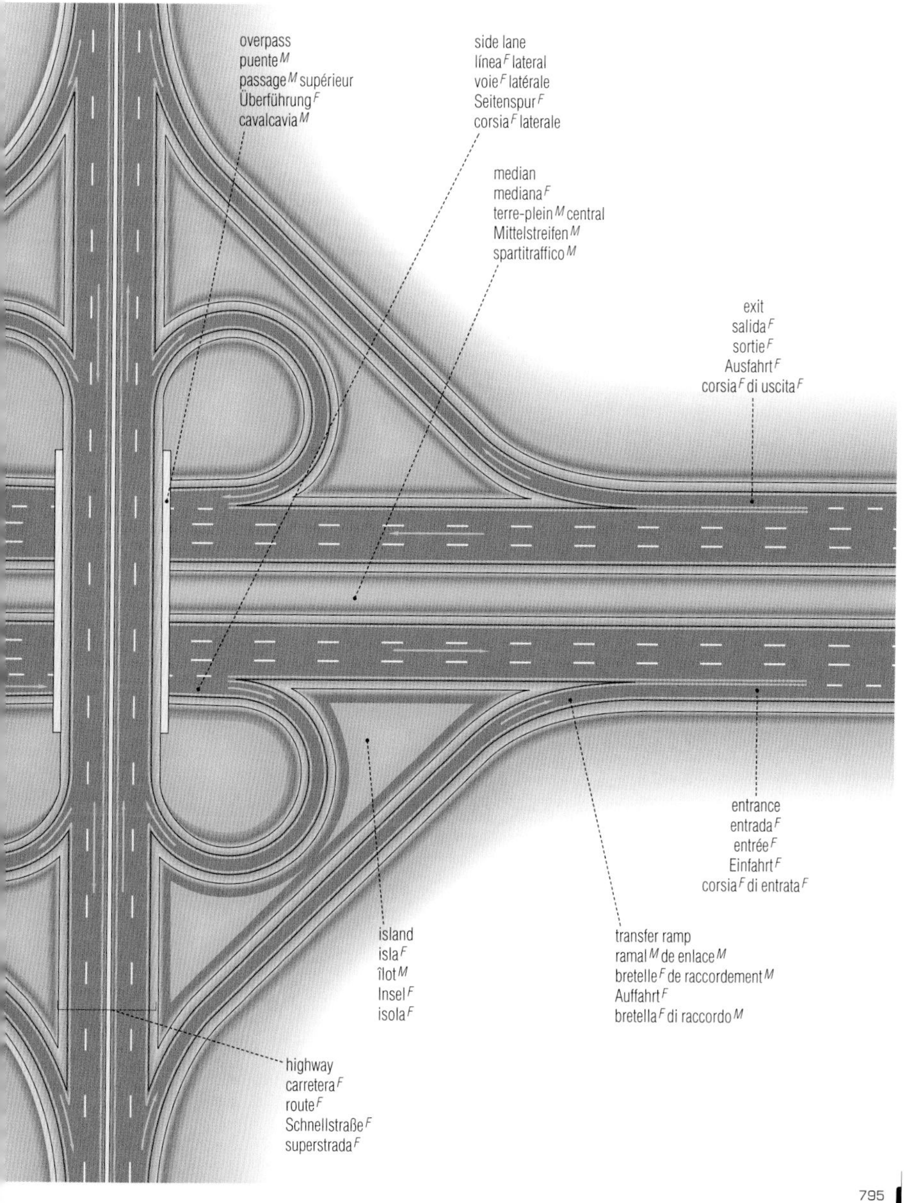
overpass
puente M
passage M supérieur
Überführung F
cavalcavia M
side lane
línea F lateral
voie F latérale
Seitenspur F
corsia F laterale
median
mediana F
terre-plein M central
Mittelstreifen M
spartitraffico M
exit
salida F
sortie F
Ausfahrt F
corsia F di uscita F
entrance
entrada F
entrée F
Einfahrt F
corsia F di entrata F
island
isla F
îlot M
Insel F
isola F
transfer ramp
ramal M de enlace M
bretelle F de raccordement M
Auffahrt F
bretella F di raccordo M
highway
carretera F
route F
Schnellstraße F
superstrada F

examples of interchanges
ejemplos M de enlaces M de carreteras F
exemples M d'échangeurs M
Beispiele N für Anschlussstellen F
esempi M di raccordo M

cloverleaf
enlace M de trébol M
échangeur M en trèfle M
Kleeblatt N
raccordo M a quadrifoglio M

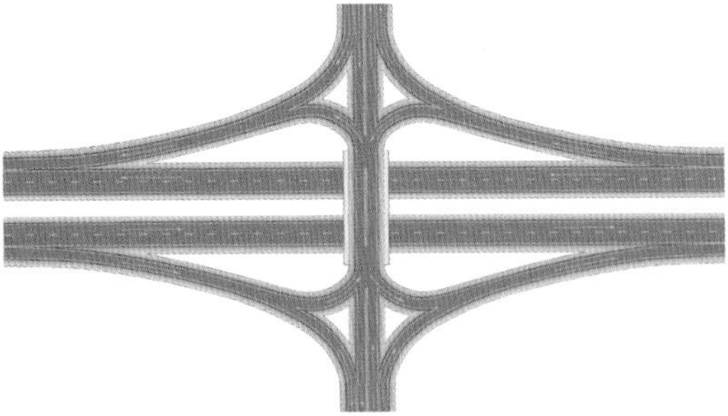

diamond interchange
enlace M de diamante M
échangeur M en losange M
Raute F
raccordo M a losanga F

traffic circle
enlace M de glorieta F
carrefour M giratoire
Verteiler M
raccordo M a rotatoria F

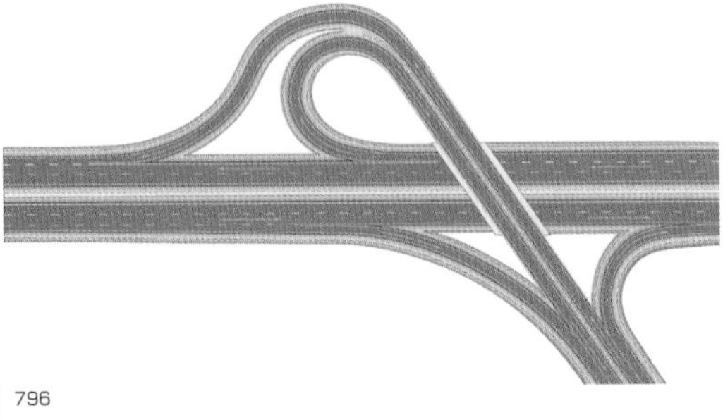

trumpet interchange
trompeta F
échangeur M en trompette F
Trompete F
raccordo M a tromba F

fixed bridges

puentes^{M} fijos | ponts^{M} fixes | starre Brücken^{F} | ponti^{M} fissi

beam bridge
puente^{M} de viga^{F}
pont^{M} à poutre^{F}
Balkenbrücke^{F}
ponte^{M} a travata^{F}

outment
ontrafuerte^{M}
ulée^{F}
iderlager^{N}
palla^{F}

overpass
paso^{M} elevado
passage^{M} supérieur
Überführung^{F}
cavalcavia^{M}

continuous beam
viga^{F} continua
poutre^{F} continue
Durchlaufträger^{M}
travata^{F} continua

parapet
parapeto^{M}
garde-corps^{M}
Geländer^{N}
parapetto^{M}

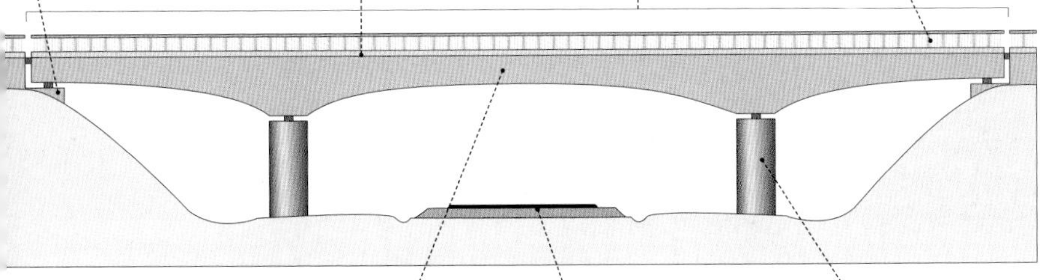

deck
tablero^{M}
tablier^{M}
Fahrbahn^{F}
impalcato^{M}

underpass
paso^{M} inferior
passage^{M} inférieur
Unterführung^{F}
sottovia^{F}

pier
pilar^{M}
pile^{F}
Pfeiler^{M}
pila^{F}

cantilever bridge
puente^{M} cantilever
pont^{M} cantilever
Auslegerbrücke^{F}
ponte^{M} a cantilever^{M}

suspended span
tramo^{M} suspendido
poutre^{F} suspendue
eingehängte Spannweite^{F}
travata^{F} appoggiata

cantilever span
viga^{F} cantilever
poutre^{F} cantilever
Kragträger^{M}
travata^{F} a cantilever^{M}

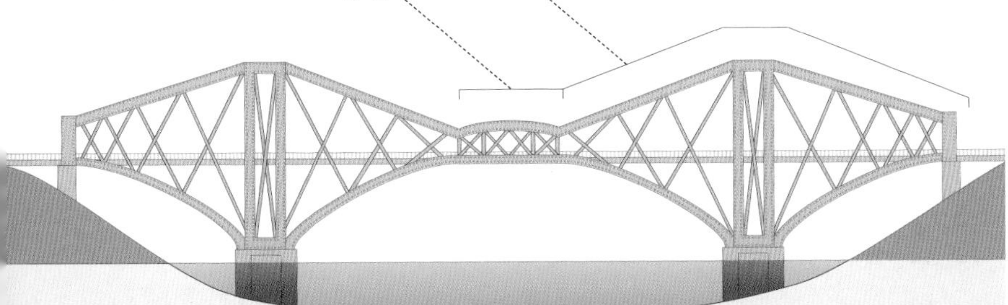

fixed bridges

arch bridge
puente^M de arco^M
pont^M en arc^M
Bogenbrücke^F
ponte^M ad arco^M

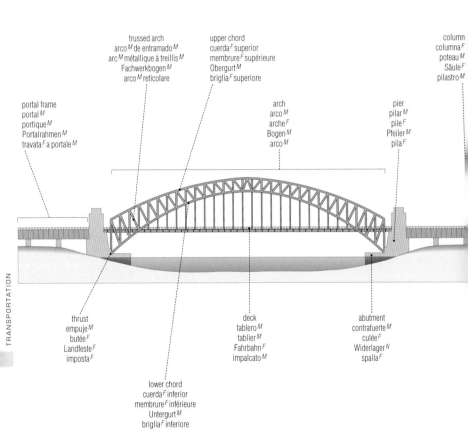

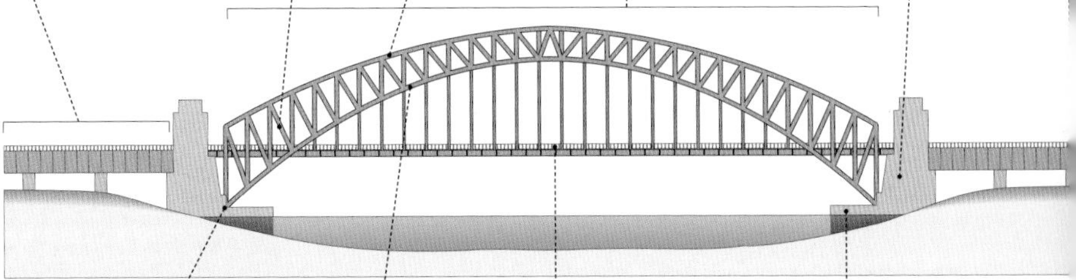
trussed arch
arco^M de entramado^M
arc^M métallique à treillis^M
Fachwerkbogen^M
arco^M reticolare
upper chord
cuerda^F superior
membrure^F supérieure
Obergurt^M
briglia^F superiore
column
columna^F
poteau^M
Säule^F
pilastro^M
portal frame
portal^M
portique^M
Portalrahmen^M
travata^F a portale^M
arch
arco^M
arche^F
Bogen^M
arco^M
pier
pilar^M
pile^F
Pfeiler^M
pila^F
thrust
empuje^M
butée^F
Landfeste^F
imposta^F
deck
tablero^M
tablier^M
Fahrbahn^F
impalcato^M
abutment
contrafuerte^M
culée^F
Widerlager^N
spalla^F
lower chord
cuerda^F inferior
membrure^F inférieure
Untergurt^M
briglia^F inferiore

suspension bridge
puente[M] colgante
pont[M] suspendu à câble[M] porteur
Hängebrücke[F]
ponte[M] sospeso

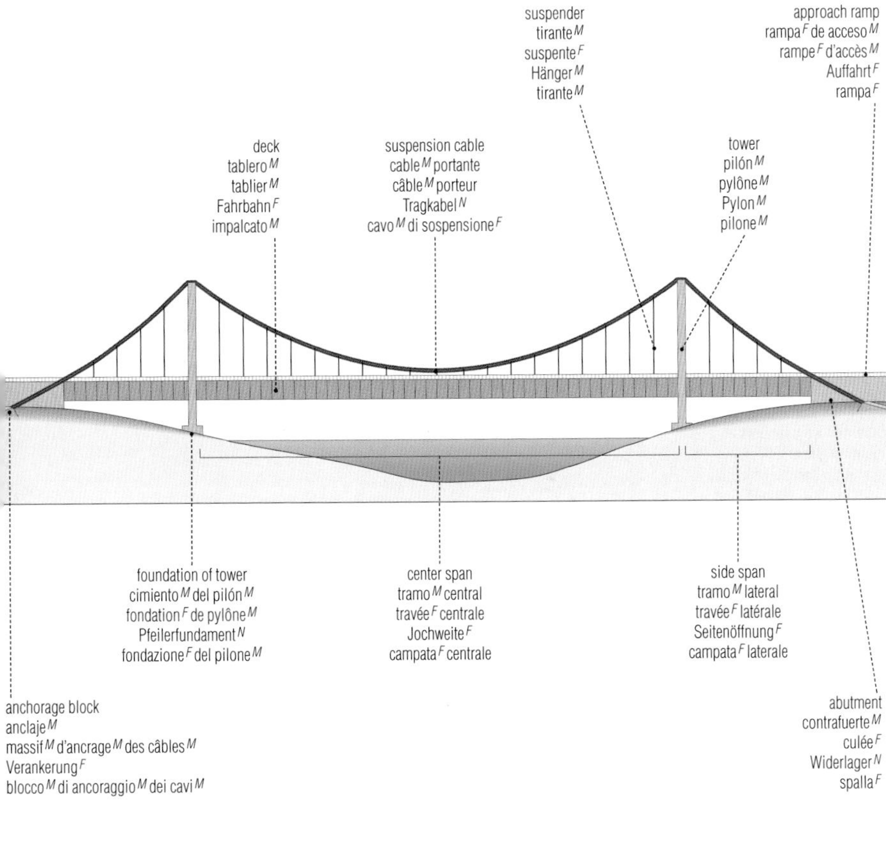
suspender
tirante[M]
suspente[F]
Hänger[M]
tirante[M]
approach ramp
rampa[F] de acceso[M]
rampe[F] d'accès[M]
Auffahrt[F]
rampa[F]
deck
tablero[M]
tablier[M]
Fahrbahn[F]
impalcato[M]
suspension cable
cable[M] portante
câble[M] porteur
Tragkabel[N]
cavo[M] di sospensione[F]
tower
pilón[M]
pylône[M]
Pylon[M]
pilone[M]
foundation of tower
cimiento[M] del pilón[M]
fondation[F] de pylône[M]
Pfeilerfundament[N]
fondazione[F] del pilone[M]
center span
tramo[M] central
travée[F] centrale
Jochweite[F]
campata[F] centrale
side span
tramo[M] lateral
travée[F] latérale
Seitenöffnung[F]
campata[F] laterale
anchorage block
anclaje[M]
massif[M] d'ancrage[M] des câbles[M]
Verankerung[F]
blocco[M] di ancoraggio[M] dei cavi[M]
abutment
contrafuerte[M]
culée[F]
Widerlager[N]
spalla[F]

movable bridges

puentes^M móviles | ponts^M mobiles | bewegliche Brücken^F | ponti^M mobili

swing bridge
puente^M giratorio
pont^M tournant
Drehbrücke^F
ponte^M girevole

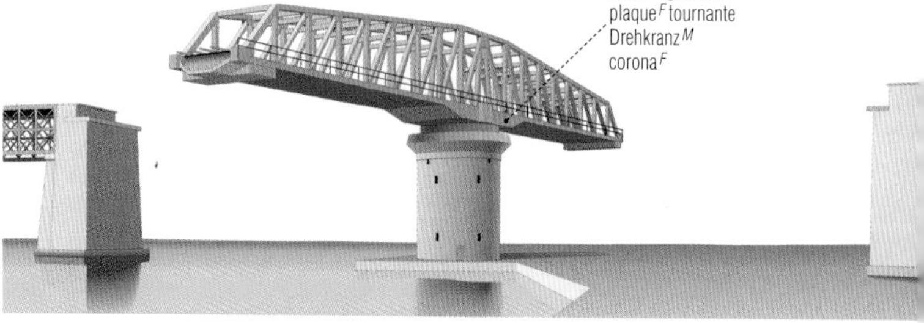
turntable
tramo^M giratorio
plaque^F tournante
Drehkranz^M
corona^F

Bailey bridge
puente^M desmontable tipo^M Bailey
pont^M Bailey
Bailey-Brücke^F
ponte^M Bailey

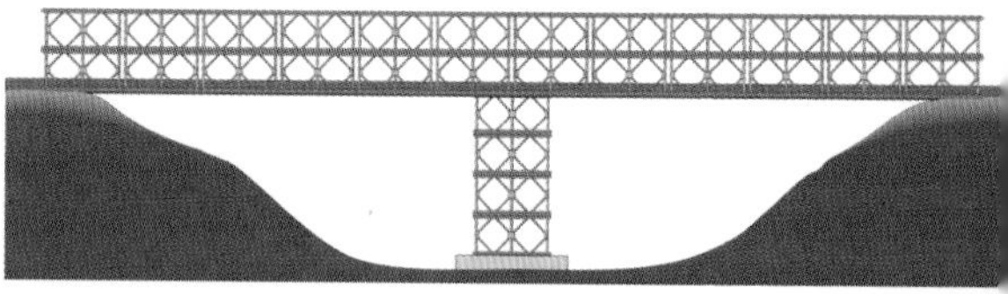

floating bridge
puente^M de pontones^M
pont^M flottant
Pontonbrücke^F
ponte^M galleggiante

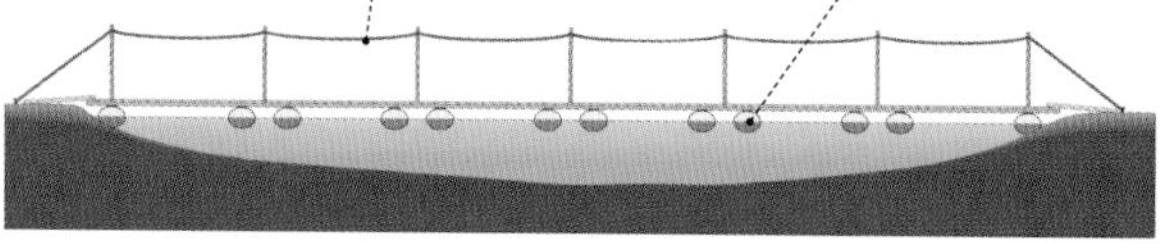
manrope
barandilla^F
garde-corps^M
Seil^N
mancorrente^M
pontoon
pontón^M
ponton^M
Ponton^M
pontone^M

transporter bridge
puente^M transbordador
pont^M transbordeur
Fährbrücke^F
ponte^M trasportatore

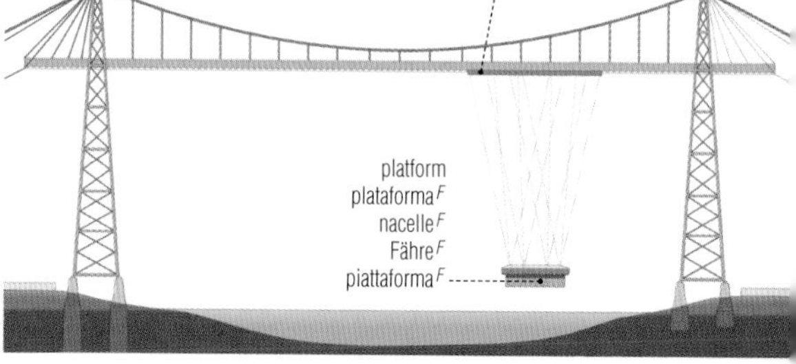
trolley
carro^M
chariot^M transbordeur
Laufkatze^F
carrello^M
platform
plataforma^F
nacelle^F
Fähre^F
piattaforma^F

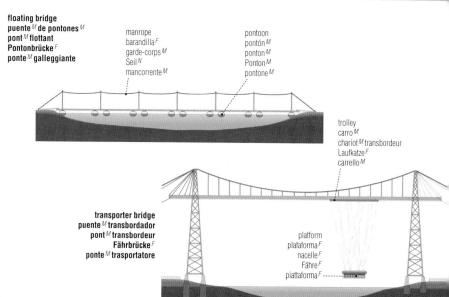

TRANSPORTATION

ouble-leaf bascule bridge
uente[M] levadizo doble
ont[M] basculant à double volée[F]
oppelklappbrücke[F]
onte[M] ribaltabile a due ali[F]

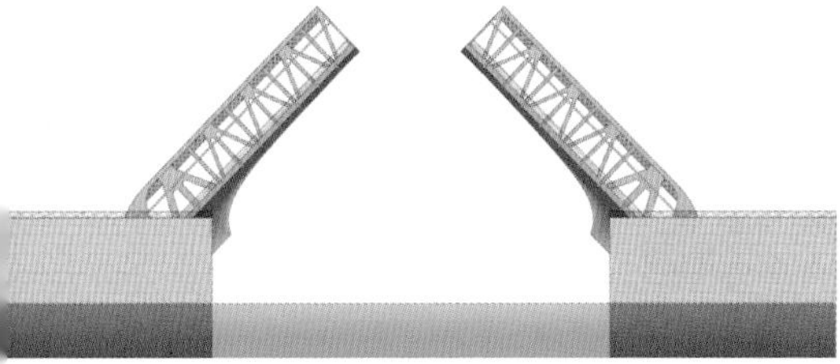

single-leaf bascule bridge
puente[M] levadizo sencillo
pont[M] basculant à simple volée[F]
einteilige Klappbrücke[F]
ponte[M] ribaltabile a un'ala[F]

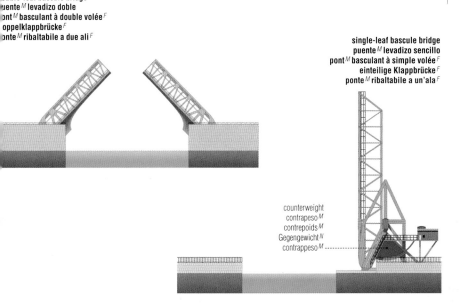

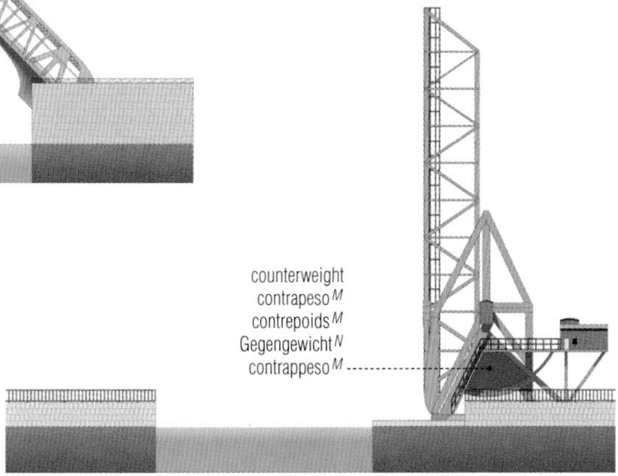
counterweight
contrapeso[M]
contrepoids[M]
Gegengewicht[N]
contrappeso[M]

lift bridge
puente[M] elevador
pont[M] levant
Hubbrücke[F]
ponte[M] sollevabile

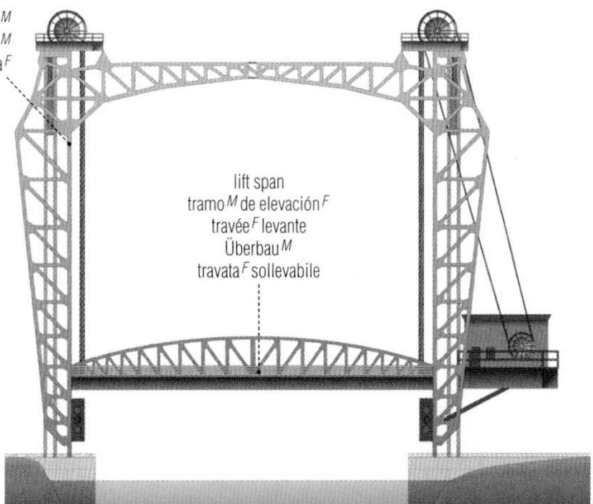
guiding tower
pilón[M] guía[M]
tour[F] de guidage[M]
Führungsturm[M]
torre[F] di guida[F]
lift span
tramo[M] de elevación[F]
travée[F] levante
Überbau[M]
travata[F] sollevabile

automobile

automóvil[M] | automobile[F] | Auto[N] | automobile[F]

examples of bodies
ejemplos[M] de carrocerías[F]
exemples[M] de carrosseries[F]
Beispiele[N] für Karosserien[F]
esempi[M] di carrozzerie[F]

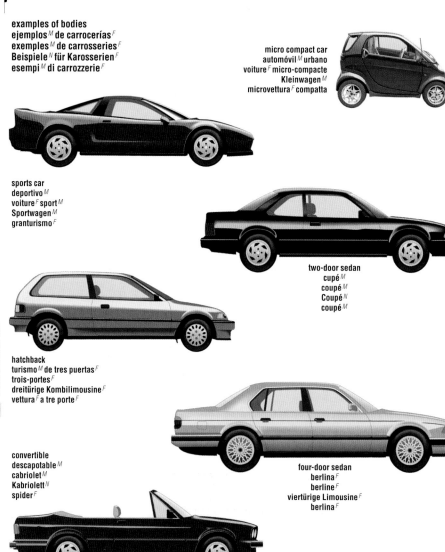

micro compact car
automóvil[M] urbano
voiture[F] micro-compacte
Kleinwagen[M]
microvettura[F] compatta

sports car
deportivo[M]
voiture[F] sport[M]
Sportwagen[M]
granturismo[F]

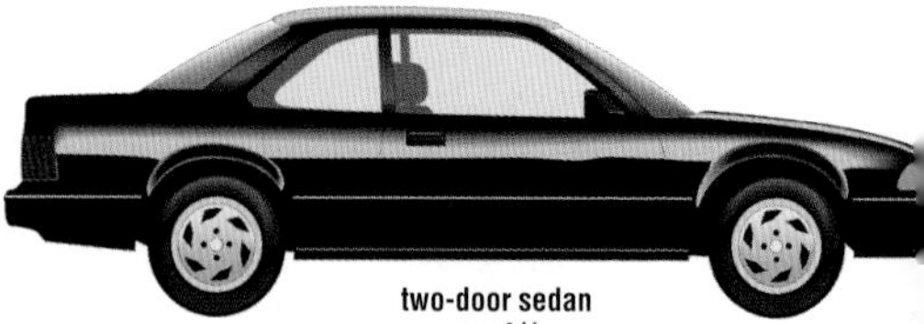

two-door sedan
cupé[M]
coupé[M]
Coupé[N]
coupé[M]

hatchback
turismo[M] de tres puertas[F]
trois-portes[F]
dreitürige Kombilimousine[F]
vettura[F] a tre porte[F]

four-door sedan
berlina[F]
berline[F]
viertürige Limousine[F]
berlina[F]

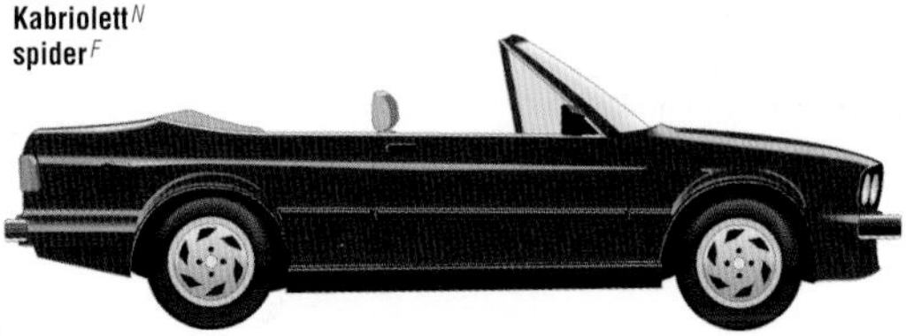

convertible
descapotable[M]
cabriolet[M]
Kabriolett[N]
spider[F]

station wagon
coche *M* familiar
break *M*
Kombi *M*
station wagon *F*

minivan
monovolumen *M*
fourgonnette *F*
Minibus *M*
monovolume *F*

sport-utility vehicle
vehículo *M* todo terreno *M*
véhicule *M* tout-terrain *M*
Geländewagen *M*
fuoristrada *M*

pickup truck
camioneta *F*
camionnette *F*
Pickup *M*
pickup *M*

limousine
limusina *F*
limousine *F*
Pullman Limousine *F*
limousine *F*

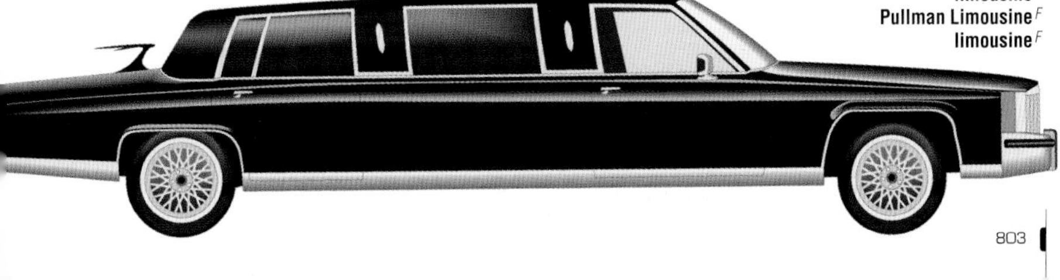

automobile

body
carrocería *F*
carrosserie *F*
Karosserie *F*
carrozzeria *F*

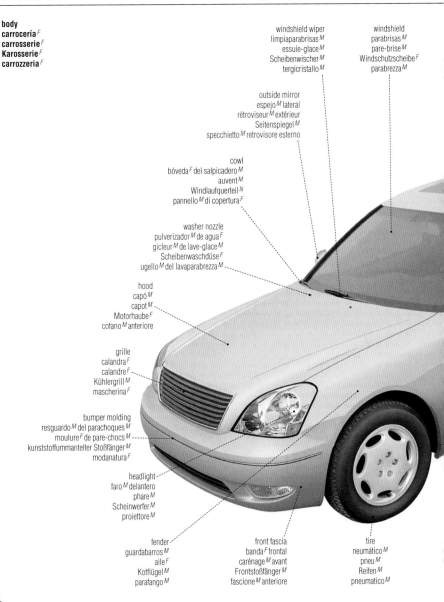

windshield wiper
limpiaparabrisas M
essuie-glace M
Scheibenwischer M
tergicristallo M
windshield
parabrisas M
pare-brise M
Windschutzscheibe F
parabrezza M
outside mirror
espejo M lateral
rétroviseur M extérieur
Seitenspiegel M
specchietto M retrovisore esterno
cowl
bóveda F del salpicadero M
auvent M
Windlaufquerteil N
pannello M di copertura F
washer nozzle
pulverizador M de agua F
gicleur M de lave-glace M
Scheibenwaschdüse F
ugello M del lavaparabrezza M
hood
capó M
capot M
Motorhaube F
cofano M anteriore
grille
calandra F
calandre F
Kühlergrill M
mascherina F
bumper molding
resguardo M del parachoques M
moulure F de pare-chocs M
kunststoffummantelter Stoßfänger M
modanatura F
headlight
faro M delantero
phare M
Scheinwerfer M
proiettore M
fender
guardabarros M
aile F
Kotflügel M
parafango M
front fascia
banda F frontal
carénage M avant
Frontstoßfänger M
fascione M anteriore
tire
neumático M
pneu M
Reifen M
pneumatico M

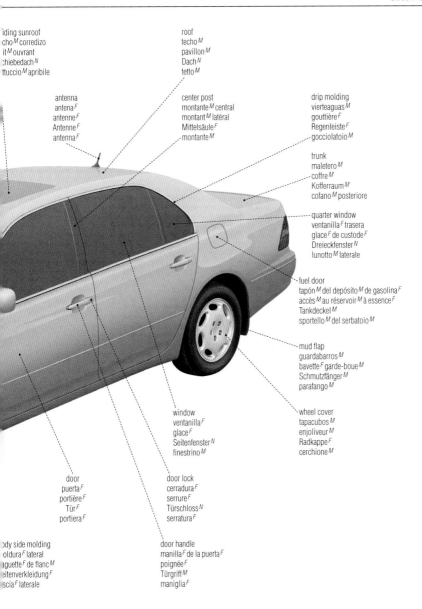

iding sunroof
cho [M] corredizo
it [M] ouvrant
chiebedach [N]
ttuccio [M] apribile

roof
techo [M]
pavillon [M]
Dach [N]
tetto [M]

antenna
antena [F]
antenne [F]
Antenne [F]
antenna [F]

center post
montante [M] central
montant [M] latéral
Mittelsäule [F]
montante [M]

drip molding
vierteaguas [M]
gouttière [F]
Regenleiste [F]
gocciolatoio [M]

trunk
maletero [M]
coffre [M]
Kofferraum [M]
cofano [M] posteriore

quarter window
ventanilla [F] trasera
glace [F] de custode [F]
Dreieckfenster [N]
lunotto [M] laterale

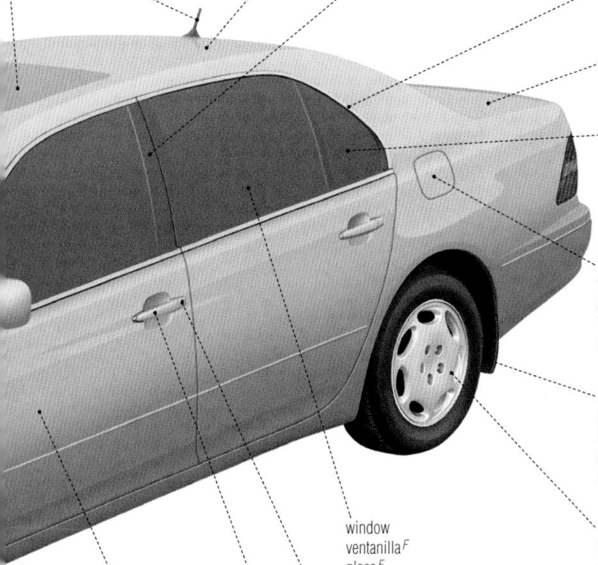

fuel door
tapón [M] del depósito [M] de gasolina [F]
accès [M] au réservoir [M] à essence [F]
Tankdeckel [M]
sportello [M] del serbatoio [M]

mud flap
guardabarros [M]
bavette [F] garde-boue [M]
Schmutzfänger [M]
parafango [M]

wheel cover
tapacubos [M]
enjoliveur [M]
Radkappe [F]
cerchione [M]

window
ventanilla [F]
glace [F]
Seitenfenster [N]
finestrino [M]

door
puerta [F]
portière [F]
Tür [F]
portiera [F]

door lock
cerradura [F]
serrure [F]
Türschloss [N]
serratura [F]

ody side molding
oldura [F] lateral
aguette [F] de flanc [M]
eitenverkleidung [F]
scia [F] laterale

door handle
manilla [F] de la puerta [F]
poignée [F]
Türgriff [M]
maniglia [F]

dashboard
salpicadero *M*
tableau *M* **de bord** *M*
Armaturenbrett *N*
plancia *F*

wiper switch
interruptor *M* del limpiaparabrisas *M*
commande *F* d'essuie-glace *M*
Scheibenwischerhebel *M*
comando *M* del tergicristallo *M*
cruise control
regulador *M* de velocidad *F*
régulateur *M* de vitesse *F*
Tempomat *M*
controllo *M* della velocità *F* di crociera *F*
ignition switch
interruptor *M* de encendido *M*
commutateur *M* d'allumage *M*
Zündschloss *N*
blocchetto *M* di accensione *F*
headlight/turn signal
palanca *F* de luces *F* e intermitentes *M*
éclairage *M*/clignotant *M*
Blinker- und Fernlichthebel *M*
comando *M* dei proiettori *M* e dell'indicatore *M* di direzione *F*
horn
claxon *M*
avertisseur *M*
Hupe *F*
clacson *M*
steering wheel
volante *M*
volant *M*
Lenkrad *N*
volante *M*
clutch pedal
pedal *M* del embrague *M*
pédale *F* de débrayage *M*
Kupplungspedal *N*
pedale *M* della frizione *F*
brake pedal
pedal *M* de los frenos *M*
pédale *F* de frein *M*
Bremspedal *N*
pedale *M* del freno *M*
gas ped
pedal *M* del acelerador
pédale *F* d'accélérateur
Gaspedal
pedale *M* dell'acceleratore

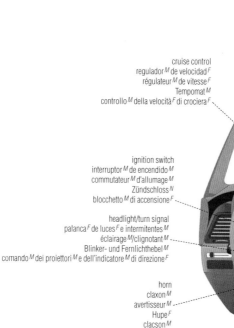

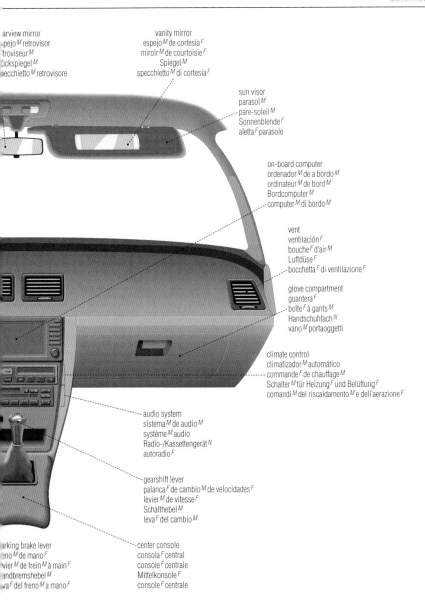

arview mirror
pejo[M] retrovisor
troviseur[M]
ückspiegel[M]
pecchietto[M] retrovisore

vanity mirror
espejo[M] de cortesía[F]
miroir[M] de courtoisie[F]
Spiegel[M]
specchietto[M] di cortesia[F]

sun visor
parasol[M]
pare-soleil[M]
Sonnenblende[F]
aletta[F] parasole

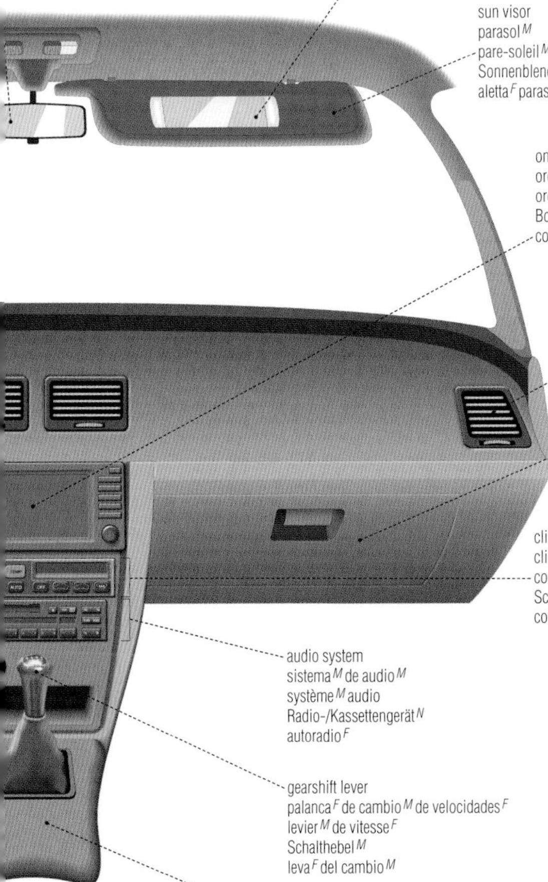

on-board computer
ordenador[M] de a bordo[M]
ordinateur[M] de bord[M]
Bordcomputer[M]
computer[M] di bordo[M]

vent
ventilación[F]
bouche[F] d'air[M]
Luftdüse[F]
bocchetta[F] di ventilazione[F]

glove compartment
guantera[F]
boîte[F] à gants[M]
Handschuhfach[N]
vano[M] portaoggetti

climate control
climatizador[M] automático
commande[F] de chauffage[M]
Schalter[M] für Heizung[F] und Belüftung[F]
comandi[M] del riscaldamento[M] e dell'aerazione[F]

audio system
sistema[M] de audio[M]
système[M] audio
Radio-/Kassettengerät[N]
autoradio[F]

gearshift lever
palanca[F] de cambio[M] de velocidades[F]
levier[M] de vitesse[F]
Schalthebel[M]
leva[F] del cambio[M]

arking brake lever
eno[M] de mano[F]
vier[M] de frein[M] à main[F]
andbremshebel[M]
va[F] del freno[M] a mano[F]

center console
consola[F] central
console[F] centrale
Mittelkonsole[F]
console[F] centrale

tire

neumático^M | pneu^M | Reifen^M | pneumatico^M

examples of tires
ejemplos^M de neumáticos^M
exemples^M de pneus^M
Reifenarten^F
esempi^M di pneumatici^M

performance tire
neumático^M de rendimiento^M
pneu^M de performance^F
Sportreifen^M
pneumatico^M sportivo

all-season tire
neumático^M de todas las estaciones^F
pneu^M toutes saisons^F
Ganzjahresreifen^M
pneumatico^M per tutte le stagioni^F

winter tire
neumático^M de invierno^M
pneu^M d'hiver^M
Winterreifen^M
pneumatico^M invernale

touring tire
neumático^M de turismo^M
pneu^M autoroutier
Touringreifen^M
pneumatico^M granturismo

studded tire
neumático^M de tacos^M
pneu^M à crampons^M
Spikereifen^M
pneumatico^M chiodato

wheel
rueda[F]
roue[F]
Rad[N]
ruota[F]

rim
llanta[F]
jante[F]
Felge[F]
cerchio[M]
rim flange
pestaña[F] de la llanta[F]
joue[F] de jante[F]
Felgenhorn[N]
bordo[M] del cerchio[M]
disk
disco[M]
voile[M]
Radschüssel[F]
disco[M]

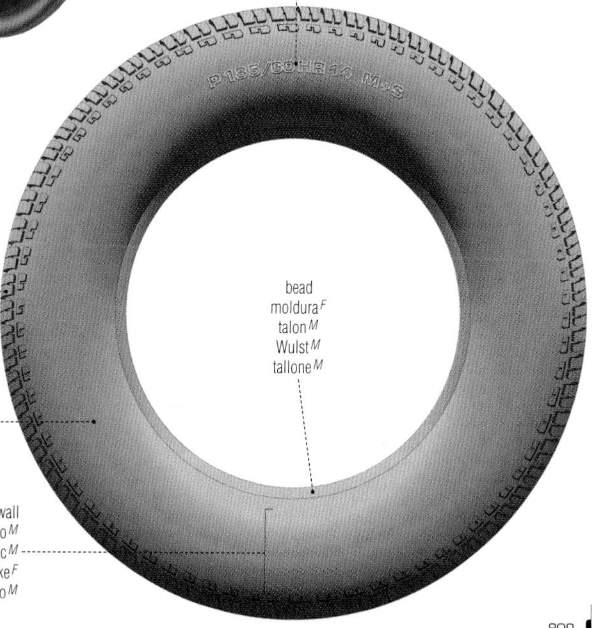
technical specifications
especificaciones[F] técnicas
spécifications[F] techniques
Kennzeichnung[F]
dati[M] tecnici
P185/60HR 14 M+S
tread design
dibujo[M] de la superficie[F] de rodadura[F]
sculptures[F]
Profil[N]
scolpitura[F] del battistrada[M]
bead
moldura[F]
talon[M]
Wulst[M]
tallone[M]
rubbing strip
banda[F] protectora
bourrelet[M]
Scheuerleiste[F]
striscia[F] antiabrasiva
rubber wall
costado[M]
flanc[M]
Reifenflanke[F]
fianco[M]

TRANSPORTATION

types of engines

tipos[M] de motores[M] | types[M] de moteurs[M] | Motortypen[M] | tipi[M] di motori[M]

gasoline engine
motor[M] de gasolina[F]
moteur[M] à essence[F]
Ottomotor[M]
motore[M] a benzina[F]

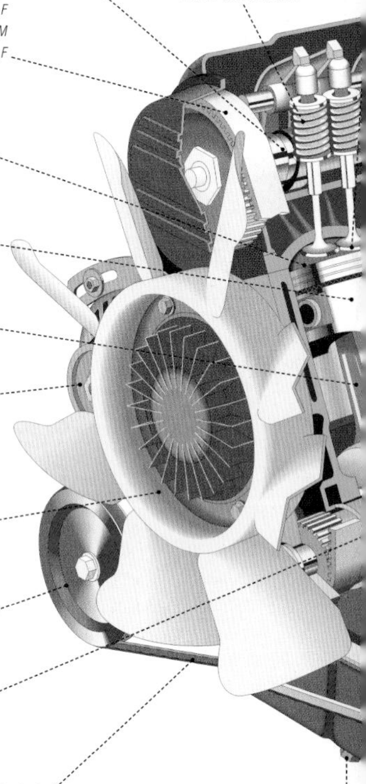
inlet va
válvula[F] de admisió
soupape[F] d'admissio
Einlassvent
valvola[F] di aspirazior
camshaft
árbol[M] de levas[F]
arbre[M] à cames[F]
Nockenwelle[F]
albero[M] a camme[F]
valve spring
resorte[M] de la válvula[F]
ressort[M] de soupape[F]
Ventilfeder[F]
molla[F] della valvola[F]
combustion chamber
cámara[F] de combustión[F]
chambre[F] de combustion[F]
Verbrennungsraum[M]
camera[F] di scoppio[M]
timing belt
correa[F] de distribución[F]
courroie[F] de distribution[F]
Antriebsriemen[M]
cinghia[F] di distribuzione[F]
piston skirt
camisa[F] de pistón[M]
jupe[F] de piston[M]
Kolbenschaft[F]
mantello[M] del pistone[M]
connecting rod
biela[F]
bielle[F]
Pleuelstange[F]
biella[F]
alternator
alternador[M]
alternateur[M]
Lichtmaschine[F]
alternatore[M]
cooling fan
ventilador[M]
ventilateur[M]
Lüfter[M]
ventilatore[M]
pulley
polea[F]
poulie[F]
Riemenscheibe[F]
puleggia[F]
crankshaft
cigüeñal[M]
vilebrequin[M]
Kurbelwelle[F]
albero[M] a gomiti[M]
fan belt
correa[F] del ventilador[M]
courroie[F] de ventilateur[M]
Keilriemen[M]
cinghia[F] del ventilatore[M]
oil drain plug
tapón[M] de vaciado[M]
bouchon[M] de vidange[F] d'huile[F]
Ölablassschraube[F]
tappo[M] di scarico[M] dell'olio[M]

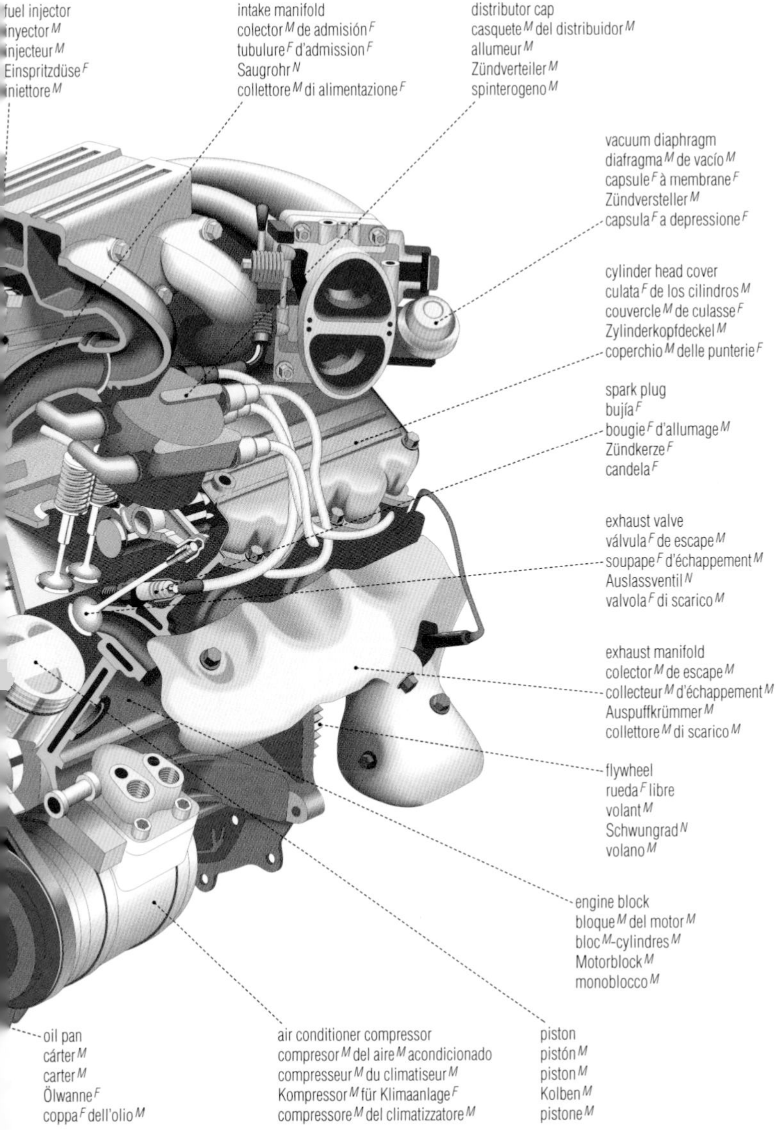
fuel injector
inyector M
injecteur M
Einspritzdüse F
iniettore M
intake manifold
colector M de admisión F
tubulure F d'admission F
Saugrohr N
collettore M di alimentazione F
distributor cap
casquete M del distribuidor M
allumeur M
Zündverteiler M
spinterogeno M
vacuum diaphragm
diafragma M de vacío M
capsule F à membrane F
Zündversteller M
capsula F a depressione F
cylinder head cover
culata F de los cilindros M
couvercle M de culasse F
Zylinderkopfdeckel M
coperchio M delle punterie F
spark plug
bujía F
bougie F d'allumage M
Zündkerze F
candela F
exhaust valve
válvula F de escape M
soupape F d'échappement M
Auslassventil N
valvola F di scarico M
exhaust manifold
colector M de escape M
collecteur M d'échappement M
Auspuffkrümmer M
collettore M di scarico M
flywheel
rueda F libre
volant M
Schwungrad N
volano M
engine block
bloque M del motor M
bloc M-cylindres M
Motorblock M
monoblocco M
oil pan
cárter M
carter M
Ölwanne F
coppa F dell'olio M
air conditioner compressor
compresor M del aire M acondicionado
compresseur M du climatiseur M
Kompressor M für Klimaanlage F
compressore M del climatizzatore M
piston
pistón M
piston M
Kolben M
pistone M

campers

caravana[F] | caravane[F] | Wohnwagen[M] | rimorchi[M] e autocaravan[M]

tent trailer
caravana[F] plegable
tente[F]-caravane[F]
Zeltwagen[M]
carrello[M] tenda[F]

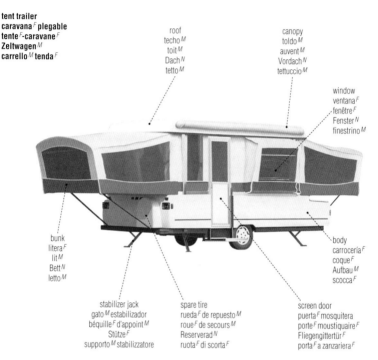

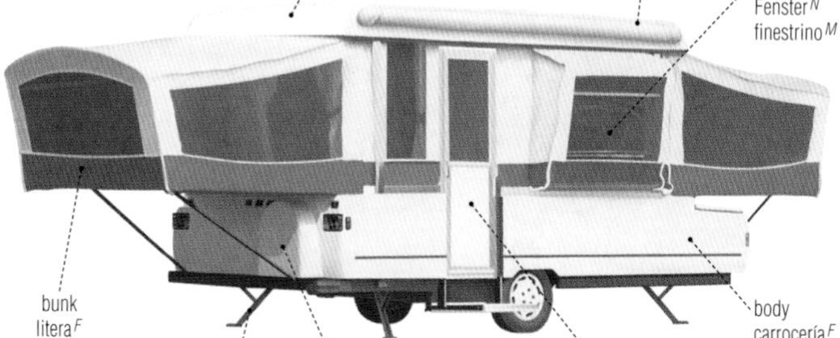
roof
techo[M]
toit[M]
Dach[N]
tetto[M]
canopy
toldo[M]
auvent[M]
Vordach[N]
tettuccio[M]
window
ventana[F]
fenêtre[F]
Fenster[N]
finestrino[M]
bunk
litera[F]
lit[M]
Bett[N]
letto[M]
body
carrocería[F]
coque[F]
Aufbau[M]
scocca[F]
stabilizer jack
gato[M] estabilizador
béquille[F] d'appoint[M]
Stütze[F]
supporto[M] stabilizzatore
spare tire
rueda[F] de repuesto[M]
roue[F] de secours[M]
Reserverad[N]
ruota[F] di scorta[F]
screen door
puerta[F] mosquitera
porte[F] moustiquaire[F]
Fliegengittertür[F]
porta[F] a zanzariera[F]

motor home
autocaravana[F]
auto[F]-caravane[F]
Wohnmobil[N]
autocaravan[M]

luggage rack
portaequipajes[M]
porte-bagages[M]
Gepäckträger[M]
portabagagli[M]
air conditioner
aire[M] acondicionado
climatiseur[M]
Klimaanlage[F]
condizionatore[M]
ladder
escalerilla[F]
échelle[F]
Leiter[F]
scala[F]

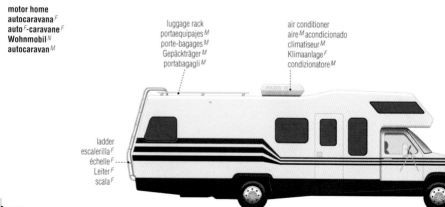

bus

autobús M | autobus M | Bus M | autobus M

double-decker bus
autocar M de dos pisos M
autobus M à impériale F
Doppeldeckerbus M
autobus M a due piani M

upper deck
piso M superior
impériale F
Oberdeck N
piano M superiore
route sign
indicador M de línea F
indicateur M de ligne F
Linienanzeige F
indicatore M di linea F

school bus
autobús M escolar
autobus M scolaire
Schulbus M
scuolabus M

outside mirror
espejo M retrovisor exterior
rétroviseur M extérieur
Außenspiegel M
specchietto M retrovisore esterno
blind spot mirror
retrovisor M de gran angular M
rétroviseur M grand-angle M
Weitwinkelspiegel M
specchietto M per il punto M cieco
flashing lights
faros M intermitentes
feux M intermittents
Blinklichter N
luci F intermittenti
crossing arm
barra F distanciadora
bras M d'éloignement M
Absperrarm M
barra F distanziatrice
crossover mirror
espejo M de cercanías F
miroir M de traversée F avant
Sicherheitsspiegel M
specchietto M anteriore di accostamento M

city bus
autobús[M] urbano
autobus[M]
Linienbus[M]
autobus[M] urbano

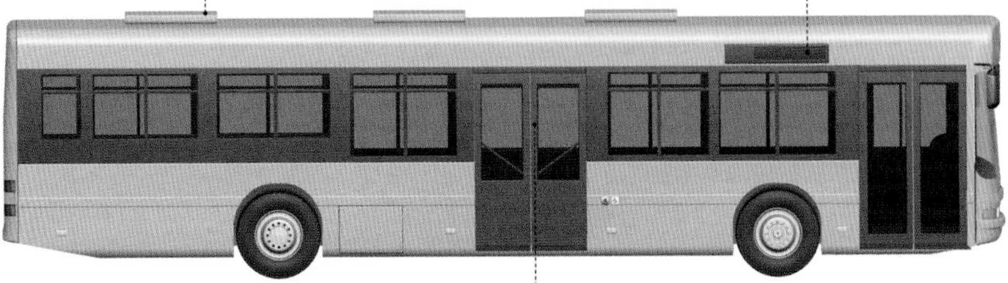
air intake
toma[F] de aire[M]
prise[F] d'air[M]
Lufteinlass[M]
presa[F] d'aria[F]
route sign
indicador[M] de línea[F]
indicateur[M] de ligne[F]
Linienanzeige[F]
indicatore[M] di linea[F]
two-leaf door
puerta[F] de dos hojas[F]
porte[F] à deux vantaux[M]
zweiflügelige Ausgangstür[F]
porta[F] a due battenti[M]

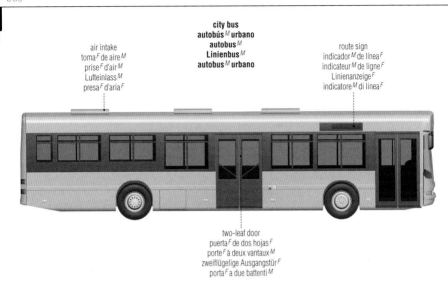

coach
autocar[M]
autocar[M]
Reisebus[M]
pullman[M]

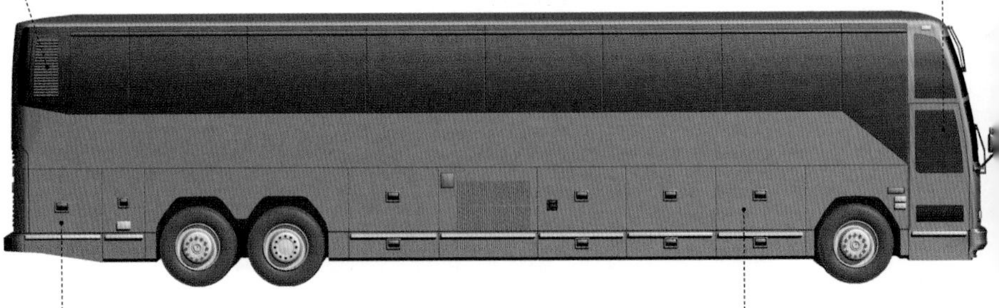
engine air intake
toma[F] de aire[M] del motor[M]
prise[F] d'air[M] du moteur[M]
Motorlufteinlass[M]
presa[F] d'aria[F] del motore[M]
entrance door
puerta[F] de entrada[F]
porte[F] d'entrée[F]
Einstiegstür[F]
porta[F] di entrata[F]
engine compartment
compartimiento[M] motor
compartiment[M] moteur[M]
Motorraum[M]
vano[M] motore[M]
baggage compartment
maletero[M]
soute[F] à bagages[M]
Gepäckraum[M]
bagagliaio[M]

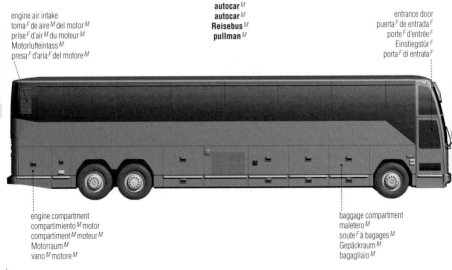

van
minibús[M]
minibus[M]
Kleinbus[M]
minibus[M]

lift door
puerta[F] de la plataforma[F] elevadora
porte[F] de l'élévateur[M]
elektrische Schiebetür[F]
porta[F] dell'elevatore[M]

West Coast mirror
espejo[M] retrovisor
rétroviseur[M]
Außenspiegel[M]
specchietto[M] retrovisore

handrail
pasamano[M]
barre[F] de maintien[M]
Haltegriff[M]
corrimano[M]

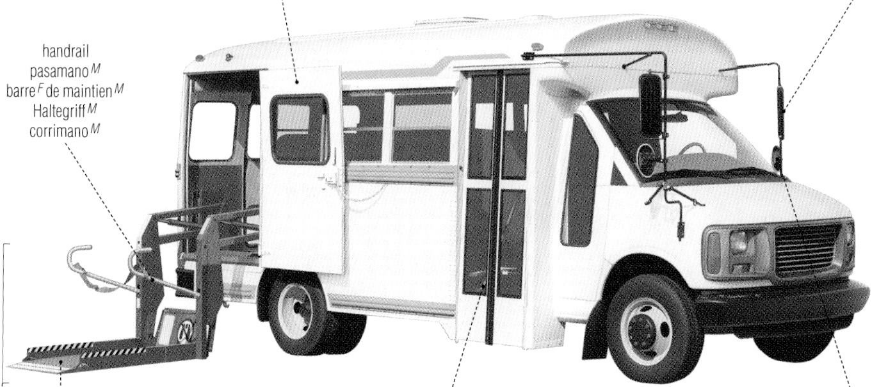

platform
plataforma[F]
plate-forme[F]
Plattform[F]
piattaforma[F]

entrance door
puerta[F] de entrada[F]
porte[F] d'entrée[F]
Einstiegstür[F]
porta[F] di entrata[F]

blind spot mirror
retrovisor[M] gran angular
rétroviseur[M] grand-angle[M]
Weitwinkelspiegel[M]
specchietto[M] per il punto[M] cieco

wheelchair lift
plataforma[F] elevadora para silla[F] de ruedas[F]
élévateur[M] pour fauteuils[M] roulants
Rollstuhllift[M]
elevatore[M] per sedie[F] a rotelle[F]

articulated bus
autobús[M] articulado
autobus[M] articulé
Gelenkbus[M]
autobus[M] articolato

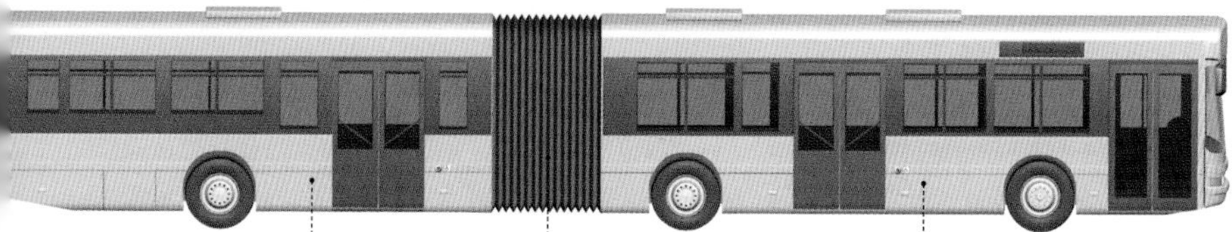

rear rigid section
remolque[M] rígido trasero
tronçon[M] rigide arrière
steifer Nachläufer[M]
sezione[F] rigida posteriore

articulated joint
sección[F] articulada
section[F] articulée
Gelenk[N]
passaggio[M] a soffietto[M]

front rigid section
sección[F] rígida de tracción[F] delantera
tronçon[M] rigide avant
steifes Vorderteil[N]
sezione[F] rigida anteriore

TRANSPORTATION

trucking

camiones M | camionnage M | Lastkraftfahrzeuge N | autoveicoli M industriali

truck tractor
camión M tractor M
tracteur M routier
Sattelschlepper M
motrice F

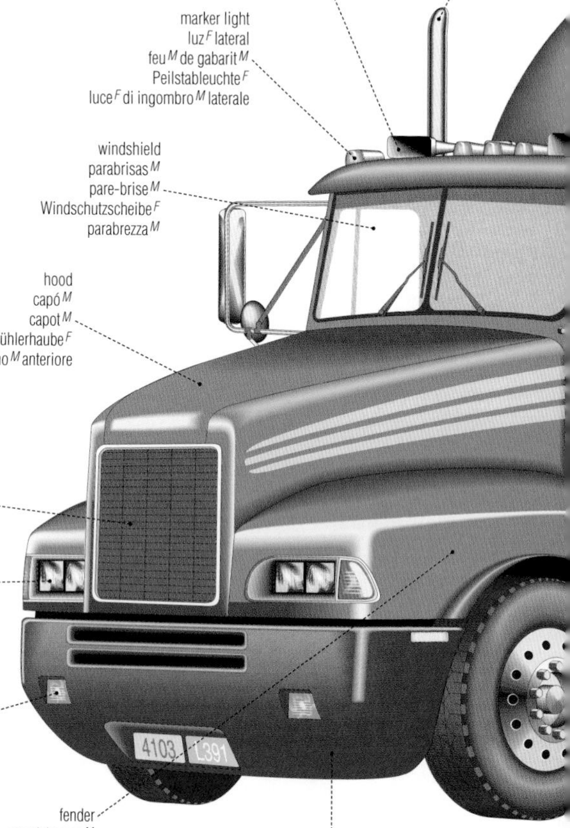
air horn
bocina F neumática
avertisseur M pneumatique
Fanfare F
avvisatore M acustico a tromba F
exhaust stack
tubo M de escape M
cheminée F d'échappement M
Auspuffrohr N
tubo M di scappamento M
marker light
luz F lateral
feu M de gabarit M
Peilstableuchte F
luce F di ingombro M laterale
windshield
parabrisas M
pare-brise M
Windschutzscheibe F
parabrezza M
hood
capó M
capot M
Kühlerhaube F
cofano M anteriore
radiator grille
calandra F
calandre F
Kühlergrill M
griglia F del radiatore M
headlight
faro M delantero
phare M
Scheinwerfer M
proiettore M
fog light
luz F antiniebla
feu M antibrouillard
Nebelscheinwerfer M
faro M fendinebbia
fender
guardabarros M
aile F
Kotflügel M
parafango F
bumper
parachoques M
pare-chocs M
Stoßfänger M
paraurti M
whe
rueda
roue
Rad
ruota

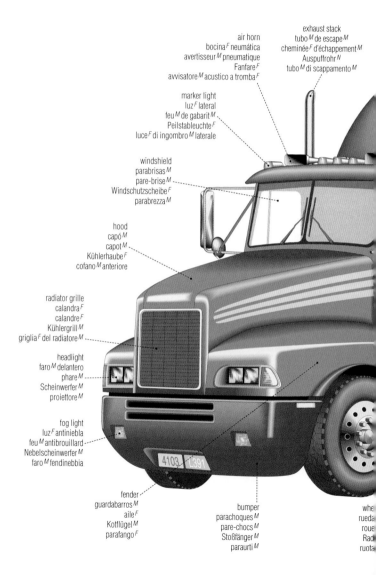

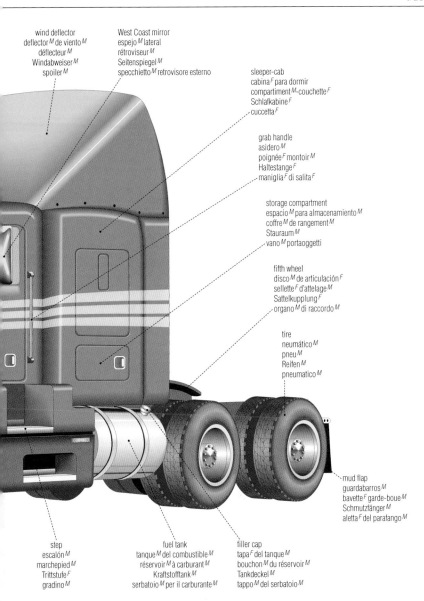

wind deflector
deflector[M] de viento[M]
déflecteur[M]
Windabweiser[M]
spoiler[M]

West Coast mirror
espejo[M] lateral
rétroviseur[M]
Seitenspiegel[M]
specchietto[M] retrovisore esterno

sleeper-cab
cabina[F] para dormir
compartiment[M]-couchette[F]
Schlafkabine[F]
cuccetta[F]

grab handle
asidero[M]
poignée[F] montoir[M]
Haltestange[F]
maniglia[F] di salita[F]

storage compartment
espacio[M] para almacenamiento[M]
coffre[M] de rangement[M]
Stauraum[M]
vano[M] portaoggetti

fifth wheel
disco[M] de articulación[F]
sellette[F] d'attelage[M]
Sattelkupplung[F]
organo[M] di raccordo[M]

tire
neumático[M]
pneu[M]
Reifen[M]
pneumatico[M]

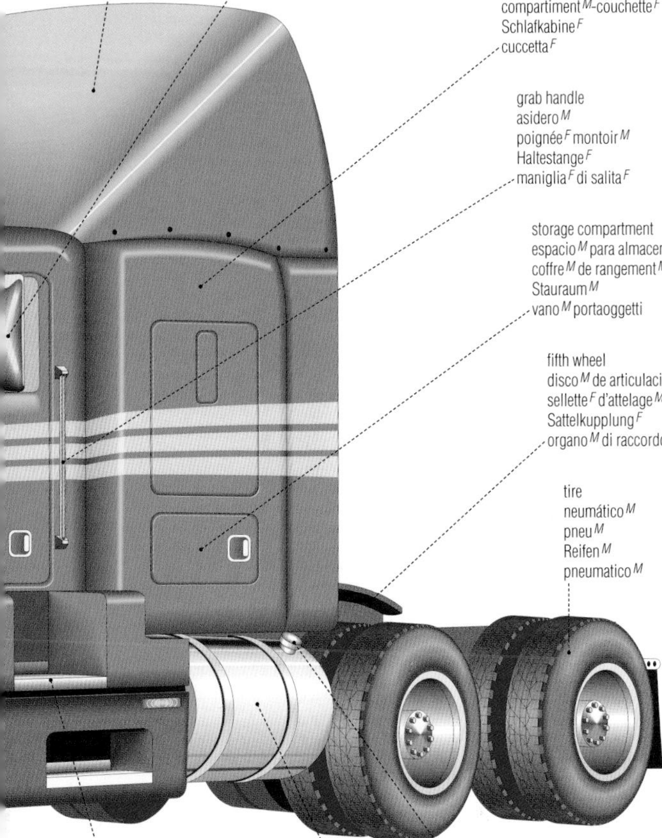

mud flap
guardabarros[M]
bavette[F] garde-boue[M]
Schmutzfänger[M]
aletta[F] del parafango[M]

step
escalón[M]
marchepied[M]
Trittstufe[F]
gradino[M]

fuel tank
tanque[M] del combustible[M]
réservoir[M] à carburant[M]
Kraftstofftank[M]
serbatoio[M] per il carburante[M]

filler cap
tapa[F] del tanque[M]
bouchon[M] du réservoir[M]
Tankdeckel[M]
tappo[M] del serbatoio[M]

refrigerated semitrailer
semirremolque^{M} frigorífico
semi-remorque^{F} frigorifique
Kühlsattelanlieger^{M}
semirimorchio^{M} frigorifero

frontwall
panel^{M} frontal
paroi^{F} avant
Stirnwand^{F}
parete^{F} anteriore

refrigeration unit
unidad^{F} de refrigeración^{F}
groupe^{M} frigorifique
Kühlaggregat^{N}
gruppo^{M} frigorifero

mud flap
guardabarros^{M}
bavette^{F} garde-boue^{M}
Schmutzfänger^{M}
alettone^{M} parafango^{M}

marker light
luz^{F} lateral
feu^{M} de gabarit^{M}
Peilstableuchte^{F}
luce^{F} di ingombro^{M} laterale

vent door
ventilador^{M}
volet^{M} d'air^{M}
Luftklappe^{F}
presa^{F} d'aria^{F}

sidewall
panel^{M} lateral
paroi^{F} latérale
Seitenwand^{F}
parete^{F} laterale

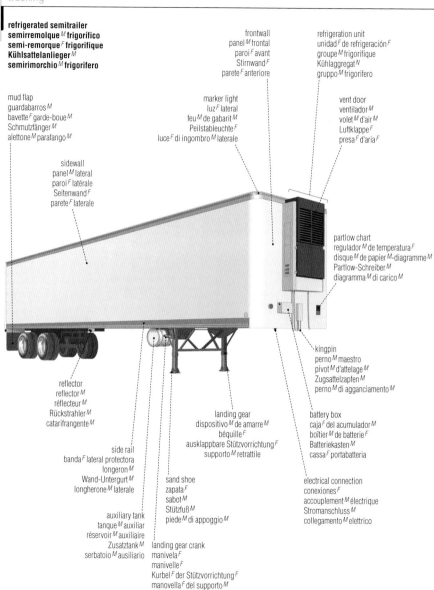

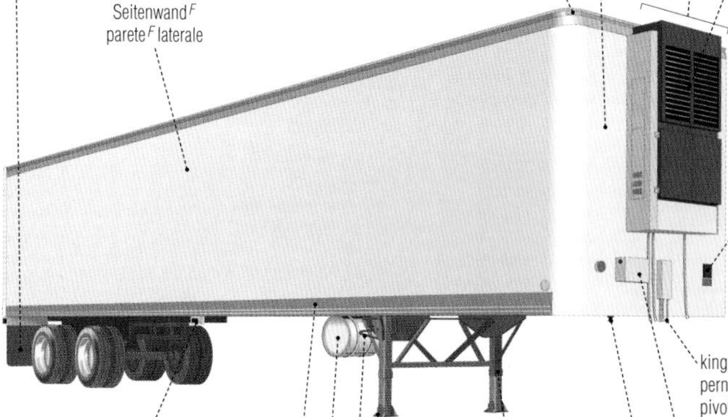

partlow chart
regulador^{M} de temperatura^{F}
disque^{M} de papier^{M}-diagramme^{M}
Partlow-Schreiber^{M}
diagramma^{M} di carico^{M}

kingpin
perno^{M} maestro
pivot^{M} d'attelage^{M}
Zugsattelzapfen^{M}
perno^{M} di agganciamento^{M}

reflector
reflector^{M}
réflecteur^{M}
Rückstrahler^{M}
catarifrangente^{M}

landing gear
dispositivo^{M} de amarre^{M}
béquille^{F}
ausklappbare Stützvorrichtung^{F}
supporto^{M} retrattile

battery box
caja^{F} del acumulador^{M}
boîtier^{M} de batterie^{F}
Batteriekasten^{M}
cassa^{F} portabatteria

side rail
banda^{F} lateral protectora
longeron^{M}
Wand-Untergurt^{M}
longherone^{M} laterale

sand shoe
zapata^{F}
sabot^{M}
Stützfuß^{M}
piede^{M} di appoggio^{M}

electrical connection
conexiones^{F}
accouplement^{M} électrique
Stromanschluss^{M}
collegamento^{M} elettrico

auxiliary tank
tanque^{M} auxiliar
réservoir^{M} auxiliaire
Zusatztank^{M}
serbatoio^{M} ausiliario

landing gear crank
manivela^{F}
manivelle^{F}
Kurbel^{F} der Stützvorrichtung^{F}
manovella^{F} del supporto^{M}

flatbed semitrailer
semirremolque [M] tipo plataforma [F]
semi-remorque [F] plateau [M]
Sattelpritschenanhänger [M]
autocarro [M] a pianale [M]

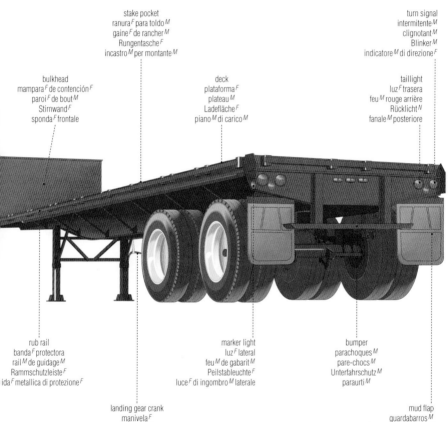

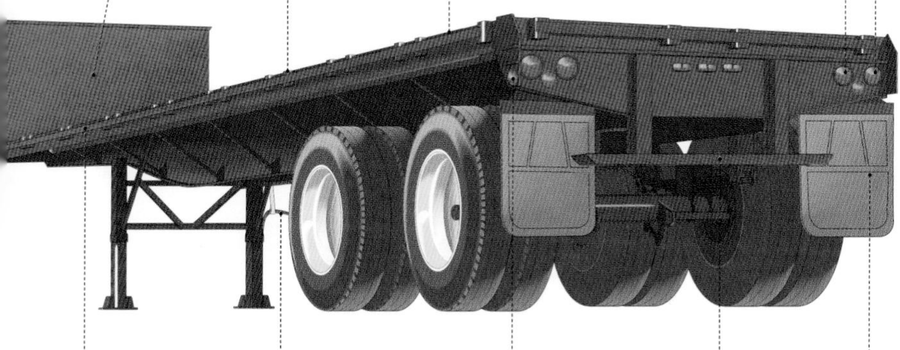
stake pocket
ranura [F] para toldo [M]
gaine [F] de rancher [M]
Rungentasche [F]
incastro [M] per montante [M]
turn signal
intermitente [M]
clignotant [M]
Blinker [M]
indicatore [M] di direzione [F]
bulkhead
mampara [F] de contención [F]
paroi [F] de bout [M]
Stirnwand [F]
sponda [F] frontale
deck
plataforma [F]
plateau [M]
Ladefläche [F]
piano [M] di carico [M]
taillight
luz [F] trasera
feu [M] rouge arrière
Rücklicht [N]
fanale [M] posteriore
rub rail
banda [F] protectora
rail [M] de guidage [M]
Rammschutzleiste [F]
ida [F] metallica di protezione [F]
marker light
luz [F] lateral
feu [M] de gabarit [M]
Peilstableuchte [F]
luce [F] di ingombro [M] laterale
bumper
parachoques [M]
pare-chocs [M]
Unterfahrschutz [M]
paraurti [M]
landing gear crank
manivela [F]
manivelle [F]
Kurbel [F] der Stützvorrichtung [F]
manovella [F] del supporto [M]
mud flap
guardabarros [M]
bavette [F] garde-boue [M]
Spritzlappen [M]
alettone [M] del parafango [M]

examples of semitrailers
ejemplos^M de camiones^M articulados
exemples^M de semi-remorques^F
Beispiele^N für Sattelkraftfahrzeuge^N
esempi^M di autoarticolati^M

tandem tractor trailer
camión^M articulado
train^M routier
Sattelzug^M
autoarticolato^M

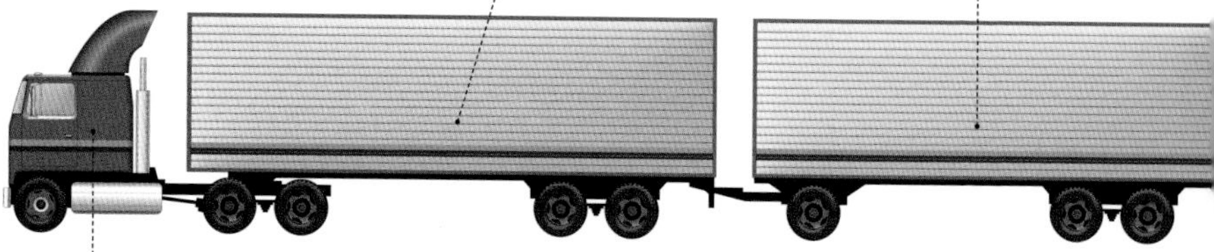
semitrailer
semirremolque^M tipo^M caja^F
semi-remorque^F
Auflieger^M
semirimorchio^M
truck trailer
remolque^M tipo^M caja^F
remorque^F
Anhänger^M
rimorchio^M
truck tractor
camión^M tractor^M
tracteur^M
Zugmaschine^F
motrice^F

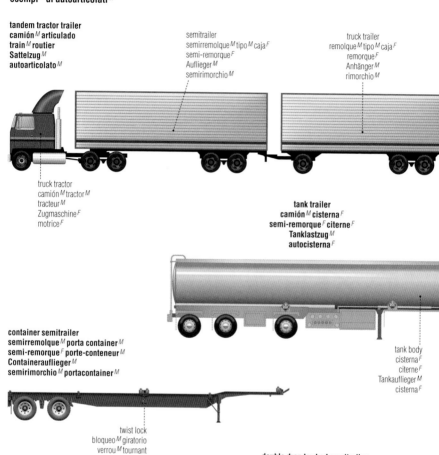

tank trailer
camión^M cisterna^F
semi-remorque^F citerne^F
Tanklastzug^M
autocisterna^F

tank body
cisterna^F
citerne^F
Tankauflieger^M
cisterna^F

container semitrailer
semirremolque^M porta container^M
semi-remorque^F porte-conteneur^M
Containerauflieger^M
semirimorchio^M portacontainer^M

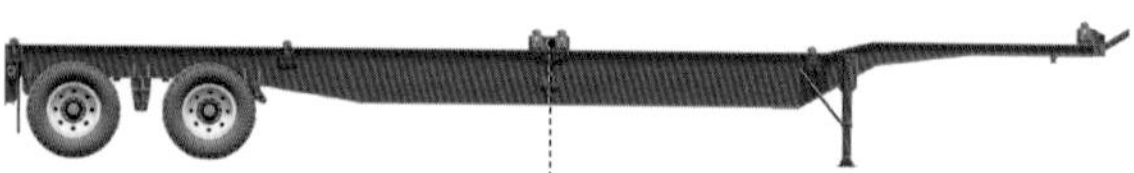
twist lock
bloqueo^M giratorio
verrou^M tournant
Drehfeststeller^M
fermo^M girevole

double drop lowbed semitrailer
semirremolque^M bajo portamáquinas^M
semi-remorque^F porte-engins^M surbaissée
Satteltiefladeanhänger^M für den Transport^M von Panzerfahrzeugen^N
semirimorchio^M ribassato per il trasporto^M di mezzi^M corazzati

TRANSPORTATION

automobile transport semitrailer
trailer *M* **para transporte** *M* **de vehículos** *M*
semi-remorque *F* **porte-véhicules** *M*
Autotransporter *M*
bisarca *F*

dump body
volquete *M* basculante
benne *F* basculante
aufgesattelter Kippanhänger *M*
cassone *M* ribaltabile

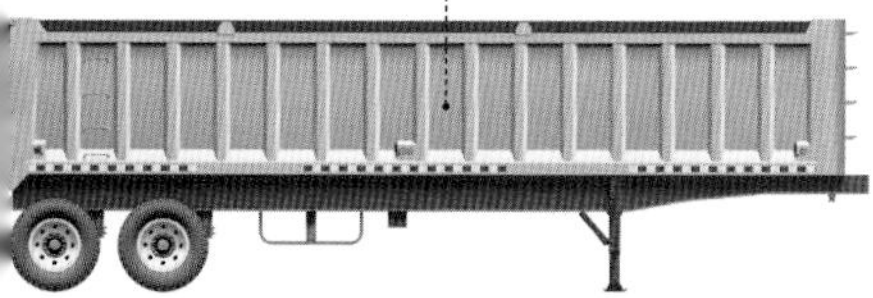

dump semitrailer
camión *M* **volquete**
semi-remorque *F* **benne** *F*
Kipplader *M*
ribaltabile *M*

chip van
semirremolque *M* **con lona** *F*
semi-remorque *F* **à copeaux** *M*
Sattelanhänger *M* **für den Spantransport** *M*
autocarro *M* **per trucioli** *M*

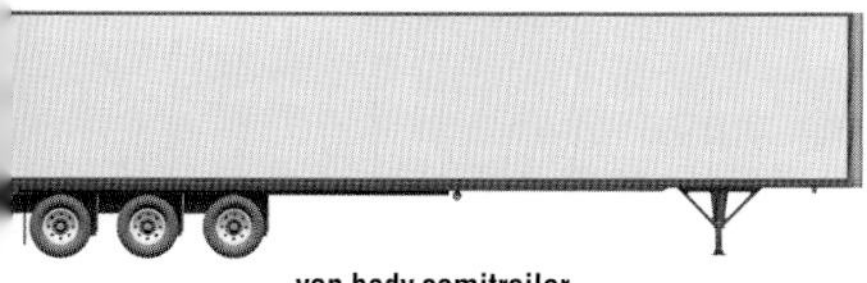

van body semitrailer
semirremolque *M* **furgón**
semi-remorque *F* **fourgon** *M*
Kofferauflieger *M*
semirimorchio *M* **furgonato**

refrigerated semitrailer
semirremolque *M* **frigorífico**
semi-remorque *F* **frigorifique**
Kühlauflieger *M*
camion *M* **frigorifero**

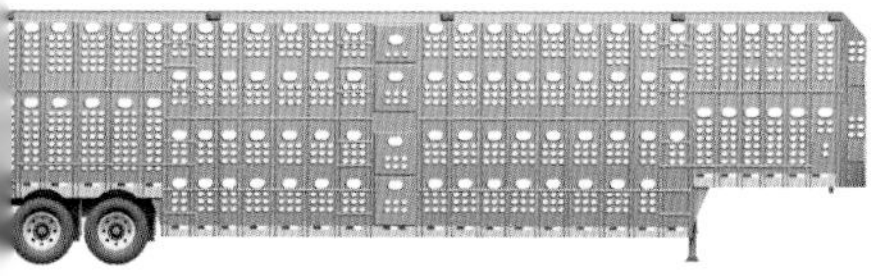

possum-belly body semitrailer
semirremolque *M* **jaula** *F* **bajo para transporte** *M* **ganadero**
semi-remorque *F* **bétaillère surbaissée**
Satteltiefladeanhänger *M* **für den Tiertransport** *M*
semirimorchio *M* **ribassato per il trasporto** *M* **del bestiame** *M*

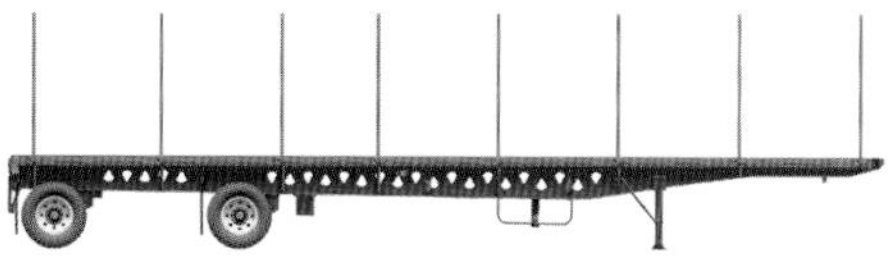

log semitrailer
semirremolque *M* **para el transporte** *M* **de troncos** *M*
semi-remorque *F* **à grumes** *F*
Sattelanhänger *M* **für den Baumstammtransport** *M*
autocarro *M* **per il trasporto** *M* **dei tronchi** *M*

trucking

examples of trucks
ejemplos^M de camiones^M
exemples^M de camions^M
Beispiele^N für Lastkraftwagen^M
esempi^M di camion^M

tow truck
grúa^F remolque
dépanneuse^F
Abschleppwagen^M
autogrù^F

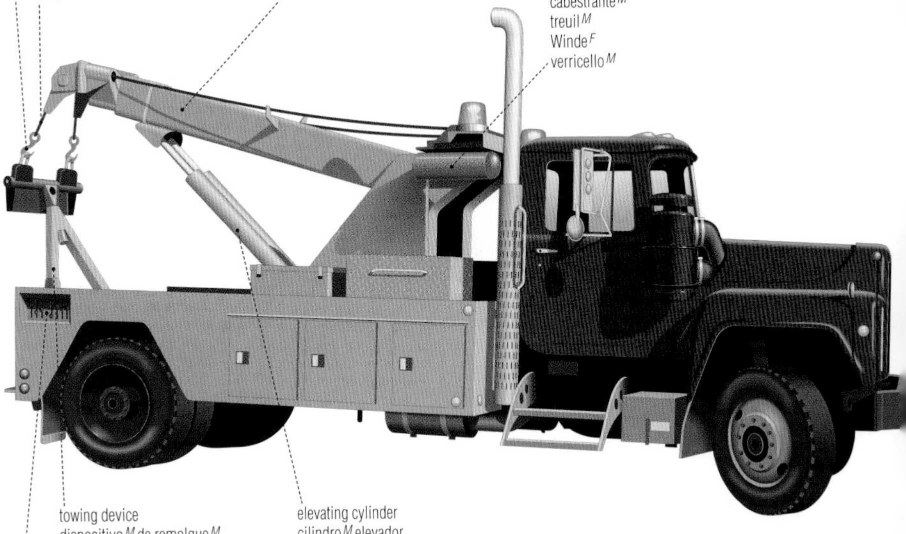
hook
gancho M
crochet M
Haken M
gancio M
cable
cable M
câble M
Kabel N
cavo M
boom
brazo M de elevación F
poutre F de levage M
Abschleppkran M
braccio M di sollevamento M
winch
cabestrante M
treuil M
Winde F
verricello M
towing device
dispositivo M de remolque M
dispositif M de remorquage M
Schleppvorrichtung F
dispositivo M di rimorchio M
elevating cylinder
cilindro M elevador
vérin M
Hubzylinder M
cilindro M di sollevamento M
winch controls
mandos M del cabestrante M
commandes F du treuil M
Windensteuerung F
comandi M del verricello M

box van
camioneta[F]
camion[M] porteur[M] fourgon[M]
Transporter[M]
furgone[M]

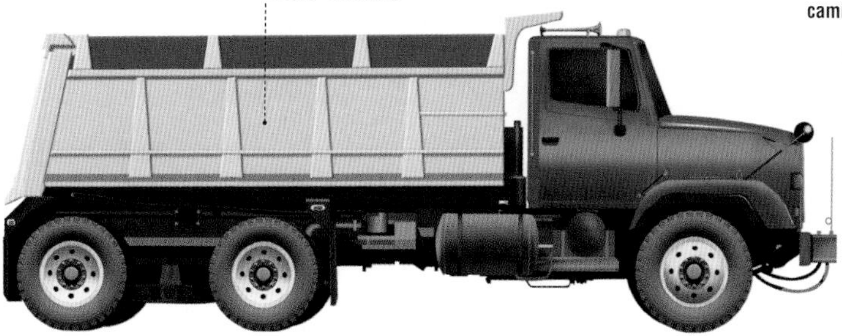
dump body
volquete[M]
benne[F] basculante
Kipppritsche[F]
cassone[M] ribaltabile

dump truck
camión[M] basculante
camion[M]-benne[F]
Kipper[M]
ribaltabile[M]

septic truck
aspiradora[F] de fangos[M]
camion[M] de vidange[F]
Saugfahrzeug[N]
camion[M] per spurghi[M]

street sweeper
barredora[F]
balayeuse[F]
Straßenkehrmaschine[F]
spazzatrice[F]

collection body
cajón[M] de basura[F]
réceptacle[M] à déchets[M]
Sammelbehälter[M]
cassone[M] di raccolta[F] dei rifiuti[M]
central brush
escoba[F] central
brosse[F] centrale
Walzenbürste[F]
spazzola[F] rotante centrale
lateral brush
escoba[F] lateral
brosse[F] latérale
Tellerbürste[F]
spazzola[F] rotante laterale
watering tube
tubo[M] de irrigación[F]
canalisation[F] d'arrosage[M]
Wassersprühdüse[F]
tubo[M] annaffiatore[M]

detachable body truck
carrocería[F] **amovible**
carrosserie[F] **amovible**
Wechselaufbau[M]
camion[M] **a cassone**[M] **amovibile**

snowblower
quitanieves[M]
chasse-neige[M] **à soufflerie**[F]
Schneefräse[F]
spazzaneve[M] **a turbina**[F]

projection device
chimenea[F] de expulsión[F]
canal[M] de projection[F]
Schleuder[F]
tubo[M] di getto[M] laterale
DANGER
worm
tornillo[M] sin fin[M]
vis[F] sans fin[F]
Schnecke[F]
vite[F] senza fine[F]

garbage truck
compactadora F
benne F **à ordures** F
Müllabfuhrwagen M
compattatore M

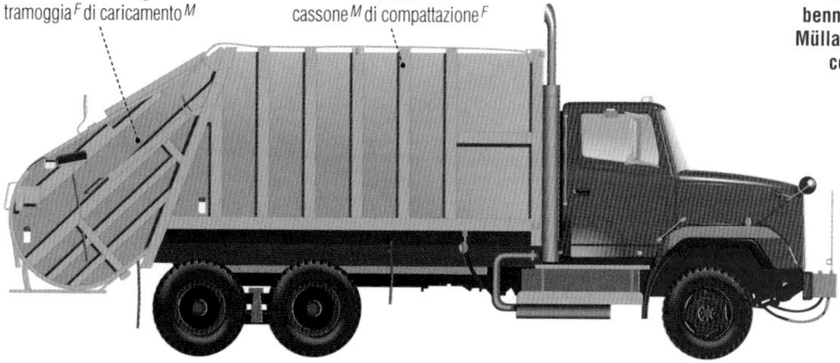
loading hopper
tolva F de carga F
trémie F de chargement M
Ladevorrichtung F
tramoggia F di caricamento M
packer body
empaquetadora F
benne F tasseuse
Verdichter M
cassone M di compattazione F

tank truck
camión M **cisterna** F
camion M**-citerne** F
Tankwagen M
autobotte F

tank body
cisterna F
citerne F
Tank M
cisterna F

cement mixer
hormigonera F
camion M**-toupie** F
Transportmischer M
betoniera F

motorcycle

motocicleta[F] | moto[F] | Motorrad[N] | motocicletta[F]

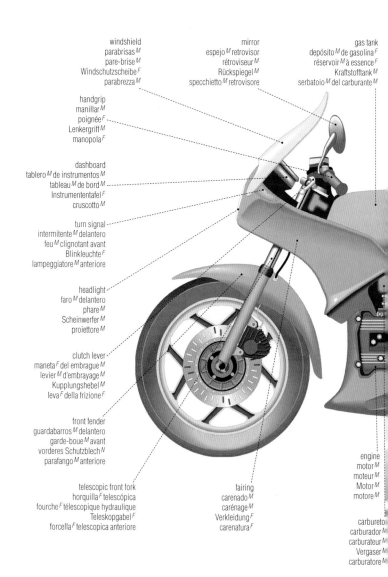

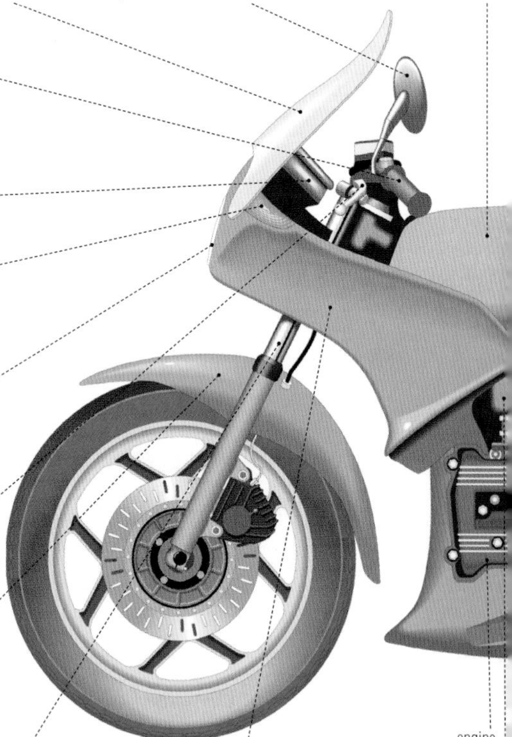
windshield
parabrisas[M]
pare-brise[M]
Windschutzscheibe[F]
parabrezza[M]
mirror
espejo[M] retrovisor
rétroviseur[M]
Rückspiegel[M]
specchietto[M] retrovisore
gas tank
depósito[M] de gasolina[F]
réservoir[M] à essence[F]
Kraftstofftank[M]
serbatoio[M] del carburante[M]
handgrip
manillar[M]
poignée[F]
Lenkergriff[M]
manopola[F]
dashboard
tablero[M] de instrumentos[M]
tableau[M] de bord[M]
Instrumententafel[F]
cruscotto[M]
turn signal
intermitente[M] delantero
feu[M] clignotant avant
Blinkleuchte[F]
lampeggiatore[M] anteriore
headlight
faro[M] delantero
phare[M]
Scheinwerfer[M]
proiettore[M]
clutch lever
maneta[F] del embrague[M]
levier[M] d'embrayage[M]
Kupplungshebel[M]
leva[F] della frizione[F]
front fender
guardabarros[M] delantero
garde-boue[M] avant
vorderes Schutzblech[N]
parafango[M] anteriore
telescopic front fork
horquilla[F] telescópica
fourche[F] télescopique hydraulique
Teleskopgabel[F]
forcella[F] telescopica anteriore
fairing
carenado[M]
carénage[M]
Verkleidung[F]
carenatura[F]
engine
motor[M]
moteur[M]
Motor[M]
motore[M]
carbureto
carburador[M]
carburateur[M]
Vergaser[M]
carburatore[M]

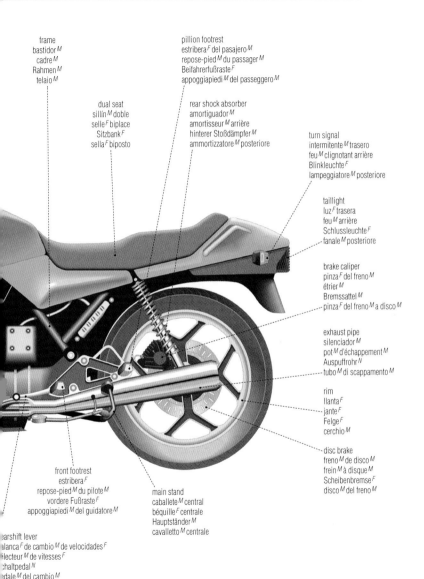

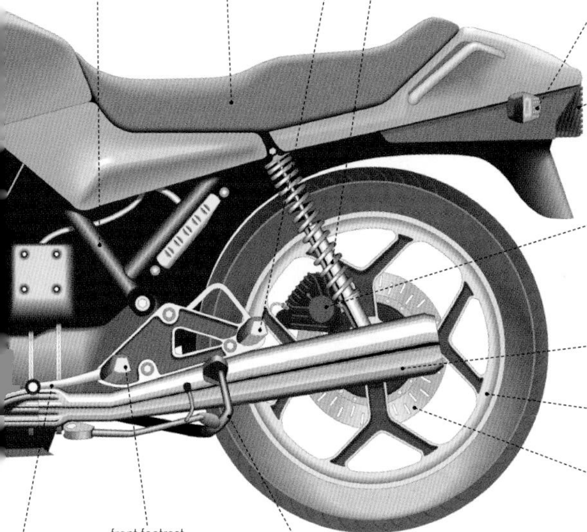
frame
bastidor [M]
cadre [M]
Rahmen [M]
telaio [M]
pillion footrest
estribera [F] del pasajero [M]
repose-pied [M] du passager [M]
Beifahrerfußraste [F]
appoggiapiedi [M] del passeggero [M]
dual seat
sillín [M] doble
selle [F] biplace
Sitzbank [F]
sella [F] biposto
rear shock absorber
amortiguador [M]
amortisseur [M] arrière
hinterer Stoßdämpfer [M]
ammortizzatore [M] posteriore
turn signal
intermitente [M] trasero
feu [M] clignotant arrière
Blinkleuchte [F]
lampeggiatore [M] posteriore
taillight
luz [F] trasera
feu [M] arrière
Schlussleuchte [F]
fanale [M] posteriore
brake caliper
pinza [F] del freno [M]
étrier [M]
Bremssattel [M]
pinza [F] del freno [M] a disco [M]
exhaust pipe
silenciador [M]
pot [M] d'échappement [M]
Auspuffrohr [N]
tubo [M] di scappamento [M]
rim
llanta [F]
jante [F]
Felge [F]
cerchio [M]
disc brake
freno [M] de disco [M]
frein [M] à disque [M]
Scheibenbremse [F]
disco [M] del freno [M]
front footrest
estribera [F]
repose-pied [M] du pilote [M]
vordere Fußraste [F]
appoggiapiedi [M] del guidatore [M]
main stand
caballete [M] central
béquille [F] centrale
Hauptständer [M]
cavalletto [M] centrale
earshift lever
alanca [F] de cambio [M] de velocidades [F]
electeur [M] de vitesses [F]
chaltpedal [N]
edale [M] del cambio [M]

motorcycle

protective helmet
casco[M] integral
casque[M] de protection[F]
Schutzhelm[M]
casco[M] di protezione[F]

bubble
casco[M]
coque[F]
Oberschale[F]
calotta[F]

visor
visera[F]
visière[F]
Visier[N]
visiera[F]

air inlet
respiradero[M]
grille[F] d'entrée[F] d'air[M]
Lufteinlass[M]
presa[F] d'aria[F]

chin protector
protector[M] de la barbilla[F]
mentonnière[F]
Kinnschutz[M]
protezione[F] del mento[M]

visor hinge
charnela[F] lateral
charnière[F] de la visière[F]
Scharnier[N]
cerniera[F] della visiera[F]

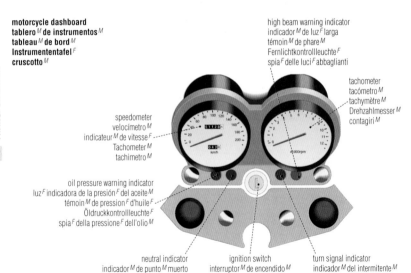

motorcycle dashboard
tablero[M] de instrumentos[M]
tableau[M] de bord[M]
Instrumententafel[F]
cruscotto[M]

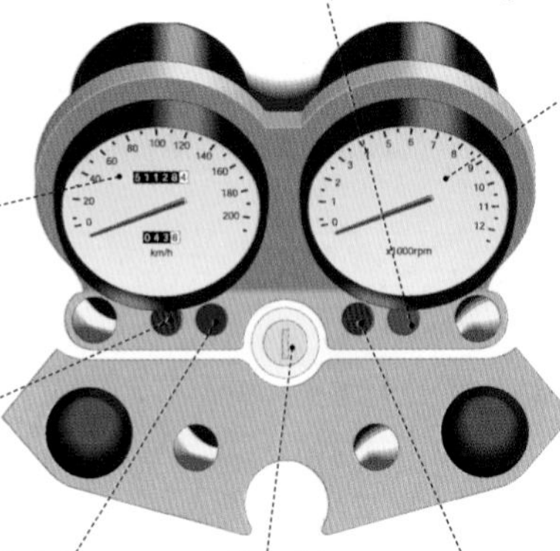

high beam warning indicator
indicador[M] de luz[F] larga
témoin[M] de phare[M]
Fernlichtkontrollleuchte[F]
spia[F] delle luci[F] abbaglianti

tachometer
tacómetro[M]
tachymètre[M]
Drehzahlmesser[M]
contagiri[M]

speedometer
velocímetro[M]
indicateur[M] de vitesse[F]
Tachometer[M]
tachimetro[M]

oil pressure warning indicator
luz[F] indicadora de la presión[F] del aceite[M]
témoin[M] de pression[F] d'huile[F]
Öldruckkontrollleuchte[F]
spia[F] della pressione[F] dell'olio[M]

neutral indicator
indicador[M] de punto[M] muerto
témoin[M] de position[F] neutre
Leerlaufanzeige[N]
spia[F] della posizione[F] di folle

ignition switch
interruptor[M] de encendido[M]
commutateur[M] d'allumage[M]
Zündschalter[M]
blocchetto[M] di avviamento[M]

turn signal indicator
indicador[M] del intermitente[M]
témoin[M] de clignotants[M]
Blinkerkontrollleuchte[F]
spia[F] dell'indicatore[M] di direzione[F]

examples of motorcycles
ejemplos^M de motocicletas^F
exemples^M de motos^F
Beispiele^N für Motorräder^N
esempi^M di motociclette^F e ciclomotore^M

off-road motorcycle
motocicleta^F todo terreno^M
moto^F tout-terrain
Geländemotorrad^N
motocicletta^F da cross^M
seat
asiento^M
selle^F
Sitz^M
sella^F
telescopic front fork
horquilla^F telescópica
fourche^F télescopique
Teleskopgabel^F
forcella^F telescopica anteriore
knobby tread tire
neumático^M de tacos^M
pneu^M à crampons^M
Stollenreifen^M
pneumatico^M scolpito

touring motorcycle
motocicleta^F de turismo^M
moto^F de tourisme^M
Touring^N-Motorrad^N
motocicletta^F da turismo^M
windshield
parabrisas^M
pare-brise^M
Windschutzscheibe^F
parabrezza^M
antenna
antena^F
antenne^F
Antenne^F
antenna^F
backrest
respaldo^M
dossier^M
Rückenlehne^F
schienale^M
top box
cofre^M
coffre^M
Topcase^N
bauletto^M
passenger seat
sillín^M del pasajero^M
selle^F passager^M
Soziussitz^M
sella^F del passeggero^M
saddlebag
maleta^F
sacoche^F
Seitenkoffer^M
borsa^F laterale
driver seat
sillín^M del conductor^M
selle^F conducteur^M
Fahrersitz^M
sella^F del guidatore^M

motor scooter
escúter *M*
scooter *M*
Motorroller *M*
scooter *M*

mirror
espejo M retrovisor
rétroviseur M
Spiegel M
specchietto M retrovisore
seat
sillín M
selle F
Sitz M
sella F
apron
salpicadero M
tablier M
Frontblech M
pannello M di protezione F
luggage rack
portaequipajes M
porte-bagages M
Gepäckträger M
portapacchi M
floorboard
reposapies M
plancher M
Fußstütze F
appoggiapiedi M

moped
ciclomotor *M*
cyclomoteur *M*
Mofa *N*
ciclomotore *M*

carrier
portaequipajes M
porte-bagages M
Gepäckträger M
portapacchi M
kickstand
soporte M
béquille F latérale
Raststütze F
cavalletto M laterale

4 X 4 all-terrain vehicle

quad^{M} | quad^{M} | 4x4-Geländemotorrad^{N} | veicolo^{M} a trazione^{F} integrale 4x4

ɜar fender
arachoques M posterior
arde-boue M arrière
interer Kotflügel M
araurti M posteriore
rear cargo rack
portaequipajes M posterior
porte-bagages M arrière
Gepäckträger M
portapacchi M posteriore
seat
sillín M
selle F
Sitz M
sella F
gas tank
depósito M de gasolina F
réservoir M à essence F
Kraftstofftank M
serbatoio M del carburante M
handgrip
manillar M
poignée F
Lenkergriff M
manopola F
bumper
parachoques M
pare-chocs M
Stoßfänger M
paraurti M
gearshift lever
palanca F de cambio M de velocidades F
sélecteur M de vitesses F
Schalthebel M
pedale M del cambio M
ffler
nciador M
M d'échappement M
puffrohr N
ɔ M di scappamento M
front shock absorber
amortiguador M delantero
amortisseur M avant
Frontstoßdämpfer M
ammortizzatore M anteriore

bicycle

bicicleta[F] | bicyclette[F] | Fahrrad[N] | bicicletta[F]

parts of a bicycle
partes[F] de una bicicleta[F]
parties[F] d'une bicyclette[F]
Teile[N] eines Fahrrads[N]
componenti[M] di una bicicletta[F]

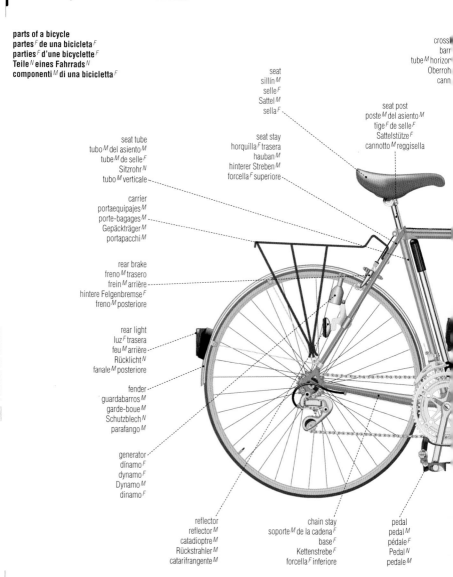

cross
barr
tube[M] horizor
Oberroh
cann
seat
sillín[M]
selle[F]
Sattel[M]
sella[F]
seat post
poste[M] del asiento[M]
tige[F] de selle[F]
Sattelstütze[F]
cannotto[M] reggisella
seat tube
tubo[M] del asiento[M]
tube[M] de selle[F]
Sitzrohr[N]
tubo[M] verticale
seat stay
horquilla[F] trasera
hauban[M]
hinterer Streben[M]
forcella[F] superiore
carrier
portaequipajes[M]
porte-bagages[M]
Gepäckträger[M]
portapacchi[M]
rear brake
freno[M] trasero
frein[M] arrière
hintere Felgenbremse[F]
freno[M] posteriore
rear light
luz[F] trasera
feu[M] arrière
Rücklicht[N]
fanale[M] posteriore
fender
guardabarros[M]
garde-boue[M]
Schutzblech[N]
parafango[M]
generator
dínamo[F]
dynamo[F]
Dynamo[M]
dinamo[F]
reflector
reflector[M]
catadioptre[M]
Rückstrahler[M]
catarifrangente[M]
chain stay
soporte[M] de la cadena[F]
base[F]
Kettenstrebe[F]
forcella[F] inferiore
pedal
pedal[M]
pédale[F]
Pedal[N]
pedale[M]

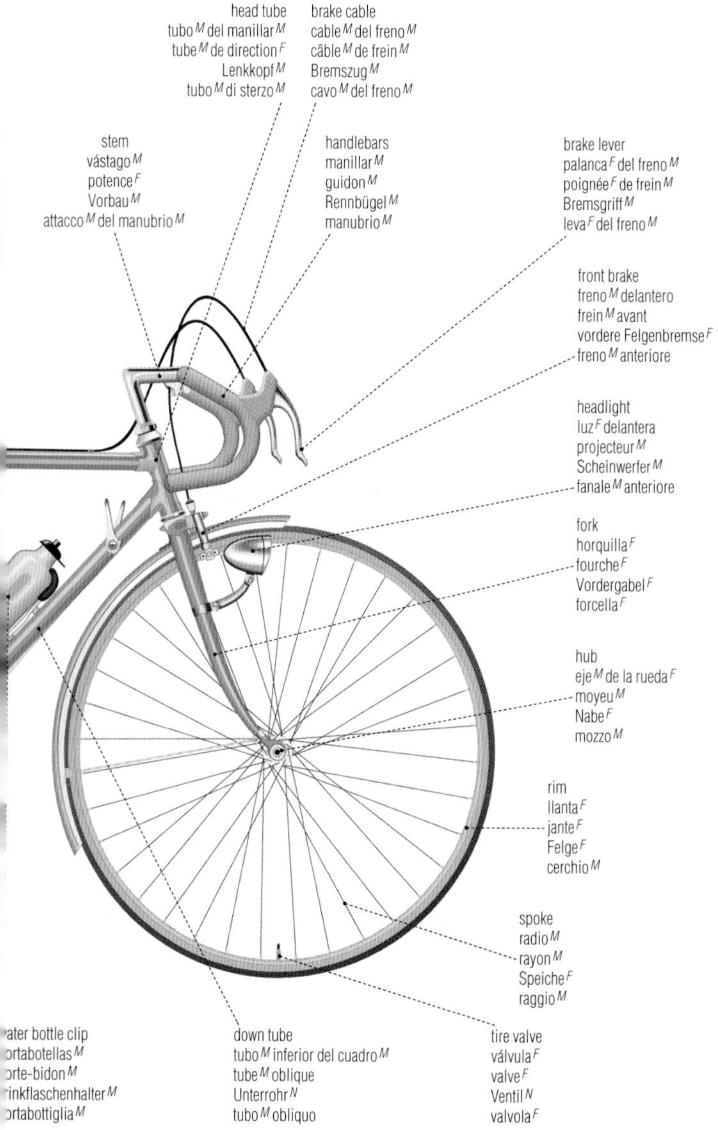
head tube
tubo M del manillar M
tube M de direction F
Lenkkopf M
tubo M di sterzo M
brake cable
cable M del freno M
câble M de frein M
Bremszug M
cavo M del freno M
stem
vástago M
potence F
Vorbau M
attacco M del manubrio M
handlebars
manillar M
guidon M
Rennbügel M
manubrio M
brake lever
palanca F del freno M
poignée F de frein M
Bremsgriff M
leva F del freno M
front brake
freno M delantero
frein M avant
vordere Felgenbremse F
freno M anteriore
headlight
luz F delantera
projecteur M
Scheinwerfer M
fanale M anteriore
fork
horquilla F
fourche F
Vordergabel F
forcella F
hub
eje M de la rueda F
moyeu M
Nabe F
mozzo M
rim
llanta F
jante F
Felge F
cerchio M
spoke
radio M
rayon M
Speiche F
raggio M
ater bottle clip
ortabotellas M
orte-bidon M
inkflaschenhalter M
ortabottiglia M
down tube
tubo M inferior del cuadro M
tube M oblique
Unterrohr N
tubo M obliquo
tire valve
válvula F
valve F
Ventil N
valvola F

examples of bicycles
ejemplos[M] de bicicletas[F]
exemples[M] de bicyclettes[F]
Beispiele[N] für Fahrräder[N]
esempi[M] di biciclette[F]

BMX bike
bicicleta[F] BMX
vélo[M] cross[M]
BMX-Rad[N], Mountainbike[N]
mountain bike[F] da cross[M]

Dutch bicycle
bicicleta[F] holandesa
bicyclette[F] hollandaise
Hollandrad[N]
bicicletta[F] olandese

city bicycle
bicicleta[F] de ciudad[F]
bicyclette[F] de ville[F]
Stadtrad[N]
city bike[F]

mountain bike
bicicleta[F] todo terreno[M]
bicyclette[F] tout-terrain
Mountain Bike[N]
mountain bike[F]

road bicycle
bicicleta F de carretera F
bicyclette F de course F
Rennrad N
bicicletta F da corsa F

touring bicycle
bicicleta F de turismo M
bicyclette F de tourisme M
Tourenrad N
bicicletta F da turismo M

child's tricycle
triciclo M
tricycle M d'enfant M
Dreirad N
triciclo M

tandem bicycle
tándem M
tandem M
Tandem N
tandem M

railroad station

estación[F] de ferrocarril[M] | gare[F] | Bahnhof[M] | stazione[F] ferroviaria

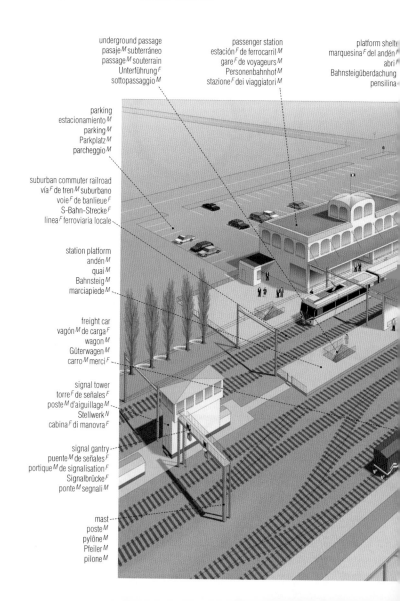

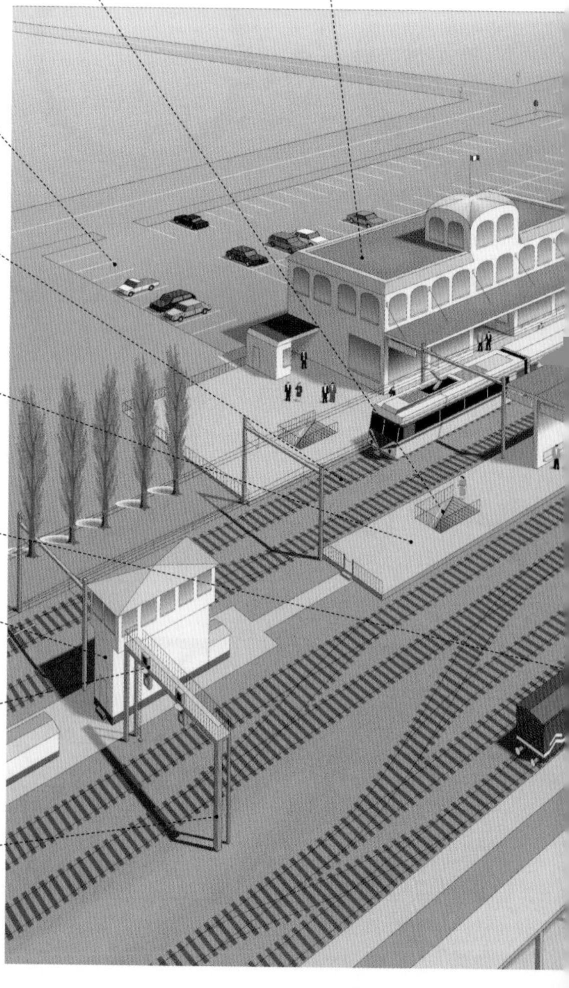
underground passage
pasaje[M] subterráneo
passage[M] souterrain
Unterführung[F]
sottopassaggio[M]
passenger station
estación[F] de ferrocarril[M]
gare[F] de voyageurs[M]
Personenbahnhof[M]
stazione[F] dei viaggiatori[M]
platform shelte
marquesina[F] del andén
abri
Bahnsteigüberdachung
pensilina
parking
estacionamiento[M]
parking[M]
Parkplatz[M]
parcheggio[M]
suburban commuter railroad
vía[F] de tren[M] suburbano
voie[F] de banlieue[F]
S-Bahn-Strecke[F]
linea[F] ferroviaria locale
station platform
andén[M]
quai[M]
Bahnsteig[M]
marciapiede[M]
freight car
vagón[M] de carga[F]
wagon[M]
Güterwagen[M]
carro[M] merci[F]
signal tower
torre[F] de señales[F]
poste[M] d'aiguillage[M]
Stellwerk[N]
cabina[F] di manovra[F]
signal gantry
puente[M] de señales[F]
portique[M] de signalisation[F]
Signalbrücke[F]
ponte[M] segnali[M]
mast
poste[M]
pylône[M]
Pfeiler[M]
pilone[M]

ommuter train
'en[M] suburbano
ain[M] de banlieue[F]
Iahverkehrszug[M]
'eno[M] locale
footbridge
pasarela[F]
passerelle[F]
Fußgängerbrücke[F]
ponte[M] pedonale
semaphore
semáforo[M]
signal[M] de voie[F]
Signal[N]
semaforo[M]
main line
vía[F] principal
grandes lignes[F]
Hauptgleis[N]
linea[F] ferroviaria principale
grade crossing
paso[M] a nivel[M]
passage[M] à niveau[M]
Bahnübergang[M]
passaggio[M] a livello[M]
bumper
tope[M]
butoir[M]
Prellbock[M]
respingente[M]
siding
vía[F] subsidiaria
voie[F] de service[M]
Nebengleis[N]
binario[M] morto
diesel shop
taller[M] de máquinas[F] diésel
atelier[M] diesel[M]
Lokschuppen[M]
officina[F] di riparazione[F] dei locomotori[M] diesel
freight station
estación[F] de carga[F]
gare[F] de marchandises[F]
Güterbahnhof[M]
scalo[M] merci[F]
switch
aguja[F] de cambio[M]
aiguillage[M]
Weiche[F]
scambio[M]
scissors crossing
carril[M] de enlace[M]
bretelle[F]
Gleiskreuzung[F]
binario[M] di raccordo[M]

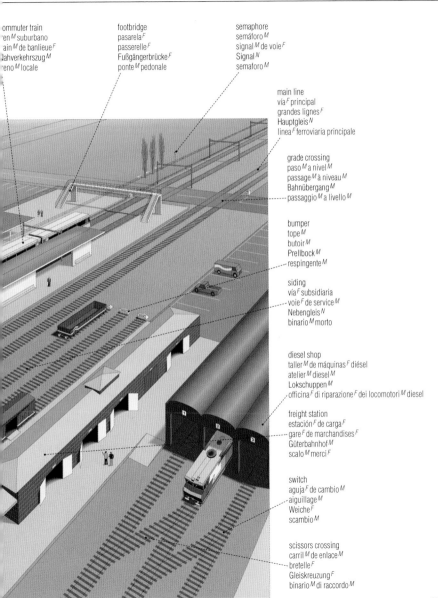

high-speed train

tren[M] de alta velocidad[F] | train[M] à grande vitesse[F] (T.G.V.) | Hochgeschwindigkeitszug[M] | treno[M] ad alta velocità[F]

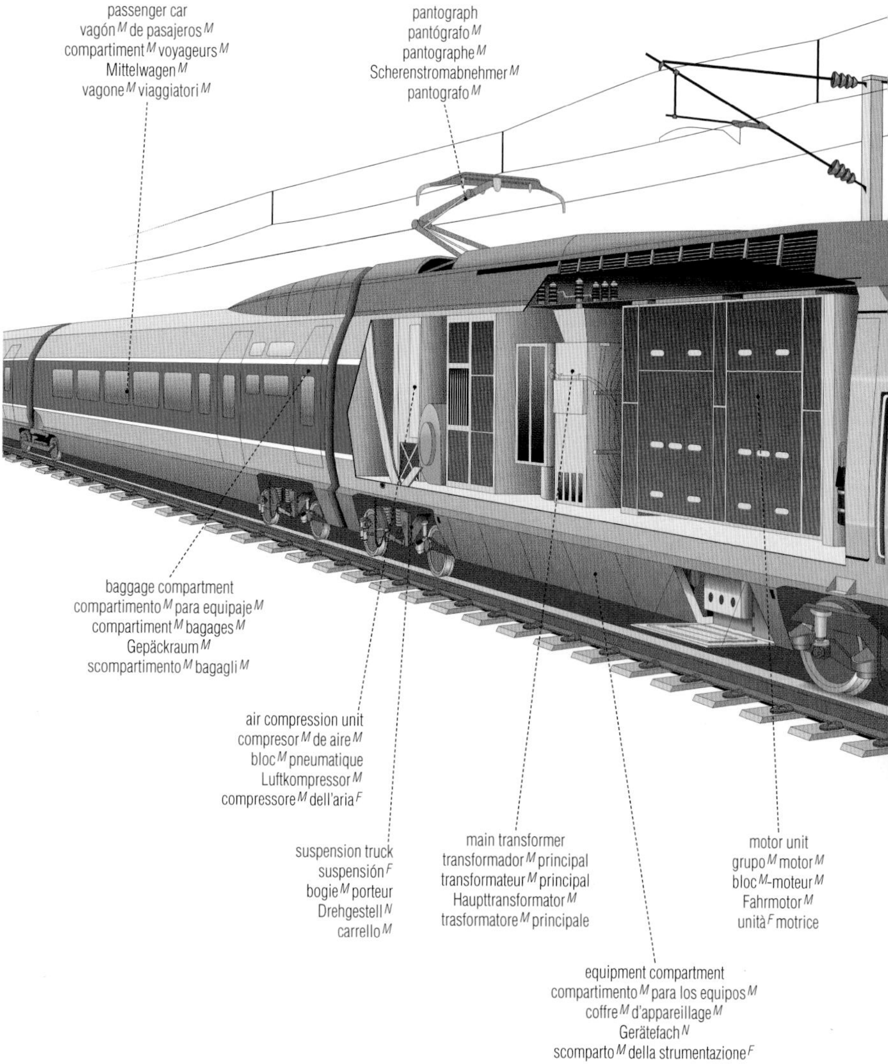
passenger car
vagón[M] de pasajeros[M]
compartiment[M] voyageurs[M]
Mittelwagen[M]
vagone[M] viaggiatori[M]
pantograph
pantógrafo[M]
pantographe[M]
Scherenstromabnehmer[M]
pantografo[M]
baggage compartment
compartimento[M] para equipaje[M]
compartiment[M] bagages[M]
Gepäckraum[M]
scompartimento[M] bagagli[M]
air compression unit
compresor[M] de aire[M]
bloc[M] pneumatique
Luftkompressor[M]
compressore[M] dell'aria[F]
suspension truck
suspensión[F]
bogie[M] porteur
Drehgestell[N]
carrello[M]
main transformer
transformador[M] principal
transformateur[M] principal
Haupttransformator[M]
trasformatore[M] principale
motor unit
grupo[M] motor[M]
bloc[M]-moteur[M]
Fahrmotor[M]
unità[F] motrice
equipment compartment
compartimento[M] para los equipos[M]
coffre[M] d'appareillage[M]
Gerätefach[N]
scomparto[M] della strumentazione[F]

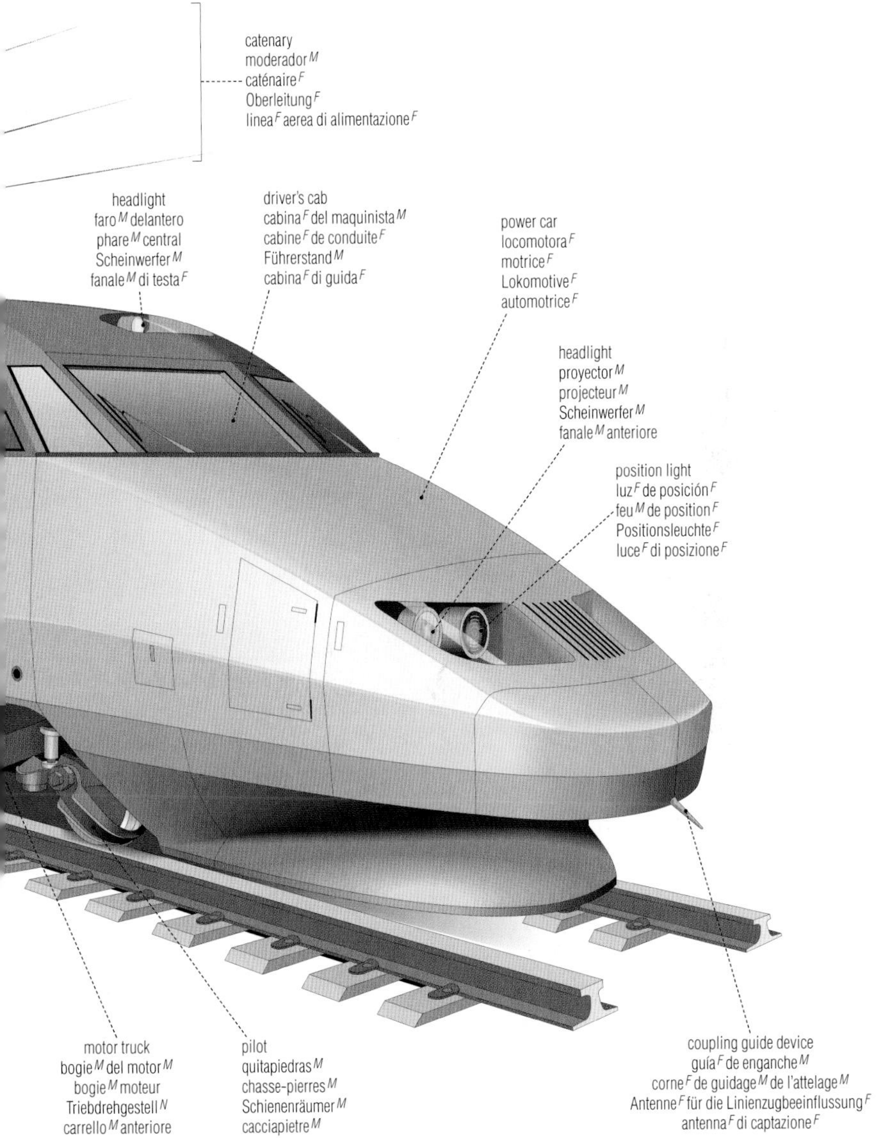
catenary
moderador M
caténaire F
Oberleitung F
linea F aerea di alimentazione F
headlight
faro M delantero
phare M central
Scheinwerfer M
fanale M di testa F
driver's cab
cabina F del maquinista M
cabine F de conduite F
Führerstand M
cabina F di guida F
power car
locomotora F
motrice F
Lokomotive F
automotrice F
headlight
proyector M
projecteur M
Scheinwerfer M
fanale M anteriore
position light
luz F de posición F
feu M de position F
Positionsleuchte F
luce F di posizione F
motor truck
bogie M del motor M
bogie M moteur
Triebdrehgestell N
carrello M anteriore
pilot
quitapiedras M
chasse-pierres M
Schienenräumer M
cacciapietre M
coupling guide device
guía F de enganche M
corne F de guidage M de l'attelage M
Antenne F für die Linienzugbeeinflussung F
antenna F di captazione F

diesel-electric locomotive

locomotora^F diésel eléctrica | locomotive^F diesel-électrique | dieselelektrische Lokomotive^F | locomotiva^F diesel-elettrica

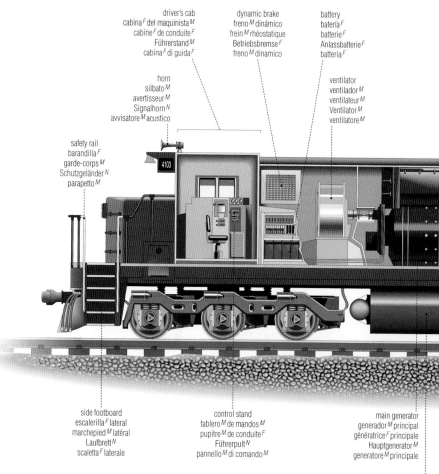

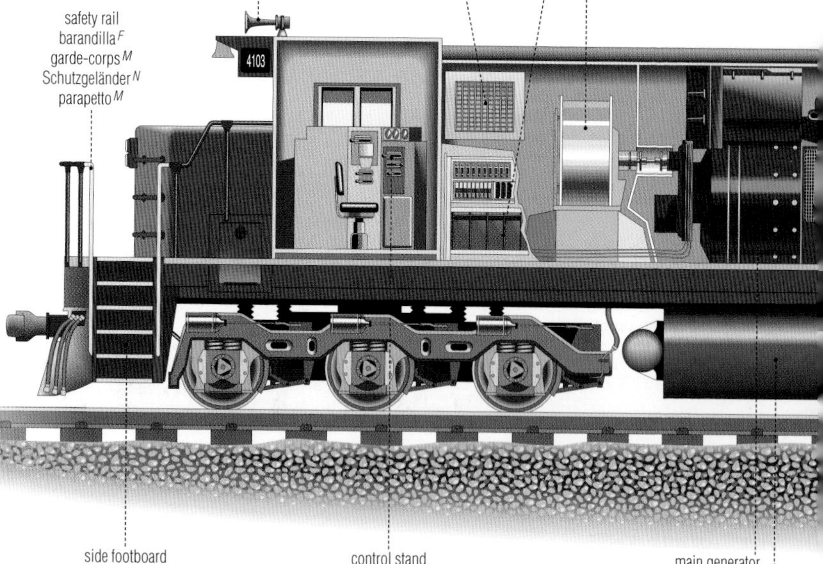
driver's cab
cabina^F del maquinista^M
cabine^F de conduite^F
Führerstand^M
cabina^F di guida^F
dynamic brake
freno^M dinámico
frein^M rhéostatique
Betriebsbremse^F
freno^M dinamico
battery
batería^F
batterie^F
Anlassbatterie^F
batteria^F
horn
silbato^M
avertisseur^M
Signalhorn^N
avvisatore^M acustico
ventilator
ventilador^M
ventilateur^M
Ventilator^M
ventilatore^M
safety rail
barandilla^F
garde-corps^M
Schutzgeländer^N
parapetto^M
4103
side footboard
escalerilla^F lateral
marchepied^M latéral
Laufbrett^N
scaletta^F laterale
control stand
tablero^M de mandos^M
pupitre^M de conduite^F
Führerpult^N
pannello^M di comando^M
main generator
generador^M principal
génératrice^F principale
Hauptgenerator^M
generatore^M principale
fuel tank
depósito^M de combustible^M
réservoir^M à carburant^M
Kraftstofftank^M
serbatoio^M del carburante^M

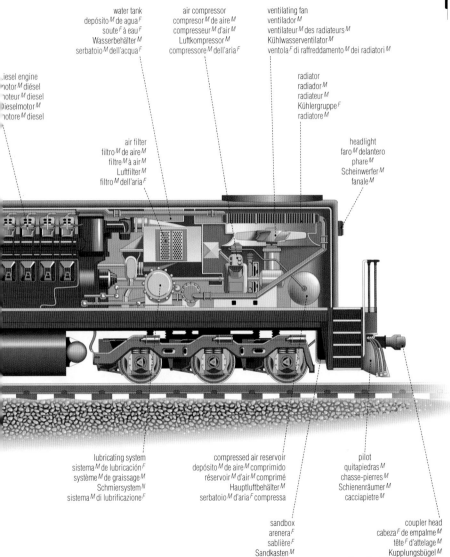

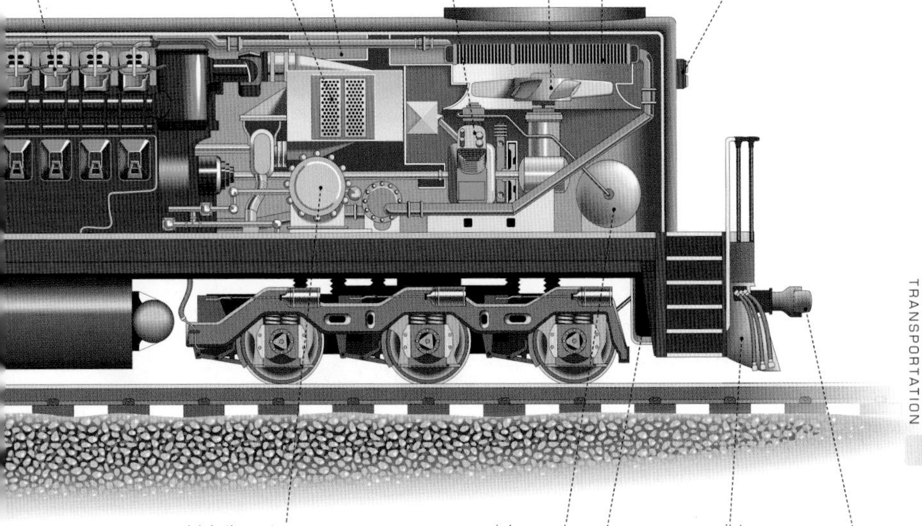
water tank
depósito M de agua F
soute F à eau F
Wasserbehälter M
serbatoio M dell'acqua F
air compressor
compresor M de aire M
compresseur M d'air M
Luftkompressor M
compressore M dell'aria F
ventilating fan
ventilador M
ventilateur M des radiateurs M
Kühlwasserventilator M
ventola F di raffreddamento M dei radiatori M
iesel engine
otor M diésel
oteur M diesel
ieselmotor M
otore M diesel
radiator
radiador M
radiateur M
Kühlergruppe F
radiatore M
air filter
filtro M de aire M
filtre M à air M
Luftfilter M
filtro M dell'aria F
headlight
faro M delantero
phare M
Scheinwerfer M
fanale M
lubricating system
sistema M de lubricación F
système M de graissage M
Schmiersystem N
sistema M di lubrificazione F
compressed air reservoir
depósito M de aire M comprimido
réservoir M d'air M comprimé
Hauptluftbehälter M
serbatoio M d'aria F compressa
pilot
quitapiedras M
chasse-pierres M
Schienenräumer M
cacciapietre M
sandbox
arenera F
sablière F
Sandkasten M
sabbiera F
coupler head
cabeza F de empalme M
tête F d'attelage M
Kupplungsbügel M
dispositivo M di agganciamento M

car

vagón[M] | wagon[M] | Waggon[M] | carro[M] merci[M]

box car
furgón[M]
wagon[M] **couvert**
Drehgestellkastenwagen[M]
carro[M] **chiuso**

corner cap
esquinera[F]
chapeau[M] d'angle[M]
Eckbeschlag[M]
testa[F] d'angolo[M]
horizontal end handhold
asidero[M] horizontal
main[F] courante
Handstange[F]
corrimano[M]
hand brake wheel
volante[M] del freno[M] manual
volant[M] de frein[M] à main[F]
Handbremsrad[N]
ruota[F] del freno[M] a mano[F]
end ladder
escalerilla[F] de estribo[M]
échelle[F] de bout[M]
Stirnwandleiter[F]
scaletta[F] posteriore
hand brake gear housing
cubierta[F] del mecanismo[M] del freno[M]
carter[M] d'engrenage[M] de frein[M] à main[F]
Schutzkasten[M] für Handbremse[F]
scatola[F] degli ingranaggi[M] del freno[M] a mano[F]
sliding channe
guía[F] corrediz
glissière
Türführungsschiene
guida[F] di scorrimento
hand brake winding lever
palanca[F] de accionamiento[M] del freno[M] de mano[F]
levier[M] de frein[M] à main[F]
Handbremshebel[M]
leva[F] di azionamento[M] del freno[M] a mano[F]
side ladder
escalerilla[F] lateral
échelle[F] latérale
Seitensprossen[F]
scaletta[F] laterale
telescoping uncoupling rod
varilla[F] telescópica de desenganche[M]
levier[M] télescopique de dételage[M]
Abkoppelvorrichtung[F]
braccio[M] telescopico di disaccoppiamento[M]
sill step
peldaño[M] inferior
marchepied[M] en étrier[M]
Bügeltritt[M]
gradino[M]

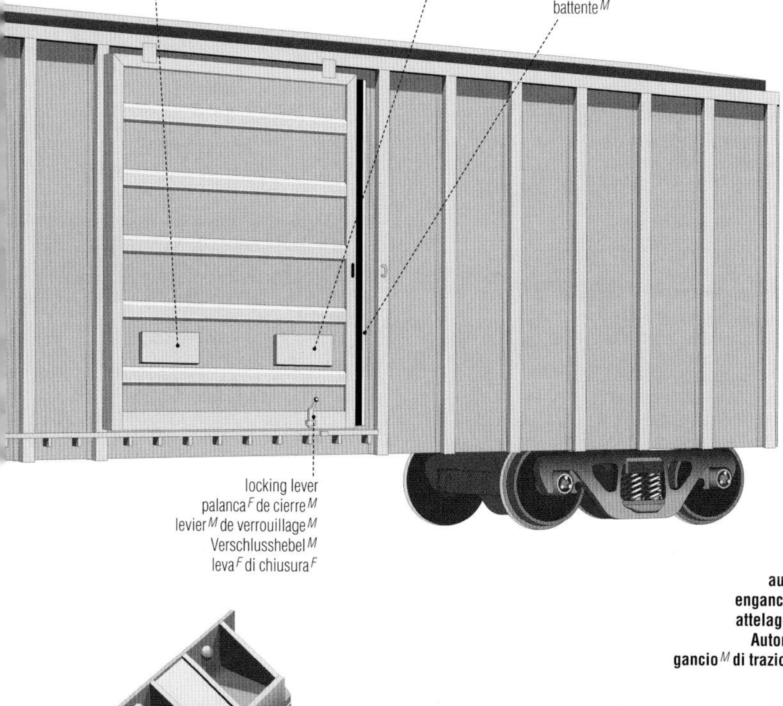
routing cardboard
tarjeta[F] de ruta[F]
porte-étiquette[M] d'acheminement[M]
Wagenlaufschild[N]
cartellino[M] indicatore[M] di destinazione[F]
placard board
tablero[M] de rótulo[M]
porte-étiquette[M]
Anschriftentafel[F]
cartellino[M] segnaletico
door stop
tope[M] de la puerta[F]
butée[F] de porte[F]
Türsäule[F]
battente[M]
locking lever
palanca[F] de cierre[M]
levier[M] de verrouillage[M]
Verschlusshebel[M]
leva[F] di chiusura[F]

automatic coupler
enganche[M] automático
attelage[M] automatique
Automatikkupplung[F]
gancio[M] di trazione[F] automatico

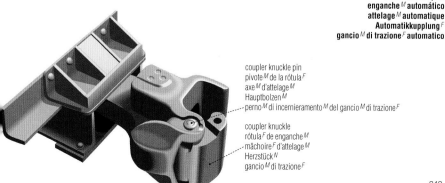

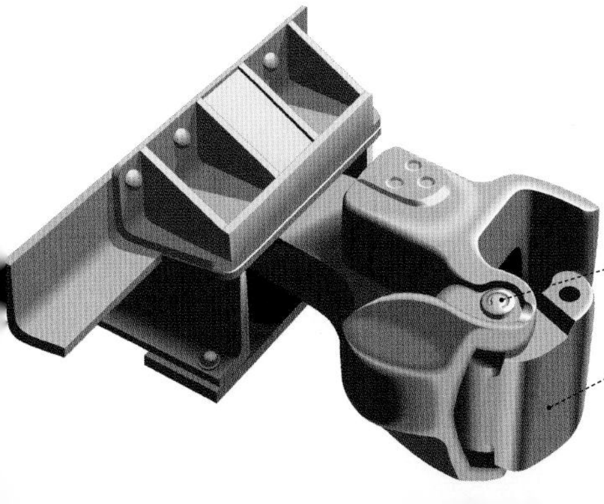
coupler knuckle pin
pivote[M] de la rótula[F]
axe[M] d'attelage[M]
Hauptbolzen[M]
perno[M] di incernieramento[M] del gancio[M] di trazione[F]
coupler knuckle
rótula[F] de enganche[M]
mâchoire[F] d'attelage[M]
Herzstück[N]
gancio[M] di trazione[F]

examples of freight cars
ejemplos *M* de vagones *M*
exemples *M* de wagons *M*
Beispiele *N* für Güterwagen *M*
esempi *M* di carri *M* merci *F*

flat car
plataforma *F*
wagon *M* plat
Drehgestellflachwagen *M*
carro *M* pianale *M*

bulkhead flat car
vagón *M* plano con retenedores *M*
wagon *M* plat à parois *F* de bout *M*
Stirnwandflachwagen *M*
carro *M* pianale *M* con stanti *M*

depressed-center flat car
plataforma *F* de piso *M* bajo
wagon *M* plat surbaissé
Tiefladewagen *M*
carro *M* pianale *M* a carrelli *M*

intermodal car
vagón *M* intermodal
wagon *M* intermodal
Wagen *M* für den Kombiverkehr *M*
vagone *M* intermodale

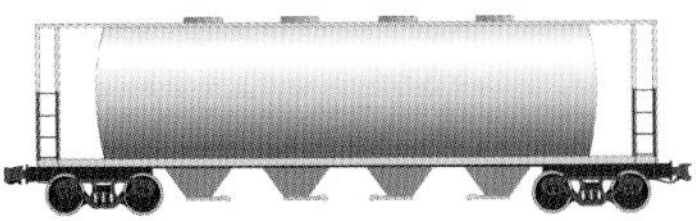

hopper car
vagón *M* tolva *F*
wagon *M*-trémie *F*
Bodenentleererwagen *M*
carro *M* a tramoggia *F*

gondola car
vagón *M* de mercancías *F*
wagon *M*-tombereau *M*
offener Güterwagen *M*
carro *M* scoperto a sponde *F* basse

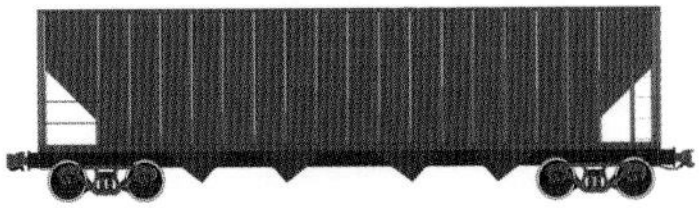

hopper ore car
vagón *M* tolva *F* para minerales *M*
wagon *M*-trémie *F* à minerai *M*
Schüttgutwagen *M*
carro *M* a tramoggia *F* per minerali *M*

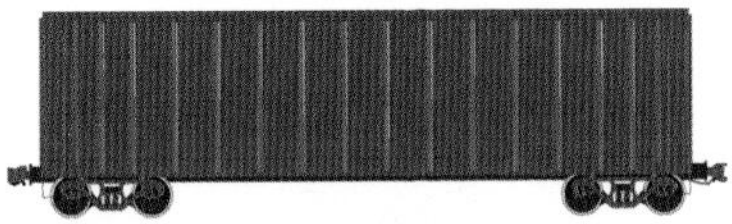

wood chip car
vagón *M* para madera *F*
wagon *M* à copeaux *M*
langer Kastenwagen *M*
carro *M* scoperto a sponde *F* alte

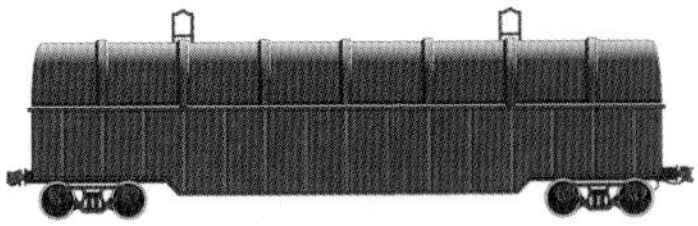

hard top gondola
vagón *M* cerrado
wagon *M*-tombereau *M* couvert
Planenwagen *M*
carro *M* chiuso con tetto *M* apribile

tank car
vagón *M* cisterna *F*
wagon *M*-citerne *F*
Kesselwagen *M*
carro *M* cisterna *F*

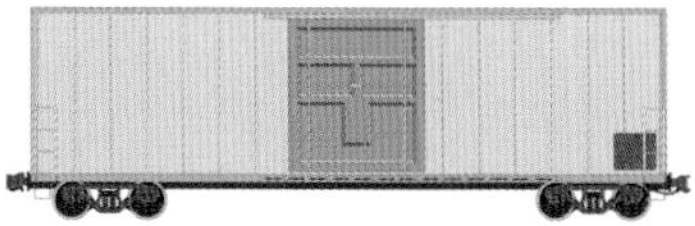

refrigerator car
vagón[M] frigorífico
wagon[M] réfrigérant
Kühlwagen[M]
carro[M] frigorifero

caboose
furgón[M] de cola[F]
wagon[M] de queue[F]
Bremswagen[M]
vagone[M] di coda[F] del personale[M] viaggiante

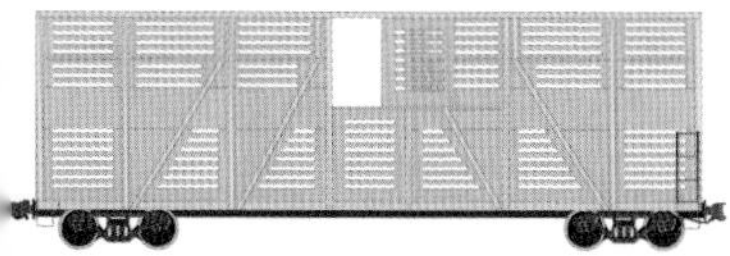

livestock car
vagón[M] para ganado[M]
wagon[M] à bestiaux[M]
Verschlagwagen[M]
carro[M] bestiame[M]

box car
vagón[M] cerrado
wagon[M] couvert
Drehgestellwaggon[M]
carro[M] merci[M] chiuso

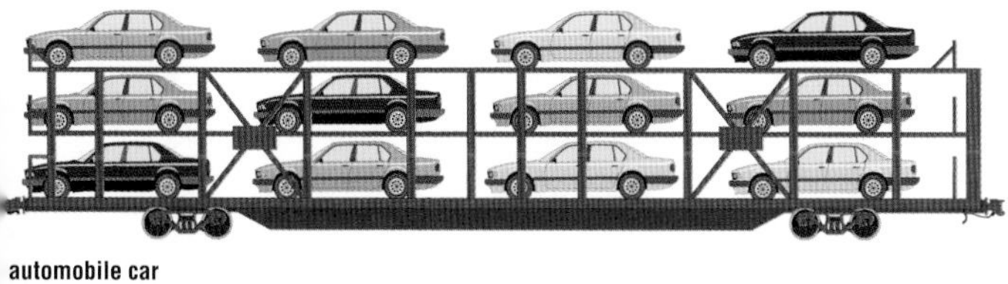

automobile car
vagón[M] para automóviles[M]
wagon[M] porte-automobiles[M]
Autotransportwagen[M]
carro[M] bisarca[F]

container car
vagón[M] para contenedores[M]
wagon[M] porte-conteneurs[M]
Containerflachwagen[M]
carro[M] pianale[M] portacontainer[M]

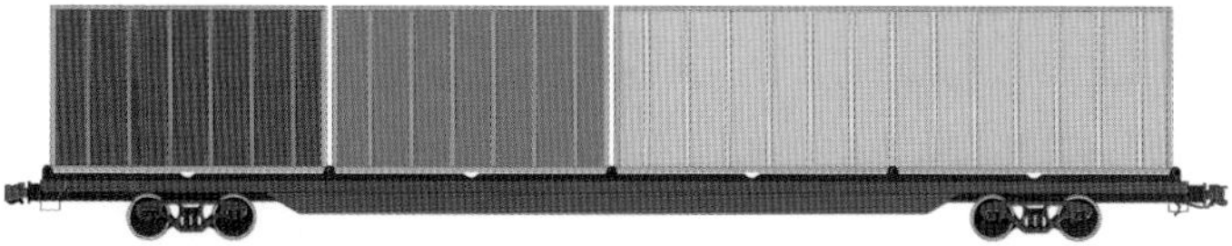

subway

metro^{M} | chemin^{M} de fer^{M} métropolitain | U-Bahn^{F} | metropolitana^{F}

subway station
estación^{F} de metro^{M}
station^{F} de métro^{M}
U-Bahn-Station^{F}
stazione^{F} della metropolitana^{F}

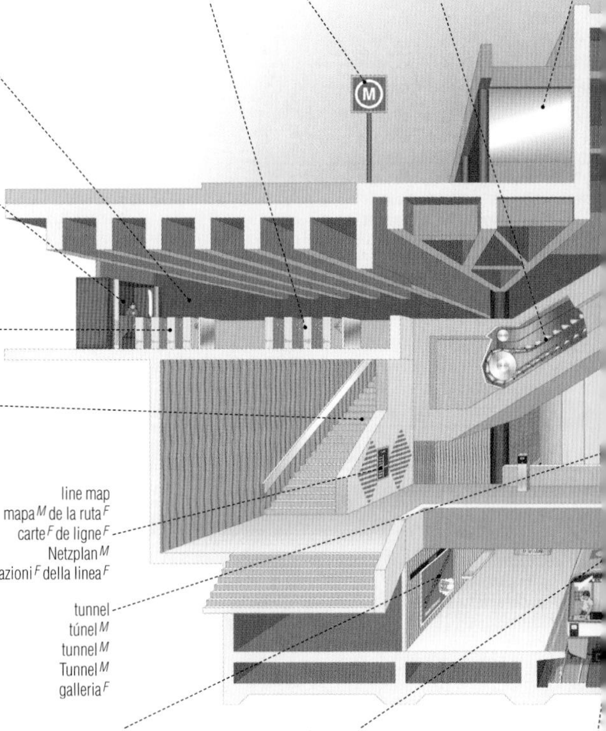

exterior sign
señal^{F} exterior
enseigne^{F} extérieure
U-Bahn-Schild^{N}
insegna^{F} esterna
station entran
entrada^{F} de la estación
édicule
Eingang
ingresso^{M} della stazione
exit turnstile
torniquete^{M} de salida^{F}
tourniquet^{M} de sortie^{F}
Ausgangssperre^{F}
tornelli^{M} di uscita^{F}
escalator
escalera^{F} mecánica
escalier^{M} mécanique
Rolltreppe^{F}
scala^{F} mobile
mezzanine
entrepiso^{M}
mezzanine^{F}
Sperrengeschoss^{N}
mezzanino^{M}
ticket collecting booth
taquilla^{F} de venta^{F} de billetes^{M}
guichet^{M} de vente^{F} des billets^{M}
Fahrkartenschalter^{M}
vendita^{F} dei biglietti^{M}
entrance turnstile
torniquete^{M} de entrada^{F}
tourniquet^{M} d'accès^{M}
Eingangssperre^{F}
tornelli^{M} di entrata^{F}
stairs
escaleras^{F}
escalier^{M}
Treppe^{F}
scale^{F}
line map
mapa^{M} de la ruta^{F}
carte^{F} de ligne^{F}
Netzplan^{M}
cartello^{M} indicatore delle stazioni^{F} della linea^{F}
tunnel
túnel^{M}
tunnel^{M}
Tunnel^{M}
galleria^{F}
advertising panel
panel^{M} de publicidad^{F}
panneau^{M} publicitaire
Werbetafel^{F}
cartello^{M} pubblicitario
subway train
tren^{M} subterráneo
rame^{F} de métro^{M}
U-Bahn-Zug^{M}
treno^{M} della metropolitana^{F}
track
vía^{F}
voie^{F}
Gleis
binario

TRANSPORTATION

transfer dispensing machine
máquina[F] expendedora de billetes[M]
distributeur[M] de correspondances[F]
Automat[M] für Umsteigekarten[F]
distributore[M] automatico di biglietti[M]

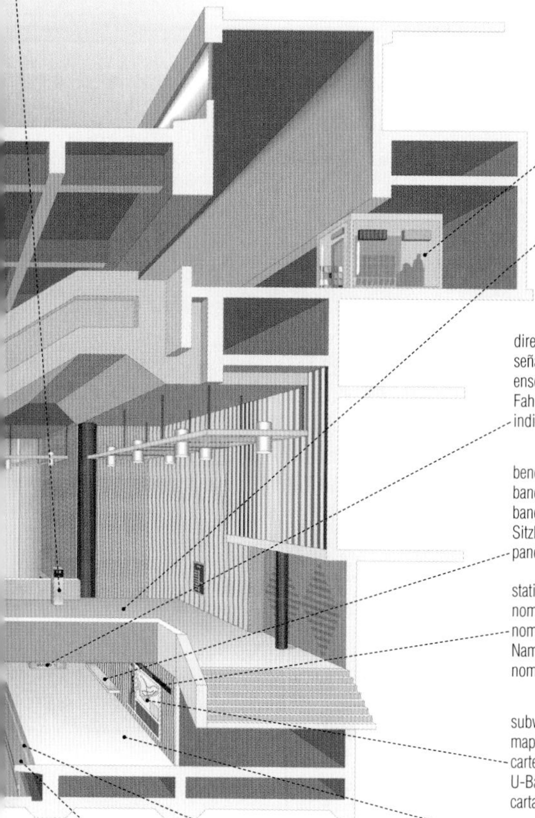

kiosk
kiosco[M]
kiosque[M]
Kiosk[M]
edicola[F]

footbridge
pasarela[F] superior
passerelle[F]
Fußgängerbrücke[F]
passerella[F]

directional sign
señal[F] de dirección[F]
enseigne[F] directionnelle
Fahrtrichtungsanzeige[F]
indicatore[M] di destinazione[F]

bench
banco[M]
banc[M]
Sitzbank[F]
panchina[F]

station name
nombre[M] de la estación[F]
nom[M] de la station[F]
Name[M] der Station[F]
nome[M] della stazione[F]

subway map
mapa[M] de rutas[F]
carte[F] de réseau[M]
U-Bahn-Netzplan[M]
carta[F] della rete[F] metropolitana

platform edge
borde[M] del andén[M]
bordure[F] de quai[M]
Bahnsteigkante[F]
margine[M] del marciapiede[M]

safety line
línea[F] de seguridad[F]
ligne[F] de sécurité[F]
Sicherheitsstreifen[M]
linea[F] di sicurezza[F]

platform
andén[M]
quai[M]
Bahnsteig[M]
marciapiede[M]

passenger car
vagón^{M} de pasajeros^{M}
voiture^{F}
Mittelwagen^{M}
carrozza^{F} passeggeri^{M}

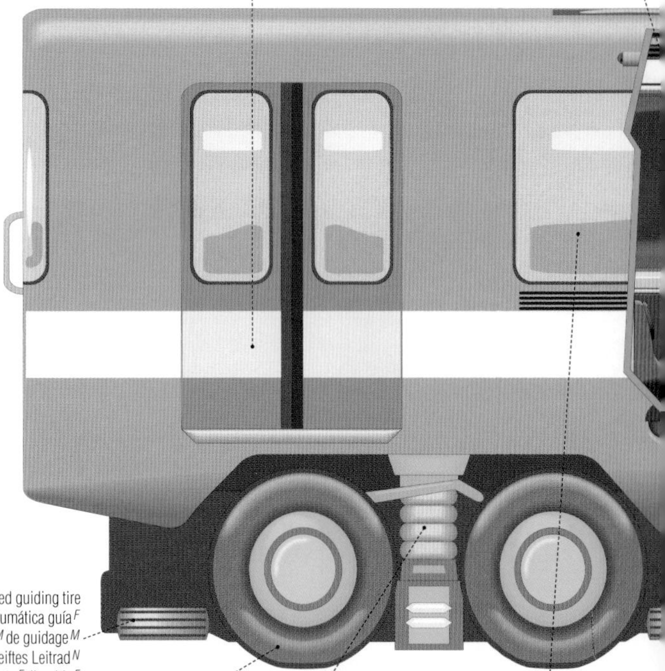
ventilator
ventilador^{M}
grille^{F} d'aération^{F}
Lüftung^{F}
griglia^{F} di aerazione^{F}
side door
puerta^{F} lateral
porte^{F} latérale
Einstiegstür^{F}
porta^{F}
light
lámpara^{F}
éclairage^{M}
Innenbeleuchtung^{F}
luce^{F}
inflated guiding tire
llanta^{F} neumática guía^{F}
pneumatique^{M} de guidage^{M}
pneubereiftes Leitrad^{N}
ruota^{F} di guida^{F}
inflated carrying tire
llanta^{F} neumática de tracción^{F}
pneumatique^{M} porteur
pneubereiftes Laufrad^{N}
ruota^{F} portante
suspension
suspensión^{F}
suspension^{F}
Federung^{F}
sospensione^{F}
window
ventanilla^{F}
fenêtre^{F}
Fenster^{N}
finestrino^{M}

dvertising sign
artel [M] comercial
fiche [F] publicitaire
Verbetafel [F]
artello [M] pubblicitario

side handrail
asidero [M] lateral
poignée [F]
Einsteigegriff [M]
maniglia [F] laterale

emergency brake
freno [M] de emergencia [F]
frein [M] d'urgence [F]
Notbremse [F]
freno [M] di emergenza [F]

communication set
altavoz [M] de comunicación [F]
poste [M] de communication [F]
Gegensprechanlage [F]
altoparlante [M]

subway map
mapa [M] de ruta [F]
carte [F] de réseau [M]
U-Bahn-Netzplan [M]
carta [F] della rete [F] metropolitana

handrail
asidero [M] vertical
colonne [F]
Handstange [F]
asta [F] di sostegno [M]

single seat
asiento [M] individual
siège [M] simple
Einzelsitz [M]
sedile [M] singolo

double seat
asiento [M] doble
siège [M] double
Doppelsitz [M]
sedile [M] doppio

heating grille
rejilla [F] de calefacción [F]
grille [F] de chauffage [M]
Heizungsgitter [N]
griglia [F] del riscaldamento [M]

TRANSPORTATION

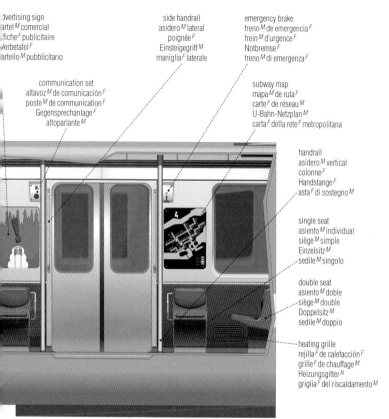

subway train
tren [M] subterráneo
rame [F] de métro [M]
U-Bahn-Zug [M]
metropolitana [F]

motor car
vagón [M] máquina [F]
motrice [F]
Triebwagen [M]
motrice [F]

trailer car
coche [M] de tracción [F]
remorque [F]
Beiwagen [M]
rimorchio [M]

motor car
vagón [M] máquina [F]
motrice [F]
Triebwagen [M]
motrice [F]

harbor

puerto[M] | port[M] maritime | Hafen[M] | porto[M] marittimo

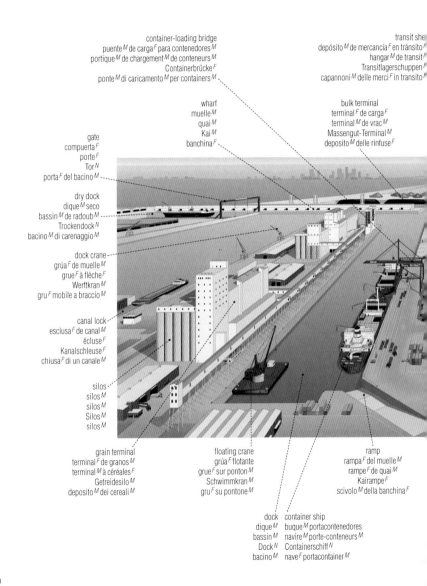

container-loading bridge
puente[M] de carga[F] para contenedores[M]
portique[M] de chargement[M] de conteneurs[M]
Containerbrücke[F]
ponte[M] di caricamento[M] per containers[M]
transit she
depósito[M] de mercancía[F] en tránsito
hangar[M] de transit
Transitlagerschuppen
capannoni[M] delle merci[F] in transito
wharf
muelle[M]
quai[M]
Kai[M]
banchina[F]
bulk terminal
terminal[F] de carga[F]
terminal[M] de vrac[M]
Massengut-Terminal[M]
deposito[M] delle rinfuse[F]
gate
compuerta[F]
porte[F]
Tor[N]
porta[F] del bacino[M]
dry dock
dique[M] seco
bassin[M] de radoub[M]
Trockendock[N]
bacino[M] di carenaggio[M]
dock crane
grúa[F] de muelle[M]
grue[F] à flèche[F]
Werftkran[M]
gru[F] mobile a braccio[M]
canal lock
esclusa[F] de canal[M]
écluse[F]
Kanalschleuse[F]
chiusa[F] di un canale[M]
silos
silos[M]
silos[M]
Silos[M]
silos[M]
grain terminal
terminal[F] de granos[M]
terminal[M] à céréales[F]
Getreidesilo[M]
deposito[M] dei cereali[M]
floating crane
grúa[F] flotante
grue[F] sur ponton[M]
Schwimmkran[M]
gru[F] su pontone[M]
ramp
rampa[F] del muelle[M]
rampe[F] de quai[M]
Kairampe[F]
scivolo[M] della banchina[F]
dock
dique[M]
bassin[M]
Dock[N]
bacino[M]
container ship
buque[M] portacontenedores
navire[M] porte-conteneurs[M]
Containerschiff[N]
nave[F] portacontainer[M]

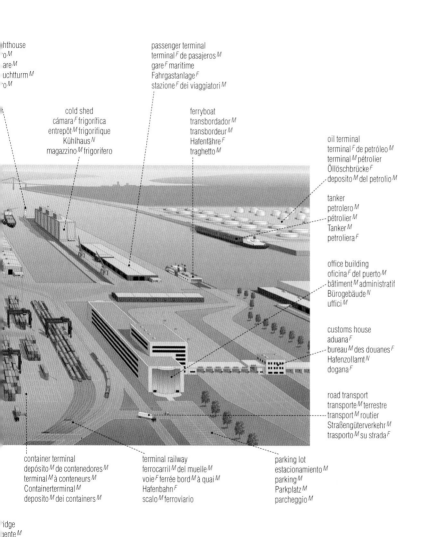

hthouse
o[M]
are[M]
uchtturm[M]
o[M]

passenger terminal
terminal[F] de pasajeros[M]
gare[F] maritime
Fahrgastanlage[F]
stazione[F] dei viaggiatori[M]

cold shed
cámara[F] frigorífica
entrepôt[M] frigorifique
Kühlhaus[N]
magazzino[M] frigorifero

ferryboat
transbordador[M]
transbordeur[M]
Hafenfähre[F]
traghetto[M]

oil terminal
terminal[F] de petróleo[M]
terminal[M] pétrolier
Öllöschbrücke[F]
deposito[M] del petrolio[M]

tanker
petrolero[M]
pétrolier[M]
Tanker[M]
petroliera[F]

office building
oficina[F] del puerto[M]
bâtiment[M] administratif
Bürogebäude[N]
uffici[M]

customs house
aduana[F]
bureau[M] des douanes[F]
Hafenzollamt[N]
dogana[F]

road transport
transporte[M] terrestre
transport[M] routier
Straßengüterverkehr[M]
trasporto[M] su strada[F]

container terminal
depósito[M] de contenedores[M]
terminal[M] à conteneurs[M]
Containerterminal[M]
deposito[M] dei containers[M]

terminal railway
ferrocarril[M] del muelle[M]
voie[F] ferrée bord[M] à quai[M]
Hafenbahn[F]
scalo[M] ferroviario

parking lot
estacionamiento[M]
parking[M]
Parkplatz[M]
parcheggio[M]

idge
uente[M]
ortique[M]
ückenlift[M]
u[F] a portale[M]

TRANSPORTATION

four-masted bark

barco^M de vela^F de cuatro palos^M | quatre-mâts^M barque^F | Viermastbark^F | veliero^M a quattro alberi^M

masting and rigging
arboladura^F y aparejos^M
mâture^F et gréement^M
Takelage^F
alberatura^F e velatura^F

mizzenmast
palo^M de mesana^F
grand mât^M arrière
Kreuzmast^M
albero^M di mezzana^F
jiggermast
contramesana^F
mât^M d'artimon^M
Besanmast^M
albero^M di contromezzana^F
mainmast
palo^M mayor
grand mât^M avant
Großmast^M
albero^M di maestra^F
foremast
palo^M de trinquete^M
mât^M de misaine^F
Fockmast^M
albero^M di trinchetto^M
gaff
botavara^F
corne^F
Gaffel^F
picco^M
shroud
obenque^M
hauban^M
Want^F
sartia^F
side
banda^F
bord^M
Seite^F
fianco^M
gaff sail boom
botavara^F de cangreja^F
gui^M
Besanbaum^M
boma^M
backstay
burda^F
galhauban^M
Pardune^F
paterazzo^M

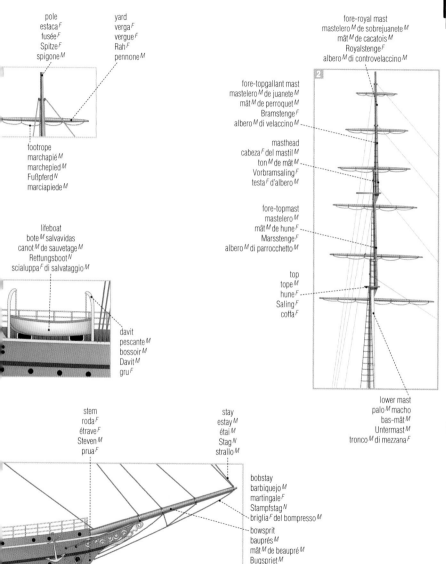

pole
estaca F
fusée F
Spitze F
spigone M

yard
verga F
vergue F
Rah F
pennone M

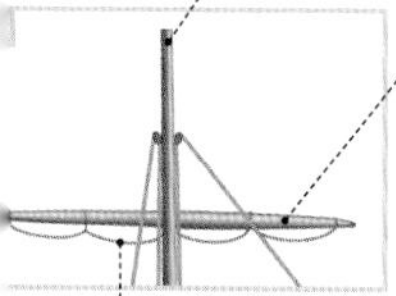

footrope
marchapié M
marchepied M
Fußpferd N
marciapiede M

fore-royal mast
mastelero M de sobrejuanete M
mât M de cacatois M
Royalstenge F
albero M di controvelaccino M

fore-topgallant mast
mastelero M de juanete M
mât M de perroquet M
Bramstenge F
albero M di velaccino M

masthead
cabeza F del mastil M
ton M de mât M
Vorbramsaling F
testa F d'albero M

fore-topmast
mastelero M
mât M de hune F
Marsstenge F
albero M di parrocchetto M

top
tope M
hune F
Saling F
coffa F

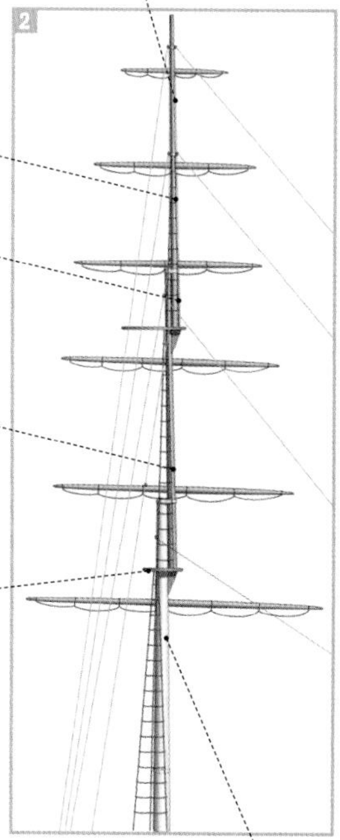

lower mast
palo M macho
bas-mât M
Untermast M
tronco M di mezzana F

lifeboat
bote M salvavidas
canot M de sauvetage M
Rettungsboot N
scialuppa F di salvataggio M

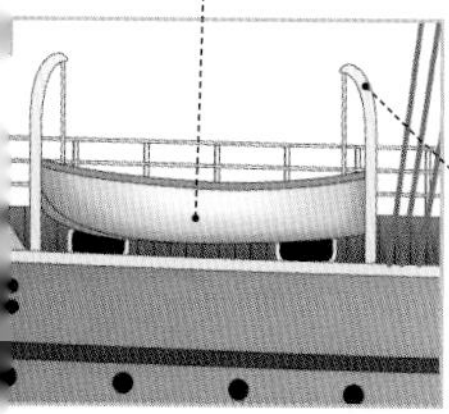

davit
pescante M
bossoir M
Davit M
gru F

stem
roda F
étrave F
Steven M
prua F

stay
estay M
étai M
Stag N
strallo M

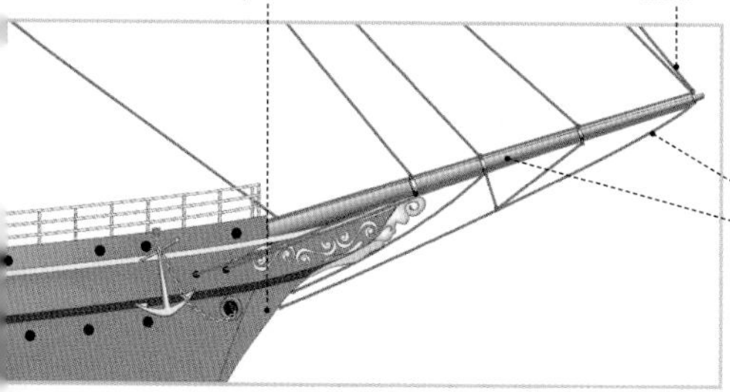

bobstay
barbiquejo M
martingale F
Stampfstag N
briglia F del bompresso M

bowsprit
bauprés M
mât M de beaupré M
Bugspriet M
bompresso M

TRANSPORTATION

four-masted bark

sails
velamen [M]
voilure [F]
Segel [N]
vele [F]

mizzen royal staysail
sobrejuanete [M] de mesana [F] de estay [M]
voile [F] d'étai [M] de grand cacatois [M] arrière
Kreuz-Royalstagsegel [N]
vela [F] di strallo [M] di controvelaccio [M]
mizzen royal brace
brazas [F] de sobrejuanete [M] de mesana [F]
bras [M] de grand cacatois [M] arrière
Kreuz-Royalbrasse [F]
braccio [M] del pennone [M] di controbelvedere [M]
mizzen topgallant staysail
juanete [M] de mesana [F] de estay [M]
voile [F] d'étai [M] de grand perroquet [M] arrière
Kreuz-Bramstagsegel [N]
vela [F] di strallo [M] di velaccio [M]
jigger topgallant staysail
aparejo [M] de juanete [M] de estay [M]
voile [F] d'étai [M] de flèche [F]
Besan-Bramstagsegel [N]
vela [F] di strallo [M] di belvedere [M]
gaff topsail
escandalosa [F]
voile [F] de flèche [F]
Besantoppsegel [N]
controranda [F]
jigger topmast staysail
aparejo [M] de mastelero [M] de estay [M]
marquise [F]
Besan-Stengestagsegel [N]
vela [F] di strallo [M] di mezzana [F]
spanker
cangreja [F] de popa [F]
brigantine [F]
Besan [M]
randa [F]
halyard
driza [F]
drisse [F]
Fall [N]
drizza [F]
sheet
escota [F]
écoute [F]
Schot [F]
scotta [F]
mizzen sail
cangreja [F] mayor popel
grand-voile [F] arrière
Kreuzsegel [N]
vela [F] di mezzana [F]
mizzen topmast stays
mastelero [M] de mesana [F] de estay
grand-voile [F] d'étai [M] arriè
Kreuz-Stengestagsege
vela [F] di strallo [M] di gabbia

TRANSPORTATION

in royal sail
rejuanete[M] mayor
nd cacatois[M] avant
ß-Royalsegel[N]
ntrovelaccio[M]

main lower topgallant sail
juanete[M] mayor bajo
grand perroquet[M] fixe avant
Groß-Unterbramsegel[N]
velaccio[M] fisso

fore royal sail
sobrejuanete[M] de proa[F]
petit cacatois[M]
Vor-Royalsegel[N]
controvelaccino[M]

main upper topgallant sail
juanete[M] mayor proel alto
grand perroquet[M] volant avant
Groß-Oberbramsegel[N]
velaccio[M] volante

upper fore topgallant sail
juanete[M] de proa[F] alto
petit perroquet[M] volant
Vor-Oberbramsegel[N]
velaccino[M] volante

main upper topsail
gavia[F] mayor alta
grand hunier[M] volant avant
Groß-Obermarssegel[N]
gabbia[F] volante

upper fore topsail
gavia[F] proel alta
petit hunier[M] volant
Vor-Obermarssegel[N]
parrocchetto[M] volante

flying jib
petifoque[M]
clinfoc[M]
Flieger[M]
controfiocco[M]

outer jib
foque[M]
grand foc[M]
Außenklüver[M]
fiocco[M]

middle jib
fofoque[M]
faux foc[M]
Binnenklüver[M]
fiocco[M] di dentro

inner jib
contrafoque[M]
petit foc[M]
Vorstenge-Stagsegel[N]
trinchettina[F]

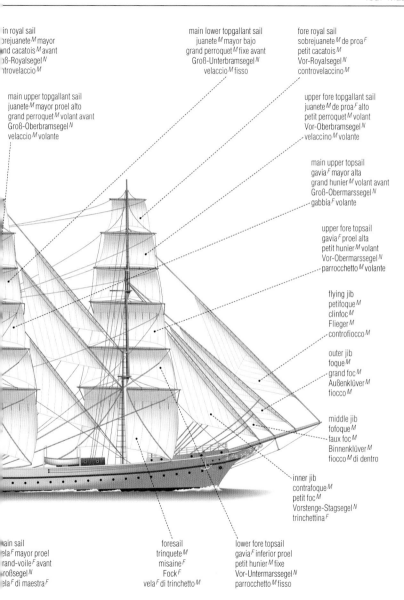

ain sail
ela[F] mayor proel
rand-voile[F] avant
roßsegel[N]
ela[F] di maestra[F]

foresail
trinquete[M]
misaine[F]
Fock[F]
vela[F] di trinchetto[M]

lower fore topsail
gavia[F] inferior proel
petit hunier[M] fixe
Vor-Untermarssegel[N]
parrocchetto[M] fisso

TRANSPORTATION

examples of boats and ships

ejemplos[M] de barcos[M] y embarcaciones[F] | exemples[M] de bateaux[M] et d'embarcations[F] | Beispiele[N] für Boote[N] und Schiffe[N] | esempi[M] di barche[F] e navi[F]

tug
remolcador[M]
remorqueur[M]
Schlepper[M]
rimorchiatore[M]

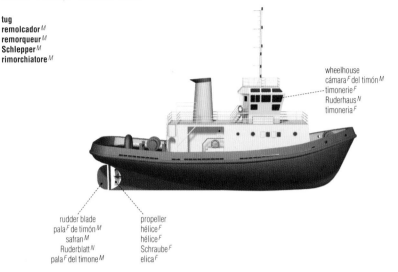

wheelhouse
cámara[F] del timón[M]
timonerie[F]
Ruderhaus[N]
timoneria[F]
rudder blade
pala[F] de timón[M]
safran[M]
Ruderblatt[N]
pala[F] del timone[M]
propeller
hélice[F]
hélice[F]
Schraube[F]
elica[F]

ice breaker
rompehielos[M]
brise-glace[M]
Eisbrecher[M]
rompighiaccio[M]

stem
proa[F]
étrave[F]
Bug[M]
prua[F]
stem propeller
hélice[F] de proa[F]
hélice[F] d'étrave[F]
Bugpropeller[M]
elica[F] di prua[F]
rear propeller
hélice[F] posterior
hélice[F] arrière
Heckpropeller[M]
elica[F] posteriore

hydrofoil boat
hidróptero[M]
hydroptère[M]
Tragflügelschiff[N]
aliscafo[M]

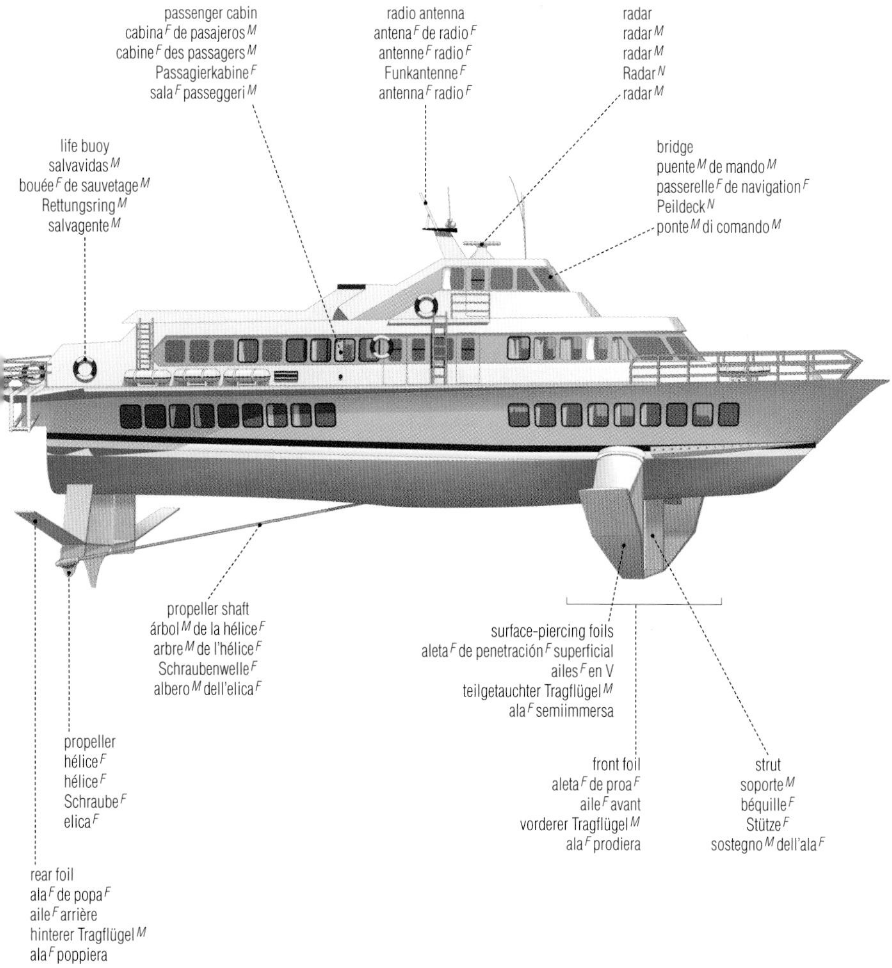
passenger cabin
cabina[F] de pasajeros[M]
cabine[F] des passagers[M]
Passagierkabine[F]
sala[F] passeggeri[M]
radio antenna
antena[F] de radio[F]
antenne[F] radio[F]
Funkantenne[F]
antenna[F] radio[F]
radar
radar[M]
radar[M]
Radar[N]
radar[M]
life buoy
salvavidas[M]
bouée[F] de sauvetage[M]
Rettungsring[M]
salvagente[M]
bridge
puente[M] de mando[M]
passerelle[F] de navigation[F]
Peildeck[N]
ponte[M] di comando[M]
propeller shaft
árbol[M] de la hélice[F]
arbre[M] de l'hélice[F]
Schraubenwelle[F]
albero[M] dell'elica[F]
surface-piercing foils
aleta[F] de penetración[F] superficial
ailes[F] en V
teilgetauchter Tragflügel[M]
ala[F] semiimmersa
propeller
hélice[F]
hélice[F]
Schraube[F]
elica[F]
front foil
aleta[F] de proa[F]
aile[F] avant
vorderer Tragflügel[M]
ala[F] prodiera
strut
soporte[M]
béquille[F]
Stütze[F]
sostegno[M] dell'ala[F]
rear foil
ala[F] de popa[F]
aile[F] arrière
hinterer Tragflügel[M]
ala[F] poppiera

examples of boats and ships

container ship
carguero *M* **portacontenedores**
navire *M* **porte-conteneurs** *M*
Containerschiff *N*
nave *F* **portacontainer** *M*

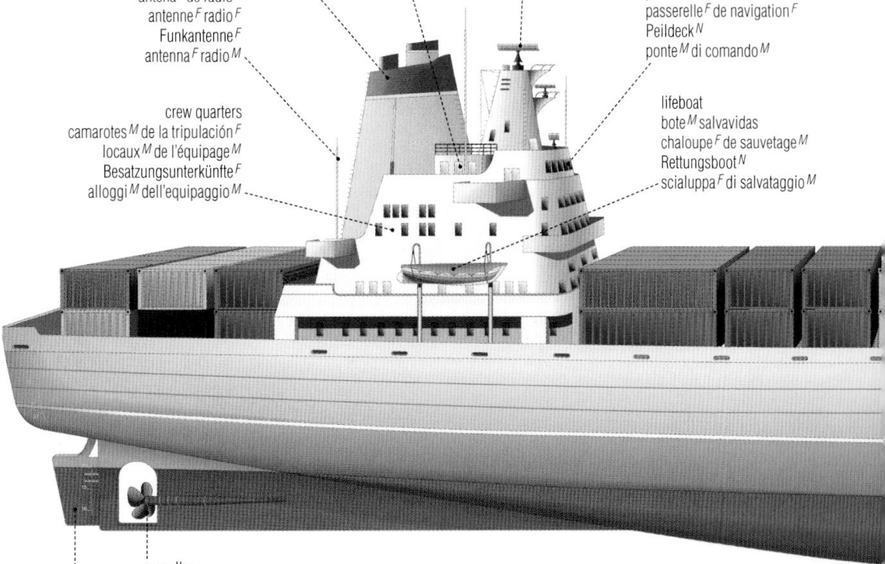

stack
chimenea F
cheminée F
Schornstein M
fumaiolo M
chart room
sala F de navegación F
salle F des cartes F
Kartenraum M
sala F nautica
radar
radar M
radar M
Radar N
radar M
radio antenna
antena F de radio F
antenne F radio F
Funkantenne F
antenna F radio M
bridge
puente M de mando M
passerelle F de navigation F
Peildeck N
ponte M di comando M
crew quarters
camarotes M de la tripulación F
locaux M de l'équipage M
Besatzungsunterkünfte F
alloggi M dell'equipaggio M
lifeboat
bote M salvavidas
chaloupe F de sauvetage M
Rettungsboot N
scialuppa F di salvataggio M
propeller
hélice F
hélice F
Schraube F
elica F
rudder
timón M
gouvernail M
Ruder N
timone M

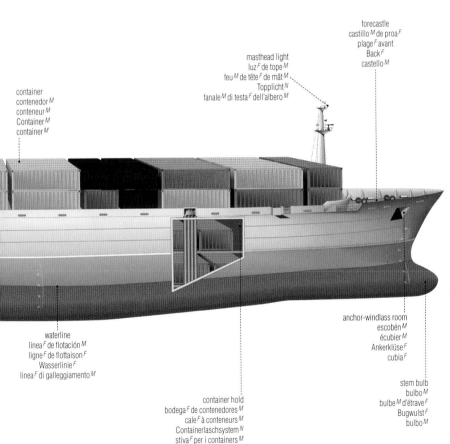

forecastle
castillo M de proa F
plage F avant
Back F
castello M
masthead light
luz F de tope M
feu M de tête F de mât M
Topplicht N
fanale M di testa F dell'albero M
container
contenedor M
conteneur M
Container M
container M
anchor-windlass room
escobén M
écubier M
Ankerklüse F
cubia F
waterline
línea F de flotación M
ligne F de flottaison F
Wasserlinie F
linea F di galleggiamento M
stem bulb
bulbo M
bulbe M d'étrave F
Bugwulst F
bulbo M
container hold
bodega F de contenedores M
cale F à conteneurs M
Containerlaschsystem N
stiva F per i containers M

hovercraft
aerodeslizador M (hovercraft M)
aéroglisseur M
Luftkissenfahrzeug N
hovercraft M

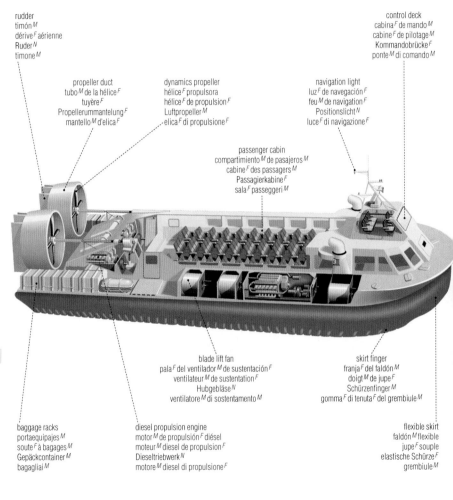

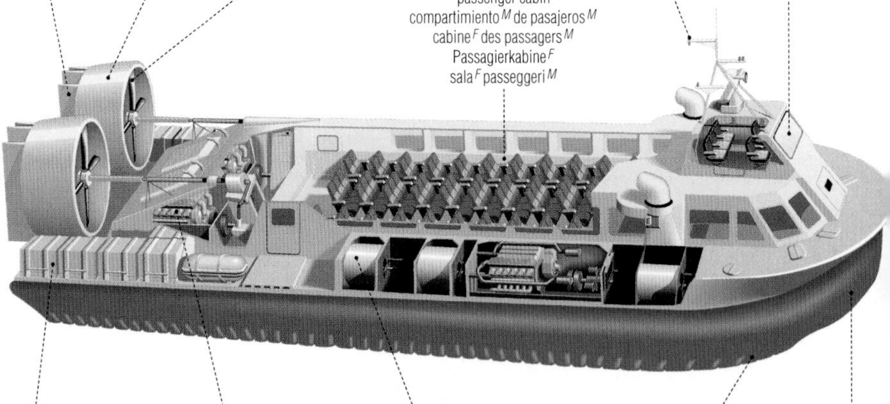
rudder
timón M
dérive F aérienne
Ruder N
timone M
control deck
cabina F de mando M
cabine F de pilotage M
Kommandobrücke F
ponte M di comando M
propeller duct
tubo M de la hélice F
tuyère F
Propellerummantelung F
mantello M d'elica F
dynamics propeller
hélice F propulsora
hélice F de propulsion F
Luftpropeller M
elica F di propulsione F
navigation light
luz F de navegación F
feu M de navigation F
Positionslicht N
luce F di navigazione F
passenger cabin
compartimiento M de pasajeros M
cabine F des passagers M
Passagierkabine F
sala F passeggeri M
blade lift fan
pala F del ventilador M de sustentación F
ventilateur M de sustentation F
Hubgebläse N
ventilatore M di sostentamento M
skirt finger
franja F del faldón M
doigt M de jupe F
Schürzenfinger M
gomma F di tenuta F del grembiule M
baggage racks
portaequipajes M
soute F à bagages M
Gepäckcontainer M
bagagliai M
diesel propulsion engine
motor M de propulsión F diésel
moteur M diesel de propulsion F
Dieseltriebwerk N
motore M diesel di propulsione F
flexible skirt
faldón M flexible
jupe F souple
elastische Schürze F
grembiule M

ferry boat
transbordador M
transbordeur M
Fähre F
nave F **traghetto** M

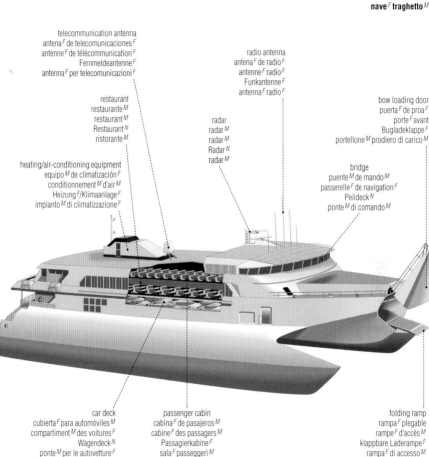

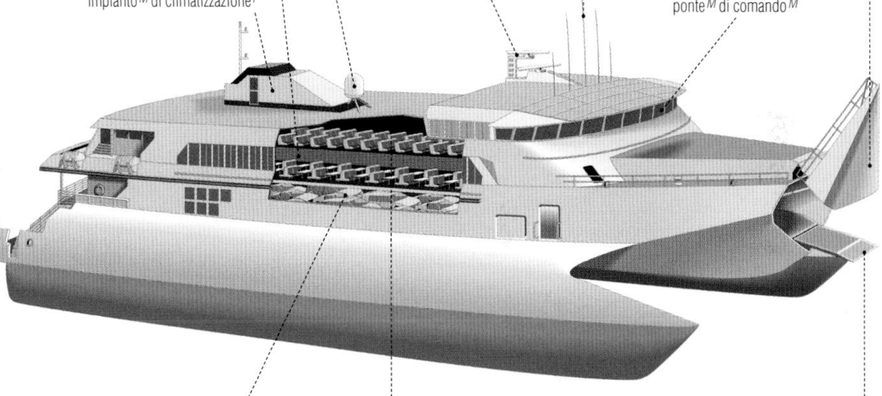
telecommunication antenna
antena F de telecomunicaciones F
antenne F de télécommunication F
Fernmeldeantenne F
antenna F per telecomunicazioni F
radio antenna
antena F de radio F
antenne F radio F
Funkantenne F
antenna F radio F
restaurant
restaurante M
restaurant M
Restaurant N
ristorante M
radar
radar M
radar M
Radar N
radar M
bow loading door
puerta F de proa F
porte F avant
Bugladeklappe F
portellone M prodiero di carico M
heating/air-conditioning equipment
equipo M de climatización F
conditionnement M d'air M
Heizung F/Klimaanlage F
impianto M di climatizzazione F
bridge
puente M de mando M
passerelle F de navigation F
Peildeck N
ponte M di comando M
car deck
cubierta F para automóviles M
compartiment M des voitures F
Wagendeck N
ponte M per le autovetture F
passenger cabin
cabina F de pasajeros M
cabine F des passagers M
Passagierkabine F
sala F passeggeri M
folding ramp
rampa F plegable
rampe F d'accès M
klappbare Laderampe F
rampa F di accesso M

examples of boats and ships

tanker
petrolero M
pétrolier M
Tanker M
nave F **cisterna** F

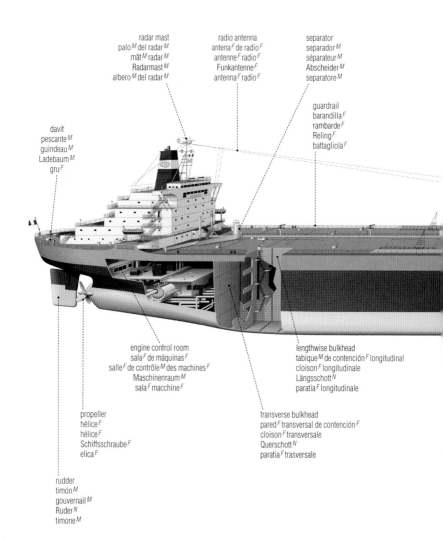

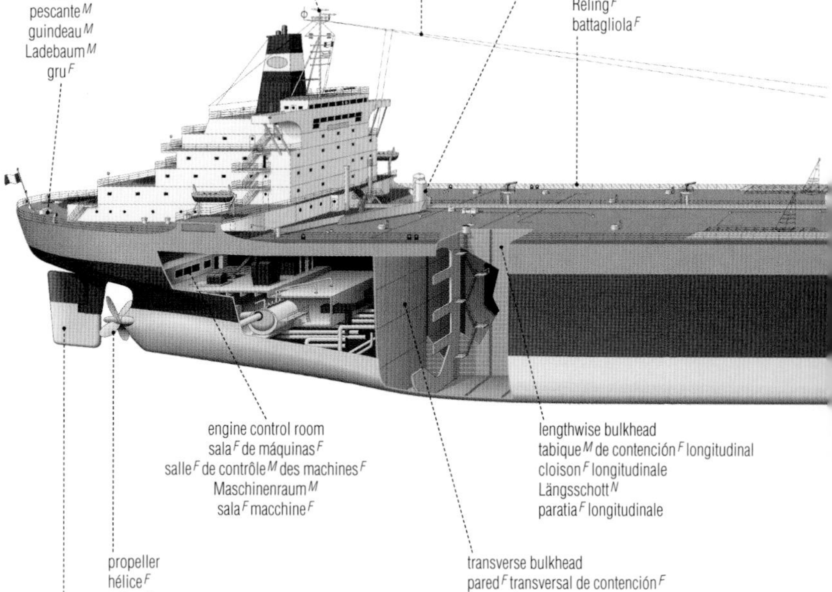
radar mast
palo M del radar M
mât M radar M
Radarmast M
albero M del radar M
radio antenna
antena F de radio F
antenne F radio F
Funkantenne F
antenna F radio F
separator
separador M
séparateur M
Abscheider M
separatore M
guardrail
barandilla F
rambarde F
Reling F
battagliola F
davit
pescante M
guindeau M
Ladebaum M
gru F
engine control room
sala F de máquinas F
salle F de contrôle M des machines F
Maschinenraum M
sala F macchine F
lengthwise bulkhead
tabique M de contención F longitudinal
cloison F longitudinale
Längsschott N
paratia F longitudinale
propeller
hélice F
hélice F
Schiffsschraube F
elica F
transverse bulkhead
pared F transversal de contención F
cloison F transversale
Querschott N
paratia F trasversale
rudder
timón M
gouvernail M
Ruder N
timone M

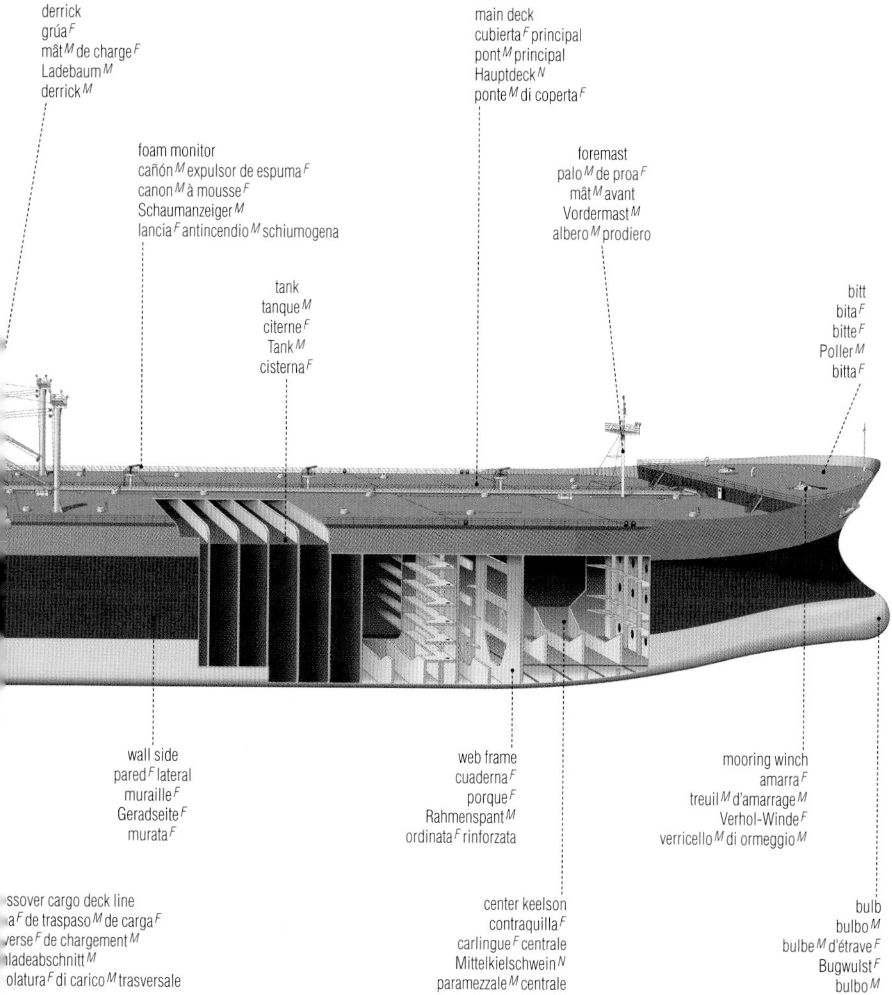
derrick
grúa F
mât M de charge F
Ladebaum M
derrick M
main deck
cubierta F principal
pont M principal
Hauptdeck N
ponte M di coperta F
foam monitor
cañón M expulsor de espuma F
canon M à mousse F
Schaumanzeiger M
lancia F antincendio M schiumogena
foremast
palo M de proa F
mât M avant
Vordermast M
albero M prodiero
tank
tanque M
citerne F
Tank M
cisterna F
bitt
bita F
bitte F
Poller M
bitta F
wall side
pared F lateral
muraille F
Geradseite F
murata F
web frame
cuaderna F
porque F
Rahmenspant M
ordinata F rinforzata
mooring winch
amarra F
treuil M d'amarrage M
Verhol-Winde F
verricello M di ormeggio M
ssover cargo deck line
a F de traspaso M de carga F
verse F de chargement M
ladeabschnitt M
olatura F di carico M trasversale
center keelson
contraquilla F
carlingue F centrale
Mittelkielschwein N
paramezzale M centrale
bulb
bulbo M
bulbe M d'étrave F
Bugwulst F
bulbo M

examples of boats and ships

passenger liner
buque[M] trasatlántico
paquebot[M]
Passagierdampfer[M]
transatlantico[M]

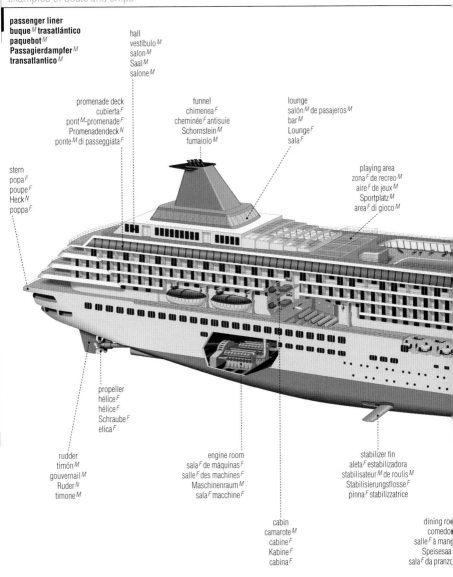

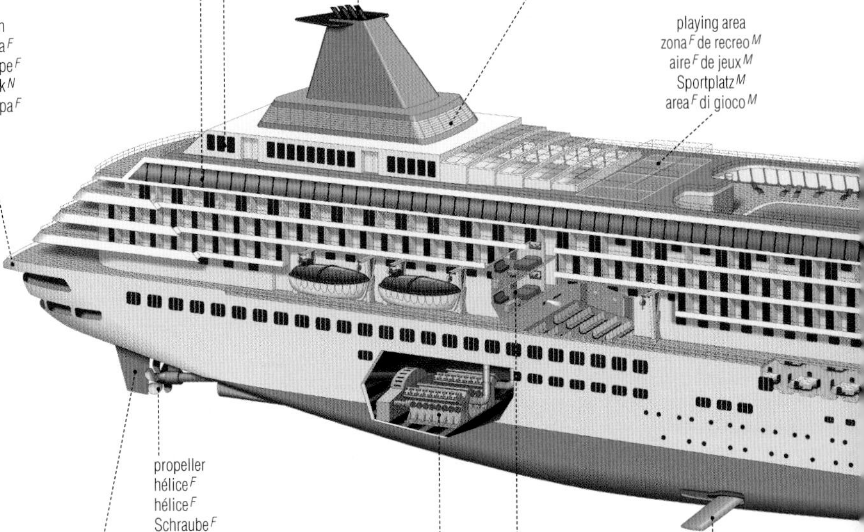
hall
vestíbulo[M]
salon[M]
Saal[M]
salone[M]
promenade deck
cubierta[F]
pont[M]-promenade[F]
Promenadendeck[N]
ponte[M] di passeggiata[F]
funnel
chimenea[F]
cheminée[F] antisuie
Schornstein[M]
fumaiolo[M]
lounge
salón[M] de pasajeros[M]
bar[M]
Lounge[F]
sala[F]
stern
popa[F]
poupe[F]
Heck[N]
poppa[F]
playing area
zona[F] de recreo[M]
aire[F] de jeux[M]
Sportplatz[M]
area[F] di gioco[M]
propeller
hélice[F]
hélice[F]
Schraube[F]
elica[F]
rudder
timón[M]
gouvernail[M]
Ruder[N]
timone[M]
engine room
sala[F] de máquinas[F]
salle[F] des machines[F]
Maschinenraum[M]
sala[F] macchine[F]
stabilizer fin
aleta[F] estabilizadora
stabilisateur[M] de roulis[M]
Stabilisierungsflosse[F]
pinna[F] stabilizzatrice
cabin
camarote[M]
cabine[F]
Kabine[F]
cabina[F]
dining ro
comedo
salle[F] à man
Speisesaa
sala[F] da pranz

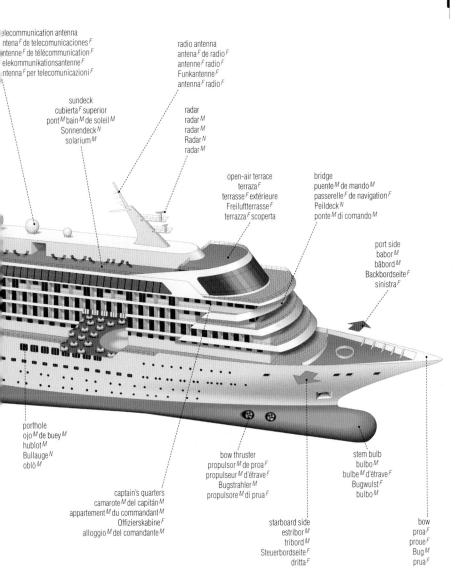

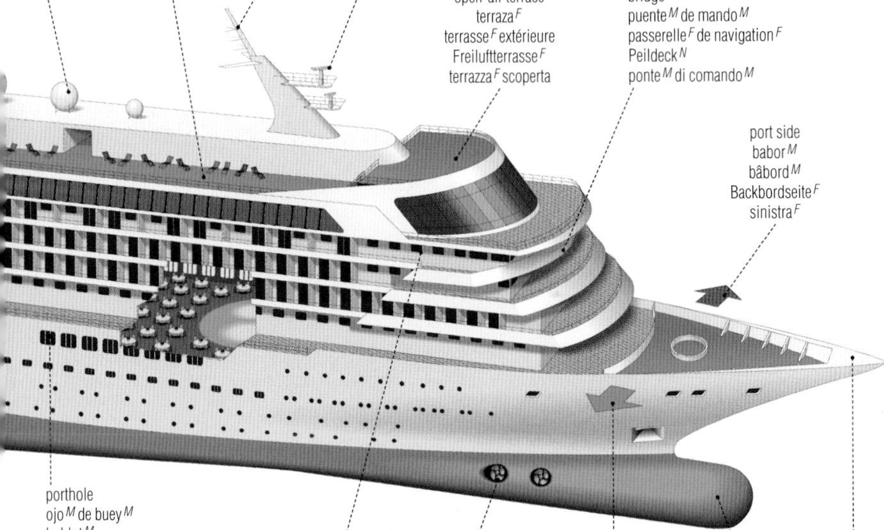
elecommunication antenna
ntena[F] de telecomunicaciones[F]
ntenne[F] de télécommunication[F]
elekommunikationsantenne[F]
ntenna[F] per telecomunicazioni[F]

radio antenna
antena[F] de radio[F]
antenne[F] radio[F]
Funkantenne[F]
antenna[F] radio[F]

sundeck
cubierta[F] superior
pont[M] bain[M] de soleil[M]
Sonnendeck[N]
solarium[M]

radar
radar[M]
radar[M]
Radar[N]
radar[M]

open-air terrace
terraza[F]
terrasse[F] extérieure
Freiluftterrasse[F]
terrazza[F] scoperta

bridge
puente[M] de mando[M]
passerelle[F] de navigation[F]
Peildeck[N]
ponte[M] di comando[M]

port side
babor[M]
bâbord[M]
Backbordseite[F]
sinistra[F]

porthole
ojo[M] de buey[M]
hublot[M]
Bullauge[N]
oblò[M]

bow thruster
propulsor[M] de proa[F]
propulseur[M] d'étrave[F]
Bugstrahler[M]
propulsore[M] di prua[F]

stem bulb
bulbo[M]
bulbe[M] d'étrave[F]
Bugwulst[F]
bulbo[M]

captain's quarters
camarote[M] del capitán[M]
appartement[M] du commandant[M]
Offizierskabine[F]
alloggio[M] del comandante[M]

starboard side
estribor[M]
tribord[M]
Steuerbordseite[F]
dritta[F]

bow
proa[F]
proue[F]
Bug[M]
prua[F]

airport

aeropuerto[M] | aéroport[M] | Flughafen[M] | aeroporto[M]

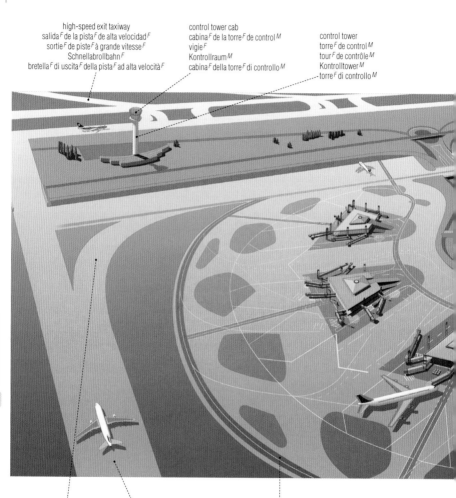

high-speed exit taxiway
salida[F] de la pista[F] de alta velocidad[F]
sortie[F] de piste[F] à grande vitesse[F]
Schnellabrollbahn[F]
bretella[F] di uscita[F] della pista[F] ad alta velocità[F]
control tower cab
cabina[F] de la torre[F] de control[M]
vigie[F]
Kontrollraum[M]
cabina[F] della torre[F] di controllo[M]
control tower
torre[F] de control[M]
tour[F] de contrôle[M]
Kontrolltower[M]
torre[F] di controllo[M]
by-pass taxiway
pista[F] de enlace[M]
bretelle[F]
Überholrollbahn[F]
pista[F] di accesso[M]
taxiway
pista[F] de rodaje[M]
voie[F] de circulation[F]
Rollbahn[F]
pista[F] di rullaggio[M]
service road
ruta[F] de servicio[M]
voie[F] de service[M]
Versorgungsstraße[M]
strada[F] di servizio[M]

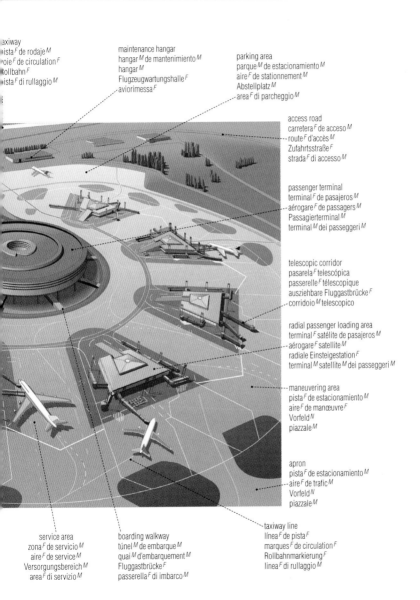

axiway
ista[F] de rodaje[M]
oie[F] de circulation[F]
ollbahn[F]
ista[F] di rullaggio[M]

maintenance hangar
hangar[M] de mantenimiento[M]
hangar[M]
Flugzeugwartungshalle[F]
aviorimessa[F]

parking area
parque[M] de estacionamiento[M]
aire[F] de stationnement[M]
Abstellplatz[M]
area[F] di parcheggio[M]

access road
carretera[F] de acceso[M]
route[F] d'accès[M]
Zufahrtsstraße[F]
strada[F] di accesso[M]

passenger terminal
terminal[F] de pasajeros[M]
aérogare[F] de passagers[M]
Passagierterminal[M]
terminal[M] dei passeggeri[M]

telescopic corridor
pasarela[F] telescópica
passerelle[F] télescopique
ausziehbare Fluggastbrücke[F]
corridoio[M] telescopico

radial passenger loading area
terminal[F] satélite de pasajeros[M]
aérogare[F] satellite[M]
radiale Einsteigestation[F]
terminal[M] satellite[M] dei passeggeri[M]

maneuvering area
pista[F] de estacionamiento[M]
aire[F] de manœuvre[F]
Vorfeld[N]
piazzale[M]

apron
pista[F] de estacionamiento[M]
aire[F] de trafic[M]
Vorfeld[N]
piazzale[M]

service area
zona[F] de servicio[M]
aire[F] de service[M]
Versorgungsbereich[M]
area[F] di servizio[M]

boarding walkway
túnel[M] de embarque[M]
quai[M] d'embarquement[M]
Fluggastbrücke[F]
passerella[F] di imbarco[M]

taxiway line
línea[F] de pista[F]
marques[F] de circulation[F]
Rollbahnmarkierung[F]
linea[F] di rullaggio[M]

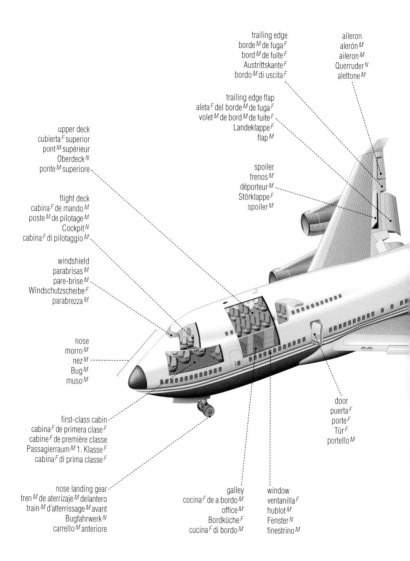

long-range jet

avión[M] turborreactor de pasajeros[M] | avion[M] long-courrier[M] | Langstrecken-Düsenflugzeug[N] | aviogetto[M] a lungo raggio[M]

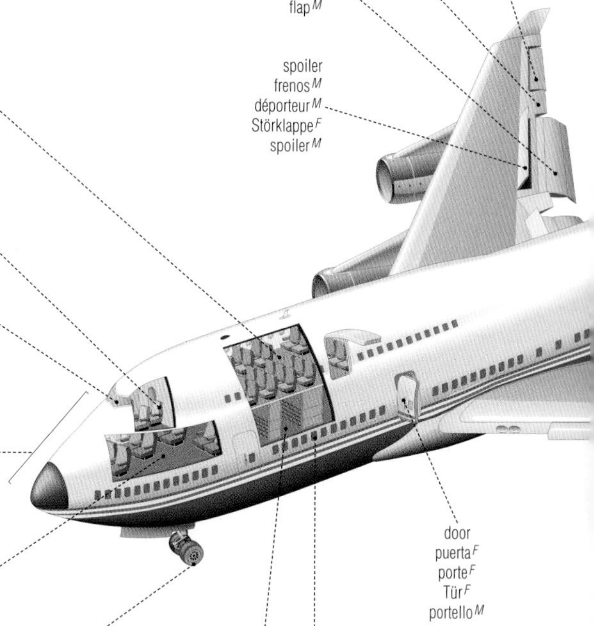

trailing edge
borde[M] de fuga[F]
bord[M] de fuite[F]
Austrittskante[F]
bordo[M] di uscita[F]
aileron
alerón[M]
aileron[M]
Querruder[N]
alettone[M]
trailing edge flap
aleta[F] del borde[M] de fuga[F]
volet[M] de bord[M] de fuite[F]
Landeklappe[F]
flap[M]
upper deck
cubierta[F] superior
pont[M] supérieur
Oberdeck[N]
ponte[M] superiore
spoiler
frenos[M]
déporteur[M]
Störklappe[F]
spoiler[M]
flight deck
cabina[F] de mando[M]
poste[M] de pilotage[M]
Cockpit[N]
cabina[F] di pilotaggio[M]
windshield
parabrisas[M]
pare-brise[M]
Windschutzscheibe[F]
parabrezza[M]
nose
morro[M]
nez[M]
Bug[M]
muso[M]
door
puerta[F]
porte[F]
Tür[F]
portello[M]
first-class cabin
cabina[F] de primera clase[F]
cabine[F] de première classe
Passagierraum[M] 1. Klasse[F]
cabina[F] di prima classe[F]
nose landing gear
tren[M] de aterrizaje[M] delantero
train[M] d'atterrissage[M] avant
Bugfahrwerk[N]
carrello[M] anteriore
galley
cocina[F] de a bordo[M]
office[M]
Bordküche[F]
cucina[F] di bordo[M]
window
ventanilla[F]
hublot[M]
Fenster[N]
finestrino[M]

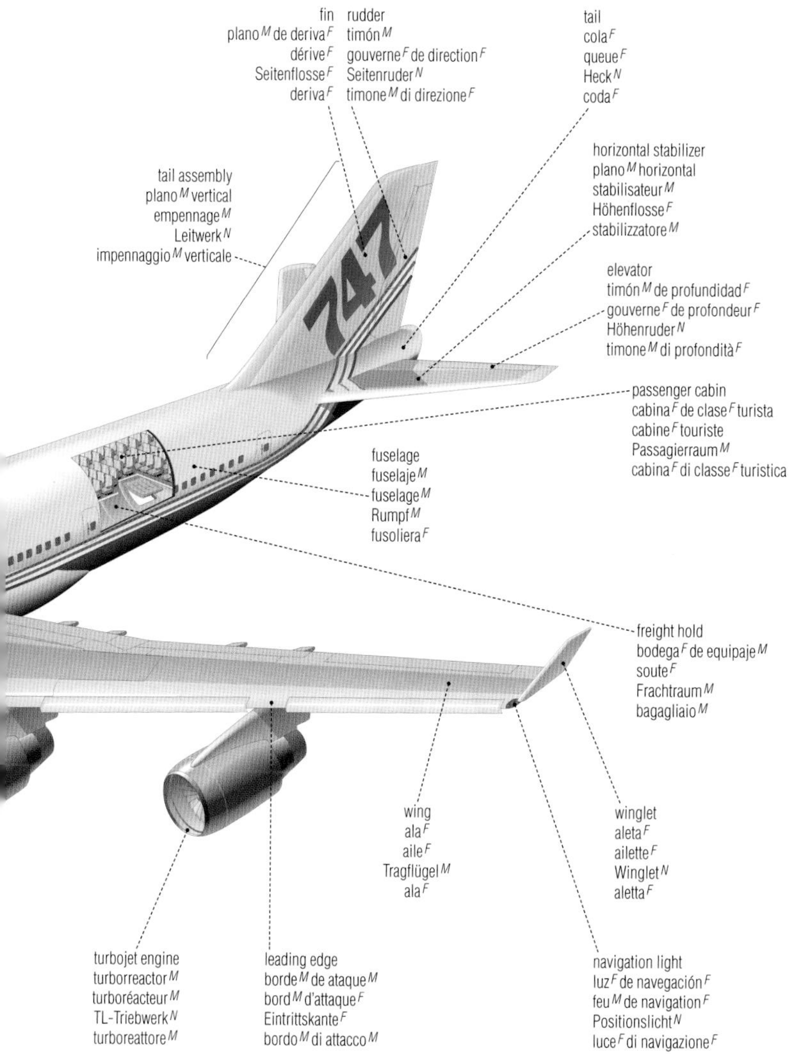
fin
plano[M] de deriva[F]
dérive[F]
Seitenflosse[F]
deriva[F]
rudder
timón[M]
gouverne[F] de direction[F]
Seitenruder[N]
timone[M] di direzione[F]
tail
cola[F]
queue[F]
Heck[N]
coda[F]
horizontal stabilizer
plano[M] horizontal
stabilisateur[M]
Höhenflosse[F]
stabilizzatore[M]
tail assembly
plano[M] vertical
empennage[M]
Leitwerk[N]
impennaggio[M] verticale
elevator
timón[M] de profundidad[F]
gouverne[F] de profondeur[F]
Höhenruder[N]
timone[M] di profondità[F]
747
passenger cabin
cabina[F] de clase[F] turista
cabine[F] touriste
Passagierraum[M]
cabina[F] di classe[F] turistica
fuselage
fuselaje[M]
fuselage[M]
Rumpf[M]
fusoliera[F]
freight hold
bodega[F] de equipaje[M]
soute[F]
Frachtraum[M]
bagagliaio[M]
wing
ala[F]
aile[F]
Tragflügel[M]
ala[F]
winglet
aleta[F]
ailette[F]
Winglet[N]
aletta[F]
turbojet engine
turborreactor[M]
turboréacteur[M]
TL-Triebwerk[N]
turboreattore[M]
leading edge
borde[M] de ataque[M]
bord[M] d'attaque[F]
Eintrittskante[F]
bordo[M] di attacco[M]
navigation light
luz[F] de navegación[F]
feu[M] de navigation[F]
Positionslicht[N]
luce[F] di navigazione[F]

examples of airplanes

ejemplos^M de aviones^M | exemples^M d'avions^M | Beispiele^N für Flugzeuge^N | esempi^M di aeroplani^M

float seaplane
hidroavión^M de flotadores^M
hydravion^M à flotteurs^M
Wasserflugzeug^N
idrovolante^M a due galleggianti^M

three-blade propeller
hélice^F de tres aspas^F
hélice^F tripale
dreiflügeliger Propeller^M
elica^F tripala
high wing
ala^F alta
aile^F haute
Tragflügel^M
ala^F alta
wing strut
montante^M
hauban^M
Flügelstrebe^F
montante^M dell'ala^F
float
flotador^M
flotteur^M
Schwimmkörper^M
galleggiante^M

biplane
biplano^M
biplan^M
Doppeldecker^M
biplano^M

upper wing
ala^F superior
aile^F supérieure
oberer Flügel^M
ala^F superiore
wings
alas^F
voilure^F
Flügel^M
ali^F
lower wing
ala^F alta
aile^F inférieure
unterer Flügel^M
ala^F inferiore

light aircraft
avión^M ligero
avion^M léger
Leichtflugzeug^N
aeroplano^M leggero

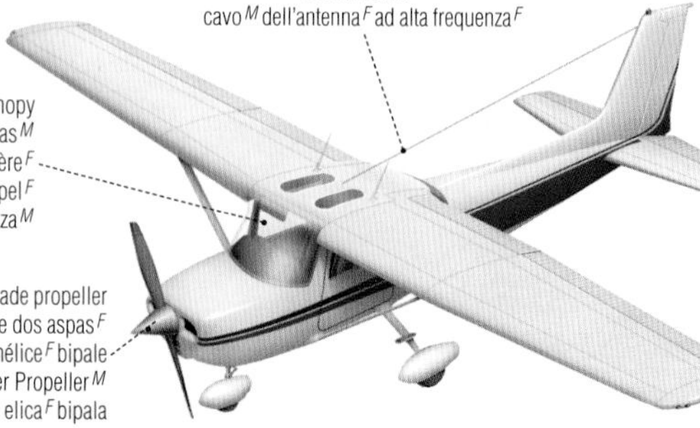
high frequency antenna cable
cable^M de la antena^F de alta frecuencia^F
câble^M de l'antenne^F haute fréquence^F
Funkantenne^F
cavo^M dell'antenna^F ad alta frequenza^F
canopy
parabrisas^M
verrière^F
Kuppel^F
parabrezza^M
two-blade propeller
hélice^F de dos aspas^F
hélice^F bipale
zweiflügeliger Propeller^M
elica^F bipala

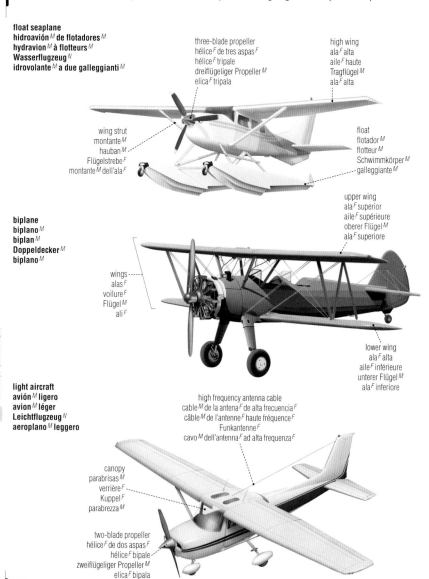

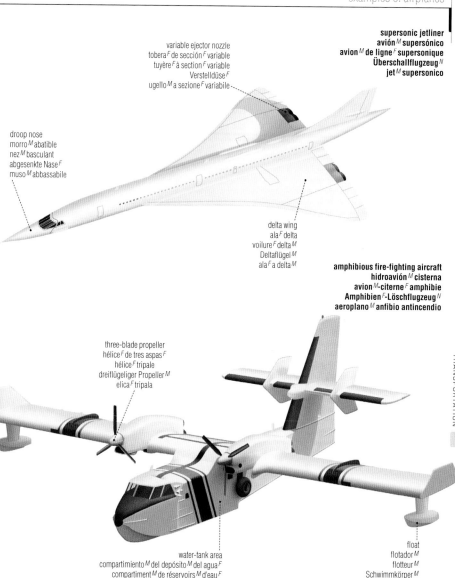

supersonic jetliner
avión[M] supersónico
avion[M] de ligne[F] supersonique
Überschallflugzeug[N]
jet[M] supersonico

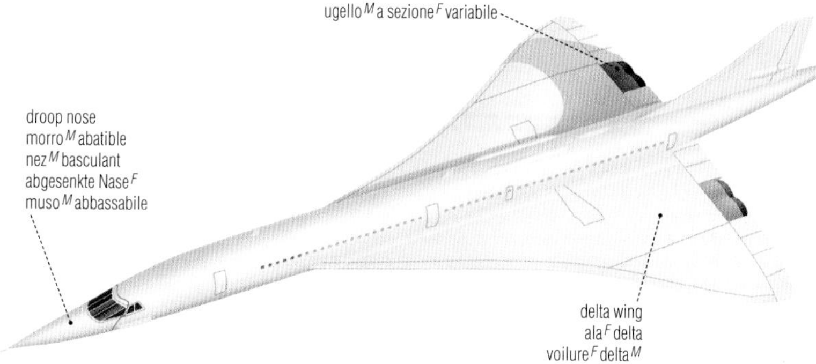
variable ejector nozzle
tobera[F] de sección[F] variable
tuyère[F] à section[F] variable
Verstelldüse[F]
ugello[M] a sezione[F] variabile
droop nose
morro[M] abatible
nez[M] basculant
abgesenkte Nase[F]
muso[M] abbassabile
delta wing
ala[F] delta
voilure[F] delta[M]
Deltaflügel[M]
ala[F] a delta[M]

amphibious fire-fighting aircraft
hidroavión[M] cisterna
avion[M]-citerne[F] amphibie
Amphibien[F]-Löschflugzeug[N]
aeroplano[M] anfibio antincendio

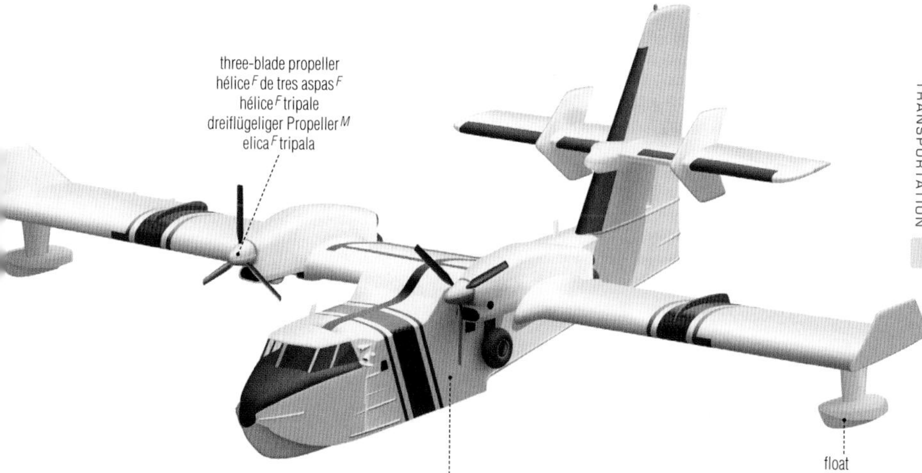
three-blade propeller
hélice[F] de tres aspas[F]
hélice[F] tripale
dreiflügeliger Propeller[M]
elica[F] tripala
water-tank area
compartimiento[M] del depósito[M] del agua[F]
compartiment[M] de réservoirs[M] d'eau[F]
Wassertank[M]
vano[M] del serbatoio[M] dell'acqua[F]
float
flotador[M]
flotteur[M]
Schwimmkörper[M]
galleggiante[M]

examples of airplanes

business aircraft
avión ᴹ particular
avion ᴹ d'affaires ᶠ
Privatflugzeug ᴺ
aeroplano ᴹ privato

winglet
aleta F
ailette F
Flosse F
aletta F

cargo aircraft
avión ᴹ de carga ᶠ
avion ᴹ-cargo ᴹ
Frachtflugzeug ᴺ
aeroplano ᴹ da carico ᴹ

superjumbo jet
avión ᴹ de gran capacidad ᶠ
avion ᴹ très gros porteur
Großraumflugzeug ᴺ
superjumbo ᴹ

examples of airplanes

vertical take-off and landing (VTOL) aircraft
avión[M] de despegue[M] y aterrizaje[M] verticales
avion[M] à décollage[M] et atterrissage[M] verticaux
Senkrechtstartflugzeug[N]
aeroplano[M] a decollo[M] e atterraggio[M] verticale

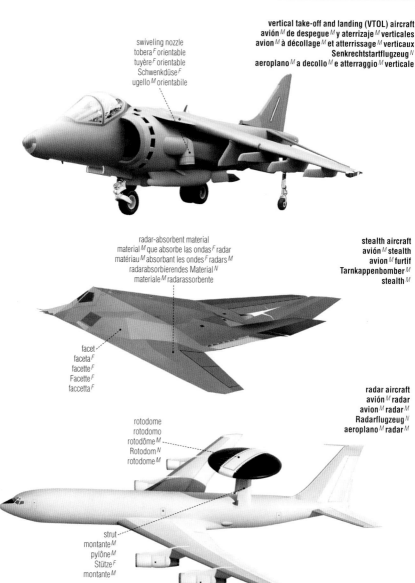

swiveling nozzle
tobera[F] orientable
tuyère[F] orientable
Schwenkdüse[F]
ugello[M] orientabile

stealth aircraft
avión[M] stealth
avion[M] furtif
Tarnkappenbomber[M]
stealth[M]

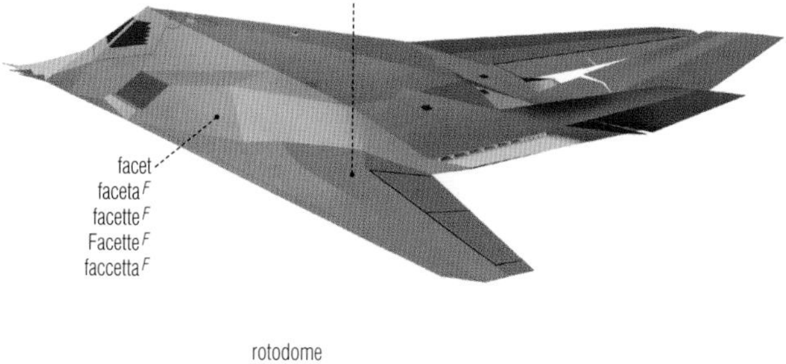
radar-absorbent material
material[M] que absorbe las ondas[F] radar
matériau[M] absorbant les ondes[F] radars[M]
radarabsorbierendes Material[N]
materiale[M] radarassorbente
facet
faceta[F]
facette[F]
Facette[F]
faccetta[F]

radar aircraft
avión[M] radar
avion[M] radar[M]
Radarflugzeug[N]
aeroplano[M] radar[M]

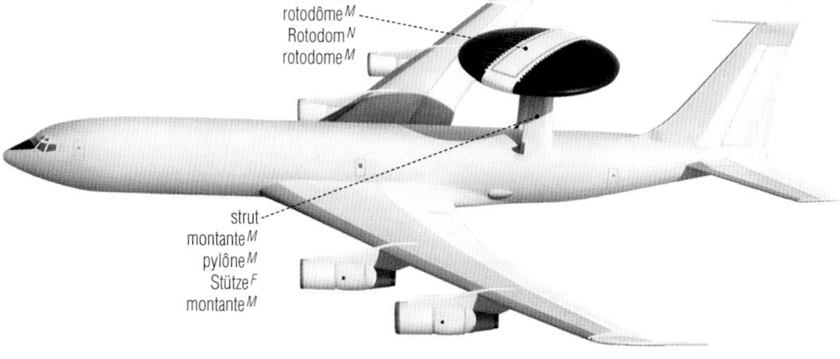
rotodome
rotodomo
rotodôme[M]
Rotodom[N]
rotodome[M]
strut
montante[M]
pylône[M]
Stütze[F]
montante[M]

TRANSPORTATION

helicopter

helicóptero M | hélicoptère M | Hubschrauber M | elicottero M

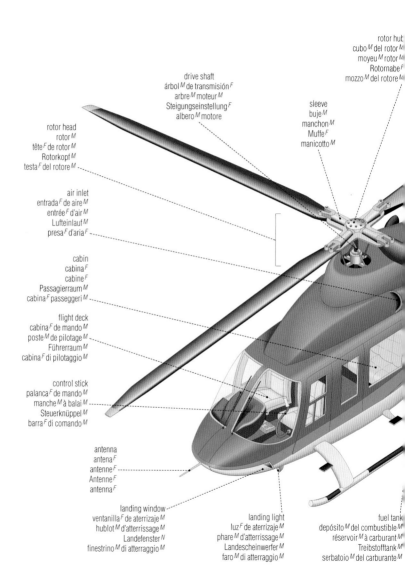

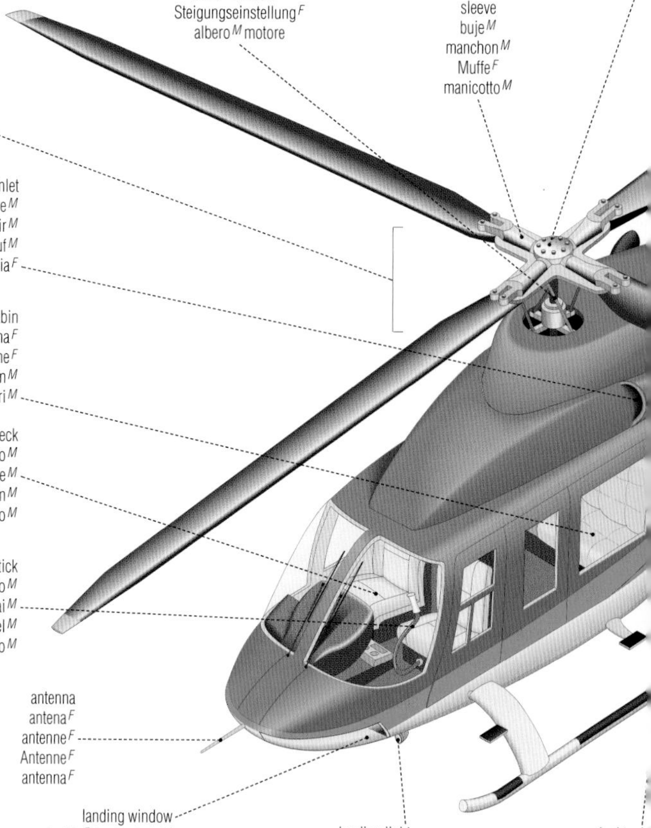
rotor huk
cubo M del rotor M
moyeu M rotor M
Rotornabe F
mozzo M del rotore M
drive shaft
árbol M de transmisión F
arbre M moteur M
Steigungseinstellung F
albero M motore
sleeve
buje M
manchon M
Muffe F
manicotto M
rotor head
rotor M
tête F de rotor M
Rotorkopf M
testa F del rotore M
air inlet
entrada F de aire M
entrée F d'air M
Lufteinlauf M
presa F d'aria F
cabin
cabina F
cabine F
Passagierraum M
cabina F passeggeri M
flight deck
cabina F de mando M
poste M de pilotage M
Führerraum M
cabina F di pilotaggio M
control stick
palanca F de mando M
manche M à balai M
Steuerknüppel M
barra F di comando M
antenna
antena F
antenne F
Antenne F
antenna F
landing window
ventanilla F de aterrizaje M
hublot M d'atterrissage M
Landefenster N
finestrino M di atterraggio M
landing light
luz F de aterrizaje M
phare M d'atterrissage M
Landescheinwerfer M
faro M di atterraggio M
fuel tank
depósito M del combustible M
réservoir M à carburant M
Treibstofftank M
serbatoio M del carburante M

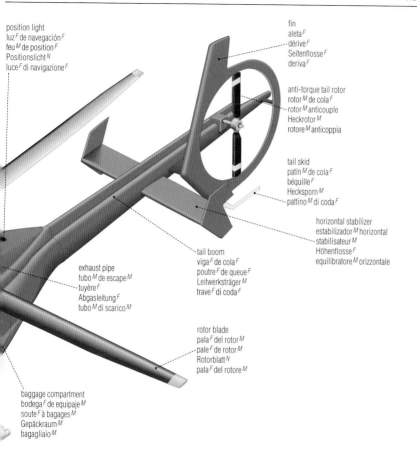

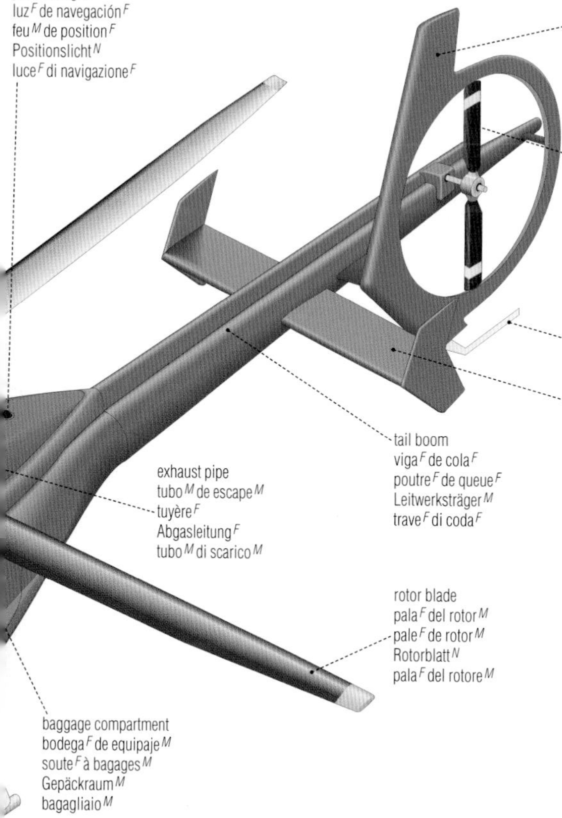
position light
luz[F] de navegación[F]
feu[M] de position[F]
Positionslicht[N]
luce[F] di navigazione[F]
fin
aleta[F]
dérive[F]
Seitenflosse[F]
deriva[F]
anti-torque tail rotor
rotor[M] de cola[F]
rotor[M] anticouple
Heckrotor[M]
rotore[M] anticoppia
tail skid
patín[M] de cola[F]
béquille[F]
Hecksporn[M]
pattino[M] di coda[F]
horizontal stabilizer
estabilizador[M] horizontal
stabilisateur[M]
Höhenflosse[F]
equilibratore[M] orizzontale
tail boom
viga[F] de cola[F]
poutre[F] de queue[F]
Leitwerksträger[M]
trave[F] di coda[F]
exhaust pipe
tubo[M] de escape[M]
tuyère[F]
Abgasleitung[F]
tubo[M] di scarico[M]
rotor blade
pala[F] del rotor[M]
pale[F] de rotor[M]
Rotorblatt[N]
pala[F] del rotore[M]
baggage compartment
bodega[F] de equipaje[M]
soute[F] à bagages[M]
Gepäckraum[M]
bagagliaio[M]
skid
patín[M] de aterrizaje[M]
patin[M]
Kufe[F]
pattino[M]

matter

materia^F | matière^F | Materie^F | materia^F

atom
átomo^M
atome^M
Atom^N
atomo^M

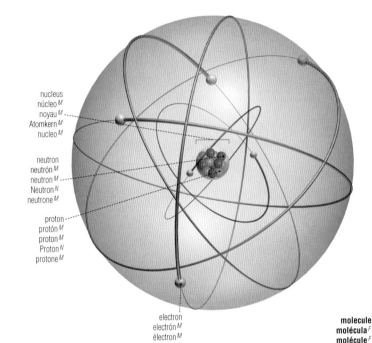

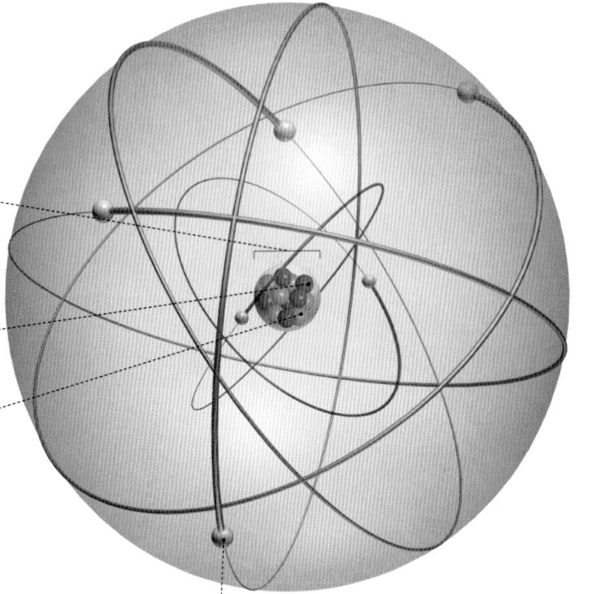
nucleus
núcleo M
noyau M
Atomkern M
nucleo M
neutron
neutrón M
neutron M
Neutron N
neutrone M
proton
protón M
proton M
Proton N
protone M
electron
electrón M
électron M
Elektron N
elettrone M

proton
protón^M
proton^M
Proton^N
protone^M

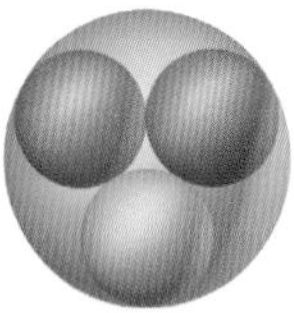

neutron
neutrón^M
neutron^M
Neutron^N
neutrone^M

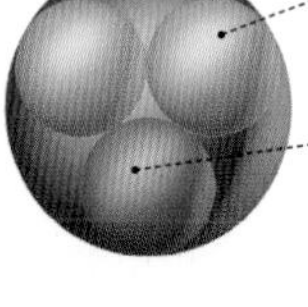
d quark
quark M d
quark M d
Down-Quark N
quark M d
u quark
quark M u
quark M u
Up-Quark N
quark M u

molecule
molécula^F
molécule^F
Molekül^N
molecola^F

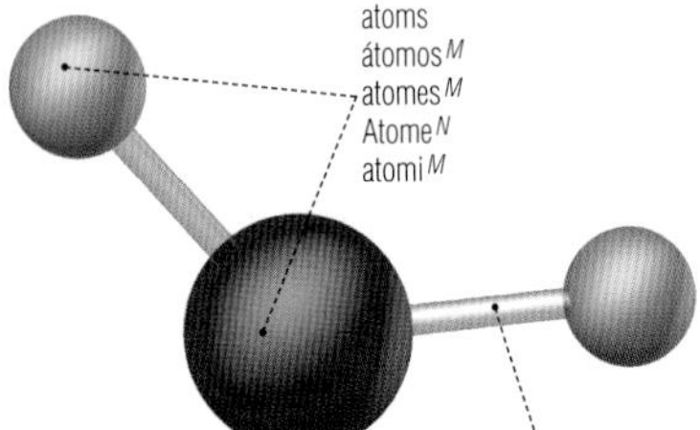
atoms
átomos M
atomes M
Atome N
atomi M
chemical bond
enlace M químico
liaison F chimique
chemische Bindung F
legame M chimico

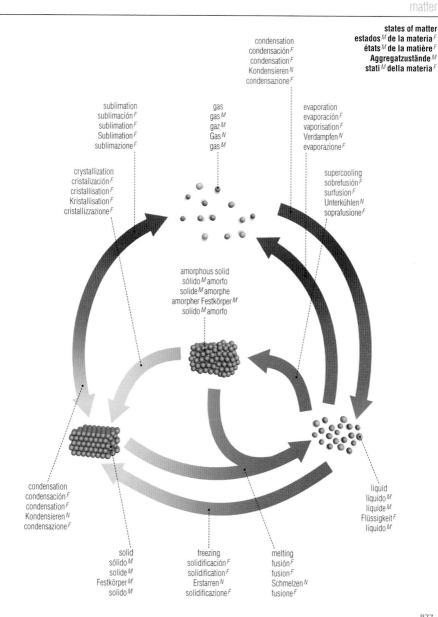

states of matter
estados^M de la materia^F
états^M de la matière^F
Aggregatzustände^M
stati^M della materia^F

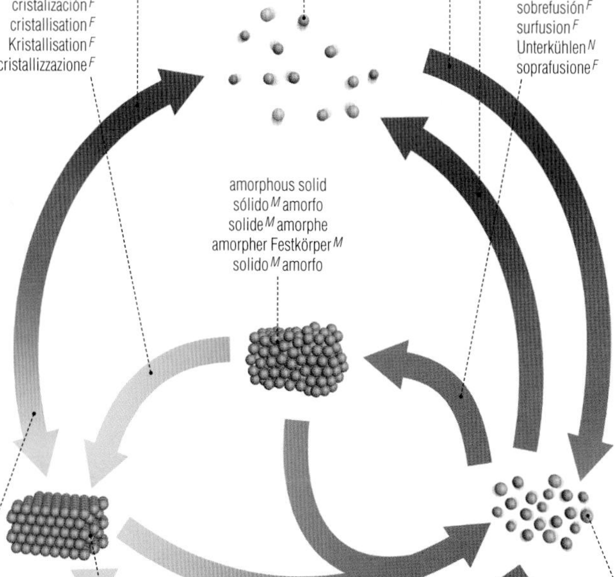
condensation
condensación^F
condensation^F
Kondensieren^N
condensazione^F
sublimation
sublimación^F
sublimation^F
Sublimation^F
sublimazione^F
gas
gas^M
gaz^M
Gas^N
gas^M
evaporation
evaporación^F
vaporisation^F
Verdampfen^N
evaporazione^F
crystallization
cristalización^F
cristallisation^F
Kristallisation^F
cristallizzazione^F
supercooling
sobrefusión^F
surfusion^F
Unterkühlen^N
soprafusione^F
amorphous solid
sólido^M amorfo
solide^M amorphe
amorpher Festkörper^M
solido^M amorfo
condensation
condensación^F
condensation^F
Kondensieren^N
condensazione^F
liquid
líquido^M
liquide^M
Flüssigkeit^F
liquido^M
solid
sólido^M
solide^M
Festkörper^M
solido^M
freezing
solidificación^F
solidification^F
Erstarren^N
solidificazione^F
melting
fusión^F
fusion^F
Schmelzen^N
fusione^F

nuclear fission
fisión[F] nuclear
fission[F] nucléaire
Kernspaltung[F]
fissione[F] nucleare

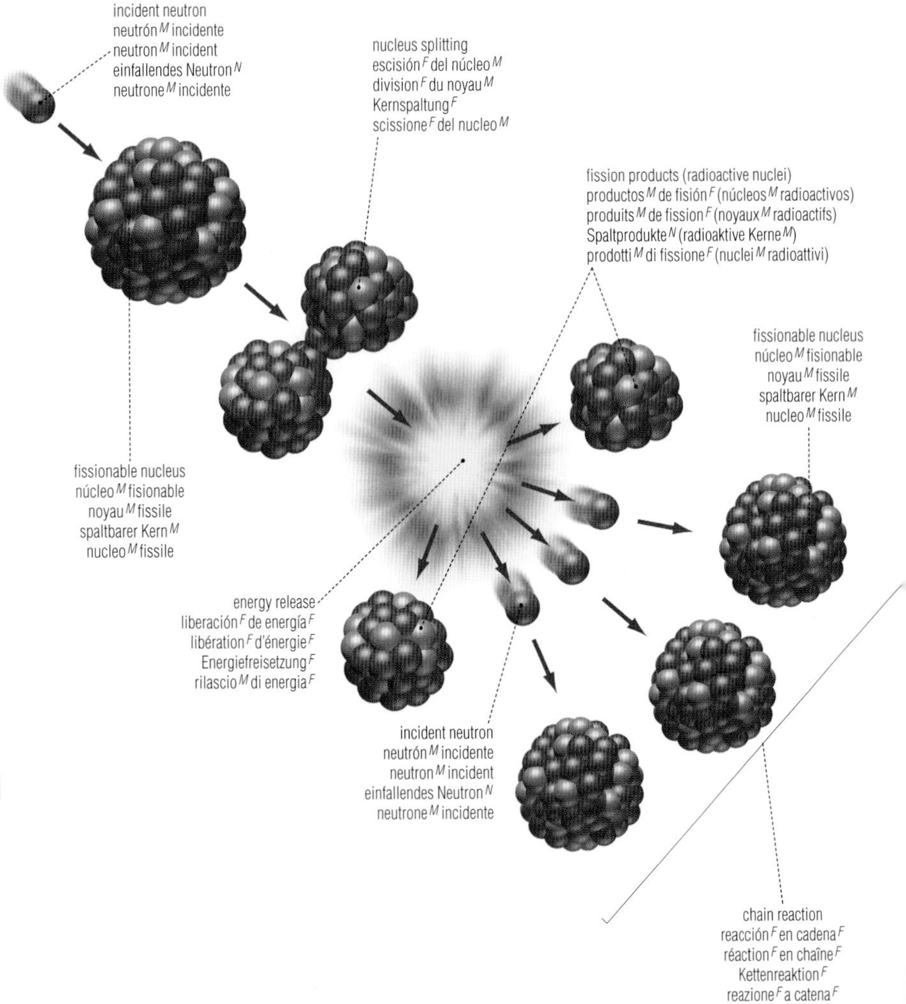
incident neutron
neutrón[M] incidente
neutron[M] incident
einfallendes Neutron[N]
neutrone[M] incidente
nucleus splitting
escisión[F] del núcleo[M]
division[F] du noyau[M]
Kernspaltung[F]
scissione[F] del nucleo[M]
fission products (radioactive nuclei)
productos[M] de fisión[F] (núcleos[M] radioactivos)
produits[M] de fission[F] (noyaux[M] radioactifs)
Spaltprodukte[N] (radioaktive Kerne[M])
prodotti[M] di fissione[F] (nuclei[M] radioattivi)
fissionable nucleus
núcleo[M] fisionable
noyau[M] fissile
spaltbarer Kern[M]
nucleo[M] fissile
fissionable nucleus
núcleo[M] fisionable
noyau[M] fissile
spaltbarer Kern[M]
nucleo[M] fissile
energy release
liberación[F] de energía[F]
libération[F] d'énergie[F]
Energiefreisetzung[F]
rilascio[M] di energia[F]
incident neutron
neutrón[M] incidente
neutron[M] incident
einfallendes Neutron[N]
neutrone[M] incidente
chain reaction
reacción[F] en cadena[F]
réaction[F] en chaîne[F]
Kettenreaktion[F]
reazione[F] a catena[F]

heat transfer
transmisión^F de calor^M
transfert^M de la chaleur^F
Wärmeübertragung^F
trasferimento^M di calore^M

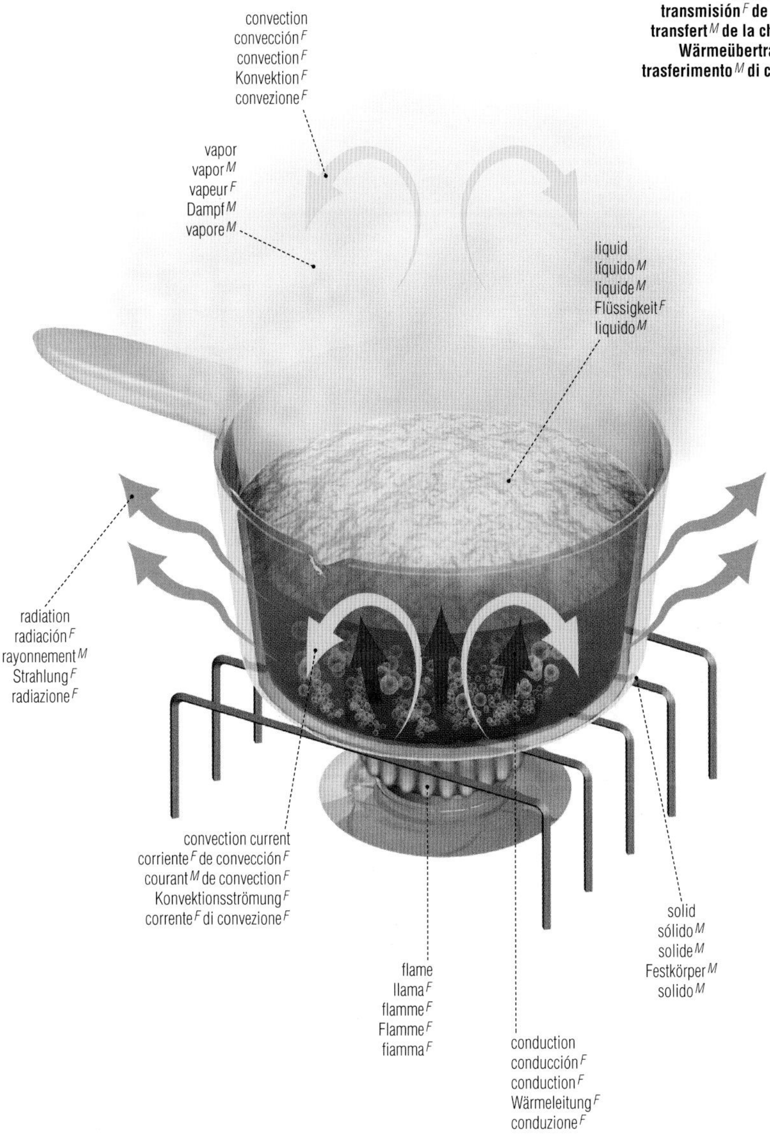
convection
convección F
convection F
Konvektion F
convezione F
vapor
vapor M
vapeur F
Dampf M
vapore M
liquid
líquido M
liquide M
Flüssigkeit F
liquido M
radiation
radiación F
rayonnement M
Strahlung F
radiazione F
convection current
corriente F de convección F
courant M de convection F
Konvektionsströmung F
corrente F di convezione F
solid
sólido M
solide M
Festkörper M
solido M
flame
llama F
flamme F
Flamme F
fiamma F
conduction
conducción F
conduction F
Wärmeleitung F
conduzione F

chemistry symbols

símbolos^M químicos | symboles^M de chimie^F | chemische Symbole^N | simboli^M chimici

$-$

negative charge
elemento^M negativo
négatif^M
negativ geladen
carica^F negativa

$+$

positive charge
elemento^M positivo
positif^M
positiv geladen
carica^F positiva

$\rightleftarrows$

reversible reaction
reacción^F
réaction^F réversible
reversible Reaktion^F
reazione^F reversibile

$\longrightarrow$

reaction direction
dirección^F
direction^F d'une réaction^F
Reaktionsrichtung^F
direzione^F della reazione^F

lever

palanca^F | levier^M | Hebel^M | leva^F

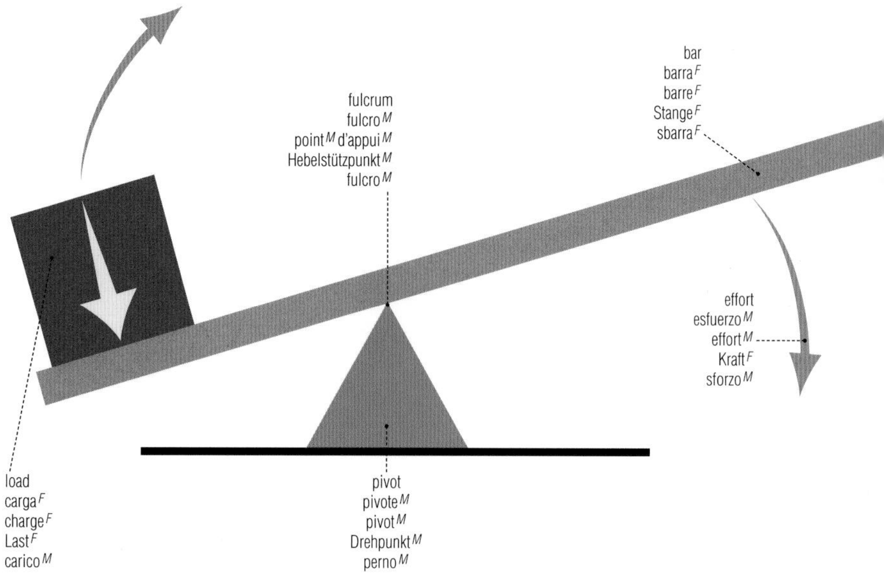
bar
barra^F
barre^F
Stange^F
sbarra^F
fulcrum
fulcro^M
point^M d'appui^M
Hebelstützpunkt^M
fulcro^M
effort
esfuerzo^M
effort^M
Kraft^F
sforzo^M
load
carga^F
charge^F
Last^F
carico^M
pivot
pivote^M
pivot^M
Drehpunkt^M
perno^M

gearing systems

sistemas[M] de engranajes[F] | engrenages[M] | Zahnradgetriebe[N] | sistemi[M] di ingranaggio[M]

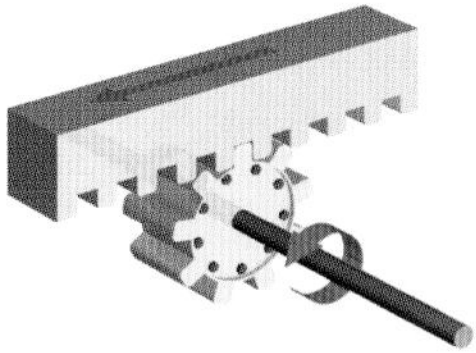

rack and pinion gear
engranaje[M] de piñón[M] y cremallera[F]
engrenage[M] à pignon[M] et crémaillère[F]
Zahnstangengetriebe[N]
ingranaggio[M] a pignone[M] e cremagliera[F]

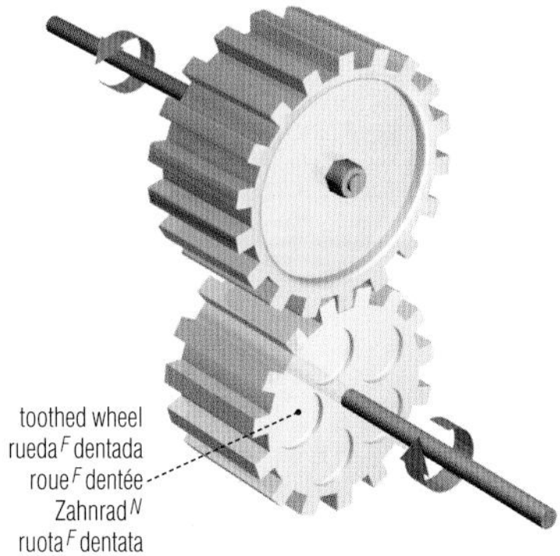
toothed wheel
rueda[F] dentada
roue[F] dentée
Zahnrad[N]
ruota[F] dentata

spur gear
rueda[F] cilíndrica de dientes[M] rectos
engrenage[M] cylindrique à denture[F] droite
Stirnradgetriebe[N]
ingranaggio[M] cilindrico a ruote[F] dentate

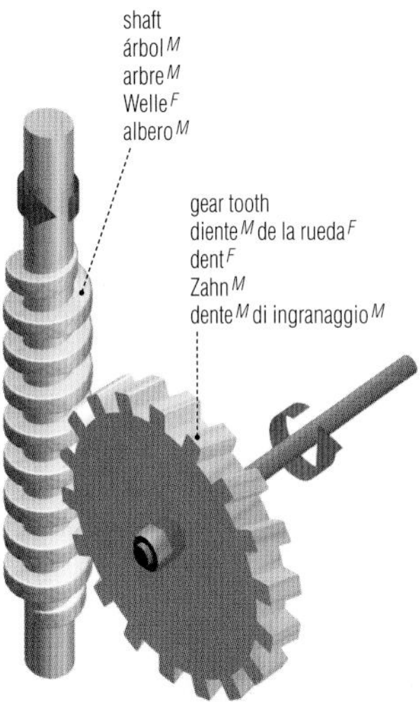
shaft
árbol[M]
arbre[M]
Welle[F]
albero[M]
gear tooth
diente[M] de la rueda[F]
dent[F]
Zahn[M]
dente[M] di ingranaggio[M]

worm gear
engranaje[M] de tornillo[M] sin fin
engrenage[M] à vis[F] sans fin[F]
Schneckengetriebe[N]
ruota[F] elicoidale

bevel gear
engranaje[M] cónico
engrenage[M] conique
Kegelradgetriebe[N]
ingranaggio[M] conico

double pulley system

sistema^F de doble polea^F | système^M à deux poulies^F | einfacher Flaschenzug^M | sistema^M a doppia puleggia^F

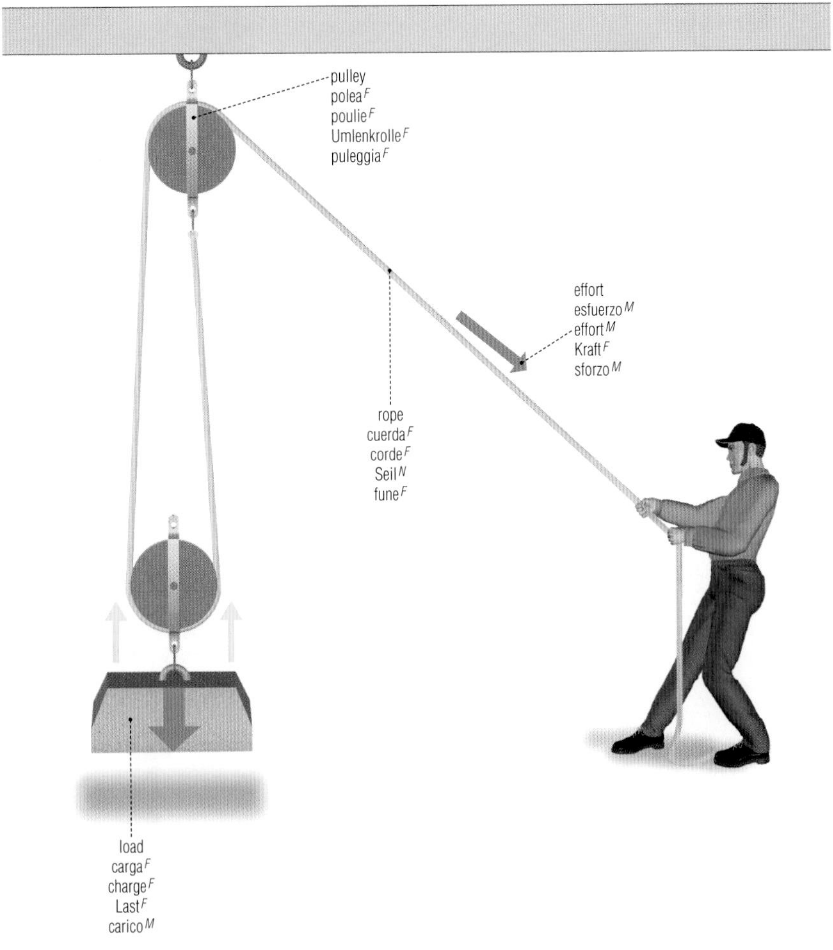
pulley
polea F
poulie F
Umlenkrolle F
puleggia F
effort
esfuerzo M
effort M
Kraft F
sforzo M
rope
cuerda F
corde F
Seil N
fune F
load
carga F
charge F
Last F
carico M

parallel electrical circuit

circuito^M eléctrico en paralelo^M | circuit^M électrique en parallèle^F | Parallelschaltung^F | circuito^M elettrico parallelo

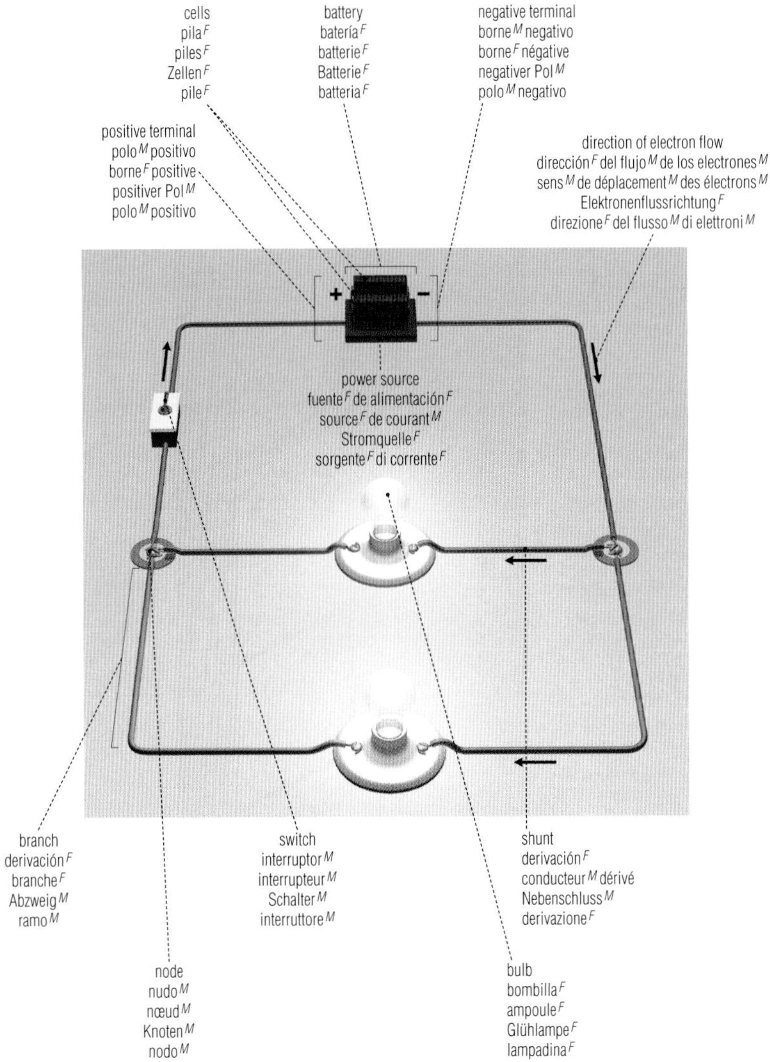
cells
pila^F
piles^F
Zellen^F
pile^F
battery
batería^F
batterie^F
Batterie^F
batteria^F
negative terminal
borne^M negativo
borne^F négative
negativer Pol^M
polo^M negativo
positive terminal
polo^M positivo
borne^F positive
positiver Pol^M
polo^M positivo
direction of electron flow
dirección^F del flujo^M de los electrones^M
sens^M de déplacement^M des électrons^M
Elektronenflussrichtung^F
direzione^F del flusso^M di elettroni^M
+
–
power source
fuente^F de alimentación^F
source^F de courant^M
Stromquelle^F
sorgente^F di corrente^F
branch
derivación^F
branche^F
Abzweig^M
ramo^M
switch
interruptor^M
interrupteur^M
Schalter^M
interruttore^M
shunt
derivación^F
conducteur^M dérivé
Nebenschluss^M
derivazione^F
node
nudo^M
nœud^M
Knoten^M
nodo^M
bulb
bombilla^F
ampoule^F
Glühlampe^F
lampadina^F

dry cells

pilas^{F} secas | piles^{F} sèches | Trockenelemente^{N} | pile^{F} a secco^{M}

carbon-zinc cell
pila^{F} de carbón^{M}-cinc^{M}
pile^{F} carbone^{M}-zinc^{M}
Kohle^{F}-Zink^{N}-Zelle^{F}
pila^{F} a carbone^{M}-zinco^{M}

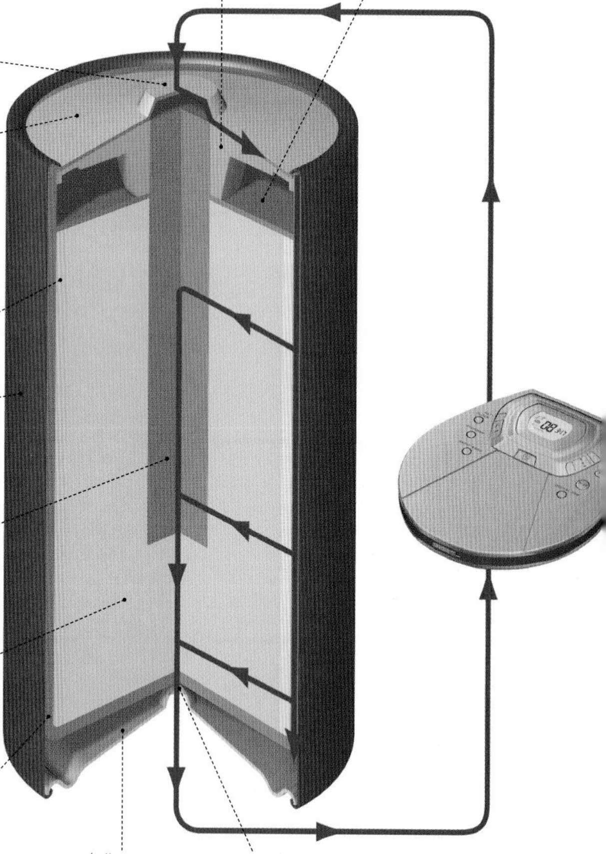

sealing plug
tapa^{F} de cierre^{M}
bouchon^{M} de scellement^{M}
Verschlussstopfen^{M}
tappo^{M} di isolamento^{M}

washer
arandela^{F}
rondelle^{F}
Abdeckscheibe^{F}
rondella^{F}

positive terminal
borne^{M} positivo
borne^{F} positive
Pluspol^{M}
polo^{M} positivo

top cap
tapa^{F} superior
couvercle^{M} supérieur
obere Abschlusskappe^{F}
coperchio^{M} superiore

electrolytic separator
separador^{M} electrolítico
séparateur^{M} électrolytique
Elektrolytseparator^{M}
separatore^{M} elettrolitico

jacket
funda^{F}
gaine^{F}
Mantel^{M}
rivestimento^{M}

carbon rod (cathode)
varilla^{F} de carbón^{M} (cátodo^{M})
tige^{F} de carbone^{M} (cathode^{F})
Kohlestab^{M} (Kathode^{F})
bastoncino^{M} di carbone^{M} (catodo^{M})

depolarizing mix
sustancia^{F} despolarizante
mélange^{M} dépolarisant
Depolarisationsgemisch^{N}
miscela^{F} di sostanze^{F} depolarizzanti

zinc can (anode)
caja^{F} de cinc^{M} (ánodo^{M})
boîte^{F} en zinc^{M} (anode^{F})
Zinkzylinder^{M} (Anode^{F})
involucro^{M} di zinco^{M} (anodo^{M})

bottom cap
tapa^{F} inferior
couvercle^{M} inférieur
untere Abschlusskappe^{F}
coperchio^{M} inferiore

negative terminal
polo^{M} negativo
borne^{F} négative
Minuspol^{M}
polo^{M} negativo

alkaline manganese-zinc cell
pila[F] alcalina de manganeso[M]-cinc[M]
pile[F] alcaline manganèse[M]-zinc[M]
alkalische Zink[N]-Mangan[N]-Zelle[F]
pila[F] alcalina a manganese[M]-zinco[M]

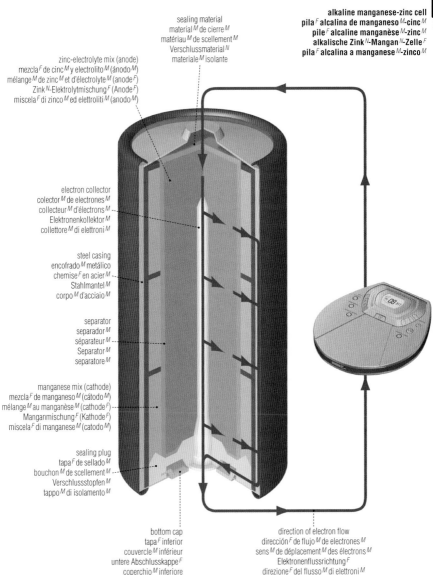

sealing material
material[M] de cierre[M]
matériau[M] de scellement[M]
Verschlussmaterial[N]
materiale[M] isolante

zinc-electrolyte mix (anode)
mezcla[F] de cinc[M] y electrolito[M] (ánodo[M])
mélange[M] de zinc[M] et d'électrolyte[M] (anode[F])
Zink[N]-Elektrolytmischung[F] (Anode[F])
miscela[F] di zinco[M] ed elettroliti[M] (anodo[M])

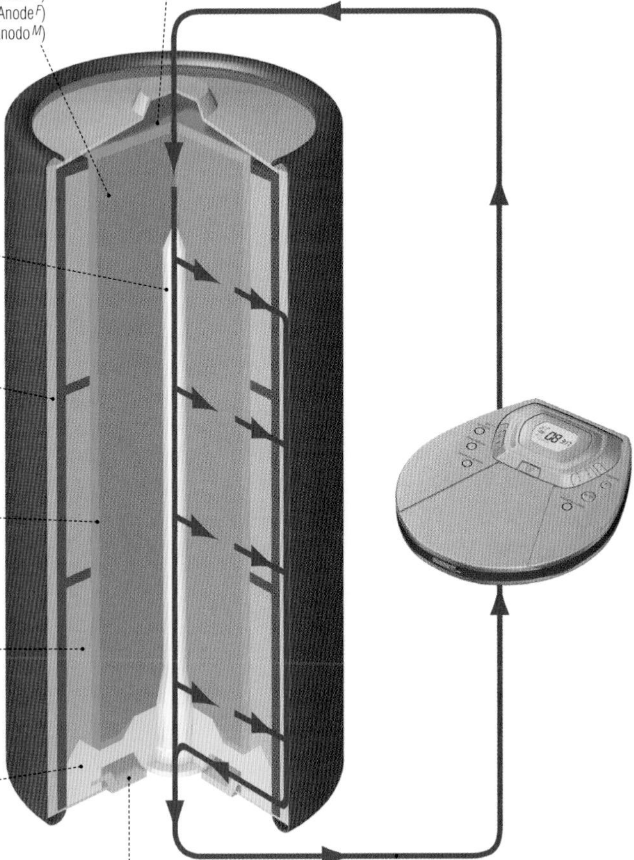

electron collector
colector[M] de electrones[M]
collecteur[M] d'électrons[M]
Elektronenkollektor[M]
collettore[M] di elettroni[M]

steel casing
encofrado[M] metálico
chemise[F] en acier[M]
Stahlmantel[M]
corpo[M] d'acciaio[M]

separator
separador[M]
séparateur[M]
Separator[M]
separatore[M]

manganese mix (cathode)
mezcla[F] de manganeso[M] (cátodo[M])
mélange[M] au manganèse[M] (cathode[F])
Manganmischung[F] (Kathode[F])
miscela[F] di manganese[M] (catodo[M])

sealing plug
tapa[F] de sellado[M]
bouchon[M] de scellement[M]
Verschlussstopfen[M]
tappo[M] di isolamento[M]

bottom cap
tapa[F] inferior
couvercle[M] inférieur
untere Abschlusskappe[F]
coperchio[M] inferiore

direction of electron flow
dirección[F] de flujo[M] de electrones[M]
sens[M] de déplacement[M] des électrons[M]
Elektronenflussrichtung[F]
direzione[F] del flusso[M] di elettroni[M]

electronics

electrónica^F | électronique^F | Elektronik^F | elettronica^F

printed circuit board
tarjeta^F de circuito^M impreso
carte^F de circuit^M imprimé
Leiterplatte^F
scheda^F del circuito^M stampato

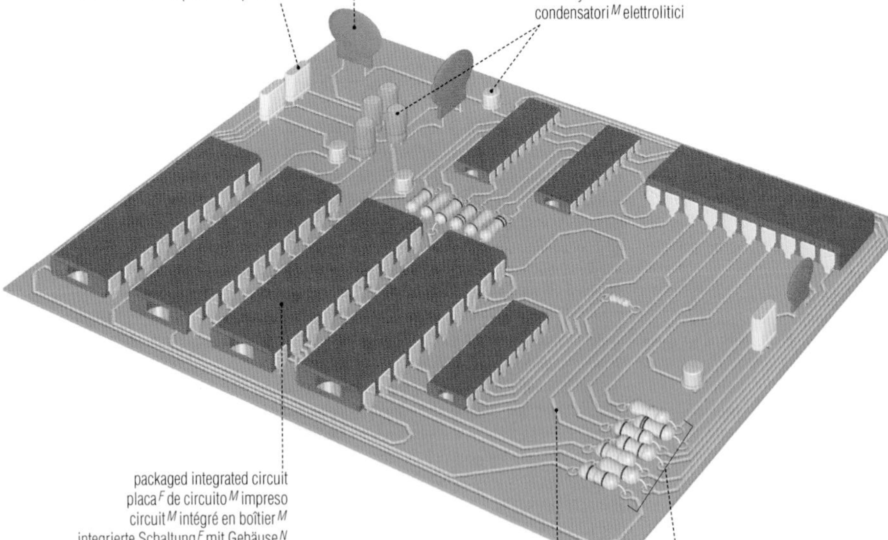
ceramic capacitor
condensador M de cerámica F
condensateur M céramique
Keramikkondensator M
condensatore M di ceramica F
plastic film capacitor
condensador M de película F plástica
condensateur M à film M plastique
Kunststoffkondensator M
condensatore M a pellicola F plastica
electrolytic capacitors
condensadores M electrolíticos
condensateurs M électrolytiques
Elektrolytkondensatoren M
condensatori M elettrolitici
packaged integrated circuit
placa F de circuito M impreso
circuit M intégré en boîtier M
integrierte Schaltung F mit Gehäuse N
circuito M integrato inscatolato
printed circuit
circuito M impreso
circuit M imprimé
gedruckte Schaltung F
circuito M stampato
resistors
resistencias F
résistances F
Widerstände M
resistenze F

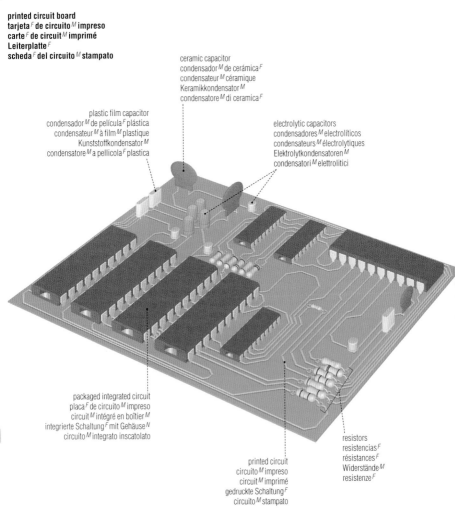

packaged integrated circuit
placa^F de circuito^M impreso
circuit^M intégré en boîtier^M
integrierte Schaltung^F mit Gehäuse^N
circuito^M integrato inscatolato

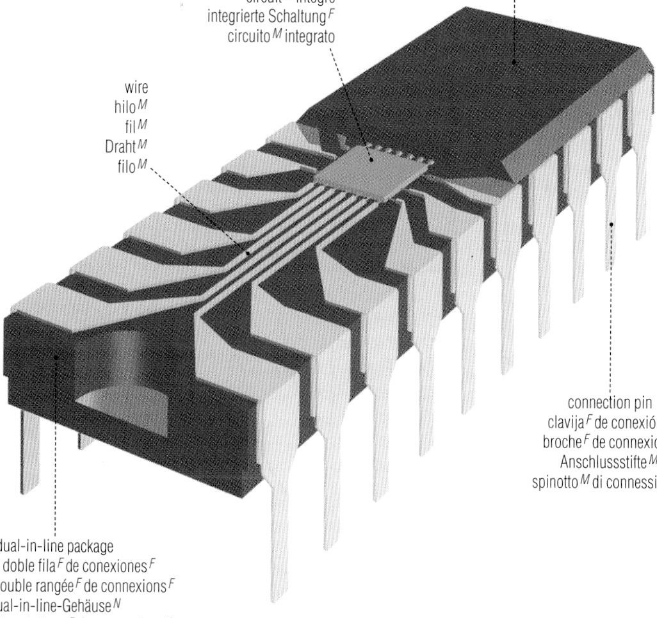
lid
tapa^F
capot^M
Verschlussdeckel^M
coperchio^M
integrated circuit
circuito^M integrado
circuit^M intégré
integrierte Schaltung^F
circuito^M integrato
wire
hilo^M
fil^M
Draht^M
filo^M
connection pin
clavija^F de conexión^F
broche^F de connexion^F
Anschlussstifte^M
spinotto^M di connessione^F
dual-in-line package
caja^F de doble fila^F de conexiones^F
boîtier^M à double rangée^F de connexions^F
Dual-in-line-Gehäuse^N
scatola^F a doppia linea^F di connessione^F

magnetism

magnetismo^{M} | magnétisme^{M} | Magnetismus^{M} | magnetismo^{M}

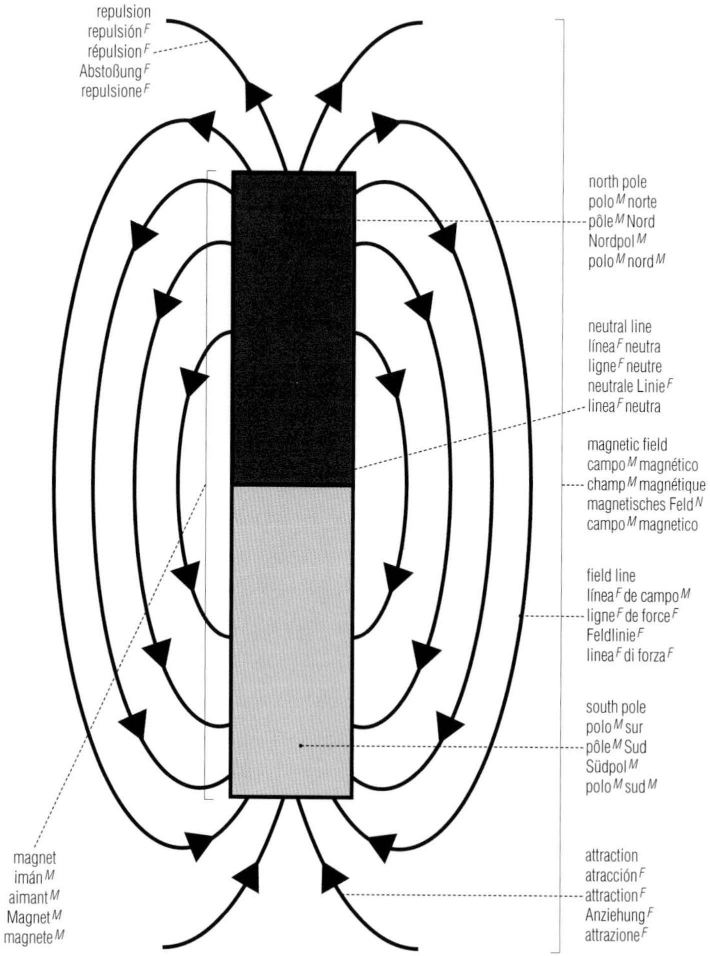
repulsion
repulsión F
répulsion F
Abstoßung F
repulsione F
north pole
polo M norte
pôle M Nord
Nordpol M
polo M nord M
neutral line
línea F neutra
ligne F neutre
neutrale Linie F
linea F neutra
magnetic field
campo M magnético
champ M magnétique
magnetisches Feld N
campo M magnetico
field line
línea F de campo M
ligne F de force F
Feldlinie F
linea F di forza F
south pole
polo M sur
pôle M Sud
Südpol M
polo M sud M
magnet
imán M
aimant M
Magnet M
magnete M
attraction
atracción F
attraction F
Anziehung F
attrazione F

wave

onda^F | onde^F | Welle^F | onda^F

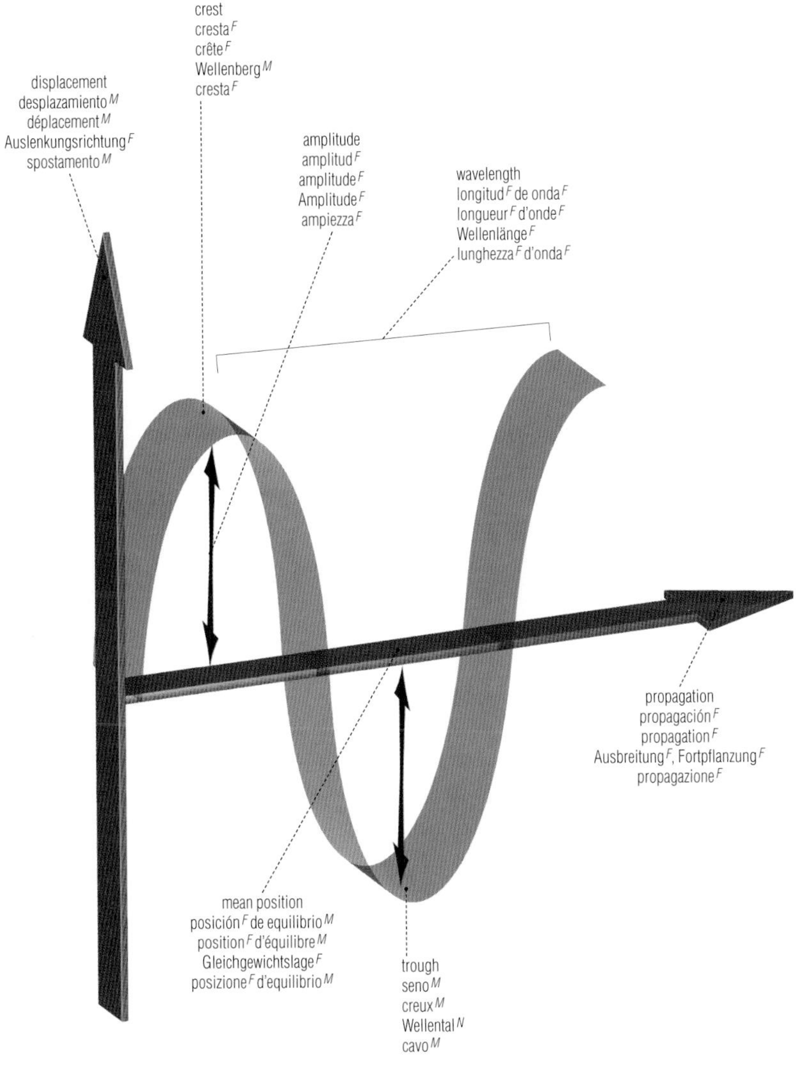
crest
cresta F
crête F
Wellenberg M
cresta F
displacement
desplazamiento M
déplacement M
Auslenkungsrichtung F
spostamento M
amplitude
amplitud F
amplitude F
Amplitude F
ampiezza F
wavelength
longitud F de onda F
longueur F d'onde F
Wellenlänge F
lunghezza F d'onda F
propagation
propagación F
propagation F
Ausbreitung F, Fortpflanzung F
propagazione F
mean position
posición F de equilibrio M
position F d'équilibre M
Gleichgewichtslage F
posizione F d'equilibrio M
trough
seno M
creux M
Wellental N
cavo M

electromagnetic spectrum

espectro[M] electromagnético | spectre[M] électromagnétique | elektromagnetisches Spektrum[N] | spettro[M] elettromagnetico

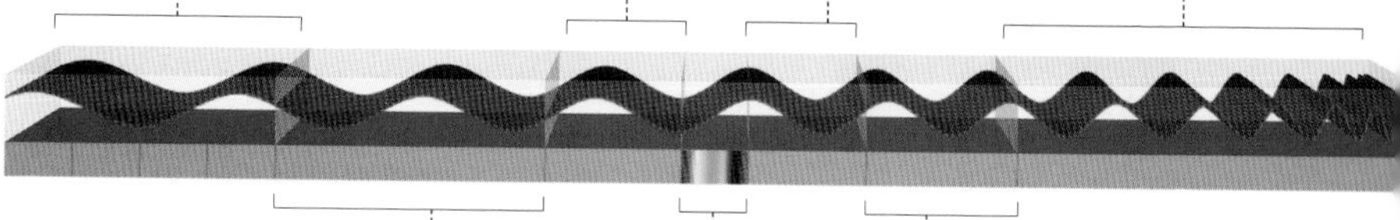
radio waves
ondas[F] radio
ondes[F] radio
Radiowellen[F]
onde[F] radio[F]
infrared radiation
radiación[F] infrarroja
rayonnement[M] infrarouge
Infrarotstrahlung[F]
radiazione[F] infrarossa
ultraviolet radiation
radiación[F] ultravioleta
rayonnement[M] ultraviolet
ultraviolette Strahlung[F]
radiazione[F] ultravioletta
gamma rays
rayos[M] gamma
rayons[M] gamma
Gammastrahlen[M]
raggi[M] gamma
microwaves
microondas[F]
micro-ondes[F]
Mikrowellen[F]
microonde[F]
visible light
luz[F] visible
lumière[F] visible
sichtbares Licht[N]
luce[F] visibile
X-rays
rayos[M] X
rayons[M] X
Röntgenstrahlen[M]
raggi[M] X

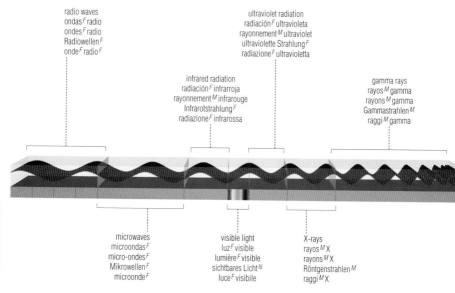

color synthesis

síntesis^{F} de los colores^{M} | synthèse^{F} des couleurs^{F} | Farbmischung^{F} | sintesi^{F} dei colori^{M}

additive color synthesis
síntesis^{F} de los colores^{M} aditivos
synthèse^{F} additive
additive Farbmischung^{F}
sintesi^{F} additiva

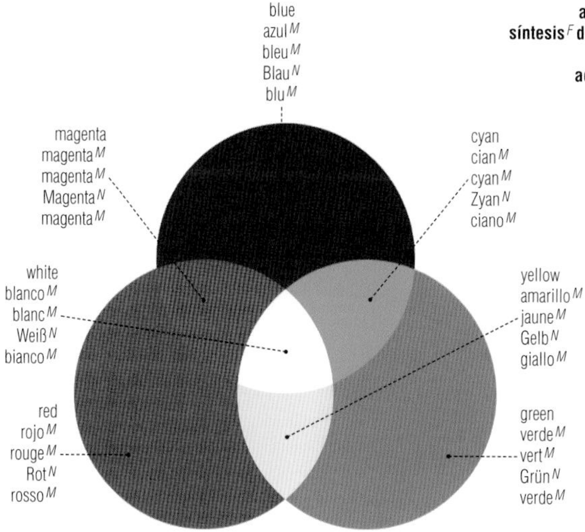

blue
azul M
bleu M
Blau N
blu M
magenta
magenta M
magenta M
Magenta N
magenta M
cyan
cian M
cyan M
Zyan N
ciano M
white
blanco M
blanc M
Weiß N
bianco M
yellow
amarillo M
jaune M
Gelb N
giallo M
red
rojo M
rouge M
Rot N
rosso M
green
verde M
vert M
Grün N
verde M

subtractive color synthesis
síntesis^{F} de los colores^{M} sustractivos
synthèse^{F} soustractive
subtraktive Farbmischung^{F}
sintesi^{F} sottrattiva

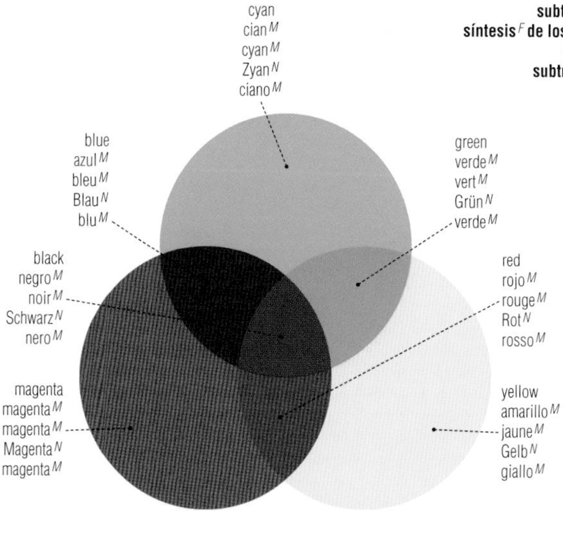

cyan
cian M
cyan M
Zyan N
ciano M
blue
azul M
bleu M
Blau N
blu M
green
verde M
vert M
Grün N
verde M
black
negro M
noir M
Schwarz N
nero M
red
rojo M
rouge M
Rot N
rosso M
magenta
magenta M
magenta M
Magenta N
magenta M
yellow
amarillo M
jaune M
Gelb N
giallo M

vision

visión^F | vision^F | Sehen^N | vista^F

normal vision
visión^F normal
vision^F normale
Normalsichtigkeit^F
vista^F normale

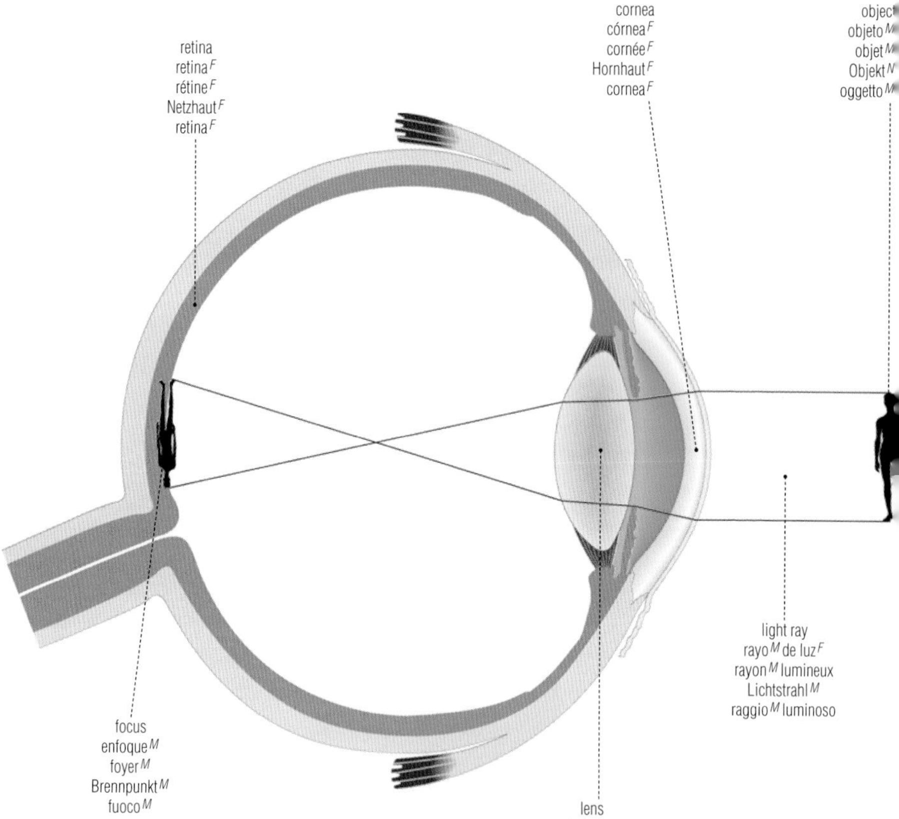
retina
retina^F
rétine^F
Netzhaut^F
retina^F
cornea
córnea^F
cornée^F
Hornhaut^F
cornea^F
objec
objeto^M
objet^M
Objekt^N
oggetto^M
light ray
rayo^M de luz^F
rayon^M lumineux
Lichtstrahl^M
raggio^M luminoso
focus
enfoque^M
foyer^M
Brennpunkt^M
fuoco^M
lens
lente^F
cristallin^M
Linse^F
cristallino^M

vision defects
defectos[M] de la visión[F]
défauts[M] de la vision[F]
Sehfehler[M]
difetti[M] della vista[F]

myopia
miopía[F]
myopie[F]
Kurzsichtigkeit[F]
miopia[F]

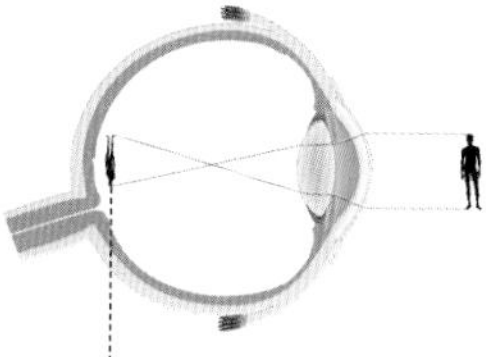

focus
enfoque[M]
foyer[M]
Brennpunkt[M]
fuoco[M]

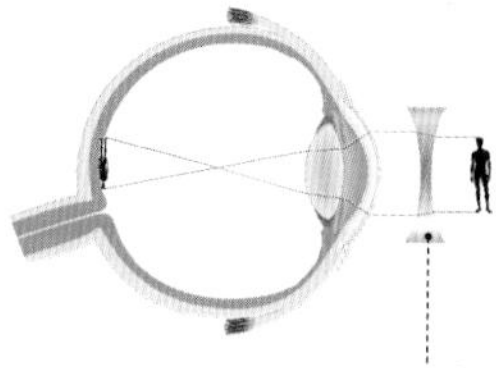

concave lens
lente[F] cóncava
lentille[F] concave
Minusglas[N]
lente[F] concava

hyperopia
hipermetropía[F]
hypermétropie[F]
Weitsichtigkeit[F]
ipermetropia[F]

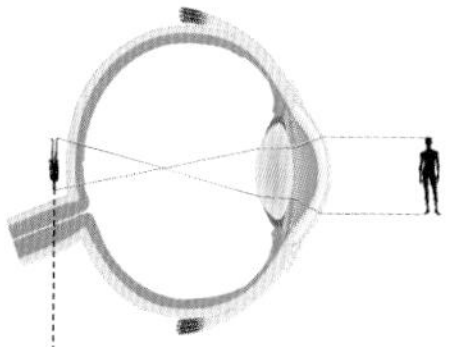

focus
enfoque[M]
foyer[M]
Brennpunkt[M]
fuoco[M]

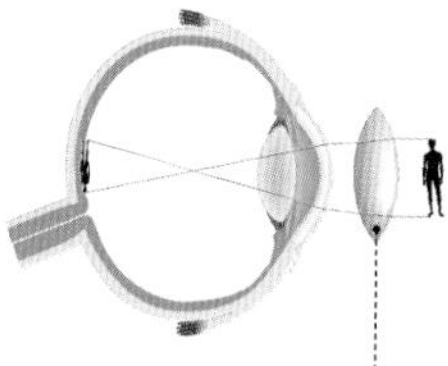

convex lens
lente[F] convexa
lentille[F] convexe
Plusglas[N]
lente[F] convessa

astigmatism
astigmatismo[M]
astigmatisme[M]
Astigmatismus[M]
astigmatismo[M]

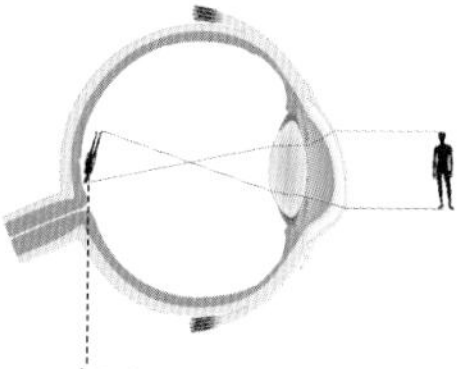

focus
foco[M]
foyer[M]
Brennpunkt[M]
fuoco[M]

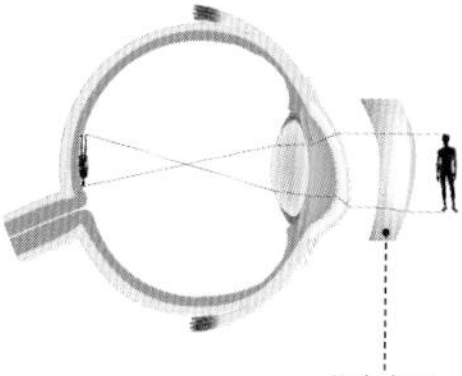

toric lens
lente[F] tórica
lentille[F] cylindrique
Zylinderglas[N]
lente[F] torica

lenses

lentes[F] | lentilles[F] | Linsen[F] | lenti[F]

converging lenses
lentes[F] convergentes
lentilles[F] convergentes
Sammellinsen[F]
lenti[F] convergenti

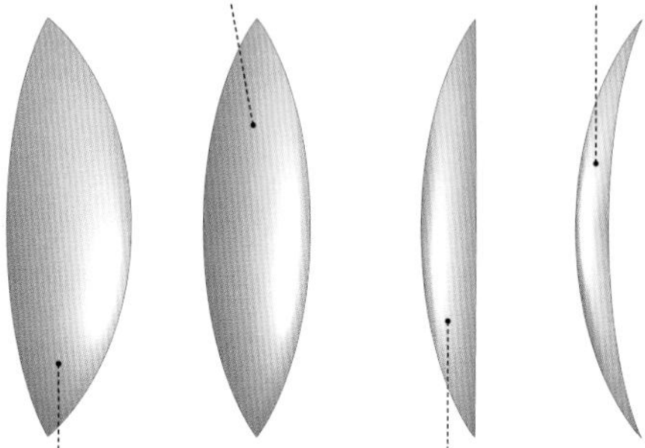
biconvex lens
lentes[F] biconvexas
lentille[F] biconvexe
bikonvexe Linse[F]
lente[F] biconvessa
positive meniscus
menisco[M] convergente
ménisque[M] convergent
konkavkonvexe Linse[F]
menisco[M] convergente
convex lens
lentes[F] convexas
lentille[F] convexe
konvexe Linse[F]
lente[F] convessa
plano-convex lens
lente[F] convexo-plana
lentille[F] plan[M]-convexe
plankonvexe Linse[F]
lente[F] piano-convessa

diverging lenses
lentes[F] divergentes
lentilles[F] divergentes
Zerstreuungslinsen[F]
lenti[F] divergenti

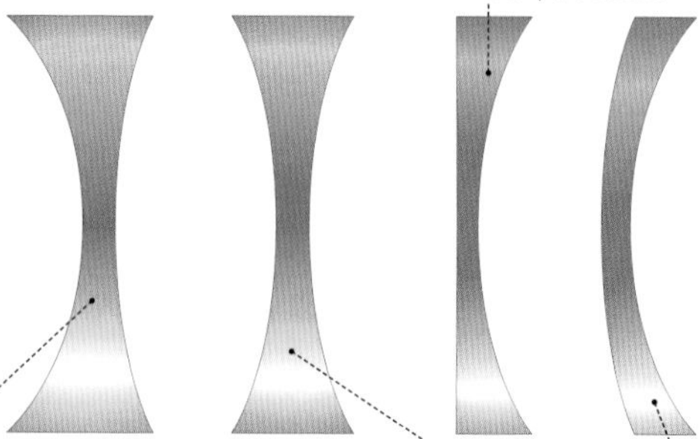
plano-concave lens
lentes[F] cóncavo-planas
lentille[F] plan[M]-concave
plankonkave Linse[F]
lente[F] piano-concava
concave lens
lentes[F] cóncavas
lentille[F] concave
konkave Linse[F]
lente[F] concava
biconcave lens
lentes[F] bicóncavas
lentille[F] biconcave
bikonkave Linse[F]
lente[F] biconcava
negative meniscus
menisco[M] divergente
ménisque[M] divergent
konvexkonkave Linse[F]
menisco[M] divergente

pulsed ruby laser

láser[M] de rubí[M] pulsado | laser[M] à rubis[M] pulsé | Rubin[M]-Impulslaser[M] | laser[M] a rubino[M] pulsato

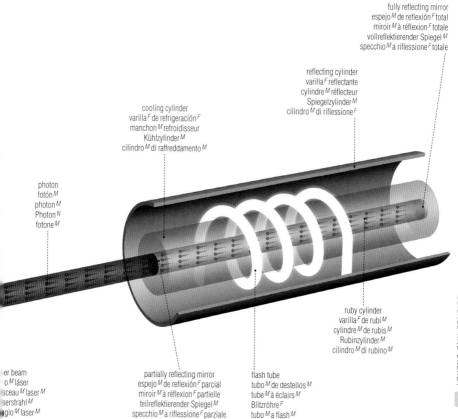

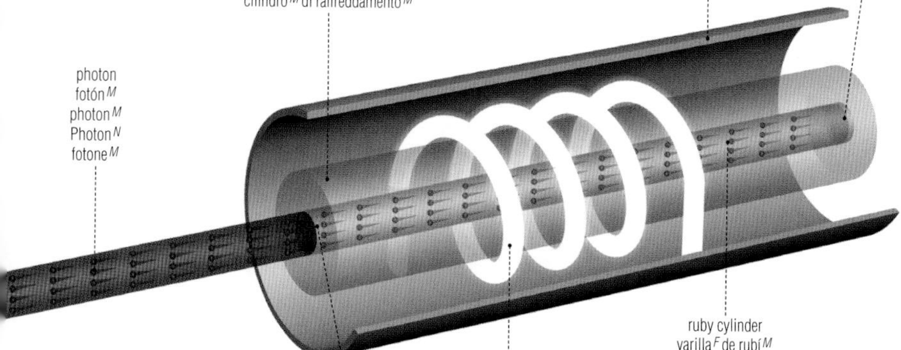
fully reflecting mirror
espejo[M] de reflexión[F] total
miroir[M] à réflexion[F] totale
vollreflektierender Spiegel[M]
specchio[M] a riflessione[F] totale
reflecting cylinder
varilla[F] reflectante
cylindre[M] réflecteur
Spiegelzylinder[M]
cilindro[M] di riflessione[F]
cooling cylinder
varilla[F] de refrigeración[F]
manchon[M] refroidisseur
Kühlzylinder[M]
cilindro[M] di raffreddamento[M]
photon
fotón[M]
photon[M]
Photon[N]
fotone[M]
ruby cylinder
varilla[F] de rubí[M]
cylindre[M] de rubis[M]
Rubinzylinder[M]
cilindro[M] di rubino[M]
er beam
o[M] láser
sceau[M] laser[M]
serstrahl[M]
gio[M] laser[M]
partially reflecting mirror
espejo[M] de reflexión[F] parcial
miroir[M] à réflexion[F] partielle
teilreflektierender Spiegel[M]
specchio[M] a riflessione[F] parziale
flash tube
tubo[M] de destellos[M]
tube[M] à éclairs[M]
Blitzröhre[F]
tubo[M] a flash[M]

prism binoculars

prismáticos^M binoculares | jumelles^F à prismes^M | Prismenfernglas^N | binocolo^M prismatico

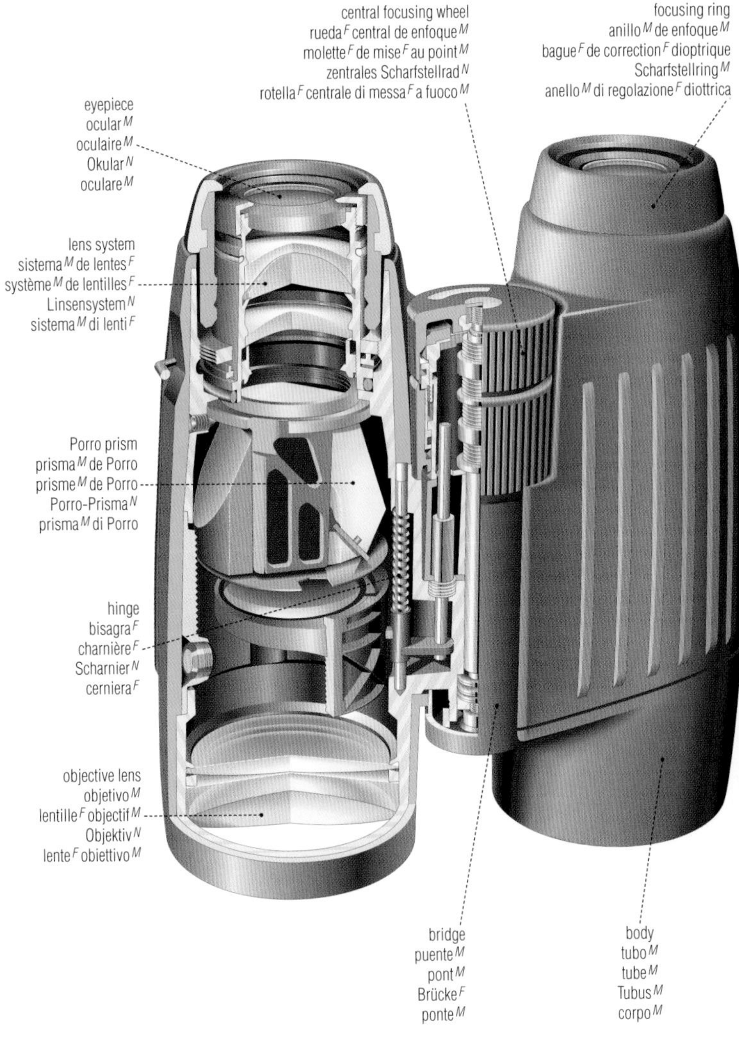
central focusing wheel
rueda^F central de enfoque^M
molette^F de mise^F au point^M
zentrales Scharfstellrad^N
rotella^F centrale di messa^F a fuoco^M
focusing ring
anillo^M de enfoque^M
bague^F de correction^F dioptrique
Scharfstellring^M
anello^M di regolazione^F diottrica
eyepiece
ocular^M
oculaire^M
Okular^N
oculare^M
lens system
sistema^M de lentes^F
système^M de lentilles^F
Linsensystem^N
sistema^M di lenti^F
Porro prism
prisma^M de Porro
prisme^M de Porro
Porro-Prisma^N
prisma^M di Porro
hinge
bisagra^F
charnière^F
Scharnier^N
cerniera^F
objective lens
objetivo^M
lentille^F objectif^M
Objektiv^N
lente^F obiettivo^M
bridge
puente^M
pont^M
Brücke^F
ponte^M
body
tubo^M
tube^M
Tubus^M
corpo^M

magnifying glass and microscopes

lupa^F y microscopios^M | loupe^F et microscopes^M | Lupe^F und Mikroskope^N | lente^F di ingrandimento^M e microscopi^M

microscope
microscopio^M
microscope^M
Mikroskop^N
microscopio^M

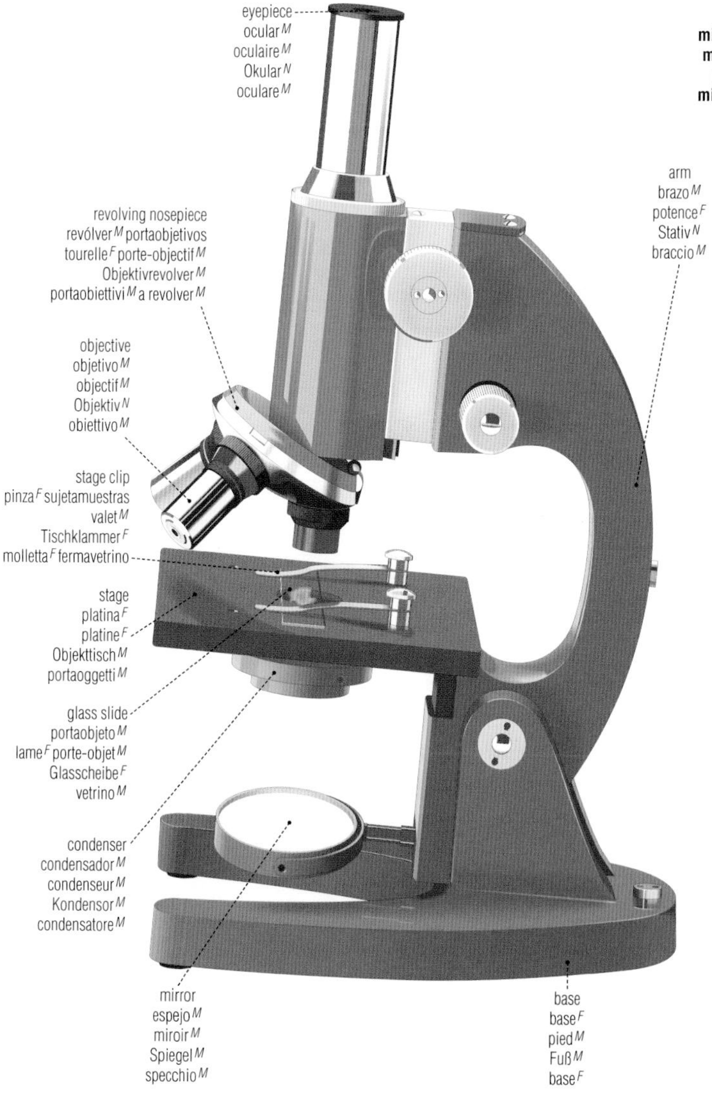
eyepiece
ocular M
oculaire M
Okular N
oculare M
arm
brazo M
potence F
Stativ N
braccio M
revolving nosepiece
revólver M portaobjetivos
tourelle F porte-objectif M
Objektivrevolver M
portaobiettivi M a revolver M
objective
objetivo M
objectif M
Objektiv N
obiettivo M
stage clip
pinza F sujetamuestras
valet M
Tischklammer F
molletta F fermavetrino
stage
platina F
platine F
Objekttisch M
portaoggetti M
glass slide
portaobjeto M
lame F porte-objet M
Glasscheibe F
vetrino M
condenser
condensador M
condenseur M
Kondensor M
condensatore M
mirror
espejo M
miroir M
Spiegel M
specchio M
base
base F
pied M
Fuß M
base F

magnifying glass and microscopes

magnifying glass
lupa F
loupe F
Lupe F
lente F **di ingrandimento** M

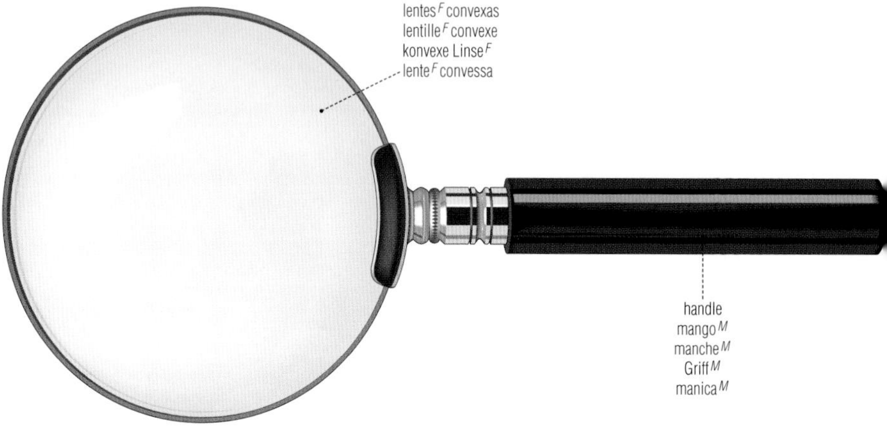
convex lens
lentes F convexas
lentille F convexe
konvexe Linse F
lente F convessa
handle
mango M
manche M
Griff M
manica M

telescopic sight

visor M telescópico | lunette F de visée F | Zielfernrohr N | cannocchiale M di mira F

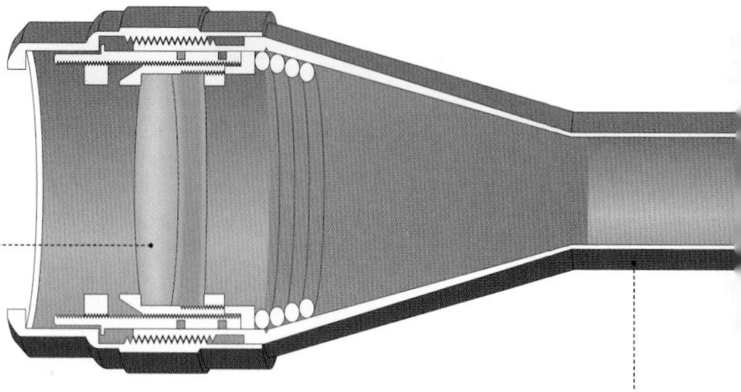
objective lens
objetivo M
lentille F objectif M
Objektiv N
lente F obiettivo M
main scope tube
tubo M principal de observación F
tube M
Tubus M
tubo M telescopico principale

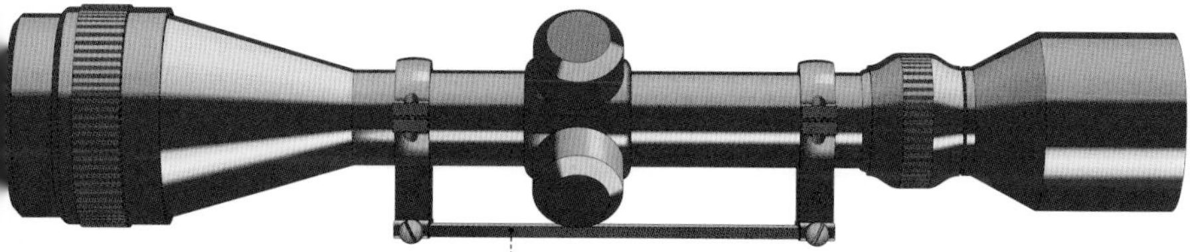
dovetail
cremallera F de fijación F
glissière F de fixation F
Befestigungsschiene F
slitta F di fissaggio M

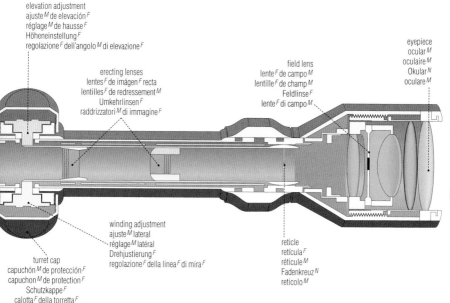

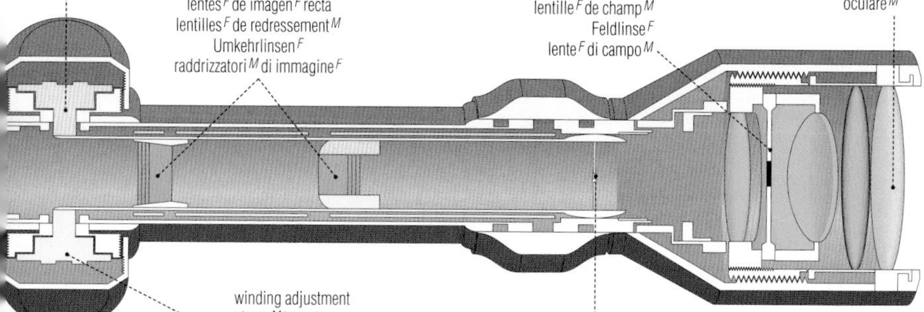
elevation adjustment
ajuste M de elevación F
réglage M de hausse F
Höheneinstellung F
regolazione F dell'angolo M di elevazione F
erecting lenses
lentes F de imágen F recta
lentilles F de redressement M
Umkehrlinsen F
raddrizzatori M di immagine F
field lens
lente F de campo M
lentille F de champ M
Feldlinse F
lente F di campo M
eyepiece
ocular M
oculaire M
Okular N
oculare M
winding adjustment
ajuste M lateral
réglage M latéral
Drehjustierung F
regolazione F della linea F di mira F
turret cap
capuchón M de protección F
capuchon M de protection F
Schutzkappe F
calotta F della torretta F
reticle
retícula F
réticule M
Fadenkreuz N
reticolo M

measure of temperature

medición^{F} de la temperatura^{F} | mesure^{F} de la température^{F} | Temperaturmessung^{F} | misura^{F} della temperatura^{F}

thermometer
termómetro^{M}
thermomètre^{M}
Thermometer^{N}
termometro^{M}

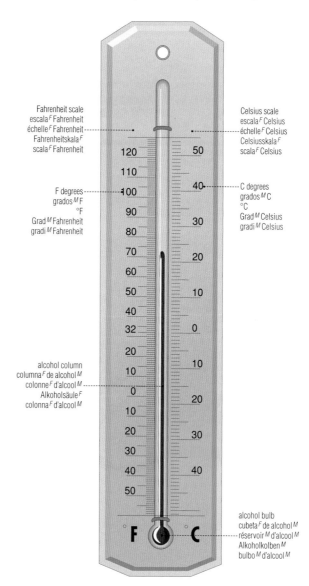

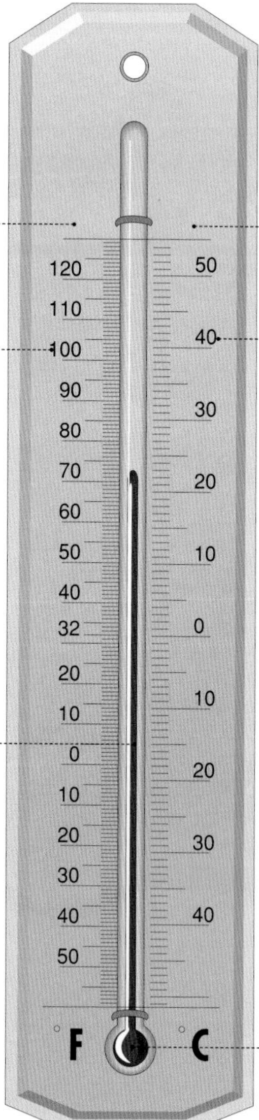
Fahrenheit scale
escala^{F} Fahrenheit
échelle^{F} Fahrenheit
Fahrenheitskala^{F}
scala^{F} Fahrenheit
Celsius scale
escala^{F} Celsius
échelle^{F} Celsius
Celsiusskala^{F}
scala^{F} Celsius
F degrees
grados^{M} F
°F
Grad^{M} Fahrenheit
gradi^{M} Fahrenheit
C degrees
grados^{M} C
°C
Grad^{M} Celsius
gradi^{M} Celsius
alcohol column
columna^{F} de alcohol^{M}
colonne^{F} d'alcool^{M}
Alkoholsäule^{F}
colonna^{F} d'alcool^{M}
alcohol bulb
cubeta^{F} de alcohol^{M}
réservoir^{M} d'alcool^{M}
Alkoholkolben^{M}
bulbo^{M} d'alcool^{M}
120
110
100
90
80
70
60
50
40
32
20
10
0
10
20
30
40
50
50
40
30
20
10
0
10
20
30
40
F
C

clinical thermometer
termómetro[M] clínico
thermomètre[M] médical
Fieberthermometer[N]
termometro[M] clinico

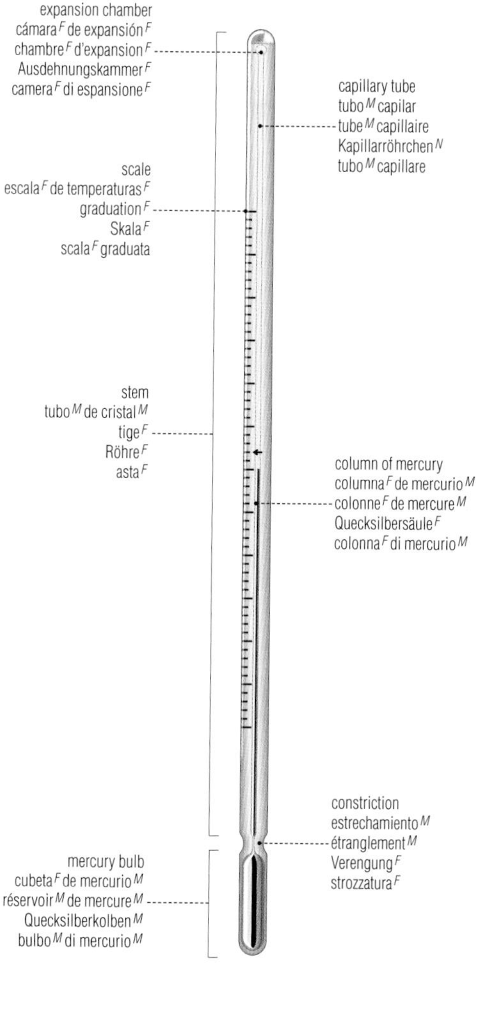
expansion chamber
cámara[F] de expansión[F]
chambre[F] d'expansion[F]
Ausdehnungskammer[F]
camera[F] di espansione[F]
capillary tube
tubo[M] capilar
tube[M] capillaire
Kapillarröhrchen[N]
tubo[M] capillare
scale
escala[F] de temperaturas[F]
graduation[F]
Skala[F]
scala[F] graduata
stem
tubo[M] de cristal[M]
tige[F]
Röhre[F]
asta[F]
column of mercury
columna[F] de mercurio[M]
colonne[F] de mercure[M]
Quecksilbersäule[F]
colonna[F] di mercurio[M]
constriction
estrechamiento[M]
étranglement[M]
Verengung[F]
strozzatura[F]
mercury bulb
cubeta[F] de mercurio[M]
réservoir[M] de mercure[M]
Quecksilberkolben[M]
bulbo[M] di mercurio[M]

measure of temperature

digital thermometer
termómetro^{M} digital
thermomètre^{M} numérique
Digitalthermometer^{N}
termometro^{M} digitale

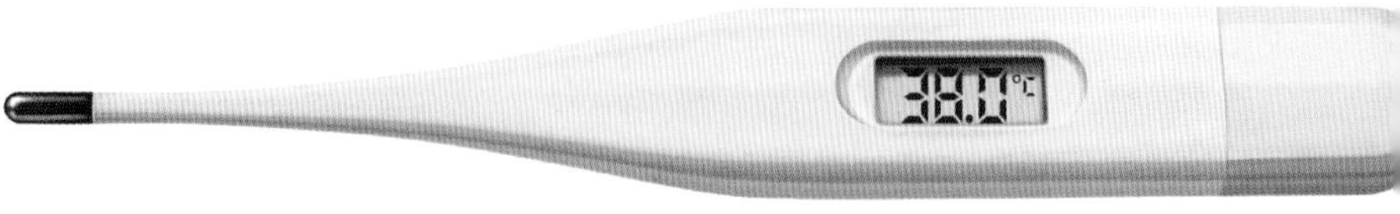
38.0°C

bimetallic thermometer
termómetro^{M} bimetálico
thermomètre^{M} bimétallique
Bimetall-Thermometer^{N}
termometro^{M} a lamina^{F} bimetallica

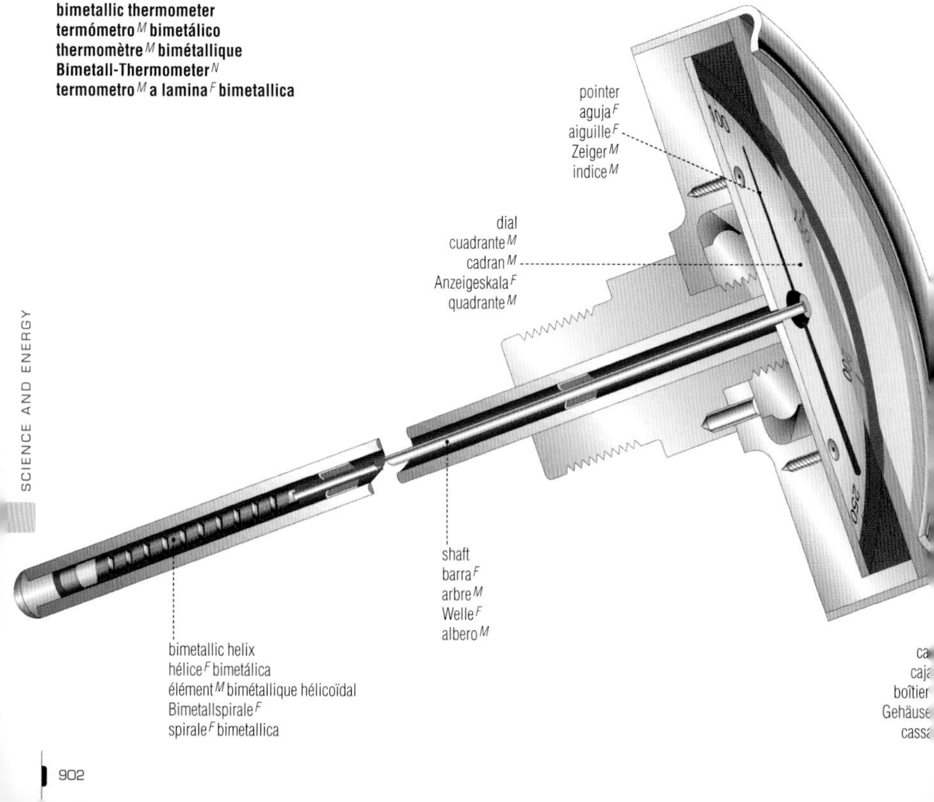
pointer
aguja^{F}
aiguille^{F}
Zeiger^{M}
indice^{M}
dial
cuadrante^{M}
cadran^{M}
Anzeigeskala^{F}
quadrante^{M}
100
200
250
shaft
barra^{F}
arbre^{M}
Welle^{F}
albero^{M}
bimetallic helix
hélice^{F} bimetálica
élément^{M} bimétallique hélicoïdal
Bimetallspirale^{F}
spirale^{F} bimetallica
ca
caj
boîtier
Gehäuse
cass

measure of time

medición[F] del tiempo[M] | mesure[F] du temps[M] | Zeitmessung[F] | misura[F] del tempo[M]

stopwatch
cronómetro[M]
chronomètre[M]
Stoppuhr[F]
cronometro[M]

start button
botón[M] de inicio[M] de marcha[F]
poussoir[M] de mise[F] en marche[F]
Startknopf[M]
pulsante[M] di partenza[F]
ring
anilla[F]
anneau[M]
Ring[M]
anello[M]
minute hand
minutero[M]
aiguille[F] des minutes[F]
Minutenzeiger[M]
lancetta[F] dei minuti[M]
reset button
botón[M] de inicio[M] del contador[M]
poussoir[M] de remise[F] à zéro[M]
Rückstellknopf[M]
pulsante[M] di azzeramento[M]
stop button
botón[M] de parada[F]
poussoir[M] d'arrêt[M]
Stoppknopf[M]
pulsante[M] di arresto[M]
55
5
50
10
45
15
40
20
35
25
30
MIN
1/10 SEC
second hand
segundero[M]
trotteuse[F]
Sekundenzeiger[M]
lancetta[F] dei secondi[M]
case
estuche[M]
boîtier[M]
Gehäuse[N]
cassa[F]
1/10 second hand
aguja[F] de décimas[F] de segundo[M]
aiguille[F] des dixièmes[M] de seconde[F]
Zehntelsekundenzeiger[M]
lancetta[F] dei decimi[M] di secondo[M]

mechanical watch
reloj^{M} **mecánico**
montre^{F} **mécanique**
mechanische Uhr^{F}
orologio^{M} **meccanico**

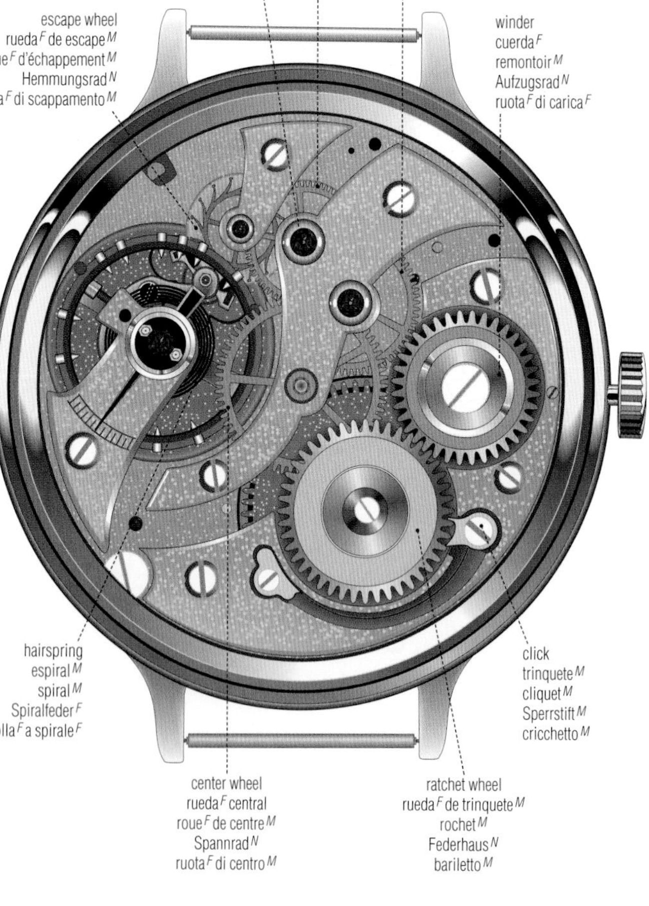
fourth wheel
rueda F de los segundos M
roue F de champ M
Ankerrad N
ruota F dei secondi M
jewel
rubí M
rubis M
Stein M
rubino M
third wheel
rueda F media
roue F petite moyenne
Antriebswerk N
ruota F intermedia
escape wheel
rueda F de escape M
roue F d'échappement M
Hemmungsrad N
ruota F di scappamento M
winder
cuerda F
remontoir M
Aufzugsrad N
ruota F di carica F
hairspring
espiral M
spiral M
Spiralfeder F
molla F a spirale F
click
trinquete M
cliquet M
Sperrstift M
cricchetto M
center wheel
rueda F central
roue F de centre M
Spannrad N
ruota F di centro M
ratchet wheel
rueda F de trinquete M
rochet M
Federhaus N
bariletto M

sundial
reloj[M] de sol[M]
cadran[M] solaire
Sonnenuhr[F]
meridiana[F]

gnomon
estilo[M]
style[M]
Gnomon[M]
gnomone[M]
shadow
sombra[F]
ombre[F]
Schatten[M]
ombra[F]
dial
cuadrante[M]
cadran[M]
Zifferblatt[N]
quadrante[M]

analog watch
reloj[M] de pulsera[F]
montre[F] à affichage[M] analogique
Analoguhr[F]
orologio[M] analogico

dial
cuadrante[M]
cadran[M]
Zifferblatt[N]
quadrante[M]
strap
correa[F]
bracelet[M]
Uhrband[N]
cinturino[M]
crown
corona[F]
couronne[F]
Krone[F]
corona[F]

igital watch
eloj[M] digital
ontre[F] à affichage[M] numérique
igitaluhr[F]
rologio[M] digitale

liquid crystal display
registro[M] de cristal[M] líquido
cristaux[M] liquides
LCD-Anzeige[F]
quadrante[M] a cristalli[M] liquidi

measure of weight

medición F del peso M | mesure F de la masse F | Wiegen N | misura F del peso M

beam balance
balanza F de astil M
balance F à fléau M
Balkenwaage F
bilancia F di precisione F

beam
astil M
fléau M
Balken M
giogo M
weight
pesa F
poids M
Gewicht N
peso M
pan
platillo M
plateau M
Waagschale F
piatto M

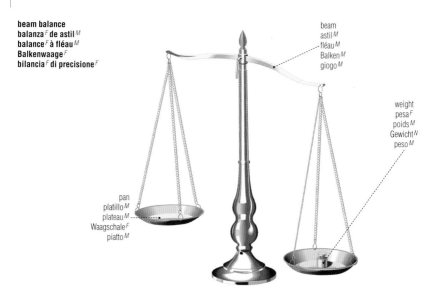

Roberval's balance
balanza F de Roberval
balance F de Roberval
Roberval-Waage F
bilancia F a sospensione F inferiore

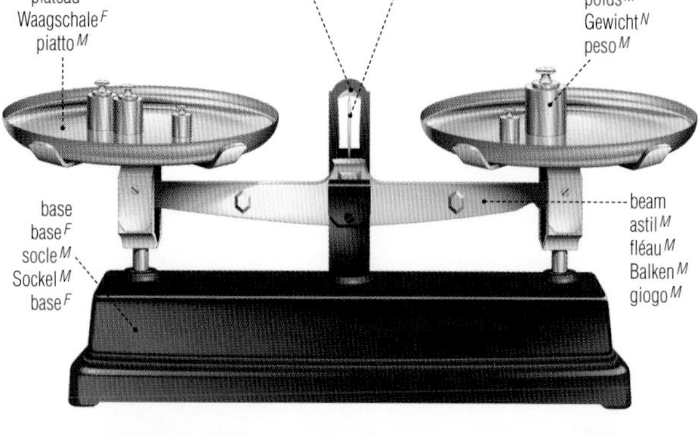
dial
esfera F
cadran M
Anzeige F
quadrante M
pointer
fiel M
aiguille F
Zeiger M
indice M
pan
platillo M
plateau M
Waagschale F
piatto M
weight
pesa F
poids M
Gewicht N
peso M
base
base F
socle M
Sockel M
base F
beam
astil M
fléau M
Balken M
giogo M

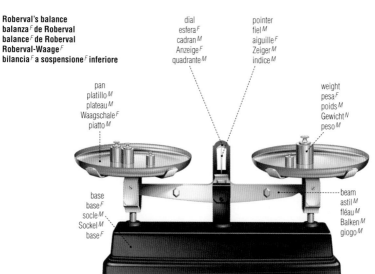

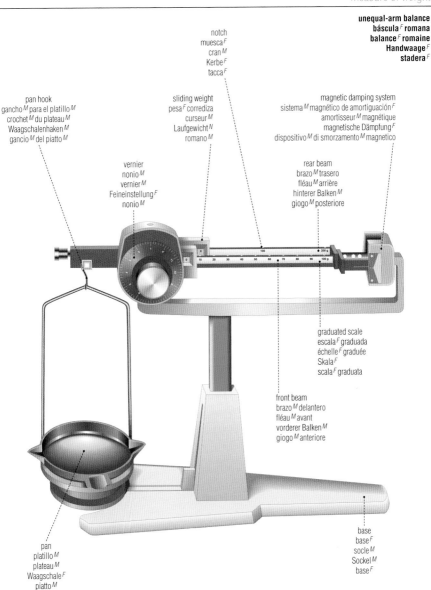

unequal-arm balance
báscula^F romana
balance^F romaine
Handwaage^F
stadera^F

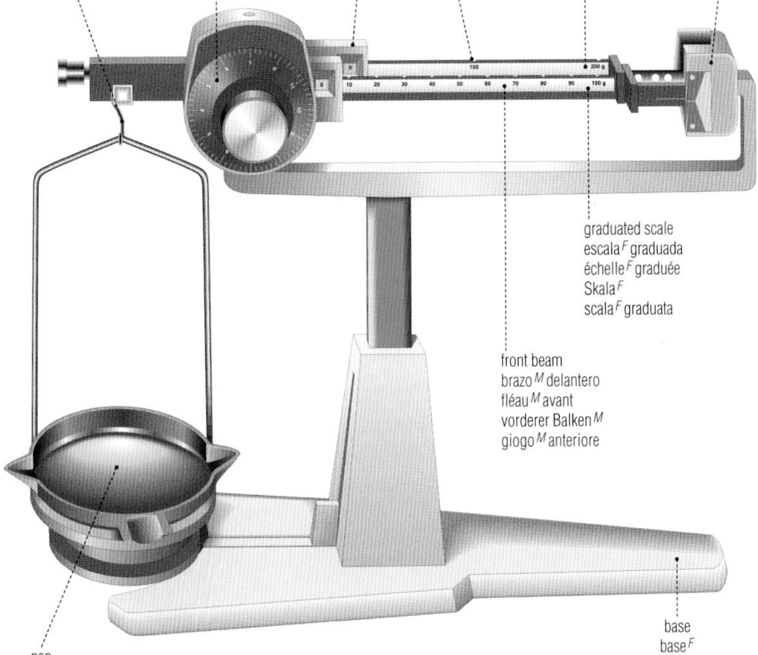
notch
muesca^F
cran^M
Kerbe^F
tacca^F
pan hook
gancho^M para el platillo^M
crochet^M du plateau^M
Waagschalenhaken^M
gancio^M del piatto^M
sliding weight
pesa^F corrediza
curseur^M
Laufgewicht^N
romano^M
magnetic damping system
sistema^M magnético de amortiguación^F
amortisseur^M magnétique
magnetische Dämpfung^F
dispositivo^M di smorzamento^M magnetico
vernier
nonio^M
vernier^M
Feineinstellung^F
nonio^M
rear beam
brazo^M trasero
fléau^M arrière
hinterer Balken^M
giogo^M posteriore
graduated scale
escala^F graduada
échelle^F graduée
Skala^F
scala^F graduata
front beam
brazo^M delantero
fléau^M avant
vorderer Balken^M
giogo^M anteriore
pan
platillo^M
plateau^M
Waagschale^F
piatto^M
base
base^F
socle^M
Sockel^M
base^F

measure of weight

electronic scale
báscula^F electrónica
balance^F électronique
elektronische Waage^F
bilancia^F elettronica

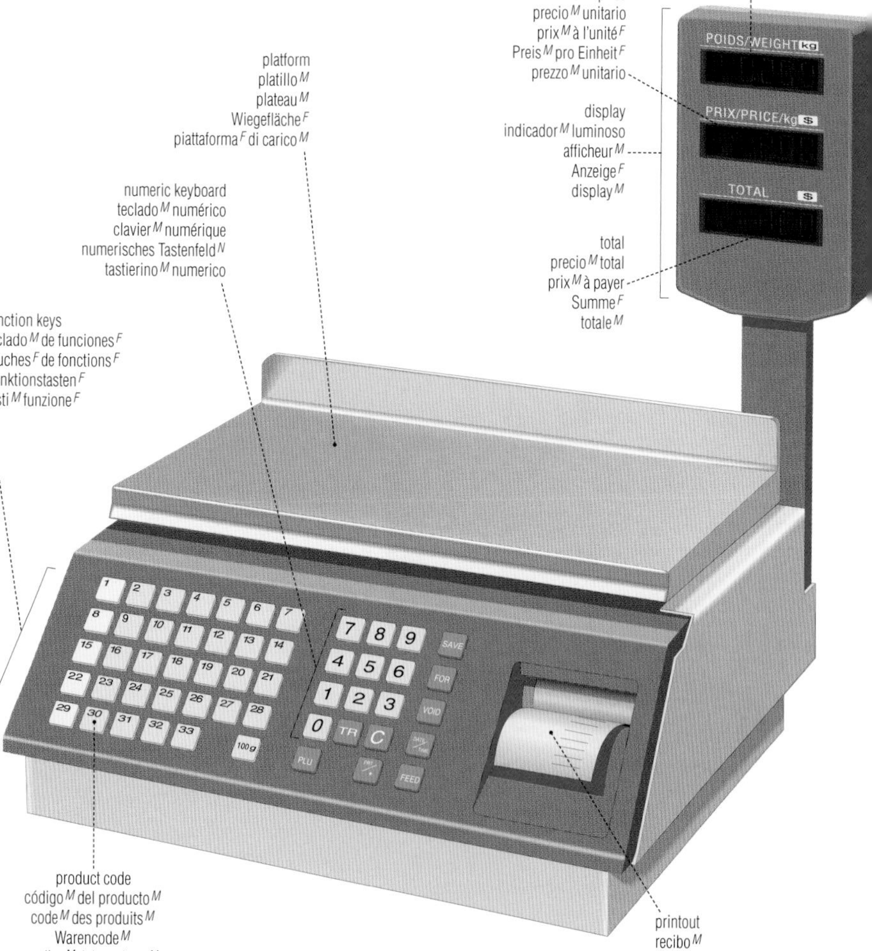
weight
peso M
poids M
Gewicht N
peso M
unit price
precio M unitario
prix M à l'unité F
Preis M pro Einheit F
prezzo M unitario
platform
platillo M
plateau M
Wiegefläche F
piattaforma F di carico M
display
indicador M luminoso
afficheur M
Anzeige F
display M
numeric keyboard
teclado M numérico
clavier M numérique
numerisches Tastenfeld N
tastierino M numerico
total
precio M total
prix M à payer
Summe F
totale M
function keys
teclado M de funciones F
touches F de fonctions F
Funktionstasten F
tasti M funzione F
POIDS/WEIGHT kg
PRIX/PRICE/kg $
TOTAL $
SAVE
FOR
VOID
PLU
FEED
TR
C
100g
product code
código M del producto M
code M des produits M
Warencode M
codice M del prodotto M
printout
recibo M
étiquette F
Wiegeetikett N
scontrino M

analytical balance
balanzaF **de precisión**F
balanceF **de précision**F
PräzisionswaageF
bilanciaF **da analisi**F

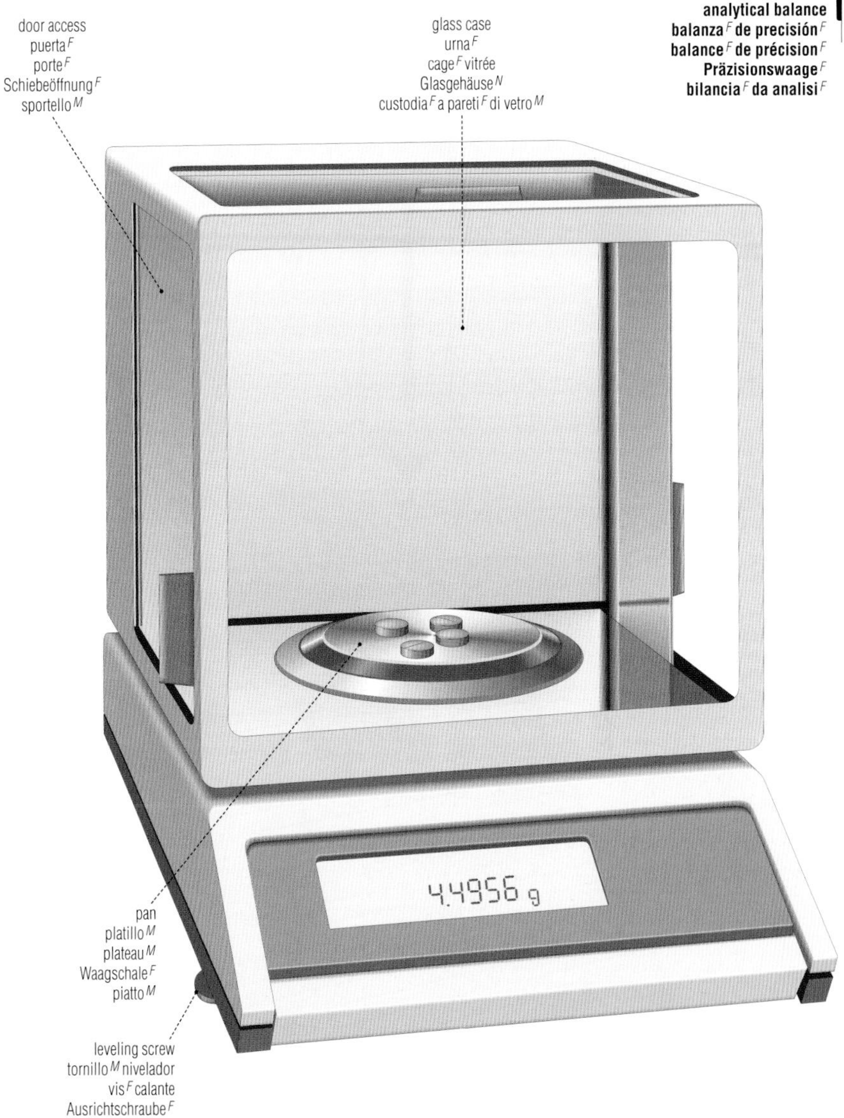
door access
puertaF
porteF
SchiebeöffnungF
sportelloM
glass case
urnaF
cageF vitrée
GlasgehäuseN
custodiaF a paretiF di vetroM
4.4956 g
pan
platilloM
plateauM
WaagschaleF
piattoM
leveling screw
tornilloM nivelador
visF calante
AusrichtschraubeF
viteF di livelloM

measure of weight

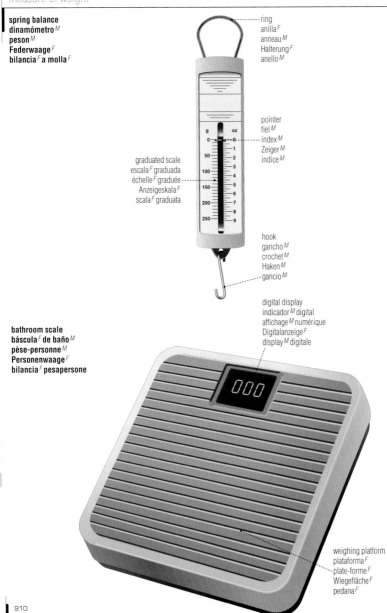

spring balance
dinamómetro *M*
peson *M*
Federwaage *F*
bilancia *F* **a molla** *F*

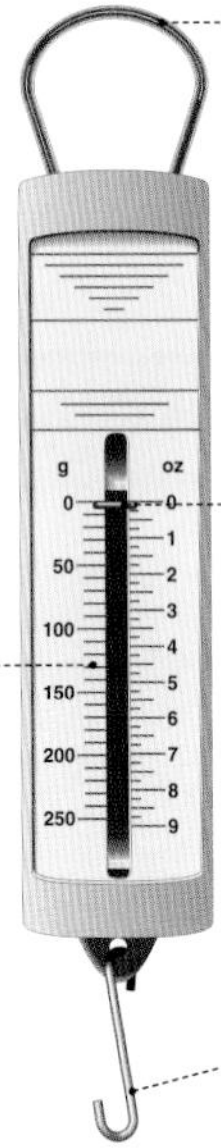
ring
anilla F
anneau M
Halterung F
anello M
pointer
fiel M
index M
Zeiger M
indice M
graduated scale
escala F graduada
échelle F graduée
Anzeigeskala F
scala F graduata
hook
gancho M
crochet M
Haken M
gancio M
g
oz
0
50
100
150
200
250
1
2
3
4
5
6
7
8
9

bathroom scale
báscula *F* **de baño** *M*
pèse-personne *M*
Personenwaage *F*
bilancia *F* **pesapersone**

digital display
indicador M digital
affichage M numérique
Digitalanzeige F
display M digitale
000
weighing platform
plataforma F
plate-forme F
Wiegefläche F
pedana F

measure of length

medición*F* de la longitud*F* | mesure*F* de la longueur*F* | Längenmessung*F* | misura*F* della lunghezza*F*

ruler
regla*F* graduada
règle*F* graduée
Lineal*N*
righello*M*

scale
escala*F* graduada
graduation*F*
Skala*F*
scala*F* graduata

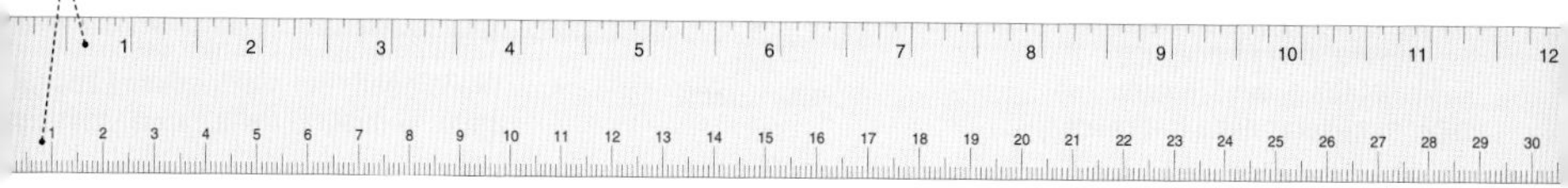
1 2 3 4 5 6 7 8 9 10 11 12
1 2 3 4 5 6 7 8 9 10 11 12 13 14 15 16 17 18 19 20 21 22 23 24 25 26 27 28 29 30

measure of distance

medición*F* de la distancia*F* | mesure*F* de la distance*F* | Entfernungsmessung*F* | misura*F* della distanza*F*

pedometer
odómetro*M*
podomètre*M*
Schrittzähler*M*, Pedometer*N*
pedometro*M*

reset button
botón*M* de inicio*M* del contador*M*
bouton*M* de remise*F* à zéro*M*
Rückstellknopf*M*
pulsante*M* di azzeramento*M*

distance traveled
distancia*F* recorrida
distance*F* parcourue
zurückgelegte Strecke*F*
distanza*F* percorsa

step setting
contador*M*
réglage*M* du pas*M*
Schrittlängeneinstellung*F*
regolazione*F* del passo*M*

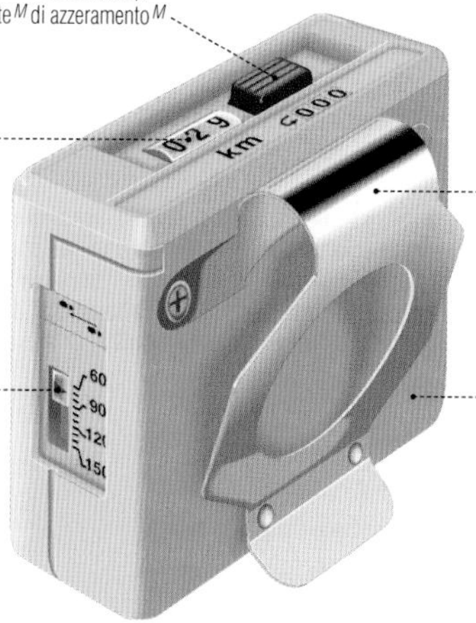
km

clip
pinza*F*
agrafe*F*
Klemme*F*
clip*F*

case
caja*F*
boîtier*M*
Gehäuse*N*
involucro*M*

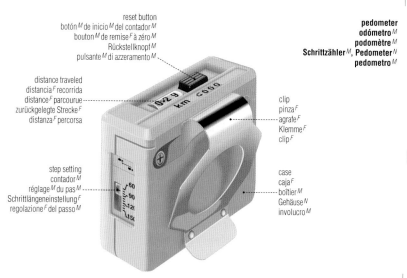

international system of units

sistema[M] internacional de unidades[F] de medida[F] | système[M] international d'unités[F] | internationales Einheitensystem[N] | sistema[M] internazionale di unità[F] di misura[F]

measurement of electric potential difference
unidad[F] de medida[F] de la diferencia[F] de potencial[M] eléctrico
mesure[F] de la différence[F] de potentiel[M] électrique
Maßeinheit[F] der elektrischen Spannung[F]
unità[F] di misura[F] della differenza[F] di potenziale[M] elettrico

V

volt
voltio[M], volt[M]
volt[M]
Volt[N]
volt[M]

measurement of frequency
unidad[F] de medida[F] de frecuencia[F]
mesure[F] de la fréquence[F]
Maßeinheit[F] der Frequenz[F]
unità[F] di misura[F] della frequenza[F]

Hz

hertz
hercio[M]
hertz[M]
Hertz[N]
hertz[M]

measurement of electric charge
unidad[F] de medida[F] de carga[F] eléctri
mesure[F] de la charge[F] électrique
Maßeinheit[F] der elektrischen Ladung
unità[F] di misura[F] della carica[F] elettri

C

coulomb
culombio[M]
coulomb[M]
Coulomb[N]
coulomb[M]

measurement of energy
unidad[F] de medida[F] de energía[F]
mesure[F] de l'énergie[F]
Maßeinheit[F] der Energie[F]
unità[F] di misura[F] dell'energia[F]

J

joule
julio[M]
joule[M]
Joule[N]
joule[M]

measurement of power
unidad[F] de medida[F] de potencia[F] eléctrica
mesure[F] de la puissance[F]
Maßeinheit[F] der Leistung[F]
unità[F] di misura[F] della potenza[F] elettrica

W

watt
vatio[M]
watt[M]
Watt[N]
watt[M]

measurement of force
unidad[F] de medida[F] de fuerza[F]
mesure[F] de la force[F]
Maßeinheit[F] der Kraft[F]
unità[F] di misura[F] della forza[F]

N

newton
newton[M]
newton[M]
Newton[N]
newton[M]

measurement of electric resistance
unidad[F] de medida[F] de resistencia[F] eléctrica
mesure[F] de la résistance[F] électrique
Maßeinheit[F] des elektrischen Widerstands[M]
unità[F] di misura[F] della resistenza[F] elettrica

Ω

ohm
ohmnio[M], ohm[M]
ohm[M]
Ohm[N]
ohm[M]

measurement of electric current
unidad[F] de medida[F] de corriente[F] eléctrica
mesure[F] du courant[M] électrique
Maßeinheit[F] der elektrischen Stromstärke[F]
unità[F] di misura[F] della corrente[F] elettrica

A

ampere
amperio[M]
ampère[M]
Ampere[N]
ampere[M]

measurement of length
unidad [F] de medida [F] de longitud [F]
mesure [F] de la longueur [F]
Maßeinheit [F] der Länge [F]
nità [F] di misura [F] della lunghezza [F]

m

meter
metro [M]
mètre [M]
Meter [M]
metro [M]

measurement of mass
unidad [F] de medida [F] de masa [F]
mesure [F] de la masse [F]
Maßeinheit [F] der Masse [F]
unità [F] di misura [F] della massa [F]

kg

kilogram
kilogramo [M]
kilogramme [M]
Kilogramm [N]
kilogrammo [M]

measurement of Celsius temperature
unidad [F] de medida [F] de la temperatura [F] Celsius
mesure [F] de la température [F] Celsius
Maßeinheit [F] der Celsius-Temperatur [F]
unità [F] di misura [F] della temperatura [F] Celsius

°C

degree Celsius
grado [M] Celsius
degré [M] Celsius
Grad [M] Celsius
grado [M] Celsius

measurement of thermodynamic temperature
dad [F] de medida [F] de temperatura [F] termodinámica
mesure [F] de la température [F] thermodynamique
aßeinheit [F] der thermodynamischen Temperatur [F]
tà [F] di misura [F] della temperatura [F] termodinamica

K

kelvin
kelvin [M]
kelvin [M]
Kelvin [N]
kelvin [M]

measurement of pressure
unidad [F] de medida [F] de presión [F]
mesure [F] de la pression [F]
Maßeinheit [F] des Drucks [M]
unità [F] di misura [F] della pressione [F]

Pa

pascal
pascal [M]
pascal [M]
Pascal [N]
pascal [M]

measurement of amount of substance
unidad [F] de medida [F] de cantidad [F] de materia [F]
mesure [F] de la quantité [F] de matière [F]
Maßeinheit [F] der Stoffmenge [F]
unità [F] di misura [F] della quantità [F] di sostanza [F]

mol

mole
mol [M]
mole [F]
Mol [N]
mole [F]

measurement of radioactivity
unidad [F] de medida [F] de radioactividad [F]
mesure [F] de la radioactivité [F]
Maßeinheit [F] der Radioaktivität [F]
unità [F] di misura [F] della radioattività [F]

Bq

becquerel
becquerel [M]
becquerel [M]
Becquerel [N]
becquerel [M]

measurement of luminous intensity
unidad [F] de medida [F] de intensidad [F] luminosa
mesure [F] de l'intensité [F] lumineuse
Maßeinheit [F] der Lichtstärke [F]
unità [F] di misura [F] dell'intensità [F] luminosa

cd

candela
candela [F]
candela [F]
Candela [F]
candela [F]

mathematics

matemáticas^{F} | mathématiques^{F} | Mathematik^{F} | matematica^{F}

$-$

minus/negative
resta^{F}
soustraction^{F}
Subtraktion^{F}
sottrazione^{F}

$+$

plus/positive
suma^{F}
addition^{F}
Addition^{F}
addizione^{F}

$\times$

multiplied by
multiplicación^{F}
multiplication^{F}
Multiplikation^{F}
moltiplicazione^{F}

$\div$

divided by
división^{F}
division^{F}
Division^{F}
divisione^{F}

$=$

equals
igual a
égale
ist gleich
uguale a

$\neq$

is not equal to
no es igual a
n'égale pas
ist ungleich
diverso da

$\approx$

is approximately equal to
casi igual a
égale à peu près
ist annähernd gleich
approssimativamente uguale a

$\sim$

is equivalent to
equivalente a
équivaut à
ist äquivalent mit
equivalente a

$\equiv$

is identical with
idéntico a
est identique à
ist identisch mit
coincide con

$\not\equiv$

is not identical with
no es idéntico a
n'est pas identique à
ist nicht identisch mit
non coincide con

$\emptyset$

empty set
conjunto^{M} vacío
ensemble^{M} vide
leere Menge^{F}
insieme^{M} vuoto

$\cup$

union of two sets
unión^{F}
réunion^{F}
Mengenvereinigung^{F}
unione^{F}

$\cap$

intersection of two sets
intersección^{F}
intersection^{F}
Mengenschnitt^{M}
intersezione^{F}

$\subset$

is included in/is a subset of
inclusión^{F}
inclusion^{F}
echte Teilmenge^{F} von
contenuto in

$\pm$

plus or minus
más [M] o menos [M]
plus ou moins
plus oder minus
più o meno

$\leqslant$

is less than or equal to
igual o menor que
égal ou plus petit que
ist gleich oder kleiner als
minore o uguale a

$>$

is greater than
mayor que
plus grand que
ist größer als
maggiore di

$\geqslant$

is greater than or equal to
igual o mayor que
égal ou plus grand que
ist gleich oder größer als
maggiore o uguale a

$<$

is less than
menor que
plus petit que
ist kleiner als
minore di

%

percent
porcentaje [M]
pourcentage [M]
Prozent [N]
percento [M]

$\in$

is an element of
pertenece a
appartenance [F]
Element [N] von
appartiene a

$\notin$

is not an element of
no pertenece a
non-appartenance [F]
nicht Element [N] von
non appartiene a

$\sum$

sum
suma [F]
sommation [F]
Summe [F]
sommatoria [F]

$\sqrt{}$

square root of
raíz [F] cuadrada de
racine [F] carrée de
Quadratwurzel [F] aus
radice [F] quadrata di

$1/2$

fraction
fracción [F]
fraction [F]
Bruch [M]
frazione [F]

∞

infinity
infinito [M]
infini [M]
unendlich
infinito [M]

$\int$

integral
integral
intégrale [F]
Integral [N]
integrale [M]

!

factorial
factorial
factorielle [F]
Fakultät [F]
fattoriale [M]

mathematics

Roman numerals
números[M] romanos
chiffres[M] romains
römische Ziffern[F]
numeri[M] romani

I
one
uno
un[M]
Eins[F]
uno[M]

V
five
cinco
cinq[M]
Fünf[F]
cinque[M]

X
ten
diez
dix[M]
Zehn[F]
dieci[M]

L
fifty
cincuenta
cinquante[M]
Fünfzig[F]
cinquanta[M]

C
one hundred
cien
cent[M]
Hundert[F]
cento[M]

D
five hundred
quinientos
cinq cents[M]
Fünfhundert[F]
cinquecento[M]

M
one thousand
mil
mille[M]
Tausend[F]
mille[M]

biology

biología[F] | biologie[F] | Biologie[F] | biologia[F]

♂
male
masculino[M]
mâle[M]
männlich
maschile

♀
female
femenino[M]
femelle[F]
weiblich
femminile

Rh+
blood factor positive
factor[M] RH positivo
facteur[M] rhésus positif
Rhesusfaktor[M] positiv
fattore[M] Rh positivo

Rh-
blood factor negative
factor[M] RH negativo
facteur[M] rhésus négatif
Rhesusfaktor[M] negativ
fattore[M] Rh negativo

†
death
muerte[F]
mort[F]
gestorben
morte[F]

*
birth
nacimiento[M]
naissance[F]
geboren
nascita[F]

geometry

geometría[F] | géométrie[F] | Geometrie[F] | geometria[F]

°

degree
grado[M]
degré[M]
Grad[M]
grado[M]

′

minute
minuto[M]
minute[F]
Bogenminute[F]
primo[M]

″

second
segundo[M]
seconde[F]
Bogensekunde[F]
secondo[M]

π

pi
pi[M]
pi[M]
Pi[N]
pi[M] greco

⊥

perpendicular
perpendicular[F]
perpendiculaire[F]
ist senkrecht zu
perpendicolare

∥

is parallel to
es paralelo a
parallèle
ist parallel zu
parallelo a

∦

is not parallel to
no es paralelo a
non parallèle
ist nicht parallel zu
non parallelo a

∟

right angle
ángulo[M] recto
angle[M] droit
rechter Winkel[M]
angolo[M] retto

obtuse angle
ángulo[M] obtuso
angle[M] obtus
stumpfer Winkel[M]
angolo[M] ottuso

∠

acute angle
ángulo[M] agudo
angle[M] aigu
spitzer Winkel[M]
angolo[M] acuto

geometrical shapes

formas[F] geométricas | formes[F] géométriques | geometrische Formen[F] | forme[F] geometriche

examples of angles
ejemplos[M] de ángulos[M]
exemples[M] d'angles[M]
Beispiele[N] für Winkel[M]
esempi[M] di angoli[M]

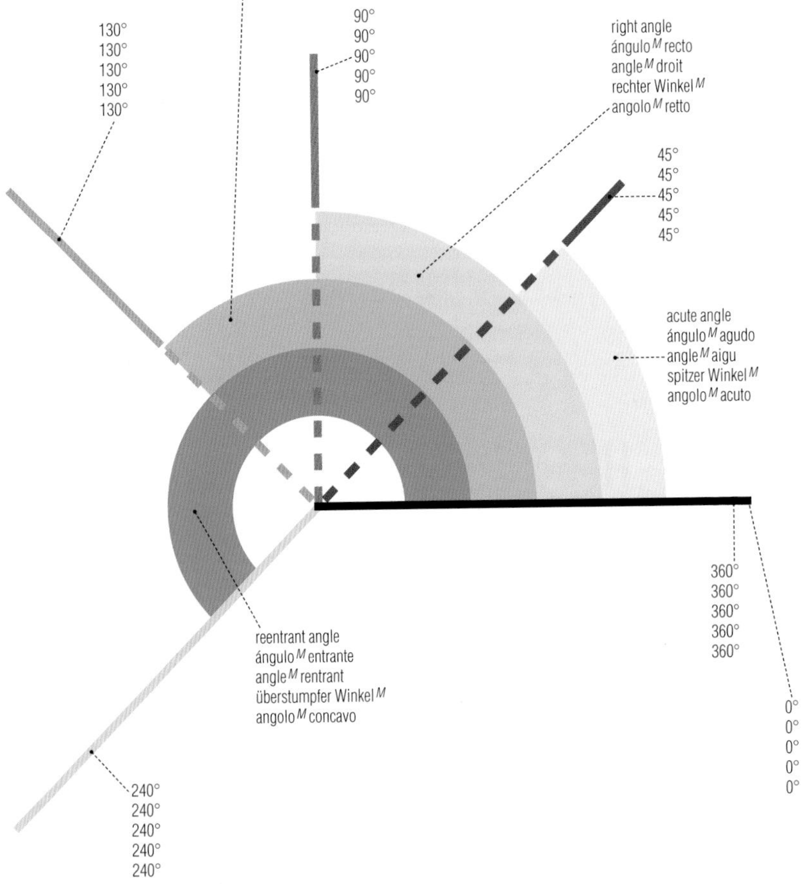
obtuse angle
ángulo[M] obtuso
angle[M] obtus
stumpfer Winkel[M]
angolo[M] ottuso
130°
130°
130°
130°
130°
90°
90°
90°
90°
90°
right angle
ángulo[M] recto
angle[M] droit
rechter Winkel[M]
angolo[M] retto
45°
45°
45°
45°
45°
acute angle
ángulo[M] agudo
angle[M] aigu
spitzer Winkel[M]
angolo[M] acuto
360°
360°
360°
360°
360°
reentrant angle
ángulo[M] entrante
angle[M] rentrant
überstumpfer Winkel[M]
angolo[M] concavo
0°
0°
0°
0°
0°
240°
240°
240°
240°
240°

plane surfaces
superficies *F*
surfaces *F*
ebene Flächen *F*
superfici *F*

parts of a circle
partes *F* **de un círculo** *M*
parties *F* **d'un cercle** *M*
Teile *M* **eines Kreises** *M*
parti *F* **di un cerchio** *M*

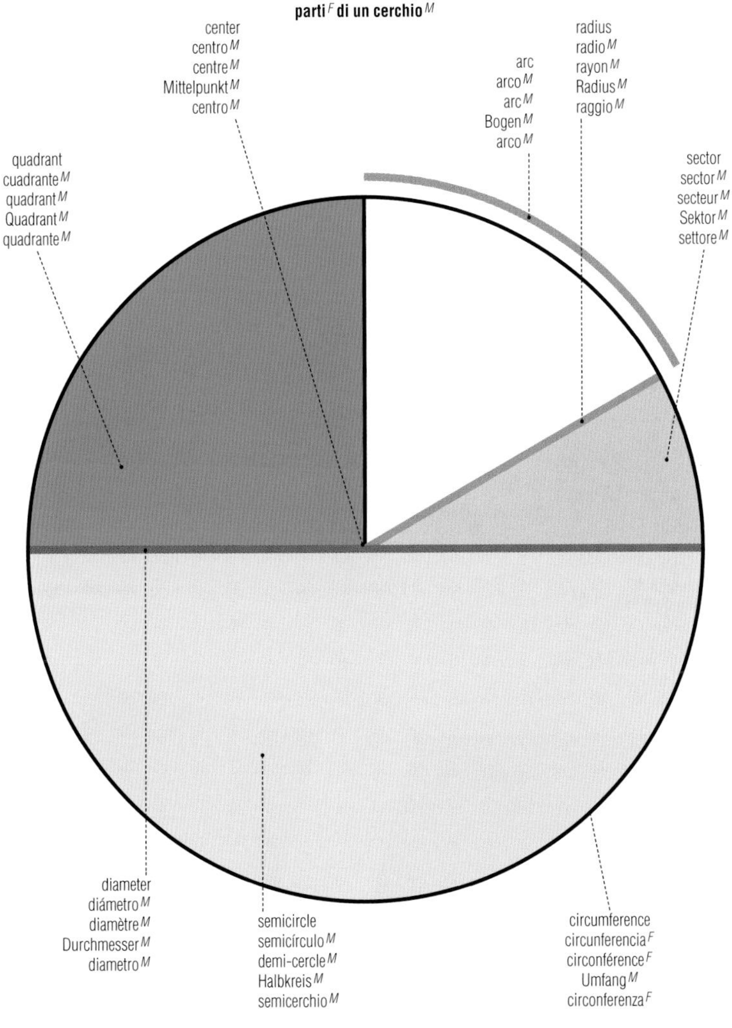
center
centro M
centre M
Mittelpunkt M
centro M
radius
radio M
rayon M
Radius M
raggio M
arc
arco M
arc M
Bogen M
arco M
quadrant
cuadrante M
quadrant M
Quadrant M
quadrante M
sector
sector M
secteur M
Sektor M
settore M
diameter
diámetro M
diamètre M
Durchmesser M
diametro M
semicircle
semicírculo M
demi-cercle M
Halbkreis M
semicerchio M
circumference
circunferencia F
circonférence F
Umfang M
circonferenza F

polygons
polígonos *M*
polygones *M*
Vielecke *N*
poligoni *M*

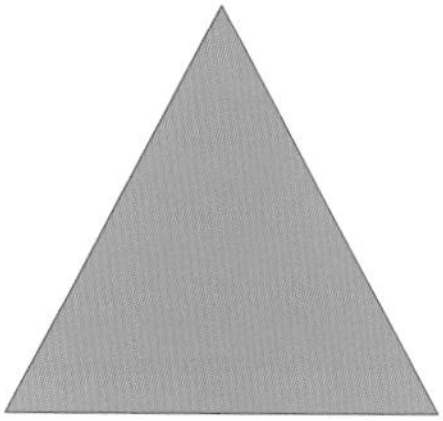

triangle
triángulo *M*
triangle *M*
Dreieck *N*
triangolo *M*

square
cuadrado *M*
carré *M*
Quadrat *N*
quadrato *M*

rectangle
rectángulo *M*
rectangle *M*
Rechteck *N*
rettangolo *M*

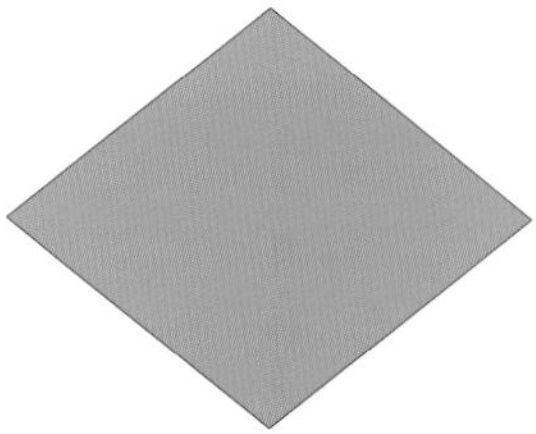

rhombus
rombo *M*
losange *M*
Rhombus *M*
rombo *M*

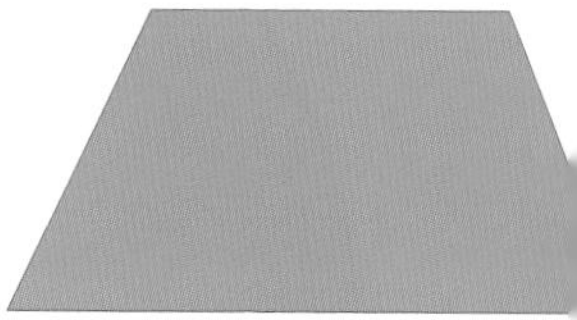

trapezoid
trapecio *M*
trapèze *M*
unregelmäßiges Trapez *N*
trapezio *M*

parallelogram
paralelogramo *M*
parallélogramme *M*
Parallelogramm *N*
parallelogramma *M*

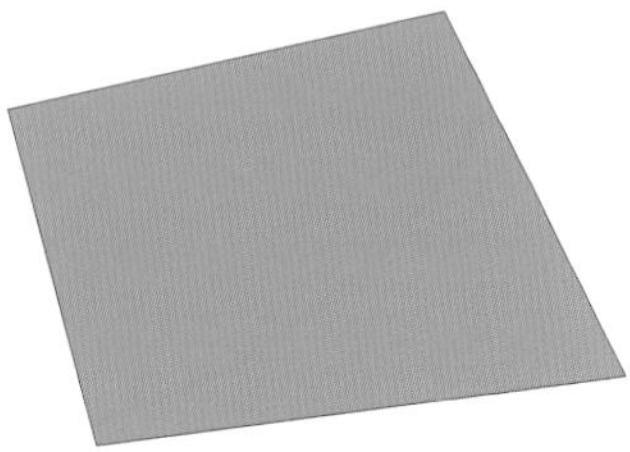

quadrilateral
cuadrilátero *M*
quadrilatère *M*
Viereck *N*
quadrilatero *M*

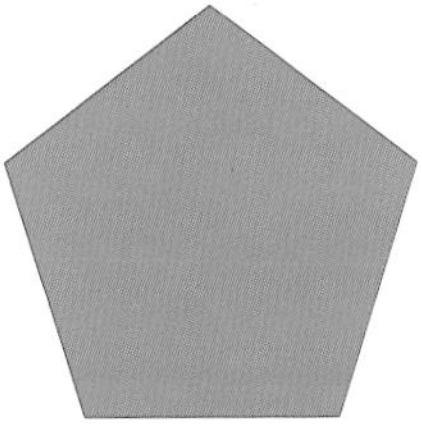

regular pentagon
pentágono[M] regular
pentagone[M] régulier
regelmäßiges Fünfeck[N]
pentagono[M] regolare

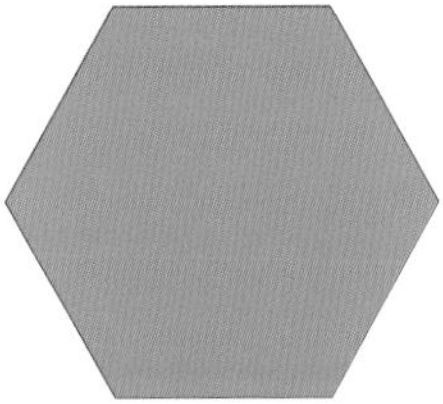

regular hexagon
hexágono[M] regular
hexagone[M] régulier
regelmäßiges Sechseck[N]
esagono[M] regolare

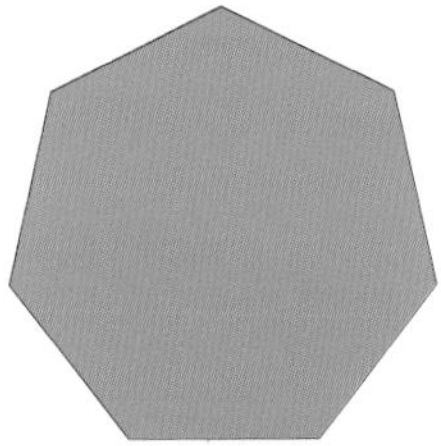

regular heptagon
heptágono[M] regular
heptagone[M] régulier
regelmäßiges Siebeneck[N]
ettagono[M] regolare

regular octagon
octágono[M] regular
octogone[M] régulier
regelmäßiges Achteck[N]
ottagono[M] regolare

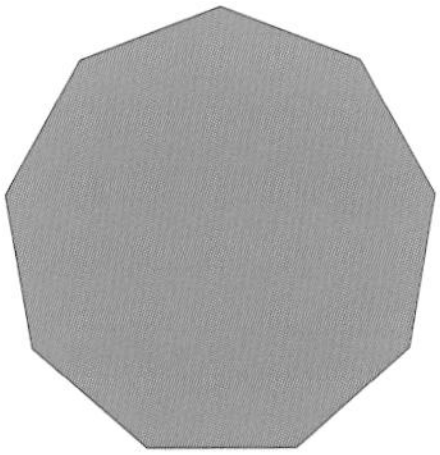

regular nonagon
nonágono[M] regular
ennéagone[M] régulier
regelmäßiges Neuneck[N]
enneagono[M] regolare

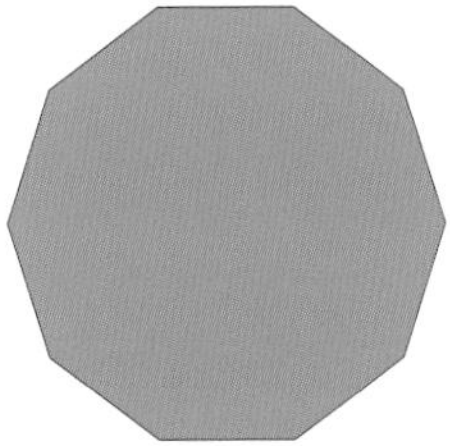

regular decagon
decágono[M] regular
décagone[M] régulier
regelmäßiges Zehneck[N]
decagono[M] regolare

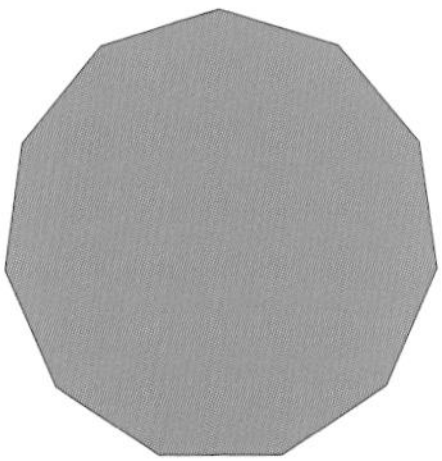

regular hendecagon
endecágono[M] regular
hendécagone[M] régulier
regelmäßiges Elfeck[N]
endecagono[M] regolare

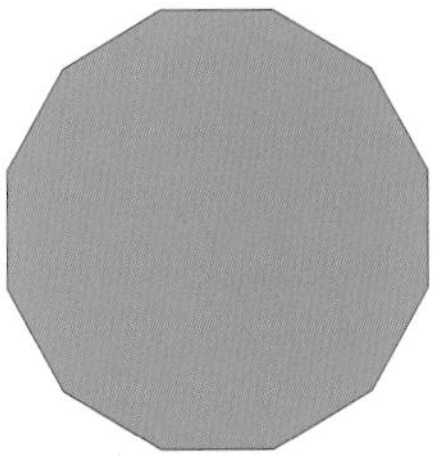

regular dodecagon
dodecágono[M] regular
dodécagone[M] régulier
regelmäßiges Zwölfeck[N]
dodecagono[M] regolare

geometrical shapes

solids
cuerpos *M* **sólidos**
volumes *M*
Körper *M*
solidi *M*

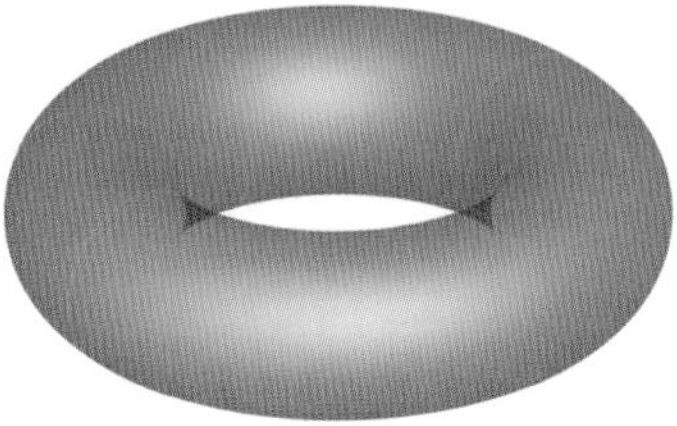

torus
toro *M*
tore *M*
Torus *M*
toro *M*

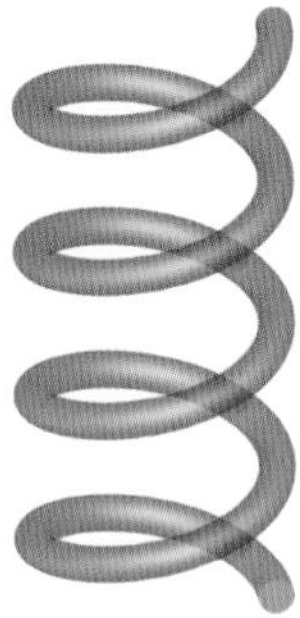

helix
hélice *F*
hélice *F*
Helix *F*
elica *F*

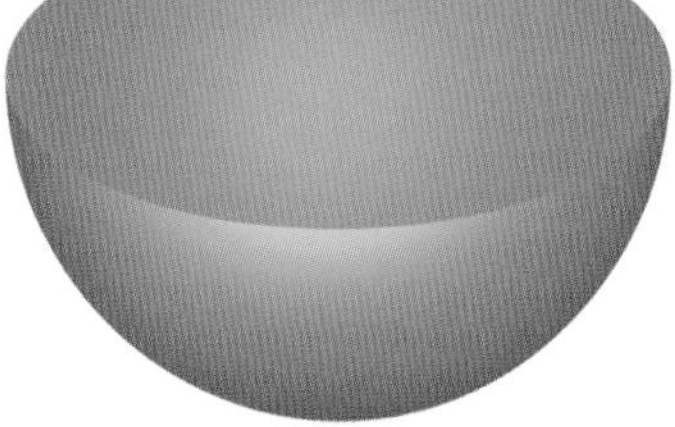

hemisphere
hemisferio *M*
hémisphère *M*
Halbkugel *F*
semisfera *F*

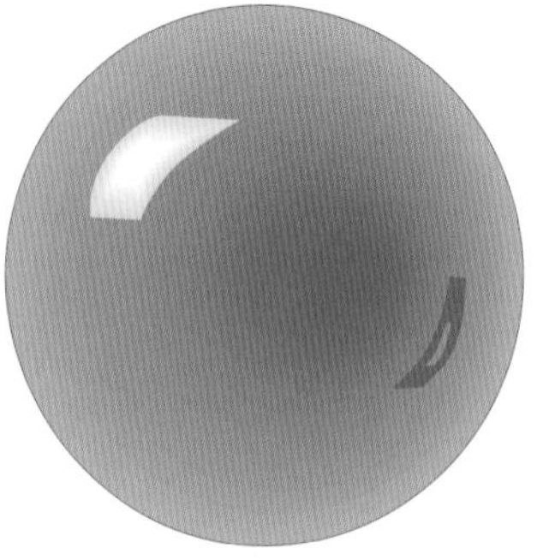

sphere
esfera *F*
sphère *F*
Kugel *F*
sfera *F*

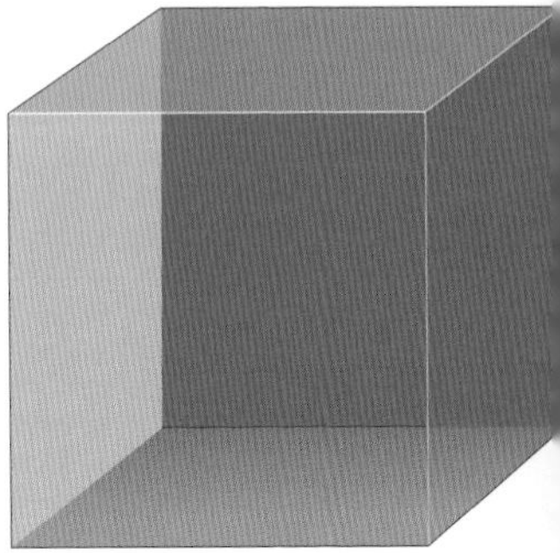

cube
cubo *M*
cube *M*
Würfel *M*
cubo *M*

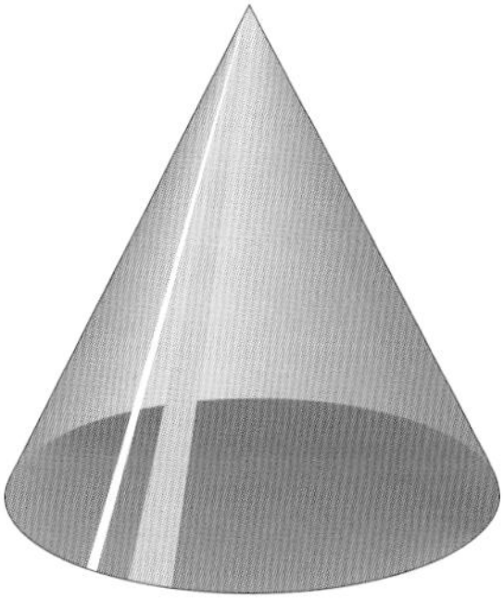

cone
cono M
cône M
Kegel M
cono M

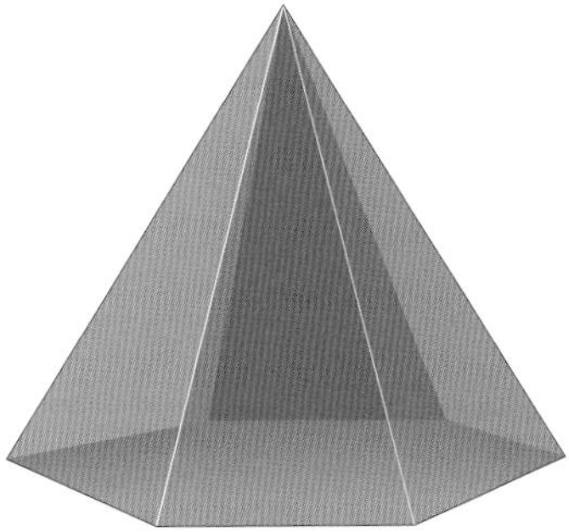

pyramid
pirámide F
pyramide F
Pyramide F
piramide F

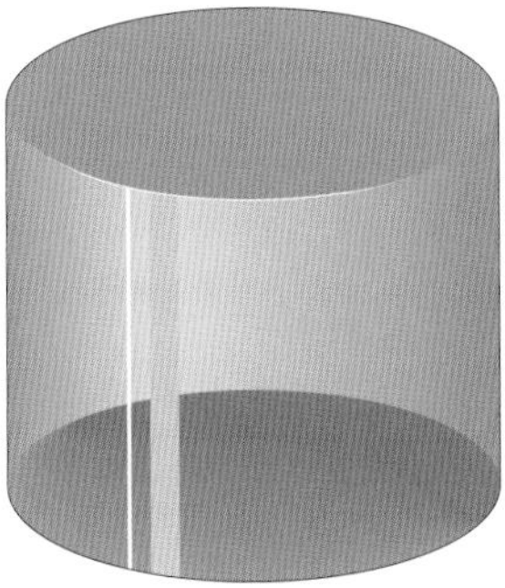

cylinder
cilindro M
cylindre M
Zylinder M
cilindro M

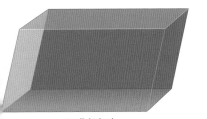

parallelepiped
paralelepípedo M
parallélépipède M
Parallelepiped N
parallelepipedo M

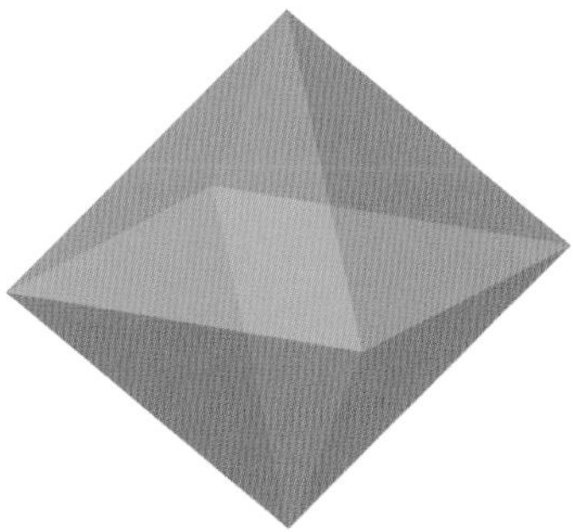

regular octahedron
octaedro M **regular**
octaèdre M **régulier**
regelmäßiges Oktaeder N
ottaedro M **regolare**

production of electricity from geothermal energy

producción[F] de electricidad[F] por energía[F] geotérmica | production[F] d'électricité[F] par énergie[F] géothermique | Elektrizitätserzeugung[F] aus geothermischer Energie[F] | produzione[F] di elettricità[F] da energia[F] geotermica

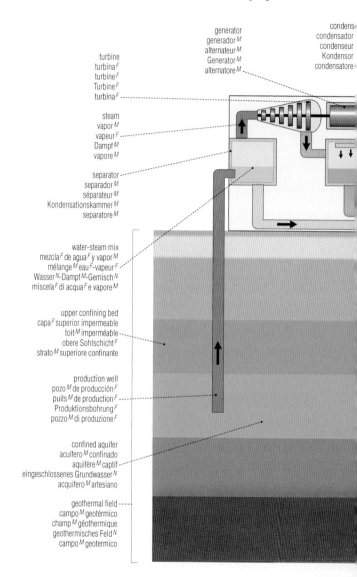

generator
generador[M]
alternateur[M]
Generator[M]
alternatore[M]

condens
condensador
condenseur
Kondensor
condensatore

turbine
turbina[F]
turbine[F]
Turbine[F]
turbina[F]

steam
vapor[M]
vapeur[F]
Dampf[M]
vapore[M]

separator
separador[M]
séparateur[M]
Kondensationskammer[M]
separatore[M]

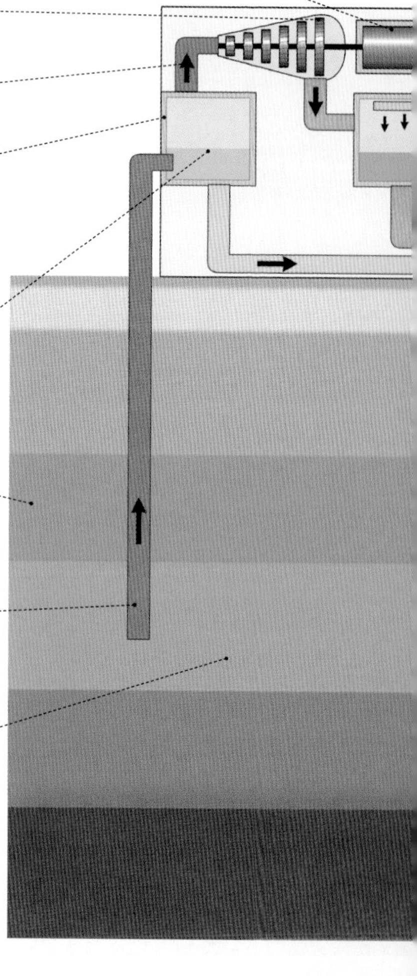

water-steam mix
mezcla[F] de agua[F] y vapor[M]
mélange[M] eau[F]-vapeur[F]
Wasser[N]-Dampf[M]-Gemisch[N]
miscela[F] di acqua[F] e vapore[M]

upper confining bed
capa[F] superior impermeable
toit[M] imperméable
obere Sohlschicht[F]
strato[M] superiore confinante

production well
pozo[M] de producción[F]
puits[M] de production[F]
Produktionsbohrung[F]
pozzo[M] di produzione[F]

confined aquifer
acuífero[M] confinado
aquifère[M] captif
eingeschlossenes Grundwasser[N]
acquifero[M] artesiano

geothermal field
campo[M] geotérmico
champ[M] géothermique
geothermisches Feld[N]
campo[M] geotermico

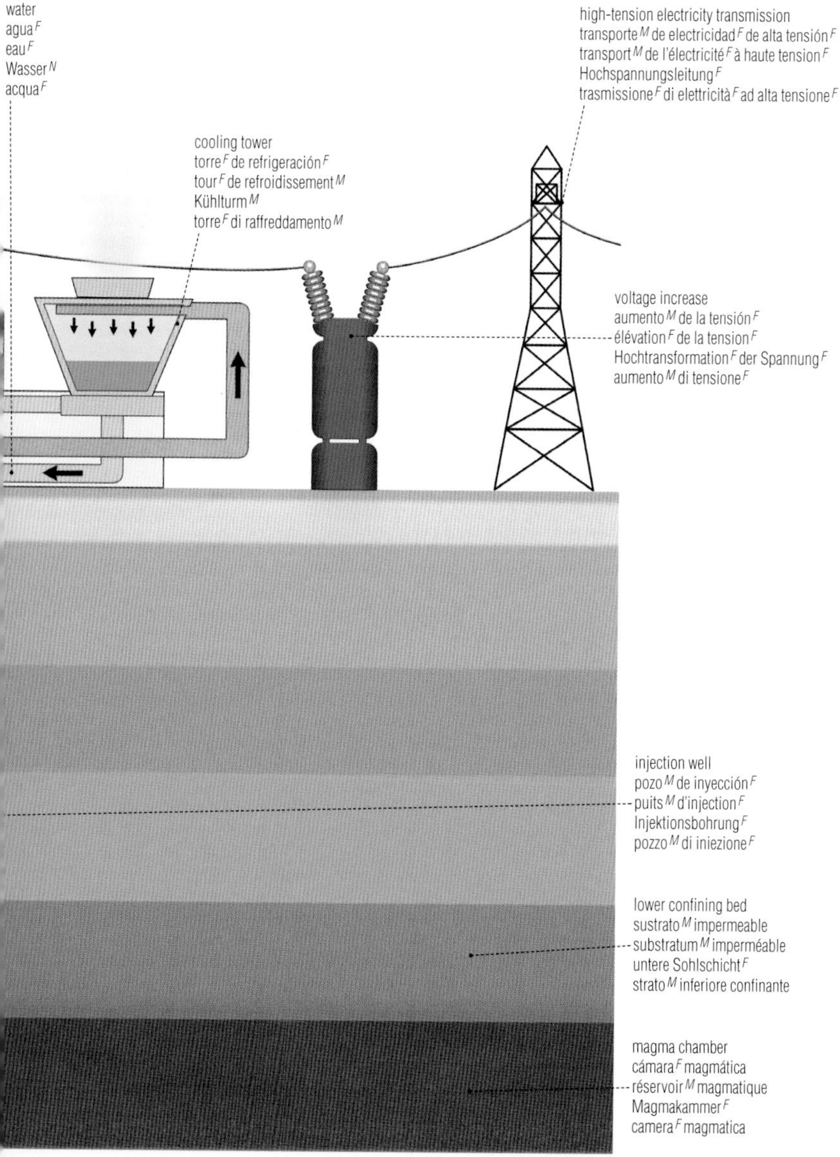
water
agua F
eau F
Wasser N
acqua F
high-tension electricity transmission
transporte M de electricidad F de alta tensión F
transport M de l'électricité F à haute tension F
Hochspannungsleitung F
trasmissione F di elettricità F ad alta tensione F
cooling tower
torre F de refrigeración F
tour F de refroidissement M
Kühlturm M
torre F di raffreddamento M
voltage increase
aumento M de la tensión F
élévation F de la tension F
Hochtransformation F der Spannung F
aumento M di tensione F
injection well
pozo M de inyección F
puits M d'injection F
Injektionsbohrung F
pozzo M di iniezione F
lower confining bed
sustrato M impermeable
substratum M imperméable
untere Sohlschicht F
strato M inferiore confinante
magma chamber
cámara F magmática
réservoir M magmatique
Magmakammer F
camera F magmatica

thermal energy

energía^F térmica | énergie^F thermique | Wärmeenergie^F | energia^F termica

production of electricity from thermal energy
producción^F de electricidad^F por energía^F térmica
production^F d'électricité^F par énergie^F thermique
Elektrizitätserzeugung^F aus Wärmeenergie^F
produzione^F di elettricità^F da energia^F termica

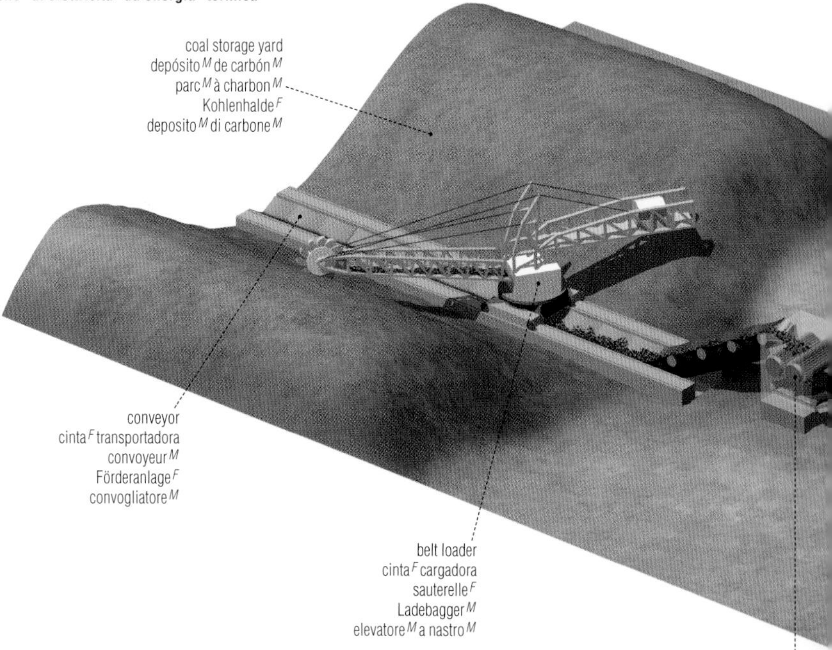

coal storage yard
depósito^M de carbón^M
parc^M à charbon^M
Kohlenhalde^F
deposito^M di carbone^M
conveyor
cinta^F transportadora
convoyeur^M
Förderanlage^F
convogliatore^M
belt loader
cinta^F cargadora
sauterelle^F
Ladebagger^M
elevatore^M a nastro^M
crusher
trituradora^F
broyeur^M
Zerkleinerungswerk^N
frantumatore^M

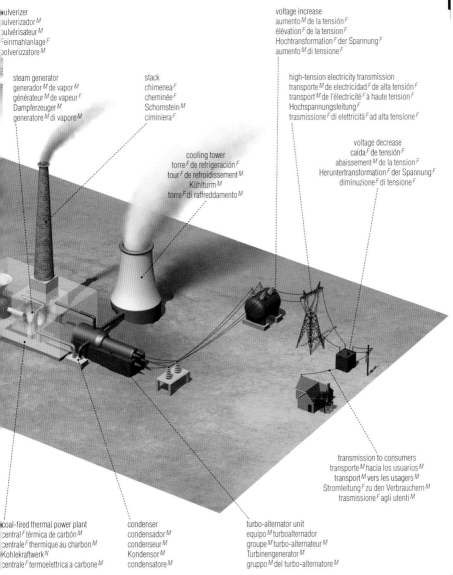

ulverizer
ulverizador[M]
ulvérisateur[M]
einmahlanlage[F]
olverizzatore[M]

voltage increase
aumento[M] de la tensión[F]
élévation[F] de la tension[F]
Hochtransformation[F] der Spannung[F]
aumento[M] di tensione[F]

steam generator
generador[M] de vapor[M]
générateur[M] de vapeur[F]
Dampferzeuger[M]
generatore[M] di vapore[M]

stack
chimenea[F]
cheminée[F]
Schornstein[M]
ciminiera[F]

high-tension electricity transmission
transporte[M] de electricidad[F] de alta tensión[F]
transport[M] de l'électricité[F] à haute tension[F]
Hochspannungsleitung[F]
trasmissione[F] di elettricità[F] ad alta tensione[F]

voltage decrease
caída[F] de tensión[F]
abaissement[M] de la tension[F]
Heruntertransformation[F] der Spannung[F]
diminuzione[F] di tensione[F]

cooling tower
torre[F] de refrigeración[F]
tour[F] de refroidissement[M]
Kühlturm[M]
torre[F] di raffreddamento[M]

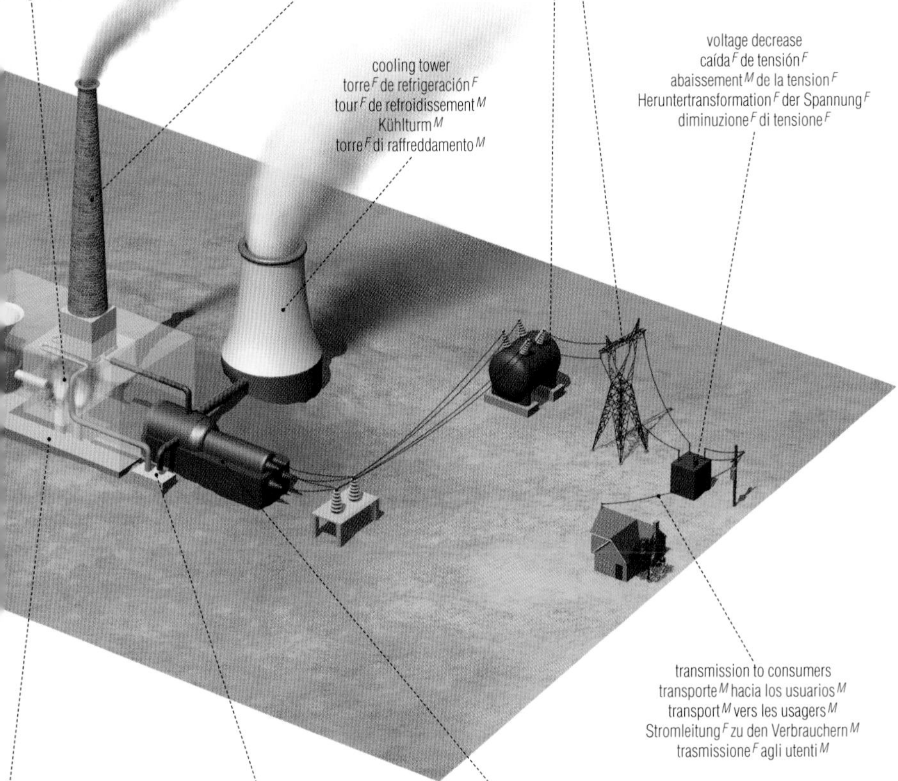

transmission to consumers
transporte[M] hacia los usuarios[M]
transport[M] vers les usagers[M]
Stromleitung[F] zu den Verbrauchern[M]
trasmissione[F] agli utenti[M]

coal-fired thermal power plant
central[F] térmica de carbón[M]
centrale[F] thermique au charbon[M]
Kohlekraftwerk[N]
centrale[F] termoelettrica a carbone[M]

condenser
condensador[M]
condenseur[M]
Kondensor[M]
condensatore[M]

turbo-alternator unit
equipo[M] turboalternador
groupe[M] turbo-alternateur[M]
Turbinengenerator[M]
gruppo[M] del turbo-alternatore[M]

coal mine

minas[F] de carbón[M] | mine[F] de charbon[M] | Kohlebergwerk[N] | miniera[F] di carbone[M]

underground mine
mina[F] subterránea
mine[F] souterraine
Grube[F]
miniera[F] sotterranea

headframe
castillete[M] de extracción[F]
chevalement[M]
Schachtgerüst[N]
castelletto[M] di testa[F] del pozzo[M]

vertical shaft
tiro[M] vertical
puits[M] vertical
Richtschacht[M]
pozzo[M] verticale

elevator
montacargas[M]
ascenseur[M]
Aufzug[M]
ascensore[M]

pillar
pilar[M]
pilier[M]
Abbaupfeiler[M]
pilastro[M]

room
cámara[F]
chambre[F]
Kammer[F]
camera[F]

chute
chimenea[F]
cheminée[F]
Rutsche[F]
fornello[M] di getto[M]

cross cut
galería[F] transversal
travers-banc[M]
Querschlag[M]
traversa[F]

manway
galería[F] de acceso[M]
galerie[F] de circulation[F]
Einstiegschacht[M]
fornello[M] di accesso[M]

drift
galería[F] de arrastre[M]
galerie[F] en direction[F]
Seitenstollen[M]
galleria[F] in direzione[F]

winze
pozo[M] ciego[M]
descenderie[F]
Blindschacht[M]
discenderia[F]

face
frente[M] de corte[M]
front[M] de taille[F]
Abbaufront[F]
fronte[M]

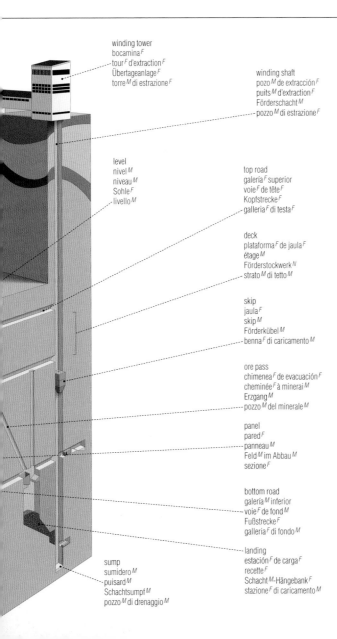

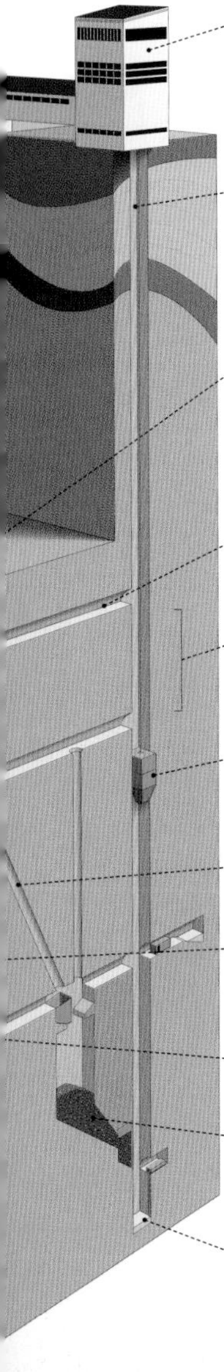

winding tower
bocamina F
tour F d'extraction F
Übertageanlage F
torre M di estrazione F

winding shaft
pozo M de extracción F
puits M d'extraction F
Förderschacht M
pozzo M di estrazione F

level
nivel M
niveau M
Sohle F
livello M

top road
galería F superior
voie F de tête F
Kopfstrecke F
galleria F di testa F

deck
plataforma F de jaula F
étage M
Förderstockwerk N
strato M di tetto M

skip
jaula F
skip M
Förderkübel M
benna F di caricamento M

ore pass
chimenea F de evacuación F
cheminée F à minerai M
Erzgang M
pozzo M del minerale M

panel
pared F
panneau M
Feld M im Abbau M
sezione F

bottom road
galería M inferior
voie F de fond M
Fußstrecke F
galleria F di fondo M

landing
estación F de carga F
recette F
Schacht M-Hängebank F
stazione F di caricamento M

sump
sumidero M
puisard M
Schachtsumpf M
pozzo M di drenaggio M

oil

petróleo M | pétrole M | Erdöl N | petrolio M

drilling rig
torre F de perforación F
appareil M de forage M
Bohranlage F
impianto M di trivellazione F

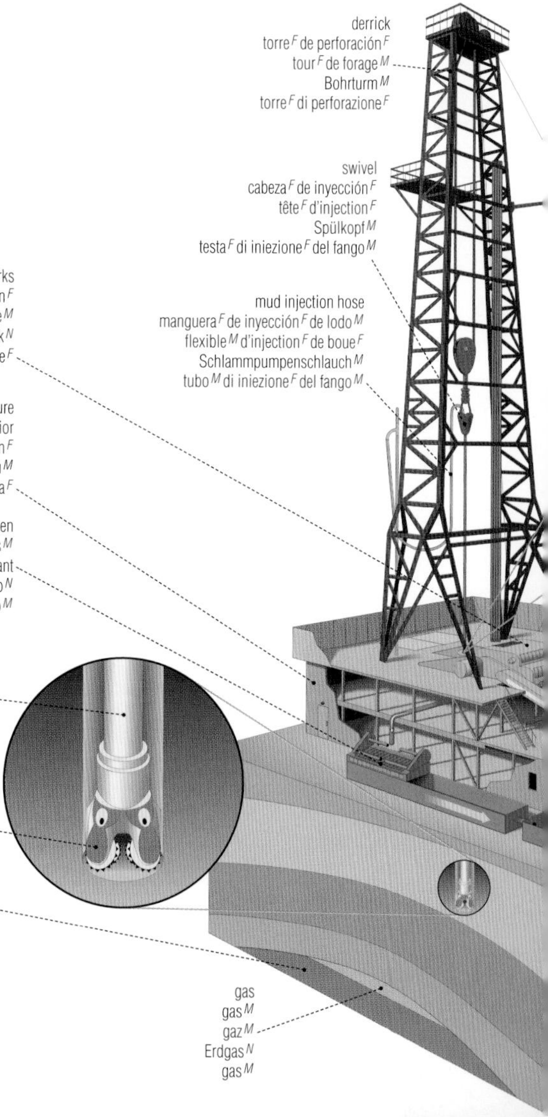
derrick
torre F de perforación F
tour F de forage M
Bohrturm M
torre F di perforazione F
swivel
cabeza F de inyección F
tête F d'injection F
Spülkopf M
testa F di iniezione F del fango M
drilling drawworks
torno M de perforación F
treuil M de forage M
Antriebs- und Hebewerk N
argani M di perforazione F
mud injection hose
manguera F de inyección F de lodo M
flexible M d'injection F de boue F
Schlammpumpenschlauch M
tubo M di iniezione F del fango M
substructure
estructura F inferior
massif M de fondation F
Unterbau M
sottostruttura F
vibrating mudscreen
tamiz M vibratorio para lodos M
tamis M vibrant
Schüttelsieb N
vibrovaglio M per la depurazione F del fango M
drill pipe
tubo M de perforación F
tige F de forage M
Bohrgestänge N
asta F di perforazione F
bit
barrena F
trépan M
Bohrkopf M
scalpello M
oil
petróleo M
pétrole M
Erdöl N
petrolio M
gas
gas M
gaz M
Erdgas N
gas M

rotary system
sistema^M rotativo
système^M rotary
Drehbohrverfahren^F
sistema^M a rotazione^F

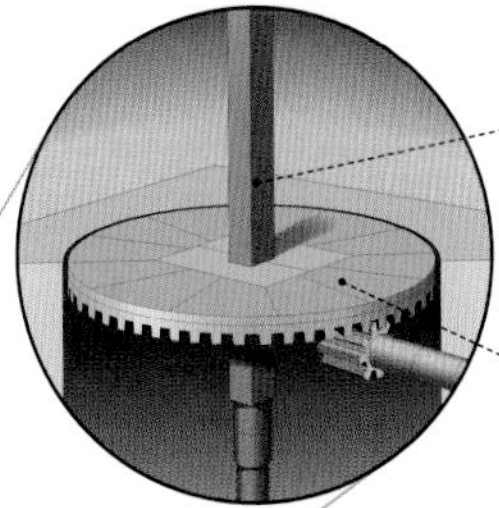

kelly
vástago^M de arrastre^M
tige^F carrée d'entraînement^M
Mitnehmerstange^F
asta^F motrice quadra

rotary table
mesa^F rotatoria
table^F de rotation^F
Drehtisch^M
tavola^F di rotazione^F

engine
motor^M
moteur^M
Motor^M
motore^M

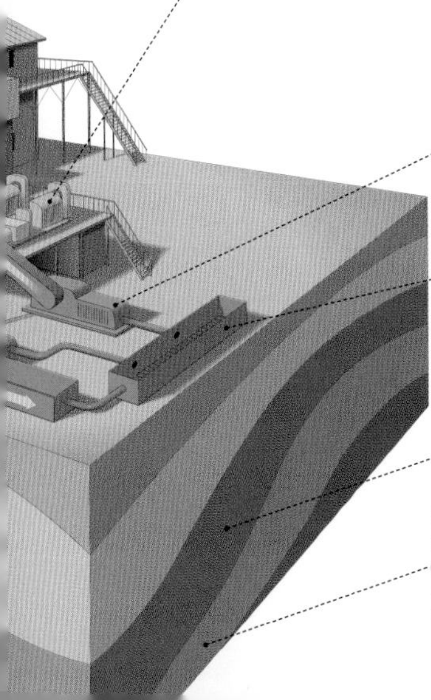

mud pump
bomba^F para lodos^M
pompe^F à boue^F
Schlammpumpe^F
pompa^F di circolazione^F del fango^M

mud pit
depósito^M de lodos^M
bac^M à boue^F
Schlammgrube^F
vasca^F del fango^M

anticline
anticlinal^M
anticlinal^M
Antiklinale^F
anticlinale^F

impervious rock
roca^F impermeable
couche^F imperméable
undurchlässiges Gestein^N
roccia^F impermeabile

crude-oil pipeline
oleoducto M para crudo M
réseau M d'oléoducs M
Rohölpipeline F
rete F di oleodotti M

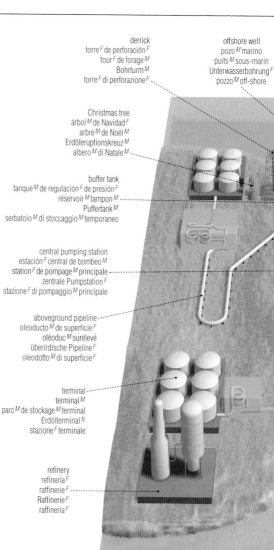

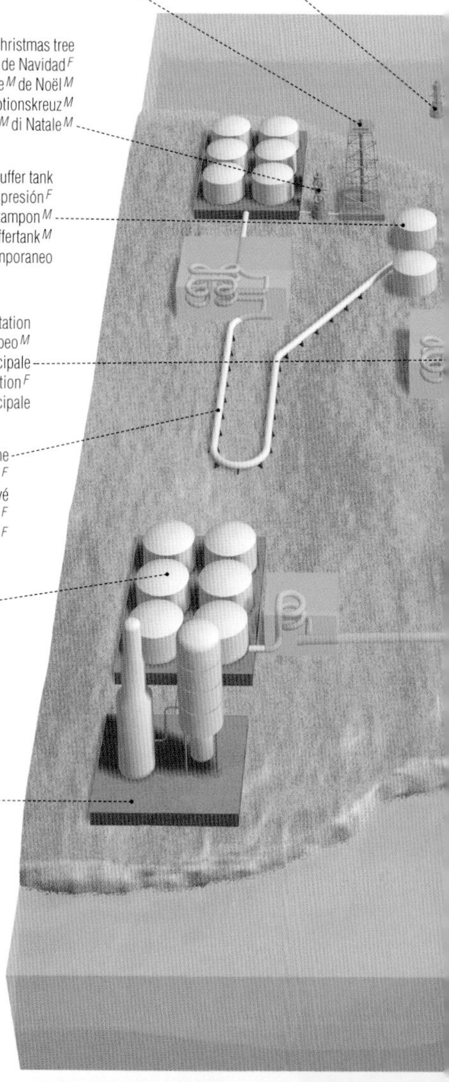
derrick
torre F de perforación F
tour F de forage M
Bohrturm M
torre F di perforazione F
offshore well
pozo M marino
puits M sous-marin
Unterwasserbohrung F
pozzo M off-shore
Christmas tree
árbol M de Navidad F
arbre M de Noël M
Erdöleruptionskreuz M
albero M di Natale M
buffer tank
tanque M de regulación F de presión F
réservoir M tampon M
Puffertank M
serbatoio M di stoccaggio M temporaneo
central pumping station
estación F central de bombeo M
station F de pompage M principale
zentrale Pumpstation F
stazione F di pompaggio M principale
aboveground pipeline
oleoducto M de superficie F
oléoduc M surélevé
überirdische Pipeline F
oleodotto M di superficie F
terminal
terminal M
parc M de stockage M terminal
Erdölterminal N
stazione F terminale
refinery
refinería F
raffinerie F
Raffinerie F
raffineria F

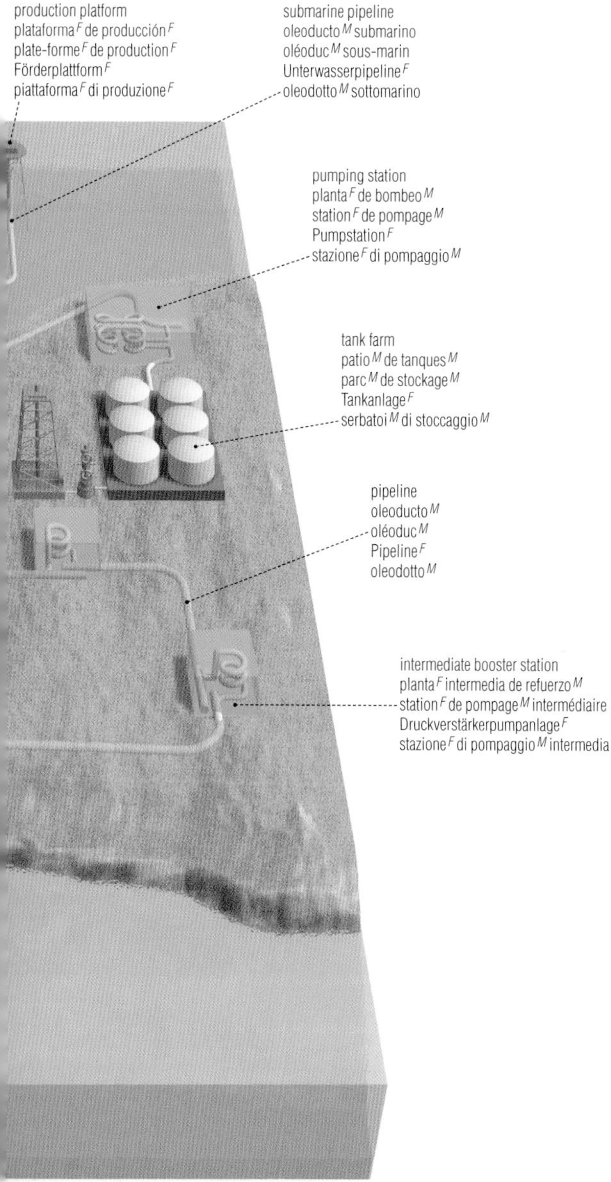
production platform
plataforma^{F} de producción^{F}
plate-forme^{F} de production^{F}
Förderplattform^{F}
piattaforma^{F} di produzione^{F}
submarine pipeline
oleoducto^{M} submarino
oléoduc^{M} sous-marin
Unterwasserpipeline^{F}
oleodotto^{M} sottomarino
pumping station
planta^{F} de bombeo^{M}
station^{F} de pompage^{M}
Pumpstation^{F}
stazione^{F} di pompaggio^{M}
tank farm
patio^{M} de tanques^{M}
parc^{M} de stockage^{M}
Tankanlage^{F}
serbatoi^{M} di stoccaggio^{M}
pipeline
oleoducto^{M}
oléoduc^{M}
Pipeline^{F}
oleodotto^{M}
intermediate booster station
planta^{F} intermedia de refuerzo^{M}
station^{F} de pompage^{M} intermédiaire
Druckverstärkerpumpanlage^{F}
stazione^{F} di pompaggio^{M} intermedia

hydroelectric complex

complejo^M hidroeléctrico | complexe^M hydroélectrique | Wasserkraftwerk^N | impianto^M idroelettrico

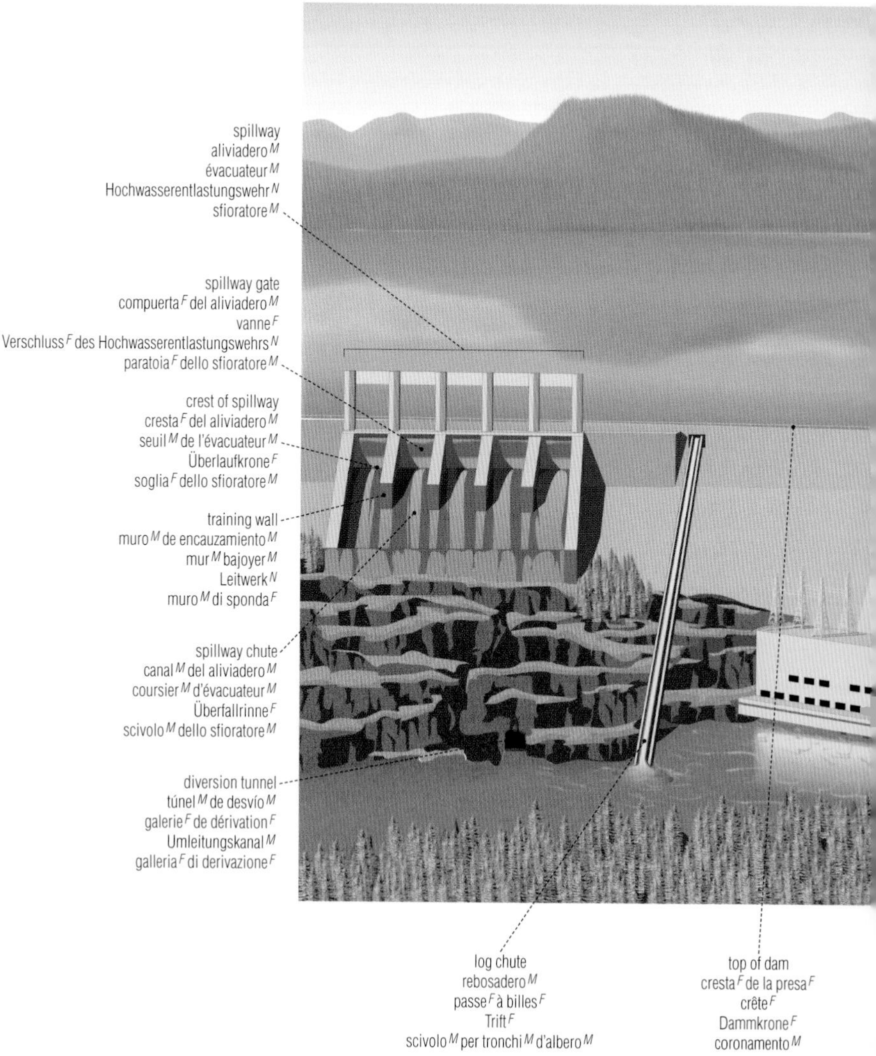
spillway
aliviadero M
évacuateur M
Hochwasserentlastungswehr N
sfioratore M
spillway gate
compuerta F del aliviadero M
vanne F
Verschluss F des Hochwasserentlastungswehrs N
paratoia F dello sfioratore M
crest of spillway
cresta F del aliviadero M
seuil M de l'évacuateur M
Überlaufkrone F
soglia F dello sfioratore M
training wall
muro M de encauzamiento M
mur M bajoyer M
Leitwerk N
muro M di sponda F
spillway chute
canal M del aliviadero M
coursier M d'évacuateur M
Überfallrinne F
scivolo M dello sfioratore M
diversion tunnel
túnel M de desvío M
galerie F de dérivation F
Umleitungskanal M
galleria F di derivazione F
log chute
rebosadero M
passe F à billes F
Trift F
scivolo M per tronchi M d'albero M
top of dam
cresta F de la presa F
crête F
Dammkrone F
coronamento M

hydroelectric complex

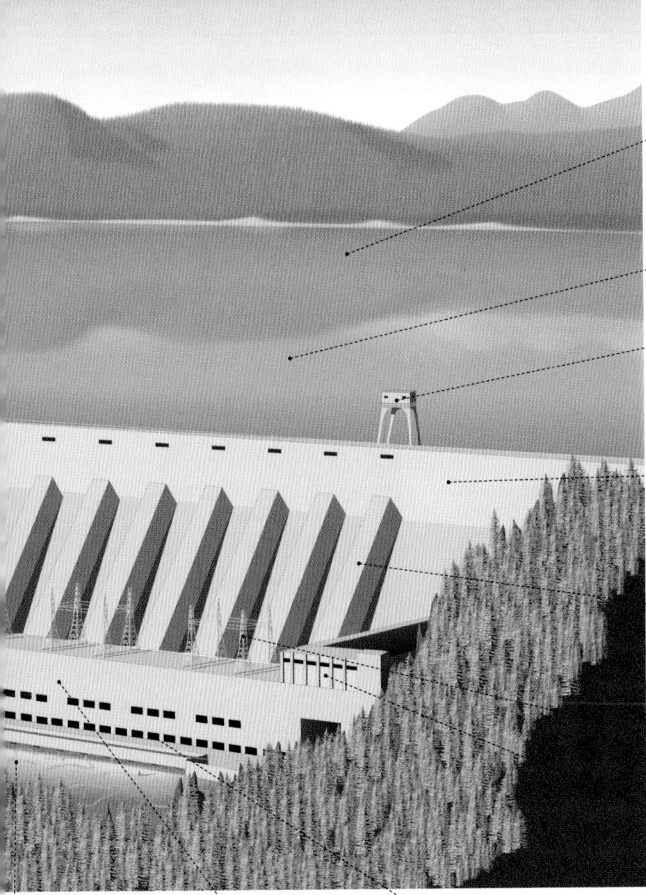

reservoir
embalse[M]
réservoir[M]
Stausee[M]
bacino[M]

headbay
embalse[M] a monte[M]
bief[M] d'amont[M]
Oberwasser[N]
bacino[M] a monte[M]

gantry crane
grúa[F] de caballete[M]
portique[M]
Bockkran[M]
gru[F] a portale[M]

dam
presa[F]
barrage[M]
Damm[M]
diga[F]

penstock
tubería[F] de carga[F]
conduite[F] forcée
Fallleitung[F]
condotta[F] forzata

bushing
boquilla[F]
traversée[F] de transformateur[M]
Durchführung[F]
stazione[F] di trasformazione[F]

control room
sala[F] de control[M]
salle[F] de commande[F]
Steuerzentrale[F]
sala[F] di controllo[M]

afterbay
embalse[M] de compensación[F]
bief[M] d'aval[M]
Ausgleichsbecken[N]
bacino[M] a valle[F]

power plant
central[F] eléctrica
centrale[F]
Speicherkraftwerk[N]
centrale[F] elettrica

machine hall
sala[F] de máquinas[F]
salle[F] des machines[F]
Maschinenhalle[F]
sala[F] macchine[F]

hydroelectric complex

cross section of a hydroelectric power plant
sección[F] transversal de una central[F] hidroeléctrica
coupe[F] d'une centrale[F] hydroélectrique
Wasserkraftwerk[N] im Querschnitt[M]
sezione[F] trasversale di una centrale[F] idroelettrica

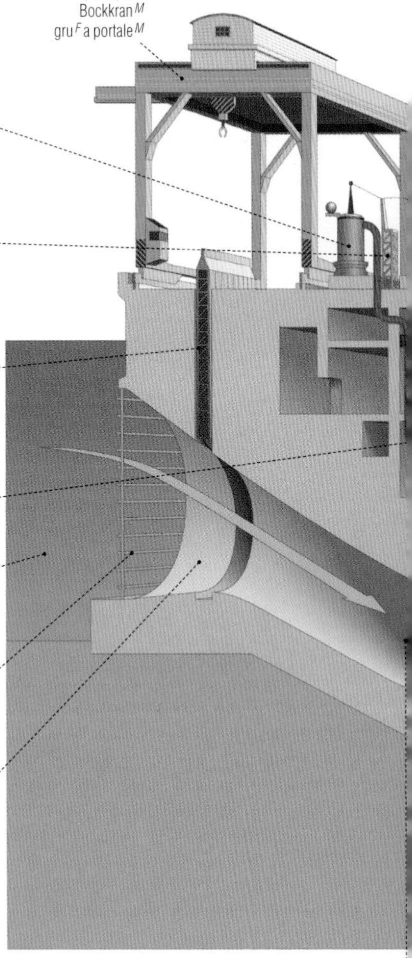
gantry crane
grúa[F] de caballete[M]
portique[M]
Bockkran[M]
gru[F] a portale[M]
transformer
transformador[M]
transformateur[M]
Transformator[M]
trasformatore[M]
circuit breaker
interruptor[M] automático
disjoncteur[M]
Sicherungsautomat[M]
interruttore[M] automatico
gate
compuerta[F]
vanne[F]
Rechen[M]
paratoia[F]
busbar
barra[F] colectora
barre[F] blindée
Sammelschiene[F]
barra[F] collettrice
reservoir
embalse[M]
réservoir[M]
Stausee[M]
bacino[M]
screen
rejilla[F]
grille[F]
Rechen[M]
griglia[F]
water intake
entrada[F] de agua[F]
prise[F] d'eau[F]
Wassereinlass[M]
presa[F] d'acqua[F]
penstoc
conducción[F] forzad
conduite[F] forcé
Fallleitung
condotta[F] forzat

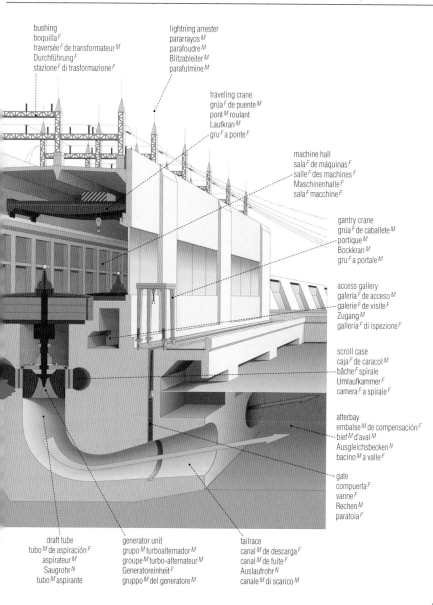

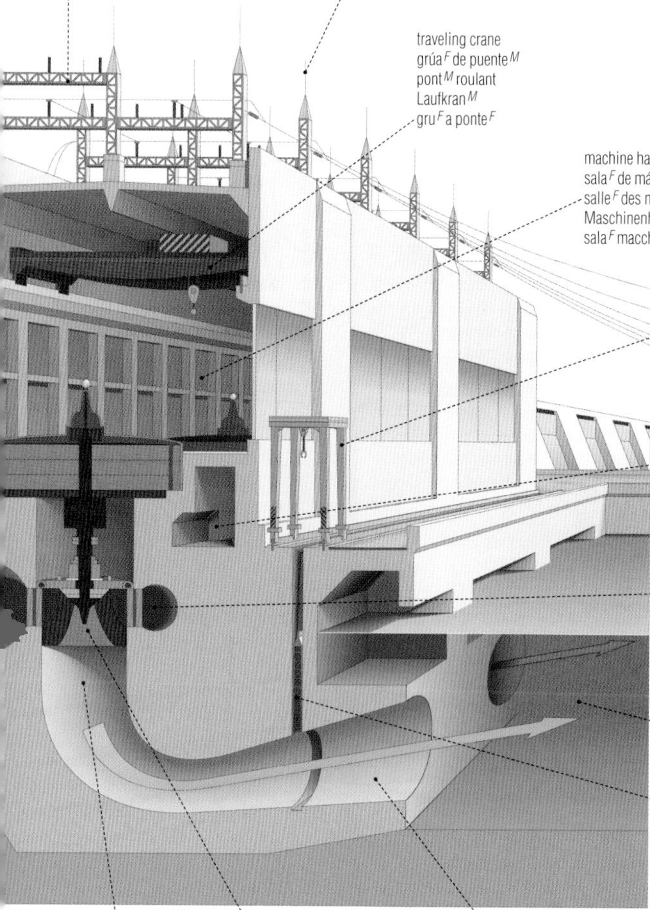
bushing
boquilla F
traversée F de transformateur M
Durchführung F
stazione F di trasformazione F
lightning arrester
pararrayos M
parafoudre M
Blitzableiter M
parafulmine M
traveling crane
grúa F de puente M
pont M roulant
Laufkran M
gru F a ponte F
machine hall
sala F de máquinas F
salle F des machines F
Maschinenhalle F
sala F macchine F
gantry crane
grúa F de caballete M
portique M
Bockkran M
gru F a portale M
access gallery
galería F de acceso M
galerie F de visite F
Zugang M
galleria F di ispezione F
scroll case
caja F de caracol M
bâche F spirale
Umlaufkammer F
camera F a spirale F
afterbay
embalse M de compensación F
bief M d'aval M
Ausgleichsbecken N
bacino M a valle F
gate
compuerta F
vanne F
Rechen M
paratoia F
draft tube
tubo M de aspiración F
aspirateur M
Saugrohr N
tubo M aspirante
generator unit
grupo M turboalternador M
groupe M turbo-alternateur M
Generatoreinheit F
gruppo M del generatore M
tailrace
canal M de descarga F
canal M de fuite F
Auslaufrohr N
canale M di scarico M

electricity transmission

transporte^M de electricidad^F | transport^M de l'électricité^F | Elektrizitätsverteilung^F | trasmissione^F di elettricità^F

overhead connection
acometida^F aérea
branchement^M aérien
Freileitung^F
connessione^F aerea

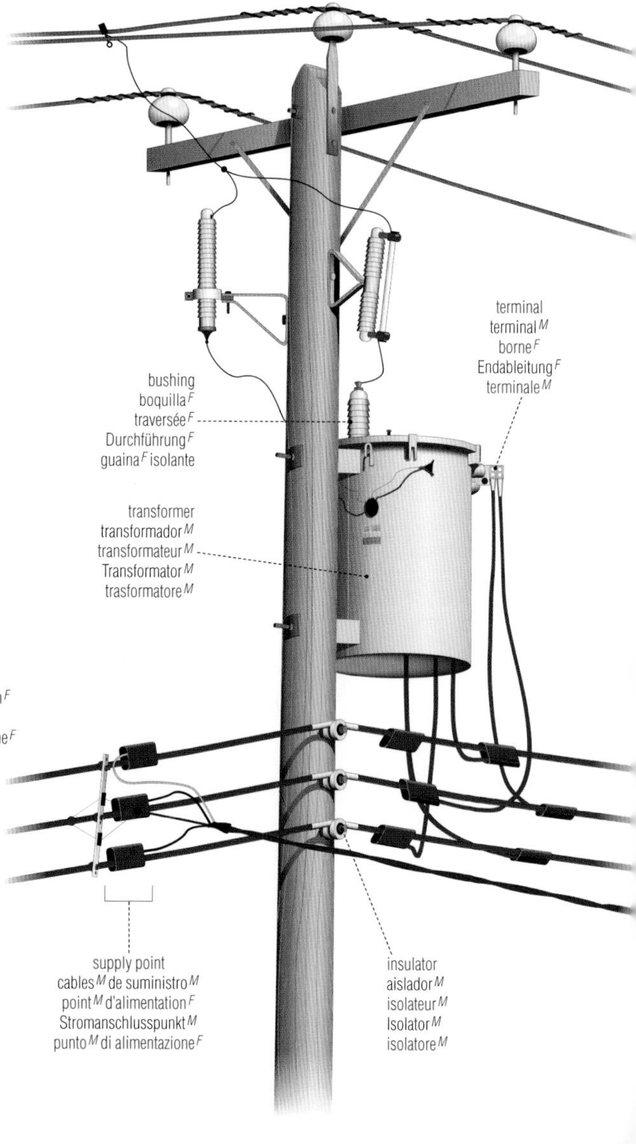

terminal
terminal^M
borne^F
Endableitung^F
terminale^M
bushing
boquilla^F
traversée^F
Durchführung^F
guaina^F isolante
transformer
transformador^M
transformateur^M
Transformator^M
trasformatore^M
low-tension distribution line
cables^M de baja tensión^F
ligne^F de distribution^F à basse tension^F
Niedrigspannungsleitung^F
linea^F di distribuzione^F a bassa tensione^F
supply point
cables^M de suministro^M
point^M d'alimentation^F
Stromanschlusspunkt^M
punto^M di alimentazione^F
insulator
aislador^M
isolateur^M
Isolator^M
isolatore^M

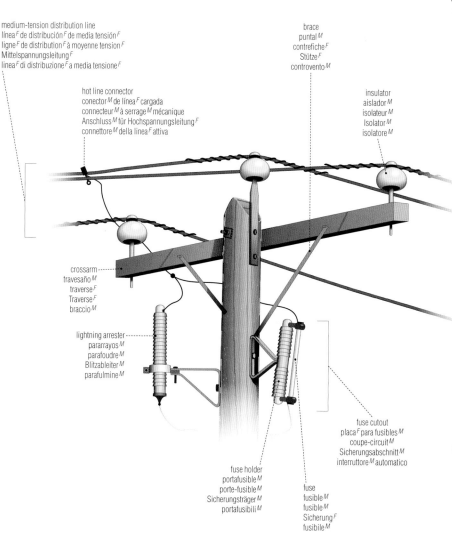

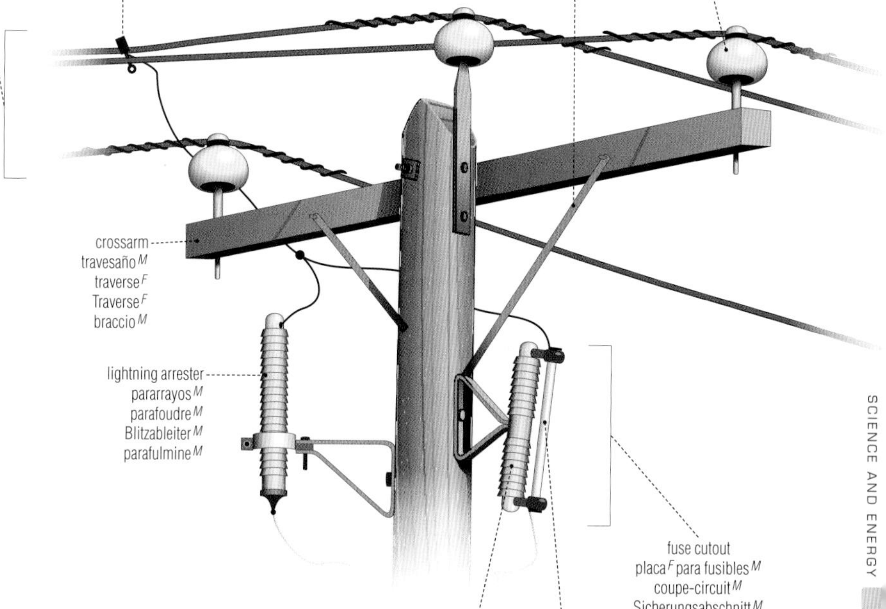
medium-tension distribution line
línea^F de distribución^F de media tensión^F
ligne^F de distribution^F à moyenne tension^F
Mittelspannungsleitung^F
linea^F di distribuzione^F a media tensione^F
brace
puntal^M
contrefiche^F
Stütze^F
controvento^M
hot line connector
conector^M de línea^F cargada
connecteur^M à serrage^M mécanique
Anschluss^M für Hochspannungsleitung^F
connettore^M della linea^F attiva
insulator
aislador^M
isolateur^M
Isolator^M
isolatore^M
crossarm
travesaño^M
traverse^F
Traverse^F
braccio^M
lightning arrester
pararrayos^M
parafoudre^M
Blitzableiter^M
parafulmine^M
fuse cutout
placa^F para fusibles^M
coupe-circuit^M
Sicherungsabschnitt^M
interruttore^M automatico
fuse holder
portafusible^M
porte-fusible^M
Sicherungsträger^M
portafusibili^M
fuse
fusible^M
fusible^M
Sicherung^F
fusibile^M

production of electricity from nuclear energy

producción^{F} de electricidad^{F} por energía^{F} nuclear | production^{F} d'électricité^{F} par énergie^{F} nucléaire | Elektrizitätserzeugung^{F} aus Kernenergie^{F} | produzione^{F} di elettricità^{F} da energia^{F} nucleare

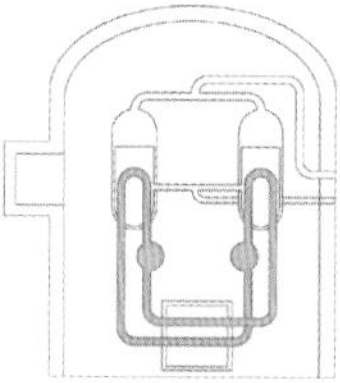

coolant
refrigerante^{M}
caloporteur^{M}
Kühlmittel^{N}
refrigerante^{M}

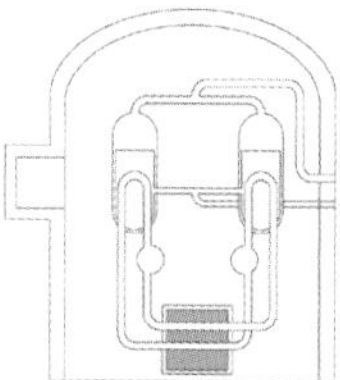

moderator
moderador^{M}
modérateur^{M}
Moderator^{M}
moderatore^{M}

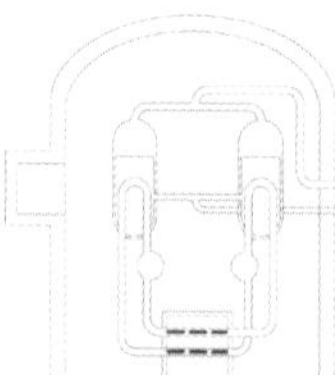

fuel
combustible^{M}
combustible^{M}
Brennstoff^{M}
combustibile^{M}

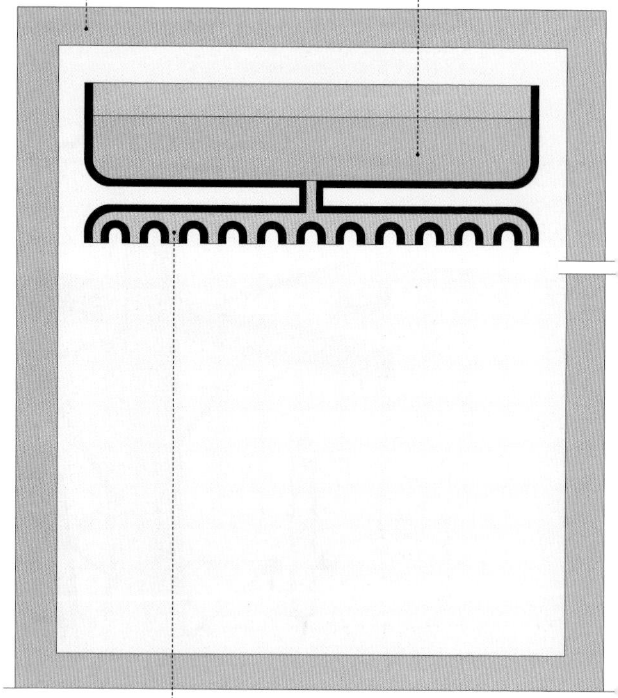

containment building
edificio^{M} de hormigón^{M}
enceinte^{F} de confinement^{M}
Sicherheitshülle^{F}
contenitore^{M} in calcestruzzo^{M}
dousing water tank
tanque^{M} de agua^{F} de rociado^{M}
réservoir^{M} d'arrosage^{M}
Kühlwassertank^{M}
serbatoio^{M} dell'acqua^{F} di raffreddamento^{M}
sprinklers
rociadores^{M}
gicleurs^{M}
Sprinkler^{M}
spruzzatori^{M}

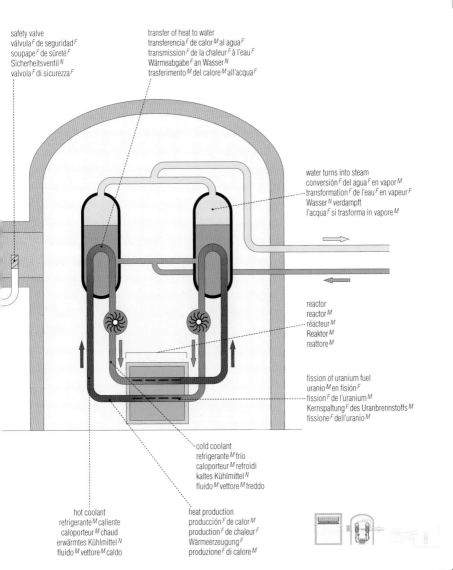

safety valve
válvula[F] de seguridad[F]
soupape[F] de sûreté[F]
Sicherheitsventil[N]
valvola[F] di sicurezza[F]

transfer of heat to water
transferencia[F] de calor[M] al agua[F]
transmission[F] de la chaleur[F] à l'eau[F]
Wärmeabgabe[F] an Wasser[N]
trasferimento[M] del calore[M] all'acqua[F]

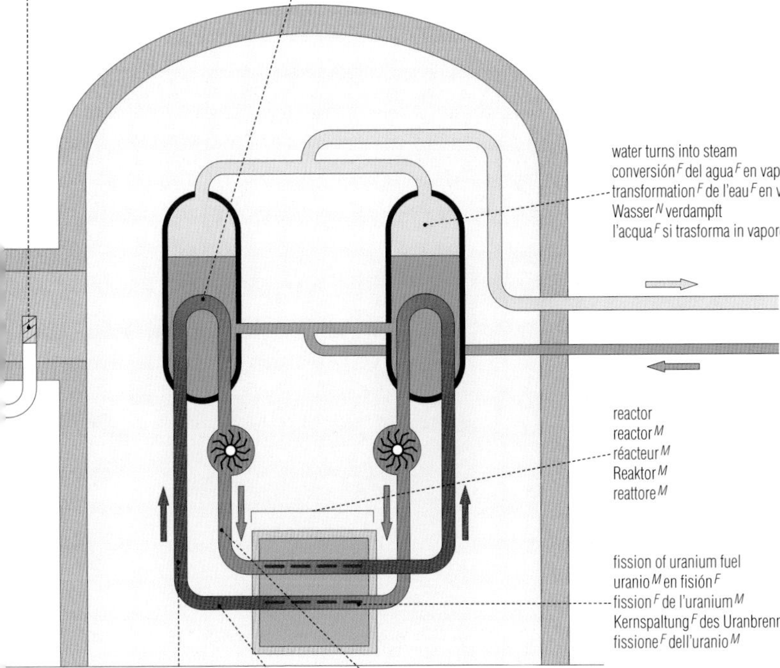

water turns into steam
conversión[F] del agua[F] en vapor[M]
transformation[F] de l'eau[F] en vapeur[F]
Wasser[N] verdampft
l'acqua[F] si trasforma in vapore[M]

reactor
reactor[M]
réacteur[M]
Reaktor[M]
reattore[M]

fission of uranium fuel
uranio[M] en fisión[F]
fission[F] de l'uranium[M]
Kernspaltung[F] des Uranbrennstoffs[M]
fissione[F] dell'uranio[M]

cold coolant
refrigerante[M] frío
caloporteur[M] refroidi
kaltes Kühlmittel[N]
fluido[M] vettore[M] freddo

hot coolant
refrigerante[M] caliente
caloporteur[M] chaud
erwärmtes Kühlmittel[N]
fluido[M] vettore[M] caldo

heat production
producción[F] de calor[M]
production[F] de chaleur[F]
Wärmeerzeugung[F]
produzione[F] di calore[M]

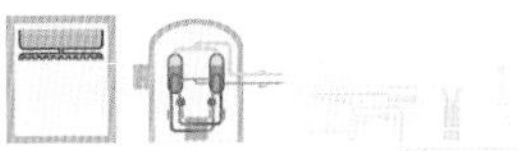

production of electricity from nuclear energy

turbine shaft turns generato
el eje[M] de la turbina[F] hace girar el generador[M]
entraînement[M] du rotor[M] de l'alternateur[M]
Turbinenwelle[F] treibt Generator[M] an
l'albero[M] della turbina[F] fa ruotare il generatore[M]

steam pressure drives turbine
la presión[F] del vapor[M] impulsa las turbinas[F]
entraînement[M] de la turbine[F] par la vapeur[F]
Dampfdruck[M] treibt Turbine[F] an
la pressione[F] del vapore[M] aziona la turbina[F]

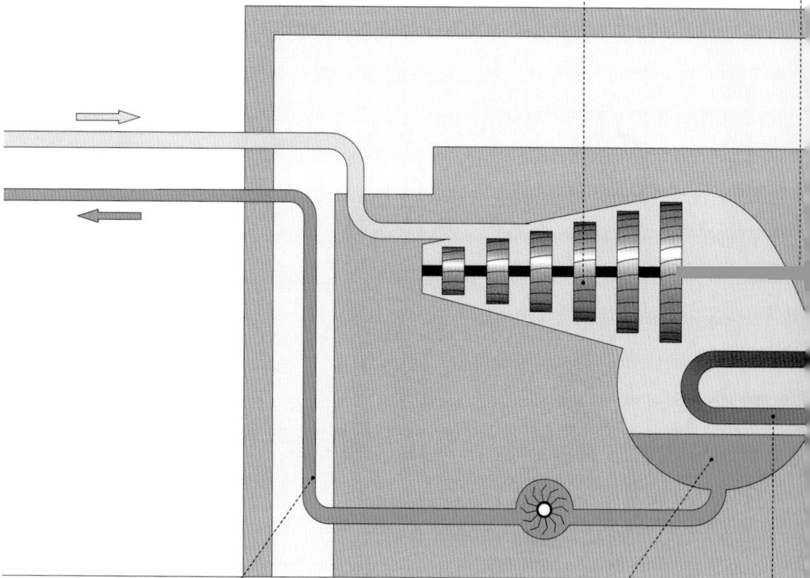

water is pumped back into the steam generator
el agua[F] regresa al generador[M] de vapor[M]
retour[M] de l'eau[F] au générateur[M] de vapeur[F]
Wasser[N] wird zum Dampfgenerator[M] zurückgepumpt
l'acqua[F] di condensazione[F] ritorna nel generatore[M] di vapore[M]

condensation of steam into water
el vapor[M] se condensa en agua[F]
condensation[F] de la vapeur[F]
Dampf[M] kondensiert zu Wasser[N]
il vapore[M] condensa in acqua[F]

water cools the used steam
el agua[F] enfría el vapor[M] utilizado
refroidissement[M] de la vapeur[F] par l'eau[F]
Wasser[N] kühlt Brauchdampf[M] ab
l'acqua[F] raffredda il vapore[M] utilizzato

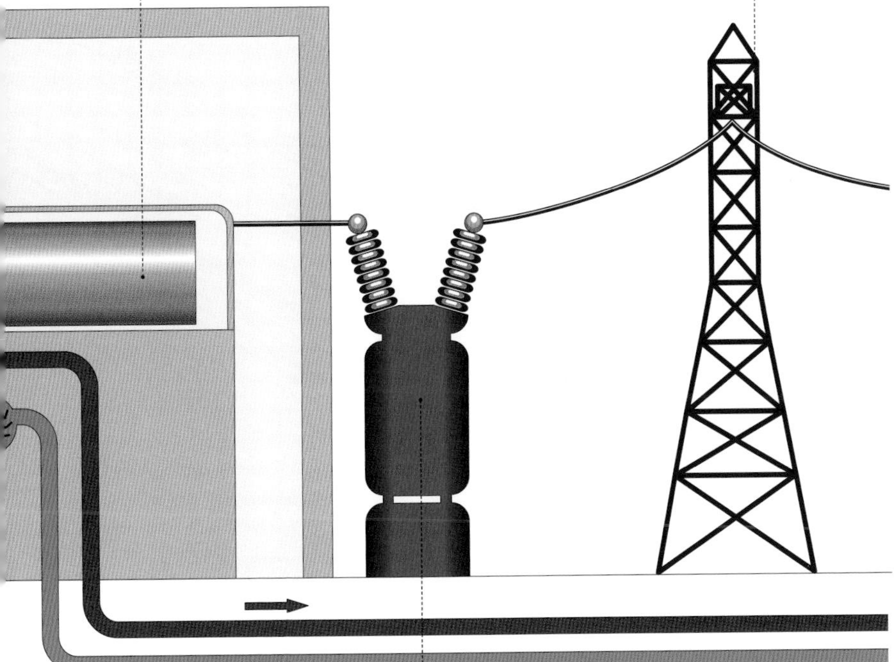
production of electricity by the generator
producción F de electricidad F por generador M
production F d'électricité F par l'alternateur M
Elektrizitätserzeugung F durch den Generator M
produzione F di elettricità F da alternatore M
electricity transmission
transmisión F de electricidad F
transport M de l'électricité F
Stromfortleitung F
trasmissione F dell'elettricità F
voltage increase
ampliación F del voltaje M
élévation F de la tension F
Hochtransformation F der Spannung F
aumento M di tensione F

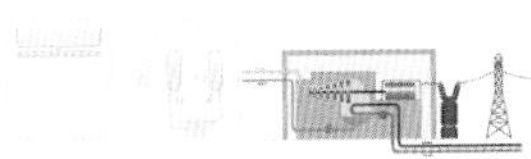

fuel bundle

elemento[M] de combustible[M] | grappe[F] de combustible[M] | Brennstabbündel[N] | elemento[M] di combustibile[M]

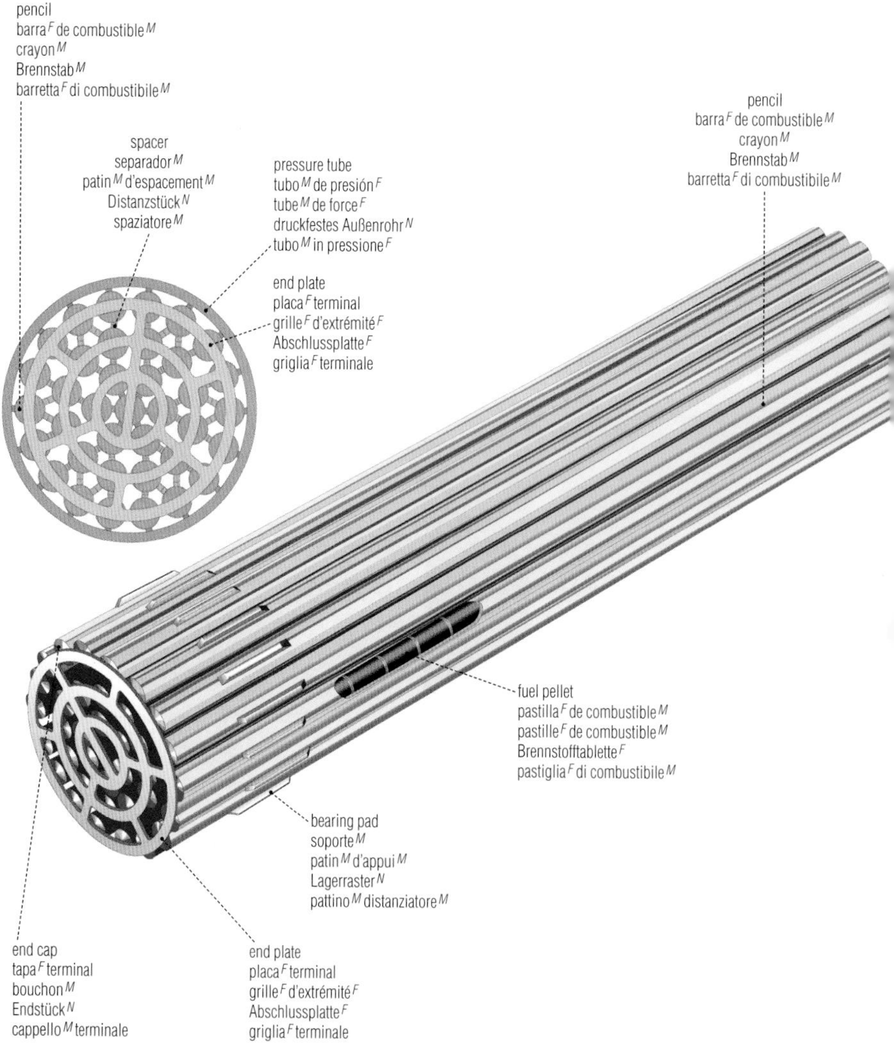
pencil
barra[F] de combustible[M]
crayon[M]
Brennstab[M]
barretta[F] di combustibile[M]
spacer
separador[M]
patin[M] d'espacement[M]
Distanzstück[N]
spaziatore[M]
pressure tube
tubo[M] de presión[F]
tube[M] de force[F]
druckfestes Außenrohr[N]
tubo[M] in pressione[F]
end plate
placa[F] terminal
grille[F] d'extrémité[F]
Abschlussplatte[F]
griglia[F] terminale
pencil
barra[F] de combustible[M]
crayon[M]
Brennstab[M]
barretta[F] di combustibile[M]
fuel pellet
pastilla[F] de combustible[M]
pastille[F] de combustible[M]
Brennstofftablette[F]
pastiglia[F] di combustibile[M]
bearing pad
soporte[M]
patin[M] d'appui[M]
Lagerraster[N]
pattino[M] distanziatore[M]
end cap
tapa[F] terminal
bouchon[M]
Endstück[N]
cappello[M] terminale
end plate
placa[F] terminal
grille[F] d'extrémité[F]
Abschlussplatte[F]
griglia[F] terminale

nuclear reactor

carga[F] del reactor[M] nuclear | réacteur[M] nucléaire | Kernreaktor[M] | reattore[M] nucleare

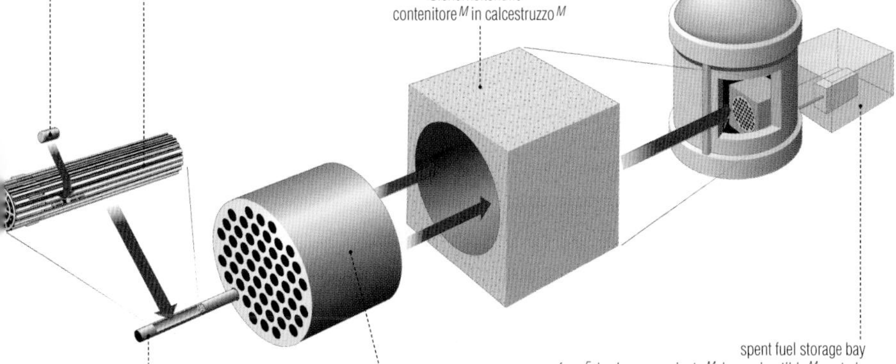
fuel pellet
pastilla[F] de combustible[M]
pastille[F] de combustible[M]
Brennstofftablette[F]
pastiglia[F] di combustibile[M]
fuel bundle
elemento[M] de combustible[M]
grappe[F] de combustible[M]
Brennstabbündel[N]
elemento[M] di combustibile[M]
reactor building
edificio[M] del reactor[M]
bâtiment[M] du réacteur[M]
Reaktorgebäude[N]
edificio[M] del reattore[M]
containment building
bloque[M] de contención[F]
enceinte[F] de confinement[M]
Sicherheitshülle[F]
contenitore[M] in calcestruzzo[M]
spent fuel storage bay
fosa[F] de almacenamiento[M] de combustible[M] agotado
piscine[F] de stockage[M] du combustible[M] irradié
Abklingbecken[N]
vasca[F] di deposito[M] del combustibile[M] esaurito
pressure tube
tubo[M] de presión[F]
tube[M] de force[F]
druckfestes Außenrohr[N]
tubo[M] in pressione[F]
reactor vessel
calandria[F]
calandre[F]
Reaktorkessel[M]
recipiente[M] del reattore[M]

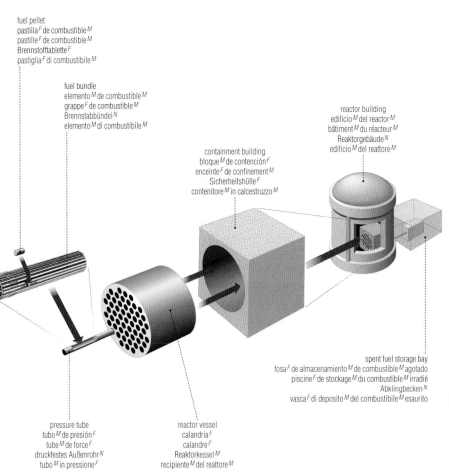

solar cell

célula^F solar | photopile^F | Solarzelle^F | cella^F solare

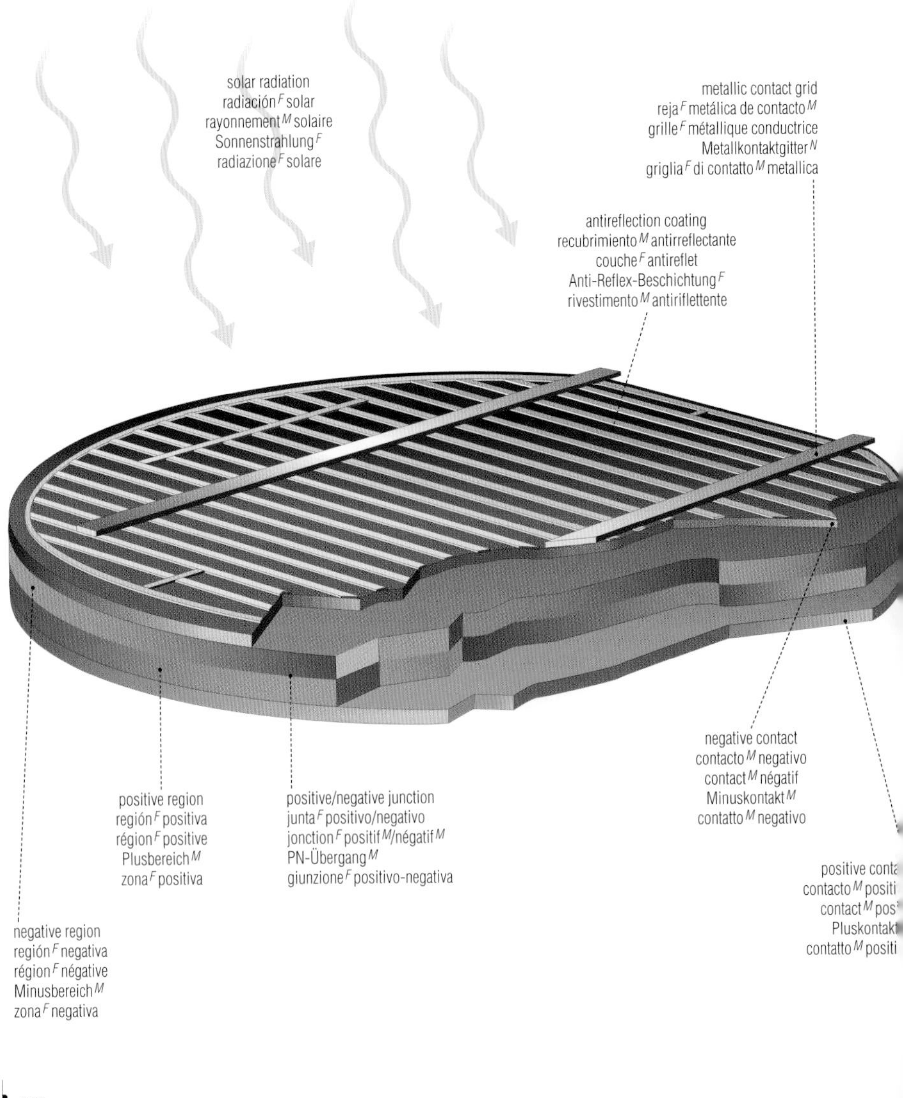
solar radiation
radiación^F solar
rayonnement^M solaire
Sonnenstrahlung^F
radiazione^F solare
metallic contact grid
reja^F metálica de contacto^M
grille^F métallique conductrice
Metallkontaktgitter^N
griglia^F di contatto^M metallica
antireflection coating
recubrimiento^M antirreflectante
couche^F antireflet
Anti-Reflex-Beschichtung^F
rivestimento^M antiriflettente
negative contact
contacto^M negativo
contact^M négatif
Minuskontakt^M
contatto^M negativo
positive region
región^F positiva
région^F positive
Plusbereich^M
zona^F positiva
positive/negative junction
junta^F positivo/negativo
jonction^F positif^M/négatif^M
PN-Übergang^M
giunzione^F positivo-negativa
positive conta
contacto^M positi
contact^M pos
Pluskontakt
contatto^M positi
negative region
región^F negativa
région^F négative
Minusbereich^M
zona^F negativa

flat-plate solar collector

colector[M] solar plano | capteur[M] solaire plan | Flachkollektor[M] | collettore[M] solare piatto

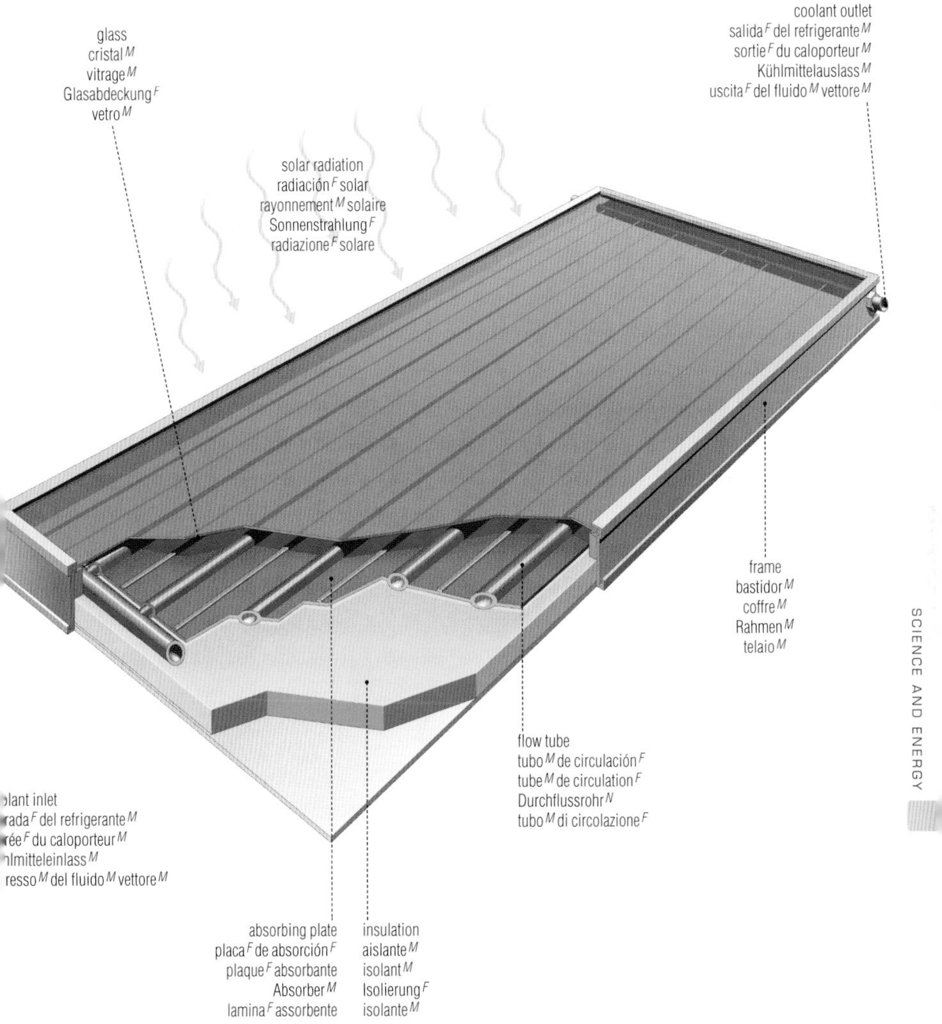

glass
cristal M
vitrage M
Glasabdeckung F
vetro M
solar radiation
radiación F solar
rayonnement M solaire
Sonnenstrahlung F
radiazione F solare
coolant outlet
salida F del refrigerante M
sortie F du caloporteur M
Kühlmittelauslass M
uscita F del fluido M vettore M
frame
bastidor M
coffre M
Rahmen M
telaio M
flow tube
tubo M de circulación F
tube M de circulation F
Durchflussrohr N
tubo M di circolazione F
absorbing plate
placa F de absorción F
plaque F absorbante
Absorber M
lamina F assorbente
insulation
aislante M
isolant M
Isolierung F
isolante M

windmill

molino[M] de viento[M] | moulin[M] à vent[M] | Windmühle[F] | mulino[M] a vento[M]

tower mill
molino[M] de torre[F]
moulin[M] tour[F]
Turmwindmühle[F]
mulino[M] a torre[F]

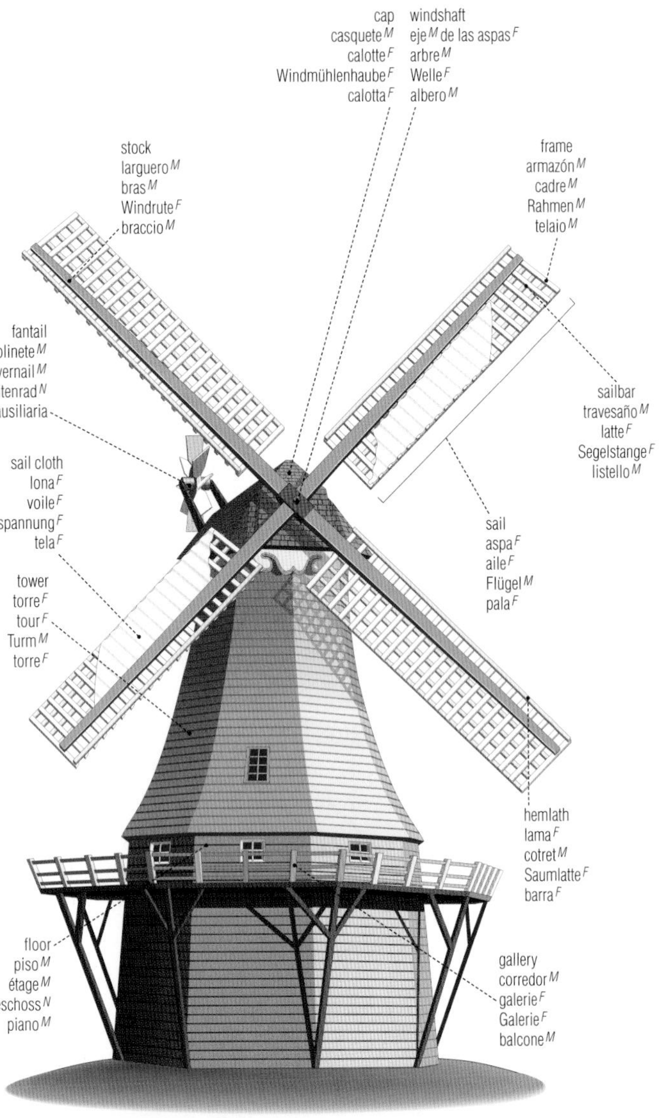

cap
casquete M
calotte F
Windmühlenhaube F
calotta F
windshaft
eje M de las aspas F
arbre M
Welle F
albero M
stock
larguero M
bras M
Windrute F
braccio M
frame
armazón M
cadre M
Rahmen M
telaio M
fantail
molinete M
gouvernail M
Seitenrad N
pala F ausiliaria
sailbar
travesaño M
latte F
Segelstange F
listello M
sail cloth
lona F
voile F
Segeltuchbespannung F
tela F
sail
aspa F
aile F
Flügel M
pala F
tower
torre F
tour F
Turm M
torre F
hemlath
lama F
cotret M
Saumlatte F
barra F
floor
piso M
étage M
Sockelgeschoss N
piano M
gallery
corredor M
galerie F
Galerie F
balcone M

wind turbines and electricity production

turbinas^F de viento^M y producción^F eléctrica | éoliennes^F et production^F d'électricité^F | Windkraftwerke^N und Elektrizitätserzeugung^F | turbine^F eoliche e produzione^F di elettricità^F

vertical-axis wind turbine
turbina^F de viento^M de eje^M vertical
éolienne^F à axe^M vertical
Windkraftwerk mit vertikaler Achse^F
turbina^F ad asse^M verticale

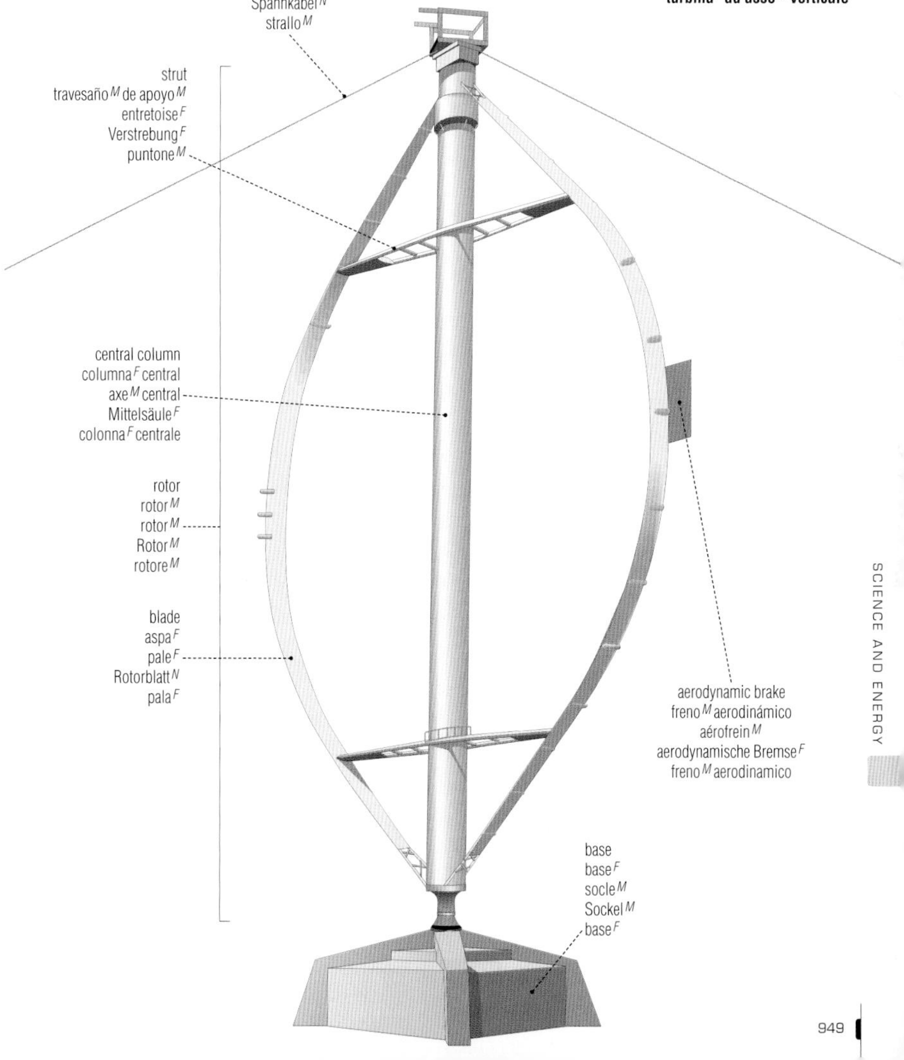
guy wire tensor^M hauban^M Spannkabel^N strallo^M
strut travesaño^M de apoyo^M entretoise^F Verstrebung^F puntone^M
central column columna^F central axe^M central Mittelsäule^F colonna^F centrale
rotor rotor^M rotor^M Rotor^M rotore^M
blade aspa^F pale^F Rotorblatt^N pala^F
aerodynamic brake freno^M aerodinámico aérofrein^M aerodynamische Bremse^F freno^M aerodinamico
base base^F socle^M Sockel^M base^F

wind turbines and electricity production

horizontal-axis wind turbine
turbina F de viento M de eje M horizontal
éolienne F à axe M horizontal
Windkraftwerk mit horizontaler Achse F
turbina F eolica ad asse M orizzontale

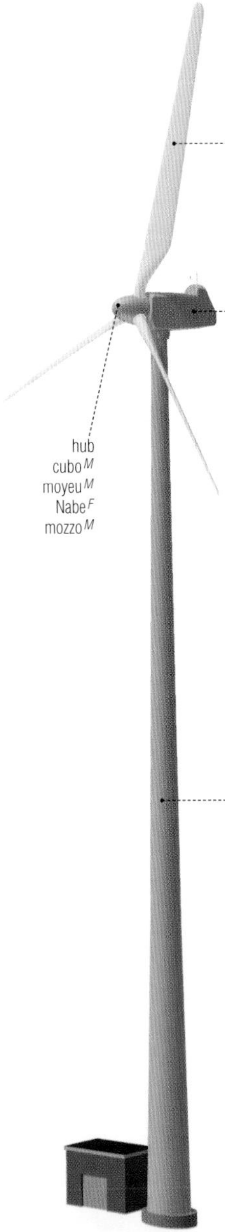
blade
aspa F
pale F
Rotorblatt N
pala F
nacelle
góndola F
nacelle F
Zelle F
navicella F
hub
cubo M
moyeu M
Nabe F
mozzo M
tower
torre F
tour F
Turm M
torre F

nacelle cross-section
sección[F] transversal de la góndola[F]
coupe[F] de la nacelle[F]
Rotorgondel[F] im Querschnitt[M]
sezione[F] trasversale di una navicella[F]

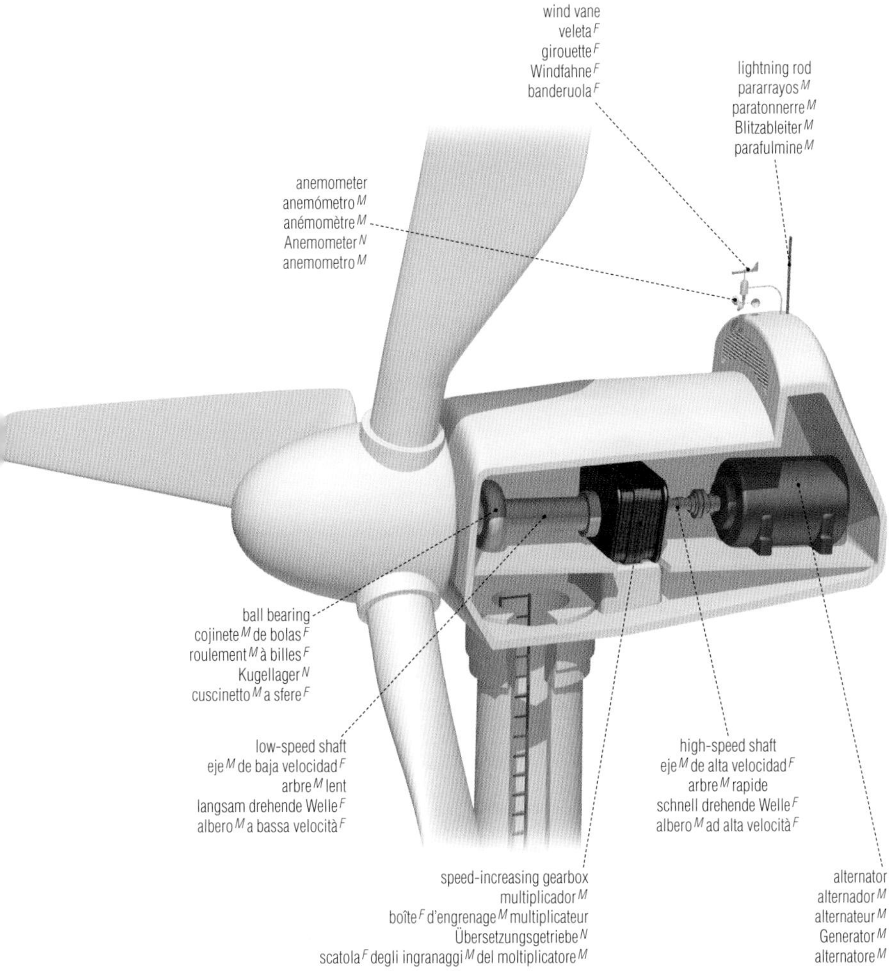
wind vane
veleta[F]
girouette[F]
Windfahne[F]
banderuola[F]
lightning rod
pararrayos[M]
paratonnerre[M]
Blitzableiter[M]
parafulmine[M]
anemometer
anemómetro[M]
anémomètre[M]
Anemometer[N]
anemometro[M]
ball bearing
cojinete[M] de bolas[F]
roulement[M] à billes[F]
Kugellager[N]
cuscinetto[M] a sfere[F]
low-speed shaft
eje[M] de baja velocidad[F]
arbre[M] lent
langsam drehende Welle[F]
albero[M] a bassa velocità[F]
high-speed shaft
eje[M] de alta velocidad[F]
arbre[M] rapide
schnell drehende Welle[F]
albero[M] ad alta velocità[F]
speed-increasing gearbox
multiplicador[M]
boîte[F] d'engrenage[M] multiplicateur
Übersetzungsgetriebe[N]
scatola[F] degli ingranaggi[M] del moltiplicatore[M]
alternator
alternador[M]
alternateur[M]
Generator[M]
alternatore[M]

arena

estadio[M] | stade[M] | Stadion[N] | stadio[M]

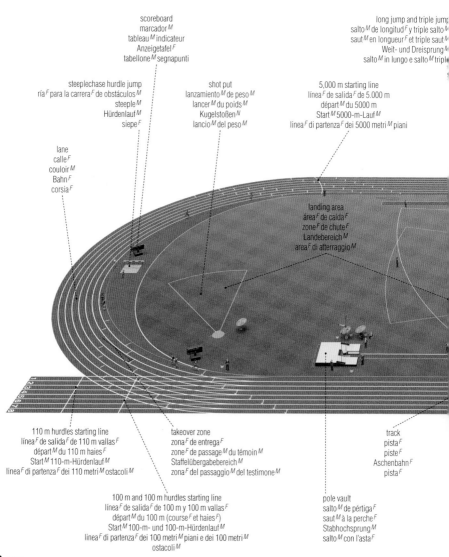

scoreboard
marcador[M]
tableau[M] indicateur
Anzeigetafel[F]
tabellone[M] segnapunti
long jump and triple jum
salto[M] de longitud[F] y triple salto
saut[M] en longueur[F] et triple saut
Weit- und Dreisprung
salto[M] in lungo e salto[M] tripl
steeplechase hurdle jump
ría[F] para la carrera[F] de obstáculos[M]
steeple[M]
Hürdenlauf[M]
siepe[F]
shot put
lanzamiento[M] de peso[M]
lancer[M] du poids[M]
Kugelstoßen[N]
lancio[M] del peso[M]
5,000 m starting line
línea[F] de salida[F] de 5.000 m
départ[M] du 5000 m
Start[M] 5000-m-Lauf[M]
linea[F] di partenza[F] dei 5000 metri[M] piani
lane
calle[F]
couloir[M]
Bahn[F]
corsia[F]
landing area
área[F] de caída[F]
zone[F] de chute[F]
Landebereich[M]
area[F] di atterraggio[M]
1 2 3 4 5 6 7 8
110 m hurdles starting line
línea[F] de salida[F] de 110 m vallas[F]
départ[M] du 110 m haies[F]
Start[M] 110-m-Hürdenlauf[M]
linea[F] di partenza[F] dei 110 metri[M] ostacoli[M]
takeover zone
zona[F] de entrega[F]
zone[F] de passage[M] du témoin[M]
Staffelübergabebereich[M]
zona[F] del passaggio[M] del testimone[M]
track
pista[F]
piste[F]
Aschenbahn[F]
pista[F]
100 m and 100 m hurdles starting line
línea[F] de salida[F] de 100 m y 100 m vallas[F]
départ[M] du 100 m (course[F] et haies[F])
Start[M] 100-m- und 100-m-Hürdenlauf[M]
linea[F] di partenza[F] dei 100 metri[M] piani e dei 100 metri[M] ostacoli[M]
pole vault
salto[M] de pértiga[F]
saut[M] à la perche[F]
Stabhochsprung[M]
salto[M] con l'asta[F]

throwing circle
círculo^{M} de lanzamiento^{M}
cercle^{M} de lancer^{M}
Wurfkreis^{M}
pedana^{F} di lancio^{M}

discus and hammer throw
lanzamiento^{M} de martillo^{M} y disco^{M}
lancer^{M} disque^{M} et marteau^{M}
Diskus- und Hammerwerfen^{N}
lancio^{M} del disco^{M} e del martello^{M}

1,500 m starting line
línea^{F} de salida^{F} de 1.500 m
départ^{M} du 1500 m
Start^{M} 1500-m-Lauf^{M}
linea^{F} di partenza^{F} dei 1500 metri^{M} piani

high jump
salto^{M} de altura^{F}
saut^{M} en hauteur^{F}
Hochsprung^{M}
salto^{M} in alto

javelin throw
lanzamiento^{M} de jabalina^{F}
lancer^{M} du javelot^{M}
Speerwurf^{M}
lancio^{M} del giavellotto^{M}

approach
pista^{F} de salto^{M}
piste^{F} d'élan^{M}
Anlaufstrecke^{F}
pista^{F} di rincorsa^{F}

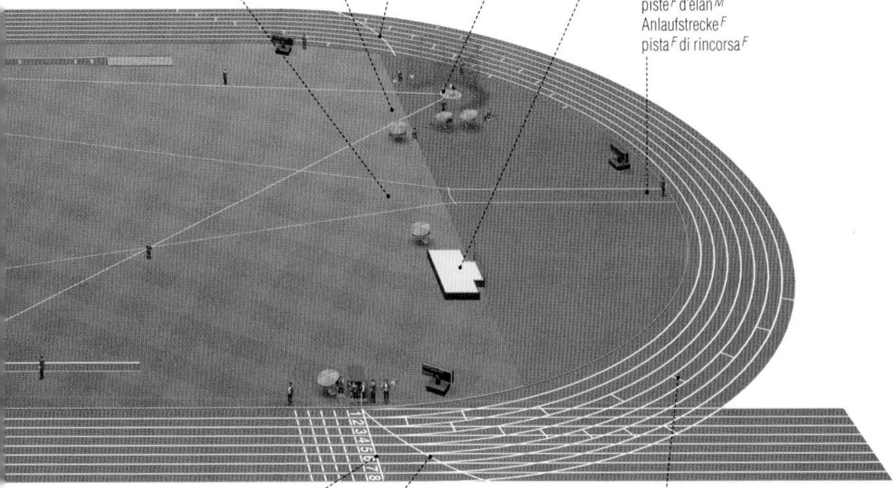
1
2
3
4
5
6
7
8

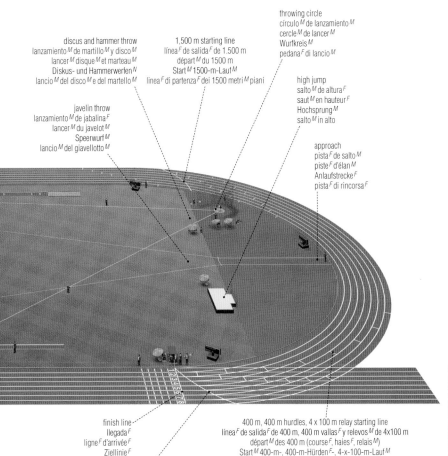

finish line
llegada^{F}
ligne^{F} d'arrivée^{F}
Ziellinie^{F}
linea^{F} del traguardo^{M}

400 m, 400 m hurdles, 4 x 100 m relay starting line
línea^{F} de salida^{F} de 400 m, 400 m vallas^{F} y relevos^{M} de 4x100 m
départ^{M} des 400 m (course^{F}, haies^{F}, relais^{M})
Start^{M} 400-m-, 400-m-Hürden^{F}-, 4-x-100-m-Lauf^{M}
linea^{F} di partenza^{F} dei 400 metri^{M} piani e a ostacoli^{M} e della staffetta^{F} 4x100 metri^{M}

10,000 m and 4 x 400 m relay starting line
línea^{F} de salida^{F} de 10.000 m y de relevos^{M} de 4 x 400 m
départ^{M} du 10 000 m et du relais^{M} 4 x 400 m
Start^{M} 10000-m- und 4-x-400-m-Lauf^{M}
linea^{F} di partenza^{F} dei 10000 metri^{M} piani e della staffetta^{F} 4 x 400 metri^{M}

soccer

fútbol M | football M | Fußball M | calcio M

playing field
campo M
terrain M
Spielfeld N
campo M **di gioco** M

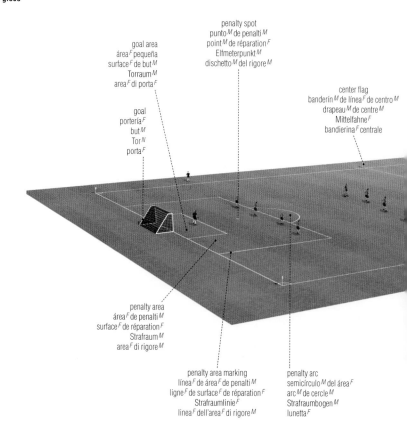

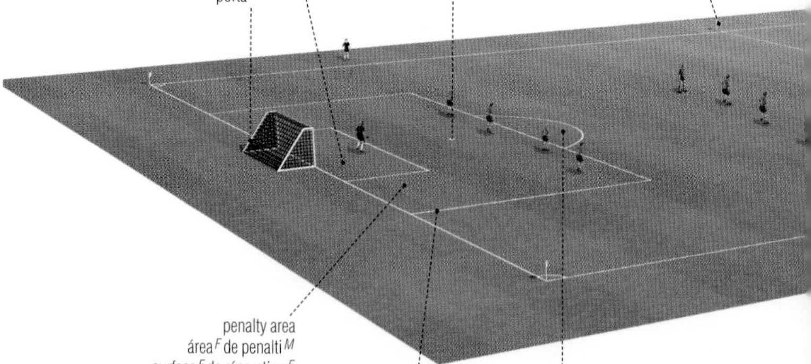
penalty spot
punto M de penalti M
point M de réparation F
Elfmeterpunkt M
dischetto M del rigore M
goal area
área F pequeña
surface F de but M
Torraum M
area F di porta F
center flag
banderín M de línea F de centro M
drapeau M de centre M
Mittelfahne F
bandierina F centrale
goal
portería F
but M
Tor N
porta F
penalty area
área F de penalti M
surface F de réparation F
Strafraum M
area F di rigore M
penalty area marking
línea F de área F de penalti M
ligne F de surface F de réparation F
Strafraumlinie F
linea F dell'area F di rigore M
penalty arc
semicírculo M del área F
arc M de cercle M
Strafraumbogen M
lunetta F

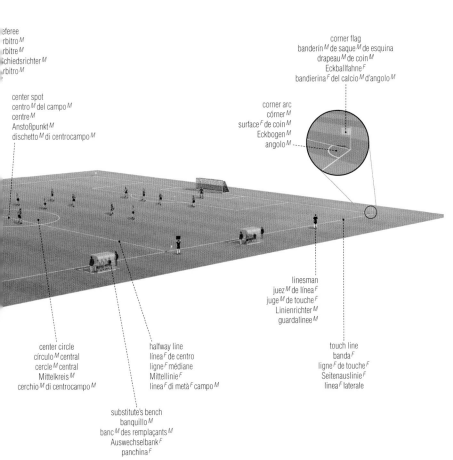

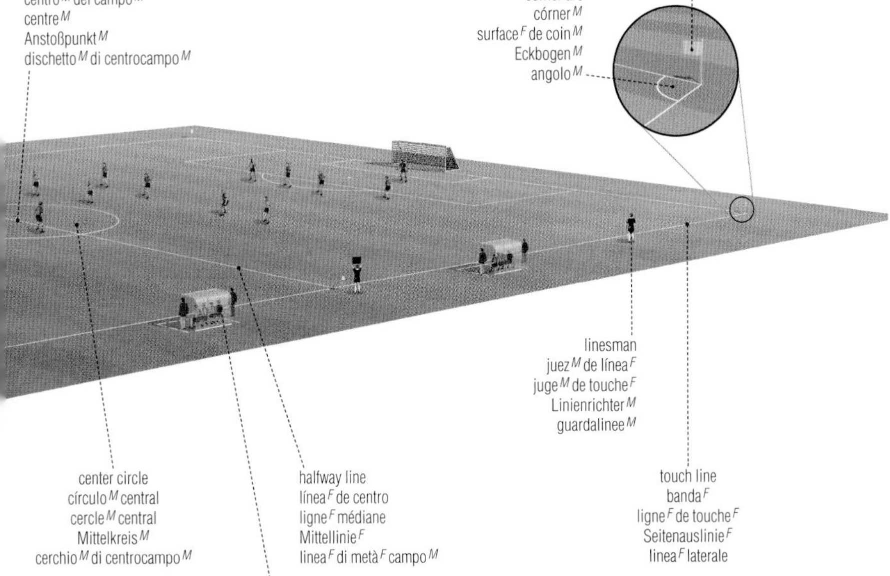
eferee
rbitro[M]
rbitre[M]
chiedsrichter[M]
rbitro[M]

corner flag
banderín[M] de saque[M] de esquina
drapeau[M] de coin[M]
Eckballfahne[F]
bandierina[F] del calcio[M] d'angolo[M]

center spot
centro[M] del campo[M]
centre[M]
Anstoßpunkt[M]
dischetto[M] di centrocampo[M]

corner arc
córner[M]
surface[F] de coin[M]
Eckbogen[M]
angolo[M]

linesman
juez[M] de línea[F]
juge[M] de touche[F]
Linienrichter[M]
guardalinee[M]

center circle
círculo[M] central
cercle[M] central
Mittelkreis[M]
cerchio[M] di centrocampo[M]

halfway line
línea[F] de centro
ligne[F] médiane
Mittellinie[F]
linea[F] di metà[F] campo[M]

touch line
banda[F]
ligne[F] de touche[F]
Seitenauslinie[F]
linea[F] laterale

substitute's bench
banquillo[M]
banc[M] des remplaçants[M]
Auswechselbank[F]
panchina[F]

soccer player
futbolista [M/F]
footballeur [M]
Fußballspieler [M]
calciatore [M]

team shirt
camiseta [F] del equipo [M]
maillot [M] d'équipe [F]
Mannschaftstrikot [N]
maglia [F] della squadra [F]
shorts
pantalones [M]
short [M]
Hose [F]
pantaloncini [M]
shin guard
espinillera [F]
protège-tibia [M]
Schienbeinschützer [M]
parastinchi [M]
sock
calcetín [M]
chaussette [F]
Stulpen [F]
calzettone [M]
soccer ball
balón [M] de fútbol [M]
ballon [M] de football [M]
Fußball [M]
pallone [M]

goalkeeper's gloves
guantes [M] **del portero** [M]
gants [M] **de gardien** [M] **de but** [M]
Torwarthandschuhe [M]
guanti [M] **del portiere** [M]

soccer shoe
bota [F] **de fútbol** [M]
chaussure [F] **de football** [M]
Fußballschuh [M]
scarpa [F]

interchangeable studs
tacos [M] de rosca [F]
crampons [M] interchangeables
Schraubstollen [M]
tacchetti [M] intercambiabili

baseball

béisbol M | baseball M | Baseball M | baseball M

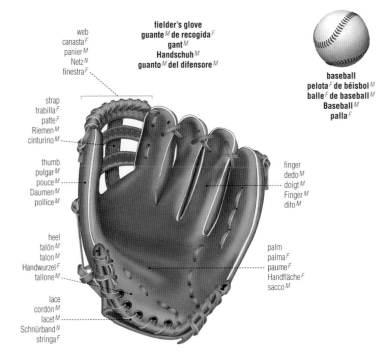

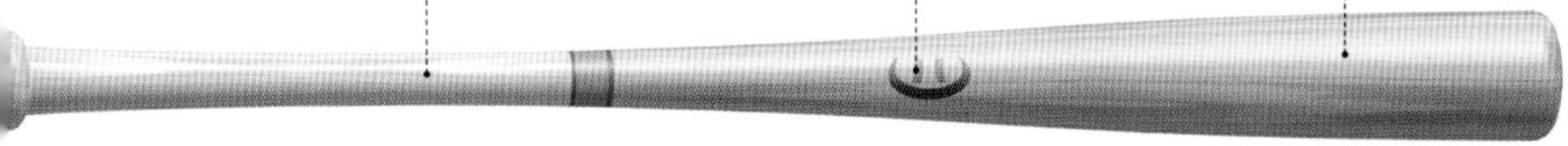
bat
bate M
bâton M
Schläger M
mazza F
crest
emblema M
écusson M
Wappen N
stemma M
nob
uño M
ommeau M
nauf M
omo M
handle
empuñadura F
manche M
Griff M
impugnatura F
hitting area
cuadro M de bateo M
surface F de frappe F
Schlagbereich M
zona F di battuta F

baseball
pelota F de béisbol M
balle F de baseball M
Baseball M
palla F

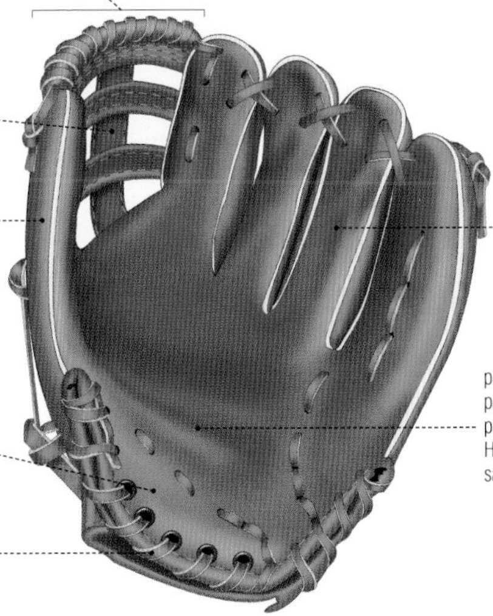
fielder's glove
guante M de recogida F
gant M
Handschuh M
guanto M del difensore M
web
canasta F
panier M
Netz N
finestra F
strap
trabilla F
patte F
Riemen M
cinturino M
thumb
pulgar M
pouce M
Daumen M
pollice M
heel
talón M
talon M
Handwurzel F
tallone M
lace
cordón M
lacet M
Schnürband N
stringa F
finger
dedo M
doigt M
Finger M
dito M
palm
palma F
paume F
Handfläche F
sacco M

baseball

field
campo M
terrain M
Spielfeld N
campo M

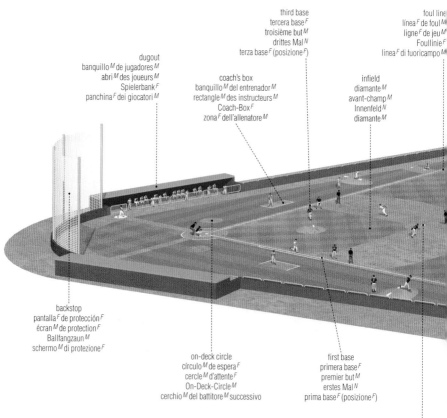

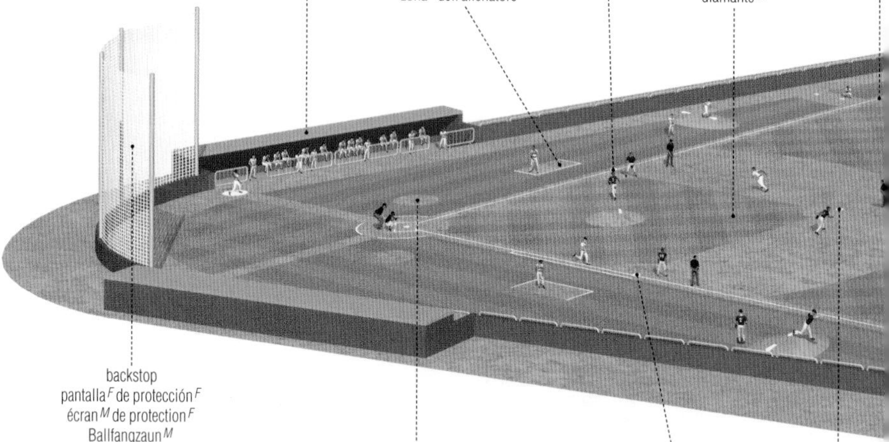
third base
tercera base F
troisième but M
drittes Mal N
terza base F (posizione F)
foul line
línea F de foul M
ligne F de jeu M
Foullinie F
linea F di fuoricampo M
dugout
banquillo M de jugadores M
abri M des joueurs M
Spielerbank F
panchina F dei giocatori M
coach's box
banquillo M del entrenador M
rectangle M des instructeurs M
Coach-Box F
zona F dell'allenatore M
infield
diamante M
avant-champ M
Innenfeld N
diamante M
backstop
pantalla F de protección F
écran M de protection F
Ballfangzaun M
schermo M di protezione F
on-deck circle
círculo M de espera F
cercle M d'attente F
On-Deck-Circle M
cerchio M del battitore M successivo
first base
primera base F
premier but M
erstes Mal N
prima base F (posizione F)
second base
segunda base F
deuxième but M
zweites Mal N
seconda base F (posizione F)

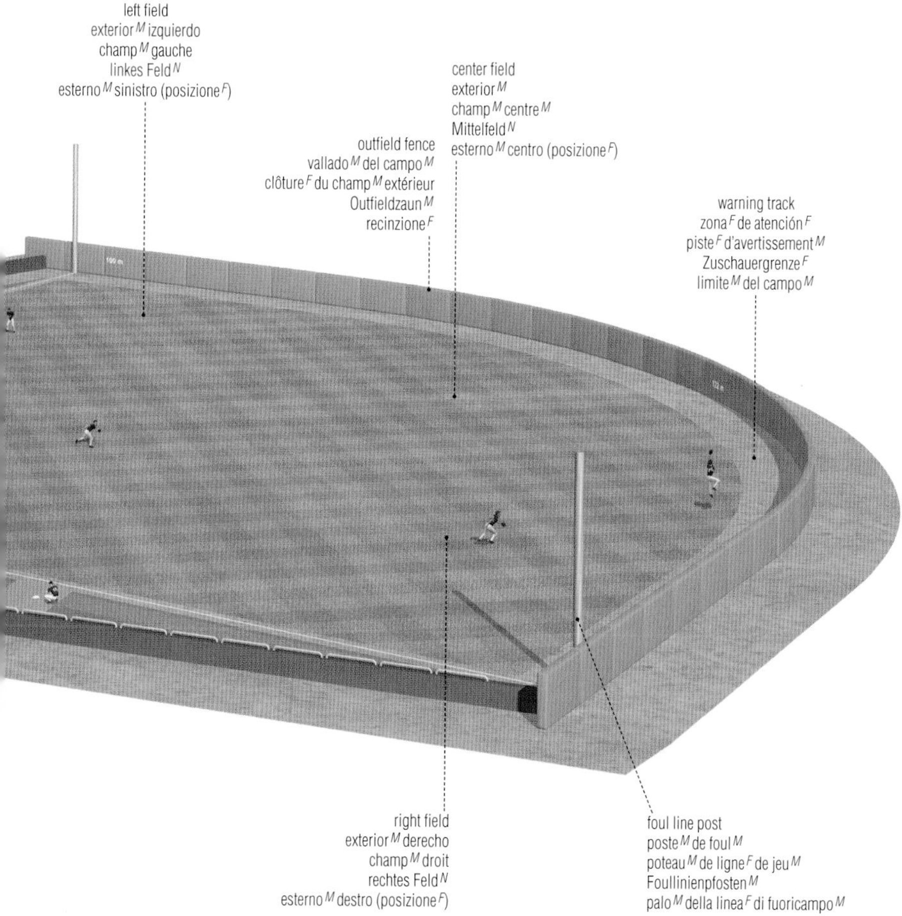
left field
exterior M izquierdo
champ M gauche
linkes Feld N
esterno M sinistro (posizione F)
center field
exterior M
champ M centre M
Mittelfeld N
esterno M centro (posizione F)
outfield fence
vallado M del campo M
clôture F du champ M extérieur
Outfieldzaun M
recinzione F
warning track
zona F de atención F
piste F d'avertissement M
Zuschauergrenze F
limite M del campo M
right field
exterior M derecho
champ M droit
rechtes Feld N
esterno M destro (posizione F)
foul line post
poste M de foul M
poteau M de ligne F de jeu M
Foullinienpfosten M
palo M della linea F di fuoricampo M

football

fútbol[M] americano | football[M] américain | American Football[M] | football[M] americano

playing field
campo[M] de juego[M] de fútbol[M] americano
terrain[M] de football[M] américain
Spielfeld[N] für American Football[M]
campo[M]

football
balón[M] de fútbol[M] americano
ballon[M] de football[M]
Football[M]
palla[F] ovale

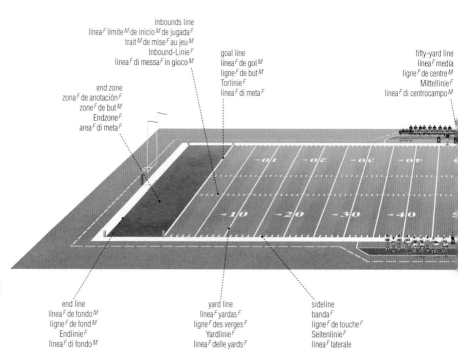

inbounds line
línea[F] límite[M] de inicio[M] de jugada[F]
trait[M] de mise[F] au jeu[M]
Inbound-Linie[F]
linea[F] di messa[F] in gioco[M]

goal line
línea[F] de gol[M]
ligne[F] de but[M]
Torlinie[F]
linea[F] di meta[F]

fifty-yard line
línea[F] media
ligne[F] de centre[M]
Mittellinie[F]
linea[F] di centrocampo[M]

end zone
zona[F] de anotación[F]
zone[F] de but[M]
Endzone[F]
area[F] di meta[F]

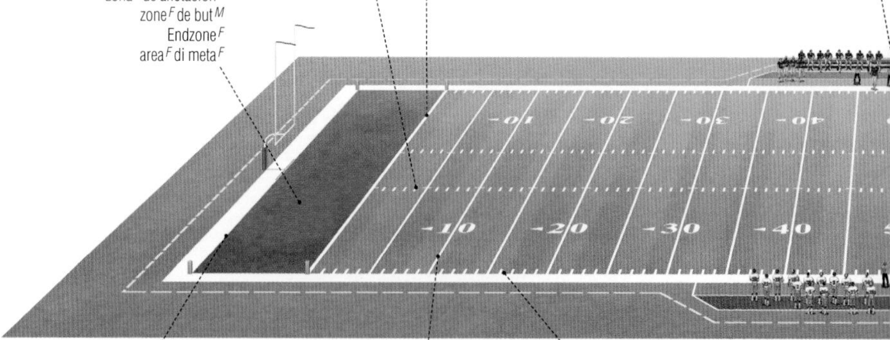
10
20
30
40

end line
línea[F] de fondo[M]
ligne[F] de fond[M]
Endlinie[F]
linea[F] di fondo[M]

yard line
línea[F] yardas[F]
ligne[F] des verges[F]
Yardlinie[F]
linea[F] delle yards[F]

sideline
banda[F]
ligne[F] de touche[F]
Seitenlinie[F]
linea[F] laterale

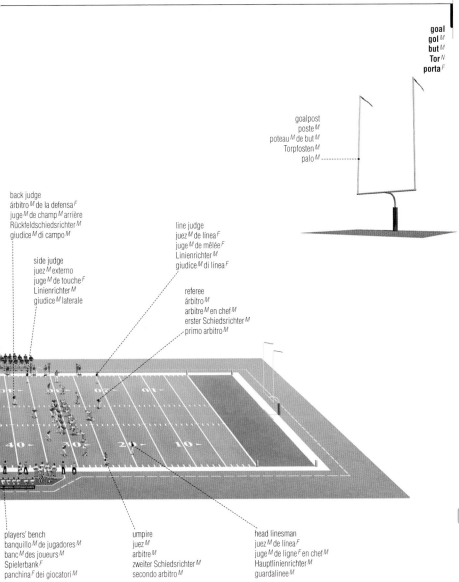

goal
gol [M]
but [M]
Tor [N]
porta [F]

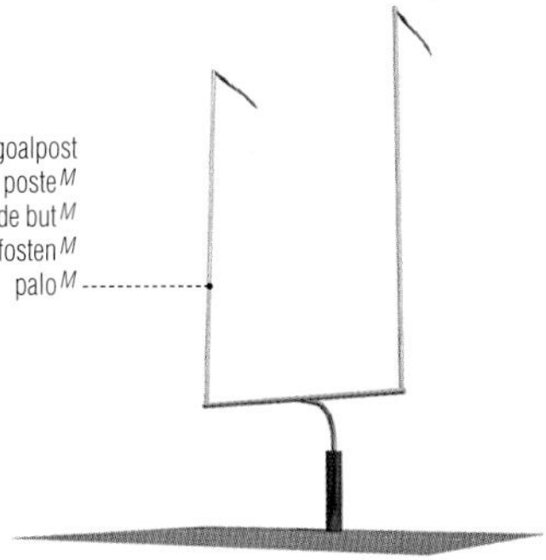
goalpost
poste [M]
poteau [M] de but [M]
Torpfosten [M]
palo [M]

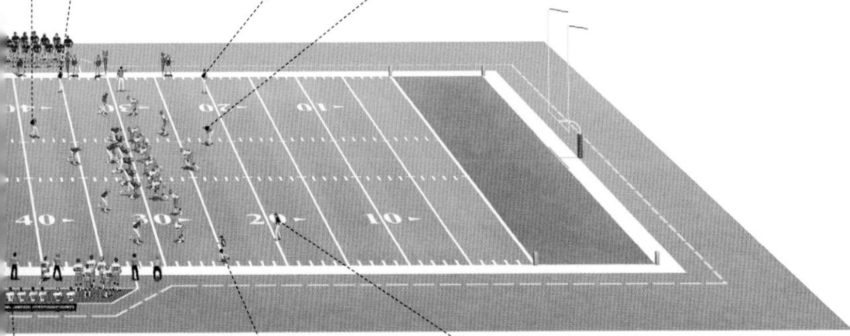
back judge
árbitro [M] de la defensa [F]
juge [M] de champ [M] arrière
Rückfeldschiedsrichter [M]
giudice [M] di campo [M]

side judge
juez [M] externo
juge [M] de touche [F]
Linienrichter [M]
giudice [M] laterale

line judge
juez [M] de línea [F]
juge [M] de mêlée [F]
Linienrichter [M]
giudice [M] di linea [F]

referee
árbitro [M]
arbitre [M] en chef [M]
erster Schiedsrichter [M]
primo arbitro [M]

players' bench
banquillo [M] de jugadores [M]
banc [M] des joueurs [M]
Spielerbank [F]
panchina [F] dei giocatori [M]

umpire
juez [M]
arbitre [M]
zweiter Schiedsrichter [M]
secondo arbitro [M]

head linesman
juez [M] de línea [F]
juge [M] de ligne [F] en chef [M]
Hauptlinienrichter [M]
guardalinee [M]

basketball

baloncesto^{M} | basketball^{M} | Basketballspiel^{N} | pallacanestro^{F}

court
cancha^{F}
terrain^{M}
Spielfeld^{N}
campo^{M}

scorer
anotador^{M}
marqueur^{M}
Anschreiber^{M}
segnapunti^{M}

clock operator
operador^{M} del reloj^{M} de 30 segundos^{M}
chronométreur^{M} des trente secondes^{F}
Uhrenmeister^{M}
addetto^{M} ai 30 secondi^{M}

timekeeper
cronometrador^{M}
chronométreur^{M}
Zeitnehmer^{M}
cronometrista^{M}

semicircle
semicírculo^{M} de la zona^{F} de tiro^{M} libre
demi-cercle^{M}
Halbkreis^{M}
lunetta^{F}

referee
árbitro^{M}
aide^{M}-arbitre^{M}
Schiedsrichter^{M}
arbitro^{M}

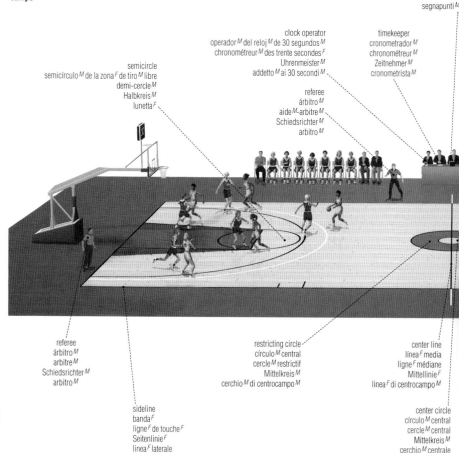

referee
árbitro^{M}
arbitre^{M}
Schiedsrichter^{M}
arbitro^{M}

restricting circle
círculo^{M} central
cercle^{M} restrictif
Mittelkreis^{M}
cerchio^{M} di centrocampo^{M}

center line
línea^{F} media
ligne^{F} médiane
Mittellinie^{F}
linea^{F} di centrocampo^{M}

sideline
banda^{F}
ligne^{F} de touche^{F}
Seitenlinie^{F}
linea^{F} laterale

center circle
círculo^{M} central
cercle^{M} central
Mittelkreis^{M}
cerchio^{M} centrale

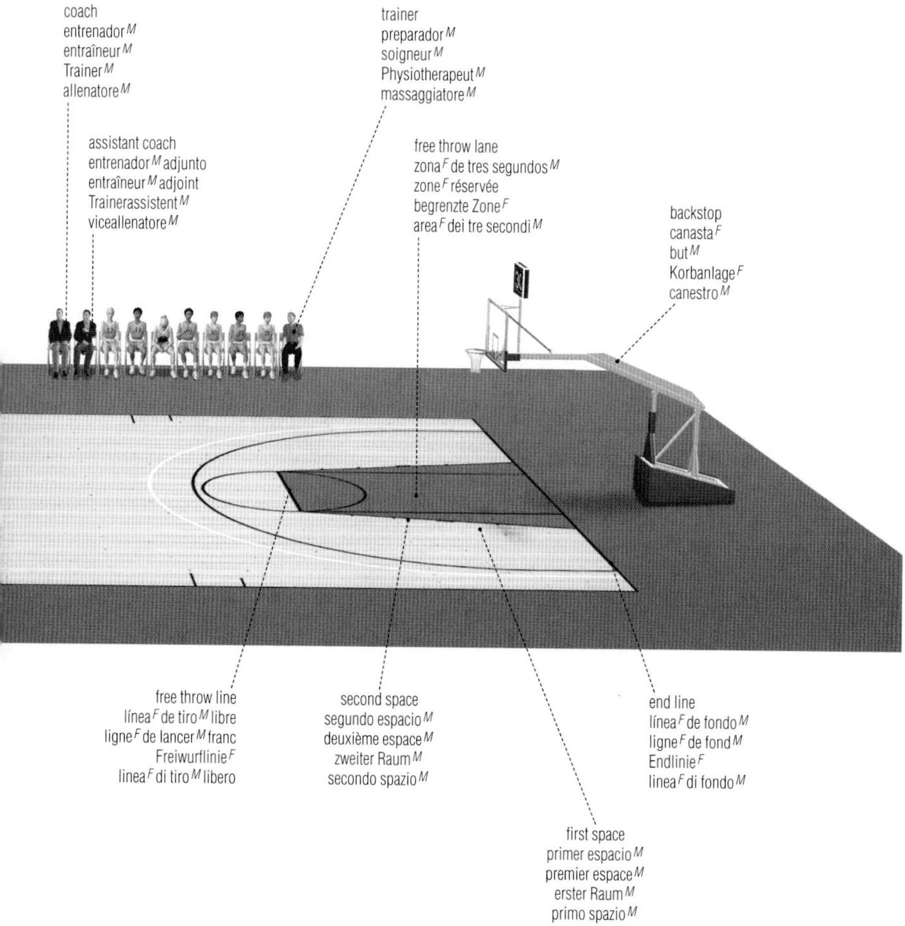
coach
entrenador[M]
entraîneur[M]
Trainer[M]
allenatore[M]
assistant coach
entrenador[M] adjunto
entraîneur[M] adjoint
Trainerassistent[M]
viceallenatore[M]
trainer
preparador[M]
soigneur[M]
Physiotherapeut[M]
massaggiatore[M]
free throw lane
zona[F] de tres segundos[M]
zone[F] réservée
begrenzte Zone[F]
area[F] dei tre secondi[M]
backstop
canasta[F]
but[M]
Korbanlage[F]
canestro[M]
free throw line
línea[F] de tiro[M] libre
ligne[F] de lancer[M] franc
Freiwurflinie[F]
linea[F] di tiro[M] libero
second space
segundo espacio[M]
deuxième espace[M]
zweiter Raum[M]
secondo spazio[M]
end line
línea[F] de fondo[M]
ligne[F] de fond[M]
Endlinie[F]
linea[F] di fondo[M]
first space
primer espacio[M]
premier espace[M]
erster Raum[M]
primo spazio[M]

volleyball

voleibol[M] | volleyball[M] | Volleyballspiel[N] | pallavolo[F]

court
cancha[F]
terrain[M]
Spielfeld[N]
campo[M]
umpire
segundo árbitro[M]
second arbitre[M]
zweiter Schiedsrichter[M]
secondo arbitro[M]
left attacker
delantero[M] izquierdo
attaquant[M] gauche
linker Außenangreifer[M]
attaccante[M] sinistro
left back
zaguero[M] izquierdo
arrière[M] gauche
linker Abwehrspieler[M]
difensore[M] sinistro
white tape
banda[F] blanca
bande[F] blanche
Netzkante[F]
nastro[M] bianco
players' bench
banquillo[M] de jugadores[M]
banc[M] des joueurs[M]
Spielerbank[F]
panchina[F] dei giocatori[M]
scorer
anotador[M]
marqueur[M]
Anschreiber[M]
segnapunti[M]
15 12
center back
zaguero[M] medio
arrière[M] centre
mittlerer Abwehrspieler[M]
difensore[M] centrale
right back
zaguero[M] derecho
arrière[M] droit
rechter Abwehrspieler[M]
difensore[M] destro
center attacker
delantero[M] medio
attaquant[M] central
Mittelangreifer[M]
attaccante[M] centrale
attack line
línea[F] de ataque[M]
ligne[F] d'attaque[F]
Angriffslinie[F]
linea[F] di attacco[M]
right attacker
delantero[M] derecho
attaquant[M] droit
rechter Außenangreifer[M]
alzatore[M] destro

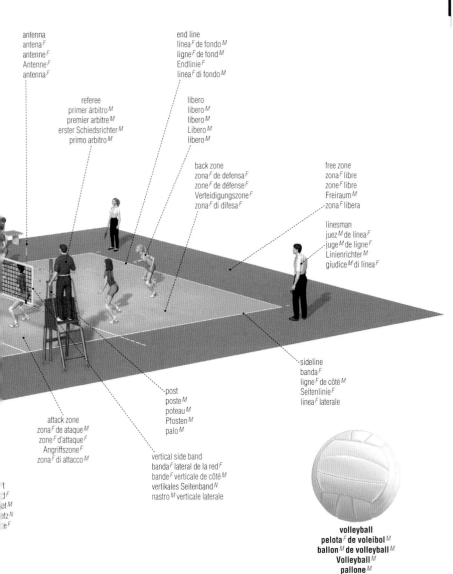

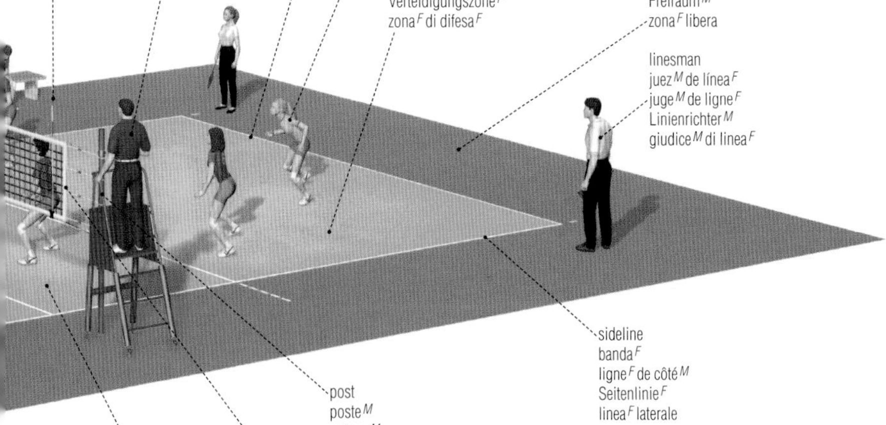
antenna
antena F
antenne F
Antenne F
antenna F
end line
línea F de fondo M
ligne F de fond M
Endlinie F
linea F di fondo M
referee
primer árbitro M
premier arbitre M
erster Schiedsrichter M
primo arbitro M
libero
libero M
libero M
Libero M
libero M
back zone
zona F de defensa F
zone F de défense F
Verteidigungszone F
zona F di difesa F
free zone
zona F libre
zone F libre
Freiraum M
zona F libera
linesman
juez M de línea F
juge M de ligne F
Linienrichter M
giudice M di linea F
sideline
banda F
ligne F de côté M
Seitenlinie F
linea F laterale
post
poste M
poteau M
Pfosten M
palo M
attack zone
zona F de ataque M
zone F d'attaque F
Angriffszone F
zona F di attacco M
vertical side band
banda F lateral de la red F
bande F verticale de côté M
vertikales Seitenband N
nastro M verticale laterale

volleyball
pelota F de voleibol M
ballon M de volleyball M
Volleyball M
pallone M

table tennis

tenis^M de mesa^F | tennis^M de table^F | Tischtennis^N | tennis^M da tavolo^M

table
mesa^F
table^F
Tischtennisplatte^F
tavolo^M

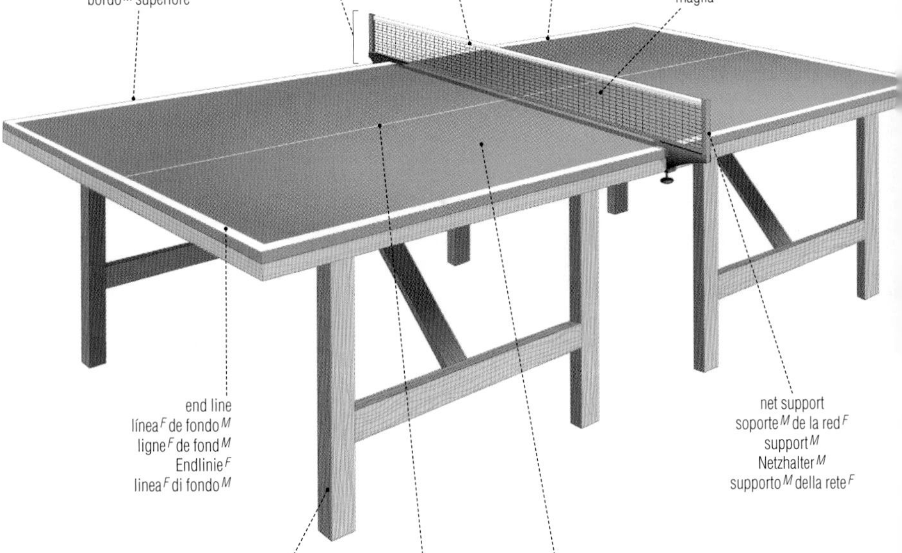
net
red^F
filet^M
Netz^N
rete^F
white tape
cinta^F
ruban^M blanc
weißes Band^N
nastro^M bianco
sideline
línea^F de banda^F
ligne^F latérale
Seitenlinie^F
linea^F laterale
upper edge
moldura^F superior
arête^F supérieure
Oberkante^F
bordo^M superiore
mesh
malla^F
maille^F
Maschen^F
maglia^F
end line
línea^F de fondo^M
ligne^F de fond^M
Endlinie^F
linea^F di fondo^M
net support
soporte^M de la red^F
support^M
Netzhalter^M
supporto^M della rete^F
leg
pata^F de la mesa^F
pied^M
Bein^N
gamba^F
center line
línea^F divisoria central
ligne^F centrale
Mittellinie^F
linea^F centrale
playing surface
superficie^F de juego^M
surface^F de jeu^M
Spielfläche^F
superficie^F di gioco^M

table tennis paddle
pala F
raquette F **de tennis** M **de table** F
Tischtennisschläger M
racchetta F

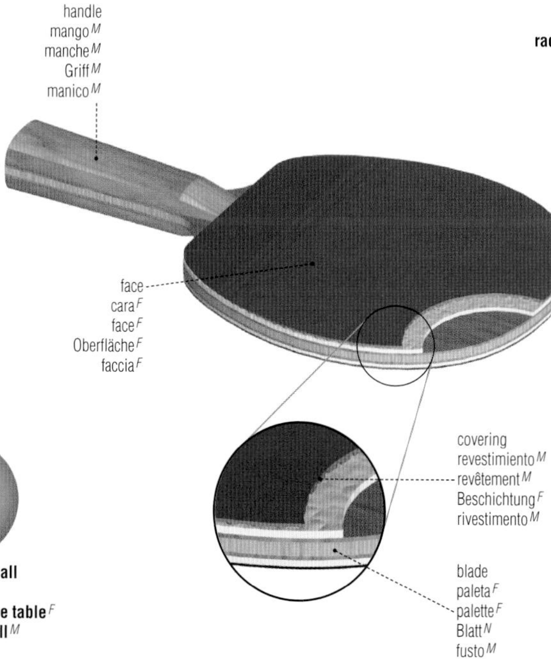
handle
mango M
manche M
Griff M
manico M
face
cara F
face F
Oberfläche F
faccia F
covering
revestimiento M
revêtement M
Beschichtung F
rivestimento M
blade
paleta F
palette F
Blatt N
fusto M

table tennis ball
pelota F
balle F **de tennis** M **de table** F
Tischtennisball M
pallina F

types of grips
formas F **de agarrar la paleta** F
types M **de prises** F
Grifftechniken F
tipi M **di impugnature** F

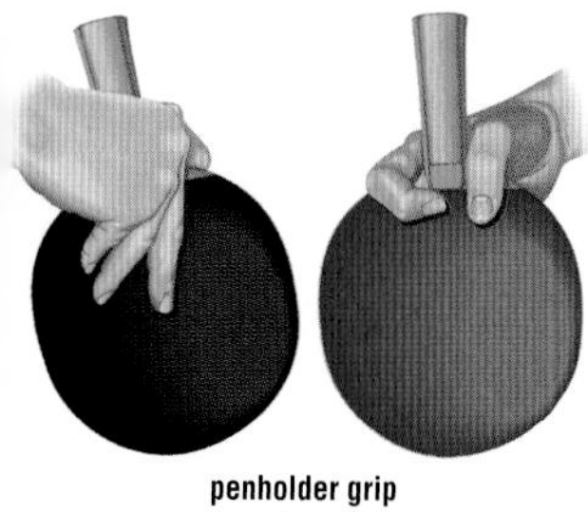

penholder grip
oriental
prise F **porte-plume** M
Penholdergriff M
impugnatura F **a penna** F

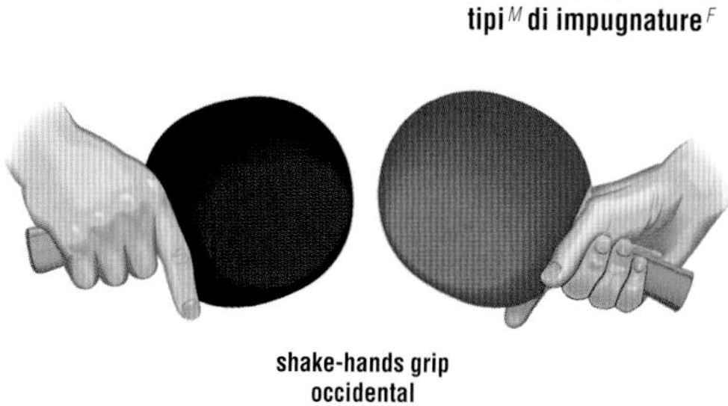

shake-hands grip
occidental
prise F **classique**
Shake-Hands-Griff M
impugnatura F **a stretta** F **di mano** F

badminton

bádminton[M] | badminton[M] | Badminton[N] | gioco[M] del volano[M]

court
cancha[F]
terrain[M]
Badmintonplatz[M]
campo[M]

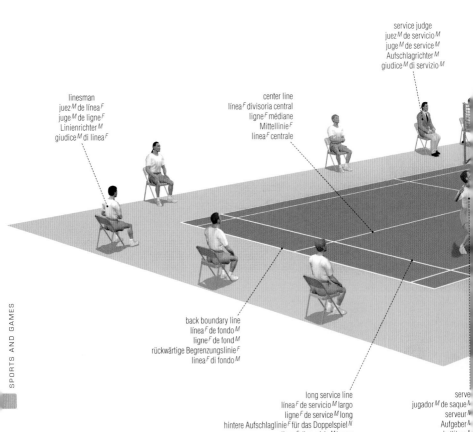

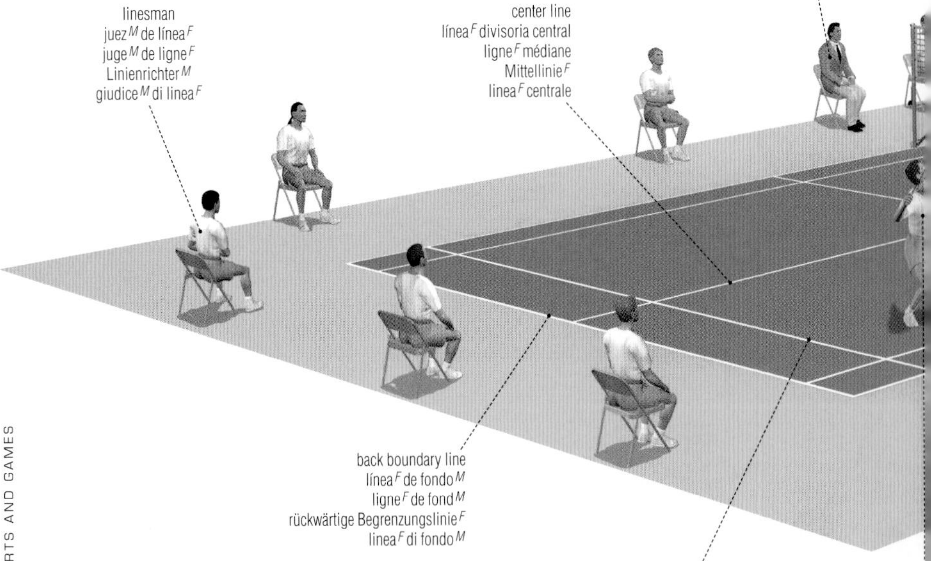
service judge
juez[M] de servicio[M]
juge[M] de service[M]
Aufschlagrichter[M]
giudice[M] di servizio[M]
linesman
juez[M] de línea[F]
juge[M] de ligne[F]
Linienrichter[M]
giudice[M] di linea[F]
center line
línea[F] divisoria central
ligne[F] médiane
Mittellinie[F]
linea[F] centrale
back boundary line
línea[F] de fondo[M]
ligne[F] de fond[M]
rückwärtige Begrenzungslinie[F]
linea[F] di fondo[M]
long service line
línea[F] de servicio[M] largo
ligne[F] de service[M] long
hintere Aufschlaglinie[F] für das Doppelspiel[N]
linea[F] di servizio[M] lungo
serve
jugador[M] de saque
serveur
Aufgeber
battitore

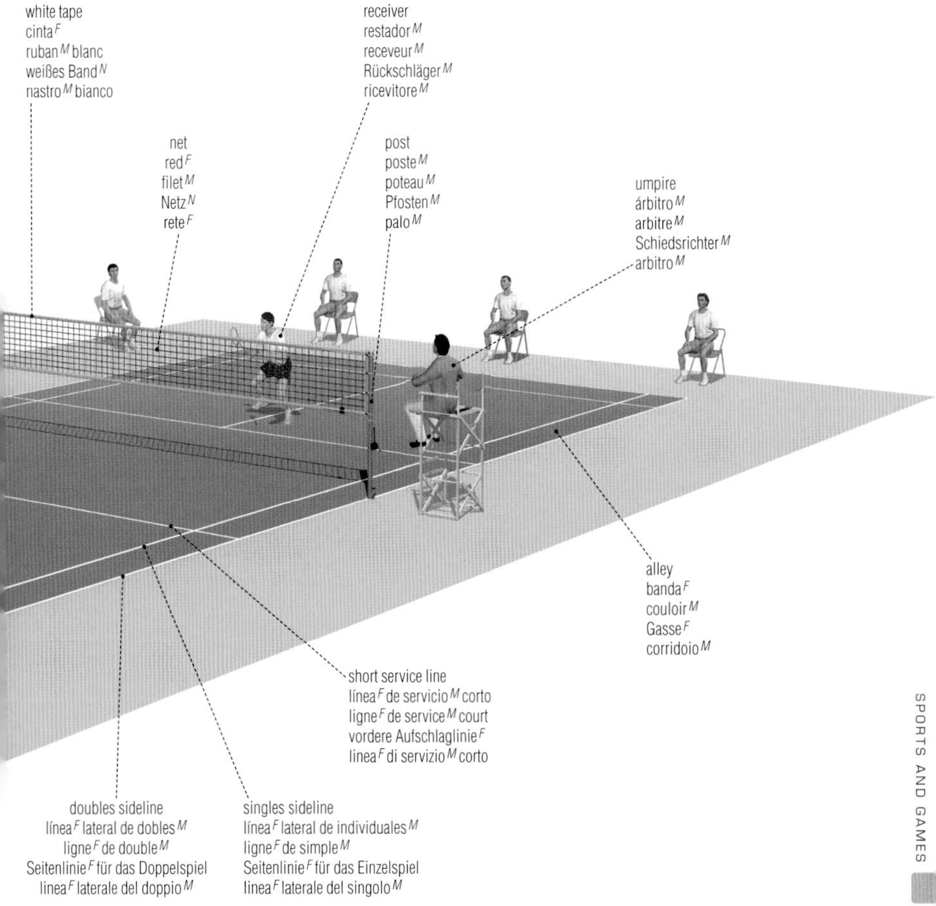
white tape
cinta F
ruban M blanc
weißes Band N
nastro M bianco
receiver
restador M
receveur M
Rückschläger M
ricevitore M
net
red F
filet M
Netz N
rete F
post
poste M
poteau M
Pfosten M
palo M
umpire
árbitro M
arbitre M
Schiedsrichter M
arbitro M
alley
banda F
couloir M
Gasse F
corridoio M
short service line
línea F de servicio M corto
ligne F de service M court
vordere Aufschlaglinie F
linea F di servizio M corto
doubles sideline
línea F lateral de dobles M
ligne F de double M
Seitenlinie F für das Doppelspiel
linea F laterale del doppio M
singles sideline
línea F lateral de individuales M
ligne F de simple M
Seitenlinie F für das Einzelspiel
linea F laterale del singolo M

badminton

badminton racket
raquetaᶠ de bádmintonᴹ
raquetteᶠ de badmintonᴹ
Badmintonschlägerᴹ
racchettaᶠ

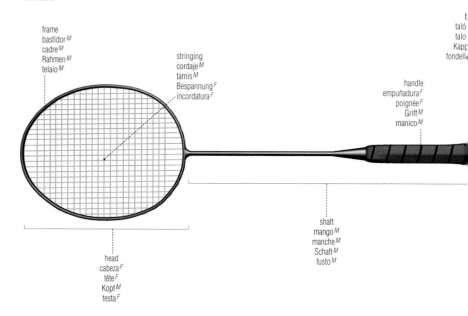

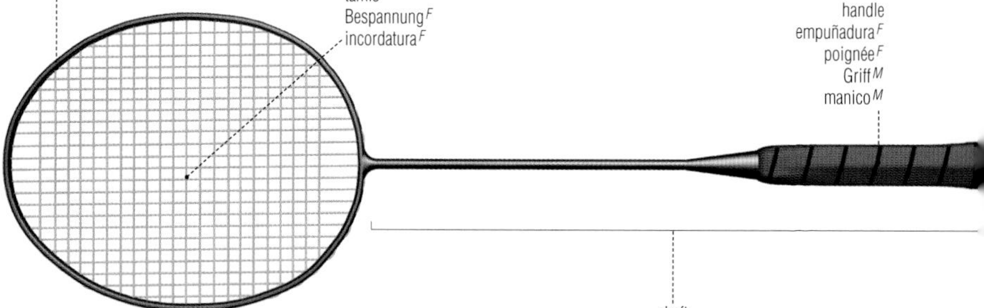
frame
bastidor M
cadre M
Rahmen M
telaio M
stringing
cordaje M
tamis M
Bespannung F
incordatura F
taló
talo
handle
empuñadura F
poignée F
Griff M
manico M
shaft
mango M
manche M
Schaft M
fusto M
head
cabeza F
tête F
Kopf M
testa F

feathered shuttlecock
volante M de plumas F
volant M de plumes F
Federball M
volano M a penne F naturali

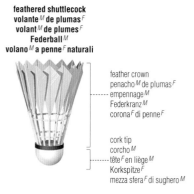

feather crown
penacho M de plumas F
empennage M
Federkranz M
corona F di penne F
cork tip
corcho M
tête F en liège M
Korkspitze F
mezza sfera F di sughero M

synthetic shuttlecock
volante M sintético
volant M synthétique
Kunststoff M-Federball M
volano M sintetico

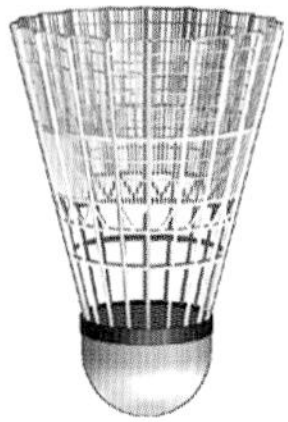

tennis

tenis[M] | tennis[M] | Tennis[N] | tennis[M]

tennis racket
raqueta[F] de tenis[M]
raquette[F] de tennis[M]
Tennisschläger[M]
racchetta[F]

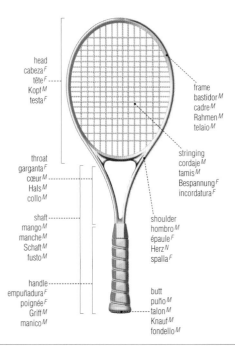

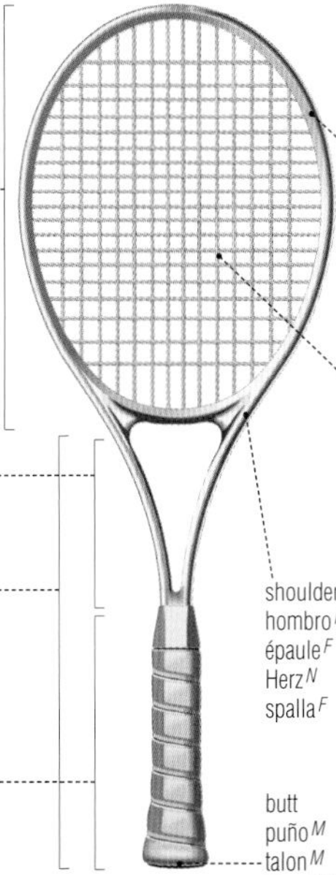
head
cabeza[F]
tête[F]
Kopf[M]
testa[F]
frame
bastidor[M]
cadre[M]
Rahmen[M]
telaio[M]
stringing
cordaje[M]
tamis[M]
Bespannung[F]
incordatura[F]
throat
garganta[F]
cœur[M]
Hals[M]
collo[M]
shaft
mango[M]
manche[M]
Schaft[M]
fusto[M]
shoulder
hombro[M]
épaule[F]
Herz[N]
spalla[F]
handle
empuñadura[F]
poignée[F]
Griff[M]
manico[M]
butt
puño[M]
talon[M]
Knauf[M]
fondello[M]

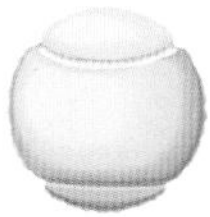

tennis ball
pelota[F] de tenis[M]
balle[F] de tennis[M]
Tennisball[M]
palla[F]

playing surfaces
superficies[F] de juego[M]
surfaces[F] de jeu[M]
Spielfeldbeläge[M]
superfici[F] di gioco[M]

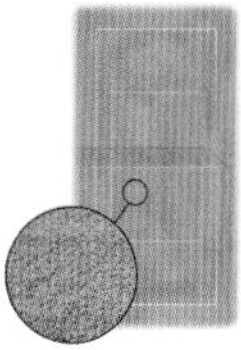

grass
hierba[F]
gazon[M]
Rasen[M]
erba[F]

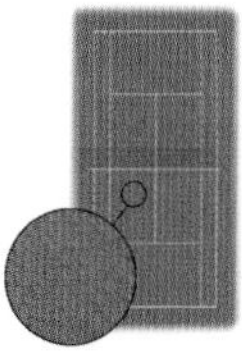

hard surface (cement)
superficie[F] dura (cemento[M])
surface[F] dure (ciment[M])
Hartplatz[M] (Zement[M])
superficie[F] dura (cemento[M])

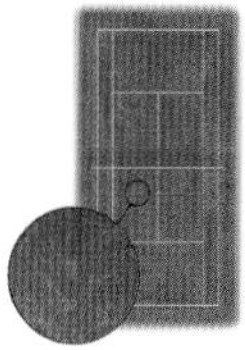

clay
tierra[F] batida
terre[F] battue
Sand[M]
terra[F] battuta

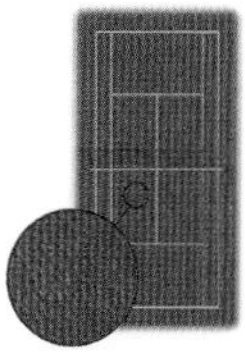

synthetic surface
superficie[F] sintética
revêtement[M] synthétique
Kunststoffboden[M]
superficie[F] sintetica

tennis

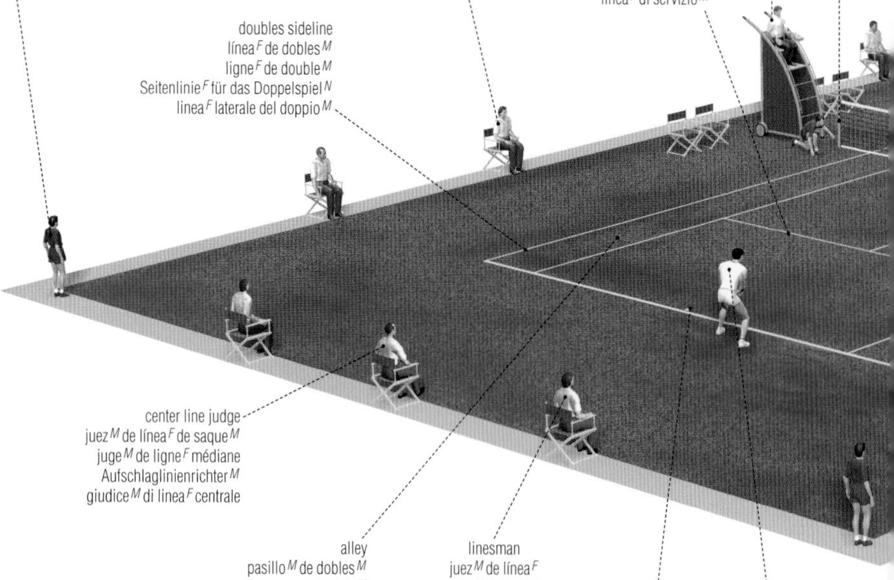
court
cancha F
court M
Tennisplatz M
campo M
pole
poste M
poteau M
Pfosten M
palo M
umpire
juez M de silla F
arbitre M
Schiedsrichter M
giudice M di sedia F
ball boy
recogepelotas M
ramasseur M
Balljunge M
raccattapalle M/F
service judge
juez M de servicio M
juge M de service M
Aufschlagrichter M
giudice M di servizio M
service line
línea F de servicio M
ligne F de service M
Aufschlaglinie F
linea F di servizio M
doubles sideline
línea F de dobles M
ligne F de double M
Seitenlinie F für das Doppelspiel N
linea F laterale del doppio M
center line judge
juez M de línea F de saque M
juge M de ligne F médiane
Aufschlaglinienrichter M
giudice M di linea F centrale
alley
pasillo M de dobles M
couloir M
Gasse F
corridoio M
linesman
juez M de línea F
juge M de ligne F
Linienrichter M
giudice M di linea F
center mark
marca F central
marque F centrale
Mittelzeichen N
segno M centrale
receiver
restador M
receveur M
Rückschläger M
ricevitore M

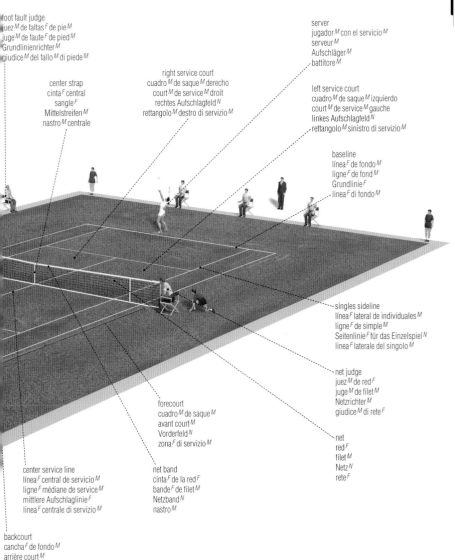

foot fault judge
juez[M] de faltas[F] de pie[M]
juge[M] de faute[F] de pied[M]
Grundlinienrichter[M]
giudice[M] del fallo[M] di piede[M]

center strap
cinta[F] central
sangle[F]
Mittelstreifen[M]
nastro[M] centrale

right service court
cuadro[M] de saque[M] derecho
court[M] de service[M] droit
rechtes Aufschlagfeld[N]
rettangolo[M] destro di servizio[M]

server
jugador[M] con el servicio[M]
serveur[M]
Aufschläger[M]
battitore[M]

left service court
cuadro[M] de saque[M] izquierdo
court[M] de service[M] gauche
linkes Aufschlagfeld[N]
rettangolo[M] sinistro di servizio[M]

baseline
línea[F] de fondo[M]
ligne[F] de fond[M]
Grundlinie[F]
linea[F] di fondo[M]

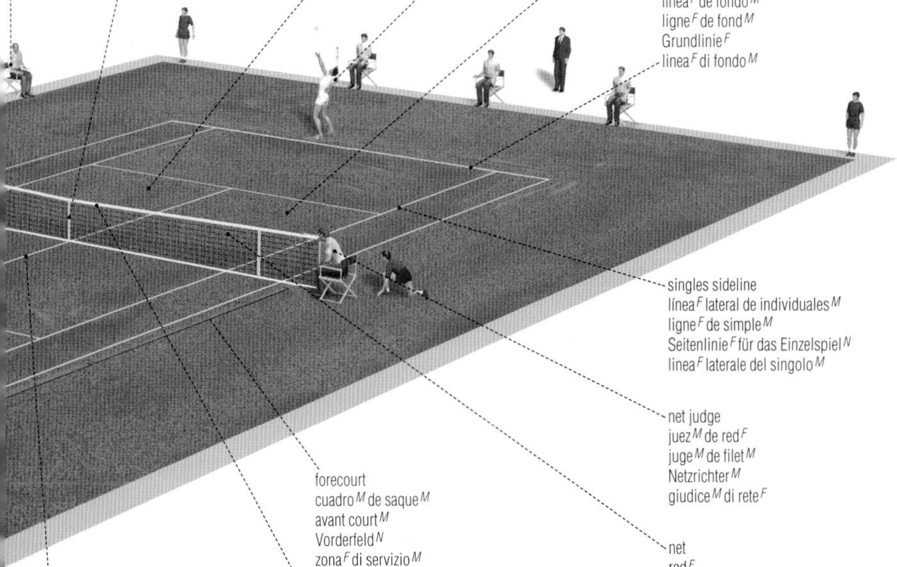

singles sideline
línea[F] lateral de individuales[M]
ligne[F] de simple[M]
Seitenlinie[F] für das Einzelspiel[N]
linea[F] laterale del singolo[M]

net judge
juez[M] de red[F]
juge[M] de filet[M]
Netzrichter[M]
giudice[M] di rete[F]

forecourt
cuadro[M] de saque[M]
avant court[M]
Vorderfeld[N]
zona[F] di servizio[M]

net
red[F]
filet[M]
Netz[N]
rete[F]

center service line
línea[F] central de servicio[M]
ligne[F] médiane de service[M]
mittlere Aufschlaglinie[F]
linea[F] centrale di servizio[M]

net band
cinta[F] de la red[F]
bande[F] de filet[M]
Netzband[N]
nastro[M]

backcourt
cancha[F] de fondo[M]
arrière court[M]
Rückfeld[N]
fondocampo[M]

gymnastics

gimnasia^F | gymnastique^F | Geräteturnen^N | ginnastica^F

event platform
área^F de competición^F
podium^M des épreuves^F
Geräteturnanlage^F
pedana^F

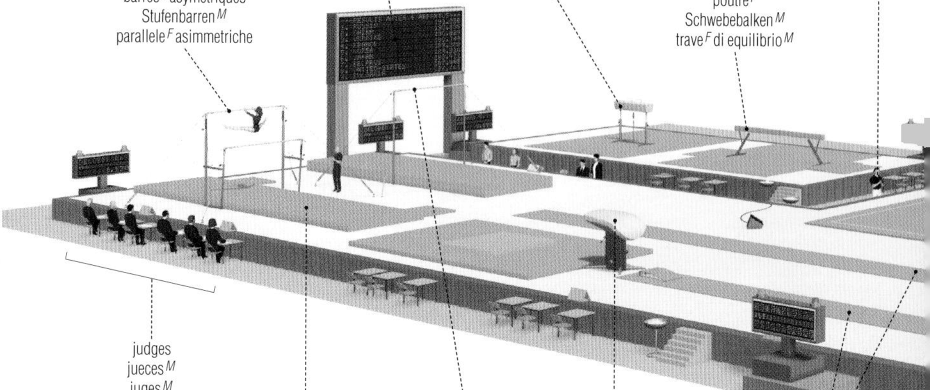

overall standings scoreboard
marcador^M de clasificación^F general
tableau^M de classement^M général
Anzeigetafel^F für das Gesamtergebnis^N
tabellone^M della classifica^F generale
pommel horse
caballo^M con arcos^M
cheval^M d'arçons^M
Seitpferd^N
cavallo^M con maniglie^F
line judge
juez^M de línea^F
juge^M de ligne^F
Linienrichter^M
giudice^M di linea^F
uneven parallel bars
barras^F paralelas asimétricas
barres^F asymétriques
Stufenbarren^M
parallele^F asimmetriche
balance beam
barra^F de equilibrio^M
poutre^F
Schwebebalken^M
trave^F di equilibrio^M
judges
jueces^M
juges^M
Kampfrichter^M
giudici^M
horizontal bar
barra^F fija
barre^F fixe
Reck^N
sbarra^F orizzontale
floor mats
colchoneta^F de recepción^F
tapis^M de réception^F
Matten^F
materassi^M
approach runs
pistas^F de carreras^F
pistes^F d'élan^M
Anlaufbahn^F
pedane^F di rincorsa^F
vaulting horse
potro^M
cheval^M sautoir^M
Sprungpferd^N
cavallo^M per volteggi^M

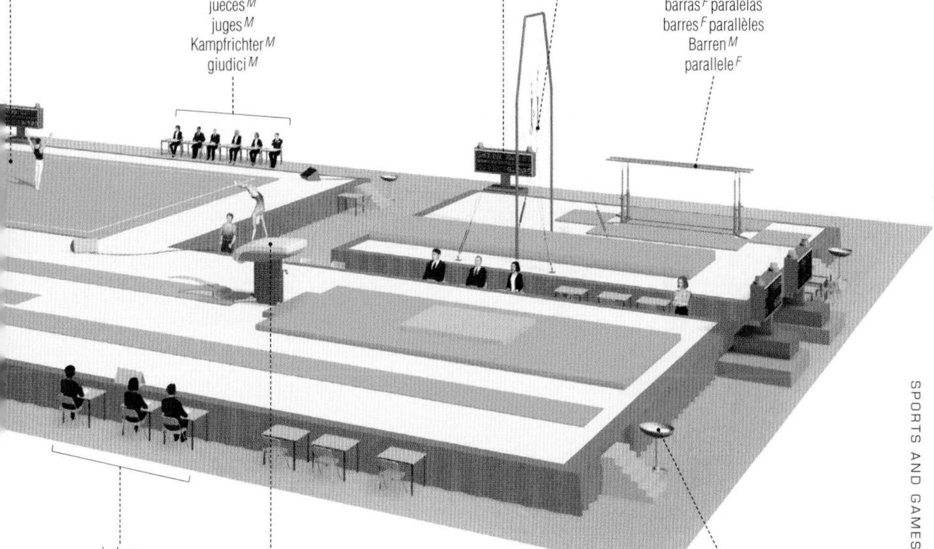
floor exercise area
practicable M para ejercicios M de suelo M
praticable M pour exercices M au sol M
Bodenturnfläche F
pedana F per il corpo M libero
current event scoreboard
marcador M del evento M en curso M
pointage M de l'épreuve F en cours M
Anzeigetafel F für die Einzeldisziplin F
tabellone M della prova F in corso
rings
anillas F
anneaux M
Ringe M
anelli M
judges
jueces M
juges M
Kampfrichter M
giudici M
parallel bars
barras F paralelas
barres F parallèles
Barren M
parallele F
judges
jueces M
juges M
Kampfrichter M
giudici M
vaulting horse
potro M
cheval M sautoir M
Sprungpferd N
cavallo M per volteggi M
magnesium powder
polvo M de magnesio M
magnésie F
Magnesia F
polvere F di magnesia F

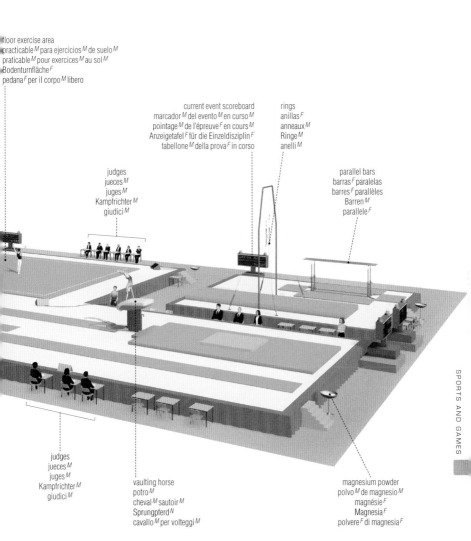

swimming

natación^F | natation^F | Schwimmen^N | nuoto^M

competitive course
piscina^F olímpica
bassin^M de compétition^F
Wettkampfbecken^N
piscina^F olimpionica

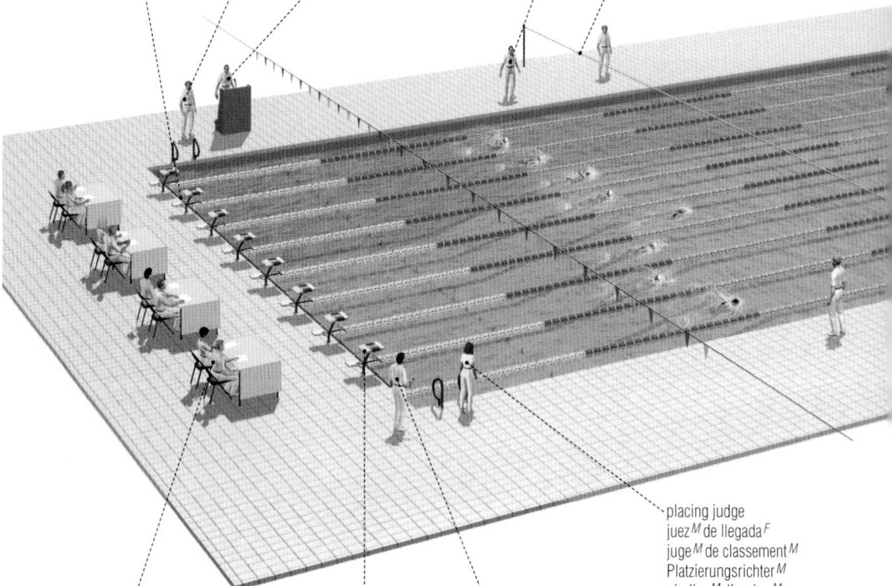
referee
árbitro^M
juge^M arbitre^M
Schiedsrichter^M
arbitro^M
stroke judge
juez^M de brazado^M
juge^M de nage^F
Zugrichter^M
giudice^M di stile^M
finish wall
muro^M de llegada^F
mur^M d'arrivée^F
Ziel^N
parete^F di arrivo^M
starter
juez^M de salida^F
juge^M de départ^M
Starter^M
starter^M
false start rope
cuerda^F de salida^F falsa
corde^F de faux départ^M
Fehlstartleine^F
fune^F di falsa partenza^F
placing judge
juez^M de llegada^F
juge^M de classement^M
Platzierungsrichter^M
giudice^M di arrivo^M
lane timekeeper
cronometrador^M de calle^F
chronométreur^M de couloir^M
Bahnzeitnehmer^M
cronometrista^M/F di corsia^F
starting block
podio^M de salida^F
plot^M de départ^M
Startblock^M
blocco^M di partenza^F
chief timekeeper
jefe^M de cronometradores^M
chronométreur^M en chef^M
Hauptzeitnehmer^M
cronometrista^M/F capo^M

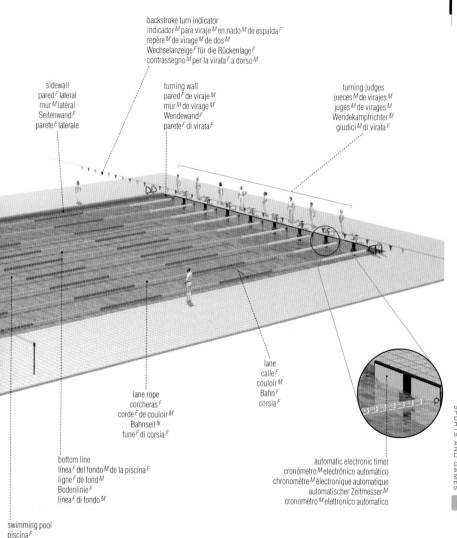

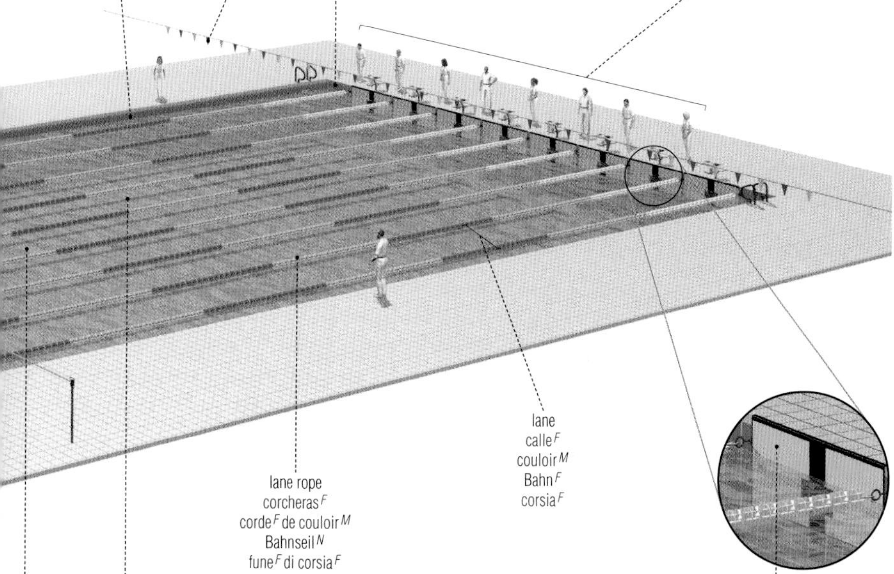
backstroke turn indicator
indicador[M] para viraje[M] en nado[M] de espalda[F]
repère[M] de virage[M] de dos[M]
Wechselanzeige[F] für die Rückenlage[F]
contrassegno[M] per la virata[F] a dorso[M]
sidewall
pared[F] lateral
mur[M] latéral
Seitenwand[F]
parete[F] laterale
turning wall
pared[F] de viraje[M]
mur[M] de virage[M]
Wendewand[F]
parete[F] di virata[F]
turning judges
jueces[M] de virajes[M]
juges[M] de virages[M]
Wendekampfrichter[M]
giudici[M] di virata[F]
lane
calle[F]
couloir[M]
Bahn[F]
corsia[F]
lane rope
corcheras[F]
corde[F] de couloir[M]
Bahnseil[N]
fune[F] di corsia[F]
bottom line
línea[F] del fondo[M] de la piscina[F]
ligne[F] de fond[M]
Bodenlinie[F]
linea[F] di fondo[M]
automatic electronic timer
cronómetro[M] electrónico automático
chronomètre[M] électronique automatique
automatischer Zeitmesser[M]
cronometro[M] elettronico automatico
swimming pool
piscina[F]
bassin[M]
Schwimmbecken[N]
vasca[F]

types of strokes
estilos [M] de natación [F]
types [M] de nages [F]
verschiedene Schwimmstile [M]
stili [M] di nuoto [M]

front crawl stroke
crol [M]
crawl [M]
Kraulen [N]
stile [M] **libero o crawl** [M]

turning wall
pared [F] de viraje [M]
mur [M] de virage [M]
Wendewand [F]
parete [F] di virata [F]

breaststroke
braza [F]
brasse [F]
Brustschwimmen [N]
rana [F]

butterfly stroke
mariposa [F]
papillon [M]
Schmetterlingsstil [M]
farfalla [F]

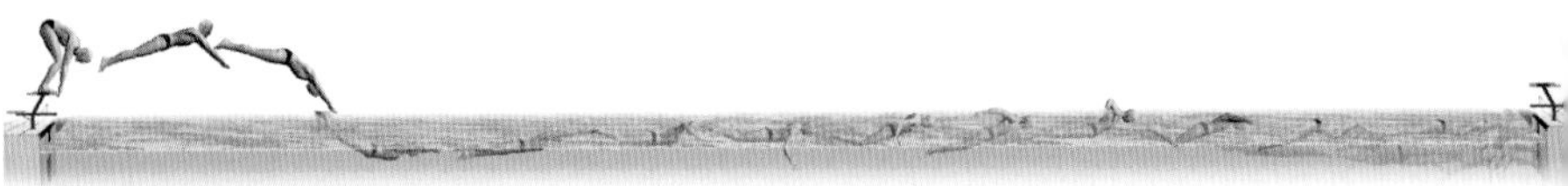

backstroke
espalda [F]
nage [F] **sur le dos** [M]
Rückenschwimmen [N]
dorso [M]

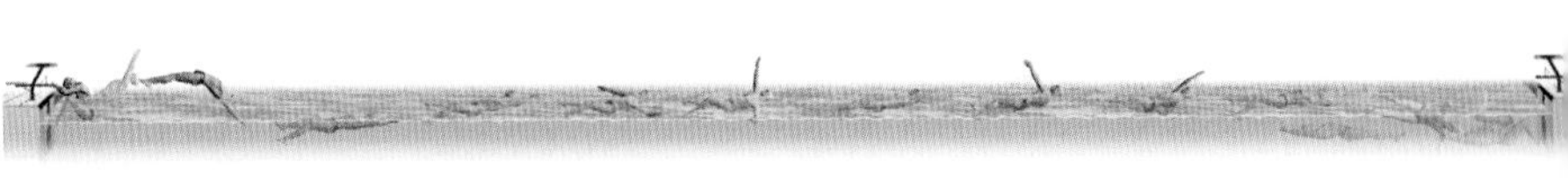

diving

saltos *M* | plongeon *M* | Kunstspringen *N* | tuffi *M*

diving installations
torre *F* de saltos *M*
plongeoir *M*
Springeinrichtungen *F*
strutture *F* per i tuffi *M*

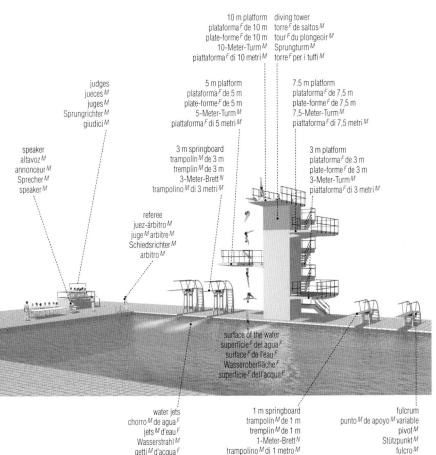

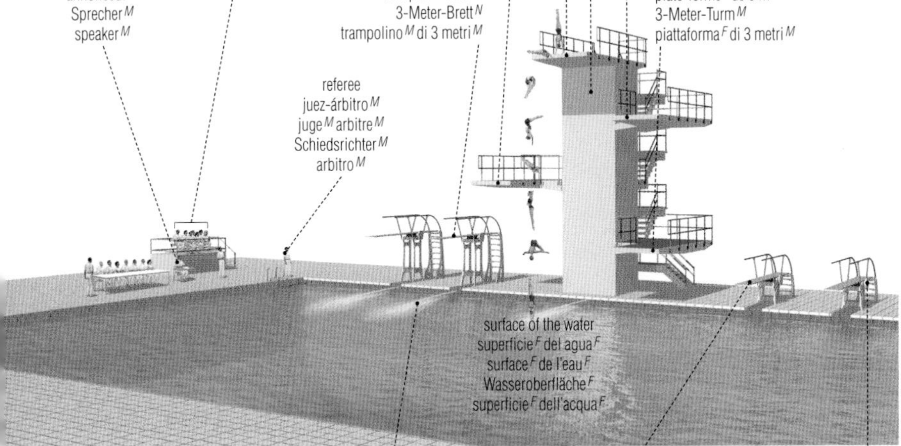
10 m platform
plataforma F de 10 m
plate-forme F de 10 m
10-Meter-Turm M
piattaforma F di 10 metri M
diving tower
torre F de saltos M
tour F du plongeoir M
Sprungturm M
torre F per i tuffi M
judges
jueces M
juges M
Sprungrichter M
giudici M
5 m platform
plataforma F de 5 m
plate-forme F de 5 m
5-Meter-Turm M
piattaforma F di 5 metri M
7.5 m platform
plataforma F de 7,5 m
plate-forme F de 7,5 m
7,5-Meter-Turm M
piattaforma F di 7,5 metri M
speaker
altavoz M
annonceur M
Sprecher M
speaker M
3 m springboard
trampolín M de 3 m
tremplin M de 3 m
3-Meter-Brett N
trampolino M di 3 metri M
3 m platform
plataforma F de 3 m
plate-forme F de 3 m
3-Meter-Turm M
piattaforma F di 3 metri M
referee
juez-árbitro M
juge M arbitre M
Schiedsrichter M
arbitro M
surface of the water
superficie F del agua F
surface F de l'eau F
Wasseroberfläche F
superficie F dell'acqua F
water jets
chorro M de agua F
jets M d'eau F
Wasserstrahl M
getti M d'acqua F
1 m springboard
trampolín M de 1 m
tremplin M de 1 m
1-Meter-Brett N
trampolino M di 1 metro M
fulcrum
punto M de apoyo M variable
pivot M
Stützpunkt M
fulcro M

sailing

vela[F] | voile[F] | Segelsport[M] | vela[F]

sailboat
velero[M]
dériveur[M]
Segelboot[N]
barca[F] **a vela**[F]

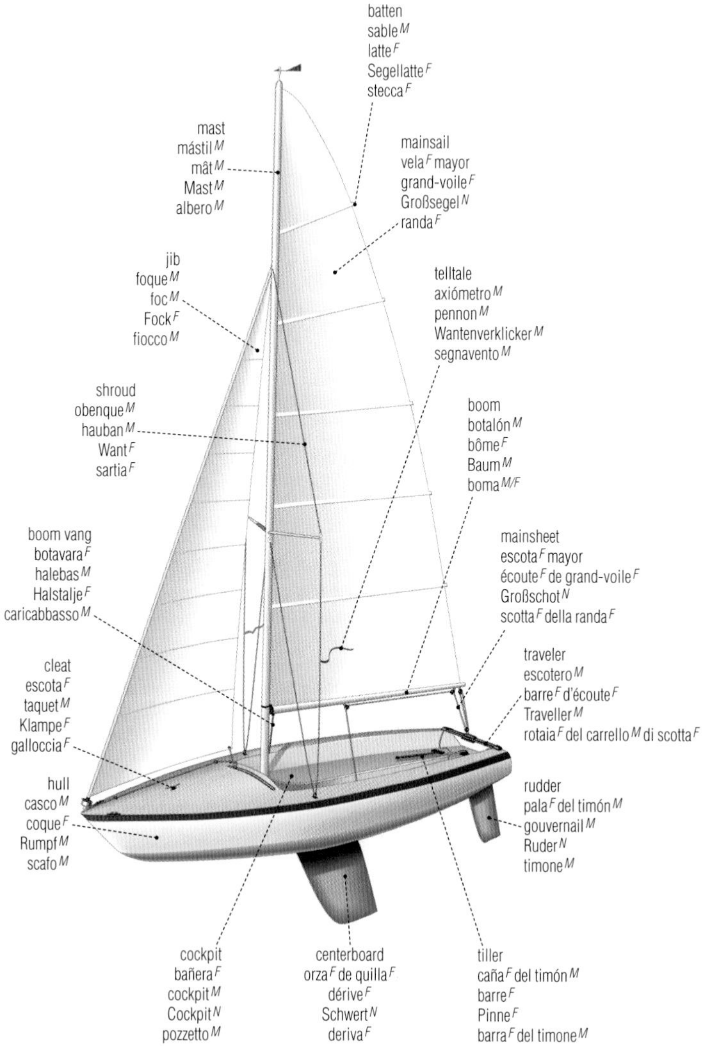

batten
sable[M]
latte[F]
Segellatte[F]
stecca[F]
mast
mástil[M]
mât[M]
Mast[M]
albero[M]
mainsail
vela[F] mayor
grand-voile[F]
Großsegel[N]
randa[F]
jib
foque[M]
foc[M]
Fock[F]
fiocco[M]
telltale
axiómetro[M]
pennon[M]
Wantenverklicker[M]
segnavento[M]
shroud
obenque[M]
hauban[M]
Want[F]
sartia[F]
boom
botalón[M]
bôme[F]
Baum[M]
boma[M/F]
boom vang
botavara[F]
halebas[M]
Halstalje[F]
caricabbasso[M]
mainsheet
escota[F] mayor
écoute[F] de grand-voile[F]
Großschot[N]
scotta[F] della randa[F]
cleat
escota[F]
taquet[M]
Klampe[F]
galloccia[F]
traveler
escotero[M]
barre[F] d'écoute[F]
Traveller[M]
rotaia[F] del carrello[M] di scotta[F]
hull
casco[M]
coque[F]
Rumpf[M]
scafo[M]
rudder
pala[F] del timón[M]
gouvernail[M]
Ruder[N]
timone[M]
cockpit
bañera[F]
cockpit[M]
Cockpit[N]
pozzetto[M]
centerboard
orza[F] de quilla[F]
dérive[F]
Schwert[N]
deriva[F]
tiller
caña[F] del timón[M]
barre[F]
Pinne[F]
barra[F] del timone[M]

sailboard

windsurf^M | planche^F à voile^F | Surfbrett^N | windsurf^M

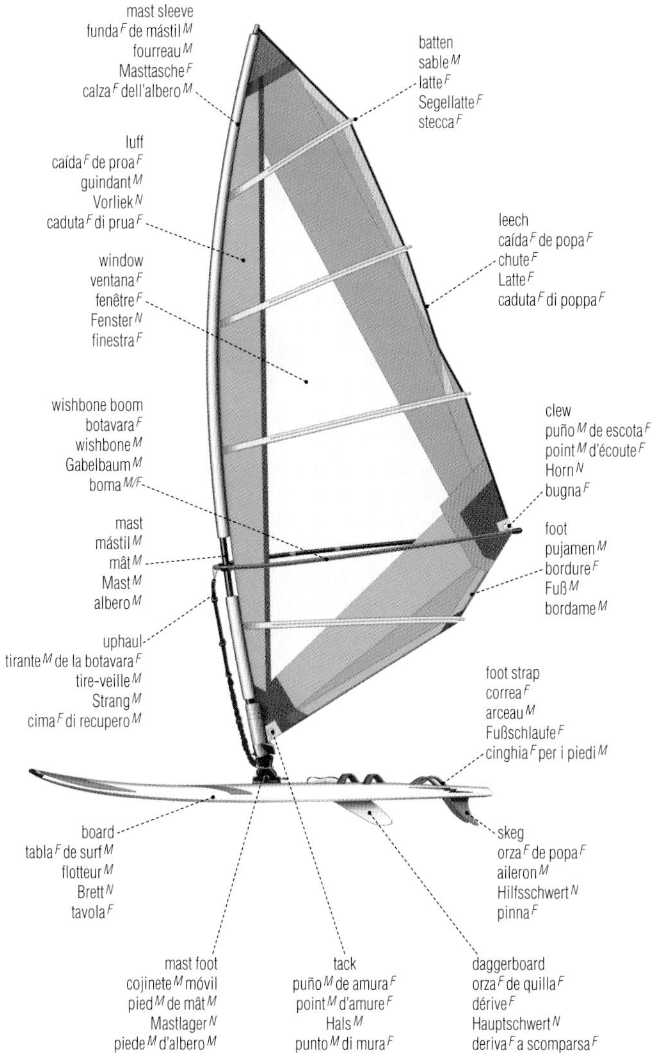
mast sleeve
funda^F de mástil^M
fourreau^M
Masttasche^F
calza^F dell'albero^M
batten
sable^M
latte^F
Segellatte^F
stecca^F
luff
caída^F de proa^F
guindant^M
Vorliek^N
caduta^F di prua^F
leech
caída^F de popa^F
chute^F
Latte^F
caduta^F di poppa^F
window
ventana^F
fenêtre^F
Fenster^N
finestra^F
wishbone boom
botavara^F
wishbone^M
Gabelbaum^M
boma^M/F
clew
puño^M de escota^F
point^M d'écoute^F
Horn^N
bugna^F
mast
mástil^M
mât^M
Mast^M
albero^M
foot
pujamen^M
bordure^F
Fuß^M
bordame^M
uphaul
tirante^M de la botavara^F
tire-veille^M
Strang^M
cima^F di recupero^M
foot strap
correa^F
arceau^M
Fußschlaufe^F
cinghia^F per i piedi^M
board
tabla^F de surf^M
flotteur^M
Brett^N
tavola^F
skeg
orza^F de popa^F
aileron^M
Hilfsschwert^N
pinna^F
mast foot
cojinete^M móvil
pied^M de mât^M
Mastlager^N
piede^M d'albero^M
tack
puño^M de amura^F
point^M d'amure^F
Hals^M
punto^M di mura^F
daggerboard
orza^F de quilla^F
dérive^F
Hauptschwert^N
deriva^F a scomparsa^F

canoe-kayak: whitewater

canoa^F-kayak^M : aguas^F bravas | canoë^M-kayak^M : eaux^F vives | Kanu^N-Kajak^M/N: Wildwasser^N | canoa^F e kayak^M: rapide^F

whitewater canoe
canoa^F
canoë^M
Kanu^N
canoa^F

single-bladed paddle
remo^M **de una sola pala**^F
pagaie^F **simple**
Stechpaddel^N
pagaia^F **a pala**^F **singola**

kayak
kayak^M
kayak^M
Kajak^M/N
kayak^M

spray skirt
cubrebañeras^M
jupe^F
Spritzschutz^M
paraspruzzi^M

31

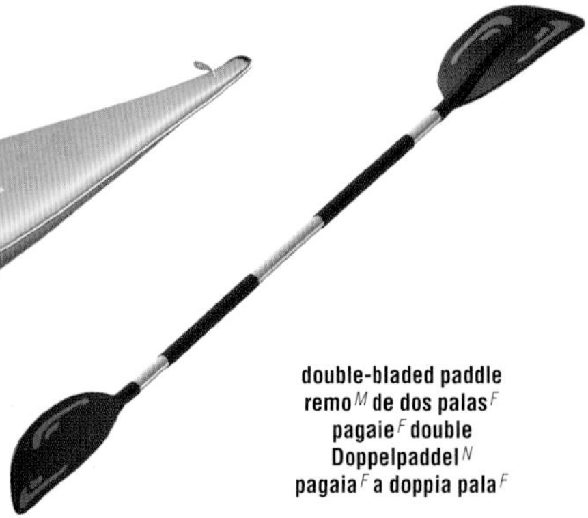

double-bladed paddle
remo^M **de dos palas**^F
pagaie^F **double**
Doppelpaddel^N
pagaia^F **a doppia pala**^F

Scuba diving

buceo^{M} | plongée^{F} sous-marine | Tauchen^{N} | pesca^{F} subacquea

scuba diver
buceador^{M}
plongeur^{M}
Taucher^{M}
sub^{M}

mask
gafas^{F}
masque^{M}
Maske^{F}
maschera^{F}

hood
caperuza^{F}
cagoule^{F}
Mütze^{F}
cappuccio^{M}

harness
correas^{F} de los aparatos^{M} de buceo^{M}
harnais^{M}
Gurtwerk^{N}
imbracatura^{F}

snorkel
tubo^{M}
tuba^{M}
Schnorchel^{M}
respiratore^{M}

regulator first stage
regulador^{M} de la 1ª etapa^{F} de descompresión^{F}
détendeur^{M} premier étage^{M}
Druckminderer^{M}
primo stadio^{M} dell'erogatore^{M}

regulator second stage
regulador^{M} de la 2ª etapa^{F} de descompresión^{F}
détendeur^{M} second étage^{M}
Druckregulierung^{F}
secondo stadio^{M} dell'erogatore^{M}

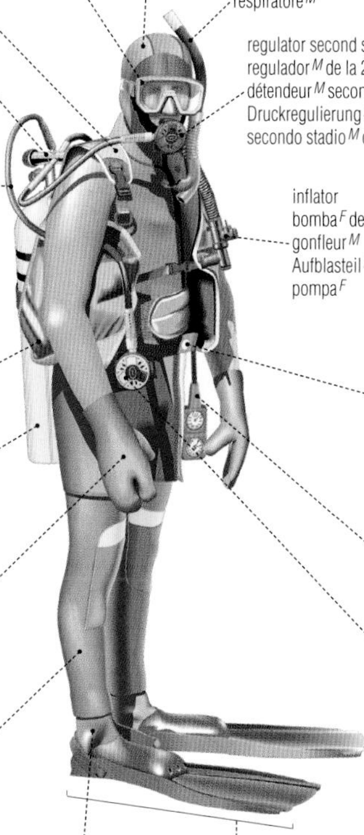

air hose
tubo^{M} de aire^{M}
tuyau^{M} d'air^{M}
Luftschlauch^{M}
tubo^{M} dell'aria^{F}

inflator
bomba^{F} de aire^{M} comprimido
gonfleur^{M}
Aufblasteil^{N}
pompa^{F}

buoyancy compensator
compensador^{M} de flotación^{F}
gilet^{M} de stabilisation^{F}
Auftriebsausgleich^{M}
giubbetto^{M} equilibratore^{M}

weight belt
cinturón^{M} lastrado
ceinture^{F} lestée
Bleigürtel^{M}
cintura^{F} da zavorra^{F}

compressed-air cylinder
tanque^{M} de aire^{M} comprimido
bouteille^{F} d'air^{M} comprimé
Druckluftflasche^{F}
bombola^{F} ad aria^{F} compressa

information console
instrumentos^{M} de inmersión^{F}
console^{F} d'instruments^{M}
Anzeigeeinheit^{F}
portastrumenti^{M}

diving glove
guante^{M} de buceo^{M}
gant^{M} de plongée^{F}
Taucherhandschuh^{M}
guanto^{M}

emergency regulator
regulador^{M} de emergencia^{F}
détendeur^{M} de secours^{M}
Notregulierung^{F}
erogatore^{M} d'emergenza^{F}

wet suit
traje^{M} isotérmico
vêtement^{M} isothermique
Tauchanzug^{M}
muta^{F}

boot
bota^{F}
bottillon^{M}
Schuh^{M}
calzare^{M}

fin
aleta^{F}
palme^{F}
Flosse^{F}
pinna^{F}

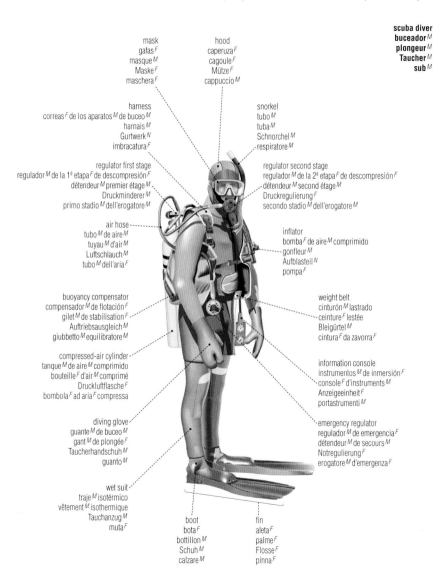

boxing

boxeo M | boxe F | Boxen N | pugilato M

ring
cuadrilátero M
ring M
Ring M
ring M

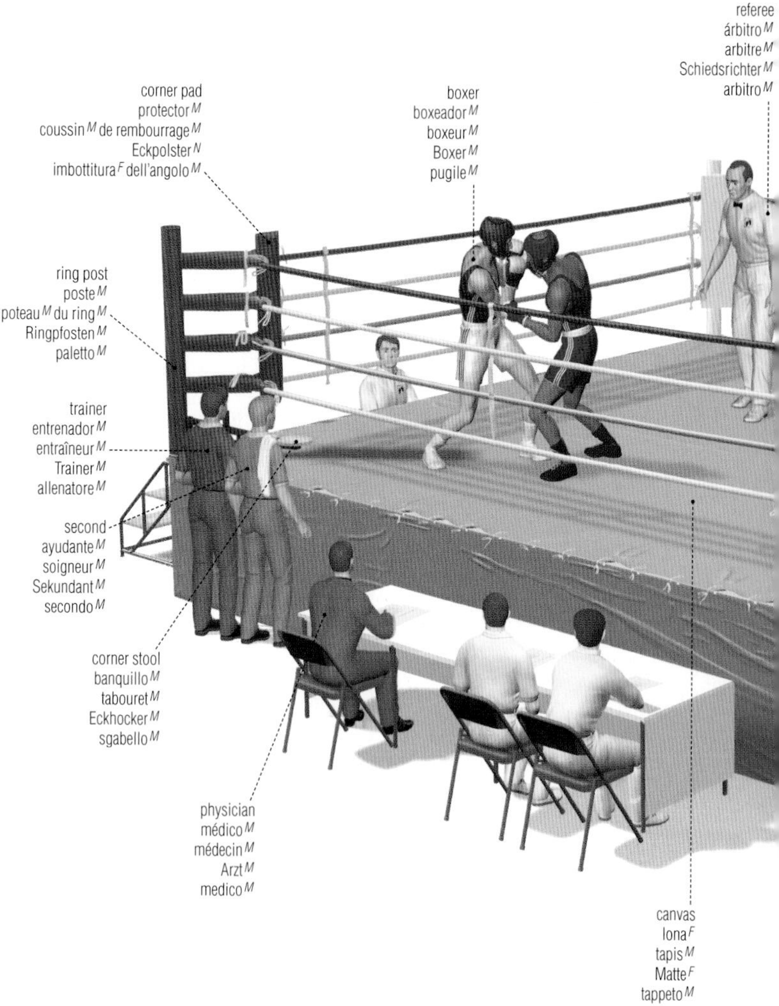

referee
árbitro M
arbitre M
Schiedsrichter M
arbitro M
corner pad
protector M
coussin M de rembourrage M
Eckpolster N
imbottitura F dell'angolo M
boxer
boxeador M
boxeur M
Boxer M
pugile M
ring post
poste M
poteau M du ring M
Ringpfosten M
paletto M
trainer
entrenador M
entraîneur M
Trainer M
allenatore M
second
ayudante M
soigneur M
Sekundant M
secondo M
corner stool
banquillo M
tabouret M
Eckhocker M
sgabello M
physician
médico M
médecin M
Arzt M
medico M
canvas
lona F
tapis M
Matte F
tappeto M

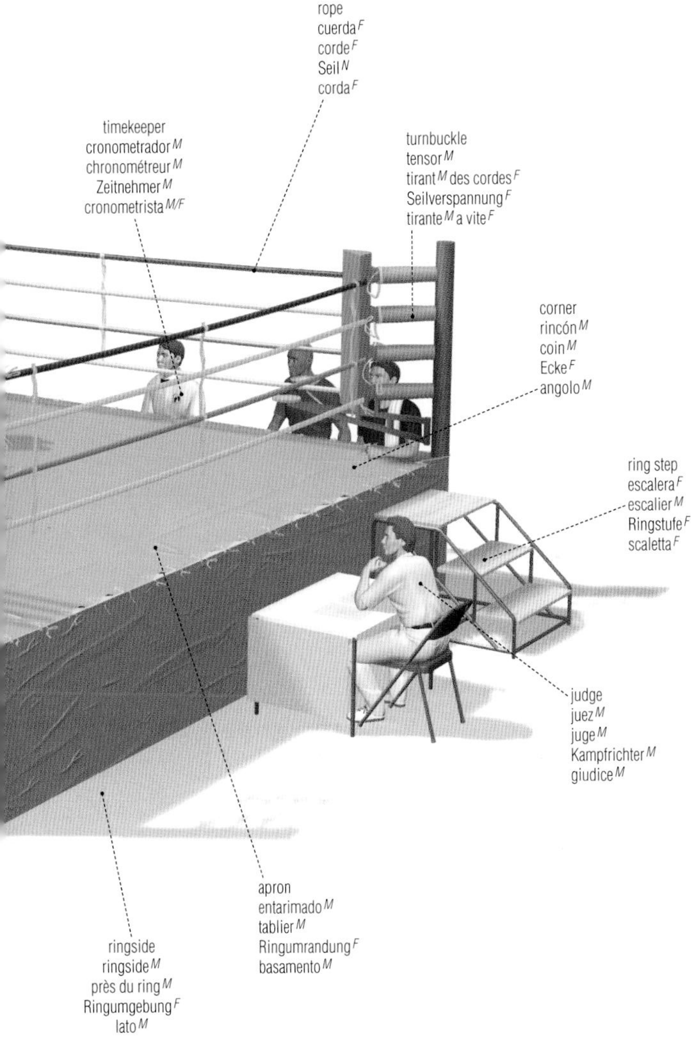
rope
cuerda F
corde F
Seil N
corda F
timekeeper
cronometrador M
chronométreur M
Zeitnehmer M
cronometrista M/F
turnbuckle
tensor M
tirant M des cordes F
Seilverspannung F
tirante M a vite F
corner
rincón M
coin M
Ecke F
angolo M
ring step
escalera F
escalier M
Ringstufe F
scaletta F
judge
juez M
juge M
Kampfrichter M
giudice M
apron
entarimado M
tablier M
Ringumrandung F
basamento M
ringside
ringside M
près du ring M
Ringumgebung F
lato M

boxing

headgear
casco M
casque M
Kopfschutz M
caschetto M
glove
guante M
gant M
Fausthandschuh M
guantone M
boxing trunks
pantalones M de boxeo M
short M de boxe F
Boxerhose F
pantaloncini M

boxer
boxeador M
boxeur M
Boxer M
pugile M

punching bag
saco M **de arena** F
sac M **de sable** M
Sandsack M
sacco M

speed ball
pera F **de maíz** M
ballon M **de boxe** F
Punchingball M
punching ball M

mouthpiece
protector M **bucal**
protège-dents M
Mundschutz M
paradenti M

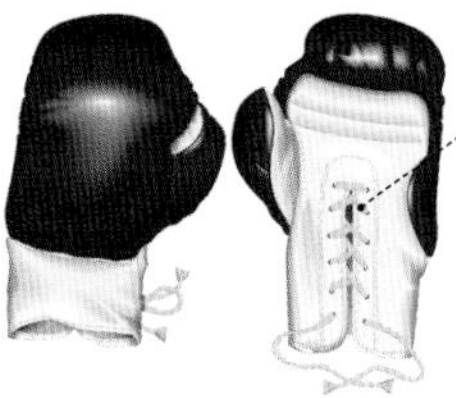
lace
cordones M
lacet M
Schnürsenkel M
stringa F

boxing gloves
guantes M **de boxeo** M
gants M **de boxe** F
Boxhandschuhe M
guantoni M

bandage
vendaje M
bandage M
Bandage F
bendaggio M

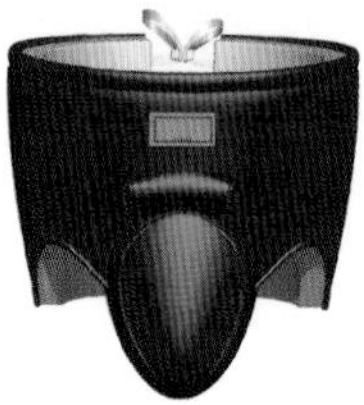

protective cup
coquilla F
coquille F **de protection** F
Suspensorium N
conchiglia F **di protezione** F

wrestling

lucha[F] | lutte[F] | Ringen[N] | lotta[F]

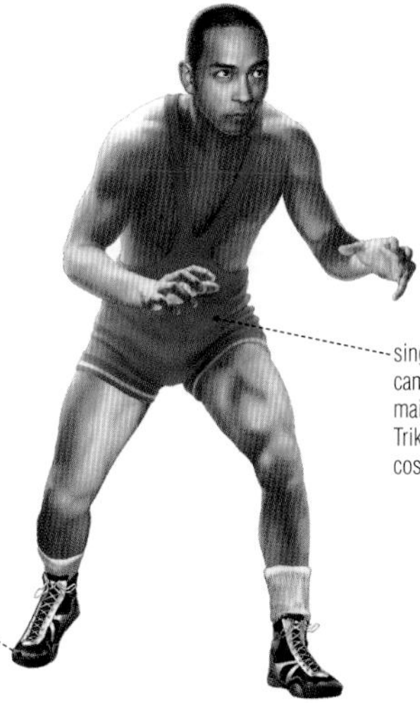
wrestler
luchador[M]
lutteur[M]
Ringer[M]
lottatore[M]
singlet
camiseta[F]
maillot[M]
Trikot[N]
costume[M]
wrestling shoe
botas[F] de lucha[F]
chaussure[F] de lutte[F]
Ringerschuh[M]
scarpa[F]

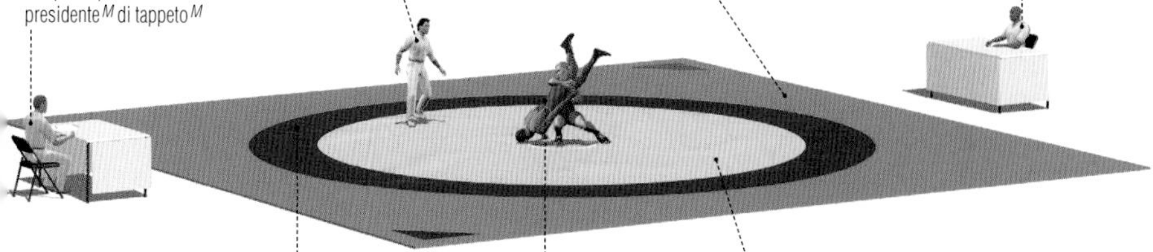
wrestling area
área[F] de lucha[F] libre
aire[F] de combat[M]
Wettkampffläche[F]
area[F] di combattimento[M]
referee
árbitro[M]
arbitre[M]
Kampfrichter[M]
arbitro[M]
protection area
superficie[F] de protección[F]
surface[F] de protection[F]
Schutzfläche[F]
area[F] di sicurezza[F]
judge
juez[M]
juge[M]
Punktrichter[M]
giudice[M]
mat chairperson
jefe[M] de tapiz[M]
chef[M] de tapis[M]
Hauptkampfrichter[M]
presidente[M] di tappeto[M]
passivity zone
zona[F] de pasividad[F]
zone[F] de passivité[F]
Passivitätszone[F]
zona[F] di passività[F]
wrestler
luchador[M]
lutteur[M]
Ringer[M]
lottatore[M]
central wrestling area
zona[F] de lucha[F]
surface[F] centrale de lutte[F]
zentrale Kampffläche[F]
superficie[F] centrale di lotta[F]

judo

judo^M | judo^M | Judo^N | judo^M

mat
tatami^M
tapis^M
Matte^F
tatami^M

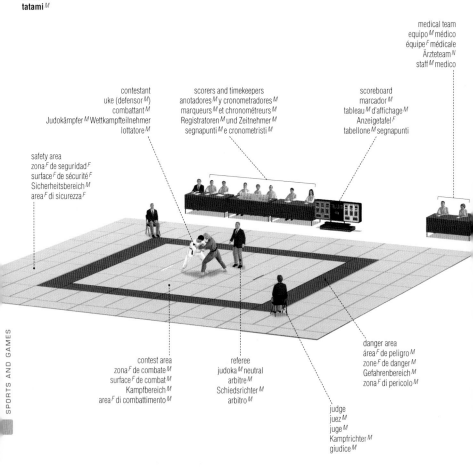

medical team
equipo^M médico
équipe^F médicale
Ärzteteam^N
staff^M medico

contestant
uke (defensor^M)
combattant^M
Judokämpfer^M Wettkampfteilnehmer
lottatore^M

scorers and timekeepers
anotadores^M y cronometradores^M
marqueurs^M et chronométreurs^M
Registratoren^M und Zeitnehmer^M
segnapunti^M e cronometristi^M

scoreboard
marcador^M
tableau^M d'affichage^M
Anzeigetafel^F
tabellone^M segnapunti

safety area
zona^F de seguridad^F
surface^F de sécurité^F
Sicherheitsbereich^M
area^F di sicurezza^F

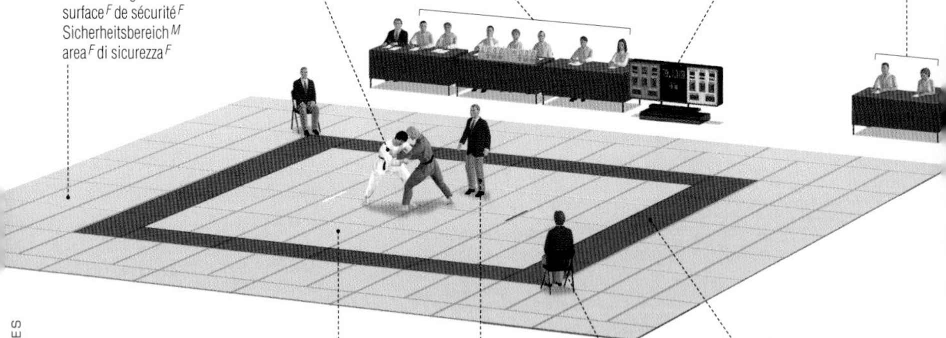

danger area
área^F de peligro^M
zone^F de danger^M
Gefahrenbereich^M
zona^F di pericolo^M

contest area
zona^F de combate^M
surface^F de combat^M
Kampfbereich^M
area^F di combattimento^M

referee
judoka^M neutral
arbitre^M
Schiedsrichter^M
arbitro^M

judge
juez^M
juge^M
Kampfrichter^M
giudice^M

examples of holds and throws
ejemplos[M] de llaves[F]
exemples[M] de prises[F]
Griff- und Wurfbeispiele[N]
esempi[M] di prese[F]

stomach throw
proyección[F] en círculo[M]
projection[F] en cercle[M]
Kopfwurf[M]
rovesciata[F] all'indietro

sweeping hip throw
proyección[F] primera de cadera[F]
hanche[F] ailée
Hüftwurf[M]
spazzata[F] d'anca[F]

holding
inmovilización[F]
immobilisation[F]
Haltegriffe[M]
presa[F] a terra[F]

major outer reaping throw
osoto-gari (gran siega[F]) exterior
grand fauchage[M] extérieur
Große Außensichel[F]
grande falciata[F] esterna

major inner reaping throw
gran siega[F] interior
grand fauchage[M] intérieur
Große Innensichel[F]
grande falciata[F] interna

naked strangle
estrangulación[F]
étranglement[M]
Halsumklammerung[F]
presa[F] di strangolamento[M]

arm lock
inmovilización[F] de brazo[M]
clé[F] de bras[M]
Armhebel[M]
presa[F] a croce[F]

one-arm shoulder throw
proyección[F] por encima del hombro[M] con una mano[F]
projection[F] d'épaule[F] par un côté[M]
einarmiger Schulterwurf[M]
proiezione[F] di spalla[F] e braccio[M]

karate

karate [M] | karaté [M] | Karate [N] | karatè [M]

karateka
karateka [M]
karatéka [F]
Karateka [M]
karateka [M/F]

karate-gi
karategi [M]
karatégi [M]
Karategi [M]
karategi [M]
obi
obi [M]
obi [F]
Obi [M]
obi [M]

competition area
zona [F] **de competición** [F]
aire [F] **de compétition** [F]
Wettkampffläche [F]
area [F] **di gara** [F]

referee
árbitro [M]
arbitre [M]
Hauptkampfrichter [M]
arbitro [M]
arbitration committee
comité [M] de arbitraje [M]
comité [M] d'arbitrage [M]
Kampfgericht [N]
collegio [M] arbitrale
corner judge
juez [M] de ángulo [M]
juge [M] de coin [M]
Seitenkampfrichter [M]
giudice [M] d'angolo [M]
scorekeeper
anotador [M]
marqueur [M]
Listenführer [M]
segnapunti [M]
karateka
karateka [M]
karatéka [M]
Karateka [M]
karateka [M]
timekeeper
cronometrador [M]
chronométreur [M]
Zeitnehmer [M]
cronometrista [M/F]

aikido

aikido^{M} | aïkido^{M} | Aikido^{N} | aikido^{M}

jo
bastón^{M}
bâton^{M}
Jo^{M}
bastone^{M}

aikidoka
aikidoka^{M}
aïkidoka^{M}
Aikidoka^{M}
aikidoka$^{M/F}$

bokken
bokken^{M}
bokken^{M}
Bokken^{M}
bokken^{M}

aikidogi
aikidogi M
aïkidogi M
Aikidogi M
aikidogi M
obi
obi M
obi F
Obi M
obi M
hakama
hakama M
hakama M
Hakama M
hakama M

kung fu

kung fu^{M} | kung-fu^{M} | Kung-Fu^{N} | kung fu^{M}

kung fu practitioner
practicante^{M}
pratiquant^{M}
Betreibender^{M}
praticante$^{M/F}$

traditional jacket
traje M tradicional
veste F traditionnelle
traditionelle Jacke F
giacca F tradizionale
sash
sash M
sash M
Sash M
sash M

weightlifting

halterofilia[F] | haltérophilie[F] | Gewichtheben[N] | sollevamento[M] pesi[M]

barbell
barra[F] con pesas[F]
haltère[M] long
Scheibenhantel[F]
bilanciere[M]
sleeveless jersey
camiseta[F] sin mangas[F]
maillot[M] de corps[M]
ärmelloses Sporthemd[N]
canottiera[F]
wristband
muñequera[F]
poignet[M] de force[F]
Handgelenksbandage[F]
polsino[M]
weightlifting belt
cinturón[M]
ceinture[F] d'haltérophilie[F]
Gewichthebergürtel[M]
cintura[F] da sollevamento[M] pesi[M]
knee wrap
rodillera[F]
genouillère[F]
Kniebandage[F]
ginocchiera[F]
trunks
pantalón[M]
culotte[F]
Hose[F]
pantaloncini[M]
strap
correa[F]
lanière[F]
Riemen[M]
cinturino[M]
weightlifting shoe
zapatilla[F]
chaussure[F] d'haltérophilie[F]
Gewichtheberschuh[M]
scarpa[F]

clean and jerk
envión[M]
épaulé[M]-jeté[M]
Stoßen[N]
slancio[M]

snatch
arranque[M]
arraché[M]
Reißen[N]
strappo[M]

fitness equipment

aparatos M de ejercicios M | appareils M de conditionnement M physique | Fitnessgeräte N | attrezzi M ginnici

stationary bicycle
bicicleta F estática
vélo M d'exercice M
Heimtrainer M
cyclette F

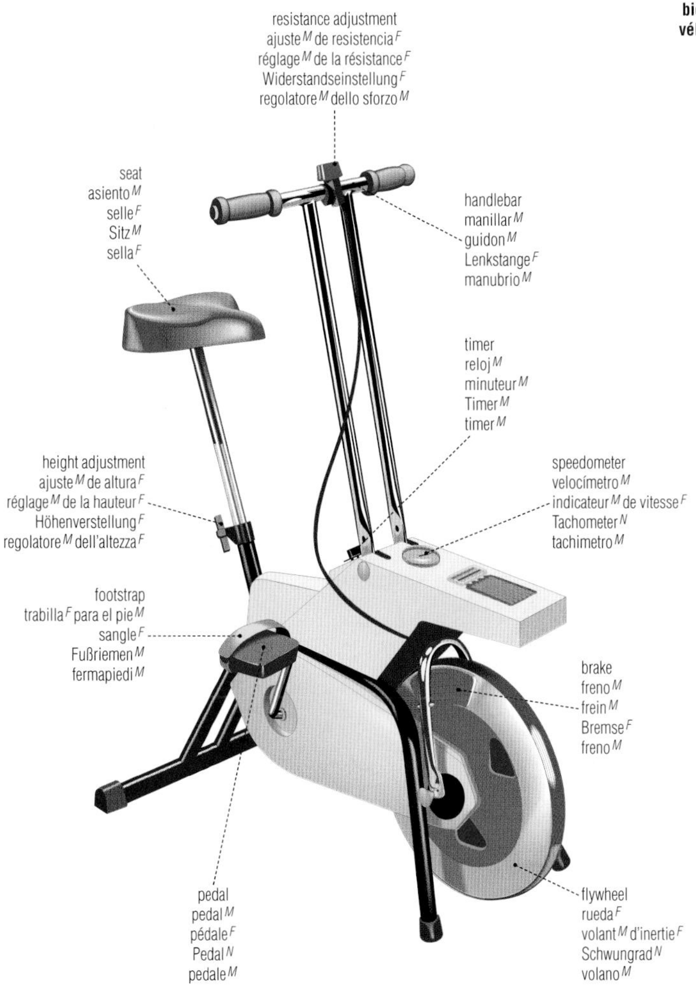
resistance adjustment
ajuste M de resistencia F
réglage M de la résistance F
Widerstandseinstellung F
regolatore M dello sforzo M
seat
asiento M
selle F
Sitz M
sella F
handlebar
manillar M
guidon M
Lenkstange F
manubrio M
timer
reloj M
minuteur M
Timer M
timer M
height adjustment
ajuste M de altura F
réglage M de la hauteur F
Höhenverstellung F
regolatore M dell'altezza F
speedometer
velocímetro M
indicateur M de vitesse F
Tachometer N
tachimetro M
footstrap
trabilla F para el pie M
sangle F
Fußriemen M
fermapiedi M
brake
freno M
frein M
Bremse F
freno M
pedal
pedal M
pédale F
Pedal N
pedale M
flywheel
rueda F
volant M d'inertie F
Schwungrad N
volano M

weight machine
unidad^F de pesas^F
banc^M de musculation^F
Multitrainer^M
attrezzo^M multiuso

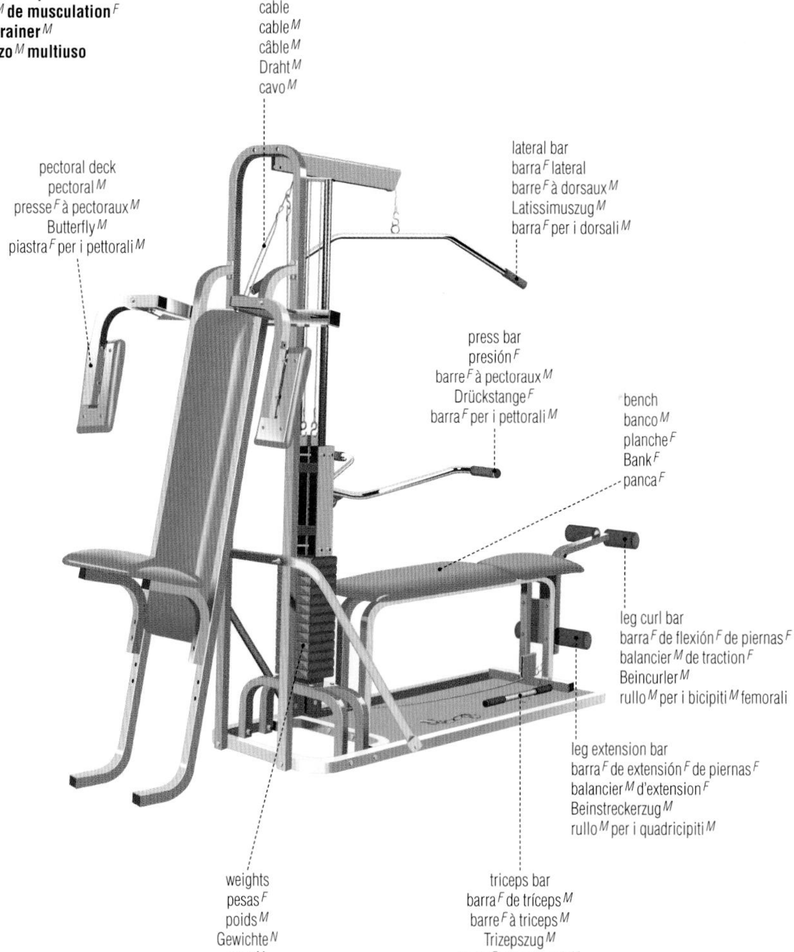
cable
cable M
câble M
Draht M
cavo M
pectoral deck
pectoral M
presse F à pectoraux M
Butterfly M
piastra F per i pettorali M
lateral bar
barra F lateral
barre F à dorsaux M
Latissimuszug M
barra F per i dorsali M
press bar
presión F
barre F à pectoraux M
Drückstange F
barra F per i pettorali M
bench
banco M
planche F
Bank F
panca F
leg curl bar
barra F de flexión F de piernas F
balancier M de traction F
Beincurler M
rullo M per i bicipiti M femorali
leg extension bar
barra F de extensión F de piernas F
balancier M d'extension F
Beinstreckerzug M
rullo M per i quadricipiti M
weights
pesas F
poids M
Gewichte N
pesi M
triceps bar
barra F de tríceps M
barre F à triceps M
Trizepszug M
barra F per i tricipiti M

ankle/wrist weight
pesas[F] para muñecas[F] y tobillos[M]
bracelet[M] lesté
Fuß-/Handgelenksgewicht[N]
cavigliera[F]/polsiera[F]

dumbbell
pesas[F]
haltère[M] court
Hantel[F]
manubrio[M]

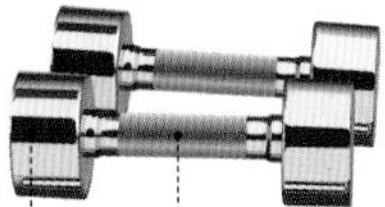
weight
pesas[F]
poids[M]
Gewicht[N]
peso[M]
bar
barra[F]
barre[F]
Griff[M]
impugnatura[F]

stair climber
escalera[F]
simulateur[M] d'escalier[M]
Climber[M]
stepper[M]

jump rope
cuerda[F]
corde[F] à sauter
Springseil[N]
corda[F]

rowing machine
remo[M]
rameur[M]
Rudergerät[N]
vogatore[M]

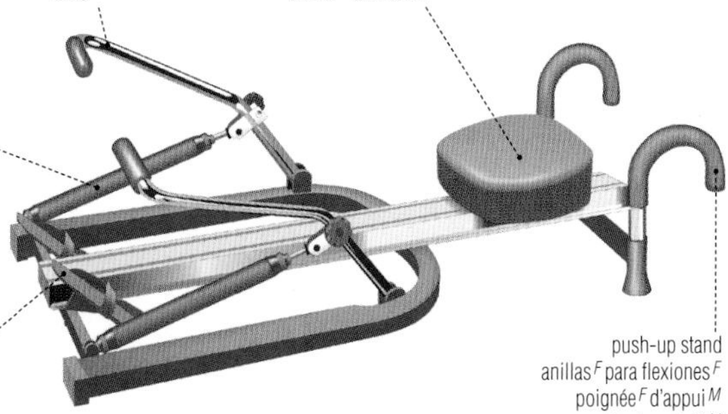
oar
remo[M]
rame[F]
Ruder[N]
remo[M]
sliding seat
asiento[M] de corredera[F]
siège[M] coulissant
freilaufender Sitz[M]
sedile[M] scorrevole
hydraulic resistance
resorte[M] hidráulico
résistance[F] hydraulique
hydraulischer Widerstand[M]
resistenza[F] idraulica
foot support
soporte[M] del pie[M]
cale-pied[M]
Fußstütze[F]
appoggiapiedi[M]
push-up stand
anillas[F] para flexiones[F]
poignée[F] d'appui[M]
Pushup-Griff[M]
ganci[M] di fissaggio[M]

billiards

billar[M] | billard[M] | Billard[N] | biliardo[M]

table
mesa[F]
table[F]
Billardtisch[M]
tavolo[M]

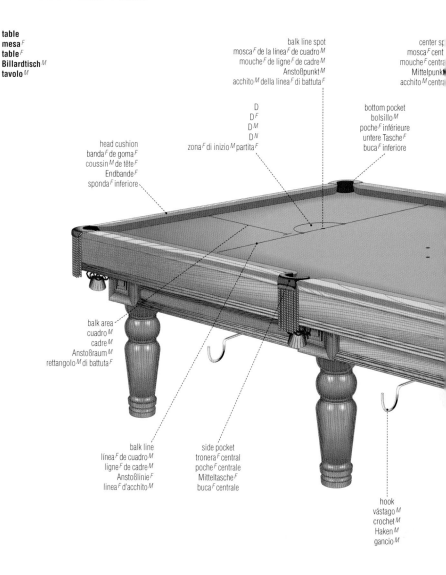

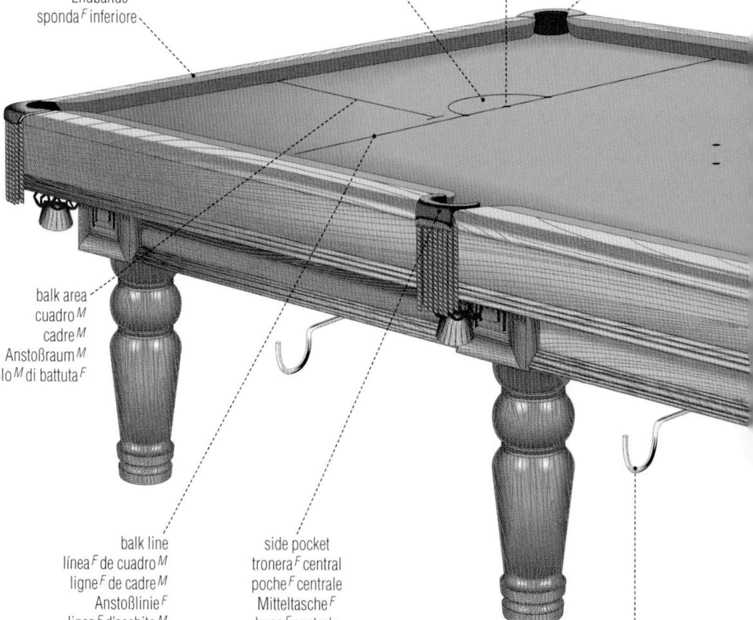
balk line spot
mosca[F] de la línea[F] de cuadro[M]
mouche[F] de ligne[F] de cadre[M]
Anstoßpunkt[M]
acchito[M] della linea[F] di battuta[F]
center sp
mosca[F] cent
mouche[F] centra
Mittelpunk
acchito[M] centra
D
D[F]
D[M]
D[N]
zona[F] di inizio[M] partita[F]
bottom pocket
bolsillo[M]
poche[F] inférieure
untere Tasche[F]
buca[F] inferiore
head cushion
banda[F] de goma[F]
coussin[M] de tête[F]
Endbande[F]
sponda[F] inferiore
balk area
cuadro[M]
cadre[M]
Anstoßraum[M]
rettangolo[M] di battuta[F]
balk line
línea[F] de cuadro[M]
ligne[F] de cadre[M]
Anstoßlinie[F]
linea[F] d'acchito[M]
side pocket
tronera[F] central
poche[F] centrale
Mitteltasche[F]
buca[F] centrale
hook
vástago[M]
crochet[M]
Haken[M]
gancio[M]

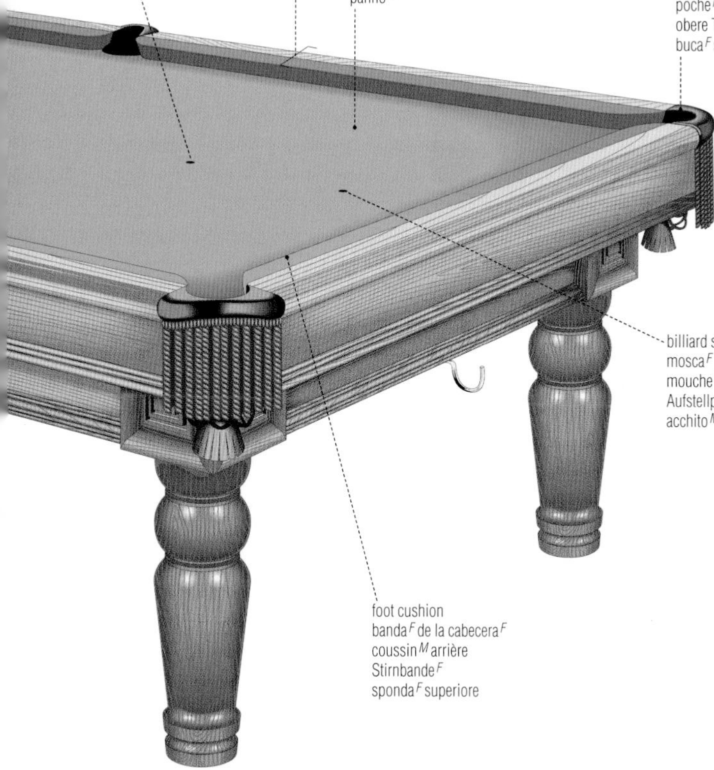
rail
baranda F
bande F
Rahmen M
sopraspondaF
pyramid spot
mosca F superior
mouche F supérieure
Aufstellpunkt M
acchito M superiore
baize
tapete M
tapis M
Bespannung F
panno M
top pocket
tronera F
poche F supérieure
obere Tasche F
buca F superiore
billiard spot
mosca F
mouche F
Aufstellpunkt M
acchito M
foot cushion
banda F de la cabecera F
coussin M arrière
Stirnbande F
sponda F superiore

billiards

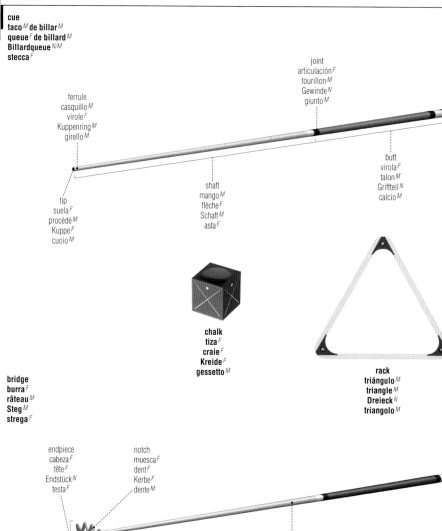

cue
taco M de billar M
queue F de billard M
Billardqueue N/M
stecca F

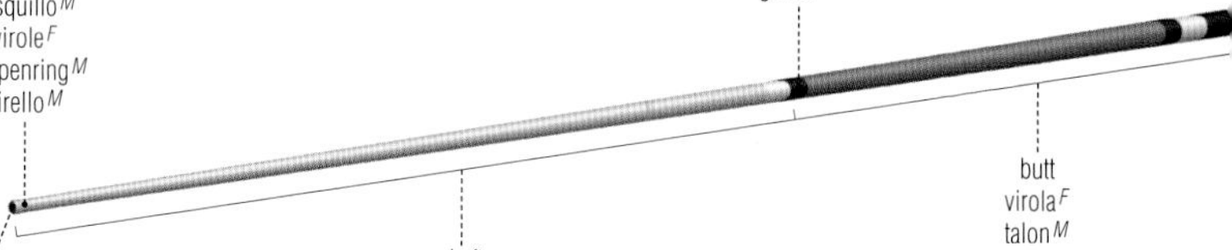
joint
articulación F
tourillon M
Gewinde N
giunto M
ferrule
casquillo M
virole F
Kuppenring M
girello M
butt
virola F
talon M
Griffteil N
calcio M
shaft
mango M
flèche F
Schaft M
asta F
tip
suela F
procédé M
Kuppe F
cuoio M

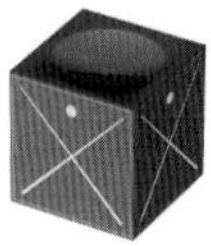

chalk
tiza F
craie F
Kreide F
gessetto M

rack
triángulo M
triangle M
Dreieck N
triangolo M

bridge
burra F
râteau M
Steg M
strega F

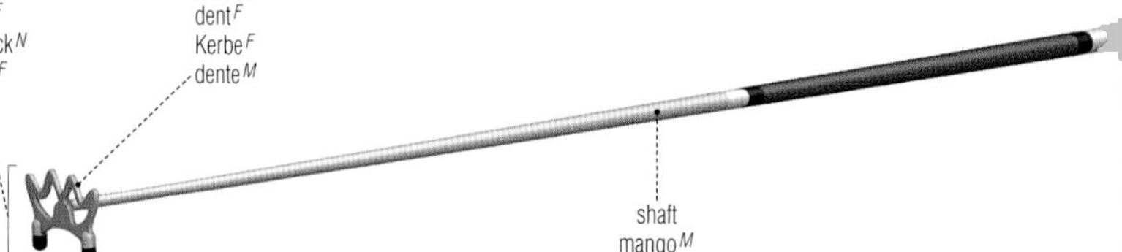
endpiece
cabeza F
tête F
Endstück N
testa F
notch
muesca F
dent F
Kerbe F
dente M
shaft
mango M
manche M
Stiel M
asta F

archery

tiro[M] con arco[M] | tir[M] à l'arc[M] | Bogenschießen[N] | tiro[M] con l'arco[M]

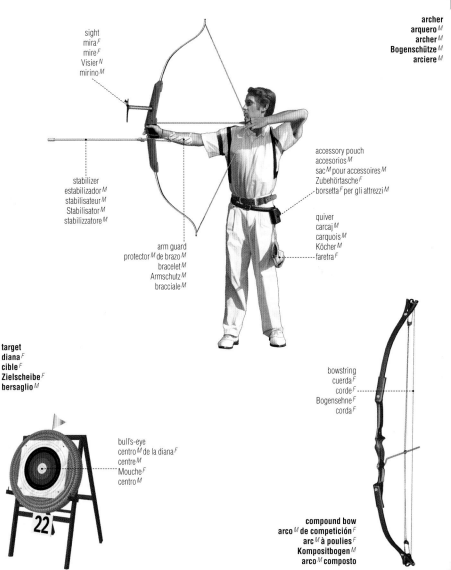

archer
arquero[M]
archer[M]
Bogenschütze[M]
arciere[M]

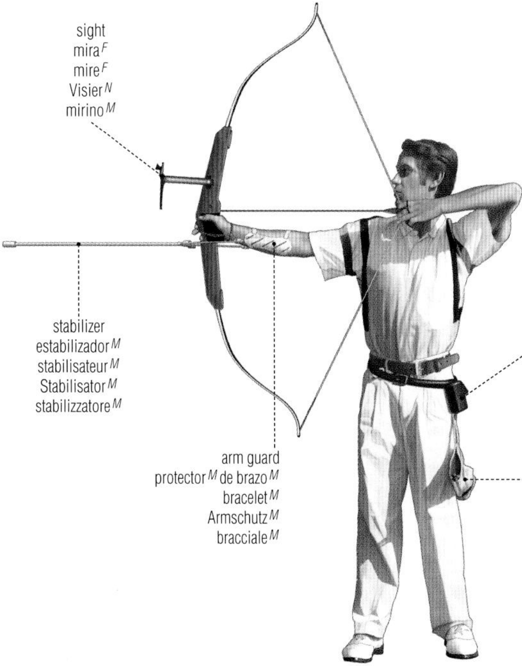

sight
mira[F]
mire[F]
Visier[N]
mirino[M]

stabilizer
estabilizador[M]
stabilisateur[M]
Stabilisator[M]
stabilizzatore[M]

arm guard
protector[M] de brazo[M]
bracelet[M]
Armschutz[M]
bracciale[M]

accessory pouch
accesorios[M]
sac[M] pour accessoires[M]
Zubehörtasche[F]
borsetta[F] per gli attrezzi[M]

quiver
carcaj[M]
carquois[M]
Köcher[M]
faretra[F]

target
diana[F]
cible[F]
Zielscheibe[F]
bersaglio[M]

22

bull's-eye
centro[M] de la diana[F]
centre[M]
Mouche[F]
centro[M]

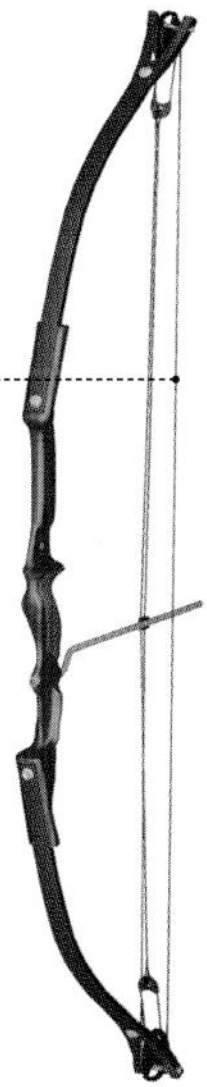

bowstring
cuerda[F]
corde[F]
Bogensehne[F]
corda[F]

compound bow
arco[M] de competición[F]
arc[M] à poulies[F]
Kompositbogen[M]
arco[M] composto

golf

accesorios[M] de golf[M] | golf[M] | Golfspiel[N] | golf[M]

par 5 hole
hoyo[M] de par 5
trou[M] de normale[F] 5
Par[N]-5-Loch[N]
buca[F] par 5

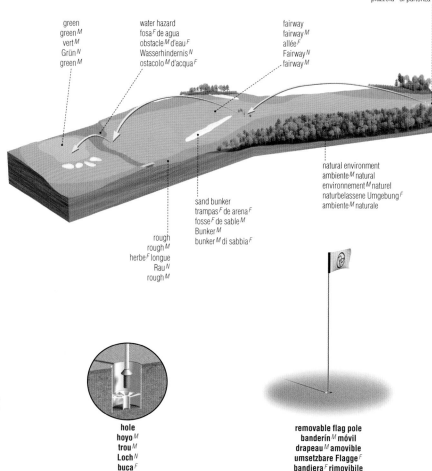

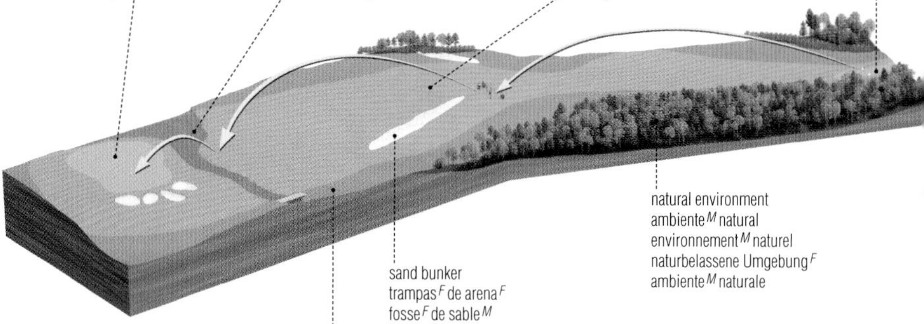
teeing ground
colina[F] de salida[F]
tertre[M] de départ[M]
Abschlagsbereich[M]
piazzola[F] di partenza[F]
green
green[M]
vert[M]
Grün[N]
green[M]
water hazard
fosa[F] de agua
obstacle[M] d'eau[F]
Wasserhindernis[N]
ostacolo[M] d'acqua[F]
fairway
fairway[M]
allée[F]
Fairway[N]
fairway[M]
natural environment
ambiente[M] natural
environnement[M] naturel
naturbelassene Umgebung[F]
ambiente[M] naturale
sand bunker
trampas[F] de arena[F]
fosse[F] de sable[M]
Bunker[M]
bunker[M] di sabbia[F]
rough
rough[M]
herbe[F] longue
Rau[N]
rough[M]

hole
hoyo[M]
trou[M]
Loch[N]
buca[F]

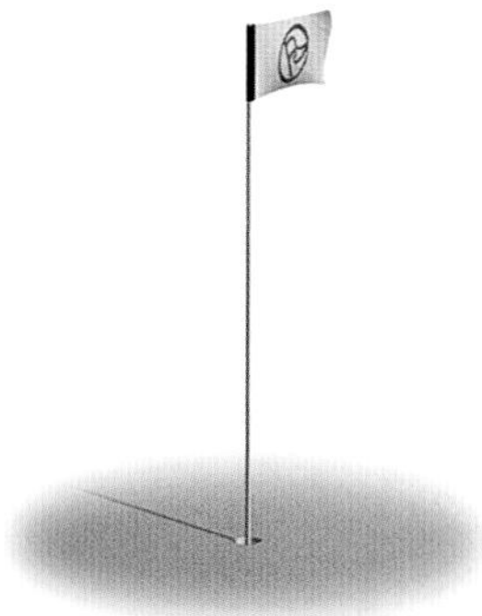

removable flag pole
banderín[M] móvil
drapeau[M] amovible
umsetzbare Flagge[F]
bandiera[F] rimovibile

golf ball
pelota^F de golf^M
balle^F de golf^M
Golfball^M
palla^F

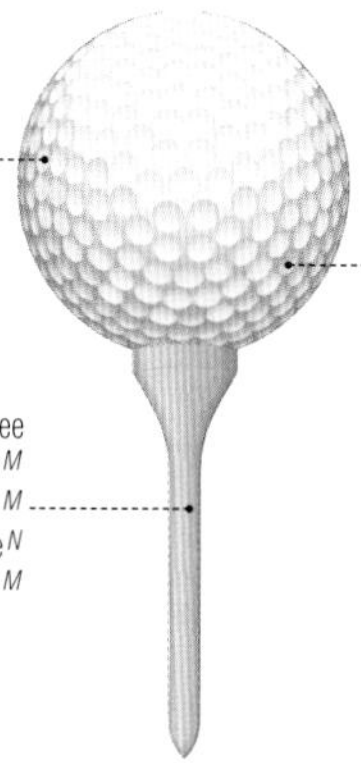
cover
revestimiento^M
enveloppe^F
Hülle^F
copertura^F
dimple
hoyuelo^M
alvéole^F
Delle^F
fossetta^F
tee
tee^M
té^M
Tee^N
tee^M

types of golf clubs
bastones^M
types^M de bâtons^M de golf^M
Arten^F von Golfschläger^M
tipi^M di mazze^F

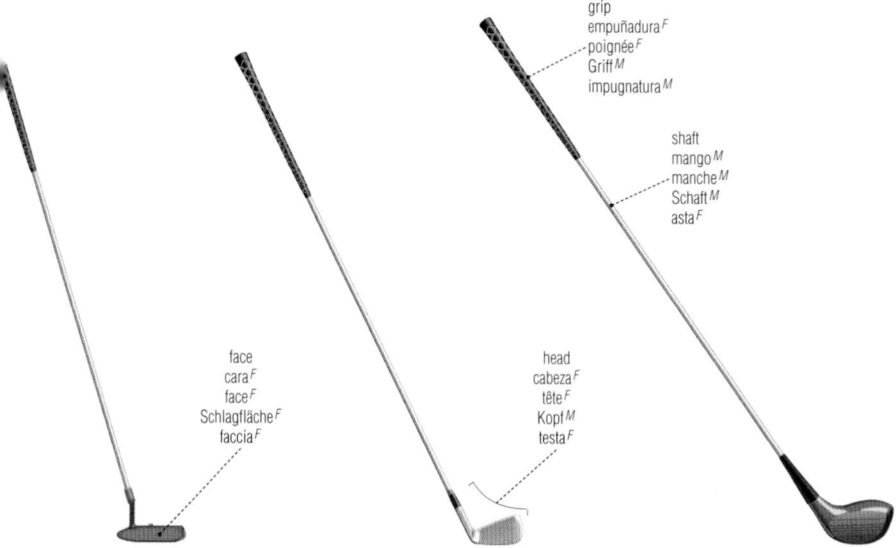
grip
empuñadura^F
poignée^F
Griff^M
impugnatura^M
shaft
mango^M
manche^M
Schaft^M
asta^F
face
cara^F
face^F
Schlagfläche^F
faccia^F
head
cabeza^F
tête^F
Kopf^M
testa^F

putter
putter^M
fer^M droit
Putter^M
putter^M

iron
hierro^M
fer^M
Eisenschläger^M
ferro^M

wood
madera^F
bois^M
Holzschläger^M
legno^M

shoulder strap
correa [F]
sangle [F]
Schultergurt [M]
tracolla [F]
pocket
bolsillo [M]
poche [F]
Seitentasche [F]
tasca [F]

golf bag
bolsa [F] de golf [M]
sac [M] de golf [M]
Golftasche [F]
sacca [F]

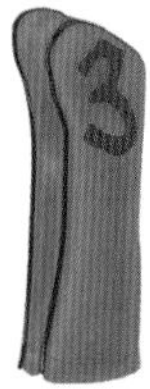

head cover
capuchón [M] de bastones [M]
capuchon [M]
Schlägerabdeckung [F]
coprilegno [M]

golf shoes
zapatos [M] de golf [M]
chaussures [F] de golf [M]
Golfschuhe [M]
scarpe [F]

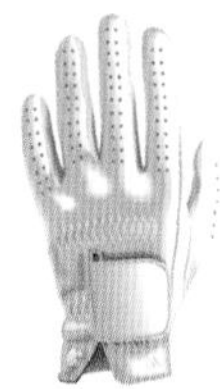

golf glove
guante [M] de golf [M]
gant [M] de golf [M]
Golfhandschuh [M]
guanto [M]

golf cart
carrito [M] de golf [M]
chariot [M]
Golfwagen [M]
carrello [M]

bag well
portabolsa [F]
porte-sac [M]
Taschenträger [M]
portasacca [M]

electric golf cart
carro [M] de golf [M] eléctrico
voiturette [F] de golf [M] électrique
elektrischer Golfwagen [M]
vettura [F] da golf [M]

BMX

ciclocross^{M} | bicross^{M} | BMX^{N} | mountain bike^{F} da cross^{M}

helmet
casco^{M}
casque^{M}
Helm^{M}
casco^{M}

handlebars
manillar^{F}
guidon^{M}
Lenkerbügel^{M}
manubrio^{M}

glove
guante^{M}
gant^{M}
Handschuh^{M}
guanto^{M}

single chain wheel
rueda^{F} posterior lenticular
plateau^{M} simple
Einfach-Kettenrad^{N}
ruota^{F} ad una sola moltiplica^{F}

foot pegs
reposapiés^{M}
repose-pieds^{M}
Fußstützen^{F}
pedane^{F}

single sprocket
piñón^{M} simple
pignon^{M} simple
Einfach-Ritzel^{M}
pignone^{M} semplice

half-pipe
halfpipe^{M}
rampe^{F}
Halfpipe^{F}
rampa^{F}

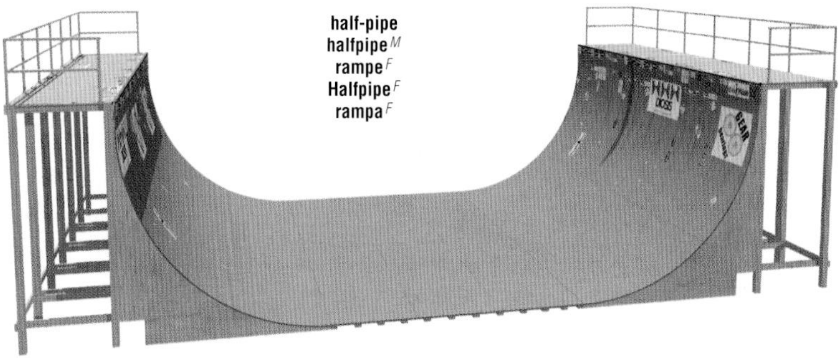

road racing

ciclismo [M] en carretera [F] | cyclisme [M] sur route [F] | Straßenradsport [M] | ciclismo [M] su strada [F]

road cycling competition
competición [F] de ciclismo [M] en carretera [F]
compétition [F] de cyclisme [M] sur route [F]
Straßenradrennen [N]
gara [F] di ciclismo [M] su strada [F]

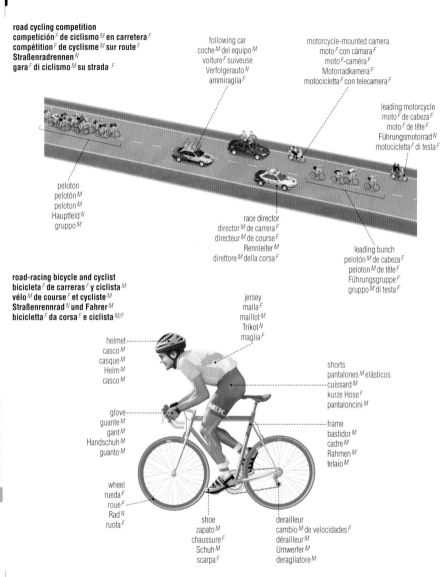

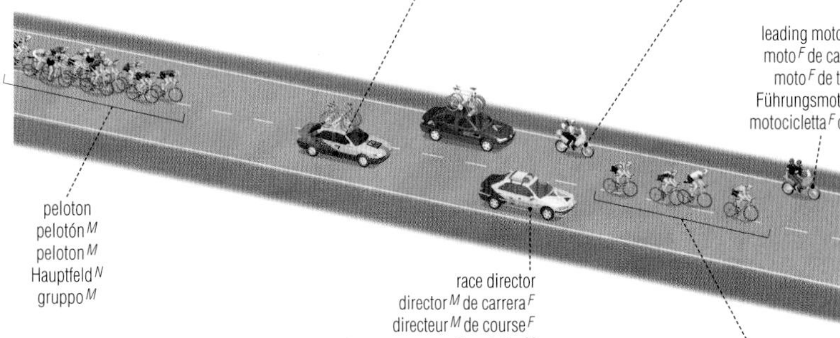
following car
coche [M] del equipo [M]
voiture [F] suiveuse
Verfolgerauto [N]
ammiraglia [F]
motorcycle-mounted camera
moto [F] con cámara [F]
moto [F]-caméra [F]
Motorradkamera [F]
motocicletta [F] con telecamera [F]
leading motorcycle
moto [F] de cabeza [F]
moto [F] de tête [F]
Führungsmotorrad [N]
motocicletta [F] di testa [F]
peloton
pelotón [M]
peloton [M]
Hauptfeld [N]
gruppo [M]
race director
director [M] de carrera [F]
directeur [M] de course [F]
Rennleiter [M]
direttore [M] della corsa [F]
leading bunch
pelotón [M] de cabeza [F]
peloton [M] de tête [F]
Führungsgruppe [F]
gruppo [M] di testa [F]

road-racing bicycle and cyclist
bicicleta [F] de carreras [F] y ciclista [M]
vélo [M] de course [F] et cycliste [M]
Straßenrennrad [N] und Fahrer [M]
bicicletta [F] da corsa [F] e ciclista [M/F]

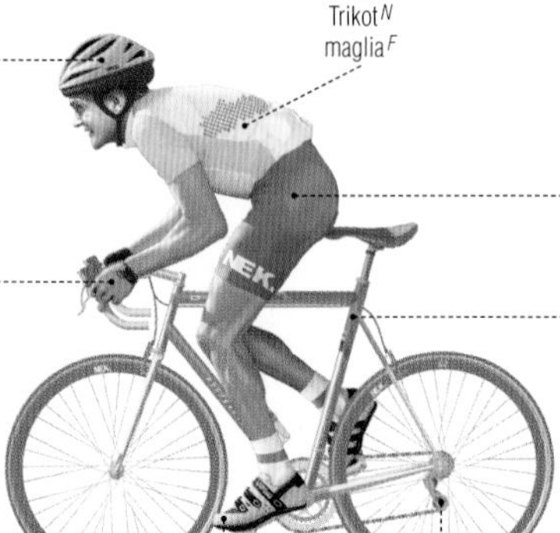
jersey
malla [F]
maillot [M]
Trikot [N]
maglia [F]
helmet
casco [M]
casque [M]
Helm [M]
casco [M]
shorts
pantalones [M] elásticos
cuissard [M]
kurze Hose [F]
pantaloncini [M]
glove
guante [M]
gant [M]
Handschuh [M]
guanto [M]
frame
bastidor [M]
cadre [M]
Rahmen [M]
telaio [M]
wheel
rueda [F]
roue [F]
Rad [N]
ruota [F]
shoe
zapato [M]
chaussure [F]
Schuh [M]
scarpa [F]
derailleur
cambio [M] de velocidades [F]
dérailleur [M]
Umwerfer [M]
deragliatore [M]

track cycling

ciclismo[M] en pista | cyclisme[M] sur piste[F] | Bahnradsport[M] | ciclismo[M] su pista[F]

pursuit bicycle and racer
bicicleta[F] de persecución[F] y corredor[M]
vélo[M] de poursuite[F] et coureur[M]
Verfolgungsrad[N] und Fahrer[M]
bicicletta[F] da inseguimento[M] e corridore[M]

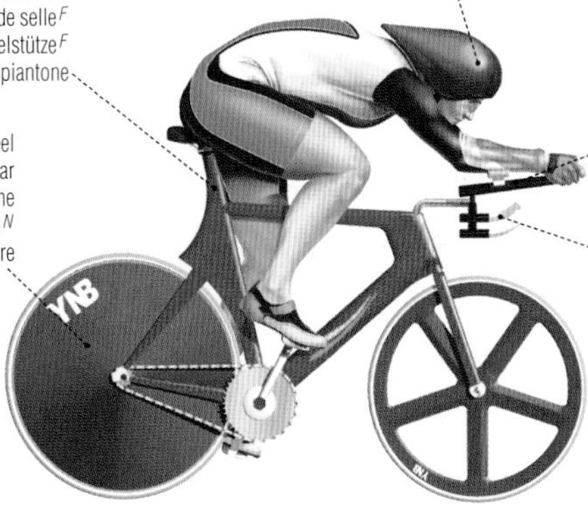
helmet
casco[M]
casque[M]
Helm[M]
casco[M] aerodinamico
seat tube
tubo[M] de sillín[M]
tube[M] de selle[F]
Sattelstütze[F]
tubo[M] piantone
solid rear wheel
rueda[F] lenticular
roue[F] arrière pleine
Scheibenhinterrad[N]
ruota[F] lenticolare
handlebar
manillar[M]
guidon[M]
Lenker[M]
manubrio[M]
handlebar grip
empuñadura[F] del manillar[M]
poignée[F] du guidon[M]
Lenkergriff[M]
manopola[F] del manubrio[M]
YNB

track
velódromo[M]
piste[F]
Radrennbahn[F]
pista[F] ciclistica

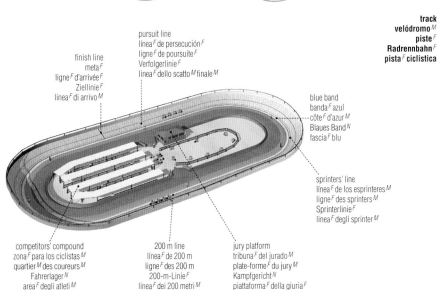

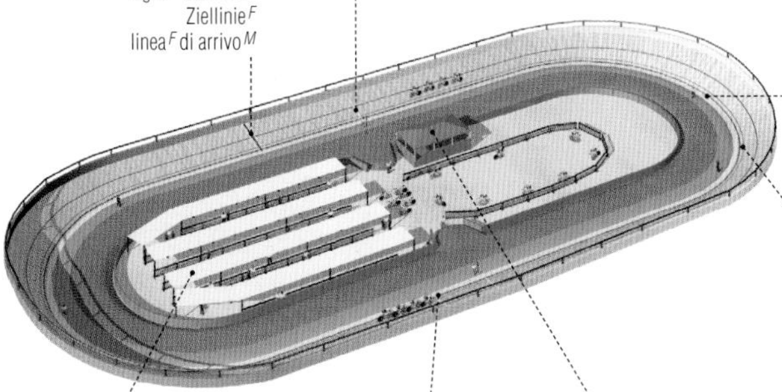
pursuit line
línea[F] de persecución[F]
ligne[F] de poursuite[F]
Verfolgerlinie[F]
linea[F] dello scatto[M] finale[M]
finish line
meta[F]
ligne[F] d'arrivée[F]
Ziellinie[F]
linea[F] di arrivo[M]
blue band
banda[F] azul
côte[F] d'azur[M]
Blaues Band[N]
fascia[F] blu
sprinters' line
línea[F] de los esprinteres[M]
ligne[F] des sprinters[M]
Sprinterlinie[F]
linea[F] degli sprinter[M]
competitors' compound
zona[F] para los ciclistas[M]
quartier[M] des coureurs[M]
Fahrerlager[N]
area[F] degli atleti[M]
200 m line
línea[F] de 200 m
ligne[F] des 200 m
200-m-Linie[F]
linea[F] dei 200 metri[M]
jury platform
tribuna[F] del jurado[M]
plate-forme[F] du jury[M]
Kampfgericht[N]
piattaforma[F] della giuria[F]

mountain biking

ciclismo^{M} de montaña^{F} | vélo^{M} de montagne^{F} | Mountainbike^{N} | mountain bike^{F}

cross-country bicycle and cyclist
bicicleta^{F} de cross^{M} y ciclista^{M}
vélo^{M} de cross-country^{M} et cycliste^{M}
Querfeldeinrad^{N} und Fahrer^{M}
bicicletta^{F} da cross-country^{M} e ciclista$^{M/F}$

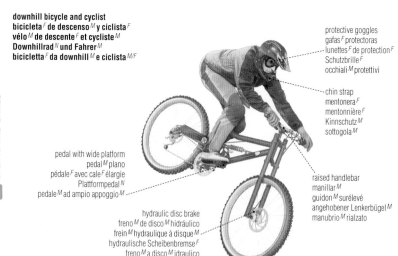

goggles
gafas^{F}
lunettes^{F}
Brille^{F}
occhiali^{M}
back suspension
suspensión^{F} trasera
suspension^{F} arrière
Stoßdämpfer^{M} hinten
sospensione^{F} posteriore
front fork
horquilla^{F} frontal
fourche^{F} avant
Radgabel^{F}
forcella^{F} anteriore
clipless pedal
pedal^{M} automático
pédale^{F} automatique
Klickpedal^{N}
pedale^{M} senza fermapiedi^{M}

downhill bicycle and cyclist
bicicleta^{F} de descenso^{M} y ciclista^{F}
vélo^{M} de descente^{F} et cycliste^{M}
Downhillrad^{N} und Fahrer^{M}
bicicletta^{F} da downhill^{M} e ciclista$^{M/F}$

protective goggles
gafas^{F} protectoras
lunettes^{F} de protection^{F}
Schutzbrille^{F}
occhiali^{M} protettivi
chin strap
mentonera^{F}
mentonnière^{F}
Kinnschutz^{M}
sottogola^{M}
pedal with wide platform
pedal^{M} plano
pédale^{F} avec cale^{F} élargie
Plattformpedal^{N}
pedale^{M} ad ampio appoggio^{M}
raised handlebar
manillar^{M}
guidon^{M} surélevé
angehobener Lenkerbügel^{M}
manubrio^{M} rialzato
hydraulic disc brake
freno^{M} de disco^{M} hidráulico
frein^{M} hydraulique à disque^{M}
hydraulische Scheibenbremse^{F}
freno^{M} a disco^{M} idraulico

car racing

carreras *F* de coches *M* | course *F* automobile | Autorennen *N* | automobilismo *M*

formula 1 car
coche *M* de fórmula *F* 1
voiture *F* de formule *F* 1
Formel-1-Auto *N*
auto *F* da formula *F* 1

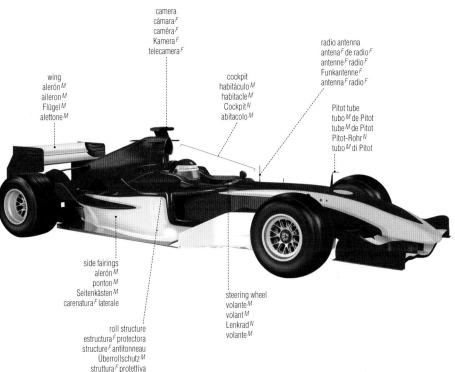

camera
cámara F
caméra F
Kamera F
telecamera F
radio antenna
antena F de radio F
antenne F radio F
Funkantenne F
antenna F radio F
wing
alerón M
aileron M
Flügel M
alettone M
cockpit
habitáculo M
habitacle M
Cockpit N
abitacolo M
Pitot tube
tubo M de Pitot
tube M de Pitot
Pitot-Rohr N
tubo M di Pitot
side fairings
alerón M
ponton M
Seitenkästen M
carenatura F laterale
steering wheel
volante M
volant M
Lenkrad N
volante M
roll structure
estructura F protectora
structure F antitonneau
Überrollschutz M
struttura F protettiva

wet-weather tire
neumático *M* de lluvia *F*
pneu *M* pluie *F*
Regenreifen *M*
gomma *F* da bagnato *M*

dry-weather tire
neumático *M* de seco *M*
pneu *M* pour temps *M* sec
Trockenreifen *M*
gomma *F* da asciutto *M*

motorcycling

motocicleta[F] | motocyclisme[M] | Motorradsport[M] | motociclismo[M]

supercross circuit
circuito[M] de supercross[M]
circuit[M] de supercross[M]
Supercross[N]-Strecke[F]
circuito[M] di supercross[M]

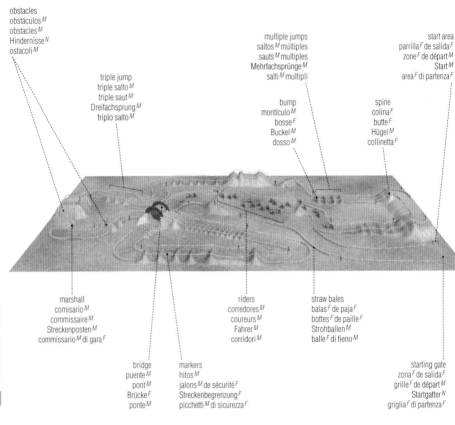

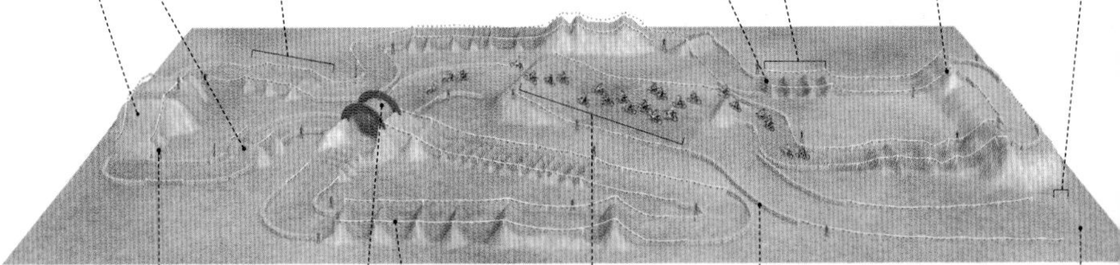
obstacles
obstáculos[M]
obstacles[M]
Hindernisse[N]
ostacoli[M]
triple jump
triple salto[M]
triple saut[M]
Dreifachsprung[M]
triplo salto[M]
multiple jumps
saltos[M] múltiples
sauts[M] multiples
Mehrfachsprünge[M]
salti[M] multipli
bump
montículo[M]
bosse[F]
Buckel[M]
dosso[M]
spine
colina[F]
butte[F]
Hügel[M]
collinetta[F]
start area
parrilla[F] de salida[F]
zone[F] de départ[M]
Start[M]
area[F] di partenza[F]
marshall
comisario[M]
commissaire[M]
Streckenposten[M]
commissario[M] di gara[F]
riders
corredores[M]
coureurs[M]
Fahrer[M]
corridori[M]
straw bales
balas[F] de paja[F]
bottes[F] de paille[F]
Strohballen[M]
balle[F] di fieno[M]
bridge
puente[M]
pont[M]
Brücke[F]
ponte[M]
markers
hitos[M]
jalons[M] de sécurité[F]
Streckenbegrenzung[F]
picchetti[M] di sicurezza[F]
starting gate
zona[F] de salida[F]
grille[F] de départ[M]
Startgatter[N]
griglia[F] di partenza[F]

motocross and supercross motorcycle
moto F de motocross M y supercross M
moto F de motocross M et supercross M
Motocross N- und Supercross N-Motorrad N
motocicletta F da motocross M e supercross M

glove
guante M
gant M
Handschuh M
guanto M
helmet
casco M
casque M
Helm M
casco M per cross M
protective suit
traje M de protección F
combinaison F de protection F
Schutzanzug M
tuta F protettiva
protective goggles
guantes M protectores
lunettes F de protection F
Schutzbrille F
occhiali M protettivi
pants
pantalones M
pantalon M
Hose F
pantaloni M
hand protector
protector M de mano F
protège-main M
Handschutz M
paramano M
number plate
placa F de número M
plaque F-numéro M
Startnummer F
numero M di gara F
fork
horquilla F
fourche F
Gabel F
forcella F
nubby tire
neumático M de tacos M
pneu M à crampons M
Stollenreifen M
pneumatico M scolpito
boot
bota F
botte F
Stiefel M
stivale M
protective plate
placa F protectora
plaque F de protection F
Schutzplatte F
piastra F di protezione F

ice hockey

hockey[M] sobre hielo[M] | hockey[M] sur glace[F] | Eishockey[N] | hockey[M] su ghiaccio[M]

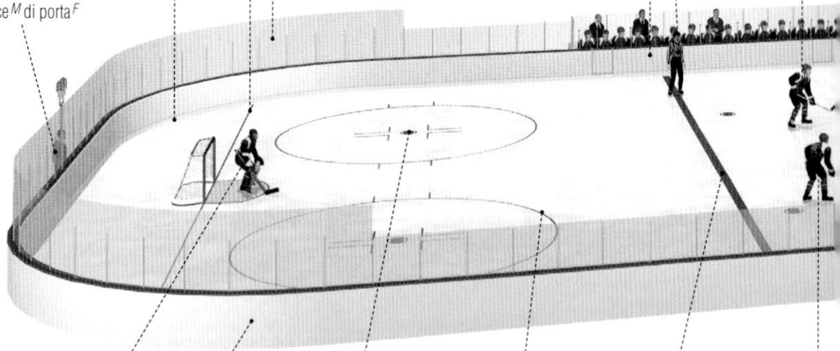
rink
pista[F]
patinoire[F]
Eisfläche[F]
campo[M]
goal line
línea[F] de gol[M]
ligne[F] de but[M]
Torlinie[F]
linea[F] di porta[F]
left defense
defensa[M] izquierdo
défenseur[M] gauche
linker Verteidiger[M]
difensore[M] sinistro
glass protector
cristal[M] de protección[M]
vitre[F] de protection[F]
Schutzwand[F]
vetro[M] di protezione[F]
linesman
juez[M] de línea[F]
juge[M] de ligne[F]
Linienrichter[M]
giudice[M] di linea[F]
rink corner
esquina[F]
coin[M] de patinoire[F]
Ecke[F]
angolo[M] della pista[F]
players' bench
banquillo[M] de los jugadores[M]
banc[M] des joueurs[M]
Spielerbank[F]
panchina[F] dei giocatori[M]
goal judge
juez[M] de gol[M]
juge[M] de but[M]
Torrichter[M]
giudice[M] di porta[F]
goalkeeper
portero[M]
gardien[M] de but[M]
Torwart[M]
portiere[M]
face-off spot
punto[M] de saque[M]
point[M] de mise[F] au jeu[M]
Anspielpunkt[M]
punto[M] di ingaggio[M]
blue line
línea[F] azul
ligne[F] bleue
blaue Linie[F]
linea[F] blu di zona[F]
boards
valla[F] de madera[F]
bande[F]
Bande[F]
balaustre[F]
face-off circle
círculo[M] de reanudación[F] del juego[M]
cercle[M] de mise[F] au jeu[M]
Anspielkreis[M]
cerchio[M] di ingaggio[M]
right defense
defensa[M] derecho
défenseur[M] droit
rechter Verteidiger[M]
difensore[M] destro

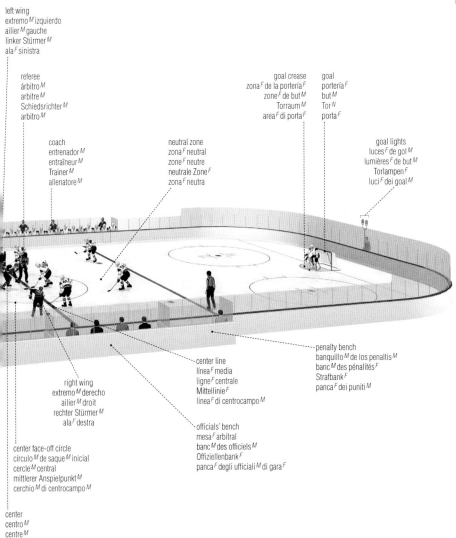

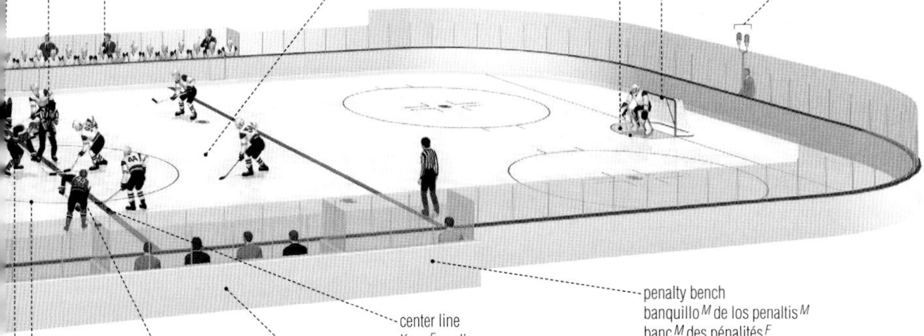
left wing
extremo^{M} izquierdo
ailier^{M} gauche
linker Stürmer^{M}
ala^{F} sinistra
referee
árbitro^{M}
arbitre^{M}
Schiedsrichter^{M}
arbitro^{M}
coach
entrenador^{M}
entraîneur^{M}
Trainer^{M}
allenatore^{M}
neutral zone
zona^{F} neutral
zone^{F} neutre
neutrale Zone^{F}
zona^{F} neutra
goal crease
zona^{F} de la portería^{F}
zone^{F} de but^{M}
Torraum^{M}
area^{F} di porta^{F}
goal
portería^{F}
but^{M}
Tor^{N}
porta^{F}
goal lights
luces^{F} de gol^{M}
lumières^{F} de but^{M}
Torlampen^{F}
luci^{F} dei goal^{M}
penalty bench
banquillo^{M} de los penaltis^{M}
banc^{M} des pénalités^{F}
Strafbank^{F}
panca^{F} dei puniti^{M}
center line
línea^{F} media
ligne^{F} centrale
Mittellinie^{F}
linea^{F} di centrocampo^{M}
right wing
extremo^{M} derecho
ailier^{M} droit
rechter Stürmer^{M}
ala^{F} destra
officials' bench
mesa^{F} arbitral
banc^{M} des officiels^{M}
Offiziellenbank^{F}
panca^{F} degli ufficiali^{M} di gara^{F}
center face-off circle
círculo^{M} de saque^{M} inicial
cercle^{M} central
mittlerer Anspielpunkt^{M}
cerchio^{M} di centrocampo^{M}
center
centro^{M}
centre^{M}
Sturmspitze^{F}
centroattacco^{M}

curling

curling^M | curling^M | Curling^N | curling^M

sheet
área^F de juego^M
piste^F
Bahn^F
campo^M

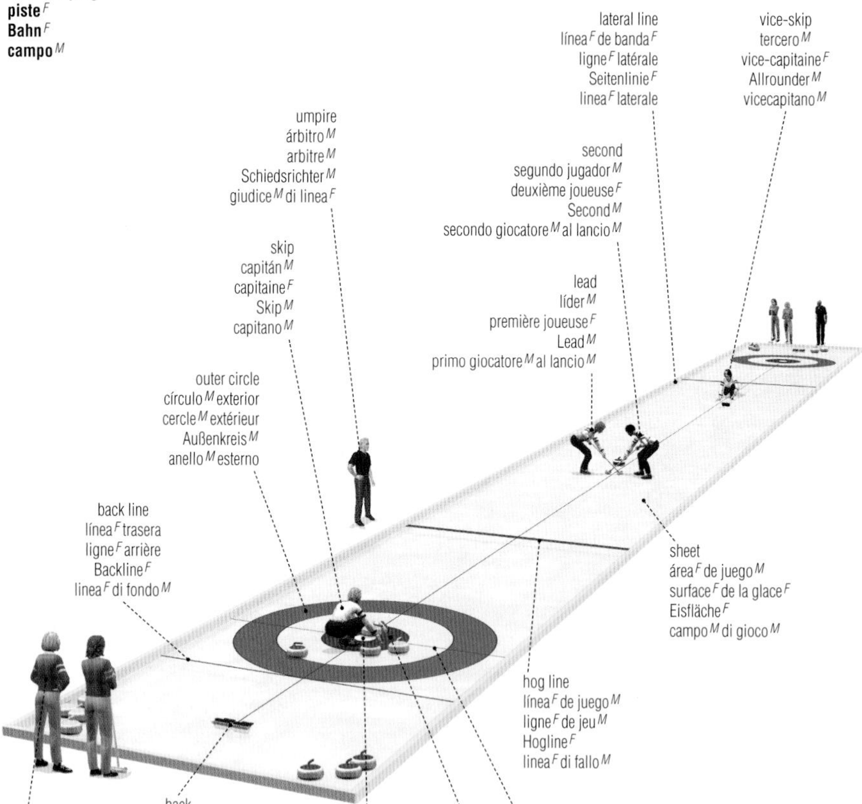
lateral line
línea^F de banda^F
ligne^F latérale
Seitenlinie^F
linea^F laterale
vice-skip
tercero^M
vice-capitaine^F
Allrounder^M
vicecapitano^M
umpire
árbitro^M
arbitre^M
Schiedsrichter^M
giudice^M di linea^F
second
segundo jugador^M
deuxième joueuse^F
Second^M
secondo giocatore^M al lancio^M
skip
capitán^M
capitaine^F
Skip^M
capitano^M
lead
líder^M
première joueuse^F
Lead^M
primo giocatore^M al lancio^M
outer circle
círculo^M exterior
cercle^M extérieur
Außenkreis^M
anello^M esterno
back line
línea^F trasera
ligne^F arrière
Backline^F
linea^F di fondo^M
sheet
área^F de juego^M
surface^F de la glace^F
Eisfläche^F
campo^M di gioco^M
hog line
línea^F de juego^M
ligne^F de jeu^M
Hogline^F
linea^F di fallo^M
hack
percha^F
appui^M-pied^M
Hack^M
staffa^F di lancio^M
tee line
línea^F de tee^M
ligne^F de balayage^M
Teeline^F
linea^F del bersaglio^M
curler
primer jugador^M
curleuse^F
Curlingstein^M
giocatore^M
tee
tee^M
centre^M
Tee^N
centro^M
inner circle
círculo^M central
cercle^M intérieur
Innenkreis^M
anello^M interno

speed skating

patinaje M de velocidad F | patinage M de vitesse F | Eisschnelllauf M | pattinaggio M di velocità F

short track
pista F corta
courte piste F
Kurzstrecke F
short track M

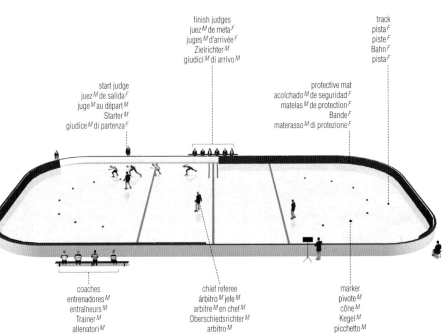

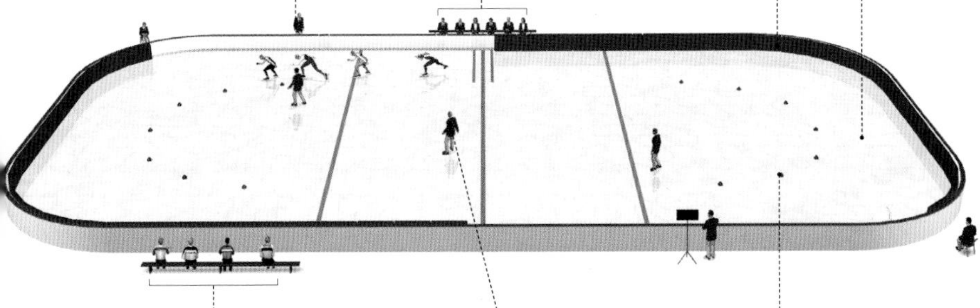
finish judges
juez M de meta F
juges M d'arrivée F
Zielrichter M
giudici M di arrivo M
track
pista F
piste F
Bahn F
pista F
start judge
juez M de salida F
juge M au départ M
Starter M
giudice M di partenza F
protective mat
acolchado M de seguridad F
matelas M de protection F
Bande F
materasso M di protezione F
coaches
entrenadores M
entraîneurs M
Trainer M
allenatori M
chief referee
árbitro M jefe M
arbitre M en chef M
Oberschiedsrichter M
arbitro M
marker
pivote M
cône M
Kegel M
picchetto M

long track
pista^F larga
longue piste^F
Eisschnelllaufbahn^F
pista^F lunga

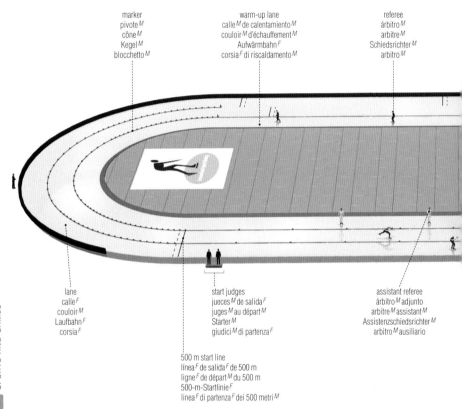

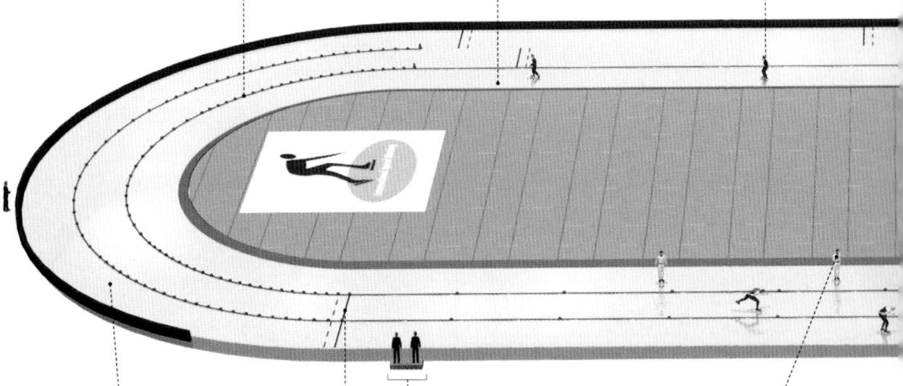
marker
pivote M
cône M
Kegel M
blocchetto M
warm-up lane
calle M de calentamiento M
couloir M d'échauffement M
Aufwärmbahn F
corsia F di riscaldamento M
referee
árbitro M
arbitre M
Schiedsrichter M
arbitro M
lane
calle F
couloir M
Laufbahn F
corsia F
start judges
jueces M de salida F
juges M au départ M
Starter M
giudici M di partenza F
assistant referee
árbitro M adjunto
arbitre M assistant M
Assistenzschiedsrichter M
arbitro M ausiliario
500 m start line
línea F de salida F de 500 m
ligne F de départ M du 500 m
500-m-Startlinie F
linea F di partenza F dei 500 metri M

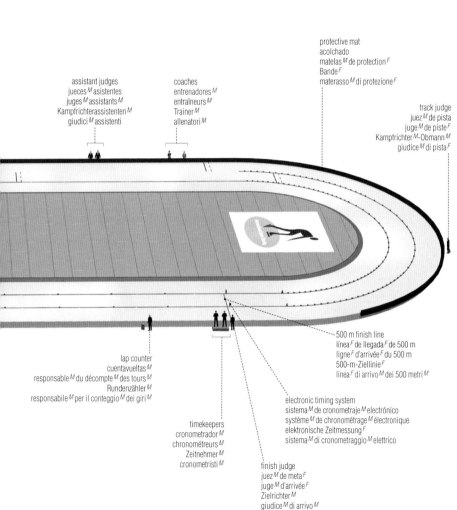

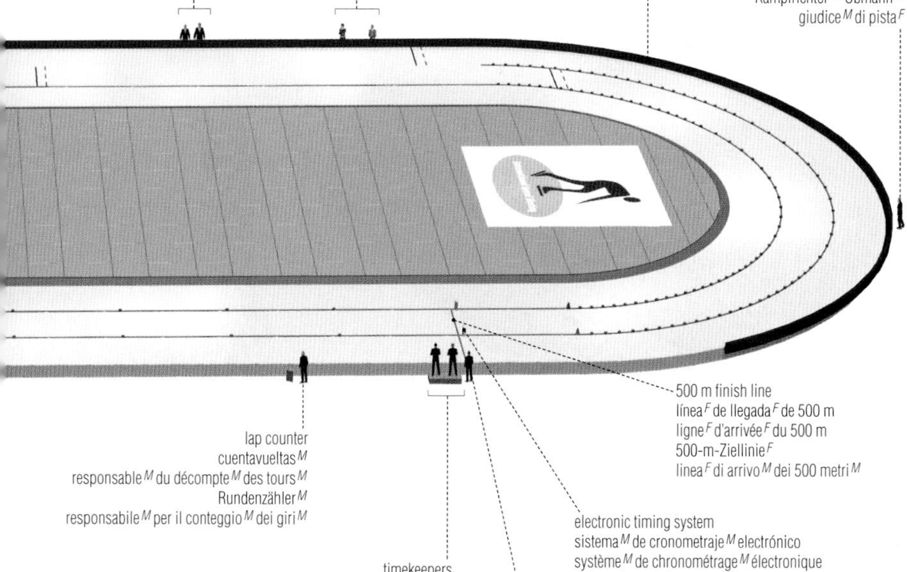
assistant judges
jueces M asistentes
juges M assistants M
Kampfrichterassistenten M
giudici M assistenti
coaches
entrenadores M
entraîneurs M
Trainer M
allenatori M
protective mat
acolchado
matelas M de protection F
Bande F
materasso M di protezione F
track judge
juez M de pista
juge M de piste F
Kampfrichter M-Obmann M
giudice M di pista F
500 m finish line
línea F de llegada F de 500 m
ligne F d'arrivée F du 500 m
500-m-Ziellinie F
linea F di arrivo M dei 500 metri M
lap counter
cuentavueltas M
responsable M du décompte M des tours M
Rundenzähler M
responsabile M per il conteggio M dei giri M
electronic timing system
sistema M de cronometraje M electrónico
système M de chronométrage M électronique
elektronische Zeitmessung F
sistema M di cronometraggio M elettrico
timekeepers
cronometrador M
chronométreurs M
Zeitnehmer M
cronometristi M
finish judge
juez M de meta F
juge M d'arrivée F
Zielrichter M
giudice M di arrivo M

speed skating

skater: short track
patinador[M] : pista[F] corta
patineur[M] : courte piste[F]
Eisschnellläufer[M]: Kurzstrecke[F]
pattinatore[M]: short track[M]

helmet
casco[M]
casque[M]
Helm[M]
casco[M]
glove
guante[M]
gant[M]
Handschuh[M]
guanto[M]

knee pad
rodillera[F]
genouillère[F]
Knieschützer[M]
ginocchiera[F]

throat protector
protector[M] de garganta[F]
protège-gorge[M]
Halsschutz[M]
paracollo[M]

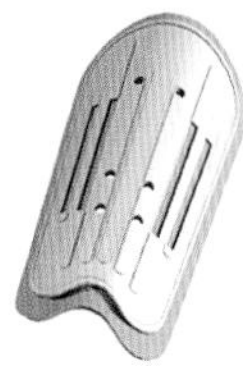

shin guard
espinillera[F]
protège-tibia[M]
Schienbeinschutz[M]
parastinchi[M]

speed skating

skater: long track
patinador M : pista F larga
patineur M : longue piste F
Eisschnellläufer M: Langstrecke F
pattinatore M: pista F lunga

hood
capuchón M
capuchon M
Kapuze F
cappuccio M
racing suit
traje M de carrera F
combinaison F de course F
Rennanzug M
tuta F

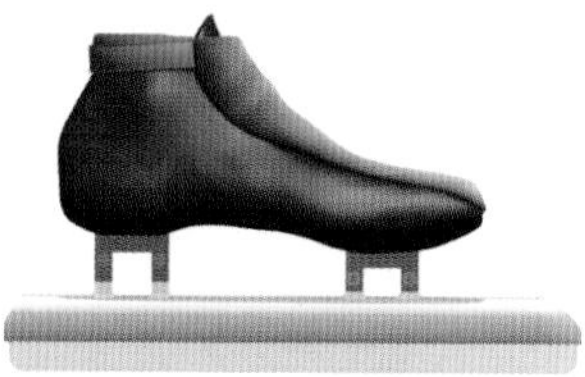

short track skate
patín M de pista F corta
patin M de courte piste F
Kurzstreckenschlittschuh M
pattino M da short track M

clapskate
patín M de pista F larga
patin M clap
Klappschlittschuh M
pattino M ad incastro M

figure skating

patinaje^M artístico | patinage^M artistique | Eiskunstlauf^M | pattinaggio^M artistico

figure skate
patín^M para figuras^F
patin^M de figure^F
Eiskunstlaufstiefel^M
pattino^M per pattinaggio^M artistico

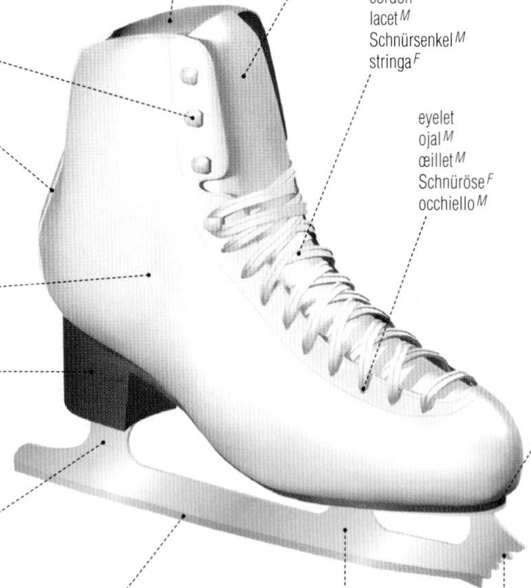
lining
forro M
doublure F
Futter N
fodera F
tongue
lengüeta F
languette F
Zunge F
linguetta F
hook
corchete M
crochet M
Schnürhaken M
gancio M
lace
cordón M
lacet M
Schnürsenkel M
stringa F
backstay
contrafuerte M
tige F
Rückenverstärkung F
rinforzo M posteriore
eyelet
ojal M
œillet M
Schnüröse F
occhiello M
boot
bota F
chaussure F
Stiefel M
scarpa F
sole
suela F
semelle F
Sohle F
suola F
heel
tacón M
talon M
Absatz M
tacco M
stanchion
montante M
montant M
Träger M
sostegno M
edge
canto M
carre F
Schneide F
lamina F
blade
hoja F de cuchilla F
lame F
Kufe F
lama F
toe pick
dientes M
dent F
Abstoßsäge F
punta F dentellata

rink
pista^{F} de patinaje^{M} sobre hielo^{M}
patinoire^{F}
Eisfläche^{F}
pista^{F} di pattinaggio^{M}

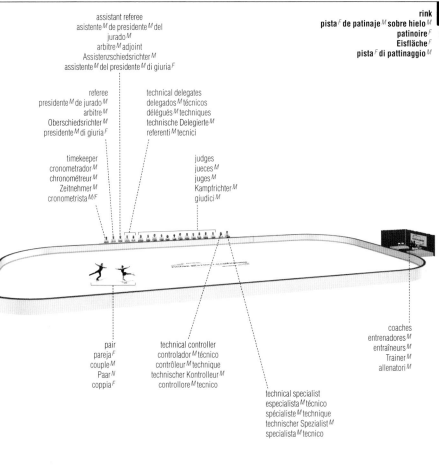

assistant referee
asistente^{M} de presidente^{M} del jurado^{M}
arbitre^{M} adjoint
Assistenzschiedsrichter^{M}
assistente^{M} del presidente^{M} di giuria^{F}

referee
presidente^{M} de jurado^{M}
arbitre^{M}
Oberschiedsrichter^{M}
presidente^{M} di giuria^{F}

technical delegates
delegados^{M} técnicos
délégués^{M} techniques
technische Delegierte^{M}
referenti^{M} tecnici

timekeeper
cronometrador^{M}
chronométreur^{M}
Zeitnehmer^{M}
cronometrista$^{M/F}$

judges
jueces^{M}
juges^{M}
Kampfrichter^{M}
giudici^{M}

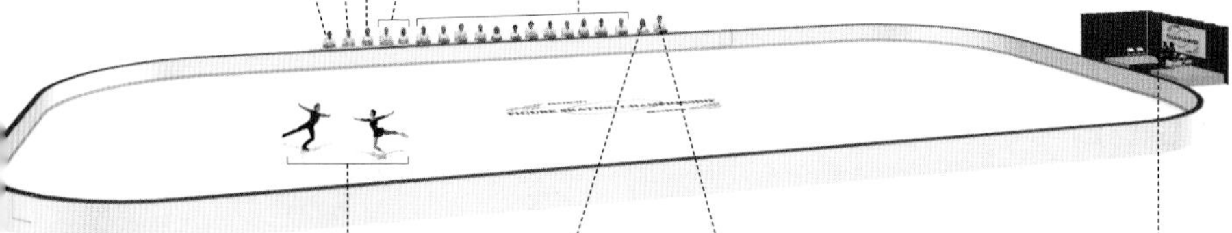

coaches
entrenadores^{M}
entraîneurs^{M}
Trainer^{M}
allenatori^{M}

pair
pareja^{F}
couple^{M}
Paar^{N}
coppia^{F}

technical controller
controlador^{M} técnico
contrôleur^{M} technique
technischer Kontrolleur^{M}
controllore^{M} tecnico

technical specialist
especialista^{M} técnico
spécialiste^{M} technique
technischer Spezialist^{M}
specialista^{M} tecnico

dance blade
cuchilla^{F} de baile^{M}
lame^{F} de danse^{F} sur glace^{F}
Eistanzkufe^{F}
lama^{F} per danza^{F}

free skating blade
cuchilla^{F} de patinaje^{M} artístico
lame^{F} pour programme^{M} libre
Eiskunstlaufkufe^{F}
lama^{F} per pattinaggio^{M} libero

snowboarding

snowboard^M | surf^M des neiges^F | Snowboarden^N | snowboard^M

snowboarder
snowboarder^M
surfeur^M
Snowboarder^M
snowboardista^M/F

helmet
casco^M
casque^M
Helm^M
casco^M
coveralls
traje^M de esquí^M
combinaison^F
Skianzug^M
tuta^F
goggles
gafas^F de esquí^M
lunettes^F
Skibrille^F
occhiali^M
glove
guante^M
gant^M
Handschuh^M
guanto^M
shin guard
tobillera^F
protège-tibia^M
Schienbeinschützer^M
parastinchi^M
snowboard
snowboard^M
surf^M des neiges^F
Snowboard^N
snowboard^M

flexible boot
bota[F] blanda
botte[F] souple
Softboots[M]
scarpone[M] morbido

hard boot
bota[F] rígida
botte[F] rigide
Hardboots[M]
scarpone[M] rigido

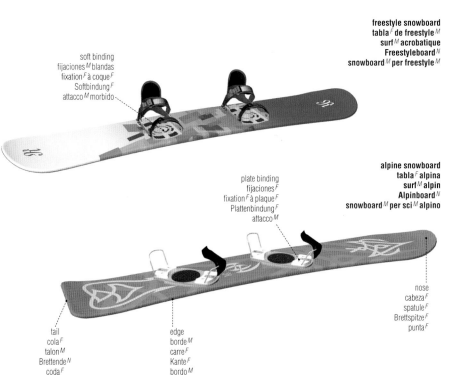

freestyle snowboard
tabla[F] de freestyle[M]
surf[M] acrobatique
Freestyleboard[N]
snowboard[M] per freestyle[M]

soft binding
fijaciones[M] blandas
fixation[F] à coque[F]
Softbindung[F]
attacco[M] morbido

alpine snowboard
tabla[F] alpina
surf[M] alpin
Alpinboard[N]
snowboard[M] per sci[M] alpino

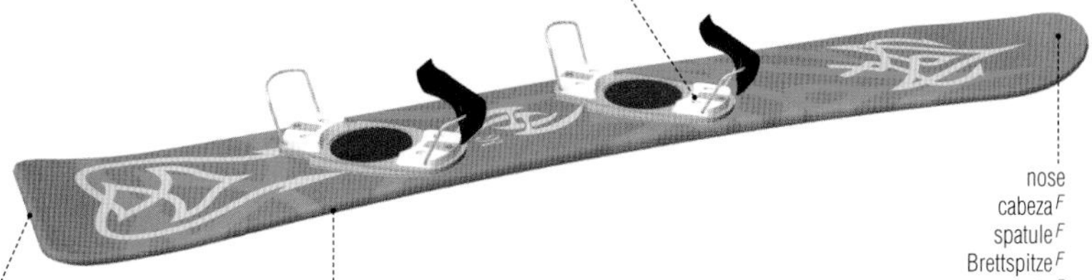

plate binding
fijaciones[F]
fixation[F] à plaque[F]
Plattenbindung[F]
attacco[M]

nose
cabeza[F]
spatule[F]
Brettspitze[F]
punta[F]

tail
cola[F]
talon[M]
Brettende[N]
coda[F]

edge
borde[M]
carre[F]
Kante[F]
bordo[M]

alpine skiing

esquí^M alpino | ski^M alpin | alpines Skilaufen^N | sci^M alpino

ski
esquí^M
ski^M
Ski^M
sci^M

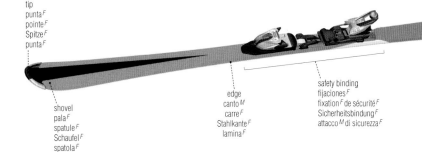

tai
cola^F
talon^M
Ende^N
coda^F
tip
punta^F
pointe^F
Spitze^F
punta^F
shovel
pala^F
spatule^F
Schaufel^F
spatola^F
edge
canto^M
carre^F
Stahlkante^F
lamina^F
safety binding
fijaciones^F
fixation^F de sécurité^F
Sicherheitsbindung^F
attacco^M di sicurezza^F

ski boot
botas^F para esquiar
chaussure^F de ski^M
Skistiefel^M
scarpone^M

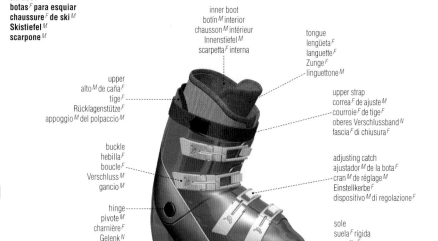

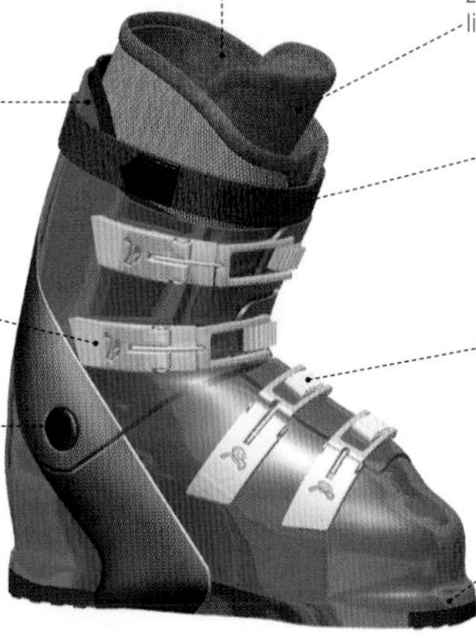
inner boot
botín^M interior
chausson^M intérieur
Innenstiefel^M
scarpetta^F interna
tongue
lengüeta^F
languette^F
Zunge^F
linguettone^M
upper
alto^M de caña^F
tige^F
Rücklagenstütze^F
appoggio^M del polpaccio^M
upper strap
correa^F de ajuste^M
courroie^F de tige^F
oberes Verschlussband^N
fascia^F di chiusura^F
buckle
hebilla^F
boucle^F
Verschluss^M
gancio^M
adjusting catch
ajustador^M de la bota^F
cran^M de réglage^M
Einstellkerbe^F
dispositivo^M di regolazione^F
hinge
pivote^M
charnière^F
Gelenk^N
snodo^M
sole
suela^F rígida
semelle^F
Sohle^F
suola^F

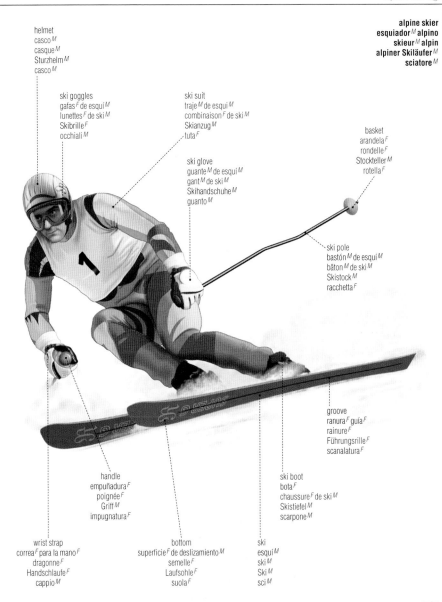

alpine skier
esquiador^{M} alpino
skieur^{M} alpin
alpiner Skiläufer^{M}
sciatore^{M}

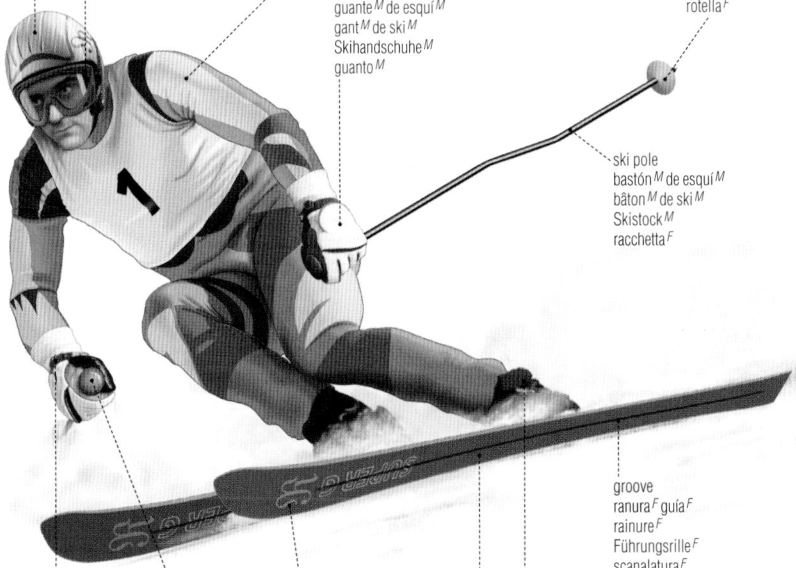
helmet
casco^{M}
casque^{M}
Sturzhelm^{M}
casco^{M}
ski goggles
gafas^{F} de esquí^{M}
lunettes^{F} de ski^{M}
Skibrille^{F}
occhiali^{M}
ski suit
traje^{M} de esqui^{M}
combinaison^{F} de ski^{M}
Skianzug^{M}
tuta^{F}
ski glove
guante^{M} de esquí^{M}
gant^{M} de ski^{M}
Skihandschuhe^{M}
guanto^{M}
basket
arandela^{F}
rondelle^{F}
Stockteller^{M}
rotella^{F}
ski pole
bastón^{M} de esquí^{M}
bâton^{M} de ski^{M}
Skistock^{M}
racchetta^{F}
groove
ranura^{F} guía^{F}
rainure^{F}
Führungsrille^{F}
scanalatura^{F}
handle
empuñadura^{F}
poignée^{F}
Griff^{M}
impugnatura^{F}
ski boot
bota^{F}
chaussure^{F} de ski^{M}
Skistiefel^{M}
scarpone^{M}
wrist strap
correa^{F} para la mano^{F}
dragonne^{F}
Handschlaufe^{F}
cappio^{M}
bottom
superficie^{F} de deslizamiento^{M}
semelle^{F}
Laufsohle^{F}
suola^{F}
ski
esquí^{M}
ski^{M}
Ski^{M}
sci^{M}

ski resort

estación^{F} de esquí^{M} | station^{F} de ski^{M} | Skigebiet^{N} | stazione^{F} sciistica

intermediate slope
pista^{F} para intermedios^{M}
pente^{F} intermédiaire
mittelschwere Piste^{F}
pista^{F} a difficoltà^{F} intermedia

gondola
teleférico^{M}
télécabine^{F}
Seilbahn^{F}
funivia^{F}

chair lift
telesilla^{M}
télésiège^{M}
Sessellift^{M}
seggiovia^{F}

easy slope
pista^{F} para principiantes^{M}
pente^{F} facile
Anfängerpiste^{F}, Idiotenhügel^{M}
pista^{F} per principianti^{M}

summit
cima^{F}
sommet^{M}
Gipfel^{M}
vetta^{F}

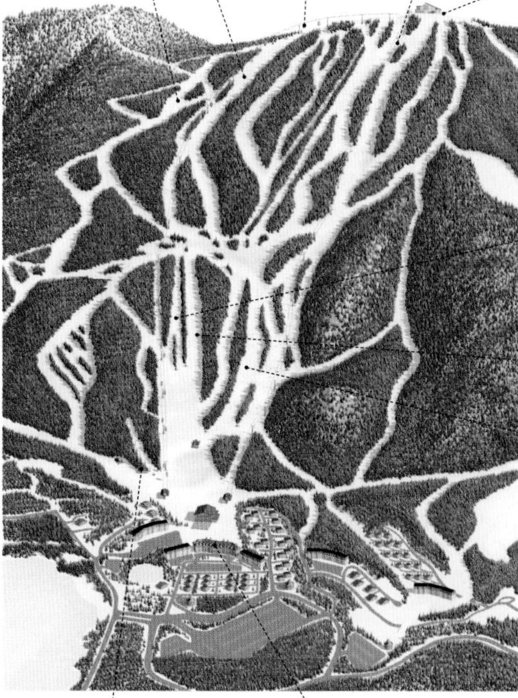

ski area
pistas^{F} de esquí^{M}
domaine^{M} skiable
Skipisten^{F}
piste^{F} da sci^{M}

expert slope
pista^{F} para expertos^{M}
pente^{F} expert^{M}
Expertenpiste^{F}
pista^{F} per esperti^{M}

difficult slope
pista^{F} para avanzados^{M}
pente^{F} difficile
schwere Piste^{F}
pista^{F} a difficoltà^{F} elevata

alpine ski trail
pista^{F} de esquí^{M} alpino
piste^{F} de ski^{M} alpin
Alpin-Skipiste^{F}
pista^{F} per sci^{M} alpino

lodging
alojamientos^{M}
hébergement^{M}
Unterkünfte^{F}
alloggi^{M}

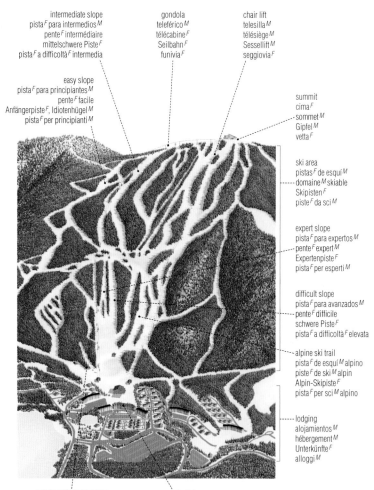

patrol and first aid station
patrulla^{F} de primeros auxilios^{M} y puesto^{M} de socorro^{M}
poste^{M} de patrouille^{F} et de secours^{M}
Bergwacht^{F}
stazione^{F} di pattugliamento^{M} e pronto soccorso^{M}

main lodge
refugio^{M} principal
chalet^{M} principal
Hauptunterkunft^{F}
rifugio^{M} principale

cross-country skiing

esquí^M de fondo^M | ski^M de fond^M | Skilanglauf^M | sci^M da fondo^M

cross-country skier
fondista^M
skieur^M de fond^M
Langläufer^M
fondista^M/F

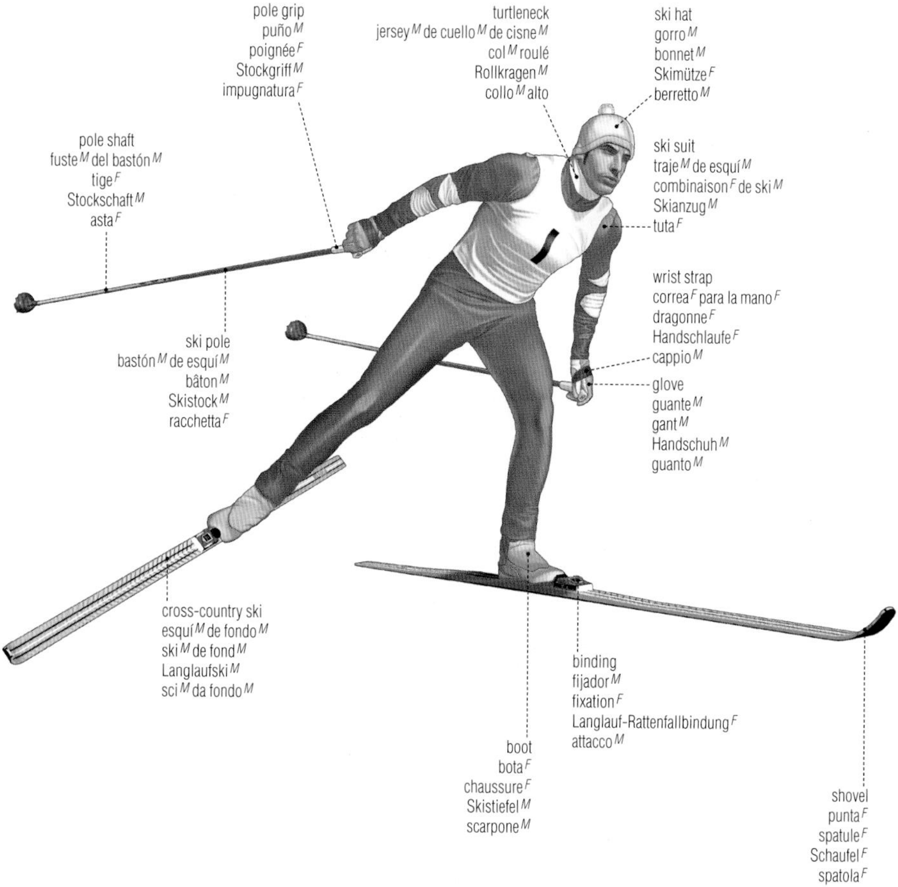
pole grip
puño M
poignée F
Stockgriff M
impugnatura F
turtleneck
jersey M de cuello M de cisne M
col M roulé
Rollkragen M
collo M alto
ski hat
gorro M
bonnet M
Skimütze F
berretto M
pole shaft
fuste M del bastón M
tige F
Stockschaft M
asta F
ski suit
traje M de esquí M
combinaison F de ski M
Skianzug M
tuta F
wrist strap
correa F para la mano F
dragonne F
Handschlaufe F
cappio M
ski pole
bastón M de esquí M
bâton M
Skistock M
racchetta F
glove
guante M
gant M
Handschuh M
guanto M
cross-country ski
esquí M de fondo M
ski M de fond M
Langlaufski M
sci M da fondo M
binding
fijador M
fixation F
Langlauf-Rattenfallbindung F
attacco M
boot
bota F
chaussure F
Skistiefel M
scarpone M
shovel
punta F
spatule F
Schaufel F
spatola F

snowshoes

raqueta^{F} | raquettes^{F} | Schneeschuh^{M} | racchetta^{F} da neve^{F}

elliptical snowshoe
raqueta^{F} elíptica
raquette^{F} elliptique
elliptischer Schneeschuh^{M}
racchetta^{F} da neve^{F} ellittica

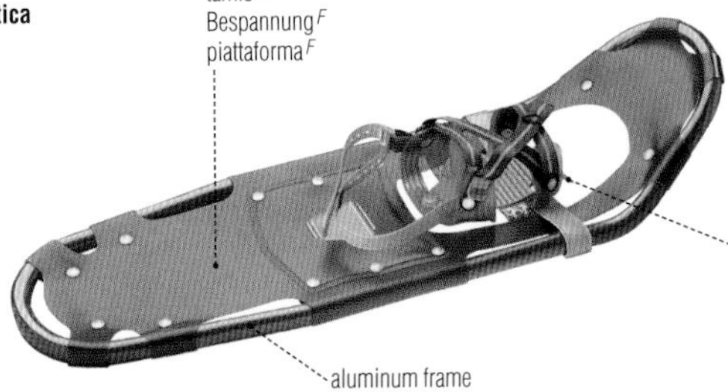
deck
tablero^{M}
tamis^{M}
Bespannung^{F}
piattaforma^{F}
crampon system
crampones^{M}
crampon^{M}
Steigeisen^{N}
rampone^{M}
aluminum frame
marco^{M} de aluminio^{M}
cadre^{M} d'aluminium^{M}
Aluminiumrahmen^{M}
struttura^{F} in alluminio^{M}

Michigan snowshoe
tipo^{M} Michigan
raquette^{F} algonquine
Michigan-Schneeschuh^{M}
racchetta^{F} Michigan

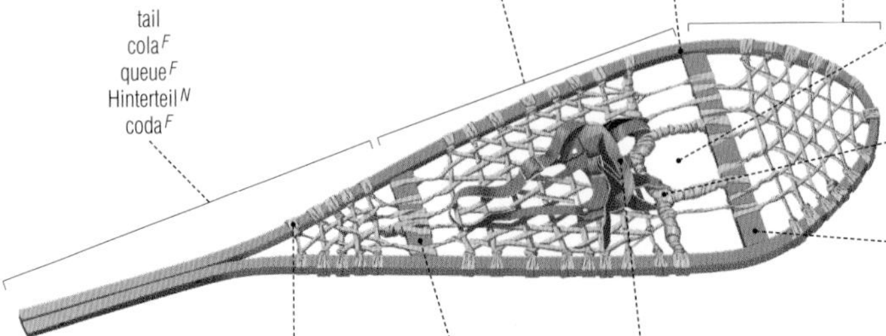
tip
cabeza^{F}
tête^{F}
Spitze^{F}
punta^{F}
body
cuerpo^{M}
pied^{M}
Korpus^{M}
corpo^{M}
frame
marco^{M}
cadre^{M}
Rahmen^{M}
telaio^{M}
toe hole
puntera^{F}
porte^{F}
Zehenloch^{N}
apertura^{F}
tail
cola^{F}
queue^{F}
Hinterteil^{N}
coda^{F}
master cord
cuerda^{F} maestra
maître^{M}-brin^{M}
Hauptband^{N}
corda^{F} principale
front crossbar
travesaño^{M} delantero
traverse^{F} avant
vordere Querleiste^{F}
traversa^{F} anteriore
lacing
cordaje^{M}
lacis^{M}
Bespannung^{F}
stringhe^{F}
back crossbar
travesaño^{M} trasero
traverse^{F} arrière
hintere Querleiste^{F}
traversa^{F} posteriore
harness
correa^{F}
harnais^{M}
Befestigungsriemen^{M}
imbracatura^{F}

in-line skating

patinaje[M] en línea[F] | patin[M] à roues[F] alignées | Inlineskating[N] | pattinaggio[M] in linea[F]

in-line skate
patín[M] en línea[F]
patin[M] à roues[F] alignées
Rollschuh[M]
pattino[M] a rotelle[F]

upper shell
bota[F] externa
coque[F] supérieure
Oberschale[F]
gambale[M]
inner boot
botín[M] interior
chausson[M] intérieur
Innenstiefel[M]
scarpetta[F] interna
adjusting buckle
hebilla[F] de ajuste[M]
boucle[F] de réglage[M]
Einstellspanner[M]
dispositivo[M] di regolazione[F]
boot
bota[F]
chaussure[F]
Stiefel[M]
scarpa[F]
heel stop
freno[M] trasero
frein[M] de talon[M]
Absatzstopper[M]
freno[M] a tampone[M]
wheel
rueda[F]
roue[F]
Rolle[F]
ruota[F]
axle
eje[M]
essieu[M]
Achse[F]
assale[M]
truck
bogie[M]
bloc[M]-essieu[M]
Wagen[M]
carrello[M]

skateboarding

skateboard^M | planche^F à roulettes^F | Skateboarding^N | skateboard^M

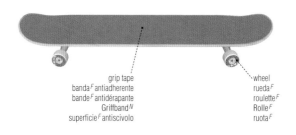

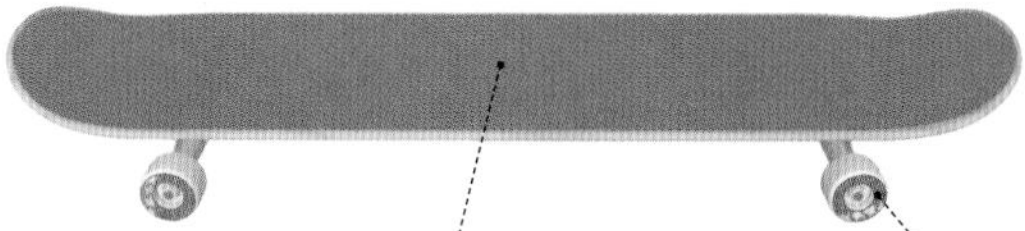
grip tape
banda^F antiadherente
bande^F antidérapante
Griffband^N
superficie^F antiscivolo
wheel
rueda^F
roulette^F
Rolle^F
ruota^F

ramp
medio tubo^M
rampe^F
Rampe^F
rampa^F

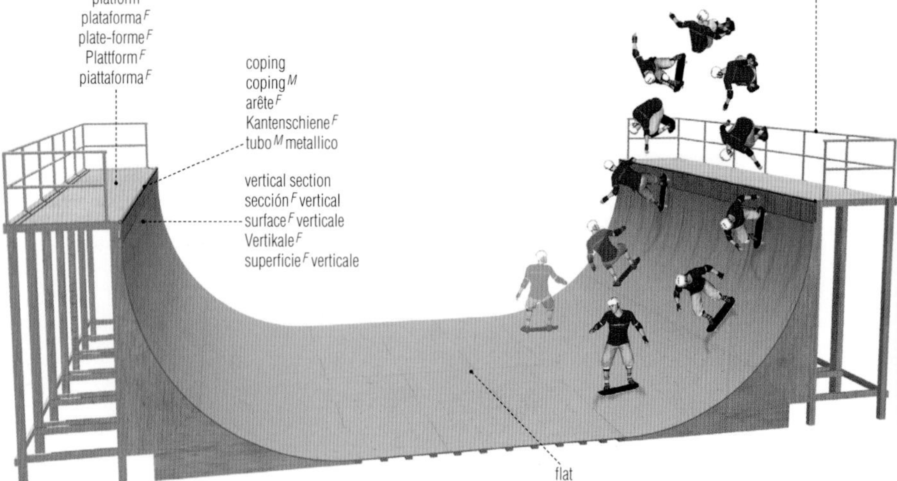
guard rail
barandilla^F
rambarde^F
Geländer^N
guardrail^M
platform
plataforma^F
plate-forme^F
Plattform^F
piattaforma^F
coping
coping^M
arête^F
Kantenschiene^F
tubo^M metallico
vertical section
sección^F vertical
surface^F verticale
Vertikale^F
superficie^F verticale
flat
piso^M
fond^M
Flachstück^N
piano^M

skateboarding

skateboard
monopatín[M]
planche[F] **à roulettes**[F]
Skateboard[N]
skateboard[M]

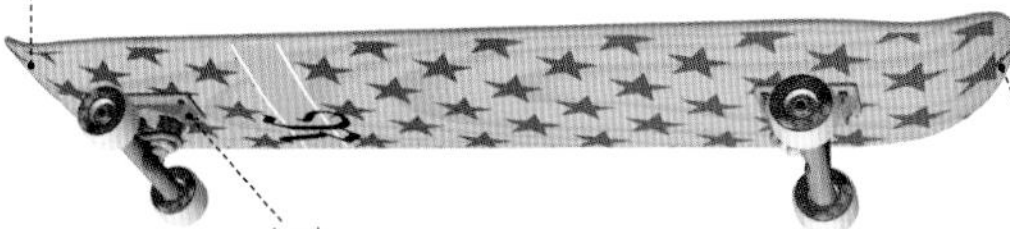
tail
cola[F]
queue[F]
Endstück[N]
coda[F]
truck
bloqueo[M] eje[M]
bloc[M]-essieu[M]
Achse[F]
attacco[M]
nose
punta[F]
nez[M]
Nase[F]
punta[F]

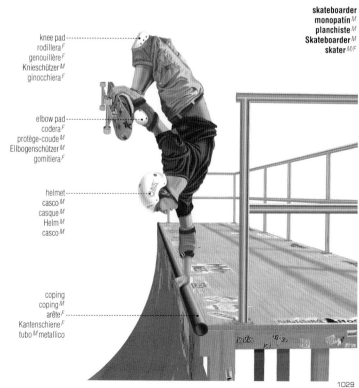

skateboarder
monopatín[M]
planchiste[M]
Skateboarder[M]
skater[M/F]

knee pad
rodillera[F]
genouillère[F]
Knieschützer[M]
ginocchiera[F]
elbow pad
codera[F]
protège-coude[M]
Ellbogenschützer[M]
gomitiera[F]
helmet
casco[M]
casque[M]
Helm[M]
casco[M]
coping
coping[M]
arête[F]
Kantenschiene[F]
tubo[M] metallico

camping

acampada F | camping M | Camping N | campeggio M

examples of tents
ejemplos M de tiendas F de campaña F
exemples M de tentes F
Beispiele N für Zelte N
esempi M di tende F

two-person tent
tienda F para dos
tente F deux places F
Zweipersonenzelt N
tenda F a due posti M

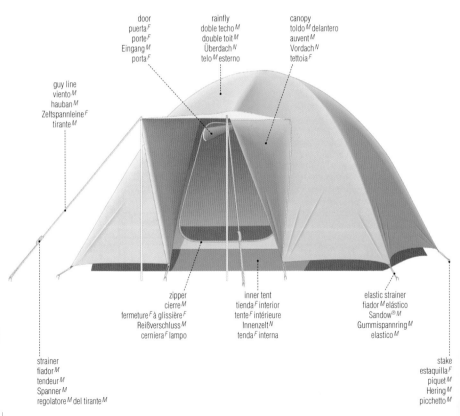

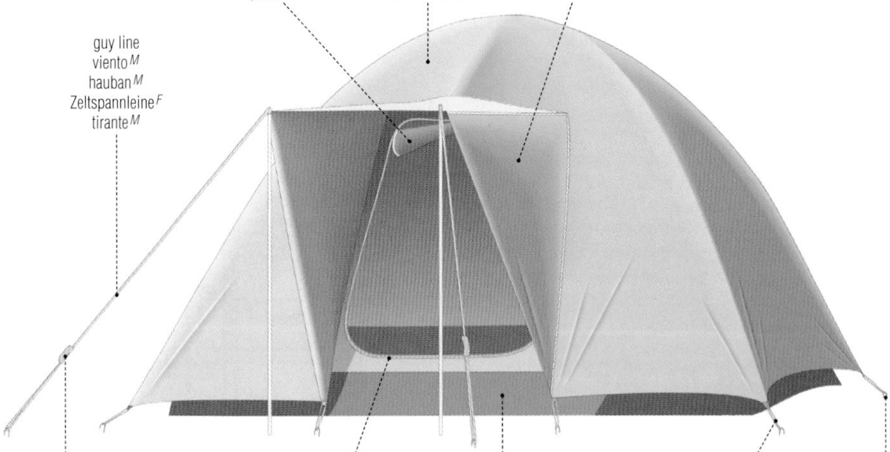
door
puerta F
porte F
Eingang M
porta F
rainfly
doble techo M
double toit M
Überdach N
telo M esterno
canopy
toldo M delantero
auvent M
Vordach N
tettoia F
guy line
viento M
hauban M
Zeltspannleine F
tirante M
zipper
cierre M
fermeture F à glissière F
Reißverschluss M
cerniera F lampo
inner tent
tienda F interior
tente F intérieure
Innenzelt N
tenda F interna
elastic strainer
fiador M elástico
Sandow® M
Gummispannring M
elastico M
strainer
fiador M
tendeur M
Spanner M
regolatore M del tirante M
stake
estaquilla F
piquet M
Hering M
picchetto M

wagon tent
tienda^{F} tipo^{M} vagón^{M}
tente^{F} grange^{F}
Mannschaftszelt^{N}
tenda^{F} da cucina^{F}

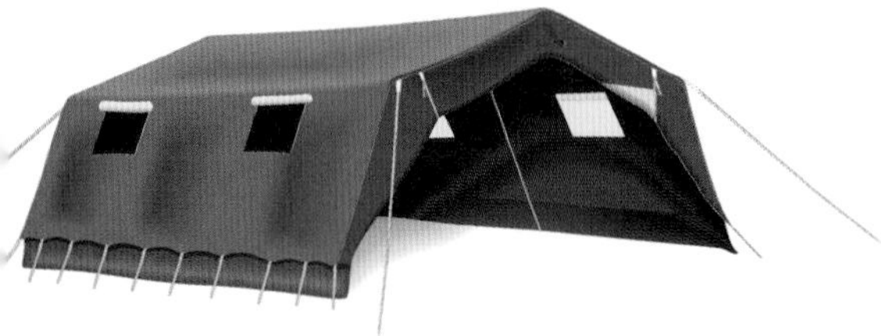

pop-up tent
tienda^{F} tipo^{M} iglú^{M}
tente^{F} igloo^{M}
Igluzelt^{N}
tenda^{F} a igloo^{M}

pup tent
tienda^{F} de campaña^{F} clásica
tente^{F} canadienne
Hauszelt^{N}
tenda^{F} canadese

one-person tent
tienda^{F} unipersonal
tente^{F} individuelle
Einpersonenzelt^{N}
tenda^{F} a un posto^{M}

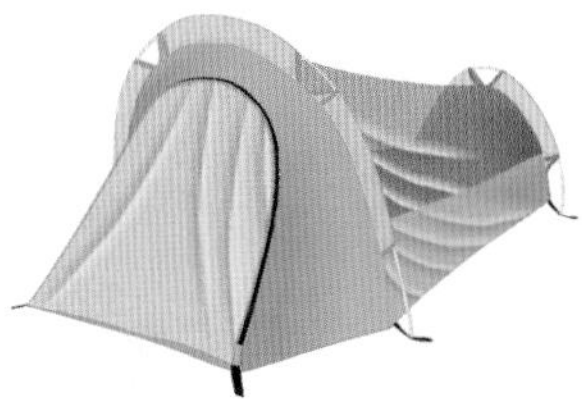

dome tent
tienda^{F} tipo^{M} domo^{M}
tente^{F} dôme^{M}
Kuppelzelt^{N}
tenda^{F} a cupola^{F}

wall tent
tienda^{F} rectangular
tente^{F} rectangulaire
Steilwandzelt^{N}
tenda^{F} da campo^{M}

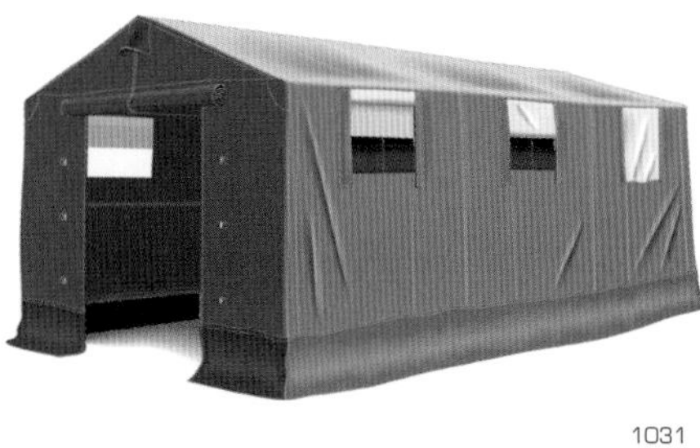

examples of sleeping bags
ejemplos[M] **de sacos**[M] **de dormir**
exemples[M] **de sacs**[M] **de couchage**[M]
Beispiele[N] **für Schlafsäcke**[M]
esempi[M] **di sacchi**[M] **a pelo**[M]

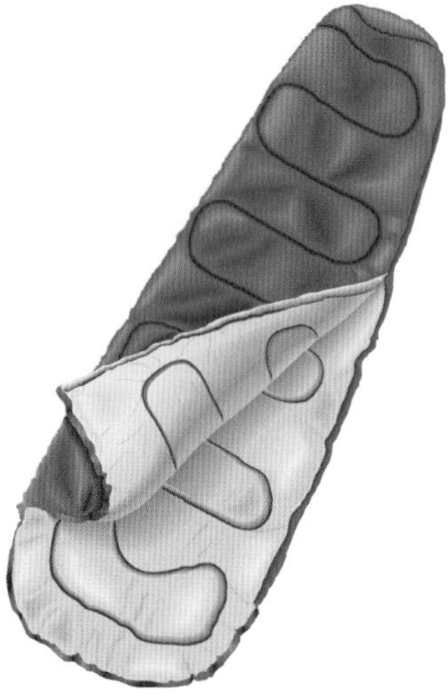

semi-mummy
saco[M] **semirrectangular**
semi-rectangulaire
Halbmumienschlafsack[M]
semi-mummia[F]

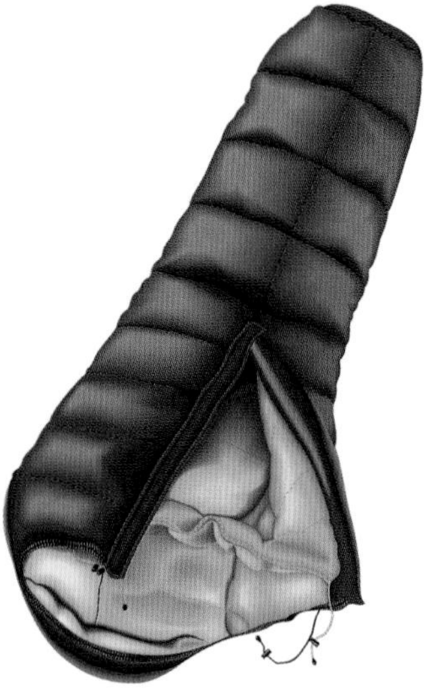

mummy
de momia[F]
à cagoule[F]
Mumienschlafsack[M]
mummia[F]

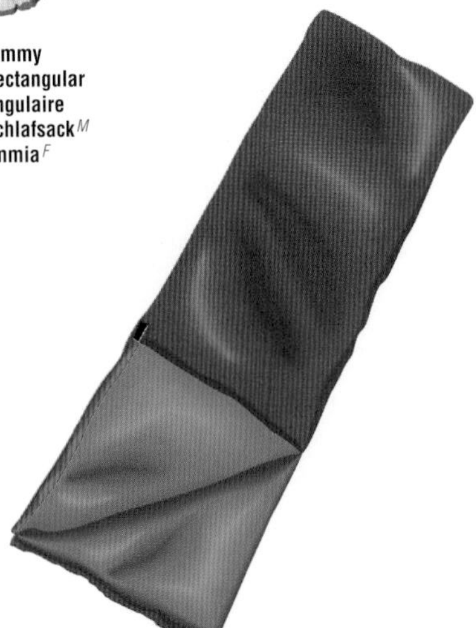

rectangular
saco[M] **rectangular**
rectangulaire
Rechteckschlafsack[M]
rettangolare

bed and mattress
camas *F* y colchonetas *F*
lit *M* et matelas *M*
Bett *N* mit Matratze *F*
branda *F* e materassino *M*

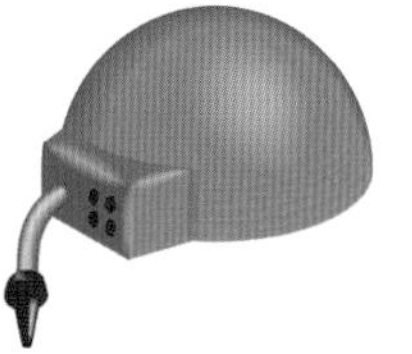

inflator
inflador *M*
gonfleur *M*
Blasebalg *M*
gonfiatore *M*

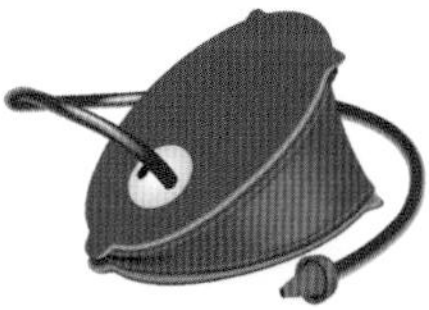

inflator-deflator
muelle *M* para inflar y desinflar
gonfleur *M*-dégonfleur *M*
Kombipumpe *F*
gonfiatore *M* a soffietto *M*

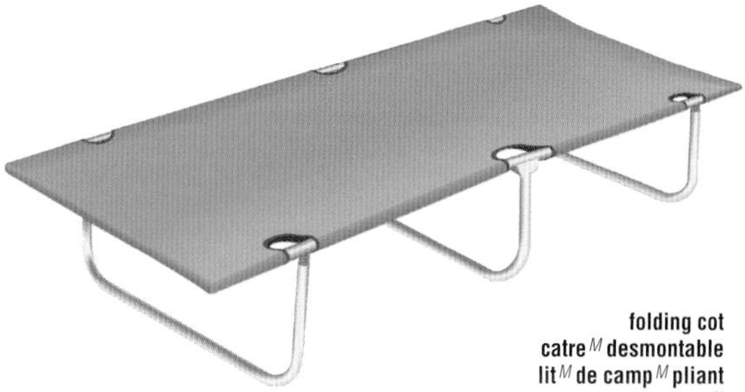

folding cot
catre *M* desmontable
lit *M* de camp *M* pliant
Feldbett *N*
brandina *F* smontabile

self-inflating mattress
colchoneta *F* aislante
matelas *M* autogonflant
selbstaufblasbare Luftmatratze *F*
materassino *M* autogonfiante

air mattress
colchoneta *F* de aire *M*
matelas *M* pneumatique
Luftmatratze *F*
materassino *M* pneumatico

foam pad
colchoneta *F* de espuma *F*
matelas *M* mousse *F*
Schaumgummimatratze *F*
materassino *M* isolante

propane or butane accessories
equipos[M] de gas[M]
accessoires[M] au propane[M] ou au butane[M]
Propan- oder Butangas-Geräte[N]
accessori[M] a propano[M] o butano[M]

single-burner camp stove
hornillo[M]
réchaud[M] à un feu[M]
einflammiger Gasbrenner[M]
fornello[M] da campo[M] con un bruciatore[M]

lantern
linterna[F]
lanterne[F]
Lampe[F]
lanterna[F]

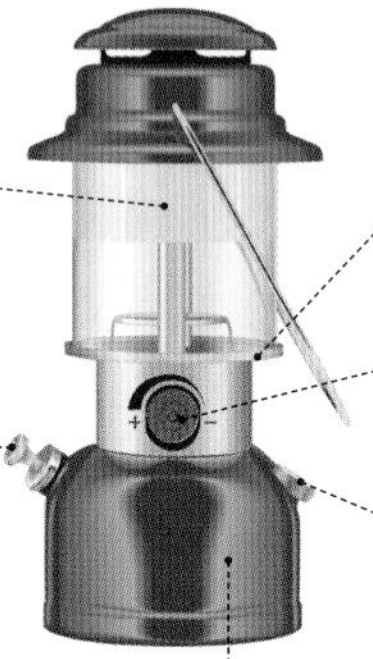
globe
globo[M]
globe[M]
Glas[N]
globo[M] di vetro[M]
pump
bomba[F]
pompe[F]
Pumpe[F]
pompa[F]
burner frame
armazón[M] del quemador[M]
bâti[M] du brûleur[M]
Brennsockel[M]
telaio[M] del bruciatore[M]
pressure regulator
regulador[M] de presión[F]
régulateur[M] de pression[F]
Gasstromregulierung[F]
regolatore[M] di luminosità[F]
leakproof cap
tapón[M] hermético
bouchon[M] antifuite
Dichtverschluss[M]
capsula[F] ermetica
tank
tanque[M]
réservoir[M]
Gasbehälter[M]
bombola[F]

double-burner camp stove
cocina[F] de campo[M]
réchaud[M] à deux feux[M]
zweiflammiger Gasbrenner[M]
fornello[M] da campo[M] a due fuochi[M]

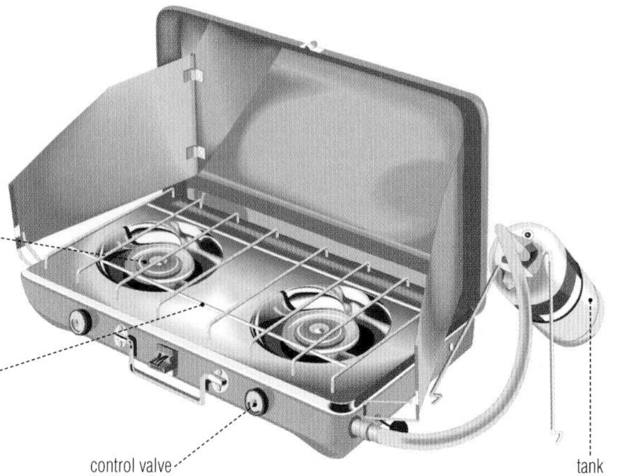
burner
quemador[M]
brûleur[M]
Brenner[M]
bruciatore[M]
wire support
parrilla[F] estabilizadora
grille[F] stabilisatrice
Metallaufsatz[M]
griglia[F]
control valve
válvula[F] de control[M]
robinet[M] relais[M]
Reglerventil[N]
manopola[F] di regolazione[F] del gas[M]
tank
bombona[F] de gas[M]
réservoir[M]
Gasbehälter[M]
bombola[F]

camping equipment
equipamiento^M para acampar
matériel^M de camping^M
Campingausrüstung^F
attrezzature^F da campeggio^M

Swiss Army knife
navaja^F multiusos suiza
couteau^M suisse
schweizer Offiziersmesser^N
temperino^M multiuso

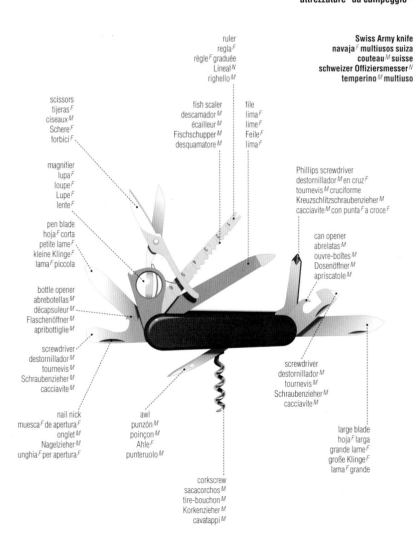

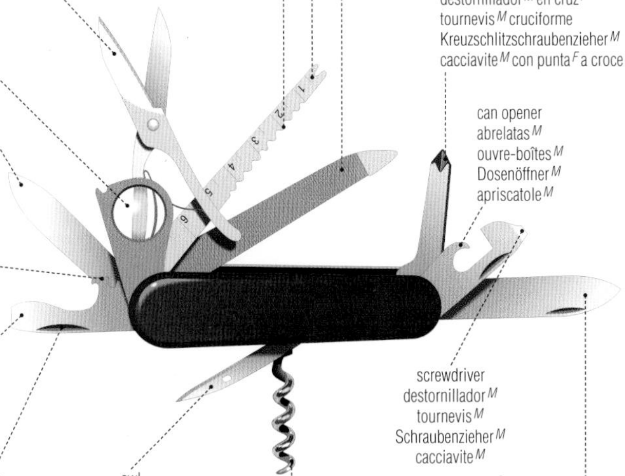
ruler
regla^F
règle^F graduée
Lineal^N
righello^M
scissors
tijeras^F
ciseaux^M
Schere^F
forbici^F
fish scaler
descamador^M
écailleur^M
Fischschupper^M
desquamatore^M
file
lima^F
lime^F
Feile^F
lima^F
magnifier
lupa^F
loupe^F
Lupe^F
lente^F
Phillips screwdriver
destornillador^M en cruz^F
tournevis^M cruciforme
Kreuzschlitzschraubenzieher^M
cacciavite^M con punta^F a croce^F
pen blade
hoja^F corta
petite lame^F
kleine Klinge^F
lama^F piccola
can opener
abrelatas^M
ouvre-boîtes^M
Dosenöffner^M
apriscatole^M
bottle opener
abrebotellas^M
décapsuleur^M
Flaschenöffner^M
apribottiglie^M
screwdriver
destornillador^M
tournevis^M
Schraubenzieher^M
cacciavite^M
screwdriver
destornillador^M
tournevis^M
Schraubenzieher^M
cacciavite^M
nail nick
muesca^F de apertura^F
onglet^M
Nagelzieher^M
unghia^F per apertura^F
awl
punzón^M
poinçon^M
Ahle^F
punteruolo^M
large blade
hoja^F larga
grande lame^F
große Klinge^F
lama^F grande
corkscrew
sacacorchos^M
tire-bouchon^M
Korkenzieher^M
cavatappi^M

SPORTS AND GAMES

camping

backpack
mochila[F]
sac[M] à dos[M]
Rucksack[M]
zaino[M]

top flap
solapa[F]
rabat[M]
Deckeltasche[F]
patta[F] di chiusura[F]

shoulder strap
espaldera[F]
bretelle[F]
Schultergurt[M]
spallaccio[M]

tightening buckle
hebilla[F] de regulación[F]
boucle[F] de réglage[M]
Schließe[F]
fibbia[F] di regolazione[F]

side compression strap
correa[F] de compresión[F]
sangle[F] de compression[F]
seitlicher Kompressionsgurt[M]
cinghia[F] di compressione[F] laterale

front compression strap
correa[F] de cierre[M]
sangle[F] de fermeture[F]
vorderer Straffergurt[M]
cinghia[F] di compressione[F] frontale

waist belt
cinturón[M]
ceinture[F]
Hüftgurt[M]
cintura[F] a vita[F]

strap loop
pasador[M]
passe-sangle[M]
Riemenschlaufe[F]
passacinghia[M]

vacuum bottle
termo[M]
bouteille[F] isolante
Thermosflasche[F]
thermos[M]

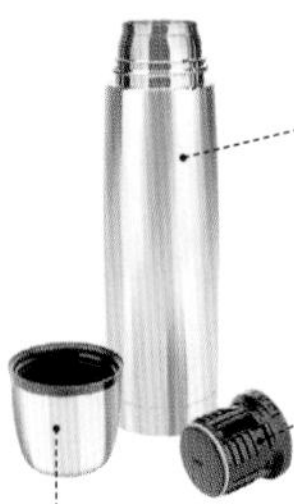

bottle
botella[F] del termo[M]
bouteille[F]
Flasche[F]
bottiglia[F]

stopper
tapón[M]
bouchon[M]
Verschluss[M]
tappo[M]

cup
taza[F]
tasse[F]
Becher[M]
bicchiere[M]

cooler
nevera[F]
glacière[F]
Kühlbox[F]
frigo[M] portatile

water carrier
termo[M] con llave[F] de servicio[M]
cruche[F]
Wasserkanister[M]
contenitore[M] termico

magnetic compass
brújula^F magnética
boussole^F magnétique
Magnetkompass^M
bussola^F magnetica

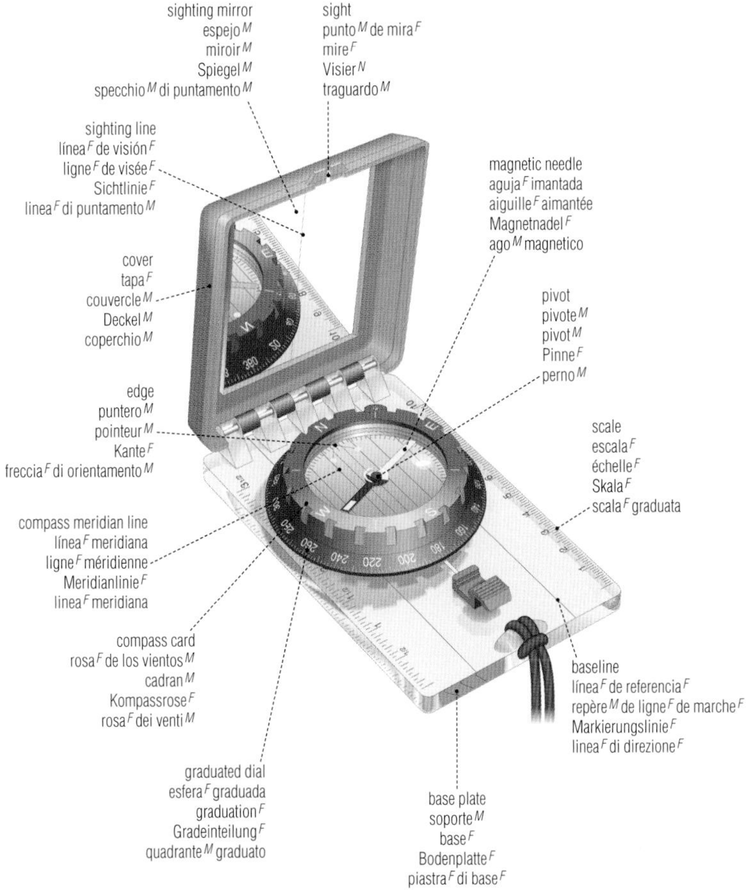
sighting mirror
espejo M
miroir M
Spiegel M
specchio M di puntamento M
sight
punto M de mira F
mire F
Visier N
traguardo M
sighting line
línea F de visión F
ligne F de visée F
Sichtlinie F
linea F di puntamento M
magnetic needle
aguja F imantada
aiguille F aimantée
Magnetnadel F
ago M magnetico
cover
tapa F
couvercle M
Deckel M
coperchio M
pivot
pivote M
pivot M
Pinne F
perno M
edge
puntero M
pointeur M
Kante F
freccia F di orientamento M
scale
escala F
échelle F
Skala F
scala F graduata
compass meridian line
línea F meridiana
ligne F méridienne
Meridianlinie F
linea F meridiana
compass card
rosa F de los vientos M
cadran M
Kompassrose F
rosa F dei venti M
baseline
línea F de referencia F
repère M de ligne F de marche F
Markierungslinie F
linea F di direzione F
graduated dial
esfera F graduada
graduation F
Gradeinteilung F
quadrante M graduato
base plate
soporte M
base F
Bodenplatte F
piastra F di base F

fishing

pesca[F] | pêche[F] | Sportfischerei[F] | pesca[F]

flyfishing
pesca[F] con mosca[F]
pêche[F] à la mouche[F]
Fliegenfischen[N]
pesca[F] a mosca[F]

fly rod
caña[F] para mosca[F]
canne[F] à mouche[F]
Fliegenrute[F]
canna[F] da mosca[F]

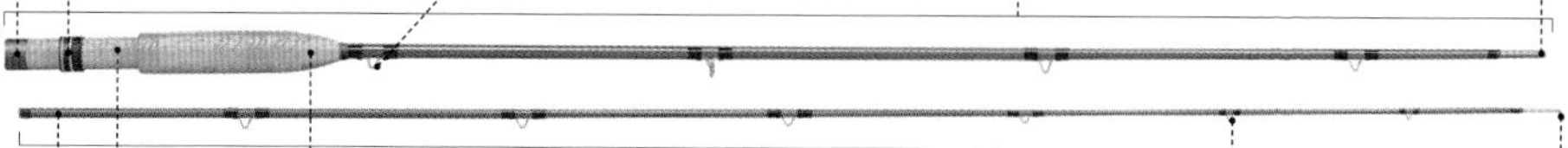
butt cap
contera[F]
embout[M]
Abschlusskappe[F]
pomello[M] in gomma[F]
butt section
talón[M]
talon[M]
Rückgrat[N]
corpo[M]
screw locking nut
tuerca[F] de sujeción[F]
écrou[M] de blocage[M]
Haltemutter[F]
vite[F] di bloccaggio[M]
keeper ring
anilla[F] de sujeción[F]
accroche-mouche[M]
Hakenhalteöse[F]
anello[M] fermamulinello
male ferrule
ensamble[M] macho[M]
virole[F] mâle
Innensteckhülse[F]
ghiera[F] maschio
handgrip
empuñadura[F]
poignée[F]
Griff[M]
impugnatura[F]
guide
anilla[F] guía[F]
anneau[M]
Führungsring[M]
anello[M] guida[F] della lenza[F]
reel seat
portacarrete[M]
porte-moulinet[M]
Rollenhalterung[F]
alloggiamento[M] del mulinello[M]
tip section
rabiza[F]
scion[M]
Spitze[F]
cimino[M]
tip-ring
guía[F] de la punta[F]
tête[F] de scion[M]
Abschlussring[M]
puntalino[M]
female ferrule
ensamble[M] hembra[F]
virole[F] femelle
Außensteckhülse[F]
ghiera[F] femmina

artificial fly
mosca[F] artificial
mouche[F] artificielle
Kunstfliege[F]
mosca[F] artificiale

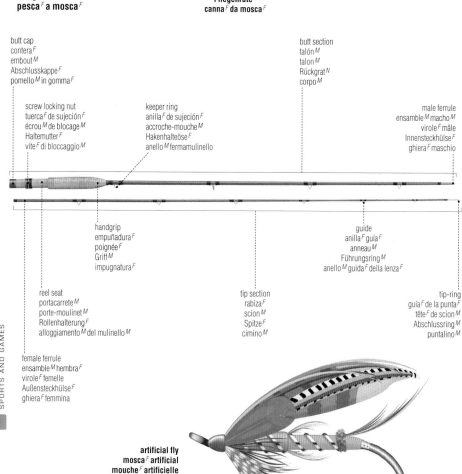

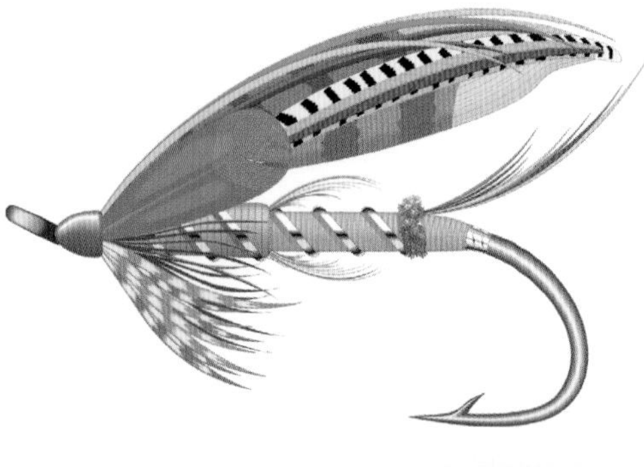

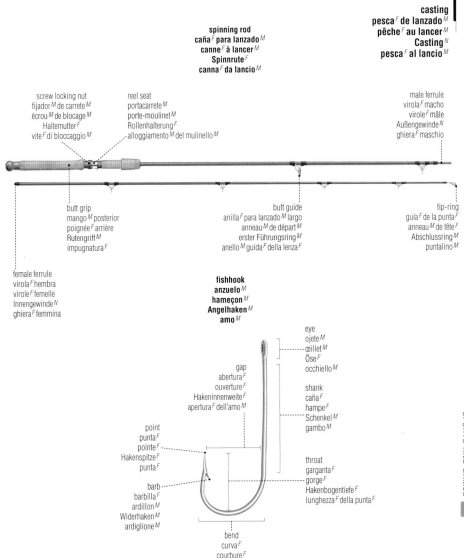

casting
pesca[F] de lanzado[M]
pêche[F] au lancer[M]
Casting[N]
pesca[F] al lancio[M]

spinning rod
caña[F] para lanzado[M]
canne[F] à lancer[M]
Spinnrute[F]
canna[F] da lancio[M]

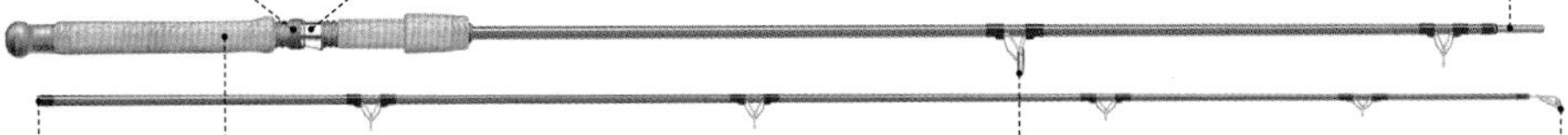
screw locking nut
fijador[M] de carrete[M]
écrou[M] de blocage[M]
Haltemutter[F]
vite[F] di bloccaggio[M]
reel seat
portacarrete[M]
porte-moulinet[M]
Rollenhalterung[F]
alloggiamento[M] del mulinello[M]
male ferrule
virola[F] macho
virole[F] mâle
Außengewinde[N]
ghiera[F] maschio
butt grip
mango[M] posterior
poignée[F] arrière
Rutengriff[M]
impugnatura[F]
butt guide
anilla[F] para lanzado[M] largo
anneau[M] de départ[M]
erster Führungsring[M]
anello[M] guida[F] della lenza[F]
tip-ring
guía[F] de la punta[F]
anneau[M] de tête[F]
Abschlussring[M]
puntalino[M]
female ferrule
virola[F] hembra
virole[F] femelle
Innengewinde[N]
ghiera[F] femmina

fishhook
anzuelo[M]
hameçon[M]
Angelhaken[M]
amo[M]

eye
ojete[M]
œillet[M]
Öse[F]
occhiello[M]
gap
abertura[F]
ouverture[F]
Hakeninnenweite[F]
apertura[F] dell'amo[M]
shank
caña[F]
hampe[F]
Schenkel[M]
gambo[M]
point
punta[F]
pointe[F]
Hakenspitze[F]
punta[F]
throat
garganta[F]
gorge[F]
Hakenbogentiefe[F]
lunghezza[F] della punta[F]
barb
barbilla[F]
ardillon[M]
Widerhaken[M]
ardiglione[M]
bend
curva[F]
courbure[F]
Hakenbogen[M]
curvatura[F]

clothing and accessories
ropa[F] y accesorios[M]
vêtements[M] et accessoires[M]
Kleidung[F] und Zubehör[N]
abbigliamento[M] e accessori[M]

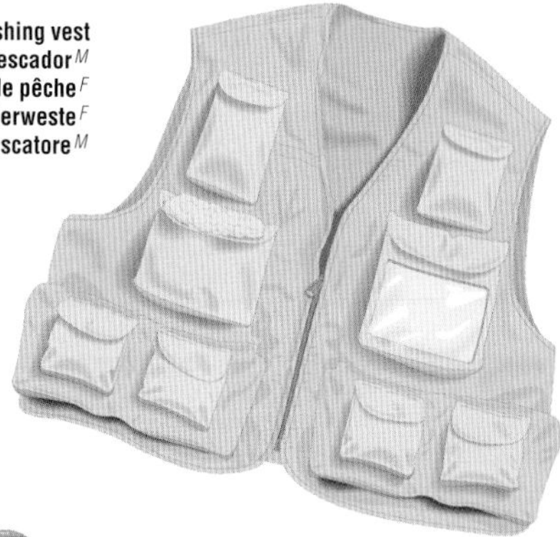

fishing vest
chaleco[M] de pescador[M]
veste[F] de pêche[F]
Anglerweste[F]
giubbotto[M] da pescatore[M]

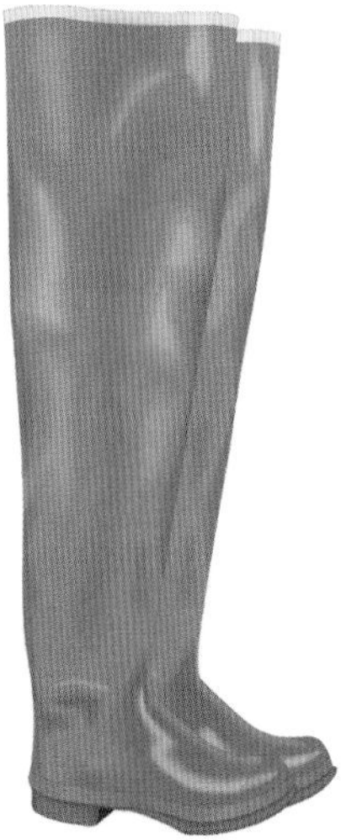

waders
botas[F] altas
cuissardes[F]
Watstiefel[M]
stivaloni[M] impermeabili

tackle box
caja[F] de pesca[F]
boîte[F] à leurres[M]
Spinnerschachtel[F]
scatola[F] portaesche

creel
cesta[F] de pescador[M]
panier[M]
Fischkorb[M]
cestino[M]

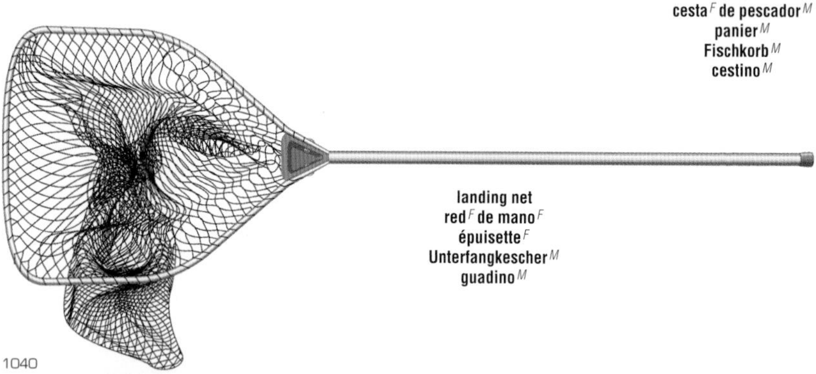

landing net
red[F] de mano[F]
épuisette[F]
Unterfangkescher[M]
guadino[M]

hunting

caza^{F} | chasse^{F} | Jagen^{N} | caccia^{F}

rifle (rifled bore)
rifle^{M}
carabine^{F} **(canon**^{M} **rayé)**
Gewehr^{N} **(gezogener Lauf**^{M}**)**
fucile^{M} **a canna**^{F} **rigata**

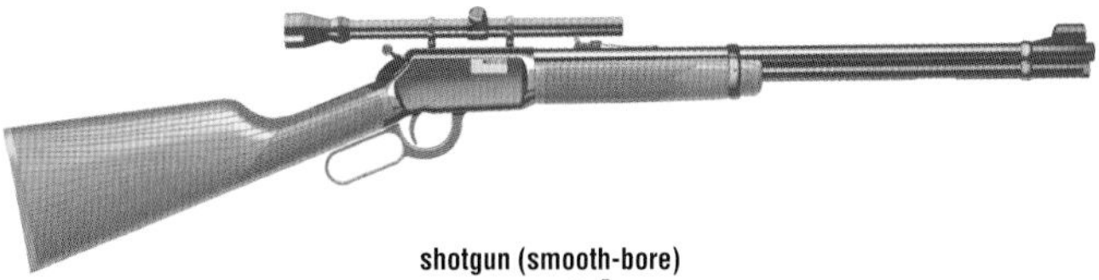

shotgun (smooth-bore)
escopeta^{F}
fusil^{M} **(canon**^{M} **lisse)**
Schrotflinte^{F} **(glatter Lauf**^{M}**)**
fucile^{M} **a canna**^{F} **liscia**

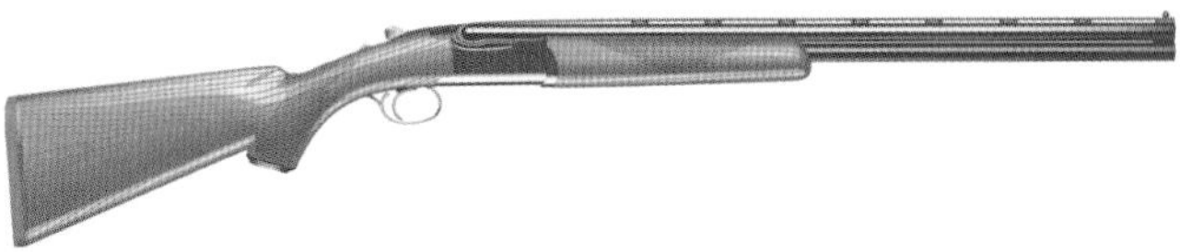

decoy
señuelo^{M}
appeau^{M}
Lockente^{F}
richiamo^{M}

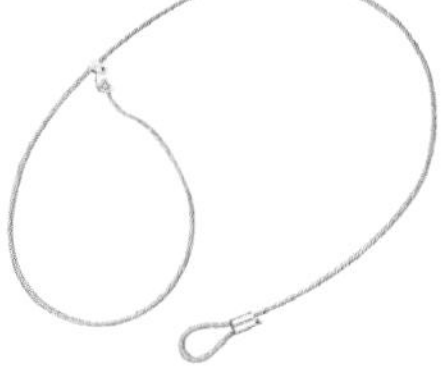

snare
lazo^{M}
collet^{M}
Schlinge^{F}
laccio^{M}

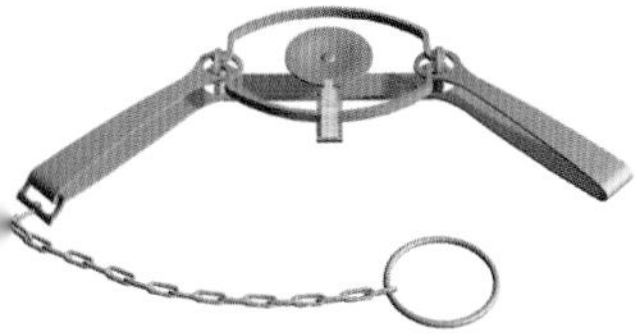

leghold trap
cepo^{M}
piège^{M} **à patte**^{F} **à mâchoires**^{F}
Tellereisen^{N}
tagliola^{F}

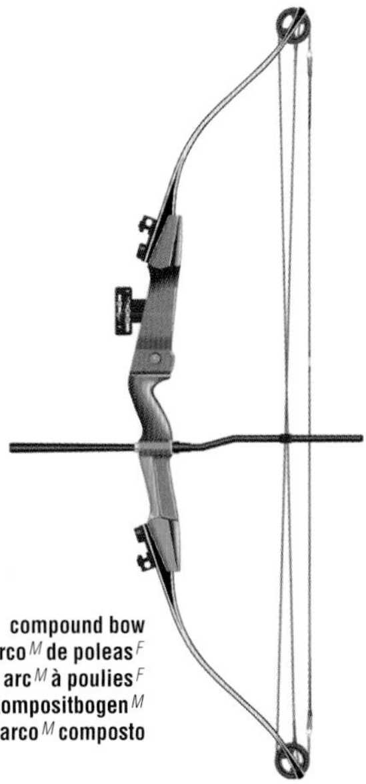

compound bow
arco^{M} **de poleas**^{F}
arc^{M} **à poulies**^{F}
Kompositbogen^{M}
arco^{M} **composto**

cards

baraja [F] | cartes [F] | Kartenspiele [N] | giochi [M] di carte [F]

symbols
símbolos [M]
symboles [M]
Farben [F]
simboli [M]

heart
corazón [M]
cœur [M]
Herz [N]
cuori [M]

diamond
diamante [M]
carreau [M]
Karo [N]
quadri [M]

club
trébol [M]
trèfle [M]
Kreuz [N]
fiori [M]

spade
espada [F]
pique [M]
Pik [N]
picche [M]

ace
as [M]
As [M]
Ass [N]
asso [M]

queen
reina [F]
Dame [F]
Dame [F]
donna [F]

joker
comodín [M]
Joker [M]
Joker [M]
jolly [M]

king
rey [M]
Roi [M]
König [M]
re [M]

jack
jota [F]
Valet [M]
Bube [M]
fante [M]

standard poker hands
manos[F] de póquer[M]
combinaisons[F] au poker[M]
normale Pokerblätter[N]
combinazioni[F] del poker[M]

high card
cartas[F] altas
carte[F] isolée
höchste Karte[F]
carta[F] più alta

one pair
un par[M]
paire[F]
ein Pärchen[N]
coppia[F]

two pairs
dobles pares[M]
double paire[F]
zwei Pärchen[N]
doppia coppia[F]

straight
escalera[F]
séquence[F]
Straße[F]
scala[F]

three-of-a-kind
trío[M]
brelan[M]
Drilling[M]
tris[M]

flush
color[M]
couleur[F]
Flush[M]
colore[M]

full house
full[M]
main[F] pleine
Full House[N]
full[M]

straight flush
escalera[F] de color[M]
quinte[F]
Straight Flush[M]
scala[F] reale

four-of-a-kind
póquer[M]
carré[M]
Vierling[M]
poker[M]

royal flush
escalera[F] real
quinte[F] royale
Royal Flush[M]
scala[F] reale massima

dice and dominoes

dados M y dominós M | dés M et dominos M | Würfel M und Dominosteine M | dadi M e domino M

dominoes
dominó M
dominos M
Dominosteine F
domino M

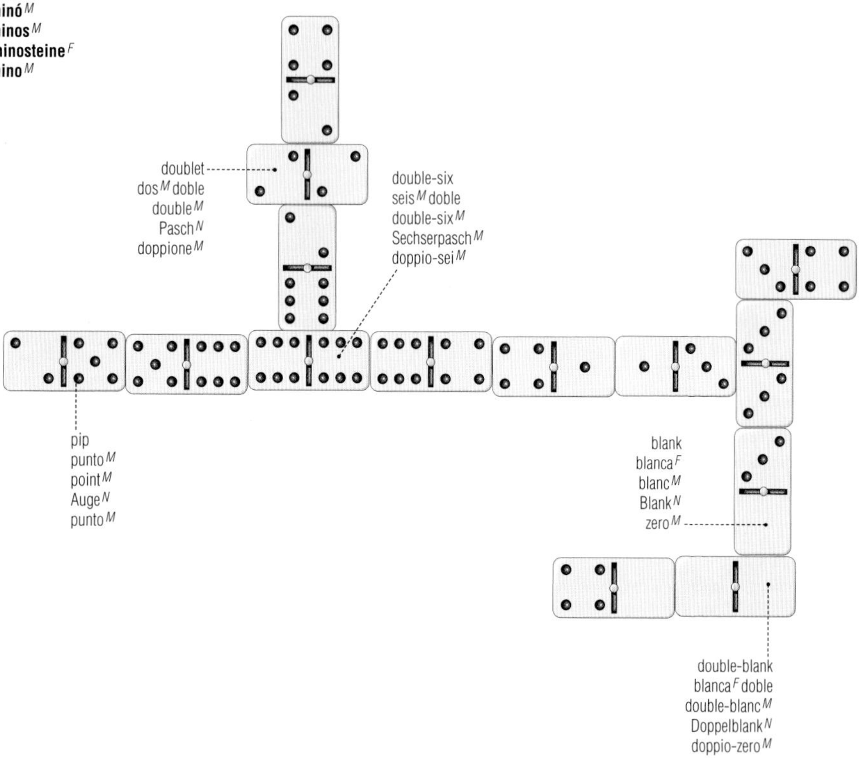
doublet
dos M doble
double M
Pasch N
doppione M
double-six
seis M doble
double-six M
Sechserpasch M
doppio-sei M
pip
punto M
point M
Auge N
punto M
blank
blanca F
blanc M
Blank N
zero M
double-blank
blanca F doble
double-blanc M
Doppelblank N
doppio-zero M

ordinary die
dado M común
dé M régulier
gewöhnlicher Würfel M
dado M comune

poker die
dado M de póquer M
dé M à poker M
Pokerwürfel M
dado M da poker M

board games

juegos M de mesa F | jeux M de plateau M | Brettspiele N | giochi M da tavola F

backgammon
backgammon M
jacquet M
Backgammon N
backgammon M

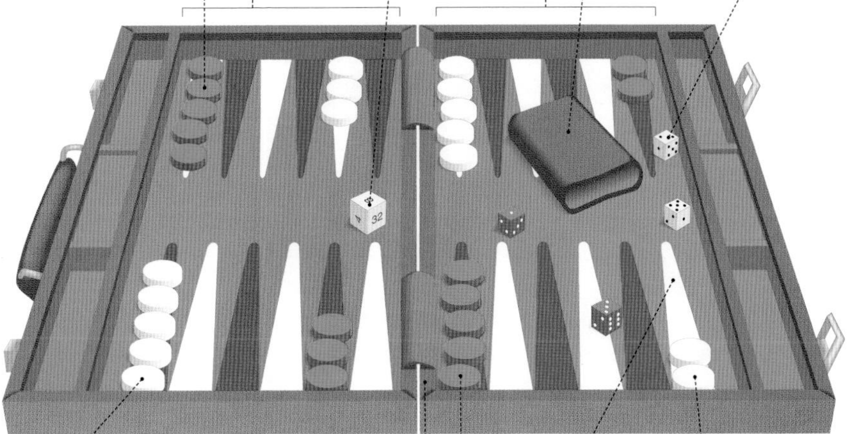
outer table
base F exterior
jan M extérieur
Außenbrett N
tavola F esterna
inner table
base F interior
jan M intérieur
Innenbrett N
tavola F interna
dice cup
cubilete M
cornet M à dés M
Würfelbecher M
bussolotto M
red
roja F
Rouges M
Rot N
rosso M
doubling die
dado M doble
dé M doubleur M
Dopplerwürfel M
dado M del raddoppio M
die
dado M
dé M
Würfel M
dado M
white
blanca F
Blancs M
Weiß N
bianco M
bar
barra F
cloison F
Bar F
barra F
point
punta F
flèche F
Feld N
punta F
checkers
dama F
dames F
Steine M
pedine F
runner
jugador M
postillon M
Läufer M
runner M

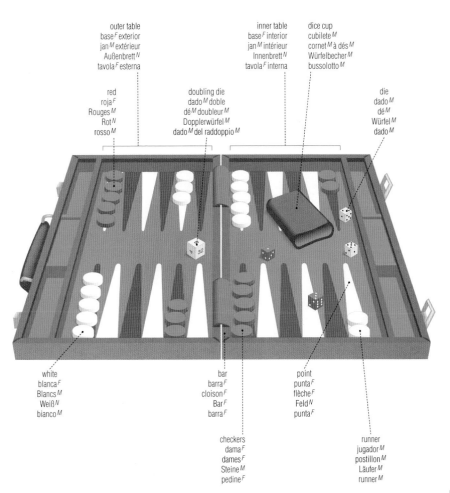

chess
ajedrez[M]
échecs[M]
Schach[N]
scacchi[M]

chessboard
tablero[M] de ajedrez[M]
échiquier[M]
Schachbrett[N]
scacchiera[F]

queen's side
lado[M] de la reina[F]
aile[F] Dame[F]
Damenflanke[F]
lato[M] della regina[F]

king's side
lado[M] del rey[M]
aile[F] Roi[M]
Königsflanke[F]
lato[M] del re[M]

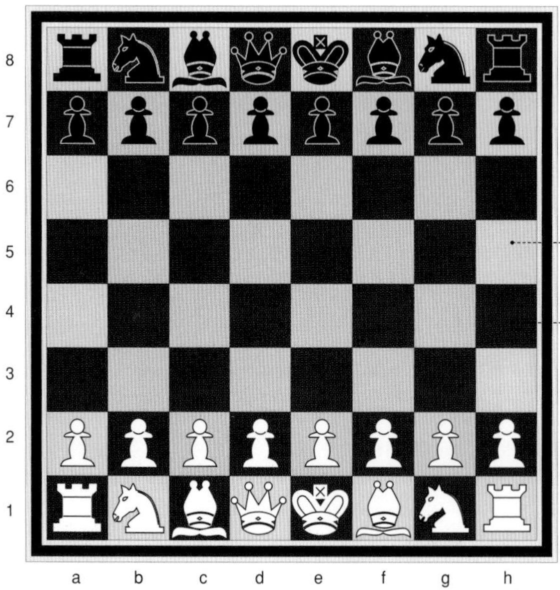

8
7
6
5
4
3
2
1
a
b
c
d
e
f
g
h

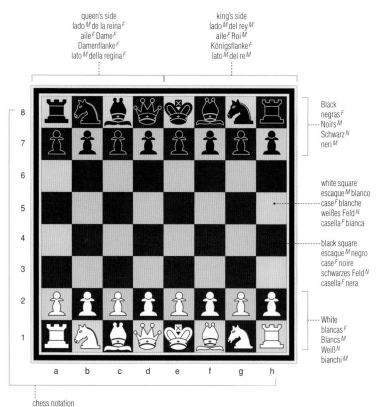

Black
negras[F]
Noirs[M]
Schwarz[N]
neri[M]

white square
escaque[M] blanco
case[F] blanche
weißes Feld[N]
casella[F] bianca

black square
escaque[M] negro
case[F] noire
schwarzes Feld[N]
casella[F] nera

White
blancas[F]
Blancs[M]
Weiß[N]
bianchi[M]

chess notation
notación[F] del ajedrez[M]
notation[F] algébrique
Notation[F]
notazione[F] degli scacchi[M]

types of movements
tipos[M] de movimientos[M]
types[M] de déplacements[M]
Zugarten[F]
tipi[M] di movimenti[M]

diagonal movement
movimiento[M] diagonal
déplacement[M] diagonal
diagonaler Zug[M]
movimento[M] diagonale

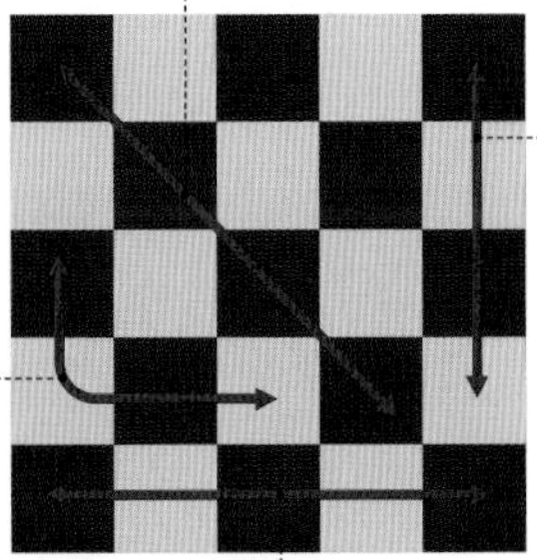

vertical movement
movimiento[M] vertical
déplacement[M] vertical
vertikaler Zug[M]
movimento[M] verticale

square movement
movimiento[M] en ángulo[M]
déplacement[M] en équerre[F]
Rösselsprung[M]
movimento[M] a L

horizontal movement
movimiento[M] horizontal
déplacement[M] horizontal
horizontaler Zug[M]
movimento[M] orizzontale

chess pieces
piezas[F]
pièces[F]
Schachfiguren[F]
pezzi[M]

pawn
peón[M]
Pion[M]
Bauer[M]
pedone[M]

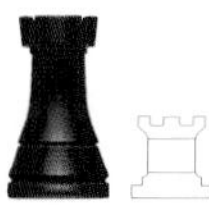

rook
torre[F]
Tour[F]
Turm[M]
torre[F]

bishop
alfil[M]
Fou[M]
Läufer[M]
alfiere[M]

knight
caballo[M]
Cavalier[M]
Springer[M]
cavallo[M]

king
rey[M]
Roi[M]
König[M]
re[M]

queen
reina[F]
Dame[F]
Dame[F]
regina[F]

video entertainment system

videojuego[M] | système[M] de jeux[M] vidéo | Videospielsystem[N] | videogioco[M]

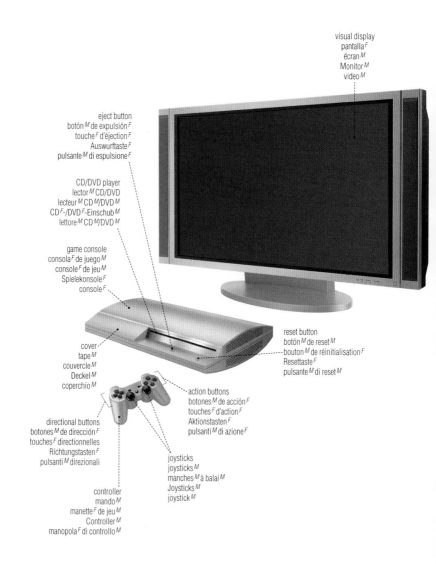

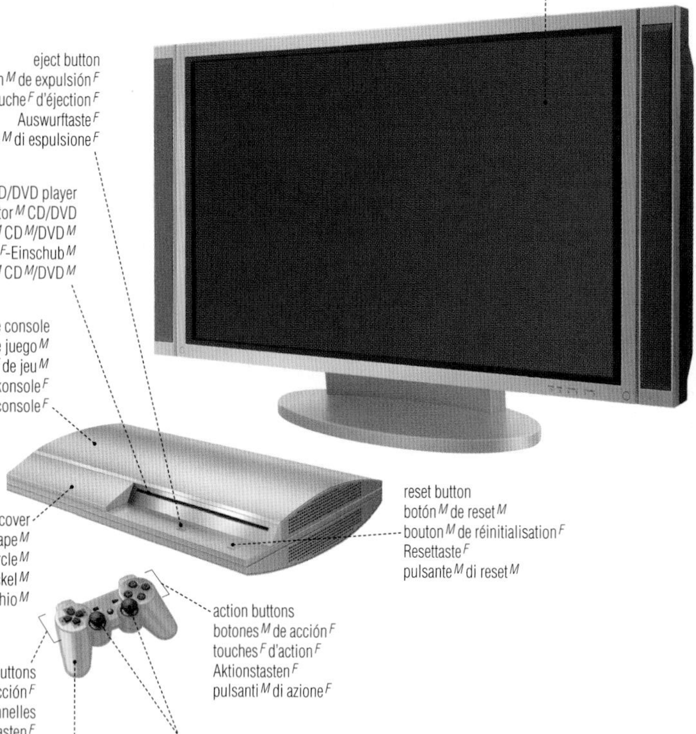
visual display
pantalla[F]
écran[M]
Monitor[M]
video[M]
eject button
botón[M] de expulsión[F]
touche[F] d'éjection[F]
Auswurftaste[F]
pulsante[M] di espulsione[F]
CD/DVD player
lector[M] CD/DVD
lecteur[M] CD[M]/DVD[M]
CD[F]-/DVD[F]-Einschub[M]
lettore[M] CD[M]/DVD[M]
game console
consola[F] de juego[M]
console[F] de jeu[M]
Spielekonsole[F]
console[F]
reset button
botón[M] de reset[M]
bouton[M] de réinitialisation[F]
Resettaste[F]
pulsante[M] di reset[M]
cover
tape[M]
couvercle[M]
Deckel[M]
coperchio[M]
action buttons
botones[M] de acción[F]
touches[F] d'action[F]
Aktionstasten[F]
pulsanti[M] di azione[F]
directional buttons
botones[M] de dirección[F]
touches[F] directionnelles
Richtungstasten[F]
pulsanti[M] direzionali
joysticks
joysticks[M]
manches[M] à balai[M]
Joysticks[M]
joystick[M]
controller
mando[M]
manette[F] de jeu[M]
Controller[M]
manopola[F] di controllo[M]

ENGLISH INDEX

B

C

D

E

F

I

J

K

L

M

P

S

T

X

Y

Z

ÍNDICE ESPAÑOL

B

D

E

F

I

J

N

Ñ

O

P

Q

R

S

T

INDEX FRANÇAIS

B

C

E

F

G

M

P

S

T

U

V

W

X

Y

Z

DEUTSCHES REGISTER

B

C

D

F

G

H

I

J

K

L

M

N

Q

R

S

T

W

INDICE DEI NOMI ITALIANI

B

C

F

G

H

I

M

N

O

P

S

T

U

V

W

X

Y

Z